The Big Picture

THE BIBLE IN 7 MINUTES A DAY

Edited by

J. Carl Laney, Jeff Schulte, and Lloyd Shadrach

Thomas Nelson Publishers
Nashville

1 2 3 4 5 6 7 8 9 – 04 03 02 01 00 99

TABLE OF CONTENTS

RANGE 11: EXILE IN BABYLON:

The Glory of God in His Discipline 424

Page

Page

PREFACE

The Bible is no ordinary book. It's the best-selling book of all time, and it's the revelation of an infinite God to a finite humanity. But it's probably the *least read* best-selling book of all time . . . go figure!

Perhaps you've tried to read the story of the Bible from Genesis to Revelation. Maybe you've even attempted the noble goal of reading through the whole Bible *in one year!*

You did great for a couple days, maybe even a few weeks. But then you missed a few days and got behind. It was also about this time that you found yourself deep in the branches of an ancient family tree like, "Enoch lived sixty-five years, and begot Methuselah" (Genesis 5:21).

Or, you persevered all the way to a mind-bending section in Leviticus. Somewhere between the "wave offering" and the "grain offering," the plot failed to thicken. Instead it disappeared while you were trying to figure how "the fat that covers the entrails and all the fat that is on the entrails, the two kidneys and the fat that is on them by the flanks, and the fatty lobe attached to the liver above the kidneys" (Leviticus 3:3-4) has anything to do with how you are going to get through your day.

Somehow the story line didn't seem to grab or hold your interest. Discouraged and de-motivated, you placed your best-selling Bible back on the shelf with all the other books you always wanted to read but never did.

Or maybe you are a regular reader of your Bible. Yet you often struggle to make sense of what you are reading because you don't grasp the "Big Picture" that makes sense of the small part you have chosen to read that day.

We've all been there at some time or another, or in one way or another. And that's why we created *WoW—The Big Picture.* What you are holding in your hands right now is your chance to succeed: to read and actually understand the entire story of the Bible over the course of a year, *in about seven minutes a day.*

Yes, you can accomplish it! It's practical, it's manageable, and it's doable.

Most people attempt to read the Bible like they're a hiker on a mountain trail, exploring each thicket, climbing each ridge, crossing streams, examining the wildflowers, turning over every interesting rock, picking up pine cones and delighting in the intricate beauty of the details.

There's nothing wrong with that, but many Bible readers following this approach to reading the story of the Bible get bogged down in the details and miss the bigger picture. They forget (or never see) that there are scenic mountain peaks to be appreciated, not just moss and meadow flowers to be examined.

But there is another way:

Have you ever flown over the Rocky Mountains in an airplane and seen what they look like from 30,000 feet? From this perspective you see the expanse and grandeur of the Continental Divide, stretching from the Canadian border into the southern reaches of Colorado. From this perspective your focus is not on the thickets, ridges, streams and wildflowers, but on the major peaks of the entire Rocky Mountain range.

If you've seen the mountains from this height you'll never forget it. The view is awesome, breathtaking. And the Bible can be read—viewed, if you will—the same way.

WoW—The Big Picture will give you a "30,000-foot view" of Scripture. You'll grasp the major themes of the Bible, from the creation account in Genesis to the end of history in Revelation. Rather than climbing each foothill, crossing each stream, and scratching your way

to each summit, you will take in every peak in the range in a sweeping panoramic view.

The story of the Bible can be likened to fifteen magnificent mountain ranges. Each range represents a historical period in the story of the Bible. In each range are a number of 14,000-foot peaks, each of which represents a particular drama, person, location, or definitive activity of God.

As you read *WoW—The Big Picture*, introductions to each of the fifteen ranges will describe how certain peaks identify major events in the story and how each mountain range combines with the others to present one Grand Story. The daily readings—which include a selection from the Psalms to direct you to worship and a Proverb to help make you wise—will lead you through the exciting story of God's plan for humanity from creation to eternity.

Also, each day ends with the question, "So What?" Ask yourself, "So what? What difference should this reading make in what I believe and how I live my life today?" This "So What?" pause will help move what you are reading from your head to your heart, so don't skip it!

This book contains the message of the Bible, not the whole Bible. By the time your journey is over, you will have read the major passages of the Bible. And most importantly, you will have a clear grasp of the "big picture" of what the Bible is all about.

It's our desire that what you experience from 30,000 feet (in about seven minutes a day), will motivate you to strap on a parachute and jump out of the plane. What you've seen from the air will encourage you to drop down and begin hiking your way through the Bible as a whole—investigating every ravine on foot, wading through each stream, riding every rapid, rappelling off each cliff, and taking the time to smell the wildflowers blooming in every meadow.

The Bible is not just the best-selling book of all time. It is also the greatest story ever told. Unlike many stories, this one was written specifically for you—and it will change your life.

So turn the page, strap yourself in, and catch an overview of "the big picture" you'll be seeing over the next 366 days.

INTRODUCTION

The Bible is the greatest story of all time. It is a story of love, war, wisdom, foolishness, mystery, prophecy, mercy, judgment, power, weakness, suffering, success, grace, glory, evil, and good. There are cosmic conflicts, bloody battles, earthshaking catastrophes, torrid romances, gut-wrenching heartbreaks, inspired beginnings, serious setbacks, awesome comebacks, and surprising finishes.

The Bible is a story about the God of the universe. It's a story that includes humankind at its best, at its worst, and every conceivable point in between. It is a story brimming with ironic twists, intriguing plots and sub-plots, courage that will make you stand up and shout, and cowardice that will make your skin crawl. It is a story that will answer the basic questions of life: Who am I? Why am I here? Where am I going? And what is life on this planet all about anyway? But don't turn the pages of the story expecting these answers to jump out at you like it's a textbook on life. Rather, read the story. Because like in any good story, you'll find the answers to these questions displayed through the lives of the characters.

While the themes of the Bible may at times feel "out there," you'll find the characters of the Bible quite down to earth. In this story you'll identify with men and women who are just trying to figure out life. You'll read about people with feet of clay, and people who are stuck in the mud—including some who seem to like it there and some who want out!

The story of the Bible begins a long time ago, back before the universe began, when the only thing that existed was God.

Think of it as a story about a King and His kingdom—a kingdom that began before anything else existed. The King not only established His kingdom, but He alone rules His kingdom for all time. That's why He is called the King of kings. The psalmist said, "The LORD is King forever and ever" (Psalm 10:16). Jeremiah declared, "He is the living God and the everlasting King" (Jeremiah 10:10).

But God could not rightly be called "King" without a recognized kingdom. As David states, "The LORD has established His throne in heaven, and His kingdom rules over all" (Psalm 103:19).

Throughout history the King has chosen to delegate aspects of His authority and rule to earthly kings, priests, and judges. This is why, as you will see, the story takes incredibly devious yet ultimately divine twists and turns.

The kingdom was at peace until the King of kings was challenged by an angelic rebel known as "Satan" or "the Devil." Satan could not directly overthrow the King or His kingdom, so he instituted a counterfeit kingdom of his own—at odds with and parallel to the kingdom of God. Satan is referred to in the story as the "god of this age" (2 Corinthians 4:4) and the "prince of the power of the air" (Ephesians 2:2).

Every ruler needs subjects, and Satan was no different. So he tempted the first human couple to join in his rebellion. The King's instruction to Adam and Eve was clear: "Of every tree of the garden you may freely eat; but of the tree of the knowledge of good and evil you shall not eat, for in the day that you eat of it you shall surely die" (Genesis 2:17). Sadly, Adam and Eve were influenced by Satan to reject the King's command. They ate of the forbidden fruit and thereby became subjects of the counterfeit kingdom.

The effect on Adam and Eve was *huge.* Their willful independence from the King destroyed their relationship with Him, producing death. They were cut off from Him spiritually. And as a result, all of their descendants became subject to the same death. The New Testament says, "Therefore, just as through one man sin entered the world, and death through sin, and thus death spread to all men, because all sinned . . ." (Romans 5:12).

What a mess! The King created a world where Adam and Eve "had it all." But they thought the King was holding out on them and foolishly traded the ultimate life for an empty promise! The King's authority was challenged. Humanity fell into sin. The rebellion took root. And it's all been unraveling ever since.

But this is where the plot thickens. How does a King who is ultimately holy, perfectly just, entirely loving, most merciful, and full of grace reestablish His kingdom authority and bring his fallen creation back to a place where they can once again enjoy the benefits of His reign? How can He display His love, His mercy, and His grace in a way that doesn't compromise His holiness and His justice? How can He demonstrate all of these qualities at once?

Most of the story of the Bible can be understood as the outworking of God's plan to do just that: reverse the curse which came on this earth because of sin by restoring fallen humankind (redemption), reestablishing His authority (kingdom), and dealing justly with sin (judgment).

REDEMPTION:

The very people that the King wanted to bless had become His enemies. Without question He would have had the right to squash their rebellion and them along with it. But because of the King's great love for His people, He amazingly chose to initiate a plan to rescue His enemies from the consequences of their rebellion. He provided them with a way they could escape the death they were facing as subjects of the counterfeit kingdom.

The story of the Bible traces this program of redemption from the King's announcement of His plan (Genesis 3:15), to its powerful and dramatic fulfillment as the King's Son is given as a sacrifice to save the rebels from destruction (2 Corinthians 5:21). The King's plan of redemption is illustrated by the sacrifices brought to His temple in Jerusalem. It is anticipated by the words of John the Baptist, "Behold! The Lamb of God who takes away the sin of the world!" (John 1:29). It is accomplished at the Cross when the Prince is killed (Romans 5:8). And it is remembered at the communion table where the love, grace, and mercy of the King is remembered (1 Corinthians 11:23-26). From Genesis to Revelation, you will see why the King's plan of redemption is called "the good news."

KINGDOM:

But the King of kings didn't stop there. He could not let His kingly authority be successfully challenged by the "counterfeit kingdom" of Satan. To do so would demonstrate that the King is not really sovereign. So He set out a plan to re-assert His authority here on this earth—the very place where it was challenged. This kingdom program involved a nation called Israel through promises made to the father of that nation, Abraham (Genesis 12:1-3) and David his descendant (2 Samuel 7:12-16). The kingdom program, revealed through these promises, was announced by Jesus when he said, "Repent, for the kingdom of heaven is at hand" (Matthew 4:17). And although the King's offer to establish His kingdom rule through Israel was initially rejected by the nation, this event moved the kingdom "underground" making it available today for all those who would place themselves under the King's rule. And some day, the Old Testament prophets predict, the kingdom authority of God will be fully restored to the earth (Zechariah 14:9).

JUDGMENT:

The final aspect of the King's plan is the judgment of sin. The mess that was made when Satan rebelled against the King, and which got worse in the Garden of Eden when humanity followed suit, required some major "cleanup." Because the King is holy, He cannot look upon sin and rebellion with indifference. And because He is just, He must execute judgment on Satan and his followers to rid the earth of the damaging effects of sin.

Like the King's plan for redemption, this aspect of God's program can be traced through the story from Genesis 3:15 to Revelation 22:3. According to the apos-

tle Peter, the earth, the place of Satan's rebellion, would need to be purged by fire in preparation for the forever Kingdom—once and for all destroying Satan's counterfeit kingdom and removing the damage to the King's creation caused by the rebellion.

A great beginning, a devastating fall, a remarkable rescue, and an indescribable future. This is the story of the Bible. This is the King's plan for the ages. This is *The Big Picture*—all by His grace and all for His glory!

MOUNTAIN RANGES

The story of the Bible can be viewed as fifteen mountain ranges with each range made up of its own major mountain peaks. Knowing what range you are in and what peak you may be viewing makes all the difference when it comes to understanding and enjoying the view.

If you've ever flown over one of the great mountain ranges in the world, or stood on one of its snow-capped peaks, you've been filled with a predictable yet overwhelming sense of awe. You've let your senses take in the picture and you've whispered to yourself, "This is awesome!"

The ranges and peaks of God's working in history evoke the same reaction. In fact, that's been the whole point—that humankind would see God in what He has revealed about Himself (in each range and on each peak) and we would respond by acknowledging, "He's awesome!" Or in biblical terms, "He's glorious!"

Like the great mountain ranges that mark our planet, there are fifteen prominent mountain ranges in the story of the Bible—each of which prompts the reader to experience the glory of God in some way.

1. Beginnings: The Glory of God in His Creation
2. A New Nation: The Glory of God in His Sovereignty
3. Slaves in Egypt: The Glory of God in His Name
4. Set Free: The Glory of God in His Redemptive Plan
5. Wandering in the Wilderness: The Glory of God in His Provision
6. Taking the Land: The Glory of God in His Faithfulness
7. Here Comes the Judge!: The Glory of God in His Righteousness
8. United We Stand: The Glory of God in His Sovereign Mercy
9. Divided We Fall: The Glory of God in His Judgments
10. Words from the Prophets: The Glory of God in His Revelation
11. Exile in Babylon: The Glory of God in His Discipline
12. There's No Place Like Home: The Glory of God in His Grace
13. The Sounds of Silence: The Glory of God in His Patience
14. The Life of Christ: The Glory of God in His Son
15. Apostles and the Church: The Glory of God in His Church

BEGINNINGS

The first mountain range on the biblical horizon is "Beginnings," taken from the Hebrew name for the first book in the Bible, Genesis. This range is called "Beginnings" because from a human perspective this is where the story really begins.

The major peaks in this range are the creation of the world, the fall of humanity, the world flood, and the promise God gave Noah.

The Creation (Genesis 1–2) reveals God as the all-powerful Creator of all things. God is good and His intent is to bless the human race along with all of His creation. It is on this peak that we see God creating humankind "in His image," with a spiritual capacity and potential to think and act as God does.

The next peak looks more like a valley—or at least it feels like one. Genesis 3 records the first man, Adam, being influenced by Satan to choose evil instead of good. This fall into sin and rebellion against God resulted in spiritual confusion, moral corruption, and divine judgment for the first couple as well as their future descendants.

The judgment of God on sinful humanity is seen from the third peak in this range. Since the earth was filled with violence and corruption, God determined it was time to wash it away and start over. For forty days and forty nights it rained, flooding the entire world and wiping out the whole human race—except for Noah and his family. God spared Noah because he trusted God and believed His promises (Genesis 6:8; Hebrews 11:7).

The last mountain peak in the "Beginnings" range is found in Genesis 8:21-22, where God promised He would never again judge the world with a flood, even though He knew the sin problem remained. Because all the descendants of Adam and Eve were born fallen and sinful, God, being just, would have to judge them again. But because of the promise made here on this peak, God would hold back the floodwaters of judgment while He brought to fruition a plan to once and for all remedy the problem of humankind's sinfulness.

The first mountain range reveals that it was God's intention to bless humanity and all creation. Sin disrupted this plan and brought all creation under a curse. But because of His grace, God began a plan to bring His sin-corrupted creation back into His blessing.

How it ALL Began
Genesis 1:1–2:24; Psalm 1:1-3; Proverbs 1:7

In the beginning God created the heavens and the earth. The earth was without form, and void; and darkness *was* on the face of the deep. And the Spirit of God was hovering over the face of the waters.

Then God said, "Let there be light"; and there was light. And God saw the light, that *it was* good; and God divided the light from the darkness. God called the light Day, and the darkness He called Night. So the evening and the morning were the first day.

Then God said, "Let there be a firmament in the midst of the waters, and let it divide the waters from the waters." Thus God made the firmament, and divided the waters which *were* under the firmament from the waters which *were* above the firmament; and it was so. And God called the firmament Heaven. So the evening and the morning were the second day.

Then God said, "Let the waters under the heavens be gathered together into one place, and let the dry *land* appear"; and it was so. And God called the dry *land* Earth, and the gathering together of the waters He called Seas. And God saw that *it was* good.

Then God said, "Let the earth bring forth grass, the herb *that* yields seed, *and* the fruit tree *that* yields fruit according to its kind, whose seed *is* in itself, on the earth"; and it was so. And the earth brought forth grass, the herb *that* yields seed according to its kind, and the tree *that* yields fruit, whose seed *is* in itself according to its kind. And God saw that *it was* good. So the evening and the morning were the third day.

Then God said, "Let there be lights in the firmament of the heavens to divide the day from the night; and let them be for signs and seasons, and for days and years; and let them be for lights in the firmament of the heavens to give light on the earth"; and it was so. Then God made two great lights: the greater light to rule the day, and the lesser light to rule the night. *He made* the stars also. God set them in the firmament of the heavens to give light on the earth, and to rule over the day and over the night, and to divide the light from the darkness. And God saw that *it was* good. So the evening and the morning were the fourth day.

Then God said, "Let the waters abound with an abundance of living creatures, and let birds fly above the earth across the face of the firmament of the heavens." So God created great sea creatures and every living thing that moves, with which the waters abounded, according to their kind, and every winged bird according to its kind. And God saw that *it was* good. And God blessed them, saying, "Be fruitful and multiply, and fill the waters in the seas, and let birds multiply on the earth." So the evening and the morning were the fifth day.

Then God said, "Let the earth bring forth the living creature according to its kind: cattle and creeping thing and beast of the earth, *each* according to its kind"; and it was so. And God made the beast of the earth according to its kind, cattle according to its kind, and everything that creeps on the earth according to its kind. And God saw that *it was* good.

Then God said, "Let Us make man in Our image, according to Our likeness; let them have dominion over the fish of the sea, over the birds of the air, and over the cattle, over all the earth and over every creeping thing that creeps on the earth." So God created man in His *own* image; in the image of God He created him; male and female He created them. Then God blessed them, and God said to them, "Be fruitful and multiply; fill the earth and subdue it; have dominion over the fish of the sea, over the birds of the air, and over every living thing that moves on the earth."

And God said, "See, I have given you every herb *that* yields seed which *is* on the face of all the earth, and every tree whose fruit yields seed; to you it shall be for food. Also, to every beast of the earth, to every bird of the air, and to everything that creeps on the earth, in which *there is* life, *I have given* every green herb for food"; and it was so. Then God saw everything that He had made, and indeed *it was* very good. So the evening and the morning were the sixth day.

Thus the heavens and the earth, and all the host of them, were finished. And on the seventh day God ended His work which He had done, and He rested on the seventh day from all His work which He had done. Then God blessed the seventh day and sanctified it, because in it He rested from all His work which God had created and made.

This *is* the history of the heavens and the earth when they were created, in the day that the LORD God made the earth and the heavens, before any plant of the field was in the earth and before any herb of the field had grown. For the LORD God had not caused it to rain on the earth, and *there was* no man to till the ground; but a mist went up from the earth and watered the whole face of the ground.

And the LORD God formed man *of* the dust of the ground, and breathed into his nostrils the breath of life; and man became a living being.

The LORD God planted a garden eastward in Eden, and there He put the man whom He had formed. And out of the ground the LORD God made every tree grow that is pleasant to the sight and good for food. The tree of life *was* also in the midst of the garden, and the tree of the knowledge of good and evil.

Now a river went out of Eden to water the garden, and from there it parted and became four riverheads. The name of the first *is* Pishon; it *is* the one which skirts the whole land of Havilah, where *there is* gold. And the gold of that land *is* good. Bdellium and the onyx stone *are* there. The name of the second river *is* Gihon; it *is* the one which goes around the whole land of Cush. The name of the third river *is* Hiddekel; it *is* the one which goes toward the east of Assyria. The fourth river *is* the Euphrates.

Then the LORD God took the man and put him in the garden of Eden to tend and keep it. And the LORD God commanded the man, saying, "Of every tree of the garden you may freely eat; but of the tree of the knowledge of good and evil you shall not eat, for in the day that you eat of it you shall surely die."

And the LORD God said, "*It is* not good that man should be alone; I will make him a helper comparable to him." Out of the ground the LORD God formed every beast of the field and every bird of the air, and brought *them* to Adam to see what he would call them. And whatever Adam called each living creature, that *was* its name. So Adam gave names to all cattle, to the birds of the air, and to every beast of the field. But for Adam there was not found a helper comparable to him.

And the LORD God caused a deep sleep to fall on Adam, and he slept; and He took one of his ribs, and closed up the flesh in its place. Then the rib

which the LORD God had taken from man He made into a woman, and He brought her to the man.

And Adam said:

"This *is* now bone of my bones
And flesh of my flesh;
She shall be called Woman,
Because she was taken out of Man."

Therefore a man shall leave his father and mother and be joined to his wife, and they shall become one flesh.

Genesis 1:1–2:24

WORSHIP

Blessed *is* the man
Who walks not in the counsel of the ungodly,
Nor stands in the path of sinners,
Nor sits in the seat of the scornful;
But his delight *is* in the law of the LORD,
And in His law he meditates day and
night.
He shall be like a tree
Planted by the rivers of water,
That brings forth its fruit in its season,
Whose leaf also shall not wither;
And whatever he does shall prosper.

Psalm 1:1-3

WISDOM

The fear of the LORD *is* the beginning of
knowledge,
But fools despise wisdom and instruction.

Proverbs 1:7

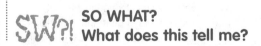

SO WHAT?
What does this tell me?

HOW IT ALL FELL APART

Genesis 3:1–4:15, 25–26; Psalm 2:1, 4–6; Proverbs 1:8-9

Now the serpent was more cunning than any beast of the field which the LORD God had made. And he said to the woman, "Has God indeed said, 'You shall not eat of every tree of the garden'?"

And the woman said to the serpent, "We may eat the fruit of the trees of the garden; but of the fruit of the tree which *is* in the midst of the garden, God has said, 'You shall not eat it, nor shall you touch it, lest you die.' "

Then the serpent said to the woman, "You will not surely die. For God knows that in the day you eat of it your eyes will be opened, and you will be like God, knowing good and evil."

So when the woman saw that the tree *was* good for food, that it *was* pleasant to the eyes, and a tree desirable to make *one* wise, she took of its fruit and ate. She also gave to her husband with her, and he ate. Then the eyes of both of them were opened, and they knew that they *were* naked; and they sewed fig leaves together and made themselves coverings.

And they heard the sound of the LORD God walking in the garden in the cool of the day, and Adam and his wife hid themselves from the presence of the LORD God among the trees of the garden.

Then the LORD God called to Adam and said to him, "Where *are* you?"

So he said, "I heard Your voice in the garden, and I was afraid because I was naked; and I hid myself."

And He said, "Who told you that you *were* naked? Have you eaten from the tree of which I commanded you that you should not eat?"

Then the man said, "The woman whom You gave *to be* with me, she gave me of the tree, and I ate."

And the LORD God said to the woman, "What *is* this you have done?"

The woman said, "The serpent deceived me, and I ate."

So the LORD God said to the serpent:

"Because you have done this,
    You *are* cursed more than all cattle,
    And more than every beast of the field;

On your belly you shall go,
And you shall eat dust
All the days of your life.
And I will put enmity
Between you and the woman,
And between your seed and her Seed;
He shall bruise your head,
And you shall bruise His heel."

To the woman He said:

"I will greatly multiply your sorrow and your
        conception;
In pain you shall bring forth children;
Your desire *shall be* for your husband,
And he shall rule over you."

Then to Adam He said, "Because you have heeded the voice of your wife, and have eaten from the tree of which I commanded you, saying, 'You shall not eat of it':

"Cursed *is* the ground for your sake;
In toil you shall eat *of* it
All the days of your life.
Both thorns and thistles it shall bring forth for
        you,
And you shall eat the herb of the field.
In the sweat of your face you shall eat bread
Till you return to the ground,
For out of it you were taken;
For dust you *are,*
And to dust you shall return."

And Adam called his wife's name Eve, because she was the mother of all living.

Also for Adam and his wife the LORD God made tunics of skin, and clothed them.

Then the LORD God said, "Behold, the man has become like one of Us, to know good and evil. And now, lest he put out his hand and take also of the tree of life, and eat, and live forever"— therefore the LORD God sent him out of the garden of Eden to till the ground from which he was taken. So He drove out the man; and He placed cherubim at the east of the garden of Eden, and a flaming sword which turned every way, to guard the way to the tree of life.

Now Adam knew Eve his wife, and she conceived and bore Cain, and said, "I have acquired a man from the LORD." Then she bore again, this time his brother Abel. Now Abel was a keeper of sheep, but Cain was a tiller of the ground. And in the process of time it came to pass that Cain brought an offering of the fruit of the ground to the LORD. Abel also brought of the firstborn of his flock and of their fat. And the LORD respected Abel and his offering, but He did not respect Cain and his offering. And Cain was very angry, and his countenance fell.

So the LORD said to Cain, "Why are you angry? And why has your countenance fallen? If you do well, will you not be accepted? And if you do not do well, sin lies at the door. And its desire *is* for you, but you should rule over it."

Now Cain talked with Abel his brother; and it came to pass, when they were in the field, that Cain rose up against Abel his brother and killed him.

Then the LORD said to Cain, "Where *is* Abel your brother?"

He said, "I do not know. *Am* I my brother's keeper?"

And He said, "What have you done? The voice of your brother's blood cries out to Me from the ground. So now you *are* cursed from the earth, which has opened its mouth to receive your brother's blood from your hand. When you till the ground, it shall no longer yield its strength to you. A fugitive and a vagabond you shall be on the earth."

And Cain said to the LORD, "My punishment *is* greater than I can bear! Surely You have driven me out this day from the face of the ground; I shall be hidden from Your face; I shall be a fugitive and a vagabond on the earth, and it will happen *that* anyone who finds me will kill me."

And the LORD said to him, "Therefore, whoever kills Cain, vengeance shall be taken on him sevenfold." And the LORD set a mark on Cain, lest anyone finding him should kill him.

And Adam knew his wife again, and she bore a son and named him Seth, "For God has appointed another seed for me instead of Abel, whom Cain killed." And as for Seth, to him also a son was born; and he named him Enosh. Then *men* began to call on the name of the LORD.

Genesis 3:1–4:15, 25-26

WORSHIP

Why do the nations rage,
And the people plot a vain thing?

He who sits in the heavens shall laugh;
The LORD shall hold them in derision.
Then He shall speak to them in His wrath,
And distress them in His deep displeasure:
"Yet I have set My King
On My holy hill of Zion."

Psalm 2:1, 4-6

WISDOM

My son, hear the instruction of your father,
And do not forsake the law of your mother;
For they *will be* a graceful ornament on your
   head,
And chains about your neck.

Proverbs 1:8-9

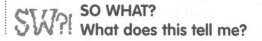

SO WHAT?
What does this tell me?

JUDGMENT BY FLOOD   Genesis 6:5–7:24; Psalm 2:10-12; Proverbs 1:10, 16

Then the LORD saw that the wickedness of man *was* great in the earth, and *that* every intent of the thoughts of his heart *was* only evil continually. And the LORD was sorry that He had made man on the earth, and He was grieved in His heart. So the LORD said, "I will destroy man whom I have created from the face of the earth, both man and beast, creeping thing and birds of the air, for I am sorry that I have made them." But Noah found grace in the eyes of the LORD.

This is the genealogy of Noah. Noah was a just man, perfect in his generations. Noah walked with God. And Noah begot three sons: Shem, Ham, and Japheth.

The earth also was corrupt before God, and the earth was filled with violence. So God looked upon the earth, and indeed it was corrupt; for all flesh had corrupted their way on the earth.

And God said to Noah, "The end of all flesh has come before Me, for the earth is filled with violence through them; and behold, I will destroy them with the earth. Make yourself an ark of gopherwood; make rooms in the ark, and cover it inside and outside with pitch. And this is how you shall make it: The length of the ark *shall be* three hundred cubits, its width fifty cubits, and its height thirty cubits. You shall make a window for the ark, and you shall finish it to a cubit from above; and set the door of the ark in its side. You shall make it *with* lower, second, and third *decks*. And behold, I Myself am bringing floodwaters on the earth, to destroy from under heaven all flesh in which *is* the breath of life; everything that *is* on the earth shall die. But I will establish My covenant with you; and you shall go into the ark—you, your sons, your wife, and your sons' wives with you. And of every living thing of all flesh you shall bring two of every *sort* into the ark, to keep *them* alive with you; they shall be male and female. Of the birds after their kind, of animals after their kind, and of every creeping thing of the earth after its kind, two of every *kind* will come to you to keep *them* alive. And you shall take for yourself of all food that is eaten, and you shall gather *it* to yourself; and it shall be food for you and for them."

Thus Noah did; according to all that God commanded him, so he did.

Then the LORD said to Noah, "Come into the ark, you and all your household, because I have seen *that* you *are* righteous before Me in this generation. You shall take with you seven each of every clean animal, a male and his female; two each of animals that *are* unclean, a male and his female; also seven each of birds of the air, male and female, to keep the species alive on the face of all the earth. For after seven more days I will cause it to rain on the earth forty days and forty nights, and I will destroy from the face of the earth all living things that I have made." And Noah did according to all that the LORD commanded him. Noah *was* six hundred years old when the floodwaters were on the earth.

So Noah, with his sons, his wife, and his sons' wives, went into the ark because of the waters of the flood. Of clean animals, of animals that *are* unclean, of birds, and of everything that creeps on the earth, two by two they went into the ark to Noah, male and female, as God had commanded Noah. And it came to pass after seven days that the waters of the flood were on the earth. In the six hundredth year of Noah's life, in the second month, the seventeenth day of the month, on that day all the fountains of the great deep were broken up, and the windows of heaven were opened. And the rain was on the earth forty days and forty nights.

On the very same day Noah and Noah's sons, Shem, Ham, and Japheth, and Noah's wife and the three wives of his sons with them, entered the ark— they and every beast after its kind, all cattle after their kind, every creeping thing that creeps on the earth after its kind, and every bird after its kind, every bird of every sort. And they went into the ark to Noah, two by two, of all flesh in which *is* the breath of life. So those that entered, male and female of all flesh, went in as God had commanded him; and the LORD shut him in.

Now the flood was on the earth forty days. The waters increased and lifted up the ark, and it rose high above the earth. The waters prevailed and greatly increased on the earth, and the ark moved about on the surface of the waters. And the waters prevailed exceedingly on the earth, and all the high

BEGINNINGS

hills under the whole heaven were covered. The waters prevailed fifteen cubits upward, and the mountains were covered. And all flesh died that moved on the earth: birds and cattle and beasts and every creeping thing that creeps on the earth, and every man. All in whose nostrils *was* the breath of the spirit of life, all that *was* on the dry *land,* died. So He destroyed all living things which were on the face of the ground: both man and cattle, creeping thing and bird of the air. They were destroyed from the earth. Only Noah and those who *were* with him in the ark remained *alive.* And the waters prevailed on the earth one hundred and fifty days.

Genesis 6:5–7:24

WORSHIP

Now therefore, be wise, O kings;
Be instructed, you judges of the earth.
Serve the LORD with fear,
And rejoice with trembling.
Kiss the Son, lest He be angry,
And you perish *in* the way,
When His wrath is kindled but a little.
Blessed *are* all those who put their trust in
Him.

Psalm 2:10-12

WISDOM

My son, if sinners entice you,
Do not consent.

For their feet run to evil,
And they make haste to shed blood.

Proverbs 1:10, 16

SW?! SO WHAT?
What does this tell me?

THE RAINBOW: A NEW BEGINNING

Genesis 8:1–9:19, 28–29;
Psalm 3:3–6; Proverbs 1:20, 23

Then God remembered Noah, and every living thing, and all the animals that *were* with him in the ark. And God made a wind to pass over the earth, and the waters subsided. The fountains of the deep and the windows of heaven were also stopped, and the rain from heaven was restrained. And the waters receded continually from the earth. At the end of the hundred and fifty days the waters decreased. Then the ark rested in the seventh month, the seventeenth day of the month, on the mountains of Ararat. And the waters decreased continually until the tenth month. In the tenth *month,* on the first *day* of the month, the tops of the mountains were seen.

So it came to pass, at the end of forty days, that Noah opened the window of the ark which he had made. Then he sent out a raven, which kept going to and fro until the waters had dried up from the earth. He also sent out from himself a dove, to see if the waters had receded from the face of the ground. But the dove found no resting place for the sole of her foot, and she returned into the ark to him, for the waters *were* on the face of the whole earth. So he put out his hand and took her, and drew her into the ark to himself. And he waited yet another seven days, and again he sent the dove out from the ark. Then the dove came to him in the evening, and behold, a freshly plucked olive leaf *was* in her mouth; and Noah knew that the waters had receded from the earth. So he waited yet another seven days and sent out the dove, which did not return again to him anymore.

And it came to pass in the six hundred and first year, in the first *month,* the first *day* of the month, that the waters were dried up from the earth; and Noah removed the covering of the ark and looked, and indeed the surface of the ground was dry. And in the second month, on the twenty-seventh day of the month, the earth was dried.

Then God spoke to Noah, saying, "Go out of the ark, you and your wife, and your sons and your sons' wives with you. Bring out with you every living thing of all flesh that *is* with you: birds and cattle and every creeping thing that creeps on the earth, so that they may abound on the earth, and be fruitful and multiply on the earth." So Noah went out, and his sons and his wife and his sons' wives with him. Every animal, every creeping thing, every bird, *and* whatever creeps on the earth, according to their families, went out of the ark.

Then Noah built an altar to the LORD, and took of every clean animal and of every clean bird, and offered burnt offerings on the altar. And the LORD smelled a soothing aroma. Then the LORD said in His heart, "I will never again curse the ground for man's sake, although the imagination of man's heart *is* evil from his youth; nor will I again destroy every living thing as I have done.

"While the earth remains,
Seedtime and harvest,
Cold and heat,
Winter and summer,
And day and night
Shall not cease."

So God blessed Noah and his sons, and said to them: "Be fruitful and multiply, and fill the earth. And the fear of you and the dread of you shall be on every beast of the earth, on every bird of the air, on all that move *on* the earth, and on all the fish of the sea. They are given into your hand. Every moving thing that lives shall be food for you. I have given you all things, even as the green herbs. But you shall not eat flesh with its life, *that is,* its blood. Surely for your lifeblood I will demand *a reckoning;* from the hand of every beast I will require it, and from the hand of man. From the hand of every man's brother I will require the life of man.

"Whoever sheds man's blood,
By man his blood shall be shed;
For in the image of God
He made man.
And as for you, be fruitful and multiply;
Bring forth abundantly in the earth
And multiply in it."

Then God spoke to Noah and to his sons with him, saying: "And as for Me, behold, I establish My covenant with you and with your descendants after you, and with every living creature that *is* with you: the birds, the cattle, and every beast of the earth with you, of all that go out of the ark, every beast of the earth. Thus I establish My covenant with you:

BEGINNINGS

Never again shall all flesh be cut off by the waters of the flood; never again shall there be a flood to destroy the earth."

And God said: "This *is* the sign of the covenant which I make between Me and you, and every living creature that *is* with you, for perpetual generations: I set My rainbow in the cloud, and it shall be for the sign of the covenant between Me and the earth. It shall be, when I bring a cloud over the earth, that the rainbow shall be seen in the cloud; and I will remember My covenant which *is* between Me and you and every living creature of all flesh; the waters shall never again become a flood to destroy all flesh. The rainbow shall be in the cloud, and I will look on it to remember the everlasting covenant between God and every living creature of all flesh that *is* on the earth." And God said to Noah, "This *is* the sign of the covenant which I have established between Me and all flesh that *is* on the earth."

Now the sons of Noah who went out of the ark were Shem, Ham, and Japheth. And Ham *was* the father of Canaan. These three *were* the sons of Noah, and from these the whole earth was populated.

And Noah lived after the flood three hundred and fifty years. So all the days of Noah were nine hundred and fifty years; and he died.

Genesis 8:1–9:19, 28-29

WORSHIP

But You, O Lord, *are* a shield for me,
My glory and the One who lifts up my head.
I cried to the Lord with my voice,
And He heard me from His holy hill.   Selah

I lay down and slept;
I awoke, for the Lord sustained me.
I will not be afraid of ten thousands of people
Who have set *themselves* against me all
    around.

Psalm 3:3–6

WISDOM

Wisdom calls aloud outside;
She raises her voice in the open squares.

Turn at my rebuke;
Surely I will pour out my spirit on you;
I will make my words known to you.

Proverbs 1:20, 23

SW?! SO WHAT?
What does this tell me?

A NEW NATION

Whereas the first mountain range dealt with the beginning of creation and God's intent to bless it, this range takes us to the birth of a new nation that would be the channel of that blessing—the nation of Israel. The four major mountain peaks in this biblical range are the lives of Israel's leaders: Abraham, Isaac, Jacob, and Joseph. Job, a contemporary of Abraham, makes up a fifth and smaller peak.

In Genesis 12:1-3, God promises He will give Abraham a land, a nation, and a blessing. Abraham's descendants would receive a land, the land of Israel. Abraham's descendants would become a great nation, the nation of Israel. Abraham would receive a blessing, and Abraham's offspring would be a blessing to the world.

Abraham and his wife Sarah had a son named Isaac. While Abraham is remembered as a man of great faith, Isaac stands out as a son who obeyed God. It took great faith for Abraham to willingly offer Isaac as a sacrifice to God. But it took an equally amazing obedience for Isaac to allow himself to be placed on that altar.

God spared Isaac's life by providing a ram for Abraham as a substitute sacrifice. Isaac grew up to marry Rebekah and together they had two sons—Esau and Jacob. Since he was the firstborn, it was the custom for Esau to be named Isaac's chief heir. But Esau didn't value this privilege and sold his birthright to Jacob for a bowl of stew. Esau's foolishness was no surprise to

God, since it was His plan all along for Jacob to be the chief heir of Isaac. Jacob's was the lineage through which God would bless the world. Jacob had his faults, but his priorities were in the right place. Above all else, He wanted the blessing of God and his father Isaac. And as Jacob's faith in God grew stronger, his name was changed to Israel, which means "strives with God" or "prince with God."

Jacob fathered many sons, but Joseph was his favorite. Out of jealousy, Joseph's brothers sold him as a slave and he was taken to Egypt. In the face of these circumstances, God prospered Joseph and he was named the prime minister of Egypt—an ironic twist in the story that enabled him to provide for his brothers and his father during a time of great famine in the land.

Joseph's life is a model of grace and integrity. When he could have sought revenge against his brothers, he blessed them. And when his supervisor's wife tried to seduce him, he ran from the temptation rather than sin against God.

A small peak at the end of this range is Job, who probably lived around the time of Abraham. Although Job suffered almost unimaginable personal loss, he maintained his faith in God. Through his suffering, Job learned that God is not bound by who we think He is, what we think He is like, or what we think He should do and not do. Job also learned that hope is not found in our circumstances but in God alone.

GOD'S PROMISE TO ABRAHAM

Genesis 10:1-2, 6, 21-22, 32; 11:1-9, 26-32; 12:1-20; Psalm 4:1-3; Proverbs 2:1-2, 5

Now this *is* the genealogy of the sons of Noah: Shem, Ham, and Japheth. And sons were born to them after the flood.

The sons of Japheth *were* Gomer, Magog, Madai, Javan, Tubal, Meshech, and Tiras.

The sons of Ham *were* Cush, Mizraim, Put, and Canaan.

And *children* were born also to Shem, the father of all the children of Eber, the brother of Japheth the elder. The sons of Shem *were* Elam, Asshur, Arphaxad, Lud, and Aram.

These *were* the families of the sons of Noah, according to their generations, in their nations; and from these the nations were divided on the earth after the flood.

Now the whole earth had one language and one speech. And it came to pass, as they journeyed from the east, that they found a plain in the land of Shinar, and they dwelt there. Then they said to one another, "Come, let us make bricks and bake *them* thoroughly." They had brick for stone, and they had asphalt for mortar. And they said, "Come, let us build ourselves a city, and a tower whose top *is* in the heavens; let us make a name for ourselves, lest we be scattered abroad over the face of the whole earth."

But the LORD came down to see the city and the tower which the sons of men had built. And the LORD said, "Indeed the people *are* one and they all have one language, and this is what they begin to do; now nothing that they propose to do will be withheld from them. Come, let Us go down and there confuse their language, that they may not understand one another's speech." So the LORD scattered them abroad from there over the face of all the earth, and they ceased building the city. Therefore its name is called Babel, because there the LORD confused the language of all the earth; and from there the LORD scattered them abroad over the face of all the earth.

Now Terah lived seventy years, and begot Abram, Nahor, and Haran.

This *is* the genealogy of Terah: Terah begot Abram, Nahor, and Haran. Haran begot Lot. And Haran died before his father Terah in his native land, in Ur of the Chaldeans. Then Abram and Nahor took wives: the name of Abram's wife *was* Sarai, and the name of Nahor's wife, Milcah, the daughter of Haran the father of Milcah and the father of Iscah. But Sarai was barren; she had no child.

And Terah took his son Abram and his grandson Lot, the son of Haran, and his daughter-in-law Sarai, his son Abram's wife, and they went out with them from Ur of the Chaldeans to go to the land of Canaan; and they came to Haran and dwelt there. So the days of Terah were two hundred and five years, and Terah died in Haran.

Now the LORD had said to Abram:

"Get out of your country,
From your family
And from your father's house,
To a land that I will show you.
I will make you a great nation;
I will bless you
And make your name great;
And you shall be a blessing.
I will bless those who bless you,
And I will curse him who curses you;
And in you all the families of the earth shall be blessed."

So Abram departed as the LORD had spoken to him, and Lot went with him. And Abram *was* seventy-five years old when he departed from Haran. Then Abram took Sarai his wife and Lot his brother's son, and all their possessions that they had gathered, and the people whom they had acquired in Haran, and they departed to go to the land of Canaan. So they came to the land of Canaan. Abram passed through the land to the place of Shechem, as far as the terebinth tree of Moreh. And the Canaanites *were* then in the land.

Then the LORD appeared to Abram and said, "To your descendants I will give this land." And there he built an altar to the LORD, who had appeared to him. And he moved from there to the mountain east of Bethel, and he pitched his tent *with* Bethel on the west and Ai on the east; there he built an altar to the LORD and called on the name of the LORD. So Abram journeyed, going on still toward the South.

A NEW NATION

Now there was a famine in the land, and Abram went down to Egypt to dwell there, for the famine *was* severe in the land. And it came to pass, when he was close to entering Egypt, that he said to Sarai his wife, "Indeed I know that you *are* a woman of beautiful countenance. Therefore it will happen, when the Egyptians see you, that they will say, 'This *is* his wife'; and they will kill me, but they will let you live. Please say you *are* my sister, that it may be well with me for your sake, and that I may live because of you."

So it was, when Abram came into Egypt, that the Egyptians saw the woman, that she *was* very beautiful. The princes of Pharaoh also saw her and commended her to Pharaoh. And the woman was taken to Pharaoh's house. He treated Abram well for her sake. He had sheep, oxen, male donkeys, male and female servants, female donkeys, and camels.

But the LORD plagued Pharaoh and his house with great plagues because of Sarai, Abram's wife. And Pharaoh called Abram and said, "What *is* this you have done to me? Why did you not tell me that she *was* your wife? Why did you say, 'She *is* my sister'? I might have taken her as my wife. Now therefore, here is your wife; take *her* and go your way." So Pharaoh commanded *his* men concerning him; and they sent him away, with his wife and all that he had.

Genesis 10:1-2, 6, 21-22, 32; 11:1-9, 26-32; 12:1-20

WORSHIP

Hear me when I call, O God of my
    righteousness!
You have relieved me in *my* distress;
Have mercy on me, and hear my prayer.

How long, O you sons of men,
Will you turn my glory to shame?
How long will you love worthlessness
And seek falsehood?   Selah
But know that the LORD has set apart for
    Himself him who is godly;
The LORD will hear when I call to Him.
Psalm 4:1-3

WISDOM

My son, if you receive my words,
And treasure my commands within you,
So that you incline your ear to wisdom,
And apply your heart to understanding;

Then you will understand the fear of the LORD,
And find the knowledge of God.
Proverbs 2:1-2, 5

SW?! **SO WHAT?**
What does this tell me?

THE STORY OF ABRAHAM AND LOT

Genesis 13–14; Psalm 4:6–8; Proverbs 2:6-7

Then Abram went up from Egypt, he and his wife and all that he had, and Lot with him, to the South. Abram *was* very rich in livestock, in silver, and in gold. And he went on his journey from the South as far as Bethel, to the place where his tent had been at the beginning, between Bethel and Ai, to the place of the altar which he had made there at first. And there Abram called on the name of the LORD.

Lot also, who went with Abram, had flocks and herds and tents. Now the land was not able to support them, that they might dwell together, for their possessions were so great that they could not dwell together. And there was strife between the herdsmen of Abram's livestock and the herdsmen of Lot's livestock. The Canaanites and the Perizzites then dwelt in the land.

So Abram said to Lot, "Please let there be no strife between you and me, and between my herdsmen and your herdsmen; for we *are* brethren. *Is* not the whole land before you? Please separate from me. If *you take* the left, then I will go to the right; or, if *you go* to the right, then I will go to the left."

And Lot lifted his eyes and saw all the plain of Jordan, that it *was* well watered everywhere (before the LORD destroyed Sodom and Gomorrah) like the garden of the LORD, like the land of Egypt as you go toward Zoar. Then Lot chose for himself all the plain of Jordan, and Lot journeyed east. And they separated from each other. Abram dwelt in the land of Canaan, and Lot dwelt in the cities of the plain and pitched *his* tent even as far as Sodom. But the men of Sodom *were* exceedingly wicked and sinful against the LORD.

And the LORD said to Abram, after Lot had separated from him: "Lift your eyes now and look from the place where you are—northward, southward, eastward, and westward; for all the land which you see I give to you and your descendants forever. And I will make your descendants as the dust of the earth; so that if a man could number the dust of the earth, *then* your descendants also could be numbered. Arise, walk in the land through its length and its width, for I give it to you."

Then Abram moved *his* tent, and went and dwelt by the terebinth trees of Mamre, which *are* in Hebron, and built an altar there to the LORD.

And it came to pass in the days of Amraphel king of Shinar, Arioch king of Ellasar, Chedorlaomer king of Elam, and Tidal king of nations, *that* they made war with Bera king of Sodom, Birsha king of Gomorrah, Shinab king of Admah, Shemeber king of Zeboiim, and the king of Bela (that is, Zoar). All these joined together in the Valley of Siddim (that is, the Salt Sea). Twelve years they served Chedorlaomer, and in the thirteenth year they rebelled.

In the fourteenth year Chedorlaomer and the kings that *were* with him came and attacked the Rephaim in Ashteroth Karnaim, the Zuzim in Ham, the Emim in Shaveh Kiriathaim, and the Horites in their mountain of Seir, as far as El Paran, which *is* by the wilderness. Then they turned back and came to En Mishpat (that *is,* Kadesh), and attacked all the country of the Amalekites, and also the Amorites who dwelt in Hazezon Tamar.

And the king of Sodom, the king of Gomorrah, the king of Admah, the king of Zeboiim, and the king of Bela (that *is,* Zoar) went out and joined together in battle in the Valley of Siddim against Chedorlaomer king of Elam, Tidal king of nations, Amraphel king of Shinar, and Arioch king of Ellasar—four kings against five. Now the Valley of Siddim *was full of* asphalt pits; and the kings of Sodom and Gomorrah fled; *some* fell there, and the remainder fled to the mountains. Then they took all the goods of Sodom and Gomorrah, and all their provisions, and went their way. They also took Lot, Abram's brother's son who dwelt in Sodom, and his goods, and departed.

Then one who had escaped came and told Abram the Hebrew, for he dwelt by the terebinth trees of Mamre the Amorite, brother of Eshcol and brother of Aner; and they *were* allies with Abram. Now when Abram heard that his brother was taken captive, he armed his three hundred and eighteen trained *servants* who were born in his own house, and went in pursuit as far as Dan. He divided his forces against them by night, and he and his servants attacked them and pursued them as far as Hobah, which *is* north of Damascus. So he brought back all the goods, and also brought back his brother Lot and his goods, as well as the women and the people.

And the king of Sodom went out to meet him at the Valley of Shaveh (that *is,* the King's Valley), after his return from the defeat of Chedorlaomer and the kings who *were* with him.

Then Melchizedek king of Salem brought out bread and wine; he *was* the priest of God Most High. And he blessed him and said:

> "Blessed be Abram of God Most High,
> Possessor of heaven and earth;
> And blessed be God Most High,
> Who has delivered your enemies into your hand."

And he gave him a tithe of all.

Now the king of Sodom said to Abram, "Give me the persons, and take the goods for yourself."

But Abram said to the king of Sodom, "I have raised my hand to the LORD, God Most High, the Possessor of heaven and earth, that I *will take* nothing, from a thread to a sandal strap, and that I will not take anything that *is* yours, lest you should say, 'I have made Abram rich'— except only what the young men have eaten, and the portion of the men who went with me: Aner, Eshcol, and Mamre; let them take their portion."

Genesis 13–14

WORSHIP

There are many who say,
"Who will show us *any* good?"
LORD, lift up the light of Your countenance upon us.
You have put gladness in my heart,
More than in the season that their grain and wine increased.
I will both lie down in peace, and sleep;
For You alone, O LORD, make me dwell in safety.

Psalm 4:6-8

WISDOM

For the LORD gives wisdom;
From His mouth *come* knowledge and understanding;
He stores up sound wisdom for the upright;
He is a shield to those who walk uprightly.

Proverbs 2:6-7

SW?! SO WHAT?
What does this tell me?

FALTERING FAITH   Genesis 15–16; Psalm 5:1-3; Proverbs 2:10-11

After these things the word of the LORD came to Abram in a vision, saying, "Do not be afraid, Abram. I *am* your shield, your exceedingly great reward."

But Abram said, "Lord GOD, what will You give me, seeing I go childless, and the heir of my house *is* Eliezer of Damascus?" Then Abram said, "Look, You have given me no offspring; indeed one born in my house is my heir!"

And behold, the word of the LORD *came* to him, saying, "This one shall not be your heir, but one who will come from your own body shall be your heir." Then He brought him outside and said, "Look now toward heaven, and count the stars if you are able to number them." And He said to him, "So shall your descendants be."

And he believed in the LORD, and He accounted it to him for righteousness.

Then He said to him, "I *am* the LORD, who brought you out of Ur of the Chaldeans, to give you this land to inherit it."

And he said, "Lord GOD, how shall I know that I will inherit it?"

So He said to him, "Bring Me a three-year-old heifer, a three-year-old female goat, a three-year-old ram, a turtledove, and a young pigeon." Then he brought all these to Him and cut them in two, down the middle, and placed each piece opposite the other; but he did not cut the birds in two. And when the vultures came down on the carcasses, Abram drove them away.

Now when the sun was going down, a deep sleep fell upon Abram; and behold, horror *and* great darkness fell upon him. Then He said to Abram: "Know certainly that your descendants will be strangers in a land *that is* not theirs, and will serve them, and they will afflict them four hundred years. And also the nation whom they serve I will judge; afterward they shall come out with great possessions. Now as for you, you shall go to your fathers in peace; you shall be buried at a good old age. But in the fourth generation they shall return here, for the iniquity of the Amorites *is* not yet complete."

And it came to pass, when the sun went down and it was dark, that behold, there appeared a smoking oven and a burning torch that passed between those pieces. On the same day the LORD made a covenant with Abram, saying:

"To your descendants I have given this land, from the river of Egypt to the great river, the River Euphrates— the Kenites, the Kenezzites, the Kadmonites, the Hittites, the Perizzites, the Rephaim, the Amorites, the Canaanites, the Girgashites, and the Jebusites."

Now Sarai, Abram's wife, had borne him no *children.* And she had an Egyptian maidservant whose name was Hagar. So Sarai said to Abram, "See now, the LORD has restrained me from bearing *children.* Please, go in to my maid; perhaps I shall obtain children by her." And Abram heeded the voice of Sarai. Then Sarai, Abram's wife, took Hagar her maid, the Egyptian, and gave her to her husband Abram to be his wife, after Abram had dwelt ten years in the land of Canaan. So he went in to Hagar, and she conceived. And when she saw that she had conceived, her mistress became despised in her eyes.

Then Sarai said to Abram, "My wrong *be* upon you! I gave my maid into your embrace; and when she saw that she had conceived, I became despised in her eyes. The LORD judge between you and me."

So Abram said to Sarai, "Indeed your maid *is* in your hand; do to her as you please." And when Sarai dealt harshly with her, she fled from her presence.

Now the Angel of the LORD found her by a spring of water in the wilderness, by the spring on the way to Shur. And He said, "Hagar, Sarai's maid, where have you come from, and where are you going?"

She said, "I am fleeing from the presence of my mistress Sarai."

The Angel of the LORD said to her, "Return to your mistress, and submit yourself under her hand." Then the Angel of the LORD said to her, "I will multiply your descendants exceedingly, so that they shall not be counted for multitude." And the Angel of the LORD said to her:

"Behold, you *are* with child,
And you shall bear a son.

A NEW NATION

You shall call his name Ishmael,
Because the LORD has heard your affliction.
He shall be a wild man;
His hand *shall be* against every man,
And every man's hand against him.
And he shall dwell in the presence of all his
    brethren."

Then she called the name of the LORD who spoke to her, You-Are-the-God-Who-Sees; for she said, "Have I also here seen Him who sees me?" Therefore the well was called Beer Lahai Roi; observe, *it is* between Kadesh and Bered.

So Hagar bore Abram a son; and Abram named his son, whom Hagar bore, Ishmael. Abram *was* eighty-six years old when Hagar bore Ishmael to Abram.

Genesis 15–16

WORSHIP

Give ear to my words, O LORD,
Consider my meditation.
Give heed to the voice of my cry,
My King and my God,
For to You I will pray.
My voice You shall hear in the morning, O
    LORD;
In the morning I will direct *it* to You,
And I will look up.

Psalm 5:1-3

WISDOM

When wisdom enters your heart,
And knowledge is pleasant to your soul,
Discretion will preserve you;
Understanding will keep you.

Proverbs 2:10-11

SW?! SO WHAT?
What does this tell me?

CONVERSATIONS WITH ABRAHAM

Genesis 17:1-21; 18:1-19; Psalm 5:11-12; Proverbs 2:21-22

When Abram was ninety-nine years old, the LORD appeared to Abram and said to him, "I am Almighty God; walk before Me and be blameless. And I will make My covenant between Me and you, and will multiply you exceedingly." Then Abram fell on his face, and God talked with him, saying: "As for Me, behold, My covenant is with you, and you shall be a father of many nations. No longer shall your name be called Abram, but your name shall be Abraham; for I have made you a father of many nations. I will make you exceedingly fruitful; and I will make nations of you, and kings shall come from you. And I will establish My covenant between Me and you and your descendants after you in their generations, for an everlasting covenant, to be God to you and your descendants after you. Also I give to you and your descendants after you the land in which you are a stranger, all the land of Canaan, as an everlasting possession; and I will be their God."

And God said to Abraham: "As for you, you shall keep My covenant, you and your descendants after you throughout their generations. This *is* My covenant which you shall keep, between Me and you and your descendants after you: Every male child among you shall be circumcised; and you shall be circumcised in the flesh of your foreskins, and it shall be a sign of the covenant between Me and you. He who is eight days old among you shall be circumcised, every male child in your generations, he who is born in your house or bought with money from any foreigner who is not your descendant. He who is born in your house and he who is bought with your money must be circumcised, and My covenant shall be in your flesh for an everlasting covenant. And the uncircumcised male child, who is not circumcised in the flesh of his foreskin, that person shall be cut off from his people; he has broken My covenant."

Then God said to Abraham, "As for Sarai your wife, you shall not call her name Sarai, but Sarah *shall be* her name. And I will bless her and also give you a son by her; then I will bless her, and she shall be *a mother of* nations; kings of peoples shall be from her."

Then Abraham fell on his face and laughed, and said in his heart, "Shall *a child* be born to a man who is one hundred years old? And shall Sarah, who is ninety years old, bear *a child?*" And Abraham said to God, "Oh, that Ishmael might live before You!"

Then God said: "No, Sarah your wife shall bear you a son, and you shall call his name Isaac; I will establish My covenant with him for an everlasting covenant, *and* with his descendants after him. And as for Ishmael, I have heard you. Behold, I have blessed him, and will make him fruitful, and will multiply him exceedingly. He shall beget twelve princes, and I will make him a great nation. But My covenant I will establish with Isaac, whom Sarah shall bear to you at this set time next year."

Then the LORD appeared to him by the terebinth trees of Mamre, as he was sitting in the tent door in the heat of the day. So he lifted his eyes and looked, and behold, three men were standing by him; and when he saw *them,* he ran from the tent door to meet them, and bowed himself to the ground, and said, "My Lord, if I have now found favor in Your sight, do not pass on by Your servant. Please let a little water be brought, and wash your feet, and rest yourselves under the tree. And I will bring a morsel of bread, that you may refresh your hearts. After that you may pass by, inasmuch as you have come to your servant."

They said, "Do as you have said."

So Abraham hurried into the tent to Sarah and said, "Quickly, make ready three measures of fine meal; knead *it* and make cakes." And Abraham ran to the herd, took a tender and good calf, gave *it* to a young man, and he hastened to prepare it. So he took butter and milk and the calf which he had prepared, and set *it* before them; and he stood by them under the tree as they ate.

Then they said to him, "Where *is* Sarah your wife?"

So he said, "Here, in the tent."

And He said, "I will certainly return to you according to the time of life, and behold, Sarah your wife shall have a son."

(Sarah was listening in the tent door which *was* behind him.) Now Abraham and Sarah were old, well advanced in age; *and* Sarah had passed

A NEW NATION

the age of childbearing. Therefore Sarah laughed within herself, saying, "After I have grown old, shall I have pleasure, my lord being old also?"

And the LORD said to Abraham, "Why did Sarah laugh, saying, 'Shall I surely bear *a child,* since I am old?' Is anything too hard for the LORD? At the appointed time I will return to you, according to the time of life, and Sarah shall have a son."

But Sarah denied *it,* saying, "I did not laugh," for she was afraid.

And He said, "No, but you did laugh!"

Then the men rose from there and looked toward Sodom, and Abraham went with them to send them on the way. And the LORD said, "Shall I hide from Abraham what I am doing, since Abraham shall surely become a great and mighty nation, and all the nations of the earth shall be blessed in him? For I have known him, in order that he may command his children and his household after him, that they keep the way of the LORD, to do righteousness and justice, that the LORD may bring to Abraham what He has spoken to him."

Genesis 17:1-21; 18:1-19

WORSHIP

But let all those rejoice who put their trust in You;
Let them ever shout for joy, because You defend them;
Let those also who love Your name
Be joyful in You.
For You, O LORD, will bless the righteous;
With favor You will surround him as *with* a shield.

Psalm 5:11-12

WISDOM

For the upright will dwell in the land,
And the blameless will remain in it;
But the wicked will be cut off from the earth,
And the unfaithful will be uprooted from it.

Proverbs 2:21-22

SW?! **SO WHAT?**
What does this tell me?

JUDGMENT OF SIN: A TALE OF TWO CITIES
Genesis 18:20–19:17, 24-29; Psalm 6:1-3; Proverbs 3:1-2

And the LORD said, "Because the outcry against Sodom and Gomorrah is great, and because their sin is very grave, I will go down now and see whether they have done altogether according to the outcry against it that has come to Me; and if not, I will know."

Then the men turned away from there and went toward Sodom, but Abraham still stood before the LORD. And Abraham came near and said, "Would You also destroy the righteous with the wicked? Suppose there were fifty righteous within the city; would You also destroy the place and not spare it for the fifty righteous that were in it? Far be it from You to do such a thing as this, to slay the righteous with the wicked, so that the righteous should be as the wicked; far be it from You! Shall not the Judge of all the earth do right?"

So the LORD said, "If I find in Sodom fifty righteous within the city, then I will spare all the place for their sakes."

Then Abraham answered and said, "Indeed now, I who am but dust and ashes have taken it upon myself to speak to the Lord: Suppose there were five less than the fifty righteous; would You destroy all of the city for lack of five?"

So He said, "If I find there forty-five, I will not destroy it."

And he spoke to Him yet again and said, "Suppose there should be forty found there?"

So He said, "I will not do it for the sake of forty."

Then he said, "Let not the Lord be angry, and I will speak: Suppose thirty should be found there?"

So He said, "I will not do it if I find thirty there."

And he said, "Indeed now, I have taken it upon myself to speak to the Lord: Suppose twenty should be found there?"

So He said, "I will not destroy it for the sake of twenty."

Then he said, "Let not the Lord be angry, and I will speak but once more: Suppose ten should be found there?"

And He said, "I will not destroy it for the

sake of ten." So the LORD went His way as soon as He had finished speaking with Abraham; and Abraham returned to his place.

Now the two angels came to Sodom in the evening, and Lot was sitting in the gate of Sodom. When Lot saw them, he rose to meet them, and he bowed himself with his face toward the ground. And he said, "Here now, my lords, please turn in to your servant's house and spend the night, and wash your feet; then you may rise early and go on your way."

And they said, "No, but we will spend the night in the open square."

But he insisted strongly; so they turned in to him and entered his house. Then he made them a feast, and baked unleavened bread, and they ate.

Now before they lay down, the men of the city, the men of Sodom, both old and young, all the people from every quarter, surrounded the house. And they called to Lot and said to him, "Where are the men who came to you tonight? Bring them out to us that we may know them carnally."

So Lot went out to them through the doorway, shut the door behind him, and said, "Please, my brethren, do not do so wickedly! See now, I have two daughters who have not known a man; please, let me bring them out to you, and you may do to them as you wish; only do nothing to these men, since this is the reason they have come under the shadow of my roof."

And they said, "Stand back!" Then they said, "This one came in to stay here, and he keeps acting as a judge; now we will deal worse with you than with them." So they pressed hard against the man Lot, and came near to break down the door. But the men reached out their hands and pulled Lot into the house with them, and shut the door. And they struck the men who were at the doorway of the house with blindness, both small and great, so that they became weary trying to find the door.

Then the men said to Lot, "Have you anyone else here? Son-in-law, your sons, your daughters, and whomever you have in the city—take them out of this place! For we will destroy this place, because the outcry against them has grown great before the face of the LORD, and the LORD has sent us to destroy it."

So Lot went out and spoke to his sons-in-law, who had married his daughters, and said, "Get up, get out of this place; for the Lord will destroy this city!" But to his sons-in-law he seemed to be joking.

When the morning dawned, the angels urged Lot to hurry, saying, "Arise, take your wife and your two daughters who are here, lest you be consumed in the punishment of the city." And while he lingered, the men took hold of his hand, his wife's hand, and the hands of his two daughters, the Lord being merciful to him, and they brought him out and set him outside the city. So it came to pass, when they had brought them outside, that he said, "Escape for your life! Do not look behind you nor stay anywhere in the plain. Escape to the mountains, lest you be destroyed."

Then the Lord rained brimstone and fire on Sodom and Gomorrah, from the Lord out of the heavens. So He overthrew those cities, all the plain, all the inhabitants of the cities, and what grew on the ground.

But his wife looked back behind him, and she became a pillar of salt.

And Abraham went early in the morning to the place where he had stood before the Lord. Then he looked toward Sodom and Gomorrah, and toward all the land of the plain; and he saw, and behold, the smoke of the land which went up like the smoke of a furnace. And it came to pass, when God destroyed the cities of the plain, that God remembered Abraham, and sent Lot out of the midst of the overthrow, when He overthrew the cities in which Lot had dwelt.

Genesis 18:20–19:17, 24-29

WORSHIP

O Lord, do not rebuke me in Your anger,
Nor chasten me in Your hot displeasure.
Have mercy on me, O Lord, for I *am* weak;
O Lord, heal me, for my bones are troubled.
My soul also is greatly troubled;
But You, O Lord—how long?

Psalm 6:1-3

WISDOM

My son, do not forget my law,
But let your heart keep my commands;
For length of days and long life
And peace they will add to you.

Proverbs 3:1-2

SW?! SO WHAT?
What does this tell me?

ABRAHAM OFFERS ISAAC

Genesis 21:1-21; 22:1-19; Psalm 6:8-10; Proverbs 3:3-4

And the Lord visited Sarah as He had said, and the Lord did for Sarah as He had spoken. For Sarah conceived and bore Abraham a son in his old age, at the set time of which God had spoken to him. And Abraham called the name of his son who was born to him—whom Sarah bore to him—Isaac. Then Abraham circumcised his son Isaac when he was eight days old, as God had commanded him. Now Abraham was one hundred years old when his son Isaac was born to him. And Sarah said, "God has made me laugh, *and* all who hear will laugh with me." She also said, "Who would have said to Abraham that Sarah would nurse children? For I have borne *him* a son in his old age."

So the child grew and was weaned. And Abraham made a great feast on the same day that Isaac was weaned.

And Sarah saw the son of Hagar the Egyptian, whom she had borne to Abraham, scoffing. Therefore she said to Abraham, "Cast out this bondwoman and her son; for the son of this bondwoman shall not be heir with my son, *namely* with Isaac." And the matter was very displeasing in Abraham's sight because of his son.

But God said to Abraham, "Do not let it be displeasing in your sight because of the lad or because of your bondwoman. Whatever Sarah has said to you, listen to her voice; for in Isaac your seed shall be called. Yet I will also make a nation of the son of the bondwoman, because he *is* your seed."

So Abraham rose early in the morning, and took bread and a skin of water; and putting *it* on her shoulder, he gave *it* and the boy to Hagar, and sent her away. Then she departed and wandered in the Wilderness of Beersheba. And the water in the skin was used up, and she placed the boy under one of the shrubs. Then she went and sat down across from *him* at a distance of about a bowshot; for she said to herself, "Let me not see the death of the boy." So she sat opposite *him*, and lifted her voice and wept.

And God heard the voice of the lad. Then the angel of God called to Hagar out of heaven, and said to her, "What ails you, Hagar? Fear not, for God has heard the voice of the lad where he *is*. Arise, lift up the lad and hold him with your hand, for I will make him a great nation."

Then God opened her eyes, and she saw a well of water. And she went and filled the skin with water, and gave the lad a drink. So God was with the lad; and he grew and dwelt in the wilderness, and became an archer. He dwelt in the Wilderness of Paran; and his mother took a wife for him from the land of Egypt.

Now it came to pass after these things that God tested Abraham, and said to him, "Abraham!"

And he said, "Here I am."

Then He said, "Take now your son, your only *son* Isaac, whom you love, and go to the land of Moriah, and offer him there as a burnt offering on one of the mountains of which I shall tell you."

So Abraham rose early in the morning and saddled his donkey, and took two of his young men with him, and Isaac his son; and he split the wood for the burnt offering, and arose and went to the place of which God had told him. Then on the third day Abraham lifted his eyes and saw the place afar off. And Abraham said to his young men, "Stay here with the donkey; the lad and I will go yonder and worship, and we will come back to you."

So Abraham took the wood of the burnt offering and laid *it* on Isaac his son; and he took the fire in his hand, and a knife, and the two of them went together. But Isaac spoke to Abraham his father and said, "My father!"

And he said, "Here I am, my son."

Then he said, "Look, the fire and the wood, but where *is* the lamb for a burnt offering?"

And Abraham said, "My son, God will provide for Himself the lamb for a burnt offering." So the two of them went together.

Then they came to the place of which God had told him. And Abraham built an altar there and placed the wood in order; and he bound Isaac his son and laid him on the altar, upon the wood. And Abraham stretched out his hand and took the knife to slay his son.

But the Angel of the Lord called to him from heaven and said, "Abraham, Abraham!"

So he said, "Here I am."

And He said, "Do not lay your hand on the lad,

or do anything to him; for now I know that you fear God, since you have not withheld your son, your only *son,* from Me."

Then Abraham lifted his eyes and looked, and there behind *him was* a ram caught in a thicket by its horns. So Abraham went and took the ram, and offered it up for a burnt offering instead of his son. And Abraham called the name of the place, The-Lord-Will-Provide; as it is said *to* this day, "In the Mount of the Lord it shall be provided."

Then the Angel of the Lord called to Abraham a second time out of heaven, and said: "By Myself I have sworn, says the Lord, because you have done this thing, and have not withheld your son, your only *son*— blessing I will bless you, and multiplying I will multiply your descendants as the stars of the heaven and as the sand which *is* on the seashore; and your descendants shall possess the gate of their enemies. In your seed all the nations of the earth shall be blessed, because you have obeyed My voice." So Abraham returned to his young men, and they rose and went together to Beersheba; and Abraham dwelt at Beersheba.

Genesis 21:1-21; 22:1-19

WORSHIP

Depart from me, all you workers of iniquity;
For the Lord has heard the voice of my
    weeping.
The Lord has heard my supplication;
The Lord will receive my prayer.
Let all my enemies be ashamed and greatly
    troubled;
Let them turn back *and* be ashamed suddenly.

Psalm 6:8-10

WISDOM

Let not mercy and truth forsake you;
Bind them around your neck,
Write them on the tablet of your heart,
And so find favor and high esteem
In the sight of God and man.

Proverbs 3:3-4

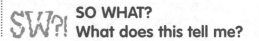

SO WHAT?
What does this tell me?

SARAH'S BURIAL; ISAAC'S MARRIAGE

Genesis 23:1-9, 17-20; 24:1-27, 61-67; Psalm 7:1-2; Proverbs 3:5-6

arah lived one hundred and twenty-seven years; *these were* the years of the life of Sarah. So Sarah died in Kirjath Arba (that *is,* Hebron) in the land of Canaan, and Abraham came to mourn for Sarah and to weep for her.

Then Abraham stood up from before his dead, and spoke to the sons of Heth, saying, "I *am* a foreigner and a visitor among you. Give me property for a burial place among you, that I may bury my dead out of my sight."

And the sons of Heth answered Abraham, saying to him, "Hear us, my lord: You *are* a mighty prince among us; bury your dead in the choicest of our burial places. None of us will withhold from you his burial place, that you may bury your dead."

Then Abraham stood up and bowed himself to the people of the land, the sons of Heth. And he spoke with them, saying, "If it is your wish that I bury my dead out of my sight, hear me, and meet with Ephron the son of Zohar for me, that he may give me the cave of Machpelah which he has, which *is* at the end of his field. Let him give it to me at the full price, as property for a burial place among you."

So the field of Ephron which *was* in Machpelah, which *was* before Mamre, the field and the cave which *was* in it, and all the trees that *were* in the field, which *were* within all the surrounding borders, were deeded to Abraham as a possession in the presence of the sons of Heth, before all who went in at the gate of his city.

And after this, Abraham buried Sarah his wife in the cave of the field of Machpelah, before Mamre (that *is,* Hebron) in the land of Canaan. So the field and the cave that *is* in it were deeded to Abraham by the sons of Heth as property for a burial place.

Now Abraham was old, well advanced in age; and the LORD had blessed Abraham in all things. So Abraham said to the oldest servant of his house, who ruled over all that he had, "Please, put your hand under my thigh, and I will make you swear by the LORD, the God of heaven and the God of the earth, that you will not take a wife for my son from

the daughters of the Canaanites, among whom I dwell; but you shall go to my country and to my family, and take a wife for my son Isaac."

And the servant said to him, "Perhaps the woman will not be willing to follow me to this land. Must I take your son back to the land from which you came?"

But Abraham said to him, "Beware that you do not take my son back there. The LORD God of heaven, who took me from my father's house and from the land of my family, and who spoke to me and swore to me, saying, 'To your descendants I give this land,' He will send His angel before you, and you shall take a wife for my son from there. And if the woman is not willing to follow you, then you will be released from this oath; only do not take my son back there." So the servant put his hand under the thigh of Abraham his master, and swore to him concerning this matter.

Then the servant took ten of his master's camels and departed, for all his master's goods *were in* his hand. And he arose and went to Mesopotamia, to the city of Nahor. And he made his camels kneel down outside the city by a well of water at evening time, the time when women go out to draw *water.* Then he said, "O LORD God of my master Abraham, please give me success this day, and show kindness to my master Abraham. Behold, *here* I stand by the well of water, and the daughters of the men of the city are coming out to draw water. Now let it be that the young woman to whom I say, 'Please let down your pitcher that I may drink,' and she says, 'Drink, and I will also give your camels a drink'—*let* her *be the one* You have appointed for Your servant Isaac. And by this I will know that You have shown kindness to my master."

And it happened, before he had finished speaking, that behold, Rebekah, who was born to Bethuel, son of Milcah, the wife of Nahor, Abraham's brother, came out with her pitcher on her shoulder. Now the young woman *was* very beautiful to behold, a virgin; no man had known her. And she went down to the well, filled her pitcher, and came up. And the servant ran to meet her and said, "Please let me drink a little water from your pitcher."

So she said, "Drink, my lord." Then she quickly

let her pitcher down to her hand, and gave him a drink. And when she had finished giving him a drink, she said, "I will draw *water* for your camels also, until they have finished drinking." Then she quickly emptied her pitcher into the trough, ran back to the well to draw *water,* and drew for all his camels. And the man, wondering at her, remained silent so as to know whether the LORD had made his journey prosperous or not.

So it was, when the camels had finished drinking, that the man took a golden nose ring weighing half a shekel, and two bracelets for her wrists weighing ten *shekels* of gold, and said, "Whose daughter *are* you? Tell me, please, is there room *in* your father's house for us to lodge?"

So she said to him, "I *am* the daughter of Bethuel, Milcah's son, whom she bore to Nahor." Moreover she said to him, "We have both straw and feed enough, and room to lodge."

Then the man bowed down his head and worshiped the LORD. And he said, "Blessed *be* the LORD God of my master Abraham, who has not forsaken His mercy and His truth toward my master. As for me, being on the way, the LORD led me to the house of my master's brethren."

Then Rebekah and her maids arose, and they rode on the camels and followed the man. So the servant took Rebekah and departed.

Now Isaac came from the way of Beer Lahai Roi, for he dwelt in the South. And Isaac went out to meditate in the field in the evening; and he lifted his eyes and looked, and there, the camels *were* coming. Then Rebekah lifted her eyes, and when she saw Isaac she dismounted from her camel; for she had said to the servant, "Who *is* this man walking in the field to meet us?"

The servant said, "It *is* my master." So she took a veil and covered herself.

And the servant told Isaac all the things that he had done. Then Isaac brought her into his mother Sarah's tent; and he took Rebekah and she became his wife, and he loved her. So Isaac was comforted after his mother's *death.*

Genesis 23:1-9, 17-20; 24:1-27, 61-67

WoRSHiP

O LORD my God, in You I put my trust;
Save me from all those who persecute me;
And deliver me,
Lest they tear me like a lion,
Rending *me* in pieces, while *there is* none to
    deliver.

Psalm 7:1-2

WiSDoM

Trust in the LORD with all your heart,
And lean not on your own understanding;
In all your ways acknowledge Him,
And He shall direct your paths.

Proverbs 3:5-6

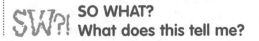

SO WHAT?
What does this tell me?

THE SALE OF A BIRTHRIGHT

Genesis 25:19–26:25; Psalm 7:6-8; Proverbs 3:7-8

This *is* the genealogy of Isaac, Abraham's son. Abraham begot Isaac. Isaac was forty years old when he took Rebekah as wife, the daughter of Bethuel the Syrian of Padan Aram, the sister of Laban the Syrian. Now Isaac pleaded with the LORD for his wife, because she *was* barren; and the LORD granted his plea, and Rebekah his wife conceived. But the children struggled together within her; and she said, "If *all is* well, why *am I like* this?" So she went to inquire of the LORD.

And the LORD said to her:

"Two nations *are* in your womb,
Two peoples shall be separated from your
    body;
One people shall be stronger than the other,
And the older shall serve the younger."

So when her days were fulfilled *for her* to give birth, indeed *there were* twins in her womb. And the first came out red. *He was* like a hairy garment all over; so they called his name Esau. Afterward his brother came out, and his hand took hold of Esau's heel; so his name was called Jacob. Isaac *was* sixty years old when she bore them.

So the boys grew. And Esau was a skillful hunter, a man of the field; but Jacob was a mild man, dwelling in tents. And Isaac loved Esau because he ate *of his* game, but Rebekah loved Jacob.

Now Jacob cooked a stew; and Esau came in from the field, and he *was* weary. And Esau said to Jacob, "Please feed me with that same red *stew,* for I *am* weary." Therefore his name was called Edom.

But Jacob said, "Sell me your birthright as of this day."

And Esau said, "Look, I *am* about to die; so what *is* this birthright to me?"

Then Jacob said, "Swear to me as of this day."

So he swore to him, and sold his birthright to Jacob. And Jacob gave Esau bread and stew of lentils; then he ate and drank, arose, and went his way. Thus Esau despised *his* birthright.

There was a famine in the land, besides the first famine that was in the days of Abraham. And Isaac went to Abimelech king of the Philistines, in Gerar.

Then the LORD appeared to him and said: "Do not go down to Egypt; live in the land of which I shall tell you. Dwell in this land, and I will be with you and bless you; for to you and your descendants I give all these lands, and I will perform the oath which I swore to Abraham your father. And I will make your descendants multiply as the stars of heaven; I will give to your descendants all these lands; and in your seed all the nations of the earth shall be blessed; because Abraham obeyed My voice and kept My charge, My commandments, My statutes, and My laws."

So Isaac dwelt in Gerar. And the men of the place asked about his wife. And he said, "She *is* my sister"; for he was afraid to say, "*She is* my wife," *because he thought,* "lest the men of the place kill me for Rebekah, because she *is* beautiful to behold." Now it came to pass, when he had been there a long time, that Abimelech king of the Philistines looked through a window, and saw, and there was Isaac, showing endearment to Rebekah his wife. Then Abimelech called Isaac and said, "Quite obviously she *is* your wife; so how could you say, 'She *is* my sister'?"

Isaac said to him, "Because I said, 'Lest I die on account of her.' "

And Abimelech said, "What *is* this you have done to us? One of the people might soon have lain with your wife, and you would have brought guilt on us." So Abimelech charged all *his* people, saying, "He who touches this man or his wife shall surely be put to death."

Then Isaac sowed in that land, and reaped in the same year a hundredfold; and the LORD blessed him. The man began to prosper, and continued prospering until he became very prosperous; for he had possessions of flocks and possessions of herds and a great number of servants. So the Philistines envied him. Now the Philistines had stopped up all the wells which his father's servants had dug in the days of Abraham his father, and they had filled them with earth. And Abimelech said to Isaac, "Go away from us, for you are much mightier than we."

Then Isaac departed from there and pitched

A NEW NATION

his tent in the Valley of Gerar, and dwelt there. And Isaac dug again the wells of water which they had dug in the days of Abraham his father, for the Philistines had stopped them up after the death of Abraham. He called them by the names which his father had called them.

Also Isaac's servants dug in the valley, and found a well of running water there. But the herdsmen of Gerar quarreled with Isaac's herdsmen, saying, "The water *is* ours." So he called the name of the well Esek, because they quarreled with him. Then they dug another well, and they quarreled over that *one* also. So he called its name Sitnah. And he moved from there and dug another well, and they did not quarrel over it. So he called its name Rehoboth, because he said, "For now the LORD has made room for us, and we shall be fruitful in the land."

Then he went up from there to Beersheba. And the LORD appeared to him the same night and said, "I *am* the God of your father Abraham; do not fear, for I *am* with you. I will bless you and multiply your descendants for My servant Abraham's sake." So he built an altar there and called on the name of the LORD, and he pitched his tent there; and there Isaac's servants dug a well.

Genesis 25:19–26:25

WORSHIP

Arise, O LORD, in Your anger;
Lift Yourself up because of the rage of my
  enemies;
Rise up for me *to* the judgment You have
  commanded!
So the congregation of the peoples shall
  surround You;
For their sakes, therefore, return on high.
The LORD shall judge the peoples;
Judge me, O LORD, according to my
  righteousness,
And according to my integrity within me.

Psalm 7:6-8

WISDOM

Do not be wise in your own eyes;
Fear the LORD and depart from evil.
It will be health to your flesh,
And strength to your bones.

Proverbs 3:7-8

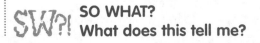

SO WHAT?
What does this tell me?

JACOB SECURES ISAAC'S BLESSING

Genesis 27:1-43; Psalm 7:10-11, 17; Proverbs 3:9-10

ow it came to pass, when Isaac was old and his eyes were so dim that he could not see, that he called Esau his older son and said to him, "My son."

And he answered him, "Here I am."

Then he said, "Behold now, I am old. I do not know the day of my death. Now therefore, please take your weapons, your quiver and your bow, and go out to the field and hunt game for me. And make me savory food, such as I love, and bring *it* to me that I may eat, that my soul may bless you before I die."

Now Rebekah was listening when Isaac spoke to Esau his son. And Esau went to the field to hunt game and to bring *it*. So Rebekah spoke to Jacob her son, saying, "Indeed I heard your father speak to Esau your brother, saying, 'Bring me game and make savory food for me, that I may eat it and bless you in the presence of the LORD before my death.' Now therefore, my son, obey my voice according to what I command you. Go now to the flock and bring me from there two choice kids of the goats, and I will make savory food from them for your father, such as he loves. Then you shall take *it* to your father, that he may eat *it,* and that he may bless you before his death."

And Jacob said to Rebekah his mother, "Look, Esau my brother *is* a hairy man, and I *am* a smooth-*skinned* man. Perhaps my father will feel me, and I shall seem to be a deceiver to him; and I shall bring a curse on myself and not a blessing."

But his mother said to him, "*Let* your curse *be* on me, my son; only obey my voice, and go, get *them* for me." And he went and got *them* and brought *them* to his mother, and his mother made savory food, such as his father loved. Then Rebekah took the choice clothes of her elder son Esau, which *were* with her in the house, and put them on Jacob her younger son. And she put the skins of the kids of the goats on his hands and on the smooth part of his neck. Then she gave the savory food and the bread, which she had prepared, into the hand of her son Jacob.

So he went to his father and said, "My father."

And he said, "Here I am. Who *are* you, my son?"

Jacob said to his father, "I *am* Esau your first-born; I have done just as you told me; please arise, sit and eat of my game, that your soul may bless me."

But Isaac said to his son, "How *is it* that you have found *it* so quickly, my son?"

And he said, "Because the LORD your God brought *it* to me."

Isaac said to Jacob, "Please come near, that I may feel you, my son, whether you *are* really my son Esau or not." So Jacob went near to Isaac his father, and he felt him and said, "The voice *is* Jacob's voice, but the hands *are* the hands of Esau." And he did not recognize him, because his hands were hairy like his brother Esau's hands; so he blessed him.

Then he said, "*Are* you really my son Esau?" He said, "I *am.*"

He said, "Bring *it* near to me, and I will eat of my son's game, so that my soul may bless you." So he brought *it* near to him, and he ate; and he brought him wine, and he drank. Then his father Isaac said to him, "Come near now and kiss me, my son." And he came near and kissed him; and he smelled the smell of his clothing, and blessed him and said:

"Surely, the smell of my son
Is like the smell of a field
Which the LORD has blessed.
Therefore may God give you
Of the dew of heaven,
Of the fatness of the earth,
And plenty of grain and wine.
Let peoples serve you,
And nations bow down to you.
Be master over your brethren,
And let your mother's sons bow down to you.
Cursed *be* everyone who curses you,
And blessed *be* those who bless you!"

Now it happened, as soon as Isaac had finished blessing Jacob, and Jacob had scarcely gone out from the presence of Isaac his father, that Esau his brother came in from his hunting. He also had made savory food, and brought it to his father, and said to his father, "Let my father arise and eat of his son's game, that your soul may bless me."

And his father Isaac said to him, "Who *are* you?"

So he said, "I *am* your son, your firstborn, Esau."

Then Isaac trembled exceedingly, and said, "Who? Where *is* the one who hunted game and brought *it* to me? I ate all *of it* before you came, and I have blessed him—*and* indeed he shall be blessed."

When Esau heard the words of his father, he cried with an exceedingly great and bitter cry, and said to his father, "Bless me—me also, O my father!"

But he said, "Your brother came with deceit and has taken away your blessing."

And *Esau* said, "Is he not rightly named Jacob? For he has supplanted me these two times. He took away my birthright, and now look, he has taken away my blessing!" And he said, "Have you not reserved a blessing for me?"

Then Isaac answered and said to Esau, "Indeed I have made him your master, and all his brethren I have given to him as servants; with grain and wine I have sustained him. What shall I do now for you, my son?"

And Esau said to his father, "Have you only one blessing, my father? Bless me—me also, O my father!" And Esau lifted up his voice and wept.

Then Isaac his father answered and said to him:

"Behold, your dwelling shall be of the fatness of the earth,
And of the dew of heaven from above.
By your sword you shall live,
And you shall serve your brother;
And it shall come to pass, when you become restless,
That you shall break his yoke from your neck."

So Esau hated Jacob because of the blessing with which his father blessed him, and Esau said in his heart, "The days of mourning for my father are at hand; then I will kill my brother Jacob."

And the words of Esau her older son were told to Rebekah. So she sent and called Jacob her younger son, and said to him, "Surely your brother Esau comforts himself concerning you *by intending* to kill you. Now therefore, my son, obey my voice: arise, flee to my brother Laban in Haran."

Genesis 27:1-43

WORSHIP

My defense *is* of God,
Who saves the upright in heart.

God *is* a just judge,
And God is angry *with the wicked* every day.

I will praise the Lord according to His righteousness,
And will sing praise to the name of the Lord Most High.

Psalm 7:10-11, 17

WISDOM

Honor the Lord with your possessions,
And with the firstfruits of all your increase;
So your barns will be filled with plenty,
And your vats will overflow with new wine.

Proverbs 3:9-10

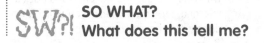

SO WHAT?
What does this tell me?

JACOB BECOMES A FAMILY MAN

Genesis 28:1-6, 10-22; 29:1-21,
26-30; Psalm 8:1-2, 9;
Proverbs 3:11-12

Then Isaac called Jacob and blessed him, and charged him, and said to him: "You shall not take a wife from the daughters of Canaan. Arise, go to Padan Aram, to the house of Bethuel your mother's father; and take yourself a wife from there of the daughters of Laban your mother's brother.

"May God Almighty bless you,
And make you fruitful and multiply you,
That you may be an assembly of peoples;
And give you the blessing of Abraham,
To you and your descendants with you,
That you may inherit the land
In which you are a stranger,
Which God gave to Abraham."

So Isaac sent Jacob away, and he went to Padan Aram, to Laban the son of Bethuel the Syrian, the brother of Rebekah, the mother of Jacob and Esau.

Esau saw that Isaac had blessed Jacob and sent him away to Padan Aram to take himself a wife from there, *and that* as he blessed him he gave him a charge, saying, "You shall not take a wife from the daughters of Canaan."

Now Jacob went out from Beersheba and went toward Haran. So he came to a certain place and stayed there all night, because the sun had set. And he took one of the stones of that place and put it at his head, and he lay down in that place to sleep. Then he dreamed, and behold, a ladder *was* set up on the earth, and its top reached to heaven; and there the angels of God were ascending and descending on it.

And behold, the LORD stood above it and said: "I *am* the LORD God of Abraham your father and the God of Isaac; the land on which you lie I will give to you and your descendants. Also your descendants shall be as the dust of the earth; you shall spread abroad to the west and the east, to the north and the south; and in you and in your seed all the families of the earth shall be blessed. Behold, I *am* with you and will keep you wherever you go, and will bring you back to this land; for I will not leave you until I have done what I have spoken to you."

Then Jacob awoke from his sleep and said, "Surely the LORD is in this place, and I did not know *it.*" And he was afraid and said, "How awesome *is* this place! This *is* none other than the house of God, and this *is* the gate of heaven!"

Then Jacob rose early in the morning, and took the stone that he had put at his head, set it up as a pillar, and poured oil on top of it. And he called the name of that place Bethel; but the name of that city had been Luz previously. Then Jacob made a vow, saying, "If God will be with me, and keep me in this way that I am going, and give me bread to eat and clothing to put on, so that I come back to my father's house in peace, then the LORD shall be my God. And this stone which I have set as a pillar shall be God's house, and of all that You give me I will surely give a tenth to You."

So Jacob went on his journey and came to the land of the people of the East. And he looked, and saw a well in the field; and behold, there *were* three flocks of sheep lying by it; for out of that well they watered the flocks. A large stone *was* on the well's mouth. Now all the flocks would be gathered there; and they would roll the stone from the well's mouth, water the sheep, and put the stone back in its place on the well's mouth.

And Jacob said to them, "My brethren, where *are* you from?"

And they said, "We *are* from Haran."

Then he said to them, "Do you know Laban the son of Nahor?"

And they said, "We know him."

So he said to them, "Is he well?"

And they said, "*He is* well. And look, his daughter Rachel is coming with the sheep."

Then he said, "Look, *it is* still high day; *it is* not time for the cattle to be gathered together. Water the sheep, and go and feed *them.*"

But they said, "We cannot until all the flocks are gathered together, and they have rolled the stone from the well's mouth; then we water the sheep."

Now while he was still speaking with them, Rachel came with her father's sheep, for she was a shepherdess. And it came to pass, when Jacob saw Rachel the daughter of Laban his mother's brother, and the sheep of Laban his mother's brother, that Jacob went near and rolled the stone from the well's mouth, and watered the flock of Laban his mother's brother. Then Jacob kissed Rachel, and lifted up his voice and wept. And Jacob told Rachel that he *was* her father's relative and that he *was* Rebekah's son. So she ran and told her father.

Then it came to pass, when Laban heard the report about Jacob his sister's son, that he ran to meet him, and embraced him and kissed him, and brought him to his house. So he told Laban all these things. And Laban said to him, "Surely you *are* my bone and my flesh." And he stayed with him for a month.

Then Laban said to Jacob, "Because you *are* my relative, should you therefore serve me for nothing? Tell me, what *should* your wages *be*?" Now Laban had two daughters: the name of the elder *was* Leah, and the name of the younger *was* Rachel. Leah's eyes *were* delicate, but Rachel was beautiful of form and appearance.

Now Jacob loved Rachel; so he said, "I will serve you seven years for Rachel your younger daughter."

And Laban said, "*It is* better that I give her to you than that I should give her to another man. Stay with me." So Jacob served seven years for Rachel, and they seemed *only* a few days to him because of the love he had for her.

Then Jacob said to Laban, "Give *me* my wife, for my days are fulfilled, that I may go in to her."

And Laban said, "It must not be done so in our country, to give the younger before the firstborn. Fulfill her week, and we will give you this one also for the service which you will serve with me still another seven years."

Then Jacob did so and fulfilled her week. So he gave him his daughter Rachel as wife also. And Laban gave his maid Bilhah to his daughter Rachel as a maid. Then *Jacob* also went in to Rachel, and he also loved Rachel more than Leah. And he served with Laban still another seven years.

Genesis 28:1-6, 10-22; 29:1-21, 26-30

WORSHIP

O Lord, our Lord,
How excellent *is* Your name in all the earth,
Who have set Your glory above the heavens!
Out of the mouth of babes and nursing infants
You have ordained strength,
Because of Your enemies,
That You may silence the enemy and the
avenger.

O Lord, our Lord,
How excellent *is* Your name in all the earth!
Psalm 8:1-2, 9

WISDOM

My son, do not despise the chastening of the
Lord,
Nor detest His correction;
For whom the Lord loves He corrects,
Just as a father the son *in whom* he delights.
Proverbs 3:11-12

SW?! **SO WHAT?**
What does this tell me?

JACOB SECRETLY DEPARTS FOR CANAAN

Genesis 31:1-42, 54-55; Psalm 9:1-2; Proverbs 3:13-14

Now *Jacob* heard the words of Laban's sons, saying, "Jacob has taken away all that was our father's, and from what was our father's he has acquired all this wealth." And Jacob saw the countenance of Laban, and indeed it *was* not *favorable* toward him as before. Then the LORD said to Jacob, "Return to the land of your fathers and to your family, and I will be with you."

So Jacob sent and called Rachel and Leah to the field, to his flock, and said to them, "I see your father's countenance, that it *is* not *favorable* toward me as before; but the God of my father has been with me. And you know that with all my might I have served your father. Yet your father has deceived me and changed my wages ten times, but God did not allow him to hurt me. If he said thus: 'The speckled shall be your wages,' then all the flocks bore speckled. And if he said thus: 'The streaked shall be your wages,' then all the flocks bore streaked. So God has taken away the livestock of your father and given *them* to me.

"And it happened, at the time when the flocks conceived, that I lifted my eyes and saw in a dream, and behold, the rams which leaped upon the flocks *were* streaked, speckled, and gray-spotted. Then the Angel of God spoke to me in a dream, saying, 'Jacob.' And I said, 'Here I am.' And He said, 'Lift your eyes now and see, all the rams which leap on the flocks *are* streaked, speckled, and gray-spotted; for I have seen all that Laban is doing to you. I *am* the God of Bethel, where you anointed the pillar *and* where you made a vow to Me. Now arise, get out of this land, and return to the land of your family.' "

Then Rachel and Leah answered and said to him, "Is there still any portion or inheritance for us in our father's house? Are we not considered strangers by him? For he has sold us, and also completely consumed our money. For all these riches which God has taken from our father are *really* ours and our children's; now then, whatever God has said to you, do it."

Then Jacob rose and set his sons and his wives on camels. And he carried away all his livestock and all his possessions which he had gained, his acquired livestock which he had gained in Padan Aram, to go to his father Isaac in the land of Canaan. Now Laban had gone to shear his sheep, and Rachel had stolen the household idols that were her father's. And Jacob stole away, unknown to Laban the Syrian, in that he did not tell him that he intended to flee. So he fled with all that he had. He arose and crossed the river, and headed toward the mountains of Gilead.

And Laban was told on the third day that Jacob had fled. Then he took his brethren with him and pursued him for seven days' journey, and he overtook him in the mountains of Gilead. But God had come to Laban the Syrian in a dream by night, and said to him, "Be careful that you speak to Jacob neither good nor bad."

So Laban overtook Jacob. Now Jacob had pitched his tent in the mountains, and Laban with his brethren pitched in the mountains of Gilead.

And Laban said to Jacob: "What have you done, that you have stolen away unknown to me, and carried away my daughters like captives *taken* with the sword? Why did you flee away secretly, and steal away from me, and not tell me; for I might have sent you away with joy and songs, with timbrel and harp? And you did not allow me to kiss my sons and my daughters. Now you have done foolishly in *so* doing. It is in my power to do you harm, but the God of your father spoke to me last night, saying, 'Be careful that you speak to Jacob neither good nor bad.' And now you have surely gone because you greatly long for your father's house, *but* why did you steal my gods?"

Then Jacob answered and said to Laban, "Because I was afraid, for I said, 'Perhaps you would take your daughters from me by force.' With whomever you find your gods, do not let him live. In the presence of our brethren, identify what I have of yours and take *it* with you." For Jacob did not know that Rachel had stolen them.

And Laban went into Jacob's tent, into Leah's tent, and into the two maids' tents, but he did not find *them*. Then he went out of Leah's tent and entered Rachel's tent. Now Rachel had taken the household idols, put them in the camel's saddle, and sat on them. And Laban searched all about the tent but did not find *them*. And she said to her father, "Let it not displease my lord that I cannot rise before you, for the manner of women *is* with me." And he searched but did not find the household idols.

Then Jacob was angry and rebuked Laban, and Jacob answered and said to Laban: "What *is* my trespass? What *is* my sin, that you have so hotly pursued me? Although you have searched all my things, what part of your household things have you found? Set *it* here before my brethren and your brethren, that they may judge between us both! These twenty years I *have been* with you; your ewes and your female goats have not miscarried their young, and I have not eaten the rams of your flock. That which was torn *by beasts* I did not bring to you; I bore the loss of it. You required it from my hand, *whether* stolen by day or stolen by night. *There* I was! In the day the drought consumed me, and the frost by night, and my sleep departed from my eyes. Thus I have been in your house twenty years; I served you fourteen years for your two daughters, and six years for your flock, and you have changed my wages ten times. Unless the God of my father, the God of Abraham and the Fear of Isaac, had been with me, surely now you would have sent me away empty-handed. God has seen my affliction and the labor of my hands, and rebuked *you* last night."

Then Jacob offered a sacrifice on the mountain, and called his brethren to eat bread. And they ate bread and stayed all night on the mountain. And early in the morning Laban arose, and kissed his sons and daughters and blessed them. Then Laban departed and returned to his place.

Genesis 31:1-42, 54-55

WORSHIP

I will praise *You*, O LORD, with my whole heart;
I will tell of all Your marvelous works.
I will be glad and rejoice in You;
I will sing praise to Your name, O Most High.

Psalm 9:1-2

WISDOM

Happy *is* the man *who* finds wisdom,
And the man *who* gains understanding;
For her proceeds *are* better than the profits of
   silver,
And her gain than fine gold.

Proverbs 3:13-14

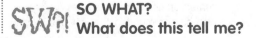

SO WHAT?
What does this tell me?

JACOB AND ESAU RECONCILED

Genesis 32:1-28; 33:1-20; Psalm 9:7-9; Proverbs 3:19-20

So Jacob went on his way, and the angels of God met him. When Jacob saw them, he said, "This *is* God's camp." And he called the name of that place Mahanaim.

Then Jacob sent messengers before him to Esau his brother in the land of Seir, the country of Edom. And he commanded them, saying, "Speak thus to my lord Esau, 'Thus your servant Jacob says: "I have dwelt with Laban and stayed there until now. I have oxen, donkeys, flocks, and male and female servants; and I have sent to tell my lord, that I may find favor in your sight." ' "

Then the messengers returned to Jacob, saying, "We came to your brother Esau, and he also is coming to meet you, and four hundred men *are* with him." So Jacob was greatly afraid and distressed; and he divided the people that *were* with him, and the flocks and herds and camels, into two companies. And he said, "If Esau comes to the one company and attacks it, then the other company which is left will escape."

Then Jacob said, "O God of my father Abraham and God of my father Isaac, the LORD who said to me, 'Return to your country and to your family, and I will deal well with you': I am not worthy of the least of all the mercies and of all the truth which You have shown Your servant; for I crossed over this Jordan with my staff, and now I have become two companies. Deliver me, I pray, from the hand of my brother, from the hand of Esau; for I fear him, lest he come and attack me *and* the mother with the children. For You said, 'I will surely treat you well, and make your descendants as the sand of the sea, which cannot be numbered for multitude.' "

So he lodged there that same night, and took what came to his hand as a present for Esau his brother: two hundred female goats and twenty male goats, two hundred ewes and twenty rams, thirty milk camels with their colts, forty cows and ten bulls, twenty female donkeys and ten foals. Then he delivered *them* to the hand of his servants, every drove by itself, and said to his servants, "Pass over before me, and put some distance between successive droves." And he commanded the first one, saying,

"When Esau my brother meets you and asks you, saying, 'To whom do you belong, and where are you going? Whose *are* these in front of you?' then you shall say, 'They *are* your servant Jacob's. It *is* a present sent to my lord Esau; and behold, he also *is* behind us.' " So he commanded the second, the third, and all who followed the droves, saying, "In this manner you shall speak to Esau when you find him; and also say, 'Behold, your servant Jacob *is* behind us.' " For he said, "I will appease him with the present that goes before me, and afterward I will see his face; perhaps he will accept me." So the present went on over before him, but he himself lodged that night in the camp.

And he arose that night and took his two wives, his two female servants, and his eleven sons, and crossed over the ford of Jabbok. He took them, sent them over the brook, and sent over what he had. Then Jacob was left alone; and a Man wrestled with him until the breaking of day. Now when He saw that He did not prevail against him, He touched the socket of his hip; and the socket of Jacob's hip was out of joint as He wrestled with him. And He said, "Let Me go, for the day breaks."

But he said, "I will not let You go unless You bless me!"

So He said to him, "What *is* your name?"

He said, "Jacob."

And He said, "Your name shall no longer be called Jacob, but Israel; for you have struggled with God and with men, and have prevailed."

Now Jacob lifted his eyes and looked, and there, Esau was coming, and with him were four hundred men. So he divided the children among Leah, Rachel, and the two maidservants. And he put the maidservants and their children in front, Leah and her children behind, and Rachel and Joseph last. Then he crossed over before them and bowed himself to the ground seven times, until he came near to his brother.

But Esau ran to meet him, and embraced him, and fell on his neck and kissed him, and they wept. And he lifted his eyes and saw the women and children, and said, "Who *are* these with you?"

So he said, "The children whom God has graciously given your servant." Then the maidservants came near, they and their children, and bowed down. And Leah also came near with her children, and they bowed down. Afterward Joseph and Rachel came near, and they bowed down.

Then Esau said, "What *do* you *mean by* all this company which I met?"

And he said, "*These are* to find favor in the sight of my lord."

But Esau said, "I have enough, my brother; keep what you have for yourself."

And Jacob said, "No, please, if I have now found favor in your sight, then receive my present from my hand, inasmuch as I have seen your face as though I had seen the face of God, and you were pleased with me. Please, take my blessing that is brought to you, because God has dealt graciously with me, and because I have enough." So he urged him, and he took *it*.

Then Esau said, "Let us take our journey; let us go, and I will go before you."

But Jacob said to him, "My lord knows that the children *are* weak, and the flocks and herds which are nursing *are* with me. And if the men should drive them hard one day, all the flock will die. Please let my lord go on ahead before his servant. I will lead on slowly at a pace which the livestock that go before me, and the children, are able to endure, until I come to my lord in Seir."

And Esau said, "Now let me leave with you *some* of the people who *are* with me."

But he said, "What need is there? Let me find favor in the sight of my lord." So Esau returned that day on his way to Seir. And Jacob journeyed to Succoth, built himself a house, and made booths for his livestock. Therefore the name of the place is called Succoth.

Then Jacob came safely to the city of Shechem, which *is* in the land of Canaan, when he came from Padan Aram; and he pitched his tent before the city. And he bought the parcel of land, where he had pitched his tent, from the children of Hamor, Shechem's father, for one hundred pieces of money. Then he erected an altar there and called it El Elohe Israel.

Genesis 32:1-28; 33:1-20

WORSHIP

But the LORD shall endure forever;
He has prepared His throne for judgment.
He shall judge the world in righteousness,
And He shall administer judgment for the
    peoples in uprightness.

The LORD also will be a refuge for the
    oppressed,
A refuge in times of trouble.

Psalm 9:7-9

WISDOM

The LORD by wisdom founded the earth;
By understanding He established the heavens;
By His knowledge the depths were broken up,
And clouds drop down the dew.

Proverbs 3:19-20

SW?! **SO WHAT?**
What does this tell me?

JACOB'S FAMILY TROUBLES

Genesis 34:1–35:7, 28-29; Psalm 9:11, 13-14; Proverbs 3:21-22

Now Dinah the daughter of Leah, whom she had borne to Jacob, went out to see the daughters of the land. And when Shechem the son of Hamor the Hivite, prince of the country, saw her, he took her and lay with her, and violated her. His soul was strongly attracted to Dinah the daughter of Jacob, and he loved the young woman and spoke kindly to the young woman. So Shechem spoke to his father Hamor, saying, "Get me this young woman as a wife."

And Jacob heard that he had defiled Dinah his daughter. Now his sons were with his livestock in the field; so Jacob held his peace until they came. Then Hamor the father of Shechem went out to Jacob to speak with him. And the sons of Jacob came in from the field when they heard *it;* and the men were grieved and very angry, because he had done a disgraceful thing in Israel by lying with Jacob's daughter, a thing which ought not to be done. But Hamor spoke with them, saying, "The soul of my son Shechem longs for your daughter. Please give her to him as a wife. And make marriages with us; give your daughters to us, and take our daughters to yourselves. So you shall dwell with us, and the land shall be before you. Dwell and trade in it, and acquire possessions for yourselves in it."

Then Shechem said to her father and her brothers, "Let me find favor in your eyes, and whatever you say to me I will give. Ask me ever so much dowry and gift, and I will give according to what you say to me; but give me the young woman as a wife."

But the sons of Jacob answered Shechem and Hamor his father, and spoke deceitfully, because he had defiled Dinah their sister. And they said to them, "We cannot do this thing, to give our sister to one who is uncircumcised, for that *would be* a reproach to us. But on this *condition* we will consent to you: If you will become as we *are,* if every male of you is circumcised, then we will give our daughters to you, and we will take your daughters to us; and we will dwell with you, and we will become one people. But if you will not heed us and be circumcised, then we will take our daughter and be gone."

And their words pleased Hamor and Shechem, Hamor's son. So the young man did not delay to do the thing, because he delighted in Jacob's daughter. He *was* more honorable than all the household of his father.

And Hamor and Shechem his son came to the gate of their city, and spoke with the men of their city, saying: "These men *are* at peace with us. Therefore let them dwell in the land and trade in it. For indeed the land *is* large enough for them. Let us take their daughters to us as wives, and let us give them our daughters. Only on this *condition* will the men consent to dwell with us, to be one people: if every male among us is circumcised as they *are* circumcised. *Will* not their livestock, their property, and every animal of theirs *be* ours? Only let us consent to them, and they will dwell with us." And all who went out of the gate of his city heeded Hamor and Shechem his son; every male was circumcised, all who went out of the gate of his city.

Now it came to pass on the third day, when they were in pain, that two of the sons of Jacob, Simeon and Levi, Dinah's brothers, each took his sword and came boldly upon the city and killed all the males. And they killed Hamor and Shechem his son with the edge of the sword, and took Dinah from Shechem's house, and went out. The sons of Jacob came upon the slain, and plundered the city, because their sister had been defiled. They took their sheep, their oxen, and their donkeys, what *was* in the city and what *was* in the field, and all their wealth. All their little ones and their wives they took captive; and they plundered even all that *was* in the houses.

Then Jacob said to Simeon and Levi, "You have troubled me by making me obnoxious among the inhabitants of the land, among the Canaanites and the Perizzites; and since I *am* few in number, they will gather themselves together against me and kill me. I shall be destroyed, my household and I."

But they said, "Should he treat our sister like a harlot?"

Then God said to Jacob, "Arise, go up to Bethel and dwell there; and make an altar there to God, who appeared to you when you fled from the face of Esau your brother."

And Jacob said to his household and to all

who *were* with him, "Put away the foreign gods that *are* among you, purify yourselves, and change your garments. Then let us arise and go up to Bethel; and I will make an altar there to God, who answered me in the day of my distress and has been with me in the way which I have gone." So they gave Jacob all the foreign gods which *were* in their hands, and the earrings which *were* in their ears; and Jacob hid them under the terebinth tree which *was* by Shechem.

And they journeyed, and the terror of God was upon the cities that *were* all around them, and they did not pursue the sons of Jacob. So Jacob came to Luz (that *is,* Bethel), which *is* in the land of Canaan, he and all the people who *were* with him. And he built an altar there and called the place El Bethel, because there God appeared to him when he fled from the face of his brother.

Now the days of Isaac were one hundred and eighty years. So Isaac breathed his last and died, and was gathered to his people, *being* old and full of days. And his sons Esau and Jacob buried him.

Genesis 34:1–35:7, 28-29

WORSHIP

Sing praises to the LORD, who dwells in Zion!
Declare His deeds among the people.

Have mercy on me, O LORD!
Consider my trouble from those who hate me,
You who lift me up from the gates of death,
That I may tell of all Your praise
In the gates of the daughter of Zion.
I will rejoice in Your salvation.

Psalm 9:11, 13-14

WISDOM

My son, let them not depart from your eyes—
Keep sound wisdom and discretion;
So they will be life to your soul
And grace to your neck.

Proverbs 3:21-22

SW?! **SO WHAT?**
What does this tell me?

Joseph SOLD into Slavery

Genesis 37; Psalm 10:3-4; Proverbs 3:25-26

Now Jacob dwelt in the land where his father was a stranger, in the land of Canaan. This *is* the history of Jacob.

Joseph, *being* seventeen years old, was feeding the flock with his brothers. And the lad *was* with the sons of Bilhah and the sons of Zilpah, his father's wives; and Joseph brought a bad report of them to his father.

Now Israel loved Joseph more than all his children, because he *was* the son of his old age. Also he made him a tunic of *many* colors. But when his brothers saw that their father loved him more than all his brothers, they hated him and could not speak peaceably to him.

Now Joseph had a dream, and he told *it* to his brothers; and they hated him even more. So he said to them, "Please hear this dream which I have dreamed: There we were, binding sheaves in the field. Then behold, my sheaf arose and also stood upright; and indeed your sheaves stood all around and bowed down to my sheaf."

And his brothers said to him, "Shall you indeed reign over us? Or shall you indeed have dominion over us?" So they hated him even more for his dreams and for his words.

Then he dreamed still another dream and told it to his brothers, and said, "Look, I have dreamed another dream. And this time, the sun, the moon, and the eleven stars bowed down to me."

So he told *it* to his father and his brothers; and his father rebuked him and said to him, "What *is* this dream that you have dreamed? Shall your mother and I and your brothers indeed come to bow down to the earth before you?" And his brothers envied him, but his father kept the matter *in mind.*

Then his brothers went to feed their father's flock in Shechem. And Israel said to Joseph, "Are not your brothers feeding *the flock* in Shechem? Come, I will send you to them."

So he said to him, "Here I am."

Then he said to him, "Please go and see if it is well with your brothers and well with the flocks, and bring back word to me." So he sent him out of the Valley of Hebron, and he went to Shechem.

Now a certain man found him, and there he was, wandering in the field. And the man asked him, saying, "What are you seeking?"

So he said, "I am seeking my brothers. Please tell me where they are feeding *their flocks.*"

And the man said, "They have departed from here, for I heard them say, 'Let us go to Dothan.' " So Joseph went after his brothers and found them in Dothan.

Now when they saw him afar off, even before he came near them, they conspired against him to kill him. Then they said to one another, "Look, this dreamer is coming! Come therefore, let us now kill him and cast him into some pit; and we shall say, 'Some wild beast has devoured him.' We shall see what will become of his dreams!"

But Reuben heard *it,* and he delivered him out of their hands, and said, "Let us not kill him." And Reuben said to them, "Shed no blood, *but* cast him into this pit which *is* in the wilderness, and do not lay a hand on him"—that he might deliver him out of their hands, and bring him back to his father.

So it came to pass, when Joseph had come to his brothers, that they stripped Joseph *of* his tunic, the tunic of *many* colors that *was* on him. Then they took him and cast him into a pit. And the pit *was* empty; *there was* no water in it.

And they sat down to eat a meal. Then they lifted their eyes and looked, and there was a company of Ishmaelites, coming from Gilead with their camels, bearing spices, balm, and myrrh, on their way to carry *them* down to Egypt. So Judah said to his brothers, "What profit *is there* if we kill our brother and conceal his blood? Come and let us sell him to the Ishmaelites, and let not our hand be upon him, for he *is* our brother *and* our flesh." And his brothers listened. Then Midianite traders passed by; so *the brothers* pulled Joseph up and lifted him out of the pit, and sold him to the Ishmaelites for twenty *shekels* of silver. And they took Joseph to Egypt.

Then Reuben returned to the pit, and indeed Joseph *was* not in the pit; and he tore his clothes. And he returned to his brothers and said, "The lad *is* no *more;* and I, where shall I go?"

So they took Joseph's tunic, killed a kid of the goats, and dipped the tunic in the blood. Then they

A NEW NATION

sent the tunic of *many* colors, and they brought *it* to their father and said, "We have found this. Do you know whether it *is* your son's tunic or not?"

And he recognized it and said, "*It is* my son's tunic. A wild beast has devoured him. Without doubt Joseph is torn to pieces." Then Jacob tore his clothes, put sackcloth on his waist, and mourned for his son many days. And all his sons and all his daughters arose to comfort him; but he refused to be comforted, and he said, "For I shall go down into the grave to my son in mourning." Thus his father wept for him.

Now the Midianites had sold him in Egypt to Potiphar, an officer of Pharaoh *and* captain of the guard.

Genesis 37

WORSHIP

For the wicked boasts of his heart's desire;
He blesses the greedy *and* renounces the
    LORD.
The wicked in his proud countenance does not
    seek *God;*
God *is* in none of his thoughts.

Psalm 10:3-4

WISDOM

Do not be afraid of sudden terror,
Nor of trouble from the wicked when it comes;
For the LORD will be your confidence,
And will keep your foot from being caught.

Proverbs 3:25-26

SW?! SO WHAT?
What does this tell me?

JOSEPH ACCUSED AND FORGOTTEN

Genesis 39–40; Psalm 10:12-14; Proverbs 3:27-28

Now Joseph had been taken down to Egypt. And Potiphar, an officer of Pharaoh, captain of the guard, an Egyptian, bought him from the Ishmaelites who had taken him down there. The LORD was with Joseph, and he was a successful man; and he was in the house of his master the Egyptian. And his master saw that the LORD *was* with him and that the LORD made all he did to prosper in his hand. So Joseph found favor in his sight, and served him. Then he made him overseer of his house, and all *that* he had he put under his authority. So it was, from the time *that* he had made him overseer of his house and all that he had, that the LORD blessed the Egyptian's house for Joseph's sake; and the blessing of the LORD was on all that he had in the house and in the field. Thus he left all that he had in Joseph's hand, and he did not know what he had except for the bread which he ate.

Now Joseph was handsome in form and appearance.

And it came to pass after these things that his master's wife cast longing eyes on Joseph, and she said, "Lie with me."

But he refused and said to his master's wife, "Look, my master does not know what *is* with me in the house, and he has committed all that he has to my hand. *There is* no one greater in this house than I, nor has he kept back anything from me but you, because you *are* his wife. How then can I do this great wickedness, and sin against God?"

So it was, as she spoke to Joseph day by day, that he did not heed her, to lie with her *or* to be with her.

But it happened about this time, when Joseph went into the house to do his work, and none of the men of the house *was* inside, that she caught him by his garment, saying, "Lie with me." But he left his garment in her hand, and fled and ran outside. And so it was, when she saw that he had left his garment in her hand and fled outside, that she called to the men of her house and spoke to them, saying, "See, he has brought in to us a Hebrew to mock us. He came in to me to lie with me, and I cried out with a loud voice. And it happened, when he heard that I lifted my voice and cried out, that he left his garment with me, and fled and went outside."

So she kept his garment with her until his master came home. Then she spoke to him with words like these, saying, "The Hebrew servant whom you brought to us came in to me to mock me; so it happened, as I lifted my voice and cried out, that he left his garment with me and fled outside."

So it was, when his master heard the words which his wife spoke to him, saying, "Your servant did to me after this manner," that his anger was aroused. Then Joseph's master took him and put him into the prison, a place where the king's prisoners *were* confined. And he was there in the prison. But the LORD was with Joseph and showed him mercy, and He gave him favor in the sight of the keeper of the prison. And the keeper of the prison committed to Joseph's hand all the prisoners who *were* in the prison; whatever they did there, it was his doing. The keeper of the prison did not look into anything *that was* under *Joseph's* authority, because the LORD was with him; and whatever he did, the LORD made *it* prosper.

It came to pass after these things *that* the butler and the baker of the king of Egypt offended their lord, the king of Egypt. And Pharaoh was angry with his two officers, the chief butler and the chief baker. So he put them in custody in the house of the captain of the guard, in the prison, the place where Joseph *was* confined. And the captain of the guard charged Joseph with them, and he served them; so they were in custody for a while.

Then the butler and the baker of the king of Egypt, who *were* confined in the prison, had a dream, both of them, each man's dream in one night *and* each man's dream with its *own* interpretation. And Joseph came in to them in the morning and looked at them, and saw that they *were* sad. So he asked Pharaoh's officers who *were* with him in the custody of his lord's house, saying, "Why do you look *so* sad today?"

And they said to him, "We each have had a dream, and *there is* no interpreter of it."

So Joseph said to them, "Do not interpretations belong to God? Tell *them* to me, please."

Then the chief butler told his dream to Joseph, and said to him, "Behold, in my dream a vine *was* before me, and in the vine *were* three branches; it *was* as though it budded, its blossoms shot forth, and its clusters brought forth ripe grapes. Then Pharaoh's cup *was* in my hand; and I took the grapes and pressed them into Pharaoh's cup, and placed the cup in Pharaoh's hand."

And Joseph said to him, "This *is* the interpretation of it: The three branches *are* three days. Now within three days Pharaoh will lift up your head and restore you to your place, and you will put Pharaoh's cup in his hand according to the former manner, when you were his butler. But remember me when it is well with you, and please show kindness to me; make mention of me to Pharaoh, and get me out of this house. For indeed I was stolen away from the land of the Hebrews; and also I have done nothing here that they should put me into the dungeon."

When the chief baker saw that the interpretation was good, he said to Joseph, "I also *was* in my dream, and there *were* three white baskets on my head. In the uppermost basket *were* all kinds of baked goods for Pharaoh, and the birds ate them out of the basket on my head."

So Joseph answered and said, "This *is* the interpretation of it: The three baskets *are* three days. Within three days Pharaoh will lift off your head from you and hang you on a tree; and the birds will eat your flesh from you."

Now it came to pass on the third day, *which was* Pharaoh's birthday, that he made a feast for all his servants; and he lifted up the head of the chief butler and of the chief baker among his servants. Then he restored the chief butler to his butlership again, and he placed the cup in Pharaoh's hand. But he hanged the chief baker, as Joseph had interpreted to them. Yet the chief butler did not remember Joseph, but forgot him.

Genesis 39–40

WoRsHiP

Arise, O Lᴏʀᴅ!
O God, lift up Your hand!
Do not forget the humble.
Why do the wicked renounce God?
He has said in his heart,
"You will not require *an account*."

But You have seen, for You observe trouble
    and grief,
To repay *it* by Your hand.
The helpless commits himself to You;
You are the helper of the fatherless.

Psalm 10:12-14

WiSdoM

Do not withhold good from those to whom it
    is due,
When it is in the power of your hand to do *so*.
Do not say to your neighbor,
"Go, and come back,
And tomorrow I will give *it*,"
When *you have* it with you.

Proverbs 3:27-28

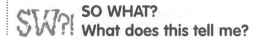

SO WHAT?
What does this tell me?

JOSEPH RISES TO POWER

Genesis 41:1–41, 45, 50–52; Psalm 10:16–18; Proverbs 3:29

Then it came to pass, at the end of two full years, that Pharaoh had a dream; and behold, he stood by the river. Suddenly there came up out of the river seven cows, fine looking and fat; and they fed in the meadow. Then behold, seven other cows came up after them out of the river, ugly and gaunt, and stood by the *other* cows on the bank of the river. And the ugly and gaunt cows ate up the seven fine looking and fat cows. So Pharaoh awoke. He slept and dreamed a second time; and suddenly seven heads of grain came up on one stalk, plump and good. Then behold, seven thin heads, blighted by the east wind, sprang up after them. And the seven thin heads devoured the seven plump and full heads. So Pharaoh awoke, and indeed, *it was* a dream. Now it came to pass in the morning that his spirit was troubled, and he sent and called for all the magicians of Egypt and all its wise men. And Pharaoh told them his dreams, but *there was* no one who could interpret them for Pharaoh.

Then the chief butler spoke to Pharaoh, saying: "I remember my faults this day. When Pharaoh was angry with his servants, and put me in custody in the house of the captain of the guard, *both* me and the chief baker, we each had a dream in one night, he and I. Each of us dreamed according to the interpretation of his *own* dream. Now there *was* a young Hebrew man with us there, a servant of the captain of the guard. And we told him, and he interpreted our dreams for us; to each man he interpreted according to his *own* dream. And it came to pass, just as he interpreted for us, so it happened. He restored me to my office, and he hanged him."

Then Pharaoh sent and called Joseph, and they brought him quickly out of the dungeon; and he shaved, changed his clothing, and came to Pharaoh. And Pharaoh said to Joseph, "I have had a dream, and *there is* no one who can interpret it. But I have heard it said of you *that* you can understand a dream, to interpret it."

So Joseph answered Pharaoh, saying, "*It is* not in me; God will give Pharaoh an answer of peace."

Then Pharaoh said to Joseph: "Behold, in my dream I stood on the bank of the river.

Suddenly seven cows came up out of the river, fine looking and fat; and they fed in the meadow. Then behold, seven other cows came up after them, poor and very ugly and gaunt, such ugliness as I have never seen in all the land of Egypt. And the gaunt and ugly cows ate up the first seven, the fat cows. When they had eaten them up, no one would have known that they had eaten them, for they *were* just as ugly as at the beginning. So I awoke. Also I saw in my dream, and suddenly seven heads came up on one stalk, full and good. Then behold, seven heads, withered, thin, *and* blighted by the east wind, sprang up after them. And the thin heads devoured the seven good heads. So I told *this* to the magicians, but *there was* no one who could explain *it* to me."

Then Joseph said to Pharaoh, "The dreams of Pharaoh *are* one; God has shown Pharaoh what He *is* about to do: The seven good cows *are* seven years, and the seven good heads *are* seven years; the dreams *are* one. And the seven thin and ugly cows which came up after them *are* seven years, and the seven empty heads blighted by the east wind are seven years of famine. This *is* the thing which I have spoken to Pharaoh. God has shown Pharaoh what He *is* about to do. Indeed seven years of great plenty will come throughout all the land of Egypt; but after them seven years of famine will arise, and all the plenty will be forgotten in the land of Egypt; and the famine will deplete the land. So the plenty will not be known in the land because of the famine following, for it *will be* very severe. And the dream was repeated to Pharaoh twice because the thing *is* established by God, and God will shortly bring it to pass.

"Now therefore, let Pharaoh select a discerning and wise man, and set him over the land of Egypt. Let Pharaoh do *this,* and let him appoint officers over the land, to collect one-fifth *of the produce* of the land of Egypt in the seven plentiful years. And let them gather all the food of those good years that are coming, and store up grain under the authority of Pharaoh, and let them keep food in the cities. Then that food shall be as a reserve for the land for the seven years of famine which shall be in the land of Egypt, that the land may not perish during the famine."

So the advice was good in the eyes of Pharaoh and in the eyes of all his servants. And Pharaoh said to his servants, "Can we find *such a one* as this, a man in whom *is* the Spirit of God?"

Then Pharaoh said to Joseph, "Inasmuch as God has shown you all this, *there is* no one as discerning and wise as you. You shall be over my house, and all my people shall be ruled according to your word; only in regard to the throne will I be greater than you." And Pharaoh said to Joseph, "See, I have set you over all the land of Egypt."

And Pharaoh called Joseph's name Zaphnath-Paaneah. And he gave him as a wife Asenath, the daughter of Poti-Pherah priest of On. So Joseph went out over *all* the land of Egypt.

And to Joseph were born two sons before the years of famine came, whom Asenath, the daughter of Poti-Pherah priest of On, bore to him. Joseph called the name of the firstborn Manasseh: "For God has made me forget all my toil and all my father's house." And the name of the second he called Ephraim: "For God has caused me to be fruitful in the land of my affliction."

Genesis 41:1-41, 45, 50-52

WORSHIP

The LORD *is* King forever and ever;
The nations have perished out of His land.
LORD, You have heard the desire of the humble;
You will prepare their heart;
You will cause Your ear to hear,
To do justice to the fatherless and the
    oppressed,
That the man of the earth may oppress no
    more.

Psalm 10:16-18

WISDOM

Do not devise evil against your neighbor,
For he dwells by you for safety's sake.

Proverbs 3:29

SW?! SO WHAT?
What does this tell me?

JOSEPH PROVIDES FOR HIS FAMILY

Genesis 42:1-30, 35-38; 43:1-14; Psalm 11:4-5, 7; Proverbs 3:30

When Jacob saw that there was grain in Egypt, Jacob said to his sons, "Why do you look at one another?" And he said, "Indeed I have heard that there is grain in Egypt; go down to that place and buy for us there, that we may live and not die."

So Joseph's ten brothers went down to buy grain in Egypt. But Jacob did not send Joseph's brother Benjamin with his brothers, for he said, "Lest some calamity befall him." And the sons of Israel went to buy *grain* among those who journeyed, for the famine was in the land of Canaan.

Now Joseph *was* governor over the land; and it was he who sold to all the people of the land. And Joseph's brothers came and bowed down before him with *their* faces to the earth. Joseph saw his brothers and recognized them, but he acted as a stranger to them and spoke roughly to them. Then he said to them, "Where do you come from?"

And they said, "From the land of Canaan to buy food."

So Joseph recognized his brothers, but they did not recognize him. Then Joseph remembered the dreams which he had dreamed about them, and said to them, "You *are* spies! You have come to see the nakedness of the land!"

And they said to him, "No, my lord, but your servants have come to buy food. We *are* all one man's sons; we *are* honest *men;* your servants are not spies."

But he said to them, "No, but you have come to see the nakedness of the land."

And they said, "Your servants *are* twelve brothers, the sons of one man in the land of Canaan; and in fact, the youngest *is* with our father today, and one *is* no more."

But Joseph said to them, "It *is* as I spoke to you, saying, 'You *are* spies!' In this *manner* you shall be tested: By the life of Pharaoh, you shall not leave this place unless your youngest brother comes here. Send one of you, and let him bring your brother; and you shall be kept in prison, that your words may be tested to see whether *there is* any truth in you; or else, by the life of Pharaoh, surely you *are* spies!" So he put them all together in prison three days.

Then Joseph said to them the third day, "Do this and live, *for* I fear God: If you *are* honest *men,* let one of your brothers be confined to your prison house; but you, go and carry grain for the famine of your houses. And bring your youngest brother to me; so your words will be verified, and you shall not die."

And they did so. Then they said to one another, "We *are* truly guilty concerning our brother, for we saw the anguish of his soul when he pleaded with us, and we would not hear; therefore this distress has come upon us."

And Reuben answered them, saying, "Did I not speak to you, saying, 'Do not sin against the boy'; and you would not listen? Therefore behold, his blood is now required of us." But they did not know that Joseph understood *them,* for he spoke to them through an interpreter. And he turned himself away from them and wept. Then he returned to them again, and talked with them. And he took Simeon from them and bound him before their eyes.

Then Joseph gave a command to fill their sacks with grain, to restore every man's money to his sack, and to give them provisions for the journey. Thus he did for them. So they loaded their donkeys with the grain and departed from there. But as one *of them* opened his sack to give his donkey feed at the encampment, he saw his money; and there it was, in the mouth of his sack. So he said to his brothers, "My money has been restored, and there it is, in my sack!" Then their hearts failed *them* and they were afraid, saying to one another, "What *is* this *that* God has done to us?"

Then they went to Jacob their father in the land of Canaan and told him all that had happened to them, saying: "The man *who is* lord of the land spoke roughly to us, and took us for spies of the country."

Then it happened as they emptied their sacks, that surprisingly each man's bundle of money *was* in his sack; and when they and their father saw the bundles of money, they were afraid. And Jacob their father said to them, "You have bereaved me: Joseph is no *more,* Simeon is no *more,* and you want to take Benjamin. All these things are against me."

Then Reuben spoke to his father, saying, "Kill my two sons if I do not bring him *back* to you; put him in my hands, and I will bring him back to you."

But he said, "My son shall not go down with you, for his brother is dead, and he is left alone. If any calamity should befall him along the way in which you go, then you would bring down my gray hair with sorrow to the grave."

Now the famine *was* severe in the land. And it came to pass, when they had eaten up the grain which they had brought from Egypt, that their father said to them, "Go back, buy us a little food."

But Judah spoke to him, saying, "The man solemnly warned us, saying, 'You shall not see my face unless your brother *is* with you.' If you send our brother with us, we will go down and buy you food. But if you will not send *him,* we will not go down; for the man said to us, 'You shall not see my face unless your brother *is* with you.' "

And Israel said, "Why did you deal *so* wrongfully with me *as* to tell the man whether you had still *another* brother?"

But they said, "The man asked us pointedly about ourselves and our family, saying, '*Is* your father still alive? Have you *another* brother?' And we told him according to these words. Could we possibly have known that he would say, 'Bring your brother down'?"

Then Judah said to Israel his father, "Send the lad with me, and we will arise and go, that we may live and not die, both we and you *and* also our little ones. I myself will be surety for him; from my hand you shall require him. If I do not bring him *back* to you and set him before you, then let me bear the blame forever. For if we had not lingered, surely by now we would have returned this second time."

And their father Israel said to them, "If *it must be* so, then do this: Take some of the best fruits of the land in your vessels and carry down a present for the man—a little balm and a little honey, spices and myrrh, pistachio nuts and almonds. Take double money in your hand, and take back in your hand the money that was returned in the mouth of your sacks; perhaps it was an oversight. Take your brother also, and arise, go back to the man. And may God Almighty give you mercy before the man, that he may release your other brother and Benjamin. If I am bereaved, I am bereaved!"

Genesis 42:1-30, 35-38; 43:1-14

WORSHIP

The LORD *is* in His holy temple,
The LORD's throne *is* in heaven;
His eyes behold,
His eyelids test the sons of men.
The LORD tests the righteous,
But the wicked and the one who loves violence
His soul hates.

For the LORD *is* righteous,
He loves righteousness;
His countenance beholds the upright.

Psalm 11:4-5, 7

WISDOM

Do not strive with a man without cause,
If he has done you no harm.

Proverbs 3:30

SO WHAT?
What does this tell me?

JOSEPH REVEALS HIS IDENTITY

Genesis 43:15-34; 45:1-28; Psalm 12:6-8; Proverbs 3:31-32

So the men took that present and Benjamin, and they took double money in their hand, and arose and went down to Egypt; and they stood before Joseph. When Joseph saw Benjamin with them, he said to the steward of his house, "Take *these* men to my home, and slaughter an animal and make ready; for *these* men will dine with me at noon." Then the man did as Joseph ordered, and the man brought the men into Joseph's house.

Now the men were afraid because they were brought into Joseph's house; and they said, "*It is* because of the money, which was returned in our sacks the first time, that we are brought in, so that he may make a case against us and seize us, to take us as slaves with our donkeys."

When they drew near to the steward of Joseph's house, they talked with him at the door of the house, and said, "O sir, we indeed came down the first time to buy food; but it happened, when we came to the encampment, that we opened our sacks, and there, *each* man's money *was* in the mouth of his sack, our money in full weight; so we have brought it back in our hand. And we have brought down other money in our hands to buy food. We do not know who put our money in our sacks."

But he said, "Peace *be* with you, do not be afraid. Your God and the God of your father has given you treasure in your sacks; I had your money." Then he brought Simeon out to them.

So the man brought the men into Joseph's house and gave *them* water, and they washed their feet; and he gave their donkeys feed. Then they made the present ready for Joseph's coming at noon, for they heard that they would eat bread there.

And when Joseph came home, they brought him the present which *was* in their hand into the house, and bowed down before him to the earth. Then he asked them about *their* well-being, and said, "*Is* your father well, the old man of whom you spoke? *Is* he still alive?"

And they answered, "Your servant our father *is* in good health; he *is* still alive." And they bowed their heads down and prostrated themselves.

Then he lifted his eyes and saw his brother Benjamin, his mother's son, and said, "*Is* this your younger brother of whom you spoke to me?" And he said, "God be gracious to you, my son." Now his heart yearned for his brother; so Joseph made haste and sought *somewhere* to weep. And he went into *his* chamber and wept there. Then he washed his face and came out; and he restrained himself, and said, "Serve the bread."

So they set him a place by himself, and them by themselves, and the Egyptians who ate with him by themselves; because the Egyptians could not eat food with the Hebrews, for that *is* an abomination to the Egyptians. And they sat before him, the firstborn according to his birthright and the youngest according to his youth; and the men looked in astonishment at one another. Then he took servings to them from before him, but Benjamin's serving was five times as much as any of theirs. So they drank and were merry with him.

Then Joseph could not restrain himself before all those who stood by him, and he cried out, "Make everyone go out from me!" So no one stood with him while Joseph made himself known to his brothers. And he wept aloud, and the Egyptians and the house of Pharaoh heard *it*.

Then Joseph said to his brothers, "I *am* Joseph; does my father still live?" But his brothers could not answer him, for they were dismayed in his presence. And Joseph said to his brothers, "Please come near to me." So they came near. Then he said: "I *am* Joseph your brother, whom you sold into Egypt. But now, do not therefore be grieved or angry with yourselves because you sold me here; for God sent me before you to preserve life. For these two years the famine *has been* in the land, and *there are* still five years in which *there will be* neither plowing nor harvesting. And God sent me before you to preserve a posterity for you in the earth, and to save your lives by a great deliverance. So now *it was* not you *who* sent me here, but God; and He has made me a father to Pharaoh, and lord of all his house, and a ruler throughout all the land of Egypt.

"Hurry and go up to my father, and say to him,

'Thus says your son Joseph: "God has made me lord of all Egypt; come down to me, do not tarry. You shall dwell in the land of Goshen, and you shall be near to me, you and your children, your children's children, your flocks and your herds, and all that you have. There I will provide for you, lest you and your household, and all that you have, come to poverty; for *there are* still five years of famine." '

"And behold, your eyes and the eyes of my brother Benjamin see that *it is* my mouth that speaks to you. So you shall tell my father of all my glory in Egypt, and of all that you have seen; and you shall hurry and bring my father down here."

Then he fell on his brother Benjamin's neck and wept, and Benjamin wept on his neck. Moreover he kissed all his brothers and wept over them, and after that his brothers talked with him.

Now the report of it was heard in Pharaoh's house, saying, "Joseph's brothers have come." So it pleased Pharaoh and his servants well. And Pharaoh said to Joseph, "Say to your brothers, 'Do this: Load your animals and depart; go to the land of Canaan. Bring your father and your households and come to me; I will give you the best of the land of Egypt, and you will eat the fat of the land. Now you are commanded—do this: Take carts out of the land of Egypt for your little ones and your wives; bring your father and come. Also do not be concerned about your goods, for the best of all the land of Egypt *is* yours.' "

Then the sons of Israel did so; and Joseph gave them carts, according to the command of Pharaoh, and he gave them provisions for the journey. He gave to all of them, to each man, changes of garments; but to Benjamin he gave three hundred *pieces* of silver and five changes of garments. And he sent to his father these *things:* ten donkeys loaded with the good things of Egypt, and ten female donkeys loaded with grain, bread, and food for his father for the journey. So he sent his brothers away, and they departed; and he said to them, "See that you do not become troubled along the way."

Then they went up out of Egypt, and came to the land of Canaan to Jacob their father. And they told him, saying, "Joseph *is* still alive, and he *is* governor over all the land of Egypt." And Jacob's heart stood still, because he did not believe them. But when they told him all the words which Joseph had said to them, and when he saw the carts which Joseph had sent to carry him, the spirit of Jacob

their father revived. Then Israel said, "*It is* enough. Joseph my son *is* still alive. I will go and see him before I die."

Genesis 43:15-34; 45:1-28

WORSHIP

The words of the LORD *are* pure words,
Like silver tried in a furnace of earth,
Purified seven times.
You shall keep them, O LORD,
You shall preserve them from this generation
    forever.

The wicked prowl on every side,
When vileness is exalted among the sons of
    men.

Psalm 12:6-8

WISDOM

Do not envy the oppressor,
And choose none of his ways;
For the perverse *person is* an abomination to
    the LORD,
But His secret counsel *is* with the upright.

Proverbs 3:31-32

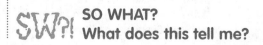

SO WHAT?
What does this tell me?

JACOB JOURNEYS TO EGYPT

Genesis 46:1–47:12; Psalm 13:1, 5-6; Proverbs 3:33

So Israel took his journey with all that he had, and came to Beersheba, and offered sacrifices to the God of his father Isaac. Then God spoke to Israel in the visions of the night, and said, "Jacob, Jacob!"

And he said, "Here I am."

So He said, "I *am* God, the God of your father; do not fear to go down to Egypt, for I will make of you a great nation there. I will go down with you to Egypt, and I will also surely bring you up *again;* and Joseph will put his hand on your eyes."

Then Jacob arose from Beersheba; and the sons of Israel carried their father Jacob, their little ones, and their wives, in the carts which Pharaoh had sent to carry him. So they took their livestock and their goods, which they had acquired in the land of Canaan, and went to Egypt, Jacob and all his descendants with him. His sons and his sons' sons, his daughters and his sons' daughters, and all his descendants he brought with him to Egypt.

Now these *were* the names of the children of Israel, Jacob and his sons, who went to Egypt: Reuben *was* Jacob's firstborn. The sons of Reuben *were* Hanoch, Pallu, Hezron, and Carmi. The sons of Simeon *were* Jemuel, Jamin, Ohad, Jachin, Zohar, and Shaul, the son of a Canaanite woman. The sons of Levi *were* Gershon, Kohath, and Merari. The sons of Judah *were* Er, Onan, Shelah, Perez, and Zerah (but Er and Onan died in the land of Canaan). The sons of Perez were Hezron and Hamul. The sons of Issachar *were* Tola, Puvah, Job, and Shimron. The sons of Zebulun *were* Sered, Elon, and Jahleel. These *were* the sons of Leah, whom she bore to Jacob in Padan Aram, with his daughter Dinah. All the persons, his sons and his daughters, *were* thirty-three.

The sons of Gad *were* Ziphion, Haggi, Shuni, Ezbon, Eri, Arodi, and Areli. The sons of Asher *were* Jimnah, Ishuah, Isui, Beriah, and Serah, their sister. And the sons of Beriah *were* Heber and Malchiel. These *were* the sons of Zilpah, whom Laban gave to Leah his daughter; and these she bore to Jacob: sixteen persons.

The sons of Rachel, Jacob's wife, *were* Joseph and Benjamin. And to Joseph in the land of Egypt were born Manasseh and Ephraim, whom Asenath, the daughter of Poti-Pherah priest of On, bore to him. The sons of Benjamin *were* Belah, Becher, Ashbel, Gera, Naaman, Ehi, Rosh, Muppim, Huppim, and Ard. These *were* the sons of Rachel, who were born to Jacob: fourteen persons in all.

The son of Dan *was* Hushim. The sons of Naphtali *were* Jahzeel, Guni, Jezer, and Shillem. These *were* the sons of Bilhah, whom Laban gave to Rachel his daughter, and she bore these to Jacob: seven persons in all.

All the persons who went with Jacob to Egypt, who came from his body, besides Jacob's sons' wives, *were* sixty-six persons in all. And the sons of Joseph who were born to him in Egypt *were* two persons. All the persons of the house of Jacob who went to Egypt were seventy.

Then he sent Judah before him to Joseph, to point out before him *the way* to Goshen. And they came to the land of Goshen. So Joseph made ready his chariot and went up to Goshen to meet his father Israel; and he presented himself to him, and fell on his neck and wept on his neck a good while.

And Israel said to Joseph, "Now let me die, since I have seen your face, because you *are* still alive."

Then Joseph said to his brothers and to his father's household, "I will go up and tell Pharaoh, and say to him, 'My brothers and those of my father's house, who *were* in the land of Canaan, have come to me. And the men *are* shepherds, for their occupation has been to feed livestock; and they have brought their flocks, their herds, and all that they have.' So it shall be, when Pharaoh calls you and says, 'What is your occupation?' that you shall say, 'Your servants' occupation has been with livestock from our youth even till now, both we *and* also our fathers,' that you may dwell in the land of Goshen; for every shepherd *is* an abomination to the Egyptians."

Then Joseph went and told Pharaoh, and said, "My father and my brothers, their flocks and their herds and all that they possess, have come from the land of Canaan; and indeed they *are* in the land of Goshen." And he took five men from among his brothers and presented them to Pharaoh. Then

Pharaoh said to his brothers, "What *is* your occupation?"

And they said to Pharaoh, "Your servants *are* shepherds, both we *and* also our fathers." And they said to Pharaoh, "We have come to dwell in the land, because your servants have no pasture for their flocks, for the famine *is* severe in the land of Canaan. Now therefore, please let your servants dwell in the land of Goshen."

Then Pharaoh spoke to Joseph, saying, "Your father and your brothers have come to you. The land of Egypt *is* before you. Have your father and brothers dwell in the best of the land; let them dwell in the land of Goshen. And if you know *any* competent men among them, then make them chief herdsmen over my livestock."

Then Joseph brought in his father Jacob and set him before Pharaoh; and Jacob blessed Pharaoh. Pharaoh said to Jacob, "How old *are* you?"

And Jacob said to Pharaoh, "The days of the years of my pilgrimage *are* one hundred and thirty years; few and evil have been the days of the years of my life, and they have not attained to the days of the years of the life of my fathers in the days of their pilgrimage." So Jacob blessed Pharaoh, and went out from before Pharaoh.

And Joseph situated his father and his brothers, and gave them a possession in the land of Egypt, in the best of the land, in the land of Rameses, as Pharaoh had commanded. Then Joseph provided his father, his brothers, and all his father's household with bread, according to the number in *their* families.

Genesis 46:1–47:12

WORSHIP

How long, O LORD? Will You forget me forever?
How long will You hide Your face from me?

But I have trusted in Your mercy;
My heart shall rejoice in Your salvation.
I will sing to the LORD,
Because He has dealt bountifully with me.

Psalm 13:1, 5-6

WISDOM

The curse of the LORD *is* on the house of the
    wicked,
But He blesses the home of the just.

Proverbs 3:33

SW?! SO WHAT?
What does this tell me?

THE DEATHS OF JACOB AND JOSEPH

Genesis 49:1-33; 50:15-26; Psalm 14:1-3; Proverbs 3:35

And Jacob called his sons and said, "Gather together, that I may tell you what shall befall you in the last days:

"Gather together and hear, you sons of Jacob,
And listen to Israel your father.

"Reuben, you are my firstborn,
My might and the beginning of my strength,
The excellency of dignity and the excellency of power.
Unstable as water, you shall not excel,
Because you went up to your father's bed;
Then you defiled *it*—
He went up to my couch.

"Simeon and Levi *are* brothers;
Instruments of cruelty *are in* their dwelling place.
Let not my soul enter their council;
Let not my honor be united to their assembly;
For in their anger they slew a man,
And in their self-will they hamstrung an ox.
Cursed *be* their anger, for *it is* fierce;
And their wrath, for it is cruel!
I will divide them in Jacob
And scatter them in Israel.

"Judah, you *are he* whom your brothers shall praise;
Your hand *shall be* on the neck of your enemies;
Your father's children shall bow down before you.
Judah *is* a lion's whelp;
From the prey, my son, you have gone up.
He bows down, he lies down as a lion;
And as a lion, who shall rouse him?
The scepter shall not depart from Judah,
Nor a lawgiver from between his feet,
Until Shiloh comes;
And to Him *shall be* the obedience of the people.
Binding his donkey to the vine,
And his donkey's colt to the choice vine,
He washed his garments in wine,
And his clothes in the blood of grapes.
His eyes *are* darker than wine,
And his teeth whiter than milk.

"Zebulun shall dwell by the haven of the sea;
He *shall become* a haven for ships,
And his border shall adjoin Sidon.

"Issachar is a strong donkey,
Lying down between two burdens;
He saw that rest *was* good,
And that the land *was* pleasant;
He bowed his shoulder to bear *a burden,*
And became a band of slaves.

"Dan shall judge his people
As one of the tribes of Israel.
Dan shall be a serpent by the way,
A viper by the path,
That bites the horse's heels
So that its rider shall fall backward.
I have waited for your salvation, O LORD!

"Gad, a troop shall tramp upon him,
But he shall triumph at last.

"Bread from Asher *shall be* rich,
And he shall yield royal dainties.

"Naphtali *is* a deer let loose;
He uses beautiful words.

"Joseph *is* a fruitful bough,
A fruitful bough by a well;
His branches run over the wall.
The archers have bitterly grieved him,
Shot *at him* and hated him.
But his bow remained in strength,
And the arms of his hands were made strong
By the hands of the Mighty *God* of Jacob
(From there *is* the Shepherd, the Stone of Israel),
By the God of your father who will help you,
And by the Almighty who will bless you
With blessings of heaven above,
Blessings of the deep that lies beneath,
Blessings of the breasts and of the womb.
The blessings of your father
Have excelled the blessings of my ancestors,
Up to the utmost bound of the everlasting hills.
They shall be on the head of Joseph,
And on the crown of the head of him who was separate from his brothers.

"Benjamin is a ravenous wolf;
In the morning he shall devour the prey,
And at night he shall divide the spoil."

All these *are* the twelve tribes of Israel, and this *is* what their father spoke to them. And he blessed them; he blessed each one according to his own blessing.

Then he charged them and said to them: "I am to be gathered to my people; bury me with my fathers in the cave that *is* in the field of Ephron the Hittite, in the cave that *is* in the field of Machpelah, which *is* before Mamre in the land of Canaan, which Abraham bought with the field of Ephron the Hittite as a possession for a burial place. There they buried Abraham and Sarah his wife, there they buried Isaac and Rebekah his wife, and there I buried Leah. The field and the cave that *is* there *were* purchased from the sons of Heth." And when Jacob had finished commanding his sons, he drew his feet up into the bed and breathed his last, and was gathered to his people.

When Joseph's brothers saw that their father was dead, they said, "Perhaps Joseph will hate us, and may actually repay us for all the evil which we did to him." So they sent *messengers* to Joseph, saying, "Before your father died he commanded, saying, 'Thus you shall say to Joseph: "I beg you, please forgive the trespass of your brothers and their sin; for they did evil to you." ' Now, please, forgive the trespass of the servants of the God of your father." And Joseph wept when they spoke to him.

Then his brothers also went and fell down before his face, and they said, "Behold, we *are* your servants."

Joseph said to them, "Do not be afraid, for *am* I in the place of God? But as for you, you meant evil against me; *but* God meant it for good, in order to bring it about as *it is* this day, to save many people alive. Now therefore, do not be afraid; I will provide for you and your little ones." And he comforted them and spoke kindly to them.

So Joseph dwelt in Egypt, he and his father's household. And Joseph lived one hundred and ten years. Joseph saw Ephraim's children to the third *generation*. The children of Machir, the son of Manasseh, were also brought up on Joseph's knees.

And Joseph said to his brethren, "I am dying; but God will surely visit you, and bring you out of this land to the land of which He swore to Abraham, to Isaac, and to Jacob." Then Joseph took an oath from the children of Israel, saying, "God will surely visit you, and you shall carry up my bones from here." So Joseph died, *being* one hundred and ten years old; and they embalmed him, and he was put in a coffin in Egypt.

Genesis 49:1-33; 50:15-26

WORSHIP

The fool has said in his heart,
"*There is* no God."
They are corrupt,
They have done abominable works,
There is none who does good.

The LORD looks down from heaven upon the children of men,
To see if there are any who understand, who seek God.
They have all turned aside,
They have together become corrupt;
There is none who does good,
No, not one.

Psalm 14:1-3

WISDOM

The wise shall inherit glory,
But shame shall be the legacy of fools.

Proverbs 3:35

 **SO WHAT?**
What does this tell me?

THE STORY OF JOB

Job 1–2; Psalm 15:1-2, 5; Proverbs 4:7

There was a man in the land of Uz, whose name *was* Job; and that man was blameless and upright, and one who feared God and shunned evil. And seven sons and three daughters were born to him. Also, his possessions were seven thousand sheep, three thousand camels, five hundred yoke of oxen, five hundred female donkeys, and a very large household, so that this man was the greatest of all the people of the East.

And his sons would go and feast *in their* houses, each on his *appointed* day, and would send and invite their three sisters to eat and drink with them. So it was, when the days of feasting had run their course, that Job would send and sanctify them, and he would rise early in the morning and offer burnt offerings *according to* the number of them all. For Job said, "It may be that my sons have sinned and cursed God in their hearts." Thus Job did regularly.

Now there was a day when the sons of God came to present themselves before the LORD, and Satan also came among them. And the LORD said to Satan, "From where do you come?"

So Satan answered the LORD and said, "From going to and fro on the earth, and from walking back and forth on it."

Then the LORD said to Satan, "Have you considered My servant Job, that *there is* none like him on the earth, a blameless and upright man, one who fears God and shuns evil?"

So Satan answered the LORD and said, "Does Job fear God for nothing? Have You not made a hedge around him, around his household, and around all that he has on every side? You have blessed the work of his hands, and his possessions have increased in the land. But now, stretch out Your hand and touch all that he has, and he will surely curse You to Your face!"

And the LORD said to Satan, "Behold, all that he has *is* in your power; only do not lay a hand on his *person.*"

So Satan went out from the presence of the LORD.

Now there was a day when his sons and daughters *were* eating and drinking wine in their oldest brother's house; and a messenger came to Job and said, "The oxen were plowing and the donkeys feeding beside them, when the Sabeans raided *them* and took them away—indeed they have killed the servants with the edge of the sword; and I alone have escaped to tell you!"

While he *was* still speaking, another also came and said, "The fire of God fell from heaven and burned up the sheep and the servants, and consumed them; and I alone have escaped to tell you!"

While he *was* still speaking, another also came and said, "The Chaldeans formed three bands, raided the camels and took them away, yes, and killed the servants with the edge of the sword; and I alone have escaped to tell you!"

While he *was* still speaking, another also came and said, "Your sons and daughters *were* eating and drinking wine in their oldest brother's house, and suddenly a great wind came from across the wilderness and struck the four corners of the house, and it fell on the young people, and they are dead; and I alone have escaped to tell you!"

Then Job arose, tore his robe, and shaved his head; and he fell to the ground and worshiped. And he said:

> "Naked I came from my mother's womb,
> And naked shall I return there.
> The LORD gave, and the LORD has taken away;
> Blessed be the name of the LORD."

In all this Job did not sin nor charge God with wrong.

Again there was a day when the sons of God came to present themselves before the LORD, and Satan came also among them to present himself before the LORD. And the LORD said to Satan, "From where do you come?"

Satan answered the LORD and said, "From going to and fro on the earth, and from walking back and forth on it."

Then the LORD said to Satan, "Have you considered My servant Job, that *there is* none like him on the earth, a blameless and upright man, one who fears God and shuns evil? And still he holds fast to his integrity, although you incited Me against him, to destroy him without cause."

A NEW NATION

So Satan answered the Lord and said, "Skin for skin! Yes, all that a man has he will give for his life. But stretch out Your hand now, and touch his bone and his flesh, and he will surely curse You to Your face!"

And the Lord said to Satan, "Behold, he *is* in your hand, but spare his life."

So Satan went out from the presence of the Lord, and struck Job with painful boils from the sole of his foot to the crown of his head. And he took for himself a potsherd with which to scrape himself while he sat in the midst of the ashes.

Then his wife said to him, "Do you still hold fast to your integrity? Curse God and die!"

But he said to her, "You speak as one of the foolish women speaks. Shall we indeed accept good from God, and shall we not accept adversity?" In all this Job did not sin with his lips.

Now when Job's three friends heard of all this adversity that had come upon him, each one came from his own place—Eliphaz the Temanite, Bildad the Shuhite, and Zophar the Naamathite. For they had made an appointment together to come and mourn with him, and to comfort him. And when they raised their eyes from afar, and did not recognize him, they lifted their voices and wept; and each one tore his robe and sprinkled dust on his head toward heaven. So they sat down with him on the ground seven days and seven nights, and no one spoke a word to him, for they saw that *his* grief was very great.

Job 1–2

WORSHIP

Lord, who may abide in Your tabernacle?
Who may dwell in Your holy hill?

He who walks uprightly,
 And works righteousness,
 And speaks the truth in his heart;

He *who* does not put out his money at usury,
 Nor does he take a bribe against the
 innocent.

He who does these *things* shall never be
 moved.

Psalm 15:1-2, 5

WISDOM

Wisdom *is* the principal thing;
Therefore get wisdom.
And in all your getting, get understanding.

Proverbs 4:7

SW?! SO WHAT?
What does this tell me?

JOB AND HIS FRIEND ELIPHAZ

Job 3:1-11, 20-26; 4:1–5:8, 17; Psalm 16:5-6; Proverbs 4:10-12

After this Job opened his mouth and cursed the day of his *birth.* And Job spoke, and said:

"May the day perish on which I was born,
And the night *in which* it was said,
'A male child is conceived.'
May that day be darkness;
May God above not seek it,
Nor the light shine upon it.
May darkness and the shadow of death claim it;
May a cloud settle on it;
May the blackness of the day terrify it.
As for that night, may darkness seize it;
May it not rejoice among the days of the year,
May it not come into the number of the months.
Oh, may that night be barren!
May no joyful shout come into it!
May those curse it who curse the day,
Those who are ready to arouse Leviathan.
May the stars of its morning be dark;
May it look for light, but *have* none,
And not see the dawning of the day;
Because it did not shut up the doors of my
        mother's womb,
Nor hide sorrow from my eyes.

"Why did I not die at birth?
Why did I *not* perish when I came from the womb?

"Why is light given to him who is in misery,
And life to the bitter of soul,
Who long for death, but it does not *come,*
And search for it more than hidden treasures;
Who rejoice exceedingly,
And are glad when they can find the grave?
Why is light given to a man whose way is hidden,
And whom God has hedged in?
For my sighing comes before I eat,
And my groanings pour out like water.
For the thing I greatly feared has come upon me,
And what I dreaded has happened to me.
I am not at ease, nor am I quiet;
I have no rest, for trouble comes."

        Then Eliphaz the Temanite answered and said:

"*If* one attempts a word with you, will you
        become weary?
But who can withhold himself from speaking?
Surely you have instructed many,
And you have strengthened weak hands.
Your words have upheld him who was
        stumbling,
And you have strengthened the feeble knees;
But now it comes upon you, and you are
        weary;
It touches you, and you are troubled.
Is not your reverence your confidence?
And the integrity of your ways your hope?

"Remember now, who *ever* perished being
        innocent?
Or where were the upright *ever* cut off?
Even as I have seen,
Those who plow iniquity
And sow trouble reap the same.
By the blast of God they perish,
And by the breath of His anger they are
        consumed.
The roaring of the lion,
The voice of the fierce lion,
And the teeth of the young lions are broken.
The old lion perishes for lack of prey,
And the cubs of the lioness are scattered.

"Now a word was secretly brought to me,
And my ear received a whisper of it.
In disquieting thoughts from the visions of the
        night,
When deep sleep falls on men,
Fear came upon me, and trembling,
Which made all my bones shake.
Then a spirit passed before my face;
The hair on my body stood up.
It stood still,
But I could not discern its appearance.
A form *was* before my eyes;
There was silence;
Then I heard a voice *saying:*
'Can a mortal be more righteous than God?
Can a man be more pure than his Maker?
If He puts no trust in His servants,
If He charges His angels with error,
How much more those who dwell in houses of
        clay,
Whose foundation is in the dust,

A NEW NATION

Who are crushed before a moth?
They are broken in pieces from morning till
        evening;
They perish forever, with no one regarding.
Does not their own excellence go away?
They die, even without wisdom.'

"Call out now;
  Is there anyone who will answer you?
  And to which of the holy ones will you turn?
  For wrath kills a foolish man,
  And envy slays a simple one.
  I have seen the foolish taking root,
  But suddenly I cursed his dwelling place.
  His sons are far from safety,
  They are crushed in the gate,
  And *there is* no deliverer.
  Because the hungry eat up his harvest,
  Taking it even from the thorns,
  And a snare snatches their substance.
  For affliction does not come from the dust,
  Nor does trouble spring from the ground;
  Yet man is born to trouble,
  As the sparks fly upward.

"But as for me, I would seek God,
  And to God I would commit my cause—

"Behold, happy *is* the man whom God corrects;
  Therefore do not despise the chastening of the
        Almighty."

Job 3:1-11, 20-26; 4:1–5:8, 17

WORSHIP

O Lord, *You are* the portion of my inheritance
      and my cup;
You maintain my lot.
The lines have fallen to me in pleasant *places;*
Yes, I have a good inheritance.

Psalm 16:5-6

WISDOM

Hear, my son, and receive my sayings,
And the years of your life will be many.
I have taught you in the way of wisdom;
I have led you in right paths.
When you walk, your steps will not be
      hindered,
And when you run, you will not stumble.

Proverbs 4:10-12

SW?! **SO WHAT?**
What does this tell me?

JOB AND HIS FRIEND BILDAD

Job 8:1–9:12, 20–33; Psalm 16:10–11; Proverbs 4:13

Then Bildad the Shuhite answered and said:

"How long will you speak these *things,*
   And the words of your mouth *be like* a strong
      wind?
Does God subvert judgment?
Or does the Almighty pervert justice?
If your sons have sinned against Him,
He has cast them away for their transgression.
If you would earnestly seek God
And make your supplication to the Almighty,
If you *were* pure and upright,
Surely now He would awake for you,
And prosper your rightful dwelling place.
Though your beginning was small,
Yet your latter end would increase abundantly.

"For inquire, please, of the former age,
   And consider the things discovered by their
      fathers;
For we *were born* yesterday, and know
      nothing,
Because our days on earth *are* a shadow.
Will they not teach you and tell you,
And utter words from their heart?

"Can the papyrus grow up without a marsh?
   Can the reeds flourish without water?
While it *is* yet green *and* not cut down,
It withers before any *other* plant.
So *are* the paths of all who forget God;
   And the hope of the hypocrite shall perish,
   Whose confidence shall be cut off,
   And whose trust *is* a spider's web.
He leans on his house, but it does not stand.
He holds it fast, but it does not endure.
He grows green in the sun,
And his branches spread out in his garden.
His roots wrap around the rock heap,
And look for a place in the stones.
If he is destroyed from his place,
Then *it* will deny him, *saying,* 'I have not
     seen you.'

"Behold, this is the joy of His way,
   And out of the earth others will grow.
Behold, God will not cast away the
     blameless,
Nor will He uphold the evildoers.
He will yet fill your mouth with laughing,
And your lips with rejoicing.

Those who hate you will be clothed with
     shame,
And the dwelling place of the wicked will come
     to nothing."

Then Job answered and said:

"Truly I know *it is* so,
   But how can a man be righteous before God?
If one wished to contend with Him,
He could not answer Him one time out of a
     thousand.
God *is* wise in heart and mighty in strength.
Who has hardened *himself* against Him and
     prospered?
He removes the mountains, and they do not
     know
When He overturns them in His anger;
He shakes the earth out of its place,
And its pillars tremble;
He commands the sun, and it does not rise;
He seals off the stars;
He alone spreads out the heavens,
And treads on the waves of the sea;
He made the Bear, Orion, and the Pleiades,
And the chambers of the south;
He does great things past finding out,
Yes, wonders without number.
If He goes by me, I do not see *Him;*
If He moves past, I do not perceive Him;
If He takes away, who can hinder Him?
Who can say to Him, 'What are You doing?'

"Though I were righteous, my own mouth
     would condemn me;
Though I *were* blameless, it would prove me
     perverse.

"I am blameless, yet I do not know myself;
I despise my life.
It *is* all one *thing;*
Therefore I say, 'He destroys the blameless
     and the wicked.'
If the scourge slays suddenly,
He laughs at the plight of the innocent.
The earth is given into the hand of the wicked.
He covers the faces of its judges.
If it is not *He,* who else could it be?

"Now my days are swifter than a runner;
They flee away, they see no good.
They pass by like swift ships,

A NEW NATION

Like an eagle swooping on its prey.
If I say, 'I will forget my complaint,
I will put off my sad face and wear a smile,'
I am afraid of all my sufferings;
I know that You will not hold me innocent.
If I am condemned,
Why then do I labor in vain?
If I wash myself with snow water,
And cleanse my hands with soap,
Yet You will plunge me into the pit,
And my own clothes will abhor me.

"For *He is* not a man, as I *am,*
That I may answer Him,
And that we should go to court together.
Nor is there any mediator between us,
Who may lay his hand on us both."

Job 8:1–9:12, 20-33

WORSHIP

For You will not leave my soul in Sheol,
Nor will You allow Your Holy One to see
corruption.
You will show me the path of life;
In Your presence *is* fullness of joy;
At Your right hand *are* pleasures forevermore.

Psalm 16:10-11

WISDOM

Take firm hold of instruction, do not let go;
Keep her, for she *is* your life.

Proverbs 4:13

SW?! SO WHAT?
What does this tell me?

JOB AND HIS FRIEND ZOPHAR

Job 11:1–12:12; 13:15-18; Psalm 17:1-3; Proverbs 4:14-15

Then Zophar the Naamathite answered and said:

"Should not the multitude of words be
    answered?
And should a man full of talk be vindicated?
Should your empty talk make men hold their
    peace?
And when you mock, should no one rebuke
    you?
For you have said,
'My doctrine *is* pure,
And I am clean in your eyes.'
But oh, that God would speak,
And open His lips against you,
That He would show you the secrets of
    wisdom!
For *they would* double *your* prudence.
Know therefore that God exacts from you
Less than your iniquity *deserves*.

"Can you search out the deep things of God?
Can you find out the limits of the Almighty?
They are higher than heaven—what can you
    do?
Deeper than Sheol—what can you know?
Their measure *is* longer than the earth
And broader than the sea.

"If He passes by, imprisons, and gathers *to*
    judgment,
Then who can hinder Him?
For He knows deceitful men;
He sees wickedness also.
Will He not then consider *it*?
For an empty-headed man will be wise,
When a wild donkey's colt is born a man.

"If you would prepare your heart,
And stretch out your hands toward Him;
If iniquity *were* in your hand, *and you* put it
    far away,
And would not let wickedness dwell in your
    tents;
Then surely you could lift up your face
    without spot;
Yes, you could be steadfast, and not fear;
Because you would forget *your* misery,
And remember *it* as waters *that have*
    passed away,

And *your* life would be brighter than noonday.
Though you were dark, you would be like the
    morning.
And you would be secure, because there is
    hope;
Yes, you would dig *around you, and* take your
    rest in safety.
You would also lie down, and no one would
    make *you* afraid;
Yes, many would court your favor.
But the eyes of the wicked will fail,
And they shall not escape,
And their hope—loss of life!"

Then Job answered and said:

"No doubt you *are* the people,
And wisdom will die with you!
But I have understanding as well as you;
I *am* not inferior to you.
Indeed, who does not *know* such things as
    these?

"I am one mocked by his friends,
Who called on God, and He answered him,
The just and blameless *who is* ridiculed.
A lamp is despised in the thought of one who
    is at ease;
It is made ready for those whose feet slip.
The tents of robbers prosper,
And those who provoke God are secure—
In what God provides by His hand.

"But now ask the beasts, and they will teach
    you;
And the birds of the air, and they will tell you;
Or speak to the earth, and it will teach you;
And the fish of the sea will explain to you.
Who among all these does not know
That the hand of the LORD has done this,
In whose hand *is* the life of every living thing,
And the breath of all mankind?
Does not the ear test words
And the mouth taste its food?
Wisdom *is* with aged men,
And with length of days, understanding.

"Though He slay me, yet will I trust Him.
Even so, I will defend my own ways before
    Him.
He also *shall* be my salvation,
For a hypocrite could not come before Him.

Listen carefully to my speech,
And to my declaration with your ears.
See now, I have prepared *my* case,
I know that I shall be vindicated."

Job 11:1–12:12; 13:15-18

WORSHIP

Hear a just cause, O LORD,
Attend to my cry;
Give ear to my prayer *which is* not from
     deceitful lips.
Let my vindication come from Your presence;
Let Your eyes look on the things that are
     upright.

You have tested my heart;
You have visited *me* in the night;
You have tried me and have found nothing;
I have purposed that my mouth shall not
     transgress.

Psalm 17:1-3

WISDOM

Do not enter the path of the wicked,
And do not walk in the way of evil.
Avoid it, do not travel on it;
Turn away from it and pass on.

Proverbs 4:14-15

SW?! SO WHAT?
What does this tell me?

Job's REFLECTIONS

Job 28:1–29:20; Psalm 17:6-8; Proverbs 4:18-19

"Surely there is a mine for silver,
And a place *where* gold is refined.
Iron is taken from the earth,
And copper *is* smelted *from* ore.
Man puts an end to darkness,
And searches every recess
For ore in the darkness and the shadow of
    death.
He breaks open a shaft away from people;
In places forgotten by feet
They hang far away from men;
They swing to and fro.
As for the earth, from it comes bread,
But underneath it is turned up as by fire;
Its stones *are* the source of sapphires,
And it contains gold dust.
That path no bird knows,
Nor has the falcon's eye seen it.
The proud lions have not trodden it,
Nor has the fierce lion passed over it.
He puts his hand on the flint;
He overturns the mountains at the roots.
He cuts out channels in the rocks,
And his eye sees every precious thing.
He dams up the streams from trickling;
What is hidden he brings forth to light.

"But where can wisdom be found?
And where *is* the place of understanding?
Man does not know its value,
    Nor is it found in the land of the living.
    The deep says, '*It is* not in me';
    And the sea says, '*It is* not with me.'
    It cannot be purchased for gold,
    Nor can silver be weighed *for* its price.
    It cannot be valued in the gold of Ophir,
    In precious onyx or sapphire.
    Neither gold nor crystal can equal it,
    Nor can it be exchanged for jewelry of fine
        gold.
    No mention shall be made of coral or
        quartz,
    For the price of wisdom *is* above rubies.
    The topaz of Ethiopia cannot equal it,
    Nor can it be valued in pure gold.

"From where then does wisdom come?
And where *is* the place of understanding?
It is hidden from the eyes of all living,
And concealed from the birds of the air.

Destruction and Death say,
'We have heard a report about it with our ears.'
God understands its way,
And He knows its place.
For He looks to the ends of the earth,
And sees under the whole heavens,
To establish a weight for the wind,
And apportion the waters by measure.
When He made a law for the rain,
And a path for the thunderbolt,
Then He saw *wisdom* and declared it;
He prepared it, indeed, He searched it out.
And to man He said,
'Behold, the fear of the Lord, that *is* wisdom,
And to depart from evil *is* understanding.' "

Job further continued his discourse, and said:

"Oh, that I were as *in* months past,
As *in* the days *when* God watched over me;
When His lamp shone upon my head,
And when by His light I walked *through*
    darkness;
Just as I was in the days of my prime,
When the friendly counsel of God *was* over my
    tent;
When the Almighty *was* yet with me,
When my children *were* around me;
When my steps were bathed with cream,
And the rock poured out rivers of oil for me!

"When I went out to the gate by the city,
When I took my seat in the open square,
The young men saw me and hid,
And the aged arose *and* stood;
The princes refrained from talking,
And put *their* hand on their mouth;
The voice of nobles was hushed,
And their tongue stuck to the roof of their
    mouth.
When the ear heard, then it blessed me,
And when the eye saw, then it approved me;
Because I delivered the poor who cried out,
The fatherless and *the one who* had no helper.
The blessing of a perishing *man* came upon
    me,
And I caused the widow's heart to sing for joy.
I put on righteousness, and it clothed me;
My justice *was* like a robe and a turban.
I *was* eyes to the blind,
And I *was* feet to the lame.

I *was* a father to the poor,
And I searched out the case *that* I did not
      know.
I broke the fangs of the wicked,
And plucked the victim from his teeth.

"Then I said, 'I shall die in my nest,
And multiply *my* days as the sand.
My root *is* spread out to the waters,
And the dew lies all night on my branch.
My glory *is* fresh within me,
And my bow is renewed in my hand.' "

Job 28:1–29:20

WORSHIP

I have called upon You, for You will hear me, O
      God;
Incline Your ear to me, *and* hear my speech.
Show Your marvelous lovingkindness by Your
      right hand,
O You who save those who trust *in You*
From those who rise up *against them.*
Keep me as the apple of Your eye;
Hide me under the shadow of Your wings.

Psalm 17:6-8

WISDOM

But the path of the just *is* like the shining sun,
That shines ever brighter unto the perfect day.
The way of the wicked *is* like darkness;
They do not know what makes them stumble.

Proverbs 4:18-19

SW?! SO WHAT?
What does this tell me?

ELIHU OFFERS AN ALTERNATIVE
Job 32:1–33:18; 36:22-23; Psalm 17:13-15; Proverbs 4:23

So these three men ceased answering Job, because he *was* righteous in his own eyes. Then the wrath of Elihu, the son of Barachel the Buzite, of the family of Ram, was aroused against Job; his wrath was aroused because he justified himself rather than God. Also against his three friends his wrath was aroused, because they had found no answer, and *yet* had condemned Job.

Now because they *were* years older than he, Elihu had waited to speak to Job. When Elihu saw that *there was* no answer in the mouth of these three men, his wrath was aroused.

So Elihu, the son of Barachel the Buzite, answered and said:

"I *am* young in years, and you *are* very old;
Therefore I was afraid,
And dared not declare my opinion to you.
I said, 'Age should speak,
And multitude of years should teach wisdom.'
But *there is* a spirit in man,
And the breath of the Almighty gives him
    understanding.
Great men are not *always* wise,
Nor do the aged *always* understand justice.

"Therefore I say, 'Listen to me,
I also will declare my opinion.'
Indeed I waited for your words,
I listened to your reasonings, while you
    searched out what to say.
I paid close attention to you;
And surely not one of you convinced Job,
Or answered his words—
Lest you say,
'We have found wisdom';
God will vanquish him, not man.
Now he has not directed *his* words against
    me;
So I will not answer him with your words.

"They are dismayed and answer no more;
Words escape them.
And I have waited, because they did not
    speak,
Because they stood still *and* answered no
    more.
I also will answer my part,
I too will declare my opinion.
For I am full of words;

The spirit within me compels me.
Indeed my belly *is* like wine *that* has no vent;
It is ready to burst like new wineskins.
I will speak, that I may find relief;
I must open my lips and answer.
Let me not, I pray, show partiality to anyone;
Nor let me flatter any man.
For I do not know how to flatter,
Else my Maker would soon take me away.

"But please, Job, hear my speech,
And listen to all my words.
Now, I open my mouth;
My tongue speaks in my mouth.
My words *come* from my upright heart;
My lips utter pure knowledge.
The Spirit of God has made me,
And the breath of the Almighty gives me life.
If you can answer me,
Set *your words* in order before me;
Take your stand.
Truly I *am* as your spokesman before God;
I also have been formed out of clay.
Surely no fear of me will terrify you,
Nor will my hand be heavy on you.

"Surely you have spoken in my hearing,
And I have heard the sound of *your* words,
        saying,
'I *am* pure, without transgression;
I *am* innocent, and *there is* no iniquity in me.
Yet He finds occasions against me,
He counts me as His enemy;
He puts my feet in the stocks,
He watches all my paths.'

"Look, *in* this you are not righteous.
I will answer you,
For God is greater than man.
Why do you contend with Him?
For He does not give an accounting of any of
        His words.
For God may speak in one way, or in another,
Yet man does not perceive it.
In a dream, in a vision of the night,
When deep sleep falls upon men,
While slumbering on their beds,
Then He opens the ears of men,
And seals their instruction.
In order to turn man *from his* deed,
And conceal pride from man,

He keeps back his soul from the Pit,
And his life from perishing by the sword.

"Behold, God is exalted by His power;
Who teaches like Him?
Who has assigned Him His way,
Or who has said, 'You have done wrong'?"
Job 32:1–33:18; 36:22-23

WORSHIP

Arise, O LORD,
Confront him, cast him down;
Deliver my life from the wicked with Your
    sword,
With Your hand from men, O LORD,
From men of the world *who have* their portion
    in *this* life,
And whose belly You fill with Your hidden
    treasure.
They are satisfied with children,
And leave the rest of their *possession* for their
    babes.
As for me, I will see Your face in
    righteousness;
I shall be satisfied when I awake in Your
    likeness.
Psalm 17:13-15

WISDOM

Keep your heart with all diligence,
For out of it *spring* the issues of life.
Proverbs 4:23

SW?! **SO WHAT?**
What does this tell me?

JOB ON THE WITNESS STAND

Job 38; Psalm 18:1-3; Proverbs 4:26-27

Then the LORD answered Job out of the whirlwind, and said:

"Who *is* this who darkens counsel
By words without knowledge?
Now prepare yourself like a man;
I will question you, and you shall answer Me.

"Where were you when I laid the foundations of
    the earth?
Tell *Me,* if you have understanding.
Who determined its measurements?
Surely you know!
Or who stretched the line upon it?
To what were its foundations fastened?
Or who laid its cornerstone,
When the morning stars sang together,
And all the sons of God shouted for joy?

"Or *who* shut in the sea with doors,
When it burst forth *and* issued from the womb;
When I made the clouds its garment,
And thick darkness its swaddling band;
When I fixed My limit for it,
And set bars and doors;
When I said,
'This far you may come, but no farther,
And here your proud waves must stop!'

"Have you commanded the morning since your
    days *began,*
And caused the dawn to know its place,
That it might take hold of the ends of the
    earth,
And the wicked be shaken out of it?
It takes on form like clay *under* a seal,
And stands out like a garment.
From the wicked their light is withheld,
And the upraised arm is broken.

"Have you entered the springs of the sea?
Or have you walked in search of the depths?
Have the gates of death been revealed to
    you?
Or have you seen the doors of the shadow
    of death?
Have you comprehended the breadth of the
    earth?
Tell *Me,* if you know all this.

"Where *is* the way *to* the dwelling of light?

And darkness, where *is* its place,
That you may take it to its territory,
That you may know the paths *to* its home?
Do you know *it,* because you were born then,
Or *because* the number of your days *is* great?

"Have you entered the treasury of snow,
Or have you seen the treasury of hail,
Which I have reserved for the time of trouble,
For the day of battle and war?
By what way is light diffused,
Or the east wind scattered over the earth?

"Who has divided a channel for the overflowing
    water,
Or a path for the thunderbolt,
To cause it to rain on a land *where there is* no
    one,
A wilderness in which *there is* no man;
To satisfy the desolate waste,
And cause to spring forth the growth of tender
    grass?
Has the rain a father?
Or who has begotten the drops of dew?
From whose womb comes the ice?
And the frost of heaven, who gives it birth?
The waters harden like stone,
And the surface of the deep is frozen.

"Can you bind the cluster of the Pleiades,
Or loose the belt of Orion?
Can you bring out Mazzaroth in its season?
Or can you guide the Great Bear with its cubs?
Do you know the ordinances of the heavens?
Can you set their dominion over the earth?

"Can you lift up your voice to the clouds,
That an abundance of water may cover you?
Can you send out lightnings, that they may go,
And say to you, 'Here we *are!*'?
Who has put wisdom in the mind?
Or who has given understanding to the heart?
Who can number the clouds by wisdom?
Or who can pour out the bottles of heaven,
When the dust hardens in clumps,
And the clods cling together?

"Can you hunt the prey for the lion,
Or satisfy the appetite of the young lions,
When they crouch in *their* dens,
Or lurk in their lairs to lie in wait?

A NEW NATION

Who provides food for the raven,
When its young ones cry to God,
And wander about for lack of food?"

Job 38

WORSHIP

I will love You, O LORD, my strength.
The LORD is my rock and my fortress and my
    deliverer;
My God, my strength, in whom I will trust;
My shield and the horn of my salvation, my
    stronghold.
I will call upon the LORD, *who is worthy* to be
    praised;
So shall I be saved from my enemies.

Psalm 18:1-3

WISDOM

Ponder the path of your feet,
And let all your ways be established.
Do not turn to the right or the left;
Remove your foot from evil.

Proverbs 4:26-27

SW?! **SO WHAT?**
What does this tell me?

JOB GETS THE POINT: GOD IS IN CONTROL

Job 40; 42; Psalm 18:4-6; Proverbs 5:1, 3-4

Moreover the LORD answered Job, and said:
"Shall the one who contends with the
    Almighty correct *Him?*
He who rebukes God, let him answer it."

Then Job answered the LORD and said:

"Behold, I am vile;
What shall I answer You?
I lay my hand over my mouth.
Once I have spoken, but I will not answer;
Yes, twice, but I will proceed no further."

Then the LORD answered Job out of the whirlwind, and said:

"Now prepare yourself like a man;
I will question you, and you shall answer Me:

"Would you indeed annul My judgment?
Would you condemn Me that you may be justified?
Have you an arm like God?
Or can you thunder with a voice like His?
Then adorn yourself *with* majesty and
    splendor,
And array yourself with glory and beauty.
Disperse the rage of your wrath;
  Look on everyone *who is* proud, and humble
    him.
  Look on everyone *who is* proud, *and* bring
    him low;
  Tread down the wicked in their place.
Hide them in the dust together,
Bind their faces in hidden *darkness.*
Then I will also confess to you
That your own right hand can save you.

"Look now at the behemoth, which I made
    along with you;
He eats grass like an ox.
See now, his strength *is* in his hips,
And his power *is* in his stomach muscles.
He moves his tail like a cedar;
The sinews of his thighs are tightly knit.
His bones *are like* beams of bronze,
His ribs like bars of iron.
He *is* the first of the ways of God;
Only He who made him can bring near His
    sword.

Surely the mountains yield food for him,
And all the beasts of the field play there.
He lies under the lotus trees,
In a covert of reeds and marsh.
The lotus trees cover him *with* their shade;
The willows by the brook surround him.
Indeed the river may rage,
Yet he is not disturbed;
He is confident, though the Jordan gushes into
    his mouth,
Though he takes it in his eyes,
Or one pierces *his* nose with a snare.

Then Job answered the LORD and said:

"I know that You can do everything,
And that no purpose *of Yours* can be withheld
    from You.
You asked, 'Who *is* this who hides counsel
    without knowledge?'
Therefore I have uttered what I did not
    understand,
Things too wonderful for me, which I did not
    know.
Listen, please, and let me speak;
You said, 'I will question you, and you shall
    answer Me.'

"I have heard of You by the hearing of the ear,
But now my eye sees You.
Therefore I abhor *myself,*
And repent in dust and ashes."

And so it was, after the LORD had spoken these words to Job, that the LORD said to Eliphaz the Temanite, "My wrath is aroused against you and your two friends, for you have not spoken of Me *what is* right, as My servant Job *has.* Now therefore, take for yourselves seven bulls and seven rams, go to My servant Job, and offer up for yourselves a burnt offering; and My servant Job shall pray for you. For I will accept him, lest I deal with you *according to your* folly; because you have not spoken of Me *what is* right, as My servant Job *has.*"

So Eliphaz the Temanite and Bildad the Shuhite *and* Zophar the Naamathite went and did as the LORD commanded them; for the LORD had accepted Job. And the LORD restored Job's losses when he prayed for his friends. Indeed the LORD gave Job twice as much as he had before. Then all his brothers, all his sisters, and all those who had been his acquaintances before, came to him and ate food with him in his house; and they consoled him and comforted him for all the adversity that the LORD had brought upon him. Each one gave him a piece of silver and each a ring of gold.

Now the LORD blessed the latter *days* of Job more than his beginning; for he had fourteen thousand sheep, six thousand camels, one thousand yoke of oxen, and one thousand female donkeys. He also had seven sons and three daughters. And he called the name of the first Jemimah, the name of the second Keziah, and the name of the third Keren-Happuch. In all the land were found no women *so* beautiful as the daughters of Job; and their father gave them an inheritance among their brothers.

After this Job lived one hundred and forty years, and saw his children and grandchildren *for* four generations. So Job died, old and full of days.

Job 40; 42

WORSHIP

The pangs of death surrounded me,
And the floods of ungodliness made me
   afraid.
The sorrows of Sheol surrounded me;
The snares of death confronted me.
In my distress I called upon the LORD,
And cried out to my God;
He heard my voice from His temple,
And my cry came before Him, *even* to His
   ears.

Psalm 18:4-6

WISDOM

My son, pay attention to my wisdom;
Lend your ear to my understanding,

For the lips of an immoral woman drip honey,
And her mouth *is* smoother than oil;
But in the end she is bitter as wormwood,
Sharp as a two-edged sword.

Proverbs 5:1, 3-4

SW?! **SO WHAT?**
What does this tell me?

SLAVES IN EGYPT

The third mountain range on the horizon is Israel's 430 years of slavery in Egypt. Jacob's family went to Egypt when Joseph helped them survive a terrible famine. But instead of returning home to Canaan when the famine was over, the Israelites stayed in Egypt. It was during this time in Egypt that they grew from a small tribe of about seventy people to a great nation of almost two million. It was evident that God was fulfilling His promise to make Abraham's descendants a great nation (Genesis 12:3).

After a long period of peace and prosperity in Egypt, Ahmose I rose to power as the pharaoh of Egypt (1580-1548 B.C.) driving out the foreign rulers (the Hyksos) and establishing Egypt's 18th dynasty. These pharaohs had no knowledge of what Joseph had done for the Egyptians. Feeling threatened by the growing size and power of the Israelite nation, the Egyptian government took measures to hinder their growth.

First Pharaoh forced the Israelites to do hard labor. Then he decreed that all male Israelite children be killed. These were brutally oppressive times for the Israelites. Mothers and fathers took extreme measures to protect their young sons from this death sentence.

It was in the midst of these dark days that an Israelite couple hid their son in a small basket in the reeds along the Nile River to keep him from being killed by Pharaoh's soldiers. Pharaoh's daughter found this baby boy and adopted him into the royal family. Named Moses, this boy would grow up to be the man God chose to lead His people out of slavery in Egypt to freedom in the Promised Land.

One of the great peaks in this action-packed narrative really does take place on a mountain, where God speaks to Moses from a burning bush. We usually remember this incident because of the bush or because God sent Moses out from there to deliver the Israelites from Egyptian bondage, but there is something even more significant to this event in the story.

After God gets Moses' attention with the burning bush, He reveals to him the meaning of His name (Exodus 3:13-15). In that day, a name was more than just what you called a person—it said something about who they were. God's name "Yahweh" (LORD) is based on the Hebrew word for "exist" and can be translated "He that is." What a revelation! In a world where so many place their faith in gods of their own creation based on their own opinions and their own limited assumptions, here is God Himself wanting to make sure we know that He is "self-existent"—not a creation of anyone or anything but Himself.

OPPRESSION IN EGYPT

Exodus 1:6–2:25; Psalm 18:16-17, 19; Proverbs 5:18-19

And Joseph died, all his brothers, and all that generation. But the children of Israel were fruitful and increased abundantly, multiplied and grew exceedingly mighty; and the land was filled with them.

Now there arose a new king over Egypt, who did not know Joseph. And he said to his people, "Look, the people of the children of Israel *are* more and mightier than we; come, let us deal shrewdly with them, lest they multiply, and it happen, in the event of war, that they also join our enemies and fight against us, and *so* go up out of the land." Therefore they set taskmasters over them to afflict them with their burdens. And they built for Pharaoh supply cities, Pithom and Raamses. But the more they afflicted them, the more they multiplied and grew. And they were in dread of the children of Israel. So the Egyptians made the children of Israel serve with rigor. And they made their lives bitter with hard bondage—in mortar, in brick, and in all manner of service in the field. All their service in which they made them serve *was* with rigor.

Then the king of Egypt spoke to the Hebrew midwives, of whom the name of one *was* Shiphrah and the name of the other Puah; and he said, "When you do the duties of a midwife for the Hebrew women, and see *them* on the birthstools, if it *is* a son, then you shall kill him; but if it *is* a daughter, then she shall live." But the midwives feared God, and did not do as the king of Egypt commanded them, but saved the male children alive. So the king of Egypt called for the midwives and said to them, "Why have you done this thing, and saved the male children alive?"

And the midwives said to Pharaoh, "Because the Hebrew women *are* not like the Egyptian women; for they *are* lively and give birth before the midwives come to them."

Therefore God dealt well with the midwives, and the people multiplied and grew very mighty. And so it was, because the midwives feared God, that He provided households for them.

So Pharaoh commanded all his people, saying, "Every son who is born you shall cast into the river, and every daughter you shall save alive."

And a man of the house of Levi went and took *as wife* a daughter of Levi. So the woman conceived and bore a son. And when she saw that he *was* a beautiful *child,* she hid him three months. But when she could no longer hide him, she took an ark of bulrushes for him, daubed it with asphalt and pitch, put the child in it, and laid *it* in the reeds by the river's bank. And his sister stood afar off, to know what would be done to him.

Then the daughter of Pharaoh came down to bathe at the river. And her maidens walked along the riverside; and when she saw the ark among the reeds, she sent her maid to get it. And when she opened *it,* she saw the child, and behold, the baby wept. So she had compassion on him, and said, "This is one of the Hebrews' children."

Then his sister said to Pharaoh's daughter, "Shall I go and call a nurse for you from the Hebrew women, that she may nurse the child for you?"

And Pharaoh's daughter said to her, "Go." So the maiden went and called the child's mother. Then Pharaoh's daughter said to her, "Take this child away and nurse him for me, and I will give *you* your wages." So the woman took the child and nursed him. And the child grew, and she brought him to Pharaoh's daughter, and he became her son. So she called his name Moses, saying, "Because I drew him out of the water."

Now it came to pass in those days, when Moses was grown, that he went out to his brethren and looked at their burdens. And he saw an Egyptian beating a Hebrew, one of his brethren. So he looked this way and that way, and when he saw no one, he killed the Egyptian and hid him in the sand. And when he went out the second day, behold, two Hebrew men were fighting, and he said to the one who did the wrong, "Why are you striking your companion?"

Then he said, "Who made you a prince and a judge over us? Do you intend to kill me as you killed the Egyptian?"

So Moses feared and said, "Surely this thing is known!" When Pharaoh heard of this matter, he sought to kill Moses. But Moses fled from the face of Pharaoh and dwelt in the land of Midian; and he sat down by a well.

Now the priest of Midian had seven daughters. And they came and drew water, and they filled the troughs to water their father's flock. Then the shepherds came and drove them away; but Moses stood up and helped them, and watered their flock.

When they came to Reuel their father, he said, "How *is it that* you have come so soon today?"

And they said, "An Egyptian delivered us from the hand of the shepherds, and he also drew enough water for us and watered the flock."

So he said to his daughters, "And where *is* he? Why *is* it *that* you have left the man? Call him, that he may eat bread."

Then Moses was content to live with the man, and he gave Zipporah his daughter to Moses. And she bore *him* a son. He called his name Gershom; for he said, "I have been a stranger in a foreign land."

Now it happened in the process of time that the king of Egypt died. Then the children of Israel groaned because of the bondage, and they cried out; and their cry came up to God because of the bondage. So God heard their groaning, and God remembered His covenant with Abraham, with Isaac, and with Jacob. And God looked upon the children of Israel, and God acknowledged *them.*

Exodus 1:6–2:25

WORSHIP

He sent from above, He took me;
He drew me out of many waters.
He delivered me from my strong enemy,
From those who hated me,
For they were too strong for me.

He also brought me out into a broad place;
He delivered me because He delighted in me.

Psalm 18:16-17, 19

WISDOM

Let your fountain be blessed,
And rejoice with the wife of your youth.
As a loving deer and a graceful doe,
Let her breasts satisfy you at all times;
And always be enraptured with her love.

Proverbs 5:18-19

SW?! **SO WHAT?**
What does this tell me?

MOSES MEETS GOD
Exodus 3:1–4:17; Psalm 18:20-21, 24; Proverbs 5:21

Now Moses was tending the flock of Jethro his father-in-law, the priest of Midian. And he led the flock to the back of the desert, and came to Horeb, the mountain of God. And the Angel of the LORD appeared to him in a flame of fire from the midst of a bush. So he looked, and behold, the bush was burning with fire, but the bush *was* not consumed. Then Moses said, "I will now turn aside and see this great sight, why the bush does not burn."

So when the LORD saw that he turned aside to look, God called to him from the midst of the bush and said, "Moses, Moses!"

And he said, "Here I am."

Then He said, "Do not draw near this place. Take your sandals off your feet, for the place where you stand *is* holy ground." Moreover He said, "I *am* the God of your father—the God of Abraham, the God of Isaac, and the God of Jacob." And Moses hid his face, for he was afraid to look upon God.

And the LORD said: "I have surely seen the oppression of My people who *are* in Egypt, and have heard their cry because of their taskmasters, for I know their sorrows. So I have come down to deliver them out of the hand of the Egyptians, and to bring them up from that land to a good and large land, to a land flowing with milk and honey, to the place of the Canaanites and the Hittites and the Amorites and the Perizzites and the Hivites and the Jebusites. Now therefore, behold, the cry of the children of Israel has come to Me, and I have also seen the oppression with which the Egyptians oppress them. Come now, therefore, and I will send you to Pharaoh that you may bring My people, the children of Israel, out of Egypt."

But Moses said to God, "Who *am* I that I should go to Pharaoh, and that I should bring the children of Israel out of Egypt?"

So He said, "I will certainly be with you. And this *shall be* a sign to you that I have sent you: When you have brought the people out of Egypt, you shall serve God on this mountain."

Then Moses said to God, "Indeed, *when* I come to the children of Israel and say

to them, 'The God of your fathers has sent me to you,' and they say to me, 'What *is* His name?' what shall I say to them?"

And God said to Moses, "I AM WHO I AM." And He said, "Thus you shall say to the children of Israel, 'I AM has sent me to you.'" Moreover God said to Moses, "Thus you shall say to the children of Israel: 'The LORD God of your fathers, the God of Abraham, the God of Isaac, and the God of Jacob, has sent me to you. This *is* My name forever, and this *is* My memorial to all generations.' Go and gather the elders of Israel together, and say to them, 'The LORD God of your fathers, the God of Abraham, of Isaac, and of Jacob, appeared to me, saying, "I have surely visited you and *seen* what is done to you in Egypt; and I have said I will bring you up out of the affliction of Egypt to the land of the Canaanites and the Hittites and the Amorites and the Perizzites and the Hivites and the Jebusites, to a land flowing with milk and honey."' Then they will heed your voice; and you shall come, you and the elders of Israel, to the king of Egypt; and you shall say to him, 'The LORD God of the Hebrews has met with us; and now, please, let us go three days' journey into the wilderness, that we may sacrifice to the LORD our God.' But I am sure that the king of Egypt will not let you go, no, not even by a mighty hand. So I will stretch out My hand and strike Egypt with all My wonders which I will do in its midst; and after that he will let you go. And I will give this people favor in the sight of the Egyptians; and it shall be, when you go, that you shall not go empty-handed. But every woman shall ask of her neighbor, namely, of her who dwells near her house, articles of silver, articles of gold, and clothing; and you shall put *them* on your sons and on your daughters. So you shall plunder the Egyptians."

Then Moses answered and said, "But suppose they will not believe me or listen to my voice; suppose they say, 'The LORD has not appeared to you.'"

So the LORD said to him, "What *is* that in your hand?"

He said, "A rod."

And He said, "Cast it on the ground." So he cast it on the ground, and it became a serpent; and Moses fled from it. Then the LORD said to Moses,

SLAVES IN EGYPT

"Reach out your hand and take *it* by the tail" (and he reached out his hand and caught it, and it became a rod in his hand), "that they may believe that the LORD God of their fathers, the God of Abraham, the God of Isaac, and the God of Jacob, has appeared to you."

Furthermore the LORD said to him, "Now put your hand in your bosom." And he put his hand in his bosom, and when he took it out, behold, his hand *was* leprous, like snow. And He said, "Put your hand in your bosom again." So he put his hand in his bosom again, and drew it out of his bosom, and behold, it was restored like his *other* flesh. "Then it will be, if they do not believe you, nor heed the message of the first sign, that they may believe the message of the latter sign. And it shall be, if they do not believe even these two signs, or listen to your voice, that you shall take water from the river and pour *it* on the dry *land*. The water which you take from the river will become blood on the dry *land*."

Then Moses said to the LORD, "O my Lord, I *am* not eloquent, neither before nor since You have spoken to Your servant; but I *am* slow of speech and slow of tongue."

So the LORD said to him, "Who has made man's mouth? Or who makes the mute, the deaf, the seeing, or the blind? *Have* not I, the LORD? Now therefore, go, and I will be with your mouth and teach you what you shall say."

But he said, "O my Lord, please send by the hand of whomever *else* You may send."

So the anger of the LORD was kindled against Moses, and He said: "Is not Aaron the Levite your brother? I know that he can speak well. And look, he is also coming out to meet you. When he sees you, he will be glad in his heart. Now you shall speak to him and put the words in his mouth. And I will be with your mouth and with his mouth, and I will teach you what you shall do. So he shall be your spokesman to the people. And he himself shall be as a mouth for you, and you shall be to him as God. And you shall take this rod in your hand, with which you shall do the signs."

Exodus 3:1–4:17

WORSHIP

The LORD rewarded me according to my righteousness;
According to the cleanness of my hands He has recompensed me.
For I have kept the ways of the LORD, And have not wickedly departed from my God.

Therefore the LORD has recompensed me according to my righteousness,
According to the cleanness of my hands in His sight.

Psalm 18:20-21, 24

WISDOM

For the ways of man *are* before the eyes of the LORD,
And He ponders all his paths.

Proverbs 5:21

SW?! SO WHAT? What does this tell me?

MOSES MEETS PHARAOH

Exodus 4:27–6:8; Psalm 18:27-29; Proverbs 6:6-8

nd the LORD said to Aaron, "Go into the wilderness to meet Moses." So he went and met him on the mountain of God, and kissed him. So Moses told Aaron all the words of the LORD who had sent him, and all the signs which He had commanded him. Then Moses and Aaron went and gathered together all the elders of the children of Israel. And Aaron spoke all the words which the LORD had spoken to Moses. Then he did the signs in the sight of the people. So the people believed; and when they heard that the LORD had visited the children of Israel and that He had looked on their affliction, then they bowed their heads and worshiped.

Afterward Moses and Aaron went in and told Pharaoh, "Thus says the LORD God of Israel: 'Let My people go, that they may hold a feast to Me in the wilderness.' "

And Pharaoh said, "Who *is* the LORD, that I should obey His voice to let Israel go? I do not know the LORD, nor will I let Israel go."

So they said, "The God of the Hebrews has met with us. Please, let us go three days' journey into the desert and sacrifice to the LORD our God, lest He fall upon us with pestilence or with the sword."

Then the king of Egypt said to them, "Moses and Aaron, why do you take the people from their work? Get *back* to your labor." And Pharaoh said, "Look, the people of the land *are* many now, and you make them rest from their labor!"

So the same day Pharaoh commanded the taskmasters of the people and their officers, saying, "You shall no longer give the people straw to make brick as before. Let them go and gather straw for themselves. And you shall lay on them the quota of bricks which they made before. You shall not reduce it. For they are idle; therefore they cry out, saying, 'Let us go *and* sacrifice to our God.' Let more work be laid on the men, that they may labor in it, and let them not regard false words."

And the taskmasters of the people and their officers went out and spoke to the people, saying, "Thus says Pharaoh: 'I will not give you straw. Go, get yourselves straw where you can find it; yet none of your work will be reduced.' " So the people were scattered abroad throughout all the land of Egypt to gather stubble instead of straw. And the taskmasters forced *them* to hurry, saying, "Fulfill your work, *your* daily quota, as when there was straw." Also the officers of the children of Israel, whom Pharaoh's taskmasters had set over them, were beaten *and* were asked, "Why have you not fulfilled your task in making brick both yesterday and today, as before?"

Then the officers of the children of Israel came and cried out to Pharaoh, saying, "Why are you dealing thus with your servants? There is no straw given to your servants, and they say to us, 'Make brick!' And indeed your servants *are* beaten, but the fault *is* in your *own* people."

But he said, "You *are* idle! Idle! Therefore you say, 'Let us go *and* sacrifice to the LORD.' Therefore go now *and* work; for no straw shall be given you, yet you shall deliver the quota of bricks." And the officers of the children of Israel saw *that* they *were* in trouble after it was said, "You shall not reduce *any* bricks from your daily quota."

Then, as they came out from Pharaoh, they met Moses and Aaron who stood there to meet them. And they said to them, "Let the LORD look on you and judge, because you have made us abhorrent in the sight of Pharaoh and in the sight of his servants, to put a sword in their hand to kill us."

So Moses returned to the LORD and said, "Lord, why have You brought trouble on this people? Why *is* it You have sent me? For since I came to Pharaoh to speak in Your name, he has done evil to this people; neither have You delivered Your people at all."

Then the LORD said to Moses, "Now you shall see what I will do to Pharaoh. For with a strong hand he will let them go, and with a strong hand he will drive them out of his land."

And God spoke to Moses and said to him: "I *am* the LORD. I appeared to Abraham, to Isaac, and to Jacob, as God Almighty, but *by* My name LORD I was not known to them. I have also established My covenant with them, to give them the land of Canaan, the land of their pilgrimage, in which they were strangers. And I have also heard the groaning of the children of Israel whom the Egyptians keep in bondage, and I have remembered My covenant. Therefore say to the children of Israel: 'I *am* the LORD; I will bring you out from under the burdens of the Egyptians, I will rescue you from their bondage, and I will redeem you with an outstretched arm and with great judgments. I will take you as My people, and I will be your God. Then you shall know that I *am* the LORD your God who brings you out from under the burdens of the Egyptians. And I will bring you into the land which I swore to give to Abraham, Isaac, and Jacob; and I will give it to you *as* a heritage: I *am* the LORD.' "

Exodus 4:27–6:8

WORSHIP

For You will save the humble people,
But will bring down haughty looks.

For You will light my lamp;
The LORD my God will enlighten my darkness.
For by You I can run against a troop,
By my God I can leap over a wall.

Psalm 18:27-29

WISDOM

Go to the ant, you sluggard!
Consider her ways and be wise,
Which, having no captain,
Overseer or ruler,
Provides her supplies in the summer,
And gathers her food in the harvest.

Proverbs 6:6-8

SW?! SO WHAT?
What does this tell me?

PLAGUES OF JUDGMENT: PART ONE

Exodus 7:1–8:24, 32; Psalm 18:30-32; Proverbs 6:9-11

So the LORD said to Moses: "See, I have made you *as* God to Pharaoh, and Aaron your brother shall be your prophet. You shall speak all that I command you. And Aaron your brother shall tell Pharaoh to send the children of Israel out of his land. And I will harden Pharaoh's heart, and multiply My signs and My wonders in the land of Egypt. But Pharaoh will not heed you, so that I may lay My hand on Egypt and bring My armies *and* My people, the children of Israel, out of the land of Egypt by great judgments. And the Egyptians shall know that I *am* the LORD, when I stretch out My hand on Egypt and bring out the children of Israel from among them."

Then Moses and Aaron did *so;* just as the LORD commanded them, so they did. And Moses *was* eighty years old and Aaron eighty-three years old when they spoke to Pharaoh.

Then the LORD spoke to Moses and Aaron, saying, "When Pharaoh speaks to you, saying, 'Show a miracle for yourselves,' then you shall say to Aaron, 'Take your rod and cast *it* before Pharaoh, *and* let it become a serpent.' " So Moses and Aaron went in to Pharaoh, and they did so, just as the LORD commanded. And Aaron cast down his rod before Pharaoh and before his servants, and it became a serpent.

But Pharaoh also called the wise men and the sorcerers; so the magicians of Egypt, they also did in like manner with their enchantments. For every man threw down his rod, and they became serpents. But Aaron's rod swallowed up their rods. And Pharaoh's heart grew hard, and he did not heed them, as the LORD had said.

So the LORD said to Moses: "Pharaoh's heart *is* hard; he refuses to let the people go. Go to Pharaoh in the morning, when he goes out to the water, and you shall stand by the river's bank to meet him; and the rod which was turned to a serpent you shall take in your hand. And you shall say to him, 'The LORD God of the Hebrews has sent me to you, saying, "Let My people go, that they may serve Me in the wilderness"; but indeed, until now you would not hear! Thus says the LORD: "By this you shall know that I *am* the LORD. Behold, I will strike the waters which *are* in the river with the rod that *is* in my hand, and they shall be turned to blood. And the fish that *are* in the river shall die, the river shall stink, and the Egyptians will loathe to drink the water of the river." ' "

Then the LORD spoke to Moses, "Say to Aaron, 'Take your rod and stretch out your hand over the waters of Egypt, over their streams, over their rivers, over their ponds, and over all their pools of water, that they may become blood. And there shall be blood throughout all the land of Egypt, both in *buckets of* wood and *pitchers of* stone.' " And Moses and Aaron did so, just as the LORD commanded. So he lifted up the rod and struck the waters that *were* in the river, in the sight of Pharaoh and in the sight of his servants. And all the waters that *were* in the river were turned to blood. The fish that *were* in the river died, the river stank, and the Egyptians could not drink the water of the river. So there was blood throughout all the land of Egypt.

Then the magicians of Egypt did so with their enchantments; and Pharaoh's heart grew hard, and he did not heed them, as the LORD had said. And Pharaoh turned and went into his house. Neither was his heart moved by this. So all the Egyptians dug all around the river for water to drink, because they could not drink the water of the river. And seven days passed after the LORD had struck the river.

And the LORD spoke to Moses, "Go to Pharaoh and say to him, 'Thus says the LORD: "Let My people go, that they may serve Me. But if you refuse to let *them* go, behold, I will smite all your territory with frogs. So the river shall bring forth frogs abundantly, which shall go up and come into your house, into your bedroom, on your bed, into the houses of your servants, on your people, into your ovens, and into your kneading bowls. And the frogs shall come up on you, on your people, and on all your servants." ' "

Then the LORD spoke to Moses, "Say to Aaron, 'Stretch out your hand with your rod over the streams, over the rivers, and over the ponds, and cause frogs to come up on the land of Egypt.' " So Aaron stretched out his hand over the waters of

Egypt, and the frogs came up and covered the land of Egypt. And the magicians did so with their enchantments, and brought up frogs on the land of Egypt.

Then Pharaoh called for Moses and Aaron, and said, "Entreat the LORD that He may take away the frogs from me and from my people; and I will let the people go, that they may sacrifice to the LORD."

And Moses said to Pharaoh, "Accept the honor of saying when I shall intercede for you, for your servants, and for your people, to destroy the frogs from you and your houses, *that* they may remain in the river only."

So he said, "Tomorrow." And he said, "*Let it be* according to your word, that you may know that *there is* no one like the LORD our God. And the frogs shall depart from you, from your houses, from your servants, and from your people. They shall remain in the river only."

Then Moses and Aaron went out from Pharaoh. And Moses cried out to the LORD concerning the frogs which He had brought against Pharaoh. So the LORD did according to the word of Moses. And the frogs died out of the houses, out of the courtyards, and out of the fields. They gathered them together in heaps, and the land stank. But when Pharaoh saw that there was relief, he hardened his heart and did not heed them, as the LORD had said.

So the LORD said to Moses, "Say to Aaron, 'Stretch out your rod, and strike the dust of the land, so that it may become lice throughout all the land of Egypt.'" And they did so. For Aaron stretched out his hand with his rod and struck the dust of the earth, and it became lice on man and beast. All the dust of the land became lice throughout all the land of Egypt.

Now the magicians so worked with their enchantments to bring forth lice, but they could not. So there were lice on man and beast. Then the magicians said to Pharaoh, "This *is* the finger of God." But Pharaoh's heart grew hard, and he did not heed them, just as the LORD had said.

And the LORD said to Moses, "Rise early in the morning and stand before Pharaoh as he comes out to the water. Then say to him, 'Thus says the LORD: "Let My people go, that they may serve Me. Or else, if you will not let My people go, behold, I will send swarms *of flies* on you and your servants, on your people and into your houses. The houses of the Egyptians shall be full of swarms *of flies,* and

also the ground on which they *stand.* And in that day I will set apart the land of Goshen, in which My people dwell, that no swarms *of flies* shall be there, in order that you may know that I *am* the LORD in the midst of the land. I will make a difference between My people and your people. Tomorrow this sign shall be." ' " And the LORD did so. Thick swarms *of flies* came into the house of Pharaoh, *into* his servants' houses, and into all the land of Egypt. The land was corrupted because of the swarms *of flies.*

But Pharaoh hardened his heart at this time also; neither would he let the people go.

Exodus 7:1–8:24, 32

WORSHIP

As for God, His way *is* perfect;
The word of the LORD is proven;
He *is* a shield to all who trust in Him.

For who *is* God, except the LORD?
And who *is* a rock, except our God?
It is God who arms me with strength,
And makes my way perfect.

Psalm 18:30-32

WISDOM

How long will you slumber, O sluggard?
When will you rise from your sleep?
A little sleep, a little slumber,
A little folding of the hands to sleep—
So shall your poverty come on you like a
    prowler,
And your need like an armed man.

Proverbs 6:9-11

SW?! SO WHAT?
What does this tell me?

PLAGUES OF JUDGMENT: PART TWO

Exodus 9:1-26, 34-35; 10:12-27; Psalm 18:39-41; Proverbs 6:16-19

Then the LORD said to Moses, "Go in to Pharaoh and tell him, 'Thus says the LORD God of the Hebrews: "Let My people go, that they may serve Me. For if you refuse to let *them* go, and still hold them, behold, the hand of the LORD will be on your cattle in the field, on the horses, on the donkeys, on the camels, on the oxen, and on the sheep—a very severe pestilence. And the LORD will make a difference between the livestock of Israel and the livestock of Egypt. So nothing shall die of all *that* belongs to the children of Israel." ' " Then the LORD appointed a set time, saying, "Tomorrow the LORD will do this thing in the land."

So the LORD did this thing on the next day, and all the livestock of Egypt died; but of the livestock of the children of Israel, not one died. Then Pharaoh sent, and indeed, not even one of the livestock of the Israelites was dead. But the heart of Pharaoh became hard, and he did not let the people go.

So the LORD said to Moses and Aaron, "Take for yourselves handfuls of ashes from a furnace, and let Moses scatter it toward the heavens in the sight of Pharaoh. And it will become fine dust in all the land of Egypt, and it will cause boils that break out in sores on man and beast throughout all the land of Egypt." Then they took ashes from the furnace and stood before Pharaoh, and Moses scattered *them* toward heaven. And *they* caused boils that break out in sores on man and beast. And the magicians could not stand before Moses because of the boils, for the boils were on the magicians and on all the Egyptians. But the LORD hardened the heart of Pharaoh; and he did not heed them, just as the LORD had spoken to Moses.

Then the LORD said to Moses, "Rise early in the morning and stand before Pharaoh, and say to him, 'Thus says the LORD God of the Hebrews: "Let My people go, that they may serve Me, for at this time I will send all My plagues to your very heart, and on your servants and on your people, that you may know that *there is* none like Me in all the earth. Now if I had stretched out My hand and struck you and your people with pesti-

lence, then you would have been cut off from the earth. But indeed for this *purpose* I have raised you up, that I may show My power *in* you, and that My name may be declared in all the earth. As yet you exalt yourself against My people in that you will not let them go. Behold, tomorrow about this time I will cause very heavy hail to rain down, such as has not been in Egypt since its founding until now. Therefore send now *and* gather your livestock and all that you have in the field, for the hail shall come down on every man and every animal which is found in the field and is not brought home; and they shall die." ' "

He who feared the word of the LORD among the servants of Pharaoh made his servants and his livestock flee to the houses. But he who did not regard the word of the LORD left his servants and his livestock in the field.

Then the LORD said to Moses, "Stretch out your hand toward heaven, that there may be hail in all the land of Egypt—on man, on beast, and on every herb of the field, throughout the land of Egypt." And Moses stretched out his rod toward heaven; and the LORD sent thunder and hail, and fire darted to the ground. And the LORD rained hail on the land of Egypt. So there was hail, and fire mingled with the hail, so very heavy that there was none like it in all the land of Egypt since it became a nation. And the hail struck throughout the whole land of Egypt, all that *was* in the field, both man and beast; and the hail struck every herb of the field and broke every tree of the field. Only in the land of Goshen, where the children of Israel *were,* there was no hail.

And when Pharaoh saw that the rain, the hail, and the thunder had ceased, he sinned yet more; and he hardened his heart, he and his servants. So the heart of Pharaoh was hard; neither would he let the children of Israel go, as the LORD had spoken by Moses.

Then the LORD said to Moses, "Stretch out your hand over the land of Egypt for the locusts, that they may come upon the land of Egypt, and eat every herb of the land—all that the hail has left." So Moses stretched out his rod over the land of Egypt, and the LORD brought an east wind on the land all that day and all *that* night. When it was morning, the east wind brought the locusts. And the locusts went up over all the land of Egypt and rested on all the territory of Egypt. *They were* very severe; previously there had been no such locusts as they, nor shall there be such after them. For they covered the face of the whole earth, so that the land was darkened; and they ate every herb of the land and all the fruit of the trees which the hail had left. So there remained nothing green on the trees or on the plants of the field throughout all the land of Egypt.

Then Pharaoh called for Moses and Aaron in haste, and said, "I have sinned against the Lord your God and against you. Now therefore, please forgive my sin only this once, and entreat the Lord your God, that He may take away from me this death only." So he went out from Pharaoh and entreated the Lord. And the Lord turned a very strong west wind, which took the locusts away and blew them into the Red Sea. There remained not one locust in all the territory of Egypt. But the Lord hardened Pharaoh's heart, and he did not let the children of Israel go.

Then the Lord said to Moses, "Stretch out your hand toward heaven, that there may be darkness over the land of Egypt, darkness *which* may even be felt." So Moses stretched out his hand toward heaven, and there was thick darkness in all the land of Egypt three days. They did not see one another; nor did anyone rise from his place for three days. But all the children of Israel had light in their dwellings.

Then Pharaoh called to Moses and said, "Go, serve the Lord; only let your flocks and your herds be kept back. Let your little ones also go with you."

But Moses said, "You must also give us sacrifices and burnt offerings, that we may sacrifice to the Lord our God. Our livestock also shall go with us; not a hoof shall be left behind. For we must take some of them to serve the Lord our God, and even we do not know with what we must serve the Lord until we arrive there."

But the Lord hardened Pharaoh's heart, and he would not let them go.

Exodus 9:1-26, 34-35; 10:12-27

WORSHIP

For You have armed me with strength for the battle;
You have subdued under me those who rose up against me.
You have also given me the necks of my enemies,
So that I destroyed those who hated me.
They cried out, but *there was* none to save;
Even to the Lord, but He did not answer them.

Psalm 18:39-41

WISDOM

These six *things* the Lord hates,
Yes, seven *are* an abomination to Him:
A proud look,
A lying tongue,
Hands that shed innocent blood,
A heart that devises wicked plans,
Feet that are swift in running to evil,
A false witness *who* speaks lies,
And one who sows discord among brethren.

Proverbs 6:16-19

SW?! SO WHAT?
What does this tell me?

FINAL PLAGUE; DEATH PASSES OVER

Exodus 11:1–12:30; Psalm 18:48–50; Proverbs 6:20–22

And the LORD said to Moses, "I will bring one more plague on Pharaoh and on Egypt. Afterward he will let you go from here. When he lets *you* go, he will surely drive you out of here altogether. Speak now in the hearing of the people, and let every man ask from his neighbor and every woman from her neighbor, articles of silver and articles of gold." And the LORD gave the people favor in the sight of the Egyptians. Moreover the man Moses *was* very great in the land of Egypt, in the sight of Pharaoh's servants and in the sight of the people.

Then Moses said, "Thus says the LORD: 'About midnight I will go out into the midst of Egypt; and all the firstborn in the land of Egypt shall die, from the firstborn of Pharaoh who sits on his throne, even to the firstborn of the female servant who *is* behind the handmill, and all the firstborn of the animals. Then there shall be a great cry throughout all the land of Egypt, such as was not like it *before,* nor shall be like it again. But against none of the children of Israel shall a dog move its tongue, against man or beast, that you may know that the LORD does make a difference between the Egyptians and Israel.' And all these your servants shall come down to me and bow down to me, saying, 'Get out, and all the people who follow you!' After that I will go out." Then he went out from Pharaoh in great anger.

But the LORD said to Moses, "Pharaoh will not heed you, so that My wonders may be multiplied in the land of Egypt." So Moses and Aaron did all these wonders before Pharaoh; and the LORD hardened Pharaoh's heart, and he did not let the children of Israel go out of his land.

Now the LORD spoke to Moses and Aaron in the land of Egypt, saying, "This month *shall be* your beginning of months; it *shall be* the first month of the year to you. Speak to all the congregation of Israel, saying: 'On the tenth of this month every man shall take for himself a lamb, according to the house of *his* father, a lamb for a household. And if the household is too small for the lamb, let him and his neighbor next to

his house take *it* according to the number of the persons; according to each man's need you shall make your count for the lamb. Your lamb shall be without blemish, a male of the first year. You may take *it* from the sheep or from the goats. Now you shall keep it until the fourteenth day of the same month. Then the whole assembly of the congregation of Israel shall kill it at twilight. And they shall take *some* of the blood and put *it* on the two doorposts and on the lintel of the houses where they eat it. Then they shall eat the flesh on that night; roasted in fire, with unleavened bread *and* with bitter *herbs* they shall eat it. Do not eat it raw, nor boiled at all with water, but roasted in fire—its head with its legs and its entrails. You shall let none of it remain until morning, and what remains of it until morning you shall burn with fire. And thus you shall eat it: *with* a belt on your waist, your sandals on your feet, and your staff in your hand. So you shall eat it in haste. It *is* the LORD's Passover.

'For I will pass through the land of Egypt on that night, and will strike all the firstborn in the land of Egypt, both man and beast; and against all the gods of Egypt I will execute judgment: I *am* the LORD. Now the blood shall be a sign for you on the houses where you *are.* And when I see the blood, I will pass over you; and the plague shall not be on you to destroy *you* when I strike the land of Egypt.

'So this day shall be to you a memorial; and you shall keep it as a feast to the LORD throughout your generations. You shall keep it as a feast by an everlasting ordinance. Seven days you shall eat unleavened bread. On the first day you shall remove leaven from your houses. For whoever eats leavened bread from the first day until the seventh day, that person shall be cut off from Israel. On the first day *there shall be* a holy convocation, and on the seventh day there shall be a holy convocation for you. No manner of work shall be done on them; but *that* which everyone must eat—that only may be prepared by you. So you shall observe *the Feast of Unleavened Bread,* for on this same day I will have brought your armies out of the land of Egypt. Therefore you shall observe this day throughout your generations as an everlasting ordinance. In the first *month,* on the fourteenth day of the month at evening, you shall eat unleavened bread, until the twenty-first day of the month at evening. For seven days no leaven shall be found in your houses, since whoever eats what is leavened, that same person shall be cut off from the congregation of Israel, whether *he is* a stranger or a native of the land. You shall eat nothing leavened; in all your dwellings you shall eat unleavened bread.' "

Then Moses called for all the elders of Israel and said to them, "Pick out and take lambs for yourselves according to your families, and kill the Passover *lamb*. And you shall take a bunch of hyssop, dip *it* in the blood that *is* in the basin, and strike the lintel and the two doorposts with the blood that *is* in the basin. And none of you shall go out of the door of his house until morning. For the LORD will pass through to strike the Egyptians; and when He sees the blood on the lintel and on the two doorposts, the LORD will pass over the door and not allow the destroyer to come into your houses to strike *you*. And you shall observe this thing as an ordinance for you and your sons forever. It will come to pass when you come to the land which the LORD will give you, just as He promised, that you shall keep this service. And it shall be, when your children say to you, 'What do you mean by this service?' that you shall say, 'It *is* the Passover sacrifice of the LORD, who passed over the houses of the children of Israel in Egypt when He struck the Egyptians and delivered our households.' " So the people bowed their heads and worshiped. Then the children of Israel went away and did *so;* just as the LORD had commanded Moses and Aaron, so they did.

And it came to pass at midnight that the LORD struck all the firstborn in the land of Egypt, from the firstborn of Pharaoh who sat on his throne to the firstborn of the captive who *was* in the dungeon, and all the firstborn of livestock. So Pharaoh rose in the night, he, all his servants, and all the Egyptians; and there was a great cry in Egypt, for *there was* not a house where *there was* not one dead.

Exodus 11:1–12:30

WORSHIP

He delivers me from my enemies.
You also lift me up above those who rise
 against me;
You have delivered me from the violent man.
Therefore I will give thanks to You, O LORD,
 among the Gentiles,
And sing praises to Your name.

Great deliverance He gives to His king,
And shows mercy to His anointed,
To David and his descendants forevermore.

Psalm 18:48-50

WISDOM

My son, keep your father's command,
And do not forsake the law of your mother.
Bind them continually upon your heart;
Tie them around your neck.
When you roam, they will lead you;
When you sleep, they will keep you;
And *when* you awake, they will speak with
 you.

Proverbs 6:20-22

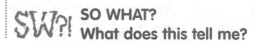

SO WHAT?
What does this tell me?

SET FREE

From a distance, we see another mountain range looming on the horizon. It is the story of how God added to His already growing reputation by setting the Israelites free from captivity in Egypt. The peaks in this range include the crossing of the Red Sea, the giving of the Law at Mount Sinai, and the erection of the tabernacle.

The Egyptians were the greatest military power on the face of the earth at this time. And the Israelites, although great in number, were no more a threat to the security of Egypt than an ant hill in your front yard. In order to convince the Egyptians they should listen to Moses and free the Israelites, God judged them with ten different plagues. None of the plagues were very pleasant but, as you saw in the last range, the tenth one was the worst. Through Moses, God warned Pharaoh that if he didn't free the Israelites, each firstborn son in Egypt would die. In order to protect the firstborn Israelite sons, each family was instructed to sacrifice a lamb and paint the doorposts of their house with the blood. That night, the homes where the blood had been applied were protected from the judgment that fell upon the Egyptians. This redemption of the Israelites by the blood of a lamb points ahead to the "Mount Everest" of the Bible, the sacrifice and death of Jesus Christ, the Lamb of God.

The Egyptians finally gave in and set the Israelites free. But after doing so, Pharaoh had a change of heart and sent his army into the desert to bring the Israelites back to Egypt. God had other plans. With the people in a panic, Moses told them to stand back and "see the salvation of the LORD which He will accomplish for you today" as God parted the Red Sea allowing them to escape to safety (Exodus 14:13). Just as the Israelites reached the opposite shore, the surging waters of the sea crashed down upon the Egyptians, thwarting their attempt to catch the Israelites. God the warrior had delivered His people.

Another peak on this mountain range is the giving of the Law. The word "law" is better understood as "instruction" and refers to the guidelines God gave Israel through Moses at Mount Sinai. These instructions were not to help the people live good enough lives to deserve God's love. God had already demonstrated His commitment to His people when He saved them from their captivity in Egypt. Rather the Law was to show the Israelites how to relate to a holy, living God. Many of the laws were specifically for Israel since they related to the priesthood and sacrifices. But much of the Law was a timeless window into God's holiness, revealing then and now how He would have us live in a love relationship with Him.

The erection of the tabernacle is another mountain peak in this range. As the people traveled about in the wilderness on their way to the land God promised Abraham in Genesis 12, God gave them instructions to build a portable, tent-like structure which would house holy objects used for religious observances. One major element in the tabernacle was the Ark of the Covenant—the place where God would meet with the High Priest.

EXIT FROM EGYPT

Exodus 12:31-40; 13:1-22; Psalm 19:1-3; Proverbs 6:23-24

Then he called for Moses and Aaron by night, and said, "Rise, go out from among my people, both you and the children of Israel. And go, serve the LORD as you have said. Also take your flocks and your herds, as you have said, and be gone; and bless me also."

And the Egyptians urged the people, that they might send them out of the land in haste. For they said, "We *shall* all *be* dead." So the people took their dough before it was leavened, having their kneading bowls bound up in their clothes on their shoulders. Now the children of Israel had done according to the word of Moses, and they had asked from the Egyptians articles of silver, articles of gold, and clothing. And the LORD had given the people favor in the sight of the Egyptians, so that they granted them *what they requested*. Thus they plundered the Egyptians.

Then the children of Israel journeyed from Rameses to Succoth, about six hundred thousand men on foot, besides children. A mixed multitude went up with them also, and flocks and herds—a great deal of livestock. And they baked unleavened cakes of the dough which they had brought out of Egypt; for it was not leavened, because they were driven out of Egypt and could not wait, nor had they prepared provisions for themselves.

Now the sojourn of the children of Israel who lived in Egypt *was* four hundred and thirty years.

Then the LORD spoke to Moses, saying, "Consecrate to Me all the firstborn, whatever opens the womb among the children of Israel, *both* of man and beast; it is Mine."

And Moses said to the people: "Remember this day in which you went out of Egypt, out of the house of bondage; for by strength of hand the LORD brought you out of this *place*. No leavened bread shall be eaten. On this day you are going out, in the month Abib. And it shall be, when the LORD brings you into the land of the Canaanites and the Hittites and the Amorites and the Hivites and the Jebusites, which He swore to your fathers to give you, a land flowing with milk and honey, that you shall keep this service in this month. Seven days you shall eat unleavened bread, and on the seventh day *there shall be* a feast to the LORD. Unleavened bread shall be eaten seven days. And no leavened bread shall be seen among you, nor shall leaven be seen among you in all your quarters. And you shall tell your son in that day, saying, '*This is done* because of what the LORD did for me when I came up from Egypt.' It shall be as a sign to you on your hand and as a memorial between your eyes, that the LORD's law may be in your mouth; for with a strong hand the LORD has brought you out of Egypt. You shall therefore keep this ordinance in its season from year to year.

"And it shall be, when the LORD brings you into the land of the Canaanites, as He swore to you and your fathers, and gives it to you, that you shall set apart to the LORD all that open the womb, that is, every firstborn that comes from an animal which you have; the males *shall be* the LORD's. But every firstborn of a donkey you shall redeem with a lamb; and if you will not redeem *it*, then you shall break its neck. And all the firstborn of man among your sons you shall redeem. So it shall be, when your son asks you in time to come, saying, 'What *is* this?' that you shall say to him, 'By strength of hand the LORD brought us out of Egypt, out of the house of bondage. And it came to pass, when Pharaoh was stubborn about letting us go, that the LORD killed all the firstborn in the land of Egypt, both the firstborn of man and the firstborn of beast. Therefore I sacrifice to the LORD all males that open the womb, but all the firstborn of my sons I redeem.' It shall be as a sign on your hand and as frontlets between your eyes, for by strength of hand the LORD brought us out of Egypt."

Then it came to pass, when Pharaoh had let the people go, that God did not lead them *by* way of the land of the Philistines, although that *was* near; for God said, "Lest perhaps the people change their minds when they see war, and return to Egypt." So God led the people around *by* way of the wilderness of the Red Sea. And the children of Israel went up in orderly ranks out of the land of Egypt.

And Moses took the bones of Joseph with him, for he had placed the children of Israel under solemn oath, saying, "God will surely visit you, and you shall carry up my bones from here with you."

SET FREE

So they took their journey from Succoth and camped in Etham at the edge of the wilderness. And the LORD went before them by day in a pillar of cloud to lead the way, and by night in a pillar of fire to give them light, so as to go by day and night. He did not take away the pillar of cloud by day or the pillar of fire by night *from* before the people.

Exodus 12:31-40; 13:1-22

The heavens declare the glory of God;
And the firmament shows His handiwork.
Day unto day utters speech,
And night unto night reveals knowledge.
There is no speech nor language
Where their voice is not heard.

Psalm 19:1-3

WISDOM

For the commandment *is* a lamp,
And the law a light;
Reproofs of instruction *are* the way of life,
To keep you from the evil woman,
From the flattering tongue of a seductress.

Proverbs 6:23-24

SW?! **SO WHAT?**
What does this tell me?

PARTING THE RED SEA

Exodus 14:5–15:18; Psalm 19:7-10; Proverbs 6:27-29

Now it was told the king of Egypt that the people had fled, and the heart of Pharaoh and his servants was turned against the people; and they said, "Why have we done this, that we have let Israel go from serving us?" So he made ready his chariot and took his people with him. Also, he took six hundred choice chariots, and all the chariots of Egypt with captains over every one of them. And the LORD hardened the heart of Pharaoh king of Egypt, and he pursued the children of Israel; and the children of Israel went out with boldness. So the Egyptians pursued them, all the horses *and* chariots of Pharaoh, his horsemen and his army, and overtook them camping by the sea beside Pi Hahiroth, before Baal Zephon.

And when Pharaoh drew near, the children of Israel lifted their eyes, and behold, the Egyptians marched after them. So they were very afraid, and the children of Israel cried out to the LORD. Then they said to Moses, "Because *there were* no graves in Egypt, have you taken us away to die in the wilderness? Why have you so dealt with us, to bring us up out of Egypt? *Is* this not the word that we told you in Egypt, saying, 'Let us alone that we may serve the Egyptians'? For *it would have been* better for us to serve the Egyptians than that we should die in the wilderness."

And Moses said to the people, "Do not be afraid. Stand still, and see the salvation of the LORD, which He will accomplish for you today. For the Egyptians whom you see today, you shall see again no more forever. The LORD will fight for you, and you shall hold your peace."

And the LORD said to Moses, "Why do you cry to Me? Tell the children of Israel to go forward. But lift up your rod, and stretch out your hand over the sea and divide it. And the children of Israel shall go on dry *ground* through the midst of the sea. And I indeed will harden the hearts of the Egyptians, and they shall follow them. So I will gain honor over Pharaoh and over all his army, his chariots, and his horsemen. Then the Egyptians shall know that I *am* the LORD, when I have gained honor for Myself over Pharaoh, his chariots, and his horsemen."

And the Angel of God, who went before the camp of Israel, moved and went behind them; and the pillar of cloud went from before them and stood behind them. So it came between the camp of the Egyptians and the camp of Israel. Thus it was a cloud and darkness *to the one,* and it gave light by night *to the other,* so that the one did not come near the other all that night.

Then Moses stretched out his hand over the sea; and the LORD caused the sea to go *back* by a strong east wind all that night, and made the sea into dry *land,* and the waters were divided. So the children of Israel went into the midst of the sea on the dry *ground,* and the waters *were* a wall to them on their right hand and on their left. And the Egyptians pursued and went after them into the midst of the sea, all Pharaoh's horses, his chariots, and his horsemen.

Now it came to pass, in the morning watch, that the LORD looked down upon the army of the Egyptians through the pillar of fire and cloud, and He troubled the army of the Egyptians. And He took off their chariot wheels, so that they drove them with difficulty; and the Egyptians said, "Let us flee from the face of Israel, for the LORD fights for them against the Egyptians."

Then the LORD said to Moses, "Stretch out your hand over the sea, that the waters may come back upon the Egyptians, on their chariots, and on their horsemen." And Moses stretched out his hand over the sea; and when the morning appeared, the sea returned to its full depth, while the Egyptians were fleeing into it. So the LORD overthrew the Egyptians in the midst of the sea. Then the waters returned and covered the chariots, the horsemen, *and* all the army of Pharaoh that came into the sea after them. Not so much as one of them remained. But the children of Israel had walked on dry *land* in the midst of the sea, and the waters *were* a wall to them on their right hand and on their left.

So the LORD saved Israel that day out of the hand of the Egyptians, and Israel saw the Egyptians dead on the seashore. Thus Israel saw the great work which the LORD had done in Egypt; so the people feared the LORD, and believed the LORD and His servant Moses.

Then Moses and the children of Israel sang this song to the LORD, and spoke, saying:

"I will sing to the LORD,
For He has triumphed gloriously!
The horse and its rider
He has thrown into the sea!
The LORD *is* my strength and song,
And He has become my salvation;
He *is* my God, and I will praise Him;
My father's God, and I will exalt Him.
The LORD *is* a man of war;
The LORD *is* His name.
Pharaoh's chariots and his army He has cast
    into the sea;
His chosen captains also are drowned in the
    Red Sea.
The depths have covered them;
They sank to the bottom like a stone.

"Your right hand, O LORD, has become glorious
    in power;
Your right hand, O LORD, has dashed the
    enemy in pieces.
And in the greatness of Your excellence
You have overthrown those who rose against
    You;
You sent forth Your wrath;
It consumed them like stubble.
And with the blast of Your nostrils
The waters were gathered together;
The floods stood upright like a heap;
The depths congealed in the heart of the sea.
The enemy said, 'I will pursue,
I will overtake,
I will divide the spoil;
My desire shall be satisfied on them.
I will draw my sword,
My hand shall destroy them.'
You blew with Your wind,
The sea covered them;
They sank like lead in the mighty waters.

"Who *is* like You, O LORD, among the gods?
Who *is* like You, glorious in holiness,
Fearful in praises, doing wonders?
You stretched out Your right hand;
The earth swallowed them.
You in Your mercy have led forth
The people whom You have redeemed;
You have guided *them* in Your strength
To Your holy habitation.

"The people will hear *and* be afraid;
Sorrow will take hold of the inhabitants of
    Philistia.
Then the chiefs of Edom will be dismayed;
The mighty men of Moab,

Trembling will take hold of them;
All the inhabitants of Canaan will melt away.
Fear and dread will fall on them;
By the greatness of Your arm
They will be *as* still as a stone,
Till Your people pass over, O LORD,
Till the people pass over
Whom You have purchased.
You will bring them in and plant them
In the mountain of Your inheritance,
In the place, O LORD, *which* You have made
For Your own dwelling,
The sanctuary, O LORD, *which* Your hands have
    established.

"The LORD shall reign forever and ever."

Exodus 14:5–15:18

WoRSHIP

The law of the LORD *is* perfect, converting the
    soul;
The testimony of the LORD *is* sure, making wise
    the simple;
The statutes of the LORD *are* right, rejoicing the
    heart;
The commandment of the LORD *is* pure,
    enlightening the eyes;
The fear of the LORD *is* clean, enduring forever;
The judgments of the LORD *are* true *and*
    righteous altogether.
More to be desired *are they* than gold,
Yea, than much fine gold;
Sweeter also than honey and the honeycomb.

Psalm 19:7-10

WiSDoM

Can a man take fire to his bosom,
And his clothes not be burned?
Can one walk on hot coals,
And his feet not be seared?
So *is* he who goes in to his neighbor's wife;
Whoever touches her shall not be innocent.

Proverbs 6:27-29

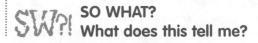 **SO WHAT?**
What does this tell me?

MOSES RECEIVES THE TEN COMMANDMENTS

Exodus 19:1-20; 20:1-17; Psalm 19:12-14; Proverbs 6:30-31

In the third month after the children of Israel had gone out of the land of Egypt, on the same day, they came *to* the Wilderness of Sinai. For they had departed from Rephidim, had come *to* the Wilderness of Sinai, and camped in the wilderness. So Israel camped there before the mountain.

And Moses went up to God, and the LORD called to him from the mountain, saying, "Thus you shall say to the house of Jacob, and tell the children of Israel: 'You have seen what I did to the Egyptians, and *how* I bore you on eagles' wings and brought you to Myself. Now therefore, if you will indeed obey My voice and keep My covenant, then you shall be a special treasure to Me above all people; for all the earth *is* Mine. And you shall be to Me a kingdom of priests and a holy nation.' These *are* the words which you shall speak to the children of Israel."

So Moses came and called for the elders of the people, and laid before them all these words which the LORD commanded him. Then all the people answered together and said, "All that the LORD has spoken we will do." So Moses brought back the words of the people to the LORD. And the LORD said to Moses, "Behold, I come to you in the thick cloud, that the people may hear when I speak with you, and believe you forever."

So Moses told the words of the people to the LORD.

Then the LORD said to Moses, "Go to the people and consecrate them today and tomorrow, and let them wash their clothes. And let them be ready for the third day. For on the third day the LORD will come down upon Mount Sinai in the sight of all the people. You shall set bounds for the people all around, saying, 'Take heed to yourselves *that* you do *not* go up to the mountain or touch its base. Whoever touches the mountain shall surely be put to death. Not a hand shall touch him, but he shall surely be stoned or shot *with an arrow*; whether man or beast, he shall not live.' When the trumpet sounds long, they shall come near the mountain."

So Moses went down from the mountain to the people and sanctified the people, and they washed their clothes. And he said to the people, "Be ready for the third day; do not come near *your* wives."

Then it came to pass on the third day, in the morning, that there were thunderings and lightnings, and a thick cloud on the mountain; and the sound of the trumpet was very loud, so that all the people who *were* in the camp trembled. And Moses brought the people out of the camp to meet with God, and they stood at the foot of the mountain. Now Mount Sinai *was* completely in smoke, because the LORD descended upon it in fire. Its smoke ascended like the smoke of a furnace, and the whole mountain quaked greatly. And when the blast of the trumpet sounded long and became louder and louder, Moses spoke, and God answered him by voice. Then the LORD came down upon Mount Sinai, on the top of the mountain. And the LORD called Moses to the top of the mountain, and Moses went up.

And God spoke all these words, saying:

"I *am* the LORD your God, who brought you out of the land of Egypt, out of the house of bondage.

"You shall have no other gods before Me.

"You shall not make for yourself a carved image—any likeness *of anything* that *is* in heaven above, or that *is* in the earth beneath, or that *is* in the water under the earth; you shall not bow down to them nor serve them. For I, the LORD your God, *am* a jealous God, visiting the iniquity of the fathers upon the children to the third and fourth *generations* of those who hate Me, but showing mercy to thousands, to those who love Me and keep My commandments.

"You shall not take the name of the LORD your God in vain, for the LORD will not hold *him* guiltless who takes His name in vain.

"Remember the Sabbath day, to keep it holy. Six days you shall labor and do all your work, but the seventh day *is* the Sabbath of the LORD your God. *In it* you shall do no work: you, nor your son, nor your daughter, nor your male servant, nor your female servant, nor your cattle, nor your stranger who *is* within your gates. For *in* six days the LORD made the heavens and the earth, the sea, and all that *is* in them, and rested the seventh day. Therefore the LORD blessed the Sabbath day and hallowed it.

"Honor your father and your mother, that your days may be long upon the land which the LORD your God is giving you.

"You shall not murder.

"You shall not commit adultery.

"You shall not steal.

"You shall not bear false witness against your neighbor.

"You shall not covet your neighbor's house; you shall not covet your neighbor's wife, nor his male servant, nor his female servant, nor his ox, nor his donkey, nor anything that *is* your neighbor's."

Exodus 19:1-20; 20:1-17

Who can understand *his* errors?
Cleanse me from secret *faults*.
Keep back Your servant also from
    presumptuous *sins;*
Let them not have dominion over me.
Then I shall be blameless,
And I shall be innocent of great transgression.

Let the words of my mouth and the meditation
    of my heart
Be acceptable in Your sight,
O LORD, my strength and my Redeemer.

Psalm 19:12-14

WISDOM

People do not despise a thief
If he steals to satisfy himself when he is
    starving.
Yet *when* he is found, he must restore
    sevenfold;
He may have to give up all the substance of
    his house.

Proverbs 6:30-31

SW?! **SO WHAT?**
What does this tell me?

APPLICATIONS OF GOD'S LAW: PART ONE

Exodus 21:1, 12-34; 22:1-22, 25; Psalm 20:1-3; Proverbs 6:32-33

"Now these *are* the judgments which you shall set before them:

"He who strikes a man so that he dies shall surely be put to death. However, if he did not lie in wait, but God delivered *him* into his hand, then I will appoint for you a place where he may flee.

"But if a man acts with premeditation against his neighbor, to kill him by treachery, you shall take him from My altar, that he may die.

"And he who strikes his father or his mother shall surely be put to death.

"He who kidnaps a man and sells him, or if he is found in his hand, shall surely be put to death.

"And he who curses his father or his mother shall surely be put to death.

"If men contend with each other, and one strikes the other with a stone or with *his* fist, and he does not die but is confined to *his* bed, if he rises again and walks about outside with his staff, then he who struck *him* shall be acquitted. He shall only pay *for* the loss of his time, and shall provide *for* him to be thoroughly healed.

"And if a man beats his male or female servant with a rod, so that he dies under his hand, he shall surely be punished. Notwithstanding, if he remains alive a day or two, he shall not be punished; for he *is* his property.

"If men fight, and hurt a woman with child, so that she gives birth prematurely, yet no harm follows, he shall surely be punished accordingly as the woman's husband imposes on him; and he shall pay as the judges *determine*. But if *any* harm follows, then you shall give life for life, eye for eye, tooth for tooth, hand for hand, foot for foot, burn for burn, wound for wound, stripe for stripe.

"If a man strikes the eye of his male or female servant, and destroys it, he shall let him go free for the sake of his eye. And if he knocks out the tooth of his male or female servant, he shall let him go free for the sake of his tooth.

"If an ox gores a man or a woman to death, then the ox shall surely be stoned, and its flesh shall not be eaten; but the owner of the ox *shall be* acquitted. But if the ox tended to thrust with its horn in times past, and it has been made known to his owner, and he has not kept it confined, so that it has killed a man or a woman, the ox shall be stoned and its owner also shall be put to death. If there is imposed on him a sum of money, then he shall pay to redeem his life, whatever is imposed on him. Whether it has gored a son or gored a daughter, according to this judgment it shall be done to him. If the ox gores a male or female servant, he shall give to their master thirty shekels of silver, and the ox shall be stoned.

"And if a man opens a pit, or if a man digs a pit and does not cover it, and an ox or a donkey falls in it, the owner of the pit shall make *it* good; he shall give money to their owner, but the dead *animal* shall be his.

"If a man steals an ox or a sheep, and slaughters it or sells it, he shall restore five oxen for an ox and four sheep for a sheep. If the thief is found breaking in, and he is struck so that he dies, *there shall be* no guilt for his bloodshed. If the sun has risen on him, *there shall be* guilt for his bloodshed. He should make full restitution; if he has nothing, then he shall be sold for his theft. If the theft is certainly found alive in his hand, whether it is an ox or donkey or sheep, he shall restore double.

"If a man causes a field or vineyard to be grazed, and lets loose his animal, and it feeds in another man's field, he shall make restitution from the best of his own field and the best of his own vineyard.

"If fire breaks out and catches in thorns, so that stacked grain, standing grain, or the field is consumed, he who kindled the fire shall surely make restitution.

"If a man delivers to his neighbor money or articles to keep, and it is stolen out of the man's house, if the thief is found, he shall pay double. If the thief is not found, then the master of the house shall be brought to the judges *to see* whether he has put his hand into his neighbor's goods.

"For any kind of trespass, *whether it concerns* an ox, a donkey, a sheep, or clothing, *or* for any kind of lost thing which *another* claims to be his, the cause of both parties shall come before the judges; *and* whomever the judges condemn shall pay double to his neighbor. If a man delivers to his neighbor a donkey, an ox, a sheep, or any animal to keep, and it dies, is hurt, or driven away, no one seeing *it, then* an oath of the LORD shall be between them both, that he has not put his hand into his neighbor's goods; and the owner of it shall accept *that,* and he shall not make *it* good. But if, in fact, it is stolen from him, he shall make restitution to the owner of it. If it is torn to pieces *by a beast, then* he shall bring it as evidence, *and* he shall not make good what was torn.

"And if a man borrows *anything* from his neighbor, and it becomes injured or dies, the owner of it not *being* with it, he shall surely make *it* good. If its owner *was* with it, he shall not make *it* good; if it *was* hired, it came for its hire.

"If a man entices a virgin who is not betrothed, and lies with her, he shall surely pay the bride-price for her *to be* his wife. If her father utterly refuses to give her to him, he shall pay money according to the bride-price of virgins.

"You shall not permit a sorceress to live.

"Whoever lies with an animal shall surely be put to death.

"He who sacrifices to *any* god, except to the LORD only, he shall be utterly destroyed.

"You shall neither mistreat a stranger nor oppress him, for you were strangers in the land of Egypt.

"You shall not afflict any widow or fatherless child.

"If you lend money to *any of* My people *who are* poor among you, you shall not be like a moneylender to him; you shall not charge him interest."

Exodus 21:1, 12-34; 22:1-22, 25

WORSHIP

May the LORD answer you in the day of trouble;
May the name of the God of Jacob defend
   you;
May He send you help from the sanctuary,
And strengthen you out of Zion;
May He remember all your offerings,
And accept your burnt sacrifice.   Selah

Psalm 20:1-3

WISDOM

Whoever commits adultery with a woman
   lacks understanding;
He *who* does so destroys his own soul.
Wounds and dishonor he will get,
And his reproach will not be wiped away.

Proverbs 6:32-33

SW?! SO WHAT?
What does this tell me?

APPLICATIONS OF GOD'S LAW: PART TWO

Exodus 23:1-25; 24:1-8, 12-18; Psalm 20:6-7; Proverbs 7:1-3

"You shall not circulate a false report. Do not put your hand with the wicked to be an unrighteous witness. You shall not follow a crowd to do evil; nor shall you testify in a dispute so as to turn aside after many to pervert *justice*. You shall not show partiality to a poor man in his dispute.

"If you meet your enemy's ox or his donkey going astray, you shall surely bring it back to him again. If you see the donkey of one who hates you lying under its burden, and you would refrain from helping it, you shall surely help him with it.

"You shall not pervert the judgment of your poor in his dispute. Keep yourself far from a false matter; do not kill the innocent and righteous. For I will not justify the wicked. And you shall take no bribe, for a bribe blinds the discerning and perverts the words of the righteous.

"Also you shall not oppress a stranger, for you know the heart of a stranger, because you were strangers in the land of Egypt.

"Six years you shall sow your land and gather in its produce, but the seventh *year* you shall let it rest and lie fallow, that the poor of your people may eat; and what they leave, the beasts of the field may eat. In like manner you shall do with your vineyard *and* your olive grove. Six days you shall do your work, and on the seventh day you shall rest, that your ox and your donkey may rest, and the son of your female servant and the stranger may be refreshed.

"And in all that I have said to you, be circumspect and make no mention of the name of other gods, nor let it be heard from your mouth.

"Three times you shall keep a feast to Me in the year: You shall keep the Feast of Unleavened Bread (you shall eat unleavened bread seven days, as I commanded you, at the time appointed in the month of Abib, for in it you came out of Egypt; none shall appear before Me empty); and the Feast of Harvest, the firstfruits of your labors which you have sown in the field; and the Feast of Ingathering at the end of the year, when you have gathered in *the fruit of* your labors from the field.

"Three times in the year all your males shall appear before the Lord GOD.

"You shall not offer the blood of My sacrifice with leavened bread; nor shall the fat of My sacrifice remain until morning. The first of the firstfruits of your land you shall bring into the house of the LORD your God. You shall not boil a young goat in its mother's milk.

"Behold, I send an Angel before you to keep you in the way and to bring you into the place which I have prepared. Beware of Him and obey His voice; do not provoke Him, for He will not pardon your transgressions; for My name *is* in Him. But if you indeed obey His voice and do all that I speak, then I will be an enemy to your enemies and an adversary to your adversaries. For My Angel will go before you and bring you in to the Amorites and the Hittites and the Perizzites and the Canaanites and the Hivites and the Jebusites; and I will cut them off. You shall not bow down to their gods, nor serve them, nor do according to their works; but you shall utterly overthrow them and completely break down their *sacred* pillars.

"So you shall serve the LORD your God, and He will bless your bread and your water. And I will take sickness away from the midst of you."

Now He said to Moses, "Come up to the LORD, you and Aaron, Nadab and Abihu, and seventy of the elders of Israel, and worship from afar. And Moses alone shall come near the LORD, but they shall not come near; nor shall the people go up with him."

So Moses came and told the people all the words of the LORD and all the judgments. And all the people answered with one voice and said, "All the words which the LORD has said we will do." And Moses wrote all the words of the LORD. And he rose early in the morning, and built an altar at the foot of the mountain, and twelve pillars according to the twelve tribes of Israel. Then he sent young men of the children of Israel, who offered burnt offerings and sacrificed peace offerings of oxen to the LORD. And Moses took half the blood and put *it* in basins, and half the blood he sprinkled on the altar. Then he took the Book of the Covenant and read in the

SET FREE

hearing of the people. And they said, "All that the LORD has said we will do, and be obedient." And Moses took the blood, sprinkled *it* on the people, and said, "This is the blood of the covenant which the LORD has made with you according to all these words."

Then the LORD said to Moses, "Come up to Me on the mountain and be there; and I will give you tablets of stone, and the law and commandments which I have written, that you may teach them."

So Moses arose with his assistant Joshua, and Moses went up to the mountain of God. And he said to the elders, "Wait here for us until we come back to you. Indeed, Aaron and Hur *are* with you. If any man has a difficulty, let him go to them." Then Moses went up into the mountain, and a cloud covered the mountain.

Now the glory of the LORD rested on Mount Sinai, and the cloud covered it six days. And on the seventh day He called to Moses out of the midst of the cloud. The sight of the glory of the LORD *was* like a consuming fire on the top of the mountain in the eyes of the children of Israel. So Moses went into the midst of the cloud and went up into the mountain. And Moses was on the mountain forty days and forty nights.

Exodus 23:1-25; 24:1-8, 12-18

WORSHIP

Now I know that the LORD saves His anointed;
He will answer him from His holy heaven
With the saving strength of His right hand.

Some *trust* in chariots, and some in horses;
But we will remember the name of the LORD
   our God.

Psalm 20:6-7

WISDOM

My son, keep my words,
And treasure my commands within you.
Keep my commands and live,
And my law as the apple of your eye.
Bind them on your fingers;
Write them on the tablet of your heart.

Proverbs 7:1-3

SW?! **SO WHAT?**
What does this tell me?

BLUEPRINTS FOR THE TABERNACLE

Exodus 25; Psalm 21:1-3; Proverbs 7:4-5

Then the LORD spoke to Moses, saying: "Speak to the children of Israel, that they bring Me an offering. From everyone who gives it willingly with his heart you shall take My offering. And this *is* the offering which you shall take from them: gold, silver, and bronze; blue, purple, and scarlet *thread,* fine linen, and goats' *hair;* ram skins dyed red, badger skins, and acacia wood; oil for the light, and spices for the anointing oil and for the sweet incense; onyx stones, and stones to be set in the ephod and in the breastplate. And let them make Me a sanctuary, that I may dwell among them. According to all that I show you, *that is,* the pattern of the tabernacle and the pattern of all its furnishings, just so you shall make *it.*

"And they shall make an ark of acacia wood; two and a half cubits *shall be* its length, a cubit and a half its width, and a cubit and a half its height. And you shall overlay it with pure gold, inside and out you shall overlay it, and shall make on it a molding of gold all around. You shall cast four rings of gold for it, and put *them* in its four corners; two rings *shall be* on one side, and two rings on the other side. And you shall make poles *of* acacia wood, and overlay them with gold. You shall put the poles into the rings on the sides of the ark, that the ark may be carried by them. The poles shall be in the rings of the ark; they shall not be taken from it. And you shall put into the ark the Testimony which I will give you.

"You shall make a mercy seat of pure gold; two and a half cubits *shall be* its length and a cubit and a half its width. And you shall make two cherubim of gold; of hammered work you shall make them at the two ends of the mercy seat. Make one cherub at one end, and the other cherub at the other end; you shall make the cherubim at the two ends of it *of one piece* with the mercy seat. And the cherubim shall stretch out *their* wings above, covering the mercy seat with their wings, and they shall face one another; the faces of the cherubim *shall be* toward the mercy seat. You shall put the mercy seat on top of the ark, and in the ark you shall put the Testimony that I will give you. And there I

will meet with you, and I will speak with you from above the mercy seat, from between the two cherubim which *are* on the ark of the Testimony, about everything which I will give you in commandment to the children of Israel.

"You shall also make a table of acacia wood; two cubits *shall be* its length, a cubit its width, and a cubit and a half its height. And you shall overlay it with pure gold, and make a molding of gold all around. You shall make for it a frame of a handbreadth all around, and you shall make a gold molding for the frame all around. And you shall make for it four rings of gold, and put the rings on the four corners that *are* at its four legs. The rings shall be close to the frame, as holders for the poles to bear the table. And you shall make the poles of acacia wood, and overlay them with gold, that the table may be carried with them. You shall make its dishes, its pans, its pitchers, and its bowls for pouring. You shall make them of pure gold. And you shall set the showbread on the table before Me always.

"You shall also make a lampstand of pure gold; the lampstand shall be of hammered work. Its shaft, its branches, its bowls, its *ornamental* knobs, and flowers shall be *of one piece.* And six branches shall come out of its sides: three branches of the lampstand out of one side, and three branches of the lampstand out of the other side. Three bowls *shall be* made like almond *blossoms* on one branch, *with* an *ornamental* knob and a flower, and three bowls made like almond *blossoms* on the other branch, *with* an *ornamental* knob and a flower—and so for the six branches that come out of the lampstand. On the lampstand itself four bowls *shall be* made like almond *blossoms, each with* its *ornamental* knob and flower. And *there shall be* a knob under the *first* two branches of the same, a knob under the *second* two branches of the same, and a knob under the *third* two branches of the same, according to the six branches that extend from the lampstand. Their knobs and their branches *shall be of one piece;* all of it *shall be* one hammered piece of pure gold. You shall make seven lamps for it, and they shall arrange its lamps so that they give light in front of it. And its wick-trimmers and their trays *shall be* of pure gold. It shall be made of a talent of pure gold, with all these utensils. And see to it that you make *them* according to the pattern which was shown you on the mountain."

Exodus 25

WORSHIP

The king shall have joy in Your strength, O LORD;
And in Your salvation how greatly shall he
    rejoice!
You have given him his heart's desire,
And have not withheld the request of his lips.
                                            Selah

For You meet him with the blessings of
    goodness;
You set a crown of pure gold upon his head.

Psalm 21:1-3

WISDOM

Say to wisdom, "You *are* my sister,"
And call understanding *your* nearest kin,
That they may keep you from the immoral
    woman,
From the seductress *who* flatters with her
    words.

Proverbs 7:4-5

SW?! **SO WHAT?**
What does this tell me?

THE PEOPLE MAKE AN IDOL

Exodus 32; Psalm 21:7, 13; Proverbs 8:1, 10-11

Now when the people saw that Moses delayed coming down from the mountain, the people gathered together to Aaron, and said to him, "Come, make us gods that shall go before us; for *as for* this Moses, the man who brought us up out of the land of Egypt, we do not know what has become of him."

And Aaron said to them, "Break off the golden earrings which *are* in the ears of your wives, your sons, and your daughters, and bring *them* to me." So all the people broke off the golden earrings which *were* in their ears, and brought *them* to Aaron. And he received *the gold* from their hand, and he fashioned it with an engraving tool, and made a molded calf.

Then they said, "This *is* your god, O Israel, that brought you out of the land of Egypt!"

So when Aaron saw *it,* he built an altar before it. And Aaron made a proclamation and said, "Tomorrow *is* a feast to the LORD." Then they rose early on the next day, offered burnt offerings, and brought peace offerings; and the people sat down to eat and drink, and rose up to play.

And the LORD said to Moses, "Go, get down! For your people whom you brought out of the land of Egypt have corrupted *themselves.* They have turned aside quickly out of the way which I commanded them. They have made themselves a molded calf, and worshiped it and sacrificed to it, and said, 'This *is* your god, O Israel, that brought you out of the land of Egypt!' " And the LORD said to Moses, "I have seen this people, and indeed it *is* a stiff-necked people! Now therefore, let Me alone, that My wrath may burn hot against them and I may consume them. And I will make of you a great nation."

Then Moses pleaded with the LORD his God, and said: "LORD, why does Your wrath burn hot against Your people whom You have brought out of the land of Egypt with great power and with a mighty hand? Why should the Egyptians speak, and say, 'He brought them out to harm them, to kill them in the mountains, and to consume them from the face of the earth'? Turn from Your fierce wrath, and relent from this harm to Your people. Remember Abraham, Isaac, and Israel, Your servants, to whom You swore by Your own self, and said to them, 'I will multiply your descendants as the stars of heaven; and all this land that I have spoken of I give to your descendants, and they shall inherit *it* forever.' " So the LORD relented from the harm which He said He would do to His people.

And Moses turned and went down from the mountain, and the two tablets of the Testimony *were* in his hand. The tablets *were* written on both sides; on the one *side* and on the other they were written. Now the tablets *were* the work of God, and the writing *was* the writing of God engraved on the tablets.

And when Joshua heard the noise of the people as they shouted, he said to Moses, "*There is* a noise of war in the camp."

But he said:

"*It is* not the noise of the shout of victory,
Nor the noise of the cry of defeat,
But the sound of singing I hear."

So it was, as soon as he came near the camp, that he saw the calf *and* the dancing. So Moses' anger became hot, and he cast the tablets out of his hands and broke them at the foot of the mountain. Then he took the calf which they had made, burned *it* in the fire, and ground *it* to powder; and he scattered *it* on the water and made the children of Israel drink *it.* And Moses said to Aaron, "What did this people do to you that you have brought *so* great a sin upon them?"

So Aaron said, "Do not let the anger of my lord become hot. You know the people, that they *are set* on evil. For they said to me, 'Make us gods that shall go before us; *as for* this Moses, the man who brought us out of the land of Egypt, we do not know what has become of him.' And I said to them, 'Whoever has any gold, let them break *it* off.' So they gave *it* to me, and I cast it into the fire, and this calf came out."

Now when Moses saw that the people *were* unrestrained (for Aaron had not restrained them, to *their* shame among their enemies), then Moses stood in the entrance of the camp, and said, "Whoever *is* on the LORD's side—*come* to me." And all the sons of Levi gathered themselves together to him.

SET FREE

And he said to them, "Thus says the LORD God of Israel: 'Let every man put his sword on his side, and go in and out from entrance to entrance throughout the camp, and let every man kill his brother, every man his companion, and every man his neighbor.'" So the sons of Levi did according to the word of Moses. And about three thousand men of the people fell that day. Then Moses said, "Consecrate yourselves today to the LORD, that He may bestow on you a blessing this day, for every man has opposed his son and his brother."

Now it came to pass on the next day that Moses said to the people, "You have committed a great sin. So now I will go up to the LORD; perhaps I can make atonement for your sin." Then Moses returned to the LORD and said, "Oh, these people have committed a great sin, and have made for themselves a god of gold! Yet now, if You will forgive their sin—but if not, I pray, blot me out of Your book which You have written."

And the LORD said to Moses, "Whoever has sinned against Me, I will blot him out of My book. Now therefore, go, lead the people to *the place* of which I have spoken to you. Behold, My Angel shall go before you. Nevertheless, in the day when I visit for punishment, I will visit punishment upon them for their sin."

So the LORD plagued the people because of what they did with the calf which Aaron made.

Exodus 32

WORSHIP

For the king trusts in the LORD,
And through the mercy of the Most High he
  shall not be moved.

Be exalted, O LORD, in Your own strength!
We will sing and praise Your power.

Psalm 21:7, 13

WISDOM

Does not wisdom cry out,
And understanding lift up her voice?

"Receive my instruction, and not silver,
And knowledge rather than choice gold;
For wisdom *is* better than rubies,
And all the things one may desire cannot be
  compared with her."

Proverbs 8:1, 10-11

SW?! SO WHAT?
What does this tell me?

THE TEN COMMANDMENTS: SECOND PRINTING

Exodus 33:7–34:17, 27-35; Psalm 22:1, 3-4; Proverbs 8:12, 17

Moses took his tent and pitched it outside the camp, far from the camp, and called it the tabernacle of meeting. And it came to pass *that* everyone who sought the LORD went out to the tabernacle of meeting which *was* outside the camp. So it was, whenever Moses went out to the tabernacle, *that* all the people rose, and each man stood *at* his tent door and watched Moses until he had gone into the tabernacle. And it came to pass, when Moses entered the tabernacle, that the pillar of cloud descended and stood *at* the door of the tabernacle, and *the* LORD talked with Moses. All the people saw the pillar of cloud standing *at* the tabernacle door, and all the people rose and worshiped, each man *in* his tent door. So the LORD spoke to Moses face to face, as a man speaks to his friend. And he would return to the camp, but his servant Joshua the son of Nun, a young man, did not depart from the tabernacle.

Then Moses said to the LORD, "See, You say to me, 'Bring up this people.' But You have not let me know whom You will send with me. Yet You have said, 'I know you by name, and you have also found grace in My sight.' Now therefore, I pray, if I have found grace in Your sight, show me now Your way, that I may know You and that I may find grace in Your sight. And consider that this nation *is* Your people."

And He said, "My Presence will go *with you,* and I will give you rest."

Then he said to Him, "If Your Presence does not go *with us,* do not bring us up from here. For how then will it be known that Your people and I have found grace in Your sight, except You go with us? So we shall be separate, Your people and I, from all the people who *are* upon the face of the earth."

So the LORD said to Moses, "I will also do this thing that you have spoken; for you have found grace in My sight, and I know you by name."

And he said, "Please, show me Your glory."

Then He said, "I will make all My goodness pass before you, and I will proclaim the name of the LORD before you. I will be gra-cious to whom I will be gracious, and I will have compassion on whom I will have compassion." But He said, "You cannot see My face; for no man shall see Me, and live." And the LORD said, "Here is a place by Me, and you shall stand on the rock. So it shall be, while My glory passes by, that I will put you in the cleft of the rock, and will cover you with My hand while I pass by. Then I will take away My hand, and you shall see My back; but My face shall not be seen."

And the LORD said to Moses, "Cut two tablets of stone like the first *ones,* and I will write on *these* tablets the words that were on the first tablets which you broke. So be ready in the morning, and come up in the morning to Mount Sinai, and present yourself to Me there on the top of the mountain. And no man shall come up with you, and let no man be seen throughout all the mountain; let neither flocks nor herds feed before that mountain."

So he cut two tablets of stone like the first *ones.* Then Moses rose early in the morning and went up Mount Sinai, as the LORD had commanded him; and he took in his hand the two tablets of stone.

Now the LORD descended in the cloud and stood with him there, and proclaimed the name of the LORD. And the LORD passed before him and proclaimed, "The LORD, the LORD God, merciful and gracious, longsuffering, and abounding in goodness and truth, keeping mercy for thousands, forgiving iniquity and transgression and sin, by no means clearing *the guilty,* visiting the iniquity of the fathers upon the children and the children's children to the third and the fourth generation."

So Moses made haste and bowed his head toward the earth, and worshiped. Then he said, "If now I have found grace in Your sight, O Lord, let my Lord, I pray, go among us, even though we *are* a stiff-necked people; and pardon our iniquity and our sin, and take us as Your inheritance."

And He said: "Behold, I make a covenant. Before all your people I will do marvels such as have not been done in all the earth, nor in any nation; and all the people among whom you *are* shall see the work of the LORD. For it *is* an awesome thing that I will do with you. Observe what I command you this day. Behold, I am driving out from before you the Amorite and the Canaanite and the Hittite and the Perizzite and the Hivite and the Jebusite. Take heed to yourself, lest you make a covenant with the inhabitants of the land where you are going, lest it be a snare in your midst. But you shall destroy their altars, break their *sacred* pillars, and cut down their wooden images (for you shall worship no other god, for the LORD, whose name *is* Jealous, *is* a jealous God), lest you make a covenant with the inhabitants of the land, and they play the harlot with their gods and make sacrifice to their gods, and *one of them* invites you and you eat of his sacrifice, and you take of his daughters for your sons, and his daughters play the harlot with their gods and make your sons play the harlot with their gods.

"You shall make no molded gods for yourselves."

Then the LORD said to Moses, "Write these words, for according to the tenor of these words I have made a covenant with you and with Israel." So he was there with the LORD forty days and forty nights; he neither ate bread nor drank water. And He wrote on the tablets the words of the covenant, the Ten Commandments.

Now it was so, when Moses came down from Mount Sinai (and the two tablets of the Testimony *were* in Moses' hand when he came down from the mountain), that Moses did not know that the skin of his face shone while he talked with Him. So when Aaron and all the children of Israel saw Moses, behold, the skin of his face shone, and they were afraid to come near him. Then Moses called to them, and Aaron and all the rulers of the congregation returned to him; and Moses talked with them. Afterward all the children of Israel came near, and he gave them as commandments all that the LORD had spoken with him on Mount Sinai. And when Moses had finished speaking with them, he put a veil on his face. But whenever Moses went in before the LORD to speak with Him, he would take the veil off until he came out; and he would come out and speak to the children of Israel whatever he had been commanded. And whenever the children of Israel saw the face of Moses, that the skin of Moses' face shone, then Moses would put the veil on his face again, until he went in to speak with Him.

Exodus 33:7–34:17, 27-35

WORSHIP

My God, My God, why have You forsaken Me?
Why are You so far from helping Me,
And from the words of My groaning?

But You *are* holy,
Enthroned in the praises of Israel.
Our fathers trusted in You;
They trusted, and You delivered them.

Psalm 22:1, 3-4

WISDOM

"I, wisdom, dwell with prudence,
And find out knowledge *and* discretion.

"I love those who love me,
And those who seek me diligently will find me."

Proverbs 8:12, 17

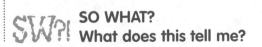

SO WHAT?
What does this tell me?

COMPLETING THE TABERNACLE

Exodus 39:32–40:35; Psalm 22:16-18; Proverbs 9:8-9

Thus all the work of the tabernacle of the tent of meeting was finished. And the children of Israel did according to all that the LORD had commanded Moses; so they did. And they brought the tabernacle to Moses, the tent and all its furnishings: its clasps, its boards, its bars, its pillars, and its sockets; the covering of ram skins dyed red, the covering of badger skins, and the veil of the covering; the ark of the Testimony with its poles, and the mercy seat; the table, all its utensils, and the showbread; the pure *gold* lampstand with its lamps (the lamps set in order), all its utensils, and the oil for light; the gold altar, the anointing oil, and the sweet incense; the screen for the tabernacle door; the bronze altar, its grate of bronze, its poles, and all its utensils; the laver with its base; the hangings of the court, its pillars and its sockets, the screen for the court gate, its cords, and its pegs; all the utensils for the service of the tabernacle, for the tent of meeting; and the garments of ministry, to minister in the holy *place:* the holy garments for Aaron the priest, and his sons' garments, to minister as priests.

According to all that the LORD had commanded Moses, so the children of Israel did all the work. Then Moses looked over all the work, and indeed they had done it; as the LORD had commanded, just so they had done it. And Moses blessed them.

Then the LORD spoke to Moses, saying: "On the first day of the first month you shall set up the tabernacle of the tent of meeting. You shall put in it the ark of the Testimony, and partition off the ark with the veil. You shall bring in the table and arrange the things that are to be set in order on it; and you shall bring in the lampstand and light its lamps. You shall also set the altar of gold for the incense before the ark of the Testimony, and put up the screen for the door of the tabernacle. Then you shall set the altar of the burnt offering before the door of the tabernacle of the tent of meeting. And you shall set the laver between the tabernacle of meeting and the altar, and put water in it. You shall set up the court all around, and hang up the screen at the court gate.

"And you shall take the anointing oil, and anoint the tabernacle and all that *is* in it;

and you shall hallow it and all its utensils, and it shall be holy. You shall anoint the altar of the burnt offering and all its utensils, and consecrate the altar. The altar shall be most holy. And you shall anoint the laver and its base, and consecrate it.

"Then you shall bring Aaron and his sons to the door of the tabernacle of meeting and wash them with water. You shall put the holy garments on Aaron, and anoint him and consecrate him, that he may minister to Me as priest. And you shall bring his sons and clothe them with tunics. You shall anoint them, as you anointed their father, that they may minister to Me as priests; for their anointing shall surely be an everlasting priesthood throughout their generations."

Thus Moses did; according to all that the LORD had commanded him, so he did.

And it came to pass in the first month of the second year, on the first *day* of the month, *that* the tabernacle was raised up. So Moses raised up the tabernacle, fastened its sockets, set up its boards, put in its bars, and raised up its pillars. And he spread out the tent over the tabernacle and put the covering of the tent on top of it, as the LORD had commanded Moses. He took the Testimony and put *it* into the ark, inserted the poles through the rings of the ark, and put the mercy seat on top of the ark. And he brought the ark into the tabernacle, hung up the veil of the covering, and partitioned off the ark of the Testimony, as the LORD had commanded Moses.

He put the table in the tabernacle of meeting, on the north side of the tabernacle, outside the veil; and he set the bread in order upon it before the LORD, as the LORD had commanded Moses. He put the lampstand in the tabernacle of meeting, across from the table, on the south side of the tabernacle; and he lit the lamps before the LORD, as the LORD had commanded Moses. He put the gold altar in the tabernacle of meeting in front of the veil; and he burned sweet incense on it, as the LORD had commanded Moses. He hung up the screen *at* the door of the tabernacle. And he put the altar of burnt offering *before* the door of the tabernacle of the tent of meeting, and offered upon it the burnt offering and the grain offering, as the LORD had commanded Moses. He set the laver between the tabernacle of meeting and the altar, and put water there for washing; and Moses, Aaron, and his sons would wash their hands and their feet *with water* from it. Whenever they went into the tabernacle of meeting, and when they came near the altar, they washed, as the LORD had commanded Moses. And he raised up the court all around the tabernacle and the altar, and hung up the screen of the court gate. So Moses finished the work.

Then the cloud covered the tabernacle of meeting, and the glory of the LORD filled the tabernacle. And Moses was not able to enter the tabernacle of meeting, because the cloud rested above it, and the glory of the LORD filled the tabernacle.

Exodus 39:32–40:35

WORSHIP

For dogs have surrounded Me;
The congregation of the wicked has enclosed Me.
They pierced My hands and My feet;
I can count all My bones.
They look *and* stare at Me.
They divide My garments among them,
And for My clothing they cast lots.

Psalm 22:16-18

WISDOM

Do not correct a scoffer, lest he hate you;
Rebuke a wise *man,* and he will love you.
Give *instruction* to a wise *man,* and he will be still wiser;
Teach a just *man,* and he will increase in learning.

Proverbs 9:8-9

SW?! SO WHAT?
What does this tell me?

THE BURNT AND GRAIN OFFERINGS

Leviticus 1–2; Psalm 22:22-24; Proverbs 9:10-12

Now the LORD called to Moses, and spoke to him from the tabernacle of meeting, saying, "Speak to the children of Israel, and say to them: 'When any one of you brings an offering to the LORD, you shall bring your offering of the livestock—of the herd and of the flock.

'If his offering is a burnt sacrifice of the herd, let him offer a male without blemish; he shall offer it of his own free will at the door of the tabernacle of meeting before the LORD. Then he shall put his hand on the head of the burnt offering, and it will be accepted on his behalf to make atonement for him. He shall kill the bull before the LORD; and the priests, Aaron's sons, shall bring the blood and sprinkle the blood all around on the altar that is by the door of the tabernacle of meeting. And he shall skin the burnt offering and cut it into its pieces. The sons of Aaron the priest shall put fire on the altar, and lay the wood in order on the fire. Then the priests, Aaron's sons, shall lay the parts, the head, and the fat in order on the wood that is on the fire upon the altar; but he shall wash its entrails and its legs with water. And the priest shall burn all on the altar as a burnt sacrifice, an offering made by fire, a sweet aroma to the LORD.

'If his offering is of the flocks—of the sheep or of the goats—as a burnt sacrifice, he shall bring a male without blemish. He shall kill it on the north side of the altar before the LORD; and the priests, Aaron's sons, shall sprinkle its blood all around on the altar. And he shall cut it into its pieces, with its head and its fat; and the priest shall lay them in order on the wood that is on the fire upon the altar; but he shall wash the entrails and the legs with water. Then the priest shall bring it all and burn it on the altar; it is a burnt sacrifice, an offering made by fire, a sweet aroma to the LORD.

'And if the burnt sacrifice of his offering to the LORD is of birds, then he shall bring his offering of turtledoves or young pigeons. The priest shall bring it to the altar, wring off its head, and burn it on the altar; its blood shall be drained out at the side of the altar. And he shall remove its crop with its feathers and cast it beside the altar on the east side, into the place for ashes. Then he shall split it at its wings, but shall not divide it completely; and the priest shall burn it on the altar, on the wood that is on the fire. It is a burnt sacrifice, an offering made by fire, a sweet aroma to the LORD.

'When anyone offers a grain offering to the LORD, his offering shall be of fine flour. And he shall pour oil on it, and put frankincense on it. He shall bring it to Aaron's sons, the priests, one of whom shall take from it his handful of fine flour and oil with all the frankincense. And the priest shall burn it as a memorial on the altar, an offering made by fire, a sweet aroma to the LORD. The rest of the grain offering shall be Aaron's and his sons'. It is most holy of the offerings to the LORD made by fire.

'And if you bring as an offering a grain offering baked in the oven, it shall be unleavened cakes of fine flour mixed with oil, or unleavened wafers anointed with oil. But if your offering is a grain offering baked in a pan, it shall be of fine flour, unleavened, mixed with oil. You shall break it in pieces and pour oil on it; it is a grain offering.

'If your offering is a grain offering baked in a covered pan, it shall be made of fine flour with oil. You shall bring the grain offering that is made of these things to the LORD. And when it is presented to the priest, he shall bring it to the altar. Then the priest shall take from the grain offering a memorial portion, and burn it on the altar. It is an offering made by fire, a sweet aroma to the LORD. And what is left of the grain offering shall be Aaron's and his sons'. It is most holy of the offerings to the LORD made by fire.

'No grain offering which you bring to the LORD shall be made with leaven, for you shall burn no leaven nor any honey in any offering to the LORD made by fire. As for the offering of the firstfruits, you shall offer them to the LORD, but they shall not be burned on the altar for a sweet aroma. And every offering of your grain offering you shall season with salt; you shall not allow the salt of the covenant of your God to be lacking from your grain offering. With all your offerings you shall offer salt.

'If you offer a grain offering of your firstfruits to the LORD, you shall offer for the grain offering of your firstfruits green heads of grain roasted on the fire, grain beaten from full heads. And you shall put oil on it, and lay frankincense on it. It *is* a grain offering. Then the priest shall burn the memorial portion: *part* of its beaten grain and *part* of its oil, with all the frankincense, as an offering made by fire to the LORD.' "

Leviticus 1–2

WORSHIP

I will declare Your name to My brethren;
In the midst of the assembly I will praise You.
You who fear the LORD, praise Him!
All you descendants of Jacob, glorify Him,
And fear Him, all you offspring of Israel!
For He has not despised nor abhorred the
    affliction of the afflicted;
Nor has He hidden His face from Him;
But when He cried to Him, He heard.

Psalm 22:22-24

WISDOM

"The fear of the LORD *is* the beginning of
    wisdom,
And the knowledge of the Holy One *is*
    understanding.
For by me your days will be multiplied,
And years of life will be added to you.
If you are wise, you are wise for yourself,
And *if* you scoff, you will bear *it* alone."

Proverbs 9:10-12

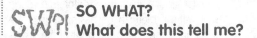

SO WHAT?
What does this tell me?

THE PEACE, SIN AND TRESPASS OFFERINGS

Leviticus 3:1-11; 4:1-20; 5:14–6:5; Psalm 22:26-28; Proverbs 10:1

" " When his offering *is* a sacrifice of a peace offering, if he offers *it* of the herd, whether male or female, he shall offer it without blemish before the LORD. And he shall lay his hand on the head of his offering, and kill it *at* the door of the tabernacle of meeting; and Aaron's sons, the priests, shall sprinkle the blood all around on the altar. Then he shall offer from the sacrifice of the peace offering an offering made by fire to the LORD. The fat that covers the entrails and all the fat that *is* on the entrails, the two kidneys and the fat that *is* on them by the flanks, and the fatty lobe *attached* to the liver above the kidneys, he shall remove; and Aaron's sons shall burn it on the altar upon the burnt sacrifice, which *is* on the wood that *is* on the fire, *as* an offering made by fire, a sweet aroma to the LORD.

'If his offering as a sacrifice of a peace offering to the LORD *is* of the flock, *whether* male or female, he shall offer it without blemish. If he offers a lamb as his offering, then he shall offer it before the LORD. And he shall lay his hand on the head of his offering, and kill it before the tabernacle of meeting; and Aaron's sons shall sprinkle its blood all around on the altar.

'Then he shall offer from the sacrifice of the peace offering, as an offering made by fire to the LORD, its fat *and* the whole fat tail which he shall remove close to the backbone. And the fat that covers the entrails and all the fat that *is* on the entrails, the two kidneys and the fat that *is* on them by the flanks, and the fatty lobe *attached* to the liver above the kidneys, he shall remove; and the priest shall burn *them* on the altar *as* food, an offering made by fire to the LORD.' "

Now the LORD spoke to Moses, saying, "Speak to the children of Israel, saying: 'If a person sins unintentionally against any of the commandments of the LORD *in anything* which ought not to be done, and does any of them, if the anointed priest sins, bringing guilt on the people, then let him offer to the LORD for his sin which he has sinned a young bull without blemish as a sin offering. He shall bring the bull to the door of the taber-

nacle of meeting before the LORD, lay his hand on the bull's head, and kill the bull before the LORD. Then the anointed priest shall take some of the bull's blood and bring it to the tabernacle of meeting. The priest shall dip his finger in the blood and sprinkle some of the blood seven times before the LORD, in front of the veil of the sanctuary. And the priest shall put some of the blood on the horns of the altar of sweet incense before the LORD, which is in the tabernacle of meeting; and he shall pour the remaining blood of the bull at the base of the altar of the burnt offering, which is at the door of the tabernacle of meeting. He shall take from it all the fat of the bull as the sin offering. The fat that covers the entrails and all the fat which *is* on the entrails, the two kidneys and the fat that *is* on them by the flanks, and the fatty lobe *attached* to the liver above the kidneys, he shall remove, as it was taken from the bull of the sacrifice of the peace offering; and the priest shall burn them on the altar of the burnt offering. But the bull's hide and all its flesh, with its head and legs, its entrails and offal—the whole bull he shall carry outside the camp to a clean place, where the ashes are poured out, and burn it on wood with fire; where the ashes are poured out it shall be burned.

'Now if the whole congregation of Israel sins unintentionally, and the thing is hidden from the eyes of the assembly, and they have done *something against* any of the commandments of the LORD *in anything* which should not be done, and are guilty; when the sin which they have committed becomes known, then the assembly shall offer a young bull for the sin, and bring it before the tabernacle of meeting. And the elders of the congregation shall lay their hands on the head of the bull before the LORD. Then the bull shall be killed before the LORD. The anointed priest shall bring some of the bull's blood to the tabernacle of meeting. Then the priest shall dip his finger in the blood and sprinkle *it* seven times before the LORD, in front of the veil. And he shall put *some* of the blood on the horns of the altar which *is* before the LORD, which *is* in the tabernacle of meeting; and he shall pour the remaining blood at the base of the altar of burnt offering, which is at the door of the tabernacle of meeting. He shall take all the fat from it and burn *it* on the altar. And he shall do with the bull as he did with the bull as a sin offering; thus he shall do with it. So the priest shall make atonement for them, and it shall be forgiven them.' "

Then the LORD spoke to Moses, saying: "If a person commits a trespass, and sins unintentionally in regard to the holy things of the LORD, then he shall bring to the LORD as his trespass offering a ram without blemish from the flocks, with your valuation in shekels of silver according to the shekel of the sanctuary, as a trespass offering. And he shall make restitution for the harm that he has done in regard to the holy thing, and shall add one-fifth to it and give it to the priest. So the priest shall make atonement for him with the ram of the trespass offering, and it shall be forgiven him.

"If a person sins, and commits any of these things which are forbidden to be done by the commandments of the LORD, though he does not know *it,* yet he is guilty and shall bear his iniquity. And he shall bring to the priest a ram without blemish from the flock, with your valuation, as a trespass offering. So the priest shall make atonement for him regarding his ignorance in which he erred and did not know *it,* and it shall be forgiven him. It is a trespass offering; he has certainly trespassed against the LORD."

And the LORD spoke to Moses, saying: "If a person sins and commits a trespass against the LORD by lying to his neighbor about what was delivered to him for safekeeping, or about a pledge, or about a robbery, or if he has extorted from his neighbor, or if he has found what was lost and lies concerning it, and swears falsely—in any one of these things that a man may do in which he sins: then it shall be, because he has sinned and is guilty, that he shall restore what he has stolen, or the thing which he has extorted, or what was delivered to him for safekeeping, or the lost thing which he found, or all that about which he has sworn falsely. He shall restore its full value, add one-fifth more to it, *and* give it to whomever it belongs, on the day of his trespass offering."

Leviticus 3:1-11; 4:1-20; 5:14–6:5

WORSHIP

The poor shall eat and be satisfied;
Those who seek Him will praise the LORD.
Let your heart live forever!

All the ends of the world
Shall remember and turn to the LORD,
And all the families of the nations
Shall worship before You.
For the kingdom *is* the LORD's,
And He rules over the nations.

Psalm 22:26-28

WISDOM

The proverbs of Solomon:

A wise son makes a glad father,
But a foolish son *is* the grief of his mother.

Proverbs 10:1

**SW?! SO WHAT?
What does this tell me?**

SETTING APART THE PRIESTS

Leviticus 8:1–9:7; Psalm 23:1-3, 6; Proverbs 10:2

And the LORD spoke to Moses, saying: "Take Aaron and his sons with him, and the garments, the anointing oil, a bull as the sin offering, two rams, and a basket of unleavened bread; and gather all the congregation together at the door of the tabernacle of meeting."

So Moses did as the LORD commanded him. And the congregation was gathered together at the door of the tabernacle of meeting. And Moses said to the congregation, "This *is* what the LORD commanded to be done."

Then Moses brought Aaron and his sons and washed them with water. And he put the tunic on him, girded him with the sash, clothed him with the robe, and put the ephod on him; and he girded him with the intricately woven band of the ephod, and with it tied *the ephod* on him. Then he put the breastplate on him, and he put the Urim and the Thummim in the breastplate. And he put the turban on his head. Also on the turban, on its front, he put the golden plate, the holy crown, as the LORD had commanded Moses.

Also Moses took the anointing oil, and anointed the tabernacle and all that *was* in it, and consecrated them. He sprinkled some of it on the altar seven times, anointed the altar and all its utensils, and the laver and its base, to consecrate them. And he poured some of the anointing oil on Aaron's head and anointed him, to consecrate him.

Then Moses brought Aaron's sons and put tunics on them, girded them with sashes, and put hats on them, as the LORD had commanded Moses.

And he brought the bull for the sin offering. Then Aaron and his sons laid their hands on the head of the bull for the sin offering, and Moses killed *it*. Then he took the blood, and put *some* on the horns of the altar all around with his finger, and purified the altar. And he poured the blood at the base of the altar, and consecrated it, to make atonement for it. Then he took all the fat that *was* on the entrails, the fatty lobe *attached to* the liver, and the two kidneys with their fat, and Moses burned *them* on the altar. But the bull, its hide, its flesh, and its offal, he burned with fire outside the camp, as the LORD had commanded Moses.

Then he brought the ram as the burnt offering. And Aaron and his sons laid their hands on the head of the ram, and Moses killed *it*. Then he sprinkled the blood all around on the altar. And he cut the ram into pieces; and Moses burned the head, the pieces, and the fat. Then he washed the entrails and the legs in water. And Moses burned the whole ram on the altar. It *was* a burnt sacrifice for a sweet aroma, an offering made by fire to the LORD, as the LORD had commanded Moses.

And he brought the second ram, the ram of consecration. Then Aaron and his sons laid their hands on the head of the ram, and Moses killed *it*. Also he took *some* of its blood and put it on the tip of Aaron's right ear, on the thumb of his right hand, and on the big toe of his right foot. Then he brought Aaron's sons. And Moses put *some* of the blood on the tips of their right ears, on the thumbs of their right hands, and on the big toes of their right feet. And Moses sprinkled the blood all around on the altar. Then he took the fat and the fat tail, all the fat that *was* on the entrails, the fatty lobe *attached to* the liver, the two kidneys and their fat, and the right thigh; and from the basket of unleavened bread that was before the LORD he took one unleavened cake, a cake of bread *anointed with* oil, and one wafer, and put *them* on the fat and on the right thigh; and he put all *these* in Aaron's hands and in his sons' hands, and waved them *as* a wave offering before the LORD. Then Moses took them from their hands and burned *them* on the altar, on the burnt offering. They *were* consecration offerings for a sweet aroma. That *was* an offering made by fire to the LORD. And Moses took the breast and waved it *as* a wave offering before the LORD. It was Moses' part of the ram of consecration, as the LORD had commanded Moses.

Then Moses took some of the anointing oil and some of the blood which *was* on the altar, and sprinkled *it* on Aaron, on his garments, on his sons, and on the garments of his sons with him; and he consecrated Aaron, his garments, his sons, and the garments of his sons with him.

And Moses said to Aaron and his sons, "Boil the flesh *at* the door of the tabernacle of meeting, and eat it there with the bread that *is* in the basket of consecration offerings, as I commanded, saying,

'Aaron and his sons shall eat it.' What remains of the flesh and of the bread you shall burn with fire. And you shall not go outside the door of the tabernacle of meeting *for* seven days, until the days of your consecration are ended. For seven days he shall consecrate you. As he has done this day, *so* the LORD has commanded to do, to make atonement for you. Therefore you shall stay *at* the door of the tabernacle of meeting day and night for seven days, and keep the charge of the LORD, so that you may not die; for so I have been commanded." So Aaron and his sons did all the things that the LORD had commanded by the hand of Moses.

It came to pass on the eighth day that Moses called Aaron and his sons and the elders of Israel. And he said to Aaron, "Take for yourself a young bull as a sin offering and a ram as a burnt offering, without blemish, and offer *them* before the LORD. And to the children of Israel you shall speak, saying, 'Take a kid of the goats as a sin offering, and a calf and a lamb, *both* of the first year, without blemish, as a burnt offering, also a bull and a ram as peace offerings, to sacrifice before the LORD, and a grain offering mixed with oil; for today the LORD will appear to you.'"

So they brought what Moses commanded before the tabernacle of meeting. And all the congregation drew near and stood before the LORD. Then Moses said, "This *is* the thing which the LORD commanded you to do, and the glory of the LORD will appear to you." And Moses said to Aaron, "Go to the altar, offer your sin offering and your burnt offering, and make atonement for yourself and for the people. Offer the offering of the people, and make atonement for them, as the LORD commanded."

Leviticus 8:1–9:7

WORSHIP

The LORD *is* my shepherd;
I shall not want.
He makes me to lie down in green pastures;
He leads me beside the still waters.
He restores my soul;
He leads me in the paths of righteousness
For His name's sake.

Surely goodness and mercy shall follow me
All the days of my life;
And I will dwell in the house of the LORD
Forever.

Psalm 23:1-3, 6

WISDOM

Treasures of wickedness profit nothing,
But righteousness delivers from death.

Proverbs 10:2

 SO WHAT?
What does this tell me?

THE FATAL SIN OF AARON'S SONS

Leviticus 9:8–10:20; Psalm 24:3-6; Proverbs 10:4

Aaron therefore went to the altar and killed the calf of the sin offering, which *was* for himself. Then the sons of Aaron brought the blood to him. And he dipped his finger in the blood, put *it* on the horns of the altar, and poured the blood at the base of the altar. But the fat, the kidneys, and the fatty lobe from the liver of the sin offering he burned on the altar, as the LORD had commanded Moses. The flesh and the hide he burned with fire outside the camp.

And he killed the burnt offering; and Aaron's sons presented to him the blood, which he sprinkled all around on the altar. Then they presented the burnt offering to him, with its pieces and head, and he burned *them* on the altar. And he washed the entrails and the legs, and burned *them* with the burnt offering on the altar.

Then he brought the people's offering, and took the goat, which *was* the sin offering for the people, and killed it and offered it for sin, like the first one. And he brought the burnt offering and offered it according to the prescribed manner. Then he brought the grain offering, took a handful of it, and burned *it* on the altar, besides the burnt sacrifice of the morning.

He also killed the bull and the ram *as* sacrifices of peace offerings, which *were* for the people. And Aaron's sons presented to him the blood, which he sprinkled all around on the altar, and the fat from the bull and the ram—the fatty tail, what covers *the entrails* and the kidneys, and the fatty lobe *attached to* the liver; and they put the fat on the breasts. Then he burned the fat on the altar; but the breasts and the right thigh Aaron waved *as* a wave offering before the LORD, as Moses had commanded.

Then Aaron lifted his hand toward the people, blessed them, and came down from offering the sin offering, the burnt offering, and peace offerings. And Moses and Aaron went into the tabernacle of meeting, and came out and blessed the people. Then the glory of the LORD appeared to all the people, and fire came out from before the LORD and consumed the burnt offering and the fat on the altar. When all the people saw *it,* they shouted and fell on their faces.

Then Nadab and Abihu, the sons of Aaron, each took his censer and put fire in it, put incense on it, and offered profane fire before the LORD, which He had not commanded them. So fire went out from the LORD and devoured them, and they died before the LORD. And Moses said to Aaron, "This is what the LORD spoke, saying:

'By those who come near Me
I must be regarded as holy;
And before all the people
I must be glorified.'

So Aaron held his peace.

Then Moses called Mishael and Elzaphan, the sons of Uzziel the uncle of Aaron, and said to them, "Come near, carry your brethren from before the sanctuary out of the camp." So they went near and carried them by their tunics out of the camp, as Moses had said.

And Moses said to Aaron, and to Eleazar and Ithamar, his sons, "Do not uncover your heads nor tear your clothes, lest you die, and wrath come upon all the people. But let your brethren, the whole house of Israel, bewail the burning which the LORD has kindled. You shall not go out from the door of the tabernacle of meeting, lest you die, for the anointing oil of the LORD *is* upon you." And they did according to the word of Moses.

Then the LORD spoke to Aaron, saying: "Do not drink wine or intoxicating drink, you, nor your sons with you, when you go into the tabernacle of meeting, lest you die. *It shall be* a statute forever throughout your generations, that you may distinguish between holy and unholy, and between unclean and clean, and that you may teach the children of Israel all the statutes which the LORD has spoken to them by the hand of Moses."

And Moses spoke to Aaron, and to Eleazar and Ithamar, his sons who were left: "Take the grain offering that remains of the offerings made by fire to the LORD, and eat it without leaven beside the altar; for it *is* most holy. You shall eat it in a holy place, because it *is* your due and your sons' due, of the sacrifices made by fire to the LORD; for so I have been commanded. The breast of the wave offering and the thigh of the heave offering you shall eat in a clean place, you, your sons, and your daughters with you; for *they are* your due and your sons' due, *which* are given from the sacrifices of peace offerings of the children of Israel. The thigh of the heave offering and the breast of the wave offering they shall bring with the offerings of fat made by fire, to offer *as* a wave offering before the LORD. And it shall be yours and your sons' with you, by a statute forever, as the LORD has commanded."

Then Moses made careful inquiry about the goat of the sin offering, and there it was—burned up. And he was angry with Eleazar and Ithamar, the sons of Aaron *who were* left, saying, "Why have you not eaten the sin offering in a holy place, since it *is* most holy, and *God* has given it to you to bear the guilt of the congregation, to make atonement for them before the LORD? See! Its blood was not brought inside the holy *place;* indeed you should have eaten it in a holy *place,* as I commanded."

And Aaron said to Moses, "Look, this day they have offered their sin offering and their burnt offering before the LORD, and such things have befallen me! *If* I had eaten the sin offering today, would it have been accepted in the sight of the LORD?" So when Moses heard *that,* he was content.

Leviticus 9:8–10:20

WORSHIP

Who may ascend into the hill of the LORD?
Or who may stand in His holy place?
He who has clean hands and a pure heart,
Who has not lifted up his soul to an idol,
Nor sworn deceitfully.
He shall receive blessing from the LORD,
And righteousness from the God of his
    salvation.
This *is* Jacob, the generation of those who
    seek Him,
Who seek Your face.   Selah
Psalm 24:3-6

WISDOM

He who has a slack hand becomes poor,
But the hand of the diligent makes rich.
Proverbs 10:4

SW?! **SO WHAT?**
What does this tell me?

THE DAY OF ATONEMENT

Leviticus 16:1–17:5, 10-14; Psalm 24:7-10; Proverbs 10:5

Now the LORD spoke to Moses after the death of the two sons of Aaron, when they offered *profane fire* before the LORD, and died; and the LORD said to Moses: "Tell Aaron your brother not to come at *just* any time into the Holy *Place* inside the veil, before the mercy seat which *is* on the ark, lest he die; for I will appear in the cloud above the mercy seat.

"Thus Aaron shall come into the Holy *Place:* with *the blood of* a young bull as a sin offering, and *of* a ram as a burnt offering. He shall put the holy linen tunic and the linen trousers on his body; he shall be girded with a linen sash, and with the linen turban he shall be attired. These *are* holy garments. Therefore he shall wash his body in water, and put them on. And he shall take from the congregation of the children of Israel two kids of the goats as a sin offering, and one ram as a burnt offering.

"Aaron shall offer the bull as a sin offering, which *is* for himself, and make atonement for himself and for his house. He shall take the two goats and present them before the LORD *at* the door of the tabernacle of meeting. Then Aaron shall cast lots for the two goats: one lot for the LORD and the other lot for the scapegoat. And Aaron shall bring the goat on which the LORD's lot fell, and offer it *as* a sin offering. But the goat on which the lot fell to be the scapegoat shall be presented alive before the LORD, to make atonement upon it, *and* to let it go as the scapegoat into the wilderness.

"And Aaron shall bring the bull of the sin offering, which is for himself, and make atonement for himself and for his house, and shall kill the bull as the sin offering which *is* for himself. Then he shall take a censer full of burning coals of fire from the altar before the LORD, with his hands full of sweet incense beaten fine, and bring *it* inside the veil. And he shall put the incense on the fire before the LORD, that the cloud of incense may cover the mercy seat that *is* on the Testimony, lest he die. He shall take some of the blood of the bull and sprinkle *it* with his finger on the mercy seat on the east *side;* and before the mercy seat he shall sprinkle some of the blood with his finger seven times.

"Then he shall kill the goat of the sin of-

fering, which *is* for the people, bring its blood inside the veil, do with that blood as he did with the blood of the bull, and sprinkle it on the mercy seat and before the mercy seat. So he shall make atonement for the Holy *Place,* because of the uncleanness of the children of Israel, and because of their transgressions, for all their sins; and so he shall do for the tabernacle of meeting which remains among them in the midst of their uncleanness. There shall be no man in the tabernacle of meeting when he goes in to make atonement in the Holy *Place,* until he comes out, that he may make atonement for himself, for his household, and for all the assembly of Israel. And he shall go out to the altar that *is* before the LORD, and make atonement for it, and shall take some of the blood of the bull and some of the blood of the goat, and put it on the horns of the altar all around. Then he shall sprinkle some of the blood on it with his finger seven times, cleanse it, and consecrate it from the uncleanness of the children of Israel.

"And when he has made an end of atoning for the Holy *Place,* the tabernacle of meeting, and the altar, he shall bring the live goat. Aaron shall lay both his hands on the head of the live goat, confess over it all the iniquities of the children of Israel, and all their transgressions, concerning all their sins, putting them on the head of the goat, and shall send *it* away into the wilderness by the hand of a suitable man. The goat shall bear on itself all their iniquities to an uninhabited land; and he shall release the goat in the wilderness.

"Then Aaron shall come into the tabernacle of meeting, shall take off the linen garments which he put on when he went into the Holy *Place,* and shall leave them there. And he shall wash his body with water in a holy place, put on his garments, come out and offer his burnt offering and the burnt offering of the people, and make atonement for himself and for the people. The fat of the sin offering he shall burn on the altar. And he who released the goat as the scapegoat shall wash his clothes and bathe his body in water, and afterward he may come into the camp. The bull *for* the sin offering and the goat *for* the sin offering, whose blood was brought in to make atonement in the Holy *Place,* shall be carried outside the camp. And they shall burn in the fire their skins, their flesh, and their of-fal. Then he who burns them shall wash his clothes and bathe his body in water, and afterward he may come into the camp.

"*This* shall be a statute forever for you: In the seventh month, on the tenth *day* of the month, you shall afflict your souls, and do no work at all, *whether* a native of your own country or a stranger who dwells among you. For on that day *the priest* shall make atonement for you, to cleanse you, *that* you may be clean from all your sins before the LORD. It *is* a sabbath of solemn rest for you, and you shall afflict your souls. *It is* a statute forever. And the priest, who is anointed and consecrated to minister as priest in his father's place, shall make atone-ment, and put on the linen clothes, the holy gar-ments; then he shall make atonement for the Holy Sanctuary, and he shall make atonement for the tabernacle of meeting and for the altar, and he shall make atonement for the priests and for all the people of the assembly. This shall be an everlasting statute for you, to make atonement for the children of Israel, for all their sins, once a year." And he did as the LORD commanded Moses.

And the LORD spoke to Moses, saying, "Speak to Aaron, to his sons, and to all the children of Is-rael, and say to them, 'This *is* the thing which the LORD has commanded, saying: "Whatever man of the house of Israel who kills an ox or lamb or goat in the camp, or who kills *it* outside the camp, and does not bring it to the door of the tabernacle of meeting to offer an offering to the LORD before the tabernacle of the LORD, the guilt of bloodshed shall be imputed to that man. He has shed blood; and that man shall be CUT off from among his people, to the end that the children of Israel may bring their sacrifices which they offer in the open field, that they may bring them to the LORD at the door of the tabernacle of meeting, to the priest, and offer them *as* peace offerings to the LORD."

'And whatever man of the house of Israel, or of the strangers who dwell among you, who eats any blood, I will set My face against that person who eats blood, and will cut him off from among his people. For the life of the flesh *is* in the blood, and I have given it to you upon the altar to make atonement for your souls; for it *is* the blood *that* makes atonement for the soul.' Therefore I said to the children of Israel, 'No one among you shall eat blood, nor shall any stranger who dwells among you eat blood.'

"Whatever man of the children of Israel, or of the strangers who dwell among you, who hunts and catches any animal or bird that may be eaten, he shall pour out its blood and cover it with dust; for *it is* the life of all flesh. Its blood sustains its life. Therefore I said to the children of Israel, 'You shall not eat the blood of any flesh, for the life of all flesh is its blood. Whoever eats it shall be cut off.' "

Leviticus 16:1–17:5, 10-14

WORSHIP

Lift up your heads, O you gates!
And be lifted up, you everlasting doors!
And the King of glory shall come in.
Who *is* this King of glory?
The LORD strong and mighty,
The LORD mighty in battle.
Lift up your heads, O you gates!
Lift up, you everlasting doors!
And the King of glory shall come in.
Who is this King of glory?
The LORD of hosts,
He *is* the King of glory. Selah

Psalm 24:7-10

WISDOM

He who gathers in summer *is* a wise son;
He who sleeps in harvest *is* a son who causes shame.

Proverbs 10:5

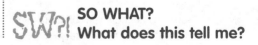

SO WHAT?
What does this tell me?

A CALL TO PERSONAL HOLINESS

Leviticus 19:1-22, 33-37; 20:1-7, 22-26; Psalm 25:4-7; Proverbs 10:9

nd the LORD spoke to Moses, saying, "Speak to all the congregation of the children of Israel, and say to them: 'You shall be holy, for I the LORD your God *am* holy.

'Every one of you shall revere his mother and his father, and keep My Sabbaths: I *am* the LORD your God.

'Do not turn to idols, nor make for yourselves molded gods: I *am* the LORD your God.

'And if you offer a sacrifice of a peace offering to the LORD, you shall offer it of your own free will. It shall be eaten the same day you offer *it,* and on the next day. And if any remains until the third day, it shall be burned in the fire. And if it is eaten at all on the third day, it *is* an abomination. It shall not be accepted. Therefore *everyone* who eats it shall bear his iniquity, because he has profaned the hallowed *offering* of the LORD; and that person shall be cut off from his people.

'When you reap the harvest of your land, you shall not wholly reap the corners of your field, nor shall you gather the gleanings of your harvest. And you shall not glean your vineyard, nor shall you gather *every* grape of your vineyard; you shall leave them for the poor and the stranger: I *am* the LORD your God.

'You shall not steal, nor deal falsely, nor lie to one another. And you shall not swear by My name falsely, nor shall you profane the name of your God: I *am* the LORD.

'You shall not cheat your neighbor, nor rob *him.* The wages of him who is hired shall not remain with you all night until morning. You shall not curse the deaf, nor put a stumbling block before the blind, but shall fear your God: I *am* the LORD.

'You shall do no injustice in judgment. You shall not be partial to the poor, nor honor the person of the mighty. In righteousness you shall judge your neighbor. You shall not go about *as* a talebearer among your people; nor shall you take a stand against the life of your neighbor: I *am* the LORD.

'You shall not hate your brother in your heart. You shall surely rebuke your neigh-bor, and not bear sin because of him. You shall not take vengeance, nor bear any grudge against the children of your people, but you shall love your neighbor as yourself: I *am* the LORD.

'You shall keep My statutes. You shall not let your livestock breed with another kind. You shall not sow your field with mixed seed. Nor shall a garment of mixed linen and wool come upon you.

'Whoever lies carnally with a woman who *is* betrothed to a man as a concubine, and who has not at all been redeemed nor given her freedom, for this there shall be scourging; *but* they shall not be put to death, because she was not free. And he shall bring his trespass offering to the LORD, to the door of the tabernacle of meeting, a ram as a trespass offering. The priest shall make atonement for him with the ram of the trespass offering before the LORD for his sin which he has committed. And the sin which he has committed shall be forgiven him.

'And if a stranger dwells with you in your land, you shall not mistreat him. The stranger who dwells among you shall be to you as one born among you, and you shall love him as yourself; for you were strangers in the land of Egypt: I *am* the LORD your God.

'You shall do no injustice in judgment, in measurement of length, weight, or volume. You shall have honest scales, honest weights, an honest ephah, and an honest hin: I *am* the LORD your God, who brought you out of the land of Egypt.

'Therefore you shall observe all My statutes and all My judgments, and perform them: I *am* the LORD.' "

Then the LORD spoke to Moses, saying, "Again, you shall say to the children of Israel: 'Whoever of the children of Israel, or of the strangers who dwell in Israel, who gives *any* of his descendants to Molech, he shall surely be put to death. The people of the land shall stone him with stones. I will set My face against that man, and will cut him off from his people, because he has given *some* of his descendants to Molech, to defile My sanctuary and profane My holy name. And if the people of the land should in any way hide their eyes from the man, when he gives *some* of his descendants to Molech, and they do not kill him, then I will set My face against that man and against his family; and I will cut him off from his people, and all who prostitute themselves with him to commit harlotry with Molech.

'And the person who turns to mediums and familiar spirits, to prostitute himself with them, I will set My face against that person and cut him off from his people. Consecrate yourselves therefore, and be holy, for I *am* the Lord your God.

'You shall therefore keep all My statutes and all My judgments, and perform them, that the land where I am bringing you to dwell may not vomit you out. And you shall not walk in the statutes of the nation which I am casting out before you; for they commit all these things, and therefore I abhor them. But I have said to you, "You shall inherit their land, and I will give it to you to possess, a land flowing with milk and honey." I *am* the Lord your God, who has separated you from the peoples. You shall therefore distinguish between clean animals and unclean, between unclean birds and clean, and you shall not make yourselves abominable by beast or by bird, or by any kind of living thing that creeps on the ground, which I have separated from you as unclean. And you shall be holy to Me, for I the Lord *am* holy, and have separated you from the peoples, that you should be Mine.' "

Leviticus 19:1-22, 33-37; 20:1-7, 22-26

WORSHIP

Show me Your ways, O Lord;
Teach me Your paths.
Lead me in Your truth and teach me,
For You *are* the God of my salvation;
On You I wait all the day.
Remember, O Lord, Your tender mercies and
Your lovingkindnesses,
For they *are* from of old.
Do not remember the sins of my youth, nor my
transgressions;
According to Your mercy remember me,
For Your goodness' sake, O Lord.

Psalm 25:4-7

WISDOM

He who walks with integrity walks securely,
But he who perverts his ways will become
known.

Proverbs 10:9

SW?! SO WHAT?
What does this tell me?

HOLY PRIESTS AND OFFERINGS

Leviticus 21:1-15; 22:17-33; Psalm 25:8-11; Proverbs 10:12

And the LORD said to Moses, "Speak to the priests, the sons of Aaron, and say to them: 'None shall defile himself for the dead among his people, except for his relatives who are nearest to him: his mother, his father, his son, his daughter, and his brother; also his virgin sister who is near to him, who has had no husband, for her he may defile himself. *Otherwise* he shall not defile himself, *being* a chief man among his people, to profane himself.

'They shall not make any bald *place* on their heads, nor shall they shave the edges of their beards nor make any cuttings in their flesh. They shall be holy to their God and not profane the name of their God, for they offer the offerings of the LORD made by fire, *and* the bread of their God; therefore they shall be holy. They shall not take a wife *who is* a harlot or a defiled woman, nor shall they take a woman divorced from her husband; for *the priest* is holy to his God. Therefore you shall consecrate him, for he offers the bread of your God. He shall be holy to you, for I the LORD, who sanctify you, *am* holy. The daughter of any priest, if she profanes herself by playing the harlot, she profanes her father. She shall be burned with fire.

'*He who is* the high priest among his brethren, on whose head the anointing oil was poured and who is consecrated to wear the garments, shall not uncover his head nor tear his clothes; nor shall he go near any dead body, nor defile himself for his father or his mother; nor shall he go out of the sanctuary, nor profane the sanctuary of his God; for the consecration of the anointing oil of his God *is* upon him: I *am* the LORD. And he shall take a wife in her virginity. A widow or a divorced woman or a defiled woman *or* a harlot—these he shall not marry; but he shall take a virgin of his own people as wife. Nor shall he profane his posterity among his people, for I the LORD sanctify him.' "

And the LORD spoke to Moses, saying, "Speak to Aaron and his sons, and to all the children of Israel, and say to them: 'Whatever man of the house of Israel, or of the strangers in Israel, who offers his sacrifice for any of his vows or for any of his freewill offerings, which they offer to the LORD as a burnt offering—*you shall offer* of your own free will a male without blemish from the cattle, from the sheep, or from the goats. Whatever has a defect, you shall not offer, for it shall not be acceptable on your behalf. And whoever offers a sacrifice of a peace offering to the LORD, to fulfill *his* vow, or a freewill offering from the cattle or the sheep, it must be perfect to be accepted; there shall be no defect in it. Those *that are* blind or broken or maimed, or have an ulcer or eczema or scabs, you shall not offer to the LORD, nor make an offering by fire of them on the altar to the LORD. Either a bull or a lamb that has any limb too long or too short you may offer *as* a freewill offering, but for a vow it shall not be accepted.

'You shall not offer to the LORD what is bruised or crushed, or torn or cut; nor shall you make *any offering of them* in your land. Nor from a foreigner's hand shall you offer any of these as the bread of your God, because their corruption *is* in them, *and* defects *are* in them. They shall not be accepted on your behalf.' "

And the LORD spoke to Moses, saying: "When a bull or a sheep or a goat is born, it shall be seven days with its mother; and from the eighth day and thereafter it shall be accepted as an offering made by fire to the LORD. *Whether it is* a cow or ewe, do not kill both her and her young on the same day. And when you offer a sacrifice of thanksgiving to the LORD, offer *it* of your own free will. On the same day it shall be eaten; you shall leave none of it until morning: I *am* the LORD.

"Therefore you shall keep My commandments, and perform them: I *am* the LORD. You shall not profane My holy name, but I will be hallowed among the children of Israel. I *am* the LORD who sanctifies you, who brought you out of the land of Egypt, to be your God: I *am* the LORD."

Leviticus 21:1-15; 22:17-33

WORSHIP

Good and upright *is* the LORD;
Therefore He teaches sinners in the way.
The humble He guides in justice,
And the humble He teaches His way.
All the paths of the LORD *are* mercy and truth,
To such as keep His covenant and His
    testimonies.
For Your name's sake, O LORD,
Pardon my iniquity, for it *is* great.

Psalm 25:8-11

WISDOM

Hatred stirs up strife,
But love covers all sins.

Proverbs 10:12

SW?! **SO WHAT?**
What does this tell me?

HOLY DAYS AND CELEBRATIONS

Leviticus 23; Psalm 25:16-18;
Proverbs 10:13

And the LORD spoke to Moses, saying, "Speak to the children of Israel, and say to them: 'The feasts of the LORD, which you shall proclaim to be holy convocations, these are My feasts.

'Six days shall work be done, but the seventh day is a Sabbath of solemn rest, a holy convocation. You shall do no work on it; it is the Sabbath of the LORD in all your dwellings.

'These are the feasts of the LORD, holy convocations which you shall proclaim at their appointed times. On the fourteenth day of the first month at twilight is the LORD's Passover. And on the fifteenth day of the same month is the Feast of Unleavened Bread to the LORD; seven days you must eat unleavened bread. On the first day you shall have a holy convocation; you shall do no customary work on it. But you shall offer an offering made by fire to the LORD for seven days. The seventh day shall be a holy convocation; you shall do no customary work on it.'"

And the LORD spoke to Moses, saying, "Speak to the children of Israel, and say to them: 'When you come into the land which I give to you, and reap its harvest, then you shall bring a sheaf of the firstfruits of your harvest to the priest. He shall wave the sheaf before the LORD, to be accepted on your behalf; on the day after the Sabbath the priest shall wave it. And you shall offer on that day, when you wave the sheaf, a male lamb of the first year, without blemish, as a burnt offering to the LORD. Its grain offering shall be two-tenths of an ephah of fine flour mixed with oil, an offering made by fire to the LORD, for a sweet aroma; and its drink offering shall be of wine, one-fourth of a hin. You shall eat neither bread nor parched grain nor fresh grain until the same day that you have brought an offering to your God; it shall be a statute forever throughout your generations in all your dwellings.

'And you shall count for yourselves from the day after the Sabbath, from the day that you brought the sheaf of the wave offering: seven Sabbaths shall be completed. Count fifty days to the day after the seventh Sabbath; then you shall offer a new grain offering to the LORD. You shall bring from your dwellings two wave loaves of two-tenths of an ephah. They shall be of fine flour; they shall be baked with leaven. They are the firstfruits to the LORD. And you shall offer with the bread seven lambs of the first year, without blemish, one young bull, and two rams. They shall be as a burnt offering to the LORD, with their grain offering and their drink offerings, an offering made by fire for a sweet aroma to the LORD. Then you shall sacrifice one kid of the goats as a sin offering, and two male lambs of the first year as a sacrifice of a peace offering. The priest shall wave them with the bread of the firstfruits as a wave offering before the LORD, with the two lambs. They shall be holy to the LORD for the priest. And you shall proclaim on the same day that it is a holy convocation to you. You shall do no customary work on it. It shall be a statute forever in all your dwellings throughout your generations.

'When you reap the harvest of your land, you shall not wholly reap the corners of your field when you reap, nor shall you gather any gleaning from your harvest. You shall leave them for the poor and for the stranger: I am the LORD your God.'"

Then the LORD spoke to Moses, saying, "Speak to the children of Israel, saying: 'In the seventh month, on the first day of the month, you shall have a sabbath-rest, a memorial of blowing of trumpets, a holy convocation. You shall do no customary work on it; and you shall offer an offering made by fire to the LORD.'"

And the LORD spoke to Moses, saying: "Also the tenth day of this seventh month shall be the Day of Atonement. It shall be a holy convocation for you; you shall afflict your souls, and offer an offering made by fire to the LORD. And you shall do no work on that same day, for it is the Day of Atonement, to make atonement for you before the LORD your God. For any person who is not afflicted in soul on that same day shall be cut off from his people. And any person who does any work on that same day, that person I will destroy from among his people. You shall do no manner of work; it shall be a statute forever throughout your generations in all your dwellings. It shall be to you a sabbath of solemn rest, and you shall afflict your souls; on the ninth day of the month at evening, from evening to evening, you shall celebrate your sabbath."

Then the LORD spoke to Moses, saying, "Speak

to the children of Israel, saying: 'The fifteenth day of this seventh month *shall be* the Feast of Tabernacles *for* seven days to the LORD. On the first day *there shall be* a holy convocation. You shall do no customary work *on it. For* seven days you shall offer an offering made by fire to the LORD. On the eighth day you shall have a holy convocation, and you shall offer an offering made by fire to the LORD. It *is* a sacred assembly, *and* you shall do no customary work *on it.*

'These *are* the feasts of the LORD which you shall proclaim *to be* holy convocations, to offer an offering made by fire to the LORD, a burnt offering and a grain offering, a sacrifice and drink offerings, everything on its day— besides the Sabbaths of the LORD, besides your gifts, besides all your vows, and besides all your freewill offerings which you give to the LORD.

'Also on the fifteenth day of the seventh month, when you have gathered in the fruit of the land, you shall keep the feast of the LORD *for* seven days; on the first day *there shall be* a sabbath-*rest,* and on the eighth day a sabbath-*rest.* And you shall take for yourselves on the first day the fruit of beautiful trees, branches of palm trees, the boughs of leafy trees, and willows of the brook; and you shall rejoice before the LORD your God for seven days. You shall keep it as a feast to the LORD for seven days in the year. *It shall be* a statute forever in your generations. You shall celebrate it in the seventh month. You shall dwell in booths for seven days. All who are native Israelites shall dwell in booths, that your generations may know that I made the children of Israel dwell in booths when I brought them out of the land of Egypt: I *am* the LORD your God.' "

So Moses declared to the children of Israel the feasts of the LORD.

Leviticus 23

WORSHIP

Turn Yourself to me, and have mercy on me,
For I *am* desolate and afflicted.
The troubles of my heart have enlarged;
Bring me out of my distresses!
Look on my affliction and my pain,
And forgive all my sins.

Psalm 25:16-18

WISDOM

Wisdom is found on the lips of him who has understanding,
But a rod *is* for the back of him who is devoid of understanding.

Proverbs 10:13

SW?! SO WHAT?
What does this tell me?

BLESSING OR JUDGMENT: IT'S UP TO YOU

Leviticus 26:1-45; Psalm 26:1-3; Proverbs 10:16

"'You shall not make idols for yourselves; neither a carved image nor a *sacred* pillar shall you rear up for yourselves;
nor shall you set up an engraved stone in your land, to bow down to it;
for I *am* the LORD your God.
You shall keep My Sabbaths and reverence My sanctuary:

I *am* the LORD.

'If you walk in My statutes and keep My commandments, and perform them,
then I will give you rain in its season, the land shall yield its produce, and the trees of the field shall yield their fruit.
Your threshing shall last till the time of vintage, and the vintage shall last till the time of sowing;
you shall eat your bread to the full, and dwell in your land safely.
I will give peace in the land, and you shall lie down, and none will make *you* afraid;
I will rid the land of evil beasts,
and the sword will not go through your land.
You will chase your enemies, and they shall fall by the sword before you.
Five of you shall chase a hundred, and a hundred of you shall put ten thousand to flight;
your enemies shall fall by the sword before you.

'For I will look on you favorably and make you fruitful, multiply you and confirm My covenant with you.
    You shall eat the old harvest, and clear out the old because of the new.
    I will set My tabernacle among you, and My soul shall not abhor you.
    I will walk among you and be your God, and you shall be My people.
    I *am* the LORD your God, who brought you out of the land of Egypt, that *you* should not be their slaves;
    I have broken the bands of your yoke and made you walk upright.

'But if you do not obey Me, and do not observe all these commandments,

and if you despise My statutes, or if your soul abhors My judgments, so that you do not perform all My commandments, *but* break My covenant,
I also will do this to you:
I will even appoint terror over you, wasting disease and fever which shall consume the eyes and cause sorrow of heart.
And you shall sow your seed in vain, for your enemies shall eat it.
I will set My face against you, and you shall be defeated by your enemies.
Those who hate you shall reign over you, and you shall flee when no one pursues you.

'And after all this, if you do not obey Me, then I will punish you seven times more for your sins.
I will break the pride of your power;
I will make your heavens like iron and your earth like bronze.
And your strength shall be spent in vain;
for your land shall not yield its produce, nor shall the trees of the land yield their fruit.

'Then, if you walk contrary to Me, and are not willing to obey Me, I will bring on you seven times more plagues, according to your sins.
I will also send wild beasts among you, which shall rob you of your children, destroy your livestock, and make you few in number;
and your highways shall be desolate.

'And if by these things you are not reformed by Me, but walk contrary to Me,
then I also will walk contrary to you, and I will punish you yet seven times for your sins.
And I will bring a sword against you that will execute the vengeance of the covenant;
when you are gathered together within your cities I will send pestilence among you;
and you shall be delivered into the hand of the enemy.
When I have cut off your supply of bread, ten women shall bake your bread in one oven, and they shall bring back your bread by weight, and you shall eat and not be satisfied.

'And after all this, if you do not obey Me, but walk contrary to Me,

then I also will walk contrary to you in fury;
and I, even I, will chastise you seven times for your sins.
You shall eat the flesh of your sons, and you shall eat the flesh of your daughters.
I will destroy your high places, cut down your incense altars, and cast your carcasses on the lifeless forms of your idols;
and My soul shall abhor you.
I will lay your cities waste and bring your sanctuaries to desolation, and I will not smell the fragrance of your sweet aromas.
I will bring the land to desolation, and your enemies who dwell in it shall be astonished at it.
I will scatter you among the nations and draw out a sword after you;
your land shall be desolate and your cities waste.
Then the land shall enjoy its sabbaths as long as it lies desolate and you *are* in your enemies' land;
then the land shall rest and enjoy its sabbaths.
As long as *it* lies desolate it shall rest—
for the time it did not rest on your sabbaths when you dwelt in it.

'And as for those of you who are left, I will send faintness into their hearts in the lands of their enemies;
the sound of a shaken leaf shall cause them to flee;
they shall flee as though fleeing from a sword, and they shall fall when no one pursues.
They shall stumble over one another, as it were before a sword, when no one pursues;
and you shall have no *power* to stand before your enemies.
You shall perish among the nations, and the land of your enemies shall eat you up.
And those of you who are left shall waste away in their iniquity in your enemies' lands;
also in their fathers' iniquities, which are with them, they shall waste away.

'But if they confess their iniquity and the iniquity of their fathers, with their unfaithfulness in which they were unfaithful to Me, and that they also have walked contrary to Me,
and *that* I also have walked contrary to them and have brought them into the land of their enemies;
if their uncircumcised hearts are humbled, and they accept their guilt—
then I will remember My covenant with Jacob, and My covenant with Isaac and My covenant with Abraham I will remember;
I will remember the land.

The land also shall be left empty by them, and will enjoy its sabbaths while it lies desolate without them;
they will accept their guilt, because they despised My judgments and because their soul abhorred My statutes.
Yet for all that, when they are in the land of their enemies, I will not cast them away, nor shall I abhor them, to utterly destroy them and break My covenant with them;
for I *am* the LORD their God.
But for their sake I will remember the covenant of their ancestors, whom I brought out of the land of Egypt in the sight of the nations, that I might be their God:
I *am* the LORD.' "

Leviticus 26:1-45

WORSHIP

Vindicate me, O LORD,
For I have walked in my integrity.
I have also trusted in the LORD;
I shall not slip.
Examine me, O LORD, and prove me;
Try my mind and my heart.
For Your lovingkindness *is* before my eyes,
And I have walked in Your truth.

Psalm 26:1-3

WISDOM

The labor of the righteous *leads* to life,
The wages of the wicked to sin.

Proverbs 10:16

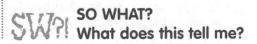

SO WHAT?
What does this tell me?

NUMBERING THE NATION

Numbers 1:1-19, 44-54; 3:1-13; Psalm 26:8, 11-12; Proverbs 10:17

Now the LORD spoke to Moses in the Wilderness of Sinai, in the tabernacle of meeting, on the first *day* of the second month, in the second year after they had come out of the land of Egypt, saying: "Take a census of all the congregation of the children of Israel, by their families, by their fathers' houses, according to the number of names, every male individually, from twenty years old and above—all who *are able to* go to war in Israel. You and Aaron shall number them by their armies. And with you there shall be a man from every tribe, each one the head of his father's house.

"These are the names of the men who shall stand with you: from Reuben, Elizur the son of Shedeur; from Simeon, Shelumiel the son of Zurishaddai; from Judah, Nahshon the son of Amminadab; from Issachar, Nethanel the son of Zuar; from Zebulun, Eliab the son of Helon; from the sons of Joseph: from Ephraim, Elishama the son of Ammihud; from Manasseh, Gamaliel the son of Pedahzur; from Benjamin, Abidan the son of Gideoni; from Dan, Ahiezer the son of Ammishaddai; from Asher, Pagiel the son of Ocran; from Gad, Eliasaph the son of Deuel; from Naphtali, Ahira the son of Enan." These *were* chosen from the congregation, leaders of their fathers' tribes, heads of the divisions in Israel.

Then Moses and Aaron took these men who had been mentioned by name, and they assembled all the congregation together on the first *day* of the second month; and they recited their ancestry by families, by their fathers' houses, according to the number of names, from twenty years old and above, each one individually. As the LORD commanded Moses, so he numbered them in the Wilderness of Sinai.

These are the ones who were numbered, whom Moses and Aaron numbered, with the leaders of Israel, twelve men, each one representing his father's house. So all who were numbered of the children of Israel, by their fathers' houses, from twenty years old and above, all who *were able to* go to war in Israel—all who were numbered were six hundred and three thousand five hundred and fifty.

But the Levites were not numbered among them by their fathers' tribe; for the LORD had spoken to Moses, saying: "Only the tribe of Levi you shall not number, nor take a census of them among the children of Israel; but you shall appoint the Levites over the tabernacle of the Testimony, over all its furnishings, and over all things that belong to it; they shall carry the tabernacle and all its furnishings; they shall attend to it and camp around the tabernacle. And when the tabernacle is to go forward, the Levites shall take it down; and when the tabernacle is to be set up, the Levites shall set it up. The outsider who comes near shall be put to death. The children of Israel shall pitch their tents, everyone by his own camp, everyone by his own standard, according to their armies; but the Levites shall camp around the tabernacle of the Testimony, that there may be no wrath on the congregation of the children of Israel; and the Levites shall keep charge of the tabernacle of the Testimony."

Thus the children of Israel did; according to all that the LORD commanded Moses, so they did.

Now these *are* the records of Aaron and Moses when the LORD spoke with Moses on Mount Sinai. And these *are* the names of the sons of Aaron: Nadab, the firstborn, and Abihu, Eleazar, and Ithamar. These *are* the names of the sons of Aaron, the anointed priests, whom he consecrated to minister as priests. Nadab and Abihu had died before the LORD when they offered profane fire before the LORD in the Wilderness of Sinai; and they had no children. So Eleazar and Ithamar ministered as priests in the presence of Aaron their father.

And the LORD spoke to Moses, saying: "Bring the tribe of Levi near, and present them before Aaron the priest, that they may serve him. And they shall attend to his needs and the needs of the whole congregation before the tabernacle of meeting, to do the work of the tabernacle. Also they shall attend to all the furnishings of the tabernacle of meeting, and to the needs of the children of Israel, to do the work of the tabernacle. And you shall give the Levites to Aaron and his sons; they *are* given entirely to him from among the children of Israel. So you shall appoint Aaron and his sons, and they shall attend to their priesthood; but the outsider who comes near shall be put to death."

Then the Lord spoke to Moses, saying: "Now behold, I Myself have taken the Levites from among the children of Israel instead of every firstborn who opens the womb among the children of Israel. Therefore the Levites shall be Mine, because all the firstborn *are* Mine. On the day that I struck all the firstborn in the land of Egypt, I sanctified to Myself all the firstborn in Israel, both man and beast. They shall be Mine: I *am* the Lord."

Numbers 1:1-19, 44-54; 3:1-13

WORSHiP

Lord, I have loved the habitation of Your house, And the place where Your glory dwells.

But as for me, I will walk in my integrity; Redeem me and be merciful to me. My foot stands in an even place; In the congregations I will bless the Lord.

Psalm 26:8, 11-12

WiSDoM

He who keeps instruction *is in* the way of life, But he who refuses correction goes astray.

Proverbs 10:17

SW?! SO WHAT?
What does this tell me?

PURITY AMONG THE ISRAELITES

Numbers 5:1-10; 6:1-27; Psalm 27:4-5; Proverbs 10:18

And the LORD spoke to Moses, saying: "Command the children of Israel that they put out of the camp every leper, everyone who has a discharge, and whoever becomes defiled by a corpse. You shall put out both male and female; you shall put them outside the camp, that they may not defile their camps in the midst of which I dwell." And the children of Israel did so, and put them outside the camp; as the LORD spoke to Moses, so the children of Israel did.

Then the LORD spoke to Moses, saying, "Speak to the children of Israel: 'When a man or woman commits any sin that men commit in unfaithfulness against the LORD, and that person is guilty, then he shall confess the sin which he has committed. He shall make restitution for his trespass in full, plus one-fifth of it, and give *it* to the one he has wronged. But if the man has no relative to whom restitution may be made for the wrong, the restitution for the wrong *must go* to the LORD for the priest, in addition to the ram of the atonement with which atonement is made for him. Every offering of all the holy things of the children of Israel, which they bring to the priest, shall be his. And every man's holy things shall be his; whatever any man gives the priest shall be his.' "

Then the LORD spoke to Moses, saying, "Speak to the children of Israel, and say to them: 'When either a man or woman consecrates an offering to take the vow of a Nazirite, to separate himself to the LORD, he shall separate himself from wine and *similar* drink; he shall drink neither vinegar made from wine nor vinegar made from *similar* drink; neither shall he drink any grape juice, nor eat fresh grapes or raisins. All the days of his separation he shall eat nothing that is produced by the grapevine, from seed to skin.

'All the days of the vow of his separation no razor shall come upon his head; until the days are fulfilled for which he separated himself to the LORD, he shall be holy. *Then* he shall let the locks of the hair of his head grow. All the days that he separates himself to the LORD he shall not go near a dead body. He shall not make himself unclean even for his father or his mother, for his brother or his sister, when they die, be-cause his separation to God *is* on his head. All the days of his separation he shall be holy to the LORD.

'And if anyone dies very suddenly beside him, and he defiles his consecrated head, then he shall shave his head on the day of his cleansing; on the seventh day he shall shave it. Then on the eighth day he shall bring two turtledoves or two young pigeons to the priest, to the door of the tabernacle of meeting; and the priest shall offer one as a sin offering and *the* other as a burnt offering, and make atonement for him, because he sinned in regard to the corpse; and he shall sanctify his head that same day. He shall consecrate to the LORD the days of his separation, and bring a male lamb in its first year as a trespass offering; but the former days shall be lost, because his separation was defiled.

'Now this *is* the law of the Nazirite: When the days of his separation are fulfilled, he shall be brought to the door of the tabernacle of meeting. And he shall present his offering to the LORD: one male lamb in its first year without blemish as a burnt offering, one ewe lamb in its first year without blemish as a sin offering, one ram without blemish as a peace offering, a basket of unleavened bread, cakes of fine flour mixed with oil, unleavened wafers anointed with oil, and their grain offering with their drink offerings.

'Then the priest shall bring *them* before the LORD and offer his sin offering and his burnt offering; and he shall offer the ram as a sacrifice of a peace offering to the LORD, with the basket of unleavened bread; the priest shall also offer its grain offering and its drink offering. Then the Nazirite shall shave his consecrated head *at* the door of the tabernacle of meeting, and shall take the hair from his consecrated head and put *it* on the fire which is under the sacrifice of the peace offering.

'And the priest shall take the boiled shoulder of the ram, one unleavened cake from the basket, and one unleavened wafer, and put *them* upon the hands of the Nazirite after he has shaved his consecrated *hair,* and the priest shall wave them as a wave offering before the LORD; they *are* holy for the priest, together with the breast of the wave offering and the thigh of the heave offering. After that the Nazirite may drink wine.'

"This is the law of the Nazirite who vows to the

LORD the offering for his separation, and besides that, whatever else his hand is able to provide; according to the vow which he takes, so he must do according to the law of his separation."

And the LORD spoke to Moses, saying: "Speak to Aaron and his sons, saying, 'This is the way you shall bless the children of Israel. Say to them:

"The LORD bless you and keep you;
The LORD make His face shine upon you,
And be gracious to you;
The LORD lift up His countenance upon you,
And give you peace." '

"So they shall put My name on the children of Israel, and I will bless them."

Numbers 5:1-10; 6:1-27

WORSHIP

One *thing* I have desired of the LORD,
That will I seek:
That I may dwell in the house of the LORD
All the days of my life,
To behold the beauty of the LORD,
And to inquire in His temple.
For in the time of trouble
He shall hide me in His pavilion;
In the secret place of His tabernacle
He shall hide me;
He shall set me high upon a rock.

Psalm 27:4-5

WISDOM

Whoever hides hatred *has* lying lips,
And whoever spreads slander *is* a fool.

Proverbs 10:18

SW?! SO WHAT?
What does this tell me?

PREPARING THE ALTAR AND THE LEVITES

Numbers 7:1-11, 84-89; 8:1-26; Psalm 27:11, 13-14; Proverbs 10:19

ow it came to pass, when Moses had finished setting up the tabernacle, that he anointed it and consecrated it and all its furnishings, and the altar and all its utensils; so he anointed them and consecrated them. Then the leaders of Israel, the heads of their fathers' houses, who *were* the leaders of the tribes and over those who were numbered, made an offering. And they brought their offering before the LORD, six covered carts and twelve oxen, a cart for *every* two of the leaders, and for each one an ox; and they presented them before the tabernacle.

Then the LORD spoke to Moses, saying, "Accept *these* from them, that they may be used in doing the work of the tabernacle of meeting; and you shall give them to the Levites, *to* every man according to his service." So Moses took the carts and the oxen, and gave them to the Levites. Two carts and four oxen he gave to the sons of Gershon, according to their service; and four carts and eight oxen he gave to the sons of Merari, according to their service, under the authority of Ithamar the son of Aaron the priest. But to the sons of Kohath he gave none, because theirs *was* the service of the holy things, *which* they carried on their shoulders.

Now the leaders offered the dedication *offering* for the altar when it was anointed; so the leaders offered their offering before the altar. For the LORD said to Moses, "They shall offer their offering, one leader each day, for the dedication of the altar."

This *was* the dedication *offering* for the altar from the leaders of Israel, when it was anointed: twelve silver platters, twelve silver bowls, and twelve gold pans. Each silver platter *weighed* one hundred and thirty *shekels* and each bowl seventy *shekels*. All the silver of the vessels *weighed* two thousand four hundred *shekels,* according to the shekel of the sanctuary. The twelve gold pans full of incense *weighed* ten *shekels* apiece, according to the shekel of the sanctuary; all the gold of the pans *weighed* one hundred and twenty *shekels*. All the oxen for the burnt offering *were* twelve young bulls,

the rams twelve, the male lambs in their first year twelve, with their grain offering, and the kids of the goats as a sin offering twelve. And all the oxen for the sacrifice of peace offerings were twenty-four bulls, the rams sixty, the male goats sixty, and the lambs in their first year sixty. This *was* the dedication *offering* for the altar after it was anointed.

Now when Moses went into the tabernacle of meeting to speak with Him, he heard the voice of One speaking to him from above the mercy seat that *was* on the ark of the Testimony, from between the two cherubim; thus He spoke to him.

And the LORD spoke to Moses, saying: "Speak to Aaron, and say to him, 'When you arrange the lamps, the seven lamps shall give light in front of the lampstand.'" And Aaron did so; he arranged the lamps to face toward the front of the lampstand, as the LORD commanded Moses. Now this workmanship of the lampstand *was* hammered gold; from its shaft to its flowers it *was* hammered work. According to the pattern which the LORD had shown Moses, so he made the lampstand.

Then the LORD spoke to Moses, saying: "Take the Levites from among the children of Israel and cleanse them *ceremonially*. Thus you shall do to them to cleanse them: Sprinkle water of purification on them, and let them shave all their body, and let them wash their clothes, and *so* make themselves clean. Then let them take a young bull with its grain offering of fine flour mixed with oil, and you shall take another young bull as a sin offering. And you shall bring the Levites before the tabernacle of meeting, and you shall gather together the whole congregation of the children of Israel. So you shall bring the Levites before the LORD, and the children of Israel shall lay their hands on the Levites; and Aaron shall offer the Levites before the LORD *like* a wave offering from the children of Israel, that they may perform the work of the LORD. Then the Levites shall lay their hands on the heads of the young bulls, and you shall offer one as a sin offering and the other as a burnt offering to the LORD, to make atonement for the Levites.

"And you shall stand the Levites before Aaron and his sons, and then offer them *like* a wave offering to the LORD. Thus you shall separate the

Levites from among the children of Israel, and the Levites shall be Mine. After that the Levites shall go in to service the tabernacle of meeting. So you shall cleanse them and offer them *like* a wave offering. For they *are* wholly given to Me from among the children of Israel; I have taken them for Myself instead of all who open the womb, the firstborn of all the children of Israel. For all the firstborn among the children of Israel *are* Mine, *both* man and beast; on the day that I struck all the firstborn in the land of Egypt I sanctified them to Myself. I have taken the Levites instead of all the firstborn of the children of Israel. And I have given the Levites as a gift to Aaron and his sons from among the children of Israel, to do the work for the children of Israel in the tabernacle of meeting, and to make atonement for the children of Israel, that there be no plague among the children of Israel when the children of Israel come near the sanctuary."

Thus Moses and Aaron and all the congregation of the children of Israel did to the Levites; according to all that the LORD commanded Moses concerning the Levites, so the children of Israel did to them. And the Levites purified themselves and washed their clothes; then Aaron presented them *like* a wave offering before the LORD, and Aaron made atonement for them to cleanse them. After that the Levites went in to do their work in the tabernacle of meeting before Aaron and his sons; as the LORD commanded Moses concerning the Levites, so they did to them.

Then the LORD spoke to Moses, saying, "This *is* what *pertains* to the Levites: From twenty-five years old and above one may enter to perform service in the work of the tabernacle of meeting; and at the age of fifty years they must cease performing this work, and shall work no more. They may minister with their brethren in the tabernacle of meeting, to attend to needs, but they *themselves* shall do no work. Thus you shall do to the Levites regarding their duties."

Numbers 7:1-11, 84-89; 8:1-26

WORSHIP

Teach me Your way, O LORD,
And lead me in a smooth path, because of my enemies.

I would have lost heart, unless I had believed
That I would see the goodness of the LORD
In the land of the living.

Wait on the LORD;
Be of good courage,
And He shall strengthen your heart;
Wait, I say, on the LORD!

Psalm 27:11, 13-14

WISDOM

In the multitude of words sin is not lacking,
But he who restrains his lips *is* wise.

Proverbs 10:19

SW?! SO WHAT?
What does this tell me?

WANDERING IN THE WILDERNESS

This mountain range in the biblical story could best be described as a dry and dusty desert, for it is on this range that we will experience Israel's forty years of wandering in the wilderness.

The journey to the land God promised His people was not a particularly difficult trek. But somewhere between Mount Sinai and the Jordan River, Israel took a wrong turn into the wilderness.

The fork in the road where the Israelites took their fateful turn was in Kadesh Barnea. Moses sent twelve spies into the Promised Land to investigate the strength of the people living there and confirm the quality of the land. But terrified by the powerful Canaanite inhabitants, most of the spies recommended going back to Egypt. Taking the land in Canaan seemed too formidable a task. Only two of the spies, Joshua and Caleb, wanted to trust God's promise and believe that He could give them victory.

Faced with two opinions, the people chose the path of fear and unbelief rather than faith and victory. They rebelled against Moses and began to map out their return trip to Egypt. God forgave the people, but they still suffered the consequences of their foolish choices. This unbelieving generation, God declared, would remain in the wilderness until every Israelite then twenty years old or more—except Caleb and Joshua—had died outside the Promised Land. For the next forty years the Israelites wandered in the wilderness of Sinai conducting funerals, each burial a reminder of God's holiness and refusal to tolerate rebellion among His people.

In spite of the discouraging nature of Israel's desert experience, there were two high points that occurred on the Plains of Moab, just across the Jordan River from Canaan. It was here that Balak, the king of Moab, hired a pagan prophet named Balaam to place a curse on Israel. While this story includes the humorous account of Balaam's conversation with his donkey, the main point of this peak in the range is profound. Back in Genesis 12:1-3, God had promised blessing for Israel. What a surprise it was to Balaam then when each time he tried to curse Israel, God turned the curse into a blessing. Nothing Balaam could do or say would thwart God's intent for His people.

The second high point that occurred on the Plains of Moab was the "Bible Review" Moses organized for the younger generation of Israelites before allowing them to cross the Jordan into Canaan. Here in the Book of Deuteronomy, Moses reminds the people of what God has done for them in bringing them out of the land of Egypt. He also reminds them that because God has shown His love for them, they should show their love for Him by obeying His commands. In a rather sobering section of Deuteronomy, God warns His people about the consequences of disobedience but assures them of the blessings that accompany obedience.

After passing the mantle of leadership to Joshua, Moses walked up Mount Nebo, where he died within view of the Promised Land. His death marked the end of the wilderness wanderings and the beginning of a new chapter in Israel's history as an emerging nation.

DEPARTURE FROM SINAI: THE CLOUD AND THE FIRE

Numbers 9:15-23; 10:11-36; Psalm 28:1-2; Proverbs 10:20

Now on the day that the tabernacle was raised up, the cloud covered the tabernacle, the tent of the Testimony; from evening until morning it was above the tabernacle like the appearance of fire. So it was always: the cloud covered it *by day,* and the appearance of fire by night. Whenever the cloud was taken up from above the tabernacle, after that the children of Israel would journey; and in the place where the cloud settled, there the children of Israel would pitch their tents. At the command of the LORD the children of Israel would journey, and at the command of the LORD they would camp; as long as the cloud stayed above the tabernacle they remained encamped. Even when the cloud continued long, many days above the tabernacle, the children of Israel kept the charge of the LORD and did not journey. So it was, when the cloud was above the tabernacle a few days: according to the command of the LORD they would remain encamped, and according to the command of the LORD they would journey. So it was, when the cloud remained only from evening until morning: when the cloud was taken up in the morning, then they would journey; whether by day or by night, whenever the cloud was taken up, they would journey. *Whether it was* two days, a month, or a year that the cloud remained above the tabernacle, the children of Israel would remain encamped and not journey; but when it was taken up, they would journey. At the command of the LORD they remained encamped, and at the command of the LORD they journeyed; they kept the charge of the LORD, at the command of the LORD by the hand of Moses.

Now it came to pass on the twentieth *day* of the second month, in the second year, that the cloud was taken up from above the tabernacle of the Testimony. And the children of Israel set out from the Wilderness of Sinai on their journeys; then the cloud settled down in the Wilderness of Paran. So they started out for the first time according to the command of the LORD by the hand of Moses.

The standard of the camp of the children of Judah set out first according to their armies; over their army was Nahshon the son of Amminadab. Over the army of the tribe of the children of Issachar *was* Nethanel the son of Zuar. And over the army of the tribe of the children of Zebulun *was* Eliab the son of Helon.

Then the tabernacle was taken down; and the sons of Gershon and the sons of Merari set out, carrying the tabernacle.

And the standard of the camp of Reuben set out according to their armies; over their army *was* Elizur the son of Shedeur. Over the army of the tribe of the children of Simeon *was* Shelumiel the son of Zurishaddai. And over the army of the tribe of the children of Gad *was* Eliasaph the son of Deuel.

Then the Kohathites set out, carrying the holy things. (The tabernacle would be prepared for their arrival.)

And the standard of the camp of the children of Ephraim set out according to their armies; over their army *was* Elishama the son of Ammihud. Over the army of the tribe of the children of Manasseh *was* Gamaliel the son of Pedahzur. And over the army of the tribe of the children of Benjamin *was* Abidan the son of Gideoni.

Then the standard of the camp of the children of Dan (the rear guard of all the camps) set out according to their armies; over their army *was* Ahiezer the son of Ammishaddai. Over the army of the tribe of the children of Asher *was* Pagiel the son of Ocran. And over the army of the tribe of the children of Naphtali *was* Ahira the son of Enan.

Thus *was* the order of march of the children of Israel, according to their armies, when they began their journey.

Now Moses said to Hobab the son of Reuel the Midianite, Moses' father-in-law, "We are setting out for the place of which the LORD said, 'I will give it to you.' Come with us, and we will treat you well; for the LORD has promised good things to Israel."

And he said to him, "I will not go, but I will depart to my *own* land and to my relatives."

So *Moses* said, "Please do not leave, inasmuch as you know how we are to camp in the wilderness, and you can be our eyes. And it shall be, if you go with us—indeed it shall be—that whatever good the LORD will do to us, the same we will do to you."

So they departed from the mountain of the LORD on a journey of three days; and the ark of the covenant of the LORD went before them for the three days' journey, to search out a resting place for them. And the cloud of the LORD *was* above them by day when they went out from the camp.

So it was, whenever the ark set out, that Moses said:

> "Rise up, O LORD!
> Let Your enemies be scattered,
> And let those who hate You flee before You."

And when it rested, he said:

> "Return, O LORD,
> *To* the many thousands of Israel."

Numbers 9:15-23; 10:11-36

WORSHIP

To You I will cry, O LORD my Rock:
Do not be silent to me,
Lest, if You *are* silent to me,
I become like those who go down to the pit.
Hear the voice of my supplications
When I cry to You,
When I lift up my hands toward Your holy
    sanctuary.

Psalm 28:1-2

WISDOM

The tongue of the righteous *is* choice silver;
The heart of the wicked *is worth* little.

Proverbs 10:20

SW?! SO WHAT?
What does this tell me?

GRUMBLING ON THE ROAD TRIP

Numbers 11:1-23, 31-35; 12:1-15;
Psalm 28:6-8; Proverbs 10:22

Now *when* the people complained, it displeased the LORD; for the LORD heard *it*, and His anger was aroused. So the fire of the LORD burned among them, and consumed *some* in the outskirts of the camp. Then the people cried out to Moses, and when Moses prayed to the LORD, the fire was quenched. So he called the name of the place Taberah, because the fire of the LORD had burned among them.

Now the mixed multitude who were among them yielded to intense craving; so the children of Israel also wept again and said: "Who will give us meat to eat? We remember the fish which we ate freely in Egypt, the cucumbers, the melons, the leeks, the onions, and the garlic; but now our whole being *is* dried up; *there is* nothing at all except this manna *before* our eyes!"

Now the manna *was* like coriander seed, and its color like the color of bdellium. The people went about and gathered *it,* ground *it* on millstones or beat *it* in the mortar, cooked *it* in pans, and made cakes of it; and its taste was like the taste of pastry prepared with oil. And when the dew fell on the camp in the night, the manna fell on it.

Then Moses heard the people weeping throughout their families, everyone at the door of his tent; and the anger of the LORD was greatly aroused; Moses also was displeased. So Moses said to the LORD, "Why have You afflicted Your servant? And why have I not found favor in Your sight, that You have laid the burden of all these people on me? Did I conceive all these people? Did I beget them, that You should say to me, 'Carry them in your bosom, as a guardian carries a nursing child,' to the land which You swore to their fathers? Where am I to get meat to give to all these people? For they weep all over me, saying, 'Give us meat, that we may eat.' I am not able to bear all these people alone, because the burden *is* too heavy for me. If You treat me like this, please kill me here and now—if I have found favor in Your sight—and do not let me see my wretchedness!"

So the LORD said to Moses: "Gather to Me seventy men of the elders of Israel, whom you know to be the elders of the people and officers over them; bring them to the tabernacle of meeting, that they may stand there with you. Then I will come down and talk with you there. I will take of the Spirit that *is* upon you and will put *the same* upon them; and they shall bear the burden of the people with you, that you may not bear *it* yourself alone. Then you shall say to the people, 'Consecrate yourselves for tomorrow, and you shall eat meat; for you have wept in the hearing of the LORD, saying, "Who will give us meat to eat? For *it was* well with us in Egypt." Therefore the LORD will give you meat, and you shall eat. You shall eat, not one day, nor two days, nor five days, nor ten days, nor twenty days, but *for* a whole month, until it comes out of your nostrils and becomes loathsome to you, because you have despised the LORD who is among you, and have wept before Him, saying, "Why did we ever come up out of Egypt?" ' "

And Moses said, "The people whom I *am* among *are* six hundred thousand men on foot; yet You have said, 'I will give them meat, that they may eat *for* a whole month.' Shall flocks and herds be slaughtered for them, to provide enough for them? Or shall all the fish of the sea be gathered together for them, to provide enough for them?"

And the LORD said to Moses, "Has the LORD's arm been shortened? Now you shall see whether what I say will happen to you or not."

Now a wind went out from the LORD, and it brought quail from the sea and left *them* fluttering near the camp, about a day's journey on this side and about a day's journey on the other side, all around the camp, and about two cubits above the surface of the ground. And the people stayed up all that day, all night, and all the next day, and gathered the quail (he who gathered least gathered ten homers); and they spread *them* out for themselves all around the camp. But while the meat *was* still between their teeth, before it was chewed, the wrath of the LORD was aroused against the people, and the LORD struck the people with a very great plague. So he called the name of that place Kibroth Hattaavah, because there they buried the people who had yielded to craving.

WILDERNESS WANDERING

From Kibroth Hattaavah the people moved to Hazeroth, and camped at Hazeroth.

Then Miriam and Aaron spoke against Moses because of the Ethiopian woman whom he had married; for he had married an Ethiopian woman. So they said, "Has the LORD indeed spoken only through Moses? Has He not spoken through us also?" And the LORD heard it. (Now the man Moses was very humble, more than all men who were on the face of the earth.)

Suddenly the LORD said to Moses, Aaron, and Miriam, "Come out, you three, to the tabernacle of meeting!" So the three came out. Then the LORD came down in the pillar of cloud and stood in the door of the tabernacle, and called Aaron and Miriam. And they both went forward. Then He said,

"Hear now My words:
If there is a prophet among you,
I, the LORD, make Myself known to him in a
    vision;
I speak to him in a dream.
Not so with My servant Moses;
He is faithful in all My house.
I speak with him face to face,
Even plainly, and not in dark sayings;
And he sees the form of the LORD.
Why then were you not afraid
To speak against My servant Moses?"

So the anger of the LORD was aroused against them, and He departed. And when the cloud departed from above the tabernacle, suddenly Miriam became leprous, as white as snow. Then Aaron turned toward Miriam, and there she was, a leper. So Aaron said to Moses, "Oh, my lord! Please do not lay this sin on us, in which we have done foolishly and in which we have sinned. Please do not let her be as one dead, whose flesh is half consumed when he comes out of his mother's womb!"

So Moses cried out to the LORD, saying, "Please heal her, O God, I pray!"

Then the LORD said to Moses, "If her father had but spit in her face, would she not be shamed seven days? Let her be shut out of the camp seven days, and afterward she may be received again." So Miriam was shut out of the camp seven days, and the people did not journey till Miriam was brought in again.

Numbers 11:1-23, 31-35; 12:1-15

WORSHIP

Blessed be the LORD,
Because He has heard the voice of my
    supplications!
The LORD is my strength and my shield;
My heart trusted in Him, and I am helped;
Therefore my heart greatly rejoices,
And with my song I will praise Him.

The LORD is their strength,
And He is the saving refuge of His anointed.
Psalm 28:6-8

WISDOM

The blessing of the LORD makes one rich,
And He adds no sorrow with it.
Proverbs 10:22

SO WHAT?
What does this tell me?

THE NATION FAILS TO WALK BY FAITH

Numbers 13:1-3, 17-33; 14:1-4, 11-31; Psalm 29:1-2; Proverbs 10:23

A
nd the LORD spoke to Moses, saying, "Send men to spy out the land of Canaan, which I am giving to the children of Israel; from each tribe of their fathers you shall send a man, every one a leader among them."

So Moses sent them from the Wilderness of Paran according to the command of the LORD, all of them men who *were* heads of the children of Israel.

Then Moses sent them to spy out the land of Canaan, and said to them, "Go up this *way* into the South, and go up to the mountains, and see what the land is like: whether the people who dwell in it *are* strong or weak, few or many; whether the land they dwell in *is* good or bad; whether the cities they inhabit *are* like camps or strongholds; whether the land *is* rich or poor; and whether there are forests there or not. Be of good courage. And bring some of the fruit of the land." Now the time *was* the season of the first ripe grapes.

So they went up and spied out the land from the Wilderness of Zin as far as Rehob, near the entrance of Hamath. And they went up through the South and came to Hebron; Ahiman, Sheshai, and Talmai, the descendants of Anak, *were* there. (Now Hebron was built seven years before Zoan in Egypt.) Then they came to the Valley of Eshcol, and there cut down a branch with one cluster of grapes; they carried it between two of them on a pole. *They* also *brought* some of the pomegranates and figs. The place was called the Valley of Eshcol, because of the cluster which the men of Israel cut down there. And they returned from spying out the land after forty days.

Now they departed and came back to Moses and Aaron and all the congregation of the children of Israel in the Wilderness of Paran, at Kadesh; they brought back word to them and to all the congregation, and showed them the fruit of the land. Then they told him, and said: "We went to the land where you sent us. It truly flows with milk and honey, and this *is* its fruit. Nevertheless the people who dwell in the land *are* strong; the cities *are* fortified *and* very large; moreover we saw the descendants of Anak there. The Amalekites dwell in the land of the South; the Hittites, the Jebusites, and the Amorites dwell in the mountains; and the Canaanites dwell by the sea and along the banks of the Jordan."

Then Caleb quieted the people before Moses, and said, "Let us go up at once and take possession, for we are well able to overcome it."

But the men who had gone up with him said, "We are not able to go up against the people, for they *are* stronger than we." And they gave the children of Israel a bad report of the land which they had spied out, saying, "The land through which we have gone as spies *is* a land that devours its inhabitants, and all the people whom we saw in it *are* men of *great* stature. There we saw the giants (the descendants of Anak came from the giants); and we were like grasshoppers in our own sight, and so we were in their sight."

So all the congregation lifted up their voices and cried, and the people wept that night. And all the children of Israel complained against Moses and Aaron, and the whole congregation said to them, "If only we had died in the land of Egypt! Or if only we had died in this wilderness! Why has the LORD brought us to this land to fall by the sword, that our wives and children should become victims? Would it not be better for us to return to Egypt?" So they said to one another, "Let us select a leader and return to Egypt."

Then the LORD said to Moses: "How long will these people reject Me? And how long will they not believe Me, with all the signs which I have performed among them? I will strike them with the pestilence and disinherit them, and I will make of you a nation greater and mightier than they."

And Moses said to the LORD: "Then the Egyptians will hear *it*, for by Your might You brought these people up from among them, and they will tell *it* to the inhabitants of this land. They have heard that You, LORD, *are* among these people; that You, LORD, are seen face to face and Your cloud stands above them, and You go before them in a pillar of cloud by day and in a pillar of fire by night. Now *if* You kill these people as one man, then the nations which have heard of Your fame will speak, saying, 'Because the LORD was not able to bring this people to the land which He swore to give them, therefore He killed them in the wilderness.' And now, I pray, let the power of my Lord be great, just as You have spoken, saying, 'The LORD is longsuffering and abundant in mercy, forgiving iniquity and transgression; but He by no means clears *the guilty,* visiting the iniquity of the fathers on the children to the third and fourth *generation.'* Pardon the iniquity of this people, I pray, according to the greatness of Your mercy, just as You have forgiven this people, from Egypt even until now."

Then the LORD said: "I have pardoned, according to your word; but truly, as I live, all the earth shall be filled with the glory of the LORD—because all these men who have seen My glory and the signs which I did in Egypt and in the wilderness, and have put Me to the test now these ten times, and have not heeded My voice, they certainly shall not see the land of which I swore to their fathers, nor shall any of those who rejected Me see it. But My servant Caleb, because he has a different spirit in him and has followed Me fully, I will bring into the land where he went, and his descendants shall inherit it. Now the Amalekites and the Canaanites dwell in the valley; tomorrow turn and move out into the wilderness by the Way of the Red Sea."

And the LORD spoke to Moses and Aaron, saying, "How long *shall I bear with* this evil congregation who complain against Me? I have heard the complaints which the children of Israel make against Me. Say to them, 'As I live,' says the LORD, 'just as you have spoken in My hearing, so I will do to you: The carcasses of you who have complained against Me shall fall in this wilderness, all of you who were numbered, according to your entire number, from twenty years old and above. Except for Caleb the son of Jephunneh and Joshua the son of Nun, you shall by no means enter the land which I swore I would make you dwell in. But your little ones, whom you said would be victims, I will bring in, and they shall know the land which you have despised.' "

Numbers 13:1-3, 17-33; 14:1-4, 11-31

WORSHIP

Give unto the LORD, O you mighty ones,
Give unto the LORD glory and strength.
Give unto the LORD the glory due to His name;
Worship the LORD in the beauty of holiness.

Psalm 29:1-2

WISDOM

To do evil *is* like sport to a fool,
But a man of understanding has wisdom.

Proverbs 10:23

SW?! SO WHAT?
What does this tell me?

REBELLION IN THE CAMP

Numbers 16:1-33, 41-50; Psalm 29:10-11; Proverbs 10:24

Now Korah the son of Izhar, the son of Kohath, the son of Levi, with Dathan and Abiram the sons of Eliab, and On the son of Peleth, sons of Reuben, took *men;* and they rose up before Moses with some of the children of Israel, two hundred and fifty leaders of the congregation, representatives of the congregation, men of renown. They gathered together against Moses and Aaron, and said to them, "*You take* too much upon yourselves, for all the congregation *is* holy, every one of them, and the LORD *is* among them. Why then do you exalt yourselves above the assembly of the LORD?"

So when Moses heard *it,* he fell on his face; and he spoke to Korah and all his company, saying, "Tomorrow morning the LORD will show who *is* His and *who is* holy, and will cause *him* to come near to Him. That one whom He chooses He will cause to come near to Him. Do this: Take censers, Korah and all your company; put fire in them and put incense in them before the LORD tomorrow, and it shall be *that* the man whom the LORD chooses *is* the holy one. *You take* too much upon yourselves, you sons of Levi!"

Then Moses said to Korah, "Hear now, you sons of Levi: *Is it* a small thing to you that the God of Israel has separated you from the congregation of Israel, to bring you near to Himself, to do the work of the tabernacle of the LORD, and to stand before the congregation to serve them; and that He has brought you near *to Himself,* you and all your brethren, the sons of Levi, with you? And are you seeking the priesthood also? Therefore you and all your company *are* gathered together against the LORD. And what *is* Aaron that you complain against him?"

And Moses sent to call Dathan and Abiram the sons of Eliab, but they said, "We will not come up! *Is it* a small thing that you have brought us up out of a land flowing with milk and honey, to kill us in the wilderness, that you should keep acting like a prince over us? Moreover you have not brought us into a land flowing with milk and honey, nor given us inheritance of fields and vineyards. Will you put out the eyes of these men? We will not come up!"

Then Moses was very angry, and said to the LORD, "Do not respect their offering. I have not taken one donkey from them, nor have I hurt one of them."

And Moses said to Korah, "Tomorrow, you and all your company be present before the LORD— you and they, as well as Aaron. Let each take his censer and put incense in it, and each of you bring his censer before the LORD, two hundred and fifty censers; both you and Aaron, each *with* his censer." So every man took his censer, put fire in it, laid incense on it, and stood at the door of the tabernacle of meeting with Moses and Aaron. And Korah gathered all the congregation against them at the door of the tabernacle of meeting. Then the glory of the LORD appeared to all the congregation.

And the LORD spoke to Moses and Aaron, saying, "Separate yourselves from among this congregation, that I may consume them in a moment."

Then they fell on their faces, and said, "O God, the God of the spirits of all flesh, shall one man sin, and You be angry with all the congregation?"

So the LORD spoke to Moses, saying, "Speak to the congregation, saying, 'Get away from the tents of Korah, Dathan, and Abiram.' "

Then Moses rose and went to Dathan and Abiram, and the elders of Israel followed him. And he spoke to the congregation, saying, "Depart now from the tents of these wicked men! Touch nothing of theirs, lest you be consumed in all their sins." So they got away from around the tents of Korah, Dathan, and Abiram; and Dathan and Abiram came out and stood at the door of their tents, with their wives, their sons, and their little children.

And Moses said: "By this you shall know that the LORD has sent me to do all these works, for *I have* not *done them* of my own will. If these men die naturally like all men, or if they are visited by the common fate of all men, *then* the LORD has not sent me. But if the LORD creates a new thing, and the earth opens its mouth and swallows them up with all that belongs to them, and they go down alive into the pit, then you will understand that these men have rejected the LORD."

Now it came to pass, as he finished speaking

all these words, that the ground split apart under them, and the earth opened its mouth and swallowed them up, with their households and all the men with Korah, with all *their* goods. So they and all those with them went down alive into the pit; the earth closed over them, and they perished from among the assembly.

On the next day all the congregation of the children of Israel complained against Moses and Aaron, saying, "You have killed the people of the LORD." Now it happened, when the congregation had gathered against Moses and Aaron, that they turned toward the tabernacle of meeting; and suddenly the cloud covered it, and the glory of the LORD appeared. Then Moses and Aaron came before the tabernacle of meeting.

And the LORD spoke to Moses, saying, "Get away from among this congregation, that I may consume them in a moment."

And they fell on their faces.

So Moses said to Aaron, "Take a censer and put fire in it from the altar, put incense *on it,* and take it quickly to the congregation and make atonement for them; for wrath has gone out from the LORD. The plague has begun." Then Aaron took *it* as Moses commanded, and ran into the midst of the assembly; and already the plague had begun among the people. So he put in the incense and made atonement for the people. And he stood between the dead and the living; so the plague was stopped. Now those who died in the plague were fourteen thousand seven hundred, besides those who died in the Korah incident. So Aaron returned to Moses at the door of the tabernacle of meeting, for the plague had stopped.

Numbers 16:1-33, 41-50

WORSHIP

The LORD sat *enthroned* at the Flood,
And the LORD sits as King forever.
The LORD will give strength to His people;
The LORD will bless His people with peace.

Psalm 29:10-11

WISDOM

The fear of the wicked will come upon him,
And the desire of the righteous will be
   granted.

Proverbs 10:24

SW?! **SO WHAT?**
What does this tell me?

MOSES LOSES HIS COOL

Numbers 20:1–21:13; Psalm 30:3–5; Proverbs 10:25

Then the children of Israel, the whole congregation, came into the Wilderness of Zin in the first month, and the people stayed in Kadesh; and Miriam died there and was buried there.

Now there was no water for the congregation; so they gathered together against Moses and Aaron. And the people contended with Moses and spoke, saying: "If only we had died when our brethren died before the LORD! Why have you brought up the assembly of the LORD into this wilderness, that we and our animals should die here? And why have you made us come up out of Egypt, to bring us to this evil place? It *is* not a place of grain or figs or vines or pomegranates; nor *is* there any water to drink." So Moses and Aaron went from the presence of the assembly to the door of the tabernacle of meeting, and they fell on their faces. And the glory of the LORD appeared to them.

Then the LORD spoke to Moses, saying, "Take the rod; you and your brother Aaron gather the congregation together. Speak to the rock before their eyes, and it will yield its water; thus you shall bring water for them out of the rock, and give drink to the congregation and their animals." So Moses took the rod from before the LORD as He commanded him.

And Moses and Aaron gathered the assembly together before the rock; and he said to them, "Hear now, you rebels! Must we bring water for you out of this rock?" Then Moses lifted his hand and struck the rock twice with his rod; and water came out abundantly, and the congregation and their animals drank.

Then the LORD spoke to Moses and Aaron, "Because you did not believe Me, to hallow Me in the eyes of the children of Israel, therefore you shall not bring this assembly into the land which I have given them."

This *was* the water of Meribah, because the children of Israel contended with the LORD, and He was hallowed among them.

Now Moses sent messengers from Kadesh to the king of Edom. "Thus says your brother Israel: 'You know all the hardship that has befallen us, how our fathers went down to Egypt, and we dwelt in Egypt a long time, and the Egyptians afflicted us and our fathers. When we cried out to the LORD, He heard our voice and sent the Angel and brought us up out of Egypt; now here we are in Kadesh, a city on the edge of your border. Please let us pass through your country. We will not pass through fields or vineyards, nor will we drink water from wells; we will go along the King's Highway; we will not turn aside to the right hand or to the left until we have passed through your territory.' "

Then Edom said to him, "You shall not pass through my *land,* lest I come out against you with the sword."

So the children of Israel said to him, "We will go by the Highway, and if I or my livestock drink any of your water, then I will pay for it; let me only pass through on foot, nothing *more.*"

Then he said, "You shall not pass through." So Edom came out against them with many men and with a strong hand. Thus Edom refused to give Israel passage through his territory; so Israel turned away from him.

Now the children of Israel, the whole congregation, journeyed from Kadesh and came to Mount Hor. And the LORD spoke to Moses and Aaron in Mount Hor by the border of the land of Edom, saying: "Aaron shall be gathered to his people, for he shall not enter the land which I have given to the children of Israel, because you rebelled against My word at the water of Meribah. Take Aaron and Eleazar his son, and bring them up to Mount Hor; and strip Aaron of his garments and put them on Eleazar his son; for Aaron shall be gathered *to his people* and die there." So Moses did just as the LORD commanded, and they went up to Mount Hor in the sight of all the congregation. Moses stripped Aaron of his garments and put them on Eleazar his son; and Aaron died there on the top of the mountain. Then Moses and Eleazar came down from the mountain. Now when all the congregation saw that Aaron was dead, all the house of Israel mourned for Aaron thirty days.

The king of Arad, the Canaanite, who dwelt in the South, heard that Israel was coming on the road to Atharim. Then he fought against Israel and

WILDERNESS WANDERING

took *some* of them prisoners. So Israel made a vow to the LORD, and said, "If You will indeed deliver this people into my hand, then I will utterly destroy their cities." And the LORD listened to the voice of Israel and delivered up the Canaanites, and they utterly destroyed them and their cities. So the name of that place was called Hormah.

Then they journeyed from Mount Hor by the Way of the Red Sea, to go around the land of Edom; and the soul of the people became very discouraged on the way. And the people spoke against God and against Moses: "Why have you brought us up out of Egypt to die in the wilderness? For *there is* no food and no water, and our soul loathes this worthless bread." So the LORD sent fiery serpents among the people, and they bit the people; and many of the people of Israel died.

Therefore the people came to Moses, and said, "We have sinned, for we have spoken against the LORD and against you; pray to the LORD that He take away the serpents from us." So Moses prayed for the people.

Then the LORD said to Moses, "Make a fiery *serpent,* and set it on a pole; and it shall be that everyone who is bitten, when he looks at it, shall live." So Moses made a bronze serpent, and put it on a pole; and so it was, if a serpent had bitten anyone, when he looked at the bronze serpent, he lived.

Now the children of Israel moved on and camped in Oboth. And they journeyed from Oboth and camped at Ije Abarim, in the wilderness which *is* east of Moab, toward the sunrise. From there they moved and camped in the Valley of Zered. From there they moved and camped on the other side of the Arnon, which *is* in the wilderness that extends from the border of the Amorites; for the Arnon *is* the border of Moab, between Moab and the Amorites.

Numbers 20:1–21:13

WORSHIP

O LORD, You brought my soul up from the grave;
You have kept me alive, that I should not go down to the pit.

Sing praise to the LORD, you saints of His,
And give thanks at the remembrance of His holy name.
For His anger *is but for* a moment,
His favor *is for* life;
Weeping may endure for a night,
But joy *comes* in the morning.

Psalm 30:3-5

WISDOM

When the whirlwind passes by, the wicked *is* no *more,*
But the righteous *has* an everlasting foundation.

Proverbs 10:25

SW?! **SO WHAT?**
What does this tell me?

GOD TURNS A CURSE INTO A BLESSING

Numbers 22:1-17, 21-35, 41; 23:1-11; Psalm 30:10-12; Proverbs 10:27

Then the children of Israel moved, and camped in the plains of Moab on the side of the Jordan *across from* Jericho.

Now Balak the son of Zippor saw all that Israel had done to the Amorites. And Moab was exceedingly afraid of the people because they *were* many, and Moab was sick with dread because of the children of Israel. So Moab said to the elders of Midian, "Now this company will lick up everything around us, as an ox licks up the grass of the field." And Balak the son of Zippor *was* king of the Moabites at that time. Then he sent messengers to Balaam the son of Beor at Pethor, which *is* near the River in the land of the sons of his people, to call him, saying: "Look, a people has come from Egypt. See, they cover the face of the earth, and are settling next to me! Therefore please come at once, curse this people for me, for they *are* too mighty for me. Perhaps I shall be able to defeat them and drive them out of the land, for I know that he whom you bless *is* blessed, and he whom you curse is cursed."

So the elders of Moab and the elders of Midian departed with the diviner's fee in their hand, and they came to Balaam and spoke to him the words of Balak. And he said to them, "Lodge here tonight, and I will bring back word to you, as the LORD speaks to me." So the princes of Moab stayed with Balaam.

Then God came to Balaam and said, "Who *are* these men with you?"

So Balaam said to God, "Balak the son of Zippor, king of Moab, has sent to me, *saying,* 'Look, a people has come out of Egypt, and they cover the face of the earth. Come now, curse them for me; perhaps I shall be able to overpower them and drive them out.' "

And God said to Balaam, "You shall not go with them; you shall not curse the people, for they *are* blessed."

So Balaam rose in the morning and said to the princes of Balak, "Go back to your land, for the LORD has refused to give me permission to go with you."

And the princes of Moab rose and went to Balak, and said, "Balaam refuses to come with us."

Then Balak again sent princes, more numerous and more honorable than they. And they came to Balaam and said to him, "Thus says Balak the son of Zippor: 'Please let nothing hinder you from coming to me; for I will certainly honor you greatly, and I will do whatever you say to me. Therefore please come, curse this people for me.' "

So Balaam rose in the morning, saddled his donkey, and went with the princes of Moab.

Then God's anger was aroused because he went, and the Angel of the LORD took His stand in the way as an adversary against him. And he was riding on his donkey, and his two servants *were* with him. Now the donkey saw the Angel of the LORD standing in the way with His drawn sword in His hand, and the donkey turned aside out of the way and went into the field. So Balaam struck the donkey to turn her back onto the road. Then the Angel of the LORD stood in a narrow path between the vineyards, *with* a wall on this side and a wall on that side. And when the donkey saw the Angel of the LORD, she pushed herself against the wall and crushed Balaam's foot against the wall; so he struck her again. Then the Angel of the LORD went further, and stood in a narrow place where there *was* no way to turn either to the right hand or to the left. And when the donkey saw the Angel of the LORD, she lay down under Balaam; so Balaam's anger was aroused, and he struck the donkey with his staff.

Then the LORD opened the mouth of the donkey, and she said to Balaam, "What have I done to you, that you have struck me these three times?"

And Balaam said to the donkey, "Because you have abused me. I wish there were a sword in my hand, for now I would kill you!"

So the donkey said to Balaam, "*Am* I not your donkey on which you have ridden, ever since *I became* yours, to this day? Was I ever disposed to do this to you?"

And he said, "No."

Then the LORD opened Balaam's eyes, and he saw the Angel of the LORD standing in the way with

His drawn sword in His hand; and he bowed his head and fell flat on his face. And the Angel of the LORD said to him, "Why have you struck your donkey these three times? Behold, I have come out to stand against you, because *your* way is perverse before Me. The donkey saw Me and turned aside from Me these three times. If she had not turned aside from Me, surely I would also have killed you by now, and let her live."

And Balaam said to the Angel of the LORD, "I have sinned, for I did not know You stood in the way against me. Now therefore, if it displeases You, I will turn back."

Then the Angel of the LORD said to Balaam, "Go with the men, but only the word that I speak to you, that you shall speak." So Balaam went with the princes of Balak.

So it was the next day, that Balak took Balaam and brought him up to the high places of Baal, that from there he might observe the extent of the people.

Then Balaam said to Balak, "Build seven altars for me here, and prepare for me here seven bulls and seven rams."

And Balak did just as Balaam had spoken, and Balak and Balaam offered a bull and a ram on *each* altar. Then Balaam said to Balak, "Stand by your burnt offering, and I will go; perhaps the LORD will come to meet me, and whatever He shows me I will tell you." So he went to a desolate height. And God met Balaam, and he said to Him, "I have prepared the seven altars, and I have offered on *each* altar a bull and a ram."

Then the LORD put a word in Balaam's mouth, and said, "Return to Balak, and thus you shall speak." So he returned to him, and there he was, standing by his burnt offering, he and all the princes of Moab.

And he took up his oracle and said:

"Balak the king of Moab has brought me from Aram,
From the mountains of the east.
'Come, curse Jacob for me,
And come, denounce Israel!'

"How shall I curse whom God has not cursed?
And how shall I denounce *whom* the LORD has not denounced?
For from the top of the rocks I see him,
And from the hills I behold him;
There! A people dwelling alone,
Not reckoning itself among the nations.

"Who can count the dust of Jacob,
Or number one-fourth of Israel?
Let me die the death of the righteous,
And let my end be like his!"

Then Balak said to Balaam, "What have you done to me? I took you to curse my enemies, and look, you have blessed *them* bountifully!"

Numbers 22:1-17, 21-35, 41; 23:1-11

WORSHIP

"Hear, O LORD, and have mercy on me;
LORD, be my helper!"

You have turned for me my mourning into dancing;
You have put off my sackcloth and clothed me with gladness,
To the end that *my* glory may sing praise to You and not be silent.
O LORD my God, I will give thanks to You forever.

Psalm 30:10-12

WISDOM

The fear of the LORD prolongs days,
But the years of the wicked will be shortened.

Proverbs 10:27

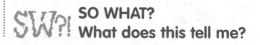

SO WHAT?
What does this tell me?

INSTRUCTIONS CONCERNING THE LAND

Numbers 33:50–34:15; 35:1-15, 29-34; Psalm 31:2-4; Proverbs 10:28

WILDERNESS WANDERING

Now the LORD spoke to Moses in the plains of Moab by the Jordan, *across from* Jericho, saying, "Speak to the children of Israel, and say to them: 'When you have crossed the Jordan into the land of Canaan, then you shall drive out all the inhabitants of the land from before you, destroy all their engraved stones, destroy all their molded images, and demolish all their high places; you shall dispossess *the inhabitants of* the land and dwell in it, for I have given you the land to possess. And you shall divide the land by lot as an inheritance among your families; to the larger you shall give a larger inheritance, and to the smaller you shall give a smaller inheritance; there everyone's *inheritance* shall be whatever falls to him by lot. You shall inherit according to the tribes of your fathers. But if you do not drive out the inhabitants of the land from before you, then it shall be that those whom you let remain *shall be* irritants in your eyes and thorns in your sides, and they shall harass you in the land where you dwell. Moreover it shall be *that* I will do to you as I thought to do to them.' "

Then the LORD spoke to Moses, saying, "Command the children of Israel, and say to them: 'When you come into the land of Canaan, this *is* the land that shall fall to you as an inheritance—the land of Canaan to its boundaries. Your southern border shall be from the Wilderness of Zin along the border of Edom; then your southern border shall extend eastward to the end of the Salt Sea; your border shall turn from the southern side of the Ascent of Akrabbim, continue to Zin, and be on the south of Kadesh Barnea; then it shall go on to Hazar Addar, and continue to Azmon; the border shall turn from Azmon to the Brook of Egypt, and it shall end at the Sea.

'As for the western border, you shall have the Great Sea for a border; this shall be your western border.

'And this shall be your northern border: From the Great Sea you shall mark out your *border* line to Mount Hor; from Mount Hor you shall mark out *your border* to the entrance of Hamath; then the direction of the border shall be toward Zedad; the border shall proceed to Ziphron, and it shall end at Hazar Enan. This shall be your northern border.

'You shall mark out your eastern border from Hazar Enan to Shepham; the border shall go down from Shepham to Riblah on the east side of Ain; the border shall go down and reach to the eastern side of the Sea of Chinnereth; the border shall go down along the Jordan, and it shall end at the Salt Sea. This shall be your land with its surrounding boundaries.' "

Then Moses commanded the children of Israel, saying: "This *is* the land which you shall inherit by lot, which the LORD has commanded to give to the nine tribes and to the half-tribe. For the tribe of the children of Reuben according to the house of their fathers, and the tribe of the children of Gad according to the house of their fathers, have received *their inheritance;* and the half-tribe of Manasseh has received its inheritance. The two tribes and the half-tribe have received their inheritance on this side of the Jordan, *across from* Jericho eastward, toward the sunrise."

And the LORD spoke to Moses in the plains of Moab by the Jordan *across from* Jericho, saying: "Command the children of Israel that they give the Levites cities to dwell in from the inheritance of their possession, and you shall *also* give the Levites common-land around the cities. They shall have the cities to dwell in; and their common-land shall be for their cattle, for their herds, and for all their animals. The common-land of the cities which you shall give the Levites *shall extend* from the wall of the city outward a thousand cubits all around. And you shall measure outside the city on the east side two thousand cubits, on the south side two thousand cubits, on the west side two thousand cubits, and on the north side two thousand cubits. The city *shall be* in the middle. This shall belong to them as common-land for the cities.

"Now among the cities which you will give to the Levites *you shall appoint* six cities of refuge, to which a manslayer may flee. And to these you shall add forty-two cities. So all the cities you will give to the Levites *shall be* forty-eight; these *you shall give* with their common-land. And the cities which you will give *shall be* from the possession of the children of Israel; from the larger *tribe* you shall give many, from the smaller you shall give few. Each shall give some of its cities to the Levites, in proportion to the inheritance that each receives."

Then the LORD spoke to Moses, saying, "Speak to the children of Israel, and say to them: 'When you cross the Jordan into the land of Canaan, then you shall appoint cities to be cities of refuge for you, that the manslayer who kills any person accidentally may flee there. They shall be cities of refuge for you from the avenger, that the manslayer may not die until he stands before the congregation in judgment. And of the cities which you give, you shall have six cities of refuge. You shall appoint three cities on this side of the Jordan, and three cities you shall appoint in the land of Canaan, *which* will be cities of refuge. These six cities shall be for refuge for the children of Israel, for the stranger, and for the sojourner among them, that anyone who kills a person accidentally may flee there.

'And these *things* shall be a statute of judgment to you throughout your generations in all your dwellings. Whoever kills a person, the murderer shall be put to death on the testimony of witnesses; but one witness is not *sufficient* testimony against a person for the death *penalty*. Moreover you shall take no ransom for the life of a murderer who *is* guilty of death, but he shall surely be put to death. And you shall take no ransom for him who has fled to his city of refuge, that he may return to dwell in the land before the death of the priest. So you shall not pollute the land where you *are*; for blood defiles the land, and no atonement can be made for the land, for the blood that is shed on it, except by the blood of him who shed it. Therefore do not defile the land which you inhabit, in the midst of which I dwell; for I the LORD dwell among the children of Israel.' "

Numbers 33:50–34:15; 35:1-15, 29-34

WoRSHiP

Bow down Your ear to me,
Deliver me speedily;
Be my rock of refuge,
A fortress of defense to save me.

For You *are* my rock and my fortress;
Therefore, for Your name's sake,
Lead me and guide me.
Pull me out of the net which they have secretly laid for me,
For You *are* my strength.

Psalm 31:2-4

WiSDoM

The hope of the righteous *will be* gladness,
But the expectation of the wicked will perish.

Proverbs 10:28

SW?! SO WHAT?
What does this tell me?

INITIAL VICTORIES AND SETTLEMENT

Deuteronomy 2:16–3:22;
Psalm 31:6-8; Proverbs 10:30

"So it was, when all the men of war had finally perished from among the people, that the LORD spoke to me, saying: 'This day you are to cross over at Ar, the boundary of Moab. And *when* you come near the people of Ammon, do not harass them or meddle with them, for I will not give you *any* of the land of the people of Ammon *as* a possession, because I have given it to the descendants of Lot *as* a possession.' "

(That was also regarded as a land of giants; giants formerly dwelt there. But the Ammonites call them Zamzummim, a people as great and numerous and tall as the Anakim. But the LORD destroyed them before them, and they dispossessed them and dwelt in their place, just as He had done for the descendants of Esau, who dwelt in Seir, when He destroyed the Horites from before them. They dispossessed them and dwelt in their place, even to this day. And the Avim, who dwelt in villages as far as Gaza—the Caphtorim, who came from Caphtor, destroyed them and dwelt in their place.)

" 'Rise, take your journey, and cross over the River Arnon. Look, I have given into your hand Sihon the Amorite, king of Heshbon, and his land. Begin to possess *it,* and engage him in battle. This day I will begin to put the dread and fear of you upon the nations under the whole heaven, who shall hear the report of you, and shall tremble and be in anguish because of you.'

"And I sent messengers from the Wilderness of Kedemoth to Sihon king of Heshbon, with words of peace, saying, 'Let me pass through your land; I will keep strictly to the road, and I will turn neither to the right nor to the left. You shall sell me food for money, that I may eat, and give me water for money, that I may drink; only let me pass through on foot, just as the descendants of Esau who dwell in Seir and the Moabites who dwell in Ar did for me, until I cross the Jordan to the land which the LORD our God is giving us.'

"But Sihon king of Heshbon would not let us pass through, for the LORD your God hardened his spirit and made his heart obstinate, that He might deliver him into your hand, as *it is* this day.

"And the LORD said to me, 'See, I have begun to give Sihon and his land over to you. Begin to possess *it,* that you may inherit his land.' Then Sihon and all his people came out against us to fight at Jahaz. And the LORD our God delivered him over to us; so we defeated him, his sons, and all his people. We took all his cities at that time, and we utterly destroyed the men, women, and little ones of every city; we left none remaining. We took only the livestock as plunder for ourselves, with the spoil of the cities which we took. From Aroer, which *is* on the bank of the River Arnon, and *from* the city that *is* in the ravine, as far as Gilead, there was not one city too strong for us; the LORD our God delivered all to us. Only you did not go near the land of the people of Ammon—anywhere along the River Jabbok, or to the cities of the mountains, or wherever the LORD our God had forbidden us.

"Then we turned and went up the road to Bashan; and Og king of Bashan came out against us, he and all his people, to battle at Edrei. And the LORD said to me, 'Do not fear him, for I have delivered him and all his people and his land into your hand; you shall do to him as you did to Sihon king of the Amorites, who dwelt at Heshbon.'

"So the LORD our God also delivered into our hands Og king of Bashan, with all his people, and we attacked him until he had no survivors remaining. And we took all his cities at that time; there was not a city which we did not take from them: sixty cities, all the region of Argob, the kingdom of Og in Bashan. All these cities *were* fortified with high walls, gates, and bars, besides a great many rural towns. And we utterly destroyed them, as we did to Sihon king of Heshbon, utterly destroying the men, women, and children of every city. But all the livestock and the spoil of the cities we took as booty for ourselves.

"And at that time we took the land from the hand of the two kings of the Amorites who *were* on this side of the Jordan, from the River Arnon to Mount Hermon (the Sidonians call Hermon Sirion, and the Amorites call it Senir), all the cities of the plain, all Gilead, and all Bashan, as far as Salcah and Edrei, cities of the kingdom of Og in Bashan.

WILDERNESS WANDERING

"For only Og king of Bashan remained of the remnant of the giants. Indeed his bedstead *was* an iron bedstead. (*Is* it not in Rabbah of the people of Ammon?) Nine cubits *is* its length and four cubits its width, according to the standard cubit.

"And this land, *which* we possessed at that time, from Aroer, which *is* by the River Arnon, and half the mountains of Gilead and its cities, I gave to the Reubenites and the Gadites. The rest of Gilead, and all Bashan, the kingdom of Og, I gave to half the tribe of Manasseh. (All the region of Argob, with all Bashan, was called the land of the giants. Jair the son of Manasseh took all the region of Argob, as far as the border of the Geshurites and the Maachathites, and called Bashan after his own name, Havoth Jair, to this day.)

"Also I gave Gilead to Machir. And to the Reubenites and the Gadites I gave from Gilead as far as the River Arnon, the middle of the river as *the* border, as far as the River Jabbok, the border of the people of Ammon; the plain also, with the Jordan as *the* border, from Chinnereth as far as the east side of the Sea of the Arabah (the Salt Sea), below the slopes of Pisgah.

"Then I commanded you at that time, saying: 'The LORD your God has given you this land to possess. All you men of valor shall cross over armed before your brethren, the children of Israel. But your wives, your little ones, and your livestock (I know that you have much livestock) shall stay in your cities which I have given you, until the LORD has given rest to your brethren as to you, and they also possess the land which the LORD your God is giving them beyond the Jordan. Then each of you may return to his possession which I have given you.'

"And I commanded Joshua at that time, saying, 'Your eyes have seen all that the LORD your God has done to these two kings; so will the LORD do to all the kingdoms through which you pass. You must not fear them, for the LORD your God Himself fights for you.' "

Deuteronomy 2:16–3:22

WoRSHiP

I have hated those who regard useless idols;
But I trust in the LORD.
I will be glad and rejoice in Your mercy,
For You have considered my trouble;
You have known my soul in adversities,
And have not shut me up into the hand of the
    enemy;
You have set my feet in a wide place.

Psalm 31:6-8

WiSDoM

The righteous will never be removed,
But the wicked will not inhabit the earth.

Proverbs 10:30

SW?! **SO WHAT?**
What does this tell me?

REMINDERS TO A NEW GENERATION

Deuteronomy 4:1-43; Psalm 31:14-16; Proverbs 10:32

"Now, O Israel, listen to the statutes and the judgments which I teach you to observe, that you may live, and go in and possess the land which the LORD God of your fathers is giving you. You shall not add to the word which I command you, nor take from it, that you may keep the commandments of the LORD your God which I command you. Your eyes have seen what the LORD did at Baal Peor; for the LORD your God has destroyed from among you all the men who followed Baal of Peor. But you who held fast to the LORD your God *are* alive today, every one of you.

"Surely I have taught you statutes and judgments, just as the LORD my God commanded me, that you should act according *to them* in the land which you go to possess. Therefore be careful to observe *them;* for this *is* your wisdom and your understanding in the sight of the peoples who will hear all these statutes, and say, 'Surely this great nation *is* a wise and understanding people.'

"For what great nation *is there* that has God *so* near to it, as the LORD our God *is* to us, for whatever *reason* we may call upon Him? And what great nation *is there* that has *such* statutes and righteous judgments as are in all this law which I set before you this day? Only take heed to yourself, and diligently keep yourself, lest you forget the things your eyes have seen, and lest they depart from your heart all the days of your life. And teach them to your children and your grandchildren, *especially concerning* the day you stood before the LORD your God in Horeb, when the LORD said to me, 'Gather the people to Me, and I will let them hear My words, that they may learn to fear Me all the days they live on the earth, and *that* they may teach their children.'

"Then you came near and stood at the foot of the mountain, and the mountain burned with fire to the midst of heaven, with darkness, cloud, and thick darkness. And the LORD spoke to you out of the midst of the fire. You heard the sound of the words, but saw no form; *you* only *heard* a voice. So He declared to you His covenant which He commanded you to perform, the Ten Commandments; and He wrote them on two tablets of stone. And the LORD commanded me at that time to teach you statutes and judgments, that you might observe them in the land which you cross over to possess.

"Take careful heed to yourselves, for you saw no form when the LORD spoke to you at Horeb out of the midst of the fire, lest you act corruptly and make for yourselves a carved image in the form of any figure: the likeness of male or female, the likeness of any animal that *is* on the earth or the likeness of any winged bird that flies in the air, the likeness of anything that creeps on the ground or the likeness of any fish that *is* in the water beneath the earth. And *take heed,* lest you lift your eyes to heaven, and *when* you see the sun, the moon, and the stars, all the host of heaven, you feel driven to worship them and serve them, which the LORD your God has given to all the peoples under the whole heaven as a heritage. But the LORD has taken you and brought you out of the iron furnace, out of Egypt, to be His people, an inheritance, as you are this day. Furthermore the LORD was angry with me for your sakes, and swore that I would not cross over the Jordan, and that I would not enter the good land which the LORD your God is giving you as an inheritance. But I must die in this land, I must not cross over the Jordan; but you shall cross over and possess that good land. Take heed to yourselves, lest you forget the covenant of the LORD your God which He made with you, and make for yourselves a carved image in the form of anything which the LORD your God has forbidden you. For the LORD your God *is* a consuming fire, a jealous God.

"When you beget children and grandchildren and have grown old in the land, and act corruptly and make a carved image in the form of anything, and do evil in the sight of the LORD your God to provoke Him to anger, I call heaven and earth to witness against you this day, that you will soon utterly perish from the land which you cross over the Jordan to possess; you will not prolong *your* days in it, but will be utterly destroyed. And the LORD will scatter you among the peoples, and you will be left few in number among the nations where the LORD will drive you. And there you will serve gods, the work of men's hands, wood and stone, which neither see nor hear nor eat nor smell. But from there you will seek the LORD your God, and you will find *Him* if you seek Him with all your heart and with all your soul. When you are in distress, and all these things come upon you in the latter days, when you turn to the LORD your God and obey His voice (for the LORD your God *is* a merciful God), He will not forsake you nor destroy you, nor forget the covenant of your fathers which He swore to them.

"For ask now concerning the days that are past, which were before you, since the day that God created man on the earth, and *ask* from one end of heaven to the other, whether *any* great *thing* like this has happened, or *anything* like it has been heard. Did *any* people *ever* hear the voice of God speaking out of the midst of the fire, as you have heard, and live? Or did God *ever* try to go *and* take for Himself a nation from the midst of *another* nation, by trials, by signs, by wonders, by war, by a mighty hand and an outstretched arm, and by great terrors, according to all that the LORD your God did for you in Egypt before your eyes? To you it was shown, that you might know that the LORD Himself *is* God; *there is* none other besides Him. Out of heaven He let you hear His voice, that He might instruct you; on earth He showed you His great fire, and you heard His words out of the midst of the fire. And because He loved your fathers, therefore He chose their descendants after them; and He brought you out of Egypt with His Presence, with His mighty power, driving out from before you nations greater and mightier than you, to bring you in, to give you their land *as* an inheritance, as *it is* this day. Therefore know this day, and consider *it* in your heart, that the LORD Himself *is* God in heaven above and on the earth beneath; *there is* no other. You shall therefore keep His statutes and His commandments which I command you today, that it may go well with you and with your children after you, and that you may prolong *your* days in the land which the LORD your God is giving you for all time."

Then Moses set apart three cities on this side of the Jordan, toward the rising of the sun, that the manslayer might flee there, who kills his neighbor unintentionally, without having hated him in time past, and that by fleeing to one of these cities he might live: Bezer in the wilderness on the plateau for the Reubenites, Ramoth in Gilead for the Gadites, and Golan in Bashan for the Manassites.

Deuteronomy 4:1-43

WORSHIP

But as for me, I trust in You, O LORD;
I say, "You *are* my God."
My times *are* in Your hand;
Deliver me from the hand of my enemies,
And from those who persecute me.
Make Your face shine upon Your servant;
Save me for Your mercies' sake.

Psalm 31:14-16

WISDOM

The lips of the righteous know what is acceptable,
But the mouth of the wicked *what is* perverse.

Proverbs 10:32

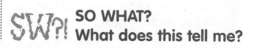

SO WHAT?
What does this tell me?

PASSING YOUR FAITH TO THE NEXT GENERATION

Deuteronomy 6:1–7:16; Psalm 31:23-24; Proverbs 11:1

"Now this *is* the commandment, *and these are* the statutes and judgments which the LORD your God has commanded to teach you, that you may observe *them* in the land which you are crossing over to possess, that you may fear the LORD your God, to keep all His statutes and His commandments which I command you, you and your son and your grandson, all the days of your life, and that your days may be prolonged. Therefore hear, O Israel, and be careful to observe *it*, that it may be well with you, and that you may multiply greatly as the LORD God of your fathers has promised you—'a land flowing with milk and honey.'

"Hear, O Israel: The LORD our God, the LORD *is* one! You shall love the LORD your God with all your heart, with all your soul, and with all your strength.

"And these words which I command you today shall be in your heart. You shall teach them diligently to your children, and shall talk of them when you sit in your house, when you walk by the way, when you lie down, and when you rise up. You shall bind them as a sign on your hand, and they shall be as frontlets between your eyes. You shall write them on the doorposts of your house and on your gates.

"So it shall be, when the LORD your God brings you into the land of which He swore to your fathers, to Abraham, Isaac, and Jacob, to give you large and beautiful cities which you did not build, houses full of all good things, which you did not fill, hewn-out wells which you did not dig, vineyards and olive trees which you did not plant—when you have eaten and are full— *then* beware, lest you forget the LORD who brought you out of the land of Egypt, from the house of bondage. You shall fear the LORD your God and serve Him, and shall take oaths in His name. You shall not go after other gods, the gods of the peoples who *are* all around you (for the LORD your God *is* a jealous God among you), lest the anger of the LORD your God be aroused against you and destroy you from the face of the earth.

"You shall not tempt the LORD your God as you tempted *Him* in Massah. You shall diligently keep the commandments of the LORD your God, His testimonies, and His statutes which He has commanded you. And you shall do *what is* right and good in the sight of the LORD, that it may be well with you, and that you may go in and possess the good land of which the LORD swore to your fathers, to cast out all your enemies from before you, as the LORD has spoken.

"When your son asks you in time to come, saying, 'What *is the meaning of* the testimonies, the statutes, and the judgments which the LORD our God has commanded you?' then you shall say to your son: 'We were slaves of Pharaoh in Egypt, and the LORD brought us out of Egypt with a mighty hand; and the LORD showed signs and wonders before our eyes, great and severe, against Egypt, Pharaoh, and all his household. Then He brought us out from there, that He might bring us in, to give us the land of which He swore to our fathers. And the LORD commanded us to observe all these statutes, to fear the LORD our God, for our good always, that He might preserve us alive, as *it is* this day. Then it will be righteousness for us, if we are careful to observe all these commandments before the LORD our God, as He has commanded us.'

"When the LORD your God brings you into the land which you go to possess, and has cast out many nations before you, the Hittites and the Girgashites and the Amorites and the Canaanites and the Perizzites and the Hivites and the Jebusites, seven nations greater and mightier than you, and when the LORD your God delivers them over to you, you shall conquer them *and* utterly destroy them. You shall make no covenant with them nor show mercy to them. Nor shall you make marriages with them. You shall not give your daughter to their son, nor take their daughter for your son. For they will turn your sons away from following Me, to serve other gods; so the anger of the LORD will be aroused against you and destroy you suddenly. But thus you shall deal with them: you shall destroy their altars, and break down their *sacred* pillars, and cut down their wooden images, and burn their carved images with fire.

WILDERNESS WANDERING

"For you *are* a holy people to the LORD your God; the LORD your God has chosen you to be a people for Himself, a special treasure above all the peoples on the face of the earth. The LORD did not set His love on you nor choose you because you were more in number than any other people, for you were the least of all peoples; but because the LORD loves you, and because He would keep the oath which He swore to your fathers, the LORD has brought you out with a mighty hand, and redeemed you from the house of bondage, from the hand of Pharaoh king of Egypt.

"Therefore know that the LORD your God, He *is* God, the faithful God who keeps covenant and mercy for a thousand generations with those who love Him and keep His commandments; and He repays those who hate Him to their face, to destroy them. He will not be slack with him who hates Him; He will repay him to his face. Therefore you shall keep the commandment, the statutes, and the judgments which I command you today, to observe them.

"Then it shall come to pass, because you listen to these judgments, and keep and do them, that the LORD your God will keep with you the covenant and the mercy which He swore to your fathers. And He will love you and bless you and multiply you; He will also bless the fruit of your womb and the fruit of your land, your grain and your new wine and your oil, the increase of your cattle and the offspring of your flock, in the land of which He swore to your fathers to give you. You shall be blessed above all peoples; there shall not be a male or female barren among you or among your livestock. And the LORD will take away from you all sickness, and will afflict you with none of the terrible diseases of Egypt which you have known, but will lay *them* on all those who hate you. Also you shall destroy all the peoples whom the LORD your God delivers over to you; your eye shall have no pity on them; nor shall you serve their gods, for that *will be* a snare to you."

Deuteronomy 6:1–7:16

WORSHIP

Oh, love the LORD, all you His saints!
For the LORD preserves the faithful,
And fully repays the proud person.
Be of good courage,
And He shall strengthen your heart,
All you who hope in the LORD.

Psalm 31:23-24

WISDOM

Dishonest scales *are* an abomination to the LORD,
But a just weight *is* His delight.

Proverbs 11:1

SW?! SO WHAT?
What does this tell me?

WHAT GOD EXPECTS OF HIS PEOPLE

Deuteronomy 10:12–11:29; Psalm 32:3–5; Proverbs 11:2

"And now, Israel, what does the LORD your God require of you, but to fear the LORD your God, to walk in all His ways and to love Him, to serve the LORD your God with all your heart and with all your soul, *and* to keep the commandments of the LORD and His statutes which I command you today for your good? Indeed heaven and the highest heavens belong to the LORD your God, *also* the earth with all that *is* in it. The LORD delighted only in your fathers, to love them; and He chose their descendants after them, you above all peoples, as *it is* this day. Therefore circumcise the foreskin of your heart, and be stiff-necked no longer. For the LORD your God *is* God of gods and Lord of lords, the great God, mighty and awesome, who shows no partiality nor takes a bribe. He administers justice for the fatherless and the widow, and loves the stranger, giving him food and clothing. Therefore love the stranger, for you were strangers in the land of Egypt. You shall fear the LORD your God; you shall serve Him, and to Him you shall hold fast, and take oaths in His name. He *is* your praise, and He *is* your God, who has done for you these great and awesome things which your eyes have seen. Your fathers went down to Egypt with seventy persons, and now the LORD your God has made you as the stars of heaven in multitude.

"Therefore you shall love the LORD your God, and keep His charge, His statutes, His judgments, and His commandments always. Know today that I *do* not *speak* with your children, who have not known and who have not seen the chastening of the LORD your God, His greatness and His mighty hand and His outstretched arm— His signs and His acts which He did in the midst of Egypt, to Pharaoh king of Egypt, and to all his land; what He did to the army of Egypt, to their horses and their chariots: how He made the waters of the Red Sea overflow them as they pursued you, and *how* the LORD has destroyed them to this day; what He did for you in the wilderness until you came to this place; and what He did to Dathan and Abiram the sons of Eliab, the son of Reuben: how the earth opened its mouth and swallowed them up, their households, their tents, and all the substance that *was* in their possession, in the midst of all Israel— but your eyes have seen every great act of the LORD which He did.

"Therefore you shall keep every commandment which I command you today, that you may be strong, and go in and possess the land which you cross over to possess, and that you may prolong *your* days in the land which the LORD swore to give your fathers, to them and their descendants, 'a land flowing with milk and honey.' For the land which you go to possess *is* not like the land of Egypt from which you have come, where you sowed your seed and watered *it* by foot, as a vegetable garden; but the land which you cross over to possess *is* a land of hills and valleys, which drinks water from the rain of heaven, a land for which the LORD your God cares; the eyes of the LORD your God *are* always on it, from the beginning of the year to the very end of the year.

'And it shall be that if you earnestly obey My commandments which I command you today, to love the LORD your God and serve Him with all your heart and with all your soul, then I will give *you* the rain for your land in its season, the early rain and the latter rain, that you may gather in your grain, your new wine, and your oil. And I will send grass in your fields for your livestock, that you may eat and be filled.' Take heed to yourselves, lest your heart be deceived, and you turn aside and serve other gods and worship them, lest the LORD's anger be aroused against you, and He shut up the heavens so that there be no rain, and the land yield no produce, and you perish quickly from the good land which the LORD is giving you.

"Therefore you shall lay up these words of mine in your heart and in your soul, and bind them as a sign on your hand, and they shall be as frontlets between your eyes. You shall teach them to your children, speaking of them when you sit in your house, when you walk by the way, when you lie down, and when you rise up. And you shall write them on the doorposts of your house and on your gates, that your days and the days of your children

(left margin) WILDERNESS WANDERING

may be multiplied in the land of which the LORD swore to your fathers to give them, like the days of the heavens above the earth.

"For if you carefully keep all these commandments which I command you to do—to love the LORD your God, to walk in all His ways, and to hold fast to Him—then the LORD will drive out all these nations from before you, and you will dispossess greater and mightier nations than yourselves. Every place on which the sole of your foot treads shall be yours: from the wilderness and Lebanon, from the river, the River Euphrates, even to the Western Sea, shall be your territory. No man shall be able to stand against you; the LORD your God will put the dread of you and the fear of you upon all the land where you tread, just as He has said to you.

"Behold, I set before you today a blessing and a curse: the blessing, if you obey the commandments of the LORD your God which I command you today; and the curse, if you do not obey the commandments of the LORD your God, but turn aside from the way which I command you today, to go after other gods which you have not known. Now it shall be, when the LORD your God has brought you into the land which you go to possess, that you shall put the blessing on Mount Gerizim and the curse on Mount Ebal."

Deuteronomy 10:12–11:29

WORSHIP

When I kept silent, my bones grew old
Through my groaning all the day long.
For day and night Your hand was heavy upon me;
My vitality was turned into the drought of summer.   Selah
I acknowledged my sin to You,
And my iniquity I have not hidden.
I said, "I will confess my transgressions to the LORD,"
And You forgave the iniquity of my sin.   Selah
Psalm 32:3-5

WISDOM

When pride comes, then comes shame;
But with the humble is wisdom.
Proverbs 11:2

SW?! SO WHAT? What does this tell me?

GUIDELINES FOR KINGS, PRIESTS AND PROPHETS

Deuteronomy 17–18; Psalm 32:10–11; Proverbs 11:3

"You shall not sacrifice to the LORD your God a bull or sheep which has any blemish *or* defect, for that *is* an abomination to the LORD your God.

"If there is found among you, within any of your gates which the LORD your God gives you, a man or a woman who has been wicked in the sight of the LORD your God, in transgressing His covenant, who has gone and served other gods and worshiped them, either the sun or moon or any of the host of heaven, which I have not commanded, and it is told you, and you hear *of it,* then you shall inquire diligently. And if *it is* indeed true *and* certain that such an abomination has been committed in Israel, then you shall bring out to your gates that man or woman who has committed that wicked thing, and shall stone to death that man or woman with stones. Whoever is deserving of death shall be put to death on the testimony of two or three witnesses; he shall not be put to death on the testimony of one witness. The hands of the witnesses shall be the first against him to put him to death, and afterward the hands of all the people. So you shall put away the evil from among you.

"If a matter arises which is too hard for you to judge, between degrees of guilt for bloodshed, between one judgment or another, or between one punishment or another, matters of controversy within your gates, then you shall arise and go up to the place which the LORD your God chooses. And you shall come to the priests, the Levites, and to the judge *there* in those days, and inquire *of them;* they shall pronounce upon you the sentence of judgment. You shall do according to the sentence which they pronounce upon you in that place which the LORD chooses. And you shall be careful to do according to all that they order you. According to the sentence of the law in which they instruct you, according to the judgment which they tell you, you shall do; you shall not turn aside *to* the right hand or *to* the left from the sentence which they pronounce upon you. Now the man who acts presump-

tuously and will not heed the priest who stands to minister there before the LORD your God, or the judge, that man shall die. So you shall put away the evil from Israel. And all the people shall hear and fear, and no longer act presumptuously.

"When you come to the land which the LORD your God is giving you, and possess it and dwell in it, and say, 'I will set a king over me like all the nations that *are* around me,' you shall surely set a king over you whom the LORD your God chooses; *one* from among your brethren you shall set as king over you; you may not set a foreigner over you, who *is* not your brother. But he shall not multiply horses for himself, nor cause the people to return to Egypt to multiply horses, for the LORD has said to you, 'You shall not return that way again.' Neither shall he multiply wives for himself, lest his heart turn away; nor shall he greatly multiply silver and gold for himself.

"Also it shall be, when he sits on the throne of his kingdom, that he shall write for himself a copy of this law in a book, from *the one* before the priests, the Levites. And it shall be with him, and he shall read it all the days of his life, that he may learn to fear the LORD his God and be careful to observe all the words of this law and these statutes, that his heart may not be lifted above his brethren, that he may not turn aside from the commandment *to* the right hand or *to* the left, and that he may prolong *his* days in his kingdom, he and his children in the midst of Israel.

"The priests, the Levites—all the tribe of Levi—shall have no part nor inheritance with Israel; they shall eat the offerings of the LORD made by fire, and His portion. Therefore they shall have no inheritance among their brethren; the LORD is their inheritance, as He said to them.

"And this shall be the priest's due from the people, from those who offer a sacrifice, whether *it is* bull or sheep: they shall give to the priest the shoulder, the cheeks, and the stomach. The firstfruits of your grain and your new wine and your oil, and the first of the fleece of your sheep, you shall give him. For the LORD your God has chosen him out of all your tribes to stand to minister in the name of the LORD, him and his sons forever.

"So if a Levite comes from any of your gates, from where he dwells among all Israel, and comes with all the desire of his mind to the place which the LORD chooses, then he may serve in the name of the LORD his God as all his brethren the Levites *do,* who stand there before the LORD. They shall have equal portions to eat, besides what comes from the sale of his inheritance.

"When you come into the land which the LORD your God is giving you, you shall not learn to follow the abominations of those nations. There shall not be found among you *anyone* who makes his son or his daughter pass through the fire, *or one* who practices witchcraft, *or* a soothsayer, or one who interprets omens, or a sorcerer, or one who con-jures spells, or a medium, or a spiritist, or one who calls up the dead. For all who do these things *are* an abomination to the LORD, and because of these abominations the LORD your God drives them out from before you. You shall be blameless before the LORD your God. For these nations which you will dis-possess listened to soothsayers and diviners; but as for you, the LORD your God has not appointed such for you.

"The LORD your God will raise up for you a Prophet like me from your midst, from your brethren. Him you shall hear, according to all you desired of the LORD your God in Horeb in the day of the assembly, saying, 'Let me not hear again the voice of the LORD my God, nor let me see this great fire anymore, lest I die.'

"And the LORD said to me: 'What they have spo-ken is good. I will raise up for them a Prophet like you from among their brethren, and will put My words in His mouth, and He shall speak to them all that I command Him. And it shall be *that* whoever will not hear My words, which He speaks in My name, I will require *it* of him. But the prophet who presumes to speak a word in My name, which I have not commanded him to speak, or who speaks in the name of other gods, that prophet shall die.' And if you say in your heart, 'How shall we know the word which the LORD has not spoken?'—when a prophet speaks in the name of the LORD, if the thing does not happen or come to pass, that *is* the thing which the LORD has not spoken; the prophet has spoken it presumptuously; you shall not be afraid of him."

Deuteronomy 17–18

WORSHIP

Many sorrows *shall be* to the wicked;
But he who trusts in the LORD, mercy shall
　　surround him.
Be glad in the LORD and rejoice, you righteous;
And shout for joy, all *you* upright in heart!

Psalm 32:10-11

WISDOM

The integrity of the upright will guide them,
But the perversity of the unfaithful will destroy
　　them.

Proverbs 11:3

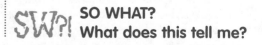

**SO WHAT?
What does this tell me?**

A CALL FOR JUSTICE
Deuteronomy 19–20; Psalm 33:1-3; Proverbs 11:4

"When the LORD your God has cut off the nations whose land the LORD your God is giving you, and you dispossess them and dwell in their cities and in their houses, you shall separate three cities for yourself in the midst of your land which the LORD your God is giving you to possess. You shall prepare roads for yourself, and divide into three parts the territory of your land which the LORD your God is giving you to inherit, that any manslayer may flee there.

"And this *is* the case of the manslayer who flees there, that he may live: Whoever kills his neighbor unintentionally, not having hated him in time past— as when *a man* goes to the woods with his neighbor to cut timber, and his hand swings a stroke with the ax to cut down the tree, and the head slips from the handle and strikes his neighbor so that he dies—he shall flee to one of these cities and live; lest the avenger of blood, while his anger is hot, pursue the manslayer and overtake him, because the way is long, and kill him, though he *was* not deserving of death, since he had not hated the victim in time past. Therefore I command you, saying, 'You shall separate three cities for yourself.'

"Now if the LORD your God enlarges your territory, as He swore to your fathers, and gives you the land which He promised to give to your fathers, and if you keep all these commandments and do them, which I command you today, to love the LORD your God and to walk always in His ways, then you shall add three more cities for yourself besides these three, lest innocent blood be shed in the midst of your land which the LORD your God is giving you *as* an inheritance, and *thus* guilt of bloodshed be upon you.

"But if anyone hates his neighbor, lies in wait for him, rises against him and strikes him mortally, so that he dies, and he flees to one of these cities, then the elders of his city shall send and bring him from there, and deliver him over to the hand of the avenger of blood, that he may die. Your eye shall not pity him, but you shall put away *the guilt of* innocent blood from Israel, that it may go well with you.

"You shall not remove your neighbor's landmark, which the men of old have set, in your inheritance which you will inherit in the land that the LORD your God is giving you to possess.

"One witness shall not rise against a man concerning any iniquity or any sin that he commits; by the mouth of two or three witnesses the matter shall be established. If a false witness rises against any man to testify against him of wrongdoing, then both men in the controversy shall stand before the LORD, before the priests and the judges who serve in those days. And the judges shall make careful inquiry, and indeed, *if* the witness *is* a false witness, who has testified falsely against his brother, then you shall do to him as he thought to have done to his brother; so you shall put away the evil from among you. And those who remain shall hear and fear, and hereafter they shall not again commit such evil among you. Your eye shall not pity: life *shall be* for life, eye for eye, tooth for tooth, hand for hand, foot for foot.

"When you go out to battle against your enemies, and see horses and chariots *and* people more numerous than you, do not be afraid of them; for the LORD your God *is* with you, who brought you up from the land of Egypt. So it shall be, when you are on the verge of battle, that the priest shall approach and speak to the people. And he shall say to them, 'Hear, O Israel: Today you are on the verge of battle with your enemies. Do not let your heart faint, do not be afraid, and do not tremble or be terrified because of them; for the LORD your God *is* He who goes with you, to fight for you against your enemies, to save you.'

"Then the officers shall speak to the people, saying: 'What man *is there* who has built a new house and has not dedicated it? Let him go and return to his house, lest he die in the battle and another man dedicate it. Also what man *is there* who has planted a vineyard and has not eaten of it? Let him go and return to his house, lest he die in the battle and another man eat of it. And what man *is there* who is betrothed to a woman and has not married her? Let him go and return to his house, lest he die in the battle and another man marry her.'

"The officers shall speak further to the people, and say, 'What man *is there who is* fearful and fainthearted? Let him go and return to his house, lest the heart of his brethren faint like his heart.' And so it shall be, when the officers have finished speaking to the people, that they shall make captains of the armies to lead the people.

"When you go near a city to fight against it, then proclaim an offer of peace to it. And it shall be that if they accept your offer of peace, and open to you, then all the people *who are* found in it shall be placed under tribute to you, and serve you. Now if *the city* will not make peace with you, but war against you, then you shall besiege it. And when the LORD your God delivers it into your hands, you shall strike every male in it with the edge of the sword. But the women, the little ones, the livestock, and all that is in the city, all its spoil, you shall plunder for yourself; and you shall eat the enemies' plunder which the LORD your God gives you. Thus you shall do to all the cities *which are* very far from you, which *are* not of the cities of these nations.

"But of the cities of these peoples which the LORD your God gives you *as* an inheritance, you shall let nothing that breathes remain alive, but you shall utterly destroy them: the Hittite and the Amorite and the Canaanite and the Perizzite and the Hivite and the Jebusite, just as the LORD your God has commanded you, lest they teach you to do according to all their abominations which they have done for their gods, and you sin against the LORD your God.

"When you besiege a city for a long time, while making war against it to take it, you shall not destroy its trees by wielding an ax against them; if you can eat of them, do not cut them down to use in the siege, for the tree of the field *is* man's *food*. Only the trees which you know *are* not trees for food you may destroy and cut down, to build siegeworks against the city that makes war with you, until it is subdued."

Deuteronomy 19–20

WORSHIP

Rejoice in the LORD, O you righteous!
For praise from the upright is beautiful.
Praise the LORD with the harp;
Make melody to Him with an instrument of ten
    strings.
Sing to Him a new song;
Play skillfully with a shout of joy.

Psalm 33:1-3

WISDOM

Riches do not profit in the day of wrath,
But righteousness delivers from death.

Proverbs 11:4

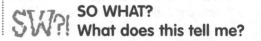 **SO WHAT?**
What does this tell me?

Laws TO Live BY

Deuteronomy 24–25; Psalm 33:6–8; Proverbs 11:5

"When a man takes a wife and marries her, and it happens that she finds no favor in his eyes because he has found some uncleanness in her, and he writes her a certificate of divorce, puts *it* in her hand, and sends her out of his house, when she has departed from his house, and goes and becomes another man's *wife, if* the latter husband detests her and writes her a certificate of divorce, puts *it* in her hand, and sends her out of his house, or if the latter husband dies who took her as his wife, *then* her former husband who divorced her must not take her back to be his wife after she has been defiled; for that *is* an abomination before the LORD, and you shall not bring sin on the land which the LORD your God is giving you *as* an inheritance.

"When a man has taken a new wife, he shall not go out to war or be charged with any business; he shall be free at home one year, and bring happiness to his wife whom he has taken.

"No man shall take the lower or the upper millstone in pledge, for he takes *one's* living in pledge.

"If a man is found kidnapping any of his brethren of the children of Israel, and mistreats him or sells him, then that kidnapper shall die; and you shall put away the evil from among you.

"Take heed in an outbreak of leprosy, that you carefully observe and do according to all that the priests, the Levites, shall teach you; just as I commanded them, *so* you shall be careful to do. Remember what the LORD your God did to Miriam on the way when you came out of Egypt!

"When you lend your brother anything, you shall not go into his house to get his pledge. You shall stand outside, and the man to whom you lend shall bring the pledge out to you. And if the man *is* poor, you shall not keep his pledge overnight. You shall in any case return the pledge to him again when the sun goes down, that he may sleep in his own garment and bless you; and it shall be righteousness to you before the LORD your God.

"You shall not oppress a hired servant *who is* poor and needy, *whether* one of your brethren or one of the aliens who *is* in your land within your gates. Each day you shall give *him* his wages, and not let the sun go down on it, for he *is* poor and has set his heart on it; lest he cry out against you to the LORD, and it be sin to you.

"Fathers shall not be put to death for *their* children, nor shall the children be put to death for *their* fathers; a person shall be put to death for his own sin.

"You shall not pervert justice due the stranger or the fatherless, nor take a widow's garment as a pledge. But you shall remember that you were a slave in Egypt, and the LORD your God redeemed you from there; therefore I command you to do this thing.

"When you reap your harvest in your field, and forget a sheaf in the field, you shall not go back to get it; it shall be for the stranger, the fatherless, and the widow, that the LORD your God may bless you in all the work of your hands. When you beat your olive trees, you shall not go over the boughs again; it shall be for the stranger, the fatherless, and the widow. When you gather the grapes of your vineyard, you shall not glean *it* afterward; it shall be for the stranger, the fatherless, and the widow. And you shall remember that you were a slave in the land of Egypt; therefore I command you to do this thing.

"If there is a dispute between men, and they come to court, that *the judges* may judge them, and they justify the righteous and condemn the wicked, then it shall be, if the wicked man deserves to be beaten, that the judge will cause him to lie down and be beaten in his presence, according to his guilt, with a certain number of blows. Forty blows he may give him *and* no more, lest he should exceed this and beat him with many blows above these, and your brother be humiliated in your sight.

"You shall not muzzle an ox while it treads out *the grain.*

"If brothers dwell together, and one of them dies and has no son, the widow of the dead man shall not be *married* to a stranger outside *the family;* her husband's brother shall go in to her, take her as his wife, and perform the duty of a husband's brother to her. And it shall be *that* the first-born son which she bears will succeed to the name of his dead brother, that his name may not be blotted out of Israel. But if the man does not want to take his brother's wife, then let his brother's wife go up to the gate to the elders, and say, 'My husband's brother refuses to raise up a name to his brother in Israel; he will not perform the duty of my husband's brother.' Then the elders of his city shall call him and speak to him. But *if* he stands firm and says, 'I do not want to take her,' then his brother's wife shall come to him in the presence of the elders, remove his sandal from his foot, spit in his face, and answer and say, 'So shall it be done to the man who will not build up his brother's house.' And his name shall be called in Israel, 'The house of him who had his sandal removed.'

"If *two* men fight together, and the wife of one draws near to rescue her husband from the hand of the one attacking him, and puts out her hand and seizes him by the genitals, then you shall cut off her hand; your eye shall not pity *her.*

"You shall not have in your bag differing weights, a heavy and a light. You shall not have in your house differing measures, a large and a small. You shall have a perfect and just weight, a perfect and just measure, that your days may be lengthened in the land which the LORD your God is giving you. For all who do such things, all who behave unrighteously, *are* an abomination to the LORD your God.

"Remember what Amalek did to you on the way as you were coming out of Egypt, how he met you on the way and attacked your rear ranks, all the stragglers at your rear, when you *were* tired and weary; and he did not fear God. Therefore it shall be, when the LORD your God has given you rest from your enemies all around, in the land which the LORD your God is giving you to possess *as* an inheritance, *that* you will blot out the remembrance of Amalek from under heaven. You shall not forget."

Deuteronomy 24–25

WORSHIP

By the word of the LORD the heavens were
    made,
And all the host of them by the breath of His
    mouth.
He gathers the waters of the sea together as a
    heap;
He lays up the deep in storehouses.

Let all the earth fear the LORD;
Let all the inhabitants of the world stand in
    awe of Him.

Psalm 33:6-8

WISDOM

The righteousness of the blameless will direct
    his way aright,
But the wicked will fall by his own wickedness.

Proverbs 11:5

SW?! **SO WHAT?**
What does this tell me?

CURSES FOR DISOBEDIENCE; BLESSINGS FOR OBEDIENCE

Deuteronomy 27:11-16; 28:1-20, 58-65; Psalm 33:13-15; Proverbs 11:6

And Moses commanded the people on the same day, saying, "These shall stand on Mount Gerizim to bless the people, when you have crossed over the Jordan: Simeon, Levi, Judah, Issachar, Joseph, and Benjamin; and these shall stand on Mount Ebal to curse: Reuben, Gad, Asher, Zebulun, Dan, and Naphtali.

"And the Levites shall speak with a loud voice and say to all the men of Israel: 'Cursed *is* the one who makes a carved or molded image, an abomination to the LORD, the work of the hands of the craftsman, and sets *it* up in secret.'

"And all the people shall answer and say, 'Amen!'

'Cursed *is* the one who treats his father or his mother with contempt.'

"And all the people shall say, 'Amen!'

"Now it shall come to pass, if you diligently obey the voice of the LORD your God, to observe carefully all His commandments which I command you today, that the LORD your God will set you high above all nations of the earth. And all these blessings shall come upon you and overtake you, because you obey the voice of the LORD your God:

"Blessed *shall* you *be* in the city, and blessed *shall* you *be* in the country.

"Blessed *shall be* the fruit of your body, the produce of your ground and the increase of your herds, the increase of your cattle and the offspring of your flocks.

"Blessed *shall be* your basket and your kneading bowl.

"Blessed *shall* you *be* when you come in, and blessed *shall* you *be* when you go out.

"The LORD will cause your enemies who rise against you to be defeated before your face; they shall come out against you one way and flee before you seven ways.

"The LORD will command the blessing on you in your storehouses and in all to which you set your hand, and He will bless you in the land which the LORD your God is giving you.

"The LORD will establish you as a holy people to Himself, just as He has sworn to you, if you keep the commandments of the LORD your God and walk in His ways. Then all peoples of the earth shall see that you are called by the name of the LORD, and they shall be afraid of you. And the LORD will grant you plenty of goods, in the fruit of your body, in the increase of your livestock, and in the produce of your ground, in the land of which the LORD swore to your fathers to give you. The LORD will open to you His good treasure, the heavens, to give the rain to your land in its season, and to bless all the work of your hand. You shall lend to many nations, but you shall not borrow. And the LORD will make you the head and not the tail; you shall be above only, and not be beneath, if you heed the commandments of the LORD your God, which I command you today, and are careful to observe *them*. So you shall not turn aside from any of the words which I command you this day, *to* the right or the left, to go after other gods to serve them.

"But it shall come to pass, if you do not obey the voice of the LORD your God, to observe carefully all His commandments and His statutes which I command you today, that all these curses will come upon you and overtake you:

"Cursed *shall* you *be* in the city, and cursed *shall* you *be* in the country.

"Cursed *shall be* your basket and your kneading bowl.

"Cursed *shall be* the fruit of your body and the produce of your land, the increase of your cattle and the offspring of your flocks.

"Cursed *shall* you *be* when you come in, and cursed *shall* you *be* when you go out.

"The LORD will send on you cursing, confusion, and rebuke in all that you set your hand to do, until you are destroyed and until you perish quickly, because of the wickedness of your doings in which you have forsaken Me.

"If you do not carefully observe all the words of

this law that are written in this book, that you may fear this glorious and awesome name, THE LORD YOUR GOD, then the LORD will bring upon you and your descendants extraordinary plagues—great and prolonged plagues—and serious and prolonged sicknesses. Moreover He will bring back on you all the diseases of Egypt, of which you were afraid, and they shall cling to you. Also every sickness and every plague, which *is* not written in this Book of the Law, will the LORD bring upon you until you are destroyed. You shall be left few in number, whereas you were as the stars of heaven in multitude, because you would not obey the voice of the LORD your God. And it shall be, *that* just as the LORD rejoiced over you to do you good and multiply you, so the LORD will rejoice over you to destroy you and bring you to nothing; and you shall be plucked from off the land which you go to possess.

"Then the LORD will scatter you among all peoples, from one end of the earth to the other, and there you shall serve other gods, which neither you nor your fathers have known—wood and stone. And among those nations you shall find no rest, nor shall the sole of your foot have a resting place; but there the LORD will give you a trembling heart, failing eyes, and anguish of soul."

Deuteronomy 27:11-16; 28:1-20, 58-65

WORSHIP

The LORD looks from heaven;
He sees all the sons of men.
From the place of His dwelling He looks
On all the inhabitants of the earth;
He fashions their hearts individually;
He considers all their works.

Psalm 33:13-15

WISDOM

The righteousness of the upright will deliver
    them,
But the unfaithful will be caught by *their* lust.

Proverbs 11:6

SW?! SO WHAT?
What does this tell me?

CHOOSE LIFE AND PROSPERITY
Deuteronomy 29:23–30:20; Psalm 33:18-20; Proverbs 11:8

" " "The whole land *is* brimstone, salt, and burning; it is not sown, nor does it bear, nor does any grass grow there, like the overthrow of Sodom and Gomorrah, Admah, and Zeboiim, which the LORD overthrew in His anger and His wrath.' All nations would say, 'Why has the LORD done so to this land? What does the heat of this great anger mean?' Then *people* would say: 'Because they have forsaken the covenant of the LORD God of their fathers, which He made with them when He brought them out of the land of Egypt; for they went and served other gods and worshiped them, gods that they did not know and that He had not given to them. Then the anger of the LORD was aroused against this land, to bring on it every curse that is written in this book. And the LORD uprooted them from their land in anger, in wrath, and in great indignation, and cast them into another land, as *it is* this day.'

"The secret *things belong* to the LORD our God, but those *things which are* revealed *belong* to us and to our children forever, that *we* may do all the words of this law.

"Now it shall come to pass, when all these things come upon you, the blessing and the curse which I have set before you, and you call *them* to mind among all the nations where the LORD your God drives you, and you return to the LORD your God and obey His voice, according to all that I command you today, you and your children, with all your heart and with all your soul, that the LORD your God will bring you back from captivity, and have compassion on you, and gather you again from all the nations where the LORD your God has scattered you. If *any* of you are driven out to the farthest *parts* under heaven, from there the LORD your God will gather you, and from there He will bring you. Then the LORD your God will bring you to the land which your fathers possessed, and you shall possess it. He will prosper you and multiply you more than your fathers. And the LORD your God will circumcise your heart and the heart of your descendants, to love the LORD your God with all your heart and with all your soul, that you may live.

"Also the LORD your God will put all these curses on your enemies and on those who hate you, who persecuted you. And you will again obey the voice of the LORD and do all His commandments which I command you today. The LORD your God will make you abound in all the work of your hand, in the fruit of your body, in the increase of your livestock, and in the produce of your land for good. For the LORD will again rejoice over you for good as He rejoiced over your fathers, if you obey the voice of the LORD your God, to keep His commandments and His statutes which are written in this Book of the Law, *and* if you turn to the LORD your God with all your heart and with all your soul.

"For this commandment which I command you today *is* not *too* mysterious for you, nor *is* it far off. It *is* not in heaven, that you should say, 'Who will ascend into heaven for us and bring it to us, that we may hear it and do it?' Nor *is* it beyond the sea, that you should say, 'Who will go over the sea for us and bring it to us, that we may hear it and do it?' But the word *is* very near you, in your mouth and in your heart, that you may do it.

"See, I have set before you today life and good, death and evil, in that I command you today to love the LORD your God, to walk in His ways, and to keep His commandments, His statutes, and His judgments, that you may live and multiply; and the LORD your God will bless you in the land which you go to possess. But if your heart turns away so that you do not hear, and are drawn away, and worship other gods and serve them, I announce to you today that you shall surely perish; you shall not prolong *your* days in the land which you cross over the Jordan to go in and possess. I call heaven and earth as witnesses today against you, *that* I have set before you life and death, blessing and cursing; therefore choose life, that both you and your descendants may live; that you may love the LORD your God, that you may obey His voice, and that you may cling to Him, for He *is* your life and the length of your days; and that you may dwell in the land which the LORD swore to your fathers, to Abraham, Isaac, and Jacob, to give them."

Deuteronomy 29:23–30:20

WILDERNESS WANDERING

WoRshiP

Behold, the eye of the LORD *is* on those who
    fear Him,
On those who hope in His mercy,
To deliver their soul from death,
And to keep them alive in famine.

Our soul waits for the LORD;
He *is* our help and our shield.

Psalm 33:18-20

WiSDoM

The righteous is delivered from trouble,
And it comes to the wicked instead.

Proverbs 11:8

SW?! **SO WHAT?**
What does this tell me?

MOSES' LAST WORDS Deuteronomy 31; 34; Psalm 34:1-3; Proverbs 11:10

Then Moses went and spoke these words to all Israel. And he said to them: "I *am* one hundred and twenty years old today. I can no longer go out and come in. Also the LORD has said to me, 'You shall not cross over this Jordan.' The LORD your God Himself crosses over before you; He will destroy these nations from before you, and you shall dispossess them. Joshua himself crosses over before you, just as the LORD has said. And the LORD will do to them as He did to Sihon and Og, the kings of the Amorites and their land, when He destroyed them. The LORD will give them over to you, that you may do to them according to every commandment which I have commanded you. Be strong and of good courage, do not fear nor be afraid of them; for the LORD your God, He *is* the One who goes with you. He will not leave you nor forsake you."

Then Moses called Joshua and said to him in the sight of all Israel, "Be strong and of good courage, for you must go with this people to the land which the LORD has sworn to their fathers to give them, and you shall cause them to inherit it. And the LORD, He *is* the One who goes before you. He will be with you, He will not leave you nor forsake you; do not fear nor be dismayed."

So Moses wrote this law and delivered it to the priests, the sons of Levi, who bore the ark of the covenant of the LORD, and to all the elders of Israel. And Moses commanded them, saying: "At the end of *every* seven years, at the appointed time in the year of release, at the Feast of Tabernacles, when all Israel comes to appear before the LORD your God in the place which He chooses, you shall read this law before all Israel in their hearing. Gather the people together, men and women and little ones, and the stranger who *is* within your gates, that they may hear and that they may learn to fear the LORD your God and carefully observe all the words of this law, and *that* their children, who have not known it, may hear and learn to fear the LORD your God as long as you live in the land which you cross the Jordan to possess."

Then the LORD said to Moses, "Behold, the days approach when you must die; call Joshua, and present yourselves in the tabernacle of meeting, that I may inaugurate him."

So Moses and Joshua went and presented themselves in the tabernacle of meeting. Now the LORD appeared at the tabernacle in a pillar of cloud, and the pillar of cloud stood above the door of the tabernacle.

And the LORD said to Moses: "Behold, you will rest with your fathers; and this people will rise and play the harlot with the gods of the foreigners of the land, where they go *to be* among them, and they will forsake Me and break My covenant which I have made with them. Then My anger shall be aroused against them in that day, and I will forsake them, and I will hide My face from them, and they shall be devoured. And many evils and troubles shall befall them, so that they will say in that day, 'Have not these evils come upon us because our God *is* not among us?' And I will surely hide My face in that day because of all the evil which they have done, in that they have turned to other gods.

"Now therefore, write down this song for yourselves, and teach it to the children of Israel; put it in their mouths, that this song may be a witness for Me against the children of Israel. When I have brought them to the land flowing with milk and honey, of which I swore to their fathers, and they have eaten and filled themselves and grown fat, then they will turn to other gods and serve them; and they will provoke Me and break My covenant. Then it shall be, when many evils and troubles have come upon them, that this song will testify against them as a witness; for it will not be forgotten in the mouths of their descendants, for I know the inclination of their behavior today, even before I have brought them to the land of which I swore *to give them.*"

Therefore Moses wrote this song the same day, and taught it to the children of Israel. Then He inaugurated Joshua the son of Nun, and said, "Be strong and of good courage; for you shall bring the children of Israel into the land of which I swore to them, and I will be with you."

So it was, when Moses had completed writing the words of this law in a book, when they were finished, that Moses commanded the Levites, who bore the ark of the covenant of the LORD, saying: "Take this

Book of the Law, and put it beside the ark of the covenant of the LORD your God, that it may be there as a witness against you; for I know your rebellion and your stiff neck. *If* today, while I am yet alive with you, you have been rebellious against the LORD, then how much more after my death? Gather to me all the elders of your tribes, and your officers, that I may speak these words in their hearing and call heaven and earth to witness against them. For I know that after my death you will become utterly corrupt, and turn aside from the way which I have commanded you. And evil will befall you in the latter days, because you will do evil in the sight of the LORD, to provoke Him to anger through the work of your hands."

Then Moses spoke in the hearing of all the assembly of Israel the words of this song until they were ended.

Then Moses went up from the plains of Moab to Mount Nebo, to the top of Pisgah, which is across from Jericho. And the LORD showed him all the land of Gilead as far as Dan, all Naphtali and the land of Ephraim and Manasseh, all the land of Judah as far as the Western Sea, the South, and the plain of the Valley of Jericho, the city of palm trees, as far as Zoar. Then the LORD said to him, "This *is* the land of which I swore to give Abraham, Isaac, and Jacob, saying, 'I will give it to your descendants.' I have caused you to see *it* with your eyes, but you shall not cross over there."

So Moses the servant of the LORD died there in the land of Moab, according to the word of the LORD. And He buried him in a valley in the land of Moab, opposite Beth Peor; but no one knows his grave to this day. Moses *was* one hundred and twenty years old when he died. His eyes were not dim nor his natural vigor diminished. And the children of Israel wept for Moses in the plains of Moab thirty days. So the days of weeping *and* mourning for Moses ended.

Now Joshua the son of Nun was full of the spirit of wisdom, for Moses had laid his hands on him; so the children of Israel heeded him, and did as the LORD had commanded Moses.

But since then there has not arisen in Israel a prophet like Moses, whom the LORD knew face to face, in all the signs and wonders which the LORD sent him to do in the land of Egypt, before Pharaoh, before all his servants, and in all his land, and by all that mighty power and all the great terror which Moses performed in the sight of all Israel.

Deuteronomy 31; 34

WORSHIP

I will bless the LORD at all times;
His praise *shall* continually *be* in my mouth.
My soul shall make its boast in the LORD;
The humble shall hear *of it* and be glad.
Oh, magnify the LORD with me,
And let us exalt His name together.

Psalm 34:1-3

WISDOM

When it goes well with the righteous, the city
  rejoices;
And when the wicked perish, *there is*
  jubilation.

Proverbs 11:10

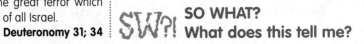

SO WHAT?
What does this tell me?

TAKING THE LAND

This mountain range demonstrates the faithfulness of God in fulfilling His promise to give Israel their land. After forty years of burying their dead and being reminded of their failure, it felt good for Israel to once again experience the thrill of victory.

After assuming leadership of the nation, Joshua immediately led them to face their first major obstacle—crossing the turbulent Jordan River. It was spring, and the melting snow from Mount Hermon filled the Jordan to overflowing. How were so many people going to cross the river into Canaan?

It took them forty years, but the Israelites learned their lesson. This time they trusted God and saw Him miraculously hold back the waters of the Jordan, allowing them to cross into the Promised Land without even getting mud on their sandals! According to Joshua, "all Israel crossed on dry ground" (Joshua 3:17). This experience was to this generation what the crossing of the Red Sea had been to their parents. The miracle demonstrated God's power and commitment to insure that His people would experience the fulfillment of His promises.

Now that that they were in the land of Canaan, the Israelites still had to deal with the Canaanites who were living there. But the people of Israel were growing in their trust of God's faithfulness to them, and the next mountain peak reflects this growing faith. The amazing thing about the overthrow of Jericho was the way it happened. This remarkable victory was accomplished solely by the power of God making it clear to the Israelites that the battle was the Lord's and that He would lead them in victory as they walked in obedience and faith.

God gave the Israelites many wonderful victories on their way to ultimate conquest of the land. After the Canaanites had been completely defeated and the land fully occupied, the land was divided among the twelve tribes of Israel. Against seemingly insurmountable odds, God fulfilled His promise to Abraham by giving Israel their promised land.

Joshua ASSUMES Leadership

Joshua 1:1–2:21; Psalm 34:8-10;
Proverbs 11:11

After the death of Moses the servant of the LORD, it came to pass that the LORD spoke to Joshua the son of Nun, Moses' assistant, saying: "Moses My servant is dead. Now therefore, arise, go over this Jordan, you and all this people, to the land which I am giving to them—the children of Israel. Every place that the sole of your foot will tread upon I have given you, as I said to Moses. From the wilderness and this Lebanon as far as the great river, the River Euphrates, all the land of the Hittites, and to the Great Sea toward the going down of the sun, shall be your territory. No man shall *be able to* stand before you all the days of your life; as I was with Moses, *so* I will be with you. I will not leave you nor forsake you. Be strong and of good courage, for to this people you shall divide as an inheritance the land which I swore to their fathers to give them. Only be strong and very courageous, that you may observe to do according to all the law which Moses My servant commanded you; do not turn from it to the right hand or to the left, that you may prosper wherever you go. This Book of the Law shall not depart from your mouth, but you shall meditate in it day and night, that you may observe to do according to all that is written in it. For then you will make your way prosperous, and then you will have good success. Have I not commanded you? Be strong and of good courage; do not be afraid, nor be dismayed, for the LORD your God *is* with you wherever you go."

Then Joshua commanded the officers of the people, saying, "Pass through the camp and command the people, saying, 'Prepare provisions for yourselves, for within three days you will cross over this Jordan, to go in to possess the land which the LORD your God is giving you to possess.' "

And to the Reubenites, the Gadites, and half the tribe of Manasseh Joshua spoke, saying, "Remember the word which Moses the servant of the LORD commanded you, saying, 'The LORD your God is giving you rest and is giving you this land.' Your wives, your little ones, and your livestock shall remain in the land which Moses gave you on this side of the Jordan. But you shall pass before your brethren armed, all your mighty men of valor, and help them, until the LORD has given your brethren rest, as He *gave* you, and they also have taken possession of the land which the LORD your God is giving them. Then you shall return to the land of your possession and enjoy it, which Moses the LORD's servant gave you on this side of the Jordan toward the sunrise."

So they answered Joshua, saying, "All that you command us we will do, and wherever you send us we will go. Just as we heeded Moses in all things, so we will heed you. Only the LORD your God be with you, as He was with Moses. Whoever rebels against your command and does not heed your words, in all that you command him, shall be put to death. Only be strong and of good courage."

Now Joshua the son of Nun sent out two men from Acacia Grove to spy secretly, saying, "Go, view the land, especially Jericho."

So they went, and came to the house of a harlot named Rahab, and lodged there. And it was told the king of Jericho, saying, "Behold, men have come here tonight from the children of Israel to search out the country."

So the king of Jericho sent to Rahab, saying, "Bring out the men who have come to you, who have entered your house, for they have come to search out all the country."

Then the woman took the two men and hid them. So she said, "Yes, the men came to me, but I did not know where they *were* from. And it happened as the gate was being shut, when it was dark, that the men went out. Where the men went I do not know; pursue them quickly, for you may overtake them." (But she had brought them up to the roof and hidden them with the stalks of flax, which she had laid in order on the roof.) Then the men pursued them by the road to the Jordan, to the fords. And as soon as those who pursued them had gone out, they shut the gate.

Now before they lay down, she came up to them on the roof, and said to the men: "I know that the LORD has given you the land, that the terror of you has fallen on us, and that all the inhabitants of the land are fainthearted because of you. For we have heard how the LORD dried up the water of the Red Sea for you when you came out of Egypt, and what you did to the two kings of the Amorites who *were* on the other side of the Jordan, Sihon and Og, whom you utterly destroyed. And as soon as we heard *these things,* our hearts melted; neither did there remain any more courage in anyone because of you, for the LORD your God, He *is* God in heaven above and on earth beneath. Now therefore, I beg you, swear to me by the LORD, since I have shown you kindness, that you also will show kindness to my father's house, and give me a true token, and spare my father, my mother, my brothers, my sisters, and all that they have, and deliver our lives from death."

So the men answered her, "Our lives for yours, if none of you tell this business of ours. And it shall be, when the LORD has given us the land, that we will deal kindly and truly with you."

Then she let them down by a rope through the window, for her house *was* on the city wall; she dwelt on the wall. And she said to them, "Get to the mountain, lest the pursuers meet you. Hide there three days, until the pursuers have returned. Afterward you may go your way."

So the men said to her: "We *will be* blameless of this oath of yours which you have made us swear, unless, *when* we come into the land, you bind this line of scarlet cord in the window through which you let us down, and unless you bring your father, your mother, your brothers, and all your father's household to your own home. So it shall be *that* whoever goes outside the doors of your house into the street, his blood *shall be* on his own head, and we *will be* guiltless. And whoever is with you in the house, his blood *shall be* on our head if a hand is laid on him. And if you tell this business of ours, then we will be free from your oath which you made us swear."

Then she said, "According to your words, so *be* it." And she sent them away, and they departed. And she bound the scarlet cord in the window.

Joshua 1:1–2:21

WORSHIP

Oh, taste and see that the LORD *is* good;
Blessed *is* the man *who* trusts in Him!
Oh, fear the LORD, you His saints!
There is no want to those who fear Him.
The young lions lack and suffer hunger;
But those who seek the LORD shall not lack any
   good *thing.*

Psalm 34:8-10

WISDOM

By the blessing of the upright the city is
   exalted,
But it is overthrown by the mouth of the
   wicked.

Proverbs 11:11

SW?! SO WHAT?
What does this tell me?

CROSSING THE JORDAN

Joshua 3:1–4:10, 19-24; Psalm 34:16-18; Proverbs 11:12

Then Joshua rose early in the morning; and they set out from Acacia Grove and came to the Jordan, he and all the children of Israel, and lodged there before they crossed over. So it was, after three days, that the officers went through the camp; and they commanded the people, saying, "When you see the ark of the covenant of the LORD your God, and the priests, the Levites, bearing it, then you shall set out from your place and go after it. Yet there shall be a space between you and it, about two thousand cubits by measure. Do not come near it, that you may know the way by which you must go, for you have not passed *this* way before."

And Joshua said to the people, "Sanctify yourselves, for tomorrow the LORD will do wonders among you." Then Joshua spoke to the priests, saying, "Take up the ark of the covenant and cross over before the people."

So they took up the ark of the covenant and went before the people.

And the LORD said to Joshua, "This day I will begin to exalt you in the sight of all Israel, that they may know that, as I was with Moses, *so* I will be with you. You shall command the priests who bear the ark of the covenant, saying, 'When you have come to the edge of the water of the Jordan, you shall stand in the Jordan.' "

So Joshua said to the children of Israel, "Come here, and hear the words of the LORD your God." And Joshua said, "By this you shall know that the living God *is* among you, and *that* He will without fail drive out from before you the Canaanites and the Hittites and the Hivites and the Perizzites and the Girgashites and the Amorites and the Jebusites: Behold, the ark of the covenant of the Lord of all the earth is crossing over before you into the Jordan. Now therefore, take for yourselves twelve men from the tribes of Israel, one man from every tribe. And it shall come to pass, as soon as the soles of the feet of the priests who bear the ark of the LORD, the Lord of all the earth, shall rest in the waters of the Jordan, *that* the waters of the Jordan shall be cut off, the waters that

come down from upstream, and they shall stand as a heap."

So it was, when the people set out from their camp to cross over the Jordan, with the priests bearing the ark of the covenant before the people, and as those who bore the ark came to the Jordan, and the feet of the priests who bore the ark dipped in the edge of the water (for the Jordan overflows all its banks during the whole time of harvest), that the waters which came down from upstream stood *still, and* rose in a heap very far away at Adam, the city that *is* beside Zaretan. So the waters that went down into the Sea of the Arabah, the Salt Sea, failed, *and* were cut off; and the people crossed over opposite Jericho. Then the priests who bore the ark of the covenant of the LORD stood firm on dry ground in the midst of the Jordan; and all Israel crossed over on dry ground, until all the people had crossed completely over the Jordan.

And it came to pass, when all the people had completely crossed over the Jordan, that the LORD spoke to Joshua, saying: "Take for yourselves twelve men from the people, one man from every tribe, and command them, saying, 'Take for yourselves twelve stones from here, out of the midst of the Jordan, from the place where the priests' feet stood firm. You shall carry them over with you and leave them in the lodging place where you lodge tonight.' "

Then Joshua called the twelve men whom he had appointed from the children of Israel, one man from every tribe; and Joshua said to them: "Cross over before the ark of the LORD your God into the midst of the Jordan, and each one of you take up a stone on his shoulder, according to the number of the tribes of the children of Israel, that this may be a sign among you when your children ask in time to come, saying, 'What do these stones *mean* to you?' Then you shall answer them that the waters of the Jordan were cut off before the ark of the covenant of the LORD; when it crossed over the Jordan, the waters of the Jordan were cut off. And these stones shall be for a memorial to the children of Israel forever."

And the children of Israel did so, just as Joshua commanded, and took up twelve stones from the midst of the Jordan, as the LORD had spoken to Joshua, according to the number of the tribes of the children of Israel, and carried them over with them to the place where they lodged, and laid them down there. Then Joshua set up twelve stones in the midst of the Jordan, in the place where the feet of the priests who bore the ark of the covenant stood; and they are there to this day.

So the priests who bore the ark stood in the midst of the Jordan until everything was finished that the LORD had commanded Joshua to speak to the people, according to all that Moses had commanded Joshua; and the people hurried and crossed over.

Now the people came up from the Jordan on the tenth *day* of the first month, and they camped in Gilgal on the east border of Jericho. And those twelve stones which they took out of the Jordan, Joshua set up in Gilgal. Then he spoke to the children of Israel, saying: "When your children ask their fathers in time to come, saying, 'What *are* these stones?' then you shall let your children know, saying, 'Israel crossed over this Jordan on dry land'; for the LORD your God dried up the waters of the Jordan before you until you had crossed over, as the LORD your God did to the Red Sea, which He dried up before us until we had crossed over, that all the peoples of the earth may know the hand of the LORD, that it *is* mighty, that you may fear the LORD your God forever."

Joshua 3:1–4:10, 19-24

WORSHIP

The face of the LORD *is* against those who do evil,
To cut off the remembrance of them from the earth.

The righteous cry out, and the LORD hears,
And delivers them out of all their troubles.
The LORD *is* near to those who have a broken heart,
And saves such as have a contrite spirit.

Psalm 34:16-18

WISDOM

He who is devoid of wisdom despises his neighbor,
But a man of understanding holds his peace.

Proverbs 11:12

SW?! **SO WHAT?**
What does this tell me?

THE WALLS FALL AT JERICHO

Joshua 5:10–6:27; Psalm 35:1–3; Proverbs 11:13

Now the children of Israel camped in Gilgal, and kept the Passover on the fourteenth day of the month at twilight on the plains of Jericho. And they ate of the produce of the land on the day after the Passover, unleavened bread and parched grain, on the very same day. Then the manna ceased on the day after they had eaten the produce of the land; and the children of Israel no longer had manna, but they ate the food of the land of Canaan that year.

And it came to pass, when Joshua was by Jericho, that he lifted his eyes and looked, and behold, a Man stood opposite him with His sword drawn in His hand. And Joshua went to Him and said to Him, "*Are* You for us or for our adversaries?"

So He said, "No, but *as* Commander of the army of the LORD I have now come."

And Joshua fell on his face to the earth and worshiped, and said to Him, "What does my Lord say to His servant?"

Then the Commander of the LORD's army said to Joshua, "Take your sandal off your foot, for the place where you stand *is* holy." And Joshua did so.

Now Jericho was securely shut up because of the children of Israel; none went out, and none came in. And the LORD said to Joshua: "See! I have given Jericho into your hand, its king, *and* the mighty men of valor. You shall march around the city, all *you* men of war; you shall go all around the city once. This you shall do six days. And seven priests shall bear seven trumpets of rams' horns before the ark. But the seventh day you shall march around the city seven times, and the priests shall blow the trumpets. It shall come to pass, when they make a long *blast* with the ram's horn, *and* when you hear the sound of the trumpet, that all the people shall shout with a great shout; then the wall of the city will fall down flat. And the people shall go up every man straight before him."

Then Joshua the son of Nun called the priests and said to them, "Take up the ark of the covenant, and let seven priests bear seven trumpets of rams' horns before the ark of the LORD." And he said to the people, "Proceed, and march around the city, and let him who is armed advance before the ark of the LORD."

So it was, when Joshua had spoken to the people, that the seven priests bearing the seven trumpets of rams' horns before the LORD advanced and blew the trumpets, and the ark of the covenant of the LORD followed them. The armed men went before the priests who blew the trumpets, and the rear guard came after the ark, while *the priests* continued blowing the trumpets. Now Joshua had commanded the people, saying, "You shall not shout or make any noise with your voice, nor shall a word proceed out of your mouth, until the day I say to you, 'Shout!' Then you shall shout." So he had the ark of the LORD circle the city, going around *it* once. Then they came into the camp and lodged in the camp.

And Joshua rose early in the morning, and the priests took up the ark of the LORD. Then seven priests bearing seven trumpets of rams' horns before the ark of the LORD went on continually and blew with the trumpets. And the armed men went before them. But the rear guard came after the ark of the LORD, while *the priests* continued blowing the trumpets. And the second day they marched around the city once and returned to the camp. So they did six days.

But it came to pass on the seventh day that they rose early, about the dawning of the day, and marched around the city seven times in the same manner. On that day only they marched around the city seven times. And the seventh time it happened, when the priests blew the trumpets, that Joshua said to the people: "Shout, for the LORD has given you the city! Now the city shall be doomed by the LORD to destruction, it and all who *are* in it. Only Rahab the harlot shall live, she and all who *are* with her in the house, because she hid the messengers that we sent. And you, by all means abstain from the accursed things, lest you become accursed when you take of the accursed things, and make the camp of Israel a curse, and trouble it. But all the silver and gold, and vessels of bronze and iron, *are* consecrated to the LORD; they shall come into the treasury of the LORD."

So the people shouted when *the priests* blew the trumpets. And it happened when the people heard the sound of the trumpet, and the people shouted with a great shout, that the wall fell down flat. Then the people went up into the city, every man straight before him, and they took the city. And they utterly destroyed all that *was* in the city, both man and woman, young and old, ox and sheep and donkey, with the edge of the sword.

But Joshua had said to the two men who had spied out the country, "Go into the harlot's house, and from there bring out the woman and all that she has, as you swore to her." And the young men who had been spies went in and brought out Rahab, her father, her mother, her brothers, and all that she had. So they brought out all her relatives and left them outside the camp of Israel. But they burned the city and all that *was* in it with fire. Only the silver and gold, and the vessels of bronze and iron, they put into the treasury of the house of the LORD. And Joshua spared Rahab the harlot, her father's household, and all that she had. So she dwells in Israel to this day, because she hid the messengers whom Joshua sent to spy out Jericho.

Then Joshua charged *them* at that time, saying, "Cursed *be* the man before the LORD who rises up and builds this city Jericho; he shall lay its foundation with his firstborn, and with his youngest he shall set up its gates."

So the LORD was with Joshua, and his fame spread throughout all the country.

Joshua 5:10–6:27

WORSHIP

Plead *my cause,* O LORD, with those who strive with me;
Fight against those who fight against me.
Take hold of shield and buckler,
And stand up for my help.
Also draw out the spear,
And stop those who pursue me.
Say to my soul,
"I *am* your salvation."

Psalm 35:1-3

WISDOM

A talebearer reveals secrets,
But he who is of a faithful spirit conceals a matter.

Proverbs 11:13

SW?! SO WHAT?
What does this tell me?

A TURNABOUT AT AI

Joshua 7:1-6, 10-26; 8:1-24; Psalm 35:9-10; Proverbs 11:14

But the children of Israel committed a trespass regarding the accursed things, for Achan the son of Carmi, the son of Zabdi, the son of Zerah, of the tribe of Judah, took of the accursed things; so the anger of the LORD burned against the children of Israel.

Now Joshua sent men from Jericho to Ai, which *is* beside Beth Aven, on the east side of Bethel, and spoke to them, saying, "Go up and spy out the country." So the men went up and spied out Ai. And they returned to Joshua and said to him, "Do not let all the people go up, but let about two or three thousand men go up and attack Ai. Do not weary all the people there, for *the people of Ai are* few." So about three thousand men went up there from the people, but they fled before the men of Ai. And the men of Ai struck down about thirty-six men, for they chased them *from* before the gate as far as Shebarim, and struck them down on the descent; therefore the hearts of the people melted and became like water.

Then Joshua tore his clothes, and fell to the earth on his face before the ark of the LORD until evening, he and the elders of Israel; and they put dust on their heads.

So the LORD said to Joshua: "Get up! Why do you lie thus on your face? Israel has sinned, and they have also transgressed My covenant which I commanded them. For they have even taken some of the accursed things, and have both stolen and deceived; and they have also put *it* among their own stuff. Therefore the children of Israel could not stand before their enemies, *but* turned *their* backs before their enemies, because they have become doomed to destruction. Neither will I be with you anymore, unless you destroy the accursed from among you. Get up, sanctify the people, and say, 'Sanctify yourselves for tomorrow, because thus says the LORD God of Israel: "*There is* an accursed thing in your midst, O Israel; you cannot stand before your enemies until you take away the accursed thing from among you." ' In the morning therefore you shall be brought according to your tribes. And it shall be *that* the tribe which the LORD takes shall come according to families; and the family which the LORD takes

shall come by households; and the household which the LORD takes shall come man by man. Then it shall be *that* he who is taken with the accursed thing shall be burned with fire, he and all that he has, because he has transgressed the covenant of the LORD, and because he has done a disgraceful thing in Israel.' "

So Joshua rose early in the morning and brought Israel by their tribes, and the tribe of Judah was taken. He brought the clan of Judah, and he took the family of the Zarhites; and he brought the family of the Zarhites man by man, and Zabdi was taken. Then he brought his household man by man, and Achan the son of Carmi, the son of Zabdi, the son of Zerah, of the tribe of Judah, was taken.

Now Joshua said to Achan, "My son, I beg you, give glory to the LORD God of Israel, and make confession to Him, and tell me now what you have done; do not hide *it* from me."

And Achan answered Joshua and said, "Indeed I have sinned against the LORD God of Israel, and this is what I have done: When I saw among the spoils a beautiful Babylonian garment, two hundred shekels of silver, and a wedge of gold weighing fifty shekels, I coveted them and took them. And there they are, hidden in the earth in the midst of my tent, with the silver under it."

So Joshua sent messengers, and they ran to the tent; and there it was, hidden in his tent, with the silver under it. And they took them from the midst of the tent, brought them to Joshua and to all the children of Israel, and laid them out before the LORD. Then Joshua, and all Israel with him, took Achan the son of Zerah, the silver, the garment, the wedge of gold, his sons, his daughters, his oxen, his donkeys, his sheep, his tent, and all that he had, and they brought them to the Valley of Achor. And Joshua said, "Why have you troubled us? The LORD will trouble you this day." So all Israel stoned him with stones; and they burned them with fire after they had stoned them with stones.

Then they raised over him a great heap of stones, still there to this day. So the LORD turned from the fierceness of His anger. Therefore the name of that place has been called the Valley of Achor to this day.

Now the LORD said to Joshua: "Do not be afraid, nor be dismayed; take all the people of war with you, and arise, go up to Ai. See, I have given into your hand the king of Ai, his people, his city, and his land. And you shall do to Ai and its king as you did to Jericho and its king. Only its spoil and its cattle you shall take as booty for yourselves. Lay an ambush for the city behind it."

So Joshua arose, and all the people of war, to go up against Ai; and Joshua chose thirty thousand mighty men of valor and sent them away by night. And he commanded them, saying: "Behold, you shall lie in ambush against the city, behind the city. Do not go very far from the city, but all of you be ready. Then I and all the people who *are* with me will approach the city; and it will come about, when they come out against us as at the first, that we shall flee before them. For they will come out after us till we have drawn them from the city, for they will say, '*They are* fleeing before us as at the first.' Therefore we will flee before them. Then you shall rise from the ambush and seize the city, for the LORD your God will deliver it into your hand. And it will be, when you have taken the city, *that* you shall set the city on fire. According to the commandment of the LORD you shall do. See, I have commanded you."

Joshua therefore sent them out; and they went to lie in ambush, and stayed between Bethel and Ai, on the west side of Ai; but Joshua lodged that night among the people. Then Joshua rose up early in the morning and mustered the people, and went up, he and the elders of Israel, before the people to Ai. And all the people of war who *were* with him went up and drew near; and they came before the city and camped on the north side of Ai. Now a valley *lay* between them and Ai. So he took about five thousand men and set them in ambush between Bethel and Ai, on the west side of the city. And when they had set the people, all the army that *was* on the north of the city, and its rear guard on the west of the city, Joshua went that night into the midst of the valley.

Now it happened, when the king of Ai saw *it,* that the men of the city hurried and rose early and went out against Israel to battle, he and all his people, at an appointed place before the plain. But he did not know that *there was* an ambush against him behind the city. And Joshua and all Israel made as if they were beaten before them, and fled by the way of the wilderness. So all the people who *were* in Ai were called together to pursue them. And they pursued Joshua and were drawn away from the city. There was not a man left in Ai or Bethel who did not go out after Israel. So they left the city open and pursued Israel.

Then the LORD said to Joshua, "Stretch out the spear that *is* in your hand toward Ai, for I will give it into your hand." And Joshua stretched out the spear that *was* in his hand toward the city. So *those in* ambush arose quickly out of their place; they ran as soon as he had stretched out his hand, and they entered the city and took it, and hurried to set the city on fire. And when the men of Ai looked behind them, they saw, and behold, the smoke of the city ascended to heaven. So they had no power to flee this way or that way, and the people who had fled to the wilderness turned back on the pursuers.

Now when Joshua and all Israel saw that the ambush had taken the city and that the smoke of the city ascended, they turned back and struck down the men of Ai. Then the others came out of the city against them; so they were *caught* in the midst of Israel, some on this side and some on that side. And they struck them down, so that they let none of them remain or escape. But the king of Ai they took alive, and brought him to Joshua.

And it came to pass when Israel had made an end of slaying all the inhabitants of Ai in the field, in the wilderness where they pursued them, and when they all had fallen by the edge of the sword until they were consumed, that all the Israelites returned to Ai and struck it with the edge of the sword.

Joshua 7:1-6, 10-26; 8:1-24

WORSHIP

And my soul shall be joyful in the LORD;
It shall rejoice in His salvation.
All my bones shall say,
"LORD, who *is* like You,
Delivering the poor from him who is too strong for him,
Yes, the poor and the needy from him who plunders him?"

Psalm 35:9-10

WISDOM

Where *there is* no counsel, the people fall;
But in the multitude of counselors *there is* safety.

Proverbs 11:14

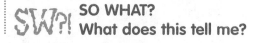 **SO WHAT?**
What does this tell me?

A DECEPTIVE ENEMY

Joshua 9:1–10:14, 42–43; Psalm 35:17-18;
Proverbs 11:15

And it came to pass when all the kings who *were* on this side of the Jordan, in the hills and in the lowland and in all the coasts of the Great Sea toward Lebanon—the Hittite, the Amorite, the Canaanite, the Perizzite, the Hivite, and the Jebusite—heard *about it,* that they gathered together to fight with Joshua and Israel with one accord.

But when the inhabitants of Gibeon heard what Joshua had done to Jericho and Ai, they worked craftily, and went and pretended to be ambassadors. And they took old sacks on their donkeys, old wineskins torn and mended, old and patched sandals on their feet, and old garments on themselves; and all the bread of their provision was dry *and* moldy. And they went to Joshua, to the camp at Gilgal, and said to him and to the men of Israel, "We have come from a far country; now therefore, make a covenant with us."

Then the men of Israel said to the Hivites, "Perhaps you dwell among us; so how can we make a covenant with you?"

But they said to Joshua, "We *are* your servants."

And Joshua said to them, "Who *are* you, and where do you come from?"

So they said to him: "From a very far country your servants have come, because of the name of the LORD your God; for we have heard of His fame, and all that He did in Egypt, and all that He did to the two kings of the Amorites who *were* beyond the Jordan—to Sihon king of Heshbon, and Og king of Bashan, who was at Ashtaroth. Therefore our elders and all the inhabitants of our country spoke to us, saying, 'Take provisions with you for the journey, and go to meet them, and say to them, "We *are* your servants; now therefore, make a covenant with us." ' This bread of ours we took hot *for* our provision from our houses on the day we departed to come to you. But now look, it is dry and moldy. And these wineskins which we filled *were* new, and see, they are torn; and these our garments and our sandals have become old because of the very long journey."

Then the men of Israel took some of their provisions; but they did not ask counsel of the LORD. So Joshua made peace with them, and made a covenant with them to let them live; and the rulers of the congregation swore to them.

And it happened at the end of three days, after they had made a covenant with them, that they heard that they *were* their neighbors who dwelt near them. Then the children of Israel journeyed and came to their cities on the third day. Now their cities *were* Gibeon, Chephirah, Beeroth, and Kirjath Jearim. But the children of Israel did not attack them, because the rulers of the congregation had sworn to them by the LORD God of Israel. And all the congregation complained against the rulers.

Then all the rulers said to all the congregation, "We have sworn to them by the LORD God of Israel; now therefore, we may not touch them. This we will do to them: We will let them live, lest wrath be upon us because of the oath which we swore to them." And the rulers said to them, "Let them live, but let them be woodcutters and water carriers for all the congregation, as the rulers had promised them."

Then Joshua called for them, and he spoke to them, saying, "Why have you deceived us, saying, 'We *are* very far from you,' when you dwell near us? Now therefore, you *are* cursed, and none of you shall be freed from being slaves—woodcutters and water carriers for the house of my God."

So they answered Joshua and said, "Because your servants were clearly told that the LORD your God commanded His servant Moses to give you all the land, and to destroy all the inhabitants of the land from before you; therefore we were very much afraid for our lives because of you, and have done this thing. And now, here we are, in your hands; do with us as it seems good and right to do to us." So he did to them, and delivered them out of the hand of the children of Israel, so that they did not kill them. And that day Joshua made them woodcutters and water carriers for the congregation and for the altar of the LORD, in the place which He would choose, even to this day.

Now it came to pass when Adoni-Zedek king of Jerusalem heard how Joshua had taken Ai and had utterly destroyed it—as he had done to Jericho and its king, so he had done to Ai and its king—and how the inhabitants of Gibeon had made peace with Israel and were among them, that they feared greatly, because Gibeon *was* a great city, like one of the royal cities, and because it *was* greater than Ai, and all its men *were* mighty. Therefore Adoni-Zedek king of Jerusalem sent to Hoham king of Hebron, Piram king of Jarmuth, Japhia king of Lachish, and Debir king of Eglon, saying, "Come up to me and help me, that we may attack Gibeon, for it has made peace with Joshua and with the children of Israel." Therefore the five kings of the Amorites, the king of Jerusalem, the king of Hebron, the king of Jarmuth, the king of Lachish, *and* the king of Eglon, gathered together and went up, they and all their armies, and camped before Gibeon and made war against it.

And the men of Gibeon sent to Joshua at the camp at Gilgal, saying, "Do not forsake your servants; come up to us quickly, save us and help us, for all the kings of the Amorites who dwell in the mountains have gathered together against us."

So Joshua ascended from Gilgal, he and all the people of war with him, and all the mighty men of valor. And the LORD said to Joshua, "Do not fear them, for I have delivered them into your hand; not a man of them shall stand before you." Joshua therefore came upon them suddenly, having marched all night from Gilgal. So the LORD routed them before Israel, killed them with a great slaughter at Gibeon, chased them along the road that goes to Beth Horon, and struck them down as far as Azekah and Makkedah. And it happened, as they fled before Israel *and* were on the descent of Beth Horon, that the LORD cast down large hailstones from heaven on them as far as Azekah, and they died. *There were* more who died from the hailstones than the children of Israel killed with the sword.

Then Joshua spoke to the LORD in the day when the LORD delivered up the Amorites before the children of Israel, and he said in the sight of Israel:

"Sun, stand still over Gibeon;
And Moon, in the Valley of Aijalon."
So the sun stood still,
And the moon stopped,
Till the people had revenge
Upon their enemies.

Is this not written in the Book of Jasher? So the sun stood still in the midst of heaven, and did not hasten to go *down* for about a whole day. And there has been no day like that, before it or after it, that the LORD heeded the voice of a man; for the LORD fought for Israel.

All these kings and their land Joshua took at one time, because the LORD God of Israel fought for Israel. Then Joshua returned, and all Israel with him, to the camp at Gilgal.

Joshua 9:1–10:14, 42-43

WORSHIP

Lord, how long will You look on?
Rescue me from their destructions,
My precious *life* from the lions.
I will give You thanks in the great assembly;
I will praise You among many people.

Psalm 35:17-18

WISDOM

He who is surety for a stranger will suffer,
But one who hates being surety is secure.

Proverbs 11:15

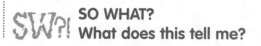

SO WHAT?
What does this tell me?

REST FROM CONQUEST

Joshua 11; 23; 24:29-33; Psalm 35:22-23, 28; Proverbs 11:17

And it came to pass, when Jabin king of Hazor heard *these things,* that he sent to Jobab king of Madon, to the king of Shimron, to the king of Achshaph, and to the kings who *were* from the north, in the mountains, in the plain south of Chinneroth, in the lowland, and in the heights of Dor on the west, to the Canaanites in the east and in the west, the Amorite, the Hittite, the Perizzite, the Jebusite in the mountains, and the Hivite below Hermon in the land of Mizpah. So they went out, they and all their armies with them, *as* many people *as* the sand that *is* on the seashore in multitude, with very many horses and chariots. And when all these kings had met together, they came and camped together at the waters of Merom to fight against Israel.

But the LORD said to Joshua, "Do not be afraid because of them, for tomorrow about this time I will deliver all of them slain before Israel. You shall hamstring their horses and burn their chariots with fire." So Joshua and all the people of war with him came against them suddenly by the waters of Merom, and they attacked them. And the LORD delivered them into the hand of Israel, who defeated them and chased them to Greater Sidon, to the Brook Misrephoth, and to the Valley of Mizpah eastward; they attacked them until they left none of them remaining. So Joshua did to them as the LORD had told him: he hamstrung their horses and burned their chariots with fire.

Joshua turned back at that time and took Hazor, and struck its king with the sword; for Hazor was formerly the head of all those kingdoms. And they struck all the people who *were* in it with the edge of the sword, utterly destroying *them.* There was none left breathing. Then he burned Hazor with fire.

So all the cities of those kings, and all their kings, Joshua took and struck with the edge of the sword. He utterly destroyed them, as Moses the servant of the LORD had commanded. But *as for* the cities that stood on their mounds, Israel burned none of them, except Hazor only, *which* Joshua burned. And all the spoil of these cities and the livestock, the children of Israel took as booty for themselves; but they struck every man with the edge of the sword until they had destroyed them, and they left none breathing. As the LORD had commanded Moses his servant, so Moses commanded Joshua, and so Joshua did. He left nothing undone of all that the LORD had commanded Moses.

Thus Joshua took all this land: the mountain country, all the South, all the land of Goshen, the lowland, and the Jordan plain—the mountains of Israel and its lowlands, from Mount Halak and the ascent to Seir, even as far as Baal Gad in the Valley of Lebanon below Mount Hermon. He captured all their kings, and struck them down and killed them. Joshua made war a long time with all those kings. There was not a city that made peace with the children of Israel, except the Hivites, the inhabitants of Gibeon. All *the others* they took in battle. For it was of the LORD to harden their hearts, that they should come against Israel in battle, that He might utterly destroy them, *and* that they might receive no mercy, but that He might destroy them, as the LORD had commanded Moses.

And at that time Joshua came and cut off the Anakim from the mountains: from Hebron, from Debir, from Anab, from all the mountains of Judah, and from all the mountains of Israel; Joshua utterly destroyed them with their cities. None of the Anakim were left in the land of the children of Israel; they remained only in Gaza, in Gath, and in Ashdod.

So Joshua took the whole land, according to all that the LORD had said to Moses; and Joshua gave it as an inheritance to Israel according to their divisions by their tribes. Then the land rested from war.

Now it came to pass, a long time after the LORD had given rest to Israel from all their enemies round about, that Joshua was old, advanced in age. And Joshua called for all Israel, for their elders, for their heads, for their judges, and for their officers, and said to them:

"I am old, advanced in age. You have seen all that the LORD your God has done to all these nations because of you, for the LORD your God *is* He who has fought for you. See, I have divided to you by lot these nations that remain, to be an inheritance for your tribes, from the Jordan, with all the nations that I have cut off, as far as the Great Sea westward. And the LORD your God will expel them from before you and drive them out of your sight. So you shall possess their land, as the LORD your God promised you. Therefore be very courageous to keep and to do all that is written in the Book of the Law of Moses, lest you turn aside from it to the right hand or to the left, *and* lest you go among these nations, these who remain among you. You shall not make mention of the name of their gods, nor cause *anyone* to swear *by them;* you shall not serve them nor bow down to them, but you shall hold fast to the LORD your God, as you have done to this day. For the LORD has driven out from before you great and strong nations; but *as for* you, no one has been able to stand against you to this day. One man of you shall chase a thousand, for the LORD your God *is* He who fights for you, as He promised you. Therefore take careful heed to yourselves, that you love the LORD your God. Or else, if indeed you do go back, and cling to the remnant of these nations— these that remain among you—and make marriages with them, and go in to them and they to you, know for certain that the LORD your God will no longer drive out these nations from before you. But they shall be snares and traps to you, and scourges on your sides and thorns in your eyes, until you perish from this good land which the LORD your God has given you.

"Behold, this day I *am* going the way of all the earth. And you know in all your hearts and in all your souls that not one thing has failed of all the good things which the LORD your God spoke concerning you. All have come to pass for you; not one word of them has failed. Therefore it shall come to pass, that as all the good things have come upon you which the LORD your God promised you, so the LORD will bring upon you all harmful things, until He has destroyed you from this good land which the LORD your God has given you. When you have transgressed the covenant of the LORD your God, which He commanded you, and have gone and served other gods, and bowed down to them, then the anger of the LORD will burn against you, and you shall perish quickly from the good land which He has given you."

Now it came to pass after these things that Joshua the son of Nun, the servant of the LORD, died, *being* one hundred and ten years old. And they buried him within the border of his inheritance at Timnath Serah, which *is* in the mountains of Ephraim, on the north side of Mount Gaash.

Israel served the LORD all the days of Joshua, and all the days of the elders who outlived Joshua, who had known all the works of the LORD which He had done for Israel.

The bones of Joseph, which the children of Israel had brought up out of Egypt, they buried at Shechem, in the plot of ground which Jacob had bought from the sons of Hamor the father of Shechem for one hundred pieces of silver, and which had become an inheritance of the children of Joseph.

And Eleazar the son of Aaron died. They buried him in a hill *belonging to* Phinehas his son, which was given to him in the mountains of Ephraim.

Joshua 11; 23; 24:29-33

WORSHIP

This You have seen, O LORD;
Do not keep silence.
O Lord, do not be far from me.
Stir up Yourself, and awake to my vindication,
To my cause, my God and my Lord.

And my tongue shall speak of Your
 righteousness
And of Your praise all the day long.

Psalm 35:22-23, 28

WISDOM

The merciful man does good for his own soul,
But *he who is* cruel troubles his own flesh.

Proverbs 11:17

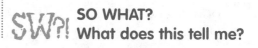

SO WHAT?
What does this tell me?

HERE COMES the JUDGE

Under the leadership of Joshua, the Israelites were on a roll. But this winning streak did not last long. Within a short period of time after inhabiting the Promised Land, the Israelites found themselves in a state of bondage worse in some ways than what they had experienced in Egypt.

This range illustrates how life can go sour when we turn our backs on God. The wisdom of Proverbs 14:34 is an appropriate summary to this mountain range: "Righteousness exalts a nation, but sin is a reproach to any people." Oppressed by their enemies and socially, politically, religiously, and morally disintegrating from within, Israel was learning the hard way that living independently of God doesn't feel much like living.

Like some sort of bungee jumper, Israel sprang up and down for 325 years, worshipping false gods like Baal, Asherah, and Anath on the way down and then repenting of their sin on the way back up. Idolatry, repentance, idolatry, repentance. Each time the people sinned they sank lower into the mess they made for themselves. Each time they repented, God raised up from their midst a judge who would lead them and deliver them from their enemies.

One of the peaks in this range occurred when God raised up Deborah to serve as judge during a time of Canaanite oppression. It was through her encouragement that Barak, the commander of Israel's forces, waged battle against their enemy and won a great victory. Gideon is another peak in this range. He led a band of just three hundred men in victory over the more powerful Midianites. Samson's leadership, another peak, was a mixed blessing for Israel. Samson had great potential as a leader when the challenge of the Philistines demanded heroic leadership. Yet his efforts were undermined to a large degree by his lack of self-control.

Undoubtedly the highest peak in this range is found in the Book of Ruth. While many Israelites were turning from God during the period of the judges, Ruth was a non-Israelite who found faith in the God of Israel. In spite of her Gentile origins, she was made a part of the nation of Israel by marriage and became an ancestor of one of Israel's greatest leaders, King David.

The birth of Samuel marks the transition from this range to the next. Samuel was the last of the judges and the first of a series of prophets who spoke for God to the people of Israel. Samuel also helped inaugurate the monarchy in Israel, anointing Israel's first two kings, Saul and then David.

ENEMY AMONG US Judges 1:1-9, 19-33; 2:1-23; Psalm 36:5-7; Proverbs 11:18

Now after the death of Joshua it came to pass that the children of Israel asked the LORD, saying, "Who shall be first to go up for us against the Canaanites to fight against them?"

And the LORD said, "Judah shall go up. Indeed I have delivered the land into his hand."

So Judah said to Simeon his brother, "Come up with me to my allotted territory, that we may fight against the Canaanites; and I will likewise go with you to your allotted territory." And Simeon went with him. Then Judah went up, and the LORD delivered the Canaanites and the Perizzites into their hand; and they killed ten thousand men at Bezek. And they found Adoni-Bezek in Bezek, and fought against him; and they defeated the Canaanites and the Perizzites. Then Adoni-Bezek fled, and they pursued him and caught him and cut off his thumbs and big toes. And Adoni-Bezek said, "Seventy kings with their thumbs and big toes cut off used to gather *scraps* under my table; as I have done, so God has repaid me." Then they brought him to Jerusalem, and there he died.

Now the children of Judah fought against Jerusalem and took it; they struck it with the edge of the sword and set the city on fire. And afterward the children of Judah went down to fight against the Canaanites who dwelt in the mountains, in the South, and in the lowland.

So the LORD was with Judah. And they drove out the mountaineers, but they could not drive out the inhabitants of the lowland, because they had chariots of iron. And they gave Hebron to Caleb, as Moses had said. Then he expelled from there the three sons of Anak. But the children of Benjamin did not drive out the Jebusites who inhabited Jerusalem; so the Jebusites dwell with the children of Benjamin in Jerusalem to this day.

And the house of Joseph also went up against Bethel, and the LORD *was* with them. So the house of Joseph sent men to spy out Bethel. (The name of the city *was* formerly Luz.) And when the spies saw a man coming out of the city, they said to him, "Please show us the entrance to the city, and we will show you mercy." So he showed them the entrance to the city, and they struck the city with the edge of the sword; but they let the man and all his family go. And the man went to the land of the Hittites, built a city, and called its name Luz, which *is* its name to this day.

However, Manasseh did not drive out *the inhabitants of* Beth Shean and its villages, or Taanach and its villages, or the inhabitants of Dor and its villages, or the inhabitants of Ibleam and its villages, or the inhabitants of Megiddo and its villages; for the Canaanites were determined to dwell in that land. And it came to pass, when Israel was strong, that they put the Canaanites under tribute, but did not completely drive them out.

Nor did Ephraim drive out the Canaanites who dwelt in Gezer; so the Canaanites dwelt in Gezer among them.

Nor did Zebulun drive out the inhabitants of Kitron or the inhabitants of Nahalol; so the Canaanites dwelt among them, and were put under tribute.

Nor did Asher drive out the inhabitants of Acco or the inhabitants of Sidon, or of Ahlab, Achzib, Helbah, Aphik, or Rehob. So the Asherites dwelt among the Canaanites, the inhabitants of the land; for they did not drive them out.

Nor did Naphtali drive out the inhabitants of Beth Shemesh or the inhabitants of Beth Anath; but they dwelt among the Canaanites, the inhabitants of the land. Nevertheless the inhabitants of Beth Shemesh and Beth Anath were put under tribute to them.

Then the Angel of the LORD came up from Gilgal to Bochim, and said: "I led you up from Egypt and brought you to the land of which I swore to your fathers; and I said, 'I will never break My covenant with you. And you shall make no covenant with the inhabitants of this land; you shall tear down their altars.' But you have not obeyed My voice. Why have you done this? Therefore I also said, 'I will not drive them out before you; but they shall be *thorns* in your side, and their gods shall be a snare to you.' " So it was, when the Angel of the LORD spoke these words to all the children of Israel, that the people lifted up their voices and wept.

Then they called the name of that place Bochim; and they sacrificed there to the LORD. And when Joshua had dismissed the people, the children of Israel went each to his own inheritance to possess the land.

So the people served the LORD all the days of Joshua, and all the days of the elders who outlived Joshua, who had seen all the great works of the LORD which He had done for Israel. Now Joshua the son of Nun, the servant of the LORD, died *when he was* one hundred and ten years old. And they buried him within the border of his inheritance at Timnath Heres, in the mountains of Ephraim, on the north side of Mount Gaash. When all that generation had been gathered to their fathers, another generation arose after them who did not know the LORD nor the work which he had done for Israel.

Then the children of Israel did evil in the sight of the LORD, and served the Baals; and they forsook the LORD God of their fathers, who had brought them out of the land of Egypt; and they followed other gods from *among* the gods of the people who *were* all around them, and they bowed down to them; and they provoked the LORD to anger. They forsook the Lord and served Baal and the Ashtoreths. And the anger of the LORD was hot against Israel. So He delivered them into the hands of plunderers who despoiled them; and He sold them into the hands of their enemies all around, so that they could no longer stand before their enemies. Wherever they went out, the hand of the Lord was against them for calamity, as the LORD had said, and as the LORD had sworn to them. And they were greatly distressed.

Nevertheless, the LORD raised up judges who delivered them out of the hand of those who plundered them. Yet they would not listen to their judges, but they played the harlot with other gods, and bowed down to them. They turned quickly from the way in which their fathers walked, in obeying the commandments of the LORD; they did not do so. And when the LORD raised up judges for them, the LORD was with the judge and delivered them out of the hand of their enemies all the days of the judge; for the LORD was moved to pity by their groaning because of those who oppressed them and harassed them. And it came to pass, when the judge was dead, that they reverted and behaved more corruptly than their fathers, by following other gods, to serve them and bow down to them. They did not cease from their own doings nor from their stubborn way.

Then the anger of the LORD was hot against Is-

rael; and He said, "Because this nation has transgressed My covenant which I commanded their fathers, and has not heeded My voice, I also will no longer drive out before them any of the nations which Joshua left when he died, so that through them I may test Israel, whether they will keep the ways of the LORD, to walk in them as their fathers kept *them,* or not." Therefore the LORD left those nations, without driving them out immediately; nor did He deliver them into the hand of Joshua.

Judges 1:1-9, 19-33; 2:1-23

WORSHIP

Your mercy, O LORD, *is* in the heavens;
Your faithfulness *reaches* to the clouds.
Your righteousness *is* like the great mountains;
Your judgments *are* a great deep;
O LORD, You preserve man and beast.

How precious *is* Your lovingkindness, O God!
Therefore the children of men put their trust
    under the shadow of Your wings.

Psalm 36:5-7

WISDOM

The wicked *man* does deceptive work,
But he who sows righteousness *will have* a
    sure reward.

Proverbs 11:18

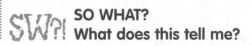

SO WHAT?
What does this tell me?

BEGINNINGS OF OPPRESSION

Judges 3:1–4:3; Psalm 36:10-12; Proverbs 11:19

Now these *are* the nations which the LORD left, that He might test Israel by them, *that is,* all who had not known any of the wars in Canaan (*this was* only so that the generations of the children of Israel might be taught to know war, at least those who had not formerly known it), *namely,* five lords of the Philistines, all the Canaanites, the Sidonians, and the Hivites who dwelt in Mount Lebanon, from Mount Baal Hermon to the entrance of Hamath. And they were *left, that He might* test Israel by them, to know whether they would obey the commandments of the LORD, which He had commanded their fathers by the hand of Moses.

Thus the children of Israel dwelt among the Canaanites, the Hittites, the Amorites, the Perizzites, the Hivites, and the Jebusites. And they took their daughters to be their wives, and gave their daughters to their sons; and they served their gods.

So the children of Israel did evil in the sight of the LORD. They forgot the LORD their God, and served the Baals and Asherahs. Therefore the anger of the LORD was hot against Israel, and He sold them into the hand of Cushan-Rishathaim king of Mesopotamia; and the children of Israel served Cushan-Rishathaim eight years. When the children of Israel cried out to the LORD, the LORD raised up a deliverer for the children of Israel, who delivered them: Othniel the son of Kenaz, Caleb's younger brother. The Spirit of the LORD came upon him, and he judged Israel. He went out to war, and the LORD delivered Cushan-Rishathaim king of Mesopotamia into his hand; and his hand prevailed over Cushan-Rishathaim. So the land had rest for forty years. Then Othniel the son of Kenaz died.

And the children of Israel again did evil in the sight of the LORD. So the LORD strengthened Eglon king of Moab against Israel, because they had done evil in the sight of the LORD. Then he gathered to himself the people of Ammon and Amalek, went and defeated Israel, and took possession of the City of Palms. So the children of Israel served Eglon king of Moab eighteen years.

But when the children of Israel cried out to the LORD, the LORD raised up a deliverer for them: Ehud the son of Gera, the Benjamite, a left-handed man. By him the children of Israel sent tribute to Eglon king of Moab. Now Ehud made himself a dagger (it was double-edged and a cubit in length) and fastened it under his clothes on his right thigh. So he brought the tribute to Eglon king of Moab. (Now Eglon *was* a very fat man.) And when he had finished presenting the tribute, he sent away the people who had carried the tribute. But he himself turned back from the stone images that *were* at Gilgal, and said, "I have a secret message for you, O king."

He said, "Keep silence!" And all who attended him went out from him.

So Ehud came to him (now he was sitting upstairs in his cool private chamber). Then Ehud said, "I have a message from God for you." So he arose from *his* seat. Then Ehud reached with his left hand, took the dagger from his right thigh, and thrust it into his belly. Even the hilt went in after the blade, and the fat closed over the blade, for he did not draw the dagger out of his belly; and his entrails came out. Then Ehud went out through the porch and shut the doors of the upper room behind him and locked them.

When he had gone out, *Eglon's* servants came to look, and *to their* surprise, the doors of the upper room were locked. So they said, "He is probably attending to his needs in the cool chamber." So they waited till they were embarrassed, and still he had not opened the doors of the upper room. Therefore they took the key and opened *them*. And there was their master, fallen dead on the floor.

But Ehud had escaped while they delayed, and passed beyond the stone images and escaped to Seirah. And it happened, when he arrived, that he blew the trumpet in the mountains of Ephraim, and the children of Israel went down with him from the mountains; and he led them. Then he said to them, "Follow *me,* for the LORD has delivered your enemies the Moabites into your hand." So they went down after him, seized the fords of the Jordan leading to Moab, and did not allow anyone to cross over. And at that time they killed about ten thousand men of Moab, all stout men of valor; not a man escaped. So Moab was subdued that day under the hand of Israel. And the land had rest for eighty years.

After him was Shamgar the son of Anath, who killed six hundred men of the Philistines with an ox goad; and he also delivered Israel.

When Ehud was dead, the children of Israel again did evil in the sight of the LORD. So the LORD sold them into the hand of Jabin king of Canaan, who reigned in Hazor. The commander of his army *was* Sisera, who dwelt in Harosheth Hagoyim. And the children of Israel cried out to the LORD; for Jabin had nine hundred chariots of iron, and for twenty years he harshly oppressed the children of Israel.

Judges 3:1–4:3

WORSHIP

Oh, continue Your lovingkindness to those who know You,
And Your righteousness to the upright in heart.
Let not the foot of pride come against me,
And let not the hand of the wicked drive me away.
There the workers of iniquity have fallen;
They have been cast down and are not able to rise.

Psalm 36:10-12

WISDOM

As righteousness *leads* to life,
So he who pursues evil *pursues it* to his own death.

Proverbs 11:19

SW?! **SO WHAT?**
What does this tell me?

DELIVERANCE THROUGH DEBORAH

Judges 4:4–5:11, 28-31; Psalm 37:3-5; Proverbs 11:20

Now Deborah, a prophetess, the wife of Lapidoth, was judging Israel at that time. And she would sit under the palm tree of Deborah between Ramah and Bethel in the mountains of Ephraim. And the children of Israel came up to her for judgment. Then she sent and called for Barak the son of Abinoam from Kedesh in Naphtali, and said to him, "Has not the LORD God of Israel commanded, 'Go and deploy *troops* at Mount Tabor; take with you ten thousand men of the sons of Naphtali and of the sons of Zebulun; and against you I will deploy Sisera, the commander of Jabin's army, with his chariots and his multitude at the River Kishon; and I will deliver him into your hand'?"

And Barak said to her, "If you will go with me, then I will go; but if you will not go with me, I will not go!"

So she said, "I will surely go with you; nevertheless there will be no glory for you in the journey you are taking, for the LORD will sell Sisera into the hand of a woman." Then Deborah arose and went with Barak to Kedesh. And Barak called Zebulun and Naphtali to Kedesh; he went up with ten thousand men under his command, and Deborah went up with him.

Now Heber the Kenite, of the children of Hobab the father-in-law of Moses, had separated himself from the Kenites and pitched his tent near the terebinth tree at Zaanaim, which *is* beside Kedesh.

And they reported to Sisera that Barak the son of Abinoam had gone up to Mount Tabor. So Sisera gathered together all his chariots, nine hundred chariots of iron, and all the people who *were* with him, from Harosheth Hagoyim to the River Kishon.

Then Deborah said to Barak, "Up! For this *is* the day in which the LORD has delivered Sisera into your hand. Has not the LORD gone out before you?" So Barak went down from Mount Tabor with ten thousand men following him. And the LORD routed Sisera and all *his* chariots and all *his* army with the edge of the sword before Barak; and Sisera alighted from *his* chariot and fled away on foot. But Barak pursued the chariots and the army as far as Harosheth Hagoyim, and all the army of Sisera fell by the edge of the sword; not a man was left.

However, Sisera had fled away on foot to the tent of Jael, the wife of Heber the Kenite; for *there was* peace between Jabin king of Hazor and the house of Heber the Kenite. And Jael went out to meet Sisera, and said to him, "Turn aside, my lord, turn aside to me; do not fear." And when he had turned aside with her into the tent, she covered him with a blanket.

Then he said to her, "Please give me a little water to drink, for I am thirsty." So she opened a jug of milk, gave him a drink, and covered him. And he said to her, "Stand at the door of the tent, and if any man comes and inquires of you, and says, 'Is there any man here?' you shall say, 'No.' "

Then Jael, Heber's wife, took a tent peg and took a hammer in her hand, and went softly to him and drove the peg into his temple, and it went down into the ground; for he was fast asleep and weary. So he died. And then, as Barak pursued Sisera, Jael came out to meet him, and said to him, "Come, I will show you the man whom you seek." And when he went into her *tent,* there lay Sisera, dead with the peg in his temple.

So on that day God subdued Jabin king of Canaan in the presence of the children of Israel. And the hand of the children of Israel grew stronger and stronger against Jabin king of Canaan, until they had destroyed Jabin king of Canaan.

Then Deborah and Barak the son of Abinoam sang on that day, saying:

"When leaders lead in Israel,
When the people willingly offer themselves,
Bless the LORD!

"Hear, O kings! Give ear, O princes!
I, *even* I, will sing to the LORD;
I will sing praise to the LORD God of Israel.

"LORD, when You went out from Seir,
When You marched from the field of Edom,
The earth trembled and the heavens poured,
The clouds also poured water;
The mountains gushed before the LORD,
This Sinai, before the LORD God of Israel.

HERE COMES THE JUDGE

"In the days of Shamgar, son of Anath,
In the days of Jael,
The highways were deserted,
And the travelers walked along the byways.
Village life ceased, it ceased in Israel,
Until I, Deborah, arose,
Arose a mother in Israel.
They chose new gods;
Then *there was* war in the gates;
Not a shield or spear was seen among forty
    thousand in Israel.
My heart *is* with the rulers of Israel
Who offered themselves willingly with the
    people.
Bless the LORD!

"Speak, you who ride on white donkeys,
Who sit in judges' attire,
And who walk along the road.
Far from the noise of the archers, among the
    watering places,
There they shall recount the righteous acts of
    the LORD,
The righteous acts *for* His villagers in Israel;
Then the people of the LORD shall go down to
    the gates.

"The mother of Sisera looked through the
    window,
And cried out through the lattice,
'Why is his chariot *so* long in coming?
Why tarries the clatter of his chariots?'
Her wisest ladies answered her,
Yes, she answered herself,
'Are they not finding and dividing the spoil:
To every man a girl *or* two;
For Sisera, plunder of dyed garments,
Plunder of garments embroidered and dyed,
Two pieces of dyed embroidery for the neck of
    the looter?'

"Thus let all Your enemies perish, O LORD!
But *let* those who love Him *be* like the sun
When it comes out in full strength."

So the land had rest for forty years.

Judges 4:4–5:11, 28-31

WORSHIP

Trust in the LORD, and do good;
Dwell in the land, and feed on His faithfulness.
Delight yourself also in the LORD,
And He shall give you the desires of your
    heart.

Commit your way to the LORD,
Trust also in Him,
And He shall bring *it* to pass.

Psalm 37:3-5

WISDOM

Those who are of a perverse heart *are* an
    abomination to the LORD,
But *the* blameless in their ways *are* His delight.

Proverbs 11:20

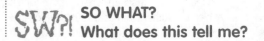 **SO WHAT?**
What does this tell me?

God's Victory THROUGH Gideon

Judges 6:1-24, 36-40; 7:1-9, 16-23; Psalm 37:7-9; Proverbs 11:21

Then the children of Israel did evil in the sight of the LORD. So the LORD delivered them into the hand of Midian for seven years, and the hand of Midian prevailed against Israel. Because of the Midianites, the children of Israel made for themselves the dens, the caves, and the strongholds which *are* in the mountains. So it was, whenever Israel had sown, Midianites would come up; also Amalekites and the people of the East would come up against them. Then they would encamp against them and destroy the produce of the earth as far as Gaza, and leave no sustenance for Israel, neither sheep nor ox nor donkey. For they would come up with their livestock and their tents, coming in as numerous as locusts; both they and their camels were without number; and they would enter the land to destroy it. So Israel was greatly impoverished because of the Midianites, and the children of Israel cried out to the LORD.

And it came to pass, when the children of Israel cried out to the LORD because of the Midianites, that the LORD sent a prophet to the children of Israel, who said to them, "Thus says the LORD God of Israel: 'I brought you up from Egypt and brought you out of the house of bondage; and I delivered you out of the hand of the Egyptians and out of the hand of all who oppressed you, and drove them out before you and gave you their land. Also I said to you, "I *am* the LORD your God; do not fear the gods of the Amorites, in whose land you dwell." But you have not obeyed My voice.' "

Now the Angel of the LORD came and sat under the terebinth tree which *was* in Ophrah, which *belonged* to Joash the Abiezrite, while his son Gideon threshed wheat in the winepress, in order to hide *it* from the Midianites. And the Angel of the LORD appeared to him, and said to him, "The LORD *is* with you, you mighty man of valor!" Gideon said to Him, "O my lord, if the LORD is with us, why then has all this happened to us? And where *are* all His miracles which our fathers told us about, saying, 'Did not the LORD bring us up from Egypt?' But

now the LORD has forsaken us and delivered us into the hands of the Midianites."

Then the LORD turned to him and said, "Go in this might of yours, and you shall save Israel from the hand of the Midianites. Have I not sent you?"

So he said to Him, "O my Lord, how can I save Israel? Indeed my clan *is* the weakest in Manasseh, and I *am* the least in my father's house."

And the LORD said to him, "Surely I will be with you, and you shall defeat the Midianites as one man."

Then he said to Him, "If now I have found favor in Your sight, then show me a sign that it is You who talk with me. Do not depart from here, I pray, until I come to You and bring out my offering and set *it* before You."

And He said, "I will wait until you come back."

So Gideon went in and prepared a young goat, and unleavened bread from an ephah of flour. The meat he put in a basket, and he put the broth in a pot; and he brought *them* out to Him under the terebinth tree and presented *them*. The Angel of God said to him, "Take the meat and the unleavened bread and lay *them* on this rock, and pour out the broth." And he did so.

Then the Angel of the LORD put out the end of the staff that *was* in His hand, and touched the meat and the unleavened bread; and fire rose out of the rock and consumed the meat and the unleavened bread. And the Angel of the LORD departed out of his sight.

Now Gideon perceived that He *was* the Angel of the LORD. So Gideon said, "Alas, O Lord GOD! For I have seen the Angel of the LORD face to face."

Then the LORD said to him, "Peace *be* with you; do not fear, you shall not die." So Gideon built an altar there to the LORD, and called it The-LORD-*Is*-Peace. To this day it *is* still in Ophrah of the Abiezrites.

So Gideon said to God, "If You will save Israel by my hand as You have said—look, I shall put a fleece of wool on the threshing floor; if there is dew on the fleece only, and *it is* dry on all the ground, then I shall know that You will save Israel by my hand, as You have said." And it was so. When he rose early the next morning and squeezed the fleece together, he wrung the dew out of the fleece, a bowlful of water. Then Gideon said to God, "Do not be angry with me, but let me speak just once more: Let me test, I pray, just once more with the fleece; let it now be dry only on the fleece, but on all the ground let there be dew." And God did so that night. It was dry on the fleece only, but there was dew on all the ground.

Then Jerubbaal (that *is,* Gideon) and all the people who *were* with him rose early and encamped beside the well of Harod, so that the camp of the Midianites was on the north side of them by the hill of Moreh in the valley.

And the LORD said to Gideon, "The people who *are* with you *are* too many for Me to give the Midianites into their hands, lest Israel claim glory for itself against Me, saying, 'My own hand has saved me.' Now therefore, proclaim in the hearing of the people, saying, 'Whoever *is* fearful and afraid, let him turn and depart at once from Mount Gilead.' " And twenty-two thousand of the people returned, and ten thousand remained.

But the LORD said to Gideon, "The people *are* still *too* many; bring them down to the water, and I will test them for you there. Then it will be, *that* of whom I say to you, 'This one shall go with you,' the same shall go with you; and of whomever I say to you, 'This one shall not go with you,' the same shall not go." So he brought the people down to the water. And the LORD said to Gideon, "Everyone who laps from the water with his tongue, as a dog laps, you shall set apart by himself; likewise everyone who gets down on his knees to drink." And the number of those who lapped, *putting* their hand to their mouth, was three hundred men; but all the rest of the people got down on their knees to drink water. Then the LORD said to Gideon, "By the three hundred men who lapped I will save you, and deliver the Midianites into your hand. Let all the *other* people go, every man to his place." So the people took provisions and their trumpets in their hands. And he sent away all *the rest of* Israel, every man to his tent, and retained those three hundred men. Now the camp of Midian was below him in the valley.

It happened on the same night that the LORD said to him, "Arise, go down against the camp, for I have delivered it into your hand."

Then he divided the three hundred men *into* three companies, and he put a trumpet into every man's hand, with empty pitchers, and torches inside the pitchers. And he said to them, "Look at me and do likewise; watch, and when I come to the edge of the camp you shall do as I do: When I blow the trumpet, I and all who *are* with me, then you also blow the trumpets on every side of the whole camp, and say, '*The sword of* the LORD and of Gideon!' "

So Gideon and the hundred men who *were* with him came to the outpost of the camp at the beginning of the middle watch, just as they had posted the watch; and they blew the trumpets and broke the pitchers that *were* in their hands. Then the three companies blew the trumpets and broke the pitchers—they held the torches in their left hands and the trumpets in their right hands for blowing—and they cried, "The sword of the LORD and of Gideon!" And every man stood in his place all around the camp; and the whole army ran and cried out and fled. When the three hundred blew the trumpets, the LORD set every man's sword against his companion throughout the whole camp; and the army fled to Beth Acacia, toward Zererah, as far as the border of Abel Meholah, by Tabbath.

And the men of Israel gathered together from Naphtali, Asher, and all Manasseh, and pursued the Midianites.

Judges 6:1-24, 36-40; 7:1-9, 16-23

WORSHIP

Rest in the LORD, and wait patiently for Him;
Do not fret because of him who prospers in his
    way,
Because of the man who brings wicked
    schemes to pass.
Cease from anger, and forsake wrath;
Do not fret—*it* only *causes* harm.

For evildoers shall be cut off;
But those who wait on the LORD,
They shall inherit the earth.

Psalm 37:7-9

WISDOM

Though they join forces, the wicked will not go
    unpunished;
But the posterity of the righteous will be
    delivered.

Proverbs 11:21

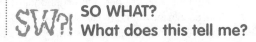 **SO WHAT?**
What does this tell me?

VICTORY THROUGH THE SON OF A HARLOT

Judges 10:6–11:11, 29-40; Psalm 37:12-15; Proverbs 11:22

Then the children of Israel again did evil in the sight of the LORD, and served the Baals and the Ashtoreths, the gods of Syria, the gods of Sidon, the gods of Moab, the gods of the people of Ammon, and the gods of the Philistines; and they forsook the LORD and did not serve Him. So the anger of the LORD was hot against Israel; and He sold them into the hands of the Philistines and into the hands of the people of Ammon. From that year they harassed and oppressed the children of Israel for eighteen years—all the children of Israel who *were* on the other side of the Jordan in the land of the Amorites, in Gilead. Moreover the people of Ammon crossed over the Jordan to fight against Judah also, against Benjamin, and against the house of Ephraim, so that Israel was severely distressed.

And the children of Israel cried out to the LORD, saying, "We have sinned against You, because we have both forsaken our God and served the Baals!"

So the LORD said to the children of Israel, "*Did I* not *deliver you* from the Egyptians and from the Amorites and from the people of Ammon and from the Philistines? Also the Sidonians and Amalekites and Maonites oppressed you; and you cried out to Me, and I delivered you from their hand. Yet you have forsaken Me and served other gods. Therefore I will deliver you no more. Go and cry out to the gods which you have chosen; let them deliver you in your time of distress."

And the children of Israel said to the LORD, "We have sinned! Do to us whatever seems best to You; only deliver us this day, we pray." So they put away the foreign gods from among them and served the LORD. And His soul could no longer endure the misery of Israel.

Then the people of Ammon gathered together and encamped in Gilead. And the children of Israel assembled together and encamped in Mizpah. And the people, the leaders of Gilead, said to one another, "Who *is* the man who will begin the fight against the people of Ammon? He shall be head over all the inhabitants of Gilead."

Now Jephthah the Gileadite was a mighty man of valor, but he *was* the son of a harlot; and Gilead begot Jephthah. Gilead's wife bore sons; and when his wife's sons grew up, they drove Jephthah out, and said to him, "You shall have no inheritance in our father's house, for you *are* the son of another woman." Then Jephthah fled from his brothers and dwelt in the land of Tob; and worthless men banded together with Jephthah and went out *raiding* with him.

It came to pass after a time that the people of Ammon made war against Israel. And so it was, when the people of Ammon made war against Israel, that the elders of Gilead went to get Jephthah from the land of Tob. Then they said to Jephthah, "Come and be our commander, that we may fight against the people of Ammon."

So Jephthah said to the elders of Gilead, "Did you not hate me, and expel me from my father's house? Why have you come to me now when you are in distress?"

And the elders of Gilead said to Jephthah, "That is why we have turned again to you now, that you may go with us and fight against the people of Ammon, and be our head over all the inhabitants of Gilead."

So Jephthah said to the elders of Gilead, "If you take me back home to fight against the people of Ammon, and the LORD delivers them to me, shall I be your head?"

And the elders of Gilead said to Jephthah, "The LORD will be a witness between us, if we do not do according to your words." Then Jephthah went with the elders of Gilead, and the people made him head and commander over them; and Jephthah spoke all his words before the LORD in Mizpah.

Then the Spirit of the LORD came upon Jephthah, and he passed through Gilead and Manasseh, and passed through Mizpah of Gilead; and from Mizpah of Gilead he advanced *toward* the people of Ammon. And Jephthah made a vow to the LORD, and said, "If You will indeed deliver the people of Ammon into my hands, then it will be that whatever comes out of the doors of my house to meet me, when I return in peace from the people of Ammon, shall surely be the LORD's, and I will offer it up as a burnt offering."

So Jephthah advanced toward the people of Ammon to fight against them, and the LORD delivered them into his hands. And he defeated them from Aroer as far as Minnith—twenty cities—and to Abel Keramim, with a very great slaughter. Thus the people of Ammon were subdued before the children of Israel.

When Jephthah came to his house at Mizpah, there was his daughter, coming out to meet him with timbrels and dancing; and she *was his* only child. Besides her he had neither son nor daughter. And it came to pass, when he saw her, that he tore his clothes, and said, "Alas, my daughter! You have brought me very low! You are among those who trouble me! For I have given my word to the LORD, and I cannot go back on it."

So she said to him, "My father, *if* you have given your word to the LORD, do to me according to what has gone out of your mouth, because the LORD has avenged you of your enemies, the people of Ammon." Then she said to her father, "Let this thing be done for me: let me alone for two months, that I may go and wander on the mountains and bewail my virginity, my friends and I."

So he said, "Go." And he sent her away *for* two months; and she went with her friends, and bewailed her virginity on the mountains. And it was so at the end of two months that she returned to her father, and he carried out his vow with her which he had vowed. She knew no man.

And it became a custom in Israel *that* the daughters of Israel went four days each year to lament the daughter of Jephthah the Gileadite.

Judges 10:6–11:11, 29–40

WORSHIP

The wicked plots against the just,
And gnashes at him with his teeth.
The Lord laughs at him,
For He sees that his day is coming.
The wicked have drawn the sword
And have bent their bow,
To cast down the poor and needy,
To slay those who are of upright conduct.
Their sword shall enter their own heart,
And their bows shall be broken.

Psalm 37:12-15

WISDOM

As a ring of gold in a swine's snout,
So is a lovely woman who lacks discretion.

Proverbs 11:22

SW?! SO WHAT?
What does this tell me?

SAMSON AND DELILAH

Judges 13:1-7, 24-25; 16:1-30; Psalm 37:16-18; Proverbs 11:23

Again the children of Israel did evil in the sight of the LORD, and the LORD delivered them into the hand of the Philistines for forty years.

Now there was a certain man from Zorah, of the family of the Danites, whose name *was* Manoah; and his wife *was* barren and had no children. And the Angel of the LORD appeared to the woman and said to her, "Indeed now, you are barren and have borne no children, but you shall conceive and bear a son. Now therefore, please be careful not to drink wine or *similar* drink, and not to eat anything unclean. For behold, you shall conceive and bear a son. And no razor shall come upon his head, for the child shall be a Nazirite to God from the womb; and he shall begin to deliver Israel out of the hand of the Philistines."

So the woman came and told her husband, saying, "A Man of God came to me, and His countenance *was* like the countenance of the Angel of God, very awesome; but I did not ask Him where He *was* from, and He did not tell me His name. And He said to me, 'Behold, you shall conceive and bear a son. Now drink no wine or *similar* drink, nor eat anything unclean, for the child shall be a Nazirite to God from the womb to the day of his death.' "

So the woman bore a son and called his name Samson; and the child grew, and the LORD blessed him. And the Spirit of the LORD began to move upon him at Mahaneh Dan between Zorah and Eshtaol.

Now Samson went to Gaza and saw a harlot there, and went in to her. *When* the Gazites *were told,* "Samson has come here!" they surrounded *the place* and lay in wait for him all night at the gate of the city. They were quiet all night, saying, "In the morning, when it is daylight, we will kill him." And Samson lay *low* till midnight; then he arose at midnight, took hold of the doors of the gate of the city and the two gateposts, pulled them up, bar and all, put *them* on his shoulders, and carried them to the top of the hill that faces Hebron.

Afterward it happened that he loved a woman in the Valley of Sorek, whose name *was* Delilah. And the lords of the Philistines came up to her and said to her, "Entice him, and find out where his great strength *lies,* and by what *means* we may overpower him, that we may bind him to afflict him; and every one of us will give you eleven hundred *pieces* of silver."

So Delilah said to Samson, "Please tell me where your great strength *lies,* and with what you may be bound to afflict you."

And Samson said to her, "If they bind me with seven fresh bowstrings, not yet dried, then I shall become weak, and be like any *other* man."

So the lords of the Philistines brought up to her seven fresh bowstrings, not yet dried, and she bound him with them. Now *men were* lying in wait, staying with her in the room. And she said to him, "The Philistines *are* upon you, Samson!" But he broke the bowstrings as a strand of yarn breaks when it touches fire. So the secret of his strength was not known.

Then Delilah said to Samson, "Look, you have mocked me and told me lies. Now, please tell me what you may be bound with."

So he said to her, "If they bind me securely with new ropes that have never been used, then I shall become weak, and be like any *other* man."

Therefore Delilah took new ropes and bound him with them, and said to him, "The Philistines *are* upon you, Samson!" And *men were* lying in wait, staying in the room. But he broke them off his arms like a thread.

Delilah said to Samson, "Until now you have mocked me and told me lies. Tell me what you may be bound with."

And he said to her, "If you weave the seven locks of my head into the web of the loom"—

So she wove *it* tightly with the batten of the loom, and said to him, "The Philistines *are* upon you, Samson!" But he awoke from his sleep, and pulled out the batten and the web from the loom.

Then she said to him, "How can you say, 'I love you,' when your heart *is* not with me? You have mocked me these three times, and have not told me where your great strength *lies.*" And it came to pass, when she pestered him daily with her words and pressed him, *so* that his soul was vexed to death, that he told her all his heart, and said to her, "No razor has ever come upon my head, for I *have been* a Nazirite to God from my mother's womb. If I am shaven, then my strength will leave me, and I shall become weak, and be like any *other* man."

When Delilah saw that he had told her all his heart, she sent and called for the lords of the Philistines, saying, "Come up once more, for he has told me all his heart." So the lords of the Philistines came up to her and brought the money in their hand. Then she lulled him to sleep on her knees, and called for a man and had him shave off the seven locks of his head. Then she began to torment him, and his strength left him. And she said, "The Philistines *are* upon you, Samson!" So he awoke from his sleep, and said, "I will go out as before, at other times, and shake myself free!" But he did not know that the LORD had departed from him.

Then the Philistines took him and put out his eyes, and brought him down to Gaza. They bound him with bronze fetters, and he became a grinder in the prison. However, the hair of his head began to grow again after it had been shaven.

Now the lords of the Philistines gathered together to offer a great sacrifice to Dagon their god, and to rejoice. And they said:

"Our god has delivered into our hands
Samson our enemy!"

When the people saw him, they praised their god; for they said:

"Our god has delivered into our hands our
        enemy,
The destroyer of our land,
And the one who multiplied our dead."

So it happened, when their hearts were merry, that they said, "Call for Samson, that he may perform for us." So they called for Samson from the prison, and he performed for them. And they stationed him between the pillars. Then Samson said to the lad who held him by the hand, "Let me feel the pillars which support the temple, so that I can lean on them." Now the temple was full of men and women. All the lords of the Philistines *were* there—about three thousand men and women on the roof watching while Samson performed.

Then Samson called to the LORD, saying, "O Lord GOD, remember me, I pray! Strengthen me, I pray, just this once, O God, that I may with one *blow* take vengeance on the Philistines for my two eyes!" And Samson took hold of the two middle pillars

which supported the temple, and he braced himself against them, one on his right and the other on his left. Then Samson said, "Let me die with the Philistines!" And he pushed with *all his* might, and the temple fell on the lords and all the people who *were* in it. So the dead that he killed at his death were more than he had killed in his life.

Judges 13:1-7, 24-25; 16:1-30

WORSHIP

A little that a righteous man has
Is better than the riches of many wicked.
For the arms of the wicked shall be broken,
But the LORD upholds the righteous.

The LORD knows the days of the upright,
And their inheritance shall be forever.

Psalm 37:16-18

WISDOM

The desire of the righteous *is* only good,
But the expectation of the wicked *is* wrath.

Proverbs 11:23

SW?! **SO WHAT?**
What does this tell me?

THE IDOLATRY OF MICAH AND DAN

Judges 17–18; 21:25; Psalm 37:23-25; Proverbs 11:24

Now there was a man from the mountains of Ephraim, whose name *was* Micah. And he said to his mother, "The eleven hundred *shekels* of silver that were taken from you, and on which you put a curse, even saying it in my ears—here *is* the silver with me; I took it."

And his mother said, "*May you be* blessed by the LORD, my son!" So when he had returned the eleven hundred *shekels* of silver to his mother, his mother said, "I had wholly dedicated the silver from my hand to the LORD for my son, to make a carved image and a molded image; now therefore, I will return it to you." Thus he returned the silver to his mother. Then his mother took two hundred *shekels* of silver and gave them to the silversmith, and he made it into a carved image and a molded image; and they were in the house of Micah.

The man Micah had a shrine, and made an ephod and household idols; and he consecrated one of his sons, who became his priest. In those days *there was* no king in Israel; everyone did *what was* right in his own eyes.

Now there was a young man from Bethlehem in Judah, of the family of Judah; he *was* a Levite, and was staying there. The man departed from the city of Bethlehem in Judah to stay wherever he could find *a place*. Then he came to the mountains of Ephraim, to the house of Micah, as he journeyed. And Micah said to him, "Where do you come from?"

So he said to him, "I *am* a Levite from Bethlehem in Judah, and I am on my way to find *a place* to stay."

Micah said to him, "Dwell with me, and be a father and a priest to me, and I will give you ten *shekels* of silver per year, a suit of clothes, and your sustenance." So the Levite went in. Then the Levite was content to dwell with the man; and the young man became like one of his sons to him. So Micah consecrated the Levite, and the young man became his priest, and lived in the house of Micah. Then Micah said, "Now I know that the LORD will be good to me, since I have a Levite as priest!"

In those days *there was* no king in Israel. And in those days the tribe of the Danites was seeking an inheritance for itself to dwell in; for until that day *their* inheritance among the tribes of Israel had not fallen to them. So the children of Dan sent five men of their family from their territory, men of valor from Zorah and Eshtaol, to spy out the land and search it. They said to them, "Go, search the land." So they went to the mountains of Ephraim, to the house of Micah, and lodged there. While they *were* at the house of Micah, they recognized the voice of the young Levite. They turned aside and said to him, "Who brought you here? What are you doing in this *place*? What do you have here?"

He said to them, "Thus and so Micah did for me. He has hired me, and I have become his priest."

So they said to him, "Please inquire of God, that we may know whether the journey on which we go will be prosperous."

And the priest said to them, "Go in peace. The presence of the LORD *be* with you on your way."

So the five men departed and went to Laish. They saw the people who *were* there, how they dwelt safely, in the manner of the Sidonians, quiet and secure. *There were* no rulers in the land who might put *them* to shame for anything. They *were* far from the Sidonians, and they had no ties with anyone.

Then *the spies* came back to their brethren at Zorah and Eshtaol, and their brethren said to them, "What *is* your *report*?"

So they said, "Arise, let us go up against them. For we have seen the land, and indeed it *is* very good. *Would* you *do* nothing? Do not hesitate to go, *and* enter to possess the land. When you go, you will come to a secure people and a large land. For God has given it into your hands, a place where *there is* no lack of anything that *is* on the earth."

And six hundred men of the family of the Danites went from there, from Zorah and Eshtaol, armed with weapons of war. Then they went up and encamped in Kirjath Jearim in Judah. (Therefore they call that place Mahaneh Dan to this day. There *it is,* west of Kirjath Jearim.) And they passed from there to the mountains of Ephraim, and came to the house of Micah.

Then the five men who had gone to spy out the country of Laish answered and said to their brethren, "Do you know that there are in these houses an ephod, household idols, a carved image, and a molded image? Now therefore, consider what you should do." So they turned aside there, and came to the house of the young Levite man—to the house of Micah—and greeted him. The six hundred men armed with their weapons of war, who *were* of the children of Dan, stood by the entrance of the gate. Then the five men who had gone to spy out the land went up. Entering there, they took the carved image, the ephod, the household idols, and the molded image. The priest stood at the entrance of the gate with the six hundred men *who were* armed with weapons of war.

When these went into Micah's house and took the carved image, the ephod, the household idols, and the molded image, the priest said to them, "What are you doing?"

And they said to him, "Be quiet, put your hand over your mouth, and come with us; be a father and a priest to us. *Is it* better for you to be a priest to the household of one man, or that you be a priest to a tribe and a family in Israel?" So the priest's heart was glad; and he took the ephod, the household idols, and the carved image, and took his place among the people.

Then they turned and departed, and put the little ones, the livestock, and the goods in front of them. When they were a good way from the house of Micah, the men who *were* in the houses near Micah's house gathered together and overtook the children of Dan. And they called out to the children of Dan. So they turned around and said to Micah, "What ails you, that you have gathered such a company?"

So he said, "You have taken away my gods which I made, and the priest, and you have gone away. Now what more do I have? How can you say to me, 'What ails you?' "

And the children of Dan said to him, "Do not let your voice be heard among us, lest angry men fall upon you, and you lose your life, with the lives of your household!" Then the children of Dan went their way. And when Micah saw that they *were* too strong for him, he turned and went back to his house.

So they took *the things* Micah had made, and the priest who had belonged to him, and went to Laish, to a people quiet and secure; and they struck them with the edge of the sword and burned the city with fire. *There was* no deliverer, because it *was* far from Sidon, and they had no ties with anyone. It was in the valley that belongs to Beth Rehob. So they rebuilt the city and dwelt there. And they called the name of the city Dan, after the name of Dan their father, who was born to Israel. However, the name of the city formerly *was* Laish.

Then the children of Dan set up for themselves the carved image; and Jonathan the son of Gershom, the son of Manasseh, and his sons were priests to the tribe of Dan until the day of the captivity of the land. So they set up for themselves Micah's carved image which he made, all the time that the house of God was in Shiloh.

In those days *there was* no king in Israel; everyone did *what was* right in his own eyes.

Judges 17–18; 21:25

WORSHIP

The steps of a *good* man are ordered by the LORD,
And He delights in his way.
Though he fall, he shall not be utterly cast down;
For the LORD upholds *him with* His hand.

I have been young, and *now* am old;
Yet I have not seen the righteous forsaken,
Nor his descendants begging bread.

Psalm 37:23-25

WISDOM

There is *one* who scatters, yet increases more;
And there is *one* who withholds more than is right,
But it *leads* to poverty.

Proverbs 11:24

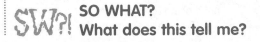

SO WHAT?
What does this tell me?

RUTH CHOOSES THE LORD

Ruth 1–2; Psalm 37:29-31; Proverbs 11:25

Now it came to pass, in the days when the judges ruled, that there was a famine in the land. And a certain man of Bethlehem, Judah, went to dwell in the country of Moab, he and his wife and his two sons. The name of the man *was* Elimelech, the name of his wife *was* Naomi, and the names of his two sons *were* Mahlon and Chilion—Ephrathites of Bethlehem, Judah. And they went to the country of Moab and remained there. Then Elimelech, Naomi's husband, died; and she was left, and her two sons. Now they took wives of the women of Moab: the name of the one *was* Orpah, and the name of the other Ruth. And they dwelt there about ten years. Then both Mahlon and Chilion also died; so the woman survived her two sons and her husband.

Then she arose with her daughters-in-law that she might return from the country of Moab, for she had heard in the country of Moab that the LORD had visited His people by giving them bread. Therefore she went out from the place where she was, and her two daughters-in-law with her; and they went on the way to return to the land of Judah. And Naomi said to her two daughters-in-law, "Go, return each to her mother's house. The LORD deal kindly with you, as you have dealt with the dead and with me. The LORD grant that you may find rest, each in the house of her husband."

So she kissed them, and they lifted up their voices and wept. And they said to her, "Surely we will return with you to your people."

But Naomi said, "Turn back, my daughters; why will you go with me? *Are* there still sons in my womb, that they may be your husbands? Turn back, my daughters, go— for I am too old to have a husband. If I should say I have hope, *if* I should have a husband tonight and should also bear sons, would you wait for them till they were grown? Would you restrain yourselves from having husbands? No, my daughters; for it grieves me very much for your sakes that the hand of the LORD has gone out against me!"

Then they lifted up their voices and wept again; and Orpah kissed her mother-in-law, but Ruth clung to her.

And she said, "Look, your sister-in-law has gone back to her people and to her gods; return after your sister-in-law."

But Ruth said:

"Entreat me not to leave you,
Or to turn back from following after you;
For wherever you go, I will go;
And wherever you lodge, I will lodge;
Your people *shall be* my people,
And your God, my God.
Where you die, I will die,
And there will I be buried.
The LORD do so to me, and more also,
If *anything but* death parts you and me."

When she saw that she was determined to go with her, she stopped speaking to her.

Now the two of them went until they came to Bethlehem. And it happened, when they had come to Bethlehem, that all the city was excited because of them; and the women said, "*Is* this Naomi?"

But she said to them, "Do not call me Naomi; call me Mara, for the Almighty has dealt very bitterly with me. I went out full, and the LORD has brought me home again empty. Why do you call me Naomi, since the LORD has testified against me, and the Almighty has afflicted me?"

So Naomi returned, and Ruth the Moabitess her daughter-in-law with her, who returned from the country of Moab. Now they came to Bethlehem at the beginning of barley harvest.

There was a relative of Naomi's husband, a man of great wealth, of the family of Elimelech. His name *was* Boaz. So Ruth the Moabitess said to Naomi, "Please let me go to the field, and glean heads of grain after *him* in whose sight I may find favor."

And she said to her, "Go, my daughter."

Then she left, and went and gleaned in the field after the reapers. And she happened to come to the part of the field *belonging* to Boaz, who *was* of the family of Elimelech.

Now behold, Boaz came from Bethlehem, and said to the reapers, "The LORD *be* with you!"

And they answered him, "The LORD bless you!"

Then Boaz said to his servant who was in charge of the reapers, "Whose young woman *is* this?"

So the servant who was in charge of the reapers answered and said, "It *is* the young Moabite woman who came back with Naomi from the country of Moab. And she said, 'Please let me glean and gather after the reapers among the sheaves.' So she came and has continued from morning until now, though she rested a little in the house."

Then Boaz said to Ruth, "You will listen, my daughter, will you not? Do not go to glean in another field, nor go from here, but stay close by my young women. *Let* your eyes *be* on the field which they reap, and go after them. Have I not commanded the young men not to touch you? And when you are thirsty, go to the vessels and drink from what the young men have drawn."

So she fell on her face, bowed down to the ground, and said to him, "Why have I found favor in your eyes, that you should take notice of me, since I *am* a foreigner?"

And Boaz answered and said to her, "It has been fully reported to me, all that you have done for your mother-in-law since the death of your husband, and *how* you have left your father and your mother and the land of your birth, and have come to a people whom you did not know before. The LORD repay your work, and a full reward be given you by the LORD God of Israel, under whose wings you have come for refuge."

Then she said, "Let me find favor in your sight, my lord; for you have comforted me, and have spoken kindly to your maidservant, though I am not like one of your maidservants."

Now Boaz said to her at mealtime, "Come here, and eat of the bread, and dip your piece of bread in the vinegar." So she sat beside the reapers, and he passed parched *grain* to her; and she ate and was satisfied, and kept some back. And when she rose up to glean, Boaz commanded his young men, saying, "Let her glean even among the sheaves, and do not reproach her. Also let *grain* from the bundles fall purposely for her; leave *it* that she may glean, and do not rebuke her."

So she gleaned in the field until evening, and beat out what she had gleaned, and it was about an ephah of barley. Then she took *it* up and went into the city, and her mother-in-law saw what she had gleaned. So she brought out and gave to her what she had kept back after she had been satisfied.

And her mother-in-law said to her, "Where have you gleaned today? And where did you work? Blessed be the one who took notice of you."

So she told her mother-in-law with whom she had worked, and said, "The man's name with whom I worked today *is* Boaz."

Then Naomi said to her daughter-in-law, "Blessed *be* he of the LORD, who has not forsaken His kindness to the living and the dead!" And Naomi said to her, "This man *is* a relation of ours, one of our close relatives."

Ruth the Moabitess said, "He also said to me, 'You shall stay close by my young men until they have finished all my harvest.'"

And Naomi said to Ruth her daughter-in-law, "*It is* good, my daughter, that you go out with his young women, and that people do not meet you in any other field." So she stayed close by the young women of Boaz, to glean until the end of barley harvest and wheat harvest; and she dwelt with her mother-in-law.

Ruth 1–2

WORSHIP

The righteous shall inherit the land,
And dwell in it forever.

The mouth of the righteous speaks wisdom,
And his tongue talks of justice.
The law of his God *is* in his heart;
None of his steps shall slide.

Psalm 37:29-31

WISDOM

The generous soul will be made rich,
And he who waters will also be watered
  himself.

Proverbs 11:25

SW?! SO WHAT?
What does this tell me?

RUTH'S CLAIM ON A KINSMAN

Ruth 3–4; Psalm 37:37-39; Proverbs 11:26

Then Naomi her mother-in-law said to her, "My daughter, shall I not seek security for you, that it may be well with you? Now Boaz, whose young women you were with, *is he* not our relative? In fact, he is winnowing barley tonight at the threshing floor. Therefore wash yourself and anoint yourself, put on your *best* garment and go down to the threshing floor; *but* do not make yourself known to the man until he has finished eating and drinking. Then it shall be, when he lies down, that you shall notice the place where he lies; and you shall go in, uncover his feet, and lie down; and he will tell you what you should do."

And she said to her, "All that you say to me I will do."

So she went down to the threshing floor and did according to all that her mother-in-law instructed her. And after Boaz had eaten and drunk, and his heart was cheerful, he went to lie down at the end of the heap of grain; and she came softly, uncovered his feet, and lay down.

Now it happened at midnight that the man was startled, and turned himself; and there, a woman was lying at his feet. And he said, "Who *are* you?"

So she answered, "I *am* Ruth, your maidservant. Take your maidservant under your wing, for you are a close relative."

Then he said, "Blessed *are* you of the LORD, my daughter! For you have shown more kindness at the end than at the beginning, in that you did not go after young men, whether poor or rich. And now, my daughter, do not fear. I will do for you all that you request, for all the people of my town know that you *are* a virtuous woman. Now it is true that I *am* a close relative; however, there is a relative closer than I. Stay this night, and in the morning it shall be *that* if he will perform the duty of a close relative for you—good; let him do it. But if he does not want to perform the duty for you, then I will perform the duty for you, *as* the LORD lives! Lie down until morning."

So she lay at his feet until morning, and she arose before one could recognize an-

other. Then he said, "Do not let it be known that the woman came to the threshing floor." Also he said, "Bring the shawl that *is* on you and hold it." And when she held it, he measured six *ephahs* of barley, and laid *it* on her. Then she went into the city.

When she came to her mother-in-law, she said, "*Is* that you, my daughter?"

Then she told her all that the man had done for her. And she said, "These six *ephahs* of barley he gave me; for he said to me, 'Do not go empty-handed to your mother-in-law.' "

Then she said, "Sit still, my daughter, until you know how the matter will turn out; for the man will not rest until he has concluded the matter this day."

Now Boaz went up to the gate and sat down there; and behold, the close relative of whom Boaz had spoken came by. So Boaz said, "Come aside, friend, sit down here." So he came aside and sat down. And he took ten men of the elders of the city, and said, "Sit down here." So they sat down. Then he said to the close relative, "Naomi, who has come back from the country of Moab, sold the piece of land which *belonged* to our brother Elimelech. And I thought to inform you, saying, 'Buy *it* back in the presence of the inhabitants and the elders of my people. If you will redeem *it*, redeem *it*; but if you will not redeem *it*, *then* tell me, that I may know; for *there is* no one but you to redeem *it*, and I *am* next after you.' "

And he said, "I will redeem *it.*"

Then Boaz said, "On the day you buy the field from the hand of Naomi, you must also buy *it* from Ruth the Moabitess, the wife of the dead, to perpetuate the name of the dead through his inheritance."

And the close relative said, "I cannot redeem *it* for myself, lest I ruin my own inheritance. You redeem my right of redemption for yourself, for I cannot redeem *it.*"

Now this *was the custom* in former times in Israel concerning redeeming and exchanging, to confirm anything: one man took off his sandal and gave *it* to the other, and this *was* a confirmation in Israel.

Therefore the close relative said to Boaz, "Buy *it* for yourself." So he took off his sandal. And Boaz said to the elders and all the people, "You *are* witnesses this day that I have bought all that was Elimelech's, and all that *was* Chilion's and Mahlon's, from the hand of Naomi. Moreover, Ruth the Moabitess, the widow of Mahlon, I have acquired as my wife, to perpetuate the name of the dead through his inheritance, that the name of the dead may not be cut off from among his brethren and from his position at the gate. You *are* witnesses this day."

And all the people who *were* at the gate, and the elders, said, "*We are* witnesses. The LORD make the woman who is coming to your house like Rachel and Leah, the two who built the house of Israel; and may you prosper in Ephrathah and be famous in Bethlehem. May your house be like the house of Perez, whom Tamar bore to Judah, because of the offspring which the LORD will give you from this young woman."

So Boaz took Ruth and she became his wife; and when he went in to her, the LORD gave her conception, and she bore a son. Then the women said to Naomi, "Blessed *be* the LORD, who has not left you this day without a close relative; and may his name be famous in Israel! And may he be to you a restorer of life and a nourisher of your old age; for your daughter-in-law, who loves you, who is better to you than seven sons, has borne him." Then Naomi took the child and laid him on her bosom, and became a nurse to him. Also the neighbor women gave him a name, saying, "There is a son born to Naomi." And they called his name Obed. He *is* the father of Jesse, the father of David.

Now this *is* the genealogy of Perez: Perez begot Hezron; Hezron begot Ram, and Ram begot Amminadab; Amminadab begot Nahshon, and Nahshon begot Salmon; Salmon begot Boaz, and Boaz begot Obed; Obed begot Jesse, and Jesse begot David.

Ruth 3–4

WoRSHiP

Mark the blameless *man,* and observe the
  upright;
For the future of *that* man *is* peace.
But the transgressors shall be destroyed
  together;
The future of the wicked shall be cut off.

But the salvation of the righteous *is* from the
  LORD;
He is their strength in the time of trouble.

Psalm 37:37-39

WiSDoM

The people will curse him who withholds
  grain,
But blessing *will be* on the head of him who
  sells *it.*

Proverbs 11:26

SW?! **SO WHAT?**
What does this tell me?

SAMUEL'S BIRTH AND GODLY HOME

1 Samuel 1:1–2:2, 11–26;
Psalm 38:1-3; Proverbs 11:27

Now there was a certain man of Ramathaim Zophim, of the mountains of Ephraim, and his name *was* Elkanah the son of Jeroham, the son of Elihu, the son of Tohu, the son of Zuph, an Ephraimite. And he had two wives: the name of one *was* Hannah, and the name of the other Peninnah. Peninnah had children, but Hannah had no children. This man went up from his city yearly to worship and sacrifice to the Lord of hosts in Shiloh. Also the two sons of Eli, Hophni and Phinehas, the priests of the Lord, *were* there. And whenever the time came for Elkanah to make an offering, he would give portions to Peninnah his wife and to all her sons and daughters. But to Hannah he would give a double portion, for he loved Hannah, although the Lord had closed her womb. And her rival also provoked her severely, to make her miserable, because the Lord had closed her womb. So it was, year by year, when she went up to the house of the Lord, that she provoked her; therefore she wept and did not eat.

Then Elkanah her husband said to her, "Hannah, why do you weep? Why do you not eat? And why is your heart grieved? *Am* I not better to you than ten sons?"

So Hannah arose after they had finished eating and drinking in Shiloh. Now Eli the priest was sitting on the seat by the doorpost of the tabernacle of the Lord. And she *was* in bitterness of soul, and prayed to the Lord and wept in anguish. Then she made a vow and said, "O Lord of hosts, if You will indeed look on the affliction of Your maidservant and remember me, and not forget Your maidservant, but will give Your maidservant a male child, then I will give him to the Lord all the days of his life, and no razor shall come upon his head."

And it happened, as she continued praying before the Lord, that Eli watched her mouth. Now Hannah spoke in her heart; only her lips moved, but her voice was not heard. Therefore Eli thought she was drunk. So Eli said to her, "How long will you be drunk? Put your wine away from you!"

And Hannah answered and said, "No, my lord, I *am* a woman of sorrowful spirit. I have drunk neither wine nor intoxicating drink, but have poured out my soul before the Lord. Do not consider your maidservant a wicked woman, for out of the abundance of my complaint and grief I have spoken until now."

Then Eli answered and said, "Go in peace, and the God of Israel grant your petition which you have asked of Him."

And she said, "Let your maidservant find favor in your sight." So the woman went her way and ate, and her face was no longer *sad*.

Then they rose early in the morning and worshiped before the Lord, and returned and came to their house at Ramah. And Elkanah knew Hannah his wife, and the Lord remembered her. So it came to pass in the process of time that Hannah conceived and bore a son, and called his name Samuel, *saying*, "Because I have asked for him from the Lord."

Now the man Elkanah and all his house went up to offer to the Lord the yearly sacrifice and his vow. But Hannah did not go up, for she said to her husband, "*Not* until the child is weaned; then I will take him, that he may appear before the Lord and remain there forever."

So Elkanah her husband said to her, "Do what seems best to you; wait until you have weaned him. Only let the Lord establish His word." So the woman stayed and nursed her son until she had weaned him.

Now when she had weaned him, she took him up with her, with three bulls, one ephah of flour, and a skin of wine, and brought him to the house of the Lord in Shiloh. And the child *was* young. Then they slaughtered a bull, and brought the child to Eli. And she said, "O my lord! As your soul lives, my lord, I *am* the woman who stood by you here, praying to the Lord. For this child I prayed, and the Lord has granted me my petition which I asked of Him. Therefore I also have lent him to the Lord; as long as he lives he shall be lent to the Lord." So they worshiped the Lord there.

And Hannah prayed and said:

"My heart rejoices in the Lord;
My horn is exalted in the Lord.
I smile at my enemies,
Because I rejoice in Your salvation.

HERE COMES THE JUDGE

"No one is holy like the Lord,
    For *there is* none besides You,
    Nor *is there* any rock like our God."

Then Elkanah went to his house at Ramah. But the child ministered to the Lord before Eli the priest.

Now the sons of Eli *were* corrupt; they did not know the Lord. And the priests' custom with the people *was that* when any man offered a sacrifice, the priest's servant would come with a three-pronged fleshhook in his hand while the meat was boiling. Then he would thrust *it* into the pan, or kettle, or caldron, or pot; and the priest would take for himself all that the fleshhook brought up. So they did in Shiloh to all the Israelites who came there. Also, before they burned the fat, the priest's servant would come and say to the man who sacrificed, "Give meat for roasting to the priest, for he will not take boiled meat from you, but raw."

And *if* the man said to him, "They should really burn the fat first; *then* you may take *as much* as your heart desires," he would then answer him, "*No,* but you must give *it* now; and if not, I will take *it* by force."

Therefore the sin of the young men was very great before the Lord, for men abhorred the offering of the Lord.

But Samuel ministered before the Lord, *even as* a child, wearing a linen ephod. Moreover his mother used to make him a little robe, and bring *it* to him year by year when she came up with her husband to offer the yearly sacrifice. And Eli would bless Elkanah and his wife, and say, "The Lord give you descendants from this woman for the loan that was given to the Lord." Then they would go to their own home.

And the Lord visited Hannah, so that she conceived and bore three sons and two daughters. Meanwhile the child Samuel grew before the Lord.

Now Eli was very old; and he heard everything his sons did to all Israel, and how they lay with the women who assembled at the door of the tabernacle of meeting. So he said to them, "Why do you do such things? For I hear of your evil dealings from all the people. No, my sons! For *it is* not a good report that I hear. You make the Lord's people transgress. If one man sins against another, God will judge him. But if a man sins against the Lord, who will intercede for him?" Nevertheless they did not heed the voice of their father, because the Lord desired to kill them.

And the child Samuel grew in stature, and in favor both with the Lord and men.

1 Samuel 1:1–2:2, 11-26

WORSHIP

O Lord, do not rebuke me in Your wrath,
Nor chasten me in Your hot displeasure!
For Your arrows pierce me deeply,
And Your hand presses me down.

There is no soundness in my flesh
Because of Your anger,
Nor *any* health in my bones
Because of my sin.

Psalm 38:1-3

WISDOM

He who earnestly seeks good finds favor,
But trouble will come to him who seeks *evil.*

Proverbs 11:27

SW?! **SO WHAT?**
What does this tell me?

SAMUEL'S CALL AS A PROPHET
1 Samuel 3–4; Psalm 38:18, 21-22; Proverbs 11:28

Now the boy Samuel ministered to the LORD before Eli. And the word of the LORD was rare in those days; *there was* no widespread revelation. And it came to pass at that time, while Eli *was* lying down in his place, and when his eyes had begun to grow so dim that he could not see, and before the lamp of God went out in the tabernacle of the LORD where the ark of God *was,* and while Samuel was lying down, that the LORD called Samuel. And he answered, "Here I am!" So he ran to Eli and said, "Here I am, for you called me."

And he said, "I did not call; lie down again." And he went and lay down.

Then the LORD called yet again, "Samuel!"

So Samuel arose and went to Eli, and said, "Here I am, for you called me." He answered, "I did not call, my son; lie down again." (Now Samuel did not yet know the LORD, nor was the word of the LORD yet revealed to him.)

And the LORD called Samuel again the third time. Then he arose and went to Eli, and said, "Here I am, for you did call me."

Then Eli perceived that the LORD had called the boy. Therefore Eli said to Samuel, "Go, lie down; and it shall be, if He calls you, that you must say, 'Speak, LORD, for Your servant hears.' " So Samuel went and lay down in his place.

Now the LORD came and stood and called as at other times, "Samuel! Samuel!"

And Samuel answered, "Speak, for Your servant hears."

Then the LORD said to Samuel: "Behold, I will do something in Israel at which both ears of everyone who hears it will tingle. In that day I will perform against Eli all that I have spoken concerning his house, from beginning to end. For I have told him that I will judge his house forever for the iniquity which he knows, because his sons made themselves vile, and he did not restrain them. And therefore I have sworn to the house of Eli that the iniquity of Eli's house shall not be atoned for by sacrifice or offering forever."

So Samuel lay down until morning, and opened the doors of the house of the LORD.

And Samuel was afraid to tell Eli the vision. Then Eli called Samuel and said, "Samuel, my son!"

He answered, "Here I am."

And he said, "What *is* the word that *the LORD* spoke to you? Please do not hide *it* from me. God do so to you, and more also, if you hide anything from me of all the things that He said to you." Then Samuel told him everything, and hid nothing from him. And he said, "It *is* the LORD. Let Him do what seems good to Him."

So Samuel grew, and the LORD was with him and let none of his words fall to the ground. And all Israel from Dan to Beersheba knew that Samuel *had been* established as a prophet of the LORD. Then the LORD appeared again in Shiloh. For the LORD revealed Himself to Samuel in Shiloh by the word of the LORD.

And the word of Samuel came to all Israel.

Now Israel went out to battle against the Philistines, and encamped beside Ebenezer; and the Philistines encamped in Aphek. Then the Philistines put themselves in battle array against Israel. And when they joined battle, Israel was defeated by the Philistines, who killed about four thousand men of the army in the field. And when the people had come into the camp, the elders of Israel said, "Why has the LORD defeated us today before the Philistines? Let us bring the ark of the covenant of the LORD from Shiloh to us, that when it comes among us it may save us from the hand of our enemies." So the people sent to Shiloh, that they might bring from there the ark of the covenant of the LORD of hosts, who dwells *between* the cherubim. And the two sons of Eli, Hophni and Phinehas, *were* there with the ark of the covenant of God.

And when the ark of the covenant of the LORD came into the camp, all Israel shouted so loudly that the earth shook. Now when the Philistines heard the noise of the shout, they said, "What *does* the sound of this great shout in the camp of the Hebrews *mean?*" Then they understood that the ark of the LORD had come into the camp. So the Philistines were afraid, for they said, "God has come into the camp!" And they said, "Woe to us! For such a thing has never happened before. Woe to us! Who will deliver us from the hand of these mighty gods? These *are* the gods who struck the Egyptians with all the plagues in the wilderness. Be strong and conduct yourselves like men, you Philistines, that you do not become servants of the Hebrews, as they have been to you. Conduct yourselves like men, and fight!"

So the Philistines fought, and Israel was defeated, and every man fled to his tent. There was a very great slaughter, and there fell of Israel thirty thousand foot soldiers. Also the ark of God was captured; and the two sons of Eli, Hophni and Phinehas, died.

Then a man of Benjamin ran from the battle line the same day, and came to Shiloh with his clothes torn and dirt on his head. Now when he came, there was Eli, sitting on a seat by the wayside watching, for his heart trembled for the ark of God. And when the man came into the city and told *it,* all the city cried out. When Eli heard the noise of the outcry, he said, "What *does* the sound of this tumult *mean?*" And the man came quickly and told Eli. Eli was ninety-eight years old, and his eyes were so dim that he could not see.

Then the man said to Eli, "I *am* he who came from the battle. And I fled today from the battle line."

And he said, "What happened, my son?"

So the messenger answered and said, "Israel has fled before the Philistines, and there has been a great slaughter among the people. Also your two sons, Hophni and Phinehas, are dead; and the ark of God has been captured."

Then it happened, when he made mention of the ark of God, that Eli fell off the seat backward by the side of the gate; and his neck was broken and he died, for the man was old and heavy. And he had judged Israel forty years.

Now his daughter-in-law, Phinehas' wife, was with child, *due* to be delivered; and when she heard the news that the ark of God was captured, and that her father-in-law and her husband were dead, she bowed herself and gave birth, for her labor pains came upon her. And about the time of her death the women who stood by her said to her, "Do not fear, for you have borne a son." But she did not answer, nor did she regard *it.* Then she named the child Ichabod, saying, "The glory has departed from Israel!" because the ark of God had been captured and because of her father-in-law and her husband. And she said, "The glory has departed from Israel, for the ark of God has been captured."

1 Samuel 3–4

WORSHIP

For I will declare my iniquity;
I will be in anguish over my sin.

Do not forsake me, O LORD;
O my God, be not far from me!
Make haste to help me,
O Lord, my salvation!

Psalm 38:18, 21-22

WISDOM

He who trusts in his riches will fall,
But the righteous will flourish like foliage.

Proverbs 11:28

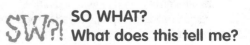

SO WHAT?
What does this tell me?

ISRAEL DEMANDS A KING

1 Samuel 7–8; Psalm 39:4-5; Proverbs 11:29

HERE COMES THE JUDGE

Then the men of Kirjath Jearim came and took the ark of the LORD, and brought it into the house of Abinadab on the hill, and consecrated Eleazar his son to keep the ark of the LORD.

So it was that the ark remained in Kirjath Jearim a long time; it was there twenty years. And all the house of Israel lamented after the LORD.

Then Samuel spoke to all the house of Israel, saying, "If you return to the LORD with all your hearts, *then* put away the foreign gods and the Ashtoreths from among you, and prepare your hearts for the LORD, and serve Him only; and He will deliver you from the hand of the Philistines." So the children of Israel put away the Baals and the Ashtoreths, and served the LORD only.

And Samuel said, "Gather all Israel to Mizpah, and I will pray to the LORD for you." So they gathered together at Mizpah, drew water, and poured *it* out before the LORD. And they fasted that day, and said there, "We have sinned against the LORD." And Samuel judged the children of Israel at Mizpah.

Now when the Philistines heard that the children of Israel had gathered together at Mizpah, the lords of the Philistines went up against Israel. And when the children of Israel heard *of it,* they were afraid of the Philistines. So the children of Israel said to Samuel, "Do not cease to cry out to the LORD our God for us, that He may save us from the hand of the Philistines."

And Samuel took a suckling lamb and offered *it as* a whole burnt offering to the LORD. Then Samuel cried out to the LORD for Israel, and the LORD answered him. Now as Samuel was offering up the burnt offering, the Philistines drew near to battle against Israel. But the LORD thundered with a loud thunder upon the Philistines that day, and so confused them that they were overcome before Israel. And the men of Israel went out of Mizpah and pursued the Philistines, and drove them back as far as below Beth Car. Then Samuel took a stone and set *it* up between Mizpah and Shen, and called its name Ebenezer, saying, "Thus far the LORD has helped us."

So the Philistines were subdued, and they did not come anymore into the territory of Israel. And the hand of the LORD was against the Philistines all the days of Samuel. Then the cities which the Philistines had taken from Israel were restored to Israel, from Ekron to Gath; and Israel recovered its territory from the hands of the Philistines. Also there was peace between Israel and the Amorites.

And Samuel judged Israel all the days of his life. He went from year to year on a circuit to Bethel, Gilgal, and Mizpah, and judged Israel in all those places. But he always returned to Ramah, for his home *was* there. There he judged Israel, and there he built an altar to the LORD.

Now it came to pass when Samuel was old that he made his sons judges over Israel. The name of his firstborn was Joel, and the name of his second, Abijah; *they were* judges in Beersheba. But his sons did not walk in his ways; they turned aside after dishonest gain, took bribes, and perverted justice.

Then all the elders of Israel gathered together and came to Samuel at Ramah, and said to him, "Look, you are old, and your sons do not walk in your ways. Now make us a king to judge us like all the nations."

But the thing displeased Samuel when they said, "Give us a king to judge us." So Samuel prayed to the LORD. And the LORD said to Samuel, "Heed the voice of the people in all that they say to you; for they have not rejected you, but they have rejected Me, that I should not reign over them. According to all the works which they have done since the day that I brought them up out of Egypt, even to this day—with which they have forsaken Me and served other gods—so they are doing to you also. Now therefore, heed their voice. However, you shall solemnly forewarn them, and show them the behavior of the king who will reign over them."

So Samuel told all the words of the LORD to the people who asked him for a king. And he said, "This will be the behavior of the king who will reign over you: He will take your sons and appoint *them* for his own chariots and *to be* his horsemen, and *some* will run before his chariots. He will appoint captains over his thousands and captains over his fifties, *will set some* to plow his ground and reap his harvest, and *some* to make his weapons of war and equipment for his chariots. He will take your daughters *to be* perfumers, cooks, and bakers. And he will take the best of your fields, your vineyards, and your olive groves, and give *them* to his servants. He will take a tenth of your grain and your vintage, and give it to his officers and servants. And he will take your male servants, your female servants, your finest young men, and your donkeys, and put *them* to his work. He will take a tenth of your sheep. And you will be his servants. And you will cry out in that day because of your king whom you have chosen for yourselves, and the LORD will not hear you in that day."

Nevertheless the people refused to obey the voice of Samuel; and they said, "No, but we will have a king over us, that we also may be like all the nations, and that our king may judge us and go out before us and fight our battles."

And Samuel heard all the words of the people, and he repeated them in the hearing of the LORD. So the LORD said to Samuel, "Heed their voice, and make them a king."

And Samuel said to the men of Israel, "Every man go to his city."

1 Samuel 7–8

WoRSHIP

"LORD, make me to know my end,
And what *is* the measure of my days,
That I may know how frail I *am*.
Indeed, You have made my days *as*
   handbreadths,
And my age *is* as nothing before You;
Certainly every man at his best state *is* but
   vapor."   Selah
Psalm 39:4-5

WiSDoM

He who troubles his own house will inherit the
   wind,
And the fool *will be* servant to the wise of
   heart.
Proverbs 11:29

SO WHAT?
What does this tell me?

UNITED WE STAND

God had ruled His people through priests, judges, and prophets, and now He would begin ruling the nation of Israel through divinely appointed kings. From the beginning of the united monarchy to the fall of Jerusalem in 586 B.C., Israel would be ruled by kings.

During the first part of the monarchy, the twelve tribes of Israel were led by a single king; first Saul, then David, and finally Solomon. In this case it really is true that "together is better," because under David the twelve tribes became a prosperous nation, and then under Solomon's rule they grew into a powerful empire.

David's great battlefield victory over the Philistine giant Goliath was a tall peak in this range. This classic event demonstrated David's spiritual and military qualifications to be king, showed that the God of Israel is a true and living God, and reaffirmed His willingness and ability to protect, defend, and deliver His people.

Another peak in the united monarchy is the great promise God gave David in 2 Samuel 7:12-16—an extension of the promise He made earlier to Abraham in Genesis 12:1-3. God assured David that he would have a son who would rule God's kingdom forever. According to Luke 1:32-33 in the New Testament, the birth of Jesus, David's descendant, was the first step toward the fulfillment of this promise to David. As sure as the first part of the promise has been fulfilled, Jesus will return and fulfill the rest of this promise when He inaugurates His future kingdom rule over God's people.

The building of Solomon's temple is the last memorable event of the united kingdom. Now that Israel had a permanent home, the temporary tabernacle the people made in the wilderness was no longer needed. So Solomon made it his goal to build a permanent temple to the glory of God. Stones were cut at the quarry and fit precisely together on the top of Mount Moriah, the highest place in Jerusalem. Floors, beams, and ivory inlays were secured with wooden pegs. The structure was so awesome and massive it took seven years to build. But when they were finished and the Ark of the Covenant was placed in the Most Holy Place in the temple, God demonstrated His approval and blessing by filling the temple with a visible sign of His presence and glory.

ISRAEL'S FIRST KING

1 Samuel 9:1–10:9, 17-24; Psalm 39:7, 12-13; Proverbs 11:30

There was a man of Benjamin whose name *was* Kish the son of Abiel, the son of Zeror, the son of Bechorath, the son of Aphiah, a Benjamite, a mighty man of power. And he had a choice and handsome son whose name *was* Saul. *There was* not a more handsome person than he among the children of Israel. From his shoulders upward *he was* taller than any of the people.

Now the donkeys of Kish, Saul's father, were lost. And Kish said to his son Saul, "Please, take one of the servants with you, and arise, go and look for the donkeys." So he passed through the mountains of Ephraim and through the land of Shalisha, but they did not find *them*. Then they passed through the land of Shaalim, and *they were* not *there*. Then he passed through the land of the Benjamites, but they did not find *them*.

When they had come to the land of Zuph, Saul said to his servant who *was* with him, "Come, let us return, lest my father cease *caring* about the donkeys and become worried about us."

And he said to him, "Look now, *there is* in this city a man of God, and *he is* an honorable man; all that he says surely comes to pass. So let us go there; perhaps he can show us the way that we should go."

Then Saul said to his servant, "But look, *if* we go, what shall we bring the man? For the bread in our vessels is all gone, and *there is* no present to bring to the man of God. What do we have?"

And the servant answered Saul again and said, "Look, I have here at hand one fourth of a shekel of silver. I will give *that* to the man of God, to tell us our way." (Formerly in Israel, when a man went to inquire of God, he spoke thus: "Come, let us go to the seer"; for *he who is* now *called* a prophet was formerly called a seer.)

Then Saul said to his servant, "Well said; come, let us go." So they went to the city where the man of God *was*.

As they went up the hill to the city, they met some young women going out to draw water, and said to them, "Is the seer here?"

And they answered them and said, "Yes, there he is, just ahead of you. Hurry now; for today he came to this city, because there is a sacrifice of the people today on the high place. As soon as you come into the city, you will surely find him before he goes up to the high place to eat. For the people will not eat until he comes, because he must bless the sacrifice; afterward those who are invited will eat. Now therefore, go up, for about this time you will find him." So they went up to the city. As they were coming into the city, there was Samuel, coming out toward them on his way up to the high place.

Now the LORD had told Samuel in his ear the day before Saul came, saying, "Tomorrow about this time I will send you a man from the land of Benjamin, and you shall anoint him commander over My people Israel, that he may save My people from the hand of the Philistines; for I have looked upon My people, because their cry has come to Me."

So when Samuel saw Saul, the LORD said to him, "There he is, the man of whom I spoke to you. This one shall reign over My people." Then Saul drew near to Samuel in the gate, and said, "Please tell me, where *is* the seer's house?"

Samuel answered Saul and said, "I *am* the seer. Go up before me to the high place, for you shall eat with me today; and tomorrow I will let you go and will tell you all that *is* in your heart. But as for your donkeys that were lost three days ago, do not be anxious about them, for they have been found. And on whom *is* all the desire of Israel? *Is it* not on you and on all your father's house?"

And Saul answered and said, "*Am* I not a Benjamite, of the smallest of the tribes of Israel, and my family the least of all the families of the tribe of Benjamin? Why then do you speak like this to me?"

Now Samuel took Saul and his servant and brought them into the hall, and had them sit in the place of honor among those who were invited; there *were* about thirty persons. And Samuel said to the cook, "Bring the portion which I gave you, of which I said to you, 'Set it apart.'" So the cook took up the thigh with its upper part and set *it* before Saul. And *Samuel* said, "Here it is, what was kept back. *It* was set apart for you. Eat; for until this time it has been kept for you, since I said I invited the people." So Saul ate with Samuel that day.

When they had come down from the high

place into the city, *Samuel* spoke with Saul on the top of the house. They arose early; and it was about the dawning of the day that Samuel called to Saul on the top of the house, saying, "Get up, that I may send you on your way." And Saul arose, and both of them went outside, he and Samuel.

As they were going down to the outskirts of the city, Samuel said to Saul, "Tell the servant to go on ahead of us." And he went on. "But you stand here awhile, that I may announce to you the word of God."

Then Samuel took a flask of oil and poured *it* on his head, and kissed him and said: "*Is it* not because the LORD has anointed you commander over His inheritance? When you have departed from me today, you will find two men by Rachel's tomb in the territory of Benjamin at Zelzah; and they will say to you, 'The donkeys which you went to look for have been found. And now your father has ceased caring about the donkeys and is worrying about you, saying, "What shall I do about my son?" ' Then you shall go on forward from there and come to the terebinth tree of Tabor. There three men going up to God at Bethel will meet you, one carrying three young goats, another carrying three loaves of bread, and another carrying a skin of wine. And they will greet you and give you two *loaves* of bread, which you shall receive from their hands. After that you shall come to the hill of God where the Philistine garrison *is*. And it will happen, when you have come there to the city, that you will meet a group of prophets coming down from the high place with a stringed instrument, a tambourine, a flute, and a harp before them; and they will be prophesying. Then the Spirit of the LORD will come upon you, and you will prophesy with them and be turned into another man. And let it be, when these signs come to you, *that* you do as the occasion demands; for God *is* with you. You shall go down before me to Gilgal; and surely I will come down to you to offer burnt offerings *and* make sacrifices of peace offerings. Seven days you shall wait, till I come to you and show you what you should do."

So it was, when he had turned his back to go from Samuel, that God gave him another heart; and all those signs came to pass that day.

Then Samuel called the people together to the LORD at Mizpah, and said to the children of Israel, "Thus says the LORD God of Israel: 'I brought up Israel out of Egypt, and delivered you from the hand of the Egyptians *and* from the hand of all kingdoms and from those who oppressed you.' But you have today rejected your God, who Himself saved you from all your adversities and your tribulations; and you have said to Him, 'No, set a king over us!' Now therefore, present yourselves before the LORD by your tribes and by your clans."

And when Samuel had caused all the tribes of Israel to come near, the tribe of Benjamin was chosen. When he had caused the tribe of Benjamin to come near by their families, the family of Matri was chosen. And Saul the son of Kish was chosen. But when they sought him, he could not be found. Therefore they inquired of the LORD further, "Has the man come here yet?"

And the LORD answered, "There he is, hidden among the equipment."

So they ran and brought him from there; and when he stood among the people, he was taller than any of the people from his shoulders upward. And Samuel said to all the people, "Do you see him whom the LORD has chosen, that *there is* no one like him among all the people?"

So all the people shouted and said, "Long live the king!"

1 Samuel 9:1–10:9, 17-24

WORSHIP

"And now, Lord, what do I wait for?
  My hope *is* in You.

"Hear my prayer, O LORD,
  And give ear to my cry;
Do not be silent at my tears;
For I *am* a stranger with You,
A sojourner, as all my fathers *were*.
Remove Your gaze from me, that I may regain
  strength,
Before I go away and am no more."

Psalm 39:7, 12-13

WISDOM

The fruit of the righteous *is a* tree of life,
And he who wins souls *is* wise.

Proverbs 11:30

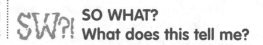

SO WHAT?
What does this tell me?

SAUL BLOWS IT BIG TIME

1 Samuel 13:1-16; 14:1-23; Psalm 40:4-5;
Proverbs 12:1

Saul reigned one year; and when he had reigned two years over Israel, Saul chose for himself three thousand *men* of Israel. Two thousand were with Saul in Michmash and in the mountains of Bethel, and a thousand were with Jonathan in Gibeah of Benjamin. The rest of the people he sent away, every man to his tent.

And Jonathan attacked the garrison of the Philistines that *was* in Geba, and the Philistines heard *of it*. Then Saul blew the trumpet throughout all the land, saying, "Let the Hebrews hear!" Now all Israel heard it said *that* Saul had attacked a garrison of the Philistines, and *that* Israel had also become an abomination to the Philistines. And the people were called together to Saul at Gilgal.

Then the Philistines gathered together to fight with Israel, thirty thousand chariots and six thousand horsemen, and people as the sand which *is* on the seashore in multitude. And they came up and encamped in Michmash, to the east of Beth Aven. When the men of Israel saw that they were in danger (for the people were distressed), then the people hid in caves, in thickets, in rocks, in holes, and in pits. And *some of* the Hebrews crossed over the Jordan to the land of Gad and Gilead.

As for Saul, he *was* still in Gilgal, and all the people followed him trembling. Then he waited seven days, according to the time set by Samuel. But Samuel did not come to Gilgal; and the people were scattered from him. So Saul said, "Bring a burnt offering and peace offerings here to me." And he offered the burnt offering. Now it happened, as soon as he had finished presenting the burnt offering, that Samuel came; and Saul went out to meet him, that he might greet him.

And Samuel said, "What have you done?"

Saul said, "When I saw that the people were scattered from me, and *that* you did not come within the days appointed, and *that* the Philistines gathered together at Michmash, then I said, 'The Philistines will now come down on me at Gilgal, and I have not made supplication to the LORD.' Therefore I felt compelled, and offered a burnt offering."

And Samuel said to Saul, "You have done foolishly. You have not kept the commandment of the LORD your God, which He commanded you. For now the LORD would have established your kingdom over Israel forever. But now your kingdom shall not continue. The LORD has sought for Himself a man after His own heart, and the LORD has commanded him *to be* commander over His people, because you have not kept what the LORD commanded you."

Then Samuel arose and went up from Gilgal to Gibeah of Benjamin. And Saul numbered the people present with him, about six hundred men.

Saul, Jonathan his son, and the people present with them remained in Gibeah of Benjamin. But the Philistines encamped in Michmash.

Now it happened one day that Jonathan the son of Saul said to the young man who bore his armor, "Come, let us go over to the Philistines' garrison that *is* on the other side." But he did not tell his father. And Saul was sitting in the outskirts of Gibeah under a pomegranate tree which *is* in Migron. The people who *were* with him *were* about six hundred men. Ahijah the son of Ahitub, Ichabod's brother, the son of Phinehas, the son of Eli, the LORD's priest in Shiloh, was wearing an ephod. But the people did not know that Jonathan had gone.

Between the passes, by which Jonathan sought to go over to the Philistines' garrison, *there was* a sharp rock on one side and a sharp rock on the other side. And the name of one *was* Bozez and the name of the other Seneh. The front of one faced northward opposite Michmash, and the other southward opposite Gibeah.

Then Jonathan said to the young man who bore his armor, "Come, let us go over to the garrison of these uncircumcised; it may be that the LORD will work for us. For nothing restrains the LORD from saving by many or by few."

So his armorbearer said to him, "Do all that is in your heart. Go then; here I am with you, according to your heart."

Then Jonathan said, "Very well, let us cross over to *these* men, and we will show ourselves to them. If they say thus to us, 'Wait until we come to you,' then we will stand still in our place and not go up to them. But if they say thus, 'Come up to us,' then we will go up. For the LORD has delivered them into our hand, and this *will be* a sign to us."

So both of them showed themselves to the garrison of the Philistines. And the Philistines said, "Look, the Hebrews are coming out of the holes where they have hidden." Then the men of the garrison called to Jonathan and his armorbearer, and said, "Come up to us, and we will show you something."

Jonathan said to his armorbearer, "Come up after me, for the LORD has delivered them into the hand of Israel." And Jonathan climbed up on his hands and knees with his armorbearer after him; and they fell before Jonathan. And as he came after him, his armorbearer killed them. That first slaughter which Jonathan and his armorbearer made was about twenty men within about half an acre of land.

And there was trembling in the camp, in the field, and among all the people. The garrison and the raiders also trembled; and the earth quaked, so that it was a very great trembling. Now the watchmen of Saul in Gibeah of Benjamin looked, and *there* was the multitude, melting away; and they went here and there. Then Saul said to the people who *were* with him, "Now call the roll and see who has gone from us." And when they had called the roll, surprisingly, Jonathan and his armorbearer *were* not *there*. And Saul said to Ahijah, "Bring the ark of God here" (for at that time the ark of God was with the children of Israel). Now it happened, while Saul talked to the priest, that the noise which *was* in the camp of the Philistines continued to increase; so Saul said to the priest, "Withdraw your hand." Then Saul and all the people who *were* with him assembled, and they went to the battle; and indeed every man's sword was against his neighbor, *and there was* very great confusion. Moreover the Hebrews *who* were with the Philistines before that time, who went up with them into the camp *from the* surrounding *country*, they also joined the Israelites who *were* with Saul and Jonathan. Likewise all the men of Israel who had hidden in the mountains of Ephraim, *when* they heard that the Philistines fled, they also followed hard after them in the battle. So the LORD saved Israel that day, and the battle shifted to Beth Aven.

1 Samuel 13:1-16; 14:1-23

WORSHIP

Blessed *is* that man who makes the LORD his trust,
And does not respect the proud, nor such as turn aside to lies.
Many, O LORD my God, *are* Your wonderful works
Which You have done;
And Your thoughts toward us
Cannot be recounted to You in order;
If I would declare and speak *of them,*
They are more than can be numbered.
Psalm 40:4-5

WISDOM

Whoever loves instruction loves knowledge,
But he who hates correction *is* stupid.
Proverbs 12:1

SW?! SO WHAT?
What does this tell me?

SAUL BLOWS IT AGAIN!

1 Samuel 15:1-23, 34-35; 16:1-14; Psalm 40:6-8; Proverbs 12:2

Samuel also said to Saul, "The LORD sent me to anoint you king over His people, over Israel. Now therefore, heed the voice of the words of the LORD. Thus says the LORD of hosts: 'I will punish Amalek *for* what he did to Israel, how he ambushed him on the way when he came up from Egypt. Now go and attack Amalek, and utterly destroy all that they have, and do not spare them. But kill both man and woman, infant and nursing child, ox and sheep, camel and donkey.' "

So Saul gathered the people together and numbered them in Telaim, two hundred thousand foot soldiers and ten thousand men of Judah. And Saul came to a city of Amalek, and lay in wait in the valley.

Then Saul said to the Kenites, "Go, depart, get down from among the Amalekites, lest I destroy you with them. For you showed kindness to all the children of Israel when they came up out of Egypt." So the Kenites departed from among the Amalekites. And Saul attacked the Amalekites, from Havilah all the way to Shur, which is east of Egypt. He also took Agag king of the Amalekites alive, and utterly destroyed all the people with the edge of the sword. But Saul and the people spared Agag and the best of the sheep, the oxen, the fatlings, the lambs, and all *that was* good, and were unwilling to utterly destroy them. But everything despised and worthless, that they utterly destroyed.

Now the word of the LORD came to Samuel, saying, "I greatly regret that I have set up Saul *as* king, for he has turned back from following Me, and has not performed My commandments." And it grieved Samuel, and he cried out to the LORD all night. So when Samuel rose early in the morning to meet Saul, it was told Samuel, saying, "Saul went to Carmel, and indeed, he set up a monument for himself; and he has gone on around, passed by, and gone down to Gilgal." Then Samuel went to Saul, and Saul said to him, "Blessed *are* you of the LORD! I have performed the commandment of the LORD."

But Samuel said, "What then *is* this bleating of the sheep in my ears, and the lowing of the oxen which I hear?"

And Saul said, "They have brought them from the Amalekites; for the people spared the best of the sheep and the oxen, to sacrifice to the LORD your God; and the rest we have utterly destroyed."

Then Samuel said to Saul, "Be quiet! And I will tell you what the LORD said to me last night."

And he said to him, "Speak on."

So Samuel said, "When you *were* little in your own eyes, *were* you not head of the tribes of Israel? And did not the LORD anoint you king over Israel? Now the LORD sent you on a mission, and said, 'Go, and utterly destroy the sinners, the Amalekites, and fight against them until they are consumed.' Why then did you not obey the voice of the LORD? Why did you swoop down on the spoil, and do evil in the sight of the LORD?"

And Saul said to Samuel, "But I have obeyed the voice of the LORD, and gone on the mission on which the LORD sent me, and brought back Agag king of Amalek; I have utterly destroyed the Amalekites. But the people took of the plunder, sheep and oxen, the best of the things which should have been utterly destroyed, to sacrifice to the LORD your God in Gilgal."

So Samuel said:

"Has the LORD *as great* delight in burnt offerings
   and sacrifices,
As in obeying the voice of the LORD?
Behold, to obey is better than sacrifice,
And to heed than the fat of rams.
For rebellion *is as* the sin of witchcraft,
And stubbornness *is as* iniquity and idolatry.
Because you have rejected the word of the
   LORD,
He also has rejected you from *being* king."

Then Samuel went to Ramah, and Saul went up to his house at Gibeah of Saul. And Samuel went no more to see Saul until the day of his death. Nevertheless Samuel mourned for Saul, and the LORD regretted that He had made Saul king over Israel.

Now the LORD said to Samuel, "How long will you mourn for Saul, seeing I have rejected him from reigning over Israel? Fill your horn with oil, and go; I am sending you to Jesse the Bethlehemite. For I have provided Myself a king among his sons."

And Samuel said, "How can I go? If Saul hears *it,* he will kill me."

And the Lord said, "Take a heifer with you, and say, 'I have come to sacrifice to the Lord.' Then invite Jesse to the sacrifice, and I will show you what you shall do; you shall anoint for Me the one I name to you."

So Samuel did what the Lord said, and went to Bethlehem. And the elders of the town trembled at his coming, and said, "Do you come peaceably?"

And he said, "Peaceably; I have come to sacrifice to the Lord. Sanctify yourselves, and come with me to the sacrifice." Then he consecrated Jesse and his sons, and invited them to the sacrifice.

So it was, when they came, that he looked at Eliab and said, "Surely the Lord's anointed *is* before Him!"

But the Lord said to Samuel, "Do not look at his appearance or at the height of his stature, because I have refused him. For *the* Lord *does* not *see* as man sees; for man looks at the outward appearance, but the Lord looks at the heart."

So Jesse called Abinadab, and made him pass before Samuel. And he said, "Neither has the Lord chosen this one." Then Jesse made Shammah pass by. And he said, "Neither has the Lord chosen this one." Thus Jesse made seven of his sons pass before Samuel. And Samuel said to Jesse, "The Lord has not chosen these." And Samuel said to Jesse, "Are all the young men here?" Then he said, "There remains yet the youngest, and there he is, keeping the sheep."

And Samuel said to Jesse, "Send and bring him. For we will not sit down till he comes here." So he sent and brought him in. Now he *was* ruddy, with bright eyes, and good-looking. And the Lord said, "Arise, anoint him; for this *is* the one!" Then Samuel took the horn of oil and anointed him in the midst of his brothers; and the Spirit of the Lord came upon David from that day forward. So Samuel arose and went to Ramah.

But the Spirit of the Lord departed from Saul, and a distressing spirit from the Lord troubled him.

1 Samuel 15:1-23, 34-35; 16:1-14

WORSHIP

Sacrifice and offering You did not desire;
My ears You have opened.
Burnt offering and sin offering You did not
  require.
Then I said, "Behold, I come;
In the scroll of the book *it is* written of me.
I delight to do Your will, O my God,
And Your law *is* within my heart."

Psalm 40:6-8

WISDOM

A good *man* obtains favor from the Lord,
But a man of wicked intentions He will
  condemn.

Proverbs 12:2

SW?! SO WHAT?
What does this tell me?

DAVID'S RISE TO FAME

1 Samuel 17:1-26, 31-51; Psalm 40:11-13; Proverbs 12:3

Now the Philistines gathered their armies together to battle, and were gathered together at Sochoh, which *belongs* to Judah; they encamped between Sochoh and Azekah, in Ephes Dammim. And Saul and the men of Israel were gathered together, and they encamped in the Valley of Elah, and drew up in battle array against the Philistines. The Philistines stood on a mountain on one side, and Israel stood on a mountain on the other side, with a valley between them.

And a champion went out from the camp of the Philistines, named Goliath, from Gath, whose height *was* six cubits and a span. *He had* a bronze helmet on his head, and he *was* armed with a coat of mail, and the weight of the coat *was* five thousand shekels of bronze. And *he had* bronze armor on his legs and a bronze javelin between his shoulders. Now the staff of his spear *was* like a weaver's beam, and his iron spearhead *weighed* six hundred shekels; and a shield-bearer went before him. Then he stood and cried out to the armies of Israel, and said to them, "Why have you come out to line up for battle? *Am* I not a Philistine, and you the servants of Saul? Choose a man for yourselves, and let him come down to me. If he is able to fight with me and kill me, then we will be your servants. But if I prevail against him and kill him, then you shall be our servants and serve us." And the Philistine said, "I defy the armies of Israel this day; give me a man, that we may fight together." When Saul and all Israel heard these words of the Philistine, they were dismayed and greatly afraid.

Now David *was* the son of that Ephrathite of Bethlehem Judah, whose name *was* Jesse, and who had eight sons. And the man was old, advanced *in years*, in the days of Saul. The three oldest sons of Jesse had gone to follow Saul to the battle. The names of his three sons who went to the battle *were* Eliab the firstborn, next to him Abinadab, and the third Shammah. David *was* the youngest. And the three oldest followed Saul. But David occasionally went and returned from Saul to feed his father's sheep at Bethlehem.

And the Philistine drew near and presented himself forty days, morning and evening.

Then Jesse said to his son David, "Take now for your brothers an ephah of this dried *grain* and these ten loaves, and run to your brothers at the camp. And carry these ten cheeses to the captain of *their* thousand, and see how your brothers fare, and bring back news of them." Now Saul and they and all the men of Israel *were* in the Valley of Elah, fighting with the Philistines.

So David rose early in the morning, left the sheep with a keeper, and took *the things* and went as Jesse had commanded him. And he came to the camp as the army was going out to the fight and shouting for the battle. For Israel and the Philistines had drawn up in battle array, army against army. And David left his supplies in the hand of the supply keeper, ran to the army, and came and greeted his brothers. Then as he talked with them, there was the champion, the Philistine of Gath, Goliath by name, coming up from the armies of the Philistines; and he spoke according to the same words. So David heard *them*. And all the men of Israel, when they saw the man, fled from him and were dreadfully afraid. So the men of Israel said, "Have you seen this man who has come up? Surely he has come up to defy Israel; and it shall be *that* the man who kills him the king will enrich with great riches, will give him his daughter, and give his father's house exemption *from taxes* in Israel."

Then David spoke to the men who stood by him, saying, "What shall be done for the man who kills this Philistine and takes away the reproach from Israel? For who *is* this uncircumcised Philistine, that he should defy the armies of the living God?"

Now when the words which David spoke were heard, they reported *them* to Saul; and he sent for him. Then David said to Saul, "Let no man's heart fail because of him; your servant will go and fight with this Philistine."

And Saul said to David, "You are not able to go against this Philistine to fight with him; for you *are* a youth, and he a man of war from his youth."

But David said to Saul, "Your servant used to keep his father's sheep, and when a lion or a bear came and took a lamb out of the flock, I went out after it and struck it, and delivered *the lamb* from its mouth; and when it arose against me, I caught *it* by its beard, and struck and killed it. Your servant has killed both lion and bear; and this uncircumcised Philistine will be like one of them, seeing he has defied the armies of the living God." Moreover David said, "The LORD, who delivered me from the paw of the lion and from the paw of the bear, He will deliver me from the hand of this Philistine."

And Saul said to David, "Go, and the LORD be with you!"

So Saul clothed David with his armor, and he put a bronze helmet on his head; he also clothed him with a coat of mail. David fastened his sword to his armor and tried to walk, for he had not tested *them.* And David said to Saul, "I cannot walk with these, for I have not tested *them.*" So David took them off.

Then he took his staff in his hand; and he chose for himself five smooth stones from the brook, and put them in a shepherd's bag, in a pouch which he had, and his sling was in his hand. And he drew near to the Philistine. So the Philistine came, and began drawing near to David, and the man who bore the shield *went* before him. And when the Philistine looked about and saw David, he disdained him; for he was *only* a youth, ruddy and good-looking. So the Philistine said to David, "*Am* I a dog, that you come to me with sticks?" And the Philistine cursed David by his gods. And the Philistine said to David, "Come to me, and I will give your flesh to the birds of the air and the beasts of the field!"

Then David said to the Philistine, "You come to me with a sword, with a spear, and with a javelin. But I come to you in the name of the LORD of hosts, the God of the armies of Israel, whom you have defied. This day the LORD will deliver you into my hand, and I will strike you and take your head from you. And this day I will give the carcasses of the camp of the Philistines to the birds of the air and the wild beasts of the earth, that all the earth may know that there is a God in Israel. Then all this assembly shall know that the LORD does not save with sword and spear; for the battle *is* the LORD's, and He will give you into our hands."

So it was, when the Philistine arose and came and drew near to meet David, that David hurried and ran toward the army to meet the Philistine. Then David put his hand in his bag and took out a stone; and he slung *it* and struck the Philistine in his

forehead, so that the stone sank into his forehead, and he fell on his face to the earth. So David prevailed over the Philistine with a sling and a stone, and struck the Philistine and killed him. But *there was* no sword in the hand of David. Therefore David ran and stood over the Philistine, took his sword and drew it out of its sheath and killed him, and cut off his head with it.

And when the Philistines saw that their champion was dead, they fled.

1 Samuel 17:1-26, 31-51

WoRSHiP

Do not withhold Your tender mercies from me,
O LORD;
Let Your lovingkindness and Your truth
continually preserve me.
For innumerable evils have surrounded me;
My iniquities have overtaken me, so that I am
not able to look up;
They are more than the hairs of my head;
Therefore my heart fails me.

Be pleased, O LORD, to deliver me;
O LORD, make haste to help me!

Psalm 40:11-13

WiSDoM

A man is not established by wickedness,
But the root of the righteous cannot be moved.

Proverbs 12:3

SW?! **SO WHAT?**
What does this tell me?

SAUL AND DAVID'S RELATIONSHIP RUPTURES

1 Samuel 18:1–19:18; Psalm 41:1-3; Proverbs 12:4

Now when he had finished speaking to Saul, the soul of Jonathan was knit to the soul of David, and Jonathan loved him as his own soul. Saul took him that day, and would not let him go home to his father's house anymore. Then Jonathan and David made a covenant, because he loved him as his own soul. And Jonathan took off the robe that *was* on him and gave it to David, with his armor, even to his sword and his bow and his belt.

So David went out wherever Saul sent him, *and* behaved wisely. And Saul set him over the men of war, and he was accepted in the sight of all the people and also in the sight of Saul's servants. Now it had happened as they were coming *home,* when David was returning from the slaughter of the Philistine, that the women had come out of all the cities of Israel, singing and dancing, to meet King Saul, with tambourines, with joy, and with musical instruments. So the women sang as they danced, and said:

"Saul has slain his thousands,
And David his ten thousands."

Then Saul was very angry, and the saying displeased him; and he said, "They have ascribed to David ten thousands, and to me they have ascribed *only* thousands. Now *what* more can he have but the kingdom?" So Saul eyed David from that day forward.

And it happened on the next day that the distressing spirit from God came upon Saul, and he prophesied inside the house. So David played *music* with his hand, as at other times; but *there was* a spear in Saul's hand. And Saul cast the spear, for he said, "I will pin David to the wall!" But David escaped his presence twice.

Now Saul was afraid of David, because the LORD was with him, but had departed from Saul. Therefore Saul removed him from his presence, and made him his captain over a thousand; and he went out and came in before the people. And David behaved wisely in all his ways, and the LORD *was* with him. Therefore, when Saul saw that he behaved very wisely, he was afraid of him. But all Israel and Judah loved David, because he went out and came in before them.

Then Saul said to David, "Here is my older daughter Merab; I will give her to you as a wife. Only be valiant for me, and fight the LORD's battles." For Saul thought, "Let my hand not be against him, but let the hand of the Philistines be against him."

So David said to Saul, "Who *am* I, and what *is* my life *or* my father's family in Israel, that I should be son-in-law to the king?" But it happened at the time when Merab, Saul's daughter, should have been given to David, that she was given to Adriel the Meholathite as a wife.

Now Michal, Saul's daughter, loved David. And they told Saul, and the thing pleased him. So Saul said, "I will give her to him, that she may be a snare to him, and that the hand of the Philistines may be against him." Therefore Saul said to David a second time, "You shall be my son-in-law today."

And Saul commanded his servants, "Communicate with David secretly, and say, 'Look, the king has delight in you, and all his servants love you. Now therefore, become the king's son-in-law.' "

So Saul's servants spoke those words in the hearing of David. And David said, "Does it seem to you *a light thing* to be a king's son-in-law, seeing I *am* a poor and lightly esteemed man?" And the servants of Saul told him, saying, "In this manner David spoke."

Then Saul said, "Thus you shall say to David: 'The king does not desire any dowry but one hundred foreskins of the Philistines, to take vengeance on the king's enemies.' " But Saul thought to make David fall by the hand of the Philistines. So when his servants told David these words, it pleased David well to become the king's son-in-law. Now the days had not expired; therefore David arose and went, he and his men, and killed two hundred men of the Philistines. And David brought their foreskins, and they gave them in full count to the king, that he might become the king's son-in-law. Then Saul gave him Michal his daughter as a wife.

Thus Saul saw and knew that the LORD *was* with David, and *that* Michal, Saul's daughter, loved him; and Saul was still more afraid of David. So Saul became David's enemy continually. Then the princes of the Philistines went out *to war.* And so it was, whenever they went out, *that* David behaved more wisely than all the servants of Saul, so that his name became highly esteemed.

Now Saul spoke to Jonathan his son and to all his servants, that they should kill David; but Jonathan, Saul's son, delighted greatly in David. So Jonathan told David, saying, "My father Saul seeks to kill you. Therefore please be on your guard until morning, and stay in a secret *place* and hide. And I will go out and stand beside my father in the field where you *are,* and I will speak with my father about you. Then what I observe, I will tell you."

Thus Jonathan spoke well of David to Saul his father, and said to him, "Let not the king sin against his servant, against David, because he has not sinned against you, and because his works *have been* very good toward you. For he took his life in his hands and killed the Philistine, and the LORD brought about a great deliverance for all Israel. You saw *it* and rejoiced. Why then will you sin against innocent blood, to kill David without a cause?"

So Saul heeded the voice of Jonathan, and Saul swore, "*As* the LORD lives, he shall not be killed." Then Jonathan called David, and Jonathan told him all these things. So Jonathan brought David to Saul, and he was in his presence as in times past.

And there was war again; and David went out and fought with the Philistines, and struck them with a mighty blow, and they fled from him.

Now the distressing spirit from the LORD came upon Saul as he sat in his house with his spear in his hand. And David was playing *music* with *his* hand. Then Saul sought to pin David to the wall with the spear, but he slipped away from Saul's presence; and he drove the spear into the wall. So David fled and escaped that night.

Saul also sent messengers to David's house to watch him and to kill him in the morning. And Michal, David's wife, told him, saying, "If you do not save your life tonight, tomorrow you will be killed." So Michal let David down through a window. And he went and fled and escaped. And Michal took an image and laid *it* in the bed, put a cover of goats' *hair* for his head, and covered *it* with clothes. So when Saul sent messengers to take David, she said, "He *is* sick."

Then Saul sent the messengers *back* to see David, saying, "Bring him up to me in the bed, that I may kill him." And when the messengers had come in, there was the image in the bed, with a cover of goats' hair for his head. Then Saul said to Michal, "Why have you deceived me like this, and sent my enemy away, so that he has escaped?"

And Michal answered Saul, "He said to me, 'Let me go! Why should I kill you?'"

So David fled and escaped, and went to Samuel at Ramah, and told him all that Saul had done to him. And he and Samuel went and stayed in Naioth.

1 Samuel 18:1–19:18

WORSHIP

Blessed *is* he who considers the poor;
The LORD will deliver him in time of trouble.
The LORD will preserve him and keep him alive,
And he will be blessed on the earth;
You will not deliver him to the will of his enemies.
The LORD will strengthen him on his bed of illness;
You will sustain him on his sickbed.

Psalm 41:1-3

WISDOM

An excellent wife *is* the crown of her husband,
But she who causes shame *is* like rottenness in his bones.

Proverbs 12:4

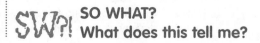

SO WHAT?
What does this tell me?

SAUL PURSUES DAVID IN THE WILDERNESS

1 Samuel 23:15–24:22; Psalm 41:12-13; Proverbs 12:5

So David saw that Saul had come out to seek his life. And David *was* in the Wilderness of Ziph in a forest. Then Jonathan, Saul's son, arose and went to David in the woods and strengthened his hand in God. And he said to him, "Do not fear, for the hand of Saul my father shall not find you. You shall be king over Israel, and I shall be next to you. Even my father Saul knows that." So the two of them made a covenant before the LORD. And David stayed in the woods, and Jonathan went to his own house.

Then the Ziphites came up to Saul at Gibeah, saying, "Is David not hiding with us in strongholds in the woods, in the hill of Hachilah, which *is* on the south of Jeshimon? Now therefore, O king, come down according to all the desire of your soul to come down; and our part *shall be* to deliver him into the king's hand."

And Saul said, "Blessed *are* you of the LORD, for you have compassion on me. Please go and find out for sure, and see the place where his hideout is, *and* who has seen him there. For I am told he is very crafty. See therefore, and take knowledge of all the lurking places where he hides; and come back to me with certainty, and I will go with you. And it shall be, if he is in the land, that I will search for him throughout all the clans of Judah."

So they arose and went to Ziph before Saul. But David and his men *were* in the Wilderness of Maon, in the plain on the south of Jeshimon. When Saul and his men went to seek *him,* they told David. Therefore he went down to the rock, and stayed in the Wilderness of Maon. And when Saul heard *that,* he pursued David in the Wilderness of Maon. Then Saul went on one side of the mountain, and David and his men on the other side of the mountain. So David made haste to get away from Saul, for Saul and his men were encircling David and his men to take them.

But a messenger came to Saul, saying, "Hurry and come, for the Philistines have invaded the land!" Therefore Saul returned from pursuing David, and went against the Philistines; so they called that place the Rock of Escape. Then David went up from there and dwelt in strongholds at En Gedi.

Now it happened, when Saul had returned from following the Philistines, that it was told him, saying, "Take note! David *is* in the Wilderness of En Gedi." Then Saul took three thousand chosen men from all Israel, and went to seek David and his men on the Rocks of the Wild Goats. So he came to the sheepfolds by the road, where there *was* a cave; and Saul went in to attend to his needs. (David and his men were staying in the recesses of the cave.) Then the men of David said to him, "This is the day of which the LORD said to you, 'Behold, I will deliver your enemy into your hand, that you may do to him as it seems good to you.' " And David arose and secretly cut off a corner of Saul's robe. Now it happened afterward that David's heart troubled him because he had cut Saul's *robe.* And he said to his men, "The LORD forbid that I should do this thing to my master, the LORD's anointed, to stretch out my hand against him, seeing he *is* the anointed of the LORD." So David restrained his servants with *these* words, and did not allow them to rise against Saul. And Saul got up from the cave and went on *his* way.

David also arose afterward, went out of the cave, and called out to Saul, saying, "My lord the king!" And when Saul looked behind him, David stooped with his face to the earth, and bowed down. And David said to Saul: "Why do you listen to the words of men who say, 'Indeed David seeks your harm'? Look, this day your eyes have seen that the LORD delivered you today into my hand in the cave, and *someone* urged *me* to kill you. But *my eye* spared you, and I said, 'I will not stretch out my hand against my lord, for he *is* the LORD's anointed.' Moreover, my father, see! Yes, see the corner of your robe in my hand! For in that I cut off the corner of your robe, and did not kill you, know and see that *there is* neither evil nor rebellion in my hand, and I have not sinned against you. Yet you hunt my life to take it. Let the LORD judge between you and me, and let the LORD avenge me on you. But my hand shall not be against you. As the proverb of the ancients says, 'Wickedness proceeds from the wicked.' But my hand shall not be against you. After whom has the king of Israel come out? Whom do you pursue? A dead dog? A flea? Therefore let the LORD be judge, and judge between you and me, and see and plead my case, and deliver me out of your hand."

So it was, when David had finished speaking these words to Saul, that Saul said, "*Is* this your voice, my son David?" And Saul lifted up his voice and wept. Then he said to David: "You *are* more righteous than I; for you have rewarded me with good, whereas I have rewarded you with evil. And you have shown this day how you have dealt well with me; for when the LORD delivered me into your hand, you did not kill me. For if a man finds his enemy, will he let him get away safely? Therefore may the LORD reward you with good for what you have done to me this day. And now I know indeed that you shall surely be king, and that the kingdom of Israel shall be established in your hand. Therefore swear now to me by the LORD that you will not cut off my descendants after me, and that you will not destroy my name from my father's house."

So David swore to Saul. And Saul went home, but David and his men went up to the stronghold.

1 Samuel 23:15–24:22

WORSHIP

As for me, You uphold me in my integrity,
And set me before Your face forever.

Blessed *be* the LORD God of Israel
From everlasting to everlasting!
Amen and Amen.

Psalm 41:12-13

WISDOM

The thoughts of the righteous *are* right,
But the counsels of the wicked *are* deceitful.

Proverbs 12:5

SW?! SO WHAT?
What does this tell me?

SAUL'S DEMISE AND DEATH

1 Samuel 28:3-19; 31:1-13; 2 Samuel 1:17-27; Psalm 42:1-3; Proverbs 12:7

Now Samuel had died, and all Israel had lamented for him and buried him in Ramah, in his own city. And Saul had put the mediums and the spiritists out of the land.

Then the Philistines gathered together, and came and encamped at Shunem. So Saul gathered all Israel together, and they encamped at Gilboa. When Saul saw the army of the Philistines, he was afraid, and his heart trembled greatly. And when Saul inquired of the LORD, the LORD did not answer him, either by dreams or by Urim or by the prophets.

Then Saul said to his servants, "Find me a woman who is a medium, that I may go to her and inquire of her."

And his servants said to him, "In fact, *there is* a woman who is a medium at En Dor."

So Saul disguised himself and put on other clothes, and he went, and two men with him; and they came to the woman by night. And he said, "Please conduct a séance for me, and bring up for me the one I shall name to you."

Then the woman said to him, "Look, you know what Saul has done, how he has cut off the mediums and the spiritists from the land. Why then do you lay a snare for my life, to cause me to die?"

And Saul swore to her by the LORD, saying, "*As* the LORD lives, no punishment shall come upon you for this thing."

Then the woman said, "Whom shall I bring up for you?"

And he said, "Bring up Samuel for me."

When the woman saw Samuel, she cried out with a loud voice. And the woman spoke to Saul, saying, "Why have you deceived me? For you *are* Saul!"

And the king said to her, "Do not be afraid. What did you see?"

And the woman said to Saul, "I saw a spirit ascending out of the earth."

So he said to her, "What *is* his form?"

And she said, "An old man is coming up, and he *is* covered with a mantle." And Saul perceived that it *was* Samuel, and he stooped with *his* face to the ground and bowed down.

Now Samuel said to Saul, "Why have you disturbed me by bringing me up?"

And Saul answered, "I am deeply distressed; for the Philistines make war against me, and God has departed from me and does not answer me anymore, neither by prophets nor by dreams. Therefore I have called you, that you may reveal to me what I should do."

Then Samuel said: "So why do you ask me, seeing the LORD has departed from you and has become your enemy? And the LORD has done for Himself as He spoke by me. For the LORD has torn the kingdom out of your hand and given it to your neighbor, David. Because you did not obey the voice of the LORD nor execute His fierce wrath upon Amalek, therefore the LORD has done this thing to you this day. Moreover the LORD will also deliver Israel with you into the hand of the Philistines. And tomorrow you and your sons *will be* with me. The LORD will also deliver the army of Israel into the hand of the Philistines."

Now the Philistines fought against Israel; and the men of Israel fled from before the Philistines, and fell slain on Mount Gilboa. Then the Philistines followed hard after Saul and his sons. And the Philistines killed Jonathan, Abinadab, and Malchishua, Saul's sons. The battle became fierce against Saul. The archers hit him, and he was severely wounded by the archers.

Then Saul said to his armorbearer, "Draw your sword, and thrust me through with it, lest these uncircumcised men come and thrust me through and abuse me."

But his armorbearer would not, for he was greatly afraid. Therefore Saul took a sword and fell on it. And when his armorbearer saw that Saul was dead, he also fell on his sword, and died with him. So Saul, his three sons, his armorbearer, and all his men died together that same day.

And when the men of Israel who *were* on the other side of the valley, and *those* who *were* on the other side of the Jordan, saw that the men of Israel had fled and that Saul and his sons were dead, they forsook the cities and fled; and the Philistines came and dwelt in them. So it happened the next day, when the Philistines came to strip the slain, that they found Saul and his three sons fallen on Mount Gilboa. And they cut off his head and stripped off his armor, and sent *word* throughout the land of the Philistines, to proclaim *it in* the temple of their idols and among the people. Then they put his armor in the temple of the Ashtoreths, and they fastened his body to the wall of Beth Shan.

Now when the inhabitants of Jabesh Gilead heard what the Philistines had done to Saul, all the valiant men arose and traveled all night, and took the body of Saul and the bodies of his sons from the wall of Beth Shan; and they came to Jabesh and burned them there. Then they took their bones and buried *them* under the tamarisk tree at Jabesh, and fasted seven days.

Then David lamented with this lamentation over Saul and over Jonathan his son, and he told *them* to teach the children of Judah *the Song of* the Bow; indeed *it is* written in the Book of Jasher:

"The beauty of Israel is slain on your high
    places!
How the mighty have fallen!
Tell *it* not in Gath,
Proclaim *it* not in the streets of Ashkelon—
Lest the daughters of the Philistines rejoice,
Lest the daughters of the uncircumcised
    triumph.

"O mountains of Gilboa,
Let there be no dew nor rain upon you,
Nor fields of offerings.
For the shield of the mighty is cast away
    there!
The shield of Saul, not anointed with oil.
From the blood of the slain,
From the fat of the mighty,
The bow of Jonathan did not turn back,
And the sword of Saul did not return empty.

"Saul and Jonathan *were* beloved and pleasant
    in their lives,
And in their death they were not divided;
They were swifter than eagles,
They were stronger than lions.

"O daughters of Israel, weep over Saul,
Who clothed you in scarlet, with luxury;
Who put ornaments of gold on your apparel.

"How the mighty have fallen in the midst of the
    battle!
Jonathan *was* slain in your high places.
I am distressed for you, my brother Jonathan;
You have been very pleasant to me;

Your love to me was wonderful,
Surpassing the love of women.

"How the mighty have fallen,
And the weapons of war perished!"
1 Samuel 28:3-19; 31:1-13; 2 Samuel 1:17-27

WORSHIP

As the deer pants for the water brooks,
So pants my soul for You, O God.
My soul thirsts for God, for the living God.
When shall I come and appear before God?
My tears have been my food day and night,
While they continually say to me,
"Where *is* your God?"

Psalm 42:1-3

WISDOM

The wicked are overthrown and *are* no more,
But the house of the righteous will stand.

Proverbs 12:7

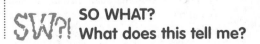

SO WHAT?
What does this tell me?

CIVIL WAR IN ISRAEL

2 Samuel 2:1–3:1; 4:5-12; Psalm 42:9-11;
Proverbs 12:8

It happened after this that David inquired of the LORD, saying, "Shall I go up to any of the cities of Judah?"

And the LORD said to him, "Go up."

David said, "Where shall I go up?"

And He said, "To Hebron."

So David went up there, and his two wives also, Ahinoam the Jezreelitess, and Abigail the widow of Nabal the Carmelite. And David brought up the men who *were* with him, every man with his household. So they dwelt in the cities of Hebron.

Then the men of Judah came, and there they anointed David king over the house of Judah. And they told David, saying, "The men of Jabesh Gilead *were the ones* who buried Saul." So David sent messengers to the men of Jabesh Gilead, and said to them, "You *are* blessed of the LORD, for you have shown this kindness to your lord, to Saul, and have buried him. And now may the LORD show kindness and truth to you. I also will repay you this kindness, because you have done this thing. Now therefore, let your hands be strengthened, and be valiant; for your master Saul is dead, and also the house of Judah has anointed me king over them."

But Abner the son of Ner, commander of Saul's army, took Ishbosheth the son of Saul and brought him over to Mahanaim; and he made him king over Gilead, over the Ashurites, over Jezreel, over Ephraim, over Benjamin, and over all Israel. Ishbosheth, Saul's son, *was* forty years old when he began to reign over Israel, and he reigned two years. Only the house of Judah followed David. And the time that David was king in Hebron over the house of Judah was seven years and six months.

Now Abner the son of Ner, and the servants of Ishbosheth the son of Saul, went out from Mahanaim to Gibeon. And Joab the son of Zeruiah, and the servants of David, went out and met them by the pool of Gibeon. So they sat down, one on one side of the pool and the other on the other side of the pool. Then Abner said to Joab, "Let the young men now arise and compete before us."

And Joab said, "Let them arise."

So they arose and went over by number, twelve from Benjamin, *followers* of Ishbosheth the son of Saul, and twelve from the servants of David. And each one grasped his opponent by the head and *thrust* his sword in his opponent's side; so they fell down together. Therefore that place was called the Field of Sharp Swords, which *is* in Gibeon. So there was a very fierce battle that day, and Abner and the men of Israel were beaten before the servants of David.

Now the three sons of Zeruiah were there: Joab and Abishai and Asahel. And Asahel *was as* fleet of foot as a wild gazelle. So Asahel pursued Abner, and in going he did not turn to the right hand or to the left from following Abner.

Then Abner looked behind him and said, "*Are* you Asahel?"

He answered, "I *am*."

And Abner said to him, "Turn aside to your right hand or to your left, and lay hold on one of the young men and take his armor for yourself." But Asahel would not turn aside from following him. So Abner said again to Asahel, "Turn aside from following me. Why should I strike you to the ground? How then could I face your brother Joab?" However, he refused to turn aside. Therefore Abner struck him in the stomach with the blunt end of the spear, so that the spear came out of his back; and he fell down there and died on the spot. So it was *that* as many as came to the place where Asahel fell down and died, stood still.

Joab and Abishai also pursued Abner. And the sun was going down when they came to the hill of Ammah, which *is* before Giah by the road to the Wilderness of Gibeon. Now the children of Benjamin gathered together behind Abner and became a unit, and took their stand on top of a hill. Then Abner called to Joab and said, "Shall the sword devour forever? Do you not know that it will be bitter in the latter end? How long will it be then until you tell the people to return from pursuing their brethren?"

And Joab said, "*As* God lives, unless you had spoken, surely then by morning all the people would have given up pursuing their brethren." So Joab blew a trumpet; and all the people stood still and did not pursue Israel anymore, nor did they fight anymore. Then Abner and his men went on all that night through the plain, crossed over the Jordan, and went through all Bithron; and they came to Mahanaim.

So Joab returned from pursuing Abner. And when he had gathered all the people together, there were missing of David's servants nineteen men and Asahel. But the servants of David had struck down, of Benjamin and Abner's men, three hundred and sixty men who died. Then they took up Asahel and buried him in his father's tomb, which *was in* Bethlehem. And Joab and his men went all night, and they came to Hebron at daybreak.

Now there was a long war between the house of Saul and the house of David. But David grew stronger and stronger, and the house of Saul grew weaker and weaker.

Then the sons of Rimmon the Beerothite, Rechab and Baanah, set out and came at about the heat of the day to the house of Ishbosheth, who was lying on his bed at noon. And they came there, all the way into the house, *as though* to get wheat, and they stabbed him in the stomach. Then Rechab and Baanah his brother escaped. For when they came into the house, he was lying on his bed in his bedroom; then they struck him and killed him, beheaded him and took his head, and were all night escaping through the plain. And they brought the head of Ishbosheth to David at Hebron, and said to the king, "Here is the head of Ishbosheth, the son of Saul your enemy, who sought your life; and the LORD has avenged my lord the king this day of Saul and his descendants."

But David answered Rechab and Baanah his brother, the sons of Rimmon the Beerothite, and said to them, "*As* the LORD lives, who has redeemed my life from all adversity, when someone told me, saying, 'Look, Saul is dead,' thinking to have brought good news, I arrested him and had him executed in Ziklag—the one who *thought* I would give him a reward for *his* news. How much more, when wicked men have killed a righteous person in his own house on his bed? Therefore, shall I not now require his blood at your hand and remove you from the earth?" So David commanded his young men, and they executed them, cut off their hands and feet, and hanged *them* by the pool in Hebron. But they took the head of Ishbosheth and buried *it* in the tomb of Abner in Hebron.

2 Samuel 2:1–3:1; 4:5-12

WORSHIP

I will say to God my Rock,
"Why have You forgotten me?
Why do I go mourning because of the
    oppression of the enemy?"
As with a breaking of my bones,
My enemies reproach me,
While they say to me all day long,
"Where *is* your God?"

Why are you cast down, O my soul?
And why are you disquieted within me?
Hope in God;
For I shall yet praise Him,
The help of my countenance and my God.

Psalm 42:9-11

WISDOM

A man will be commended according to his
    wisdom,
But he who is of a perverse heart will be
    despised.

Proverbs 12:8

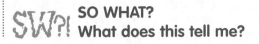

SO WHAT?
What does this tell me?

DAVID'S CAPITAL ESTABLISHED IN JERUSALEM

2 Samuel 5:1–21; 6:1–23; Psalm 43:3–4; Proverbs 12:9

Then all the tribes of Israel came to David at Hebron and spoke, saying, "Indeed we *are* your bone and your flesh. Also, in time past, when Saul was king over us, you were the one who led Israel out and brought them in; and the LORD said to you, 'You shall shepherd My people Israel, and be ruler over Israel.' " Therefore all the elders of Israel came to the king at Hebron, and King David made a covenant with them at Hebron before the LORD. And they anointed David king over Israel. David *was* thirty years old when he began to reign, *and* he reigned forty years. In Hebron he reigned over Judah seven years and six months, and in Jerusalem he reigned thirty-three years over all Israel and Judah.

And the king and his men went to Jerusalem against the Jebusites, the inhabitants of the land, who spoke to David, saying, "You shall not come in here; but the blind and the lame will repel you," thinking, "David cannot come in here." Nevertheless David took the stronghold of Zion (that *is,* the City of David).

Now David said on that day, "Whoever climbs up by way of the water shaft and defeats the Jebusites (the lame and the blind, *who are* hated by David's soul), *he shall be chief and captain.*" Therefore they say, "The blind and the lame shall not come into the house."

Then David dwelt in the stronghold, and called it the City of David. And David built all around from the Millo and inward. So David went on and became great, and the LORD God of hosts *was* with him.

Then Hiram king of Tyre sent messengers to David, and cedar trees, and carpenters and masons. And they built David a house. So David knew that the LORD had established him as king over Israel, and that He had exalted His kingdom for the sake of His people Israel.

And David took more concubines and wives from Jerusalem, after he had come from Hebron. Also more sons and daughters were born to David. Now these *are* the names of those who were born to him in Jerusalem: Shammua, Shobab, Nathan, Solomon, Ibhar, Elishua, Nepheg, Japhia, Elishama, Eliada, and Eliphelet.

Now when the Philistines heard that they had anointed David king over Israel, all the Philistines went up to search for David. And David heard *of it* and went down to the stronghold. The Philistines also went and deployed themselves in the Valley of Rephaim. So David inquired of the LORD, saying, "Shall I go up against the Philistines? Will You deliver them into my hand?"

And the LORD said to David, "Go up, for I will doubtless deliver the Philistines into your hand."

So David went to Baal Perazim, and David defeated them there; and he said, "The LORD has broken through my enemies before me, like a breakthrough of water." Therefore he called the name of that place Baal Perazim. And they left their images there, and David and his men carried them away.

Again David gathered all *the* choice *men* of Israel, thirty thousand. And David arose and went with all the people who *were* with him from Baale Judah to bring up from there the ark of God, whose name is called by the Name, the LORD of Hosts, who dwells *between* the cherubim. So they set the ark of God on a new cart, and brought it out of the house of Abinadab, which *was* on the hill; and Uzzah and Ahio, the sons of Abinadab, drove the new cart. And they brought it out of the house of Abinadab, which *was* on the hill, accompanying the ark of God; and Ahio went before the ark. Then David and all the house of Israel played *music* before the LORD on all kinds of *instruments of* fir wood, on harps, on stringed instruments, on tambourines, on sistrums, and on cymbals.

And when they came to Nachon's threshing floor, Uzzah put out *his hand* to the ark of God and took hold of it, for the oxen stumbled. Then the anger of the LORD was aroused against Uzzah, and God struck him there for *his* error; and he died there by the ark of God. And David became angry because of the LORD's outbreak against Uzzah; and he called the name of the place Perez Uzzah to this day.

David was afraid of the LORD that day; and he said, "How can the ark of the LORD come to me?" So

David would not move the ark of the LORD with him into the City of David; but David took it aside into the house of Obed-Edom the Gittite. The ark of the LORD remained in the house of Obed-Edom the Gittite three months. And the LORD blessed Obed-Edom and all his household.

Now it was told King David, saying, "The LORD has blessed the house of Obed-Edom and all that *belongs* to him, because of the ark of God." So David went and brought up the ark of God from the house of Obed-Edom to the City of David with gladness. And so it was, when those bearing the ark of the LORD had gone six paces, that he sacrificed oxen and fatted sheep. Then David danced before the LORD with all *his* might; and David *was* wearing a linen ephod. So David and all the house of Israel brought up the ark of the LORD with shouting and with the sound of the trumpet.

Now as the ark of the LORD came into the City of David, Michal, Saul's daughter, looked through a window and saw King David leaping and whirling before the LORD; and she despised him in her heart. So they brought the ark of the LORD, and set it in its place in the midst of the tabernacle that David had erected for it. Then David offered burnt offerings and peace offerings before the LORD. And when David had finished offering burnt offerings and peace offerings, he blessed the people in the name of the LORD of hosts. Then he distributed among all the people, among the whole multitude of Israel, both the women and the men, to everyone a loaf of bread, a piece *of meat,* and a cake of raisins. So all the people departed, everyone to his house.

Then David returned to bless his household. And Michal the daughter of Saul came out to meet David, and said, "How glorious was the king of Israel today, uncovering himself today in the eyes of the maids of his servants, as one of the base fellows shamelessly uncovers himself!"

So David said to Michal, "*It was* before the LORD, who chose me instead of your father and all his house, to appoint me ruler over the people of the LORD, over Israel. Therefore I will play *music* before the LORD. And I will be even more undignified than this, and will be humble in my own sight. But as for the maidservants of whom you have spoken, by them I will be held in honor."

Therefore Michal the daughter of Saul had no children to the day of her death.

2 Samuel 5:1-21; 6:1-23

WoRSHiP

Oh, send out Your light and Your truth!
Let them lead me;
Let them bring me to Your holy hill
And to Your tabernacle.
Then I will go to the altar of God,
To God my exceeding joy;
And on the harp I will praise You,
O God, my God.

Psalm 43:3-4

WiSDoM

Better *is the one* who is slighted but has a
    servant,
Than he who honors himself but lacks bread.

Proverbs 12:9

SW?! SO WHAT?
What does this tell me?

DAVID'S COVENANT AND KINDNESS

2 Samuel 7; 9; Psalm 44:6–8; Proverbs 12:10

Now it came to pass when the king was dwelling in his house, and the LORD had given him rest from all his enemies all around, that the king said to Nathan the prophet, "See now, I dwell in a house of cedar, but the ark of God dwells inside tent curtains."

Then Nathan said to the king, "Go, do all that *is* in your heart, for the LORD *is* with you."

But it happened that night that the word of the LORD came to Nathan, saying, "Go and tell My servant David, 'Thus says the LORD: "Would you build a house for Me to dwell in? For I have not dwelt in a house since the time that I brought the children of Israel up from Egypt, even to this day, but have moved about in a tent and in a tabernacle. Wherever I have moved about with all the children of Israel, have I ever spoken a word to anyone from the tribes of Israel, whom I commanded to shepherd My people Israel, saying, 'Why have you not built Me a house of cedar?' " ' Now therefore, thus shall you say to My servant David, 'Thus says the LORD of hosts: "I took you from the sheepfold, from following the sheep, to be ruler over My people, over Israel. And I have been with you wherever you have gone, and have cut off all your enemies from before you, and have made you a great name, like the name of the great men who *are* on the earth. Moreover I will appoint a place for My people Israel, and will plant them, that they may dwell in a place of their own and move no more; nor shall the sons of wickedness oppress them anymore, as previously, since the time that I commanded judges *to be* over My people Israel, and have caused you to rest from all your enemies. Also the LORD tells you that He will make you a house.

"When your days are fulfilled and you rest with your fathers, I will set up your seed after you, who will come from your body, and I will establish his kingdom. He shall build a house for My name, and I will establish the throne of his kingdom forever. I will be his Father, and he shall be My son. If he commits iniquity, I will chasten him with the rod of men and with the blows of the sons of men. But My mercy shall not depart from him, as I took *it* from Saul, whom I removed from before you. And your house and your kingdom shall be established forever before you. Your throne shall be established forever." ' "

According to all these words and according to all this vision, so Nathan spoke to David.

Then King David went in and sat before the LORD; and he said: "Who *am* I, O Lord GOD? And what is my house, that You have brought me this far? And yet this was a small thing in Your sight, O Lord GOD; and You have also spoken of Your servant's house for a great while to come. *Is* this the manner of man, O Lord GOD? Now what more can David say to You? For You, Lord GOD, know Your servant. For Your word's sake, and according to Your own heart, You have done all these great things, to make Your servant know *them*. Therefore You are great, O Lord GOD. For *there is* none like You, nor *is there any* God besides You, according to all that we have heard with our ears. And who *is* like Your people, like Israel, the one nation on the earth whom God went to redeem for Himself as a people, to make for Himself a name—and to do for Youself great and awesome deeds for Your land—before Your people whom You redeemed for Yourself from Egypt, the nations, and their gods? For You have made Your people Israel Your very own people forever; and You, LORD, have become their God.

"Now, O LORD God, the word which You have spoken concerning Your servant and concerning his house, establish *it* forever and do as You have said. So let Your name be magnified forever, saying, 'The LORD of hosts *is* the God over Israel.' And let the house of Your servant David be established before You. For You, O LORD of hosts, God of Israel, have revealed *this* to Your servant, saying, 'I will build you a house.' Therefore Your servant has found it in his heart to pray this prayer to You.

"And now, O Lord GOD, You are God, and Your words are true, and You have promised this goodness to Your servant. Now therefore, let it please You to bless the house of Your servant, that it may continue before You forever; for You, O Lord GOD, have spoken *it*, and with Your blessing let the house of Your servant be blessed forever."

Now David said, "Is there still anyone who is left of the house of Saul, that I may show him kindness for Jonathan's sake?"

And *there was* a servant of the house of Saul whose name *was* Ziba. So when they had called him to David, the king said to him, "*Are* you Ziba?"

He said, "At your service!"

Then the king said, "*Is* there not still someone of the house of Saul, to whom I may show the kindness of God?"

And Ziba said to the king, "There is still a son of Jonathan *who is* lame in *his* feet."

So the king said to him, "Where *is* he?"

And Ziba said to the king, "Indeed he *is* in the house of Machir the son of Ammiel, in Lo Debar."

Then King David sent and brought him out of the house of Machir the son of Ammiel, from Lo Debar.

Now when Mephibosheth the son of Jonathan, the son of Saul, had come to David, he fell on his face and prostrated himself. Then David said, "Mephibosheth?"

And he answered, "Here is your servant!"

So David said to him, "Do not fear, for I will surely show you kindness for Jonathan your father's sake, and will restore to you all the land of Saul your grandfather; and you shall eat bread at my table continually."

Then he bowed himself, and said, "What *is* your servant, that you should look upon such a dead dog as I?"

And the king called to Ziba, Saul's servant, and said to him, "I have given to your master's son all that belonged to Saul and to all his house. You therefore, and your sons and your servants, shall work the land for him, and you shall bring in *the harvest,* that your master's son may have food to eat. But Mephibosheth your master's son shall eat bread at my table always." Now Ziba had fifteen sons and twenty servants.

Then Ziba said to the king, "According to all that my lord the king has commanded his servant, so will your servant do."

"As for Mephibosheth," *said the king,* "he shall eat at my table like one of the king's sons." Mephibosheth had a young son whose name *was* Micha. And all who dwelt in the house of Ziba *were* servants of Mephibosheth. So Mephibosheth dwelt in Jerusalem, for he ate continually at the king's table. And he was lame in both his feet.

2 Samuel 7; 9

WORSHIP

For I will not trust in my bow,
Nor shall my sword save me.
But You have saved us from our enemies,
And have put to shame those who hated us.
In God we boast all day long,
And praise Your name forever.   Selah
Psalm 44:6-8

WISDOM

A righteous *man* regards the life of his animal,
But the tender mercies of the wicked *are* cruel.
Proverbs 12:10

SW?! SO WHAT?
What does this tell me?

DAVID'S ADULTERY AND ATTEMPTED COVER-UP

2 Samuel 11:1–12:13; Psalm 44:15, 17–18; Proverbs 12:11

It happened in the spring of the year, at the time when kings go out *to battle,* that David sent Joab and his servants with him, and all Israel; and they destroyed the people of Ammon and besieged Rabbah. But David remained at Jerusalem.

Then it happened one evening that David arose from his bed and walked on the roof of the king's house. And from the roof he saw a woman bathing, and the woman *was* very beautiful to behold. So David sent and inquired about the woman. And *someone* said, "*Is* this not Bathsheba, the daughter of Eliam, the wife of Uriah the Hittite?" Then David sent messengers, and took her; and she came to him, and he lay with her, for she was cleansed from her impurity; and she returned to her house. And the woman conceived; so she sent and told David, and said, "I *am* with child."

Then David sent to Joab, *saying,* "Send me Uriah the Hittite." And Joab sent Uriah to David. When Uriah had come to him, David asked how Joab was doing, and how the people were doing, and how the war prospered. And David said to Uriah, "Go down to your house and wash your feet." So Uriah departed from the king's house, and a gift *of food* from the king followed him. But Uriah slept at the door of the king's house with all the servants of his lord, and did not go down to his house. So when they told David, saying, "Uriah did not go down to his house," David said to Uriah, "Did you not come from a journey? Why did you not go down to your house?"

And Uriah said to David, "The ark and Israel and Judah are dwelling in tents, and my lord Joab and the servants of my lord are encamped in the open fields. Shall I then go to my house to eat and drink, and to lie with my wife? *As* you live, and *as* your soul lives, I will not do this thing."

Then David said to Uriah, "Wait here today also, and tomorrow I will let you depart." So Uriah remained in Jerusalem that day and the next. Now when David called him, he ate and drank before him; and he made him drunk. And at evening he went out to lie on his bed with the servants of his lord, but he did not go down to his house.

In the morning it happened that David wrote a letter to Joab and sent *it* by the hand of Uriah. And he wrote in the letter, saying, "Set Uriah in the forefront of the hottest battle, and retreat from him, that he may be struck down and die." So it was, while Joab besieged the city, that he assigned Uriah to a place where he knew there *were* valiant men. Then the men of the city came out and fought with Joab. And *some* of the people of the servants of David fell; and Uriah the Hittite died also.

Then Joab sent and told David all the things concerning the war, and charged the messenger, saying, "When you have finished telling the matters of the war to the king, if it happens that the king's wrath rises, and he says to you: 'Why did you approach so near to the city when you fought? Did you not know that they would shoot from the wall? Who struck Abimelech the son of Jerubbesheth? Was it not a woman who cast a piece of a millstone on him from the wall, so that he died in Thebez? Why did you go near the wall?'—then you shall say, 'Your servant Uriah the Hittite is dead also.' "

So the messenger went, and came and told David all that Joab had sent by him. And the messenger said to David, "Surely the men prevailed against us and came out to us in the field; then we drove them back as far as the entrance of the gate. The archers shot from the wall at your servants; and *some* of the king's servants are dead, and your servant Uriah the Hittite is dead also."

Then David said to the messenger, "Thus you shall say to Joab: 'Do not let this thing displease you, for the sword devours one as well as another. Strengthen your attack against the city, and overthrow it.' So encourage him."

When the wife of Uriah heard that Uriah her husband was dead, she mourned for her husband. And when her mourning was over, David sent and brought her to his house, and she became his wife and bore him a son. But the thing that David had done displeased the LORD.

Then the LORD sent Nathan to David. And he came to him, and said to him: "There were two men in one city, one rich and the other poor. The rich *man* had exceedingly many flocks and herds. But the poor *man* had nothing, except one little ewe lamb which he had bought and nourished; and it grew up together with him and with his children. It ate of his own food and drank from his own cup and lay in his bosom; and it was like a daughter to him. And a traveler came to the rich man, who refused to take from his own flock and from his own herd to prepare one for the wayfaring man who had come to him; but he took the poor man's lamb and prepared it for the man who had come to him."

So David's anger was greatly aroused against the man, and he said to Nathan, "*As* the L ORD lives, the man who has done this shall surely die! And he shall restore fourfold for the lamb, because he did this thing and because he had no pity."

Then Nathan said to David, "You *are* the man! Thus says the L ORD God of Israel: 'I anointed you king over Israel, and I delivered you from the hand of Saul. I gave you your master's house and your master's wives into your keeping, and gave you the house of Israel and Judah. And if *that had been* too little, I also would have given you much more! Why have you despised the commandment of the L ORD, to do evil in His sight? You have killed Uriah the Hittite with the sword; you have taken his wife *to be* your wife, and have killed him with the sword of the people of Ammon. Now therefore, the sword shall never depart from your house, because you have despised Me, and have taken the wife of Uriah the Hittite to be your wife.' Thus says the L ORD: 'Behold, I will raise up adversity against you from your own house; and I will take your wives before your eyes and give *them* to your neighbor, and he shall lie with your wives in the sight of this sun. For you did *it* secretly, but I will do this thing before all Israel, before the sun.' "

So David said to Nathan, "I have sinned against the L ORD."

And Nathan said to David, "The L ORD also has put away your sin; you shall not die."

2 Samuel 11:1–12:13

WO R SHIP

My dishonor *is* continually before me,
And the shame of my face has covered me.

All this has come upon us;
But we have not forgotten You,
Nor have we dealt falsely with Your covenant.
Our heart has not turned back,
Nor have our steps departed from Your way.
Psalm 44:15, 17-18

WI S DoM

He who tills his land will be satisfied with bread,
But he who follows frivolity *is* devoid of understanding.
Proverbs 12:11

SW?! SO WHAT?
What does this tell me?

DAVID'S FAMILY TROUBLES

2 Samuel 13:1–14:1, 21-25, 28; Psalm 44:20-21; Proverbs 12:12

After this Absalom the son of David had a lovely sister, whose name *was* Tamar; and Amnon the son of David loved her. Amnon was so distressed over his sister Tamar that he became sick; for she *was* a virgin. And it was improper for Amnon to do anything to her. But Amnon had a friend whose name *was* Jonadab the son of Shimeah, David's brother. Now Jonadab *was* a very crafty man. And he said to him, "Why *are* you, the king's son, becoming thinner day after day? Will you not tell me?"

Amnon said to him, "I love Tamar, my brother Absalom's sister."

So Jonadab said to him, "Lie down on your bed and pretend to be ill. And when your father comes to see you, say to him, 'Please let my sister Tamar come and give me food, and prepare the food in my sight, that I may see *it* and eat it from her hand.'" Then Amnon lay down and pretended to be ill; and when the king came to see him, Amnon said to the king, "Please let Tamar my sister come and make a couple of cakes for me in my sight, that I may eat from her hand."

And David sent home to Tamar, saying, "Now go to your brother Amnon's house, and prepare food for him." So Tamar went to her brother Amnon's house; and he was lying down. Then she took flour and kneaded *it,* made cakes in his sight, and baked the cakes. And she took the pan and placed *them* out before him, but he refused to eat. Then Amnon said, "Have everyone go out from me." And they all went out from him. Then Amnon said to Tamar, "Bring the food into the bedroom, that I may eat from your hand." And Tamar took the cakes which she had made, and brought *them* to Amnon her brother in the bedroom. Now when she had brought *them* to him to eat, he took hold of her and said to her, "Come, lie with me, my sister."

And she answered him, "No, my brother, do not force me, for no such thing should be done in Israel. Do not do this disgraceful thing! And I, where could I take my shame? And as for you, you would be like one of the fools in Israel. Now therefore, please speak to the king; for he will not withhold me from you." However, he would not heed her voice; and being stronger than she, he forced her and lay with her.

Then Amnon hated her exceedingly, so that the hatred with which he hated her *was* greater than the love with which he had loved her. And Amnon said to her, "Arise, be gone!"

So she said to him, "No, indeed! This evil of sending me away *is* worse than the other that you did to me."

But he would not listen to her. Then he called his servant who attended him, and said, "Here! Put this *woman* out, away from me, and bolt the door behind her." Now she had on a robe of many colors, for the king's virgin daughters wore such apparel. And his servant put her out and bolted the door behind her.

Then Tamar put ashes on her head, and tore her robe of many colors that *was* on her, and laid her hand on her head and went away crying bitterly. And Absalom her brother said to her, "Has Amnon your brother been with you? But now hold your peace, my sister. He *is* your brother; do not take this thing to heart." So Tamar remained desolate in her brother Absalom's house.

But when King David heard of all these things, he was very angry. And Absalom spoke to his brother Amnon neither good nor bad. For Absalom hated Amnon, because he had forced his sister Tamar.

And it came to pass, after two full years, that Absalom had sheepshearers in Baal Hazor, which *is* near Ephraim; so Absalom invited all the king's sons. Then Absalom came to the king and said, "Kindly note, your servant has sheepshearers; please, let the king and his servants go with your servant."

But the king said to Absalom, "No, my son, let us not all go now, lest we be a burden to you." Then he urged him, but he would not go; and he blessed him.

Then Absalom said, "If not, please let my brother Amnon go with us."

And the king said to him, "Why should he go with you?" But Absalom urged him; so he let Amnon and all the king's sons go with him.

Now Absalom had commanded his servants, saying, "Watch now, when Amnon's heart is merry with wine, and when I say to you, 'Strike Amnon!' then kill him. Do not be afraid. Have I not commanded you? Be courageous and valiant." So the servants of Absalom did to Amnon as Absalom had commanded. Then all the king's sons arose, and each one got on his mule and fled.

And it came to pass, while they were on the way, that news came to David, saying, "Absalom has killed all the king's sons, and not one of them is left!" So the king arose and tore his garments and lay on the ground, and all his servants stood by with their clothes torn. Then Jonadab the son of Shimeah, David's brother, answered and said, "Let not my lord suppose they have killed all the young men, the king's sons, for only Amnon is dead. For by the command of Absalom this has been determined from the day that he forced his sister Tamar. Now therefore, let not my lord the king take the thing to his heart, to think that all the king's sons are dead. For only Amnon is dead."

Then Absalom fled. And the young man who was keeping watch lifted his eyes and looked, and there, many people were coming from the road on the hillside behind him. And Jonadab said to the king, "Look, the king's sons are coming; as your servant said, so it is." So it was, as soon as he had finished speaking, that the king's sons indeed came, and they lifted up their voice and wept. Also the king and all his servants wept very bitterly.

But Absalom fled and went to Talmai the son of Ammihud, king of Geshur. And *David* mourned for his son every day. So Absalom fled and went to Geshur, and was there three years. And King David longed to go to Absalom. For he had been comforted concerning Amnon, because he was dead.

So Joab the son of Zeruiah perceived that the king's heart *was* concerned about Absalom.

And the king said to Joab, "All right, I have granted this thing. Go therefore, bring back the young man Absalom."

Then Joab fell to the ground on his face and bowed himself, and thanked the king. And Joab said, "Today your servant knows that I have found favor in your sight, my lord, O king, in that the king has fulfilled the request of his servant." So Joab arose and went to Geshur, and brought Absalom to Jerusalem. And the king said, "Let him return to his own house, but do not let him see my face." So Absalom returned to his own house, but did not see the king's face.

Now in all Israel there was no one who was praised as much as Absalom for his good looks. From the sole of his foot to the crown of his head there was no blemish in him.

And Absalom dwelt two full years in Jerusalem, but did not see the king's face.

2 Samuel 13:1–14:1, 21-25, 28

WORSHIP

If we had forgotten the name of our God,
Or stretched out our hands to a foreign god,
Would not God search this out?
For He knows the secrets of the heart.

Psalm 44:20-21

WISDOM

The wicked covet the catch of evil *men*,
But the root of the righteous yields *fruit*.

Proverbs 12:12

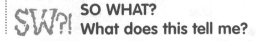

SO WHAT?
What does this tell me?

ABSALOM'S REBELLION

2 Samuel 15:1-30; 18:1-15; Psalm 44:24-26; Proverbs 12:15

A fter this it happened that Absalom provided himself with chariots and horses, and fifty men to run before him. Now Absalom would rise early and stand beside the way to the gate. So it was, whenever anyone who had a lawsuit came to the king for a decision, that Absalom would call to him and say, "What city *are* you from?" And he would say, "Your servant *is* from such and such a tribe of Israel." Then Absalom would say to him, "Look, your case *is* good and right; but *there is* no deputy of the king to hear you." Moreover Absalom would say, "Oh, that I were made judge in the land, and everyone who has any suit or cause would come to me; then I would give him justice." And *so* it was, whenever anyone came near to bow down to him, that he would put out his hand and take him and kiss him. In this manner Absalom acted toward all Israel who came to the king for judgment. So Absalom stole the hearts of the men of Israel.

Now it came to pass after forty years that Absalom said to the king, "Please, let me go to Hebron and pay the vow which I made to the LORD. For your servant took a vow while I dwelt at Geshur in Syria, saying, 'If the LORD indeed brings me back to Jerusalem, then I will serve the LORD.' "

And the king said to him, "Go in peace." So he arose and went to Hebron.

Then Absalom sent spies throughout all the tribes of Israel, saying, "As soon as you hear the sound of the trumpet, then you shall say, 'Absalom reigns in Hebron!' " And with Absalom went two hundred men invited from Jerusalem, and they went along innocently and did not know anything. Then Absalom sent for Ahithophel the Gilonite, David's counselor, from his city—from Giloh—while he offered sacrifices. And the conspiracy grew strong, for the people with Absalom continually increased in number.

Now a messenger came to David, saying, "The hearts of the men of Israel are with Absalom."

So David said to all his servants who *were* with him at Jerusalem, "Arise, and let us flee; or we shall not escape from Absalom. Make haste to depart, lest he overtake us suddenly and bring disaster upon us, and strike the city with the edge of the sword."

And the king's servants said to the king, "We *are* your servants, *ready to do* whatever my lord the king commands." Then the king went out with all his household after him. But the king left ten women, concubines, to keep the house. And the king went out with all the people after him, and stopped at the outskirts. Then all his servants passed before him; and all the Cherethites, all the Pelethites, and all the Gittites, six hundred men who had followed him from Gath, passed before the king.

Then the king said to Ittai the Gittite, "Why are you also going with us? Return and remain with the king. For you *are* a foreigner and also an exile from your own place. In fact, you came *only* yesterday. Should I make you wander up and down with us today, since I go I know not where? Return, and take your brethren back. Mercy and truth *be* with you."

And Ittai answered the king and said, "*As* the LORD lives, and *as* my lord the king lives, surely in whatever place my lord the king shall be, whether in death or life, even there also your servant will be."

So David said to Ittai, "Go, and cross over." Then Ittai the Gittite and all his men and all the little ones who *were* with him crossed over. And all the country wept with a loud voice, and all the people crossed over. The king himself also crossed over the Brook Kidron, and all the people crossed over toward the way of the wilderness.

There was Zadok also, and all the Levites with him, bearing the ark of the covenant of God. And they set down the ark of God, and Abiathar went up until all the people had finished crossing over from the city. Then the king said to Zadok, "Carry the ark of God back into the city. If I find favor in the eyes of the LORD, He will bring me back and show me *both* it and His dwelling place. But if He says thus: 'I have no delight in you,' here I am, let Him do to me as seems good to Him." The king also said to Zadok the priest, "*Are* you *not* a seer? Return to the city in peace, and your two sons with you, Ahimaaz your son, and Jonathan the son of Abiathar. See, I will wait in the plains of the wilderness until word comes from you to inform me." Therefore Zadok and Abiathar carried the ark of God back to Jerusalem. And they remained there.

So David went up by the Ascent of the *Mount of Olives*, and wept as he went up; and he had his head covered and went barefoot. And all the people who *were* with him covered their heads and went up, weeping as they went up.

And David numbered the people who *were* with him, and set captains of thousands and captains of hundreds over them. Then David sent out one third of the people under the hand of Joab, one third under the hand of Abishai the son of Zeruiah, Joab's brother, and one third under the hand of Ittai the Gittite. And the king said to the people, "I also will surely go out with you myself."

But the people answered, "You shall not go out! For if we flee away, they will not care about us; nor if half of us die, will they care about us. But *you are* worth ten thousand of us now. For you are now more help to us in the city."

Then the king said to them, "Whatever seems best to you I will do." So the king stood beside the gate, and all the people went out by hundreds and by thousands. Now the king had commanded Joab, Abishai, and Ittai, saying, "*Deal* gently for my sake with the young man Absalom." And all the people heard when the king gave all the captains orders concerning Absalom.

So the people went out into the field of battle against Israel. And the battle was in the woods of Ephraim. The people of Israel were overthrown there before the servants of David, and a great slaughter of twenty thousand took place there that day. For the battle there was scattered over the face of the whole countryside, and the woods devoured more people that day than the sword devoured.

Then Absalom met the servants of David. Absalom rode on a mule. The mule went under the thick boughs of a great terebinth tree, and his head caught in the terebinth; so he was left hanging between heaven and earth. And the mule which *was* under him went on. Now a certain man saw *it* and told Joab, and said, "I just saw Absalom hanging in a terebinth tree!"

So Joab said to the man who told him, "You just saw *him*! And why did you not strike him there to the ground? I would have given you ten *shekels* of silver and a belt."

But the man said to Joab, "Though I were to receive a thousand *shekels* of silver in my hand, I would not raise my hand against the king's son. For

in our hearing the king commanded you and Abishai and Ittai, saying, 'Beware lest anyone *touch* the young man Absalom!' Otherwise I would have dealt falsely against my own life. For there is nothing hidden from the king, and you yourself would have set yourself against *me*."

Then Joab said, "I cannot linger with you." And he took three spears in his hand and thrust them through Absalom's heart, while he was *still* alive in the midst of the terebinth tree. And ten young men who bore Joab's armor surrounded Absalom, and struck and killed him.

2 Samuel 15:1-30; 18:1-15

WORSHIP

Why do You hide Your face,
And forget our affliction and our oppression?
For our soul is bowed down to the dust;
Our body clings to the ground.
Arise for our help,
And redeem us for Your mercies' sake.

Psalm 44:24-26

WISDOM

The way of a fool *is* right in his own eyes,
But he who heeds counsel *is* wise.

Proverbs 12:15

**SW?! SO WHAT?
What does this tell me?**

DAVID'S LAST WORDS AND ACTS
2 Samuel 23:1-7; 24:1-25; Psalm 45:1-2; Proverbs 12:16

Now these *are* the last words of David.

Thus says David the son of Jesse;
Thus says the man raised up on high,
The anointed of the God of Jacob,
And the sweet psalmist of Israel:

"The Spirit of the Lord spoke by me,
And His word *was* on my tongue.
The God of Israel said,
The Rock of Israel spoke to me:
'He who rules over men *must be* just,
Ruling in the fear of God.
And *he shall be* like the light of the morning
    when the sun rises,
A morning without clouds,
Like the tender grass *springing* out of the
    earth,
By clear shining after rain.'

"Although my house *is* not so with God,
Yet He has made with me an everlasting
    covenant,
Ordered in all *things* and secure.
For *this is* all my salvation and all *my* desire;
    Will He not make *it* increase?
    But *the sons* of rebellion *shall* all *be* as
        thorns thrust away,
    Because they cannot be taken with hands.
    But the man *who* touches them
    Must be armed with iron and the shaft of
        a spear,
    And they shall be utterly burned with fire
        in *their* place."

Again the anger of the Lord was aroused against Israel, and He moved David against them to say, "Go, number Israel and Judah."

So the king said to Joab the commander of the army who *was* with him, "Now go throughout all the tribes of Israel, from Dan to Beersheba, and count the people, that I may know the number of the people."

And Joab said to the king, "Now may the Lord your God add to the people a hundred times more than there are, and may the eyes of my lord the king see *it*. But why does my lord the king desire this thing?"

Nevertheless the king's word prevailed against Joab and against the captains of the army. Therefore Joab and the captains of the army went out from the presence of the king to count the people of Israel.

And they crossed over the Jordan and camped in Aroer, on the right side of the town which *is* in the midst of the ravine of Gad, and toward Jazer. Then they came to Gilead and to the land of Tahtim Hodshi; they came to Dan Jaan and around to Sidon; and they came to the stronghold of Tyre and to all the cities of the Hivites and the Canaanites. Then they went out to South Judah *as far as* Beersheba. So when they had gone through all the land, they came to Jerusalem at the end of nine months and twenty days. Then Joab gave the sum of the number of the people to the king. And there were in Israel eight hundred thousand valiant men who drew the sword, and the men of Judah were five hundred thousand men.

And David's heart condemned him after he had numbered the people. So David said to the Lord, "I have sinned greatly in what I have done; but now, I pray, O Lord, take away the iniquity of Your servant, for I have done very foolishly."

Now when David arose in the morning, the word of the Lord came to the prophet Gad, David's seer, saying, "Go and tell David, 'Thus says the Lord: "I offer you three *things*; choose one of them for yourself, that I may do *it* to you."'" So Gad came to David and told him; and he said to him, "Shall seven years of famine come to you in your land? Or shall you flee three months before your enemies, while they pursue you? Or shall there be three days' plague in your land? Now consider and see what answer I should take back to Him who sent me."

And David said to Gad, "I am in great distress. Please let us fall into the hand of the Lord, for His mercies *are* great; but do not let me fall into the hand of man."

So the Lord sent a plague upon Israel from the morning till the appointed time. From Dan to Beersheba seventy thousand men of the people died. And when the angel stretched out His hand over Jerusalem to destroy it, the Lord relented from the destruction, and said to the angel who was destroying the people, "It is enough; now restrain your hand." And the angel of the LORD was by the threshing floor of Araunah the Jebusite.

Then David spoke to the LORD when he saw the angel who was striking the people, and said, "Surely I have sinned, and I have done wickedly; but these sheep, what have they done? Let Your hand, I pray, be against me and against my father's house."

And Gad came that day to David and said to him, "Go up, erect an altar to the LORD on the threshing floor of Araunah the Jebusite." So David, according to the word of Gad, went up as the LORD commanded. Now Araunah looked, and saw the king and his servants coming toward him. So Araunah went out and bowed before the king with his face to the ground.

Then Araunah said, "Why has my lord the king come to his servant?"

And David said, "To buy the threshing floor from you, to build an altar to the LORD, that the plague may be withdrawn from the people."

Now Araunah said to David, "Let my lord the king take and offer up whatever *seems* good to him. Look, *here are* oxen for burnt sacrifice, and threshing implements and the yokes of the oxen for wood. All these, O king, Araunah has given to the king."

And Araunah said to the king, "May the LORD your God accept you."

Then the king said to Araunah, "No, but I will surely buy *it* from you for a price; nor will I offer burnt offerings to the LORD my God with that which costs me nothing." So David bought the threshing floor and the oxen for fifty shekels of silver. And David built there an altar to the LORD, and offered burnt offerings and peace offerings. So the LORD heeded the prayers for the land, and the plague was withdrawn from Israel.

2 Samuel 23:1-7; 24:1-25

WORSHIP

My heart is overflowing with a good theme;
I recite my composition concerning the King;
My tongue *is* the pen of a ready writer.

You are fairer than the sons of men;
Grace is poured upon Your lips;
Therefore God has blessed You forever.

Psalm 45:1-2

WISDOM

A fool's wrath is known at once,
But a prudent *man* covers shame.

Proverbs 12:16

SW?! SO WHAT?
What does this tell me?

SOLOMON SUCCEEDS DAVID AS KING
1 Kings 1:1-43, 49-53; Psalm 45:3-5; Proverbs 12:17

Now King David was old, advanced in years; and they put covers on him, but he could not get warm. Therefore his servants said to him, "Let a young woman, a virgin, be sought for our lord the king, and let her stand before the king, and let her care for him; and let her lie in your bosom, that our lord the king may be warm." So they sought for a lovely young woman throughout all the territory of Israel, and found Abishag the Shunammite, and brought her to the king. The young woman *was* very lovely; and she cared for the king, and served him; but the king did not know her.

Then Adonijah the son of Haggith exalted himself, saying, "I will be king"; and he prepared for himself chariots and horsemen, and fifty men to run before him. (And his father had not rebuked him at any time by saying, "Why have you done so?" He *was* also very good-looking. *His mother* had borne him after Absalom.) Then he conferred with Joab the son of Zeruiah and with Abiathar the priest, and they followed and helped Adonijah. But Zadok the priest, Benaiah the son of Jehoiada, Nathan the prophet, Shimei, Rei, and the mighty men who *belonged* to David were not with Adonijah.

And Adonijah sacrificed sheep and oxen and fattened cattle by the stone of Zoheleth, which *is* by En Rogel; he also invited all his brothers, the king's sons, and all the men of Judah, the king's servants. But he did not invite Nathan the prophet, Benaiah, the mighty men, or Solomon his brother.

So Nathan spoke to Bathsheba the mother of Solomon, saying, "Have you not heard that Adonijah the son of Haggith has become king, and David our lord does not know *it?* Come, please, let me now give you advice, that you may save your own life and the life of your son Solomon. Go immediately to King David and say to him, 'Did you not, my lord, O king, swear to your maidservant, saying, "Assuredly your son Solomon shall reign after me, and he shall sit on my throne"? Why then has Adonijah become king?' Then, while you are still talking there with the king, I also will come in after you and confirm your words."

So Bathsheba went into the chamber to the king. (Now the king was very old, and Abishag the Shunammite was serving the king.) And Bathsheba bowed and did homage to the king. Then the king said, "What is your wish?"

Then she said to him, "My lord, you swore by the LORD your God to your maidservant, *saying,* 'Assuredly Solomon your son shall reign after me, and he shall sit on my throne.' So now, look! Adonijah has become king; and now, my lord the king, you do not know about *it*. He has sacrificed oxen and fattened cattle and sheep in abundance, and has invited all the sons of the king, Abiathar the priest, and Joab the commander of the army; but Solomon your servant he has not invited. And as for you, my lord, O king, the eyes of all Israel *are* on you, that you should tell them who will sit on the throne of my lord the king after him. Otherwise it will happen, when my lord the king rests with his fathers, that I and my son Solomon will be counted as offenders."

And just then, while she was still talking with the king, Nathan the prophet also came in. So they told the king, saying, "Here is Nathan the prophet." And when he came in before the king, he bowed down before the king with his face to the ground. And Nathan said, "My lord, O king, have you said, 'Adonijah shall reign after me, and he shall sit on my throne'? For he has gone down today, and has sacrificed oxen and fattened cattle and sheep in abundance, and has invited all the king's sons, and the commanders of the army, and Abiathar the priest; and look! They are eating and drinking before him; and they say, '*Long* live King Adonijah!' But he has not invited me—me your servant—nor Zadok the priest, nor Benaiah the son of Jehoiada, nor your servant Solomon. Has this thing been done by my lord the king, and you have not told your servant who should sit on the throne of my lord the king after him?"

Then King David answered and said, "Call Bathsheba to me." So she came into the king's presence and stood before the king. And the king took an oath and said, "*As* the LORD lives, who has redeemed my life from every distress, just as I swore to you by the LORD God of Israel, saying, 'Assuredly Solomon your son shall be king after me, and he shall sit on my throne in my place,' so I certainly will do this day."

Then Bathsheba bowed with *her* face to the earth, and paid homage to the king, and said, "Let my lord King David live forever!"

And King David said, "Call to me Zadok the priest, Nathan the prophet, and Benaiah the son of Jehoiada." So they came before the king. The king also said to them, "Take with you the servants of your lord, and have Solomon my son ride on my own mule, and take him down to Gihon. There let Zadok the priest and Nathan the prophet anoint him king over Israel; and blow the horn, and say, '*Long* live King Solomon!' Then you shall come up after him, and he shall come and sit on my throne, and he shall be king in my place. For I have appointed him to be ruler over Israel and Judah."

Benaiah the son of Jehoiada answered the king and said, "Amen! May the LORD God of my lord the king say so *too*. As the LORD has been with my lord the king, even so may He be with Solomon, and make his throne greater than the throne of my lord King David."

So Zadok the priest, Nathan the prophet, Benaiah the son of Jehoiada, the Cherethites, and the Pelethites went down and had Solomon ride on King David's mule, and took him to Gihon. Then Zadok the priest took a horn of oil from the tabernacle and anointed Solomon. And they blew the horn, and all the people said, "*Long* live King Solomon!" And all the people went up after him; and the people played the flutes and rejoiced with great joy, so that the earth *seemed to* split with their sound.

Now Adonijah and all the guests who *were* with him heard *it* as they finished eating. And when Joab heard the sound of the horn, he said, "Why *is* the city in such a noisy uproar?" While he was still speaking, there came Jonathan, the son of Abiathar the priest. And Adonijah said to him, "Come in, for you *are* a prominent man, and bring good news."

Then Jonathan answered and said to Adonijah, "No! Our lord King David has made Solomon king."

So all the guests who were with Adonijah were afraid, and arose, and each one went his way.

Now Adonijah was afraid of Solomon; so he arose, and went and took hold of the horns of the altar. And it was told Solomon, saying, "Indeed Adonijah is afraid of King Solomon; for look, he has taken hold of the horns of the altar, saying, 'Let King Solomon swear to me today that he will not put his servant to death with the sword.'"

Then Solomon said, "If he proves himself a worthy man, not one hair of him shall fall to the earth; but if wickedness is found in him, he shall die." So King Solomon sent them to bring him down from the altar. And he came and fell down before King Solomon; and Solomon said to him, "Go to your house."

1 Kings 1:1-43, 49-53

WORSHIP

Gird Your sword upon *Your* thigh, O Mighty
    One,
With Your glory and Your majesty.
And in Your majesty ride prosperously
    because of truth, humility, *and*
    righteousness;
And Your right hand shall teach You awesome
    things.
Your arrows *are* sharp in the heart of the
    King's enemies;
The peoples fall under You.

Psalm 45:3-5

WISDOM

He *who* speaks truth declares righteousness,
But a false witness, deceit.

Proverbs 12:17

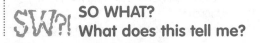

SO WHAT?
What does this tell me?

SOLOMON DEALS WITH HIS ENEMIES

1 Kings 2; Psalm 45:6-7; Proverbs 12:18

Now the days of David drew near that he should die, and he charged Solomon his son, saying: "I go the way of all the earth; be strong, therefore, and prove yourself a man. And keep the charge of the LORD your God: to walk in His ways, to keep His statutes, His commandments, His judgments, and His testimonies, as it is written in the Law of Moses, that you may prosper in all that you do and wherever you turn; that the LORD may fulfill His word which He spoke concerning me, saying, 'If your sons take heed to their way, to walk before Me in truth with all their heart and with all their soul,' He said, 'you shall not lack a man on the throne of Israel.'

"Moreover you know also what Joab the son of Zeruiah did to me, *and* what he did to the two commanders of the armies of Israel, to Abner the son of Ner and Amasa the son of Jether, whom he killed. And he shed the blood of war in peacetime, and put the blood of war on his belt that *was* around his waist, and on his sandals that *were* on his feet. Therefore do according to your wisdom, and do not let his gray hair go down to the grave in peace.

"But show kindness to the sons of Barzillai the Gileadite, and let them be among those who eat at your table, for so they came to me when I fled from Absalom your brother.

"And see, *you have* with you Shimei the son of Gera, a Benjamite from Bahurim, who cursed me with a malicious curse in the day when I went to Mahanaim. But he came down to meet me at the Jordan, and I swore to him by the LORD, saying, 'I will not put you to death with the sword.' Now therefore, do not hold him guiltless, for you *are* a wise man and know what you ought to do to him; but bring his gray hair down to the grave with blood."

So David rested with his fathers, and was buried in the City of David. The period that David reigned over Israel *was* forty years; seven years he reigned in Hebron, and in Jerusalem he reigned thirty-three years. Then Solomon sat on the throne of his father David; and his kingdom was firmly established.

Now Adonijah the son of Haggith came to Bathsheba the mother of Solomon. So she said, "Do you come peaceably?"

And he said, "Peaceably." Moreover he said, "I have something *to say* to you."

And she said, "Say it."

Then he said, "You know that the kingdom was mine, and all Israel had set their expectations on me, that I should reign. However, the kingdom has been turned over, and has become my brother's; for it was his from the LORD. Now I ask one petition of you; do not deny me."

And she said to him, "Say it."

Then he said, "Please speak to King Solomon, for he will not refuse you, that he may give me Abishag the Shunammite as wife."

So Bathsheba said, "Very well, I will speak for you to the king."

Bathsheba therefore went to King Solomon, to speak to him for Adonijah. And the king rose up to meet her and bowed down to her, and sat down on his throne and had a throne set for the king's mother; so she sat at his right hand. Then she said, "I desire one small petition of you; do not refuse me."

And the king said to her, "Ask it, my mother, for I will not refuse you."

So she said, "Let Abishag the Shunammite be given to Adonijah your brother as wife."

And King Solomon answered and said to his mother, "Now why do you ask Abishag the Shunammite for Adonijah? Ask for him the kingdom also—for he *is* my older brother—for him, and for Abiathar the priest, and for Joab the son of Zeruiah." Then King Solomon swore by the LORD, saying, "May God do so to me, and more also, if Adonijah has not spoken this word against his own life! Now therefore, *as* the LORD lives, who has confirmed me and set me on the throne of David my father, and who has established a house for me, as He promised, Adonijah shall be put to death today!"

So King Solomon sent by the hand of Benaiah the son of Jehoiada; and he struck him down, and he died.

And to Abiathar the priest the king said, "Go to Anathoth, to your own fields, for you *are* deserving of death; but I will not put you to death at this time, because you carried the ark of the Lord God before my father David, and because you were afflicted every time my father was afflicted." So Solomon removed Abiathar from being priest to the LORD, that he might fulfill the word of the LORD which He spoke concerning the house of Eli at Shiloh.

Then news came to Joab, for Joab had defected to Adonijah, though he had not defected to Absalom. So Joab fled to the tabernacle of the LORD, and took hold of the horns of the altar. And King Solomon was told, "Joab has fled to the tabernacle of the LORD; there *he is,* by the altar." Then Solomon sent Benaiah the son of Jehoiada, saying, "Go, strike him down." So Benaiah went to the tabernacle of the LORD, and said to him, "Thus says the king, 'Come out!' "

And he said, "No, but I will die here." And Benaiah brought back word to the king, saying, "Thus said Joab, and thus he answered me."

Then the king said to him, "Do as he has said, and strike him down and bury him, that you may take away from me and from the house of my father the innocent blood which Joab shed. So the LORD will return his blood on his head, because he struck down two men more righteous and better than he, and killed them with the sword—Abner the son of Ner, the commander of the army of Israel, and Amasa the son of Jether, the commander of the army of Judah—though my father David did not know *it.* Their blood shall therefore return upon the head of Joab and upon the head of his descendants forever. But upon David and his descendants, upon his house and his throne, there shall be peace forever from the LORD."

So Benaiah the son of Jehoiada went up and struck and killed him; and he was buried in his own house in the wilderness. The king put Benaiah the son of Jehoiada in his place over the army, and the king put Zadok the priest in the place of Abiathar.

Then the king sent and called for Shimei, and said to him, "Build yourself a house in Jerusalem and dwell there, and do not go out from there anywhere. For it shall be, on the day you go out and cross the Brook Kidron, know for certain you shall surely die; your blood shall be on your own head."

And Shimei said to the king, "The saying *is* good. As my lord the king has said, so your servant will do." So Shimei dwelt in Jerusalem many days.

Now it happened at the end of three years, that two slaves of Shimei ran away to Achish the son of Maachah, king of Gath. And they told Shimei,

saying, "Look, your slaves *are* in Gath!" So Shimei arose, saddled his donkey, and went to Achish at Gath to seek his slaves. And Shimei went and brought his slaves from Gath. And Solomon was told that Shimei had gone from Jerusalem to Gath and had come back. Then the king sent and called for Shimei, and said to him, "Did I not make you swear by the LORD, and warn you, saying, 'Know for certain that on the day you go out and travel anywhere, you shall surely die'? And you said to me, 'The word I have heard *is* good.' Why then have you not kept the oath of the LORD and the commandment that I gave you?" The king said moreover to Shimei, "You know, as your heart acknowledges, all the wickedness that you did to my father David; therefore the LORD will return your wickedness on your own head. But King Solomon *shall be* blessed, and the throne of David shall be established before the LORD forever."

So the king commanded Benaiah the son of Jehoiada; and he went out and struck him down, and he died. Thus the kingdom was established in the hand of Solomon.

1 Kings 2

WORSHIP

Your throne, O God, *is* forever and ever;
A scepter of righteousness *is* the scepter of
   Your kingdom.
You love righteousness and hate wickedness;
Therefore God, Your God, has anointed You
With the oil of gladness more than Your
   companions.

Psalm 45:6-7

WISDOM

There is one who speaks like the piercings of a
   sword,
But the tongue of the wise *promotes* health.

Proverbs 12:18

 SO WHAT?
What does this tell me?

SOLOMON'S WISDOM AND BLESSING
1 Kings 3:1-28; 4:21-34;
Psalm 46:4-7; Proverbs 12:19

Now Solomon made a treaty with Pharaoh king of Egypt, and married Pharaoh's daughter; then he brought her to the City of David until he had finished building his own house, and the house of the LORD, and the wall all around Jerusalem. Meanwhile the people sacrificed at the high places, because there was no house built for the name of the LORD until those days. And Solomon loved the LORD, walking in the statutes of his father David, except that he sacrificed and burned incense at the high places.

Now the king went to Gibeon to sacrifice there, for that *was* the great high place: Solomon offered a thousand burnt offerings on that altar. At Gibeon the LORD appeared to Solomon in a dream by night; and God said, "Ask! What shall I give you?"

And Solomon said: "You have shown great mercy to Your servant David my father, because he walked before You in truth, in righteousness, and in uprightness of heart with You; You have continued this great kindness for him, and You have given him a son to sit on his throne, as *it is* this day. Now, O LORD my God, You have made Your servant king instead of my father David, but I *am* a little child; I do not know *how* to go out or come in. And Your servant *is* in the midst of Your people whom You have chosen, a great people, too numerous to be numbered or counted. Therefore give to Your servant an understanding heart to judge Your people, that I may discern between good and evil. For who is able to judge this great people of Yours?"

The speech pleased the LORD, that Solomon had asked this thing. Then God said to him: "Because you have asked this thing, and have not asked long life for yourself, nor have asked riches for yourself, nor have asked the life of your enemies, but have asked for yourself understanding to discern justice, behold, I have done according to your words; see, I have given you a wise and understanding heart, so that there has not been anyone like you before you, nor shall any like you arise after you. And I have also given you what you have not asked: both riches and honor, so that there

shall not be anyone like you among the kings all your days. So if you walk in My ways, to keep My statutes and My commandments, as your father David walked, then I will lengthen your days."

Then Solomon awoke; and indeed it had been a dream. And he came to Jerusalem and stood before the ark of the covenant of the LORD, offered up burnt offerings, offered peace offerings, and made a feast for all his servants.

Now two women *who were* harlots came to the king, and stood before him. And one woman said, "O my lord, this woman and I dwell in the same house; and I gave birth while she *was* in the house. Then it happened, the third day after I had given birth, that this woman also gave birth. And we *were* together; no one *was* with us in the house, except the two of us in the house. And this woman's son died in the night, because she lay on him. So she arose in the middle of the night and took my son from my side, while your maidservant slept, and laid him in her bosom, and laid her dead child in my bosom. And when I rose in the morning to nurse my son, there he was, dead. But when I had examined him in the morning, indeed, he was not my son whom I had borne."

Then the other woman said, "No! But the living one *is* my son, and the dead one *is* your son."

And the first woman said, "No! But the dead one *is* your son, and the living one *is* my son."

Thus they spoke before the king.

And the king said, "The one says, 'This *is* my son, who lives, and your son *is* the dead one'; and the other says, 'No! But your son *is* the dead one, and my son *is* the living one.' " Then the king said, "Bring me a sword." So they brought a sword before the king. And the king said, "Divide the living child in two, and give half to one, and half to the other."

Then the woman whose son *was* living spoke to the king, for she yearned with compassion for her son; and she said, "O my lord, give her the living child, and by no means kill him!"

But the other said, "Let him be neither mine nor yours, *but* divide *him*."

So the king answered and said, "Give the first woman the living child, and by no means kill him; she *is* his mother."

And all Israel heard of the judgment which the king had rendered; and they feared the king, for they saw that the wisdom of God *was* in him to administer justice.

So Solomon reigned over all kingdoms from the River *to* the land of the Philistines, as far as the border of Egypt. *They* brought tribute and served Solomon all the days of his life.

Now Solomon's provision for one day was thirty kors of fine flour, sixty kors of meal, ten fatted oxen, twenty oxen from the pastures, and one hundred sheep, besides deer, gazelles, roebucks, and fatted fowl.

For he had dominion over all *the region* on this side of the River from Tiphsah even to Gaza, namely over all the kings on this side of the River; and he had peace on every side all around him. And Judah and Israel dwelt safely, each man under his vine and his fig tree, from Dan as far as Beersheba, all the days of Solomon.

Solomon had forty thousand stalls of horses for his chariots, and twelve thousand horsemen. And these governors, each man in his month, provided food for King Solomon and for all who came to King Solomon's table. There was no lack in their supply. They also brought barley and straw to the proper place, for the horses and steeds, each man according to his charge.

And God gave Solomon wisdom and exceedingly great understanding, and largeness of heart like the sand on the seashore. Thus Solomon's wisdom excelled the wisdom of all the men of the East and all the wisdom of Egypt. For he was wiser than all men—than Ethan the Ezrahite, and Heman, Chalcol, and Darda, the sons of Mahol; and his fame was in all the surrounding nations. He spoke three thousand proverbs, and his songs were one thousand and five. Also he spoke of trees, from the cedar tree of Lebanon even to the hyssop that springs out of the wall; he spoke also of animals, of birds, of creeping things, and of fish. And men of all nations, from all the kings of the earth who had heard of his wisdom, came to hear the wisdom of Solomon.

1 Kings 3:1-28; 4:21-34

WORSHIP

There is a river whose streams shall make glad the city of God,
The holy *place* of the tabernacle of the Most High.
God *is* in the midst of her, she shall not be moved;
God shall help her, just at the break of dawn.
The nations raged, the kingdoms were moved;
He uttered His voice, the earth melted.

The LORD of hosts *is* with us;
The God of Jacob *is* our refuge.   Selah
Psalm 46:4-7

WISDOM

The truthful lip shall be established forever,
But a lying tongue *is* but for a moment.
Proverbs 12:19

SW?! **SO WHAT?**
What does this tell me?

SOLOMON'S LOVE AND MARRIAGE

Song of Songs 1:1–2:3; 4:1–5:1; Psalm 46:8-10; Proverbs 12:20

The song of songs, which *is* Solomon's.

THE SHULAMITE

Let him kiss me with the kisses of his mouth—
For your love *is* better than wine.
Because of the fragrance of your good
    ointments,
Your name *is* ointment poured forth;
Therefore the virgins love you.
Draw me away!

THE DAUGHTERS OF JERUSALEM

We will run after you.

THE SHULAMITE

The king has brought me into his chambers.

THE DAUGHTERS OF JERUSALEM

We will be glad and rejoice in you.

We will remember your love more than wine.

THE SHULAMITE

Rightly do they love you.

I *am* dark, but lovely,
O daughters of Jerusalem,
Like the tents of Kedar,
Like the curtains of Solomon.
Do not look upon me, because I *am* dark,
Because the sun has tanned me.
My mother's sons were angry with me;
They made me the keeper of the vineyards,
But my own vineyard I have not kept.

(TO HER BELOVED)

Tell me, O you whom I love,
Where you feed *your flock*,
Where you make *it* rest at noon.
For why should I be as one who veils herself
By the flocks of your companions?

THE BELOVED

If you do not know, O fairest among women,
Follow in the footsteps of the flock,
And feed your little goats
Beside the shepherds' tents.
I have compared you, my love,
To my filly among Pharaoh's chariots.
Your cheeks are lovely with ornaments,
Your neck with chains *of gold*.

THE DAUGHTERS OF JERUSALEM

We will make you ornaments of gold
With studs of silver.

THE SHULAMITE

While the king *is* at his table,
My spikenard sends forth its fragrance.
A bundle of myrrh *is* my beloved to me,
That lies all night between my breasts.
My beloved *is* to me a cluster of henna *blooms*
In the vineyards of En Gedi.

THE BELOVED

Behold, you *are* fair, my love!
Behold, you *are* fair!
You *have* dove's eyes.

THE SHULAMITE

Behold, you *are* handsome, my beloved!
Yes, pleasant!
Also our bed *is* green.
The beams of our houses *are* cedar,
And our rafters of fir.
I *am* the rose of Sharon,
And the lily of the valleys.

THE BELOVED

Like a lily among thorns,
So is my love among the daughters.

THE SHULAMITE

Like an apple tree among the trees of the
    woods,
So *is* my beloved among the sons.
I sat down in his shade with great delight,
And his fruit *was* sweet to my taste.

THE BELOVED

Behold, you *are* fair, my love!
Behold, you *are* fair!
You *have* dove's eyes behind your veil.
Your hair *is* like a flock of goats,
Going down from Mount Gilead.
Your teeth *are* like a flock of shorn *sheep*
Which have come up from the washing,
Every one of which bears twins,
And none *is* barren among them.
Your lips *are* like a strand of scarlet,
And your mouth is lovely.
Your temples behind your veil

Are like a piece of pomegranate.
Your neck *is* like the tower of David,
Built for an armory,
On which hang a thousand bucklers,
All shields of mighty men.
Your two breasts *are* like two fawns,
Twins of a gazelle,
Which feed among the lilies.

Until the day breaks
And the shadows flee away,
I will go my way to the mountain of myrrh
And to the hill of frankincense.

You *are* all fair, my love,
And *there is* no spot in you.
Come with me from Lebanon, *my* spouse,
With me from Lebanon.
Look from the top of Amana,
From the top of Senir and Hermon,
From the lions' dens,
From the mountains of the leopards.

You have ravished my heart,
My sister, *my* spouse;
You have ravished my heart
With one *look* of your eyes,
With one link of your necklace.
How fair is your love,
My sister, *my* spouse!
How much better than wine is your love,
And the scent of your perfumes
Than all spices!
Your lips, O *my* spouse,
Drip as the honeycomb;
Honey and milk *are* under your tongue;
And the fragrance of your garments
Is like the fragrance of Lebanon.

A garden enclosed
Is my sister, *my* spouse,
A spring shut up,
A fountain sealed.
Your plants *are* an orchard of pomegranates
With pleasant fruits,
Fragrant henna with spikenard,
Spikenard and saffron,
Calamus and cinnamon,
With all trees of frankincense,
Myrrh and aloes,
With all the chief spices—
A fountain of gardens,
A well of living waters,
And streams from Lebanon.

THE SHULAMITE

Awake, O north *wind,*
And come, O south!
Blow upon my garden,
That its spices may flow out.
Let my beloved come to his garden
And eat its pleasant fruits.

THE BELOVED

I have come to my garden, my sister, *my*
    spouse;
I have gathered my myrrh with my spice;
I have eaten my honeycomb with my honey;
I have drunk my wine with my milk.

(TO HIS FRIENDS)

Eat, O friends!
Drink, yes, drink deeply,
O beloved ones!
Song of Songs 1:1–2:3; 4:1–5:1

WORSHIP

Come, behold the works of the LORD,
Who has made desolations in the earth.
He makes wars cease to the end of the earth;
He breaks the bow and cuts the spear in two;
He burns the chariot in the fire.

Be still, and know that I *am* God;
I will be exalted among the nations,
I will be exalted in the earth!
Psalm 46:8-10

WISDOM

Deceit is in the heart of those who devise evil,
But counselors of peace have joy.
Proverbs 12:20

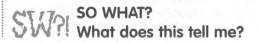

SO WHAT?
What does this tell me?

SOLOMON AND THE SHULAMITE

Song of Songs 5:9–6:13; 7:10-13;
Psalm 47:6-8; Proverbs 12:21

THE DAUGHTERS OF JERUSALEM

What *is* your beloved
More than *another* beloved,
O fairest among women?
What *is* your beloved
More than *another* beloved,
That you so charge us?

THE SHULAMITE

My beloved *is* white and ruddy,
Chief among ten thousand.
His head *is like* the finest gold;
His locks *are* wavy,
And black as a raven.
His eyes *are* like doves
By the rivers of waters,
Washed with milk,
And fitly set.
His cheeks *are* like a bed of spices,
Banks of scented herbs.
His lips *are* lilies,
Dripping liquid myrrh.

His hands *are* rods of gold
  Set with beryl.
  His body *is* carved ivory
  Inlaid *with* sapphires.
  His legs *are* pillars of marble
  Set on bases of fine gold.
  His countenance *is* like Lebanon,
  Excellent as the cedars.
  His mouth *is* most sweet,
  Yes, he *is* altogether lovely.
  This *is* my beloved,
  And this *is* my friend,
  O daughters of Jerusalem!

THE DAUGHTERS OF JERUSALEM

Where has your beloved gone,
O fairest among women?
Where has your beloved turned aside,
That we may seek him with you?

THE SHULAMITE

My beloved has gone to his garden,
To the beds of spices,
To feed *his flock* in the gardens,
And to gather lilies.
I *am* my beloved's,

And my beloved *is* mine.
He feeds *his flock* among the lilies.

THE BELOVED

O my love, you *are as* beautiful as Tirzah,
Lovely as Jerusalem,
Awesome as *an army* with banners!
Turn your eyes away from me,
For they have overcome me.
Your hair *is* like a flock of goats
Going down from Gilead.
Your teeth *are* like a flock of sheep
Which have come up from the washing;
Every one bears twins,
And none *is* barren among them.
Like a piece of pomegranate
Are your temples behind your veil.

There are sixty queens
And eighty concubines,
And virgins without number.
My dove, my perfect one,
Is the only one,
The only one of her mother,
The favorite of the one who bore her.
The daughters saw her
And called her blessed,
The queens and the concubines,
And they praised her.

Who is she who looks forth as the morning,
Fair as the moon,
Clear as the sun,
Awesome as *an army* with banners?

THE SHULAMITE

I went down to the garden of nuts
To see the verdure of the valley,
To see whether the vine had budded
And the pomegranates had bloomed.
Before I was even aware,
My soul had made me
As the chariots of my noble people.

THE BELOVED AND HIS FRIENDS

Return, return, O Shulamite;
Return, return, that we may look upon you!

THE SHULAMITE

What would you see in the Shulamite—
As it were, the dance of the two camps?

THE SHULAMITE

I *am* my beloved's,
And his desire *is* toward me.

Come, my beloved,
Let us go forth to the field;
Let us lodge in the villages.
Let us get up early to the vineyards;
Let us see if the vine has budded,
Whether the grape blossoms are open,
And the pomegranates are in bloom.
There I will give you my love.
The mandrakes give off a fragrance,
And at our gates *are* pleasant *fruits,*
All manner, new and old,
Which I have laid up for you, my beloved.

Song of Songs 5:9–6:13; 7:10-13

WORSHIP

Sing praises to God, sing praises!
Sing praises to our King, sing praises!
For God *is* the King of all the earth;
Sing praises with understanding.

God reigns over the nations;
God sits on His holy throne.

Psalm 47:6-8

WISDOM

No grave trouble will overtake the righteous,
But the wicked shall be filled with evil.

Proverbs 12:21

SW?! SO WHAT?
What does this tell me?

SOLOMON'S TEMPLE AND HOUSE

1 Kings 6:1–7:8; Psalm 48:1–3; Proverbs 12:22

And it came to pass in the four hundred and eightieth year after the children of Israel had come out of the land of Egypt, in the fourth year of Solomon's reign over Israel, in the month of Ziv, which *is* the second month, that he began to build the house of the LORD. Now the house which King Solomon built for the LORD, its length *was* sixty cubits, its width twenty, and its height thirty cubits. The vestibule in front of the sanctuary of the house *was* twenty cubits long across the width of the house, *and* the width of *the vestible extended* ten cubits from the front of the house. And he made for the house windows with beveled frames.

Against the wall of the temple he built chambers all around, *against* the walls of the temple, all around the sanctuary and the inner sanctuary. Thus he made side chambers all around it. The lowest chamber *was* five cubits wide, the middle *was* six cubits wide, and the third *was* seven cubits wide; for he made narrow ledges around the outside of the temple, so that *the support beams* would not be fastened into the walls of the temple. And the temple, when it was being built, was built with stone finished at the quarry, so that no hammer or chisel *or* any iron tool was heard in the temple while it was being built. The doorway for the middle story *was* on the right side of the temple. They went up by stairs to the middle *story,* and from the middle to the third.

So he built the temple and finished it, and he paneled the temple with beams and boards of cedar. And he built side chambers against the entire temple, each five cubits high; they were attached to the temple with cedar beams.

Then the word of the LORD came to Solomon, saying: "*Concerning* this temple which you are building, if you walk in My statutes, execute My judgments, keep all My commandments, and walk in them, then I will perform My word with you, which I spoke to your father David. And I will dwell among the children of Israel, and will not forsake My people Israel."

So Solomon built the temple and finished it. And he built the inside walls of the temple with cedar boards; from the floor of the temple to the ceiling he paneled the inside with wood; and he covered the floor of the temple with planks of cypress. Then he built the twenty-cubit room at the rear of the temple, from floor to ceiling, with cedar boards; he built *it* inside as the inner sanctuary, as the Most Holy *Place.* And in front of it the temple sanctuary was forty cubits *long.* The inside of the temple was cedar, carved with ornamental buds and open flowers. All *was* cedar; there was no stone *to be* seen.

And he prepared the inner sanctuary inside the temple, to set the ark of the covenant of the LORD there. The inner sanctuary *was* twenty cubits long, twenty cubits wide, and twenty cubits high. He overlaid it with pure gold, and overlaid the altar of cedar. So Solomon overlaid the inside of the temple with pure gold. He stretched gold chains across the front of the inner sanctuary, and overlaid it with gold. The whole temple he overlaid with gold, until he had finished all the temple; also he overlaid with gold the entire altar that *was* by the inner sanctuary.

Inside the inner sanctuary he made two cherubim *of* olive wood, *each* ten cubits high. One wing of the cherub *was* five cubits, and the other wing of the cherub five cubits: ten cubits from the tip of one wing to the tip of the other. And the other cherub *was* ten cubits; both cherubim *were* of the same size and shape. The height of one cherub *was* ten cubits, and so *was* the other cherub. Then he set the cherubim inside the inner room; and they stretched out the wings of the cherubim so that the wing of the one touched *one* wall, and the wing of the other cherub touched the other wall. And their wings touched each other in the middle of the room. Also he overlaid the cherubim with gold.

Then he carved all the walls of the temple all around, both the inner and outer *sanctuaries,* with carved figures of cherubim, palm trees, and open flowers. And the floor of the temple he overlaid with gold, both the inner and outer *sanctuaries.*

For the entrance of the inner sanctuary he made doors *of* olive wood; the lintel *and* doorposts *were* one-fifth *of the wall.* The two doors *were of* olive wood; and he carved on them figures of cherubim, palm trees, and open flowers, and overlaid *them* with gold; and he spread gold on the cherubim and on the palm trees. So for the door of the sanctuary he also made doorposts *of* olive wood, one-fourth *of the wall.* And the two doors *were of* cypress wood; two panels *comprised* one folding door, and two panels *comprised* the other folding door. Then he carved cherubim, palm trees, and open flowers *on them,* and overlaid *them* with gold applied evenly on the carved work.

And he built the inner court with three rows of hewn stone and a row of cedar beams.

In the fourth year the foundation of the house of the LORD was laid, in the month of Ziv. And in the eleventh year, in the month of Bul, which is the eighth month, the house was finished in all its details and according to all its plans. So he was seven years in building it.

But Solomon took thirteen years to build his own house; so he finished all his house.

He also built the House of the Forest of Lebanon; its length *was* one hundred cubits, its width fifty cubits, and its height thirty cubits, with four rows of cedar pillars, and cedar beams on the pillars. And *it was* paneled with cedar above the beams that *were* on forty-five pillars, fifteen *to a* row. *There were* windows *with beveled frames in* three rows, and window *was* opposite window *in* three tiers. And all the doorways and doorposts *had* rectangular frames; and window *was* opposite window *in* three tiers.

He also made the Hall of Pillars: its length *was* fifty cubits, and its width thirty cubits; and in front of them *was* a portico with pillars, and a canopy *was* in front of them.

Then he made a hall for the throne, the Hall of Judgment, where he might judge; and *it was* paneled with cedar from floor to ceiling.

And the house where he dwelt *had* another court inside the hall, of like workmanship. Solomon also made a house like this hall for Pharaoh's daughter, whom he had taken *as wife.*

1 Kings 6:1–7:8

WORSHIP

Great *is* the LORD, and greatly to be praised
In the city of our God,
In His holy mountain.
Beautiful in elevation,
The joy of the whole earth,
Is Mount Zion *on* the sides of the north,
The city of the great King.
God *is* in her palaces;
He is known as her refuge.

Psalm 48:1-3

WISDOM

Lying lips *are* an abomination to the LORD,
But those who deal truthfully *are* His delight.

Proverbs 12:22

SW?! **SO WHAT?**
What does this tell me?

DEDICATION OF GOD'S HOUSE

1 Kings 8:1-40, 54-56, 63; Psalm 48:12-14; Proverbs 12:23

Now Solomon assembled the elders of Israel and all the heads of the tribes, the chief fathers of the children of Israel, to King Solomon in Jerusalem, that they might bring up the ark of the covenant of the LORD from the City of David, which *is* Zion. Therefore all the men of Israel assembled with King Solomon at the feast in the month of Ethanim, which *is* the seventh month. So all the elders of Israel came, and the priests took up the ark. Then they brought up the ark of the LORD, the tabernacle of meeting, and all the holy furnishings that *were* in the tabernacle. The priests and the Levites brought them up. Also King Solomon, and all the congregation of Israel who were assembled with him, *were* with him before the ark, sacrificing sheep and oxen that could not be counted or numbered for multitude. Then the priests brought in the ark of the covenant of the LORD to its place, into the inner sanctuary of the temple, to the Most Holy *Place,* under the wings of the cherubim. For the cherubim spread *their* two wings over the place of the ark, and the cherubim overshadowed the ark and its poles. The poles extended so that the ends of the poles could be seen from the holy *place,* in front of the inner sanctuary; but they could not be seen from outside. And they are there to this day. Nothing *was* in the ark except the two tablets of stone which Moses put there at Horeb, when the LORD made *a covenant* with the children of Israel, when they came out of the land of Egypt.

And it came to pass, when the priests came out of the holy *place,* that the cloud filled the house of the LORD, so that the priests could not continue ministering because of the cloud; for the glory of the LORD filled the house of the LORD.

Then Solomon spoke:

"The LORD said He would dwell in the dark cloud.
I have surely built You an exalted house,
And a place for You to dwell in forever."

Then the king turned around and blessed the whole assembly of Israel, while all the assembly of Israel was standing. And he said: "Blessed *be* the LORD God of Israel, who spoke with His mouth to my father David, and with His hand has fulfilled *it,* saying, 'Since the day that I brought My people Israel out of Egypt, I have chosen no city from any tribe of Israel *in which* to build a house, that My name might be there; but I chose David to be over My people Israel.' Now it was in the heart of my father David to build a temple for the name of the LORD God of Israel. But the LORD said to my father David, 'Whereas it was in your heart to build a temple for My name, you did well that it was in your heart. Nevertheless you shall not build the temple, but your son who will come from your body, he shall build the temple for My name.' So the LORD has fulfilled His word which He spoke; and I have filled the position of my father David, and sit on the throne of Israel, as the LORD promised; and I have built a temple for the name of the LORD God of Israel. And there I have made a place for the ark, in which *is* the covenant of the LORD which He made with our fathers, when He brought them out of the land of Egypt."

Then Solomon stood before the altar of the LORD in the presence of all the assembly of Israel, and spread out his hands toward heaven; and he said: "LORD God of Israel, *there is* no God in heaven above or on earth below like You, who keep *Your* covenant and mercy with Your servants who walk before You with all their hearts. You have kept what You promised Your servant David my father; You have both spoken with Your mouth and fulfilled *it* with Your hand, as *it is* this day. Therefore, LORD God of Israel, now keep what You promised Your servant David my father, saying, 'You shall not fail to have a man sit before Me on the throne of Israel, only if your sons take heed to their way, that they walk before Me as you have walked before Me.' And now I pray, O God of Israel, let Your word come true, which You have spoken to Your servant David my father.

"But will God indeed dwell on the earth? Behold, heaven and the heaven of heavens cannot contain You. How much less this temple which I have built! Yet regard the prayer of Your servant and his supplication, O LORD my God, and listen to the cry and the prayer which Your servant is praying before You today: that Your eyes may be open toward this temple night and day, toward the place of which You said, 'My name shall be there,' that You may hear the prayer which Your servant makes toward this place. And may You hear the supplication of Your servant and of Your people Israel, when they pray toward this place. Hear in heaven Your dwelling place; and when You hear, forgive.

"When anyone sins against his neighbor, and is forced to take an oath, and comes *and* takes an oath before Your altar in this temple, then hear in heaven, and act, and judge Your servants, condemning the wicked, bringing his way on his head, and justifying the righteous by giving him according to his righteousness.

"When Your people Israel are defeated before an enemy because they have sinned against You, and when they turn back to You and confess Your name, and pray and make supplication to You in this temple, then hear in heaven, and forgive the sin of Your people Israel, and bring them back to the land which You gave to their fathers.

"When the heavens are shut up and there is no rain because they have sinned against You, when they pray toward this place and confess Your name, and turn from their sin because You afflict them, then hear in heaven, and forgive the sin of Your servants, Your people Israel, that You may teach them the good way in which they should walk; and send rain on Your land which You have given to Your people as an inheritance.

"When there is famine in the land, pestilence *or* blight *or* mildew, locusts *or* grasshoppers; when their enemy besieges them in the land of their cities; whatever plague or whatever sickness *there is;* whatever prayer, whatever supplication is made by anyone, *or* by all Your people Israel, when each one knows the plague of his own heart, and spreads out his hands toward this temple: then hear in heaven Your dwelling place, and forgive, and act, and give to everyone according to all his ways, whose heart You know (for You alone know the hearts of all the sons of men), that they may fear You all the days that they live in the land which You gave to our fathers."

And so it was, when Solomon had finished praying all this prayer and supplication to the LORD, that he arose from before the altar of the LORD, from kneeling on his knees with his hands spread up to heaven. Then he stood and blessed all the assembly of Israel with a loud voice, saying: "Blessed *be* the LORD, who has given rest to His people Israel, according to all that He promised. There has not

failed one word of all His good promise, which He promised through His servant Moses."

And Solomon offered a sacrifice of peace offerings, which he offered to the LORD, twenty-two thousand bulls and one hundred and twenty thousand sheep. So the king and all the children of Israel dedicated the house of the LORD.

1 Kings 8:1-40, 54-56, 63

WORSHIP

Walk about Zion,
And go all around her.
Count her towers;
Mark well her bulwarks;
Consider her palaces;
That you may tell *it* to the generation following.
For this *is* God,
Our God forever and ever;
He will be our guide
Even to death.

Psalm 48:12-14

WISDOM

A prudent man conceals knowledge,
But the heart of fools proclaims foolishness.

Proverbs 12:23

SO WHAT?
What does this tell me?

SOLOMON'S WISDOM, WEALTH AND WIVES

1 Kings 10:1–11:13; Psalm 49:7–9; Proverbs 12:24

Now when the queen of Sheba heard of the fame of Solomon concerning the name of the LORD, she came to test him with hard questions. She came to Jerusalem with a very great retinue, with camels that bore spices, very much gold, and precious stones; and when she came to Solomon, she spoke with him about all that was in her heart. So Solomon answered all her questions; there was nothing so difficult for the king that he could not explain *it* to her. And when the queen of Sheba had seen all the wisdom of Solomon, the house that he had built, the food on his table, the seating of his servants, the service of his waiters and their apparel, his cupbearers, and his entryway by which he went up to the house of the LORD, there was no more spirit in her. Then she said to the king: "It was a true report which I heard in my own land about your words and your wisdom. However I did not believe the words until I came and saw with my own eyes; and indeed the half was not told me. Your wisdom and prosperity exceed the fame of which I heard. Happy *are* your men and happy *are* these your servants, who stand continually before you *and* hear your wisdom! Blessed be the LORD your God, who delighted in you, setting you on the throne of Israel! Because the LORD has loved Israel forever, therefore He made you king, to do justice and righteousness."

Then she gave the king one hundred and twenty talents of gold, spices in great quantity, and precious stones. There never again came such abundance of spices as the queen of Sheba gave to King Solomon. Also, the ships of Hiram, which brought gold from Ophir, brought great *quantities* of almug wood and precious stones from Ophir. And the king made steps of the almug wood for the house of the LORD and for the king's house, also harps and stringed instruments for singers. There never again came such almug wood, nor has the like been seen to this day.

Now King Solomon gave the queen of Sheba all she desired, whatever she asked, besides what Solomon had given her according to the royal generosity. So she turned and went to her own country, she and her servants.

The weight of gold that came to Solomon yearly was six hundred and sixty-six talents of gold, besides *that* from the traveling merchants, from income of traders, from all the kings of Arabia, and from the governors of the country.

And King Solomon made two hundred large shields *of* hammered gold; six hundred *shekels* of gold went into each shield. He also *made* three hundred shields *of* hammered gold; three minas of gold went into each shield. The king put them in the House of the Forest of Lebanon.

Moreover the king made a great throne of ivory, and overlaid it with pure gold. The throne had six steps, and the top of the throne *was* round at the back; *there were* armrests on either side of the place of the seat, and two lions stood beside the armrests. Twelve lions stood there, one on each side of the six steps; nothing like *this* had been made for any *other* kingdom.

All King Solomon's drinking vessels *were* gold, and all the vessels of the House of the Forest of Lebanon *were* pure gold. Not *one was* silver, for this was accounted as nothing in the days of Solomon. For the king had merchant ships at sea with the fleet of Hiram. Once every three years the merchant ships came bringing gold, silver, ivory, apes, and monkeys. So King Solomon surpassed all the kings of the earth in riches and wisdom.

Now all the earth sought the presence of Solomon to hear his wisdom, which God had put in his heart. Each man brought his present: articles of silver and gold, garments, armor, spices, horses, and mules, at a set rate year by year.

And Solomon gathered chariots and horsemen; he had one thousand four hundred chariots and twelve thousand horsemen, whom he stationed in the chariot cities and with the king in Jerusalem. The king made silver *as common* in Jerusalem as stones, and he made cedar trees as abundant as the sycamores which *are* in the lowland.

Also Solomon had horses imported from Egypt and Keveh; the king's merchants bought them in Keveh at the *current* price. Now a chariot that was imported from Egypt cost six hundred *shekels* of silver, and a horse one hundred and fifty; and thus, through their agents, they exported *them* to all the kings of the Hittites and the kings of Syria.

But King Solomon loved many foreign women, as well as the daughter of Pharaoh: women of the Moabites, Ammonites, Edomites, Sidonians, *and* Hittites— from the nations of whom the LORD had said to the children of Israel, "You shall not intermarry with them, nor they with you. Surely they will turn away your hearts after their gods." Solomon clung to these in love. And he had seven hundred wives, princesses, and three hundred concubines; and his wives turned away his heart. For it was so, when Solomon was old, that his wives turned his heart after other gods; and his heart was not loyal to the LORD his God, as *was* the heart of his father David. For Solomon went after Ashtoreth the goddess of the Sidonians, and after Milcom the abomination of the Ammonites. Solomon did evil in the sight of the LORD, and did not fully follow the LORD, as *did* his father David. Then Solomon built a high place for Chemosh the abomination of Moab, on the hill that *is* east of Jerusalem, and for Molech the abomination of the people of Ammon. And he did likewise for all his foreign wives, who burned incense and sacrificed to their gods.

So the LORD became angry with Solomon, because his heart had turned from the LORD God of Israel, who had appeared to him twice, and had commanded him concerning this thing, that he should not go after other gods; but he did not keep what the LORD had commanded. Therefore the LORD said to Solomon, "Because you have done this, and have not kept My covenant and My statutes, which I have commanded you, I will surely tear the kingdom away from you and give it to your servant. Nevertheless I will not do it in your days, for the sake of your father David; I will tear it out of the hand of your son. However I will not tear away the whole kingdom; I will give one tribe to your son for the sake of my servant David, and for the sake of Jerusalem which I have chosen."

1 Kings 10:1–11:13

WoRSHiP

None *of them* can by any means redeem *his* brother,
Nor give to God a ransom for him—
For the redemption of their souls *is* costly,
And it shall cease forever—
That he should continue to live eternally,
And not see the Pit.

Psalm 49:7-9

WiSDoM

The hand of the diligent will rule,
But the lazy *man* will be put to forced labor.

Proverbs 12:24

SW?! SO WHAT?
What does this tell me?

SOLOMON'S PHILOSOPHY OF LIFE

Ecclesiastes 1:1–2:26; Psalm 49:13-15; Proverbs 12:25

The words of the Preacher, the son of David, king in Jerusalem.

"Vanity of vanities," says the Preacher;
"Vanity of vanities, all *is* vanity."

What profit has a man from all his labor
In which he toils under the sun?
One generation passes away, and *another*
    generation comes;
But the earth abides forever.
The sun also rises, and the sun goes down,
And hastens to the place where it arose.
The wind goes toward the south,
And turns around to the north;
The wind whirls about continually,
And comes again on its circuit.
All the rivers run into the sea,
Yet the sea *is* not full;
To the place from which the rivers come,
There they return again.
All things *are* full of labor;
Man cannot express *it*.
The eye is not satisfied with seeing,
Nor the ear filled with hearing.

That which has been *is* what will be,
That which *is* done is what will be done,
And *there is* nothing new under the sun.
Is there anything of which it may be said,
"See, this *is* new"?
It has already been in ancient times before
    us.
There is no remembrance of former *things,*
Nor will there be any remembrance of
    things that are to come
By *those* who will come after.

I, the Preacher, was king over Israel in Jerusalem. And I set my heart to seek and search out by wisdom concerning all that is done under heaven; this burdensome task God has given to the sons of man, by which they may be exercised. I have seen all the works that are done under the sun; and indeed, all *is* vanity and grasping for the wind.

What is crooked cannot be made straight,
And what is lacking cannot be numbered.

I communed with my heart, saying, "Look, I have attained greatness, and have gained more wisdom than all who were before me in Jerusalem. My heart has understood great wisdom and knowledge." And I set my heart to know wisdom and to know madness and folly. I perceived that this also is grasping for the wind.

For in much wisdom *is* much grief,
And he who increases knowledge increases
    sorrow.

I said in my heart, "Come now, I will test you with mirth; therefore enjoy pleasure"; but surely, this also *was* vanity. I said of laughter—"Madness!"; and of mirth, "What does it accomplish?" I searched in my heart *how* to gratify my flesh with wine, while guiding my heart with wisdom, and how to lay hold on folly, till I might see what *was* good for the sons of men to do under heaven all the days of their lives. I made my works great, I built myself houses, and planted myself vineyards. I made myself gardens and orchards, and I planted all *kinds* of fruit trees in them. I made myself water pools from which to water the growing trees of the grove. I acquired male and female servants, and had servants born in my house. Yes, I had greater possessions of herds and flocks than all who were in Jerusalem before me. I also gathered for myself silver and gold and the special treasures of kings and of the provinces. I acquired male and female singers, the delights of the sons of men, *and* musical instruments of all kinds.

So I became great and excelled more than all who were before me in Jerusalem. Also my wisdom remained with me.

Whatever my eyes desired I did not keep from
    them.
I did not withhold my heart from any pleasure,
For my heart rejoiced in all my labor;
And this was my reward from all my labor.
Then I looked on all the works that my hands
    had done
And on the labor in which I had toiled;
And indeed all *was* vanity and grasping for the
    wind.
There was no profit under the sun.
Then I turned myself to consider wisdom and
    madness and folly;

For what *can* the man *do* who succeeds the
    king?—
Only what he has already done.
Then I saw that wisdom excels folly
As light excels darkness.
The wise man's eyes *are* in his head,
But the fool walks in darkness.
Yet I myself perceived
That the same event happens to them all.

So I said in my heart,
"As it happens to the fool,
It also happens to me,
And why was I then more wise?"
Then I said in my heart,
"This also *is* vanity."
For *there is* no more remembrance of the wise
    than of the fool forever,
Since all that now *is* will be forgotten in the
    days to come.
And how does a wise *man* die?
As the fool!

Therefore I hated life because the work that was
done under the sun *was* distressing to me, for all *is*
vanity and grasping for the wind.

Then I hated all my labor in which I had toiled
under the sun, because I must leave it to the man
who will come after me. And who knows whether
he will be wise or a fool? Yet he will rule over all my
labor in which I toiled and in which I have shown
myself wise under the sun. This also *is* vanity.
Therefore I turned my heart and despaired of all the
labor in which I had toiled under the sun. For there
is a man whose labor *is* with wisdom, knowledge,
and skill; yet he must leave his heritage to a man
who has not labored for it. This also *is* vanity and a
great evil. For what has man for all his labor, and
for the striving of his heart with which he has toiled
under the sun? For all his days *are* sorrowful, and
his work burdensome; even in the night his heart
takes no rest. This also is vanity.

Nothing *is* better for a man *than* that he
should eat and drink, and *that* his soul should enjoy good in his labor. This also, I saw, was from the
hand of God. For who can eat, or who can have en-
joyment, more than I? For *God* gives wisdom and
knowledge and joy to a man who *is* good in His
sight; but to the sinner He gives the work of gathering and collecting, that he may give to *him who is*
good before God. This also *is* vanity and grasping
for the wind.

Ecclesiastes 1:1–2:26

WORSHIP

This is the way of those who *are* foolish,
And of their posterity who approve their
    sayings.   Selah
Like sheep they are laid in the grave;
Death shall feed on them;
The upright shall have dominion over them in
    the morning;
And their beauty shall be consumed in the
    grave, far from their dwelling.
But God will redeem my soul from the power
    of the grave,
For He shall receive me.   Selah
Psalm 49:13-15

WISDOM

Anxiety in the heart of man causes
    depression,
But a good word makes it glad.
Proverbs 12:25

SO WHAT?
What does this tell me?

SOLOMON'S SAGE ADVICE

Ecclesiastes 9:7-18; 11:1–12:14;
Psalm 49:16-17, 20; Proverbs 12:26

Go, eat your bread with joy,
And drink your wine with a merry heart;
For God has already accepted your works.
Let your garments always be white,
And let your head lack no oil.

Live joyfully with the wife whom you love all the days of your vain life which He has given you under the sun, all your days of vanity; for that *is* your portion in life, and in the labor which you perform under the sun.

Whatever your hand finds to do, do *it* with your might; for *there is* no work or device or knowledge or wisdom in the grave where you are going.

I returned and saw under the sun that—

The race *is* not to the swift,
Nor the battle to the strong,
Nor bread to the wise,
Nor riches to men of understanding,
Nor favor to men of skill;
But time and chance happen to them all.
For man also does not know his time:
Like fish taken in a cruel net,
Like birds caught in a snare,
So the sons of men *are* snared in an evil time,
When it falls suddenly upon them.

This wisdom I have also seen under the sun, and it *seemed* great to me: *There was* a little city with few men in it; and a great king came against it, besieged it, and built great snares around it. Now there was found in it a poor wise man, and he by his wisdom delivered the city. Yet no one remembered that same poor man.

Then I said:

"Wisdom *is* better than strength.
Nevertheless the poor man's wisdom *is* despised,
And his words are not heard.
Words of the wise, *spoken* quietly, *should be* heard
Rather than the shout of a ruler of fools.
Wisdom *is* better than weapons of war;
But one sinner destroys much good."

Cast your bread upon the waters,
For you will find it after many days.
Give a serving to seven, and also to eight,

For you do not know what evil will be on the earth.

If the clouds are full of rain,
They empty *themselves* upon the earth;
And if a tree falls to the south or the north,
In the place where the tree falls, there it shall lie.
He who observes the wind will not sow,
And he who regards the clouds will not reap.

As you do not know what *is* the way of the wind,
Or how the bones *grow* in the womb of her who is with child,
So you do not know the works of God who makes everything.
In the morning sow your seed,
And in the evening do not withhold your hand;
For you do not know which will prosper,
Either this or that,
Or whether both alike *will be* good.

Truly the light is sweet,
And *it is* pleasant for the eyes to behold the sun;
But if a man lives many years
And rejoices in them all,
Yet let him remember the days of darkness,
For they will be many.
All that is coming *is* vanity.

Rejoice, O young man, in your youth,
And let your heart cheer you in the days of your youth;
Walk in the ways of your heart,
And in the sight of your eyes;
But know that for all these
God will bring you into judgment.
Therefore remove sorrow from your heart,
And put away evil from your flesh,
For childhood and youth *are* vanity.

Remember now your Creator in the days of your youth,
Before the difficult days come,
And the years draw near when you say,
"I have no pleasure in them":
While the sun and the light,
The moon and the stars,
Are not darkened,

And the clouds do not return after the rain;
In the day when the keepers of the house
    tremble,
And the strong men bow down;
When the grinders cease because they are
    few,
And those that look through the windows grow
    dim;
When the doors are shut in the streets,
And the sound of grinding is low;
When one rises up at the sound of a bird,
And all the daughters of music are brought
    low;
Also they are afraid of height,
And of terrors in the way;
When the almond tree blossoms,
The grasshopper is a burden,
And desire fails.
For man goes to his eternal home,
And the mourners go about the streets.

Remember your Creator before the silver cord
    is loosed,
Or the golden bowl is broken,
Or the pitcher shattered at the fountain,
Or the wheel broken at the well.
Then the dust will return to the earth as it was,
And the spirit will return to God who gave it.

"Vanity of vanities," says the Preacher,
"All *is* vanity."

And moreover, because the Preacher was wise, he still taught the people knowledge; yes, he pondered and sought out *and* set in order many proverbs. The Preacher sought to find acceptable words; and *what was* written *was* upright—words of truth. The words of the wise are like goads, and the words of scholars are like well-driven nails, given by one Shepherd. And further, my son, be admonished by these. Of making many books *there is* no end, and much study *is* wearisome to the flesh.
Let us hear the conclusion of the whole matter:

Fear God and keep His commandments,
For this is man's all.
For God will bring every work into judgment,
Including every secret thing,
Whether good or evil.

Ecclesiastes 9:7-18; 11:1–12:14

WORSHIP

Do not be afraid when one becomes rich,
When the glory of his house is increased;
For when he dies he shall carry nothing away;
His glory shall not descend after him.

A man *who is* in honor, yet does not
    understand,
Is like the beasts *that* perish.

Psalm 49:16-17, 20

WISDOM

The righteous should choose his friends
    carefully,
For the way of the wicked leads them astray.

Proverbs 12:26

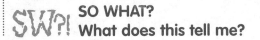

SO WHAT?
What does this tell me?

DIVIDED WE FALL

When Solomon died in 931 B.C., the dynasty that began under Saul, was built under David, and reached its high point under Solomon began to crumble.

Led by a former member of Solomon's administration, the northern tribes of Israel revolted against the Davidic dynasty— starting a civil war that resulted in a divided monarchy. With the northern kingdom (now called Israel) independent from the southern kingdom (now called Judah), Jeroboam, the leader of the northern tribes, established golden calf worship centers at Dan and Bethel, sending the northern kingdom into a spiritual slide.

While Israel in the north was coming apart spiritually, the South was not faring any better. Rehoboam, Solomon's son, took the throne of Jerusalem in the south and promptly reestablished Canaanite worship in Judah.

It wasn't until two generations later that Asa, the grandson of Rehoboam, ascended to the throne and reversed Judah's spiritual slide by doing away with the spiritual apostasy initiated by his grandfather. Elijah and Elisha were also heroes on this mountain range, representing God and calling the nation to account for violating their covenant with God. One other event of note was Elijah's confrontation with the prophets of Baal on Mount Carmel, where the impotent Baal proved to be no match for the power of the living God.

The rise of the Assyrians added another element to this part of the story, as Israel found itself in a weakened and vulnerable state. Assyrian expansion led to the capture of Galilee and eventually the fall of Samaria. Although Jerusalem was attacked, it was spared from being overthrown when the Angel of the Lord struck down 185,000 soldiers of Sennacherib's army.

King Josiah's reforms were the last mountain peak before Jerusalem was finally overthrown in 586 B.C. by the fierce Babylonian king Nebuchadnezzar. The southern kingdom of Judah was then taken into captivity for seventy years.

DIVISION OF THE MONARCHY

1 Kings 11:26–12:20; Psalm 50:1-3; Proverbs 12:27

Then Solomon's servant, Jeroboam the son of Nebat, an Ephraimite from Zereda, whose mother's name was Zeruah, a widow, also rebelled against the king.

And this *is* what caused him to rebel against the king: Solomon had built the Millo *and* repaired the damages to the City of David his father. The man Jeroboam *was* a mighty man of valor; and Solomon, seeing that the young man was industrious, made him the officer over all the labor force of the house of Joseph.

Now it happened at that time, when Jeroboam went out of Jerusalem, that the prophet Ahijah the Shilonite met him on the way; and he had clothed himself with a new garment, and the two *were* alone in the field. Then Ahijah took hold of the new garment that *was* on him, and tore it *into* twelve pieces. And he said to Jeroboam, "Take for yourself ten pieces, for thus says the LORD, the God of Israel: 'Behold, I will tear the kingdom out of the hand of Solomon and will give ten tribes to you (but he shall have one tribe for the sake of My servant David, and for the sake of Jerusalem, the city which I have chosen out of all the tribes of Israel), because they have forsaken Me, and worshiped Ashtoreth the goddess of the Sidonians, Chemosh the god of the Moabites, and Milcom the god of the people of Ammon, and have not walked in My ways to do *what is* right in My eyes and *keep* My statutes and My judgments, as *did* his father David. However I will not take the whole kingdom out of his hand, because I have made him ruler all the days of his life for the sake of My servant David, whom I chose because he kept My commandments and My statutes. But I will take the kingdom out of his son's hand and give it to you—ten tribes. And to his son I will give one tribe, that My servant David may always have a lamp before Me in Jerusalem, the city which I have chosen for Myself, to put My name there. So I will take you, and you shall reign over all your heart desires, and you shall be king over Israel. Then it shall be, if you heed all that I command you, walk in My ways, and do *what is* right in My sight, to keep My statutes and My commandments, as My

servant David did, then I will be with you and build for you an enduring house, as I built for David, and will give Israel to you. And I will afflict the descendants of David because of this, but not forever.'"

Solomon therefore sought to kill Jeroboam. But Jeroboam arose and fled to Egypt, to Shishak king of Egypt, and was in Egypt until the death of Solomon.

Now the rest of the acts of Solomon, all that he did, and his wisdom, *are* they not written in the book of the acts of Solomon? And the period that Solomon reigned in Jerusalem over all Israel *was* forty years. Then Solomon rested with his fathers, and was buried in the City of David his father. And Rehoboam his son reigned in his place.

And Rehoboam went to Shechem, for all Israel had gone to Shechem to make him king. So it happened, when Jeroboam the son of Nebat heard *it* (he was still in Egypt, for he had fled from the presence of King Solomon and had been dwelling in Egypt), that they sent and called him. Then Jeroboam and the whole assembly of Israel came and spoke to Rehoboam, saying, "Your father made our yoke heavy; now therefore, lighten the burdensome service of your father, and his heavy yoke which he put on us, and we will serve you."

So he said to them, "Depart *for* three days, then come back to me." And the people departed.

Then King Rehoboam consulted the elders who stood before his father Solomon while he still lived, and he said, "How do you advise *me* to answer these people?"

And they spoke to him, saying, "If you will be a servant to these people today, and serve them, and answer them, and speak good words to them, then they will be your servants forever."

But he rejected the advice which the elders had given him, and consulted the young men who had grown up with him, who stood before him. And he said to them, "What advice do you give? How should we answer this people who have spoken to me, saying, 'Lighten the yoke which your father put on us'?"

Then the young men who had grown up with him spoke to him, saying, "Thus you should speak to this people who have spoken to you, saying, 'Your father made our yoke heavy, but you make *it* lighter on us'—thus you shall say to them: 'My little *finger* shall be thicker than my father's waist! And now, whereas my father put a heavy yoke on you, I will add to your yoke; my father chastised you with whips, but I will chastise you with scourges!' "

So Jeroboam and all the people came to Rehoboam the third day, as the king had directed, saying, "Come back to me the third day." Then the king answered the people roughly, and rejected the advice which the elders had given him; and he spoke to them according to the advice of the young men, saying, "My father made your yoke heavy, but I will add to your yoke; my father chastised you with whips, but I will chastise you with scourges!" So the king did not listen to the people; for the turn *of events* was from the LORD, that He might fulfill His word, which the LORD had spoken by Ahijah the Shilonite to Jeroboam the son of Nebat.

Now when all Israel saw that the king did not listen to them, the people answered the king, saying:

"What share have we in David?
We have no inheritance in the son of Jesse.
To your tents, O Israel!
Now, see to your own house, O David!"

So Israel departed to their tents. But Rehoboam reigned over the children of Israel who dwelt in the cities of Judah.

Then King Rehoboam sent Adoram, who *was* in charge of the revenue; but all Israel stoned him with stones, and he died. Therefore King Rehoboam mounted his chariot in haste to flee to Jerusalem. So Israel has been in rebellion against the house of David to this day.

Now it came to pass when all Israel heard that Jeroboam had come back, they sent for him and called him to the congregation, and made him king over all Israel. There was none who followed the house of David, but the tribe of Judah only.

1 Kings 11:26–12:20

WoRSHiP

The Mighty One, God the LORD,
Has spoken and called the earth
From the rising of the sun to its going down.
Out of Zion, the perfection of beauty,
God will shine forth.
Our God shall come, and shall not keep silent;
A fire shall devour before Him,
And it shall be very tempestuous all around
    Him.

Psalm 50:1-3

WiSDoM

The lazy *man* does not roast what he took in
    hunting,
But diligence *is* man's precious possession.

Proverbs 12:27

SW?! SO WHAT?
What does this tell me?

JEROBOAM'S BAD NEWS

1 Kings 12:25-33; 14:1-20; Psalm 50:7, 14-15; Proverbs 12:28

Then Jeroboam built Shechem in the mountains of Ephraim, and dwelt there. Also he went out from there and built Penuel. And Jeroboam said in his heart, "Now the kingdom may return to the house of David: If these people go up to offer sacrifices in the house of the LORD at Jerusalem, then the heart of this people will turn back to their lord, Rehoboam king of Judah, and they will kill me and go back to Rehoboam king of Judah."

Therefore the king asked advice, made two calves of gold, and said to the people, "It is too much for you to go up to Jerusalem. Here are your gods, O Israel, which brought you up from the land of Egypt!" And he set up one in Bethel, and the other he put in Dan. Now this thing became a sin, for the people went *to worship* before the one as far as Dan. He made shrines on the high places, and made priests from every class of people, who were not of the sons of Levi.

Jeroboam ordained a feast on the fifteenth day of the eighth month, like the feast that *was* in Judah, and offered sacrifices on the altar. So he did at Bethel, sacrificing to the calves that he had made. And at Bethel he installed the priests of the high places which he had made. So he made offerings on the altar which he had made at Bethel on the fifteenth day of the eighth month, in the month which he had devised in his own heart. And he ordained a feast for the children of Israel, and offered sacrifices on the altar and burned incense.

At that time Abijah the son of Jeroboam became sick. And Jeroboam said to his wife, "Please arise, and disguise yourself, that they may not recognize you as the wife of Jeroboam, and go to Shiloh. Indeed, Ahijah the prophet *is* there, who told me that *I would be* king over this people. Also take with you ten loaves, *some* cakes, and a jar of honey, and go to him; he will tell you what will become of the child." And Jeroboam's wife did so; she arose and went to Shiloh, and came to the house of Ahijah. But Ahijah could not see, for his eyes were glazed by reason of his age.

Now the LORD had said to Ahijah, "Here is the wife of Jeroboam, coming to ask you something about her son, for he *is* sick. Thus and thus you shall say to her; for it will be, when she comes in, that she will pretend *to be* another *woman*."

And so it was, when Ahijah heard the sound of her footsteps as she came through the door, he said, "Come in, wife of Jeroboam. Why do you pretend *to be* another *person*? For I *have been* sent to you *with* bad *news*. Go, tell Jeroboam, 'Thus says the LORD God of Israel: "Because I exalted you from among the people, and made you ruler over My people Israel, and tore the kingdom away from the house of David, and gave it to you; and *yet* you have not been as My servant David, who kept My commandments and who followed Me with all his heart, to do only *what was* right in My eyes; but you have done more evil than all who were before you, for you have gone and made for yourself other gods and molded images to provoke Me to anger, and have cast Me behind your back—therefore behold! I will bring disaster on the house of Jeroboam, and will cut off from Jeroboam every male in Israel, bond and free; I will take away the remnant of the house of Jeroboam, as one takes away refuse until it is all gone. The dogs shall eat whoever belongs to Jeroboam and dies in the city, and the birds of the air shall eat whoever dies in the field; for the LORD has spoken!" ' Arise therefore, go to your own house. When your feet enter the city, the child shall die. And all Israel shall mourn for him and bury him, for he is the only one of Jeroboam who shall come to the grave, because in him there is found something good toward the LORD God of Israel in the house of Jeroboam.

"Moreover the LORD will raise up for Himself a king over Israel who shall cut off the house of Jeroboam; this is the day. What? Even now! For the LORD will strike Israel, as a reed is shaken in the water. He will uproot Israel from this good land which He gave to their fathers, and will scatter them beyond the River, because they have made their wooden images, provoking the LORD to anger. And He will give Israel up because of the sins of Jeroboam, who sinned and who made Israel sin."

Then Jeroboam's wife arose and departed, and came to Tirzah. When she came to the threshold of the house, the child died. And they buried

DIVIDED WE FALL

him; and all Israel mourned for him, according to the word of the LORD which He spoke through His servant Ahijah the prophet.

Now the rest of the acts of Jeroboam, how he made war and how he reigned, indeed they *are* written in the book of the chronicles of the kings of Israel. The period that Jeroboam reigned *was* twenty-two years. So he rested with his fathers. Then Nadab his son reigned in his place.

1 Kings 12:25-33; 14:1-20

WORSHIP

"Hear, O My people, and I will speak,
O Israel, and I will testify against you;
I *am* God, your God!

Offer to God thanksgiving,
And pay your vows to the Most High.
Call upon Me in the day of trouble;
I will deliver you, and you shall glorify Me."

Psalm 50:7, 14-15

WISDOM

In the way of righteousness *is* life,
And in *its* pathway *there is* no death.

Proverbs 12:28

SW?! SO WHAT?
What does this tell me?

REHOBOAM AND ASA—DOING WRONG AND DOING RIGHT

1 Kings 14:21–15:24; Psalm 50:22-23; Proverbs 13:1

And Rehoboam the son of Solomon reigned in Judah. Rehoboam *was* forty-one years old when he became king. He reigned seventeen years in Jerusalem, the city which the LORD had chosen out of all the tribes of Israel, to put His name there. His mother's name *was* Naamah, an Ammonitess. Now Judah did evil in the sight of the LORD, and they provoked Him to jealousy with their sins which they committed, more than all that their fathers had done. For they also built for themselves high places, *sacred* pillars, and wooden images on every high hill and under every green tree. And there were also perverted persons in the land. They did according to all the abominations of the nations which the LORD had cast out before the children of Israel.

It happened in the fifth year of King Rehoboam *that* Shishak king of Egypt came up against Jerusalem. And he took away the treasures of the house of the LORD and the treasures of the king's house; he took away everything. He also took away all the gold shields which Solomon had made. Then King Rehoboam made bronze shields in their place, and committed *them* to the hands of the captains of the guard, who guarded the doorway of the king's house. And whenever the king entered the house of the LORD, the guards carried them, then brought them back into the guardroom.

Now the rest of the acts of Rehoboam, and all that he did, *are* they not written in the book of the chronicles of the kings of Judah? And there was war between Rehoboam and Jeroboam all *their* days. So Rehoboam rested with his fathers, and was buried with his fathers in the City of David. His mother's name *was* Naamah, an Ammonitess. Then Abijam his son reigned in his place.

In the eighteenth year of King Jeroboam the son of Nebat, Abijam became king over Judah. He reigned three years in Jerusalem. His mother's name *was* Maa-

chah the granddaughter of Abishalom. And he walked in all the sins of his father, which he had done before him; his heart was not loyal to the LORD his God, as was the heart of his father David. Nevertheless for David's sake the LORD his God gave him a lamp in Jerusalem, by setting up his son after him and by establishing Jerusalem; because David did *what was* right in the eyes of the LORD, and had not turned aside from anything that He commanded him all the days of his life, except in the matter of Uriah the Hittite. And there was war between Rehoboam and Jeroboam all the days of his life. Now the rest of the acts of Abijam, and all that he did, *are* they not written in the book of the chronicles of the kings of Judah? And there was war between Abijam and Jeroboam.

So Abijam rested with his fathers, and they buried him in the City of David. Then Asa his son reigned in his place.

In the twentieth year of Jeroboam king of Israel, Asa became king over Judah. And he reigned forty-one years in Jerusalem. His grandmother's name *was* Maachah the granddaughter of Abishalom. Asa did *what was* right in the eyes of the LORD, as *did* his father David. And he banished the perverted persons from the land, and removed all the idols that his fathers had made. Also he removed Maachah his grandmother from *being* queen mother, because she had made an obscene image of Asherah. And Asa cut down her obscene image and burned *it* by the Brook Kidron. But the high places were not removed. Nevertheless Asa's heart was loyal to the LORD all his days. He also brought into the house of the LORD the things which his father had dedicated, and the things which he himself had dedicated: silver and gold and utensils.

Now there was war between Asa and Baasha king of Israel all their days. And Baasha king of Israel came up against Judah, and built Ramah, that he might let none go out or come in to Asa king of Judah. Then Asa took all the silver and gold *that was* left in the treasuries of the house of the LORD and the treasuries of the king's house, and delivered them into the hand of his servants. And King Asa sent them to Ben-Hadad the son of Tabrimmon, the son of Hezion, king of Syria, who dwelt in Damascus, saying, "*Let there be* a treaty between you and me, as there was between my father and your father. See, I have sent you a present of silver and gold. Come and break your treaty with Baasha king of Israel, so that he will withdraw from me."

So Ben-Hadad heeded King Asa, and sent the captains of his armies against the cities of Israel. He attacked Ijon, Dan, Abel Beth Maachah, and all Chinneroth, with all the land of Naphtali. Now it happened, when Baasha heard *it,* that he stopped building Ramah, and remained in Tirzah.

Then King Asa made a proclamation throughout all Judah; none *was* exempted. And they took away the stones and timber of Ramah, which Baasha had used for building; and with them King Asa built Geba of Benjamin, and Mizpah.

The rest of all the acts of Asa, all his might, all that he did, and the cities which he built, *are* they not written in the book of the chronicles of the kings of Judah? But in the time of his old age he was diseased in his feet. So Asa rested with his fathers, and was buried with his fathers in the City of David his father. Then Jehoshaphat his son reigned in his place.

1 Kings 14:21–15:24

WORSHIP

"Now consider this, you who forget God,
Lest I tear *you* in pieces,
And *there be* none to deliver:
Whoever offers praise glorifies Me;
And to him who orders *his* conduct *aright*
I will show the salvation of God."

Psalm 50:22-23

WISDOM

A wise son *heeds* his father's instruction,
But a scoffer does not listen to rebuke.

Proverbs 13:1

SW?! SO WHAT?
What does this tell me?

EVIL KINGS OF ISRAEL 1 Kings 15:25–16:28; Psalm 51:1-3; Proverbs 13:3

Now Nadab the son of Jeroboam became king over Israel in the second year of Asa king of Judah, and he reigned over Israel two years. And he did evil in the sight of the LORD, and walked in the way of his father, and in his sin by which he had made Israel sin.

Then Baasha the son of Ahijah, of the house of Issachar, conspired against him. And Baasha killed him at Gibbethon, which *belonged* to the Philistines, while Nadab and all Israel laid siege to Gibbethon. Baasha killed him in the third year of Asa king of Judah, and reigned in his place. And it was so, when he became king, *that* he killed all the house of Jeroboam. He did not leave to Jeroboam anyone that breathed, until he had destroyed him, according to the word of the LORD which He had spoken by His servant Ahijah the Shilonite, because of the sins of Jeroboam, which he had sinned and by which he had made Israel sin, because of his provocation with which he had provoked the LORD God of Israel to anger.

Now the rest of the acts of Nadab, and all that he did, *are* they not written in the book of the chronicles of the kings of Israel? And there was war between Asa and Baasha king of Israel all their days.

In the third year of Asa king of Judah, Baasha the son of Ahijah became king over all Israel in Tirzah, and *reigned* twenty-four years. He did evil in the sight of the LORD, and walked in the way of Jeroboam, and in his sin by which he had made Israel sin.

Then the word of the LORD came to Jehu the son of Hanani, against Baasha, saying: "Inasmuch as I lifted you out of the dust and made you ruler over My people Israel, and you have walked in the way of Jeroboam, and have made My people Israel sin, to provoke Me to anger with their sins, surely I will take away the posterity of Baasha and the posterity of his house, and I will make your house like the house of Jeroboam the son of Nebat. The dogs shall eat whoever belongs to Baasha and dies in the city, and the birds of the air shall eat whoever dies in the fields."

Now the rest of the acts of Baasha, what he did, and his might, *are* they not written in the book of the chronicles of the kings of Israel? So Baasha rested with his fathers and was buried in Tirzah. Then Elah his son reigned in his place.

And also the word of the LORD came by the prophet Jehu the son of Hanani against Baasha and his house, because of all the evil that he did in the sight of the LORD in provoking Him to anger with the work of his hands, in being like the house of Jeroboam, and because he killed them.

In the twenty-sixth year of Asa king of Judah, Elah the son of Baasha became king over Israel, *and reigned* two years in Tirzah. Now his servant Zimri, commander of half *his* chariots, conspired against him as he was in Tirzah drinking himself drunk in the house of Arza, steward of *his* house in Tirzah. And Zimri went in and struck him and killed him in the twenty-seventh year of Asa king of Judah, and reigned in his place.

Then it came to pass, when he began to reign, as soon as he was seated on his throne, *that* he killed all the household of Baasha; he did not leave him one male, neither of his relatives nor of his friends. Thus Zimri destroyed all the household of Baasha, according to the word of the LORD, which He spoke against Baasha by Jehu the prophet, for all the sins of Baasha and the sins of Elah his son, by which they had sinned and by which they had made Israel sin, in provoking the LORD God of Israel to anger with their idols.

Now the rest of the acts of Elah, and all that he did, *are* they not written in the book of the chronicles of the kings of Israel?

In the twenty-seventh year of Asa king of Judah, Zimri had reigned in Tirzah seven days. And the people *were* encamped against Gibbethon, which *belonged* to the Philistines. Now the people *who were* encamped heard it said, "Zimri has conspired and also has killed the king." So all Israel made Omri, the commander of the army, king over Israel that day in the camp. Then Omri and all Israel with him went up from Gibbethon, and they besieged Tirzah. And it happened, when Zimri saw that the city was taken, that he went into the citadel of the king's house and burned the king's house down upon himself with fire, and died, because of the sins which he had committed in doing evil in the sight of the LORD, in walking in the way of Jeroboam, and in his sin which he had committed to make Israel sin.

Now the rest of the acts of Zimri, and the treason he committed, *are* they not written in the book of the chronicles of the kings of Israel?

Then the people of Israel were divided into two parts: half of the people followed Tibni the son of Ginath, to make him king, and half followed Omri. But the people who followed Omri prevailed over the people who followed Tibni the son of Ginath. So Tibni died and Omri reigned. In the thirty-first year of Asa king of Judah, Omri became king over Israel, *and reigned* twelve years. Six years he reigned in Tirzah. And he bought the hill of Samaria from Shemer for two talents of silver; then he built on the hill, and called the name of the city which he built, Samaria, after the name of Shemer, owner of the hill. Omri did evil in the eyes of the LORD, and did worse than all who *were* before him. For he walked in all the ways of Jeroboam the son of Nebat, and in his sin by which he had made Israel sin, provoking the LORD God of Israel to anger with their idols.

Now the rest of the acts of Omri which he did, and the might that he showed, *are* they not written in the book of the chronicles of the kings of Israel?

So Omri rested with his fathers and was buried in Samaria. Then Ahab his son reigned in his place.

1 Kings 15:25–16:28

WORSHIP

Have mercy upon me, O God,
According to Your lovingkindness;
According to the multitude of Your tender
  mercies,
Blot out my transgressions.
Wash me thoroughly from my iniquity,
And cleanse me from my sin.

For I acknowledge my transgressions,
And my sin *is* always before me.

Psalm 51:1-3

WISDOM

He who guards his mouth preserves his life,
But he who opens wide his lips shall have
  destruction.

Proverbs 13:3

SW?! **SO WHAT?**
What does this tell me?

WICKED AHAB SEARCHES FOR ELIJAH

1 Kings 16:29–18:15; Psalm 51:10-12; Proverbs 13:4

In the thirty-eighth year of Asa king of Judah, Ahab the son of Omri became king over Israel; and Ahab the son of Omri reigned over Israel in Samaria twenty-two years. Now Ahab the son of Omri did evil in the sight of the LORD, more than all who *were* before him. And it came to pass, as though it had been a trivial thing for him to walk in the sins of Jeroboam the son of Nebat, that he took as wife Jezebel the daughter of Ethbaal, king of the Sidonians; and he went and served Baal and worshiped him. Then he set up an altar for Baal in the temple of Baal, which he had built in Samaria. And Ahab made a wooden image. Ahab did more to provoke the LORD God of Israel to anger than all the kings of Israel who were before him. In his days Hiel of Bethel built Jericho. He laid its foundation with Abiram his firstborn, and with his youngest *son* Segub he set up its gates, according to the word of the LORD, which He had spoken through Joshua the son of Nun.

And Elijah the Tishbite, of the inhabitants of Gilead, said to Ahab, "*As* the LORD God of Israel lives, before whom I stand, there shall not be dew nor rain these years, except at my word."

Then the word of the LORD came to him, saying, "Get away from here and turn eastward, and hide by the Brook Cherith, which flows into the Jordan. And it will be *that* you shall drink from the brook, and I have commanded the ravens to feed you there."

So he went and did according to the word of the LORD, for he went and stayed by the Brook Cherith, which flows into the Jordan. The ravens brought him bread and meat in the morning, and bread and meat in the evening; and he drank from the brook. And it happened after a while that the brook dried up, because there had been no rain in the land.

Then the word of the LORD came to him, saying, "Arise, go to Zarephath, which *belongs* to Sidon, and dwell there. See, I have commanded a widow there to provide for you." So he arose and went to Zarephath. And when he came to the gate of the city, indeed a widow *was* there gathering sticks. And he called to her and said, "Please bring me a little water in a cup, that I may drink." And as she was going to get *it,* he called to her and said, "Please bring me a morsel of bread in your hand."

So she said, "As the LORD your God lives, I do not have bread, only a handful of flour in a bin, and a little oil in a jar; and see, I *am* gathering a couple of sticks that I may go in and prepare it for myself and my son, that we may eat it, and die."

And Elijah said to her, "Do not fear; go *and* do as you have said, but make me a small cake from it first, and bring *it* to me; and afterward make *some* for yourself and your son. For thus says the LORD God of Israel: 'The bin of flour shall not be used up, nor shall the jar of oil run dry, until the day the LORD sends rain on the earth.'"

So she went away and did according to the word of Elijah; and she and he and her household ate for *many* days. The bin of flour was not used up, nor did the jar of oil run dry, according to the word of the LORD which He spoke by Elijah.

Now it happened after these things *that* the son of the woman who owned the house became sick. And his sickness was so serious that there was no breath left in him. So she said to Elijah, "What have I to do with you, O man of God? Have you come to me to bring my sin to remembrance, and to kill my son?"

And he said to her, "Give me your son." So he took him out of her arms and carried him to the upper room where he was staying, and laid him on his own bed. Then he cried out to the LORD and said, "O LORD my God, have You also brought tragedy on the widow with whom I lodge, by killing her son?" And he stretched himself out on the child three times, and cried out to the LORD and said, "O LORD my God, I pray, let this child's soul come back to him." Then the LORD heard the voice of Elijah; and the soul of the child came back to him, and he revived.

And Elijah took the child and brought him down from the upper room into the house, and gave him to his mother. And Elijah said, "See, your son lives!"

Then the woman said to Elijah, "Now by this I know that you *are* a man of God, *and* that the word of the LORD in your mouth *is* the truth."

And it came to pass *after* many days that the

word of the LORD came to Elijah, in the third year, saying, "Go, present yourself to Ahab, and I will send rain on the earth."

So Elijah went to present himself to Ahab; and *there was* a severe famine in Samaria. And Ahab had called Obadiah, who *was* in charge of *his* house. (Now Obadiah feared the LORD greatly. For so it was, while Jezebel massacred the prophets of the LORD, that Obadiah had taken one hundred prophets and hidden them, fifty to a cave, and had fed them with bread and water.) And Ahab had said to Obadiah, "Go into the land to all the springs of water and to all the brooks; perhaps we may find grass to keep the horses and mules alive, so that we will not have to kill any livestock." So they divided the land between them to explore it; Ahab went one way by himself, and Obadiah went another way by himself.

Now as Obadiah was on his way, suddenly Elijah met him; and he recognized him, and fell on his face, and said, "*Is* that you, my lord Elijah?"

And he answered him, "*It is* I. Go, tell your master, 'Elijah *is here.*'

So he said, "How have I sinned, that you are delivering your servant into the hand of Ahab, to kill me? *As* the LORD your God lives, there is no nation or kingdom where my master has not sent someone to hunt for you; and when they said, 'He *is* not *here,*' he took an oath from the kingdom or nation that they could not find you. And now you say, 'Go, tell your master, "Elijah *is here*"'! And it shall come to pass, *as soon as* I am gone from you, that the Spirit of the LORD will carry you to a place I do not know; so when I go and tell Ahab, and he cannot find you, he will kill me. But I your servant have feared the LORD from my youth. Was it not reported to my lord what I did when Jezebel killed the prophets of the LORD, how I hid one hundred men of the LORD's prophets, fifty to a cave, and fed them with bread and water? And now you say, 'Go, tell your master, "Elijah *is here.*"' He will kill me!"

Then Elijah said, "*As* the LORD of hosts lives, before whom I stand, I will surely present myself to him today."

1 Kings 16:29–18:15

WORSHIP

Create in me a clean heart, O God,
And renew a steadfast spirit within me.
Do not cast me away from Your presence,
And do not take Your Holy Spirit from me.

Restore to me the joy of Your salvation,
And uphold me *by Your* generous Spirit.
Psalm 51:10-12

WISDOM

The soul of a lazy *man* desires, and *has* nothing;
But the soul of the diligent shall be made rich.
Proverbs 13:4

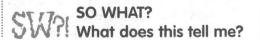

SO WHAT?
What does this tell me?

CONFRONTATION ON MOUNT CARMEL

1 Kings 18:16–19:16; Psalm 51:15-17; Proverbs 13:6

So Obadiah went to meet Ahab, and told him; and Ahab went to meet Elijah.

Then it happened, when Ahab saw Elijah, that Ahab said to him, "*Is that* you, O troubler of Israel?"

And he answered, "I have not troubled Israel, but you and your father's house *have,* in that you have forsaken the commandments of the LORD and have followed the Baals. Now therefore, send *and* gather all Israel to me on Mount Carmel, the four hundred and fifty prophets of Baal, and the four hundred prophets of Asherah, who eat at Jezebel's table."

So Ahab sent for all the children of Israel, and gathered the prophets together on Mount Carmel. And Elijah came to all the people, and said, "How long will you falter between two opinions? If the LORD *is* God, follow Him; but if Baal, follow him." But the people answered him not a word. Then Elijah said to the people, "I alone am left a prophet of the LORD; but Baal's prophets *are* four hundred and fifty men. Therefore let them give us two bulls; and let them choose one bull for themselves, cut it in pieces, and lay *it* on the wood, but put no fire *under it;* and I will prepare the other bull, and lay *it* on the wood, but put no fire *under it.* Then you call on the name of your gods, and I will call on the name of the LORD; and the God who answers by fire, He is God."

So all the people answered and said, "It is well spoken."

Now Elijah said to the prophets of Baal, "Choose one bull for yourselves and prepare *it* first, for you *are* many; and call on the name of your god, but put no fire *under it.*"

So they took the bull which was given them, and they prepared *it,* and called on the name of Baal from morning even till noon, saying, "O Baal, hear us!" But *there was* no voice; no one answered. Then they leaped about the altar which they had made.

And so it was, at noon, that Elijah mocked them and said, "Cry aloud, for he *is* a god; either he is meditating, or he is busy, or he is on a journey, *or* perhaps he is sleep-

ing and must be awakened." So they cried aloud, and cut themselves, as was their custom, with knives and lances, until the blood gushed out on them. And when midday was past, they prophesied until the *time* of the offering of the *evening* sacrifice. But *there was* no voice; no one answered, no one paid attention.

Then Elijah said to all the people, "Come near to me." So all the people came near to him. And he repaired the altar of the LORD *that was* broken down. And Elijah took twelve stones, according to the number of the tribes of the sons of Jacob, to whom the word of the LORD had come, saying, "Israel shall be your name." Then with the stones he built an altar in the name of the LORD; and he made a trench around the altar large enough to hold two seahs of seed. And he put the wood in order, cut the bull in pieces, and laid *it* on the wood, and said, "Fill four waterpots with water, and pour *it* on the burnt sacrifice and on the wood." Then he said, "Do *it* a second time," and they did *it* a second time; and he said, "Do *it* a third time," and they did *it* a third time. So the water ran all around the altar; and he also filled the trench with water.

And it came to pass, at *the time of* the offering of the *evening* sacrifice, that Elijah the prophet came near and said, "LORD God of Abraham, Isaac, and Israel, let it be known this day that You *are* God in Israel and I *am* Your servant, and *that* I have done all these things at Your word. Hear me, O LORD, hear me, that this people may know that You *are* the LORD God, and *that* You have turned their hearts back *to You* again."

Then the fire of the LORD fell and consumed the burnt sacrifice, and the wood and the stones and the dust, and it licked up the water that *was* in the trench. Now when all the people saw *it,* they fell on their faces; and they said, "The LORD, He *is* God! The LORD, He *is* God!"

And Elijah said to them, "Seize the prophets of Baal! Do not let one of them escape!" So they seized them; and Elijah brought them down to the Brook Kishon and executed them there.

Then Elijah said to Ahab, "Go up, eat and drink; for *there is* the sound of abundance of rain." So Ahab went up to eat and drink. And Elijah went up to the top of Carmel; then he bowed down on the ground, and put his face between his knees, and said to his servant, "Go up now, look toward the sea."

So he went up and looked, and said, "*There is* nothing." And seven times he said, "Go again."

Then it came to pass the seventh *time,* that he said, "There is a cloud, as small as a man's hand, rising out of the sea!" So he said, "Go up, say to Ahab, 'Prepare *your chariot,* and go down before the rain stops you.'"

Now it happened in the meantime that the sky became black with clouds and wind, and there was a heavy rain. So Ahab rode away and went to Jezreel. Then the hand of the LORD came upon Elijah; and he girded up his loins and ran ahead of Ahab to the entrance of Jezreel.

And Ahab told Jezebel all that Elijah had done, also how he had executed all the prophets with the sword. Then Jezebel sent a messenger to Elijah, saying, "So let the gods do *to me,* and more also, if I do not make your life as the life of one of them by tomorrow about this time." And when he saw *that,* he arose and ran for his life, and went to Beersheba, which *belongs* to Judah, and left his servant there.

But he himself went a day's journey into the wilderness, and came and sat down under a broom tree. And he prayed that he might die, and said, "It is enough! Now, LORD, take my life, for I *am* no better than my fathers!"

Then as he lay and slept under a broom tree, suddenly an angel touched him, and said to him, "Arise *and* eat." Then he looked, and there by his head *was* a cake baked on coals, and a jar of water. So he ate and drank, and lay down again. And the angel of the LORD came back the second time, and touched him, and said, "Arise *and* eat, because the journey *is* too great for you." So he arose, and ate and drank; and he went in the strength of that food forty days and forty nights as far as Horeb, the mountain of God.

And there he went into a cave, and spent the night in that place; and behold, the word of the LORD *came* to him, and He said to him, "What are you doing here, Elijah?"

So he said, "I have been very zealous for the LORD God of hosts; for the children of Israel have forsaken Your covenant, torn down Your altars, and killed Your prophets with the sword. I alone am left; and they seek to take my life."

Then He said, "Go out, and stand on the mountain before the LORD." And behold, the LORD passed by, and a great and strong wind tore into the mountains and broke the rocks in pieces before the LORD, *but* the LORD *was* not in the wind; and after the wind an earthquake, *but* the LORD *was* not in the earthquake; and after the earthquake a fire, *but* the LORD *was* not in the fire; and after the fire a still small voice.

So it was, when Elijah heard *it,* that he wrapped his face in his mantle and went out and stood in the entrance of the cave. Suddenly a voice *came* to him, and said, "What are you doing here, Elijah?"

And he said, "I have been very zealous for the LORD God of hosts; because the children of Israel have forsaken Your covenant, torn down Your altars, and killed Your prophets with the sword. I alone am left; and they seek to take my life."

Then the LORD said to him: "Go, return on your way to the Wilderness of Damascus; and when you arrive, anoint Hazael *as* king over Syria. Also you shall anoint Jehu the son of Nimshi *as* king over Israel. And Elisha the son of Shaphat of Abel Meholah you shall anoint *as* prophet in your place."

1 Kings 18:16–19:16

WoRSHIP

O Lord, open my lips,
And my mouth shall show forth Your praise.
For You do not desire sacrifice, or else I would
   give *it;*
You do not delight in burnt offering.
The sacrifices of God *are* a broken spirit,
A broken and a contrite heart—
These, O God, You will not despise.

Psalm 51:15-17

WiSDoM

Righteousness guards *him whose* way is
   blameless,
But wickedness overthrows the sinner.

Proverbs 13:6

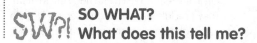 **SO WHAT?**
What does this tell me?

AHAB'S SIN AND DEATH

1 Kings 21:1-29; 22:29-40; Psalm 52:7-9; Proverbs 13:7

And it came to pass after these things *that* Naboth the Jezreelite had a vineyard which *was* in Jezreel, next to the palace of Ahab king of Samaria. So Ahab spoke to Naboth, saying, "Give me your vineyard, that I may have it for a vegetable garden, because it *is* near, next to my house; and for it I will give you a vineyard better than it. *Or,* if it seems good to you, I will give you its worth in money."

But Naboth said to Ahab, "The Lord forbid that I should give the inheritance of my fathers to you!"

So Ahab went into his house sullen and displeased because of the word which Naboth the Jezreelite had spoken to him; for he had said, "I will not give you the inheritance of my fathers." And he lay down on his bed, and turned away his face, and would eat no food. But Jezebel his wife came to him, and said to him, "Why is your spirit so sullen that you eat no food?"

He said to her, "Because I spoke to Naboth the Jezreelite, and said to him, 'Give me your vineyard for money; or else, if it pleases you, I will give you *another* vineyard for it.' And he answered, 'I will not give you my vineyard.'"

Then Jezebel his wife said to him, "You now exercise authority over Israel! Arise, eat food, and let your heart be cheerful; I will give you the vineyard of Naboth the Jezreelite."

And she wrote letters in Ahab's name, sealed *them* with his seal, and sent the letters to the elders and the nobles who *were* dwelling in the city with Naboth. She wrote in the letters, saying,

> Proclaim a fast, and seat Naboth with high honor among the people; and seat two men, scoundrels, before him to bear witness against him, saying, "You have blasphemed God and the king." *Then* take him out, and stone him, that he may die.

So the men of his city, the elders and nobles who were inhabitants of his city, did as Jezebel had sent to them, as it *was* written in the letters which she had sent to them. They proclaimed a fast, and seated Naboth with high honor among the people. And two men, scoundrels, came in and sat before him; and the scoundrels witnessed against him, against Naboth, in the presence of the people, saying, "Naboth has blasphemed God and the king!" Then they took him outside the city and stoned him with stones, so that he died. Then they sent to Jezebel, saying, "Naboth has been stoned and is dead."

And it came to pass, when Jezebel heard that Naboth had been stoned and was dead, that Jezebel said to Ahab, "Arise, take possession of the vineyard of Naboth the Jezreelite, which he refused to give you for money; for Naboth is not alive, but dead." So it was, when Ahab heard that Naboth was dead, that Ahab got up and went down to take possession of the vineyard of Naboth the Jezreelite.

Then the word of the Lord came to Elijah the Tishbite, saying, "Arise, go down to meet Ahab king of Israel, who *lives* in Samaria. There *he is*, in the vineyard of Naboth, where he has gone down to take possession of it. You shall speak to him, saying, 'Thus says the Lord: "Have you murdered and also taken possession?"' And you shall speak to him, saying, 'Thus says the Lord: "In the place where dogs licked the blood of Naboth, dogs shall lick your blood, even yours."'"

So Ahab said to Elijah, "Have you found me, O my enemy?"

And he answered, "I have found *you*, because you have sold yourself to do evil in the sight of the Lord: 'Behold, I will bring calamity on you. I will take away your posterity, and will cut off from Ahab every male in Israel, both bond and free. I will make your house like the house of Jeroboam the son of Nebat, and like the house of Baasha the son of Ahijah, because of the provocation with which you have provoked *Me* to anger, and made Israel sin.' And concerning Jezebel the Lord also spoke, saying, 'The dogs shall eat Jezebel by the wall of Jezreel.' The dogs shall eat whoever belongs to Ahab and dies in the city, and the birds of the air shall eat whoever dies in the field."

But there was no one like Ahab who sold himself to do wickedness in the sight of the Lord, because Jezebel his wife stirred him up. And he behaved very abominably in following idols, according to all *that* the Amorites had done, whom the Lord had cast out before the children of Israel.

So it was, when Ahab heard those words, that he tore his clothes and put sackcloth on his body, and fasted and lay in sackcloth, and went about mourning.

And the word of the LORD came to Elijah the Tishbite, saying, "See how Ahab has humbled himself before Me? Because he has humbled himself before Me, I will not bring the calamity in his days. In the days of his son I will bring the calamity on his house."

So the king of Israel and Jehoshaphat the king of Judah went up to Ramoth Gilead. And the king of Israel said to Jehoshaphat, "I will disguise myself and go into battle; but you put on your robes." So the king of Israel disguised himself and went into battle.

Now the king of Syria had commanded the thirty-two captains of his chariots, saying, "Fight with no one small or great, but only with the king of Israel." So it was, when the captains of the chariots saw Jehoshaphat, that they said, "Surely it *is* the king of Israel!" Therefore they turned aside to fight against him, and Jehoshaphat cried out. And it happened, when the captains of the chariots saw that it *was* not the king of Israel, that they turned back from pursuing him. Now a *certain* man drew a bow at random, and struck the king of Israel between the joints of his armor. So he said to the driver of his chariot, "Turn around and take me out of the battle, for I am wounded."

The battle increased that day; and the king was propped up in his chariot, facing the Syrians, and died at evening. The blood ran out from the wound onto the floor of the chariot. Then, as the sun was going down, a shout went throughout the army, saying, "Every man to his city, and every man to his own country!"

So the king died, and was brought to Samaria. And they buried the king in Samaria. Then *someone* washed the chariot at a pool in Samaria, and the dogs licked up his blood while the harlots bathed, according to the word of the LORD which He had spoken.

Now the rest of the acts of Ahab, and all that he did, the ivory house which he built and all the cities that he built, *are* they not written in the book of the chronicles of the kings of Israel? So Ahab rested with his fathers. Then Ahaziah his son reigned in his place.

1 Kings 21:1-29; 22:29-40

WORSHIP

"Here is the man *who* did not make God his
strength,
But trusted in the abundance of his riches,
And strengthened himself in his wickedness."

But I *am* like a green olive tree in the house of
God;
I trust in the mercy of God forever and ever.
I will praise You forever,
Because You have done *it;*
And in the presence of Your saints
I will wait on Your name, for *it is* good.

Psalm 52:7-9

WISDOM

There is one who makes himself rich, yet *has*
nothing;
And one who makes himself poor, yet *has*
great riches.

Proverbs 13:7

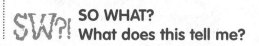

SO WHAT?
What does this tell me?

ELISHA SUCCEEDS ELIJAH

2 Kings 2:1-25; 5:1-14; Psalm 53:1-3; Proverbs 13:9

And it came to pass, when the LORD was about to take up Elijah into heaven by a whirlwind, that Elijah went with Elisha from Gilgal. Then Elijah said to Elisha, "Stay here, please, for the LORD has sent me on to Bethel."

But Elisha said, "*As* the LORD lives, and *as* your soul lives, I will not leave you!" So they went down to Bethel.

Now the sons of the prophets who *were* at Bethel came out to Elisha, and said to him, "Do you know that the LORD will take away your master from over you today?"

And he said, "Yes, I know; keep silent!"

Then Elijah said to him, "Elisha, stay here, please, for the LORD has sent me on to Jericho."

But he said, "*As* the LORD lives, and *as* your soul lives, I will not leave you!" So they came to Jericho.

Now the sons of the prophets who *were* at Jericho came to Elisha and said to him, "Do you know that the LORD will take away your master from over you today?"

So he answered, "Yes, I know; keep silent!"

Then Elijah said to him, "Stay here, please, for the LORD has sent me on to the Jordan."

But he said, "*As* the LORD lives, and *as* your soul lives, I will not leave you!" So the two of them went on. And fifty men of the sons of the prophets went and stood facing *them* at a distance, while the two of them stood by the Jordan. Now Elijah took his mantle, rolled *it* up, and struck the water; and it was divided this way and that, so that the two of them crossed over on dry ground.

And so it was, when they had crossed over, that Elijah said to Elisha, "Ask! What may I do for you, before I am taken away from you?"

Elisha said, "Please let a double portion of your spirit be upon me."

So he said, "You have asked a hard thing. *Nevertheless,* if you see me *when I am* taken from you, it shall be so for you; but if not, it shall not be *so.*" Then it happened, as they continued on and talked, that suddenly a chariot of fire *appeared* with horses of fire, and separated the two of them; and Elijah went up by a whirlwind into heaven.

And Elisha saw *it,* and he cried out, "My father, my father, the chariot of Israel and its horsemen!" So he saw him no more. And he took hold of his own clothes and tore them into two pieces. He also took up the mantle of Elijah that had fallen from him, and went back and stood by the bank of the Jordan. Then he took the mantle of Elijah that had fallen from him, and struck the water, and said, "Where *is* the LORD God of Elijah?" And when he also had struck the water, it was divided this way and that; and Elisha crossed over.

Now when the sons of the prophets who *were* from Jericho saw him, they said, "The spirit of Elijah rests on Elisha." And they came to meet him, and bowed to the ground before him. Then they said to him, "Look now, there are fifty strong men with your servants. Please let them go and search for your master, lest perhaps the Spirit of the LORD has taken him up and cast him upon some mountain or into some valley."

And he said, "You shall not send anyone."

But when they urged him till he was ashamed, he said, "Send *them!*" Therefore they sent fifty men, and they searched for three days but did not find him. And when they came back to him, for he had stayed in Jericho, he said to them, "Did I not say to you, 'Do not go'?"

Then the men of the city said to Elisha, "Please notice, the situation of this city *is* pleasant, as my lord sees; but the water *is* bad, and the ground barren."

And he said, "Bring me a new bowl, and put salt in it." So they brought *it* to him. Then he went out to the source of the water, and cast in the salt there, and said, "Thus says the LORD: 'I have healed this water; from it there shall be no more death or barrenness.'" So the water remains healed to this day, according to the word of Elisha which he spoke.

Then he went up from there to Bethel; and as he was going up the road, some youths came from the city and mocked him, and said to him, "Go up, you baldhead! Go up, you baldhead!"

So he turned around and looked at them, and pronounced a curse on them in the name of the LORD. And two female bears came out of the woods and mauled forty-two of the youths.

Then he went from there to Mount Carmel, and from there he returned to Samaria.

Now Naaman, commander of the army of the king of Syria, was a great and honorable man in the eyes of his master, because by him the LORD had given victory to Syria. He was also a mighty man of valor, *but* a leper. And the Syrians had gone out on raids, and had brought back captive a young girl from the land of Israel. She waited on Naaman's wife. Then she said to her mistress, "If only my master *were* with the prophet who *is* in Samaria! For he would heal him of his leprosy." And *Naaman* went in and told his master, saying, "Thus and thus said the girl who *is* from the land of Israel."

Then the king of Syria said, "Go now, and I will send a letter to the king of Israel."

So he departed and took with him ten talents of silver, six thousand *shekels* of gold, and ten changes of clothing. Then he brought the letter to the king of Israel, which said,

> Now be advised, when this letter comes to you, that I have sent Naaman my servant to you, that you may heal him of his leprosy.

And it happened, when the king of Israel read the letter, that he tore his clothes and said, "*Am* I God, to kill and make alive, that this man sends a man to me to heal him of his leprosy? Therefore please consider, and see how he seeks a quarrel with me."

So it was, when Elisha the man of God heard that the king of Israel had torn his clothes, that he sent to the king, saying, "Why have you torn your clothes? Please let him come to me, and he shall know that there is a prophet in Israel."

Then Naaman went with his horses and chariot, and he stood at the door of Elisha's house. And Elisha sent a messenger to him, saying, "Go and wash in the Jordan seven times, and your flesh shall be restored to you, and *you shall* be clean." But Naaman became furious, and went away and said, "Indeed, I said to myself, 'He will surely come out *to me,* and stand and call on the name of the LORD his God, and wave his hand over the place, and heal the leprosy.' *Are* not the Abanah and the Pharpar, the rivers of Damascus, better than all the waters of Israel? Could I not wash in them and be clean?" So he turned and went away in a rage. And his servants came near and spoke to him, and said, "My father, *if* the prophet had told you *to do* something great, would you not have done *it?* How much more then, when he says to you, 'Wash, and be clean'?" So he went down and dipped seven

times in the Jordan, according to the saying of the man of God; and his flesh was restored like the flesh of a little child, and he was clean.

2 Kings 2:1-25; 5:1-14

WORSHIP

The fool has said in his heart,
"*There is* no God."
They are corrupt, and have done abominable iniquity;
There is none who does good.

God looks down from heaven upon the children of men,
To see if there are *any* who understand, who seek God.
Every one of them has turned aside;
They have together become corrupt;
There is none who does good,
No, not one.

Psalm 53:1-3

WISDOM

The light of the righteous rejoices,
But the lamp of the wicked will be put out.

Proverbs 13:9

SW?! SO WHAT?
What does this tell me?

ELISHA'S PROPHETIC MINISTRY

2 Kings 6:1-7, 24-33; 7:1-20;
Psalm 54:4, 6-7; Proverbs 13:10

And the sons of the prophets said to Elisha, "See now, the place where we dwell with you is too small for us. Please, let us go to the Jordan, and let every man take a beam from there, and let us make there a place where we may dwell."

So he answered, "Go."

Then one said, "Please consent to go with your servants."

And he answered, "I will go." So he went with them. And when they came to the Jordan, they cut down trees. But as one was cutting down a tree, the iron *ax head* fell into the water; and he cried out and said, "Alas, master! For it was borrowed."

So the man of God said, "Where did it fall?" And he showed him the place. So he cut off a stick, and threw *it* in there; and he made the iron float. Therefore he said, "Pick *it* up for yourself." So he reached out his hand and took it.

And it happened after this that Ben-Hadad king of Syria gathered all his army, and went up and besieged Samaria. And there was a great famine in Samaria; and indeed they besieged it until a donkey's head was *sold* for eighty *shekels* of silver, and one-fourth of a kab of dove droppings for five *shekels* of silver.

Then, as the king of Israel was passing by on the wall, a woman cried out to him, saying, "Help, my lord, O king!"

And he said, "If the LORD does not help you, where can I find help for you? From the threshing floor or from the winepress?" Then the king said to her, "What is troubling you?"

And she answered, "This woman said to me, 'Give your son, that we may eat him today, and we will eat my son tomorrow.' So we boiled my son, and ate him. And I said to her on the next day, 'Give your son, that we may eat him'; but she has hidden her son."

Now it happened, when the king heard the words of the woman, that he tore his clothes; and as he passed by on the wall, the people looked, and there underneath *he had* sackcloth on his body. Then he said, "God do so to me and more also, if the head of Elisha the son of Shaphat remains on him today!"

But Elisha was sitting in his house, and the elders were sitting with him. And *the king* sent a man ahead of him, but before the messenger came to him, he said to the elders, "Do you see how this son of a murderer has sent someone to take away my head? Look, when the messenger comes, shut the door, and hold him fast at the door. *Is* not the sound of his master's feet behind him?" And while he was still talking with them, there was the messenger, coming down to him; and then *the king* said, "Surely this calamity *is* from the LORD; why should I wait for the LORD any longer?"

Then Elisha said, "Hear the word of the LORD. Thus says the LORD: 'Tomorrow about this time a seah of fine flour *shall be sold* for a shekel, and two seahs of barley for a shekel, at the gate of Samaria.' "

So an officer on whose hand the king leaned answered the man of God and said, "Look, *if* the LORD would make windows in heaven, could this thing be?"

And he said, "In fact, you shall see *it* with your eyes, but you shall not eat of it."

Now there were four leprous men at the entrance of the gate; and they said to one another, "Why are we sitting here until we die? If we say, 'We will enter the city,' the famine *is* in the city, and we shall die there. And if we sit here, we die also. Now therefore, come, let us surrender to the army of the Syrians. If they keep us alive, we shall live; and if they kill us, we shall only die." And they rose at twilight to go to the camp of the Syrians; and when they had come to the outskirts of the Syrian camp, to their surprise no one *was* there. For the LORD had caused the army of the Syrians to hear the noise of chariots and the noise of horses—the noise of a great army; so they said to one another, "Look, the king of Israel has hired against us the kings of the Hittites and the kings of the Egyptians to attack us!" Therefore they arose and fled at twilight, and left the camp intact—their tents, their horses, and their donkeys—and they fled for their lives. And when these lepers came to the outskirts of the camp, they went into one tent and ate and drank, and carried from it silver and gold and clothing, and went and hid *them;* then they came back and entered another tent, and carried *some* from there *also,* and went and hid *it.*

Then they said to one another, "We are not doing right. This day *is* a day of good news, and we remain silent. If we wait until morning light, some punishment will come upon us. Now therefore, come, let us go and tell the king's household." So they went and called to the gatekeepers of the city, and told them, saying, "We went to the Syrian camp, and surprisingly no one *was* there, not a human sound—only horses and donkeys tied, and the tents intact." And the gatekeepers called out, and they told *it* to the king's household inside.

So the king arose in the night and said to his servants, "Let me now tell you what the Syrians have done to us. They know that we *are* hungry; therefore they have gone out of the camp to hide themselves in the field, saying, 'When they come out of the city, we shall catch them alive, and get into the city.' "

And one of his servants answered and said, "Please, let several *men* take five of the remaining horses which are left in the city. Look, they *may either become* like all the multitude of Israel that are left in it; or indeed, *I say,* they *may become* like all the multitude of Israel left from those who are consumed; so let us send them and see." Therefore they took two chariots with horses; and the king sent them in the direction of the Syrian army, saying, "Go and see." And they went after them to the Jordan; and indeed all the road *was* full of garments and weapons which the Syrians had thrown away in their haste. So the messengers returned and told the king. Then the people went out and plundered the tents of the Syrians. So a seah of fine flour was *sold* for a shekel, and two seahs of barley for a shekel, according to the word of the LORD.

Now the king had appointed the officer on whose hand he leaned to have charge of the gate. But the people trampled him in the gate, and he died, just as the man of God had said, who spoke when the king came down to him. So it happened just as the man of God had spoken to the king, saying, "Two seahs of barley for a shekel, and a seah of fine flour for a shekel, shall be *sold* tomorrow about this time in the gate of Samaria."

Then that officer had answered the man of God, and said, "Now look, *if* the LORD would make windows in heaven, could such a thing be?"

And he had said, "In fact, you shall see *it* with your eyes, but you shall not eat of it." And so it happened to him, for the people trampled him in the gate, and he died.

2 Kings 6:1-7, 24-33; 7:1-20

WORSHIP

Behold, God *is* my helper;
The Lord *is* with those who uphold my life.

I will freely sacrifice to You;
I will praise Your name, O LORD, for *it is* good.
For He has delivered me out of all trouble;
And my eye has seen *its desire* upon my
    enemies.

Psalm 54:4, 6-7

WISDOM

By pride comes nothing but strife,
But with the well-advised *is* wisdom.

Proverbs 13:10

SO WHAT?
What does this tell me?

JEHU'S BLOODBATH

2 Kings 9:1-37; 10:12-17; Psalm 55:1-3; Proverbs 13:11

And Elisha the prophet called one of the sons of the prophets, and said to him, "Get yourself ready, take this flask of oil in your hand, and go to Ramoth Gilead. Now when you arrive at that place, look there for Jehu the son of Jehoshaphat, the son of Nimshi, and go in and make him rise up from among his associates, and take him to an inner room. Then take the flask of oil, and pour *it* on his head, and say, 'Thus says the LORD: "I have anointed you king over Israel." ' Then open the door and flee, and do not delay."

So the young man, the servant of the prophet, went to Ramoth Gilead. And when he arrived, there *were* the captains of the army sitting; and he said, "I have a message for you, Commander."

Jehu said, "For which *one* of us?"

And he said, "For you, Commander." Then he arose and went into the house. And he poured the oil on his head, and said to him, "Thus says the LORD God of Israel: 'I have anointed you king over the people of the LORD, over Israel. You shall strike down the house of Ahab your master, that I may avenge the blood of My servants the prophets, and the blood of all the servants of the LORD, at the hand of Jezebel. For the whole house of Ahab shall perish; and I will cut off from Ahab all the males in Israel, both bond and free. So I will make the house of Ahab like the house of Jeroboam the son of Nebat, and like the house of Baasha the son of Ahijah. The dogs shall eat Jezebel on the plot *of ground* at Jezreel, and *there shall be* none to bury her.' " And he opened the door and fled.

Then Jehu came out to the servants of his master, and *one* said to him, "*Is* all well? Why did this madman come to you?"

And he said to them, "You know the man and his babble."

And they said, "A lie! Tell us now."

So he said, "Thus and thus he spoke to me, saying, 'Thus says the LORD: "I have anointed you king over Israel." ' "

Then each man hastened to take his garment and put *it* under him on the top of the steps; and they blew trumpets, saying, "Jehu is king!"

So Jehu the son of Jehoshaphat, the son of Nimshi, conspired against Joram. (Now Joram had been defending Ramoth Gilead, he and all Israel, against Hazael king of Syria. But King Joram had returned to Jezreel to recover from the wounds which the Syrians had inflicted on him when he fought with Hazael king of Syria.) And Jehu said, "If you are so minded, let no one leave *or* escape from the city to go and tell *it* in Jezreel." So Jehu rode in a chariot and went to Jezreel, for Joram was laid up there; and Ahaziah king of Judah had come down to see Joram.

Now a watchman stood on the tower in Jezreel, and he saw the company of Jehu as he came, and said, "I see a company of men."

And Joram said, "Get a horseman and send him to meet them, and let him say, '*Is it* peace?' "

So the horseman went to meet him, and said, "Thus says the king: '*Is it* peace?' "

And Jehu said, "What have you to do with peace? Turn around and follow me."

So the watchman reported, saying, "The messenger went to them, but is not coming back."

Then he sent out a second horseman who came to them, and said, "Thus says the king: '*Is it* peace?' "

And Jehu answered, "What have you to do with peace? Turn around and follow me."

So the watchman reported, saying, "He went up to them and is not coming back; and the driving *is* like the driving of Jehu the son of Nimshi, for he drives furiously!"

Then Joram said, "Make ready." And his chariot was made ready. Then Joram king of Israel and Ahaziah king of Judah went out, each in his chariot; and they went out to meet Jehu, and met him on the property of Naboth the Jezreelite. Now it happened, when Joram saw Jehu, that he said, "*Is it* peace, Jehu?"

So he answered, "What peace, as long as the harlotries of your mother Jezebel and her witchcraft *are so* many?"

Then Joram turned around and fled, and said to Ahaziah, "Treachery, Ahaziah!" Now Jehu drew his bow with full strength and shot Jehoram between his arms; and the arrow came out at his heart, and he sank down in his chariot. Then *Jehu* said to Bidkar his captain, "Pick *him* up, *and* throw

DIVIDED WE FALL

him into the tract of the field of Naboth the Jezreelite; for remember, when you and I were riding together behind Ahab his father, that the LORD laid this burden upon him: 'Surely I saw yesterday the blood of Naboth and the blood of his sons,' says the LORD, 'and I will repay you in this plot,' says the LORD. Now therefore, take *and* throw him on the plot *of ground,* according to the word of the LORD."

But when Ahaziah king of Judah saw *this,* he fled by the road to Beth Haggan. So Jehu pursued him, and said, "Shoot him also in the chariot." *And they shot him* at the Ascent of Gur, which is by Ibleam. Then he fled to Megiddo, and died there. And his servants carried him in the chariot to Jerusalem, and buried him in his tomb with his fathers in the City of David. In the eleventh year of Joram the son of Ahab, Ahaziah had become king over Judah.

Now when Jehu had come to Jezreel, Jezebel heard *of it;* and she put paint on her eyes and adorned her head, and looked through a window. Then, as Jehu entered at the gate, she said, "*Is it* peace, Zimri, murderer of your master?"

And he looked up at the window, and said, "Who *is* on my side? Who?" So two *or* three eunuchs looked out at him. Then he said, "Throw her down." So they threw her down, and *some* of her blood spattered on the wall and on the horses; and he trampled her underfoot. And when he had gone in, he ate and drank. Then he said, "Go now, see to this accursed *woman,* and bury her, for she was a king's daughter." So they went to bury her, but they found no more of her than the skull and the feet and the palms of *her* hands. Therefore they came back and told him. And he said, "This *is* the word of the LORD, which He spoke by His servant Elijah the Tishbite, saying, 'On the plot *of ground* at Jezreel dogs shall eat the flesh of Jezebel; and the corpse of Jezebel shall be as refuse on the surface of the field, in the plot at Jezreel, so that they shall not say, "Here *lies* Jezebel." ' "

And he arose and departed and went to Samaria. On the way, at Beth Eked of the Shepherds, Jehu met with the brothers of Ahaziah king of Judah, and said, "Who *are* you?"

So they answered, "We *are* the brothers of Ahaziah; we have come down to greet the sons of the king and the sons of the queen mother."

And he said, "Take them alive!" So they took them alive, and killed them at the well of Beth Eked, forty-two men; and he left none of them.

Now when he departed from there, he met Jehonadab the son of Rechab, *coming* to meet him; and he greeted him and said to him, "Is your heart right, as my heart *is* toward your heart?"

And Jehonadab answered, "It is."

Jehu said, "If it is, give *me* your hand." So he gave *him* his hand, and he took him up to him into the chariot. Then he said, "Come with me, and see my zeal for the LORD." So they had him ride in his chariot. And when he came to Samaria, he killed all who remained to Ahab in Samaria, till he had destroyed them, according to the word of the LORD which He spoke to Elijah.

2 Kings 9:1-37; 10:12-17

WORSHIP

Give ear to my prayer, O God,
And do not hide Yourself from my supplication.
Attend to me, and hear me;
I am restless in my complaint, and moan
   noisily,
Because of the voice of the enemy,
Because of the oppression of the wicked;
For they bring down trouble upon me,
And in wrath they hate me.

Psalm 55:1-3

WISDOM

Wealth *gained by* dishonesty will be
   diminished,
But he who gathers by labor will increase.

Proverbs 13:11

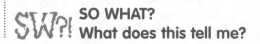

SO WHAT?
What does this tell me?

A WICKED QUEEN AND A YOUNG KING

2 Kings 11–12; Psalm 55:4–6; Proverbs 13:12

When Athaliah the mother of Ahaziah saw that her son was dead, she arose and destroyed all the royal heirs. But Jehosheba, the daughter of King Joram, sister of Ahaziah, took Joash the son of Ahaziah, and stole him away from among the king's sons *who were* being murdered; and they hid him and his nurse in the bedroom, from Athaliah, so that he was not killed. So he was hidden with her in the house of the LORD for six years, while Athaliah reigned over the land.

In the seventh year Jehoiada sent and brought the captains of hundreds—of the bodyguards and the escorts—and brought them into the house of the LORD to him. And he made a covenant with them and took an oath from them in the house of the LORD, and showed them the king's son. Then he commanded them, saying, "This *is* what you shall do: One-third of you who come on duty on the Sabbath shall be keeping watch over the king's house, one-third *shall be* at the gate of Sur, and one-third at the gate behind the escorts. You shall keep the watch of the house, lest it be broken down. The two contingents of you who go off duty on the Sabbath shall keep the watch of the house of the LORD for the king. But you shall surround the king on all sides, every man with his weapons in his hand; and whoever comes within range, let him be put to death. You are to be with the king as he goes out and as he comes in."

So the captains of the hundreds did according to all that Jehoiada the priest commanded. Each of them took his men who were to be on duty on the Sabbath, with those who were going off duty on the Sabbath, and came to Jehoiada the priest. And the priest gave the captains of hundreds the spears and shields which *had belonged* to King David, that were in the temple of the LORD. Then the escorts stood, every man with his weapons in his hand, all around the king, from the right side of the temple to the left side of the temple, by the altar and the house. And he brought out the king's son, put the crown on him, and *gave him* the Testimony; they made him king and anointed him, and they clapped their hands and said, "Long live the king!"

Now when Athaliah heard the noise of the escorts *and* the people, she came to the people *in* the temple of the LORD. When she looked, there was the king standing by a pillar according to custom; and the leaders and the trumpeters were by the king. All the people of the land were rejoicing and blowing trumpets. So Athaliah tore her clothes and cried out, "Treason! Treason!"

And Jehoiada the priest commanded the captains of the hundreds, the officers of the army, and said to them, "Take her outside under guard, and slay with the sword whoever follows her." For the priest had said, "Do not let her be killed in the house of the LORD." So they seized her; and she went by way of the horses' entrance *into* the king's house, and there she was killed.

Then Jehoiada made a covenant between the LORD, the king, and the people, that they should be the LORD's people, and *also* between the king and the people. And all the people of the land went to the temple of Baal, and tore it down. They thoroughly broke in pieces its altars and images, and killed Mattan the priest of Baal before the altars. And the priest appointed officers over the house of the LORD. Then he took the captains of hundreds, the bodyguards, the escorts, and all the people of the land; and they brought the king down from the house of the LORD, and went by way of the gate of the escorts to the king's house. Then he sat on the throne of the kings. So all the people of the land rejoiced; and the city was quiet, for they had slain Athaliah with the sword *in* the king's house. Jehoash *was* seven years old when he became king.

In the seventh year of Jehu, Jehoash became king, and he reigned forty years in Jerusalem. His mother's name *was* Zibiah of Beersheba. Jehoash did *what was* right in the sight of the LORD all the days in which Jehoiada the priest instructed him. But the high places were not taken away; the people still sacrificed and burned incense on the high places.

And Jehoash said to the priests, "All the money of the dedicated gifts that are brought into the house of the LORD—each man's census money, each man's assessment money—*and* all the money that a man purposes in his heart to bring into the house of the LORD, let the priests take *it* themselves, each from his constituency; and let them repair the damages of the temple, wherever any dilapidation is found."

Now it was so, by the twenty-third year of King Jehoash, *that* the priests had not repaired the damages of the temple. So King Jehoash called Jehoiada the priest and the *other* priests, and said to them, "Why have you not repaired the damages of the temple? Now therefore, do not take *more* money from your constituency, but deliver it for repairing the damages of the temple." And the priests agreed that they would neither receive *more* money from the people, nor repair the damages of the temple.

Then Jehoiada the priest took a chest, bored a hole in its lid, and set it beside the altar, on the right side as one comes into the house of the LORD; and the priests who kept the door put there all the money brought into the house of the LORD. So it was, whenever they saw that *there was* much money in the chest, that the king's scribe and the high priest came up and put it in bags, and counted the money that was found in the house of the LORD. Then they gave the money, which had been apportioned, into the hands of those who did the work, who had the oversight of the house of the LORD; and they paid it out to the carpenters and builders who worked on the house of the LORD, and to masons and stonecutters, and for buying timber and hewn stone, to repair the damage of the house of the LORD, and for all that was paid out to repair the temple. However there were not made for the house of the LORD basins of silver, trimmers, sprinkling-bowls, trumpets, any articles of gold or articles of silver, from the money brought into the house of the LORD. But they gave that to the workmen, and they repaired the house of the LORD with it. Moreover they did not require an account from the men into whose hand they delivered the money to be paid to workmen, for they dealt faithfully. The money from the trespass offerings and the money from the sin offerings was not brought into the house of the LORD. It belonged to the priests.

Hazael king of Syria went up and fought against Gath, and took it; then Hazael set his face to go up to Jerusalem. And Jehoash king of Judah took all the sacred things that his fathers, Jehoshaphat and Jehoram and Ahaziah, kings of Judah, had dedicated, and his own sacred things, and all the gold found in the treasuries of the house of the LORD and in the king's house, and sent *them* to Hazael king of Syria. Then he went away from Jerusalem.

Now the rest of the acts of Joash, and all that he did, *are* they not written in the book of the chronicles of the kings of Judah?

And his servants arose and formed a conspiracy, and killed Joash in the house of the Millo, which goes down to Silla. For Jozachar the son of Shimeath and Jehozabad the son of Shomer, his servants, struck him. So he died, and they buried him with his fathers in the City of David. Then Amaziah his son reigned in his place.

2 Kings 11–12

WORSHIP

My heart is severely pained within me,
And the terrors of death have fallen upon me.
Fearfulness and trembling have come upon
   me,
And horror has overwhelmed me.
So I said, "Oh, that I had wings like a dove!
I would fly away and be at rest."

Psalm 55:4-6

WISDOM

Hope deferred makes the heart sick,
But *when* the desire comes, *it is* a tree of life.

Proverbs 13:12

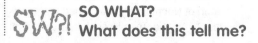

SO WHAT?
What does this tell me?

RISE OF ASSYRIA

2 Kings 15:17–16:20; Psalm 55:16-18; Proverbs 13:13

In the thirty-ninth year of Azariah king of Judah, Menahem the son of Gadi became king over Israel, *and reigned* ten years in Samaria. And he did evil in the sight of the LORD; he did not depart all his days from the sins of Jeroboam the son of Nebat, who had made Israel sin. Pul king of Assyria came against the land; and Menahem gave Pul a thousand talents of silver, that his hand might be with him to strengthen the kingdom under his control. And Menahem exacted the money from Israel, from all the very wealthy, from each man fifty shekels of silver, to give to the king of Assyria. So the king of Assyria turned back, and did not stay there in the land.

Now the rest of the acts of Menahem, and all that he did, *are* they not written in the book of the chronicles of the kings of Israel? So Menahem rested with his fathers. Then Pekahiah his son reigned in his place.

In the fiftieth year of Azariah king of Judah, Pekahiah the son of Menahem became king over Israel in Samaria, *and reigned* two years. And he did evil in the sight of the LORD; he did not depart from the sins of Jeroboam the son of Nebat, who had made Israel sin. Then Pekah the son of Remaliah, an officer of his, conspired against him and killed him in Samaria, in the citadel of the king's house, along with Argob and Arieh; and with him were fifty men of Gilead. He killed him and reigned in his place.

Now the rest of the acts of Pekahiah, and all that he did, indeed they *are* written in the book of the chronicles of the kings of Israel.

In the fifty-second year of Azariah king of Judah, Pekah the son of Remaliah became king over Israel in Samaria, *and reigned* twenty years. And he did evil in the sight of the LORD; he did not depart from the sins of Jeroboam the son of Nebat, who had made Israel sin. In the days of Pekah king of Israel, Tiglath-Pileser king of Assyria came and took Ijon, Abel Beth Maachah, Janoah, Kedesh, Hazor, Gilead, and Galilee, all the land of Naphtali; and he carried them captive to Assyria. Then Hoshea the son of Elah

led a conspiracy against Pekah the son of Remaliah, and struck and killed him; so he reigned in his place in the twentieth year of Jotham the son of Uzziah.

Now the rest of the acts of Pekah, and all that he did, indeed they *are* written in the book of the chronicles of the kings of Israel.

In the second year of Pekah the son of Remaliah, king of Israel, Jotham the son of Uzziah, king of Judah, began to reign. He was twenty-five years old when he became king, and he reigned sixteen years in Jerusalem. His mother's name *was* Jerusha the daughter of Zadok. And he did *what was* right in the sight of the LORD; he did according to all that his father Uzziah had done. However the high places were not removed; the people still sacrificed and burned incense on the high places. He built the Upper Gate of the house of the LORD.

Now the rest of the acts of Jotham, and all that he did, *are* they not written in the book of the chronicles of the kings of Judah? In those days the LORD began to send Rezin king of Syria and Pekah the son of Remaliah against Judah. So Jotham rested with his fathers, and was buried with his fathers in the City of David his father. Then Ahaz his son reigned in his place.

In the seventeenth year of Pekah the son of Remaliah, Ahaz the son of Jotham, king of Judah, began to reign. Ahaz *was* twenty years old when he became king, and he reigned sixteen years in Jerusalem; and he did not do *what was* right in the sight of the LORD his God, as his father David *had done*. But he walked in the way of the kings of Israel; indeed he made his son pass through the fire, according to the abominations of the nations whom the LORD had cast out from before the children of Israel. And he sacrificed and burned incense on the high places, on the hills, and under every green tree.

Then Rezin king of Syria and Pekah the son of Remaliah, king of Israel, came up to Jerusalem to *make* war; and they besieged Ahaz but could not overcome *him*. At that time Rezin king of Syria captured Elath for Syria, and drove the men of Judah from Elath. Then the Edomites went to Elath, and dwell there to this day.

So Ahaz sent messengers to Tiglath-Pileser king of Assyria, saying, "I *am* your servant and your son. Come up and save me from the hand of the king of Syria and from the hand of the king of Israel, who rise up against me." And Ahaz took the silver and gold that was found in the house of the LORD, and in the treasuries of the king's house, and sent *it as* a present to the king of Assyria. So the king of Assyria heeded him; for the king of Assyria went up against Damascus and took it, carried *its people* captive to Kir, and killed Rezin.

Now King Ahaz went to Damascus to meet Tiglath-Pileser king of Assyria, and saw an altar that *was* at Damascus; and King Ahaz sent to Urijah the priest the design of the altar and its pattern, according to all its workmanship. Then Urijah the priest built an altar according to all that King Ahaz had sent from Damascus. So Urijah the priest made *it* before King Ahaz came back from Damascus. And when the king came back from Damascus, the king saw the altar; and the king approached the altar and made offerings on it. So he burned his burnt offering and his grain offering; and he poured his drink offering and sprinkled the blood of his peace offerings on the altar. He also brought the bronze altar which *was* before the LORD, from the front of the temple—from between the *new* altar and the house of the LORD—and put it on the north side of the *new* altar. Then King Ahaz commanded Urijah the priest, saying, "On the great *new* altar burn the morning burnt offering, the evening grain offering, the king's burnt sacrifice, and his grain offering, with the burnt offering of all the people of the land, their grain offering, and their drink offerings; and sprinkle on it all the blood of the burnt offering and all the blood of the sacrifice. And the bronze altar shall be for me to inquire *by*." Thus did Urijah the priest, according to all that King Ahaz commanded.

And King Ahaz cut off the panels of the carts, and removed the lavers from them; and he took down the Sea from the bronze oxen that *were* under it, and put it on a pavement of stones. Also he removed the Sabbath pavilion which they had built in the temple, and he removed the king's outer entrance from the house of the LORD, on account of the king of Assyria.

Now the rest of the acts of Ahaz which he did, *are* they not written in the book of the chronicles of the kings of Judah? So Ahaz rested with his fathers, and was buried with his fathers in the City of David. Then Hezekiah his son reigned in his place.

2 Kings 15:17–16:20

WORSHIP

As for me, I will call upon God,
And the LORD shall save me.
Evening and morning and at noon
I will pray, and cry aloud,
And He shall hear my voice.
He has redeemed my soul in peace from the
    battle *that was* against me,
For there were many against me.

Psalm 55:16-18

WISDOM

He who despises the word will be destroyed,
But he who fears the commandment will be
    rewarded.

Proverbs 13:13

SW?! **SO WHAT?**
What does this tell me?

CAPTIVITY OF SAMARIA 2 Kings 17; Psalm 55:22-23; Proverbs 13:14

In the twelfth year of Ahaz king of Judah, Hoshea the son of Elah became king of Israel in Samaria, *and he reigned* nine years. And he did evil in the sight of the LORD, but not as the kings of Israel who were before him. Shalmaneser king of Assyria came up against him; and Hoshea became his vassal, and paid him tribute money. And the king of Assyria uncovered a conspiracy by Hoshea; for he had sent messengers to So, king of Egypt, and brought no tribute to the king of Assyria, as *he had done* year by year. Therefore the king of Assyria shut him up, and bound him in prison.

Now the king of Assyria went throughout all the land, and went up to Samaria and besieged it for three years. In the ninth year of Hoshea, the king of Assyria took Samaria and carried Israel away to Assyria, and placed them in Halah and by the Habor, the River of Gozan, and in the cities of the Medes.

For so it was that the children of Israel had sinned against the LORD their God, who had brought them up out of the land of Egypt, from under the hand of Pharaoh king of Egypt; and they had feared other gods, and had walked in the statutes of the nations whom the LORD had cast out from before the children of Israel, and of the kings of Israel, which they had made. Also the children of Israel secretly did against the LORD their God things that *were* not right, and they built for themselves high places in all their cities, from watchtower to fortified city. They set up for themselves *sacred* pillars and wooden images on every high hill and under every green tree. There they burned incense on all the high places, like the nations whom the LORD had carried away before them; and they did wicked things to provoke the LORD to anger, for they served idols, of which the LORD had said to them, "You shall not do this thing."

Yet the LORD testified against Israel and against Judah, by all of His prophets, every seer, saying, "Turn from your evil ways, and keep My commandments *and* My statutes, according to all the law which I commanded your fathers, and which I sent to you by My servants the prophets." Nevertheless they would not hear, but stiffened their necks, like the necks of their fathers, who did not believe in the LORD their God. And they rejected His statutes and His covenant that He had made with their fathers, and His testimonies which He had testified against them; they followed idols, became idolaters, and *went* after the nations who *were* all around them, *concerning* whom the LORD had charged them that they should not do like them. So they left all the commandments of the LORD their God, made for themselves a molded image *and* two calves, made a wooden image and worshiped all the host of heaven, and served Baal. And they caused their sons and daughters to pass through the fire, practiced witchcraft and soothsaying, and sold themselves to do evil in the sight of the LORD, to provoke Him to anger. Therefore the LORD was very angry with Israel, and removed them from His sight; there was none left but the tribe of Judah alone.

Also Judah did not keep the commandments of the LORD their God, but walked in the statutes of Israel which they made. And the LORD rejected all the descendants of Israel, afflicted them, and delivered them into the hand of plunderers, until He had cast them from His sight. For He tore Israel from the house of David, and they made Jeroboam the son of Nebat king. Then Jeroboam drove Israel from following the LORD, and made them commit a great sin. For the children of Israel walked in all the sins of Jeroboam which he did; they did not depart from them, until the LORD removed Israel out of His sight, as He had said by all His servants the prophets. So Israel was carried away from their own land to Assyria, *as it is* to this day.

Then the king of Assyria brought *people* from Babylon, Cuthah, Ava, Hamath, and from Sepharvaim, and placed *them* in the cities of Samaria instead of the children of Israel; and they took possession of Samaria and dwelt in its cities. And it was so, at the beginning of their dwelling there, *that* they did not fear the LORD; therefore the LORD sent lions among them, which killed *some* of them. So they spoke to the king of Assyria, saying, "The nations whom you have removed and placed in the cities of Samaria do not know the rituals of the God of the land; therefore He has sent lions among them, and indeed, they are killing them because they do not know the rituals of the God of the land." Then the king of Assyria commanded, saying, "Send there one of the priests whom you brought from there; let him go and dwell there, and let him teach them the rituals of the God of the land." Then one of the priests whom they had carried away from Samaria came and dwelt in Bethel, and taught them how they should fear the LORD.

However every nation continued to make gods of its own, and put *them* in the shrines on the high places which the Samaritans had made, *every* nation in the cities where they dwelt. The men of Babylon made Succoth Benoth, the men of Cuth made Nergal, the men of Hamath made Ashima, and the Avites made Nibhaz and Tartak; and the Sepharvites burned their children in fire to Adrammelech and Anammelech, the gods of Sepharvaim. So they feared the LORD, and from every class they appointed for themselves priests of the high places, who sacrificed for them in the shrines of the high places. They feared the LORD, yet served their own gods—according to the rituals of the nations from among whom they were carried away.

To this day they continue practicing the former rituals; they do not fear the LORD, nor do they follow their statutes or their ordinances, or the law and commandment which the LORD had commanded the children of Jacob, whom He named Israel, with whom the LORD had made a covenant and charged them, saying: "You shall not fear other gods, nor bow down to them nor serve them nor sacrifice to them; but the LORD, who brought you up from the land of Egypt with great power and an outstretched arm, Him you shall fear, Him you shall worship, and to Him you shall offer sacrifice. And the statutes, the ordinances, the law, and the commandment which He wrote for you, you shall be careful to observe forever; you shall not fear other gods. And the covenant that I have made with you, you shall not forget, nor shall you fear other gods. But the LORD your God you shall fear; and He will deliver you from the hand of all your enemies." However they did not obey, but they followed their former rituals. So these nations feared the LORD, yet served their carved images; also their children and their children's children have continued doing as their fathers did, even to this day.

2 Kings 17

WORSHIP

Cast your burden on the LORD,
And He shall sustain you;
He shall never permit the righteous to be moved.

But You, O God, shall bring them down to the pit of destruction;
Bloodthirsty and deceitful men shall not live out half their days;
But I will trust in You.

Psalm 55:22-23

WISDOM

The law of the wise *is* a fountain of life,
To turn *one* away from the snares of death.

Proverbs 13:14

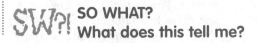

SO WHAT?
What does this tell me?

ASSYRIA ATTACKS JERUSALEM

2 Kings 18:1-8, 13-18, 26-37; 19:1-7, 32-37; Psalm 56:2-4; Proverbs 13:15

Now it came to pass in the third year of Hoshea the son of Elah, king of Israel, *that* Hezekiah the son of Ahaz, king of Judah, began to reign. He was twenty-five years old when he became king, and he reigned twenty-nine years in Jerusalem. His mother's name *was* Abi the daughter of Zechariah. And he did *what was* right in the sight of the LORD, according to all that his father David had done.

He removed the high places and broke the *sacred* pillars, cut down the wooden image and broke in pieces the bronze serpent that Moses had made; for until those days the children of Israel burned incense to it, and called it Nehushtan. He trusted in the LORD God of Israel, so that after him was none like him among all the kings of Judah, nor who were before him. For he held fast to the LORD; he did not depart from following Him, but kept His commandments, which the LORD had commanded Moses. The LORD was with him; he prospered wherever he went. And he rebelled against the king of Assyria and did not serve him. He subdued the Philistines, as far as Gaza and its territory, from watchtower to fortified city.

And in the fourteenth year of King Hezekiah, Sennacherib king of Assyria came up against all the fortified cities of Judah and took them. Then Hezekiah king of Judah sent to the king of Assyria at Lachish, saying, "I have done wrong; turn away from me; whatever you impose on me I will pay." And the king of Assyria assessed Hezekiah king of Judah three hundred talents of silver and thirty talents of gold. So Hezekiah gave *him* all the silver that was found in the house of the LORD and in the treasuries of the king's house. At that time Hezekiah stripped *the gold from* the doors of the temple of the LORD, and *from* the pillars which Hezekiah king of Judah had overlaid, and gave it to the king of Assyria.

Then the king of Assyria sent *the* Tartan, *the* Rabsaris, *and the* Rabshakeh from Lachish, with a great army against Jerusalem, to King Hezekiah. And they went up and came to Jerusalem. When they had come up, they went and stood by the aque-

duct from the upper pool, which *was* on the highway to the Fuller's Field. And when they had called to the king, Eliakim the son of Hilkiah, who *was* over the household, Shebna the scribe, and Joah the son of Asaph, the recorder, came out to them.

Then Eliakim the son of Hilkiah, Shebna, and Joah said to *the* Rabshakeh, "Please speak to your servants in Aramaic, for we understand *it;* and do not speak to us in Hebrew in the hearing of the people who *are* on the wall."

But *the* Rabshakeh said to them, "Has my master sent me to your master and to you to speak these words, and not to the men who sit on the wall, who will eat and drink their own waste with you?"

Then *the* Rabshakeh stood and called out with a loud voice in Hebrew, and spoke, saying, "Hear the word of the great king, the king of Assyria! Thus says the king: 'Do not let Hezekiah deceive you, for he shall not be able to deliver you from his hand; nor let Hezekiah make you trust in the LORD, saying, "The LORD will surely deliver us; this city shall not be given into the hand of the king of Assyria." ' Do not listen to Hezekiah; for thus says the king of Assyria: 'Make *peace* with me by a present and come out to me; and every one of you eat from his own vine and every one from his own fig tree, and every one of you drink the waters of his own cistern; until I come and take you away to a land like your own land, a land of grain and new wine, a land of bread and vineyards, a land of olive groves and honey, that you may live and not die. But do not listen to Hezekiah, lest he persuade you, saying, "The LORD will deliver us." Has any of the gods of the nations at all delivered its land from the hand of the king of Assyria? Where *are* the gods of Hamath and Arpad? Where *are* the gods of Sepharvaim and Hena and Ivah? Indeed, have they delivered Samaria from my hand? Who among all the gods of the lands have delivered their countries from my hand, that the LORD should deliver Jerusalem from my hand?' "

But the people held their peace and answered him not a word; for the king's commandment was, "Do not answer him." Then Eliakim the son of Hilkiah, who *was* over the household, Shebna the scribe, and Joah the son of Asaph, the recorder, came to Hezekiah with *their* clothes torn, and told him the words of *the* Rabshakeh.

And so it was, when King Hezekiah heard *it,* that he tore his clothes, covered himself with sack-cloth, and went into the house of the LORD. Then he sent Eliakim, who *was* over the household, Shebna the scribe, and the elders of the priests, covered with sackcloth, to Isaiah the prophet, the son of Amoz. And they said to him, "Thus says Hezekiah: 'This day *is* a day of trouble, and rebuke, and blas-phemy; for the children have come to birth, but *there is* no strength to bring them forth. It may be that the LORD your God will hear all the words of *the* Rabshakeh, whom his master the king of Assyria has sent to reproach the living God, and will rebuke the words which the LORD your God has heard. Therefore lift up *your* prayer for the remnant that is left.' "

So the servants of King Hezekiah came to Isa-iah. And Isaiah said to them, "Thus you shall say to your master, 'Thus says the LORD: "Do not be afraid of the words which you have heard, with which the servants of the king of Assyria have blasphemed Me. Surely I will send a spirit upon him, and he shall hear a rumor and return to his own land; and I will cause him to fall by the sword in his own land." ' "

"Therefore thus says the LORD concerning the king of Assyria:

'He shall not come into this city,
Nor shoot an arrow there,
Nor come before it with shield,
Nor build a siege mound against it.
By the way that he came,
By the same shall he return;
And he shall not come into this city,'
Says the LORD.
'For I will defend this city, to save it
For My own sake and for My servant David's
    sake.' "

And it came to pass on a certain night that the angel of the LORD went out, and killed in the camp of the Assyrians one hundred and eighty-five thou-sand; and when *people* arose early in the morning, there were the corpses—all dead. So Sennacherib king of Assyria departed and went away, returned *home,* and remained at Nineveh. Now it came to pass, as he was worshiping in the temple of Nis-roch his god, that his sons Adrammelech and Sharezer struck him down with the sword; and they escaped into the land of Ararat. Then Esarhaddon

his son reigned in his place.
2 Kings 18:1-8, 13-18, 26-37; 19:1-7, 32-37

WORSHIP

My enemies would hound *me* all day,
For *there are* many who fight against me, O
    Most High.

Whenever I am afraid,
I will trust in You.
In God (I will praise His word),
In God I have put my trust;
I will not fear.
What can flesh do to me?

Psalm 56:2-4

WISDOM

Good understanding gains favor,
But the way of the unfaithful *is* hard.

Proverbs 13:15

SW?!

SO WHAT?
What does this tell me?

JOSIAH'S REFORMS

2 Kings 22:1-20; 23:21-37; Psalm 56:11-13;
Proverbs 13:16

Josiah *was* eight years old when he became king, and he reigned thirty-one years in Jerusalem. His mother's name *was* Jedidah the daughter of Adaiah of Bozkath. And he did *what was* right in the sight of the LORD, and walked in all the ways of his father David; he did not turn aside to the right hand or to the left.

Now it came to pass, in the eighteenth year of King Josiah, *that* the king sent Shaphan the scribe, the son of Azaliah, the son of Meshullam, to the house of the LORD, saying: "Go up to Hilkiah the high priest, that he may count the money which has been brought into the house of the LORD, which the doorkeepers have gathered from the people. And let them deliver it into the hand of those doing the work, who are the overseers in the house of the LORD; let them give it to those who *are* in the house of the LORD doing the work, to repair the damages of the house—to carpenters and builders and masons—and to buy timber and hewn stone to repair the house. However there need be no accounting made with them of the money delivered into their hand, because they deal faithfully."

Then Hilkiah the high priest said to Shaphan the scribe, "I have found the Book of the Law in the house of the LORD." And Hilkiah gave the book to Shaphan, and he read it. So Shaphan the scribe went to the king, bringing the king word, saying, "Your servants have gathered the money that was found in the house, and have delivered it into the hand of those who do the work, who oversee the house of the LORD." Then Shaphan the scribe showed the king, saying, "Hilkiah the priest has given me a book." And Shaphan read it before the king.

Now it happened, when the king heard the words of the Book of the Law, that he tore his clothes. Then the king commanded Hilkiah the priest, Ahikam the son of Shaphan, Achbor the son of Michaiah, Shaphan the scribe, and Asaiah a servant of the king, saying, "Go, inquire of the LORD for me, for the people and for all Judah, concerning the words of this book that has been found; for great *is* the wrath of the LORD that is aroused against us, because our fathers have not obeyed the words of this book, to do according to all that is written concerning us."

So Hilkiah the priest, Ahikam, Achbor, Shaphan, and Asaiah went to Huldah the prophetess, the wife of Shallum the son of Tikvah, the son of Harhas, keeper of the wardrobe. (She dwelt in Jerusalem in the Second Quarter.) And they spoke with her. Then she said to them, "Thus says the LORD God of Israel, 'Tell the man who sent you to Me, "Thus says the LORD: 'Behold, I will bring calamity on this place and on its inhabitants—all the words of the book which the king of Judah has read—because they have forsaken Me and burned incense to other gods, that they might provoke Me to anger with all the works of their hands. Therefore My wrath shall be aroused against this place and shall not be quenched.' " ' But as for the king of Judah, who sent you to inquire of the LORD, in this manner you shall speak to him, 'Thus says the LORD God of Israel: "*Concerning* the words which you have heard—because your heart was tender, and you humbled yourself before the LORD when you heard what I spoke against this place and against its inhabitants, that they would become a desolation and a curse, and you tore your clothes and wept before Me, I also have heard *you*," says the LORD. "Surely, therefore, I will gather you to your fathers, and you shall be gathered to your grave in peace; and your eyes shall not see all the calamity which I will bring on this place." ' " So they brought back word to the king.

Then the king commanded all the people, saying, "Keep the Passover to the LORD your God, as *it is* written in this Book of the Covenant." Such a Passover surely had never been held since the days of the judges who judged Israel, nor in all the days of the kings of Israel and the kings of Judah. But in the eighteenth year of King Josiah this Passover was held before the LORD in Jerusalem. Moreover Josiah put away those who consulted mediums and spiritists, the household gods and idols, all the abominations that were seen in the land of Judah and in Jerusalem, that he might perform the words of the law which were written in the book that Hilkiah the priest found in the house of the LORD. Now before him there was no king like him, who turned to the LORD with all his heart, with all his soul, and with all his might, according to all the Law of Moses; nor after him did *any* arise like him.

Nevertheless the LORD did not turn from the fierceness of His great wrath, with which His anger was aroused against Judah, because of all the provocations with which Manasseh had provoked Him. And the LORD said, "I will also remove Judah from My sight, as I have removed Israel, and will cast off this city Jerusalem which I have chosen, and the house of which I said, 'My name shall be there.' "

Now the rest of the acts of Josiah, and all that he did, *are* they not written in the book of the chronicles of the kings of Judah? In his days Pharaoh Necho king of Egypt went to the aid of the king of Assyria, to the River Euphrates; and King Josiah went against him. And *Pharaoh Necho* killed him at Megiddo when he confronted him. Then his servants moved his body in a chariot from Megiddo, brought him to Jerusalem, and buried him in his own tomb. And the people of the land took Jehoahaz the son of Josiah, anointed him, and made him king in his father's place.

Jehoahaz *was* twenty-three years old when he became king, and he reigned three months in Jerusalem. His mother's name *was* Hamutal the daughter of Jeremiah of Libnah. And he did evil in the sight of the LORD, according to all that his fathers had done. Now Pharaoh Necho put him in prison at Riblah in the land of Hamath, that he might not reign in Jerusalem; and he imposed on the land a tribute of one hundred talents of silver and a talent of gold. Then Pharaoh Necho made Eliakim the son of Josiah king in place of his father Josiah, and changed his name to Jehoiakim. And *Pharaoh* took Jehoahaz and went to Egypt, and he died there.

So Jehoiakim gave the silver and gold to Pharaoh; but he taxed the land to give money according to the command of Pharaoh; he exacted the silver and gold from the people of the land, from every one according to his assessment, to give *it* to Pharaoh Necho. Jehoiakim *was* twenty-five years old when he became king, and he reigned eleven years in Jerusalem. His mother's name *was* Zebudah the daughter of Pedaiah of Rumah. And he did evil in the sight of the LORD, according to all that his fathers had done.

2 Kings 22:1-20; 23:21-37

WORSHIP

In God I have put my trust;
I will not be afraid.
What can man do to me?

Vows *made* to You *are binding* upon me, O
    God;
I will render praises to You,
For You have delivered my soul from death.
Have You not *kept* my feet from falling,
That I may walk before God
In the light of the living?

Psalm 56:11-13

WISDOM

Every prudent *man* acts with knowledge,
But a fool lays open *his* folly.

Proverbs 13:16

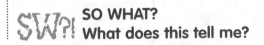

SO WHAT?
What does this tell me?

BABYLONIAN CAPTIVITY

2 Kings 24:1–25:21, 27-30;
Psalm 57:1-3; Proverbs 13:17

In his days Nebuchadnezzar king of Babylon came up, and Jehoiakim became his vassal *for* three years. Then he turned and rebelled against him. And the LORD sent against him *raiding* bands of Chaldeans, bands of Syrians, bands of Moabites, and bands of the people of Ammon; He sent them against Judah to destroy it, according to the word of the LORD which He had spoken by His servants the prophets. Surely at the commandment of the LORD *this* came upon Judah, to remove *them* from His sight because of the sins of Manasseh, according to all that he had done, and also because of the innocent blood that he had shed; for he had filled Jerusalem with innocent blood, which the LORD would not pardon.

Now the rest of the acts of Jehoiakim, and all that he did, *are* they not written in the book of the chronicles of the kings of Judah? So Jehoiakim rested with his fathers. Then Jehoiachin his son reigned in his place.

And the king of Egypt did not come out of his land anymore, for the king of Babylon had taken all that belonged to the king of Egypt from the Brook of Egypt to the River Euphrates.

Jehoiachin *was* eighteen years old when he became king, and he reigned in Jerusalem three months. His mother's name *was* Nehushta the daughter of Elnathan of Jerusalem. And he did evil in the sight of the LORD, according to all that his father had done.

At that time the servants of Nebuchadnezzar king of Babylon came up against Jerusalem, and the city was besieged. And Nebuchadnezzar king of Babylon came against the city, as his servants were besieging it. Then Jehoiachin king of Judah, his mother, his servants, his princes, and his officers went out to the king of Babylon; and the king of Babylon, in the eighth year of his reign, took him prisoner.

And he carried out from there all the treasures of the house of the LORD and the treasures of the king's house, and he cut in pieces all the articles of gold which Solomon king of Israel had made in the temple of the LORD, as the LORD had said. Also he carried

into captivity all Jerusalem: all the captains and all the mighty men of valor, ten thousand captives, and all the craftsmen and smiths. None remained except the poorest people of the land. And he carried Jehoiachin captive to Babylon. The king's mother, the king's wives, his officers, and the mighty of the land he carried into captivity from Jerusalem to Babylon. All the valiant men, seven thousand, and craftsmen and smiths, one thousand, all *who were* strong *and* fit for war, these the king of Babylon brought captive to Babylon.

Then the king of Babylon made Mattaniah, *Jehoiachin's* uncle, king in his place, and changed his name to Zedekiah.

Zedekiah *was* twenty-one years old when he became king, and he reigned eleven years in Jerusalem. His mother's name *was* Hamutal the daughter of Jeremiah of Libnah. He also did evil in the sight of the LORD, according to all that Jehoiakim had done. For because of the anger of the LORD *this* happened in Jerusalem and Judah, that He finally cast them out from His presence. Then Zedekiah rebelled against the king of Babylon.

Now it came to pass in the ninth year of his reign, in the tenth month, on the tenth *day* of the month, *that* Nebuchadnezzar king of Babylon and all his army came against Jerusalem and encamped against it; and they built a siege wall against it all around. So the city was besieged until the eleventh year of King Zedekiah. By the ninth *day* of the *fourth* month the famine had become so severe in the city that there was no food for the people of the land.

Then the city wall was broken through, and all the men of war *fled* at night by way of the gate between two walls, which was by the king's garden, even though the Chaldeans *were* still encamped all around against the city. And *the king* went by way of the plain. But the army of the Chaldeans pursued the king, and they overtook him in the plains of Jericho. All his army was scattered from him. So they took the king and brought him up to the king of Babylon at Riblah, and they pronounced judgment on him. Then they killed the sons of Zedekiah before his eyes, put out the eyes of Zedekiah, bound him with bronze fetters, and took him to Babylon.

And in the fifth month, on the seventh *day* of

the month (which *was* the nineteenth year of King Nebuchadnezzar king of Babylon), Nebuzaradan the captain of the guard, a servant of the king of Babylon, came to Jerusalem. He burned the house of the LORD and the king's house; all the houses of Jerusalem, that is, all the houses of the great, he burned with fire. And all the army of the Chaldeans who *were with* the captain of the guard broke down the walls of Jerusalem all around.

Then Nebuzaradan the captain of the guard carried away captive the rest of the people *who* remained in the city and the defectors who had deserted to the king of Babylon, with the rest of the multitude. But the captain of the guard left *some* of the poor of the land as vinedressers and farmers. The bronze pillars that *were* in the house of the LORD, and the carts and the bronze Sea that *were* in the house of the LORD, the Chaldeans broke in pieces, and carried their bronze to Babylon. They also took away the pots, the shovels, the trimmers, the spoons, and all the bronze utensils with which the priests ministered. The firepans and the basins, the things of solid gold and solid silver, the captain of the guard took away. The two pillars, one Sea, and the carts, which Solomon had made for the house of the LORD, the bronze of all these articles was beyond measure. The height of one pillar *was* eighteen cubits, and the capital on it *was* of bronze. The height of the capital was three cubits, and the network and pomegranates all around the capital were all of bronze. The second pillar was the same, with a network.

And the captain of the guard took Seraiah the chief priest, Zephaniah the second priest, and the three doorkeepers. He also took out of the city an officer who had charge of the men of war, five men of the king's close associates who were found in the city, the chief recruiting officer of the army, who mustered the people of the land, and sixty men of the people of the land *who were* found in the city. So Nebuzaradan, captain of the guard, took these and brought them to the king of Babylon at Riblah. Then the king of Babylon struck them and put them to death at Riblah in the land of Hamath. Thus Judah was carried away captive from its own land.

Now it came to pass in the thirty-seventh year of the captivity of Jehoiachin king of Judah, in the twelfth month, on the twenty-seventh *day* of the month, *that* Evil-Merodach king of Babylon, in the year that he began to reign, released Jehoiachin king of Judah from prison. He spoke kindly to him, and gave him a more prominent seat than those of the kings who *were* with him in Babylon. So Jehoiachin changed from his prison garments, and he ate bread regularly before the king all the days of his life. And as for his provisions, *there was* a regular ration given him by the king, a portion for each day, all the days of his life.

2 Kings 24:1–25:21, 27-30

WORSHIP

Be merciful to me, O God, be merciful to me!
For my soul trusts in You;
And in the shadow of Your wings I will make
        my refuge,
Until *these* calamities have passed by.

I will cry out to God Most High,
To God who performs *all things* for me.
He shall send from heaven and save me;
He reproaches the one who would swallow
        me up.   Selah
God shall send forth His mercy and His truth.

Psalm 57:1-3

WISDOM

A wicked messenger falls into trouble,
But a faithful ambassador *brings* health.

Proverbs 13:17

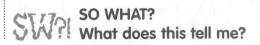

SO WHAT?
What does this tell me?

WORDS FROM THE PROPHETS

A prophet was a person who spoke for God—giving God's message to the people and sometimes announcing or warning about a future event. The period of Israel's monarchy was rich in prophetic revelation. And while the prophets appear at various times through the history of the monarchy, it's easier to grasp the big picture if we view them as one major mountain range of divine revelation.

Obadiah, probably the earliest of the writing prophets, announced bad news for Edom, the descendants of Jacob's brother Esau. The prophet Joel used the imagery of a locust swarm to announce an even more devastating day of the Lord's judgment yet future. The prophet Jonah demonstrated that God's mercy and compassion extend to all people, even Gentiles like those in Nineveh. Amos was called from tending sheep to warn of God's righteous judgment on the northern kingdom. And Hosea's marriage to an unfaithful wife named Gomer illustrated God's unceasing love for His unfaithful people.

The prophet Isaiah condemned Judah and Jerusalem for breaking God's covenant, but also announced comfort and blessings for the future. Isaiah's prophecies of the coming of Immanuel, which means "God with us" (Isaiah 7:14; 9:6-7; 11:1), and the Servant of the Lord (Isaiah 42:1-9; 49:1-13; 50:4-9; 52:13–53:12) constitute twin peaks of God's Old Testament revelation concerning Jesus. Micah warned of coming judgment on both the northern and southern kingdoms and the deliverance to be brought about one day by the coming of the Messiah. Nahum announced the divine judgment and destruction of Nineveh, the defiant capital of the Assyrian Empire. And Zephaniah returns to the theme of the Day of the Lord—a day of universal judgment and salvation for the faithful remnant of God's people.

Jeremiah, "the weeping prophet," warned of the inevitable judgment to come on Judah and announced the Babylonian captivity. His announcement of a New Covenant which will replace the old one broken by Israel (Jeremiah 31:31-34) was a massive peak in the range of the prophets. The New Covenant amplifies the blessings of the Abrahamic promise (Genesis 12:1-3) and is the basis of all the spiritual blessings followers of Jesus Christ enjoy in their relationship with Him. Habakkuk, a perplexed prophet, questioned God's holiness in light of His plan to use the wicked Chaldeans to judge His own people. And after the fall of Jerusalem in 586 B.C., Jeremiah wrote a book called Lamentations which expresses his sorrow over the destruction of the city.

BAD NEWS FOR EDOM Obadiah; Psalm 57:9-11; Proverbs 13:18

The vision of Obadiah.

Thus says the Lord GOD concerning Edom
(We have heard a report from the LORD,
And a messenger has been sent among the
    nations, *saying,*
"Arise, and let us rise up against her for battle"):

"Behold, I will make you small among the
    nations;
You shall be greatly despised.
The pride of your heart has deceived you,
    You who dwell in the clefts of the rock,
    Whose habitation is high;
    You who say in your heart, 'Who will bring
        me down to the ground?'
    Though you ascend *as* high as the eagle,
    And though you set your nest among the
        stars,
    From there I will bring you down," says the
        LORD.

"If thieves had come to you,
If robbers by night—
Oh, how you will be cut off!—
Would they not have stolen till they had
    enough?
If grape-gatherers had come to you,
Would they not have left *some* gleanings?

"Oh, how Esau shall be searched out!
How his hidden treasures shall be sought
    after!
All the men in your confederacy
Shall force you to the border;
The men at peace with you
Shall deceive you *and* prevail against you.
Those who eat your bread shall lay a trap for
    you.
No one is aware of it.

"Will I not in that day," says the LORD,
"Even destroy the wise *men* from Edom,
And understanding from the mountains of
    Esau?
Then your mighty men, O Teman, shall be
    dismayed,
To the end that everyone from the mountains
    of Esau
May be cut off by slaughter.

"For violence against your brother Jacob,
Shame shall cover you,

And you shall be cut off forever.
In the day that you stood on the other side—
In the day that strangers carried captive his
    forces,
When foreigners entered his gates
And cast lots for Jerusalem—
Even you *were* as one of them.

But you should not have gazed on the day of
    your brother
In the day of his captivity;
Nor should you have rejoiced over the children
    of Judah
In the day of their destruction;
Nor should you have spoken proudly
In the day of distress.
You should not have entered the gate of My
    people
In the day of their calamity.
Indeed, you should not have gazed on their
    affliction
In the day of their calamity,
Nor laid *hands* on their substance
In the day of their calamity.
You should not have stood at the crossroads
To cut off those among them who escaped;
Nor should you have delivered up those
    among them who remained
In the day of distress.

"For the day of the LORD upon all the nations *is*
    near;
As you have done, it shall be done to you;
Your reprisal shall return upon your own head.
For as you drank on My holy mountain,
So shall all the nations drink continually;
Yes, they shall drink, and swallow,
And they shall be as though they had never
    been.

"But on Mount Zion there shall be deliverance,
And there shall be holiness;
The house of Jacob shall possess their
    possessions.
The house of Jacob shall be a fire,
And the house of Joseph a flame;
But the house of Esau *shall be* stubble;
They shall kindle them and devour them,
And no survivor shall *remain* of the house of
    Esau,"
For the LORD has spoken.

The South shall possess the mountains of
   Esau,
And the Lowland shall possess Philistia.
They shall possess the fields of Ephraim
And the fields of Samaria.
Benjamin *shall possess* Gilead.
And the captives of this host of the children of
   Israel
Shall possess the land of the Canaanites
As far as Zarephath.
The captives of Jerusalem who are in
   Sepharad
Shall possess the cities of the South.
Then saviors shall come to Mount Zion
To judge the mountains of Esau,
And the kingdom shall be the LORD's.

Obadiah

WoRShiP

I will praise You, O Lord, among the peoples;
I will sing to You among the nations.
For Your mercy reaches unto the heavens,
And Your truth unto the clouds.

Be exalted, O God, above the heavens;
Let Your glory *be* above all the earth.

Psalm 57:9-11

WiSDoM

Poverty and shame *will come* to him who
   disdains correction,
But he who regards a rebuke will be honored.

Proverbs 13:18

SW?! SO WHAT?
What does this tell me?

JUDGMENT HAS COME... AND IS COMING AGAIN!

Joel 1:1–2:17; Psalm 58:1-3; Proverbs 13:19

The word of the LORD that came to Joel the son of Pethuel.

Hear this, you elders,
And give ear, all you inhabitants of the land!
Has *anything like* this happened in your days,
Or even in the days of your fathers?
Tell your children about it,
Let your children *tell* their children,
And their children another generation.

What the chewing locust left, the swarming
    locust has eaten;
  What the swarming locust left, the crawling
      locust has eaten;
  And what the crawling locust left, the
      consuming locust has eaten.

Awake, you drunkards, and weep;
And wail, all you drinkers of wine,
Because of the new wine,
For it has been cut off from your mouth.
For a nation has come up against My land,
Strong, and without number;
His teeth *are* the teeth of a lion,
And he has the fangs of a fierce lion.
He has laid waste My vine,
And ruined My fig tree;
He has stripped it bare and thrown *it* away;
Its branches are made white.

Lament like a virgin girded with sackcloth
For the husband of her youth.
The grain offering and the drink offering
Have been cut off from the house of the LORD;
The priests mourn, who minister to the LORD.
The field is wasted,
The land mourns;
For the grain is ruined,
The new wine is dried up,
The oil fails.

Be ashamed, you farmers,
Wail, you vinedressers,
For the wheat and the barley;
Because the harvest of the field has perished.
The vine has dried up,
And the fig tree has withered;
The pomegranate tree,
The palm tree also,

And the apple tree—
All the trees of the field are withered;
Surely joy has withered away from the sons of
    men.

Gird yourselves and lament, you priests;
Wail, you who minister before the altar;
Come, lie all night in sackcloth,
You who minister to my God;
For the grain offering and the drink offering
Are withheld from the house of your God.
Consecrate a fast,
Call a sacred assembly;
Gather the elders
And all the inhabitants of the land
Into the house of the LORD your God,
And cry out to the LORD.

Alas for the day!
For the day of the LORD *is* at hand;
It shall come as destruction from the Almighty.
Is not the food cut off before our eyes,
Joy and gladness from the house of our God?
The seed shrivels under the clods,
Storehouses are in shambles;
Barns are broken down,
For the grain has withered.
How the animals groan!
The herds of cattle are restless,
Because they have no pasture;
Even the flocks of sheep suffer punishment.

O LORD, to You I cry out;
For fire has devoured the open pastures,
And a flame has burned all the trees of the
    field.
The beasts of the field also cry out to You,
For the water brooks are dried up,
And fire has devoured the open pastures.

Blow the trumpet in Zion,
And sound an alarm in My holy mountain!
Let all the inhabitants of the land tremble;
For the day of the LORD is coming,
For it is at hand:
A day of darkness and gloominess,
A day of clouds and thick darkness,
Like the morning *clouds* spread over the
    mountains.

WORDS FROM THE PROPHETS

A people *come,* great and strong,
The like of whom has never been;
Nor will there ever be any *such* after them,
Even for many successive generations.

A fire devours before them,
And behind them a flame burns;
The land *is* like the Garden of Eden before them,
And behind them a desolate wilderness;
Surely nothing shall escape them.
Their appearance is like the appearance of
    horses;
And like swift steeds, so they run.
With a noise like chariots
Over mountaintops they leap,
Like the noise of a flaming fire that devours the
    stubble,
Like a strong people set in battle array.

Before them the people writhe in pain;
All faces are drained of color.
They run like mighty men,
They climb the wall like men of war;
Every one marches in formation,
And they do not break ranks.
They do not push one another;
Every one marches in his own column.
Though they lunge between the weapons,
They are not cut down.
They run to and fro in the city,
They run on the wall;
They climb into the houses,
They enter at the windows like a thief.

The earth quakes before them,
The heavens tremble;
The sun and moon grow dark,
And the stars diminish their brightness.
The LORD gives voice before His army,
For His camp is very great;
For strong *is the One* who executes His word.
For the day of the LORD *is* great and very terrible;
Who can endure it?

"Now, therefore," says the LORD,
"Turn to Me with all your heart,
With fasting, with weeping, and with mourning."
So rend your heart, and not your garments;
Return to the LORD your God,
For He *is* gracious and merciful,
Slow to anger, and of great kindness;
And He relents from doing harm.
Who knows *if* He will turn and relent,
And leave a blessing behind Him—
A grain offering and a drink offering
For the LORD your God?

Blow the trumpet in Zion,
Consecrate a fast,
Call a sacred assembly;
Gather the people,
Sanctify the congregation,
Assemble the elders,
Gather the children and nursing babes;
Let the bridegroom go out from his chamber,
And the bride from her dressing room.
Let the priests, who minister to the LORD,
Weep between the porch and the altar;
Let them say, "Spare Your people, O LORD,
And do not give Your heritage to reproach,
That the nations should rule over them.
Why should they say among the peoples,
'Where *is* their God?' "

Joel 1:1–2:17

WORSHIP

Do you indeed speak righteousness, you silent
    ones?
Do you judge uprightly, you sons of men?
No, in heart you work wickedness;
You weigh out the violence of your hands in the
    earth.

The wicked are estranged from the womb;
They go astray as soon as they are born,
    speaking lies.

Psalm 58:1-3

WISDOM

A desire accomplished is sweet to the soul,
But *it is* an abomination to fools to depart from
    evil.

Proverbs 13:19

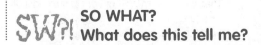

SO WHAT?
What does this tell me?

THE PROMISE OF THE SPIRIT

Joel 2:18–3:21; Psalm 58:10-11; Proverbs 13:20

Then the LORD will be zealous for His land,
And pity His people.
The LORD will answer and say to His people,
"Behold, I will send you grain and new wine and
    oil,
And you will be satisfied by them;
I will no longer make you a reproach among
    the nations.

"But I will remove far from you the northern
    army,
And will drive him away into a barren and
    desolate land,
    With his face toward the eastern sea
    And his back toward the western sea;
    His stench will come up,
    And his foul odor will rise,
    Because he has done monstrous things."

Fear not, O land;
Be glad and rejoice,
For the LORD has done marvelous things!
Do not be afraid, you beasts of the field;
For the open pastures are springing up,
And the tree bears its fruit;
The fig tree and the vine yield their strength.
Be glad then, you children of Zion,
And rejoice in the LORD your God;
For He has given you the former rain faith-
    fully,
And He will cause the rain to come down for
    you—
The former rain,
And the latter rain in the first *month*.
The threshing floors shall be full of wheat,
And the vats shall overflow with new wine
    and oil.

"So I will restore to you the years that the
    swarming locust has eaten,
The crawling locust,
The consuming locust,
And the chewing locust,
My great army which I sent among you.
You shall eat in plenty and be satisfied,
And praise the name of the LORD your God,
Who has dealt wondrously with you;
And My people shall never be put to shame.
Then you shall know that I *am* in the midst of
    Israel:
I *am* the LORD your God

And there is no other.
My people shall never be put to shame.

"And it shall come to pass afterward
That I will pour out My Spirit on all flesh;
Your sons and your daughters shall prophesy,
Your old men shall dream dreams,
Your young men shall see visions.
And also on *My* menservants and on *My*
    maidservants
I will pour out My Spirit in those days.

"And I will show wonders in the heavens and in
    the earth:
Blood and fire and pillars of smoke.
The sun shall be turned into darkness,
And the moon into blood,
Before the coming of the great and
    awesome day of the LORD.
And it shall come to pass
That whoever calls on the name of the LORD
Shall be saved.
For in Mount Zion and in Jerusalem there shall
    be deliverance,
As the LORD has said,
Among the remnant whom the LORD calls.

"For behold, in those days and at that time,
When I bring back the captives of Judah and
    Jerusalem,
I will also gather all nations,
And bring them down to the Valley of
    Jehoshaphat;
And I will enter into judgment with them there
On account of My people, My heritage Israel,
Whom they have scattered among the nations;
They have also divided up My land.
They have cast lots for My people,
Have given a boy *as payment* for a harlot,
And sold a girl for wine, that they may drink.

"Indeed, what have you to do with Me,
O Tyre and Sidon, and all the coasts of Philistia?
Will you retaliate against Me?
But if you retaliate against Me,
Swiftly and speedily I will return your retaliation
    upon your own head;
Because you have taken My silver and My
    gold,
And have carried into your temples My prized
    possessions.

Also the people of Judah and the people of
    Jerusalem
You have sold to the Greeks,
That you may remove them far from their
    borders.

"Behold, I will raise them
Out of the place to which you have sold them,
And will return your retaliation upon your own
    head.
I will sell your sons and your daughters
Into the hand of the people of Judah,
And they will sell them to the Sabeans,
To a people far off;
For the LORD has spoken."

Proclaim this among the nations:
"Prepare for war!
Wake up the mighty men,
Let all the men of war draw near,
Let them come up.
Beat your plowshares into swords
And your pruning hooks into spears;
Let the weak say, 'I *am* strong.' "
Assemble and come, all you nations,
And gather together all around.
Cause Your mighty ones to go down there, O
    LORD.

"Let the nations be wakened, and come up to
    the Valley of Jehoshaphat;
For there I will sit to judge all the surrounding
    nations.
Put in the sickle, for the harvest is ripe.
Come, go down;
For the winepress is full,
The vats overflow—
For their wickedness *is* great."

Multitudes, multitudes in the valley of decision!
For the day of the LORD *is* near in the valley of
    decision.
The sun and moon will grow dark,
And the stars will diminish their brightness.
The LORD also will roar from Zion,
And utter His voice from Jerusalem;
The heavens and earth will shake;
But the LORD will be a shelter for His people,
And the strength of the children of Israel.

"So you shall know that I *am* the LORD your
    God,
Dwelling in Zion My holy mountain.
Then Jerusalem shall be holy,
And no aliens shall ever pass through her
    again."

And it will come to pass in that day
That the mountains shall drip with new wine,
The hills shall flow with milk,
And all the brooks of Judah shall be flooded
    with water;
A fountain shall flow from the house of the
    LORD
And water the Valley of Acacias.

"Egypt shall be a desolation,
And Edom a desolate wilderness,
Because of violence *against* the people of
    Judah,
For they have shed innocent blood in their
    land.
But Judah shall abide forever,
And Jerusalem from generation to generation.
For I will acquit them of the guilt of bloodshed,
    whom I had not acquitted;
For the LORD dwells in Zion."

Joel 2:18–3:21

The righteous shall rejoice when he sees the
    vengeance;
He shall wash his feet in the blood of the
    wicked,
So that men will say,
"Surely *there is* a reward for the righteous;
Surely He is God who judges in the earth."

Psalm 58:10-11

WISDOM

He who walks with wise *men* will be wise,
But the companion of fools will be destroyed.

Proverbs 13:20

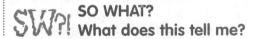

SO WHAT?
What does this tell me?

A WHALE OF A TALE

Jonah 1:1–2:2, 10; 3–4; Psalm 59:1–3;
Proverbs 13:21

Now the word of the LORD came to Jonah the son of Amittai, saying, "Arise, go to Nineveh, that great city, and cry out against it; for their wickedness has come up before Me." But Jonah arose to flee to Tarshish from the presence of the LORD. He went down to Joppa, and found a ship going to Tarshish; so he paid the fare, and went down into it, to go with them to Tarshish from the presence of the LORD.

But the LORD sent out a great wind on the sea, and there was a mighty tempest on the sea, so that the ship was about to be broken up.

Then the mariners were afraid; and every man cried out to his god, and threw the cargo that *was* in the ship into the sea, to lighten the load. But Jonah had gone down into the lowest parts of the ship, had lain down, and was fast asleep.

So the captain came to him, and said to him, "What do you mean, sleeper? Arise, call on your God; perhaps your God will consider us, so that we may not perish."

And they said to one another, "Come, let us cast lots, that we may know for whose cause this trouble *has come* upon us." So they cast lots, and the lot fell on Jonah. Then they said to him, "Please tell us! For whose cause *is* this trouble upon us? What is your occupation? And where do you come from? What is your country? And of what people are you?"

So he said to them, "I *am* a Hebrew; and I fear the LORD, the God of heaven, who made the sea and the dry *land*."

Then the men were exceedingly afraid, and said to him, "Why have you done this?" For the men knew that he fled from the presence of the LORD, because he had told them. Then they said to him, "What shall we do to you that the sea may be calm for us?"—for the sea was growing more tempestuous.

And he said to them, "Pick me up and throw me into the sea; then the sea will become calm for you. For I know that this great tempest *is* because of me."

Nevertheless the men rowed hard to return to land, but they could not, for the sea continued to grow more tempestuous

against them. Therefore they cried out to the LORD and said, "We pray, O LORD, please do not let us perish for this man's life, and do not charge us with innocent blood; for You, O LORD, have done as it pleased You." So they picked up Jonah and threw him into the sea, and the sea ceased from its raging. Then the men feared the LORD exceedingly, and offered a sacrifice to the LORD and took vows.

Now the LORD had prepared a great fish to swallow Jonah. And Jonah was in the belly of the fish three days and three nights.

Then Jonah prayed to the LORD his God from the fish's belly. And he said:

"I cried out to the LORD because of my affliction,
And He answered me.

"Out of the belly of Sheol I cried,
And You heard my voice.

So the LORD spoke to the fish, and it vomited Jonah onto dry *land*.

Now the word of the LORD came to Jonah the second time, saying, "Arise, go to Nineveh, that great city, and preach to it the message that I tell you." So Jonah arose and went to Nineveh, according to the word of the LORD. Now Nineveh was an exceedingly great city, a three-day journey *in extent*. And Jonah began to enter the city on the first day's walk. Then he cried out and said, "Yet forty days, and Nineveh shall be overthrown!"

So the people of Nineveh believed God, proclaimed a fast, and put on sackcloth, from the greatest to the least of them. Then word came to the king of Nineveh; and he arose from his throne and laid aside his robe, covered *himself* with sackcloth and sat in ashes. And he caused *it* to be proclaimed and published throughout Nineveh by the decree of the king and his nobles, saying,

Let neither man nor beast, herd nor flock, taste anything; do not let them eat, or drink water. But let man and beast be covered with sackcloth, and cry mightily to God; yes, let every one turn from his evil way and from the violence that is in his hands. Who can tell *if* God will turn and relent, and turn away from His fierce anger, so that we may not perish?

Then God saw their works, that they turned from their evil way; and God relented from the disaster that He had said He would bring upon them, and He did not do it.

But it displeased Jonah exceedingly, and he became angry. So he prayed to the LORD, and said, "Ah, LORD, was not this what I said when I was still in my country? Therefore I fled previously to Tarshish; for I know that You *are* a gracious and merciful God, slow to anger and abundant in lovingkindness, One who relents from doing harm. Therefore now, O LORD, please take my life from me, for *it is* better for me to die than to live!"

Then the LORD said, "*Is it* right for you to be angry?"

So Jonah went out of the city and sat on the east side of the city. There he made himself a shelter and sat under it in the shade, till he might see what would become of the city. And the LORD God prepared a plant and made it come up over Jonah, that it might be shade for his head to deliver him from his misery. So Jonah was very grateful for the plant. But as morning dawned the next day God prepared a worm, and it *so* damaged the plant that it withered. And it happened, when the sun arose, that God prepared a vehement east wind; and the sun beat on Jonah's head, so that he grew faint. Then he wished death for himself, and said, "*It is* better for me to die than to live."

Then God said to Jonah, "*Is it* right for you to be angry about the plant?"

And he said, "*It is* right for me to be angry, even to death!"

But the LORD said, "You have had pity on the plant for which you have not labored, nor made it grow, which came up in a night and perished in a night. And should I not pity Nineveh, that great city, in which are more than one hundred and twenty thousand persons who cannot discern between their right hand and their left—and much livestock?"

Jonah 1:1–2:2, 10; 3–4

WORSHIP

Deliver me from my enemies, O my God;
Defend me from those who rise up against
  me.
Deliver me from the workers of iniquity,
And save me from bloodthirsty men.

For look, they lie in wait for my life;
The mighty gather against me,
Not *for* my transgression nor *for* my sin, O
  LORD.

Psalm 59:1-3

WISDOM

Evil pursues sinners,
But to the righteous, good shall be repaid.

Proverbs 13:21

SW?! **SO WHAT?**
What does this tell me?

JUDGMENT ON ALL NATIONS
Amos 1–2; Psalm 59:9-10; Proverbs 13:22

The words of Amos, who was among the sheepbreeders of Tekoa, which he saw concerning Israel in the days of Uzziah king of Judah, and in the days of Jeroboam the son of Joash, king of Israel, two years before the earthquake. And he said:

"The LORD roars from Zion,
And utters His voice from Jerusalem;
The pastures of the shepherds mourn,
And the top of Carmel withers."

Thus says the LORD:

"For three transgressions of Damascus,
and for four,
I will not turn away its *punishment,*
Because they have threshed Gilead with
implements of iron.
But I will send a fire into the house of
Hazael,
Which shall devour the palaces of
Ben-Hadad.
I will also break the *gate* bar of
Damascus,
And cut off the inhabitant from the Valley
of Aven,
And the one who holds the scepter from
Beth Eden.
The people of Syria shall go captive to
Kir,"
Says the LORD.

Thus says the LORD:

"For three transgressions of Gaza, and for
four,
I will not turn away its *punishment,*
Because they took captive the whole
captivity
To deliver *them* up to Edom.
But I will send a fire upon the wall of
Gaza,
Which shall devour its palaces.
I will cut off the inhabitant from Ashdod,
And the one who holds the scepter from
Ashkelon;
I will turn My hand against Ekron,
And the remnant of the Philistines shall
perish,"
Says the Lord GOD.

Thus says the LORD:

"For three transgressions of Tyre, and for four,
I will not turn away its *punishment,*
Because they delivered up the whole
captivity to Edom,
And did not remember the covenant of
brotherhood.
But I will send a fire upon the wall of Tyre,
Which shall devour its palaces."

Thus says the LORD:

"For three transgressions of Edom, and for four,
I will not turn away its *punishment,*
Because he pursued his brother with the
sword,
And cast off all pity;
His anger tore perpetually,
And he kept his wrath forever.
But I will send a fire upon Teman,
Which shall devour the palaces of Bozrah."

Thus says the LORD:

"For three transgressions of the people of
Ammon, and for four,
I will not turn away its *punishment,*
Because they ripped open the women with
child in Gilead,
That they might enlarge their territory.
But I will kindle a fire in the wall of Rabbah,
And it shall devour its palaces,
Amid shouting in the day of battle,
And a tempest in the day of the whirlwind.
Their king shall go into captivity,
He and his princes together,"
Says the LORD.

Thus says the LORD:

"For three transgressions of Moab, and for four,
I will not turn away its *punishment,*
Because he burned the bones of the king of
Edom to lime.
But I will send a fire upon Moab,
And it shall devour the palaces of Kerioth;
Moab shall die with tumult,
With shouting *and* trumpet sound.
And I will cut off the judge from its midst,
And slay all its princes with him,"
Says the LORD.

Thus says the LORD:

"For three transgressions of Judah, and for four,
I will not turn away its *punishment,*
Because they have despised the law of the
    LORD,
And have not kept His commandments.
Their lies lead them astray,
Lies which their fathers followed.
But I will send a fire upon Judah,
And it shall devour the palaces of Jerusalem."

Thus says the LORD:

"For three transgressions of Israel, and for four,
I will not turn away its *punishment,*
Because they sell the righteous for silver,
And the poor for a pair of sandals.
They pant after the dust of the earth *which is*
    on the head of the poor,
And pervert the way of the humble.
A man and his father go in to the *same* girl,
To defile My holy name.
They lie down by every altar on clothes taken
    in pledge,
And drink the wine of the condemned *in* the
    house of their god.

"Yet *it was* I *who* destroyed the Amorite before
    them,
Whose height *was* like the height of the
    cedars,
And he *was as* strong as the oaks;
Yet I destroyed his fruit above
And his roots beneath.
Also *it was* I *who* brought you up from the land
    of Egypt,
And led you forty years through the
    wilderness,
To possess the land of the Amorite.
I raised up some of your sons as prophets,
And some of your young men as Nazirites.
Is it not so, O you children of Israel?"
Says the LORD.
"But you gave the Nazirites wine to drink,
And commanded the prophets saying,
'Do not prophesy!'

"Behold, I am weighed down by you,
As a cart full of sheaves is weighed down.
Therefore flight shall perish from the swift,
The strong shall not strengthen his power,
Nor shall the mighty deliver himself;
He shall not stand who handles the bow,
The swift of foot shall not escape,
Nor shall he who rides a horse deliver himself.

The most courageous men of might
Shall flee naked in that day,"
Says the LORD.

Amos 1–2

WORSHIP

I will wait for You, O You his Strength;
For God *is* my defense.
My God of mercy shall come to meet me;
God shall let me see *my desire* on my
    enemies.

Psalm 59:9-10

WISDOM

A good *man* leaves an inheritance to his
    children's children,
But the wealth of the sinner is stored up for the
    righteous.

Proverbs 13:22

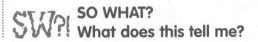 **SO WHAT?**
What does this tell me?

SERMONS AGAINST ISRAEL

Amos 3–4; 5:21-24; Psalm 59:16-17; Proverbs 13:24

Hear this word that the LORD has spoken against you, O children of Israel, against the whole family which I brought up from the land of Egypt, saying:

"You only have I known of all the families of the earth;
Therefore I will punish you for all your iniquities."

Can two walk together, unless they are agreed?
Will a lion roar in the forest, when he has no prey?
Will a young lion cry out of his den, if he has caught nothing?
Will a bird fall into a snare on the earth, where there is no trap for it?
Will a snare spring up from the earth, if it has caught nothing at all?
If a trumpet is blown in a city, will not the people be afraid?
If there is calamity in a city, will not the LORD have done it?

Surely the Lord GOD does nothing,
Unless He reveals His secret to His servants the prophets.
A lion has roared!
Who will not fear?
The Lord GOD has spoken!
Who can but prophesy?

"Proclaim in the palaces at Ashdod,
And in the palaces in the land of Egypt, and say:
'Assemble on the mountains of Samaria;
See great tumults in her midst,
And the oppressed within her.
For they do not know to do right,'
Says the LORD,
'Who store up violence and robbery in their palaces.' "

Therefore thus says the Lord GOD:

"An adversary *shall be* all around the land;
He shall sap your strength from you,
And your palaces shall be plundered."

Thus says the LORD:

"As a shepherd takes from the mouth of a lion

Two legs or a piece of an ear,
So shall the children of Israel be taken out
Who dwell in Samaria—
In the corner of a bed and on the edge of a couch!
Hear and testify against the house of Jacob,"
Says the Lord GOD, the God of hosts,
"That in the day I punish Israel for their transgressions,
I will also visit *destruction* on the altars of Bethel;
And the horns of the altar shall be cut off
And fall to the ground.
I will destroy the winter house along with the summer house;
The houses of ivory shall perish,
And the great houses shall have an end,"
Says the LORD.

Hear this word, you cows of Bashan, who *are* on the mountain of Samaria,
Who oppress the poor,
Who crush the needy,
Who say to your husbands, "Bring *wine,* let us drink!"
The Lord GOD has sworn by His holiness:
"Behold, the days shall come upon you
When He will take you away with fishhooks,
And your posterity with fishhooks.
You will go out *through* broken *walls,*
Each one straight ahead of her,
And you will be cast into Harmon,"
Says the LORD.

"Come to Bethel and transgress,
At Gilgal multiply transgression;
Bring your sacrifices every morning,
Your tithes every three days.
Offer a sacrifice of thanksgiving with leaven,
Proclaim *and* announce the freewill offerings;
For this you love,
You children of Israel!"
Says the Lord GOD.

"Also I gave you cleanness of teeth in all your cities.
And lack of bread in all your places;
Yet you have not returned to Me,"
Says the LORD.

"I also withheld rain from you,

When *there were* still three months to the
    harvest.
I made it rain on one city,
I withheld rain from another city.
One part was rained upon,
And where it did not rain the part withered.
So two *or* three cities wandered to another city
    to drink water,
But they were not satisfied;
Yet you have not returned to Me,"
Says the LORD.

"I blasted you with blight and mildew.
 When your gardens increased,
 Your vineyards,
 Your fig trees,
 And your olive trees,
 The locust devoured *them;*
 Yet you have not returned to Me,"
Says the LORD.

"I sent among you a plague after the manner of
    Egypt;
 Your young men I killed with a sword,
 Along with your captive horses;
 I made the stench of your camps come up into
    your nostrils;
 Yet you have not returned to Me,"
Says the LORD.

"I overthrew *some* of you,
 As God overthrew Sodom and Gomorrah,
 And you were like a firebrand plucked from
    the burning;
 Yet you have not returned to Me,"
Says the LORD.

"Therefore thus will I do to you, O Israel;
 Because I will do this to you,
 Prepare to meet your God, O Israel!"

For behold,
He who forms mountains,
And creates the wind,
Who declares to man what his thought *is,*
And makes the morning darkness,
Who treads the high places of the earth—
The LORD God of hosts *is* His name.

"I hate, I despise your feast days,
 And I do not savor your sacred assemblies.
 Though you offer Me burnt offerings and your
    grain offerings,
 I will not accept *them,*
 Nor will I regard your fattened peace
    offerings.
 Take away from Me the noise of your songs,

For I will not hear the melody of your stringed
    instruments.
But let justice run down like water,
And righteousness like a mighty stream."

                     Amos 3–4; 5:21-24

WORSHIP

But I will sing of Your power;
Yes, I will sing aloud of Your mercy in the
    morning;
For You have been my defense
And refuge in the day of my trouble.
To You, O my Strength, I will sing praises;
For God *is* my defense,
My God of mercy.

                     Psalm 59:16-17

WISDOM

He who spares his rod hates his son,
But he who loves him disciplines him promptly.

                     Proverbs 13:24

SW?! **SO WHAT?**
What does this tell me?

THE PLUMBLINE OF GOD

Amos 7:7–9; 8:1-12; 9:1-15;
Psalm 60:3-5; Proverbs 13:25

Thus He showed me: Behold, the Lord stood on a wall *made* with a plumb line, with a plumb line in His hand. And the LORD said to me, "Amos, what do you see?"

And I said, "A plumb line."

Then the Lord said:

"Behold, I am setting a plumb line
In the midst of My people Israel;
I will not pass by them anymore.
The high places of Isaac shall be desolate,
And the sanctuaries of Israel shall be laid
waste.
I will rise with the sword against the house
of Jeroboam."

Thus the Lord GOD showed me: Behold, a basket of summer fruit. And He said, "Amos, what do you see?"

So I said, "A basket of summer fruit."

Then the LORD said to me:

"The end has come upon My people
Israel;
I will not pass by them anymore.
And the songs of the temple
Shall be wailing in that day,"
Says the Lord GOD—
"Many dead bodies everywhere,
They shall be thrown out in silence."

Hear this, you who swallow up the
needy,
And make the poor of the land fail,

Saying:

"When will the New Moon be past,
That we may sell grain?
And the Sabbath,
That we may trade wheat?
Making the ephah small and the
shekel large,
Falsifying the scales by deceit,
That we may buy the poor for silver,
And the needy for a pair of sandals—
Even sell the bad wheat?"

The LORD has sworn by the pride of
Jacob:
"Surely I will never forget any of their
works.
Shall the land not tremble for this,

And everyone mourn who dwells in it?
All of it shall swell like the River,
Heave and subside
Like the River of Egypt.

"And it shall come to pass in that day," says the
Lord GOD,
"That I will make the sun go down at noon,
And I will darken the earth in broad daylight;
I will turn your feasts into mourning,
And all your songs into lamentation;
I will bring sackcloth on every waist,
And baldness on every head;
I will make it like mourning for an only *son*,
And its end like a bitter day.

"Behold, the days are coming," says the Lord
GOD,
"That I will send a famine on the land,
Not a famine of bread,
Nor a thirst for water,
But of hearing the words of the LORD.
They shall wander from sea to sea,
And from north to east;
They shall run to and fro, seeking the word of
the LORD,
But shall not find *it*.

I saw the Lord standing by the altar, and He
said:

"Strike the doorposts, that the thresholds may
shake,
And break them on the heads of them all.
I will slay the last of them with the sword.
He who flees from them shall not get away,
And he who escapes from them shall not be
delivered.

"Though they dig into hell,
From there My hand shall take them;
Though they climb up to heaven,
From there I will bring them down;
And though they hide themselves on top of
Carmel,
From there I will search and take them;
Though they hide from My sight at the bottom
of the sea,
From there I will command the serpent, and it
shall bite them;
Though they go into captivity before their
enemies,

From there I will command the sword,
And it shall slay them.
I will set My eyes on them for harm and not for
good."

The Lord GOD of hosts,
He who touches the earth and it melts,
And all who dwell there mourn;
All of it shall swell like the River,
And subside like the River of Egypt.
He who builds His layers in the sky,
And has founded His strata in the earth;
Who calls for the waters of the sea,
And pours them out on the face of the earth—
The LORD *is* His name.

"*Are* you not like the people of Ethiopia to Me,
O children of Israel?" says the LORD.
"Did I not bring up Israel from the land of Egypt,
The Philistines from Caphtor,
And the Syrians from Kir?

"Behold, the eyes of the Lord GOD *are* on the
sinful kingdom,
And I will destroy it from the face of the earth;
Yet I will not utterly destroy the house of
Jacob,"
Says the LORD.

"For surely I will command,
And will sift the house of Israel among all
nations,
As *grain* is sifted in a sieve;
Yet not the smallest grain shall fall to the
ground.
All the sinners of My people shall die by the
sword,
Who say, 'The calamity shall not overtake nor
confront us.'

"On that day I will raise up
The tabernacle of David, which has fallen down,
And repair its damages;
I will raise up its ruins,
And rebuild it as in the days of old;
That they may possess the remnant of Edom,
And all the Gentiles who are called by My
name,"
Says the LORD who does this thing.

"Behold, the days are coming," says the LORD,
"When the plowman shall overtake the reaper,
And the treader of grapes him who sows
seed;
The mountains shall drip with sweet wine,
And all the hills shall flow *with it.*

I will bring back the captives of My people
Israel;
They shall build the waste cities and inhabit
them;
They shall plant vineyards and drink wine from
them;
They shall also make gardens and eat fruit
from them.
I will plant them in their land,
And no longer shall they be pulled up
From the land I have given them,"
Says the LORD your God.
Amos 7:7–9; 8:1-12; 9:1-15

WoRSHiP

You have shown Your people hard things;
You have made us drink the wine of confusion.

You have given a banner to those who fear
You,
That it may be displayed because of the truth.
Selah

That Your beloved may be delivered,
Save *with* Your right hand, and hear me.
Psalm 60:3-5

WiSDoM

The righteous eats to the satisfying of his soul,
But the stomach of the wicked shall be in
want.
Proverbs 13:25

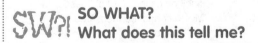

SO WHAT?
What does this tell me?

THE PROPHET WHO LOVED A SINFUL WOMAN

Hosea 1–2; Psalm 60:10-12; Proverbs 14:1

The word of the LORD that came to Hosea the son of Beeri, in the days of Uzziah, Jotham, Ahaz, *and* Hezekiah, kings of Judah, and in the days of Jeroboam the son of Joash, king of Israel. When the LORD began to speak by Hosea, the LORD said to Hosea:

"Go, take yourself a wife of harlotry
And children of harlotry,
For the land has committed great harlotry
By *departing* from the LORD."

So he went and took Gomer the daughter of Diblaim, and she conceived and bore him a son. Then the LORD said to him:

"Call his name Jezreel,
For in a little *while*
I will avenge the bloodshed of Jezreel on the house of Jehu,
And bring an end to the kingdom of the house of Israel.
It shall come to pass in that day
That I will break the bow of Israel in the Valley of Jezreel."

And she conceived again and bore a daughter. Then *God* said to him:

"Call her name Lo-Ruhamah,
For I will no longer have mercy on the house of Israel,
But I will utterly take them away.
Yet I will have mercy on the house of Judah,
Will save them by the LORD their God,
And will not save them by bow,
Nor by sword or battle,
By horses or horsemen."

Now when she had weaned Lo-Ruhamah, she conceived and bore a son. Then *God* said:

"Call his name Lo-Ammi,
For you *are* not My people,
And I will not be your *God.*

"Yet the number of the children of Israel
Shall be as the sand of the sea,
Which cannot be measured or numbered.

And it shall come to pass
In the place where it was said to them,
'You *are* not My people,'
There it shall be said to them,
'*You are* sons of the living God.'
Then the children of Judah and the children of Israel
Shall be gathered together,
And appoint for themselves one head;
And they shall come up out of the land,
For great *will be* the day of Jezreel!
Say to your brethren, 'My people,'
And to your sisters, 'Mercy *is shown.*'

"Bring charges against your mother, bring charges;
For she *is* not My wife, nor *am* I her Husband!
Let her put away her harlotries from her sight,
And her adulteries from between her breasts;
Lest I strip her naked
And expose her, as in the day she was born,
And make her like a wilderness,
And set her like a dry land,
And slay her with thirst.

"I will not have mercy on her children,
For they *are* the children of harlotry.
For their mother has played the harlot;
She who conceived them has behaved shamefully.
For she said, 'I will go after my lovers,
Who give *me* my bread and my water,
My wool and my linen,
My oil and my drink.'

"Therefore, behold,
I will hedge up your way with thorns,
And wall her in,
So that she cannot find her paths.
She will chase her lovers,
But not overtake them;
Yes, she will seek them, but not find *them.*
Then she will say,
'I will go and return to my first husband,
For then *it was* better for me than now.'
For she did not know
That I gave her grain, new wine, and oil,
And multiplied her silver and gold—
Which they prepared for Baal.

"Therefore I will return and take away
My grain in its time
And My new wine in its season,
And will take back My wool and My linen,
Given to cover her nakedness.
Now I will uncover her lewdness in the sight of
her lovers,
And no one shall deliver her from My hand.
I will also cause all her mirth to cease,
Her feast days,
Her New Moons,
Her Sabbaths—
All her appointed feasts.

"And I will destroy her vines and her fig trees,
Of which she has said,
'These *are* my wages that my lovers have given
me.'
So I will make them a forest,
And the beasts of the field shall eat them.
I will punish her
For the days of the Baals to which she burned
incense.
She decked herself with her earrings and
jewelry,
And went after her lovers;
But Me she forgot," says the LORD.

"Therefore, behold, I will allure her,
Will bring her into the wilderness,
And speak comfort to her.
I will give her her vineyards from there,
And the Valley of Achor as a door of hope;
She shall sing there,
As in the days of her youth,
As in the day when she came up from the land
of Egypt.

"And it shall be, in that day,"
Says the LORD,
"*That* you will call Me 'My Husband,'
And no longer call Me 'My Master,'
For I will take from her mouth the names of the
Baals,
And they shall be remembered by their name
no more.
In that day I will make a covenant for them
With the beasts of the field,
With the birds of the air,
And *with* the creeping things of the ground.
Bow and sword of battle I will shatter from the
earth,
To make them lie down safely.

"I will betroth you to Me forever;
Yes, I will betroth you to Me

In righteousness and justice,
In lovingkindness and mercy;
I will betroth you to Me in faithfulness,
And you shall know the LORD.

"It shall come to pass in that day
That I will answer," says the LORD;
"I will answer the heavens,
And they shall answer the earth.
The earth shall answer
With grain,
With new wine,
And with oil;
They shall answer Jezreel.
Then I will sow her for Myself in the earth,
And I will have mercy on *her who had* not
obtained mercy;
Then I will say to *those who were* not My
people,
'You *are* My people!'
And they shall say, '*You are* my God!'"

Hosea 1–2

WORSHIP

Is it not You, O God, *who* cast us off?
And You, O God, *who* did not go out with our
armies?
Give us help from trouble,
For the help of man *is* useless.
Through God we will do valiantly,
For *it is* He *who* shall tread down our enemies.

Psalm 60:10-12

WISDOM

The wise woman builds her house,
But the foolish pulls it down with her hands.

Proverbs 14:1

 **SO WHAT?**
What does this tell me?

THE GOD WHO LOVED A SINFUL PEOPLE

Hosea 3–4; 6:4-6; 11:1-11; Psalm 61:2-4; Proverbs 14:2

Then the LORD said to me, "Go again, love a woman *who is* loved by a lover and is committing adultery, just like the love of the LORD for the children of Israel, who look to other gods and love *the* raisin cakes *of the pagans.*"

So I bought her for myself for fifteen *shekels* of silver, and one and one-half homers of barley. And I said to her, "You shall stay with me many days; you shall not play the harlot, nor shall you have a man—so, too, *will* I *be* toward you."

For the children of Israel shall abide many days without king or prince, without sacrifice or *sacred* pillar, without ephod or teraphim. Afterward the children of Israel shall return and seek the LORD their God and David their king. They shall fear the LORD and His goodness in the latter days.

Hear the word of the LORD,
You children of Israel,
For the LORD *brings* a charge against the
inhabitants of the land:

"There is no truth or mercy
Or knowledge of God in the land.
By swearing and lying,
Killing and stealing and committing
adultery,
They break all restraint,
With bloodshed upon bloodshed.
Therefore the land will mourn;
And everyone who dwells there will
waste away
With the beasts of the field
And the birds of the air;
Even the fish of the sea will be taken
away.

"Now let no man contend, or rebuke
another;
For your people *are* like those who
contend with the priest.
Therefore you shall stumble in the day;
The prophet also shall stumble with you
in the night;
And I will destroy your mother.
My people are destroyed for lack of
knowledge.

Because you have rejected knowledge,
I also will reject you from being priest for Me;
Because you have forgotten the law of your
God,
I also will forget your children.

"The more they increased,
The more they sinned against Me;
I will change their glory into shame.
They eat up the sin of My people;
They set their heart on their iniquity.
And it shall be: like people, like priest.
So I will punish them for their ways,
And reward them for their deeds.
For they shall eat, but not have enough;
They shall commit harlotry, but not increase;
Because they have ceased obeying the LORD.

"Harlotry, wine, and new wine enslave the
heart.
My people ask counsel from their wooden
idols,
And their staff informs them.
For the spirit of harlotry has caused *them* to
stray,
And they have played the harlot against their
God.
They offer sacrifices on the mountaintops,
And burn incense on the hills,
Under oaks, poplars, and terebinths,
Because their shade *is* good.
Therefore your daughters commit harlotry,
And your brides commit adultery.

"I will not punish your daughters when they
commit harlotry,
Nor your brides when they commit adultery;
For *the men* themselves go apart with harlots,
And offer sacrifices with a ritual harlot.
Therefore people *who* do not understand will
be trampled.

"Though you, Israel, play the harlot,
Let not Judah offend.
Do not come up to Gilgal,
Nor go up to Beth Aven,
Nor swear an oath, *saying,* 'As the LORD
lives'—

"For Israel is stubborn
Like a stubborn calf;

Now the LORD will let them forage
Like a lamb in open country.

"Ephraim *is* joined to idols,
Let him alone.
Their drink is rebellion,
They commit harlotry continually.
Her rulers dearly love dishonor.
The wind has wrapped her up in its wings,
And they shall be ashamed because of their
     sacrifices.

"O Ephraim, what shall I do to you?
O Judah, what shall I do to you?
For your faithfulness is like a morning cloud,
And like the early dew it goes away.
Therefore I have hewn *them* by the prophets,
I have slain them by the words of My mouth;
And your judgments *are like* light *that* goes
     forth.
For I desire mercy and not sacrifice,
And the knowledge of God more than burnt
     offerings.

"When Israel *was* a child, I loved him,
And out of Egypt I called My son.
As they called them,
So they went from them;
They sacrificed to the Baals,
And burned incense to carved images.

"I taught Ephraim to walk,
Taking them by their arms;
But they did not know that I healed them.
I drew them with gentle cords,
With bands of love,
And I was to them as those who take the yoke
     from their neck.
I stooped *and* fed them.

"He shall not return to the land of Egypt;
But the Assyrian shall be his king,
Because they refused to repent.
And the sword shall slash in his cities,
Devour his districts,
And consume *them,*
Because of their own counsels.
My people are bent on backsliding from Me.
Though they call to the Most High,
None at all exalt *Him.*

"How can I give you up, Ephraim?
How can I hand you over, Israel?
How can I make you like Admah?
How can I set you like Zeboiim?
My heart churns within Me;

My sympathy is stirred.
I will not execute the fierceness of My anger;
I will not again destroy Ephraim.
For I *am* God, and not man,
The Holy One in your midst;
And I will not come with terror.

"They shall walk after the LORD.
He will roar like a lion.
When He roars,
Then *His* sons shall come trembling from the
     west;
They shall come trembling like a bird from
     Egypt,
Like a dove from the land of Assyria.
And I will let them dwell in their houses,"
Says the LORD.

Hosea 3–4; 6:4-6; 11:1-11

From the end of the earth I will cry to You,
When my heart is overwhelmed;
Lead me to the rock that is higher than I.

For You have been a shelter for me,
A strong tower from the enemy.
I will abide in Your tabernacle forever;
I will trust in the shelter of Your wings.   Selah
Psalm 61:2-4

WISDOM

He who walks in his uprightness fears the
     LORD,
But *he who is* perverse in his ways despises
     Him.

Proverbs 14:2

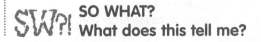

SO WHAT?
What does this tell me?

CALLED TO THE COURTROOM   Isaiah 1; Psalm 62:5-7; Proverbs 14:3

The vision of Isaiah the son of Amoz, which he saw concerning Judah and Jerusalem in the days of Uzziah, Jotham, Ahaz, *and* Hezekiah, kings of Judah.

Hear, O heavens, and give ear, O earth!
For the LORD has spoken:
"I have nourished and brought up children,
And they have rebelled against Me;
The ox knows its owner
And the donkey its master's crib;
But Israel does not know,
My people do not consider."

Alas, sinful nation,
A people laden with iniquity,
A brood of evildoers,
Children who are corrupters!
They have forsaken the LORD,
They have provoked to anger
The Holy One of Israel,
They have turned away backward.

Why should you be stricken again?
You will revolt more and more.
The whole head is sick,
And the whole heart faints.
From the sole of the foot even to the head,
There is no soundness in it,
But wounds and bruises and putrefying
    sores;
They have not been closed or bound up,
Or soothed with ointment.

Your country *is* desolate,
Your cities *are* burned with fire;
Strangers devour your land in your presence;
And *it is* desolate, as overthrown by
    strangers.
So the daughter of Zion is left as a booth in
    a vineyard,
As a hut in a garden of cucumbers,
As a besieged city.
Unless the LORD of hosts
Had left to us a very small remnant,
We would have become like Sodom,
We would have been made like Gomorrah.

Hear the word of the LORD,
You rulers of Sodom;
Give ear to the law of our God,
You people of Gomorrah:
"To what purpose *is* the multitude of your
    sacrifices to Me?"
Says the LORD.
"I have had enough of burnt offerings of rams
And the fat of fed cattle.
I do not delight in the blood of bulls,
Or of lambs or goats.

"When you come to appear before Me,
Who has required this from your hand,
To trample My courts?
Bring no more futile sacrifices;
Incense is an abomination to Me.
The New Moons, the Sabbaths, and the calling
    of assemblies—
I cannot endure iniquity and the sacred
    meeting.
Your New Moons and your appointed feasts
My soul hates;
They are a trouble to Me,
I am weary of bearing *them*.
When you spread out your hands,
I will hide My eyes from you;
Even though you make many prayers,
I will not hear.
Your hands are full of blood.

"Wash yourselves, make yourselves clean;
Put away the evil of your doings from before
    My eyes.
Cease to do evil,
Learn to do good;
Seek justice,
Rebuke the oppressor;
Defend the fatherless,
Plead for the widow.

"Come now, and let us reason together,"
Says the LORD,
"Though your sins are like scarlet,
They shall be as white as snow;
Though they are red like crimson,
They shall be as wool.
If you are willing and obedient,
You shall eat the good of the land;
But if you refuse and rebel,
You shall be devoured by the sword";
For the mouth of the LORD has spoken.

How the faithful city has become a harlot!
It was full of justice;
Righteousness lodged in it,
But now murderers.
Your silver has become dross,
Your wine mixed with water.
Your princes *are* rebellious,
And companions of thieves;
Everyone loves bribes,
And follows after rewards.
They do not defend the fatherless,
Nor does the cause of the widow come before
    them.

Therefore the Lord says,
The LORD of hosts, the Mighty One of Israel,
"Ah, I will rid Myself of My adversaries,
And take vengeance on My enemies.
I will turn My hand against you,
And thoroughly purge away your dross,
And take away all your alloy.
I will restore your judges as at the first,
And your counselors as at the beginning.
Afterward you shall be called the city of
    righteousness, the faithful city."

Zion shall be redeemed with justice,
And her penitents with righteousness.
The destruction of transgressors and of sinners
    shall be together,
And those who forsake the LORD shall be
    consumed.
For they shall be ashamed of the terebinth
    trees
Which you have desired;
And you shall be embarrassed because of the
    gardens
Which you have chosen.
For you shall be as a terebinth whose leaf
    fades,
And as a garden that has no water.
The strong shall be as tinder,
And the work of it as a spark;
Both will burn together,
And no one shall quench *them.*

Isaiah 1

WORSHIP

My soul, wait silently for God alone,
For my expectation *is* from Him.
He only *is* my rock and my salvation;
He is my defense;
I shall not be moved.
In God *is* my salvation and my glory;
The rock of my strength,
And my refuge, *is* in God.

Psalm 62:5-7

WISDOM

In the mouth of a fool *is* a rod of pride,
But the lips of the wise will preserve them.

Proverbs 14:3

SW?! SO WHAT?
What does this tell me?

JUDGMENT FOLLOWED BY BLESSING

Isaiah 3–4; Psalm 62:10-12; Proverbs 14:4

For behold, the Lord, the LORD of hosts,
Takes away from Jerusalem and from Judah
The stock and the store,
The whole supply of bread and the whole
supply of water;
The mighty man and the man of war,
The judge and the prophet,
And the diviner and the elder;
The captain of fifty and the honorable man,
The counselor and the skillful artisan,
And the expert enchanter.

"I will give children *to be* their princes,
And babes shall rule over them.
The people will be oppressed,
Every one by another and every one by his
neighbor;
The child will be insolent toward the elder,
And the base toward the honorable."

When a man takes hold of his brother
In the house of his father, *saying,*
"You have clothing;
You be our ruler,
And *let* these ruins *be* under your power,"
In that day he will protest, saying,
"I cannot cure *your* ills,
For in my house *is* neither food nor clothing;
Do not make me a ruler of the people."

For Jerusalem stumbled,
And Judah is fallen,
Because their tongue and their doings
Are against the LORD,
To provoke the eyes of His glory.
The look on their countenance witnesses
against them,
And they declare their sin as Sodom;
They do not hide *it.*
Woe to their soul!
For they have brought evil upon themselves.

"Say to the righteous that *it shall be* well *with
them,*
For they shall eat the fruit of their doings.
Woe to the wicked! *It shall be* ill *with him,*
For the reward of his hands shall be given
him.
As for My people, children *are* their
oppressors,
And women rule over them.

O My people! Those who lead you cause *you*
to err,
And destroy the way of your paths."

The LORD stands up to plead,
And stands to judge the people.
The LORD will enter into judgment
With the elders of His people
And His princes:
"For you have eaten up the vineyard;
The plunder of the poor *is* in your houses.
What do you mean by crushing My people
And grinding the faces of the poor?"
Says the Lord GOD of hosts.

Moreover the LORD says:

"Because the daughters of Zion are haughty,
And walk with outstretched necks
And wanton eyes,
Walking and mincing *as* they go,
Making a jingling with their feet,
Therefore the Lord will strike with a scab
The crown of the head of the daughters of
Zion,
And the LORD will uncover their secret parts."

In that day the Lord will take away the finery:
The jingling anklets, the scarves, and the
crescents;
The pendants, the bracelets, and the veils;
The headdresses, the leg ornaments, and the
headbands;
The perfume boxes, the charms, and the rings;
The nose jewels, the festal apparel, and the
mantles;
The outer garments, the purses, and the
mirrors;
The fine linen, the turbans, and the robes.

And so it shall be:

Instead of a sweet smell there will be a stench;
Instead of a sash, a rope;
Instead of well-set hair, baldness;
Instead of a rich robe, a girding of sackcloth;
And branding instead of beauty.
Your men shall fall by the sword,
And your mighty in the war.

Her gates shall lament and mourn,
And she *being* desolate shall sit on the
ground.

And in that day seven women shall take hold
of one man, saying,

"We will eat our own food and wear our own
apparel;
Only let us be called by your name,
To take away our reproach."

In that day the Branch of the LORD shall be
beautiful and glorious;
And the fruit of the earth *shall be* excellent and
appealing
For those of Israel who have escaped.

And it shall come to pass that *he who is* left in
Zion and remains in Jerusalem will be called
holy—everyone who is recorded among the living
in Jerusalem. When the Lord has washed away the
filth of the daughters of Zion, and purged the blood
of Jerusalem from her midst, by the spirit of judgment and by the spirit of burning, then the LORD will
create above every dwelling place of Mount Zion,
and above her assemblies, a cloud and smoke by
day and the shining of a flaming fire by night. For
over all the glory there *will be* a covering. And there
will be a tabernacle for shade in the daytime from
the heat, for a place of refuge, and for a shelter
from storm and rain.

Isaiah 3–4

WORSHIP

Do not trust in oppression,
Nor vainly hope in robbery;
If riches increase,
Do not set *your* heart *on them.*

God has spoken once,
Twice I have heard this:
That power *belongs* to God.
Also to You, O Lord, *belongs* mercy;
For You render to each one according to his
work.

Psalm 62:10-12

WISDOM

Where no oxen *are,* the trough *is* clean;
But much increase *comes* by the strength of
an ox.

Proverbs 14:4

SW?! SO WHAT?
What does this tell me?

THE SONG OF THE VINEYARD Isaiah 5; Psalm 63:3-5; Proverbs 14:5

Now let me sing to my Well-beloved
A song of my Beloved regarding His vineyard:

My Well-beloved has a vineyard
On a very fruitful hill.
He dug it up and cleared out its stones,
And planted it with the choicest vine.
He built a tower in its midst,
And also made a winepress in it;
So He expected *it* to bring forth *good* grapes,
But it brought forth wild grapes.

"And now, O inhabitants of Jerusalem and men
    of Judah,
    Judge, please, between Me and My
        vineyard.
    What more could have been done to My
        vineyard
    That I have not done in it?
    Why then, when I expected *it* to bring forth
        good grapes,
    Did it bring forth wild grapes?
    And now, please let Me tell you what I will
        do to My vineyard:
    I will take away its hedge, and it shall be
        burned;
    And break down its wall, and it shall be
        trampled down.
    I will lay it waste;
    It shall not be pruned or dug,
    But there shall come up briers and thorns.
    I will also command the clouds
    That they rain no rain on it."

For the vineyard of the LORD of hosts *is* the
    house of Israel,
And the men of Judah are His pleasant
    plant.
He looked for justice, but behold,
    oppression;
For righteousness, but behold, a cry *for help.*

Woe to those who join house to house;
They add field to field,
Till *there is* no place
Where they may dwell alone in the midst of
    the land!
In my hearing the LORD of hosts *said,*
"Truly, many houses shall be desolate,
Great and beautiful ones, without inhabitant.

For ten acres of vineyard shall yield one bath,
And a homer of seed shall yield one ephah."

Woe to those who rise early in the morning,
That they may follow intoxicating drink;
Who continue until night, *till* wine inflames
    them!
The harp and the strings,
The tambourine and flute,
And wine are in their feasts;
But they do not regard the work of the LORD,
Nor consider the operation of His hands.

Therefore my people have gone into captivity,
Because *they have* no knowledge;
Their honorable men *are* famished,
And their multitude dried up with thirst.
Therefore Sheol has enlarged itself
And opened its mouth beyond measure;
Their glory and their multitude and their pomp,
And he who is jubilant, shall descend into it.
People shall be brought down,
Each man shall be humbled,
And the eyes of the lofty shall be humbled.
But the LORD of hosts shall be exalted in
    judgment,
And God who is holy shall be hallowed in
    righteousness.
Then the lambs shall feed in their pasture,
And in the waste places of the fat ones
    strangers shall eat.

Woe to those who draw iniquity with cords of
    vanity,
And sin as if with a cart rope;
That say, "Let Him make speed *and* hasten His
    work,
That we may see *it*;
And let the counsel of the Holy One of Israel
    draw near and come,
That we may know *it*."

Woe to those who call evil good, and good
    evil;
Who put darkness for light, and light for
    darkness;
Who put bitter for sweet, and sweet for bitter!

Woe to *those who are* wise in their own eyes,
And prudent in their own sight!

Woe to men mighty at drinking wine,
Woe to men valiant for mixing intoxicating
  drink,
Who justify the wicked for a bribe,
And take away justice from the righteous man!

Therefore, as the fire devours the stubble,
And the flame consumes the chaff,
So their root will be as rottenness,
And their blossom will ascend like dust;
Because they have rejected the law of the LORD
  of hosts,
And despised the word of the Holy One of
  Israel.
Therefore the anger of the LORD is aroused
  against His people;
He has stretched out His hand against them
And stricken them,
And the hills trembled.
Their carcasses *were* as refuse in the midst of
  the streets.

For all this His anger is not turned away,
But His hand *is* stretched out still.

He will lift up a banner to the nations from
  afar,
And will whistle to them from the end of the
  earth;
Surely they shall come with speed, swiftly.
No one will be weary or stumble among them,
No one will slumber or sleep;
Nor will the belt on their loins be loosed,
Nor the strap of their sandals be broken;
Whose arrows *are* sharp,
And all their bows bent;
Their horses' hooves will seem like flint,
And their wheels like a whirlwind.
Their roaring *will be* like a lion,
They will roar like young lions;
Yes, they will roar
And lay hold of the prey;
They will carry *it* away safely,
And no one will deliver.
In that day they will roar against them
Like the roaring of the sea.
And if *one* looks to the land,
Behold, darkness *and* sorrow;
And the light is darkened by the clouds.

Isaiah 5

WORSHIP

Because Your lovingkindness *is* better than life,
My lips shall praise You.
Thus I will bless You while I live;
I will lift up my hands in Your name.
My soul shall be satisfied as with marrow and
  fatness,
And my mouth shall praise *You* with joyful lips.

Psalm 63:3-5

WISDOM

A faithful witness does not lie,
But a false witness will utter lies.

Proverbs 14:5

SW?! **SO WHAT?**
      What does this tell me?

THE CALL OF A PROPHET   Isaiah 6; Psalm 63:6-8; Proverbs 14:6

In the year that King Uzziah died, I saw the Lord sitting on a throne, high and lifted up, and the train of His *robe* filled the temple. Above it stood seraphim; each one had six wings: with two he covered his face, with two he covered his feet, and with two he flew. And one cried to another and said:

"Holy, holy, holy *is* the LORD of hosts;
The whole earth *is* full of His glory!"

And the posts of the door were shaken by the voice of him who cried out, and the house was filled with smoke.

So I said:

"Woe *is* me, for I am undone!
Because I *am* a man of unclean lips,
And I dwell in the midst of a people of unclean lips;
For my eyes have seen the King,
The LORD of hosts."

Then one of the seraphim flew to me, having in his hand a live coal *which* he had taken with the tongs from the altar. And he touched my mouth *with it,* and said:

"Behold, this has touched your lips;
Your iniquity is taken away,
And your sin purged."

Also I heard the voice of the Lord, saying:

"Whom shall I send,
And who will go for Us?"

Then I said, "Here *am* I! Send me."
And He said, "Go, and tell this people:

'Keep on hearing, but do not understand;
Keep on seeing, but do not perceive.'

"Make the heart of this people dull,
And their ears heavy,
And shut their eyes;
Lest they see with their eyes,
And hear with their ears,
And understand with their heart,
And return and be healed."

Then I said, "Lord, how long?"
And He answered:

"Until the cities are laid waste and without inhabitant,
The houses are without a man,
The land is utterly desolate,
The LORD has removed men far away,
And the forsaken places *are* many in the midst of the land.
But yet a tenth *will be* in it,
And will return and be for consuming,
As a terebinth tree or as an oak,
Whose stump *remains* when it is cut down.
So the holy seed *shall be* its stump."

Isaiah 6

WORSHIP

When I remember You on my bed,
I meditate on You in the *night* watches.
Because You have been my help,
Therefore in the shadow of Your wings I will
    rejoice.
My soul follows close behind You;
Your right hand upholds me.

Psalm 63:6-8

WISDOM

A scoffer seeks wisdom and does not *find it,*
But knowledge *is* easy to him who
    understands.

Proverbs 14:6

SW?! **SO WHAT?**
What does this tell me?

THE SIGN OF IMMANUEL'S COMING

Now it came to pass in the days of Ahaz the son of Jotham, the son of Uzziah, king of Judah, *that* Rezin king of Syria and Pekah the son of Remaliah, king of Israel, went up to Jerusalem to *make* war against it, but could not prevail against it. And it was told to the house of David, saying, "Syria's forces are deployed in Ephraim." So his heart and the heart of his people were moved as the trees of the woods are moved with the wind.

Then the LORD said to Isaiah, "Go out now to meet Ahaz, you and Shear-Jashub your son, at the end of the aqueduct from the upper pool, on the highway to the Fuller's Field, and say to him: 'Take heed, and be quiet; do not fear or be fainthearted for these two stubs of smoking firebrands, for the fierce anger of Rezin and Syria, and the son of Remaliah. Because Syria, Ephraim, and the son of Remaliah have plotted evil against you, saying, "Let us go up against Judah and trouble it, and let us make a gap in its wall for ourselves, and set a king over them, the son of Tabel"—thus says the Lord GOD:

"It shall not stand,
   Nor shall it come to pass.
   For the head of Syria *is* Damascus,
   And the head of Damascus *is* Rezin.
   Within sixty-five years Ephraim will be
      broken,
   So that it will not *be* a people.
   The head of Ephraim *is* Samaria,
   And the head of Samaria *is* Remaliah's son.
   If you will not believe,
   Surely you shall not be established." ' "

Moreover the LORD spoke again to Ahaz, saying, "Ask a sign for yourself from the LORD your God; ask it either in the depth or in the height above."

But Ahaz said, "I will not ask, nor will I test the LORD!"

Then he said, "Hear now, O house of David! *Is it* a small thing for you to weary men, but will you weary my God also? Therefore the Lord Himself will give you a sign: Behold, the virgin shall conceive and bear a Son, and shall call His name Im-manuel. Curds and honey He shall eat, that He may know to refuse the evil and choose the good. For before the Child shall know to refuse the evil and choose the good, the land that you dread will be forsaken by both her kings. The LORD will bring the king of Assyria upon you and your people and your father's house—days that have not come since the day that Ephraim departed from Judah."

And it shall come to pass in that day
That the LORD will whistle for the fly
That *is* in the farthest part of the rivers of Egypt,
And for the bee that *is* in the land of Assyria.
They will come, and all of them will rest
In the desolate valleys and in the clefts of the
      rocks,
And on all thorns and in all pastures.

In the same day the Lord will shave with a
      hired razor,
With those from beyond the River, with the king
      of Assyria,
The head and the hair of the legs,
And will also remove the beard.

It shall be in that day
That a man will keep alive a young cow and
      two sheep;
So it shall be, from the abundance of milk they
      give,
That he will eat curds;
For curds and honey everyone will eat who is
      left in the land.

It shall happen in that day,
That wherever there could be a thousand vines
Worth a thousand *shekels* of silver,
It will be for briers and thorns.
With arrows and bows men will come there,
Because all the land will become briers and
      thorns.

And to any hill which could be dug with the
      hoe,
You will not go there for fear of briers and
      thorns;
But it will become a range for oxen
And a place for sheep to roam.

Moreover the LORD said to me, "Take a large scroll, and write on it with a man's pen concerning Maher-Shalal-Hash-Baz. And I will take for Myself faithful witnesses to record, Uriah the priest and Zechariah the son of Jeberechiah."

Then I went to the prophetess, and she conceived and bore a son. Then the LORD said to me, "Call his name Maher-Shalal-Hash-Baz; for before the child shall have knowledge to cry 'My father' and 'My mother,' the riches of Damascus and the spoil of Samaria will be taken away before the king of Assyria."

The LORD also spoke to me again, saying:

"Inasmuch as these people refused
The waters of Shiloah that flow softly,
And rejoice in Rezin and in Remaliah's son;
Now therefore, behold, the Lord brings up over
 them
The waters of the River, strong and mighty—
The king of Assyria and all his glory;
He will go up over all his channels
And go over all his banks.
He will pass through Judah,
He will overflow and pass over,
He will reach up to the neck;
And the stretching out of his wings
Will fill the breadth of Your land, O Immanuel.

"Be shattered, O you peoples, and be broken in
 pieces!
Give ear, all you from far countries.
Gird yourselves, but be broken in pieces;
Gird yourselves, but be broken in pieces.
Take counsel together, but it will come to
 nothing;
Speak the word, but it will not stand,
For God *is* with us."

Isaiah 7:1–8:10

WORSHIP

Hear my voice, O God, in my meditation;
Preserve my life from fear of the enemy.
Hide me from the secret plots of the wicked,
From the rebellion of the workers of iniquity,
Who sharpen their tongue like a sword,
And bend *their bows to shoot* their arrows—
 bitter words.

Psalm 64:1-3

WISDOM

Go from the presence of a foolish man,
When you do not perceive *in him* the lips of
 knowledge.

Proverbs 14:7

SW?! **SO WHAT?**
What does this tell me?

THE COMING MESSIANIC KING

Isaiah 8:19–9:21; Psalm 64:7, 9-10; Proverbs 14:8

And when they say to you, "Seek those who are mediums and wizards, who whisper and mutter," should not a people seek their God? *Should they seek* the dead on behalf of the living? To the law and to the testimony! If they do not speak according to this word, *it is* because *there is* no light in them.

They will pass through it hard-pressed and hungry; and it shall happen, when they are hungry, that they will be enraged and curse their king and their God, and look upward. Then they will look to the earth, and see trouble and darkness, gloom of anguish; and *they will be* driven into darkness.

Nevertheless the gloom *will* not *be* upon
   her who *is* distressed,
As when at first He lightly esteemed
The land of Zebulun and the land of
   Naphtali,
And afterward more heavily oppressed *her,*
By the way of the sea, beyond the Jordan,
In Galilee of the Gentiles.
The people who walked in darkness
Have seen a great light;
Those who dwelt in the land of the
   shadow of death,
Upon them a light has shined.

You have multiplied the nation
And increased its joy;
They rejoice before You
According to the joy of harvest,
As *men* rejoice when they divide the spoil.
For You have broken the yoke of his burden
And the staff of his shoulder,
The rod of his oppressor,
As in the day of Midian.
For every warrior's sandal from the noisy
   battle,
And garments rolled in blood,
Will be used for burning *and* fuel of fire.

For unto us a Child is born,
Unto us a Son is given;
And the government will be upon His
   shoulder.
And His name will be called
Wonderful, Counselor, Mighty God,
Everlasting Father, Prince of Peace.

Of the increase of *His* government and peace
There will be no end,
Upon the throne of David and over His
   kingdom,
To order it and establish it with judgment and
   justice
From that time forward, even forever.
The zeal of the Lord of hosts will perform this.

The Lord sent a word against Jacob,
And it has fallen on Israel.
All the people will know—
Ephraim and the inhabitant of Samaria—
Who say in pride and arrogance of heart:
"The bricks have fallen down,
But we will rebuild with hewn stones;
The sycamores are cut down,
But we will replace *them* with cedars."
Therefore the LORD shall set up
The adversaries of Rezin against him,
And spur his enemies on,
The Syrians before and the Philistines behind;
And they shall devour Israel with an open
   mouth.

For all this His anger is not turned away,
But His hand *is* stretched out still.

For the people do not turn to Him who strikes
   them,
Nor do they seek the LORD of hosts.
Therefore the LORD will cut off head and tail
   from Israel,
Palm branch and bulrush in one day.
The elder and honorable, he *is* the head;
The prophet who teaches lies, he *is* the tail.
For the leaders of this people cause *them* to
   err,
And *those who are* led by them are destroyed.
Therefore the Lord will have no joy in their
   young men,
Nor have mercy on their fatherless and
   widows;
For everyone *is* a hypocrite and an evildoer,
And every mouth speaks folly.

For all this His anger is not turned away,
But His hand *is* stretched out still.

For wickedness burns as the fire;
It shall devour the briers and thorns,
And kindle in the thickets of the forest;

They shall mount up *like* rising smoke.
Through the wrath of the LORD of hosts
The land is burned up,
And the people shall be as fuel for the fire;
No man shall spare his brother.
And he shall snatch on the right hand
And be hungry;
He shall devour on the left hand
And not be satisfied;
Every man shall eat the flesh of his own arm.
Manasseh *shall devour* Ephraim, and Ephraim
　　Manasseh;
Together they *shall be* against Judah.

For all this His anger is not turned away,
But His hand *is* stretched out still.

Isaiah 8:19–9:21

WORSHIP

But God shall shoot at them *with* an arrow;
Suddenly they shall be wounded.

All men shall fear,
And shall declare the work of God;
For they shall wisely consider His doing.

The righteous shall be glad in the LORD, and
　　trust in Him.
And all the upright in heart shall glory.

Psalm 64:7, 9-10

WISDOM

The wisdom of the prudent *is* to understand
　　his way,
But the folly of fools *is* deceit.

Proverbs 14:8

SW?! **SO WHAT?**
What does this tell me?

THE GLORY OF MESSIAH'S KINGDOM

Isaiah 11–12; Psalm 65:2-4; Proverbs 14:10

There shall come forth a Rod from the stem of
    Jesse,
And a Branch shall grow out of his roots.
The Spirit of the LORD shall rest upon Him,
The Spirit of wisdom and understanding,
The Spirit of counsel and might,
The Spirit of knowledge and of the fear of the
    LORD.

His delight *is* in the fear of the LORD,
And He shall not judge by the sight of His
    eyes,
    Nor decide by the hearing of His ears;
    But with righteousness He shall judge the
    poor,
    And decide with equity for the meek of the
    earth;
He shall strike the earth with the rod of His
    mouth,
    And with the breath of His lips He shall slay
    the wicked.
Righteousness shall be the belt of His loins,
And faithfulness the belt of His waist.

"The wolf also shall dwell with the lamb,
The leopard shall lie down with the young
    goat,
The calf and the young lion and the fatling
    together;
And a little child shall lead them.
The cow and the bear shall graze;
Their young ones shall lie down together;
And the lion shall eat straw like the ox.
The nursing child shall play by the cobra's
    hole,
And the weaned child shall put his hand in
    the viper's den.
They shall not hurt nor destroy in all My holy
    mountain,
For the earth shall be full of the knowledge
    of the LORD
As the waters cover the sea.

"And in that day there shall be a Root of
    Jesse,
Who shall stand as a banner to the people;
For the Gentiles shall seek Him,
And His resting place shall be glorious."

It shall come to pass in that day
That the Lord shall set His hand again the
    second time
To recover the remnant of His people who are
    left,
From Assyria and Egypt,
From Pathros and Cush,
From Elam and Shinar,
From Hamath and the islands of the sea.

He will set up a banner for the nations,
And will assemble the outcasts of Israel,
And gather together the dispersed of Judah
From the four corners of the earth.
Also the envy of Ephraim shall depart,
And the adversaries of Judah shall be cut off;
Ephraim shall not envy Judah,
And Judah shall not harass Ephraim.
But they shall fly down upon the shoulder of
    the Philistines toward the west;
Together they shall plunder the people of the
    East;
They shall lay their hand on Edom and Moab;
And the people of Ammon shall obey them.
The LORD will utterly destroy the tongue of the
    Sea of Egypt;
With His mighty wind He will shake His fist
    over the River,
And strike it in the seven streams,
And make *men* cross over dryshod.
There will be a highway for the remnant of His
    people
Who will be left from Assyria,
As it was for Israel
In the day that he came up from the land of
    Egypt.

And in that day you will say:

"O LORD, I will praise You;
Though You were angry with me,
Your anger is turned away, and You comfort me.
Behold, God *is* my salvation,
I will trust and not be afraid;
'For YAH, the LORD, *is* my strength and song;
He also has become my salvation.' "

Therefore with joy you will draw water
From the wells of salvation.

And in that day you will say:

"Praise the LORD, call upon His name;
Declare His deeds among the peoples,
Make mention that His name is exalted.
Sing to the LORD,
For He has done excellent things;
This *is* known in all the earth.
Cry out and shout, O inhabitant of Zion,
For great *is* the Holy One of Israel in your
    midst!"

Isaiah 11–12

WORSHIP

O You who hear prayer,
To You all flesh will come.
Iniquities prevail against me;
As for our transgressions,
You will provide atonement for them.

Blessed *is the man* You choose,
And cause to approach *You,*
That he may dwell in Your courts.
We shall be satisfied with the goodness of
    Your house,
Of Your holy temple.

Psalm 65:2-4

WISDOM

The heart knows its own bitterness,
And a stranger does not share its joy.

Proverbs 14:10

SW?! SO WHAT? What does this tell me?

THE COMING ATTACK ON JERUSALEM

Isaiah 22; Psalm 65:5-8;
Proverbs 14:11

The burden against the Valley of Vision.

What ails you now, that you have all gone
    up to the housetops,
You who are full of noise,
A tumultuous city, a joyous city?
Your slain *men are* not slain with the sword,
Nor dead in battle.
All your rulers have fled together;
They are captured by the archers.
All who are found in you are bound together;
They have fled from afar.
Therefore I said, "Look away from me,
    I will weep bitterly;
    Do not labor to comfort me
    Because of the plundering of the daughter of
        my people."

For *it is* a day of trouble and treading down
    and perplexity
By the Lord GOD of hosts
In the Valley of Vision—
Breaking down the walls
And of crying to the mountain.
Elam bore the quiver
With chariots of men *and* horsemen,
And Kir uncovered the shield.
It shall come to pass *that* your choicest
    valleys
Shall be full of chariots,
And the horsemen shall set themselves in
    array at the gate.

He removed the protection of Judah.
You looked in that day to the armor of the
    House of the Forest;
You also saw the damage to the city of
    David,
That it was great;
And you gathered together the waters of the
    lower pool.
You numbered the houses of Jerusalem,
And the houses you broke down
To fortify the wall.
You also made a reservoir between the two
    walls
For the water of the old pool.
But you did not look to its Maker,
Nor did you have respect for Him who
    fashioned it long ago.

And in that day the Lord GOD of hosts
Called for weeping and for mourning,
For baldness and for girding with sackcloth.
But instead, joy and gladness,
Slaying oxen and killing sheep,
Eating meat and drinking wine:
"Let us eat and drink, for tomorrow we die!"

Then it was revealed in my hearing by the LORD
    of hosts,
"Surely for this iniquity there will be no
    atonement for you,
    Even to your death," says the Lord GOD of
    hosts.

Thus says the Lord GOD of hosts:

"Go, proceed to this steward,
    To Shebna, who *is* over the house, *and say:*
'What have you here, and whom have you
        here,
    That you have hewn a sepulcher here,
As he who hews himself a sepulcher on high,
Who carves a tomb for himself in a rock?
Indeed, the LORD will throw you away violently,
O mighty man,
And will surely seize you.
He will surely turn violently and toss you like a
    ball
Into a large country;
There you shall die, and there your glorious
    chariots
Shall be the shame of your master's house.
So I will drive you out of your office,
And from your position he will pull you down.

'Then it shall be in that day,
That I will call My servant Eliakim the son of
    Hilkiah;
I will clothe him with your robe
And strengthen him with your belt;
I will commit your responsibility into his hand.
He shall be a father to the inhabitants of
    Jerusalem
And to the house of Judah.
The key of the house of David
I will lay on his shoulder;
So he shall open, and no one shall shut;
And he shall shut, and no one shall open.
I will fasten him *as* a peg in a secure place,

And he will become a glorious throne to his father's house.

'They will hang on him all the glory of his father's house, the offspring and the posterity, all vessels of small quantity, from the cups to all the pitchers. In that day,' says the LORD of hosts, 'the peg that is fastened in the secure place will be removed and be cut down and fall, and the burden that *was* on it will be cut off; for the LORD has spoken.' "

Isaiah 22

WORSHIP

By awesome deeds in righteousness You will answer us,
O God of our salvation,
You who are the confidence of all the ends of the earth,
And of the far-off seas;
Who established the mountains by His strength,
Being clothed with power;
You who still the noise of the seas,
The noise of their waves,
And the tumult of the peoples.
They also who dwell in the farthest parts are afraid of Your signs;
You make the outgoings of the morning and evening rejoice.

Psalm 65:5-8

WISDOM

The house of the wicked will be overthrown,
But the tent of the upright will flourish.

Proverbs 14:11

SW?! **SO WHAT?**
What does this tell me?

UNIVERSAL JUDGMENT AND BLESSING

Isaiah 24:1–25:9; Psalm 66:5-7; Proverbs 14:12

Behold, the LORD makes the earth empty and
    makes it waste,
Distorts its surface
And scatters abroad its inhabitants.
And it shall be:
As with the people, so with the priest;
As with the servant, so with his master;
As with the maid, so with her mistress;
As with the buyer, so with the seller;
As with the lender, so with the borrower;
As with the creditor, so with the debtor.
The land shall be entirely emptied and utterly
    plundered,
    For the LORD has spoken this word.

The earth mourns *and* fades away,
The world languishes *and* fades away;
The haughty people of the earth languish.
The earth is also defiled under its
    inhabitants,
Because they have transgressed the
    laws,
Changed the ordinance,
Broken the everlasting covenant.
Therefore the curse has devoured the earth,
And those who dwell in it are desolate.
Therefore the inhabitants of the earth are
    burned,
And few men *are* left.

The new wine fails, the vine languishes,
All the merry-hearted sigh.
The mirth of the tambourine ceases,
The noise of the jubilant ends,
The joy of the harp ceases.
They shall not drink wine with a song;
Strong drink is bitter to those who drink it.
The city of confusion is broken down;
Every house is shut up, so that none may go
    in.
There is a cry for wine in the streets,
All joy is darkened,
The mirth of the land is gone.
In the city desolation is left,
And the gate is stricken with destruction.
When it shall be thus in the midst of the land
    among the people,
It shall be like the shaking of an olive tree,
Like the gleaning of grapes when the vintage
    is done.

They shall lift up their voice, they shall sing;
For the majesty of the LORD
They shall cry aloud from the sea.
Therefore glorify the LORD in the dawning light,
The name of the LORD God of Israel in the
    coastlands of the sea.
From the ends of the earth we have heard
    songs:
"Glory to the righteous!"
But I said, "I am ruined, ruined!
Woe to me!
The treacherous dealers have dealt
    treacherously,
Indeed, the treacherous dealers have dealt
    very treacherously."

Fear and the pit and the snare
Are upon you, O inhabitant of the earth.
And it shall be
That he who flees from the noise of the fear
Shall fall into the pit,
And he who comes up from the midst of the
    pit
Shall be caught in the snare;
For the windows from on high are open,
And the foundations of the earth are shaken.

The earth is violently broken,
The earth is split open,
The earth is shaken exceedingly.
The earth shall reel to and fro like a drunkard,
And shall totter like a hut;
Its transgression shall be heavy upon it,
And it will fall, and not rise again.

It shall come to pass in that day
That the LORD will punish on high the host of
    exalted ones,
And on the earth the kings of the earth.
They will be gathered together,
As prisoners are gathered in the pit,
And will be shut up in the prison;
After many days they will be punished.
Then the moon will be disgraced
And the sun ashamed;
For the LORD of hosts will reign
On Mount Zion and in Jerusalem
And before His elders, gloriously.

O LORD, You *are* my God.
I will exalt You,

I will praise Your name,
For You have done wonderful *things;*
Your counsels of old *are* faithfulness *and* truth.
For You have made a city a ruin,
A fortified city a ruin,
A palace of foreigners to be a city no more;
It will never be rebuilt.
Therefore the strong people will glorify You;
The city of the terrible nations will fear You.
For You have been a strength to the poor,
A strength to the needy in his distress,
A refuge from the storm,
A shade from the heat;
For the blast of the terrible ones *is* as a storm
        against the wall.
You will reduce the noise of aliens,
As heat in a dry place;
As heat in the shadow of a cloud,
The song of the terrible ones will be
        diminished.

And in this mountain
The LORD of hosts will make for all people
A feast of choice pieces,
A feast of wines on the lees,
Of fat things full of marrow,
Of well-refined wines on the lees.
And He will destroy on this mountain
The surface of the covering cast over all
        people,
And the veil that is spread over all nations.
He will swallow up death forever,
And the Lord GOD will wipe away tears from all
        faces;
The rebuke of His people
He will take away from all the earth;
For the LORD has spoken.

And it will be said in that day:
"Behold, this *is* our God;
We have waited for Him, and He will save us.
This *is* the LORD;
We have waited for Him;
We will be glad and rejoice in His salvation."
                                Isaiah 24:1–25:9

WORSHIP

Come and see the works of God;
He is awesome *in His* doing toward the sons of
        men.
He turned the sea into dry *land;*
They went through the river on foot.
There we will rejoice in Him.
He rules by His power forever;
His eyes observe the nations;
Do not let the rebellious exalt themselves.
                                            Selah
                                Psalm 66:5-7

WISDOM

There is a way *that seems* right to a man,
But its end *is* the way of death.
                                Proverbs 14:12

SO WHAT?
What does this tell me?

COMING JUDGMENT ON JERUSALEM

Isaiah 29; Psalm 66:8-10;
Proverbs 14:13

"Woe to Ariel, to Ariel, the city *where* David
dwelt!
Add year to year;
Let feasts come around.
Yet I will distress Ariel;
There shall be heaviness and sorrow,
And it shall be to Me as Ariel.
I will encamp against you all around,
I will lay siege against you with a mound,
And I will raise siegeworks against you.
You shall be brought down,
You shall speak out of the ground;
Your speech shall be low, out of the dust;
Your voice shall be like a medium's, out of
the ground;
And your speech shall whisper out of the
dust.

"Moreover the multitude of your foes
Shall be like fine dust,
And the multitude of the terrible ones
Like chaff that passes away;
Yes, it shall be in an instant, suddenly.
You will be punished by the LORD of hosts
With thunder and earthquake and great
noise,
With storm and tempest
And the flame of devouring fire.
The multitude of all the nations who fight
against Ariel,
Even all who fight against her and her
fortress,
And distress her,
Shall be as a dream of a night vision.
It shall even be as when a hungry man
dreams,
And look—he eats;
But he awakes, and his soul is still empty;
Or as when a thirsty man dreams,
And look—he drinks;
But he awakes, and indeed *he is* faint,
And his soul still craves:
So the multitude of all the nations shall be,
Who fight against Mount Zion."

Pause and wonder!
Blind yourselves and be blind!
They are drunk, but not with wine;
They stagger, but not with intoxicating drink.
For the LORD has poured out on you

The spirit of deep sleep,
And has closed your eyes, namely, the
prophets;
And He has covered your heads, *namely,* the
seers.

The whole vision has become to you like the
words of a book that is sealed, which *men* deliver
to one who is literate, saying, "Read this, please."
And he says, "I cannot, for it *is* sealed."
Then the book is delivered to one who is illiterate, saying, "Read this, please."
And he says, "I am not literate."
Therefore the Lord said:

"Inasmuch as these people draw near with
their mouths
And honor Me with their lips,
But have removed their hearts far from Me,
And their fear toward Me is taught by the
commandment of men,
Therefore, behold, I will again do a marvelous
work
Among this people,
A marvelous work and a wonder;
For the wisdom of their wise *men* shall perish,
And the understanding of their prudent *men*
shall be hidden."

Woe to those who seek deep to hide their
counsel far from the LORD,
And their works are in the dark;
They say, "Who sees us?" and, "Who knows
us?"
Surely you have things turned around!
Shall the potter be esteemed as the clay;
For shall the thing made say of him who made
it,
"He did not make me"?
Or shall the thing formed say of him who
formed it,
"He has no understanding"?

Is it not yet a very little while
Till Lebanon shall be turned into a fruitful field,
And the fruitful field be esteemed as a forest?
In that day the deaf shall hear the words of the
book,
And the eyes of the blind shall see out of
obscurity and out of darkness.

The humble also shall increase *their* joy in the
    LORD,
And the poor among men shall rejoice
In the Holy One of Israel.
For the terrible one is brought to nothing,
The scornful one is consumed,
And all who watch for iniquity are cut off—
Who make a man an offender by a word,
And lay a snare for him who reproves in the
    gate,
And turn aside the just by empty words.

Therefore thus says the LORD, who redeemed
Abraham, concerning the house of Jacob:

"Jacob shall not now be ashamed,
Nor shall his face now grow pale;
But when he sees his children,
The work of My hands, in his midst,
They will hallow My name,
And hallow the Holy One of Jacob,
And fear the God of Israel.
These also who erred in spirit will come to
    understanding,
And those who complained will learn
    doctrine."

Isaiah 29

WORSHIP

Oh, bless our God, you peoples!
And make the voice of His praise to be heard,
Who keeps our soul among the living,
And does not allow our feet to be moved.
For You, O God, have tested us;
You have refined us as silver is refined.

Psalm 66:8-10

WISDOM

Even in laughter the heart may sorrow,
And the end of mirth *may be* grief.

Proverbs 14:13

SW?! SO WHAT?
What does this tell me?

DON'T LOOK TO EGYPT FOR HELP

Isaiah 30:1-5, 12-26; 31:1-9; Psalm
66:16-17, 20; Proverbs 14:14

"Woe to the rebellious children," says the
LORD,
"Who take counsel, but not of Me,
And who devise plans, but not of My Spirit,
That they may add sin to sin;
Who walk to go down to Egypt,
And have not asked My advice,
To strengthen themselves in the strength of
Pharaoh,
And to trust in the shadow of Egypt!
Therefore the strength of Pharaoh
Shall be your shame,
And trust in the shadow of Egypt
Shall be *your* humiliation.
For his princes were at Zoan,
And his ambassadors came to Hanes.
They were all ashamed of a people *who*
could not benefit them,
Or be help or benefit,
But a shame and also a reproach."

Therefore thus says the Holy One of
Israel:

"Because you despise this word,
And trust in oppression and perversity,
And rely on them,
Therefore this iniquity shall be to you
Like a breach ready to fall,
A bulge in a high wall,
Whose breaking comes suddenly, in an
instant.
And He shall break it like the breaking of
the potter's vessel,
Which is broken in pieces;
He shall not spare.
So there shall not be found among its
fragments
A shard to take fire from the hearth,
Or to take water from the cistern."

For thus says the Lord God, the Holy
One of Israel:

"In returning and rest you shall be saved;
In quietness and confidence shall be your
strength."
But you would not,
And you said, "No, for we will flee on
horses"—
Therefore you shall flee!

And, "We will ride on swift *horses*"—
Therefore those who pursue you shall be swift!

One thousand *shall flee* at the threat of one,
At the threat of five you shall flee,
Till you are left as a pole on top of a mountain
And as a banner on a hill.

Therefore the LORD will wait, that He may be
gracious to you;
And therefore He will be exalted, that He may
have mercy on you.
For the LORD *is* a God of justice;
Blessed *are* all those who wait for Him.

For the people shall dwell in Zion at
Jerusalem;
You shall weep no more.
He will be very gracious to you at the sound of
your cry;
When He hears it, He will answer you.
And *though* the Lord gives you
The bread of adversity and the water of
affliction,
Yet your teachers will not be moved into a
corner anymore,
But your eyes shall see your teachers.
Your ears shall hear a word behind you,
saying,
"This *is* the way, walk in it,"
Whenever you turn to the right hand
Or whenever you turn to the left.
You will also defile the covering of your images
of silver,
And the ornament of your molded images of
gold.
You will throw them away as an unclean thing;
You will say to them, "Get away!"

Then He will give the rain for your seed
With which you sow the ground,
And bread of the increase of the earth;
It will be fat and plentiful.
In that day your cattle will feed
In large pastures.
Likewise the oxen and the young donkeys that
work the ground
Will eat cured fodder,
Which has been winnowed with the shovel
and fan.
There will be on every high mountain

And on every high hill
Rivers *and* streams of waters,
In the day of the great slaughter,
When the towers fall.
Moreover the light of the moon will be as the
    light of the sun,
And the light of the sun will be sevenfold,
As the light of seven days,
In the day that the LORD binds up the bruise of
    His people
And heals the stroke of their wound.

Woe to those who go down to Egypt for help,
And rely on horses,
Who trust in chariots because *they are* many,
And in horsemen because they are very
    strong,
But who do not look to the Holy One of Israel,
Nor seek the LORD!
Yet He also *is* wise and will bring disaster,
And will not call back His words,
But will arise against the house of evildoers,
And against the help of those who work
    iniquity.
Now the Egyptians *are* men, and not God;
And their horses are flesh, and not spirit.
When the LORD stretches out His hand,
Both he who helps will fall,
And he who is helped will fall down;
They all will perish together.

For thus the LORD has spoken to me:

"As a lion roars,
And a young lion over his prey
(When a multitude of shepherds is summoned
    against him,
He will not be afraid of their voice
Nor be disturbed by their noise),
So the LORD of hosts will come down
To fight for Mount Zion and for its hill.
Like birds flying about,
So will the LORD of hosts defend Jerusalem.
Defending, He will also deliver *it;*
Passing over, He will preserve *it.*"

Return *to Him* against whom the children of Israel have deeply revolted. For in that day every man
shall throw away his idols of silver and his idols of
gold—sin, which your own hands have made for
yourselves.

"Then Assyria shall fall by a sword not of man,
And a sword not of mankind shall devour him.
But he shall flee from the sword,
And his young men shall become forced labor.

He shall cross over to his stronghold for fear,
And his princes shall be afraid of the banner,"
Says the LORD,
Whose fire *is* in Zion
And whose furnace *is* in Jerusalem.

Isaiah 30:1-5, 12-26; 31:1-9

WORSHIP

Come *and* hear, all you who fear God,
And I will declare what He has done for my
    soul.
I cried to Him with my mouth,
And He was extolled with my tongue.

Blessed *be* God,
Who has not turned away my prayer,
Nor His mercy from me!

Psalm 66:16-17, 20

WISDOM

The backslider in heart will be filled with his
    own ways,
But a good man *will be satisfied* from above.

Proverbs 14:14

SW?! SO WHAT?
What does this tell me?

THE BLESSINGS OF MESSIAH'S REIGN

Isaiah 32; 33:17-24; Psalm 67:1-3, 7; Proverbs 14:15

Behold, a king will reign in righteousness,
And princes will rule with justice.
A man will be as a hiding place from the
wind,
And a cover from the tempest,
As rivers of water in a dry place,
As the shadow of a great rock in a weary land.
The eyes of those who see will not be dim,
And the ears of those who hear will listen.
Also the heart of the rash will understand
knowledge,
And the tongue of the stammerers will be
ready to speak plainly.

The foolish person will no longer be called
generous,
Nor the miser said to be bountiful;
For the foolish person will speak foolishness,
And his heart will work iniquity:
To practice ungodliness,
To utter error against the LORD,
To keep the hungry unsatisfied,
And he will cause the drink of the thirsty to
fail.
Also the schemes of the schemer are evil;
He devises wicked plans
To destroy the poor with lying words,
Even when the needy speaks justice.
But a generous man devises generous
things,
And by generosity he shall stand.

Rise up, you women who are at ease,
Hear my voice;
You complacent daughters,
Give ear to my speech.
In a year and some days
You will be troubled, you complacent
women;
For the vintage will fail,
The gathering will not come.
Tremble, you women who are at ease;
Be troubled, you complacent ones;
Strip yourselves, make yourselves bare,
And gird sackcloth on your waists.

People shall mourn upon their breasts
For the pleasant fields, for the fruitful vine.
On the land of my people will come up
thorns and briers,

Yes, on all the happy homes in the joyous city;
Because the palaces will be forsaken,
The bustling city will be deserted.
The forts and towers will become lairs forever,
A joy of wild donkeys, a pasture of flocks—
Until the Spirit is poured upon us from on high,
And the wilderness becomes a fruitful field,
And the fruitful field is counted as a forest.

Then justice will dwell in the wilderness,
And righteousness remain in the fruitful field.
The work of righteousness will be peace,
And the effect of righteousness, quietness and
assurance forever.
My people will dwell in a peaceful habitation,
In secure dwellings, and in quiet resting
places,
Though hail comes down on the forest,
And the city is brought low in humiliation.

Blessed are you who sow beside all waters,
Who send out freely the feet of the ox and the
donkey.

Your eyes will see the King in His beauty;
They will see the land that is very far off.
Your heart will meditate on terror:
"Where is the scribe?
Where is he who weighs?
Where is he who counts the towers?"
You will not see a fierce people,
A people of obscure speech, beyond
perception,
Of a stammering tongue that you cannot
understand.

Look upon Zion, the city of our appointed
feasts;
Your eyes will see Jerusalem, a quiet home,
A tabernacle that will not be taken down;
Not one of its stakes will ever be removed,
Nor will any of its cords be broken.
But there the majestic LORD will be for us
A place of broad rivers and streams,
In which no galley with oars will sail,
Nor majestic ships pass by
(For the LORD is our Judge,
The LORD is our Lawgiver,
The LORD is our King;
He will save us);
Your tackle is loosed,

They could not strengthen their mast,
They could not spread the sail.

Then the prey of great plunder is divided;
The lame take the prey.
And the inhabitant will not say, "I am sick";
The people who dwell in it *will be* forgiven *their*
     iniquity.

Isaiah 32; 33:17-24

WORSHIP

God be merciful to us and bless us,
And cause His face to shine upon us,   Selah
That Your way may be known on earth,
Your salvation among all nations.

Let the peoples praise You, O God;
Let all the peoples praise You.

God shall bless us,
And all the ends of the earth shall fear Him.

Psalm 67:1-3, 7

WISDOM

The simple believes every word,
But the prudent considers well his steps.

Proverbs 14:15

SW?! **SO WHAT?**
What does this tell me?

FUTURE JUDGMENTS AND BLESSINGS

Isaiah 34–35; Psalm
68:4–6; Proverbs 14:16

Come near, you nations, to hear;
And heed, you people!
Let the earth hear, and all that is in it,
The world and all things that come forth from
    it.
For the indignation of the LORD *is* against all
    nations,
And *His* fury against all their armies;
He has utterly destroyed them,
He has given them over to the slaughter.
Also their slain shall be thrown out;
Their stench shall rise from their corpses,
    And the mountains shall be melted with their
        blood.
All the host of heaven shall be dissolved,
And the heavens shall be rolled up like a
    scroll;
All their host shall fall down
As the leaf falls from the vine,
And as *fruit* falling from a fig tree.

"For My sword shall be bathed in heaven;
Indeed it shall come down on Edom,
And on the people of My curse, for
    judgment.
The sword of the LORD is filled with blood,
It is made overflowing with fatness,
With the blood of lambs and goats,
With the fat of the kidneys of rams.
For the LORD has a sacrifice in Bozrah,
And a great slaughter in the land of Edom.
The wild oxen shall come down with them,
And the young bulls with the mighty bulls;
Their land shall be soaked with blood,
And their dust saturated with fatness."

For *it is* the day of the LORD's vengeance,
The year of recompense for the cause of
    Zion.
Its streams shall be turned into pitch,
And its dust into brimstone;
Its land shall become burning pitch.
It shall not be quenched night or day;
Its smoke shall ascend forever.
From generation to generation it shall lie
    waste;
No one shall pass through it forever and
    ever.
But the pelican and the porcupine shall
    possess it,

Also the owl and the raven shall dwell in it.
And He shall stretch out over it
The line of confusion and the stones of
    emptiness.
They shall call its nobles to the kingdom,
But none *shall be* there, and all its princes
    shall be nothing.

And thorns shall come up in its palaces,
Nettles and brambles in its fortresses;
It shall be a habitation of jackals,
A courtyard for ostriches.
The wild beasts of the desert shall also meet
    with the jackals,
And the wild goat shall bleat to its companion;
Also the night creature shall rest there,
And find for herself a place of rest.
There the arrow snake shall make her nest
    and lay *eggs*
And hatch, and gather *them* under her
    shadow;
There also shall the hawks be gathered,
Every one with her mate.

"Search from the book of the LORD, and read:
Not one of these shall fail;
Not one shall lack her mate.
For My mouth has commanded it, and His
    Spirit has gathered them.
He has cast the lot for them,
And His hand has divided it among them with
    a measuring line.
They shall possess it forever;
From generation to generation they shall dwell
    in it."

The wilderness and the wasteland shall be
    glad for them,
And the desert shall rejoice and blossom as
    the rose;
It shall blossom abundantly and rejoice,
Even with joy and singing.
The glory of Lebanon shall be given to it,
The excellence of Carmel and Sharon.
They shall see the glory of the LORD,
The excellency of our God.

Strengthen the weak hands,
And make firm the feeble knees.
Say to those *who are* fearful-hearted,
"Be strong, do not fear!

Behold, your God will come *with* vengeance,
With the recompense of God;
He will come and save you."

Then the eyes of the blind shall be opened,
And the ears of the deaf shall be unstopped.
Then the lame shall leap like a deer,
And the tongue of the dumb sing.
For waters shall burst forth in the wilderness,
And streams in the desert.
The parched ground shall become a pool,
And the thirsty land springs of water;
In the habitation of jackals, where each lay,
There shall be grass with reeds and rushes.

A highway shall be there, and a road,
And it shall be called the Highway of Holiness.
The unclean shall not pass over it,
But it *shall be* for others.
Whoever walks the road, although a fool,
Shall not go astray.
No lion shall be there,
Nor shall *any* ravenous beast go up on it;
It shall not be found there.
But the redeemed shall walk *there,*
And the ransomed of the LORD shall return,
And come to Zion with singing,
With everlasting joy on their heads.
They shall obtain joy and gladness,
And sorrow and sighing shall flee away.

Isaiah 34–35

WoRsHiP

Sing to God, sing praises to His name;
Extol Him who rides on the clouds,
By His name YAH,
And rejoice before Him.

A father of the fatherless, a defender of
    widows,
Is God in His holy habitation.
God sets the solitary in families;
He brings out those who are bound into
    prosperity;
But the rebellious dwell in a dry *land.*

Psalm 68:4-6

WiSDoM

A wise *man* fears and departs from evil,
But a fool rages and is self-confident.

Proverbs 14:16

SW?! **SO WHAT?**
What does this tell me?

WORDS FROM THE PROPHETS

DELIVERANCE FROM SENNACHERIB

Isaiah 36:1–37:7, 30–35;
Psalm 68:7-9; Proverbs 14:17

Now it came to pass in the fourteenth year of King Hezekiah *that* Sennacherib king of Assyria came up against all the fortified cities of Judah and took them. Then the king of Assyria sent *the* Rabshakeh with a great army from Lachish to King Hezekiah at Jerusalem. And he stood by the aqueduct from the upper pool, on the highway to the Fuller's Field. And Eliakim the son of Hilkiah, who was over the household, Shebna the scribe, and Joah the son of Asaph, the recorder, came out to him.

Then *the* Rabshakeh said to them, "Say now to Hezekiah, 'Thus says the great king, the king of Assyria: "What confidence is this in which you trust? I say you speak of having plans and power for war; but *they are* mere words. Now in whom do you trust, that you rebel against me? Look! You are trusting in the staff of this broken reed, Egypt, on which if a man leans, it will go into his hand and pierce it. So *is* Pharaoh king of Egypt to all who trust in him.

"But if you say to me, 'We trust in the LORD our God,' *is it* not He whose high places and whose altars Hezekiah has taken away, and said to Judah and Jerusalem, 'You shall worship before this altar'?" ' Now therefore, I urge you, give a pledge to my master the king of Assyria, and I will give you two thousand horses—if you are able on your part to put riders on them! How then will you repel one captain of the least of my master's servants, and put your trust in Egypt for chariots and horsemen? Have I now come up without the LORD against this land to destroy it? The LORD said to me, 'Go up against this land, and destroy it.' "

Then Eliakim, Shebna, and Joah said to *the* Rabshakeh, "Please speak to your servants in Aramaic, for we understand *it;* and do not speak to us in Hebrew in the hearing of the people who *are* on the wall."

But *the* Rabshakeh said, "Has my master sent me to your master and to you to speak these words, and not to the men who sit on the wall, who will eat and drink their own waste with you?"

Then *the* Rabshakeh stood and called out with a loud voice in Hebrew, and said, "Hear the words of the great king, the king of Assyria! Thus says the king: 'Do not let Hezekiah deceive you, for he will not be able to deliver you; nor let Hezekiah make you trust in the LORD, saying, "The LORD will surely deliver us; this city will not be given into the hand of the king of Assyria." ' Do not listen to Hezekiah; for thus says the king of Assyria: 'Make *peace* with me *by a* present and come out to me; and every one of you eat from his own vine and every one from his own fig tree, and every one of you drink the waters of his own cistern; until I come and take you away to a land like your own land, a land of grain and new wine, a land of bread and vineyards. *Beware* lest Hezekiah persuade you, saying, "The LORD will deliver us." Has any one of the gods of the nations delivered its land from the hand of the king of Assyria? Where *are* the gods of Hamath and Arpad? Where *are* the gods of Sepharvaim? Indeed, have they delivered Samaria from my hand? Who among all the gods of these lands have delivered their countries from my hand, that the LORD should deliver Jerusalem from my hand?' "

But they held their peace and answered him not a word; for the king's commandment was, "Do not answer him." Then Eliakim the son of Hilkiah, who *was* over the household, Shebna the scribe, and Joah the son of Asaph, the recorder, came to Hezekiah with *their* clothes torn, and told him the words of *the* Rabshakeh.

And so it was, when King Hezekiah heard *it,* that he tore his clothes, covered himself with sackcloth, and went into the house of the LORD. Then he sent Eliakim, who *was* over the household, Shebna the scribe, and the elders of the priests, covered with sackcloth, to Isaiah the prophet, the son of Amoz. And they said to him, "Thus says Hezekiah: 'This day *is* a day of trouble and rebuke and blasphemy; for the children have come to birth, but *there is* no strength to bring them forth. It may be that the LORD your God will hear the words of *the* Rabshakeh, whom his master the king of Assyria has sent to reproach the living God, and will rebuke the words which the LORD your God has heard. Therefore lift up *your* prayer for the remnant that is left.' "

So the servants of King Hezekiah came to Isaiah. And Isaiah said to them, "Thus you shall say to your master, 'Thus says the LORD: "Do not be afraid of the words which you have heard, with which the servants of the king of Assyria have blasphemed Me. Surely I will send a spirit upon him, and he shall hear a rumor and return to his own land; and I will cause him to fall by the sword in his own land." ' "

"This *shall be* a sign to you:

You shall eat this year such as grows of itself,
And the second year what springs from the
    same;
Also in the third year sow and reap,
Plant vineyards and eat the fruit of them.
And the remnant who have escaped of the
    house of Judah
Shall again take root downward,
And bear fruit upward.
For out of Jerusalem shall go a remnant,
And those who escape from Mount Zion.
The zeal of the LORD of hosts will do this.

"Therefore thus says the LORD concerning the king of Assyria:

'He shall not come into this city,
Nor shoot an arrow there,
Nor come before it with shield,
Nor build a siege mound against it.
By the way that he came,
By the same shall he return;
And he shall not come into this city,'
Says the LORD.
'For I will defend this city, to save it
For My own sake and for My servant David's
    sake.' "

Isaiah 36:1–37:7, 30-35

WORSHIP

O God, when You went out before Your
    people,
When You marched through the wilderness,
                                        Selah
The earth shook;
The heavens also dropped *rain* at the
    presence of God;
Sinai itself *was moved* at the presence of God,
    the God of Israel.
You, O God, sent a plentiful rain,
Whereby You confirmed Your inheritance,
When it was weary.

Psalm 68:7-9

WISDOM

A quick-tempered *man* acts foolishly,
And a man of wicked intentions is hated.

Proverbs 14:17

SW?! **SO WHAT?**
What does this tell me?

HEZEKIAH'S FOOLISH HOSPITALITY

Isaiah 38–39; Psalm 68:19-20; Proverbs 14:18

In those days Hezekiah was sick and near death. And Isaiah the prophet, the son of Amoz, went to him and said to him, "Thus says the LORD: 'Set your house in order, for you shall die and not live.' "

Then Hezekiah turned his face toward the wall, and prayed to the LORD, and said, "Remember now, O LORD, I pray, how I have walked before You in truth and with a loyal heart, and have done *what is* good in Your sight." And Hezekiah wept bitterly.

And the word of the LORD came to Isaiah, saying, "Go and tell Hezekiah, 'Thus says the LORD, the God of David your father: "I have heard your prayer, I have seen your tears; surely I will add to your days fifteen years. I will deliver you and this city from the hand of the king of Assyria, and I will defend this city." ' And this *is* the sign to you from the LORD, that the LORD will do this thing which He has spoken: Behold, I will bring the shadow on the sundial, which has gone down with the sun on the sundial of Ahaz, ten degrees backward." So the sun returned ten degrees on the dial by which it had gone down.

This is the writing of Hezekiah king of Judah, when he had been sick and had recovered from his sickness:

I said,
"In the prime of my life
I shall go to the gates of Sheol;
I am deprived of the remainder of my years."
I said,
"I shall not see YAH,
The LORD in the land of the living;
I shall observe man no more among the
    inhabitants of the world.
My life span is gone,
Taken from me like a shepherd's tent;
I have cut off my life like a weaver.
He cuts me off from the loom;
From day until night You make an end of me.
I have considered until morning—
Like a lion,
So He breaks all my bones;
From day until night You make an end of me.
Like a crane *or* a swallow, so I chattered;
I mourned like a dove;
My eyes fail *from looking* upward.

O LORD, I am oppressed;
Undertake for me!

"What shall I say?
He has both spoken to me,
And He Himself has done *it*.
I shall walk carefully all my years
In the bitterness of my soul.
O Lord, by these *things men* live;
And in all these *things is* the life of my spirit;
So You will restore me and make me live.
Indeed *it was* for *my own* peace
That I had great bitterness;
But You have lovingly *delivered* my soul from
    the pit of corruption,
For You have cast all my sins behind Your
    back.
For Sheol cannot thank You,
Death cannot praise You;
Those who go down to the pit cannot hope for
    Your truth.
The living, the living man, he shall praise You,
As I *do* this day;
The father shall make known Your truth to the
    children.

"The LORD *was ready* to save me;
Therefore we will sing my songs with stringed
    instruments
All the days of our life, in the house of the
    LORD."

Now Isaiah had said, "Let them take a lump of figs, and apply *it* as a poultice on the boil, and he shall recover."

And Hezekiah had said, "What *is* the sign that I shall go up to the house of the LORD?"

At that time Merodach-Baladan the son of Baladan, king of Babylon, sent letters and a present to Hezekiah, for he heard that he had been sick and had recovered. And Hezekiah was pleased with them, and showed them the house of his treasures—the silver and gold, the spices and precious ointment, and all his armory—all that was found among his treasures. There was nothing in his house or in all his dominion that Hezekiah did not show them.

Then Isaiah the prophet went to King Hezekiah, and said to him, "What did these men say, and from where did they come to you?"

So Hezekiah said, "They came to me from a far country, from Babylon."

And he said, "What have they seen in your house?"

So Hezekiah answered, "They have seen all that *is* in my house; there is nothing among my treasures that I have not shown them."

Then Isaiah said to Hezekiah, "Hear the word of the LORD of hosts: 'Behold, the days are coming when all that *is* in your house, and what your fathers have accumulated until this day, shall be carried to Babylon; nothing shall be left,' says the LORD. 'And they shall take away *some* of your sons who will descend from you, whom you will beget; and they shall be eunuchs in the palace of the king of Babylon.' "

So Hezekiah said to Isaiah, "The word of the LORD which you have spoken *is* good!" For he said, "At least there will be peace and truth in my days."

Isaiah 38–39

WORSHIP

Blessed *be* the Lord,
Who daily loads us *with benefits,*
The God of our salvation!   Selah
Our God *is* the God of salvation;
And to GOD the Lord *belong* escapes from
    death.

Psalm 68:19-20

WISDOM

The simple inherit folly,
But the prudent are crowned with knowledge.

Proverbs 14:18

SW?! SO WHAT?
What does this tell me?

THE COMFORT OF KNOWING GOD

"Comfort, yes, comfort My people!"
Says your God.
"Speak comfort to Jerusalem, and cry
out to her,
That her warfare is ended,
That her iniquity is pardoned;
For she has received from the LORD's hand
Double for all her sins."

The voice of one crying in the wilderness:
"Prepare the way of the LORD;
Make straight in the desert
A highway for our God.
    Every valley shall be exalted
    And every mountain and hill brought low;
    The crooked places shall be made straight
    And the rough places smooth;
    The glory of the LORD shall be revealed,
    And all flesh shall see it together;
    For the mouth of the LORD has spoken."

The voice said, "Cry out!"
And he said, "What shall I cry?"

"All flesh is grass,
    And all its loveliness is like the flower of the
        field.
The grass withers, the flower fades,
Because the breath of the LORD blows upon it;
Surely the people are grass.
The grass withers, the flower fades,
But the word of our God stands forever."

O Zion,
You who bring good tidings,
Get up into the high mountain;
O Jerusalem,
You who bring good tidings,
Lift up your voice with strength,
Lift it up, be not afraid;
Say to the cities of Judah, "Behold your God!"

Behold, the Lord GOD shall come with a
        strong hand,
And His arm shall rule for Him;
Behold, His reward is with Him,
And His work before Him.
He will feed His flock like a shepherd;
He will gather the lambs with His arm,
And carry them in His bosom,
And gently lead those who are with young.

Who has measured the waters in the hollow of
        His hand,
Measured heaven with a span
And calculated the dust of the earth in a
        measure?
Weighed the mountains in scales
And the hills in a balance?
Who has directed the Spirit of the LORD,
Or as His counselor has taught Him?
With whom did He take counsel, and who
        instructed Him,
And taught Him in the path of justice?
Who taught Him knowledge,
And showed Him the way of understanding?

Behold, the nations are as a drop in a bucket,
And are counted as the small dust on the
        scales;
Look, He lifts up the isles as a very little thing.
And Lebanon is not sufficient to burn,
Nor its beasts sufficient for a burnt offering.
All nations before Him are as nothing,
And they are counted by Him less than nothing
        and worthless.

To whom then will you liken God?
Or what likeness will you compare to Him?
The workman molds an image,
The goldsmith overspreads it with gold,
And the silversmith casts silver chains.
Whoever is too impoverished for such a
        contribution
Chooses a tree that will not rot;
He seeks for himself a skillful workman
To prepare a carved image that will not totter.

Have you not known?
Have you not heard?
Has it not been told you from the beginning?
Have you not understood from the foundations
        of the earth?
It is He who sits above the circle of the earth,
And its inhabitants are like grasshoppers,
Who stretches out the heavens like a curtain,
And spreads them out like a tent to dwell in.
He brings the princes to nothing;
He makes the judges of the earth useless.

Scarcely shall they be planted,
Scarcely shall they be sown,
Scarcely shall their stock take root in the earth,

When He will also blow on them,
And they will wither,
And the whirlwind will take them away like
     stubble.

"To whom then will you liken Me,
Or *to whom* shall I be equal?" says the Holy
     One.
Lift up your eyes on high,
And see who has created these *things,*
Who brings out their host by number;
He calls them all by name,
By the greatness of His might
And the strength of *His* power;
Not one is missing.

Why do you say, O Jacob,
And speak, O Israel:
"My way is hidden from the LORD,
And my just claim is passed over by my God"?
Have you not known?
Have you not heard?
The everlasting God, the LORD,
The Creator of the ends of the earth,
Neither faints nor is weary.
His understanding is unsearchable.
He gives power to the weak,
And to *those who have* no might He increases
     strength.
Even the youths shall faint and be weary,
And the young men shall utterly fall,
But those who wait on the LORD
Shall renew *their* strength;
They shall mount up with wings like eagles,
They shall run and not be weary,
They shall walk and not faint.

Isaiah 40

WoRshiP

Sing to God, you kingdoms of the earth;
Oh, sing praises to the Lord,   Selah
To Him who rides on the heaven of heavens,
     which were of old!
Indeed, He sends out His voice, a mighty
     voice.

Psalm 68:32-33

WiSdoM

The evil will bow before the good,
And the wicked at the gates of the righteous.

Proverbs 14:19

SW?! **SO WHAT?**
What does this tell me?

THE COMING MESSIAH-SERVANT

Isaiah 42; Psalm 68:34-35;
Proverbs 14:20

"Behold! My Servant whom I uphold,
My Elect One *in whom* My soul delights!
I have put My Spirit upon Him;
He will bring forth justice to the Gentiles.
He will not cry out, nor raise *His voice,*
Nor cause His voice to be heard in the street.
A bruised reed He will not break,
And smoking flax He will not quench;
He will bring forth justice for truth.
He will not fail nor be discouraged,
Till He has established justice in the earth;
And the coastlands shall wait for His law."

Thus says God the LORD,
Who created the heavens and stretched
them out,
Who spread forth the earth and that which
comes from it,
Who gives breath to the people on it,
And spirit to those who walk on it:
"I, the LORD, have called You in
righteousness,
And will hold Your hand;
I will keep You and give You as a covenant
to the people,
As a light to the Gentiles,
To open blind eyes,
To bring out prisoners from the prison,
Those who sit in darkness from the prison
house.
I *am* the LORD, that *is* My name;
And My glory I will not give to another,
Nor My praise to carved images.
Behold, the former things have come to
pass,
And new things I declare;
Before they spring forth I tell you of them."

Sing to the LORD a new song,
And His praise from the ends of the earth,
You who go down to the sea, and all that is
in it,
You coastlands and you inhabitants of them!
Let the wilderness and its cities lift up *their
voice,*
The villages *that* Kedar inhabits.
Let the inhabitants of Sela sing,
Let them shout from the top of the
mountains.
Let them give glory to the LORD,

And declare His praise in the coastlands.
The LORD shall go forth like a mighty man;
He shall stir up *His* zeal like a man of war.
He shall cry out, yes, shout aloud;
He shall prevail against His enemies.

"I have held My peace a long time,
I have been still and restrained Myself.
Now I will cry like a woman in labor,
I will pant and gasp at once.
I will lay waste the mountains and hills,
And dry up all their vegetation;
I will make the rivers coastlands,
And I will dry up the pools.
I will bring the blind by a way they did not
know;
I will lead them in paths they have not known.
I will make darkness light before them,
And crooked places straight.
These things I will do for them,
And not forsake them.
They shall be turned back,
They shall be greatly ashamed,
Who trust in carved images,
Who say to the molded images,
'You *are* our gods.'

"Hear, you deaf;
And look, you blind, that you may see.
Who *is* blind but My servant,
Or deaf as My messenger *whom* I send?
Who *is* blind as *he who is* perfect,
And blind as the LORD's servant?
Seeing many things, but you do not observe;
Opening the ears, but he does not hear."

The LORD is well pleased for His righteousness'
sake;
He will exalt the law and make *it* honorable.
But this *is* a people robbed and plundered;
All of them are snared in holes,
And they are hidden in prison houses;
They are for prey, and no one delivers;
For plunder, and no one says, "Restore!"

Who among you will give ear to this?
Who will listen and hear for the time to come?
Who gave Jacob for plunder, and Israel to the
robbers?
Was it not the LORD,
He against whom we have sinned?

For they would not walk in His ways,
Nor were they obedient to His law.
Therefore He has poured on him the fury of
    His anger
And the strength of battle;
It has set him on fire all around,
Yet he did not know;
And it burned him,
Yet he did not take *it* to heart.

Isaiah 42

WORSHIP

Ascribe strength to God;
His excellence *is* over Israel,
And His strength *is* in the clouds.
O God, *You are* more awesome than Your holy
    places.
The God of Israel *is* He who gives strength and
    power to *His* people.

Blessed *be* God!

Psalm 68:34-35

WISDOM

The poor *man* is hated even by his own
    neighbor,
But the rich *has* many friends.

Proverbs 14:20

SW?! **SO WHAT?**
What does this tell me?

JUDAH'S DELIVERANCE THROUGH CYRUS

Isaiah 44:28–45:25; Psalm 69:1-3; Proverbs 14:21

"Who says of Cyrus, '*He is* My shepherd,
And he shall perform all My pleasure,
Saying to Jerusalem, "You shall be built,"
And to the temple, "Your foundation shall be
laid." '

"Thus says the LORD to His anointed,
To Cyrus, whose right hand I have held—
To subdue nations before him
And loose the armor of kings,
To open before him the double doors,
So that the gates will not be shut:
  'I will go before you
  And make the crooked places straight;
  I will break in pieces the gates of bronze
  And cut the bars of iron.
  I will give you the treasures of darkness
  And hidden riches of secret places,
  That you may know that I, the LORD,
  Who call *you* by your name,
  Am the God of Israel.
  For Jacob My servant's sake,
  And Israel My elect,
  I have even called you by your name;
  I have named you, though you have not
    known Me.
  I *am* the LORD, and *there is* no other;
  There is no God besides Me.
  I will gird you, though you have not known Me,
  That they may know from the rising of the
    sun to its setting
  That *there is* none besides Me.
  I *am* the LORD, and *there is* no other;
  I form the light and create darkness,
  I make peace and create calamity;
  I, the LORD, do all these *things*.'

"Rain down, you heavens, from above,
  And let the skies pour down righteousness;
  Let the earth open, let them bring forth
    salvation,
  And let righteousness spring up together.
  I, the LORD, have created it.

"Woe to him who strives with his Maker!
  Let the potsherd *strive* with the potsherds of
    the earth!
  Shall the clay say to him who forms it, 'What
    are you making?'

Or shall your handiwork *say,* 'He has no
  hands'?
Woe to him who says to *his* father, 'What are
  you begetting?'
Or to the woman, 'What have you brought
  forth?' "

Thus says the LORD,
The Holy One of Israel, and his Maker:
"Ask Me of things to come concerning My sons;
And concerning the work of My hands, you
  command Me.
I have made the earth,
And created man on it.
I—My hands— stretched out the heavens,
And all their host I have commanded.
I have raised him up in righteousness,
And I will direct all his ways;
He shall build My city
And let My exiles go free,
Not for price nor reward,"
Says the LORD of hosts.

Thus says the LORD:

"The labor of Egypt and merchandise of Cush
  And of the Sabeans, men of stature,
  Shall come over to you, and they shall be
    yours;
  They shall walk behind you,
  They shall come over in chains;
  And they shall bow down to you.
  They will make supplication to you, *saying,*
    'Surely God *is* in you,
  And *there is* no other;
  There is no other God.' "

Truly You *are* God, who hide Yourself,
O God of Israel, the Savior!
They shall be ashamed
And also disgraced, all of them;
They shall go in confusion together,
Who are makers of idols.
But Israel shall be saved by the LORD
With an everlasting salvation;
You shall not be ashamed or disgraced
Forever and ever.

For thus says the LORD,
Who created the heavens,

Who is God,
Who formed the earth and made it,
Who has established it,
Who did not create it in vain,
Who formed it to be inhabited:
"I *am* the LORD, and *there is* no other.
I have not spoken in secret,
In a dark place of the earth;
I did not say to the seed of Jacob,
'Seek Me in vain';
I, the LORD, speak righteousness,
I declare things that are right.

"Assemble yourselves and come;
Draw near together,
You *who have* escaped from the nations.
They have no knowledge,
Who carry the wood of their carved image,
And pray to a god *that* cannot save.
Tell and bring forth *your case;*
Yes, let them take counsel together.
Who has declared this from ancient time?
Who has told it from that time?
Have not I, the LORD?
And *there is* no other God besides Me,
A just God and a Savior;
There is none besides Me.

"Look to Me, and be saved,
All you ends of the earth!
For I *am* God, and *there is* no other.
I have sworn by Myself;
The word has gone out of My mouth *in*
    righteousness,
And shall not return,
That to Me every knee shall bow,
Every tongue shall take an oath.
He shall say,
'Surely in the LORD I have righteousness and
    strength.
To Him *men* shall come,
And all shall be ashamed
Who are incensed against Him.
In the LORD all the descendants of Israel
Shall be justified, and shall glory.' "
                                Isaiah 44:28–45:25

WORSHIP

Save me, O God!
For the waters have come up to *my* neck.
I sink in deep mire,
Where *there is* no standing;
I have come into deep waters,
Where the floods overflow me.
I am weary with my crying;
My throat is dry;
My eyes fail while I wait for my God.
                                Psalm 69:1-3

WISDOM

He who despises his neighbor sins;
But he who has mercy on the poor, happy *is*
  he.
                                Proverbs 14:21

SW?! SO WHAT?
What does this tell me?

BABYLON'S IMMINENT FALL

Isaiah 46–47; Psalm 69:13-15;
Proverbs 14:22

Bel bows down, Nebo stoops;
Their idols were on the beasts and on the
    cattle.
Your carriages *were* heavily loaded,
A burden to the weary *beast*.
They stoop, they bow down together;
They could not deliver the burden,
But have themselves gone into captivity.

"Listen to Me, O house of Jacob,
And all the remnant of the house of Israel,
Who have been upheld *by Me* from birth,
Who have been carried from the womb:
    Even to *your* old age, I *am* He,
    And *even* to gray hairs I will carry *you!*
    I have made, and I will bear;
    Even I will carry, and will deliver *you*.

"To whom will you liken Me, and make *Me*
    equal
And compare Me, that we should be alike?
They lavish gold out of the bag,
And weigh silver on the scales;
They hire a goldsmith, and he makes it a
    god;
They prostrate themselves, yes, they
    worship.
They bear it on the shoulder, they carry it
And set it in its place, and it stands;
From its place it shall not move.
Though *one* cries out to it, yet it cannot
    answer
Nor save him out of his trouble.

"Remember this, and show yourselves
    men;
Recall to mind, O you transgressors.
Remember the former things of old,
For I *am* God, and *there is* no other;
I am God, and *there is* none like Me,
Declaring the end from the beginning,
And from ancient times *things* that are not
    yet done,
Saying, 'My counsel shall stand,
And I will do all My pleasure,'
Calling a bird of prey from the east,
The man who executes My counsel, from a
    far country.
Indeed I have spoken *it*;
I will also bring it to pass.

I have purposed *it*;
I will also do it.

"Listen to Me, you stubborn-hearted,
Who *are* far from righteousness:
I bring My righteousness near, it shall not be
    far off;
My salvation shall not linger.
And I will place salvation in Zion,
For Israel My glory.

"Come down and sit in the dust,
O virgin daughter of Babylon;
Sit on the ground without a throne,
O daughter of the Chaldeans!
For you shall no more be called
Tender and delicate.
Take the millstones and grind meal.
Remove your veil,
Take off the skirt,
Uncover the thigh,
Pass through the rivers.
Your nakedness shall be uncovered,
Yes, your shame will be seen;
I will take vengeance,
And I will not arbitrate with a man."

As for our Redeemer, the LORD of hosts *is* His
    name,
The Holy One of Israel.

"Sit in silence, and go into darkness,
O daughter of the Chaldeans;
For you shall no longer be called
The Lady of Kingdoms.
I was angry with My people;
I have profaned My inheritance,
And given them into your hand.
You showed them no mercy;
On the elderly you laid your yoke very heavily.
And you said, 'I shall be a lady forever,'
So that you did not take these *things* to heart,
Nor remember the latter end of them.

"Therefore hear this now, *you who are* given to
    pleasures,
Who dwell securely,
Who say in your heart, 'I *am,* and *there is* no
    one else besides me;
I shall not sit *as* a widow,
Nor shall I know the loss of children';

But these two *things* shall come to you
In a moment, in one day:
The loss of children, and widowhood.
They shall come upon you in their fullness
Because of the multitude of your sorceries,
For the great abundance of your
enchantments.

"For you have trusted in your wickedness;
You have said, 'No one sees me';
Your wisdom and your knowledge have
warped you;
And you have said in your heart,
'I *am,* and *there is* no one else besides me.'
Therefore evil shall come upon you;
You shall not know from where it arises.
And trouble shall fall upon you;
You will not be able to put it off.
And desolation shall come upon you suddenly,
Which you shall not know.

"Stand now with your enchantments
And the multitude of your sorceries,
In which you have labored from your youth—
Perhaps you will be able to profit,
Perhaps you will prevail.
You are wearied in the multitude of your
counsels;
Let now the astrologers, the stargazers,
And the monthly prognosticators
Stand up and save you
From what shall come upon you.
Behold, they shall be as stubble,
The fire shall burn them;
They shall not deliver themselves
From the power of the flame;
It shall not *be* a coal to be warmed by,
Nor a fire to sit before!
Thus shall they be to you
With whom you have labored,
Your merchants from your youth;
They shall wander each one to his quarter.
No one shall save you."

Isaiah 46–47

WoRSHiP

But as for me, my prayer *is* to You,
O LORD, *in* the acceptable time;
O God, in the multitude of Your mercy,
Hear me in the truth of Your salvation.
Deliver me out of the mire,
And let me not sink;
Let me be delivered from those who hate me,
And out of the deep waters.
Let not the floodwater overflow me,
Nor let the deep swallow me up;
And let not the pit shut its mouth on me.

Psalm 69:13-15

WiSDoM

Do they not go astray who devise evil?
But mercy and truth *belong* to those who
devise good.

Proverbs 14:22

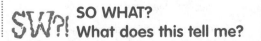 **SO WHAT?**
What does this tell me?

MESSIAH'S MISSION TO BRING SALVATION
Isaiah 49; Psalm 69:16-18; Proverbs 14:23

"Listen, O coastlands, to Me,
  And take heed, you peoples from afar!
  The LORD has called Me from the womb;
From the matrix of My mother He has made
    mention of My name.
And He has made My mouth like a sharp
    sword;
In the shadow of His hand He has hidden Me,
And made Me a polished shaft;
In His quiver He has hidden Me."

"And He said to me,
 'You *are* My servant, O Israel,
  In whom I will be glorified.'
  Then I said, 'I have labored in vain,
  I have spent my strength for nothing and in
    vain;
  Yet surely my just reward *is* with the LORD,
  And my work with my God.' "

"And now the LORD says,
  Who formed Me from the womb *to be* His
    Servant,
  To bring Jacob back to Him,
  So that Israel is gathered to Him
  (For I shall be glorious in the eyes of the LORD,
  And My God shall be My strength),
  Indeed He says,
  'It is too small a thing that You should be My
    Servant
  To raise up the tribes of Jacob,
  And to restore the preserved ones of Israel;
  I will also give You as a light to the Gentiles,
  That You should be My salvation to the ends
    of the earth.' "

Thus says the LORD,
  The Redeemer of Israel, their Holy One,
  To Him whom man despises,
  To Him whom the nation abhors,
  To the Servant of rulers:
"Kings shall see and arise,
  Princes also shall worship,
  Because of the LORD who is faithful,
  The Holy One of Israel;
  And He has chosen You."

Thus says the LORD:

"In an acceptable time I have heard You,
And in the day of salvation I have helped You;
I will preserve You and give You
As a covenant to the people,
To restore the earth,
To cause them to inherit the desolate
    heritages;
That You may say to the prisoners, 'Go forth,'
To those who *are* in darkness, 'Show
    yourselves.'

"They shall feed along the roads,
  And their pastures *shall be* on all desolate
    heights.
They shall neither hunger nor thirst,
Neither heat nor sun shall strike them;
For He who has mercy on them will lead them,
Even by the springs of water He will guide them.
I will make each of My mountains a road,
And My highways shall be elevated.
Surely these shall come from afar;
Look! Those from the north and the west,
And these from the land of Sinim."

Sing, O heavens!
Be joyful, O earth!
And break out in singing, O mountains!
For the LORD has comforted His people,
And will have mercy on His afflicted.

But Zion said, "The LORD has forsaken me,
And my Lord has forgotten me."

"Can a woman forget her nursing child,
  And not have compassion on the son of her
    womb?
Surely they may forget,
Yet I will not forget you.
See, I have inscribed you on the palms *of My
    hands;*
Your walls *are* continually before Me.
Your sons shall make haste;
Your destroyers and those who laid you waste
Shall go away from you.
Lift up your eyes, look around and see;
All these gather together *and* come to you.
As I live," says the LORD,
"You shall surely clothe yourselves with them
    all as an ornament,
And bind them *on you* as a bride *does.*

"For your waste and desolate places,
  And the land of your destruction,
  Will even now be too small for the inhabitants;
  And those who swallowed you up will be far
    away.
  The children you will have,
  After you have lost the others,
  Will say again in your ears,
  'The place *is* too small for me;
  Give me a place where I may dwell.'
  Then you will say in your heart,
  'Who has begotten these for me,
  Since I have lost my children and am desolate,
  A captive, and wandering to and fro?
  And who has brought these up?
  There I was, left alone;
  But these, where *were* they?' "

Thus says the Lord GOD:

"Behold, I will lift My hand in an oath to the
    nations,
  And set up My standard for the peoples;
  They shall bring your sons in *their* arms,
  And your daughters shall be carried on *their*
    shoulders;
  Kings shall be your foster fathers,
  And their queens your nursing mothers;
  They shall bow down to you with *their* faces to
    the earth,
  And lick up the dust of your feet.
  Then you will know that I *am* the LORD,
  For they shall not be ashamed who wait for
    Me."

Shall the prey be taken from the mighty,
Or the captives of the righteous be delivered?

But thus says the LORD:

"Even the captives of the mighty shall be taken
    away,
  And the prey of the terrible be delivered;
  For I will contend with him who contends with
    you,
  And I will save your children.
  I will feed those who oppress you with their
    own flesh,
  And they shall be drunk with their own blood
    as with sweet wine.
  All flesh shall know
  That I, the LORD, *am* your Savior,
  And your Redeemer, the Mighty One of Jacob."

Isaiah 49

WORSHIP

Hear me, O LORD, for Your lovingkindness *is*
    good;
Turn to me according to the multitude of Your
    tender mercies.
And do not hide Your face from Your servant,
For I am in trouble;
Hear me speedily.
Draw near to my soul, *and* redeem it;
Deliver me because of my enemies.

Psalm 69:16-18

WISDOM

In all labor there is profit,
But idle chatter *leads* only to poverty.

Proverbs 14:23

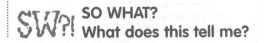 **SO WHAT?**
What does this tell me?

MESSIAH'S EARTHLY EDUCATION

Isaiah 50:4–51:8, 12-16; Psalm 69:30-33; Proverbs 14:25

"The Lord GOD has given Me
The tongue of the learned,
That I should know how to speak
A word in season to *him who is* weary.
He awakens Me morning by morning,
He awakens My ear
To hear as the learned.
The Lord GOD has opened My ear;
And I was not rebellious,
Nor did I turn away.
I gave My back to those who struck *Me*,
And My cheeks to those who plucked out the
    beard;
  I did not hide My face from shame and
    spitting.

"For the Lord GOD will help Me;
Therefore I will not be disgraced;
Therefore I have set My face like a flint,
And I know that I will not be ashamed.
He is near who justifies Me;
Who will contend with Me?
Let us stand together.
Who *is* My adversary?
Let him come near Me.
Surely the Lord GOD will help Me;
Who *is* he *who* will condemn Me?
Indeed they will all grow old like a garment;
The moth will eat them up.

"Who among you fears the LORD?
Who obeys the voice of His Servant?
Who walks in darkness
And has no light?
Let him trust in the name of the LORD
And rely upon his God.
Look, all you who kindle a fire,
Who encircle *yourselves* with sparks:
Walk in the light of your fire and in the
    sparks you have kindled—
This you shall have from My hand:
You shall lie down in torment.

"Listen to Me, you who follow after
    righteousness,
You who seek the LORD:
Look to the rock *from which* you were hewn,
And to the hole of the pit *from which* you
    were dug.
Look to Abraham your father,
And to Sarah *who* bore you;

For I called him alone,
And blessed him and increased him."

For the LORD will comfort Zion,
He will comfort all her waste places;
He will make her wilderness like Eden,
And her desert like the garden of the LORD;
Joy and gladness will be found in it,
Thanksgiving and the voice of melody.

"Listen to Me, My people;
And give ear to Me, O My nation:
For law will proceed from Me,
And I will make My justice rest
As a light of the peoples.
My righteousness *is* near,
My salvation has gone forth,
And My arms will judge the peoples;
The coastlands will wait upon Me,
And on My arm they will trust.
Lift up your eyes to the heavens,
And look on the earth beneath.
For the heavens will vanish away like smoke,
The earth will grow old like a garment,
And those who dwell in it will die in like
    manner;
But My salvation will be forever,
And My righteousness will not be abolished.

"Listen to Me, you who know righteousness,
You people in whose heart *is* My law:
Do not fear the reproach of men,
Nor be afraid of their insults.
For the moth will eat them up like a garment,
And the worm will eat them like wool;
But My righteousness will be forever,
And My salvation from generation to
    generation."

"I, *even* I, *am* He who comforts you.
Who *are* you that you should be afraid
Of a man *who* will die,
And of the son of a man *who* will be made like
    grass?
And you forget the LORD your Maker,
Who stretched out the heavens
And laid the foundations of the earth;
You have feared continually every day
Because of the fury of the oppressor,
When *he has* prepared to destroy.
And where *is* the fury of the oppressor?

The captive exile hastens, that he may be
    loosed,
That he should not die in the pit,
And that his bread should not fail.
But I *am* the LORD your God,
Who divided the sea whose waves roared—
The LORD of hosts *is* His name.
And I have put My words in your mouth;
I have covered you with the shadow of My
    hand,
That I may plant the heavens,
Lay the foundations of the earth,
And say to Zion, 'You *are* My people.' "
Isaiah 50:4–51:8, 12-16

WORSHIP

I will praise the name of God with a song,
And will magnify Him with thanksgiving.
This also shall please the LORD better than an
    ox *or* bull,
Which has horns and hooves.
The humble shall see *this and* be glad;
And you who seek God, your hearts shall live.
For the LORD hears the poor,
And does not despise His prisoners.
Psalm 69:30-33

WISDOM

A true witness delivers souls,
But a deceitful *witness* speaks lies.
Proverbs 14:25

SW?! **SO WHAT?**
What does this tell me?

MESSIAH'S REJECTION AND DEATH

Isaiah 52:13–53:12; Psalm 69:34-36; Proverbs 14:26

Behold, My Servant shall deal prudently;
He shall be exalted and extolled and be very
high.
Just as many were astonished at you,
So His visage was marred more than any
man,
And His form more than the sons of men;
So shall He sprinkle many nations.
Kings shall shut their mouths at Him;
For what had not been told them they shall
see,
And what they had not heard they shall
consider.

Who has believed our report?
And to whom has the arm of the LORD been
revealed?
For He shall grow up before Him as a tender
plant,
And as a root out of dry ground.
He has no form or comeliness;
And when we see Him,
There is no beauty that we should desire
Him.
He is despised and rejected by men,
A Man of sorrows and acquainted with grief.
And we hid, as it were, *our* faces from Him;
He was despised, and we did not esteem
Him.

Surely He has borne our griefs
And carried our sorrows;
Yet we esteemed Him stricken,
Smitten by God, and afflicted.
But He *was* wounded for our transgressions,
He was bruised for our iniquities;
The chastisement for our peace *was* upon
Him,
And by His stripes we are healed.
All we like sheep have gone astray;
We have turned, every one, to his own way;
And the LORD has laid on Him the iniquity of
us all.

He was oppressed and He was afflicted,
Yet He opened not His mouth;
He was led as a lamb to the slaughter,
And as a sheep before its shearers is silent,
So He opened not His mouth.
He was taken from prison and from
judgment,

And who will declare His generation?
For He was cut off from the land of the living;
For the transgressions of My people He was
stricken.
And they made His grave with the wicked—
But with the rich at His death,
Because He had done no violence,
Nor *was any* deceit in His mouth.

Yet it pleased the LORD to bruise Him;
He has put *Him* to grief.
When You make His soul an offering for sin,
He shall see *His* seed, He shall prolong *His*
days,
And the pleasure of the LORD shall prosper in
His hand.
He shall see the labor of His soul, *and* be
satisfied.
By His knowledge My righteous Servant shall
justify many,
For He shall bear their iniquities.
Therefore I will divide Him a portion with the
great,
And He shall divide the spoil with the strong,
Because He poured out His soul unto death,
And He was numbered with the transgressors,
And He bore the sin of many,
And made intercession for the transgressors.

Isaiah 52:13–53:12

WORSHIP

Let heaven and earth praise Him,
The seas and everything that moves in them.
For God will save Zion
And build the cities of Judah,
That they may dwell there and possess it.
Also, the descendants of His servants shall
    inherit it,
And those who love His name shall dwell in it.

Psalm 69:34-36

WISDOM

In the fear of the LORD *there is* strong
    confidence,
And His children will have a place of refuge.

Proverbs 14:26

SW?! **SO WHAT?**
What does this tell me?

GOD'S INVITATION TO SALVATION

Isaiah 55:1–56:8; 57:14–21;
Psalm 70:4-5; Proverbs 14:27

"Ho! Everyone who thirsts,
Come to the waters;
And you who have no money,
Come, buy and eat.
Yes, come, buy wine and milk
Without money and without price.
Why do you spend money for *what is* not
bread,
And your wages for *what* does not satisfy?
Listen carefully to Me, and eat *what is* good,
And let your soul delight itself in abundance.
Incline your ear, and come to Me.
Hear, and your soul shall live;
And I will make an everlasting covenant with
you—
The sure mercies of David.
Indeed I have given him *as* a witness to the
people,
A leader and commander for the people.
Surely you shall call a nation you do not
know,
And nations *who* do not know you shall run
to you,
Because of the LORD your God,
And the Holy One of Israel;
For He has glorified you."

Seek the LORD while He may be found,
Call upon Him while He is near.
Let the wicked forsake his way,
And the unrighteous man his thoughts;
Let him return to the LORD,
And He will have mercy on him;
And to our God,
For He will abundantly pardon.

"For My thoughts *are* not your thoughts,
Nor *are* your ways My ways," says the
LORD.
"For *as* the heavens are higher than the
earth,
So are My ways higher than your ways,
And My thoughts than your thoughts.

"For as the rain comes down, and the snow
from heaven,
And do not return there,
But water the earth,
And make it bring forth and bud,
That it may give seed to the sower
And bread to the eater,

So shall My word be that goes forth from My
mouth;
It shall not return to Me void,
But it shall accomplish what I please,
And it shall prosper *in the thing* for which I
sent it.

"For you shall go out with joy,
And be led out with peace;
The mountains and the hills
Shall break forth into singing before you,
And all the trees of the field shall clap *their*
hands.
Instead of the thorn shall come up the cypress
tree,
And instead of the brier shall come up the
myrtle tree;
And it shall be to the LORD for a name,
For an everlasting sign *that* shall not be cut
off."

Thus says the LORD:

"Keep justice, and do righteousness,
For My salvation *is* about to come,
And My righteousness to be revealed.
Blessed *is* the man *who* does this,
And the son of man *who* lays hold on it;
Who keeps from defiling the Sabbath,
And keeps his hand from doing any evil."

Do not let the son of the foreigner
Who has joined himself to the LORD
Speak, saying,
"The LORD has utterly separated me from His
people";
Nor let the eunuch say,
"Here I am, a dry tree."
For thus says the LORD:
"To the eunuchs who keep My Sabbaths,
And choose what pleases Me,
And hold fast My covenant,
Even to them I will give in My house
And within My walls a place and a name
Better than that of sons and daughters;
I will give them an everlasting name
That shall not be cut off.

"Also the sons of the foreigner
Who join themselves to the LORD, to serve Him,
And to love the name of the LORD, to be His
servants—

Everyone who keeps from defiling the Sabbath,
And holds fast My covenant—
Even them I will bring to My holy mountain,
And make them joyful in My house of prayer.
Their burnt offerings and their sacrifices
Will be accepted on My altar;
For My house shall be called a house of prayer
    for all nations."
The Lord GOD, who gathers the outcasts of
    Israel, says,
"Yet I will gather to him
Others besides those who are gathered to
    him."

And one shall say,
"Heap it up! Heap it up!
Prepare the way,
Take the stumbling block out of the way of My
    people."

For thus says the High and Lofty One
Who inhabits eternity, whose name *is* Holy:
"I dwell in the high and holy *place,*
With him *who* has a contrite and humble spirit,
To revive the spirit of the humble,
And to revive the heart of the contrite ones.
For I will not contend forever,
Nor will I always be angry;
For the spirit would fail before Me,
And the souls *which* I have made.
For the iniquity of his covetousness
I was angry and struck him;
I hid and was angry,
And he went on backsliding in the way of his
    heart.
I have seen his ways, and will heal him;
I will also lead him,
And restore comforts to him
And to his mourners.

"I create the fruit of the lips:
Peace, peace to *him who is* far off and to *him
    who is* near,"
Says the LORD,
"And I will heal him."
But the wicked *are* like the troubled sea,
When it cannot rest,
Whose waters cast up mire and dirt.

"*There is* no peace,"
Says my God, "for the wicked."
                        Isaiah 55:1–56:8; 57:14-21

WORSHIP

Let all those who seek You rejoice and be
    glad in You;
And let those who love Your salvation say
    continually,
"Let God be magnified!"

But I *am* poor and needy;
Make haste to me, O God!
You *are* my help and my deliverer;
O LORD, do not delay.
                        Psalm 70:4-5

WISDOM

The fear of the LORD *is* a fountain of life,
To turn *one* away from the snares of death.
                        Proverbs 14:27

SW?! SO WHAT?
What does this tell me?

FALSE AND TRUE PIETY

Isaiah 58:1–59:8, 15-20; Psalm 71:4-6;
Proverbs 14:29

"Cry aloud, spare not;
Lift up your voice like a trumpet;
Tell My people their transgression,
And the house of Jacob their sins.
Yet they seek Me daily,
And delight to know My ways,
As a nation that did righteousness,
And did not forsake the ordinance of their God.
They ask of Me the ordinances of justice;
They take delight in approaching God.
'Why have we fasted,' they say, 'and You have not seen?
Why have we afflicted our souls, and You take no notice?'

"In fact, in the day of your fast you find pleasure,
And exploit all your laborers.
Indeed you fast for strife and debate,
And to strike with the fist of wickedness.
You will not fast as you do this day,
To make your voice heard on high.
Is it a fast that I have chosen,
A day for a man to afflict his soul?
Is it to bow down his head like a bulrush,
And to spread out sackcloth and ashes?
Would you call this a fast,
And an acceptable day to the LORD?

"Is this not the fast that I have chosen:
To loose the bonds of wickedness,
To undo the heavy burdens,
To let the oppressed go free,
And that you break every yoke?
Is it not to share your bread with the hungry,
And that you bring to your house the poor who are cast out;
When you see the naked, that you cover him,
And not hide yourself from your own flesh?
Then your light shall break forth like the morning,
Your healing shall spring forth speedily,
And your righteousness shall go before you;
The glory of the LORD shall be your rear guard.
Then you shall call, and the LORD will answer;
You shall cry, and He will say, 'Here I am.'

"If you take away the yoke from your midst,
The pointing of the finger, and speaking wickedness,

If you extend your soul to the hungry
And satisfy the afflicted soul,
Then your light shall dawn in the darkness,
And your darkness shall be as the noonday.
The LORD will guide you continually,
And satisfy your soul in drought,
And strengthen your bones;
You shall be like a watered garden,
And like a spring of water, whose waters do not fail.
Those from among you
Shall build the old waste places;
You shall raise up the foundations of many generations;
And you shall be called the Repairer of the Breach,
The Restorer of Streets to Dwell In.

"If you turn away your foot from the Sabbath,
From doing your pleasure on My holy day,
And call the Sabbath a delight,
The holy day of the LORD honorable,
And shall honor Him, not doing your own ways,
Nor finding your own pleasure,
Nor speaking your own words,
Then you shall delight yourself in the LORD;
And I will cause you to ride on the high hills of the earth,
And feed you with the heritage of Jacob your father.
The mouth of the LORD has spoken."

Behold, the LORD's hand is not shortened,
That it cannot save;
Nor His ear heavy,
That it cannot hear.
But your iniquities have separated you from your God;
And your sins have hidden His face from you,
So that He will not hear.
For your hands are defiled with blood,
And your fingers with iniquity;
Your lips have spoken lies,
Your tongue has muttered perversity.

No one calls for justice,
Nor does any plead for truth.
They trust in empty words and speak lies;
They conceive evil and bring forth iniquity.

They hatch vipers' eggs and weave the
spider's web;
He who eats of their eggs dies,
And *from* that which is crushed a viper breaks
out.

Their webs will not become garments,
Nor will they cover themselves with their
works;
Their works *are* works of iniquity,
And the act of violence *is* in their hands.
Their feet run to evil,
And they make haste to shed innocent blood;
Their thoughts *are* thoughts of iniquity;
Wasting and destruction *are* in their paths.
The way of peace they have not known,
And *there is* no justice in their ways;
They have made themselves crooked paths;
Whoever takes that way shall not know peace.

So truth fails,
And he *who* departs from evil makes himself a
prey.

Then the LORD saw *it,* and it displeased Him
That *there was* no justice.
He saw that *there was* no man,
And wondered that *there was* no intercessor;
Therefore His own arm brought salvation for
Him;
And His own righteousness, it sustained Him.
For He put on righteousness as a breastplate,
And a helmet of salvation on His head;
He put on the garments of vengeance for
clothing,
And was clad with zeal as a cloak.
According to *their* deeds, accordingly He will
repay,
Fury to His adversaries,
Recompense to His enemies;
The coastlands He will fully repay.
So shall they fear
The name of the LORD from the west,
And His glory from the rising of the sun;
When the enemy comes in like a flood,
The Spirit of the LORD will lift up a standard
against him.

"The Redeemer will come to Zion,
And to those who turn from transgression in
Jacob,"
Says the LORD.

Isaiah 58:1–59:8, 15-20

WORSHIP

Deliver me, O my God, out of the hand of the
wicked,
Out of the hand of the unrighteous and cruel
man.
For You are my hope, O Lord GOD;
You are my trust from my youth.
By You I have been upheld from birth;
You are He who took me out of my mother's
womb.
My praise *shall be* continually of You.

Psalm 71:4-6

WISDOM

He who is slow to wrath has great
understanding,
But *he who is* impulsive exalts folly.

Proverbs 14:29

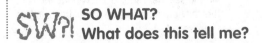

SO WHAT?
What does this tell me?

JERUSALEM'S FUTURE BLESSING

Isaiah 61–62; Psalm 71:9-11;
Proverbs 14:30

"The Spirit of the Lord GOD *is* upon Me,
Because the LORD has anointed Me
To preach good tidings to the poor;
He has sent Me to heal the brokenhearted,
To proclaim liberty to the captives,
And the opening of the prison to *those who are*
  bound;
To proclaim the acceptable year of the LORD,
And the day of vengeance of our God;
To comfort all who mourn,
To console those who mourn in Zion,
To give them beauty for ashes,
  The oil of joy for mourning,
  The garment of praise for the spirit of
    heaviness;
  That they may be called trees of
    righteousness,
  The planting of the LORD, that He may be
    glorified."

And they shall rebuild the old ruins,
They shall raise up the former desolations,
And they shall repair the ruined cities,
The desolations of many generations.
Strangers shall stand and feed your flocks,
And the sons of the foreigner
Shall be your plowmen and your vinedressers.
But you shall be named the priests of the LORD,
They shall call you the servants of our God.
You shall eat the riches of the Gentiles,
And in their glory you shall boast.
Instead of your shame *you shall have* double
  honor,
And *instead of* confusion they shall rejoice in
  their portion.
Therefore in their land they shall possess
  double;
Everlasting joy shall be theirs.

"For I, the LORD, love justice;
I hate robbery for burnt offering;
I will direct their work in truth,
And will make with them an everlasting
  covenant.
Their descendants shall be known among the
  Gentiles,
And their offspring among the people.
All who see them shall acknowledge them,
That they *are* the posterity *whom* the LORD has
  blessed."

I will greatly rejoice in the LORD,
My soul shall be joyful in my God;
For He has clothed me with the garments of
  salvation,
He has covered me with the robe of
  righteousness,
As a bridegroom decks *himself* with ornaments,
And as a bride adorns *herself* with her jewels.
For as the earth brings forth its bud,
As the garden causes the things that are sown
  in it to spring forth,
So the Lord GOD will cause righteousness and
  praise to spring forth before all the nations.

For Zion's sake I will not hold My peace,
And for Jerusalem's sake I will not rest,
Until her righteousness goes forth as brightness,
And her salvation as a lamp *that* burns.
The Gentiles shall see your righteousness,
And all kings your glory.
You shall be called by a new name,
Which the mouth of the LORD will name.
You shall also be a crown of glory
In the hand of the LORD,
And a royal diadem
In the hand of your God.
You shall no longer be termed Forsaken,
Nor shall your land any more be termed
  Desolate;
But you shall be called Hephzibah, and your
  land Beulah;
For the LORD delights in you,
And your land shall be married.
For *as* a young man marries a virgin,
So shall your sons marry you;
And *as* the bridegroom rejoices over the bride,
So shall your God rejoice over you.

I have set watchmen on your walls, O
  Jerusalem;
They shall never hold their peace day or night.
You who make mention of the LORD, do not keep
  silent,
And give Him no rest till He establishes
And till He makes Jerusalem a praise in the
  earth.

The LORD has sworn by His right hand
And by the arm of His strength:
"Surely I will no longer give your grain
As food for your enemies;

And the sons of the foreigner shall not drink your
    new wine,
For which you have labored.
But those who have gathered it shall eat it,
And praise the Lord;
Those who have brought it together shall drink it
    in My holy courts."

Go through,
Go through the gates!
Prepare the way for the people;
Build up,
Build up the highway!
Take out the stones,
Lift up a banner for the peoples!

Indeed the Lord has proclaimed
To the end of the world:
"Say to the daughter of Zion,
'Surely your salvation is coming;
Behold, His reward *is* with Him,
And His work before Him.' "
And they shall call them The Holy People,
The Redeemed of the Lord;
And you shall be called Sought Out,
A City Not Forsaken.

Isaiah 61–62

WoRSHiP

Do not cast me off in the time of old age;
Do not forsake me when my strength fails.
For my enemies speak against me;
And those who lie in wait for my life take
    counsel together,
Saying, "God has forsaken him;
Pursue and take him, for *there is* none to deliver
    him."

Psalm 71:9-11

WiSDoM

A sound heart *is* life to the body,
But envy *is* rottenness to the bones.

Proverbs 14:30

SW?! SO WHAT?
What does this tell me?

THE NEW HEAVENS AND NEW EARTH

"For behold, I create new heavens and a
  new earth;
  And the former shall not be remembered
  or come to mind.
But be glad and rejoice forever in what I
  create;
For behold, I create Jerusalem as a rejoicing,
And her people a joy.
I will rejoice in Jerusalem,
And joy in My people;
The voice of weeping shall no longer be heard
  in her,
  Nor the voice of crying.

  "No more shall an infant from there live but a
  few days,
  Nor an old man who has not fulfilled his
  days;
  For the child shall die one hundred years
  old,
  But the sinner being one hundred years old
  shall be accursed.
They shall build houses and inhabit them;
They shall plant vineyards and eat their fruit.
They shall not build and another inhabit;
They shall not plant and another eat;
For as the days of a tree, so shall be the
  days of My people,
And My elect shall long enjoy the work of
  their hands.
They shall not labor in vain,
Nor bring forth children for trouble;
For they shall be the descendants of the
  blessed of the LORD,
And their offspring with them.

"It shall come to pass
That before they call, I will answer;
And while they are still speaking, I will hear.
The wolf and the lamb shall feed together,
The lion shall eat straw like the ox,
And dust shall be the serpent's food.
They shall not hurt nor destroy in all My holy
  mountain,"
Says the LORD.

Thus says the LORD:

"Heaven is My throne,
And earth is My footstool.
Where is the house that you will build Me?

And where is the place of My rest?
For all those things My hand has made,
And all those things exist,"
Says the LORD.
"But on this one will I look:
On him who is poor and of a contrite spirit,
And who trembles at My word.

"He who kills a bull is as if he slays a man;
He who sacrifices a lamb, as if he breaks a
  dog's neck;
He who offers a grain offering, as if he offers
  swine's blood;
He who burns incense, as if he blesses an
  idol.
Just as they have chosen their own ways,
And their soul delights in their abominations,
So will I choose their delusions,
And bring their fears on them;
Because, when I called, no one answered,
When I spoke they did not hear;
But they did evil before My eyes,
And chose that in which I do not delight."

Hear the word of the LORD,
You who tremble at His word:
"Your brethren who hated you,
Who cast you out for My name's sake, said,
'Let the LORD be glorified,
That we may see your joy.'
But they shall be ashamed."

The sound of noise from the city!
A voice from the temple!
The voice of the LORD,
Who fully repays His enemies!

"Before she was in labor, she gave birth;
Before her pain came,
She delivered a male child.
Who has heard such a thing?
Who has seen such things?
Shall the earth be made to give birth in one
  day?
Or shall a nation be born at once?
For as soon as Zion was in labor,
She gave birth to her children.
Shall I bring to the time of birth, and not cause
  delivery?" says the LORD.
"Shall I who cause delivery shut up the womb?"
  says your God.

"Rejoice with Jerusalem,
 And be glad with her, all you who love her;
 Rejoice for joy with her, all you who mourn for
   her;
 That you may feed and be satisfied
 With the consolation of her bosom,
 That you may drink deeply and be delighted
 With the abundance of her glory."

For thus says the LORD:

"Behold, I will extend peace to her like a river,
 And the glory of the Gentiles like a flowing
   stream.
 Then you shall feed;
 On *her* sides shall you be carried,
 And be dandled on *her* knees.
 As one whom his mother comforts,
 So I will comfort you;
 And you shall be comforted in Jerusalem."

When you see *this,* your heart shall rejoice,
 And your bones shall flourish like grass;
 The hand of the LORD shall be known to His
   servants,
 And *His* indignation to His enemies.
 For behold, the LORD will come with fire
 And with His chariots, like a whirlwind,
 To render His anger with fury,
 And His rebuke with flames of fire.
 For by fire and by His sword
 The LORD will judge all flesh;
 And the slain of the LORD shall be many.

"Those who sanctify themselves and purify
   themselves,
 To go to the gardens
 After an *idol* in the midst,
 Eating swine's flesh and the abomination and
   the mouse,
 Shall be consumed together," says the LORD.

"For I *know* their works and their thoughts. It shall be that I will gather all nations and tongues; and they shall come and see My glory. I will set a sign among them; and those among them who escape I will send to the nations: *to* Tarshish and Pul and Lud, who draw the bow, and Tubal and Javan, *to* the coastlands afar off who have not heard My fame nor seen My glory. And they shall declare My glory among the Gentiles. Then they shall bring all your brethren for an offering to the LORD out of all nations, on horses and in chariots and in litters, on mules and on camels, to My holy mountain Jerusalem," says the LORD, "as the children of Israel bring an offering in a clean vessel into the house of the LORD. And I will also take some of them for priests *and* Levites," says the LORD.

"For as the new heavens and the new earth
 Which I will make shall remain before Me,"
   says the LORD,
"So shall your descendants and your name
   remain.
 And it shall come to pass
 That from one New Moon to another,
 And from one Sabbath to another,
 All flesh shall come to worship before Me,"
   says the LORD.

"And they shall go forth and look
 Upon the corpses of the men
 Who have transgressed against Me.
 For their worm does not die,
 And their fire is not quenched.
 They shall be an abhorrence to all flesh."
                              Isaiah 65:17–66:24

WORSHIP

But I will hope continually,
And will praise You yet more and more.
My mouth shall tell of Your righteousness
And Your salvation all the day,
For I do not know *their* limits.
I will go in the strength of the Lord GOD;
I will make mention of Your righteousness, of
   Yours only.
                              Psalm 71:14-16

WISDOM

He who oppresses the poor reproaches his
   Maker,
But he who honors Him has mercy on the
   needy.
                              Proverbs 14:31

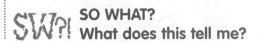

SO WHAT?
What does this tell me?

COMING JUDGMENT ON ISRAEL AND JUDAH

Micah 1:1–9; 2–3; Psalm 71:20, 22–23; Proverbs 14:34

The word of the LORD that came to Micah of Moresheth in the days of Jotham, Ahaz, *and* Hezekiah, kings of Judah, which he saw concerning Samaria and Jerusalem.

> Hear, all you peoples!
> Listen, O earth, and all that is in it!
> Let the Lord GOD be a witness against you,
> The Lord from His holy temple.
>
> For behold, the LORD is coming out of His place;
> He will come down
>   And tread on the high places of the earth.
>   The mountains will melt under Him,
>   And the valleys will split
>   Like wax before the fire,
>   Like waters poured down a steep place.
> All this is for the transgression of Jacob
> And for the sins of the house of Israel.
> What *is* the transgression of Jacob?
> *Is it* not Samaria?
> And what *are* the high places of Judah?
> *Are they* not Jerusalem?
>
> "Therefore I will make Samaria a heap of
>   ruins in the field,
>   Places for planting a vineyard;
> I will pour down her stones into the valley,
> And I will uncover her foundations.
> All her carved images shall be beaten to
>   pieces,
> And all her pay as a harlot shall be burned
>   with the fire;
> All her idols I will lay desolate,
> For she gathered *it* from the pay of a harlot,
> And they shall return to the pay of a harlot."
>
> Therefore I will wail and howl,
> I will go stripped and naked;
> I will make a wailing like the jackals
> And a mourning like the ostriches,
> For her wounds *are* incurable.
> For it has come to Judah;
> It has come to the gate of My people—
> To Jerusalem.
>
> Woe to those who devise iniquity,
> And work out evil on their beds!
> At morning light they practice it,
> Because it is in the power of their hand.

> They covet fields and take *them* by violence,
> Also houses, and seize *them*.
> So they oppress a man and his house,
> A man and his inheritance.
>
> Therefore thus says the LORD:
>
> "Behold, against this family I am devising
>   disaster,
> From which you cannot remove your necks;
> Nor shall you walk haughtily,
> For this *is* an evil time.
> In that day *one* shall take up a proverb against
>   you,
> And lament with a bitter lamentation, saying:
> 'We are utterly destroyed!
> He has changed the heritage of my people;
> How He has removed *it* from me!
> To a turncoat He has divided our fields.' "
>
> Therefore you will have no one to determine
>   boundaries by lot
> In the assembly of the LORD.
>
> "Do not prattle," *you say to those* who
>   prophesy.
>   So they shall not prophesy to you;
>   They shall not return insult for insult.
>   *You who are* named the house of Jacob:
> "Is the Spirit of the LORD restricted?
>   *Are* these His doings?
>   Do not My words do good
> To him who walks uprightly?
>
> "Lately My people have risen up as an enemy—
>   You pull off the robe with the garment
> From those who trust *you*, as they pass by,
>   Like men returned from war.
> The women of My people you cast out
> From their pleasant houses;
> From their children
> You have taken away My glory forever.
>
> "Arise and depart,
>   For this *is* not *your* rest;
> Because it is defiled, it shall destroy,
>   Yes, with utter destruction.
> If a man should walk in a false spirit
>   And speak a lie, *saying,*
> 'I will prophesy to you of wine and drink,'
> Even he would be the prattler of this people.

"I will surely assemble all of you, O Jacob,
I will surely gather the remnant of Israel;
I will put them together like sheep of the fold,
Like a flock in the midst of their pasture;
They shall make a loud noise because of *so
     many* people.
The one who breaks open will come up before
     them;
They will break out,
Pass through the gate,
And go out by it;
Their king will pass before them,
With the LORD at their head."

And I said:

"Hear now, O heads of Jacob,
And you rulers of the house of Israel:
Is it not for you to know justice?
You who hate good and love evil;
Who strip the skin from My people,
And the flesh from their bones;
Who also eat the flesh of My people,
Flay their skin from them,
Break their bones,
And chop *them* in pieces
Like *meat* for the pot,
Like flesh in the caldron."

Then they will cry to the LORD,
But He will not hear them;
He will even hide His face from them at that
     time,
Because they have been evil in their deeds.

Thus says the LORD concerning the prophets
Who make my people stray;
Who chant "Peace"
While they chew with their teeth,
But who prepare war against him
Who puts nothing into their mouths:
"Therefore you shall have night without vision,
And you shall have darkness without
     divination;
The sun shall go down on the prophets,
And the day shall be dark for them.
So the seers shall be ashamed,
And the diviners abashed;
Indeed they shall all cover their lips;
For *there is* no answer from God."

But truly I am full of power by the Spirit of the
     LORD,
And of justice and might,
To declare to Jacob his transgression
And to Israel his sin.

Now hear this,
You heads of the house of Jacob
And rulers of the house of Israel,
Who abhor justice
And pervert all equity,
Who build up Zion with bloodshed
And Jerusalem with iniquity:
Her heads judge for a bribe,
Her priests teach for pay,
And her prophets divine for money.
Yet they lean on the LORD, and say,
"Is not the LORD among us?
No harm can come upon us."
Therefore because of you
Zion shall be plowed *like* a field,
Jerusalem shall become heaps of ruins,
And the mountain of the temple
Like the bare hills of the forest.

Micah 1:1-9; 2–3

WORSHIP

You, who have shown me great and severe
     troubles,
Shall revive me again,
And bring me up again from the depths of the
     earth.

Also with the lute I will praise you—
And Your faithfulness, O my God!
To You I will sing with the harp,
O Holy One of Israel.
My lips shall greatly rejoice when I sing to You,
And my soul, which You have redeemed.

Psalm 71:20, 22-23

WISDOM

Righteousness exalts a nation,
But sin *is* a reproach to *any* people.

Proverbs 14:34

SO WHAT?
What does this tell me?

TRIUMPH OF GOD'S GRACE
Micah 4:1-8; 5:1–6:8; 7:18; Psalm 72:1-4; Proverbs 15:1

Now it shall come to pass in the latter days
That the mountain of the LORD's house
Shall be established on the top of the
mountains,
And shall be exalted above the hills;
And peoples shall flow to it.
Many nations shall come and say,
"Come, and let us go up to the mountain of the
LORD,
To the house of the God of Jacob;
He will teach us His ways,
And we shall walk in His paths."
  For out of Zion the law shall go forth,
  And the word of the LORD from Jerusalem.
  He shall judge between many peoples,
  And rebuke strong nations afar off;
  They shall beat their swords into
  plowshares,
  And their spears into pruning hooks;
  Nation shall not lift up sword against nation,
  Neither shall they learn war any more.

But everyone shall sit under his vine and
  under his fig tree,
And no one shall make *them* afraid;
For the mouth of the LORD of hosts has
  spoken.
For all people walk each in the name of his
  god,
But we will walk in the name of the LORD our
  God
Forever and ever.

"In that day," says the LORD,
"I will assemble the lame,
I will gather the outcast
And those whom I have afflicted;
I will make the lame a remnant,
And the outcast a strong nation;
So the LORD will reign over them in Mount
  Zion
From now on, even forever.
And you, O tower of the flock,
The stronghold of the daughter of Zion,
To you shall it come,
Even the former dominion shall come,
The kingdom of the daughter of Jerusalem."

Now gather yourself in troops,
O daughter of troops;

He has laid siege against us;
They will strike the judge of Israel with a rod on
  the cheek.

"But you, Bethlehem Ephrathah,
Though you are little among the thousands of
  Judah,
Yet out of you shall come forth to Me
The One to be Ruler in Israel,
Whose goings forth *are* from of old,
From everlasting."

Therefore He shall give them up,
Until the time *that* she who is in labor has
  given birth;
Then the remnant of His brethren
Shall return to the children of Israel.
And He shall stand and feed *His flock*
In the strength of the LORD,
In the majesty of the name of the LORD His God;
And they shall abide,
For now He shall be great
To the ends of the earth;
And this *One* shall be peace.

When the Assyrian comes into our land,
And when he treads in our palaces,
Then we will raise against him
Seven shepherds and eight princely men.
They shall waste with the sword the land of
  Assyria,
And the land of Nimrod at its entrances;
Thus He shall deliver *us* from the Assyrian,
When he comes into our land
And when he treads within our borders.

Then the remnant of Jacob
Shall be in the midst of many peoples,
Like dew from the LORD,
Like showers on the grass,
That tarry for no man
Nor wait for the sons of men.
And the remnant of Jacob
Shall be among the Gentiles,
In the midst of many peoples,
Like a lion among the beasts of the forest,
Like a young lion among flocks of sheep,
Who, if he passes through,
Both treads down and tears in pieces,
And none can deliver.

WORDS FROM THE PROPHETS

Your hand shall be lifted against your
    adversaries,
And all your enemies shall be cut off.

"And it shall be in that day," says the LORD,
"That I will cut off your horses from your midst
And destroy your chariots.
I will cut off the cities of your land
And throw down all your strongholds.
I will cut off sorceries from your hand,
And you shall have no soothsayers.
Your carved images I will also cut off,
And your sacred pillars from your midst;
You shall no more worship the work of your
    hands;
I will pluck your wooden images from your
    midst;
Thus I will destroy your cities.
And I will execute vengeance in anger and
    fury
On the nations that have not heard."

Hear now what the LORD says:

"Arise, plead your case before the mountains,
And let the hills hear your voice.
Hear, O you mountains, the LORD's complaint,
And you strong foundations of the earth;
For the LORD has a complaint against His
    people,
And He will contend with Israel.

"O My people, what have I done to you?
And how have I wearied you?
Testify against Me.
For I brought you up from the land of Egypt,
I redeemed you from the house of bondage;
And I sent before you Moses, Aaron, and
    Miriam.
O My people, remember now
What Balak king of Moab counseled,
And what Balaam the son of Beor answered
    him,
From Acacia Grove to Gilgal,
That you may know the righteousness of the
    LORD."

With what shall I come before the LORD,
And bow myself before the High God?
Shall I come before Him with burnt offerings,
With calves a year old?
Will the LORD be pleased with thousands of
    rams,
Ten thousand rivers of oil?
Shall I give my firstborn *for* my transgression,
The fruit of my body *for* the sin of my soul?

He has shown you, O man, what *is* good;
And what does the LORD require of you
But to do justly,
To love mercy,
And to walk humbly with your God?

Who *is* a God like You,
Pardoning iniquity
And passing over the transgression of the
    remnant of His heritage?

He does not retain His anger forever,
Because He delights *in* mercy.
        Micah 4:1-8; 5:1–6:8; 7:18

WORSHIP

Give the king Your judgments, O God,
And Your righteousness to the king's Son.
He will judge Your people with righteousness,
And Your poor with justice.
The mountains will bring peace to the people,
And the little hills, by righteousness.
He will bring justice to the poor of the people;
He will save the children of the needy,
And will break in pieces the oppressor.
        Psalm 72:1-4

WISDOM

A soft answer turns away wrath,
But a harsh word stirs up anger.

        Proverbs 15:1

SW?! **SO WHAT?**
What does this tell me?

BAD NEWS FOR NINEVEH

Nahum 1:1-8; 2:1–3:15; Psalm 72:5-7; Proverbs 15:2

The burden against Nineveh. The book of the vision of Nahum the Elkoshite.

God *is* jealous, and the LORD avenges;
The LORD avenges and *is* furious.
The LORD will take vengeance on His
    adversaries,
And He reserves *wrath* for His enemies;
The LORD *is* slow to anger and great in power,
And will not at all acquit *the wicked.*

The LORD has His way
In the whirlwind and in the storm,
And the clouds *are* the dust of His feet.
  He rebukes the sea and makes it dry,
  And dries up all the rivers.
  Bashan and Carmel wither,
  And the flower of Lebanon wilts.
  The mountains quake before Him,
  The hills melt,
  And the earth heaves at His presence,
  Yes, the world and all who dwell in it.

Who can stand before His indignation?
And who can endure the fierceness of His
    anger?
His fury is poured out like fire,
And the rocks are thrown down by Him.

The LORD *is* good,
A stronghold in the day of trouble;
And He knows those who trust in Him.
But with an overflowing flood
He will make an utter end of its place,
And darkness will pursue His enemies.

He who scatters has come up before your
    face.
Man the fort!
Watch the road!
Strengthen *your* flanks!
Fortify *your* power mightily.

For the LORD will restore the excellence of
    Jacob
Like the excellence of Israel,
For the emptiers have emptied them out
And ruined their vine branches.

The shields of his mighty men *are* made red,
The valiant men *are* in scarlet.
The chariots *come* with flaming torches
In the day of his preparation,

And the spears are brandished.
The chariots rage in the streets,
They jostle one another in the broad roads;
They seem like torches,
They run like lightning.

He remembers his nobles;
They stumble in their walk;
They make haste to her walls,
And the defense is prepared.
The gates of the rivers are opened,
And the palace is dissolved.
It is decreed:
She shall be led away captive,
She shall be brought up;
And her maidservants shall lead *her* as with
    the voice of doves,
Beating their breasts.

Though Nineveh of old *was* like a pool of
    water,
Now they flee away.
"Halt! Halt!" *they cry;*
But no one turns back.
Take spoil of silver!
Take spoil of gold!
There is no end of treasure,
Or wealth of every desirable prize.
She is empty, desolate, and waste!
The heart melts, and the knees shake;
Much pain *is* in every side,
And all their faces are drained of color.

Where *is* the dwelling of the lions,
And the feeding place of the young lions,
Where the lion walked, the lioness *and* lion's
    cub,
And no one made *them* afraid?
The lion tore in pieces enough for his cubs,
Killed for his lionesses,
Filled his caves with prey,
And his dens with flesh.

"Behold, I *am* against you," says the LORD of hosts, "I will burn your chariots in smoke, and the sword shall devour your young lions; I will cut off your prey from the earth, and the voice of your messengers shall be heard no more."

Woe to the bloody city!
It *is* all full of lies *and* robbery.
Its victim never departs.

The noise of a whip
And the noise of rattling wheels,
Of galloping horses,
Of clattering chariots!
Horsemen charge with bright sword and
glittering spear.
There is a multitude of slain,
A great number of bodies,
Countless corpses—
They stumble over the corpses—
Because of the multitude of harlotries of the
seductive harlot,
The mistress of sorceries,
Who sells nations through her harlotries,
And families through her sorceries.

"Behold, I *am* against you," says the LORD of
hosts;
"I will lift your skirts over your face,
I will show the nations your nakedness,
And the kingdoms your shame.
I will cast abominable filth upon you,
Make you vile,
And make you a spectacle.
It shall come to pass *that* all who look upon
you
Will flee from you, and say,
'Nineveh is laid waste!
Who will bemoan her?'
Where shall I seek comforters for you?"

Are you better than No Amon
That was situated by the River,
That had the waters around her,
Whose rampart *was* the sea,
Whose wall *was* the sea?
Ethiopia and Egypt *were* her strength,
And *it was* boundless;
Put and Lubim were your helpers.
Yet she *was* carried away,
She went into captivity;
Her young children also were dashed to
pieces
At the head of every street;
They cast lots for her honorable men,
And all her great men were bound in chains.
You also will be drunk;
You will be hidden;
You also will seek refuge from the enemy.

All your strongholds *are* fig trees with ripened
figs:
If they are shaken,
They fall into the mouth of the eater.
Surely, your people in your midst *are* women!

The gates of your land are wide open for your
enemies;
Fire shall devour the bars of your *gates*.

Draw your water for the siege!
Fortify your strongholds!
Go into the clay and tread the mortar!
Make strong the brick kiln!
There the fire will devour you,
The sword will cut you off;
It will eat you up like a locust.

Make yourself many—like the locust!
Make yourself many—like the *swarming*
locusts!

Nahum 1:1-8; 2:1–3:15

WORSHIP

They shall fear You
As long as the sun and moon endure,
Throughout all generations.
He shall come down like rain upon the grass
before mowing,
Like showers *that* water the earth.
In His days the righteous shall flourish,
And abundance of peace,
Until the moon is no more.

Psalm 72:5-7

WISDOM

The tongue of the wise uses knowledge rightly,
But the mouth of fools pours forth foolishness.

Proverbs 15:2

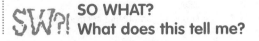 **SO WHAT?**
What does this tell me?

THE COMING DAY OF THE LORD

Zephaniah 1:1–2:3; 3:14-20;
Psalm 72:18-19; Proverbs 15:3

The word of the LORD which came to Zephaniah the son of Cushi, the son of Gedaliah, the son of Amariah, the son of Hezekiah, in the days of Josiah the son of Amon, king of Judah.

"I will utterly consume everything
From the face of the land,"
Says the LORD;
"I will consume man and beast;
I will consume the birds of the heavens,
The fish of the sea,
And the stumbling blocks along with the
    wicked.
    I will cut off man from the face of the land,"
Says the LORD.

"I will stretch out My hand against Judah,
And against all the inhabitants of Jerusalem.
I will cut off every trace of Baal from this
    place,
The names of the idolatrous priests with the
    pagan priests—
Those who worship the host of heaven on
    the housetops;
Those who worship and swear *oaths* by the
    LORD,
But who *also* swear by Milcom;
Those who have turned back from *following*
    the LORD,
And have not sought the LORD, nor inquired
    of Him."

Be silent in the presence of the Lord GOD;
For the day of the LORD *is* at hand,
For the LORD has prepared a sacrifice;
He has invited His guests.

"And it shall be,
In the day of the LORD's sacrifice,
That I will punish the princes and the king's
    children,
And all such as are clothed with foreign
    apparel.
In the same day I will punish
All those who leap over the threshold,
Who fill their masters' houses with violence
    and deceit.

"And there shall be on that day," says the
    LORD,
"The sound of a mournful cry from the Fish
    Gate,

A wailing from the Second Quarter,
And a loud crashing from the hills.
Wail, you inhabitants of Maktesh!
For all the merchant people are cut down;
All those who handle money are cut off.

"And it shall come to pass at that time
That I will search Jerusalem with lamps,
And punish the men
Who are settled in complacency,
Who say in their heart,
'The LORD will not do good,
Nor will He do evil.'
Therefore their goods shall become booty,
And their houses a desolation;
They shall build houses, but not inhabit *them*;
They shall plant vineyards, but not drink their
    wine."

The great day of the LORD *is* near;
It is near and hastens quickly.
The noise of the day of the LORD is bitter;
There the mighty men shall cry out.
That day *is* a day of wrath,
A day of trouble and distress,
A day of devastation and desolation,
A day of darkness and gloominess,
A day of clouds and thick darkness,
A day of trumpet and alarm
Against the fortified cities
And against the high towers.

"I will bring distress upon men,
And they shall walk like blind men,
Because they have sinned against the LORD;
Their blood shall be poured out like dust,
And their flesh like refuse."

Neither their silver nor their gold
Shall be able to deliver them
In the day of the LORD's wrath;
But the whole land shall be devoured
By the fire of His jealousy,
For He will make speedy riddance
Of all those who dwell in the land.

Gather yourselves together, yes, gather
    together,
O undesirable nation,
Before the decree is issued,
Or the day passes like chaff,
Before the LORD's fierce anger comes upon you,

Before the day of the LORD's anger comes upon
    you!
Seek the LORD, all you meek of the earth,
Who have upheld His justice.
Seek righteousness, seek humility.
It may be that you will be hidden
In the day of the LORD's anger.

Sing, O daughter of Zion!
Shout, O Israel!
Be glad and rejoice with all *your* heart,
O daughter of Jerusalem!
The LORD has taken away your judgments,
He has cast out your enemy.
The King of Israel, the LORD, *is* in your midst;
You shall see disaster no more.

In that day it shall be said to Jerusalem:
"Do not fear;
Zion, let not your hands be weak.
The LORD your God in your midst,
The Mighty One, will save;
He will rejoice over you with gladness,
He will quiet *you* with His love,
He will rejoice over you with singing."

"I will gather those who sorrow over the
    appointed assembly,
Who are among you,
To whom its reproach *is* a burden.
Behold, at that time
I will deal with all who afflict you;
I will save the lame,
And gather those who were driven out;
I will appoint them for praise and fame
In every land where they were put to shame.
At that time I will bring you back,
Even at the time I gather you;
For I will give you fame and praise
Among all the peoples of the earth,
When I return your captives before your eyes,"
Says the LORD.

Zephaniah 1:1–2:3; 3:14-20

WORSHIP

Blessed *be* the LORD God, the God of Israel,
Who only does wondrous things!
And blessed *be* His glorious name forever!
And let the whole earth be filled *with* His glory.
Amen and Amen.

Psalm 72:18-19

WISDOM

The eyes of the LORD *are* in every place,
Keeping watch on the evil and the good.

Proverbs 15:3

SW?! SO WHAT?
What does this tell me?

HABAKKUK, THE PERPLEXED PROPHET

Habakkuk 1:1–2:4; 3:1-7, 16-19; Psalm 73:1-3; Proverbs 15:4

The burden which the prophet Habakkuk saw.

O LORD, how long shall I cry,
And You will not hear?
Even cry out to You, "Violence!"
And You will not save.
Why do You show me iniquity,
And cause *me* to see trouble?
For plundering and violence *are* before me;
There is strife, and contention arises.
Therefore the law is powerless,
And justice never goes forth.
  For the wicked surround the righteous;
  Therefore perverse judgment proceeds.

"Look among the nations and watch—
Be utterly astounded!
For *I will* work a work in your days
Which you would not believe, though it were
   told *you.*
For indeed I am raising up the Chaldeans,
A bitter and hasty nation
Which marches through the breadth of the
   earth,
To possess dwelling places *that are* not
   theirs.
They are terrible and dreadful;
Their judgment and their dignity proceed
   from themselves.
Their horses also are swifter than leopards,
And more fierce than evening wolves.
Their chargers charge ahead;
Their cavalry comes from afar;
They fly as the eagle *that* hastens to eat.

"They all come for violence;
Their faces are set *like* the east wind.
They gather captives like sand.
They scoff at kings,
And princes are scorned by them.
They deride every stronghold,
For they heap up earthen *mounds* and seize
   it.
Then *his* mind changes, and he
   transgresses;
He commits offense,
Ascribing this power to his god."

Are You not from everlasting,
O LORD my God, my Holy One?

We shall not die.
O LORD, You have appointed them for
   judgment;
O Rock, You have marked them for
   correction.
You are of purer eyes than to behold evil,
And cannot look on wickedness.
Why do You look on those who deal
   treacherously,
And hold Your tongue when the wicked
   devours
A *person* more rightous than he?
Why do You make men like fish of the sea,
Like creeping things *that have* no ruler over
   them?

They take up all of them with a hook,
They catch them in their net,
And gather them in their dragnet.
Therefore they rejoice and are glad.
Therefore they sacrifice to their net,
And burn incense to their dragnet;
Because by them their share *is* sumptuous
And their food plentiful.
Shall they therefore empty their net,
And continue to slay nations without pity?

I will stand my watch
And set myself on the rampart,
And watch to see what He will say to me,
And what I will answer when I am corrected.

Then the LORD answered me and said:

"Write the vision
And make *it* plain on tablets,
That he may run who reads it.
For the vision *is* yet for an appointed time;
But at the end it will speak, and it will not lie.
Though it tarries, wait for it;
Because it will surely come,
It will not tarry.

"Behold the proud,
His soul is not upright in him;
But the just shall live by his faith.

A prayer of Habakkuk the prophet, on Shi-
gionoth.

O LORD, I have heard your speech *and* was
   afraid;

O Lord, revive Your work in the midst of the
      years!
In the midst of the years make *it* known;
In wrath remember mercy.

God came from Teman,
The Holy One from Mount Paran.   Selah

His glory covered the heavens,
And the earth was full of His praise.
His brightness was like the light;
He had rays *flashing* from His hand,
And there His power *was* hidden.
Before Him went pestilence,
And fever followed at His feet.

He stood and measured the earth;
He looked and startled the nations.
And the everlasting mountains were scattered,
The perpetual hills bowed.
His ways *are* everlasting.
I saw the tents of Cushan in affliction;
The curtains of the land of Midian trembled.

When I heard, my body trembled;
My lips quivered at *the* voice;
Rottenness entered my bones;
And I trembled in myself,
That I might rest in the day of trouble.
When he comes up to the people,
He will invade them with his troops.

Though the fig tree may not blossom,
Nor fruit be on the vines;
Though the labor of the olive may fail,
And the fields yield no food;
Though the flock may be cut off from the fold,
And there be no herd in the stalls—
Yet I will rejoice in the Lord,
I will joy in the God of my salvation.

The Lord God is my strength;
He will make my feet like deer's *feet*,
And He will make me walk on my high hills.

To the Chief Musician. With my stringed instruments.

Habakkuk 1:1–2:4; 3:1-7, 16-19

WORSHIP

Truly God *is* good to Israel,
To such as are pure in heart.
But as for me, my feet had almost stumbled;
My steps had nearly slipped.
For I *was* envious of the boastful,
When I saw the prosperity of the wicked.

Psalm 73:1-3

WISDOM

A wholesome tongue *is* a tree of life,
But perverseness in it breaks the spirit.

Proverbs 15:4

SW?! SO WHAT?
What does this tell me?

JEREMIAH'S CALL AND COMMISSIONING

Jeremiah 1:1-19; 16:1-9; Psalm 73:12-14; Proverbs 15:5

The words of Jeremiah the son of Hilkiah, of the priests who *were* in Anathoth in the land of Benjamin, to whom the word of the LORD came in the days of Josiah the son of Amon, king of Judah, in the thirteenth year of his reign. It came also in the days of Jehoiakim the son of Josiah, king of Judah, until the end of the eleventh year of Zedekiah the son of Josiah, king of Judah, until the carrying away of Jerusalem captive in the fifth month.

Then the word of the LORD came to me, saying:

"Before I formed you in the womb I knew you;
Before you were born I sanctified you;
I ordained you a prophet to the nations."

Then said I:

"Ah, Lord GOD!
Behold, I cannot speak, for I *am* a youth."

But the LORD said to me:

"Do not say, 'I *am* a youth,'
For you shall go to all to whom I send you,
And whatever I command you, you shall speak.
Do not be afraid of their faces,
For I *am* with you to deliver you," says the LORD.

Then the LORD put forth His hand and touched my mouth, and the LORD said to me:

"Behold, I have put My words in your mouth.
See, I have this day set you over the nations and over the kingdoms,
To root out and to pull down,
To destroy and to throw down,
To build and to plant."

Moreover the word of the LORD came to me, saying, "Jeremiah, what do you see?"
And I said, "I see a branch of an almond tree."
Then the LORD said to me, "You have seen well, for I am ready to perform My word."
And the word of the LORD came to me the second time, saying, "What do you see?"
And I said, "I see a boiling pot, and it is facing away from the north."

Then the LORD said to me:

"Out of the north calamity shall break forth
On all the inhabitants of the land.
For behold, I am calling
All the families of the kingdoms of the north," says the LORD;
"They shall come and each one set his throne
At the entrance of the gates of Jerusalem,
Against all its walls all around,
And against all the cities of Judah.
I will utter My judgments
Against them concerning all their wickedness,
Because they have forsaken Me,
Burned incense to other gods,
And worshiped the works of their own hands.

"Therefore prepare yourself and arise,
And speak to them all that I command you.
Do not be dismayed before their faces,
Lest I dismay you before them.
For behold, I have made you this day
A fortified city and an iron pillar,
And bronze walls against the whole land—
Against the kings of Judah,
Against its princes,
Against its priests,
And against the people of the land.
They will fight against you,
But they shall not prevail against you.
For I *am* with you," says the LORD, "to deliver you."

The word of the LORD also came to me, saying, "You shall not take a wife, nor shall you have sons or daughters in this place." For thus says the LORD concerning the sons and daughters who are born in this place, and concerning their mothers who bore them and their fathers who begot them in this land: "They shall die gruesome deaths; they shall not be lamented nor shall they be buried, *but* they shall be like refuse on the face of the earth. They shall be consumed by the sword and by famine, and their corpses shall be meat for the birds of heaven and for the beasts of the earth."

For thus says the LORD: "Do not enter the house of mourning, nor go to lament or bemoan them; for I have taken away My peace from this people," says the LORD, "lovingkindness and mercies. Both the great and the small shall die in this land. They shall not be buried; neither shall men lament for them, cut themselves, nor make themselves bald for them. Nor shall *men* break *bread* in mourning for them, to comfort them for the dead; nor shall *men* give them the cup of consolation to drink for their father or their mother. Also you shall not go into the house of feasting to sit with them, to eat and drink."

For thus says the LORD of hosts, the God of Israel: "Behold, I will cause to cease from this place, before your eyes and in your days, the voice of mirth and the voice of gladness, the voice of the bridegroom and the voice of the bride."

Jeremiah 1:1-19; 16:1-9

WORSHIP

Behold, these *are* the ungodly,
Who are always at ease;
They increase *in* riches.
Surely I have cleansed my heart *in* vain,
And washed my hands in innocence.
For all day long I have been plagued,
And chastened every morning.

Psalm 73:12-14

WISDOM

A fool despises his father's instruction,
But he who receives correction is prudent.

Proverbs 15:5

SW?! SO WHAT?
What does this tell me?

JUDAH'S TURNING FROM THE LORD

Jeremiah 2:1-32; Psalm 73:22-24; Proverbs 15:6

Moreover the word of the LORD came to me, saying, "Go and cry in the hearing of Jerusalem, saying, 'Thus says the LORD:

"I remember you,
The kindness of your youth,
The love of your betrothal,
When you went after Me in the wilderness,
In a land not sown.
Israel *was* holiness to the LORD,
The firstfruits of His increase.
All that devour him will offend;
Disaster will come upon them," says the LORD.' "

Hear the word of the LORD, O house of Jacob and all the families of the house of Israel. Thus says the LORD:

"What injustice have your fathers found in Me,
That they have gone far from Me,
Have followed idols,
And have become idolaters?
Neither did they say, 'Where *is* the LORD,
Who brought us up out of the land of Egypt,
Who led us through the wilderness,
Through a land of deserts and pits,
Through a land of drought and the shadow of death,
Through a land that no one crossed
And where no one dwelt?'
I brought you into a bountiful country,
To eat its fruit and its goodness.
But when you entered, you defiled My land
And made My heritage an abomination.
The priests did not say, 'Where *is* the LORD?'
And those who handle the law did not know Me;
The rulers also transgressed against Me;
The prophets prophesied by Baal,
And walked after *things that* do not profit.

"Therefore I will yet bring charges against you," says the LORD,
"And against your children's children I will bring charges.
For pass beyond the coasts of Cyprus and see,
Send to Kedar and consider diligently,
And see if there has been such *a thing.*
Has a nation changed *its* gods,

Which *are* not gods?
But My people have changed their Glory
For *what* does not profit.
Be astonished, O heavens, at this,
And be horribly afraid;
Be very desolate," says the LORD.
"For My people have committed two evils:
They have forsaken Me, the fountain of living waters,
And hewn themselves cisterns—broken cisterns that can hold no water.

"*Is* Israel a servant?
Is he a homeborn *slave?*
Why is he plundered?
The young lions roared at him, *and* growled;
They made his land waste;
His cities are burned, without inhabitant.
Also the people of Noph and Tahpanhes
Have broken the crown of your head.
Have you not brought this on yourself,
In that you have forsaken the LORD your God
When He led you in the way?
And now why take the road to Egypt,
To drink the waters of Sihor?
Or why take the road to Assyria,
To drink the waters of the River?
Your own wickedness will correct you,
And your backslidings will rebuke you.
Know therefore and see that *it is* an evil and bitter *thing*
That you have forsaken the LORD your God,
And the fear of Me *is* not in you,"
Says the Lord GOD of hosts.

"For of old I have broken your yoke *and* burst your bonds;
And you said, 'I will not transgress,'
When on every high hill and under every green tree
You lay down, playing the harlot.
Yet I had planted you a noble vine, a seed of highest quality.
How then have you turned before Me
Into the degenerate plant of an alien vine?
For though you wash yourself with lye, and use much soap,
Yet your iniquity is marked before Me," says the Lord GOD.

"How can you say, 'I am not polluted,
   I have not gone after the Baals'?
See your way in the valley;
Know what you have done:
You are a swift dromedary breaking loose in
      her ways,
A wild donkey used to the wilderness,
That sniffs at the wind in her desire;
In her time of mating, who can turn her away?
All those who seek her will not weary
      themselves;
In her month they will find her.
Withhold your foot from being unshod, and
      your throat from thirst.
But you said, 'There is no hope.
No! For I have loved aliens, and after them I
   will go.'

"As the thief is ashamed when he is found out,
So is the house of Israel ashamed;
They and their kings and their princes, and
      their priests and their prophets,
Saying to a tree, 'You *are* my father,'
And to a stone, 'You gave birth to me.'
For they have turned *their* back to Me, and not
      their face.
But in the time of their trouble
They will say, 'Arise and save us.'
But where *are* your gods that you have made
      for yourselves?
Let them arise,
If they can save you in the time of your trouble;
For *according to* the number of your cities
Are your gods, O Judah.

"Why will you plead with Me?
You all have transgressed against Me," says
      the LORD.
"In vain I have chastened your children;
They received no correction.
Your sword has devoured your prophets
Like a destroying lion.

"O generation, see the word of the LORD!
Have I been a wilderness to Israel,
Or a land of darkness?
Why do My people say, 'We are lords;
We will come no more to You'?
Can a virgin forget her ornaments,
Or a bride her attire?
Yet My people have forgotten Me days without
      number.

Jeremiah 2:1-32

WORSHIP

I *was* so foolish and ignorant;
I was *like* a beast before You.
Nevertheless I *am* continually with You;
You hold *me* by my right hand.
You will guide me with Your counsel,
And afterward receive me *to* glory.

Psalm 73:22-24

WISDOM

In the house of the righteous *there is* much
      treasure,
But in the revenue of the wicked is trouble.

Proverbs 15:6

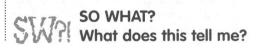

SO WHAT?
What does this tell me?

ISRAEL'S EXAMPLE OF UNFAITHFULNESS

Jeremiah 3:6–4:4; Psalm 73:26–28; Proverbs 15:7

The LORD said also to me in the days of Josiah the king: "Have you seen what backsliding Israel has done? She has gone up on every high mountain and under every green tree, and there played the harlot. And I said, after she had done all these *things,* 'Return to Me.' But she did not return. And her treacherous sister Judah saw it. Then I saw that for all the causes for which backsliding Israel had committed adultery, I had put her away and given her a certificate of divorce; yet her treacherous sister Judah did not fear, but went and played the harlot also. So it came to pass, through her casual harlotry, that she defiled the land and committed adultery with stones and trees. And yet for all this her treacherous sister Judah has not turned to Me with her whole heart, but in pretense," says the LORD.

Then the LORD said to me, "Backsliding Israel has shown herself more righteous than treacherous Judah. Go and proclaim these words toward the north, and say:

'Return, backsliding Israel,' says the LORD;
'I will not cause My anger to fall on you.
For I *am* merciful,' says the LORD;
'I will not remain angry forever.
Only acknowledge your iniquity,
That you have transgressed against the
    LORD your God,
And have scattered your charms
To alien deities under every green tree,
And you have not obeyed My voice,' says
    the LORD.

"Return, O backsliding children," says the LORD; "for I am married to you. I will take you, one from a city and two from a family, and I will bring you to Zion. And I will give you shepherds according to My heart, who will feed you with knowledge and understanding.

"Then it shall come to pass, when you are multiplied and increased in the land in those days," says the LORD, "that they will say no more, 'The ark of the covenant of the LORD.' It shall not come to mind, nor shall they remember it, nor shall they visit *it,* nor shall it be made anymore.

"At that time Jerusalem shall be called The Throne of the LORD, and all the nations shall be gathered to it, to the name of the LORD, to Jerusalem. No more shall they follow the dictates of their evil hearts.

"In those days the house of Judah shall walk with the house of Israel, and they shall come together out of the land of the north to the land that I have given as an inheritance to your fathers.

"But I said:

'How can I put you among the children
    And give you a pleasant land,
    A beautiful heritage of the hosts of nations?'

"And I said:

'You shall call Me, "My Father,"
    And not turn away from Me.'
Surely, *as* a wife treacherously departs from
        her husband,
So have you dealt treacherously with Me,
O house of Israel," says the LORD.

A voice was heard on the desolate heights,
Weeping *and* supplications of the children of
        Israel.
For they have perverted their way;
They have forgotten the LORD their God.

"Return, you backsliding children,
    And I will heal your backslidings."

"Indeed we do come to You,
    For You are the LORD our God.
Truly, in vain *is salvation hoped for* from the
        hills,
And from the multitude of mountains;
Truly, in the LORD our God
Is the salvation of Israel.
For shame has devoured
The labor of our fathers from our youth—
Their flocks and their herds,
Their sons and their daughters.
We lie down in our shame,
And our reproach covers us.
For we have sinned against the LORD our
        God,
We and our fathers,
From our youth even to this day,

And have not obeyed the voice of the LORD our
  God."

"If you will return, O Israel," says the LORD,
"Return to Me;
  And if you will put away your abominations out
    of My sight,
  Then you shall not be moved.
  And you shall swear, 'The LORD lives,'
  In truth, in judgment, and in righteousness;
  The nations shall bless themselves in Him,
  And in Him they shall glory."

For thus says the LORD to the men of Judah and
Jerusalem:

  "Break up your fallow ground,
  And do not sow among thorns.
  Circumcise yourselves to the LORD,
  And take away the foreskins of your hearts,
  You men of Judah and inhabitants of
    Jerusalem,
  Lest My fury come forth like fire,
  And burn so that no one can quench it,
  Because of the evil of your doings."

Jeremiah 3:6–4:4

WORSHIP

My flesh and my heart fail;
But God *is* the strength of my heart and my
  portion forever.

For indeed, those who are far from You shall
  perish;
You have destroyed all those who desert You
  for harlotry.
But *it is* good for me to draw near to God;
I have put my trust in the Lord GOD,
That I may declare all Your works.

Psalm 73:26-28

WISDOM

The lips of the wise disperse knowledge,
But the heart of the fool *does* not *do* so.

Proverbs 15:7

SW?! **SO WHAT?**
What does this tell me?

REASONS FOR GOD'S JUDGMENT

Jeremiah 5; Psalm 74:1-2;
Proverbs 15:8

"Run to and fro through the streets of
    Jerusalem;
    See now and know;
And seek in her open places
If you can find a man,
If there is *anyone* who executes judgment,
Who seeks the truth,
And I will pardon her.
Though they say, '*As* the LORD lives,'
Surely they swear falsely."

O LORD, *are* not Your eyes on the truth?
You have stricken them,
    But they have not grieved;
    You have consumed them,
    But they have refused to receive correction.
    They have made their faces harder than
        rock;
    They have refused to return.

Therefore I said, "Surely these *are* poor.
They are foolish;
For they do not know the way of the LORD,
The judgment of their God.
I will go to the great men and speak to
    them,
For they have known the way of the LORD,
The judgment of their God."

But these have altogether broken the yoke
And burst the bonds.
Therefore a lion from the forest shall slay
    them,
A wolf of the deserts shall destroy them;
A leopard will watch over their cities.
Everyone who goes out from there shall be
    torn in pieces,
Because their transgressions are many;
Their backslidings have increased.

"How shall I pardon you for this?
Your children have forsaken Me
And sworn by *those that are* not gods.
When I had fed them to the full,
Then they committed adultery
And assembled themselves by troops in the
    harlots' houses.
They were *like* well-fed lusty stallions;
Every one neighed after his neighbor's wife.
Shall I not punish *them* for these *things*?"
    says the LORD.

"And shall I not avenge Myself on such a nation
    as this?

"Go up on her walls and destroy,
    But do not make a complete end.
    Take away her branches,
    For they *are* not the LORD's.
    For the house of Israel and the house of
        Judah
    Have dealt very treacherously with Me," says
        the LORD.

They have lied about the LORD,
And said, "*It is* not He.
Neither will evil come upon us,
Nor shall we see sword or famine.
And the prophets become wind,
For the word *is* not in them.
Thus shall it be done to them."

Therefore thus says the LORD God of hosts:

"Because you speak this word,
    Behold, I will make My words in your mouth
        fire,
    And this people wood,
    And it shall devour them.
    Behold, I will bring a nation against you from
        afar,
    O house of Israel," says the LORD.
"It *is* a mighty nation,
    It *is* an ancient nation,
    A nation whose language you do not know,
    Nor can you understand what they say.
    Their quiver *is* like an open tomb;
    They *are* all mighty men.
    And they shall eat up your harvest and your
        bread,
    Which your sons and daughters should eat.
    They shall eat up your flocks and your herds;
    They shall eat up your vines and your fig trees;
    They shall destroy your fortified cities,
    In which you trust, with the sword.

"Nevertheless in those days," says the LORD, "I
will not make a complete end of you. And it will be
when you say, 'Why does the LORD our God do all
these *things* to us?' then you shall answer them,
'Just as you have forsaken Me and served foreign
gods in your land, so you shall serve aliens in a
land *that is* not yours.'

"Declare this in the house of Jacob
And proclaim it in Judah, saying,
'Hear this now, O foolish people,
Without understanding,
Who have eyes and see not,
And who have ears and hear not:
Do you not fear Me?' says the LORD.
'Will you not tremble at My presence,
Who have placed the sand as the bound of the
     sea,
By a perpetual decree, that it cannot pass
     beyond it?
And though its waves toss to and fro,
Yet they cannot prevail;
Though they roar, yet they cannot pass over it.
But this people has a defiant and rebellious
     heart;
They have revolted and departed.
They do not say in their heart,
"Let us now fear the LORD our God,
Who gives rain, both the former and the latter,
     in its season.
He reserves for us the appointed weeks of the
     harvest."
Your iniquities have turned these *things* away,
And your sins have withheld good from you.

'For among My people are found wicked *men*;
They lie in wait as one who sets snares;
They set a trap;
They catch men.
As a cage is full of birds,
So their houses *are* full of deceit.
Therefore they have become great and grown
     rich.
They have grown fat, they are sleek;
Yes, they surpass the deeds of the wicked;
They do not plead the cause,
The cause of the fatherless;
Yet they prosper,
And the right of the needy they do not defend.
Shall I not punish *them* for these *things?'* says
     the LORD.
'Shall I not avenge Myself on such a nation as
     this?'

"An astonishing and horrible thing
Has been committed in the land:
The prophets prophesy falsely,
And the priests rule by their *own* power;
And My people love *to have it* so.
But what will you do in the end?

Jeremiah 5

WORSHIP

O God, why have You cast *us* off forever?
Why does Your anger smoke against the
     sheep of Your pasture?
Remember Your congregation, *which* You
     have purchased of old,
The tribe of Your inheritance, *which* You have
     redeemed—
This Mount Zion where You have dwelt.

Psalm 74:1-2

WISDOM

The sacrifice of the wicked *is* an abomination
     to the LORD,
But the prayer of the upright *is* His delight.

Proverbs 15:8

SW?! **SO WHAT?**
What does this tell me?

TEMPLE RITUAL WON'T SAVE YOU!

WORDS FROM THE PROPHETS

The word that came to Jeremiah from the LORD, saying, "Stand in the gate of the LORD's house, and proclaim there this word, and say, 'Hear the word of the LORD, all *you of* Judah who enter in at these gates to worship the LORD!' " Thus says the LORD of hosts, the God of Israel: "Amend your ways and your doings, and I will cause you to dwell in this place. Do not trust in these lying words, saying, 'The temple of the LORD, the temple of the LORD, the temple of the LORD *are* these.'

"For if you thoroughly amend your ways and your doings, if you thoroughly execute judgment between a man and his neighbor, *if* you do not oppress the stranger, the fatherless, and the widow, and do not shed innocent blood in this place, or walk after other gods to your hurt, then I will cause you to dwell in this place, in the land that I gave to your fathers forever and ever.

"Behold, you trust in lying words that cannot profit. Will you steal, murder, commit adultery, swear falsely, burn incense to Baal, and walk after other gods whom you do not know, and *then* come and stand before Me in this house which is called by My name, and say, 'We are delivered to do all these abominations'? Has this house, which is called by My name, become a den of thieves in your eyes? Behold, I, even I, have seen *it*," says the LORD.

"But go now to My place which *was* in Shiloh, where I set My name at the first, and see what I did to it because of the wickedness of My people Israel. And now, because you have done all these works," says the LORD, "and I spoke to you, rising up early and speaking, but you did not hear, and I called you, but you did not answer, therefore I will do to the house which is called by My name, in which you trust, and to this place which I gave to you and your fathers, as I have done to Shiloh. And I will cast you out of My sight, as I have cast out all your brethren—the whole posterity of Ephraim.

"Therefore do not pray for this people, nor lift up a cry or prayer for them, nor make intercession to Me; for I will not hear you. Do you not see what they do in the cities of Judah and in the streets of Jerusalem? The children gather wood, the fathers kindle the fire, and the women knead dough, to make cakes for the queen of heaven; and *they* pour out drink offerings to other gods, that they may provoke Me to anger. Do they provoke Me to anger?" says the LORD. "*Do they* not *provoke* themselves, to the shame of their own faces?"

Therefore thus says the Lord GOD: "Behold, My anger and My fury will be poured out on this place—on man and on beast, on the trees of the field and on the fruit of the ground. And it will burn and not be quenched."

Thus says the LORD of hosts, the God of Israel: "Add your burnt offerings to your sacrifices and eat meat. For I did not speak to your fathers, or command them in the day that I brought them out of the land of Egypt, concerning burnt offerings or sacrifices. But this is what I commanded them, saying, 'Obey My voice, and I will be your God, and you shall be My people. And walk in all the ways that I have commanded you, that it may be well with you.' Yet they did not obey or incline their ear, but followed the counsels *and* the dictates of their evil hearts, and went backward and not forward. Since the day that your fathers came out of the land of Egypt until this day, I have even sent to you all My servants the prophets, daily rising up early and sending *them*. Yet they did not obey Me or incline their ear, but stiffened their neck. They did worse than their fathers.

"Therefore you shall speak all these words to them, but they will not obey you. You shall also call to them, but they will not answer you.

"So you shall say to them, 'This *is* a nation that does not obey the voice of the LORD their God nor receive correction. Truth has perished and has been cut off from their mouth. Cut off your hair and cast *it* away, and take up a lamentation on the desolate heights; for the LORD has rejected and forsaken the generation of His wrath.' For the children of Judah have done evil in My sight," says the LORD. "They have set their abominations in the house which is called by My name, to pollute it. And they have built the high places of Tophet, which *is* in the Valley of the Son of Hinnom, to burn their sons and their daughters in the fire, which I did not command, nor did it come into My heart.

"Therefore behold, the days are coming," says the LORD, "when it will no more be called Tophet, or the Valley of the Son of Hinnom, but the Valley of Slaughter; for they will bury in Tophet until there is no room. The corpses of this people will be food for the birds of the heaven and for the beasts of the earth. And no one will frighten *them away*. Then I will cause to cease from the cities of Judah and from the streets of Jerusalem the voice of mirth and the voice of gladness, the voice of the bridegroom and the voice of the bride. For the land shall be desolate.

"At that time," says the LORD, "they shall bring out the bones of the kings of Judah, and the bones of its princes, and the bones of the priests, and the bones of the prophets, and the bones of the inhabitants of Jerusalem, out of their graves. They shall spread them before the sun and the moon and all the host of heaven, which they have loved and which they have served and after which they have walked, which they have sought and which they have worshiped. They shall not be gathered nor buried; they shall be like refuse on the face of the earth. Then death shall be chosen rather than life by all the residue of those who remain of this evil family, who remain in all the places where I have driven them," says the LORD of hosts.

Jeremiah 7:1–8:3

WORSHIP

For God *is* my King from of old,
Working salvation in the midst of the earth.
You divided the sea by Your strength;
You broke the heads of the sea serpents in the
    waters.

You have set all the borders of the earth;
You have made summer and winter.

Psalm 74:12-13, 17

WISDOM

The way of the wicked *is* an abomination to
    the LORD,
But He loves him who follows righteousness.

Proverbs 15:9

SO WHAT?
What does this tell me?

JEREMIAH'S LAMENT OVER ZION

Jeremiah 8:18–9:26; Psalm 74:19-21; Proverbs 15:10

I would comfort myself in sorrow;
  My heart *is* faint in me.
  Listen! The voice,
  The cry of the daughter of my people
  From a far country:
  "*Is* not the LORD in Zion?
  Is not her King in her?"

"Why have they provoked Me to anger
  With their carved images—
  With foreign idols?"

"The harvest is past,
    The summer is ended,
    And we are not saved!"

  For the hurt of the daughter of my people I
    am hurt.
  I am mourning;
  Astonishment has taken hold of me.
  Is there no balm in Gilead,
  Is there no physician there?
  Why then is there no recovery
  For the health of the daughter of my people?

  Oh, that my head were waters,
  And my eyes a fountain of tears,
  That I might weep day and night
  For the slain of the daughter of my people!
  Oh, that I had in the wilderness
  A lodging place for travelers;
  That I might leave my people,
  And go from them!
  For they *are* all adulterers,
  An assembly of treacherous men.

"And *like* their bow they have bent their
    tongues *for* lies.
  They are not valiant for the truth on the
    earth.
  For they proceed from evil to evil,
  And they do not know Me," says the LORD.
"Everyone take heed to his neighbor,
  And do not trust any brother;
  For every brother will utterly supplant,
  And every neighbor will walk with
    slanderers.
  Everyone will deceive his neighbor,
  And will not speak the truth;
  They have taught their tongue to speak lies;
  They weary themselves to commit iniquity.

Your dwelling place *is* in the midst of deceit;
  Through deceit they refuse to know Me," says
    the LORD.

Therefore thus says the LORD of hosts:

"Behold, I will refine them and try them;
  For how shall I deal with the daughter of My
    people?
  Their tongue *is* an arrow shot out;
  It speaks deceit;
  One speaks peaceably to his neighbor with his
    mouth,
  But in his heart he lies in wait.
  Shall I not punish them for these *things*?" says
    the LORD.
"Shall I not avenge Myself on such a nation as
    this?"

I will take up a weeping and wailing for the
    mountains,
  And for the dwelling places of the wilderness a
    lamentation,
  Because they are burned up,
  So that no one can pass through;
  Nor can *men* hear the voice of the cattle.
  Both the birds of the heavens and the beasts
    have fled;
  They are gone.

"I will make Jerusalem a heap of ruins, a den of
    jackals.
  I will make the cities of Judah desolate, without
    an inhabitant."

Who *is* the wise man who may understand
this? And *who is he* to whom the mouth of the LORD
has spoken, that he may declare it? Why does the
land perish *and* burn up like a wilderness, so that
no one can pass through?

And the LORD said, "Because they have forsaken My law which I set before them, and have
not obeyed My voice, nor walked according to it,
but they have walked according to the dictates of
their own hearts and after the Baals, which their fathers taught them," therefore thus says the LORD of
hosts, the God of Israel: "Behold, I will feed them,
this people, with wormwood, and give them water
of gall to drink. I will scatter them also among the
Gentiles, whom neither they nor their fathers have

known. And I will send a sword after them until I
have consumed them."

Thus says the LORD of hosts:

"Consider and call for the mourning women,
That they may come;
And send for skillful wailing women,
That they may come.
Let them make haste
And take up a wailing for us,
That our eyes may run with tears,
And our eyelids gush with water.
For a voice of wailing is heard from Zion:
'How we are plundered!
We are greatly ashamed,
Because we have forsaken the land,
Because we have been cast out of our
dwellings.' "

Yet hear the word of the LORD, O women,
And let your ear receive the word of His mouth;
Teach your daughters wailing,
And everyone her neighbor a lamentation.
For death has come through our windows,
Has entered our palaces,
To kill off the children—*no longer to be*
outside!
And the young men—*no longer* on the streets!

Speak, "Thus says the LORD:

'Even the carcasses of men shall fall as refuse
on the open field,
Like cuttings after the harvester,
And no one shall gather *them.*' "

Thus says the LORD:

"Let not the wise *man* glory in his wisdom,
Let not the mighty *man* glory in his might,
Nor let the rich *man* glory in his riches;
But let him who glories glory in this,
That he understands and knows Me,
That I *am* the LORD, exercising lovingkindness,
judgment, and righteousness in the
earth.
For in these I delight," says the LORD.

"Behold, the days are coming," says the LORD,
"that I will punish all *who are* circumcised with the
uncircumcised— Egypt, Judah, Edom, the people of
Ammon, Moab, and all *who are* in the farthest corners, who dwell in the wilderness. For all *these* nations *are* uncircumcised, and all the house of Israel
are uncircumcised in the heart."

Jeremiah 8:18–9:26

WORSHIP

Oh, do not deliver the life of Your turtledove to
the wild beast!
Do not forget the life of Your poor forever.
Have respect to the covenant;
For the dark places of the earth are full of the
haunts of cruelty.
Oh, do not let the oppressed return ashamed!
Let the poor and needy praise Your name.

Psalm 74:19-21

WISDOM

Harsh discipline *is* for him who forsakes the
way,
And he who hates correction will die.

Proverbs 15:10

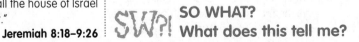

SO WHAT?
What does this tell me?

A PLOT AGAINST THE PROPHET

Jeremiah 11; Psalm 75:1-2, 10; Proverbs 15:11

The word that came to Jeremiah from the LORD, saying, "Hear the words of this covenant, and speak to the men of Judah and to the inhabitants of Jerusalem; and say to them, 'Thus says the LORD God of Israel: "Cursed is the man who does not obey the words of this covenant which I commanded your fathers in the day I brought them out of the land of Egypt, from the iron furnace, saying, 'Obey My voice, and do according to all that I command you; so shall you be My people, and I will be your God,' that I may establish the oath which I have sworn to your fathers, to give them 'a land flowing with milk and honey,' as it is this day." ' "

And I answered and said, "So be it, LORD."

Then the LORD said to me, "Proclaim all these words in the cities of Judah and in the streets of Jerusalem, saying: 'Hear the words of this covenant and do them. For I earnestly exhorted your fathers in the day I brought them up out of the land of Egypt, until this day, rising early and exhorting, saying, "Obey My voice." Yet they did not obey or incline their ear, but everyone followed the dictates of his evil heart; therefore I will bring upon them all the words of this covenant, which I commanded them to do, but which they have not done.' "

And the LORD said to me, "A conspiracy has been found among the men of Judah and among the inhabitants of Jerusalem. They have turned back to the iniquities of their forefathers who refused to hear My words, and they have gone after other gods to serve them; the house of Israel and the house of Judah have broken My covenant which I made with their fathers."

Therefore thus says the LORD: "Behold, I will surely bring calamity on them which they will not be able to escape; and though they cry out to Me, I will not listen to them. Then the cities of Judah and the inhabitants of Jerusalem will go and cry out to the gods to whom they offer incense, but they will not save them at all in the time of their trouble. For according to the number of your cities were your gods, O Judah; and according to the number of the streets of Jerusalem you have set up altars to that shameful thing, altars to burn incense to Baal.

"So do not pray for this people, or lift up a cry or prayer for them; for I will not hear them in the time that they cry out to Me because of their trouble.

"What has My beloved to do in My house,
Having done lewd deeds with many?
And the holy flesh has passed from you.
When you do evil, then you rejoice.
The LORD called your name,
Green Olive Tree, Lovely and of Good Fruit.
With the noise of a great tumult
He has kindled fire on it,
And its branches are broken.

"For the LORD of hosts, who planted you, has pronounced doom against you for the evil of the house of Israel and of the house of Judah, which they have done against themselves to provoke Me to anger in offering incense to Baal."

Now the LORD gave me knowledge of it, and I know it; for You showed me their doings. But I was like a docile lamb brought to the slaughter; and I did not know that they had devised schemes against me, saying, "Let us destroy the tree with its fruit, and let us cut him off from the land of the living, that his name may be remembered no more."

But, O LORD of hosts,
You who judge righteously,
Testing the mind and the heart,
Let me see Your vengeance on them,
For to You I have revealed my cause.

"Therefore thus says the LORD concerning the men of Anathoth who seek your life, saying, 'Do not prophesy in the name of the LORD, lest you die by our hand'— therefore thus says the LORD of hosts: 'Behold, I will punish them. The young men shall die by the sword, their sons and their daughters shall die by famine; and there shall be no remnant of them, for I will bring catastrophe on the men of Anathoth, even the year of their punishment.' "

Jeremiah 11

WORSHIP

We give thanks to You, O God, we give
thanks!
For Your wondrous works declare *that* Your
name is near.

"When I choose the proper time,
I will judge uprightly.

"All the horns of the wicked I will also cut off,
But the horns of the righteous shall be
exalted."

Psalm 75:1-2, 10

WISDOM

Hell and Destruction *are* before the LORD;
So how much more the hearts of the sons of
men.

Proverbs 15:11

SW?! **SO WHAT?**
What does this tell me?

THE LESSON OF THE RUINED WAISTBAND

Jeremiah 13; Psalm 76:1-3; Proverbs 15:12

Thus the LORD said to me: "Go and get yourself a linen sash, and put it around your waist, but do not put it in water." So I got a sash according to the word of the LORD, and put *it* around my waist.

And the word of the LORD came to me the second time, saying, "Take the sash that you acquired, which *is* around your waist, and arise, go to the Euphrates, and hide it there in a hole in the rock." So I went and hid it by the Euphrates, as the LORD commanded me.

Now it came to pass after many days that the LORD said to me, "Arise, go to the Euphrates, and take from there the sash which I commanded you to hide there." Then I went to the Euphrates and dug, and I took the sash from the place where I had hidden it; and there was the sash, ruined. It was profitable for nothing.

Then the word of the LORD came to me, saying, "Thus says the LORD: 'In this manner I will ruin the pride of Judah and the great pride of Jerusalem. This evil people, who refuse to hear My words, who follow the dictates of their hearts, and walk after other gods to serve them and worship them, shall be just like this sash which is profitable for nothing. For as the sash clings to the waist of a man, so I have caused the whole house of Israel and the whole house of Judah to cling to Me,' says the LORD, 'that they may become My people, for renown, for praise, and for glory; but they would not hear.'

"Therefore you shall speak to them this word: 'Thus says the LORD God of Israel: "Every bottle shall be filled with wine." '

"And they will say to you, 'Do we not certainly know that every bottle will be filled with wine?'

"Then you shall say to them, 'Thus says the LORD: "Behold, I will fill all the inhabitants of this land—even the kings who sit on David's throne, the priests, the prophets, and all the inhabitants of Jerusalem—with drunkenness! And I will dash them one against another, even the fathers and the sons together," says the LORD. "I will not pity nor spare nor have mercy, but will destroy them." ' "

Hear and give ear:
Do not be proud,
For the LORD has spoken.
Give glory to the LORD your God
Before He causes darkness,
And before your feet stumble
On the dark mountains,
And while you are looking for light,
He turns it into the shadow of death
And makes *it* dense darkness.
But if you will not hear it,
My soul will weep in secret for *your* pride;
My eyes will weep bitterly
And run down with tears,
Because the LORD's flock has been taken
    captive.

Say to the king and to the queen mother,
"Humble yourselves;
Sit down,
For your rule shall collapse, the crown of your
    glory."
The cities of the South shall be shut up,
And no one shall open *them;*
Judah shall be carried away captive, all of it;
It shall be wholly carried away captive.

Lift up your eyes and see
Those who come from the north.
Where *is* the flock *that* was given to you,
Your beautiful sheep?
What will you say when He punishes you?
For you have taught them
To be chieftains, to be head over you.
Will not pangs seize you,
Like a woman in labor?
And if you say in your heart,
"Why have these things come upon me?"
For the greatness of your iniquity
Your skirts have been uncovered,
Your heels made bare.
Can the Ethiopian change his skin or the
    leopard its spots?
Then may you also do good who are
    accustomed to do evil.

"Therefore I will scatter them like stubble
That passes away by the wind of the wilderness.

This is your lot,
The portion of your measures from Me," says
    the LORD,
"Because you have forgotten Me
And trusted in falsehood.
Therefore I will uncover your skirts over your
    face,
That your shame may appear.
I have seen your adulteries
And your *lustful* neighings,
The lewdness of your harlotry,
Your abominations on the hills in the fields.
Woe to you, O Jerusalem!
Will you still not be made clean?"

Jeremiah 13

WORSHIP

In Judah God *is* known;
His name *is* great in Israel.
In Salem also is His tabernacle,
And His dwelling place in Zion.
There He broke the arrows of the bow,
The shield and sword of battle.   Selah

Psalm 76:1-3

WISDOM

A scoffer does not love one who corrects him,
Nor will he go to the wise.

Proverbs 15:12

SW?! **SO WHAT?**
What does this tell me?

THE LESSON OF THE POTTER AND THE CLAY

Jeremiah 18; Psalm 76:8–10; Proverbs 15:13

he word which came to Jeremiah from the LORD, saying: "Arise and go down to the potter's house, and there I will cause you to hear My words." Then I went down to the potter's house, and there he was, making something at the wheel. And the vessel that he made of clay was marred in the hand of the potter; so he made it again into another vessel, as it seemed good to the potter to make.

Then the word of the LORD came to me, saying: "O house of Israel, can I not do with you as this potter?" says the LORD. "Look, as the clay *is* in the potter's hand, so *are* you in My hand, O house of Israel! The instant I speak concerning a nation and concerning a kingdom, to pluck up, to pull down, and to destroy *it,* if that nation against whom I have spoken turns from its evil, I will relent of the disaster that I thought to bring upon it. And the instant I speak concerning a nation and concerning a kingdom, to build and to plant *it,* if it does evil in My sight so that it does not obey My voice, then I will relent concerning the good with which I said I would benefit it.

"Now therefore, speak to the men of Judah and to the inhabitants of Jerusalem, saying, 'Thus says the LORD: "Behold, I am fashioning a disaster and devising a plan against you. Return now every one from his evil way, and make your ways and your doings good." ' "

And they said, "That is hopeless! So we will walk according to our own plans, and we will every one obey the dictates of his evil heart."

Therefore thus says the LORD:

"Ask now among the Gentiles,
Who has heard such things?
The virgin of Israel has done a very
    horrible thing.
Will *a man* leave the snow water of
    Lebanon,
Which comes from the rock of the field?
Will the cold flowing waters be forsaken
    for strange waters?

"Because My people have forgotten Me,
They have burned incense to worthless idols.
And they have caused themselves to stumble
    in their ways,
From the ancient paths,
To walk in pathways and not on a highway,
To make their land desolate *and* a perpetual
    hissing;
Everyone who passes by it will be astonished
And shake his head.
I will scatter them as with an east wind before
    the enemy;
I will show them the back and not the face
In the day of their calamity."

Then they said, "Come and let us devise plans against Jeremiah; for the law shall not perish from the priest, nor counsel from the wise, nor the word from the prophet. Come and let us attack him with the tongue, and let us not give heed to any of his words."

Give heed to me, O LORD,
And listen to the voice of those who contend
    with me!
Shall evil be repaid for good?
For they have dug a pit for my life.
Remember that I stood before You
To speak good for them,
To turn away Your wrath from them.
Therefore deliver up their children to the
    famine,
And pour out their *blood*
By the force of the sword;
Let their wives *become* widows
And bereaved of their children.
Let their men be put to death,
Their young men *be* slain
By the sword in battle.
Let a cry be heard from their houses,
When You bring a troop suddenly upon them;
For they have dug a pit to take me,
And hidden snares for my feet.
Yet, LORD, You know all their counsel
Which is against me, to slay *me.*
Provide no atonement for their iniquity,
Nor blot out their sin from Your sight;
But let them be overthrown before You.

Deal *thus* with them
In the time of Your anger.

Jeremiah 18

WORSHIP

You caused judgment to be heard from
heaven;
The earth feared and was still,
When God arose to judgment,
To deliver all the oppressed of the earth.

Selah

Surely the wrath of man shall praise You;
With the remainder of wrath You shall gird
Yourself.

Psalm 76:8-10

WISDOM

A merry heart makes a cheerful countenance,
But by sorrow of the heart the spirit is broken.

Proverbs 15:13

SW?! SO WHAT?
What does this tell me?

JEREMIAH'S JAR AND COMPLAINT

Jeremiah 19–20; Psalm 77:1-2;
Proverbs 15:14

Thus says the LORD: "Go and get a potter's earthen flask, and *take* some of the elders of the people and some of the elders of the priests. And go out to the Valley of the Son of Hinnom, which *is* by the entry of the Potsherd Gate; and proclaim there the words that I will tell you, and say, 'Hear the word of the LORD, O kings of Judah and inhabitants of Jerusalem. Thus says the LORD of hosts, the God of Israel: "Behold, I will bring such a catastrophe on this place, that whoever hears of it, his ears will tingle.

"Because they have forsaken Me and made this an alien place, because they have burned incense in it to other gods whom neither they, their fathers, nor the kings of Judah have known, and have filled this place with the blood of the innocents (they have also built the high places of Baal, to burn their sons with fire *for* burnt offerings to Baal, which I did not command or speak, nor did it come into My mind), therefore behold, the days are coming," says the LORD, "that this place shall no more be called Tophet or the Valley of the Son of Hinnom, but the Valley of Slaughter. And I will make void the counsel of Judah and Jerusalem in this place, and I will cause them to fall by the sword before their enemies and by the hands of those who seek their lives; their corpses I will give as meat for the birds of the heaven and for the beasts of the earth. I will make this city desolate and a hissing; everyone who passes by it will be astonished and hiss because of all its plagues. And I will cause them to eat the flesh of their sons and the flesh of their daughters, and everyone shall eat the flesh of his friend in the siege and in the desperation with which their enemies and those who seek their lives shall drive them to despair." '

"Then you shall break the flask in the sight of the men who go with you, and say to them, 'Thus says the LORD of hosts: "Even so I will break this people and this city, as *one* breaks a potter's vessel, which cannot be made whole again; and they shall bury *them* in Tophet till *there is* no place to bury.

Thus I will do to this place," says the LORD, "and to its inhabitants, and make this city like Tophet. And the houses of Jerusalem and the houses of the kings of Judah shall be defiled like the place of Tophet, because of all the houses on whose roofs they have burned incense to all the host of heaven, and poured out drink offerings to other gods." ' "

Then Jeremiah came from Tophet, where the LORD had sent him to prophesy; and he stood in the court of the Lord's house and said to all the people, "Thus says the LORD of hosts, the God of Israel: 'Behold, I will bring on this city and on all her towns all the doom that I have pronounced against it, because they have stiffened their necks that they might not hear My words.' "

Now Pashhur the son of Immer, the priest who *was* also chief governor in the house of the LORD, heard that Jeremiah prophesied these things. Then Pashhur struck Jeremiah the prophet, and put him in the stocks that *were* in the high gate of Benjamin, which *was* by the house of the LORD.

And it happened on the next day that Pashhur brought Jeremiah out of the stocks. Then Jeremiah said to him, "The LORD has not called your name Pashhur, but Magor-Missabib. For thus says the LORD: 'Behold, I will make you a terror to yourself and to all your friends; and they shall fall by the sword of their enemies, and your eyes shall see *it*. I will give all Judah into the hand of the king of Babylon, and he shall carry them captive to Babylon and slay them with the sword. Moreover I will deliver all the wealth of this city, all its produce, and all its precious things; all the treasures of the kings of Judah I will give into the hand of their enemies, who will plunder them, seize them, and carry them to Babylon. And you, Pashhur, and all who dwell in your house, shall go into captivity. You shall go to Babylon, and there you shall die, and be buried there, you and all your friends, to whom you have prophesied lies.' "

O LORD, You induced me, and I was
  persuaded;
You are stronger than I, and have prevailed.
I am in derision daily;
Everyone mocks me.
For when I spoke, I cried out;
I shouted, "Violence and plunder!"

Because the word of the LORD was made to me
A reproach and a derision daily.
Then I said, "I will not make mention of Him,
Nor speak anymore in His name."
But *His word* was in my heart like a burning
fire
Shut up in my bones;
I was weary of holding *it* back,
And I could not.
For I heard many mocking:
"Fear on every side!"
"Report," *they say,* "and we will report it!"
All my acquaintances watched for my
stumbling, *saying,*
"Perhaps he can be induced;
Then we will prevail against him,
And we will take our revenge on him."

But the LORD *is* with me as a mighty, awesome
One.
Therefore my persecutors will stumble, and will
not prevail.
They will be greatly ashamed, for they will not
prosper.
Their everlasting confusion will never be
forgotten.
But, O LORD of hosts,
You who test the righteous,
And see the mind and heart,
Let me see Your vengeance on them;
For I have pleaded my cause before You.

Sing to the LORD! Praise the LORD!
For He has delivered the life of the poor
From the hand of evildoers.

Cursed *be* the day in which I was born!
Let the day not be blessed in which my mother
bore me!
Let the man *be* cursed
Who brought news to my father, saying,
"A male child has been born to you!"
Making him very glad.
And let that man be like the cities
Which the LORD overthrew, and did not relent;
Let him hear the cry in the morning
And the shouting at noon,
Because he did not kill me from the womb,
That my mother might have been my grave,
And her womb always enlarged *with me.*
Why did I come forth from the womb to see
labor and sorrow,
That my days should be consumed with
shame?

Jeremiah 19–20

WORSHIP

I cried out to God with my voice—
To God with my voice;
And He gave ear to me.
In the day of my trouble I sought the Lord;
My hand was stretched out in the night
without ceasing;
My soul refused to be comforted.

Psalm 77:1-2

WISDOM

The heart of him who has understanding
seeks knowledge,
But the mouth of fools feeds on foolishness.

Proverbs 15:14

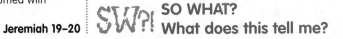

SO WHAT?
What does this tell me?

THE FALSE PROPHETS DENOUNCED

Jeremiah 23:9-40; Psalm 77:7-9; Proverbs 15:15

My heart within me is broken
Because of the prophets;
All my bones shake.
I am like a drunken man,
And like a man whom wine has overcome,
Because of the LORD,
And because of His holy words.
For the land is full of adulterers;
For because of a curse the land mourns.
The pleasant places of the wilderness are
    dried up.
Their course of life is evil,
And their might *is* not right.

"For both prophet and priest are profane;
Yes, in My house I have found their
    wickedness," says the LORD.
"Therefore their way shall be to them
Like slippery *ways;*
In the darkness they shall be driven on
And fall in them;
For I will bring disaster on them,
The year of their punishment," says the LORD.
"And I have seen folly in the prophets of
    Samaria:
They prophesied by Baal
And caused My people Israel to err.
Also I have seen a horrible thing in the
    prophets of Jerusalem:
They commit adultery and walk in lies;
They also strengthen the hands of evildoers,
So that no one turns back from his
    wickedness.
All of them are like Sodom to Me,
And her inhabitants like Gomorrah.

    "Therefore thus says the LORD of hosts
concerning the prophets:

'Behold, I will feed them with wormwood,
And make them drink the water of gall;
For from the prophets of Jerusalem
Profaneness has gone out into all the land.'"

    Thus says the LORD of hosts:

"Do not listen to the words of the prophets
    who prophesy to you.
They make you worthless;
They speak a vision of their own heart,

Not from the mouth of the LORD.
They continually say to those who despise Me,
'The LORD has said, "You shall have peace" ';
And *to* everyone who walks according to the
    dictates of his own heart, they say,
'No evil shall come upon you.' "

For who has stood in the counsel of the LORD,
And has perceived and heard His word?
Who has marked His word and heard *it*?
Behold, a whirlwind of the LORD has gone forth
    in fury—
A violent whirlwind!
It will fall violently on the head of the wicked.
The anger of the LORD will not turn back
Until He has executed and performed the
    thoughts of His heart.
In the latter days you will understand it
    perfectly.

"I have not sent these prophets, yet they ran.
I have not spoken to them, yet they
    prophesied.
But if they had stood in My counsel,
And had caused My people to hear My words,
Then they would have turned them from their
    evil way
And from the evil of their doings.

"*Am* I a God near at hand," says the LORD,
"And not a God afar off?
Can anyone hide himself in secret places,
So I shall not see him?" says the LORD;
"Do I not fill heaven and earth?" says the LORD.

    "I have heard what the prophets have said
who prophesy lies in My name, saying, 'I have
dreamed, I have dreamed!' How long will *this* be in
the heart of the prophets who prophesy lies? Indeed *they are* prophets of the deceit of their own
heart, who try to make My people forget My name
by their dreams which everyone tells his neighbor,
as their fathers forgot My name for Baal.

    "The prophet who has a dream, let him tell a
        dream;
And he who has My word, let him speak My
        word faithfully.
What *is* the chaff to the wheat?" says the LORD.
"*Is* not My word like a fire?" says the LORD,

"And like a hammer *that* breaks the rock in pieces?

"Therefore behold, I *am* against the prophets," says the LORD, "who steal My words every one from his neighbor. Behold, I *am* against the prophets," says the LORD, "who use their tongues and say, 'He says.' Behold, I *am* against those who prophesy false dreams," says the LORD, "and tell them, and cause My people to err by their lies and by their recklessness. Yet I did not send them or command them; therefore they shall not profit this people at all," says the LORD.

"So when these people or the prophet or the priest ask you, saying, 'What is the oracle of the LORD?' you shall then say to them, 'What oracle?' I will even forsake you," says the LORD. "And *as for* the prophet and the priest and the people who say, 'The oracle of the LORD!' I will even punish that man and his house. Thus every one of you shall say to his neighbor, and every one to his brother, 'What has the LORD answered?' and, 'What has the LORD spoken?' And the oracle of the LORD you shall mention no more. For every man's word will be his oracle, for you have perverted the words of the living God, the LORD of hosts, our God. Thus you shall say to the prophet, 'What has the LORD answered you?' and, 'What has the LORD spoken?' But since you say, 'The oracle of the LORD!' therefore thus says the LORD: 'Because you say this word, "The oracle of the LORD!" and I have sent to you, saying, "Do not say, 'The oracle of the LORD!'" therefore behold, I, even I, will utterly forget you and forsake you, and the city that I gave you and your fathers, and *will cast you* out of My presence. And I will bring an everlasting reproach upon you, and a perpetual shame, which shall not be forgotten.'"

Jeremiah 23:9-40

WORSHIP

Will the Lord cast off forever?
And will He be favorable no more?
Has His mercy ceased forever?
Has *His* promise failed forevermore?
Has God forgotten to be gracious?
Has He in anger shut up His tender mercies?
Selah
Psalm 77:7-9

WISDOM

All the days of the afflicted *are* evil,
But he who is of a merry heart *has* a continual feast.

Proverbs 15:15

SW?! SO WHAT?
What does this tell me?

JUDAH'S CAPTIVITY TO BABYLON

Jeremiah 24:1–25:13; Psalm 77:11-13; Proverbs 15:16

The LORD showed me, and there were two baskets of figs set before the temple of the LORD, after Nebuchadnezzar king of Babylon had carried away captive Jeconiah the son of Jehoiakim, king of Judah, and the princes of Judah with the craftsmen and smiths, from Jerusalem, and had brought them to Babylon. One basket *had* very good figs, like the figs *that are* first ripe; and the other basket *had* very bad figs which could not be eaten, they were so bad. Then the LORD said to me, "What do you see, Jeremiah?"

And I said, "Figs, the good figs, very good; and the bad, very bad, which cannot be eaten, they are so bad."

Again the word of the LORD came to me, saying, "Thus says the LORD, the God of Israel: 'Like these good figs, so will I acknowledge those who are carried away captive from Judah, whom I have sent out of this place for *their own* good, into the land of the Chaldeans. For I will set My eyes on them for good, and I will bring them back to this land; I will build them and not pull *them* down, and I will plant them and not pluck *them* up. Then I will give them a heart to know Me, that I *am* the LORD; and they shall be My people, and I will be their God, for they shall return to Me with their whole heart.

'And as the bad figs which cannot be eaten, they are so bad'—surely thus says the LORD—'so will I give up Zedekiah the king of Judah, his princes, the residue of Jerusalem who remain in this land, and those who dwell in the land of Egypt. I will deliver them to trouble into all the kingdoms of the earth, for *their* harm, *to be* a reproach and a byword, a taunt and a curse, in all places where I shall drive them. And I will send the sword, the famine, and the pestilence among them, till they are consumed from the land that I gave to them and their fathers.' "

The word that came to Jeremiah concerning all the people of Judah, in the fourth year of Jehoiakim the son of Josiah, king of Judah (which *was* the first year of Nebuchadnezzar king of Babylon), which Jeremiah the prophet spoke to all the people of Judah and to all the inhabitants of Jerusalem, saying: "From the thirteenth year of Josiah the son of Amon, king of Judah, even to this day, this *is* the twenty-third year in which the word of the LORD has come to me; and I have spoken to you, rising early and speaking, but you have not listened. And the LORD has sent to you all His servants the prophets, rising early and sending *them,* but you have not listened nor inclined your ear to hear. They said, 'Repent now everyone of his evil way and his evil doings, and dwell in the land that the LORD has given to you and your fathers forever and ever. Do not go after other gods to serve them and worship them, and do not provoke Me to anger with the works of your hands; and I will not harm you.' Yet you have not listened to Me," says the LORD, "that you might provoke Me to anger with the works of your hands to your own hurt.

"Therefore thus says the LORD of hosts: 'Because you have not heard My words, behold, I will send and take all the families of the north,' says the LORD, 'and Nebuchadnezzar the king of Babylon, My servant, and will bring them against this land, against its inhabitants, and against these nations all around, and will utterly destroy them, and make them an astonishment, a hissing, and perpetual desolations. Moreover I will take from them the voice of mirth and the voice of gladness, the voice of the bridegroom and the voice of the bride, the sound of the millstones and the light of the lamp. And this whole land shall be a desolation *and* an astonishment, and these nations shall serve the king of Babylon seventy years.

'Then it will come to pass, when seventy years are completed, *that* I will punish the king of Babylon and that nation, the land of the Chaldeans, for their iniquity,' says the LORD; 'and I will make it a perpetual desolation. So I will bring on that land all My words which I have pronounced against it, all that is written in this book, which Jeremiah has prophesied concerning all the nations.' "

Jeremiah 24:1–25:13

WORSHIP

I will remember the works of the LORD;
Surely I will remember Your wonders of old.
I will also meditate on all Your work,
And talk of Your deeds.
Your way, O God, *is* in the sanctuary;
Who *is* so great a God as *our* God?

Psalm 77:11-13

WISDOM

Better *is* a little with the fear of the LORD,
Than great treasure with trouble.

Proverbs 15:16

SW?! **SO WHAT?**
What does this tell me?

THE EXAMPLE OF THE RECHABITES

Jeremiah 35; Psalm 78:5-7; Proverbs 15:17

The word which came to Jeremiah from the LORD in the days of Jehoiakim the son of Josiah, king of Judah, saying, "Go to the house of the Rechabites, speak to them, and bring them into the house of the LORD, into one of the chambers, and give them wine to drink."

Then I took Jaazaniah the son of Jeremiah, the son of Habazziniah, his brothers and all his sons, and the whole house of the Rechabites, and I brought them into the house of the LORD, into the chamber of the sons of Hanan the son of Igdaliah, a man of God, which *was* by the chamber of the princes, above the chamber of Maaseiah the son of Shallum, the keeper of the door. Then I set before the sons of the house of the Rechabites bowls full of wine, and cups; and I said to them, "Drink wine."

But they said, "We will drink no wine, for Jonadab the son of Rechab, our father, commanded us, saying, 'You shall drink no wine, you nor your sons, forever. You shall not build a house, sow seed, plant a vineyard, nor have *any of these;* but all your days you shall dwell in tents, that you may live many days in the land where you are sojourners.' Thus we have obeyed the voice of Jonadab the son of Rechab, our father, in all that he charged us, to drink no wine all our days, we, our wives, our sons, or our daughters, nor to build ourselves houses to dwell in; nor do we have vineyard, field, or seed. But we have dwelt in tents, and have obeyed and done according to all that Jonadab our father commanded us. But it came to pass, when Nebuchadnezzar king of Babylon came up into the land, that we said, 'Come, let us go to Jerusalem for fear of the army of the Chaldeans and for fear of the army of the Syrians.' So we dwell at Jerusalem."

Then came the word of the LORD to Jeremiah, saying, "Thus says the LORD of hosts, the God of Israel: 'Go and tell the men of Judah and the inhabitants of Jerusalem, "Will you not receive instruction to obey My words?" says the LORD. "The words of Jonadab the son of Rechab, which he com-

manded his sons, not to drink wine, are performed; for to this day they drink none, and obey their father's commandment. But although I have spoken to you, rising early and speaking, you did not obey Me. I have also sent to you all My servants the prophets, rising up early and sending *them,* saying, 'Turn now everyone from his evil way, amend your doings, and do not go after other gods to serve them; then you will dwell in the land which I have given you and your fathers.' But you have not inclined your ear, nor obeyed Me. Surely the sons of Jonadab the son of Rechab have performed the commandment of their father, which he commanded them, but this people has not obeyed Me." '

"Therefore thus says the LORD God of hosts, the God of Israel: 'Behold, I will bring on Judah and on all the inhabitants of Jerusalem all the doom that I have pronounced against them; because I have spoken to them but they have not heard, and I have called to them but they have not answered.' "

And Jeremiah said to the house of the Rechabites, "Thus says the LORD of hosts, the God of Israel: 'Because you have obeyed the commandment of Jonadab your father, and kept all his precepts and done according to all that he commanded you, therefore thus says the LORD of hosts, the God of Israel: "Jonadab the son of Rechab shall not lack a man to stand before Me forever." ' "

Jeremiah 35

WORSHIP

For He established a testimony in Jacob,
And appointed a law in Israel,
Which He commanded our fathers,
That they should make them known to their
　　children;
That the generation to come might know *them*,
The children *who* would be born,
That they may arise and declare *them* to their
　　children,
That they may set their hope in God,
And not forget the works of God,
But keep His commandments.

Psalm 78:5-7

WISDOM

Better *is* a dinner of herbs where love is,
Than a fatted calf with hatred.

Proverbs 15:17

SW?! **SO WHAT?**
What does this tell me?

JEHOIAKIM'S CONTEMPT FOR GOD'S WORD

Jeremiah 36; Psalm 78:9-11; Proverbs 15:18

Now it came to pass in the fourth year of Jehoiakim the son of Josiah, king of Judah, *that* this word came to Jeremiah from the LORD, saying: "Take a scroll of a book and write on it all the words that I have spoken to you against Israel, against Judah, and against all the nations, from the day I spoke to you, from the days of Josiah even to this day. It may be that the house of Judah will hear all the adversities which I purpose to bring upon them, that everyone may turn from his evil way, that I may forgive their iniquity and their sin."

Then Jeremiah called Baruch the son of Neriah; and Baruch wrote on a scroll of a book, at the instruction of Jeremiah, all the words of the LORD which He had spoken to him. And Jeremiah commanded Baruch, saying, "I *am* confined, I cannot go into the house of the LORD. You go, therefore, and read from the scroll which you have written at my instruction, the words of the LORD, in the hearing of the people in the LORD's house on the day of fasting. And you shall also read them in the hearing of all Judah who come from their cities. It may be that they will present their supplication before the LORD, and everyone will turn from his evil way. For great *is* the anger and the fury that the LORD has pronounced against this people." And Baruch the son of Neriah did according to all that Jeremiah the prophet commanded him, reading from the book the words of the LORD in the LORD's house.

Now it came to pass in the fifth year of Jehoiakim the son of Josiah, king of Judah, in the ninth month, *that* they proclaimed a fast before the LORD to all the people in Jerusalem, and to all the people who came from the cities of Judah to Jerusalem. Then Baruch read from the book the words of Jeremiah in the house of the LORD, in the chamber of Gemariah the son of Shaphan the scribe, in the upper court at the entry of the New Gate of the LORD's house, in the hearing of all the people.

When Michaiah the son of Gemariah, the son of Shaphan, heard all the words of the LORD from the book, he then went down to the king's house, into the scribe's chamber; and there all the princes were sitting—Elishama the scribe, Delaiah the son of Shemaiah, Elnathan the son of Achbor, Gemariah the son of Shaphan, Zedekiah the son of Hananiah, and all the princes. Then Michaiah declared to them all the words that he had heard when Baruch read the book in the hearing of the people. Therefore all the princes sent Jehudi the son of Nethaniah, the son of Shelemiah, the son of Cushi, to Baruch, saying, "Take in your hand the scroll from which you have read in the hearing of the people, and come." So Baruch the son of Neriah took the scroll in his hand and came to them. And they said to him, "Sit down now, and read it in our hearing." So Baruch read *it* in their hearing.

Now it happened, when they had heard all the words, that they looked in fear from one to another, and said to Baruch, "We will surely tell the king of all these words." And they asked Baruch, saying, "Tell us now, how did you write all these words—at his instruction?"

So Baruch answered them, "He proclaimed with his mouth all these words to me, and I wrote *them* with ink in the book."

Then the princes said to Baruch, "Go and hide, you and Jeremiah; and let no one know where you are."

And they went to the king, into the court; but they stored the scroll in the chamber of Elishama the scribe, and told all the words in the hearing of the king. So the king sent Jehudi to bring the scroll, and he took it from Elishama the scribe's chamber. And Jehudi read it in the hearing of the king and in the hearing of all the princes who stood beside the king. Now the king was sitting in the winter house in the ninth month, with *a fire* burning on the hearth before him. And it happened, when Jehudi had read three or four columns, *that the king* cut it with the scribe's knife and cast *it* into the fire that *was* on the hearth, until all the scroll was consumed in the fire that *was* on the hearth. Yet they were not afraid, nor did they tear their garments, the king nor any of his servants who heard all these words. Nevertheless Elnathan, Delaiah, and Gemariah implored the king not to burn the scroll; but he would not listen to them. And the king commanded Jerahmeel the king's son, Seraiah the son of Azriel, and Shelemiah the son of Abdeel, to seize Baruch the scribe and Jeremiah the prophet, but the LORD hid them.

Now after the king had burned the scroll with the words which Baruch had written at the instruction of Jeremiah, the word of the LORD came to Jeremiah, saying: "Take yet another scroll, and write on it all the former words that were in the first scroll which Jehoiakim the king of Judah has burned. And you shall say to Jehoiakim king of Judah, 'Thus says the LORD: "You have burned this scroll, saying, 'Why have you written in it that the king of Babylon will certainly come and destroy this land, and cause man and beast to cease from here?' " Therefore thus says the LORD concerning Jehoiakim king of Judah: "He shall have no one to sit on the throne of David, and his dead body shall be cast out to the heat of the day and the frost of the night. I will punish him, his family, and his servants for their iniquity; and I will bring on them, on the inhabitants of Jerusalem, and on the men of Judah all the doom that I have pronounced against them; but they did not heed." ' "

Then Jeremiah took another scroll and gave it to Baruch the scribe, the son of Neriah, who wrote on it at the instruction of Jeremiah all the words of the book which Jehoiakim king of Judah had burned in the fire. And besides, there were added to them many similar words.

Jeremiah 36

WORSHIP

The children of Ephraim, *being* armed *and* carrying bows,
Turned back in the day of battle.
They did not keep the covenant of God;
They refused to walk in His law,
And forgot His works
And His wonders that He had shown them.

Psalm 78:9-11

WISDOM

A wrathful man stirs up strife,
But *he who is* slow to anger allays contention.

Proverbs 15:18

SW?! SO WHAT?
What does this tell me?

THE SIGN OF THE WOODEN YOKE

Jeremiah 27:1-15; 28:1-17; Psalm 78:17-20; Proverbs 15:19

In the beginning of the reign of Jehoiakim the son of Josiah, king of Judah, this word came to Jeremiah from the LORD, saying, "Thus says the LORD to me: 'Make for yourselves bonds and yokes, and put them on your neck, and send them to the king of Edom, the king of Moab, the king of the Ammonites, the king of Tyre, and the king of Sidon, by the hand of the messengers who come to Jerusalem to Zedekiah king of Judah. And command them to say to their masters, "Thus says the LORD of hosts, the God of Israel—thus you shall say to your masters: 'I have made the earth, the man and the beast that *are* on the ground, by My great power and by My outstretched arm, and have given it to whom it seemed proper to Me. And now I have given all these lands into the hand of Nebuchadnezzar the king of Babylon, My servant; and the beasts of the field I have also given him to serve him. So all nations shall serve him and his son and his son's son, until the time of his land comes; and then many nations and great kings shall make him serve them. And it shall be, *that* the nation and kingdom which will not serve Nebuchadnezzar the king of Babylon, and which will not put its neck under the yoke of the king of Babylon, that nation I will punish,' says the LORD, 'with the sword, the famine, and the pestilence, until I have consumed them by his hand. Therefore do not listen to your prophets, your diviners, your dreamers, your soothsayers, or your sorcerers, who speak to you, saying, "You shall not serve the king of Babylon." For they prophesy a lie to you, to remove you far from your land; and I will drive you out, and you will perish. But the nations that bring their necks under the yoke of the king of Babylon and serve him, I will let them remain in their own land,' says the LORD, 'and they shall till it and dwell in it.' " ' "

I also spoke to Zedekiah king of Judah according to all these words, saying, "Bring your necks under the yoke of the king of Babylon, and serve him and his people, and live! Why will you die, you and your people, by the sword, by the famine, and by the pestilence, as the LORD has spoken against the nation that will not serve the king of Babylon? Therefore do not listen to the words of the prophets who speak to you, saying, 'You shall not serve the king of Babylon,' for they prophesy a lie to you; for I have not sent them," says the LORD, "yet they prophesy a lie in My name, that I may drive you out, and that you may perish, you and the prophets who prophesy to you."

And it happened in the same year, at the beginning of the reign of Zedekiah king of Judah, in the fourth year *and* in the fifth month, *that* Hananiah the son of Azur the prophet, who *was* from Gibeon, spoke to me in the house of the LORD in the presence of the priests and of all the people, saying, "Thus speaks the LORD of hosts, the God of Israel, saying: 'I have broken the yoke of the king of Babylon. Within two full years I will bring back to this place all the vessels of the LORD's house, that Nebuchadnezzar king of Babylon took away from this place and carried to Babylon. And I will bring back to this place Jeconiah the son of Jehoiakim, king of Judah, with all the captives of Judah who went to Babylon,' says the LORD, 'for I will break the yoke of the king of Babylon.' "

Then the prophet Jeremiah spoke to the prophet Hananiah in the presence of the priests and in the presence of all the people who stood in the house of the LORD, and the prophet Jeremiah said, "Amen! The LORD do so; the LORD perform your words which you have prophesied, to bring back the vessels of the LORD's house and all who were carried away captive, from Babylon to this place. Nevertheless hear now this word that I speak in your hearing and in the hearing of all the people: The prophets who have been before me and before you of old prophesied against many countries and great kingdoms—of war and disaster and pestilence. As for the prophet who prophesies of peace, when the word of the prophet comes to pass, the prophet will be known *as* one whom the LORD has truly sent."

Then Hananiah the prophet took the yoke off the prophet Jeremiah's neck and broke it. And Hananiah spoke in the presence of all the people, saying, "Thus says the LORD: 'Even so I will break the yoke of Nebuchadnezzar king of Babylon from the neck of all nations within the space of two full years.'" And the prophet Jeremiah went his way.

Now the word of the LORD came to Jeremiah, after Hananiah the prophet had broken the yoke from the neck of the prophet Jeremiah, saying, "Go and tell Hananiah, saying, 'Thus says the LORD: "You have broken the yokes of wood, but you have made in their place yokes of iron." For thus says the LORD of hosts, the God of Israel: "I have put a yoke of iron on the neck of all these nations, that they may serve Nebuchadnezzar king of Babylon; and they shall serve him. I have given him the beasts of the field also." ' "

Then the prophet Jeremiah said to Hananiah the prophet, "Hear now, Hananiah, the LORD has not sent you, but you make this people trust in a lie. Therefore thus says the LORD: 'Behold, I will cast you from the face of the earth. This year you shall die, because you have taught rebellion against the LORD.' "

So Hananiah the prophet died the same year in the seventh month.

Jeremiah 27:1–15; 28:1–17

WORSHIP

But they sinned even more against Him
By rebelling against the Most High in the
     wilderness.
And they tested God in their heart
By asking for the food of their fancy.
Yes, they spoke against God:
They said, "Can God prepare a table in the
     wilderness?
Behold, He struck the rock,
So that the waters gushed out,
And the streams overflowed.
Can He give bread also?
Can He provide meat for His people?"

Psalm 78:17-20

WISDOM

The way of the lazy *man is* like a hedge of
     thorns,
But the way of the upright *is* a highway.

Proverbs 15:19

SW?! SO WHAT?
What does this tell me?

Jeremiah's Letter To The Exiles

Jeremiah 29; Psalm 78:21-24; Proverbs 15:20

Now these *are* the words of the letter that Jeremiah the prophet sent from Jerusalem to the remainder of the elders who were carried away captive—to the priests, the prophets, and all the people whom Nebuchadnezzar had carried away captive from Jerusalem to Babylon. (This happened after Jeconiah the king, the queen mother, the eunuchs, the princes of Judah and Jerusalem, the craftsmen, and the smiths had departed from Jerusalem.) *The letter was sent* by the hand of Elasah the son of Shaphan, and Gemariah the son of Hilkiah, whom Zedekiah king of Judah sent to Babylon, to Nebuchadnezzar king of Babylon, saying,

Thus says the LORD of hosts, the God of Israel, to all who were carried away captive, whom I have caused to be carried away from Jerusalem to Babylon:

Build houses and dwell *in them;* plant gardens and eat their fruit. Take wives and beget sons and daughters; and take wives for your sons and give your daughters to husbands, so that they may bear sons and daughters—that you may be increased there, and not diminished. And seek the peace of the city where I have caused you to be carried away captive, and pray to the LORD for it; for in its peace you will have peace. For thus says the LORD of hosts, the God of Israel: Do not let your prophets and your diviners who are in your midst deceive you, nor listen to your dreams which you cause to be dreamed. For they prophesy falsely to you in My name; I have not sent them, says the LORD.

For thus says the LORD: After seventy years are completed at Babylon, I will visit you and perform My good word toward you, and cause you to return to this place. For I know the thoughts that I think toward you, says the LORD, thoughts of peace and not of evil, to give you a future and a hope. Then

you will call upon Me and go and pray to Me, and I will listen to you. And you will seek Me and find *Me,* when you search for Me with all your heart. I will be found by you, says the LORD, and I will bring you back from your captivity; I will gather you from all the nations and from all the places where I have driven you, says the LORD, and I will bring you to the place from which I cause you to be carried away captive.

Because you have said, "The LORD has raised up prophets for us in Babylon"—therefore thus says the LORD concerning the king who sits on the throne of David, concerning all the people who dwell in this city, and concerning your brethren who have not gone out with you into captivity—thus says the LORD of hosts: Behold, I will send on them the sword, the famine, and the pestilence, and will make them like rotten figs that cannot be eaten, they are so bad. And I will pursue them with the sword, with famine, and with pestilence; and I will deliver them to trouble among all the kingdoms of the earth—to be a curse, an astonishment, a hissing, and a reproach among all the nations where I have driven them, because they have not heeded My words, says the LORD, which I sent to them by My servants the prophets, rising up early and sending *them;* neither would you heed, says the LORD. Therefore hear the word of the LORD, all you of the captivity, whom I have sent from Jerusalem to Babylon.

Thus says the LORD of hosts, the God of Israel, concerning Ahab the son of Kolaiah, and Zedekiah the son of Maaseiah, who prophesy a lie to you in My name: Behold, I will deliver them into the hand of Nebuchadnezzar king of Babylon, and he shall slay them before your eyes. And because of them a curse shall be taken up by all the captivity of Judah

WORDS FROM THE PROPHETS

who *are* in Babylon, saying, "The LORD make you like Zedekiah and Ahab, whom the king of Babylon roasted in the fire"; because they have done disgraceful things in Israel, have committed adultery with their neighbors' wives, and have spoken lying words in My name, which I have not commanded them. Indeed I know, and *am* a witness, says the LORD.

You shall also speak to Shemaiah the Nehelamite, saying, Thus speaks the LORD of hosts, the God of Israel, saying: You have sent letters in your name to all the people who *are* at Jerusalem, to Zephaniah the son of Maaseiah the priest, and to all the priests, saying, "The LORD has made you priest instead of Jehoiada the priest, so that there should be officers *in* the house of the LORD over every man *who* is demented and considers himself a prophet, that you should put him in prison and in the stocks. Now therefore, why have you not reproved Jeremiah of Anathoth who makes himself a prophet to you? For he has sent to us *in* Babylon, saying, 'This *captivity is* long; build houses and dwell *in them,* and plant gardens and eat their fruit.' "

Now Zephaniah the priest read this letter in the hearing of Jeremiah the prophet. Then the word of the LORD came to Jeremiah, saying: Send to all those in captivity, saying, Thus says the LORD concerning Shemaiah the Nehelamite: Because Shemaiah has prophesied to you, and I have not sent him, and he has caused you to trust in a lie—therefore thus says the LORD: Behold, I will punish Shemaiah the Nehelamite and his family: he shall not have anyone to dwell among this people, nor shall he see the good that I will do for My people, says the LORD, because he has taught rebellion against the LORD.

Jeremiah 29

WORSHIP

Therefore the LORD heard *this* and was furious;
So a fire was kindled against Jacob,
And anger also came up against Israel,
Because they did not believe in God,
And did not trust in His salvation.
Yet He had commanded the clouds above,
And opened the doors of heaven,
Had rained down manna on them to eat,
And given them of the bread of heaven.

Psalm 78:21-24

WISDOM

A wise son makes a father glad,
But a foolish man despises his mother.

Proverbs 15:20

SW?! SO WHAT?
What does this tell me?

GOD'S PROMISE OF A NEW COVENANT

"At the same time," says the LORD, "I will be the God of all the families of Israel, and they shall be My people."

Thus says the LORD:

"The people who survived the sword
Found grace in the wilderness—
Israel, when I went to give him rest."

The LORD has appeared of old to me, *saying:*
"Yes, I have loved you with an everlasting love;
Therefore with lovingkindness I have drawn
    you.
    Again I will build you, and you shall be
        rebuilt,
    O virgin of Israel!
    You shall again be adorned with your
        tambourines,
    And shall go forth in the dances of those
        who rejoice.
    You shall yet plant vines on the mountains
        of Samaria;
    The planters shall plant and eat *them* as
        ordinary food.
    For there shall be a day
    When the watchmen will cry on Mount
        Ephraim,
    'Arise, and let us go up *to* Zion,
    To the LORD our God.'"

    For thus says the LORD:

"Sing with gladness for Jacob,
    And shout among the chief of the nations;
    Proclaim, give praise, and say,
    'O LORD, save Your people,
    The remnant of Israel!'
    Behold, I will bring them from the north country,
    And gather them from the ends of the
        earth,
    Among them the blind and the lame,
    The woman with child
    And the one who labors with child, together;
    A great throng shall return there.
    They shall come with weeping,
    And with supplications I will lead them.
    I will cause them to walk by the rivers of
        waters,
    In a straight way in which they shall not
        stumble;
    For I am a Father to Israel,
    And Ephraim *is* My firstborn.

"Hear the word of the LORD, O nations,
    And declare *it* in the isles afar off, and say,
    'He who scattered Israel will gather him,
    And keep him as a shepherd *does* his flock.'
    For the LORD has redeemed Jacob,
    And ransomed him from the hand of one
        stronger than he.
    Therefore they shall come and sing in the
        height of Zion,
    Streaming to the goodness of the LORD—
    For wheat and new wine and oil,
    For the young of the flock and the herd;
    Their souls shall be like a well-watered
        garden,
    And they shall sorrow no more at all.

"Then shall the virgin rejoice in the dance,
    And the young men and the old, together;
    For I will turn their mourning to joy,
    Will comfort them,
    And make them rejoice rather than sorrow.
    I will satiate the soul of the priests with
        abundance,
    And My people shall be satisfied with My
        goodness, says the LORD."

Thus says the LORD:

"A voice was heard in Ramah,
    Lamentation *and* bitter weeping,
    Rachel weeping for her children,
    Refusing to be comforted for her children,
    Because they *are* no more."

Thus says the LORD:

"Refrain your voice from weeping,
    And your eyes from tears;
    For your work shall be rewarded, says the
        LORD,
    And they shall come back from the land of the
        enemy.
    There is hope in your future, says the LORD,
    That *your* children shall come back to their
        own border.

"I have surely heard Ephraim bemoaning
        himself:
    'You have chastised me, and I was chastised,
    Like an untrained bull;
    Restore me, and I will return,
    For You *are* the LORD my God.
    Surely, after my turning, I repented;

And after I was instructed, I struck myself on
    the thigh;
I was ashamed, yes, even humiliated,
Because I bore the reproach of my youth.'
Is Ephraim My dear son?
Is he a pleasant child?
For though I spoke against him,
I earnestly remember him still;
Therefore My heart yearns for him;
I will surely have mercy on him, says the LORD.

"Set up signposts,
Make landmarks;
Set your heart toward the highway,
The way in *which* you went.
Turn back, O virgin of Israel,
Turn back to these your cities.
How long will you gad about,
O you backsliding daughter?
For the LORD has created a new thing in the
    earth—
A woman shall encompass a man."

Thus says the LORD of hosts, the God of Israel:
"They shall again use this speech in the land of Judah and in its cities, when I bring back their captivity: 'The LORD bless you, O home of justice, *and* mountain of holiness!' And there shall dwell in Judah itself, and in all its cities together, farmers and those going out with flocks. For I have satiated the weary soul, and I have replenished every sorrowful soul."

After this I awoke and looked around, and my sleep was sweet to me.

"Behold, the days are coming, says the LORD, that I will sow the house of Israel and the house of Judah with the seed of man and the seed of beast. And it shall come to pass, *that* as I have watched over them to pluck up, to break down, to throw down, to destroy, and to afflict, so I will watch over them to build and to plant, says the LORD. In those days they shall say no more:

'The fathers have eaten sour grapes,
And the children's teeth are set on edge.'

But every one shall die for his own iniquity; every man who eats the sour grapes, his teeth shall be set on edge.

"Behold, the days are coming, says the LORD, when I will make a new covenant with the house of Israel and with the house of Judah— not according to the covenant that I made with their fathers in the day *that* I took them by the hand to lead them out of the land of Egypt, My covenant which they broke, though I was a husband to them, says the LORD. But this *is* the covenant that I will make with the house of Israel after those days, says the LORD: I will put My law in their minds, and write it on their hearts; and I will be their God, and they shall be My people. No more shall every man teach his neighbor, and every man his brother, saying, 'Know the LORD,' for they all shall know Me, from the least of them to the greatest of them, says the LORD. For I will forgive their iniquity, and their sin I will remember no more."

Jeremiah 31:1-34

WoRSHiP

For their heart was not steadfast with Him,
Nor were they faithful in His covenant.
But He, *being* full of compassion, forgave *their*
    iniquity,
And did not destroy *them*.
Yes, many a time He turned His anger away,
And did not stir up all His wrath;
For He remembered that they *were but* flesh,
A breath that passes away and does not come
    again.

Psalm 78:37-39

WiSDoM

Folly *is* joy *to him who is* destitute of
    discernment,
But a man of understanding walks uprightly.

Proverbs 15:21

SW?! SO WHAT?
What does this tell me?

JEREMIAH PURCHASES A FIELD

The word that came to Jeremiah from the LORD in the tenth year of Zedekiah king of Judah, which was the eighteenth year of Nebuchadnezzar. For then the king of Babylon's army besieged Jerusalem, and Jeremiah the prophet was shut up in the court of the prison, which *was in* the king of Judah's house. For Zedekiah king of Judah had shut him up, saying, "Why do you prophesy and say, 'Thus says the LORD: "Behold, I will give this city into the hand of the king of Babylon, and he shall take it; and Zedekiah king of Judah shall not escape from the hand of the Chaldeans, but shall surely be delivered into the hand of the king of Babylon, and shall speak with him face to face, and see him eye to eye; then he shall lead Zedekiah to Babylon, and there he shall be until I visit him," says the LORD; "though you fight with the Chaldeans, you shall not succeed" '?"

And Jeremiah said, "The word of the LORD came to me, saying, 'Behold, Hanamel the son of Shallum your uncle will come to you, saying, "Buy my field which *is* in Anathoth, for the right of redemption *is* yours to buy *it*." ' Then Hanamel my uncle's son came to me in the court of the prison according to the word of the LORD, and said to me, 'Please buy my field that *is* in Anathoth, which *is* in the country of Benjamin; for the right of inheritance *is* yours, and the redemption yours; buy *it* for yourself.' Then I knew that this was the word of the LORD. So I bought the field from Hanamel, the son of my uncle who *was* in Anathoth, and weighed *out to* him the money—seventeen shekels of silver. And I signed the deed and sealed *it*, took witnesses, and weighed the money on the scales. So I took the purchase deed, *both* that which was sealed *according* to the law and custom, and that which was open; and I gave the purchase deed to Baruch the son of Neriah, son of Mahseiah, in the presence of Hanamel my uncle's *son,* and in the presence of the witnesses who signed the purchase deed, before all the Jews who sat in the court of the prison.

"Then I charged Baruch before them, saying, 'Thus says the LORD of hosts, the God of Israel: "Take these deeds, both this purchase deed which is sealed and this deed which is open, and put them in an earthen vessel, that they may last many days." For thus says the LORD of hosts, the God of Israel: "Houses and fields and vineyards shall be possessed again in this land." '

"Now when I had delivered the purchase deed to Baruch the son of Neriah, I prayed to the LORD, saying: 'Ah, Lord GOD! Behold, You have made the heavens and the earth by Your great power and outstretched arm. There is nothing too hard for You. *You* show lovingkindness to thousands, and repay the iniquity of the fathers into the bosom of their children after them—the Great, the Mighty God, whose name *is* the LORD of hosts. *You are* great in counsel and mighty in work, for your eyes *are* open to all the ways of the sons of men, to give everyone according to his ways and according to the fruit of his doings. You have set signs and wonders in the land of Egypt, to this day, and in Israel and among *other* men; and You have made Yourself a name, as it is this day. You have brought Your people Israel out of the land of Egypt with signs and wonders, with a strong hand and an outstretched arm, and with great terror; You have given them this land, of which You swore to their fathers to give them—"a land flowing with milk and honey." And they came in and took possession of it, but they have not obeyed Your voice or walked in Your law. They have done nothing of all that You commanded them to do; therefore You have caused all this calamity to come upon them.

'Look, the siege mounds! They have come to the city to take it; and the city has been given into the hand of the Chaldeans who fight against it, because of the sword and famine and pestilence. What You have spoken has happened; there You see *it*! And You have said to me, O Lord GOD, "Buy the field for money, and take witnesses"!—yet the city has been given into the hand of the Chaldeans.' "

Then the word of the LORD came to Jeremiah, saying, "Behold, I *am* the LORD, the God of all flesh. Is there anything too hard for Me? Therefore thus says the LORD: 'Behold, I will give this city into the hand of the Chaldeans, into the hand of Nebuchadnezzar king of Babylon, and he shall take it. And the Chaldeans who fight against this city shall come and set fire to this city and burn it, with the houses on whose roofs they have offered incense to Baal and poured out drink offerings to other gods, to provoke Me to anger; because the children of Israel and the children of Judah have done only evil before Me from their youth. For the children of Israel have provoked Me only to anger with the work of their hands,' says the LORD. 'For this city has been to Me *a provocation of* My anger and My fury from the day that they built it, even to this day; so I will remove it from before My face because of all the evil of the children of Israel and the children of Judah, which they have done to provoke Me to anger—they, their kings, their princes, their priests, their prophets, the men of Judah, and the inhabitants of Jerusalem. And they have turned to Me the back, and not the face; though I taught them, rising up early and teaching *them,* yet they have not listened to receive instruction. But they set their abominations in the house which is called by My name, to defile it. And they built the high places of Baal which *are* in the Valley of the Son of Hinnom, to cause their sons and their daughters to pass through *the fire* to Molech, which I did not command them, nor did it come into My mind that they should do this abomination, to cause Judah to sin.' "

Jeremiah 32:1-35

WORSHIP

How often they provoked Him in the
  wilderness,
And grieved Him in the desert!
Yes, again and again they tempted God,
And limited the Holy One of Israel.
They did not remember His power:
The day when He redeemed them from the
  enemy.

Psalm 78:40-42

WISDOM

Without counsel, plans go awry,
But in the multitude of counselors they are
  established.

Proverbs 15:22

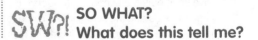

SO WHAT?
What does this tell me?

RESTORATION AFTER JUDGMENT

Jeremiah 32:36–33:26; Psalm 78:52-53; Proverbs 15:23

"Now therefore, thus says the LORD, the God of Israel, concerning this city of which you say, 'It shall be delivered into the hand of the king of Babylon by the sword, by the famine, and by the pestilence: Behold, I will gather them out of all countries where I have driven them in My anger, in My fury, and in great wrath; I will bring them back to this place, and I will cause them to dwell safely. They shall be My people, and I will be their God; then I will give them one heart and one way, that they may fear Me forever, for the good of them and their children after them. And I will make an everlasting covenant with them, that I will not turn away from doing them good; but I will put My fear in their hearts so that they will not depart from Me. Yes, I will rejoice over them to do them good, and I will assuredly plant them in this land, with all My heart and with all My soul.'

"For thus says the LORD: 'Just as I have brought all this great calamity on this people, so I will bring on them all the good that I have promised them. And fields will be bought in this land of which you say, "It is desolate, without man or beast; it has been given into the hand of the Chaldeans." Men will buy fields for money, sign deeds and seal *them,* and take witnesses, in the land of Benjamin, in the places around Jerusalem, in the cities of Judah, in the cities of the mountains, in the cities of the lowland, and in the cities of the South; for I will cause their captives to return,' says the LORD."

Moreover the word of the LORD came to Jeremiah a second time, while he was still shut up in the court of the prison, saying, "Thus says the LORD who made it, the LORD who formed it to establish it (the LORD *is* His name): 'Call to Me, and I will answer you, and show you great and mighty things, which you do not know.'

"For thus says the LORD, the God of Israel, concerning the houses of this city and the houses of the kings of Judah, which have been pulled down *to fortify* against the siege mounds and the sword: 'They come to fight with the Chaldeans, but *only* to fill their

places with the dead bodies of men whom I will slay in My anger and My fury, all for whose wickedness I have hidden My face from this city. Behold, I will bring it health and healing; I will heal them and reveal to them the abundance of peace and truth. And I will cause the captives of Judah and the captives of Israel to return, and will rebuild those places as at the first. I will cleanse them from all their iniquity by which they have sinned against Me, and I will pardon all their iniquities by which they have sinned and by which they have transgressed against Me. Then it shall be to Me a name of joy, a praise, and an honor before all nations of the earth, who shall hear all the good that I do to them; they shall fear and tremble for all the goodness and all the prosperity that I provide for it.'

"Thus says the LORD: 'Again there shall be heard in this place—of which you say, "It *is* desolate, without man and without beast"—in the cities of Judah, in the streets of Jerusalem that are desolate, without man and without inhabitant and without beast, the voice of joy and the voice of gladness, the voice of the bridegroom and the voice of the bride, the voice of those who will say:

"Praise the LORD of hosts,
 For the LORD *is* good,
 For His mercy *endures* forever"—

and of those *who will* bring the sacrifice of praise into the house of the LORD. For I will cause the captives of the land to return as at the first,' says the LORD.

"Thus says the LORD of hosts: 'In this place which is desolate, without man and without beast, and in all its cities, there shall again be a dwelling place of shepherds causing *their* flocks to lie down. In the cities of the mountains, in the cities of the lowland, in the cities of the South, in the land of Benjamin, in the places around Jerusalem, and in the cities of Judah, the flocks shall again pass under the hands of him who counts *them,*' says the LORD.

'Behold, the days are coming,' says the LORD, 'that I will perform that good thing which I have promised to the house of Israel and to the house of Judah:

'In those days and at that time
 I will cause to grow up to David

A Branch of righteousness;
He shall execute judgment and righteousness
in the earth.
In those days Judah will be saved,
And Jerusalem will dwell safely.
And this *is the name* by which she will be
called:

THE LORD OUR RIGHTEOUSNESS.'

"For thus says the LORD: 'David shall never lack a man to sit on the throne of the house of Israel; nor shall the priests, the Levites, lack a man to offer burnt offerings before Me, to kindle grain offerings, and to sacrifice continually.' "

And the word of the LORD came to Jeremiah, saying, "Thus says the LORD: 'If you can break My covenant with the day and My covenant with the night, so that there will not be day and night in their season, then My covenant may also be broken with David My servant, so that he shall not have a son to reign on his throne, and with the Levites, the priests, My ministers. As the host of heaven cannot be numbered, nor the sand of the sea measured, so will I multiply the descendants of David My servant and the Levites who minister to Me.' "

Moreover the word of the LORD came to Jeremiah, saying, "Have you not considered what these people have spoken, saying, 'The two families which the LORD has chosen, He has also cast them off'? Thus they have despised My people, as if they should no more be a nation before them.

"Thus says the LORD: 'If My covenant *is* not with day and night, *and if* I have not appointed the ordinances of heaven and earth, then I will cast away the descendants of Jacob and David My servant, *so* that I will not take *any* of his descendants *to be* rulers over the descendants of Abraham, Isaac, and Jacob. For I will cause their captives to return, and will have mercy on them.' "

Jeremiah 32:36–33:26

WORSHIP

But He made His own people go forth like
sheep,
And guided them in the wilderness like a flock;
And He led them on safely, so that they did not
fear;
But the sea overwhelmed their enemies.

Psalm 78:52-53

WISDOM

A man has joy by the answer of his mouth,
And a word *spoken* in due season, how good
it is!

Proverbs 15:23

SW?! SO WHAT?
What does this tell me?

JEREMIAH'S LAST MEETING WITH ZEDEKIAH

Jeremiah 38; Psalm 78:54-56; Proverbs 15:24

Now Shephatiah the son of Mattan, Gedaliah the son of Pashhur, Jucal the son of Shelemiah, and Pashhur the son of Malchiah heard the words that Jeremiah had spoken to all the people, saying, "Thus says the LORD: 'He who remains in this city shall die by the sword, by famine, and by pestilence; but he who goes over to the Chaldeans shall live; his life shall be as a prize to him, and he shall live.' Thus says the LORD: 'This city shall surely be given into the hand of the king of Babylon's army, which shall take it.' "

Therefore the princes said to the king, "Please, let this man be put to death, for thus he weakens the hands of the men of war who remain in this city, and the hands of all the people, by speaking such words to them. For this man does not seek the welfare of this people, but their harm."

Then Zedekiah the king said, "Look, he *is* in your hand. For the king can *do* nothing against you." So they took Jeremiah and cast him into the dungeon of Malchiah the king's son, which *was* in the court of the prison, and they let Jeremiah down with ropes. And in the dungeon *there was* no water, but mire. So Jeremiah sank in the mire.

Now Ebed-Melech the Ethiopian, one of the eunuchs, who was in the king's house, heard that they had put Jeremiah in the dungeon. When the king was sitting at the Gate of Benjamin, Ebed-Melech went out of the king's house and spoke to the king, saying: "My lord the king, these men have done evil in all that they have done to Jeremiah the prophet, whom they have cast into the dungeon, and he is likely to die from hunger in the place where he is. For *there is* no more bread in the city." Then the king commanded Ebed-Melech the Ethiopian, saying, "Take from here thirty men with you, and lift Jeremiah the prophet out of the dungeon before he dies." So Ebed-Melech took the men with him and went into the house of the king under the treasury, and took from there old clothes and old rags, and let them down by ropes into the dungeon to Jeremiah. Then

Ebed-Melech the Ethiopian said to Jeremiah, "Please put these old clothes and rags under your armpits, under the ropes." And Jeremiah did so. So they pulled Jeremiah up with ropes and lifted him out of the dungeon. And Jeremiah remained in the court of the prison.

Then Zedekiah the king sent and had Jeremiah the prophet brought to him at the third entrance of the house of the LORD. And the king said to Jeremiah, "I will ask you something. Hide nothing from me."

Jeremiah said to Zedekiah, "If I declare *it* to you, will you not surely put me to death? And if I give you advice, you will not listen to me."

So Zedekiah the king swore secretly to Jeremiah, saying, "*As* the LORD lives, who made our very souls, I will not put you to death, nor will I give you into the hand of these men who seek your life."

Then Jeremiah said to Zedekiah, "Thus says the LORD, the God of hosts, the God of Israel: 'If you surely surrender to the king of Babylon's princes, then your soul shall live; this city shall not be burned with fire, and you and your house shall live. But if you do not surrender to the king of Babylon's princes, then this city shall be given into the hand of the Chaldeans; they shall burn it with fire, and you shall not escape from their hand.' "

And Zedekiah the king said to Jeremiah, "I am afraid of the Jews who have defected to the Chaldeans, lest they deliver me into their hand, and they abuse me."

But Jeremiah said, "They shall not deliver *you*. Please, obey the voice of the LORD which I speak to you. So it shall be well with you, and your soul shall live. But if you refuse to surrender, this *is* the word that the LORD has shown me: 'Now behold, all the women who are left in the king of Judah's house *shall be* surrendered to the king of Babylon's princes, and those *women* shall say:

"Your close friends have set upon you
And prevailed against you;
Your feet have sunk in the mire,
And they have turned away again."

'So they shall surrender all your wives and children to the Chaldeans. You shall not escape from their hand, but shall be taken by the hand of the king of Babylon. And you shall cause this city to be burned with fire.' "

Then Zedekiah said to Jeremiah, "Let no one know of these words, and you shall not die. But if the princes hear that I have talked with you, and they come to you and say to you, 'Declare to us now what you have said to the king, and also what the king said to you; do not hide *it* from us, and we will not put you to death,' then you shall say to them, 'I presented my request before the king, that he would not make me return to Jonathan's house to die there.' "

Then all the princes came to Jeremiah and asked him. And he told them according to all these words that the king had commanded. So they stopped speaking with him, for the conversation had not been heard. Now Jeremiah remained in the court of the prison until the day that Jerusalem was taken. And he was *there* when Jerusalem was taken.

Jeremiah 38

WORSHIP

And He brought them to His holy border,
This mountain *which* His right hand had
　　acquired.
He also drove out the nations before them,
Allotted them an inheritance by survey,
And made the tribes of Israel dwell in their
　　tents.
Yet they tested and provoked the Most High
　　God,
And did not keep His testimonies.

Psalm 78:54-56

WISDOM

The way of life *winds* upward for the wise,
That he may turn away from hell below.

Proverbs 15:24

SW?! SO WHAT?
What does this tell me?

THE CAPTURE OF JERUSALEM AND BURNING OF THE TEMPLE

Jeremiah 39:1-18; 52:12-23; Psalm 78:70-72; Proverbs 15:25

In the ninth year of Zedekiah king of Judah, in the tenth month, Nebuchadnezzar king of Babylon and all his army came against Jerusalem, and besieged it. In the eleventh year of Zedekiah, in the fourth month, on the ninth *day* of the month, the city was penetrated.

Then all the princes of the king of Babylon came in and sat in the Middle Gate: Nergal-Sharezer, Samgar-Nebo, Sarsechim, Rabsaris, Nergal-Sarezer, Rabmag, with the rest of the princes of the king of Babylon.

So it was, when Zedekiah the king of Judah and all the men of war saw them, that they fled and went out of the city by night, by way of the king's garden, by the gate between the two walls. And he went out by way of the plain. But the Chaldean army pursued them and overtook Zedekiah in the plains of Jericho. And when they had captured him, they brought him up to Nebuchadnezzar king of Babylon, to Riblah in the land of Hamath, where he pronounced judgment on him. Then the king of Babylon killed the sons of Zedekiah before his eyes in Riblah; the king of Babylon also killed all the nobles of Judah. Moreover he put out Zedekiah's eyes, and bound him with bronze fetters to carry him off to Babylon. And the Chaldeans burned the king's house and the houses of the people with fire, and broke down the walls of Jerusalem. Then Nebuzaradan the captain of the guard carried away captive to Babylon the remnant of the people who remained in the city and those who defected to him, with the rest of the people who remained. But Nebuzaradan the captain of the guard left in the land of Judah the poor people, who had nothing, and gave them vineyards and fields at the same time.

Now Nebuchadnezzar king of Babylon gave charge concerning Jeremiah to Nebuzaradan the captain of the guard, saying, "Take him and look after him, and do him no harm; but do to him just as he says to you." So Nebuzaradan the captain of the guard sent Nebushasban, Rabsaris, Nergal-Sharezer, Rabmag, and all the king of Babylon's chief officers; then they sent *someone* to take Jeremiah from the court of the prison, and committed him to Gedaliah the son of Ahikam, the son of Shaphan, that he should take him home. So he dwelt among the people.

Meanwhile the word of the Lord had come to Jeremiah while he was shut up in the court of the prison, saying, "Go and speak to Ebed-Melech the Ethiopian, saying, 'Thus says the Lord of hosts, the God of Israel: "Behold, I will bring My words upon this city for adversity and not for good, and they shall be *performed* in that day before you. But I will deliver you in that day," says the Lord, "and you shall not be given into the hand of the men of whom you *are* afraid. For I will surely deliver you, and you shall not fall by the sword; but your life shall be as a prize to you, because you have put your trust in Me," says the Lord.' "

Now in the fifth month, on the tenth *day* of the month (which *was* the nineteenth year of King Nebuchadnezzar king of Babylon), Nebuzaradan, the captain of the guard, *who* served the king of Babylon, came to Jerusalem. He burned the house of the Lord and the king's house; all the houses of Jerusalem, that is, all the houses of the great, he burned with fire. And all the army of the Chaldeans who *were* with the captain of the guard broke down all the walls of Jerusalem all around. Then Nebuzaradan the captain of the guard carried away captive *some* of the poor people, the rest of the people who remained in the city, the defectors who had deserted to the king of Babylon, and the rest of the craftsmen. But Nebuzaradan the captain of the guard left *some* of the poor of the land as vinedressers and farmers.

The bronze pillars that *were* in the house of the Lord, and the carts and the bronze Sea that *were* in the house of the Lord, the Chaldeans broke in pieces, and carried all their bronze to Babylon. They also took away the pots, the shovels, the trimmers, the bowls, the spoons, and all the bronze utensils with which the priests ministered. The basins, the firepans, the bowls, the pots, the lampstands, the spoons, and the cups, whatever *was* solid gold and whatever *was* solid silver, the captain of the guard took away. The two pillars, one Sea, the twelve bronze bulls which *were* under *it, and* the carts, which King Solomon had made for the house of the LORD—the bronze of all these articles was beyond measure. Now *concerning* the pillars: the height of one pillar *was* eighteen cubits, a measuring line of twelve cubits could measure its circumference, and its thickness *was* four fingers; *it was* hollow. A capital of bronze *was* on it; and the height of one capital *was* five cubits, with a network and pomegranates all around the capital, all of bronze. The second pillar, with pomegranates was the same. There were ninety-six pomegranates on the sides; all the pomegranates, all around on the network, *were* one hundred.

Jeremiah 39:1-18; 52:12-23

WORSHIP

He also chose David His servant,
And took him from the sheepfolds;
From following the ewes that had young He
  brought him,
To shepherd Jacob His people,
And Israel His inheritance.
So he shepherded them according to the
  integrity of his heart,
And guided them by the skillfulness of his
  hands.

Psalm 78:70-72

WISDOM

The LORD will destroy the house of the proud,
But He will establish the boundary of the
  widow.

Proverbs 15:25

SW?! **SO WHAT?**
What does this tell me?

GOVERNOR GEDALIAH KILLED

Jeremiah 40:7–41:18; Psalm 79:8-10; Proverbs 15:26

And when all the captains of the armies who *were* in the fields, they and their men, heard that the king of Babylon had made Gedaliah the son of Ahikam governor in the land, and had committed to him men, women, children, and the poorest of the land who had not been carried away captive to Babylon, then they came to Gedaliah at Mizpah—Ishmael the son of Nethaniah, Johanan and Jonathan the sons of Kareah, Seraiah the son of Tanhumeth, the sons of Ephai the Netophathite, and Jezaniah the son of a Maachathite, they and their men. And Gedaliah the son of Ahikam, the son of Shaphan, took an oath before them and their men, saying, "Do not be afraid to serve the Chaldeans. Dwell in the land and serve the king of Babylon, and it shall be well with you. As for me, I will indeed dwell at Mizpah and serve the Chaldeans who come to us. But you, gather wine and summer fruit and oil, put *them* in your vessels, and dwell in your cities that you have taken." Likewise, when all the Jews who *were* in Moab, among the Ammonites, in Edom, and who *were* in all the countries, heard that the king of Babylon had left a remnant of Judah, and that he had set over them Gedaliah the son of Ahikam, the son of Shaphan, then all the Jews returned out of all places where they had been driven, and came to the land of Judah, to Gedaliah at Mizpah, and gathered wine and summer fruit in abundance.

Moreover Johanan the son of Kareah and all the captains of the forces that *were* in the fields came to Gedaliah at Mizpah, and said to him, "Do you certainly know that Baalis the king of the Ammonites has sent Ishmael the son of Nethaniah to murder you?" But Gedaliah the son of Ahikam did not believe them.

Then Johanan the son of Kareah spoke secretly to Gedaliah in Mizpah, saying, "Let me go, please, and I will kill Ishmael the son of Nethaniah, and no one will know *it*. Why should he murder you, so that all the Jews who are gathered to you would be scattered, and the remnant in Judah perish?" But Gedaliah the son of Ahikam said to Johanan the son of Kareah, "You shall not do this thing, for you speak falsely concerning Ishmael."

Now it came to pass in the seventh month *that* Ishmael the son of Nethaniah, the son of Elishama, of the royal family and of the officers of the king, came with ten men to Gedaliah the son of Ahikam, at Mizpah. And there they ate bread together in Mizpah. Then Ishmael the son of Nethaniah, and the ten men who were with him, arose and struck Gedaliah the son of Ahikam, the son of Shaphan, with the sword, and killed him whom the king of Babylon had made governor over the land. Ishmael also struck down all the Jews who were with him, *that is,* with Gedaliah at Mizpah, and the Chaldeans who were found there, the men of war.

And it happened, on the second day after he had killed Gedaliah, when as yet no one knew *it,* that certain men came from Shechem, from Shiloh, and from Samaria, eighty men with their beards shaved and their clothes torn, having cut themselves, with offerings and incense in their hand, to bring *them* to the house of the LORD. Now Ishmael the son of Nethaniah went out from Mizpah to meet them, weeping as he went along; and it happened as he met them that he said to them, "Come to Gedaliah the son of Ahikam!" So it was, when they came into the midst of the city, that Ishmael the son of Nethaniah killed them *and cast them* into the midst of a pit, he and the men who were with him. But ten men were found among them who said to Ishmael, "Do not kill us, for we have treasures of wheat, barley, oil, and honey in the field." So he desisted and did not kill them among their brethren. Now the pit into which Ishmael had cast all the dead bodies of the men whom he had slain, because of Gedaliah, *was* the same one Asa the king had made for fear of Baasha king of Israel. Ishmael the son of Nethaniah filled it with *the* slain. Then Ishmael carried away captive all the rest of the people who *were* in Mizpah, the king's daughters and all the people who remained in Mizpah, whom Nebuzaradan the captain of the guard had committed to Gedaliah the son of Ahikam. And Ishmael the son of Nethaniah carried them away captive and departed to go over to the Ammonites.

But when Johanan the son of Kareah and all the captains of the forces that *were* with him heard of all the evil that Ishmael the son of Nethaniah had done, they took all the men and went to fight with Ishmael the son of Nethaniah; and they found him by the great pool that *is* in Gibeon. So it was, when all the people who *were* with Ishmael saw Johanan the son of Kareah, and all the captains of the forces who *were* with him, that they were glad. Then all the people whom Ishmael had carried away captive from Mizpah turned around and came back, and went to Johanan the son of Kareah. But Ishmael the son of Nethaniah escaped from Johanan with eight men and went to the Ammonites.

Then Johanan the son of Kareah, and all the captains of the forces that were with him, took from Mizpah all the rest of the people whom he had recovered from Ishmael the son of Nethaniah after he had murdered Gedaliah the son of Ahikam—the mighty men of war and the women and the children and the eunuchs, whom he had brought back from Gibeon. And they departed and dwelt in the habitation of Chimham, which is near Bethlehem, as they went on their way to Egypt, because of the Chaldeans; for they were afraid of them, because Ishmael the son of Nethaniah had murdered Gedaliah the son of Ahikam, whom the king of Babylon had made governor in the land.

Jeremiah 40:7–41:18

WoRSHiP

Oh, do not remember former iniquities
    against us!
Let Your tender mercies come speedily to
    meet us,
For we have been brought very low.
Help us, O God of our salvation,
For the glory of Your name;
And deliver us, and provide atonement for
    our sins,
For Your name's sake!
Why should the nations say,
"Where *is* their God?"
Let there be known among the nations in our
    sight
The avenging of the blood of Your servants
    which has been shed.

Psalm 79:8-10

WiSDoM

The thoughts of the wicked *are* an
    abomination to the LORD,
But *the words* of the pure *are* pleasant.

Proverbs 15:26

SW?! **SO WHAT?**
What does this tell me?

JEREMIAH TAKEN TO EGYPT

Jeremiah 42:1–43:7; Psalm 79:11-13; Proverbs 15:27

Now all the captains of the forces, Johanan the son of Kareah, Jezaniah the son of Hoshaiah, and all the people, from the least to the greatest, came near and said to Jeremiah the prophet, "Please, let our petition be acceptable to you, and pray for us to the LORD your God, for all this remnant (since we are left *but* a few of many, as you can see), that the LORD your God may show us the way in which we should walk and the thing we should do."

Then Jeremiah the prophet said to them, "I have heard. Indeed, I will pray to the LORD your God according to your words, and it shall be, *that* whatever the LORD answers you, I will declare *it* to you. I will keep nothing back from you."

So they said to Jeremiah, "Let the LORD be a true and faithful witness between us, if we do not do according to everything which the LORD your God sends us by you. Whether *it is* pleasing or displeasing, we will obey the voice of the LORD our God to whom we send you, that it may be well with us when we obey the voice of the LORD our God."

And it happened after ten days that the word of the LORD came to Jeremiah. Then he called Johanan the son of Kareah, all the captains of the forces which *were* with him, and all the people from the least even to the greatest, and said to them, "Thus says the LORD, the God of Israel, to whom you sent me to present your petition before Him: 'If you will still remain in this land, then I will build you and not pull *you* down, and I will plant you and not pluck *you* up. For I relent concerning the disaster that I have brought upon you. Do not be afraid of the king of Babylon, of whom you are afraid; do not be afraid of him,' says the LORD, 'for I *am* with you, to save you and deliver you from his hand. And I will show you mercy, that he may have mercy on you and cause you to return to your own land.'

"But if you say, 'We will not dwell in this land,' disobeying the voice of the LORD your God, saying, 'No, but we will go to the land of Egypt where we shall see no war, nor hear the sound of the trumpet, nor be hungry for bread, and there we will dwell'— Then hear now the word of the LORD, O remnant of Judah! Thus says the LORD of hosts, the God of Israel: 'If you wholly set your faces to enter Egypt, and go to dwell there, then it shall be *that* the sword which you feared shall overtake you there in the land of Egypt; the famine of which you were afraid shall follow close after you there *in* Egypt; and there you shall die. So shall it be with all the men who set their faces to go to Egypt to dwell there. They shall die by the sword, by famine, and by pestilence. And none of them shall remain or escape from the disaster that I will bring upon them.'

"For thus says the LORD of hosts, the God of Israel: 'As My anger and My fury have been poured out on the inhabitants of Jerusalem, so will My fury be poured out on you when you enter Egypt. And you shall be an oath, an astonishment, a curse, and a reproach; and you shall see this place no more.'

"The LORD has said concerning you, O remnant of Judah, 'Do not go to Egypt!' Know certainly that I have admonished you this day. For you were hypocrites in your hearts when you sent me to the LORD your God, saying, 'Pray for us to the LORD our God, and according to all that the LORD your God says, so declare to us and we will do *it*.' And I have this day declared *it* to you, but you have not obeyed the voice of the LORD your God, or anything which He has sent you by me. Now therefore, know certainly that you shall die by the sword, by famine, and by pestilence in the place where you desire to go to dwell."

Now it happened, when Jeremiah had stopped speaking to all the people all the words of the LORD their God, for which the LORD their God had sent him to them, all these words, that Azariah the son of Hoshaiah, Johanan the son of Kareah, and all the proud men spoke, saying to Jeremiah, "You speak falsely! The LORD our God has not sent you to say, 'Do not go to Egypt to dwell there.' But Baruch the son of Neriah has set you against us, to deliver us into the hand of the Chaldeans, that they may put us to death or carry us away captive to Babylon." So Johanan the son of Kareah, all the captains of the forces, and all the people would not obey the voice of the LORD, to remain in the land of Judah. But Johanan the son of Kareah and all the captains of the forces took all the remnant of Judah who had returned to dwell in the land of Judah, from all nations where they had been driven— men, women, children, the king's daughters, and every person whom Nebuzaradan the captain of the guard had left with Gedaliah the son of Ahikam, the son of Shaphan, and Jeremiah the prophet and Baruch the son of Neriah. So they went to the land of Egypt, for they did not obey the voice of the LORD. And they went as far as Tahpanhes.

Jeremiah 42:1–43:7

WORSHIP

Let the groaning of the prisoner come before
   You;
According to the greatness of Your power
Preserve those who are appointed to die;
And return to our neighbors sevenfold into
   their bosom
Their reproach with which they have
   reproached You, O Lord.

So we, Your people and sheep of Your
   pasture,
Will give You thanks forever;
We will show forth Your praise to all
   generations.

Psalm 79:11-13

WISDOM

He who is greedy for gain troubles his own
   house,
But he who hates bribes will live.

Proverbs 15:27

SW?! **SO WHAT?**
What does this tell me?

JEREMIAH PREDICTS THE CONQUEST OF EGYPT
Jeremiah 44; Psalm 80:1-3; Proverbs 15:28

The word that came to Jeremiah concerning all the Jews who dwell in the land of Egypt, who dwell at Migdol, at Tahpanhes, at Noph, and in the country of Pathros, saying, "Thus says the LORD of hosts, the God of Israel: 'You have seen all the calamity that I have brought on Jerusalem and on all the cities of Judah; and behold, this day they *are* a desolation, and no one dwells in them, because of their wickedness which they have committed to provoke Me to anger, in that they went to burn incense *and* to serve other gods whom they did not know, they nor you nor your fathers. However I have sent to you all My servants the prophets, rising early and sending *them*, saying, "Oh, do not do this abominable thing that I hate!" But they did not listen or incline their ear to turn from their wickedness, to burn no incense to other gods. So My fury and My anger were poured out and kindled in the cities of Judah and in the streets of Jerusalem; and they are wasted *and* desolate, as it is this day.'

"Now therefore, thus says the LORD, the God of hosts, the God of Israel: 'Why do you commit *this* great evil against yourselves, to cut off from you man and woman, child and infant, out of Judah, leaving none to remain, in that you provoke Me to wrath with the works of your hands, burning incense to other gods in the land of Egypt where you have gone to dwell, that you may cut yourselves off and be a curse and a reproach among all the nations of the earth? Have you forgotten the wickedness of your fathers, the wickedness of the kings of Judah, the wickedness of their wives, your own wickedness, and the wickedness of your wives, which they committed in the land of Judah and in the streets of Jerusalem? They have not been humbled, to this day, nor have they feared; they have not walked in My law or in My statutes that I set before you and your fathers.'

"Therefore thus says the LORD of hosts, the God of Israel: 'Behold, I will set My face against you for catastrophe and for cutting off all Judah. And I will take the remnant of Judah who have set their faces to go into the land of Egypt to dwell there, and they shall all be consumed *and* fall in the land of Egypt. They shall be consumed by the sword *and* by famine. They shall die, from the least to the greatest, by the sword and by famine; and they shall be an oath, an astonishment, a curse and a reproach! For I will punish those who dwell in the land of Egypt, as I have punished Jerusalem, by the sword, by famine, and by pestilence, so that none of the remnant of Judah who have gone into the land of Egypt to dwell there shall escape or survive, lest they return to the land of Judah, to which they desire to return and dwell. For none shall return except those who escape.' "

Then all the men who knew that their wives had burned incense to other gods, with all the women who stood by, a great multitude, and all the people who dwelt in the land of Egypt, in Pathros, answered Jeremiah, saying: "*As for* the word that you have spoken to us in the name of the LORD, we will not listen to you! But we will certainly do whatever has gone out of our own mouth, to burn incense to the queen of heaven and pour out drink offerings to her, as we have done, we and our fathers, our kings and our princes, in the cities of Judah and in the streets of Jerusalem. For *then* we had plenty of food, were well-off, and saw no trouble. But since we stopped burning incense to the queen of heaven and pouring out drink offerings to her, we have lacked everything and have been consumed by the sword and by famine."

The women also said, "And when we burned incense to the queen of heaven and poured out drink offerings to her, did we make cakes for her, to worship her, and pour out drink offerings to her without our husbands' *permission*?"

Then Jeremiah spoke to all the people—the men, the women, and all the people who had given him *that* answer—saying: "The incense that you burned in the cities of Judah and in the streets of Jerusalem, you and your fathers, your kings and your princes, and the people of the land, did not the LORD remember them, and did it *not* come into His mind? So the LORD could no longer bear *it*, because of the evil of your doings *and* because of the abominations which you committed. Therefore your land is a desolation, an astonishment, a curse, and without an inhabitant, as *it is* this day. Because you have burned incense and because you have sinned against the LORD, and have not obeyed the voice of the LORD or walked in His law, in His statutes or in His testimonies, therefore this calamity has happened to you, as *at* this day."

Moreover Jeremiah said to all the people and to all the women, "Hear the word of the LORD, all Judah who *are* in the land of Egypt! Thus says the LORD of hosts, the God of Israel, saying: 'You and your wives have spoken with your mouths and fulfilled with your hands, saying, "We will surely keep our vows that we have made, to burn incense to the queen of heaven and pour out drink offerings to her." You will surely keep your vows and perform your vows!' Therefore hear the word of the LORD, all Judah who dwell in the land of Egypt: 'Behold, I have sworn by My great name,' says the LORD, 'that My name shall no more be named in the mouth of any man of Judah in all the land of Egypt, saying, "The Lord GOD lives." Behold, I will watch over them for adversity and not for good. And all the men of Judah who *are* in the land of Egypt shall be consumed by the sword and by famine, until there is an end to them. Yet a small number who escape the sword shall return from the land of Egypt to the land of Judah; and all the remnant of Judah, who have gone to the land of Egypt to dwell there, shall know whose words will stand, Mine or theirs. And this *shall be* a sign to you,' says the LORD, 'that I will punish you in this place, that you may know that My words will surely stand against you for adversity.'

"Thus says the LORD: 'Behold, I will give Pharaoh Hophra king of Egypt into the hand of his enemies and into the hand of those who seek his life, as I gave Zedekiah king of Judah into the hand of Nebuchadnezzar king of Babylon, his enemy who sought his life.' "

Jeremiah 44

WORSHIP

Give ear, O Shepherd of Israel,
You who lead Joseph like a flock;
You who dwell *between* the cherubim, shine
    forth!
Before Ephraim, Benjamin, and Manasseh,
Stir up Your strength,
And come *and* save us!

Restore us, O God;
Cause Your face to shine,
And we shall be saved!

Psalm 80:1-3

WISDOM

The heart of the righteous studies how to
    answer,
But the mouth of the wicked pours forth evil.

Proverbs 15:28

SW?! SO WHAT?
What does this tell me?

BABYLON TO BE DESTROYED

Jeremiah 51:1-5, 15-26, 49-58;
Psalm 80:4-7; Proverbs 15:29

Thus says the LORD:

"Behold, I will raise up against Babylon,
Against those who dwell in Leb Kamai,
A destroying wind.
And I will send winnowers to Babylon,
Who shall winnow her and empty her land.
For in the day of doom
They shall be against her all around.
Against *her* let the archer bend his bow,
And lift himself up against *her* in his armor.
Do not spare her young men;
Utterly destroy all her army.

Thus the slain shall fall in the land of the
Chaldeans,
And *those* thrust through in her streets.
For Israel is not forsaken, nor Judah,
By his God, the LORD of hosts,
Though their land was filled with sin against
the Holy One of Israel."

He has made the earth by His power;
He has established the world by His
wisdom,
And stretched out the heaven by His
understanding.
When He utters *His* voice—
There is a multitude of waters in the
heavens:
"He causes the vapors to ascend from the
ends of the earth;
He makes lightnings for the rain;
He brings the wind out of His treasuries."

Everyone is dull-hearted, without knowledge;
Every metalsmith is put to shame by the
carved image;
For his molded image *is* falsehood,
And *there is* no breath in them.
They *are* futile, a work of errors;
In the time of their punishment they shall
perish.
The Portion of Jacob *is* not like them,
For He *is* the Maker of all things;
And *Israel is* the tribe of His inheritance.
The LORD of hosts *is* His name.

"You *are* My battle-ax *and* weapons of war:
For with you I will break the nation in pieces;
With you I will destroy kingdoms;
With you I will break in pieces the horse and
its rider;

With you I will break in pieces the chariot and
its rider;
With you also I will break in pieces man and
woman;
With you I will break in pieces old and young;
With you I will break in pieces the young man
and the maiden;
With you also I will break in pieces the
shepherd and his flock;
With you I will break in pieces the farmer and
his yoke of oxen;
And with you I will break in pieces governors
and rulers.

"And I will repay Babylon
And all the inhabitants of Chaldea
For all the evil they have done
In Zion in your sight," says the LORD.

"Behold, I *am* against you, O destroying
mountain,
Who destroys all the earth," says the LORD.
"And I will stretch out My hand against you,
Roll you down from the rocks,
And make you a burnt mountain.
They shall not take from you a stone for a
corner
Nor a stone for a foundation,
But you shall be desolate forever," says the
LORD.

As Babylon *has caused* the slain of Israel to
fall,
So at Babylon the slain of all the earth shall
fall.
You who have escaped the sword,
Get away! Do not stand still!
Remember the LORD afar off,
And let Jerusalem come to your mind.

We are ashamed because we have heard
reproach.
Shame has covered our faces,
For strangers have come into the sanctuaries
of the LORD's house.

"Therefore behold, the days are coming," says
the LORD,
"That I will bring judgment on her carved
images,
And throughout all her land the wounded shall
groan.

Though Babylon were to mount up to heaven,
And though she were to fortify the height of
    her strength,
Yet from Me plunderers would come to her,"
    says the LORD.

The sound of a cry *comes* from Babylon,
And great destruction from the land of the
    Chaldeans,
Because the LORD is plundering Babylon
And silencing her loud voice,
Though her waves roar like great waters,
And the noise of their voice is uttered,
Because the plunderer comes against her,
    against Babylon,
And her mighty men are taken.
Every one of their bows is broken;
For the LORD *is* the God of recompense,
He will surely repay.

"And I will make drunk
  Her princes and wise men,
  Her governors, her deputies, and her mighty
    men.
  And they shall sleep a perpetual sleep
  And not awake," says the King,
  Whose name *is* the LORD of hosts.

Thus says the LORD of hosts:

"The broad walls of Babylon shall be utterly
    broken,
  And her high gates shall be burned with fire;
  The people will labor in vain,
  And the nations, because of the fire;
  And they shall be weary."
                Jeremiah 51:1-5, 15-26, 49-58

WORSHIP

O LORD God of hosts,
How long will You be angry
Against the prayer of Your people?
You have fed them with the bread of tears,
And given them tears to drink in great
    measure.
You have made us a strife to our neighbors,
And our enemies laugh among themselves.

Restore us, O God of hosts;
Cause Your face to shine,
And we shall be saved!
                Psalm 80:4-7

WISDOM

The LORD *is* far from the wicked,
But He hears the prayer of the righteous.
                Proverbs 15:29

SW?! **SO WHAT?**
What does this tell me?

JEREMIAH WEEPS OVER JERUSALEM

Lamentations 1:1-22; 3:21-32; Psalm 80:17-19; Proverbs 15:30

How lonely sits the city
That was full of people!
How like a widow is she,
Who *was* great among the nations!
The princess among the provinces
Has become a slave!

She weeps bitterly in the night,
Her tears *are* on her cheeks;
Among all her lovers
She has none to comfort *her*.
All her friends have dealt treacherously with
    her;
They have become her enemies.

Judah has gone into captivity,
Under affliction and hard servitude;
She dwells among the nations,
She finds no rest;
All her persecutors overtake her in dire
    straits.

The roads to Zion mourn
Because no one comes to the set feasts.
All her gates are desolate;
Her priests sigh,
Her virgins are afflicted,
And she *is* in bitterness.

Her adversaries have become the
    master,
Her enemies prosper;
For the LORD has afflicted her
Because of the multitude of her
    transgressions.
Her children have gone into captivity before
    the enemy.

And from the daughter of Zion
All her splendor has departed.
Her princes have become like deer
That find no pasture,
That flee without strength
Before the pursuer.

In the days of her affliction and roaming,
Jerusalem remembers all her pleasant
    things
That she had in the days of old.
When her people fell into the hand of the
    enemy,

With no one to help her,
The adversaries saw her
And mocked at her downfall.

Jerusalem has sinned gravely,
Therefore she has become vile.
All who honored her despise her
Because they have seen her nakedness;
Yes, she sighs and turns away.

Her uncleanness *is* in her skirts;
She did not consider her destiny;
Therefore her collapse was awesome;
She had no comforter.
"O LORD, behold my affliction,
For *the* enemy is exalted!"

The adversary has spread his hand
Over all her pleasant things;
For she has seen the nations enter her
    sanctuary,
Those whom You commanded
Not to enter Your assembly.

All her people sigh,
They seek bread;
They have given their valuables for food to
    restore life.
"See, O LORD, and consider,
For I am scorned."

"*Is it* nothing to you, all you who pass by?
Behold and see
If there is any sorrow like my sorrow,
Which has been brought on me,
Which the LORD has inflicted
In the day of His fierce anger.

"From above He has sent fire into my bones,
And it overpowered them;
He has spread a net for my feet
And turned me back;
He has made me desolate
And faint all the day.

"The yoke of my transgressions was bound;
They were woven together by His hands,
And thrust upon my neck.
He made my strength fail;
The Lord delivered me into the hands of *those*
    whom I am not able to withstand.

"The Lord has trampled underfoot all my mighty
    men in my midst;
He has called an assembly against me
To crush my young men;
The Lord trampled as in a winepress
The virgin daughter of Judah.

"For these things I weep;
  My eye, my eye overflows with water;
Because the comforter, who should restore my
    life,
Is far from me.
My children are desolate
Because the enemy prevailed."

Zion spreads out her hands,
But no one comforts her;
The Lord has commanded concerning Jacob
That those around him become his
    adversaries;
Jerusalem has become an unclean thing
    among them.

"The Lord is righteous,
  For I rebelled against His commandment.
Hear now, all peoples,
And behold my sorrow;
My virgins and my young men
Have gone into captivity.

"I called for my lovers,
But they deceived me;
My priests and my elders
Breathed their last in the city,
While they sought food
To restore their life.

"See, O Lord, that I am in distress;
  My soul is troubled;
My heart is overturned within me,
For I have been very rebellious.
Outside the sword bereaves,
At home it is like death.

"They have heard that I sigh,
But no one comforts me.
All my enemies have heard of my trouble;
They are glad that You have done it.
Bring on the day You have announced,
That they may become like me.

"Let all their wickedness come before You,
  And do to them as You have done to me
For all my transgressions;
For my sighs are many,
And my heart is faint."

This I recall to my mind,
Therefore I have hope.

Through the Lord's mercies we are not
    consumed,
Because His compassions fail not.
They are new every morning;
Great is Your faithfulness.
"The Lord is my portion," says my soul,
"Therefore I hope in Him!"

The Lord is good to those who wait for Him,
To the soul who seeks Him.
It is good that one should hope and wait
    quietly
For the salvation of the Lord.
It is good for a man to bear
The yoke in his youth.

Let him sit alone and keep silent,
Because God has laid it on him;
Let him put his mouth in the dust—
There may yet be hope.
Let him give his cheek to the one who strikes
    him,
And be full of reproach.

For the Lord will not cast off forever.
Though He causes grief,
Yet He will show compassion
According to the multitude of His mercies.
Lamentations 1:1-22; 3:21-32

WORSHIP

Let Your hand be upon the man of Your right
    hand,
Upon the son of man whom You made strong
    for Yourself.
Then we will not turn back from You;
Revive us, and we will call upon Your name.

Restore us, O Lord God of hosts;
Cause Your face to shine,
And we shall be saved!
Psalm 80:17-19

WISDOM

The light of the eyes rejoices the heart,
And a good report makes the bones healthy.
Proverbs 15:30

SO WHAT?
What does this tell me?

JEREMIAH PRAYS FOR RESTORATION

How the gold has become dim!
How changed the fine gold!
The stones of the sanctuary are scattered
At the head of every street.

The precious sons of Zion,
Valuable as fine gold,
How they are regarded as clay pots,
The work of the hands of the potter!

Even the jackals present their breasts
To nurse their young;
But the daughter of my people *is* cruel,
   Like ostriches in the wilderness.

   The tongue of the infant clings
   To the roof of its mouth for thirst;
   The young children ask for bread,
   But no one breaks *it* for them.

Those who ate delicacies
Are desolate in the streets;
Those who were brought up in scarlet
Embrace ash heaps.

The punishment of the iniquity of the
   daughter of my people
Is greater than the punishment of the sin of
   Sodom,
Which was overthrown in a moment,
With no hand to help her!

Her Nazirites were brighter than snow
And whiter than milk;
They were more ruddy in body than rubies,
Like sapphire in their appearance.

Now their appearance is blacker than
   soot;
They go unrecognized in the streets;
Their skin clings to their bones,
It has become as dry as wood.

Those slain by the sword are better off
Than *those* who die of hunger;
For these pine away,
Stricken *for lack* of the fruits of the field.

The hands of the compassionate women
Have cooked their own children;
They became food for them
In the destruction of the daughter of my
   people.

The LORD has fulfilled His fury,
He has poured out His fierce anger.
He kindled a fire in Zion,
And it has devoured its foundations.

The kings of the earth,
And all inhabitants of the world,
Would not have believed
That the adversary and the enemy
Could enter the gates of Jerusalem—

Because of the sins of her prophets
And the iniquities of her priests,
Who shed in her midst
The blood of the just.

They wandered blind in the streets;
They have defiled themselves with blood,
So that no one would touch their garments.

They cried out to them,
"Go away, unclean!
Go away, go away,
Do not touch us!"
When they fled and wandered,
Those among the nations said,
"They shall no longer dwell *here*."

The face of the LORD scattered them;
He no longer regards them.
The people do not respect the priests
Nor show favor to the elders.

Still our eyes failed us,
Watching vainly for our help;
In our watching we watched
For a nation *that* could not save *us*.

They tracked our steps
So that we could not walk in our streets.
Our end was near;
Our days were over,
For our end had come.

Our pursuers were swifter
Than the eagles of the heavens.
They pursued us on the mountains
And lay in wait for us in the wilderness.

The breath of our nostrils, the anointed of the
   LORD,
Was caught in their pits,
Of whom we said, "Under his shadow
We shall live among the nations."

Rejoice and be glad, O daughter of Edom,
You who dwell in the land of Uz!
The cup shall also pass over to you
And you shall become drunk and make
  yourself naked.

The punishment of your iniquity is
  accomplished,
O daughter of Zion;
He will no longer send you into captivity.
He will punish your iniquity,
O daughter of Edom;
He will uncover your sins!

Remember, O Lord, what has come upon us;
Look, and behold our reproach!
Our inheritance has been turned over to aliens,
And our houses to foreigners.
We have become orphans and waifs,
Our mothers *are* like widows.

We pay for the water we drink,
And our wood comes at a price.
They pursue at our heels;
We labor *and* have no rest.
We have given our hand *to* the Egyptians
And the Assyrians, to be satisfied with bread.

Our fathers sinned *and are* no more,
But we bear their iniquities.
Servants rule over us;
There is none to deliver *us* from their hand.
We get our bread *at the risk* of our lives,
Because of the sword in the wilderness.

Our skin is hot as an oven,
Because of the fever of famine.
They ravished the women in Zion,
The maidens in the cities of Judah.
Princes were hung up by their hands,
And elders were not respected.
Young men ground at the millstones;
Boys staggered under *loads of* wood.
The elders have ceased *gathering at* the gate,
And the young men from their music.

The joy of our heart has ceased;
Our dance has turned into mourning.
The crown has fallen *from* our head.
Woe to us, for we have sinned!
Because of this our heart is faint;
Because of these *things* our eyes grow dim;
Because of Mount Zion which is desolate,
With foxes walking about on it.

You, O Lord, remain forever;
Your throne from generation to generation.

Why do You forget us forever,
And forsake us for so long a time?
Turn us back to You, O Lord, and we will be
  restored;
Renew our days as of old,
Unless You have utterly rejected us,
And are very angry with us!

Lamentations 4–5

WORSHIP

Sing aloud to God our strength;
Make a joyful shout to the God of Jacob.
Raise a song and strike the timbrel,
The pleasant harp with the lute.

Blow the trumpet at the time of the New Moon,
At the full moon, on our solemn feast day.
For this *is* a statute for Israel,
A law of the God of Jacob.

Psalm 81:1-4

WISDOM

The ear that hears the rebukes of life
Will abide among the wise.

Proverbs 15:31

SW?! **SO WHAT?**
What does this tell me?

EXILE in BABYLON

Daniel was taken captive in 605 B.C. by King Nebuchadnezzar to help prepare for the administration and supervision of Judeans who would be exiled in Babylon after the fall of Jerusalem several years later. Daniel was assigned to eat his meals from the king's table. But being a man of integrity with strict Jewish upbringing, and faced with the choice whether or not to compromise his convictions, Daniel "purposed in his heart that he would not defile himself with the portion of the king's delicacies, nor with the wine which he drank" (Daniel 1:8).

This decision was a fork in the road for Daniel that established a pattern which characterized his service in Babylon. When told to bow down to a golden image of the Babylonian king, Daniel's three friends refused and were thrown into a fiery furnace, but they were kept from harm. On another occasion, Daniel refused to stop praying to God and was forced to spend the night in a lions' den.

While Daniel carried out his ministry in the royal court, Ezekiel ministered among the thousands of Jewish exiles being held captive. He was taken captive in 597 B.C. along with King Jehoiachin and thousands of other Judeans. Ezekiel was a prophet of pantomime. He was made mute for the first years of his ministry, so he communicated with the people through symbolic actions—baking bread, cutting his hair, and packing his luggage. After the fall of Jerusalem, his tongue was set free and he spent his last years announcing the future restoration of Jerusalem and the rebuilding of the temple. His "tour of the temple" is one of the highlights of his later ministry.

The Book of Esther takes place near the end of the Babylonian captivity. It tells a classic story of how God sovereignly elevated a Jewish girl to the position of queen in Persia, in order to provide a means of deliverance from the destruction planned by Haman, the wicked enemy of the Jews.

DANIEL'S LIFE IN BABYLON

Daniel 1:1–2:23; Psalm 81:11-13; Proverbs 15:32

In the third year of the reign of Jehoiakim king of Judah, Nebuchadnezzar king of Babylon came to Jerusalem and besieged it. And the Lord gave Jehoiakim king of Judah into his hand, with some of the articles of the house of God, which he carried into the land of Shinar to the house of his god; and he brought the articles into the treasure house of his god.

Then the king instructed Ashpenaz, the master of his eunuchs, to bring some of the children of Israel and some of the king's descendants and some of the nobles, young men in whom *there was* no blemish, but good-looking, gifted in all wisdom, possessing knowledge and quick to understand, who *had* ability to serve in the king's palace, and whom they might teach the language and literature of the Chaldeans. And the king appointed for them a daily provision of the king's delicacies and of the wine which he drank, and three years of training for them, so that at the end of *that time* they might serve before the king. Now from among those of the sons of Judah were Daniel, Hananiah, Mishael, and Azariah. To them the chief of the eunuchs gave names: he gave Daniel *the name* Belteshazzar; to Hananiah, Shadrach; to Mishael, Meshach; and to Azariah, Abed-Nego.

But Daniel purposed in his heart that he would not defile himself with the portion of the king's delicacies, nor with the wine which he drank; therefore he requested of the chief of the eunuchs that he might not defile himself. Now God had brought Daniel into the favor and goodwill of the chief of the eunuchs. And the chief of the eunuchs said to Daniel, "I fear my lord the king, who has appointed your food and drink. For why should he see your faces looking worse than the young men who *are* your age? Then you would endanger my head before the king."

So Daniel said to the steward whom the chief of the eunuchs had set over Daniel, Hananiah, Mishael, and Azariah, "Please test your servants for ten days, and let them give us vegetables to eat and water to drink. Then let our appearance be examined before you, and the appearance of the young men who eat the portion of the king's deli-

cacies; and as you see fit, *so* deal with your servants." So he consented with them in this matter, and tested them ten days.

And at the end of ten days their features appeared better and fatter in flesh than all the young men who ate the portion of the king's delicacies. Thus the steward took away their portion of delicacies and the wine that they were to drink, and gave them vegetables.

As for these four young men, God gave them knowledge and skill in all literature and wisdom; and Daniel had understanding in all visions and dreams.

Now at the end of the days, when the king had said that they should be brought in, the chief of the eunuchs brought them in before Nebuchadnezzar. Then the king interviewed them, and among them all none was found like Daniel, Hananiah, Mishael, and Azariah; therefore they served before the king. And in all matters of wisdom *and* understanding about which the king examined them, he found them ten times better than all the magicians *and* astrologers who *were* in all his realm. Thus Daniel continued until the first year of King Cyrus.

Now in the second year of Nebuchadnezzar's reign, Nebuchadnezzar had dreams; and his spirit was *so* troubled that his sleep left him. Then the king gave the command to call the magicians, the astrologers, the sorcerers, and the Chaldeans to tell the king his dreams. So they came and stood before the king. And the king said to them, "I have had a dream, and my spirit is anxious to know the dream."

Then the Chaldeans spoke to the king in Aramaic, "O king, live forever! Tell your servants the dream, and we will give the interpretation."

The king answered and said to the Chaldeans, "My decision is firm: if you do not make known the dream to me, and its interpretation, you shall be cut in pieces, and your houses shall be made an ash heap. However, if you tell the dream and its interpretation, you shall receive from me gifts, rewards, and great honor. Therefore tell me the dream and its interpretation."

They answered again and said, "Let the king tell his servants the dream, and we will give its interpretation."

The king answered and said, "I know for certain that you would gain time, because you see that my decision is firm: if you do not make known the dream to me, *there is only* one decree for you! For you have agreed to speak lying and corrupt words before me till the time has changed. Therefore tell me the dream, and I shall know that you can give me its interpretation."

The Chaldeans answered the king, and said, "There is not a man on earth who can tell the king's matter; therefore no king, lord, or ruler has *ever* asked such things of any magician, astrologer, or Chaldean. *It is* a difficult thing that the king requests, and there is no other who can tell it to the king except the gods, whose dwelling is not with flesh."

For this reason the king was angry and very furious, and gave the command to destroy all the wise *men* of Babylon. So the decree went out, and they began killing the wise *men;* and they sought Daniel and his companions, to kill *them.*

Then with counsel and wisdom Daniel answered Arioch, the captain of the king's guard, who had gone out to kill the wise *men* of Babylon; he answered and said to Arioch the king's captain, "Why is the decree from the king so urgent?" Then Arioch made the decision known to Daniel.

So Daniel went in and asked the king to give him time, that he might tell the king the interpretation. Then Daniel went to his house, and made the decision known to Hananiah, Mishael, and Azariah, his companions, that they might seek mercies from the God of heaven concerning this secret, so that Daniel and his companions might not perish with the rest of the wise *men* of Babylon. Then the secret was revealed to Daniel in a night vision. So Daniel blessed the God of heaven.

Daniel answered and said:

"Blessed be the name of God forever and ever,
For wisdom and might are His.
And He changes the times and the seasons;
He removes kings and raises up kings;
He gives wisdom to the wise
And knowledge to those who have
    understanding.
He reveals deep and secret things;
He knows what *is* in the darkness,
And light dwells with Him.

"I thank You and praise You,
O God of my fathers;

You have given me wisdom and might,
And have now made known to me what we
    asked of You,
For You have made known to us the king's
    demand."

Daniel 1:1–2:23

WORSHIP

"But My people would not heed My voice,
And Israel would *have* none of Me.
So I gave them over to their own stubborn
    heart,
To walk in their own counsels.

"Oh, that My people would listen to Me,
That Israel would walk in My ways!"

Psalm 81:11-13

WISDOM

He who disdains instruction despises his own
    soul,
But he who heeds rebuke gets understanding.

Proverbs 15:32

SW?! **SO WHAT?**
What does this tell me?

THREE FRIENDS IN A FURNACE

Daniel 3; Psalm 82:1-4;
Proverbs 15:33

Nebuchadnezzar the king made an image of gold, whose height *was* sixty cubits *and* its width six cubits. He set it up in the plain of Dura, in the province of Babylon. And King Nebuchadnezzar sent *word* to gather together the satraps, the administrators, the governors, the counselors, the treasurers, the judges, the magistrates, and all the officials of the provinces, to come to the dedication of the image which King Nebuchadnezzar had set up. So the satraps, the administrators, the governors, the counselors, the treasurers, the judges, the magistrates, and all the officials of the provinces gathered together for the dedication of the image that King Nebuchadnezzar had set up; and they stood before the image that Nebuchadnezzar had set up. Then a herald cried aloud: "To you it is commanded, O peoples, nations, and languages, *that* at the time you hear the sound of the horn, flute, harp, lyre, *and* psaltery, in symphony with all kinds of music, you shall fall down and worship the gold image that King Nebuchadnezzar has set up; and whoever does not fall down and worship shall be cast immediately into the midst of a burning fiery furnace."

So at that time, when all the people heard the sound of the horn, flute, harp, *and* lyre, in symphony with all kinds of music, all the people, nations, and languages fell down *and* worshiped the gold image which King Nebuchadnezzar had set up.

Therefore at that time certain Chaldeans came forward and accused the Jews. They spoke and said to King Nebuchadnezzar, "O king, live forever! You, O king, have made a decree that everyone who hears the sound of the horn, flute, harp, lyre, *and* psaltery, in symphony with all kinds of music, shall fall down and worship the gold image; and whoever does not fall down and worship shall be cast into the midst of a burning fiery furnace. There are certain Jews whom you have set over the affairs of the province of Babylon: Shadrach, Meshach, and Abed-Nego; these men, O king, have not paid due regard to you. They do not serve your gods or worship the gold image which you have set up."

Then Nebuchadnezzar, in rage and fury, gave the command to bring Shadrach, Meshach, and Abed-Nego. So they brought these men before the king. Nebuchadnezzar spoke, saying to them, "*Is it true*, Shadrach, Meshach, and Abed-Nego, *that* you do not serve my gods or worship the gold image which I have set up? Now if you are ready at the time you hear the sound of the horn, flute, harp, lyre, *and* psaltery, in symphony with all kinds of music, and you fall down and worship the image which I have made, *good!* But if you do not worship, you shall be cast immediately into the midst of a burning fiery furnace. And who *is* the god who will deliver you from my hands?"

Shadrach, Meshach, and Abed-Nego answered and said to the king, "O Nebuchadnezzar, we have no need to answer you in this matter. If that *is the case,* our God whom we serve is able to deliver us from the burning fiery furnace, and He will deliver *us* from your hand, O king. But if not, let it be known to you, O king, that we do not serve your gods, nor will we worship the gold image which you have set up."

Then Nebuchadnezzar was full of fury, and the expression on his face changed toward Shadrach, Meshach, and Abed-Nego. He spoke and commanded that they heat the furnace seven times more than it was usually heated. And he commanded certain mighty men of valor who *were* in his army to bind Shadrach, Meshach, and Abed-Nego, *and* cast *them* into the burning fiery furnace. Then these men were bound in their coats, their trousers, their turbans, and their *other* garments, and were cast into the midst of the burning fiery furnace. Therefore, because the king's command was urgent, and the furnace exceedingly hot, the flame of the fire killed those men who took up Shadrach, Meshach, and Abed-Nego. And these three men, Shadrach, Meshach, and Abed-Nego, fell down bound into the midst of the burning fiery furnace.

Then King Nebuchadnezzar was astonished; and he rose in haste *and* spoke, saying to his counselors, "Did we not cast three men bound into the midst of the fire?"

They answered and said to the king, "True, O king."

"Look!" he answered, "I see four men loose, walking in the midst of the fire; and they are not hurt, and the form of the fourth is like the Son of God."

Then Nebuchadnezzar went near the mouth of the burning fiery furnace *and* spoke, saying, "Shadrach, Meshach, and Abed-Nego, servants of the Most High God, come out, and come *here*." Then Shadrach, Meshach, and Abed-Nego came from the midst of the fire. And the satraps, administrators, governors, and the king's counselors gathered together, and they saw these men on whose bodies the fire had no power; the hair of their head was not singed nor were their garments affected, and the smell of fire was not on them.

Nebuchadnezzar spoke, saying, "Blessed be the God of Shadrach, Meshach, and Abed-Nego, who sent His Angel and delivered His servants who trusted in Him, and they have frustrated the king's word, and yielded their bodies, that they should not serve nor worship any god except their own God! Therefore I make a decree that any people, nation, or language which speaks anything amiss against the God of Shadrach, Meshach, and Abed-Nego shall be cut in pieces, and their houses shall be made an ash heap; because there is no other God who can deliver like this."

Then the king promoted Shadrach, Meshach, and Abed-Nego in the province of Babylon.

Daniel 3

WORSHIP

God stands in the congregation of the mighty;
He judges among the gods.
How long will you judge unjustly,
And show partiality to the wicked?   Selah
Defend the poor and fatherless;
Do justice to the afflicted and needy.
Deliver the poor and needy;
Free *them* from the hand of the wicked.

Psalm 82:1-4

WISDOM

The fear of the LORD *is* the instruction of
    wisdom,
And before honor *is* humility.

Proverbs 15:33

SW?! SO WHAT?
What does this tell me?

NEBUCHADNEZZAR LEARNS A LESSON

Daniel 4; Psalm 83:1–3; Proverbs 16:1

Nebuchadnezzar the king,

To all peoples, nations, and languages that dwell in all the earth:

Peace be multiplied to you.

I thought it good to declare the signs and wonders that the Most High God has worked for me.

How great *are* His signs,
And how mighty His wonders!
His kingdom *is* an everlasting kingdom,
And His dominion *is* from generation to
    generation.

I, Nebuchadnezzar, was at rest in my house, and flourishing in my palace. I saw a dream which made me afraid, and the thoughts on my bed and the visions of my head troubled me. Therefore I issued a decree to bring in all the wise *men* of Babylon before me, that they might make known to me the interpretation of the dream. Then the magicians, the astrologers, the Chaldeans, and the soothsayers came in, and I told them the dream; but they did not make known to me its interpretation. But at last Daniel came before me (his name *is* Belteshazzar, according to the name of my god; in him *is* the Spirit of the Holy God), and I told the dream before him, *saying:* "Belteshazzar, chief of the magicians, because I know that the Spirit of the Holy God *is* in you, and no secret troubles you, explain to me the visions of my dream that I have seen, and its interpretation.

"These *were* the visions of my head *while* on my bed:

I was looking, and behold,
A tree in the midst of the earth,
And its height was great.
The tree grew and became strong;
Its height reached to the heavens,
And it could be seen to the ends of all the earth.
Its leaves *were* lovely,
Its fruit abundant,
And in it *was* food for all.
The beasts of the field found shade under it,
The birds of the heavens dwelt in its branches,
And all flesh was fed from it.

"I saw in the visions of my head *while* on my bed, and there was a watcher, a holy one, coming down from heaven. He cried aloud and said thus:

'Chop down the tree and cut off its branches,
Strip off its leaves and scatter its fruit.
Let the beasts get out from under it,
And the birds from its branches.
Nevertheless leave the stump and roots in the
    earth,
Bound with a band of iron and bronze,
In the tender grass of the field.
Let it be wet with the dew of heaven,
And *let* him graze with the beasts
On the grass of the earth.
Let his heart be changed from *that of* a man,
Let him be given the heart of a beast,
And let seven times pass over him.

'This decision *is* by the decree of the watchers,
And the sentence by the word of the holy ones,
In order that the living may know
That the Most High rules in the kingdom of
    men,
Gives it to whomever He will,
And sets over it the lowest of men.'

"This dream I, King Nebuchadnezzar, have seen. Now you, Belteshazzar, declare its interpretation, since all the wise *men* of my kingdom are not able to make known to me the interpretation; but you *are* able, for the Spirit of the Holy God *is* in you."

Then Daniel, whose name was Belteshazzar, was astonished for a time, and his thoughts troubled him. *So* the king spoke, and said, "Belteshazzar, do not let the dream or its interpretation trouble you."

Belteshazzar answered and said, "My lord, may the dream concern those who hate you, and its interpretation concern your enemies!

"The tree that you saw, which grew and became strong, whose height reached to the heavens and which *could be seen* by all the earth, whose leaves *were* lovely and its fruit abundant, in which *was* food for all, under which the beasts of the field dwelt, and in whose branches the birds of the heaven had their home— it *is* you, O king, who have grown and become strong; for your greatness has grown and reaches to the heavens, and your dominion to the end of the earth.

"And inasmuch as the king saw a watcher, a holy one, coming down from heaven and saying, 'Chop down the tree and destroy it, but leave its stump and roots in the earth, *bound* with a band of iron and bronze in the tender grass of the field; let it be wet with the dew of heaven, and let him graze with the beasts of the field, till seven times pass over him'; this is the interpretation, O king, and this is the decree of the Most High, which has come upon my lord the king: They shall drive you from men, your dwelling shall be with the beasts of the field, and they shall make you eat grass like oxen. They shall wet you with the dew of heaven, and seven times shall pass over you, till you know that the Most High rules in the kingdom of men, and gives it to whomever He chooses.

"And inasmuch as they gave the command to leave the stump *and* roots of the tree, your kingdom shall be assured to you, after you come to know that Heaven rules. Therefore, O king, let my advice be acceptable to you; break off your sins by *being* righteous, and your iniquities by showing mercy to *the* poor. Perhaps there may be a lengthening of your prosperity."

All *this* came upon King Nebuchadnezzar. At the end of the twelve months he was walking about the royal palace of Babylon. The king spoke, saying, "Is not this great Babylon, that I have built for a royal dwelling by my mighty power and for the honor of my majesty?"

While the word *was still* in the king's mouth, a voice fell from heaven: "King Nebuchadnezzar, to you it is spoken: the kingdom has departed from you! And they shall drive you from men, and your dwelling *shall be* with the beasts of the field. They shall make you eat grass like oxen; and seven times shall pass over you, until you know that the Most High rules in the kingdom of men, and gives it to whomever He chooses."

That very hour the word was fulfilled concerning Nebuchadnezzar; he was driven from men and ate grass like oxen; his body was wet with the dew of heaven till his hair had grown like eagles' *feathers* and his nails like birds' *claws*.

And at the end of the time I, Nebuchadnezzar, lifted my eyes to heaven, and my understanding returned to me; and I blessed the Most High and praised and honored Him who lives forever:

For His dominion *is* an everlasting dominion,
And His kingdom *is* from generation to
generation.
All the inhabitants of the earth *are* reputed as
nothing;
He does according to His will in the army of
heaven
And *among* the inhabitants of the earth.
No one can restrain His hand
Or say to Him, "What have You done?"

At the same time my reason returned to me, and for the glory of my kingdom, my honor and splendor returned to me. My counselors and nobles resorted to me, I was restored to my kingdom, and excellent majesty was added to me. Now I, Nebuchadnezzar, praise and extol and honor the King of heaven, all of whose works *are* truth, and His ways justice. And those who walk in pride He is able to put down.

Daniel 4

Do not keep silent, O God!
Do not hold Your peace,
And do not be still, O God!
For behold, Your enemies make a tumult;
And those who hate You have lifted up their
head.
They have taken crafty counsel against Your
people,
And consulted together against Your sheltered
ones.

Psalm 83:1-3

WiSDoM

The preparations of the heart *belong* to man,
But the answer of the tongue *is* from the LORD.

Proverbs 16:1

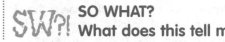

SO WHAT?
What does this tell me?

DANIEL LIVES HIS FAITH IN GOD

Daniel 5:1, 3-9, 13-14, 17-30;
6:1-23; Psalm 83:16-18;
Proverbs 16:2

Belshazzar the king made a great feast for a thousand of his lords, and drank wine in the presence of the thousand.

Then they brought the gold vessels that had been taken from the temple of the house of God which *had been* in Jerusalem; and the king and his lords, his wives, and his concubines drank from them. They drank wine, and praised the gods of gold and silver, bronze and iron, wood and stone.

In the same hour the fingers of a man's hand appeared and wrote opposite the lampstand on the plaster of the wall of the king's palace; and the king saw the part of the hand that wrote. Then the king's countenance changed, and his thoughts troubled him, so that the joints of his hips were loosened and his knees knocked against each other. The king cried aloud to bring in the astrologers, the Chaldeans, and the soothsayers. The king spoke, saying to the wise *men* of Babylon, "Whoever reads this writing, and tells me its interpretation, shall be clothed with purple and *have* a chain of gold around his neck; and he shall be the third ruler in the kingdom." Now all the king's wise *men* came, but they could not read the writing, or make known to the king its interpretation. Then King Belshazzar was greatly troubled, his countenance was changed, and his lords were astonished.

Then Daniel was brought in before the king. The king spoke, and said to Daniel, "*Are* you that Daniel who is one of the captives from Judah, whom my father the king brought from Judah? I have heard of you, that the Spirit of God *is* in you, and *that* light and understanding and excellent wisdom are found in you."

Then Daniel answered, and said before the king, "Let your gifts be for yourself, and give your rewards to another; yet I will read the writing to the king, and make known to him the interpretation. O king, the Most High God gave Nebuchadnezzar your father a kingdom and majesty, glory and honor. And because of the majesty that He gave him, all peoples, nations, and languages trembled and feared before him.

Whomever he wished, he executed; whomever he wished, he kept alive; whomever he wished, he set up; and whomever he wished, he put down. But when his heart was lifted up, and his spirit was hardened in pride, he was deposed from his kingly throne, and they took his glory from him. Then he was driven from the sons of men, his heart was made like the beasts, and his dwelling *was* with the wild donkeys. They fed him with grass like oxen, and his body was wet with the dew of heaven, till he knew that the Most High God rules in the kingdom of men, and appoints over it whomever He chooses.

"But you his son, Belshazzar, have not humbled your heart, although you knew all this. And you have lifted yourself up against the Lord of heaven. They have brought the vessels of His house before you, and you and your lords, your wives and your concubines, have drunk wine from them. And you have praised the gods of silver and gold, bronze and iron, wood and stone, which do not see or hear or know; and the God who *holds* your breath in His hand and owns all your ways, you have not glorified. Then the fingers of the hand were sent from Him, and this writing was written.

"And this is the inscription that was written:

MENE, MENE, TEKEL, UPHARSIN.

This *is* the interpretation of *each* word. Mene: God has numbered your kingdom, and finished it; Tekel: You have been weighed in the balances, and found wanting; Peres: Your kingdom has been divided, and given to the Medes and Persians." Then Belshazzar gave the command, and they clothed Daniel with purple and *put* a chain of gold around his neck, and made a proclamation concerning him that he should be the third ruler in the kingdom.

That very night Belshazzar, king of the Chaldeans, was slain.

It pleased Darius to set over the kingdom one hundred and twenty satraps, to be over the whole kingdom; and over these, three governors, of whom Daniel *was* one, that the satraps might give account to them, so that the king would suffer no loss. Then this Daniel distinguished himself above the governors and satraps, because an excellent spirit *was* in him; and the king gave thought to setting him over the whole realm. So the governors and satraps sought to find *some* charge against Daniel concerning the kingdom; but they could find no charge or fault, because he *was* faithful; nor was there any error or fault found in him. Then these men said, "We shall not find any charge against this Daniel unless we find *it* against him concerning the law of his God."

So these governors and satraps thronged before the king, and said thus to him: "King Darius, live forever! All the governors of the kingdom, the administrators and satraps, the counselors and advisors, have consulted together to establish a royal statute and to make a firm decree, that whoever petitions any god or man for thirty days, except you, O king, shall be cast into the den of lions. Now, O king, establish the decree and sign the writing, so that it cannot be changed, according to the law of the Medes and Persians, which does not alter." Therefore King Darius signed the written decree.

Now when Daniel knew that the writing was signed, he went home. And in his upper room, with his windows open toward Jerusalem, he knelt down on his knees three times that day, and prayed and gave thanks before his God, as was his custom since early days.

Then these men assembled and found Daniel praying and making supplication before his God. And they went before the king, and spoke concerning the king's decree: "Have you not signed a decree that every man who petitions any god or man within thirty days, except you, O king, shall be cast into the den of lions?"

The king answered and said, "The thing *is* true, according to the law of the Medes and Persians, which does not alter."

So they answered and said before the king, "That Daniel, who is one of the captives from Judah, does not show due regard for you, O king, or for the decree that you have signed, but makes his petition three times a day."

And the king, when he heard *these* words, was greatly displeased with himself, and set *his* heart on Daniel to deliver him; and he labored till the going down of the sun to deliver him. Then these men approached the king, and said to the king, "Know, O king, that *it is* the law of the Medes and Persians that no decree or statute which the king establishes may be changed."

So the king gave the command, and they brought Daniel and cast *him* into the den of lions. *But* the king spoke, saying to Daniel, "Your God, whom you serve continually, He will deliver you." Then a stone was brought and laid on the mouth of the den, and the king sealed it with his own signet ring and with the signets of his lords, that the purpose concerning Daniel might not be changed.

Now the king went to his palace and spent the night fasting; and no musicians were brought before him. Also his sleep went from him. Then the king arose very early in the morning and went in haste to the den of lions. And when he came to the den, he cried out with a lamenting voice to Daniel. The king spoke, saying to Daniel, "Daniel, servant of the living God, has your God, whom you serve continually, been able to deliver you from the lions?"

Then Daniel said to the king, "O king, live forever! My God sent His angel and shut the lions' mouths, so that they have not hurt me, because I was found innocent before Him; and also, O king, I have done no wrong before you."

Now the king was exceedingly glad for him, and commanded that they should take Daniel up out of the den. So Daniel was taken up out of the den, and no injury whatever was found on him, because he believed in his God.

Daniel 5:1, 3-9, 13-14, 17-30; 6:1-23

Fill their faces with shame,
That they may seek Your name, O LORD.
Let them be confounded and dismayed
    forever;
Yes, let them be put to shame and perish,
That they may know that You, whose name
    alone *is* the LORD,
Are the Most High over all the earth.

Psalm 83:16-18

WiSDOM

All the ways of a man *are* pure in his own
    eyes,
But the LORD weighs the spirits.

Proverbs 16:2

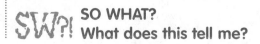

SO WHAT?
What does this tell me?

DANIEL SEES THE FUTURE

Daniel 7; Psalm 84:1-2, 4; Proverbs 16:3

EXILE IN BABYLON

In the first year of Belshazzar king of Babylon, Daniel had a dream and visions of his head *while* on his bed. Then he wrote down the dream, telling the main facts.

Daniel spoke, saying, "I saw in my vision by night, and behold, the four winds of heaven were stirring up the Great Sea. And four great beasts came up from the sea, each different from the other. The first *was* like a lion, and had eagle's wings. I watched till its wings were plucked off; and it was lifted up from the earth and made to stand on two feet like a man, and a man's heart was given to it.

"And suddenly another beast, a second, like a bear. It was raised up on one side, and *had* three ribs in its mouth between its teeth. And they said thus to it: 'Arise, devour much flesh!'

"After this I looked, and there was another, like a leopard, which had on its back four wings of a bird. The beast also had four heads, and dominion was given to it.

"After this I saw in the night visions, and behold, a fourth beast, dreadful and terrible, exceedingly strong. It had huge iron teeth; it was devouring, breaking in pieces, and trampling the residue with its feet. It *was* different from all the beasts that *were* before it, and it had ten horns. I was considering the horns, and there was another horn, a little one, coming up among them, before whom three of the first horns were plucked out by the roots. And there, in this horn, *were* eyes like the eyes of a man, and a mouth speaking pompous words.

"I watched till thrones were put in place,
And the Ancient of Days was seated;
His garment *was* white as snow,
And the hair of His head *was* like pure wool.
His throne *was* a fiery flame,
Its wheels a burning fire;
A fiery stream issued
And came forth from before Him.
A thousand thousands ministered to Him;
Ten thousand times ten thousand stood
   before Him.
The court was seated,
And the books were opened.

"I watched then because of the sound of the pompous words which the horn was speaking; I watched till the beast was slain, and its body destroyed and given to the burning flame. As for the rest of the beasts, they had their dominion taken away, yet their lives were prolonged for a season and a time.

"I was watching in the night visions,
And behold, *One* like the Son of Man,
Coming with the clouds of heaven!
He came to the Ancient of Days,
And they brought Him near before Him.
Then to Him was given dominion and glory
   and a kingdom,
That all peoples, nations, and languages
   should serve Him.
His dominion *is* an everlasting dominion,
Which shall not pass away,
And His kingdom *the one*
Which shall not be destroyed.

"I, Daniel, was grieved in my spirit within *my* body, and the visions of my head troubled me. I came near to one of those who stood by, and asked him the truth of all this. So he told me and made known to me the interpretation of these things: 'Those great beasts, which are four, *are* four kings *which* arise out of the earth. But the saints of the Most High shall receive the kingdom, and possess the kingdom forever, even forever and ever.'

"Then I wished to know the truth about the fourth beast, which was different from all the others, exceedingly dreadful, *with* its teeth of iron and its nails of bronze, *which* devoured, broke in pieces, and trampled the residue with its feet; and the ten horns that *were* on its head, and the other *horn* which came up, before which three fell, namely, that horn which had eyes and a mouth which spoke pompous words, whose appearance *was* greater than his fellows.

"I was watching; and the same horn was making war against the saints, and prevailing against them, until the Ancient of Days came, and a judgment was made *in favor* of the saints of the Most High, and the time came for the saints to possess the kingdom.

"Thus he said:

'The fourth beast shall be
A fourth kingdom on earth,
Which shall be different from all *other*
	kingdoms,
And shall devour the whole earth,
Trample it and break it in pieces.
The ten horns *are* ten kings
Who shall arise from this kingdom.
And another shall rise after them;
He shall be different from the first *ones,*
And shall subdue three kings.
He shall speak *pompous* words against the
	Most High,
Shall persecute the saints of the Most High,
And shall intend to change times and law.
Then *the saints* shall be given into his hand
For a time and times and half a time.

'But the court shall be seated,
And they shall take away his dominion,
To consume and destroy *it* forever.
Then the kingdom and dominion,
And the greatness of the kingdoms under the
	whole heaven,
Shall be given to the people, the saints of the
	Most High.
His kingdom *is* an everlasting kingdom,
And all dominions shall serve and obey Him.'

"This *is* the end of the account. As for me, Daniel, my thoughts greatly troubled me, and my countenance changed; but I kept the matter in my heart."

Daniel 7

WORSHIP

How lovely *is* Your tabernacle,
O Lord of hosts!
My soul longs, yes, even faints
For the courts of the Lord;
My heart and my flesh cry out for the living
	God.

Blessed *are* those who dwell in Your house;
They will still be praising You.   Selah
Psalm 84:1-2, 4

WISDOM

Commit your works to the Lord,
And your thoughts will be established.
Proverbs 16:3

SW?! **SO WHAT?**
What does this tell me?

THE TIME OF THE END

**Daniel 9:1-7, 16-27; 10:12-14; 11:36–12:3;
Psalm 84:8-10; Proverbs 16:4**

In the first year of Darius the son of Ahasuerus, of the lineage of the Medes, who was made king over the realm of the Chaldeans—in the first year of his reign I, Daniel, understood by the books the number of the years *specified* by the word of the LORD through Jeremiah the prophet, that He would accomplish seventy years in the desolations of Jerusalem.

Then I set my face toward the Lord God to make request by prayer and supplications, with fasting, sackcloth, and ashes. And I prayed to the LORD my God, and made confession, and said, "O Lord, great and awesome God, who keeps His covenant and mercy with those who love Him, and with those who keep His commandments, we have sinned and committed iniquity, we have done wickedly and rebelled, even by departing from Your precepts and Your judgments. Neither have we heeded Your servants the prophets, who spoke in Your name to our kings and our princes, to our fathers and all the people of the land. O Lord, righteousness *belongs* to You, but to us shame of face, as *it is* this day—to the men of Judah, to the inhabitants of Jerusalem and all Israel, those near and those far off in all the countries to which You have driven them, because of the unfaithfulness which they have committed against You.

"O Lord, according to all Your righteousness, I pray, let Your anger and Your fury be turned away from Your city Jerusalem, Your holy mountain; because for our sins, and for the iniquities of our fathers, Jerusalem and Your people *are* a reproach to all *those* around us. Now therefore, our God, hear the prayer of Your servant, and his supplications, and for the Lord's sake cause Your face to shine on Your sanctuary, which is desolate. O my God, incline Your ear and hear; open Your eyes and see our desolations, and the city which is called by Your name; for we do not present our supplications before You because of our righteous deeds, but because of Your great mercies. O Lord, hear! O Lord, forgive! O Lord, listen and act! Do not delay for Your own sake, my God, for Your city and Your people are called by Your name."

Now while I *was* speaking, praying, and confessing my sin and the sin of my people Israel, and presenting my supplication before the LORD my God for the holy mountain of my God, yes, while I *was* speaking in prayer, the man Gabriel, whom I had seen in the vision at the beginning, being caused to fly swiftly, reached me about the time of the evening offering. And he informed *me,* and talked with me, and said, "O Daniel, I have now come forth to give you skill to understand. At the beginning of your supplications the command went out, and I have come to tell *you,* for you *are* greatly beloved; therefore consider the matter, and understand the vision:

"Seventy weeks are determined
For your people and for your holy city,
To finish the transgression,
To make an end of sins,
To make reconciliation for iniquity,
To bring in everlasting righteousness,
To seal up vision and prophecy,
And to anoint the Most Holy.

"Know therefore and understand,
That from the going forth of the command
To restore and build Jerusalem
Until Messiah the Prince,
There shall be seven weeks and sixty-two
    weeks;
The street shall be built again, and the wall,
Even in troublesome times.

"And after the sixty-two weeks
Messiah shall be cut off, but not for Himself;
And the people of the prince who is to come
Shall destroy the city and the sanctuary.
The end of it *shall be* with a flood,
And till the end of the war desolations are
    determined.
Then he shall confirm a covenant with many
    for one week;
But in the middle of the week
He shall bring an end to sacrifice and offering.
And on the wing of abominations shall be one
    who makes desolate,
Even until the consummation, which is
    determined,
Is poured out on the desolate."

Then he said to me, "Do not fear, Daniel, for from the first day that you set your heart to understand, and to humble yourself before your God, your words were heard; and I have come because of your words. But the prince of the kingdom of Persia withstood me twenty-one days; and behold, Michael, one of the chief princes, came to help me, for I had been left alone there with the kings of Persia. Now I have come to make you understand what will happen to your people in the latter days, for the vision *refers* to *many* days yet *to come*."

"Then the king shall do according to his own will: he shall exalt and magnify himself above every god, shall speak blasphemies against the God of gods, and shall prosper till the wrath has been accomplished; for what has been determined shall be done. He shall regard neither the God of his fathers nor the desire of women, nor regard any god; for he shall exalt himself above *them* all. But in their place he shall honor a god of fortresses; and a god which his fathers did not know he shall honor with gold and silver, with precious stones and pleasant things. Thus he shall act against the strongest fortresses with a foreign god, which he shall acknowledge, *and* advance *its* glory; and he shall cause them to rule over many, and divide the land for gain.

"At the time of the end the king of the South shall attack him; and the king of the North shall come against him like a whirlwind, with chariots, horsemen, and with many ships; and he shall enter the countries, overwhelm *them,* and pass through. He shall also enter the Glorious Land, and many *countries* shall be overthrown; but these shall escape from his hand: Edom, Moab, and the prominent people of Ammon. He shall stretch out his hand against the countries, and the land of Egypt shall not escape. He shall have power over the treasures of gold and silver, and over all the precious things of Egypt; also the Libyans and Ethiopians *shall follow* at his heels. But news from the east and the north shall trouble him; therefore he shall go out with great fury to destroy and annihilate many. And he shall plant the tents of his palace between the seas and the glorious holy mountain; yet he shall come to his end, and no one will help him.

"At that time Michael shall stand up,
The great prince who stands *watch* over the
    sons of your people;
And there shall be a time of trouble,
Such as never was since there was a nation,

Even to that time.
And at that time your people shall be
    delivered,
Every one who is found written in the book.
And many of those who sleep in the dust of
    the earth shall awake,
Some to everlasting life,
Some to shame *and* everlasting contempt.
Those who are wise shall shine
Like the brightness of the firmament,
And those who turn many to righteousness
Like the stars forever and ever.
Daniel 9:1-7, 16-27; 10:12-14; 11:36–12:3

WORSHIP

O LORD God of hosts, hear my prayer;
Give ear, O God of Jacob!   Selah
O God, behold our shield,
And look upon the face of Your anointed.

For a day in Your courts *is* better than a
    thousand.
I would rather be a doorkeeper in the house of
    my God
Than dwell in the tents of wickedness.
Psalm 84:8-10

WISDOM

The LORD has made all for Himself,
Yes, even the wicked for the day of doom.
Proverbs 16:4

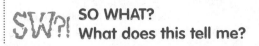

SO WHAT?
What does this tell me?

EZEKIEL'S VISION OF GOD'S GLORY

Ezekiel 1; Psalm 84:11-12; Proverbs 16:5

Now it came to pass in the thirtieth year, in the fourth *month,* on the fifth *day* of the month, as I *was* among the captives by the River Chebar, *that* the heavens were opened and I saw visions of God. On the fifth *day* of the month, which *was* in the fifth year of King Jehoiachin's captivity, the word of the LORD came expressly to Ezekiel the priest, the son of Buzi, in the land of the Chaldeans by the River Chebar; and the hand of the LORD was upon him there.

Then I looked, and behold, a whirlwind was coming out of the north, a great cloud with raging fire engulfing itself; and brightness *was* all around it and radiating out of its midst like the color of amber, out of the midst of the fire. Also from within it *came* the likeness of four living creatures. And this *was* their appearance: they had the likeness of a man. Each one had four faces, and each one had four wings. Their legs *were* straight, and the soles of their feet *were* like the soles of calves' feet. They sparkled like the color of burnished bronze. The hands of a man *were* under their wings on their four sides; and each of the four had faces and wings. Their wings touched one another. *The creatures* did not turn when they went, but each one went straight forward.

As for the likeness of their faces, *each* had the face of a man; each of the four had the face of a lion on the right side, each of the four had the face of an ox on the left side, and each of the four had the face of an eagle. Thus *were* their faces. Their wings stretched upward; two *wings* of each one touched one another, and two covered their bodies. And each one went straight forward; they went wherever the spirit wanted to go, and they did not turn when they went.

As for the likeness of the living creatures, their appearance *was* like burning coals of fire, like the appearance of torches going back and forth among the living creatures. The fire was bright, and out of the fire went lightning. And the living creatures ran back and forth, in appearance like a flash of lightning.

Now as I looked at the living creatures, behold, a wheel *was* on the earth beside each living creature with its four faces. The appearance of the wheels and their workings *was* like the color of beryl, and all four had the same likeness. The appearance of their workings *was,* as it were, a wheel in the middle of a wheel. When they moved, they went toward any one of four directions; they did not turn aside when they went. As for their rims, they were so high they were awesome; and their rims *were* full of eyes, all around the four of them. When the living creatures went, the wheels went beside them; and when the living creatures were lifted up from the earth, the wheels were lifted up. Wherever the spirit wanted to go, they went, *because* there the spirit went; and the wheels were lifted together with them, for the spirit of the living creatures *was* in the wheels. When those went, *these* went; when those stood, *these* stood; and when those were lifted up from the earth, the wheels were lifted up together with them, for the spirit of the living creatures *was* in the wheels.

The likeness of the firmament above the heads of the living creatures *was* like the color of an awesome crystal, stretched out over their heads. And under the firmament their wings *spread out* straight, one toward another. Each one had two which covered one side, and each one had two which covered the other side of the body. When they went, I heard the noise of their wings, like the noise of many waters, like the voice of the Almighty, a tumult like the noise of an army; and when they stood still, they let down their wings. A voice came from above the firmament that *was* over their heads; whenever they stood, they let down their wings.

And above the firmament over their heads *was* the likeness of a throne, in appearance like a sapphire stone; on the likeness of the throne *was* a likeness with the appearance of a man high above it. Also from the appearance of His waist and upward I saw, as it were, the color of amber with the appearance of fire all around within it; and from the appearance of His waist and downward I saw, as it were, the appearance of fire with brightness all around. Like the appearance of a rainbow in a cloud on a rainy day, so *was* the appearance of the brightness all around it. This *was* the appearance of the likeness of the glory of the LORD.

So when I saw *it,* I fell on my face, and I heard a voice of One speaking.

Ezekiel 1

WoRSHiP

For the LORD God *is* a sun and shield;
The LORD will give grace and glory;
No good *thing* will He withhold
From those who walk uprightly.

O LORD of hosts,
Blessed *is* the man who trusts in You!

Psalm 84:11-12

WiSDoM

Everyone proud in heart *is* an abomination to
the LORD;
Though they join forces, none will go
unpunished.

Proverbs 16:5

SW?! **SO WHAT?**
What does this tell me?

EZEKIEL COMMISSIONED AS A PROPHET

Ezekiel 2–3; Psalm 85:4-7; Proverbs 16:6

And He said to me, "Son of man, stand on your feet, and I will speak to you." Then the Spirit entered me when He spoke to me, and set me on my feet; and I heard Him who spoke to me. And He said to me: "Son of man, I am sending you to the children of Israel, to a rebellious nation that has rebelled against Me; they and their fathers have transgressed against Me to this very day. For *they are* impudent and stubborn children. I am sending you to them, and you shall say to them, 'Thus says the Lord GOD.' As for them, whether they hear or whether they refuse—for they *are* a rebellious house—yet they will know that a prophet has been among them.

"And you, son of man, do not be afraid of them nor be afraid of their words, though briers and thorns *are* with you and you dwell among scorpions; do not be afraid of their words or dismayed by their looks, though they *are* a rebellious house. You shall speak My words to them, whether they hear or whether they refuse, for they *are* rebellious. But you, son of man, hear what I say to you. Do not be rebellious like that rebellious house; open your mouth and eat what I give you."

Now when I looked, there was a hand stretched out to me; and behold, a scroll of a book *was* in it. Then He spread it before me; and *there was* writing on the inside and on the outside, and written on it *were* lamentations and mourning and woe.

Moreover He said to me, "Son of man, eat what you find; eat this scroll, and go, speak to the house of Israel." So I opened my mouth, and He caused me to eat that scroll.

And He said to me, "Son of man, feed your belly, and fill your stomach with this scroll that I give you." So I ate, and it was in my mouth like honey in sweetness.

Then He said to me: "Son of man, go to the house of Israel and speak with My words to them. For you *are* not sent to a people of unfamiliar speech and of hard language, *but* to the house of Israel, not to many people of unfamiliar speech and of hard language, whose words you cannot

understand. Surely, had I sent you to them, they would have listened to you. But the house of Israel will not listen to you, because they will not listen to Me; for all the house of Israel *are* impudent and hard-hearted. Behold, I have made your face strong against their faces, and your forehead strong against their foreheads. Like adamant stone, harder than flint, I have made your forehead; do not be afraid of them, nor be dismayed at their looks, though they *are* a rebellious house."

Moreover He said to me: "Son of man, receive into your heart all My words that I speak to you, and hear with your ears. And go, get to the captives, to the children of your people, and speak to them and tell them, 'Thus says the Lord GOD,' whether they hear, or whether they refuse."

Then the Spirit lifted me up, and I heard behind me a great thunderous voice: "Blessed *is* the glory of the LORD from His place!" *I* also *heard* the noise of the wings of the living creatures that touched one another, and the noise of the wheels beside them, and a great thunderous noise. So the Spirit lifted me up and took me away, and I went in bitterness, in the heat of my spirit; but the hand of the LORD was strong upon me. Then I came to the captives at Tel Abib, who dwelt by the River Chebar; and I sat where they sat, and remained there astonished among them seven days.

Now it came to pass at the end of seven days that the word of the LORD came to me, saying, "Son of man, I have made you a watchman for the house of Israel; therefore hear a word from My mouth, and give them warning from Me: When I say to the wicked, 'You shall surely die,' and you give him no warning, nor speak to warn the wicked from his wicked way, to save his life, that same wicked *man* shall die in his iniquity; but his blood I will require at your hand. Yet, if you warn the wicked, and he does not turn from his wickedness, nor from his wicked way, he shall die in his iniquity; but you have delivered your soul.

"Again, when a righteous *man* turns from his righteousness and commits iniquity, and I lay a stumbling block before him, he shall die; because you did not give him warning, he shall die in his sin, and his righteousness which he has done shall not be remembered; but his blood I will require at your hand. Nevertheless if you warn the righteous *man* that the righteous should not sin, and he does not sin, he shall surely live because he took warning; also you will have delivered your soul."

Then the hand of the LORD was upon me there, and He said to me, "Arise, go out into the plain, and there I shall talk with you."

So I arose and went out into the plain, and behold, the glory of the LORD stood there, like the glory which I saw by the River Chebar; and I fell on my face. Then the Spirit entered me and set me on my feet, and spoke with me and said to me: "Go, shut yourself inside your house. And you, O son of man, surely they will put ropes on you and bind you with them, so that you cannot go out among them. I will make your tongue cling to the roof of your mouth, so that you shall be mute and not be one to rebuke them, for they *are* a rebellious house. But when I speak with you, I will open your mouth, and you shall say to them, 'Thus says the Lord GOD.' He who hears, let him hear; and he who refuses, let him refuse; for they *are* a rebellious house."

Ezekiel 2–3

WORSHIP

Restore us, O God of our salvation,
And cause Your anger toward us to cease.
Will You be angry with us forever?
Will You prolong Your anger to all
    generations?
Will You not revive us again,
That Your people may rejoice in You?
Show us Your mercy, LORD,
And grant us Your salvation.

Psalm 85:4-7

WISDOM

In mercy and truth
Atonement is provided for iniquity;
And by the fear of the LORD *one* departs from
    evil.

Proverbs 16:6

SW?! SO WHAT?
What does this tell me?

EZEKIEL, PROPHET OF PANTOMIME

Ezekiel 4–5; Psalm 85:9-11; Proverbs 16:7

"You also, son of man, take a clay tablet and lay it before you, and portray on it a city, Jerusalem. Lay siege against it, build a siege wall against it, and heap up a mound against it; set camps against it also, and place battering rams against it all around. Moreover take for yourself an iron plate, and set it *as* an iron wall between you and the city. Set your face against it, and it shall be besieged, and you shall lay siege against it. This *will be* a sign to the house of Israel.

"Lie also on your left side, and lay the iniquity of the house of Israel upon it. *According* to the number of the days that you lie on it, you shall bear their iniquity. For I have laid on you the years of their iniquity, according to the number of the days, three hundred and ninety days; so you shall bear the iniquity of the house of Israel. And when you have completed them, lie again on your right side; then you shall bear the iniquity of the house of Judah forty days. I have laid on you a day for each year.

"Therefore you shall set your face toward the siege of Jerusalem; your arm *shall be* uncovered, and you shall prophesy against it. And surely I will restrain you so that you cannot turn from one side to another till you have ended the days of your siege.

"Also take for yourself wheat, barley, beans, lentils, millet, and spelt; put them into one vessel, and make bread of them for yourself. *During* the number of days that you lie on your side, three hundred and ninety days, you shall eat it. And your food which you eat *shall be* by weight, twenty shekels a day; from time to time you shall eat it. You shall also drink water by measure, one-sixth of a hin; from time to time you shall drink. And you shall eat it *as* barley cakes; and bake it using fuel of human waste in their sight."

Then the LORD said, "So shall the children of Israel eat their defiled bread among the Gentiles, where I will drive them."

So I said, "Ah, Lord GOD! Indeed I have never defiled myself from my youth till now; I have never eaten what died of itself or was torn by beasts, nor has abominable flesh ever come into my mouth."

Then He said to me, "See, I am giving you cow dung instead of human waste, and you shall prepare your bread over it."

Moreover He said to me, "Son of man, surely I will cut off the supply of bread in Jerusalem; they shall eat bread by weight and with anxiety, and shall drink water by measure and with dread, that they may lack bread and water, and be dismayed with one another, and waste away because of their iniquity.

"And you, son of man, take a sharp sword, take it as a barber's razor, and pass *it* over your head and your beard; then take scales to weigh and divide the hair. You shall burn with fire one-third in the midst of the city, when the days of the siege are finished; then you shall take one-third and strike around *it* with the sword, and one-third you shall scatter in the wind: I will draw out a sword after them. You shall also take a small number of them and bind them in the edge of your *garment*. Then take some of them again and throw them into the midst of the fire, and burn them in the fire. From there a fire will go out into all the house of Israel.

"Thus says the Lord GOD: 'This *is* Jerusalem; I have set her in the midst of the nations and the countries all around her. She has rebelled against My judgments by doing wickedness more than the nations, and against My statutes more than the countries that *are* all around her; for they have refused My judgments, and they have not walked in My statutes.' Therefore thus says the Lord GOD: 'Because you have multiplied *disobedience* more than the nations that *are* all around you, have not walked in My statutes nor kept My judgments, nor even done according to the judgments of the nations that *are* all around you'—therefore thus says the Lord GOD: 'Indeed I, even I, *am* against you and will execute judgments in your midst in the sight of the nations. And I will do among you what I have never done, and the like of which I will never do again, because of all your abominations. Therefore fathers shall eat *their* sons in your midst, and sons shall eat their fathers; and I will execute judgments among you, and all of you who remain I will scatter to all the winds.

'Therefore, *as* I live,' says the Lord GOD, 'surely, because you have defiled My sanctuary with all your detestable things and with all your abominations, therefore I will also diminish *you;* My eye will not spare, nor will I have any pity. One-third of you shall die of the pestilence, and be consumed with famine in your midst; and one-third shall fall by the sword all around you; and I will scatter another third to all the winds, and I will draw out a sword after them.

'Thus shall My anger be spent, and I will cause My fury to rest upon them, and I will be avenged; and they shall know that I, the LORD, have spoken *it* in My zeal, when I have spent My fury upon them. Moreover I will make you a waste and a reproach among the nations that *are* all around you, in the sight of all who pass by.

'So it shall be a reproach, a taunt, a lesson, and an astonishment to the nations that *are* all around you, when I execute judgments among you in anger and in fury and in furious rebukes. I, the LORD, have spoken. When I send against them the terrible arrows of famine which shall be for destruction, which I will send to destroy you, I will increase the famine upon you and cut off your supply of bread. So I will send against you famine and wild beasts, and they will bereave you. Pestilence and blood shall pass through you, and I will bring the sword against you. I, the LORD, have spoken.'"

Ezekiel 4–5

WORSHIP

Surely His salvation *is* near to those who fear
  Him,
That glory may dwell in our land.

Mercy and truth have met together;
Righteousness and peace have kissed.
Truth shall spring out of the earth,
And righteousness shall look down from
  heaven.

Psalm 85:9-11

WISDOM

When a man's ways please the LORD,
He makes even his enemies to be at peace
  with him.

Proverbs 16:7

SW?! **SO WHAT?**
What does this tell me?

THE IMMINENT DOWNFALL OF JUDAH

Ezekiel 7; Psalm 86:7-10; Proverbs 16:8

Moreover the word of the LORD came to me, saying, "And you, son of man, thus says the Lord GOD to the land of Israel:

'An end! The end has come upon the four
    corners of the land.
Now the end *has come* upon you,
And I will send My anger against you;
I will judge you according to your ways,
And I will repay you for all your abominations.
My eye will not spare you,
Nor will I have pity;
But I will repay your ways,
And your abominations will be in your midst;
Then you shall know that I *am* the LORD!'

"Thus says the Lord GOD:

'A disaster, a singular disaster;
Behold, it has come!
An end has come,
The end has come;
It has dawned for you;
Behold, it has come!
    Doom has come to you, you who dwell in
        the land;
    The time has come,
    A day of trouble *is* near,
    And not of rejoicing in the mountains.
    Now upon you I will soon pour out My fury,
    And spend My anger upon you;
    I will judge you according to your ways,
    And I will repay you for all your
        abominations.

'My eye will not spare,
Nor will I have pity;
I will repay you according to your ways,
And your abominations will be in your midst.
Then you shall know that I *am* the LORD who
    strikes.

'Behold, the day!
Behold, it has come!
Doom has gone out;
The rod has blossomed,
Pride has budded.
Violence has risen up into a rod of
    wickedness;
None of them *shall remain,*
None of their multitude,
None of them;

Nor *shall there be* wailing for them.
The time has come,
The day draws near.

'Let not the buyer rejoice,
Nor the seller mourn,
For wrath *is* on their whole multitude.
For the seller shall not return to what has been
    sold,
Though he may still be alive;
For the vision concerns the whole multitude,
And it shall not turn back;
No one will strengthen himself
Who lives in iniquity.

'They have blown the trumpet and made
    everyone ready,
But no one goes to battle;
For My wrath *is* on all their multitude.
The sword *is* outside,
And the pestilence and famine within.
Whoever *is* in the field
Will die by the sword;
And whoever *is* in the city,
Famine and pestilence will devour him.

'Those who survive will escape and be on the
    mountains
Like doves of the valleys,
All of them mourning,
Each for his iniquity.
Every hand will be feeble,
And every knee will be *as* weak *as* water.
They will also be girded with sackcloth;
Horror will cover them;
Shame *will be* on every face,
Baldness on all their heads.

'They will throw their silver into the streets,
And their gold will be like refuse;
Their silver and their gold will not be able to
    deliver them
In the day of the wrath of the LORD;
They will not satisfy their souls,
Nor fill their stomachs,
Because it became their stumbling block of
    iniquity.

'As for the beauty of his ornaments,
He set it in majesty;
But they made from it
The images of their abominations—

Their detestable things;
Therefore I have made it
Like refuse to them.
I will give it as plunder
Into the hands of strangers,
And to the wicked of the earth as spoil;
And they shall defile it.
I will turn My face from them,
And they will defile My secret place;
For robbers shall enter it and defile it.

'Make a chain,
For the land is filled with crimes of blood,
And the city is full of violence.
Therefore I will bring the worst of the Gentiles,
And they will possess their houses;
I will cause the pomp of the strong to cease,
And their holy places shall be defiled.
Destruction comes;
They will seek peace, but *there shall be* none.
Disaster will come upon disaster,
And rumor will be upon rumor.
Then they will seek a vision from a prophet;
But the law will perish from the priest,
And counsel from the elders.

'The king will mourn,
The prince will be clothed with desolation,
And the hands of the common people will
      tremble.
I will do to them according to their way,
And according to what they deserve I will
      judge them;
Then they shall know that I *am* the LORD!' "

Ezekiel 7

WORSHIP

In the day of my trouble I will call upon You,
For You will answer me.

Among the gods *there is* none like You, O
      Lord;
Nor *are there any works* like Your works.
All nations whom You have made
Shall come and worship before You, O Lord,
And shall glorify Your name.
For You *are* great, and do wondrous things;
You alone *are* God.

Psalm 86:7-10

WISDOM

Better *is* a little with righteousness,
Than vast revenues without justice.

Proverbs 16:8

SW?! SO WHAT?
What does this tell me?

EZEKIEL'S VISION OF JERUSALEM'S IDOLATRY

Ezekiel 8–9; Psalm 86:11-13; Proverbs 16:9

And it came to pass in the sixth year, in the sixth *month,* on the fifth *day* of the month, as I sat in my house with the elders of Judah sitting before me, that the hand of the Lord GOD fell upon me there. Then I looked, and there was a likeness, like the appearance of fire—from the appearance of His waist and downward, fire; and from His waist and upward, like the appearance of brightness, like the color of amber. He stretched out the form of a hand, and took me by a lock of my hair; and the Spirit lifted me up between earth and heaven, and brought me in visions of God to Jerusalem, to the door of the north gate of the inner *court,* where the seat of the image of jealousy *was,* which provokes to jealousy. And behold, the glory of the God of Israel *was* there, like the vision that I saw in the plain.

Then He said to me, "Son of man, lift your eyes now toward the north." So I lifted my eyes toward the north, and there, north of the altar gate, was this image of jealousy in the entrance.

Furthermore He said to me, "Son of man, do you see what they are doing, the great abominations that the house of Israel commits here, to make Me go far away from My sanctuary? Now turn again, you will see greater abominations." So He brought me to the door of the court; and when I looked, there was a hole in the wall. Then He said to me, "Son of man, dig into the wall"; and when I dug into the wall, there was a door.

And He said to me, "Go in, and see the wicked abominations which they are doing there." So I went in and saw, and there—every sort of creeping thing, abominable beasts, and all the idols of the house of Israel, portrayed all around on the walls. And there stood before them seventy men of the elders of the house of Israel, and in their midst stood Jaazaniah the son of Shaphan. Each man had a censer in his hand, and a thick cloud of incense went up. Then He said to me, "Son of man, have you seen what the elders of the house of Israel do in the dark, every man in the room of his idols? For they say, 'The LORD does not see us, the LORD has forsaken the land.' "

And He said to me, "Turn again, *and* you will see greater abominations that they are doing." So He brought me to the door of the north gate of the LORD's house; and to my dismay, women were sitting there weeping for Tammuz.

Then He said to me, "Have you seen *this,* O son of man? Turn again, you will see greater abominations than these." So He brought me into the inner court of the LORD's house; and there, at the door of the temple of the LORD, between the porch and the altar, *were* about twenty-five men with their backs toward the temple of the LORD and their faces toward the east, and they were worshiping the sun toward the east.

And He said to me, "Have you seen *this,* O son of man? Is it a trivial thing to the house of Judah to commit the abominations which they commit here? For they have filled the land with violence; then they have returned to provoke Me to anger. Indeed they put the branch to their nose. Therefore I also will act in fury. My eye will not spare nor will I have pity; and though they cry in My ears with a loud voice, I will not hear them."

Then He called out in my hearing with a loud voice, saying, "Let those who have charge over the city draw near, each *with* a deadly weapon in his hand." And suddenly six men came from the direction of the upper gate, which faces north, each with his battle-ax in his hand. One man among them *was* clothed with linen and had a writer's inkhorn at his side. They went in and stood beside the bronze altar.

Now the glory of the God of Israel had gone up from the cherub, where it had been, to the threshold of the temple. And He called to the man clothed with linen, who *had* the writer's inkhorn at his side; and the LORD said to him, "Go through the midst of the city, through the midst of Jerusalem, and put a mark on the foreheads of the men who sigh and cry over all the abominations that are done within it."

To the others He said in my hearing, "Go after him through the city and kill; do not let your eye spare, nor have any pity. Utterly slay old *and* young men, maidens and little children and women; but do not come near anyone on whom *is* the mark;

and begin at My sanctuary." So they began with the elders who *were* before the temple. Then He said to them, "Defile the temple, and fill the courts with the slain. Go out!" And they went out and killed in the city.

So it was, that while they were killing them, I was left *alone;* and I fell on my face and cried out, and said, "Ah, Lord GOD! Will You destroy all the remnant of Israel in pouring out Your fury on Jerusalem?"

Then He said to me, "The iniquity of the house of Israel and Judah *is* exceedingly great, and the land is full of bloodshed, and the city full of perversity; for they say, 'The LORD has forsaken the land, and the LORD does not see!' And as for Me also, My eye will neither spare, nor will I have pity, *but* I will recompense their deeds on their own head."

Just then, the man clothed with linen, who *had* the inkhorn at his side, reported back and said, "I have done as You commanded me."

Ezekiel 8–9

WORSHIP

Teach me Your way, O LORD;
I will walk in Your truth;
Unite my heart to fear Your name.
I will praise You, O Lord my God, with all my
    heart,
And I will glorify Your name forevermore.
For great *is* Your mercy toward me,
And You have delivered my soul from the
    depths of Sheol.

Psalm 86:11-13

WISDOM

A man's heart plans his way,
But the LORD directs his steps.

Proverbs 16:9

SW?! SO WHAT?
What does this tell me?

GOD'S GLORY DEPARTS FROM JERUSALEM

Ezekiel 10:1-5, 18-22; 11:1-25; Psalm 86:14-16; Proverbs 16:11

A nd I looked, and there in the firmament that was above the head of the cherubim, there appeared something like a sapphire stone, having the appearance of the likeness of a throne. Then He spoke to the man clothed with linen, and said, "Go in among the wheels, under the cherub, fill your hands with coals of fire from among the cherubim, and scatter *them* over the city." And he went in as I watched.

Now the cherubim were standing on the south side of the temple when the man went in, and the cloud filled the inner court. Then the glory of the LORD went up from the cherub, *and paused* over the threshold of the temple; and the house was filled with the cloud, and the court was full of the brightness of the LORD's glory. And the sound of the wings of the cherubim was heard *even* in the outer court, like the voice of Almighty God when He speaks.

Then the glory of the LORD departed from the threshold of the temple and stood over the cherubim. And the cherubim lifted their wings and mounted up from the earth in my sight. When they went out, the wheels *were* beside them; and they stood at the door of the east gate of the LORD's house, and the glory of the God of Israel *was* above them.

This *is* the living creature I saw under the God of Israel by the River Chebar, and I knew they *were* cherubim. Each one had four faces and each one four wings, and the likeness of the hands of a man *was* under their wings. And the likeness of their faces *was* the same *as* the faces which I had seen by the River Chebar, their appearance and their persons. They each went straight forward.

Then the Spirit lifted me up and brought me to the East Gate of the LORD's house, which faces eastward; and there at the door of the gate were twenty-five men, among whom I saw Jaazaniah the son of Azzur, and Pelatiah the son of Benaiah, princes of the people. And He said to me: "Son of man, these *are* the men who devise iniquity and give wicked counsel in this city, who say,

'*The time is* not near to build houses; this *city is* the caldron, and we *are* the meat.' Therefore prophesy against them, prophesy, O son of man!"

Then the Spirit of the LORD fell upon me, and said to me, "Speak! 'Thus says the LORD: "Thus you have said, O house of Israel; for I know the things that come into your mind. You have multiplied your slain in this city, and you have filled its streets with the slain." Therefore thus says the Lord GOD: "Your slain whom you have laid in its midst, they *are* the meat, and this *city is* the caldron; but I shall bring you out of the midst of it. You have feared the sword; and I will bring a sword upon you," says the Lord GOD. "And I will bring you out of its midst, and deliver you into the hands of strangers, and execute judgments on you. You shall fall by the sword. I will judge you at the border of Israel. Then you shall know that I *am* the LORD. This *city* shall not be your caldron, nor shall you be the meat in its midst. I will judge you at the border of Israel. And you shall know that I *am* the LORD; for you have not walked in My statutes nor executed My judgments, but have done according to the customs of the Gentiles which *are* all around you." ' "

Now it happened, while I was prophesying, that Pelatiah the son of Benaiah died. Then I fell on my face and cried with a loud voice, and said, "Ah, Lord GOD! Will You make a complete end of the remnant of Israel?"

Again the word of the LORD came to me, saying, "Son of man, your brethren, your relatives, your countrymen, and all the house of Israel in its entirety, *are* those about whom the inhabitants of Jerusalem have said, 'Get far away from the LORD; this land has been given to us as a possession.' Therefore say, 'Thus says the Lord GOD: "Although I have cast them far off among the Gentiles, and although I have scattered them among the countries, yet I shall be a little sanctuary for them in the countries where they have gone." ' Therefore say, 'Thus says the Lord GOD: "I will gather you from the peoples, assemble you from the countries where you have been scattered, and I will give you the land of Israel." ' And they will go there, and they will take away all its detestable things and all its abominations from there. Then I will give them one heart, and I will put a new spirit within them, and take the stony heart out of their flesh, and give them a heart of flesh, that they may walk in My statutes and keep My judgments and do them; and they shall be My people, and I will be their God. But *as for those* whose hearts follow the desire for their detestable things and their abominations, I will recompense their deeds on their own heads," says the Lord God.

So the cherubim lifted up their wings, with the wheels beside them, and the glory of the God of Israel *was* high above them. And the glory of the Lord went up from the midst of the city and stood on the mountain, which *is* on the east side of the city.

Then the Spirit took me up and brought me in a vision by the Spirit of God into Chaldea, to those in captivity. And the vision that I had seen went up from me. So I spoke to those in captivity of all the things the Lord had shown me.

Ezekiel 10:1-5, 18-22; 11:1-25

WORSHIP

O God, the proud have risen against me,
And a mob of violent *men* have sought my life,
And have not set You before them.
But You, O Lord, *are* a God full of compassion,
    and gracious,
Longsuffering and abundant in mercy and
    truth.

Oh, turn to me, and have mercy on me!
Give Your strength to Your servant,
And save the son of Your maidservant.

Psalm 86:14-16

WISDOM

Honest weights and scales *are* the Lord's;
All the weights in the bag *are* His work.

Proverbs 16:11

SW?! **SO WHAT?**
What does this tell me?

Packing For the Move To Babylon

Ezekiel 12; Psalm 87:1-3; Proverbs 16:12

Now the word of the Lord came to me, saying: "Son of man, you dwell in the midst of a rebellious house, which has eyes to see but does not see, and ears to hear but does not hear; for they *are* a rebellious house.

"Therefore, son of man, prepare your belongings for captivity, and go into captivity by day in their sight. You shall go from your place into captivity to another place in their sight. It may be that they will consider, though they *are* a rebellious house. By day you shall bring out your belongings in their sight, as though going into captivity; and at evening you shall go in their sight, like those who go into captivity. Dig through the wall in their sight, and carry your belongings out through it. In their sight you shall bear *them* on *your* shoulders *and* carry *them* out at twilight; you shall cover your face, so that you cannot see the ground, for I have made you a sign to the house of Israel."

So I did as I was commanded. I brought out my belongings by day, as though going into captivity, and at evening I dug through the wall with my hand. I brought *them* out at twilight, *and* I bore *them* on *my* shoulder in their sight.

And in the morning the word of the Lord came to me, saying, "Son of man, has not the house of Israel, the rebellious house, said to you, 'What are you doing?' Say to them, 'Thus says the Lord God: "This burden *concerns* the prince in Jerusalem and all the house of Israel who are among them."' Say, 'I *am* a sign to you. As I have done, so shall it be done to them; they shall be carried away into captivity.' And the prince who *is* among them shall bear *his belongings* on *his* shoulder at twilight and go out. They shall dig through the wall to carry *them* out through it. He shall cover his face, so that he cannot see the ground with *his* eyes. I will also spread My net over him, and he shall be caught in My snare. I will bring him to Babylon, *to* the land of the Chaldeans; yet he shall not see it, though he shall die there. I will scatter to every wind all who *are* around him to help him, and all his troops; and I will draw out the sword after them.

"Then they shall know that I *am* the Lord, when I scatter them among the nations and disperse them throughout the countries. But I will spare a few of their men from the sword, from famine, and from pestilence, that they may declare all their abominations among the Gentiles wherever they go. Then they shall know that I *am* the Lord."

Moreover the word of the Lord came to me, saying, "Son of man, eat your bread with quaking, and drink your water with trembling and anxiety. And say to the people of the land, 'Thus says the Lord God to the inhabitants of Jerusalem *and* to the land of Israel: "They shall eat their bread with anxiety, and drink their water with dread, so that her land may be emptied of all who are in it, because of the violence of all those who dwell in it. Then the cities that are inhabited shall be laid waste, and the land shall become desolate; and you shall know that I *am* the Lord."'"

And the word of the Lord came to me, saying, "Son of man, what *is* this proverb *that* you *people* have about the land of Israel, which says, 'The days are prolonged, and every vision fails'? Tell them therefore, 'Thus says the Lord God: "I will lay this proverb to rest, and they shall no more use it as a proverb in Israel."' But say to them, 'The days are at hand, and the fulfillment of every vision. For no more shall there be any false vision or flattering divination within the house of Israel. For I *am* the Lord. I speak, and the word which I speak will come to pass; it will no more be postponed; for in your days, O rebellious house, I will say the word and perform it," says the Lord God.'"

Again the word of the Lord came to me, saying, "Son of man, look, the house of Israel is saying, 'The vision that he sees *is* for many days *from now*, and he prophesies of times far off.' Therefore say to them, 'Thus says the Lord God: "None of My words will be postponed any more, but the word which I speak will be done," says the Lord God.'"

Ezekiel 12

WORSHIP

His foundation *is* in the holy mountains.
The LORD loves the gates of Zion
More than all the dwellings of Jacob.
Glorious things are spoken of you,
O city of God!   Selah
Psalm 87:1-3

WISDOM

It is an abomination for kings to commit
    wickedness,
For a throne is established by righteousness.
Proverbs 16:12

SW?! SO WHAT?
What does this tell me?

Idols in THEIR HEARTS Ezekiel 14–15; Psalm 88:1-3; Proverbs 16:16

Now some of the elders of Israel came to me and sat before me. And the word of the LORD came to me, saying, "Son of man, these men have set up their idols in their hearts, and put before them that which causes them to stumble into iniquity. Should I let Myself be inquired of at all by them?

"Therefore speak to them, and say to them, 'Thus says the Lord GOD: "Everyone of the house of Israel who sets up his idols in his heart, and puts before him what causes him to stumble into iniquity, and then comes to the prophet, I the LORD will answer him who comes, according to the multitude of his idols, that I may seize the house of Israel by their heart, because they are all estranged from Me by their idols." '

"Therefore say to the house of Israel, 'Thus says the Lord GOD: "Repent, turn away from your idols, and turn your faces away from all your abominations. For anyone of the house of Israel, or of the strangers who dwell in Israel, who separates himself from Me and sets up his idols in his heart and puts before him what causes him to stumble into iniquity, then comes to a prophet to inquire of him concerning Me, I the LORD will answer him by Myself. I will set My face against that man and make him a sign and a proverb, and I will cut him off from the midst of My people. Then you shall know that I am the LORD.

"And if the prophet is induced to speak anything, I the LORD have induced that prophet, and I will stretch out My hand against him and destroy him from among My people Israel. And they shall bear their iniquity; the punishment of the prophet shall be the same as the punishment of the one who inquired, that the house of Israel may no longer stray from Me, nor be profaned anymore with all their transgressions, but that they may be My people and I may be their God," says the Lord GOD.' "

The word of the LORD came again to me, saying: "Son of man, when a land sins against Me by persistent unfaithfulness, I will stretch out My hand against it; I will cut off its supply of bread, send famine on it, and cut off man and beast from it. Even if these three men, Noah, Daniel, and Job, were in it, they would deliver only themselves by their righteousness," says the Lord GOD.

"If I cause wild beasts to pass through the land, and they empty it, and make it so desolate that no man may pass through because of the beasts, even though these three men were in it, as I live," says the Lord GOD, "they would deliver neither sons nor daughters; only they would be delivered, and the land would be desolate.

"Or if I bring a sword on that land, and say, 'Sword, go through the land,' and I cut off man and beast from it, even though these three men were in it, as I live," says the Lord GOD, "they would deliver neither sons nor daughters, but only they themselves would be delivered.

"Or if I send a pestilence into that land and pour out My fury on it in blood, and cut off from it man and beast, even though Noah, Daniel, and Job were in it, as I live," says the Lord GOD, "they would deliver neither son nor daughter; they would deliver only themselves by their righteousness."

For thus says the Lord GOD: "How much more it shall be when I send My four severe judgments on Jerusalem—the sword and famine and wild beasts and pestilence—to cut off man and beast from it? Yet behold, there shall be left in it a remnant who will be brought out, both sons and daughters; surely they will come out to you, and you will see their ways and their doings. Then you will be comforted concerning the disaster that I have brought upon Jerusalem, all that I have brought upon it. And they will comfort you, when you see their ways and their doings; and you shall know that I have done nothing without cause that I have done in it," says the LORD GOD.

Then the word of the LORD came to me, saying: "Son of man, how is the wood of the vine better than any other wood, the vine branch which is among the trees of the forest? Is wood taken from it to make any object? Or can men make a peg from it to hang any vessel on? Instead, it is thrown into the fire for fuel; the fire devours both ends of it, and its middle is burned. Is it useful for any work? Indeed, when it was whole, no object could be made from it. How much less will it be useful for *any* work when the fire has devoured it, and it is burned?

"Therefore thus says the Lord GOD: 'Like the wood of the vine among the trees of the forest, which I have given to the fire for fuel, so I will give up the inhabitants of Jerusalem; and I will set My face against them. They will go out from *one* fire, but *another* fire shall devour them. Then you shall know that I *am* the LORD, when I set My face against them. Thus I will make the land desolate, because they have persisted in unfaithfulness,' says the Lord GOD."

Ezekiel 14–15

WORSHIP

O LORD, God of my salvation,
I have cried out day and night before You.
Let my prayer come before You;
Incline Your ear to my cry.

For my soul is full of troubles,
And my life draws near to the grave.

Psalm 88:1-3

WISDOM

How much better to get wisdom than gold!
And to get understanding is to be chosen
       rather than silver.

Proverbs 16:16

SW?! SO WHAT?
What does this tell me?

THE STORY OF THE ADULTEROUS WIFE
Ezekiel 16:1-43, 60-63; Psalm 88:8-9; Proverbs 16:17

Again the word of the LORD came to me, saying, "Son of man, cause Jerusalem to know her abominations, and say, 'Thus says the Lord GOD to Jerusalem: "Your birth and your nativity *are* from the land of Canaan; your father *was* an Amorite and your mother a Hittite. *As for* your nativity, on the day you were born your navel cord was not cut, nor were you washed in water to cleanse *you;* you were not rubbed with salt nor wrapped in swaddling cloths. No eye pitied you, to do any of these things for you, to have compassion on you; but you were thrown out into the open field, when you yourself were loathed on the day you were born.

"And when I passed by you and saw you struggling in your own blood, I said to you in your blood, 'Live!' Yes, I said to you in your blood, 'Live!' I made you thrive like a plant in the field; and you grew, matured, and became very beautiful. *Your* breasts were formed, your hair grew, but you *were* naked and bare.

"When I passed by you again and looked upon you, indeed your time *was* the time of love; so I spread My wing over you and covered your nakedness. Yes, I swore an oath to you and entered into a covenant with you, and you became Mine," says the Lord GOD.

"Then I washed you in water; yes, I thoroughly washed off your blood, and I anointed you with oil. I clothed you in embroidered cloth and gave you sandals of badger skin; I clothed you with fine linen and covered you with silk. I adorned you with ornaments, put bracelets on your wrists, and a chain on your neck. And I put a jewel in your nose, earrings in your ears, and a beautiful crown on your head. Thus you were adorned with gold and silver, and your clothing *was of* fine linen, silk, and embroidered cloth. You ate *pastry of* fine flour, honey, and oil. You were exceedingly beautiful, and succeeded to royalty. Your fame went out among the nations because of your beauty, for it *was* perfect through My splendor which I had bestowed on you," says the Lord GOD.

"But you trusted in your own beauty, played the harlot because of your fame, and poured out your harlotry on everyone passing by who *would have* it. You took some of your garments and adorned multicolored high places for yourself, and played the harlot on them. *Such* things should not happen, nor be. You have also taken your beautiful jewelry from My gold and My silver, which I had given you, and made for yourself male images and played the harlot with them. You took your embroidered garments and covered them, and you set My oil and My incense before them. Also My food which I gave you—the pastry of fine flour, oil, and honey *which* I fed you—you set it before them as sweet incense; and *so* it was," says the Lord GOD.

"Moreover you took your sons and your daughters, whom you bore to Me, and these you sacrificed to them to be devoured. *Were* your *acts* of harlotry a small matter, that you have slain My children and offered them up to them by causing them to pass through *the fire?* And in all your abominations and acts of harlotry you did not remember the days of your youth, when you were naked and bare, struggling in your blood.

"Then it was so, after all your wickedness—'Woe, woe to you!' says the Lord GOD—*that* you also built for yourself a shrine, and made a high place for yourself in every street. You built your high places at the head of every road, and made your beauty to be abhorred. You offered yourself to everyone who passed by, and multiplied your acts of harlotry. You also committed harlotry with the Egyptians, your very fleshly neighbors, and increased your acts of harlotry to provoke Me to anger.

"Behold, therefore, I stretched out My hand against you, diminished your allotment, and gave you up to the will of those who hate you, the daughters of the Philistines, who were ashamed of your lewd behavior. You also played the harlot with the Assyrians, because you were insatiable; indeed you played the harlot with them and still were not satisfied. Moreover you multiplied your acts of harlotry as far as the land of the trader, Chaldea; and even then you were not satisfied.

"How degenerate is your heart!" says the Lord GOD, "seeing you do all these *things,* the deeds of a brazen harlot.

"You erected your shrine at the head of every road, and built your high place in every street. Yet you were not like a harlot, because you scorned payment. *You are* an adulterous wife, *who* takes strangers instead of her husband. Men make payment to all harlots, but you made your payments to all your lovers, and hired them to come to you from all around for your harlotry. You are the opposite of *other* women in your harlotry, because no one solicited you to be a harlot. In that you gave payment but no payment was given you, therefore you are the opposite."

'Now then, O harlot, hear the word of the LORD! Thus says the Lord GOD: "Because your filthiness was poured out and your nakedness uncovered in your harlotry with your lovers, and with all your abominable idols, and because of the blood of your children which you gave to them, surely, therefore, I will gather all your lovers with whom you took pleasure, all those you loved, *and* all those you hated; I will gather them from all around against you and will uncover your nakedness to them, that they may see all your nakedness. And I will judge you as women who break wedlock or shed blood are judged; I will bring blood upon you in fury and jealousy. I will also give you into their hand, and they shall throw down your shrines and break down your high places. They shall also strip you of your clothes, take your beautiful jewelry, and leave you naked and bare.

"They shall also bring up an assembly against you, and they shall stone you with stones and thrust you through with their swords. They shall burn your houses with fire, and execute judgments on you in the sight of many women; and I will make you cease playing the harlot, and you shall no longer hire lovers. So I will lay to rest My fury toward you, and My jealousy shall depart from you. I will be quiet, and be angry no more. Because you did not remember the days of your youth, but agitated Me with all these *things,* surely I will also recompense your deeds on *your own* head," says the Lord GOD. "And you shall not commit lewdness in addition to all your abominations.

"Nevertheless I will remember My covenant with you in the days of your youth, and I will establish an everlasting covenant with you. Then you will remember your ways and be ashamed, when you receive your older and your younger sisters; for I will give them to you for daughters, but not because of My covenant with you. And I will establish My covenant with you. Then you shall know that I *am* the LORD, that you may remember and be ashamed, and never open your mouth anymore because of your shame, when I provide you an atonement for all you have done," says the Lord GOD.' "

Ezekiel 16:1-43, 60-63

WORSHIP

You have put away my acquaintances far from
    me;
You have made me an abomination to them;
I am shut up, and I cannot get out;
My eye wastes away because of affliction.

LORD, I have called daily upon You;
I have stretched out my hands to You.

Psalm 88:8-9

WISDOM

The highway of the upright *is* to depart from
    evil;
He who keeps his way preserves his soul.

Proverbs 16:17

SO WHAT?
What does this tell me?

THE PARABLE OF THE EAGLES

Ezekiel 17; Psalm 88:11-13; Proverbs 16:18

And the word of the LORD came to me, saying, "Son of man, pose a riddle, and speak a parable to the house of Israel, and say, 'Thus says the Lord GOD:

"A great eagle with large wings and long pinions,
Full of feathers of various colors,
Came to Lebanon
And took from the cedar the highest branch.
He cropped off its topmost young twig
And carried it to a land of trade;
He set it in a city of merchants.
Then he took some of the seed of the land
And planted it in a fertile field;
He placed *it* by abundant waters
And set it like a willow tree.
And it grew and became a spreading vine of
   low stature;
Its branches turned toward him,
But its roots were under it.
So it became a vine,
Brought forth branches,
And put forth shoots.

"But there was another great eagle with
   large wings and many feathers;
And behold, this vine bent its roots toward
   him,
And stretched its branches toward him,
From the garden terrace where it had
   been planted,
That he might water it.
It was planted in good soil by many waters,
To bring forth branches, bear fruit,
And become a majestic vine." '

"Say, 'Thus says the Lord GOD:

"Will it thrive?
Will he not pull up its roots,
Cut off its fruit,
And leave it to wither?
All of its spring leaves will wither,
And no great power or many people
Will be needed to pluck it up by its roots.
Behold, *it is* planted,
Will it thrive?
Will it not utterly wither when the east wind
   touches it?
It will wither in the garden terrace where it
   grew." ' "

Moreover the word of the LORD came to me, saying, "Say now to the rebellious house: 'Do you not know what these *things mean?*' Tell *them*, 'Indeed the king of Babylon went to Jerusalem and took its king and princes, and led them with him to Babylon. And he took the king's offspring, made a covenant with him, and put him under oath. He also took away the mighty of the land, that the kingdom might be brought low and not lift itself up, *but* that by keeping his covenant it might stand. But he rebelled against him by sending his ambassadors to Egypt, that they might give him horses and many people. Will he prosper? Will he who does such *things* escape? Can he break a covenant and still be delivered?

'As I live,' says the Lord GOD, 'surely in the place *where* the king *dwells* who made him king, whose oath he despised and whose covenant he broke—with him in the midst of Babylon he shall die. Nor will Pharaoh with *his* mighty army and great company do anything in the war, when they heap up a siege mound and build a wall to cut off many persons. Since he despised the oath by breaking the covenant, and in fact gave his hand and still did all these *things,* he shall not escape.' "

Therefore thus says the Lord GOD: "As I live, surely My oath which he despised, and My covenant which he broke, I will recompense on his own head. I will spread My net over him, and he shall be taken in My snare. I will bring him to Babylon and try him there for the treason which he committed against Me. All his fugitives with all his troops shall fall by the sword, and those who remain shall be scattered to every wind; and you shall know that I, the LORD, have spoken."

Thus says the Lord GOD: "I will take also *one* of the highest branches of the high cedar and set *it* out. I will crop off from the topmost of its young twigs a tender one, and will plant *it* on a high and prominent mountain. On the mountain height of Israel I will plant it; and it will bring forth boughs, and bear fruit, and be a majestic cedar. Under it will dwell birds of every sort; in the shadow of its branches they will dwell. And all the trees of the field shall know that I, the LORD, have brought down the high tree and exalted the low tree, dried up the green tree and made the dry tree flourish; I, the LORD, have spoken and have done *it.*"

Ezekiel 17

WoRSHiP

Shall Your lovingkindness be declared in the
        grave?
Or Your faithfulness in the place of
        destruction?
Shall Your wonders be known in the dark?
And Your righteousness in the land of
        forgetfulness?

But to You I have cried out, O LORD,
And in the morning my prayer comes before
        You.

Psalm 88:11-13

WiSDoM

Pride *goes* before destruction,
And a haughty spirit before a fall.

Proverbs 16:18

SW?! SO WHAT?
What does this tell me?

THE PRINCIPLE OF PERSONAL RESPONSIBILITY

Ezekiel 18; Psalm 89:1-4; Proverbs 16:19

The word of the LORD came to me again, saying, "What do you mean when you use this proverb concerning the land of Israel, saying:

'The fathers have eaten sour grapes,
And the children's teeth are set on edge'?

"As I live," says the Lord GOD, "you shall no longer use this proverb in Israel.

"Behold, all souls are Mine;
The soul of the father
As well as the soul of the son is Mine;
The soul who sins shall die.
But if a man is just
And does what is lawful and right;
If he has not eaten on the mountains,
Nor lifted up his eyes to the idols of the house
    of Israel,
Nor defiled his neighbor's wife,
Nor approached a woman during her impurity;
If he has not oppressed anyone,
But has restored to the debtor his pledge;
    Has robbed no one by violence,
    But has given his bread to the hungry
    And covered the naked with clothing;
If he has not exacted usury
Nor taken any increase,
But has withdrawn his hand from iniquity
And executed true judgment between man
    and man;
If he has walked in My statutes
And kept My judgments faithfully—
He is just;
He shall surely live!"
Says the Lord GOD.

"If he begets a son who is a robber
Or a shedder of blood,
Who does any of these things
And does none of those duties,
But has eaten on the mountains
Or defiled his neighbor's wife;
If he has oppressed the poor and needy,
Robbed by violence,
Not restored the pledge,
Lifted his eyes to the idols,
Or committed abomination;
If he has exacted usury
Or taken increase—

Shall he then live?
He shall not live!
If he has done any of these abominations,
He shall surely die;
His blood shall be upon him.

"If, however, he begets a son
Who sees all the sins which his father has
    done,
And considers but does not do likewise;
Who has not eaten on the mountains,
Nor lifted his eyes to the idols of the house of
    Israel,
Nor defiled his neighbor's wife;
Has not oppressed anyone,
Nor withheld a pledge,
Nor robbed by violence,
But has given his bread to the hungry
And covered the naked with clothing;
Who has withdrawn his hand from the poor
And not received usury or increase,
But has executed My judgments
And walked in My statutes—
He shall not die for the iniquity of his father;
He shall surely live!

"As for his father,
Because he cruelly oppressed,
Robbed his brother by violence,
And did what is not good among his people,
Behold, he shall die for his iniquity.

"Yet you say, 'Why should the son not bear the guilt of the father?' Because the son has done what is lawful and right, and has kept all My statutes and observed them, he shall surely live. The soul who sins shall die. The son shall not bear the guilt of the father, nor the father bear the guilt of the son. The righteousness of the righteous shall be upon himself, and the wickedness of the wicked shall be upon himself.

"But if a wicked man turns from all his sins which he has committed, keeps all My statutes, and does what is lawful and right, he shall surely live; he shall not die. None of the transgressions which he has committed shall be remembered against him; because of the righteousness which he has done, he shall live. Do I have any pleasure at all that the wicked should die?" says the Lord GOD, "*and* not that he should turn from his ways and live?

"But when a righteous man turns away from his righteousness and commits iniquity, and does according to all the abominations that the wicked *man* does, shall he live? All the righteousness which he has done shall not be remembered; because of the unfaithfulness of which he is guilty and the sin which he has committed, because of them he shall die.

"Yet you say, 'The way of the Lord is not fair.' Hear now, O house of Israel, is it not My way which is fair, and your ways which are not fair? When a righteous *man* turns away from his righteousness, commits iniquity, and dies in it, it is because of the iniquity which he has done that he dies. Again, when a wicked *man* turns away from the wickedness which he committed, and does what is lawful and right, he preserves himself alive. Because he considers and turns away from all the transgressions which he committed, he shall surely live; he shall not die. Yet the house of Israel says, 'The way of the Lord is not fair.' O house of Israel, is it not My ways which are fair, and your ways which are not fair?

"Therefore I will judge you, O house of Israel, every one according to his ways," says the Lord GOD. "Repent, and turn from all your transgressions, so that iniquity will not be your ruin. Cast away from you all the transgressions which you have committed, and get yourselves a new heart and a new spirit. For why should you die, O house of Israel? For I have no pleasure in the death of one who dies," says the Lord GOD. "Therefore turn and live!"

Ezekiel 18

WoRSHiP

I will sing of the mercies of the LORD forever;
With my mouth will I make known Your
  faithfulness to all generations.
For I have said, "Mercy shall be built up
  forever;
Your faithfulness You shall establish in the
  very heavens."

"I have made a covenant with My chosen,
 I have sworn to My servant David:
'Your seed I will establish forever,
 And build up your throne to all generations.' "
Selah
Psalm 89:1-4

WiSDoM

Better *to be* of a humble spirit with the lowly,
Than to divide the spoil with the proud.
Proverbs 16:19

SW?! **SO WHAT?**
What does this tell me?

THE REASONS FOR JUDGMENT ON JERUSALEM

Ezekiel 22; Psalm 89:5-7; Proverbs 16:20

Moreover the word of the LORD came to me, saying, "Now, son of man, will you judge, will you judge the bloody city? Yes, show her all her abominations! Then say, 'Thus says the Lord GOD: "The city sheds blood in her own midst, that her time may come; and she makes idols within herself to defile herself. You have become guilty by the blood which you have shed, and have defiled yourself with the idols which you have made. You have caused your days to draw near, and have come to *the end of* your years; therefore I have made you a reproach to the nations, and a mockery to all countries. *Those* near and *those* far from you will mock you as infamous *and* full of tumult.

"Look, the princes of Israel: each one has used his power to shed blood in you. In you they have made light of father and mother; in your midst they have oppressed the stranger; in you they have mistreated the fatherless and the widow. You have despised My holy things and profaned My Sabbaths. In you are men who slander to cause bloodshed; in you are those who eat on the mountains; in your midst they commit lewdness. In you men uncover their fathers' nakedness; in you they violate women who are set apart during their impurity. One commits abomination with his neighbor's wife; another lewdly defiles his daughter-in-law; and another in you violates his sister, his father's daughter. In you they take bribes to shed blood; you take usury and increase; you have made profit from your neighbors by extortion, and have forgotten Me," says the Lord GOD.

"Behold, therefore, I beat My fists at the dishonest profit which you have made, and at the bloodshed which has been in your midst. Can your heart endure, or can your hands remain strong, in the days when I shall deal with you? I, the LORD, have spoken, and will do *it*. I will scatter you among the nations, disperse you throughout the countries, and remove your filthiness completely from you. You shall defile yourself in the sight of the nations; then you shall know that I *am* the LORD." ' "

The word of the LORD came to me, saying, "Son of man, the house of Israel has become dross to Me; they *are* all bronze, tin, iron, and lead, in the midst of a furnace; they have become dross from silver. Therefore thus says the Lord GOD: 'Because you have all become dross, therefore behold, I will gather you into the midst of Jerusalem. *As men* gather silver, bronze, iron, lead, and tin into the midst of a furnace, to blow fire on it, to melt *it;* so I will gather *you* in My anger and in My fury, and I will leave *you there* and melt you. Yes, I will gather you and blow on you with the fire of My wrath, and you shall be melted in its midst. As silver is melted in the midst of a furnace, so shall you be melted in its midst; then you shall know that I, the LORD, have poured out My fury on you.' "

And the word of the LORD came to me, saying, "Son of man, say to her: 'You *are* a land that is not cleansed or rained on in the day of indignation.' The conspiracy of her prophets in her midst is like a roaring lion tearing the prey; they have devoured people; they have taken treasure and precious things; they have made many widows in her midst. Her priests have violated My law and profaned My holy things; they have not distinguished between the holy and unholy, nor have they made known *the difference* between the unclean and the clean; and they have hidden their eyes from My Sabbaths, so that I am profaned among them. Her princes in her midst *are* like wolves tearing the prey, to shed blood, to destroy people, and to get dishonest gain. Her prophets plastered them with untempered *mortar,* seeing false visions, and divining lies for them, saying, 'Thus says the Lord GOD,' when the LORD had not spoken. The people of the land have used oppressions, committed robbery, and mistreated the poor and needy; and they wrongfully oppress the stranger. So I sought for a man among them who would make a wall, and stand in the gap before Me on behalf of the land, that I should not destroy it; but I found no one. Therefore I have poured out My indignation on them; I have consumed them with the fire of My wrath; and I have recompensed their deeds on their own heads," says the Lord GOD.

Ezekiel 22

WORSHIP

And the heavens will praise Your wonders, O
LORD;
Your faithfulness also in the assembly of the
saints.
For who in the heavens can be compared to
the LORD?
Who among the sons of the mighty can be
likened to the LORD?
God is greatly to be feared in the assembly of
the saints,
And to be held in reverence by all *those*
around Him.

Psalm 89:5-7

WISDOM

He who heeds the word wisely will find good,
And whoever trusts in the LORD, happy *is* he.

Proverbs 16:20

SW?! **SO WHAT?**
What does this tell me?

THE DEATH OF EZEKIEL'S WIFE

Ezekiel 24; Psalm 89:14-16; Proverbs 16:21

Again, in the ninth year, in the tenth month, on the tenth *day* of the month, the word of the LORD came to me, saying, "Son of man, write down the name of the day, this very day—the king of Babylon started his siege against Jerusalem this very day. And utter a parable to the rebellious house, and say to them, 'Thus says the Lord GOD:

"Put on a pot, set *it* on,
And also pour water into it.
Gather pieces *of meat* in it,
Every good piece,
The thigh and the shoulder.
Fill *it* with choice cuts;
Take the choice of the flock.
Also pile *fuel* bones under it,
Make it boil well,
And let the cuts simmer in it."

'Therefore thus says the Lord GOD:

"Woe to the bloody city,
To the pot whose scum *is* in it,
    And whose scum is not gone from it!
        Bring it out piece by piece,
        On which no lot has fallen.
        For her blood is in her midst;
        She set it on top of a rock;
        She did not pour it on the ground,
        To cover it with dust.
        That it may raise up fury and take
            vengeance,
        I have set her blood on top of a rock,
        That it may not be covered."

'Therefore thus says the Lord GOD:

"Woe to the bloody city!
I too will make the pyre great.
Heap on the wood,
Kindle the fire;
Cook the meat well,
Mix in the spices,
And let the cuts be burned up.

"Then set the pot empty on the coals,
That it may become hot and its bronze
    may burn,
That its filthiness may be melted in it,
That its scum may be consumed.
She has grown weary with lies,

And her great scum has not gone from her.
Let her scum *be* in the fire!
In your filthiness *is* lewdness.
Because I have cleansed you, and you were
    not cleansed,
You will not be cleansed of your filthiness
    anymore,
Till I have caused My fury to rest upon you.
I, the LORD, have spoken *it*;
It shall come to pass, and I will do *it*;
I will not hold back,
Nor will I spare,
Nor will I relent;
According to your ways
And according to your deeds
They will judge you,"
Says the Lord GOD.' "

Also the word of the LORD came to me, saying, "Son of man, behold, I take away from you the desire of your eyes with one stroke; yet you shall neither mourn nor weep, nor shall your tears run down. Sigh in silence, make no mourning for the dead; bind your turban on your head, and put your sandals on your feet; do not cover *your* lips, and do not eat man's bread *of sorrow*."

So I spoke to the people in the morning, and at evening my wife died; and the next morning I did as I was commanded.

And the people said to me, "Will you not tell us what these *things signify* to us, that you behave so?"

Then I answered them, "The word of the LORD came to me, saying, 'Speak to the house of Israel, "Thus says the Lord GOD: 'Behold, I will profane My sanctuary, your arrogant boast, the desire of your eyes, the delight of your soul; and your sons and daughters whom you left behind shall fall by the sword. And you shall do as I have done; you shall not cover *your* lips nor eat man's bread *of sorrow*. Your turbans shall be on your heads and your sandals on your feet; you shall neither mourn nor weep, but you shall pine away in your iniquities and mourn with one another. Thus Ezekiel is a sign to you; according to all that he has done you shall do; and when this comes, you shall know that I *am* the Lord GOD.' "

'And you, son of man—*will it* not *be* in the day

when I take from them their stronghold, their joy and their glory, the desire of their eyes, and that on which they set their minds, their sons and their daughters: on that day one who escapes will come to you to let *you* hear *it* with *your* ears; on that day your mouth will be opened to him who has escaped; you shall speak and no longer be mute. Thus you will be a sign to them, and they shall know that I *am* the LORD.' "

Ezekiel 24

WORSHIP

Righteousness and justice *are* the foundation
    of Your throne;
Mercy and truth go before Your face.
Blessed *are* the people who know the joyful
    sound!
They walk, O LORD, in the light of Your
    countenance.
In Your name they rejoice all day long,
And in Your righteousness they are exalted.

Psalm 89:14-16

WISDOM

The wise in heart will be called prudent,
And sweetness of the lips increases learning.

Proverbs 16:21

SW?! SO WHAT?
What does this tell me?

EZEKIEL'S WORK AS A WATCHMAN

Ezekiel 33; Psalm 89:20, 28-29; Proverbs 16:22

Again the word of the LORD came to me, saying, "Son of man, speak to the children of your people, and say to them: 'When I bring the sword upon a land, and the people of the land take a man from their territory and make him their watchman, when he sees the sword coming upon the land, if he blows the trumpet and warns the people, then whoever hears the sound of the trumpet and does not take warning, if the sword comes and takes him away, his blood shall be on his *own* head. He heard the sound of the trumpet, but did not take warning; his blood shall be upon himself. But he who takes warning will save his life. But if the watchman sees the sword coming and does not blow the trumpet, and the people are not warned, and the sword comes and takes *any* person from among them, he is taken away in his iniquity; but his blood I will require at the watchman's hand.'

"So you, son of man: I have made you a watchman for the house of Israel; therefore you shall hear a word from My mouth and warn them for Me. When I say to the wicked, 'O wicked *man,* you shall surely die!' and you do not speak to warn the wicked from his way, that wicked *man* shall die in his iniquity; but his blood I will require at your hand. Nevertheless if you warn the wicked to turn from his way, and he does not turn from his way, he shall die in his iniquity; but you have delivered your soul.

"Therefore you, O son of man, say to the house of Israel: 'Thus you say, "If our transgressions and our sins *lie* upon us, and we pine away in them, how can we then live?"' Say to them: '*As* I live,' says the Lord GOD, 'I have no pleasure in the death of the wicked, but that the wicked turn from his way and live. Turn, turn from your evil ways! For why should you die, O house of Israel?'

"Therefore you, O son of man, say to the children of your people: 'The righteousness of the righteous man shall not deliver him in the day of his transgression; as for the wickedness of the wicked, he shall not fall because of it in the day that he turns from his wickedness; nor shall the righteous be able to live because of *his righteousness* in the day that he sins.' When I say to the righteous *that* he shall surely live, but he trusts in his own righteousness and commits iniquity, none of his righteous works shall be remembered; but because of the iniquity that he has committed, he shall die. Again, when I say to the wicked, 'You shall surely die,' if he turns from his sin and does what is lawful and right, *if* the wicked restores the pledge, gives back what he has stolen, and walks in the statutes of life without committing iniquity, he shall surely live; he shall not die. None of his sins which he has committed shall be remembered against him; he has done what is lawful and right; he shall surely live.

"Yet the children of your people say, 'The way of the LORD is not fair.' But it is their way which is not fair! When the righteous turns from his righteousness and commits iniquity, he shall die because of it. But when the wicked turns from his wickedness and does what is lawful and right, he shall live because of it. Yet you say, 'The way of the LORD is not fair.' O house of Israel, I will judge every one of you according to his own ways."

And it came to pass in the twelfth year of our captivity, in the tenth *month,* on the fifth *day* of the month, *that* one who had escaped from Jerusalem came to me and said, "The city has been captured!" Now the hand of the LORD had been upon me the evening before the man came who had escaped. And He had opened my mouth; so when he came to me in the morning, my mouth was opened, and I was no longer mute.

Then the word of the LORD came to me, saying: "Son of man, they who inhabit those ruins in the land of Israel are saying, 'Abraham was only one, and he inherited the land. But we *are* many; the land has been given to us as a possession.'

"Therefore say to them, 'Thus says the Lord GOD: "You eat *meat* with blood, you lift up your eyes toward your idols, and shed blood. Should you then possess the land? You rely on your sword, you commit abominations, and you defile one another's wives. Should you then possess the land?"'

"Say thus to them, 'Thus says the Lord GOD: "*As* I live, surely those who *are* in the ruins shall fall by the sword, and the one who *is* in the open field I will give to the beasts to be devoured, and those who *are* in the strongholds and caves shall die of the pestilence. For I will make the land most desolate, her arrogant strength shall cease, and the mountains of Israel shall be so desolate that no one will pass through. Then they shall know that I *am* the Lord, when I have made the land most desolate because of all their abominations which they have committed." '

"As for you, son of man, the children of your people are talking about you beside the walls and in the doors of the houses; and they speak to one another, everyone saying to his brother, 'Please come and hear what the word is that comes from the Lord.' So they come to you as people do, they sit before you *as* My people, and they hear your words, but they do not do them; for with their mouth they show much love, *but* their hearts pursue their *own* gain. Indeed you *are* to them as a very lovely song of one who has a pleasant voice and can play well on an instrument; for they hear your words, but they do not do them. And when this comes to pass—surely it will come—then they will know that a prophet has been among them."

Ezekiel 33

WORSHIP

I have found My servant David;
With My holy oil I have anointed him.

My mercy I will keep for him forever,
And My covenant shall stand firm with him.
His seed also I will make *to endure* forever,
And his throne as the days of heaven.

Psalm 89:20, 28-29

WISDOM

Understanding *is* a wellspring of life to him
    who has it.
But the correction of fools *is* folly.

Proverbs 16:22

SW?! SO WHAT?
What does this tell me?

WOE TO THE SHEPHERD LEADERS OF ISRAEL

Ezekiel 34; Psalm 89:34-37; Proverbs 16:23

And the word of the LORD came to me, saying, "Son of man, prophesy against the shepherds of Israel, prophesy and say to them, 'Thus says the Lord GOD to the shepherds: "Woe to the shepherds of Israel who feed themselves! Should not the shepherds feed the flocks? You eat the fat and clothe yourselves with the wool; you slaughter the fatlings, *but* you do not feed the flock. The weak you have not strengthened, nor have you healed those who were sick, nor bound up the broken, nor brought back what was driven away, nor sought what was lost; but with force and cruelty you have ruled them. So they were scattered because *there was* no shepherd; and they became food for all the beasts of the field when they were scattered. My sheep wandered through all the mountains, and on every high hill; yes, My flock was scattered over the whole face of the earth, and no one was seeking or searching *for them*."

'Therefore, you shepherds, hear the word of the LORD: "*As* I live," says the Lord GOD, "surely because My flock became a prey, and My flock became food for every beast of the field, because *there was* no shepherd, nor did My shepherds search for My flock, but the shepherds fed themselves and did not feed My flock"—therefore, O shepherds, hear the word of the LORD! Thus says the Lord GOD: "Behold, I *am* against the shepherds, and I will require My flock at their hand; I will cause them to cease feeding the sheep, and the shepherds shall feed themselves no more; for I will deliver My flock from their mouths, that they may no longer be food for them."

'For thus says the Lord GOD: "Indeed I Myself will search for My sheep and seek them out. As a shepherd seeks out his flock on the day he is among his scattered sheep, so will I seek out My sheep and deliver them from all the places where they were scattered on a cloudy and dark day. And I will bring them out from the peoples and gather them from the countries, and will bring them to their own land; I will feed them on the mountains of Israel, in the valleys and in all the inhabited places of the country. I will feed them in good pasture, and their fold shall be on the high mountains of Israel. There they shall lie down in a good fold and feed in rich pasture on the mountains of Israel. I will feed My flock, and I will make them lie down," says the Lord GOD. "I will seek what was lost and bring back what was driven away, bind up the broken and strengthen what was sick; but I will destroy the fat and the strong, and feed them in judgment."

'And *as for* you, O My flock, thus says the Lord GOD: "Behold, I shall judge between sheep and sheep, between rams and goats. *Is it* too little for you to have eaten up the good pasture, that you must tread down with your feet the residue of your pasture—and to have drunk of the clear waters, that you must foul the residue with your feet? And *as for* My flock, they eat what you have trampled with your feet, and they drink what you have fouled with your feet."

'Therefore thus says the Lord GOD to them: "Behold, I Myself will judge between the fat and the lean sheep. Because you have pushed with side and shoulder, butted all the weak ones with your horns, and scattered them abroad, therefore I will save My flock, and they shall no longer be a prey; and I will judge between sheep and sheep. I will establish one shepherd over them, and he shall feed them—My servant David. He shall feed them and be their shepherd. And I, the LORD, will be their God, and My servant David a prince among them; I, the LORD, have spoken.

"I will make a covenant of peace with them, and cause wild beasts to cease from the land; and they will dwell safely in the wilderness and sleep in the woods. I will make them and the places all around My hill a blessing; and I will cause showers to come down in their season; there shall be showers of blessing. Then the trees of the field shall yield their fruit, and the earth shall yield her increase. They shall be safe in their land; and they shall know that I *am* the LORD, when I have broken the bands of their yoke and delivered them from the hand of those who enslaved them. And they shall no longer be a prey for the nations, nor shall beasts of the land devour them; but they shall dwell safely, and no one shall make *them* afraid. I will raise up for them a garden of renown, and they shall no longer be consumed with hunger in the land, nor bear the shame of the Gentiles anymore. Thus they shall know that I, the LORD their God, *am* with them, and they, the house of Israel, *are* My people," says the Lord GOD.' "

"You are My flock, the flock of My pasture; you *are* men, *and* I *am* your God," says the Lord GOD.

Ezekiel 34

WORSHIP

"My covenant I will not break,
Nor alter the word that has gone out of My lips.
Once I have sworn by My holiness;
I will not lie to David:
His seed shall endure forever,
And his throne as the sun before Me;
It shall be established forever like the moon,
Even *like* the faithful witness in the sky." Selah

Psalm 89:34-37

WISDOM

The heart of the wise teaches his mouth,
And adds learning to his lips.

Proverbs 16:23

SW?! SO WHAT?
What does this tell me?

THE FUTURE RESTORATION OF ISRAEL

Ezekiel 36; Psalm 89:46-48; Proverbs 16:24

"And you, son of man, prophesy to the mountains of Israel, and say, 'O mountains of Israel, hear the word of the LORD! Thus says the Lord GOD: "Because the enemy has said of you, 'Aha! The ancient heights have become our possession,' " ' therefore prophesy, and say, 'Thus says the Lord GOD: "Because they made *you* desolate and swallowed you up on every side, so that you became the possession of the rest of the nations, and you are taken up by the lips of talkers and slandered by the people"—therefore, O mountains of Israel, hear the word of the Lord GOD! Thus says the Lord GOD to the mountains, the hills, the rivers, the valleys, the desolate wastes, and the cities that have been forsaken, which became plunder and mockery to the rest of the nations all around—therefore thus says the Lord GOD: "Surely I have spoken in My burning jealousy against the rest of the nations and against all Edom, who gave My land to themselves as a possession, with wholehearted joy *and* spiteful minds, in order to plunder its open country." '

"Therefore prophesy concerning the land of Israel, and say to the mountains, the hills, the rivers, and the valleys, 'Thus says the Lord GOD: "Behold, I have spoken in My jealousy and My fury, because you have borne the shame of the nations." Therefore thus says the Lord GOD: "I have raised My hand in an oath that surely the nations that *are* around you shall bear their own shame. But you, O mountains of Israel, you shall shoot forth your branches and yield your fruit to My people Israel, for they are about to come. For indeed I *am* for you, and I will turn to you, and you shall be tilled and sown. I will multiply men upon you, all the house of Israel, all of it; and the cities shall be inhabited and the ruins rebuilt. I will multiply upon you man and beast; and they shall increase and bear young; I will make you inhabited as in former times, and do better *for you* than at your beginnings. Then you shall know that I *am* the LORD. Yes, I will cause men to walk on you, My people Israel; they shall take possession of you, and you shall be their inheritance; no more shall you bereave them *of children*."

'Thus says the Lord GOD: "Because they say to you, 'You devour men and bereave your nation *of children*,' therefore you shall devour men no more, nor bereave your nation anymore," says the Lord GOD. Nor will I let you hear the taunts of the nations anymore, nor bear the reproach of the peoples anymore, nor shall you cause your nation to stumble anymore," says the Lord GOD.' "

Moreover the word of the LORD came to me, saying: "Son of man, when the house of Israel dwelt in their own land, they defiled it by their own ways and deeds; to Me their way was like the uncleanness of a woman in her customary impurity. Therefore I poured out My fury on them for the blood they had shed on the land, and for their idols *with which* they had defiled it. So I scattered them among the nations, and they were dispersed throughout the countries; I judged them according to their ways and their deeds. When they came to the nations, wherever they went, they profaned My holy name—when they said of them, 'These *are* the people of the LORD, *and* yet they have gone out of His land.' But I had concern for My holy name, which the house of Israel had profaned among the nations wherever they went.

"Therefore say to the house of Israel, 'Thus says the Lord GOD: "I do not do *this* for your sake, O house of Israel, but for My holy name's sake, which you have profaned among the nations wherever you went. And I will sanctify My great name, which has been profaned among the nations, which you have profaned in their midst; and the nations shall know that I *am* the LORD," says the Lord GOD, "when I am hallowed in you before their eyes. For I will take you from among the nations, gather you out of all countries, and bring you into your own land. Then I will sprinkle clean water on you, and you shall be clean; I will cleanse you from all your filthiness and from all your idols. I will give you a new heart and put a new spirit within you; I will take the heart of stone out of your flesh and give you a heart of flesh. I will put My Spirit within you and cause you to walk in My statutes, and you will keep My judgments and do *them*. Then you shall dwell in the land that I gave to your fathers; you shall be My people, and I will be your God. I will deliver you from all your uncleannesses. I will call for the grain and multiply it, and bring no famine upon you. And I will multiply the fruit of your trees and the increase of your fields, so that you need never again bear the reproach of famine among the nations. Then you will remember your evil ways and your deeds that *were* not good; and you will loathe yourselves in your own sight, for your iniquities and your abominations. Not for your sake do I do *this*," says the Lord GOD, "let it be known to you. Be ashamed and confounded for your own ways, O house of Israel!"

'Thus says the Lord GOD: "On the day that I cleanse you from all your iniquities, I will also enable *you* to dwell in the cities, and the ruins shall be rebuilt. The desolate land shall be tilled instead of lying desolate in the sight of all who pass by. So they will say, 'This land that was desolate has become like the garden of Eden; and the wasted, desolate, and ruined cities *are now* fortified *and* inhabited.' Then the nations which are left all around you shall know that I, the LORD, have rebuilt the ruined places *and* planted what was desolate. I, the LORD, have spoken *it,* and I will do *it.*"

'Thus says the Lord GOD: "I will also let the house of Israel inquire of Me to do this for them: I will increase their men like a flock. Like a flock *offered as* holy *sacrifices,* like the flock at Jerusalem on its feast days, so shall the ruined cities be filled with flocks of men. Then they shall know that I *am* the LORD." ' "

Ezekiel 36

WORSHIP

How long, LORD?
Will You hide Yourself forever?
Will Your wrath burn like fire?
Remember how short my time is;
For what futility have You created all the
    children of men?
What man can live and not see death?
Can he deliver his life from the power of the
    grave?   Selah
Psalm 89:46-48

WISDOM

Pleasant words *are like* a honeycomb,
Sweetness to the soul and health to the bones.
Proverbs 16:24

**SW?! SO WHAT?
What does this tell me?**

THE SPIRIT WORKS ON DRY BONES

Ezekiel 37; Psalm 89:49-51; Proverbs 16:25

The hand of the LORD came upon me and brought me out in the Spirit of the LORD, and set me down in the midst of the valley; and it *was* full of bones. Then He caused me to pass by them all around, and behold, *there were* very many in the open valley; and indeed *they were* very dry. And He said to me, "Son of man, can these bones live?"

So I answered, "O Lord GOD, You know."

Again He said to me, "Prophesy to these bones, and say to them, 'O dry bones, hear the word of the LORD! Thus says the Lord GOD to these bones: "Surely I will cause breath to enter into you, and you shall live. I will put sinews on you and bring flesh upon you, cover you with skin and put breath in you; and you shall live. Then you shall know that I *am* the LORD." ' "

So I prophesied as I was commanded; and as I prophesied, there was a noise, and suddenly a rattling; and the bones came together, bone to bone. Indeed, as I looked, the sinews and the flesh came upon them, and the skin covered them over; but *there was* no breath in them.

Also He said to me, "Prophesy to the breath, prophesy, son of man, and say to the breath, 'Thus says the Lord GOD: "Come from the four winds, O breath, and breathe on these slain, that they may live." ' " So I prophesied as He commanded me, and breath came into them, and they lived, and stood upon their feet, an exceedingly great army.

Then He said to me, "Son of man, these bones are the whole house of Israel. They indeed say, 'Our bones are dry, our hope is lost, and we ourselves are cut off!' Therefore prophesy and say to them, 'Thus says the Lord GOD: "Behold, O My people, I will open your graves and cause you to come up from your graves, and bring you into the land of Israel. Then you shall know that I *am* the LORD, when I have opened your graves, O My people, and brought you up from your graves. I will put My Spirit in you, and you shall live, and I will place you in your own land. Then you shall know that I, the LORD, have spoken *it* and performed *it*," says the LORD.' "

Again the word of the LORD came to me, saying, "As for you, son of man, take a stick for yourself and write on it: 'For Judah and for the children of Israel, his companions.' Then take another stick and write on it, 'For Joseph, the stick of Ephraim, and *for* all the house of Israel, his companions.' Then join them one to another for yourself into one stick, and they will become one in your hand.

"And when the children of your people speak to you, saying, 'Will you not show us what you *mean* by these?'— say to them, 'Thus says the Lord GOD: "Surely I will take the stick of Joseph, which *is* in the hand of Ephraim, and the tribes of Israel, his companions; and I will join them with it, with the stick of Judah, and make them one stick, and they will be one in My hand." ' And the sticks on which you write will be in your hand before their eyes.

"Then say to them, 'Thus says the Lord GOD: "Surely I will take the children of Israel from among the nations, wherever they have gone, and will gather them from every side and bring them into their own land; and I will make them one nation in the land, on the mountains of Israel; and one king shall be king over them all; they shall no longer be two nations, nor shall they ever be divided into two kingdoms again. They shall not defile themselves anymore with their idols, nor with their detestable things, nor with any of their transgressions; but I will deliver them from all their dwelling places in which they have sinned, and will cleanse them. Then they shall be My people, and I will be their God.

"David My servant *shall be* king over them, and they shall all have one shepherd; they shall also walk in My judgments and observe My statutes, and do them. Then they shall dwell in the land that I have given to Jacob My servant, where your fathers dwelt; and they shall dwell there, they, their children, and their children's children, forever; and My servant David *shall be* their prince forever. Moreover I will make a covenant of peace with them, and it shall be an everlasting covenant with them; I will establish them and multiply them, and I will set My sanctuary in their midst forevermore. My tabernacle also shall be with them; indeed I will be their God, and they shall be My people. The nations also will know that I, the LORD, sanctify Israel, when My sanctuary is in their midst forevermore." ' "

Ezekiel 37

WORSHIP

Lord, where *are* Your former lovingkindnesses,
Which You swore to David in Your truth?
Remember, Lord, the reproach of Your
    servants—
How I bear in my bosom *the reproach of* all
    the many peoples,
With which Your enemies have reproached, O
    LORD,
With which they have reproached the footsteps
    of Your anointed.

Psalm 89:49-51

WISDOM

There is a way *that seems* right to a man,
But its end *is* the way of death.

Proverbs 16:25

SW?! **SO WHAT?**
What does this tell me?

THE DESTRUCTION OF AN EVIL FOE

"Therefore, son of man, prophesy and say to Gog, 'Thus says the Lord GOD: "On that day when My people Israel dwell safely, will you not know *it?* Then you will come from your place out of the far north, you and many peoples with you, all of them riding on horses, a great company and a mighty army. You will come up against My people Israel like a cloud, to cover the land. It will be in the latter days that I will bring you against My land, so that the nations may know Me, when I am hallowed in you, O Gog, before their eyes." Thus says the Lord GOD: "Are *you* he of whom I have spoken in former days by My servants the prophets of Israel, who prophesied for years in those days that I would bring you against them?

"And it will come to pass at the same time, when Gog comes against the land of Israel," says the Lord GOD, "*that* My fury will show in My face. For in My jealousy *and* in the fire of My wrath I have spoken: 'Surely in that day there shall be a great earthquake in the land of Israel, so that the fish of the sea, the birds of the heavens, the beasts of the field, all creeping things that creep on the earth, and all men who *are* on the face of the earth shall shake at My presence. The mountains shall be thrown down, the steep places shall fall, and every wall shall fall to the ground.' I will call for a sword against Gog throughout all My mountains," says the Lord GOD. "Every man's sword will be against his brother. And I will bring him to judgment with pestilence and bloodshed; I will rain down on him, on his troops, and on the many peoples who *are* with him, flooding rain, great hailstones, fire, and brimstone. Thus I will magnify Myself and sanctify Myself, and I will be known in the eyes of many nations. Then they shall know that I *am* the LORD." '

"And you, son of man, prophesy against Gog, and say, 'Thus says the Lord GOD: "Behold, I *am* against you, O Gog, the prince of Rosh, Meshech, and Tubal; and I will turn you around and lead you on, bringing you up from the far north, and bring you against the mountains of Israel. Then I will knock the bow out of your left hand, and cause the arrows to fall out of your right hand. You shall fall upon the mountains of Israel, you and all your troops and the peoples who *are* with you; I will give you to birds of prey of every sort and *to* the beasts of the field to be devoured. You shall fall on the open field; for I have spoken," says the Lord GOD. "And I will send fire on Magog and on those who live in security in the coastlands. Then they shall know that I *am* the LORD. So I will make My holy name known in the midst of My people Israel, and I will not *let them* profane My holy name anymore. Then the nations shall know that *I am* the LORD, the Holy One in Israel. Surely it is coming, and it shall be done," says the Lord GOD. "This *is* the day of which I have spoken.

"Then those who dwell in the cities of Israel will go out and set on fire and burn the weapons, both the shields and bucklers, the bows and arrows, the javelins and spears; and they will make fires with them for seven years. They will not take wood from the field nor cut down *any* from the forests, because they will make fires with the weapons; and they will plunder those who plundered them, and pillage those who pillaged them," says the Lord GOD.

"It will come to pass in that day *that* I will give Gog a burial place there in Israel, the valley of those who pass by east of the sea; and it will obstruct travelers, because there they will bury Gog and all his multitude. Therefore they will call *it* the Valley of Hamon Gog. For seven months the house of Israel will be burying them, in order to cleanse the land. Indeed all the people of the land will be burying, and they will gain renown for it on the day that I am glorified," says the Lord GOD. "They will set apart men regularly employed, with the help of a search party, to pass through the land and bury those bodies remaining on the ground, in order to cleanse it. At the end of seven months they will make a search. The search party will pass through the land; and *when anyone* sees a man's bone, he shall set up a marker by it, till the buriers have buried it in the Valley of Hamon Gog. *The* name of *the* city *will* also *be* Hamonah. Thus they shall cleanse the land." '

"And as for you, son of man, thus says the Lord GOD, 'Speak to every sort of bird and to every beast of the field:

"Assemble yourselves and come;
    Gather together from all sides to My sacrificial
      meal
    Which I am sacrificing for you,
    A great sacrificial meal on the mountains of
      Israel,
    That you may eat flesh and drink blood.
    You shall eat the flesh of the mighty,
    Drink the blood of the princes of the earth,
    Of rams and lambs,
    Of goats and bulls,
    All of them fatlings of Bashan.
    You shall eat fat till you are full,
    And drink blood till you are drunk,
    At My sacrificial meal
    Which I am sacrificing for you.
    You shall be filled at My table
    With horses and riders,
    With mighty men
    And with all the men of war," says the Lord
      God.

"I will set My glory among the nations; all the nations shall see My judgment which I have executed, and My hand which I have laid on them. So the house of Israel shall know that I *am* the LORD their God from that day forward. The Gentiles shall know that the house of Israel went into captivity for their iniquity; because they were unfaithful to Me, therefore I hid My face from them. I gave them into the hand of their enemies, and they all fell by the sword. According to their uncleanness and according to their transgressions I have dealt with them, and hidden My face from them." '

"Therefore thus says the Lord GOD: 'Now I will bring back the captives of Jacob, and have mercy on the whole house of Israel; and I will be jealous for My holy name—after they have borne their shame, and all their unfaithfulness in which they were unfaithful to Me, when they dwelt safely in their *own* land and no one made *them* afraid. When I have brought them back from the peoples and gathered them out of their enemies' lands, and I am hallowed in them in the sight of many nations, then they shall know that I *am* the LORD their God, who sent them into captivity among the nations, but also brought them back to their land, and left none of them captive any longer. And I will not hide My face from them anymore; for I shall have poured out My Spirit on the house of Israel,' says the Lord GOD."

Ezekiel 38:14–39:29

WORSHIP

LORD, You have been our dwelling place in all
    generations.
Before the mountains were brought forth,
Or ever You had formed the earth and the
    world,
Even from everlasting to everlasting, You *are*
    God.

Psalm 90:1-2

WISDOM

An ungodly man digs up evil,
And *it is* on his lips like a burning fire.

Proverbs 16:27

SW?! SO WHAT?
What does this tell me?

A TOUR OF THE FUTURE TEMPLE

Ezekiel 40; Psalm 90:10-12; Proverbs 16:28

In the twenty-fifth year of our captivity, at the beginning of the year, on the tenth *day* of the month, in the fourteenth year after the city was captured, on the very same day the hand of the LORD was upon me; and He took me there. In the visions of God He took me into the land of Israel and set me on a very high mountain; on it toward the south *was* something like the structure of a city. He took me there, and behold, *there was* a man whose appearance *was* like the appearance of bronze. He had a line of flax and a measuring rod in his hand, and he stood in the gateway.

And the man said to me, "Son of man, look with your eyes and hear with your ears, and fix your mind on everything I show you; for you *were* brought here so that I might show *them* to you. Declare to the house of Israel everything you see." Now there was a wall all around the outside of the temple. In the man's hand was a measuring rod six cubits *long, each being a* cubit and a handbreadth; and he measured the width of the wall structure, one rod; and the height, one rod.

Then he went to the gateway which faced east; and he went up its stairs and measured the threshold of the gateway, *which was* one rod wide, and the other threshold *was* one rod wide. Each gate chamber *was* one rod long and one rod wide; between the gate chambers *was a space of* five cubits; and the threshold of the gateway by the vestibule of the inside gate *was* one rod. He also measured the vestibule of the inside gate, one rod. Then he measured the vestibule of the gateway, eight cubits; and the gateposts, two cubits. The vestibule of the gate *was* on the inside. In the eastern gateway *were* three gate chambers on one side and three on the other; the three *were* all the same size; also the gateposts were of the same size on this side and that side.

He measured the width of the entrance to the gateway, ten cubits; *and* the length of the gate, thirteen cubits. *There was* a space in front of the gate chambers, one cubit *on this side* and one cubit on that side; the gate chambers *were* six cubits on this side and six cubits on that side. Then he measured the gateway from the roof of *one* gate chamber to the roof of the other; the width *was* twenty-five cubits, as door faces door. He measured the gateposts, sixty cubits high, and the court all around the gateway *extended* to the gatepost. *From* the front of the entrance gate to the front of the vestibule of the inner gate *was* fifty cubits. *There were* beveled window *frames* in the gate chambers and in their intervening archways on the inside of the gateway all around, and likewise in the vestibules. *There were* windows all around on the inside. And on each gatepost *were* palm trees.

Then he brought me into the outer court; and *there were* chambers and a pavement made all around the court; thirty chambers faced the pavement. The pavement was by the side of the gateways, corresponding to the length of the gateways; *this was* the lower pavement. Then he measured the width from the front of the lower gateway to the front of the inner court exterior, one hundred cubits toward the east and the north.

On the outer court was also a gateway facing north, and he measured its length and its width. Its gate chambers, three on this side and three on that side, its gateposts and its archways, had the same measurements as the first gate; its length *was* fifty cubits and its width twenty-five cubits. Its windows and those of its archways, and also its palm trees, *had* the same measurements as the gateway facing east; it was ascended by seven steps, and its archway *was* in front of it. A gate of the inner court was opposite the northern gateway, just as the eastern *gateway;* and he measured from gateway to gateway, one hundred cubits.

After that he brought me toward the south, and there a gateway was facing south; and he measured its gateposts and archways according to these same measurements. *There were* windows in it and in its archways all around like those windows; its length *was* fifty cubits and its width twenty-five cubits. Seven steps led up to it, and its archway *was* in front of them; and it had palm trees on its gateposts, one on this side and one on that side. *There was* also a gateway on the inner court, facing south; and he measured from gateway to gateway toward the south, one hundred cubits.

Then he brought me to the inner court through the southern gateway; he measured the southern gateway according to these same measurements. Also its gate chambers, its gateposts, and its archways *were* according to these same measurements; *there were* windows in it and in its archways all around; *it was* fifty cubits long and twenty-five cubits wide. *There were* archways all around, twenty-five cubits long and five cubits wide. Its archways faced the outer court, palm trees *were* on its gateposts, and going up to it *were* eight steps.

And he brought me into the inner court facing east; he measured the gateway according to these same measurements. Also its gate chambers, its gateposts, and its archways *were* according to these same measurements; and *there were* windows in it and in its archways all around; *it was* fifty cubits long and twenty-five cubits wide. Its archways faced the outer court, and palm trees *were* on its gateposts on this side and on that side; and going up to it *were* eight steps.

Then he brought me to the north gateway and measured *it* according to these same measurements— also its gate chambers, its gateposts, and its archways. It had windows all around; its length *was* fifty cubits and its width twenty-five cubits. Its gateposts faced the outer court, palm trees *were* on its gateposts on this side and on that side, and going up to it *were* eight steps.

There was a chamber and its entrance by the gateposts of the gateway, where they washed the burnt offering. In the vestibule of the gateway *were* two tables on this side and two tables on that side, on which to slay the burnt offering, the sin offering, and the trespass offering. At the outer side of the vestibule, as one goes up to the entrance of the northern gateway, *were* two tables; and on the other side of the vestibule of the gateway *were* two tables. Four tables *were* on this side and four tables on that side, by the side of the gateway, eight tables on which they slaughtered *the sacrifices. There were* also four tables of hewn stone for the burnt offering, one cubit and a half long, one cubit and a half wide, and one cubit high; on these they laid the instruments with which they slaughtered the burnt offering and the sacrifice. Inside *were* hooks, a handbreadth wide, fastened all around; and the flesh of the sacrifices *was* on the tables.

Outside the inner gate *were* the chambers for the singers in the inner court, one facing south at the side of the northern gateway, and the other facing north at the side of the southern gateway. Then he said to me, "This chamber which faces south *is* for the priests who have charge of the temple. The chamber which faces north *is* for the priests who have charge of the altar; these *are* the sons of Zadok, from the sons of Levi, who come near the Lord to minister to Him."

And he measured the court, one hundred cubits long and one hundred cubits wide, foursquare. The altar *was* in front of the temple. Then he brought me to the vestibule of the temple and measured the doorposts of the vestibule, five cubits on this side and five cubits on that side; and the width of the gateway was three cubits on this side and three cubits on that side. The length of the vestibule *was* twenty cubits, and the width eleven cubits; and by the steps which led up to it *there were* pillars by the doorposts, one on this side and another on that side.

Ezekiel 40

WORSHIP

The days of our lives *are* seventy years;
And if by reason of strength *they are* eighty years,
Yet their boast *is* only labor and sorrow;
For it is soon cut off, and we fly away.
Who knows the power of Your anger?
For as the fear of You, *so is* Your wrath.
So teach *us* to number our days,
That we may gain a heart of wisdom.

Psalm 90:10-12

WISDOM

A perverse man sows strife,
And a whisperer separates the best of friends.

Proverbs 16:28

SO WHAT?
What does this tell me?

THE RETURN OF GOD'S GLORY

Afterward he brought me to the gate, the gate that faces toward the east. And behold, the glory of the God of Israel came from the way of the east. His voice *was* like the sound of many waters; and the earth shone with His glory. *It was* like the appearance of the vision which I saw—like the vision which I saw when I came to destroy the city. The visions *were* like the vision which I saw by the River Chebar; and I fell on my face. And the glory of the LORD came into the temple by way of the gate which faces toward the east. The Spirit lifted me up and brought me into the inner court; and behold, the glory of the LORD filled the temple.

Then I heard *Him* speaking to me from the temple, while a man stood beside me. And He said to me, "Son of man, *this is* the place of My throne and the place of the soles of My feet, where I will dwell in the midst of the children of Israel forever. No more shall the house of Israel defile My holy name, they nor their kings, by their harlotry or with the carcasses of their kings on their high places. When they set their threshold by My threshold, and their doorpost by My doorpost, with a wall between them and Me, they defiled My holy name by the abominations which they committed; therefore I have consumed them in My anger. Now let them put their harlotry and the carcasses of their kings far away from Me, and I will dwell in their midst forever.

"Son of man, describe the temple to the house of Israel, that they may be ashamed of their iniquities; and let them measure the pattern. And if they are ashamed of all that they have done, make known to them the design of the temple and its arrangement, its exits and its entrances, its entire design and all its ordinances, all its forms and all its laws. Write *it* down in their sight, so that they may keep its whole design and all its ordinances, and perform them. This *is* the law of the temple: The whole area surrounding the mountaintop *is* most holy. Behold, this *is* the law of the temple.

"These are the measurements of the altar in cubits (the *cubit is* one cubit and a handbreadth): the base one cubit high and one cubit wide, with a rim all around its edge of one span. This *is* the height of the altar: from the base on the ground to the lower ledge, two cubits; the width of the ledge, one cubit; from the smaller ledge to the larger ledge, four cubits; and the width of the ledge, *one* cubit. The altar hearth *is* four cubits high, with four horns extending upward from the hearth. The altar hearth *is* twelve cubits long, twelve wide, square at its four corners; the ledge, fourteen *cubits* long and fourteen wide on its four sides, with a rim of half a cubit around it; its base, one cubit all around; and its steps face toward the east."

And He said to me, "Son of man, thus says the Lord GOD: 'These *are* the ordinances for the altar on the day when it is made, for sacrificing burnt offerings on it, and for sprinkling blood on it. You shall give a young bull for a sin offering to the priests, the Levites, who are of the seed of Zadok, who approach Me to minister to Me,' says the Lord GOD. 'You shall take some of its blood and put *it* on the four horns of the altar, on the four corners of the ledge, and on the rim around it; thus you shall cleanse it and make atonement for it. Then you shall also take the bull of the sin offering, and burn it in the appointed place of the temple, outside the sanctuary. On the second day you shall offer a kid of the goats without blemish for a sin offering; and they shall cleanse the altar, as they cleansed *it* with the bull. When you have finished cleansing *it,* you shall offer a young bull without blemish, and a ram from the flock without blemish. When you offer them before the LORD, the priests shall throw salt on them, and they will offer them up *as* a burnt offering to the LORD. Every day for seven days you shall prepare a goat *for* a sin offering; they shall also prepare a young bull and a ram from the flock, both without blemish. Seven days they shall make atonement for the altar and purify it, and so consecrate *it.* When these days are over it shall be, on the eighth day and thereafter, that the priests shall offer your burnt offerings and your peace offerings on the altar; and I will accept you,' says the Lord GOD."

Ezekiel 43

WORSHIP

Return, O LORD!
How long?
And have compassion on Your servants.
Oh, satisfy us early with Your mercy,
That we may rejoice and be glad all our days!

And let the beauty of the LORD our God be
    upon us,
And establish the work of our hands for us;
Yes, establish the work of our hands.

Psalm 90:13-14, 17

WISDOM

The silver-haired head *is* a crown of glory,
If it is found in the way of righteousness.

Proverbs 16:31

SW?! **SO WHAT?**
What does this tell me?

WORSHIP IN GOD'S KINGDOM

Ezekiel 44:1-31; 46:1-3; Psalm 91:1-4; Proverbs 16:32

Then He brought me back to the outer gate of the sanctuary which faces toward the east, but it *was* shut. And the LORD said to me, "This gate shall be shut; it shall not be opened, and no man shall enter by it, because the LORD God of Israel has entered by it; therefore it shall be shut. *As for* the prince, *because* he *is* the prince, he may sit in it to eat bread before the LORD; he shall enter by way of the vestibule of the gateway, and go out the same way."

Also He brought me by way of the north gate to the front of the temple; so I looked, and behold, the glory of the LORD filled the house of the LORD; and I fell on my face. And the LORD said to me, "Son of man, mark well, see with your eyes and hear with your ears, all that I say to you concerning all the ordinances of the house of the LORD and all its laws. Mark well who may enter the house and all who go out from the sanctuary.

"Now say to the rebellious, to the house of Israel, 'Thus says the Lord GOD: "O house of Israel, let Us have no more of all your abominations. When you brought in foreigners, uncircumcised in heart and uncircumcised in flesh, to be in My sanctuary to defile it—My house—and when you offered My food, the fat and the blood, then they broke My covenant because of all your abominations. And you have not kept charge of My holy things, but you have set *others* to keep charge of My sanctuary for you." Thus says the Lord GOD: "No foreigner, uncircumcised in heart or uncircumcised in flesh, shall enter My sanctuary, including any foreigner who *is* among the children of Israel.

"And the Levites who went far from Me, when Israel went astray, who strayed away from Me after their idols, they shall bear their iniquity. Yet they shall be ministers in My sanctuary, *as* gatekeepers of the house and ministers of the house; they shall slay the burnt offering and the sacrifice for the people, and they shall stand before them to minister to them. Because they ministered to them before their idols and caused the house of Israel to fall into iniquity, therefore I have raised My hand in an oath against

them," says the Lord GOD, "that they shall bear their iniquity. And they shall not come near Me to minister to Me as priest, nor come near any of My holy things, nor into the Most Holy *Place;* but they shall bear their shame and their abominations which they have committed. Nevertheless I will make them keep charge of the temple, for all its work, and for all that has to be done in it.

"But the priests, the Levites, the sons of Zadok, who kept charge of My sanctuary when the children of Israel went astray from Me, they shall come near Me to minister to Me; and they shall stand before Me to offer to Me the fat and the blood," says the Lord GOD. "They shall enter My sanctuary, and they shall come near My table to minister to Me, and they shall keep My charge. And it shall be, whenever they enter the gates of the inner court, that they shall put on linen garments; no wool shall come upon them while they minister within the gates of the inner court or within the house. They shall have linen turbans on their heads and linen trousers on their bodies; they shall not clothe themselves with *anything that causes* sweat. When they go out to the outer court, to the *outer* court to the people, they shall take off their garments in which they have ministered, leave them in the holy chambers, and put on other garments; and in their holy garments they shall not sanctify the people.

"They shall neither shave their heads, nor let their hair grow long, but they shall keep their hair well trimmed. No priest shall drink wine when he enters the inner court. They shall not take as wife a widow or a divorced woman, but take virgins of the descendants of the house of Israel, or widows of priests.

"And they shall teach My people *the difference* between the holy and the unholy, and cause them to discern between the unclean and the clean. In controversy they shall stand as judges, *and* judge it according to My judgments. They shall keep My laws and My statutes in all My appointed meetings, and they shall hallow My Sabbaths.

"They shall not defile *themselves* by coming near a dead person. Only for father or mother, for son or daughter, for brother or unmarried sister may they defile themselves. After he is cleansed, they shall count seven days for him. And on the day that he goes to the sanctuary to minister in the sanctuary, he must offer his sin offering in the inner court," says the Lord GOD.

"It shall be, in regard to their inheritance, *that I am* their inheritance. You shall give them no possession in Israel, for I *am* their possession. They shall eat the grain offering, the sin offering, and the trespass offering; every dedicated thing in Israel shall be theirs. The best of all firstfruits of any kind, and every sacrifice of any kind from all your sacrifices, shall be the priest's; also you shall give to the priest the first of your ground meal, to cause a blessing to rest on your house. The priests shall not eat anything, bird or beast, that died naturally or was torn *by wild beasts.*

Thus says the Lord GOD: "The gateway of the inner court that faces toward the east shall be shut the six working days; but on the Sabbath it shall be opened, and on the day of the New Moon it shall be opened. The prince shall enter by way of the vestibule of the gateway from the outside, and stand by the gatepost. The priests shall prepare his burnt offering and his peace offerings. He shall worship at the threshold of the gate. Then he shall go out, but the gate shall not be shut until evening. Likewise the people of the land shall worship at the entrance to this gateway before the LORD on the Sabbaths and the New Moons." ' "

Ezekiel 44:1-31; 46:1-3

WORSHIP

He who dwells in the secret place of the Most High
Shall abide under the shadow of the Almighty.
I will say of the LORD, "*He is* my refuge and my fortress;
My God, in Him I will trust."
Surely He shall deliver you from the snare of the fowler
And from the perilous pestilence.
He shall cover you with His feathers,
And under His wings you shall take refuge;
His truth *shall be your* shield and buckler.

Psalm 91:1-4

WISDOM

He who is slow to anger *is* better than the mighty,
And he who rules his spirit than he who takes a city.

Proverbs 16:32

SW?! **SO WHAT?**
What does this tell me?

BLESSINGS FROM A DEEP RIVER

Ezekiel 47:1-23; 48:30-35; Psalm 91:11-13; Proverbs 17:1

Then he brought me back to the door of the temple; and there was water, flowing from under the threshold of the temple toward the east, for the front of the temple faced east; the water was flowing from under the right side of the temple, south of the altar. He brought me out by way of the north gate, and led me around on the outside to the outer gateway that faces east; and there was water, running out on the right side.

And when the man went out to the east with the line in his hand, he measured one thousand cubits, and he brought me through the waters; the water *came up to my* ankles. Again he measured one thousand and brought me through the waters; the water *came up to my* knees. Again he measured one thousand and brought me through; the water *came up to my* waist. Again he measured one thousand, *and it was* a river that I could not cross; for the water was too deep, water in which one must swim, a river that could not be crossed. He said to me, "Son of man, have you seen *this?*" Then he brought me and returned me to the bank of the river.

When I returned, there, along the bank of the river, *were* very many trees on one side and the other. Then he said to me: "This water flows toward the eastern region, goes down into the valley, and enters the sea. *When it* reaches the sea, *its* waters are healed. And it shall be *that* every living thing that moves, wherever the rivers go, will live. There will be a very great multitude of fish, because these waters go there; for they will be healed, and everything will live wherever the river goes. It shall be *that* fishermen will stand by it from En Gedi to En Eglaim; they will be *places* for spreading their nets. Their fish will be of the same kinds as the fish of the Great Sea, exceedingly many. But its swamps and marshes will not be healed; they will be given over to salt. Along the bank of the river, on this side and that, will grow all *kinds of* trees used for food; their leaves will not wither, and their fruit will not fail. They will bear fruit every month, because their water flows from the sanctuary. Their fruit will be for food, and their leaves for medicine."

Thus says the Lord GOD: "These *are* the borders by which you shall divide the land as an inheritance among the twelve tribes of Israel. Joseph *shall have two* portions. You shall inherit it equally with one another; for I raised My hand in an oath to give it to your fathers, and this land shall fall to you as your inheritance.

"This *shall be* the border of the land on the north: from the Great Sea, *by* the road to Hethlon, as one goes to Zedad, Hamath, Berothah, Sibraim (which *is* between the border of Damascus and the border of Hamath), to Hazar Hatticon (which *is* on the border of Hauran). Thus the boundary shall be from the Sea to Hazar Enan, the border of Damascus; and as for the north, northward, it is the border of Hamath. *This is* the north side.

"On the east side you shall mark out the border from between Hauran and Damascus, and between Gilead and the land of Israel, along the Jordan, and along the eastern side of the sea. *This is* the east side.

"The south side, toward the South, *shall be* from Tamar to the waters of Meribah by Kadesh, along the brook to the Great Sea. *This is* the south side, toward the South.

"The west side *shall be* the Great Sea, from the *southern* boundary until one comes to a point opposite Hamath. This *is* the west side.

"Thus you shall divide this land among yourselves according to the tribes of Israel. It shall be that you will divide it by lot as an inheritance for yourselves, and for the strangers who dwell among you and who bear children among you. They shall be to you as native-born among the children of Israel; they shall have an inheritance with you among the tribes of Israel. And it shall be *that* in whatever tribe the stranger dwells, there you shall give *him* his inheritance," says the Lord GOD.

"These *are* the exits of the city. On the north side, measuring four thousand five hundred *cubits* (the gates of the city *shall be* named after the tribes of Israel), the three gates northward: one gate for Reuben, one gate for Judah, and one gate for Levi; on the east side, four thousand five hundred *cubits,* three gates: one gate for Joseph, one gate for Benjamin, and one gate for Dan; on the south side, measuring four thousand five hundred *cubits,* three gates: one gate for Simeon, one gate for Issachar, and one gate for Zebulun; on the west side, four thousand five hundred *cubits* with their three gates: one gate for Gad, one gate for Asher, and one gate for Naphtali. All the way around *shall be* eighteen thousand cubits; and the name of the city from *that* day *shall be:* THE LORD *IS* THERE."

Ezekiel 47:1-23; 48:30-35

WORSHIP

For He shall give His angels charge over you,
To keep you in all your ways.
In *their* hands they shall bear you up,
Lest you dash your foot against a stone.
You shall tread upon the lion and the cobra,
The young lion and the serpent you shall
    trample underfoot.

Psalm 91:11-13

WISDOM

Better *is* a dry morsel with quietness,
Than a house full of feasting *with* strife.

Proverbs 17:1

SO WHAT?
What does this tell me?

THE STORY OF ESTHER: A LESSON IN GOD'S SOVEREIGNTY

Esther 1–2; Psalm 92:1-4; Proverbs 17:2

Now it came to pass in the days of Ahasuerus (this *was* the Ahasuerus who reigned over one hundred and twenty-seven provinces, from India to Ethiopia), in those days when King Ahasuerus sat on the throne of his kingdom, which *was* in Shushan the citadel, *that* in the third year of his reign he made a feast for all his officials and servants—the powers of Persia and Media, the nobles, and the princes of the provinces *being* before him—when he showed the riches of his glorious kingdom and the splendor of his excellent majesty for many days, one hundred and eighty days *in all*.

And when these days were completed, the king made a feast lasting seven days for all the people who were present in Shushan the citadel, from great to small, in the court of the garden of the king's palace. *There were* white and blue linen *curtains* fastened with cords of fine linen and purple on silver rods and marble pillars; *and the* couches *were* of gold and silver on a *mosaic* pavement of alabaster, turquoise, and white and black marble. And they served drinks in golden vessels, each vessel being different from the other, with royal wine in abundance, according to the generosity of the king. In accordance with the law, the drinking was not compulsory; for so the king had ordered all the officers of his household, that they should do according to each man's pleasure.

Queen Vashti also made a feast for the women *in* the royal palace which *belonged* to King Ahasuerus.

On the seventh day, when the heart of the king was merry with wine, he commanded Mehuman, Biztha, Harbona, Bigtha, Abagtha, Zethar, and Carcas, seven eunuchs who served in the presence of King Ahasuerus, to bring Queen Vashti before the king, *wearing* her royal crown, in order to show her beauty to the people and the officials, for she *was* beautiful to behold. But Queen Vashti refused to come at the king's command *brought* by *his* eunuchs; therefore the king was furious, and his anger burned within him.

Then the king said to the wise men who understood the times (for this *was* the king's

manner toward all who knew law and justice, those closest to him *being* Carshena, Shethar, Admatha, Tarshish, Meres, Marsena, and Memucan, the seven princes of Persia and Media, who had access to the king's presence, *and* who ranked highest in the kingdom): "What *shall* we do to Queen Vashti, according to law, because she did not obey the command of King Ahasuerus *brought to her* by the eunuchs?"

And Memucan answered before the king and the princes: "Queen Vashti has not only wronged the king, but also all the princes, and all the people who *are* in all the provinces of King Ahasuerus. For the queen's behavior will become known to all women, so that they will despise their husbands in their eyes, when they report, 'King Ahasuerus commanded Queen Vashti to be brought in before him, but she did not come.' This very day the *noble* ladies of Persia and Media will say to all the king's officials that they have heard of the behavior of the queen. Thus *there will be* excessive contempt and wrath. If it pleases the king, let a royal decree go out from him, and let it be recorded in the laws of the Persians and the Medes, so that it will not be altered, that Vashti shall come no more before King Ahasuerus; and let the king give her royal position to another who is better than she. When the king's decree which he will make is proclaimed throughout all his empire (for it is great), all wives will honor their husbands, both great and small."

And the reply pleased the king and the princes, and the king did according to the word of Memucan. Then he sent letters to all the king's provinces, to each province in its own script, and to every people in their own language, that each man should be master in his own house, and speak in the language of his own people.

After these things, when the wrath of King Ahasuerus subsided, he remembered Vashti, what she had done, and what had been decreed against her. Then the king's servants who attended him said: "Let beautiful young virgins be sought for the king; and let the king appoint officers in all the provinces of his kingdom, that they may gather all the beautiful young virgins to Shushan the citadel, into the women's quarters, under the custody of Hegai the king's eunuch, custodian of the women. And let beauty preparations be given *them*. Then let the young woman who pleases the king be queen instead of Vashti."

This thing pleased the king, and he did so.

In Shushan the citadel there was a certain Jew whose name *was* Mordecai the son of Jair, the son of Shimei, the son of Kish, a Benjamite. *Kish* had been carried away from Jerusalem with the captives who had been captured with Jeconiah king of Judah, whom Nebuchadnezzar the king of Babylon had carried away. And *Mordecai* had brought up Hadassah, that *is*, Esther, his uncle's daughter, for she had neither father nor mother. The young woman *was* lovely and beautiful. When her father and mother died, Mordecai took her as his own daughter.

So it was, when the king's command and decree were heard, and when many young women were gathered at Shushan the citadel, *under* the custody of Hegai, that Esther also was taken to the king's palace, into the care of Hegai the custodian of the women. Now the young woman pleased him, and she obtained his favor; so he readily gave beauty preparations to her, besides her allowance. Then seven choice maidservants were provided for her from the king's palace, and he moved her and her maidservants to the best *place* in the house of the women.

Esther had not revealed her people or family, for Mordecai had charged her not to reveal *it*. And every day Mordecai paced in front of the court of the women's quarters, to learn of Esther's welfare and what was happening to her.

Each young woman's turn came to go in to King Ahasuerus after she had completed twelve months' preparation, according to the regulations for the women, for thus were the days of their preparation apportioned: six months with oil of myrrh, and six months with perfumes and preparations for beautifying women. Thus *prepared, each* young woman went to the king, and she was given whatever she desired to take with her from the women's quarters to the king's palace. In the evening she went, and in the morning she returned to the second house of the women, to the custody of Shaashgaz, the king's eunuch who kept the concubines. She would not go in to the king again unless the king delighted in her and called for her by name.

Now when the turn came for Esther the daughter of Abihail the uncle of Mordecai, who had taken her as his daughter, to go in to the king, she requested nothing but what Hegai the king's eunuch, the custodian of the women, advised. And Esther obtained favor in the sight of all who saw her. So Esther

was taken to King Ahasuerus, into his royal palace, in the tenth month, which *is* the month of Tebeth, in the seventh year of his reign. The king loved Esther more than all the *other* women, and she obtained grace and favor in his sight more than all the virgins; so he set the royal crown upon her head and made her queen instead of Vashti. Then the king made a great feast, the Feast of Esther, for all his officials and servants; and he proclaimed a holiday in the provinces and gave gifts according to the generosity of a king.

When virgins were gathered together a second time, Mordecai sat within the king's gate. *Now* Esther had not revealed her family and her people, just as Mordecai had charged her, for Esther obeyed the command of Mordecai as when she was brought up by him.

In those days, while Mordecai sat within the king's gate, two of the king's eunuchs, Bigthan and Teresh, doorkeepers, became furious and sought to lay hands on King Ahasuerus. So the matter became known to Mordecai, who told Queen Esther, and Esther informed the king in Mordecai's name. And when an inquiry was made into the matter, it was confirmed, and both were hanged on a gallows; and it was written in the book of the chronicles in the presence of the king.

Esther 1–2

WORSHIP

It is good to give thanks to the LORD,
And to sing praises to Your name, O Most High;
To declare Your lovingkindness in the morning,
And Your faithfulness every night,
On an instrument of ten strings,
On the lute,
And on the harp,
With harmonious sound.
For You, LORD, have made me glad through Your work;
I will triumph in the works of Your hands.

Psalm 92:1–4

WISDOM

A wise servant will rule over a son who causes shame,
And will share an inheritance among the brothers.

Proverbs 17:2

 SO WHAT?
What does this tell me?

HAMAN, THE WICKED ENEMY OF THE JEWS

Esther 3–4; Psalm 92:12-14; Proverbs 17:3

After these things King Ahasuerus promoted Haman, the son of Hammedatha the Agagite, and advanced him and set his seat above all the princes who *were* with him. And all the king's servants who *were* within the king's gate bowed and paid homage to Haman, for so the king had commanded concerning him. But Mordecai would not bow or pay homage. Then the king's servants who *were* within the king's gate said to Mordecai, "Why do you transgress the king's command?" Now it happened, when they spoke to him daily and he would not listen to them, that they told *it* to Haman, to see whether Mordecai's words would stand; for *Mordecai* had told them that he *was* a Jew. When Haman saw that Mordecai did not bow or pay him homage, Haman was filled with wrath. But he disdained to lay hands on Mordecai alone, for they had told him of the people of Mordecai. Instead, Haman sought to destroy all the Jews who *were* throughout the whole kingdom of Ahasuerus—the people of Mordecai.

In the first month, which is the month of Nisan, in the twelfth year of King Ahasuerus, they cast Pur (that *is,* the lot), before Haman to determine the day and the month, until *it fell on the* twelfth *month,* which *is* the month of Adar.

Then Haman said to King Ahasuerus, "There is a certain people scattered and dispersed among the people in all the provinces of your kingdom; their laws *are* different from all *other* people's, and they do not keep the king's laws. Therefore it *is* not fitting for the king to let them remain. If it pleases the king, let *a* decree be written that they be destroyed, and I will pay ten thousand talents of silver into the hands of those who do the work, to bring *it* into the king's treasuries."

So the king took his signet ring from his hand and gave it to Haman, the son of Hammedatha the Agagite, the enemy of the Jews. And the king said to Haman, "The money and the people *are* given to you, to do with them as seems good to you."

Then the king's scribes were called on the thirteenth day of the first month, and a *decree* was written according to all that Haman commanded—to the king's satraps, to the governors who *were* over each province, to the officials of all people, to every province according to its script, and to every people in their language. In the name of King Ahasuerus it was written, and sealed with the king's signet ring. And the letters were sent by couriers into all the king's provinces, to destroy, to kill, and to annihilate all the Jews, both young and old, little children and women, in one day, on the thirteenth *day* of the twelfth *month,* which *is* the month of Adar, and to plunder their possessions. A copy of the document was to be issued as law in every province, being published for all people, that they should be ready for that day. The couriers went out, hastened by the king's command; and the decree was proclaimed in Shushan the citadel. So the king and Haman sat down to drink, but the city of Shushan was perplexed.

When Mordecai learned all that had happened, he tore his clothes and put on sackcloth and ashes, and went out into the midst of the city. He cried out with a loud and bitter cry. He went as far as the front of the king's gate, for no one *might* enter the king's gate clothed with sackcloth. And in every province where the king's command and decree arrived, *there was* great mourning among the Jews, with fasting, weeping, and wailing; and many lay in sackcloth and ashes.

So Esther's maids and eunuchs came and told her, and the queen was deeply distressed. Then she sent garments to clothe Mordecai and take his sackcloth away from him, but he would not accept *them.* Then Esther called Hathach, *one* of the king's eunuchs whom he had appointed to attend her, and she gave him a command concerning Mordecai, to learn what and why this *was.* So Hathach went out to Mordecai in the city square that *was* in front of the king's gate. And Mordecai told him all that had happened to him, and the sum of money that Haman had promised to pay into the king's treasuries to destroy the Jews. He also gave him a copy of the written decree for their destruction, which was given at Shushan, that he might show it to Esther and explain it to her, and that he might command her to go in to the king to make supplication to him and plead before him for her people.

So Hathach returned and told Esther the words of Mordecai.

Then Esther spoke to Hathach, and gave him a command for Mordecai: "All the king's servants and the people of the king's provinces know that any man or woman who goes into the inner court to the king, who has not been called, *he has* but one law: put *all* to death, except the one to whom the king holds out the golden scepter, that he may live. Yet I myself have not been called to go in to the king these thirty days." So they told Mordecai Esther's words.

And Mordecai told *them* to answer Esther: "Do not think in your heart that you will escape in the king's palace any more than all the other Jews. For if you remain completely silent at this time, relief and deliverance will arise for the Jews from another place, but you and your father's house will perish. Yet who knows whether you have come to the kingdom for *such* a time as this?"

Then Esther told *them* to reply to Mordecai: "Go, gather all the Jews who are present in Shushan, and fast for me; neither eat nor drink for three days, night or day. My maids and I will fast likewise. And so I will go to the king, which *is* against the law; and if I perish, I perish!"

So Mordecai went his way and did according to all that Esther commanded him.

Esther 3–4

WORSHIP

The righteous shall flourish like a palm tree,
He shall grow like a cedar in Lebanon.
Those who are planted in the house of the Lord
Shall flourish in the courts of our God.
They shall still bear fruit in old age;
They shall be fresh and flourishing.

Psalm 92:12-14

WISDOM

The refining pot *is* for silver and the furnace for gold,
But the Lord tests the hearts.

Proverbs 17:3

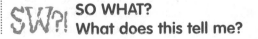

SO WHAT?
What does this tell me?

ESTHER'S INTERVENTION FOR HER PEOPLE

Esther 5–7; Psalm 93:1-2; Proverbs 17:4

Now it happened on the third day that Esther put on *her* royal *robes* and stood in the inner court of the king's palace, across from the king's house, while the king sat on his royal throne in the royal house, facing the entrance of the house. So it was, when the king saw Queen Esther standing in the court, *that* she found favor in his sight, and the king held out to Esther the golden scepter that *was* in his hand. Then Esther went near and touched the top of the scepter.

And the king said to her, "What do you wish, Queen Esther? What *is* your request? It shall be given to you—up to half the kingdom!"

So Esther answered, "If it pleases the king, let the king and Haman come today to the banquet that I have prepared for him."

Then the king said, "Bring Haman quickly, that he may do as Esther has said." So the king and Haman went to the banquet that Esther had prepared.

At the banquet of wine the king said to Esther, "What *is* your petition? It shall be granted you. What *is* your request, up to half the kingdom? It shall be done!"

Then Esther answered and said, "My petition and request *is this:* If I have found favor in the sight of the king, and if it pleases the king to grant my petition and fulfill my request, then let the king and Haman come to the banquet which I will prepare for them, and tomorrow I will do as the king has said."

So Haman went out that day joyful and with a glad heart; but when Haman saw Mordecai in the king's gate, and that he did not stand or tremble before him, he was filled with indignation against Mordecai. Nevertheless Haman restrained himself and went home, and he sent and called for his friends and his wife Zeresh. Then Haman told them of his great riches, the multitude of his children, everything in which the king had promoted him, and how he had advanced him above the officials and servants of the king.

Moreover Haman said, "Besides, Queen Esther invited no one but me to come in with the king to the banquet that she pre-pared; and tomorrow I am again invited by her, along with the king. Yet all this avails me nothing, so long as I see Mordecai the Jew sitting at the king's gate."

Then his wife Zeresh and all his friends said to him, "Let a gallows be made, fifty cubits high, and in the morning suggest to the king that Mordecai be hanged on it; then go merrily with the king to the banquet."

And the thing pleased Haman; so he had the gallows made.

That night the king could not sleep. So one was commanded to bring the book of the records of the chronicles; and they were read before the king. And it was found written that Mordecai had told of Bigthana and Teresh, two of the king's eunuchs, the doorkeepers who had sought to lay hands on King Ahasuerus. Then the king said, "What honor or dignity has been bestowed on Mordecai for this?"

And the king's servants who attended him said, "Nothing has been done for him."

So the king said, "Who *is* in the court?" Now Haman had *just* entered the outer court of the king's palace to suggest that the king hang Mordecai on the gallows that he had prepared for him.

The king's servants said to him, "Haman is there, standing in the court."

And the king said, "Let him come in."

So Haman came in, and the king asked him, "What shall be done for the man whom the king delights to honor?"

Now Haman thought in his heart, "Whom would the king delight to honor more than me?" And Haman answered the king, "*For* the man whom the king delights to honor, let a royal robe be brought which the king has worn, and a horse on which the king has ridden, which has a royal crest placed on its head. Then let this robe and horse be delivered to the hand of one of the king's most noble princes, that he may array the man whom the king delights to honor. Then parade him on horseback through the city square, and proclaim before him: 'Thus shall it be done to the man whom the king delights to honor!'"

Then the king said to Haman, "Hurry, take the robe and the horse, as you have suggested, and do so for Mordecai the Jew who sits within the king's gate! Leave nothing undone of all that you have spoken."

So Haman took the robe and the horse, arrayed Mordecai and led him on horseback through the city square, and proclaimed before him, "Thus shall it be done to the man whom the king delights to honor!"

Afterward Mordecai went back to the king's gate. But Haman hurried to his house, mourning and with his head covered. When Haman told his wife Zeresh and all his friends everything that had happened to him, his wise men and his wife Zeresh said to him, "If Mordecai, before whom you have begun to fall, is of Jewish descent, you will not prevail against him but will surely fall before him."

While they *were* still talking with him, the king's eunuchs came, and hastened to bring Haman to the banquet which Esther had prepared.

So the king and Haman went to dine with Queen Esther. And on the second day, at the banquet of wine, the king again said to Esther, "What *is* your petition, Queen Esther? It shall be granted you. And what *is* your request, up to half the kingdom? It shall be done!"

Then Queen Esther answered and said, "If I have found favor in your sight, O king, and if it pleases the king, let my life be given me at my petition, and my people at my request. For we have been sold, my people and I, to be destroyed, to be killed, and to be annihilated. Had we been sold as male and female slaves, I would have held my tongue, although the enemy could never compensate for the king's loss."

So King Ahasuerus answered and said to Queen Esther, "Who is he, and where is he, who would dare presume in his heart to do such a thing?"

And Esther said, "The adversary and enemy *is* this wicked Haman!"

So Haman was terrified before the king and queen.

Then the king arose in his wrath from the banquet of wine *and went* into the palace garden; but Haman stood before Queen Esther, pleading for his life, for he saw that evil was determined against him by the king. When the king returned from the palace garden to the place of the banquet of wine, Haman had fallen across the couch where Esther *was*. Then the king said, "Will he also assault the queen while I *am* in the house?"

As the word left the king's mouth, they covered Haman's face. Now Harbonah, one of the eunuchs, said to the king, "Look! The gallows, fifty cubits high, which Haman made for Mordecai, who spoke good on the king's behalf, is standing at the house of Haman."

Then the king said, "Hang him on it!"

So they hanged Haman on the gallows that he had prepared for Mordecai. Then the king's wrath subsided.

Esther 5–7

WORSHIP

The LORD reigns, He is clothed with majesty;
The LORD is clothed,
He has girded Himself with strength.
Surely the world is established, so that it
　　cannot be moved.
Your throne *is* established from of old;
You *are* from everlasting.

Psalm 93:1-2

WISDOM

An evildoer gives heed to false lips;
A liar listens eagerly to a spiteful tongue.

Proverbs 17:4

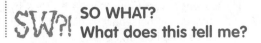

**SO WHAT?
What does this tell me?**

A NEW EDICT AND DELIVERANCE!

**Esther 8:1–9:5, 13-32;
Psalm 94:1-3; Proverbs 17:5**

On that day King Ahasuerus gave Queen Esther the house of Haman, the enemy of the Jews. And Mordecai came before the king, for Esther had told how he *was related* to her. So the king took off his signet ring, which he had taken from Haman, and gave it to Mordecai; and Esther appointed Mordecai over the house of Haman.

Now Esther spoke again to the king, fell down at his feet, and implored him with tears to counteract the evil of Haman the Agagite, and the scheme which he had devised against the Jews. And the king held out the golden scepter toward Esther. So Esther arose and stood before the king, and said, "If it pleases the king, and if I have found favor in his sight and the thing *seems* right to the king and I am pleasing in his eyes, let it be written to revoke the letters devised by Haman, the son of Hammedatha the Agagite, which he wrote to annihilate the Jews who *are* in all the king's provinces. For how can I endure to see the evil that will come to my people? Or how can I endure to see the destruction of my countrymen?"

Then King Ahasuerus said to Queen Esther and Mordecai the Jew, "Indeed, I have given Esther the house of Haman, and they have hanged him on the gallows because he *tried to* lay his hand on the Jews. You yourselves write *a decree* concerning the Jews, as you please, in the king's name, and seal *it* with the king's signet ring; for whatever is written in the king's name and sealed with the king's signet ring no one can revoke."

So the king's scribes were called at that time, in the third month, which *is* the month of Sivan, on the twenty-third *day;* and it was written, according to all that Mordecai commanded, to the Jews, the satraps, the governors, and the princes of the provinces from India to Ethiopia, one hundred and twenty-seven provinces *in all,* to every province in its own script, to every people in their own language, and to the Jews in their own script and language. And he wrote in the name of King Ahasuerus, sealed *it* with the king's signet ring, and sent letters by couriers on horseback, riding on royal horses bred from swift steeds.

By these letters the king permitted the Jews who *were* in every city to gather together and protect their lives—to destroy, kill, and annihilate all the forces of any people or province that would assault them, *both* little children and women, and to plunder their possessions, on one day in all the provinces of King Ahasuerus, on the thirteenth *day* of the twelfth month, which *is* the month of Adar. A copy of the document was to be issued as a decree in every province and published for all people, so that the Jews would be ready on that day to avenge themselves on their enemies. The couriers who rode on royal horses went out, hastened and pressed on by the king's command. And the decree was issued in Shushan the citadel.

So Mordecai went out from the presence of the king in royal apparel of blue and white, with a great crown of gold and a garment of fine linen and purple; and the city of Shushan rejoiced and was glad. The Jews had light and gladness, joy and honor. And in every province and city, wherever the king's command and decree came, the Jews had joy and gladness, a feast and a holiday. Then many of the people of the land became Jews, because fear of the Jews fell upon them.

Now in the twelfth month, that *is,* the month of Adar, on the thirteenth day, *the time* came for the king's command and his decree to be executed. On the day that the enemies of the Jews had hoped to overpower them, the opposite occurred, in that the Jews themselves overpowered those who hated them. The Jews gathered together in their cities throughout all the provinces of King Ahasuerus to lay hands on those who sought their harm. And no one could withstand them, because fear of them fell upon all people. And all the officials of the provinces, the satraps, the governors, and all those doing the king's work, helped the Jews, because the fear of Mordecai fell upon them. For Mordecai *was* great in the king's palace, and his fame spread throughout all the provinces; for this man Mordecai became increasingly prominent. Thus the Jews defeated all their enemies with the stroke of the sword, with slaughter and destruction, and did what they pleased with those who hated them.

Then Esther said, "If it pleases the king, let it be granted to the Jews who *are* in Shushan to do again tomorrow according to today's decree, and let Haman's ten sons be hanged on the gallows."

So the king commanded this to be done; the decree was issued in Shushan, and they hanged Haman's ten sons.

And the Jews who *were* in Shushan gathered together again on the fourteenth day of the month of Adar and killed three hundred men at Shushan; but they did not lay a hand on the plunder.

The remainder of the Jews in the king's provinces gathered together and protected their lives, had rest from their enemies, and killed seventy-five thousand of their enemies; but they did not lay a hand on the plunder. *This was* on the thirteenth day of the month of Adar. And on the fourteenth of *the month* they rested and made it a day of feasting and gladness.

But the Jews who *were* at Shushan assembled together on the thirteenth *day*, as well as on the fourteenth; and on the fifteenth of *the month* they rested, and made it a day of feasting and gladness. Therefore the Jews of the villages who dwelt in the unwalled towns celebrated the fourteenth day of the month of Adar *with* gladness and feasting, as a holiday, and for sending presents to one another.

And Mordecai wrote these things and sent letters to all the Jews, near and far, who *were* in all the provinces of King Ahasuerus, to establish among them that they should celebrate yearly the fourteenth and fifteenth days of the month of Adar, as the days on which the Jews had rest from their enemies, as the month which was turned from sorrow to joy for them, and from mourning to a holiday; that they should make them days of feasting and joy, of sending presents to one another and gifts to the poor. So the Jews accepted the custom which they had begun, as Mordecai had written to them, because Haman, the son of Hammedatha the Agagite, the enemy of all the Jews, had plotted against the Jews to annihilate them, and had cast Pur (that *is,* the lot), to consume them and destroy them; but when *Esther* came before the king, he commanded by letter that this wicked plot which *Haman* had devised against the Jews should return on his own head, and that he and his sons should be hanged on the gallows.

So they called these days Purim, after the name Pur. Therefore, because of all the words of this letter, what they had seen concerning this matter, and what had happened to them, the Jews established and imposed it upon themselves and

their descendants and all who would join them, that without fail they should celebrate these two days every year, according to the written *instructions* and according to the *prescribed* time, *that* these days *should be* remembered and kept throughout every generation, every family, every province, and every city, that these days of Purim should not fail *to be observed* among the Jews, and *that* the memory of them should not perish among their descendants.

Then Queen Esther, the daughter of Abihail, with Mordecai the Jew, wrote with full authority to confirm this second letter about Purim. And *Mordecai* sent letters to all the Jews, to the one hundred and twenty-seven provinces of the kingdom of Ahasuerus, *with* words of peace and truth, to confirm these days of Purim at their *appointed* time, as Mordecai the Jew and Queen Esther had prescribed for them, and as they had decreed for themselves and their descendants concerning matters of their fasting and lamenting. So the decree of Esther confirmed these matters of Purim, and it was written in the book.

Esther 8:1–9:5, 13–32

O LORD God, to whom vengeance belongs—
O God, to whom vengeance belongs, shine
     forth!
Rise up, O Judge of the earth;
Render punishment to the proud.
LORD, how long will the wicked,
How long will the wicked triumph?

Psalm 94:1-3

WISDOM

He who mocks the poor reproaches his
     Maker;
He who is glad at calamity will not go
     unpunished.

Proverbs 17:5

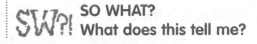

SO WHAT?
What does this tell me?

THERE'S NO PLACE LIKE HOME

The Glory of God in His Grace

After seventy years of captivity in a foreign land, the Lord raised up Cyrus, king of Persia, to conquer Babylon and decree the return of the Jews to their land. Here we see the glory of God in His gracious restoration of His people.

The restoration period offered God's people a unique opportunity to "start over." By rebuilding the temple and re-establishing worship, this fresh start could be based on lasting spiritual foundations. However, as you will discover, a fresh start doesn't necessarily mean a good finish. Several significant mountain peaks rise skyward as the people of God go home.

The first peak is the return to Jerusalem to rebuild the temple. Unfortunately, the returned exiles became distracted and began repairing their own homes instead of working on the temple. It wasn't until God raised up the prophets Haggai and Zechariah that the people got their priorities in order and completed the work on the temple.

A second mountain peak in the restoration period is the return of Ezra, a scribe and teacher of the Law, to enhance worship in the temple. Under his leadership, a group of Jews returned to Jerusalem to offer sacrifices and teach the people. Ezra also brought back to Jerusalem many of the gold and silver worship utensils that had been taken by the Babylonians.

Nehemiah's return to Jerusalem to rebuild the walls of the city marks a third peak in the restoration. Nehemiah, cupbearer to King Artaxerxes, learned that although the temple had been rebuilt, the city of Jerusalem was still in ruins and vulnerable to attack. Under Nehemiah's leadership—which was challenged in ways you'll have to read to believe—the walls of Jerusalem were rebuilt in a remarkable 52 days!

After completing the wall, Nehemiah served for 12 years as governor of Jerusalem before returning to Babylon to report to Artaxerxes. After he left, the priests became lax in their duties and the people began to neglect their giving. To address these problems, God raised up the prophet Malachi to remind the people that repentance was necessary in order to enjoy God's blessing. The ministry of Malachi represents the last mountain peak in this final mountain range of the Old Testament.

THE EXILES RETURN TO REBUILD

Ezra 1:1-11; 3:1–4:5, 24;
Psalm 94:12-14; Proverbs 17:6

Now in the first year of Cyrus king of Persia, that the word of the LORD by the mouth of Jeremiah might be fulfilled, the LORD stirred up the spirit of Cyrus king of Persia, so that he made a proclamation throughout all his kingdom, and also *put it in writing*, saying,

Thus says Cyrus king of Persia: All the kingdoms of the earth the LORD God of heaven has given me. And He has commanded me to build Him a house at Jerusalem which *is* in Judah. Who *is* among you of all His people? May his God be with him, and let him go up to Jerusalem which *is* in Judah, and build the house of the LORD God of Israel (He *is* God), which *is* in Jerusalem. And whoever is left in any place where he dwells, let the men of his place help him with silver and gold, with goods and livestock, besides the freewill offerings for the house of God which *is* in Jerusalem.

Then the heads of the fathers' *houses* of Judah and Benjamin, and the priests and the Levites, with all whose spirits God had moved, arose to go up and build the house of the LORD which *is* in Jerusalem. And all those who *were* around them encouraged them with articles of silver and gold, with goods and livestock, and with precious things, besides all *that* was willingly offered. King Cyrus also brought out the articles of the house of the LORD, which Nebuchadnezzar had taken from Jerusalem and put in the temple of his gods; and Cyrus king of Persia brought them out by the hand of Mithredath the treasurer, and counted them out to Sheshbazzar the prince of Judah. This *is* the number of them: thirty gold platters, one thousand silver platters, twenty-nine knives, thirty gold basins, four hundred and ten silver basins of a similar *kind, and* one thousand other articles. All the articles of gold and silver *were* five thousand four hundred. All *these* Sheshbazzar took with the captives who were brought from Babylon to Jerusalem.

And when the seventh month had come, and the children of Israel *were* in the cities, the people gathered together as one man to Jerusalem. Then Jeshua the son of Jozadak and his brethren the priests, and Zerubbabel the son of Shealtiel and his brethren, arose and built the altar of the God of Israel, to offer burnt offerings on it, as *it is* written in the Law of Moses the man of God. Though fear *had come* upon them because of the people of those countries, they set the altar on its bases; and they offered burnt offerings on it to the LORD, *both* the morning and evening burnt offerings. They also kept the Feast of Tabernacles, as *it is* written, and *offered* the daily burnt offerings in the number required by ordinance for each day. Afterwards *they offered* the regular burnt offering, and *those* for New Moons and for all the appointed feasts of the LORD that were consecrated, and *those* of everyone who willingly offered a freewill offering to the LORD. From the first day of the seventh month they began to offer burnt offerings to the LORD, although the foundation of the temple of the LORD had not been laid. They also gave money to the masons and the carpenters, and food, drink, and oil to the people of Sidon and Tyre to bring cedar logs from Lebanon to the sea, to Joppa, according to the permission which they had from Cyrus king of Persia.

Now in the second month of the second year of their coming to the house of God at Jerusalem, Zerubbabel the son of Shealtiel, Jeshua the son of Jozadak, and the rest of their brethren the priests and the Levites, and all those who had come out of the captivity to Jerusalem, began *work* and appointed the Levites from twenty years old and above to oversee the work of the house of the LORD. Then Jeshua *with* his sons and brothers, Kadmiel *with* his sons, and the sons of Judah, arose as one to oversee those working on the house of God: the sons of Henadad *with* their sons and their brethren the Levites.

When the builders laid the foundation of the temple of the LORD, the priests stood in their apparel with trumpets, and the Levites, the sons of Asaph, with cymbals, to praise the LORD, according to the ordinance of David king of Israel. And they sang responsively, praising and giving thanks to the LORD:

"For *He is* good,
For His mercy *endures* forever toward Israel."

Then all the people shouted with a great shout, when they praised the LORD, because the foundation of the house of the LORD was laid.

But many of the priests and Levites and heads of the fathers' *houses,* old men who had seen the first temple, wept with a loud voice when the foundation of this temple was laid before their eyes. Yet many shouted aloud for joy, so that the people could not discern the noise of the shout of joy from the noise of the weeping of the people, for the people shouted with a loud shout, and the sound was heard afar off.

Now when the adversaries of Judah and Benjamin heard that the descendants of the captivity were building the temple of the LORD God of Israel, they came to Zerubbabel and the heads of the fathers' *houses,* and said to them, "Let us build with you, for we seek your God as you *do;* and we have sacrificed to Him since the days of Esarhaddon king of Assyria, who brought us here." But Zerubbabel and Jeshua and the rest of the heads of the fathers' *houses* of Israel said to them, "You may do nothing with us to build a house for our God; but we alone will build to the LORD God of Israel, as King Cyrus the king of Persia has commanded us." Then the people of the land tried to discourage the people of Judah. They troubled them in building, and hired counselors against them to frustrate their purpose all the days of Cyrus king of Persia, even until the reign of Darius king of Persia.

Thus the work of the house of God which *is* at Jerusalem ceased, and it was discontinued until the second year of the reign of Darius king of Persia.

Ezra 1:1-11; 3:1–4:5, 24

WORSHIP

Blessed *is* the man whom You instruct, O LORD,
And teach out of Your law,
That You may give him rest from the days of
    adversity,
Until the pit is dug for the wicked.
For the LORD will not cast off His people,
Nor will He forsake His inheritance.

Psalm 94:12-14

WISDOM

Children's children *are* the crown of old men,
And the glory of children *is* their father.

Proverbs 17:6

SW?! SO WHAT?
What does this tell me?

A PROBLEM OF PRIORITIES   Haggai 1–2; Psalm 94:17-19; Proverbs 17:7

In the second year of King Darius, in the sixth month, on the first day of the month, the word of the LORD came by Haggai the prophet to Zerubbabel the son of Shealtiel, governor of Judah, and to Joshua the son of Jehozadak, the high priest, saying, "Thus speaks the LORD of hosts, saying: 'This people says, "The time has not come, the time that the LORD's house should be built." ' "

Then the word of the LORD came by Haggai the prophet, saying, "*Is it* time for you yourselves to dwell in your paneled houses, and this temple *to lie* in ruins?" Now therefore, thus says the LORD of hosts: "Consider your ways!

"You have sown much, and bring in little;
You eat, but do not have enough;
You drink, but you are not filled with drink;
You clothe yourselves, but no one is warm;
And he who earns wages,
Earns wages *to put* into a bag with holes."

Thus says the LORD of hosts: "Consider your ways! Go up to the mountains and bring wood and build the temple, that I may take pleasure in it and be glorified," says the LORD. "*You* looked for much, but indeed *it came to* little; and when you brought it home, I blew it away. Why?" says the LORD of hosts. "Because of My house that *is in* ruins, while every one of you runs to his own house. Therefore the heavens above you withhold the dew, and the earth withholds its fruit. For I called for a drought on the land and the mountains, on the grain and the new wine and the oil, on whatever the ground brings forth, on men and livestock, and on all the labor of *your* hands."

Then Zerubbabel the son of Shealtiel, and Joshua the son of Jehozadak, the high priest, with all the remnant of the people, obeyed the voice of the LORD their God, and the words of Haggai the prophet, as the LORD their God had sent him; and the people feared the presence of the LORD. Then Haggai, the LORD's messenger, spoke the LORD's message to the people, saying, "I *am* with you, says the LORD." So the LORD stirred up the spirit of Zerubbabel the son of Shealtiel, governor of Judah, and the spirit of Joshua the son of Jehozadak, the high priest, and the spirit of all the remnant of the people; and they came and worked on the house of the LORD of hosts, their God, on the twenty-fourth day of the sixth month, in the second year of King Darius.

In the seventh *month,* on the twenty-first of the month, the word of the LORD came by Haggai the prophet, saying: "Speak now to Zerubbabel the son of Shealtiel, governor of Judah, and to Joshua the son of Jehozadak, the high priest, and to the remnant of the people, saying: 'Who is left among you who saw this temple in its former glory? And how do you see it now? In comparison with it, *is this* not in your eyes as nothing? Yet now be strong, Zerubbabel,' says the LORD; 'and be strong, Joshua, son of Jehozadak, the high priest; and be strong, all you people of the land,' says the LORD, 'and work; for I *am* with you,' says the LORD of hosts. '*According to* the word that I covenanted with you when you came out of Egypt, so My Spirit remains among you; do not fear!'

"For thus says the LORD of hosts: 'Once more (it *is* a little while) I will shake heaven and earth, the sea and dry land; and I will shake all nations, and they shall come to the Desire of All Nations, and I will fill this temple with glory,' says the LORD of hosts. 'The silver *is* Mine, and the gold *is* Mine,' says the LORD of hosts. 'The glory of this latter temple shall be greater than the former,' says the LORD of hosts. 'And in this place I will give peace,' says the LORD of hosts."

On the twenty-fourth *day* of the ninth *month,* in the second year of Darius, the word of the LORD came by Haggai the prophet, saying, "Thus says the LORD of hosts: 'Now, ask the priests *concerning the* law, saying, "If one carries holy meat in the fold of his garment, and with the edge he touches bread or stew, wine or oil, or any food, will it become holy?" ' "

Then the priests answered and said, "No."

And Haggai said, "If *one who is* unclean *because* of a dead body touches any of these, will it be unclean?"

So the priests answered and said, "It shall be unclean."

Then Haggai answered and said, " 'So is this people, and so is this nation before Me,' says the

Lord, 'and so is every work of their hands; and what they offer there is unclean.

'And now, carefully consider from this day forward: from before stone was laid upon stone in the temple of the Lord—since those *days,* when *one* came to a heap of twenty ephahs, there were *but* ten; when *one* came to the wine vat to draw out fifty baths from the press, there were *but* twenty. I struck you with blight and mildew and hail in all the labors of your hands; yet you did not *turn* to Me,' says the Lord. 'Consider now from this day forward, from the twenty-fourth day of the ninth month, from the day that the foundation of the Lord's temple was laid—consider it: Is the seed still in the barn? As yet the vine, the fig tree, the pomegranate, and the olive tree have not yielded *fruit. But* from this day I will bless *you.' "*

And again the word of the Lord came to Haggai on the twenty-fourth day of the month, saying, "Speak to Zerubbabel, governor of Judah, saying:

'I will shake heaven and earth.
I will overthrow the throne of kingdoms;
I will destroy the strength of the Gentile
    kingdoms.
I will overthrow the chariots
And those who ride in them;
The horses and their riders shall come down,
Every one by the sword of his brother.

'In that day,' says the Lord of hosts, 'I will take you, Zerubbabel My servant, the son of Shealtiel,' says the Lord, 'and will make you like a signet *ring;* for I have chosen you,' says the Lord of hosts."

Haggai 1–2

WORSHIP

Unless the Lord *had been* my help,
My soul would soon have settled in silence.
If I say, "My foot slips,"
Your mercy, O Lord, will hold me up.
In the multitude of my anxieties within me,
Your comforts delight my soul.

Psalm 94:17-19

WISDOM

Excellent speech is not becoming to a fool,
Much less lying lips to a prince.

Proverbs 17:7

SW?! **SO WHAT?**
What does this tell me?

A FUTURE FOR JERUSALEM AND THE TEMPLE
Zechariah 1:1–3:5; Psalm 95:1–3; Proverbs 17:9

In the eighth month of the second year of Darius, the word of the LORD came to Zechariah the son of Berechiah, the son of Iddo the prophet, saying, "The LORD has been very angry with your fathers. Therefore say to them, 'Thus says the LORD of hosts: "Return to Me," says the LORD of hosts, "and I will return to you," says the LORD of hosts. "Do not be like your fathers, to whom the former prophets preached, saying, 'Thus says the LORD of hosts: "Turn now from your evil ways and your evil deeds." ' But they did not hear nor heed Me," says the LORD.

"Your fathers, where *are* they?
And the prophets, do they live forever?
Yet surely My words and My statutes,
Which I commanded My servants the
    prophets,
Did they not overtake your fathers?

"So they returned and said:

'Just as the LORD of hosts determined to do
    to us,
According to our ways and according to
    our deeds,
So He has dealt with us.' " ' "

On the twenty-fourth day of the eleventh month, which is the month Shebat, in the second year of Darius, the word of the LORD came to Zechariah the son of Berechiah, the son of Iddo the prophet: I saw by night, and behold, a man riding on a red horse, and it stood among the myrtle trees in the hollow; and behind him *were* horses: red, sorrel, and white. Then I said, "My lord, what *are* these?" So the angel who talked with me said to me, "I will show you what they *are*."

And the man who stood among the myrtle trees answered and said, "These *are the ones* whom the LORD has sent to walk to and fro throughout the earth."

So they answered the Angel of the LORD, who stood among the myrtle trees, and said, "We have walked to and fro throughout the earth, and behold, all the earth is resting quietly."

Then the Angel of the LORD answered and said, "O LORD of hosts, how long will You not have mercy on Jerusalem and on the cities of Judah, against which You were angry these seventy years?"

And the LORD answered the angel who talked to me, *with* good *and* comforting words. So the angel who spoke with me said to me, "Proclaim, saying, 'Thus says the LORD of hosts:

"I am zealous for Jerusalem
And for Zion with great zeal.
I am exceedingly angry with the nations at
    ease;
For I was a little angry,
And they helped—*but* with evil *intent*."

'Therefore thus says the LORD:

"I am returning to Jerusalem with mercy;
My house shall be built in it," says the LORD of
    hosts,
"And a *surveyor*'s line shall be stretched out
    over Jerusalem." '

"Again proclaim, saying, 'Thus says the LORD of hosts:

"My cities shall again spread out through
    prosperity;
The LORD will again comfort Zion,
And will again choose Jerusalem." ' "

Then I raised my eyes and looked, and there *were* four horns. And I said to the angel who talked with me, "What *are* these?"

So he answered me, "These *are* the horns that have scattered Judah, Israel, and Jerusalem."

Then the LORD showed me four craftsmen. And I said, "What are these coming to do?"

So he said, "These *are* the horns that scattered Judah, so that no one could lift up his head; but the craftsmen are coming to terrify them, to cast out the horns of the nations that lifted up *their* horn against the land of Judah to scatter it."

Then I raised my eyes and looked, and behold, a man with a measuring line in his hand. So I said, "Where are you going?"

And he said to me, "To measure Jerusalem, to see what *is* its width and what *is* its length."

And there *was* the angel who talked with me, going out; and another angel was coming out to meet him, who said to him, "Run, speak to this young man, saying: 'Jerusalem shall be inhabited *as* towns without walls, because of the multitude of men and livestock in it. For I,' says the LORD, 'will be a wall of fire all around her, and I will be the glory in her midst.' "

"Up, up! Flee from the land of the north," says the LORD; "for I have spread you abroad like the four winds of heaven," says the LORD. "Up, Zion! Escape, you who dwell with the daughter of Babylon."

For thus says the LORD of hosts: "He sent Me after glory, to the nations which plunder you; for he who touches you touches the apple of His eye. For surely I will shake My hand against them, and they shall become spoil for their servants. Then you will know that the LORD of hosts has sent Me.

"Sing and rejoice, O daughter of Zion! For behold, I am coming and I will dwell in your midst," says the LORD. "Many nations shall be joined to the LORD in that day, and they shall become My people. And I will dwell in your midst. Then you will know that the LORD of hosts has sent Me to you. And the LORD will take possession of Judah as His inheritance in the Holy Land, and will again choose Jerusalem. Be silent, all flesh, before the LORD, for He is aroused from His holy habitation!"

Then he showed me Joshua the high priest standing before the Angel of the LORD, and Satan standing at his right hand to oppose him. And the LORD said to Satan, "The LORD rebuke you, Satan! The LORD who has chosen Jerusalem rebuke you! *Is* this not a brand plucked from the fire?"

Now Joshua was clothed with filthy garments, and was standing before the Angel.

Then He answered and spoke to those who stood before Him, saying, "Take away the filthy garments from him." And to him He said, "See, I have removed your iniquity from you, and I will clothe you with rich robes."

And I said, "Let them put a clean turban on his head."

So they put a clean turban on his head, and they put the clothes on him. And the Angel of the LORD stood by.

Zechariah 1:1–3:5

WORSHIP

Oh come, let us sing to the LORD!
Let us shout joyfully to the Rock of our salvation.
Let us come before His presence with thanksgiving;
Let us shout joyfully to Him with psalms.
For the LORD *is* the great God,
And the great King above all gods.

Psalm 95:1-3

WISDOM

He who covers a transgression seeks love,
But he who repeats a matter separates friends.

Proverbs 17:9

SW?! SO WHAT?
What does this tell me?

FASTING TURNS TO FEASTING

Zechariah 7–8; Psalm 95:6–7; Proverbs 17:10

Now in the fourth year of King Darius it came to pass *that* the word of the LORD came to Zechariah, on the fourth day of the ninth month, Chislev, when *the people* sent Sherezer, with Regem-Melech and his men, *to* the house of God, to pray before the LORD, *and* to ask the priests who *were* in the house of the LORD of hosts, and the prophets, saying, "Should I weep in the fifth month and fast as I have done for so many years?"

Then the word of the LORD of hosts came to me, saying, "Say to all the people of the land, and to the priests: 'When you fasted and mourned in the fifth and seventh *months* during those seventy years, did you really fast for Me—for Me? When you eat and when you drink, do you not eat and drink *for yourselves*? *Should you* not *have obeyed* the words which the LORD proclaimed through the former prophets when Jerusalem and the cities around it were inhabited and prosperous, and the South and the Lowland were inhabited?' "

Then the word of the LORD came to Zechariah, saying, "Thus says the LORD of hosts:

'Execute true justice,
Show mercy and compassion
Everyone to his brother.
Do not oppress the widow or the fatherless,
The alien or the poor.
Let none of you plan evil in his heart
Against his brother.'

"But they refused to heed, shrugged their shoulders, and stopped their ears so that they could not hear. Yes, they made their hearts like flint, refusing to hear the law and the words which the LORD of hosts had sent by His Spirit through the former prophets. Thus great wrath came from the LORD of hosts. Therefore it happened, *that* just as He proclaimed and they would not hear, so they called out and I would not listen," says the LORD of hosts. "But I scattered them with a whirlwind among all the nations which they had not known. Thus the land became desolate after them, so that no one

passed through or returned; for they made the pleasant land desolate."

Again the word of the LORD of hosts came, saying, "Thus says the LORD of hosts:

'I am zealous for Zion with great zeal;
With great fervor I am zealous for her.'

"Thus says the LORD:

'I will return to Zion,
And dwell in the midst of Jerusalem.
Jerusalem shall be called the City of Truth,
The Mountain of the LORD of hosts,
The Holy Mountain.'

"Thus says the LORD of hosts:

'Old men and old women shall again sit
In the streets of Jerusalem,
Each one with his staff in his hand
Because of great age.
The streets of the city
Shall be full of boys and girls
Playing in its streets.'

"Thus says the LORD of hosts:

'If it is marvelous in the eyes of the remnant of
this people in these days,
Will it also be marvelous in My eyes?'
Says the LORD of hosts.

"Thus says the LORD of hosts:

'Behold, I will save My people from the land of
the east
And from the land of the west;
I will bring them *back,*
And they shall dwell in the midst of Jerusalem.
They shall be My people
And I will be their God,
In truth and righteousness.'

"Thus says the LORD of hosts:

'Let your hands be strong,
You who have been hearing in these days
These words by the mouth of the prophets,
Who *spoke* in the day the foundation was laid
For the house of the LORD of hosts,
That the temple might be built.
For before these days
There were no wages for man nor any hire for
beast;

THERE'S NO PLACE LIKE HOME

There was no peace from the enemy for
whoever went out or came in;
For I set all men, everyone, against his
neighbor.

But now I *will* not *treat* the remnant of this people as in the former days,' says the LORD of hosts.

'For the seed *shall be* prosperous,
The vine shall give its fruit,
The ground shall give her increase,
And the heavens shall give their dew—
I will cause the remnant of this people
To possess all these.
And it shall come to pass
That just as you were a curse among the
nations,
O house of Judah and house of Israel,
So I will save you, and you shall be a
blessing.
Do not fear,
Let your hands be strong.'

"For thus says the LORD of hosts:

'Just as I determined to punish you
When your fathers provoked Me to wrath,'
Says the LORD of hosts,
'And I would not relent,
So again in these days
I am determined to do good
To Jerusalem and to the house of Judah.
Do not fear.
These *are* the things you shall do:
Speak each man the truth to his neighbor;
Give judgment in your gates for truth, justice,
and peace;
Let none of you think evil in your heart against
your neighbor;
And do not love a false oath.
For all these *are things* that I hate,'
Says the LORD."

Then the word of the LORD of hosts came to me, saying, "Thus says the LORD of hosts:

'The fast of the fourth *month,*
The fast of the fifth,
The fast of the seventh,
And the fast of the tenth,
Shall be joy and gladness and cheerful feasts
For the house of Judah.
Therefore love truth and peace.'

"Thus says the LORD of hosts:

'Peoples shall yet come,
Inhabitants of many cities;

The inhabitants of one *city* shall go to another,
saying,
"Let us continue to go and pray before the LORD,
And seek the LORD of hosts.
I myself will go also."
Yes, many peoples and strong nations
Shall come to seek the LORD of hosts in
Jerusalem,
And to pray before the LORD.'

"Thus says the LORD of hosts: 'In those days ten men from every language of the nations shall grasp the sleeve of a Jewish man, saying, "Let us go with you, for we have heard *that* God *is* with you." ' "

Zechariah 7–8

WORSHIP

Oh come, let us worship and bow down;
Let us kneel before the LORD our Maker.
For He *is* our God,
And we *are* the people of His pasture,
And the sheep of His hand.

Psalm 95:6-7

WISDOM

Rebuke is more effective for a wise *man*
Than a hundred blows on a fool.

Proverbs 17:10

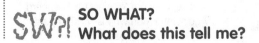

SO WHAT?
What does this tell me?

Israel's SPIRITUAL FUTURE
Zechariah 12:10–14:21; Psalm 96:1-4; Proverbs 17:12

"And I will pour on the house of David and on the inhabitants of Jerusalem the Spirit of grace and supplication; then they will look on Me whom they pierced. Yes, they will mourn for Him as one mourns for *his* only *son*, and grieve for Him as one grieves for a firstborn. In that day there shall be a great mourning in Jerusalem, like the mourning at Hadad Rimmon in the plain of Megiddo. And the land shall mourn, every family by itself: the family of the house of David by itself, and their wives by themselves; the family of the house of Nathan by itself, and their wives by themselves; the family of the house of Levi by itself, and their wives by themselves; the family of Shimei by itself, and their wives by themselves; all the families that remain, every family by itself, and their wives by themselves.

"In that day a fountain shall be opened for the house of David and for the inhabitants of Jerusalem, for sin and for uncleanness.

"It shall be in that day," says the LORD of hosts, "that I will cut off the names of the idols from the land, and they shall no longer be remembered. I will also cause the prophets and the unclean spirit to depart from the land. It shall come to pass *that* if anyone still prophesies, then his father and mother who begot him will say to him, 'You shall not live, because you have spoken lies in the name of the LORD.' And his father and mother who begot him shall thrust him through when he prophesies.

"And it shall be in that day *that* every prophet will be ashamed of his vision when he prophesies; they will not wear a robe of coarse hair to deceive. But he will say, 'I *am* no prophet, I *am* a farmer; for a man taught me to keep cattle from my youth.' And *one* will say to him, 'What are these wounds between your arms?' Then he will answer, '*Those* with which I was wounded in the house of my friends.'

"Awake, O sword, against My Shepherd,
Against the Man who is My Companion,"
Says the LORD of hosts.

"Strike the Shepherd,
And the sheep will be scattered;
Then I will turn My hand against the little ones.
And it shall come to pass in all the land,"
Says the LORD,
"*That* two-thirds in it shall be cut off *and* die,
But *one*-third shall be left in it:
I will bring the *one-third* through the fire,
Will refine them as silver is refined,
And test them as gold is tested.
They will call on My name,
And I will answer them.
I will say, 'This *is* My people';
And each one will say, 'The LORD *is* my God.' "

Behold, the day of the LORD is coming,
And your spoil will be divided in your midst.
For I will gather all the nations to battle against Jerusalem;
The city shall be taken,
The houses rifled,
And the women ravished.
Half of the city shall go into captivity,
But the remnant of the people shall not be cut off from the city.

Then the LORD will go forth
And fight against those nations,
As He fights in the day of battle.
And in that day His feet will stand on the Mount of Olives,
Which faces Jerusalem on the east.
And the Mount of Olives shall be split in two,
From east to west,
Making a very large valley;
Half of the mountain shall move toward the north
And half of it toward the south.

Then you shall flee *through* My mountain valley,
For the mountain valley shall reach to Azal.
Yes, you shall flee
As you fled from the earthquake
In the days of Uzziah king of Judah.

Thus the LORD my God will come,
And all the saints with You.

It shall come to pass in that day
That there will be no light;
The lights will diminish.

It shall be one day
Which is known to the LORD—
Neither day nor night.
But at evening time it shall happen
That it will be light.

And in that day it shall be
That living waters shall flow from Jerusalem,
Half of them toward the eastern sea
And half of them toward the western sea;
In both summer and winter it shall occur.
And the LORD shall be King over all the earth.
In that day it shall be—
"The LORD *is* one,"
And His name one.

All the land shall be turned into a plain from Geba to Rimmon south of Jerusalem. *Jerusalem* shall be raised up and inhabited in her place from Benjamin's Gate to the place of the First Gate and the Corner Gate, and *from* the Tower of Hananeel to the king's winepresses.

The people shall dwell in it;
And no longer shall there be utter destruction,
But Jerusalem shall be safely inhabited.

And this shall be the plague with which the LORD will strike all the people who fought against Jerusalem:

Their flesh shall dissolve while they stand on
their feet,
Their eyes shall dissolve in their sockets,
And their tongues shall dissolve in their
mouths.

It shall come to pass in that day
That a great panic from the LORD will be among
them.
Everyone will seize the hand of his neighbor,
And raise his hand against his neighbor's
hand;
Judah also will fight at Jerusalem.
And the wealth of all the surrounding nations
Shall be gathered together:
Gold, silver, and apparel in great abundance.

Such also shall be the plague
On the horse *and* the mule,
On the camel and the donkey,
And on all the cattle that will be in those
camps.
So *shall* this plague *be*.

And it shall come to pass *that* everyone who is left of all the nations which came against Jerusalem shall go up from year to year to worship the King, the LORD of hosts, and to keep the Feast of Tabernacles. And it shall be *that* whichever of the families of the earth do not come up to Jerusalem to worship the King, the LORD of hosts, on them there will be no rain. If the family of Egypt will not come up and enter in, they *shall have* no *rain;* they shall receive the plague with which the LORD strikes the nations who do not come up to keep the Feast of Tabernacles. This shall be the punishment of Egypt and the punishment of all the nations that do not come up to keep the Feast of Tabernacles.

In that day "HOLINESS TO THE LORD" shall be *engraved* on the bells of the horses. The pots in the LORD's house shall be like the bowls before the altar. Yes, every pot in Jerusalem and Judah shall be holiness to the LORD of hosts. Everyone who sacrifices shall come and take them and cook in them. In that day there shall no longer be a Canaanite in the house of the LORD of hosts.

Zechariah 12:10–14:21

WORSHIP

Oh, sing to the LORD a new song!
Sing to the LORD, all the earth.
Sing to the LORD, bless His name;
Proclaim the good news of His salvation from
day to day.
Declare His glory among the nations,
His wonders among all peoples.

For the LORD *is* great and greatly to be praised;
He *is* to be feared above all gods.

Psalm 96:1-4

WISDOM

Let a man meet a bear robbed of her cubs,
Rather than a fool in his folly.

Proverbs 17:12

 SO WHAT?
What does this tell me?

Against ALL odds, THE Temple Completed

Ezra 5–6; Psalm 96:8-10; Proverbs 17:13

Then the prophet Haggai and Zechariah the son of Iddo, prophets, prophesied to the Jews who *were* in Judah and Jerusalem, in the name of the God of Israel, *who was* over them. So Zerubbabel the son of Shealtiel and Jeshua the son of Jozadak rose up and began to build the house of God which *is* in Jerusalem; and the prophets of God *were* with them, helping them.

At the same time Tattenai the governor of *the region* beyond the River and Shethar-Boznai and their companions came to them and spoke thus to them: "Who has commanded you to build this temple and finish this wall?" Then, accordingly, we told them the names of the men who were constructing this building. But the eye of their God was upon the elders of the Jews, so that they could not make them cease till a report could go to Darius. Then a written answer was returned concerning this *matter*. This is a copy of the letter that Tattenai sent:

The governor of *the region* beyond the River, and Shethar-Boznai, and his companions, the Persians who *were in the region* beyond the River, to Darius the king.

(They sent a letter to him, in which was written thus)

To Darius the king:

All peace.

Let it be known to the king that we went into the province of Judea, to the temple of the great God, which is being built with heavy stones, and timber is being laid in the walls; and this work goes on diligently and prospers in their hands.

Then we asked those elders, *and* spoke thus to them: "Who commanded you to build this temple and to finish these walls?" We also asked them their names to inform you, that we might write the names of the men who *were* chief among them.

And thus they returned us an answer, saying: "We are the servants of the God of heaven and earth, and we are rebuilding the temple that was built many years ago, which a great king of Israel built and completed. But because our fathers provoked the God of heaven to wrath, He gave them into the hand of Nebuchadnezzar king of Babylon, the Chaldean, *who* destroyed this temple and carried the people away to Babylon. However, in the first year of Cyrus king of Babylon, King Cyrus issued a decree to build this house of God. Also, the gold and silver articles of the house of God, which Nebuchadnezzar had taken from the temple that *was* in Jerusalem and carried into the temple of Babylon—those King Cyrus took from the temple of Babylon, and they were given to one named Sheshbazzar, whom he had made governor. And he said to him, 'Take these articles; go, carry them to the temple *site* that *is* in Jerusalem, and let the house of God be rebuilt on its former site.' Then the same Sheshbazzar came *and* laid the foundation of the house of God which *is* in Jerusalem; but from that time even until now it has been under construction, and it is not finished."

Now therefore, if *it seems* good to the king, let a search be made in the king's treasure house, which *is* there in Babylon, whether it is *so* that a decree was issued by King Cyrus to build this house of God at Jerusalem, and let the king send us his pleasure concerning this *matter*.

Then King Darius issued a decree, and a search was made in the archives, where the treasures were stored in Babylon. And at Achmetha, in the palace that *is* in the province of Media, a scroll was found, and in it a record *was* written thus:

In the first year of King Cyrus, King Cyrus issued a decree *concerning* the house of God at Jerusalem: "Let the house be rebuilt, the place where they offered sacrifices; and let the foundations of it be firmly laid, its height sixty cubits *and* its width sixty cubits, *with* three rows of heavy stones and one row of new timber. Let the expenses be paid from the king's treasury. Also let the gold and silver articles of the house of God, which Nebuchadnezzar took from the temple which *is* in Jerusalem and brought to Babylon, be restored and taken back to the temple which *is* in Jerusalem, *each* to its place; and deposit *them* in the house of God"—

Now *therefore*, Tattenai, governor of *the region* beyond the River, and Shethar-Boznai, and your companions the Persians who *are* beyond the River, keep yourselves far from there. Let the work of this house of God alone; let the governor of the Jews and the elders of the Jews build this house of God on its site.

Moreover I issue a decree *as to* what you shall do for the elders of these Jews, for the building of this house of God: Let the cost be paid at the king's expense from taxes *on the region* beyond the River; this is to be given immediately to these men, so that they are not hindered. And whatever they need—young bulls, rams, and lambs for the burnt offerings of the God of heaven, wheat, salt, wine, and oil, according to the request of the priests who *are* in Jerusalem—let it be given them day by day without fail, that they may offer sacrifices of sweet aroma to the God of heaven, and pray for the life of the king and his sons.

Also I issue a decree that whoever alters this edict, let a timber be pulled from his house and erected, and let him be hanged on it; and let his house be made a refuse heap because of this. And may the God who causes His name to dwell there destroy any king or people who put their hand to alter it, or to destroy this house of God which is in Jerusalem. I Darius issue a decree; let it be done diligently.

Then Tattenai, governor of *the region* beyond the River, Shethar-Boznai, and their companions diligently did according to what King Darius had sent. So the elders of the Jews built, and they prospered through the prophesying of Haggai the prophet and Zechariah the son of Iddo. And they built and finished *it*, according to the commandment of the God of Israel, and according to the command of Cyrus, Darius, and Artaxerxes king of Persia. Now the temple was finished on the third day of the month of Adar, which was in the sixth year of the reign of King Darius. Then the children of Israel, the priests and the Levites and the rest of the descendants of the captivity, celebrated the dedication of this house of God with joy. And they offered sacrifices at the dedication of this house of God, one hundred bulls, two hundred rams, four hundred lambs, and as a sin offering for all Israel twelve male goats, according to the number of the tribes of Israel. They assigned the priests to their divisions and the Levites to their divisions, over the service of God in Jerusalem, as it is written in the Book of Moses.

And the descendants of the captivity kept the Passover on the fourteenth *day* of the first month. For the priests and the Levites had purified themselves; all of them *were ritually* clean. And they slaughtered the Passover *lambs* for all the descendants of the captivity, for their brethren the priests, and for themselves. Then the children of Israel who had returned from the captivity ate together with all who had separated themselves from the filth of the nations of the land in order to seek the LORD God of Israel. And they kept the Feast of Unleavened Bread seven days with joy; for the LORD made them joyful, and turned the heart of the king of Assyria toward them, to strengthen their hands in the work of the house of God, the God of Israel.

Ezra 5–6

WORSHIP

Give to the LORD the glory *due* His name;
Bring an offering, and come into His courts.
Oh, worship the LORD in the beauty of holiness!
Tremble before Him, all the earth.

Say among the nations, "The LORD reigns;
The world also is firmly established,
It shall not be moved;
He shall judge the peoples righteously."

Psalm 96:8-10

WISDOM

Whoever rewards evil for good,
Evil will not depart from his house.

Proverbs 17:13

SW?! SO WHAT?
What does this tell me?

EZRA'S RETURN TO JERUSALEM

Ezra 7:1-28; 8:31—9:6; 10:1-5, 10-12;
Psalm 97:7-9; Proverbs 17:14

Now after these things, in the reign of Artaxerxes king of Persia, Ezra the son of Seraiah, the son of Azariah, the son of Hilkiah, the son of Shallum, the son of Zadok, the son of Ahitub, the son of Amariah, the son of Azariah, the son of Meraioth, the son of Zerahiah, the son of Uzzi, the son of Bukki, the son of Abishua, the son of Phinehas, the son of Eleazar, the son of Aaron the chief priest—this Ezra came up from Babylon; and he *was* a skilled scribe in the Law of Moses, which the LORD God of Israel had given. The king granted him all his request, according to the hand of the LORD his God upon him. *Some* of the children of Israel, the priests, the Levites, the singers, the gatekeepers, and the Nethinim came up to Jerusalem in the seventh year of King Artaxerxes. And Ezra came to Jerusalem in the fifth month, which *was* in the seventh year of the king. On the first *day* of the first month he began *his* journey from Babylon, and on the first *day* of the fifth month he came to Jerusalem, according to the good hand of his God upon him. For Ezra had prepared his heart to seek the Law of the LORD, and to do *it,* and to teach statutes and ordinances in Israel.

This *is* a copy of the letter that King Artaxerxes gave Ezra the priest, the scribe, expert in the words of the commandments of the LORD, and of His statutes to Israel:

Artaxerxes, king of kings,

To Ezra the priest, a scribe of the Law of the God of heaven:

Perfect *peace,* and so forth.

I issue a decree that all those of the people of Israel and the priests and Levites in my realm, who volunteer to go up to Jerusalem, may go with you. And whereas you are being sent by the king and his seven counselors to inquire concerning Judah and Jerusalem, with regard to the Law of your God which *is* in your hand; and *whereas you are* to carry the silver and gold which the king and his counselors have freely offered to the God of Israel, whose dwelling *is* in Jerusalem; and *whereas* all the silver and gold that you may find in all

the province of Babylon, along with the freewill offering of the people and the priests, *are to be* freely offered for the house of their God in Jerusalem— now therefore, be careful to buy with this money bulls, rams, and lambs, with their grain offerings and their drink offerings, and offer them on the altar of the house of your God in Jerusalem.

And whatever seems good to you and your brethren to do with the rest of the silver and the gold, do it according to the will of your God. Also the articles that are given to you for the service of the house of your God, deliver in full before the God of Jerusalem. And whatever more may be needed for the house of your God, which you may have occasion to provide, pay *for it* from the king's treasury.

And I, *even* I, Artaxerxes the king, issue a decree to all the treasurers who *are in the region* beyond the River, that whatever Ezra the priest, the scribe of the Law of the God of heaven, may require of you, let it be done diligently, up to one hundred talents of silver, one hundred kors of wheat, one hundred baths of wine, one hundred baths of oil, and salt without prescribed limit. Whatever is commanded by the God of heaven, let it diligently be done for the house of the God of heaven. For why should there be wrath against the realm of the king and his sons?

Also we inform you that it shall not be lawful to impose tax, tribute, or custom *on* any of the priests, Levites, singers, gatekeepers, Nethinim, or servants of this house of God. And you, Ezra, according to your God-given wisdom, set magistrates and judges who may judge all the people who *are in the region* beyond the River, all such as know the laws of your God; and teach those who do not know *them.* Whoever will not observe the law of your God and the law of the king, let judgment be executed speedily on him, whether *it be* death, or banishment, or confiscation of goods, or imprisonment.

Blessed *be* the LORD God of our fathers, who has put *such a thing* as this in the king's heart, to beautify the house of the LORD which *is* in Jerusalem, and has extended mercy to me before the king and his counselors, and before all the king's mighty princes.

So I was encouraged, as the hand of the LORD my God *was* upon me; and I gathered leading men of Israel to go up with me.

Then we departed from the river of Ahava on the twelfth *day* of the first month, to go to Jerusalem. And the hand of our God was upon us, and He delivered us from the hand of the enemy and from ambush along the road. So we came to Jerusalem, and stayed there three days.

Now on the fourth day the silver and the gold and the articles were weighed in the house of our God by the hand of Meremoth the son of Uriah the priest, and with him *was* Eleazar the son of Phinehas; with them *were* the Levites, Jozabad the son of Jeshua and Noadiah the son of Binnui, with the number *and* weight of everything. All the weight was written down at that time.

The children of those who had been carried away captive, who had come from the captivity, offered burnt offerings to the God of Israel: twelve bulls for all Israel, ninety-six rams, seventy-seven lambs, and twelve male goats *as* a sin offering. All *this was* a burnt offering to the LORD.

And they delivered the king's orders to the king's satraps and the governors *in the region* beyond the River. So they gave support to the people and the house of God.

When these things were done, the leaders came to me, saying, "The people of Israel and the priests and the Levites have not separated themselves from the peoples of the lands, with respect to the abominations of the Canaanites, the Hittites, the Perizzites, the Jebusites, the Ammonites, the Moabites, the Egyptians, and the Amorites. For they have taken some of their daughters *as wives* for themselves and their sons, so that the holy seed is mixed with the peoples of *those* lands. Indeed, the hand of the leaders and rulers has been foremost in this trespass." So when I heard this thing, I tore my garment and my robe, and plucked out some of the hair of my head and beard, and sat down astonished. Then everyone who trembled at the words of the God of Israel assembled to me, because of the transgression of those who had been carried away captive, and I sat astonished until the evening sacrifice.

At the evening sacrifice I arose from my fasting; and having torn my garment and my robe, I fell on my knees and spread out my hands to the LORD my God. And I said: "O my God, I am too ashamed and humiliated to lift up my face to You, my God; for our iniquities have risen higher than *our* heads, and our guilt has grown up to the heavens."

Now while Ezra was praying, and while he was confessing, weeping, and bowing down before the house of God, a very large assembly of men, women, and children gathered to him from Israel; for the people wept very bitterly. And Shechaniah the son of Jehiel, *one* of the sons of Elam, spoke up and said to Ezra, "We have trespassed against our God, and have taken pagan wives from the peoples of the land; yet now there is hope in Israel in spite of this. Now therefore, let us make a covenant with our God to put away all these wives and those who have been born to them, according to the advice of my master and of those who tremble at the commandment of our God; and let it be done according to the law. Arise, for *this* matter *is* your *responsibility*. We also *are* with you. Be of good courage, and do *it*."

Then Ezra arose, and made the leaders of the priests, the Levites, and all Israel swear an oath that they would do according to this word. So they swore an oath.

Then Ezra the priest stood up and said to them, "You have transgressed and have taken pagan wives, adding to the guilt of Israel. Now therefore, make confession to the LORD God of your fathers, and do His will; separate yourselves from the peoples of the land, and from the pagan wives."

Then all the assembly answered and said with a loud voice, "Yes! As you have said, so we must do."

Ezra 7:1-28; 8:31–9:6; 10:1-5, 10-12

WORSHIP

Let all be put to shame who serve carved
    images,
Who boast of idols.
Worship Him, all *you* gods.
Zion hears and is glad,
And the daughters of Judah rejoice
Because of Your judgments, O LORD.
For You, LORD, *are* most high above all the earth;
You are exalted far above all gods.

Psalm 97:7-9

WISDOM

The beginning of strife *is like* releasing water;
Therefore stop contention before a quarrel
    starts.

Proverbs 17:14

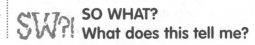 **SO WHAT?**
What does this tell me?

NEHEMIAH'S RETURN TO REBUILD
Nehemiah 1–2; 4:7-20; Psalm 97:10-12; Proverbs 17:15

The words of Nehemiah the son of Hachaliah. It came to pass in the month of Chislev, *in* the twentieth year, as I was in Shushan the citadel, that Hanani one of my brethren came with men from Judah; and I asked them concerning the Jews who had escaped, who had survived the captivity, and concerning Jerusalem. And they said to me, "The survivors who are left from the captivity in the province *are* there in great distress and reproach. The wall of Jerusalem *is* also broken down, and its gates *are* burned with fire."

So it was, when I heard these words, that I sat down and wept, and mourned *for many* days; I was fasting and praying before the God of heaven.

And I said: "I pray, LORD God of heaven, O great and awesome God, *You* who keep *Your* covenant and mercy with those who love You and observe Your commandments, please let Your ear be attentive and Your eyes open, that You may hear the prayer of Your servant which I pray before You now, day and night, for the children of Israel Your servants, and confess the sins of the children of Israel which we have sinned against You. Both my father's house and I have sinned. We have acted very corruptly against You, and have not kept the commandments, the statutes, nor the ordinances which You commanded Your servant Moses. Remember, I pray, the word that You commanded Your servant Moses, saying, 'If you are unfaithful, I will scatter you among the nations; but *if* you return to Me, and keep My commandments and do them, though some of you were cast out to the farthest part of the heavens, *yet* I will gather them from there, and bring them to the place which I have chosen as a dwelling for My name.' Now these *are* Your servants and Your people, whom You have redeemed by Your great power, and by Your strong hand. O Lord, I pray, please let Your ear be attentive to the prayer of Your servant, and to the prayer of Your servants who desire to fear Your name; and let Your servant prosper this day, I pray, and grant him mercy in the sight of this man."

For I was the king's cupbearer.

And it came to pass in the month of Nisan, in the twentieth year of King Artaxerxes, *when* wine *was* before him, that I took the wine and gave it to the king. Now I had never been sad in his presence before. Therefore the king said to me, "Why *is* your face sad, since you *are* not sick? This *is* nothing but sorrow of heart."

So I became dreadfully afraid, and said to the king, "May the king live forever! Why should my face not be sad, when the city, the place of my fathers' tombs, *lies* waste, and its gates are burned with fire?"

Then the king said to me, "What do you request?"

So I prayed to the God of heaven. And I said to the king, "If it pleases the king, and if your servant has found favor in your sight, I ask that you send me to Judah, to the city of my fathers' tombs, that I may rebuild it."

Then the king said to me (the queen also sitting beside him), "How long will your journey be? And when will you return?" So it pleased the king to send me; and I set him a time.

Furthermore I said to the king, "If it pleases the king, let letters be given to me for the governors *of the region* beyond the River, that they must permit me to pass through till I come to Judah, and a letter to Asaph the keeper of the king's forest, that he must give me timber to make beams for the gates of the citadel which *pertains* to the temple, for the city wall, and for the house that I will occupy." And the king granted *them* to me according to the good hand of my God upon me.

Then I went to the governors *in the region* beyond the River, and gave them the king's letters. Now the king had sent captains of the army and horsemen with me. When Sanballat the Horonite and Tobiah the Ammonite official heard *of it,* they were deeply disturbed that a man had come to seek the well-being of the children of Israel.

So I came to Jerusalem and was there three days. Then I arose in the night, I and a few men with me; I told no one what my God had put in my heart to do at Jerusalem; nor was there any animal with me, except the one on which I rode. And I went out by night through the Valley Gate to the Serpent Well and the Refuse Gate, and viewed the walls of Jerusalem which were broken down and its gates which were burned with fire. Then I went on to the Fountain Gate and to the King's Pool, but *there was* no room for the animal under me to pass. So I went up in the night by the valley, and viewed the wall; then I turned back and entered by the Valley Gate, and so returned. And the officials did not know where I had gone or what I had done; I had not yet told the Jews, the priests, the nobles, the officials, or the others who did the work.

Then I said to them, "You see the distress that we *are* in, how Jerusalem *lies* waste, and its gates are burned with fire. Come and let us build the wall of Jerusalem, that we may no longer be a reproach." And I told them of the hand of my God which had been good upon me, and also of the king's words that he had spoken to me.

So they said, "Let us rise up and build." Then they set their hands to *this* good *work.*

But when Sanballat the Horonite, Tobiah the Ammonite official, and Geshem the Arab heard *of it,* they laughed at us and despised us, and said, "What *is* this thing that you are doing? Will you rebel against the king?"

So I answered them, and said to them, "The God of heaven Himself will prosper us; therefore we His servants will arise and build, but you have no heritage or right or memorial in Jerusalem."

Now it happened, when Sanballat, Tobiah, the Arabs, the Ammonites, and the Ashdodites heard that the walls of Jerusalem were being restored and the gaps were beginning to be closed, that they became very angry, and all of them conspired together to come *and* attack Jerusalem and create confusion. Nevertheless we made our prayer to our God, and because of them we set a watch against them day and night.

Then Judah said, "The strength of the laborers is failing, and *there is* so much rubbish that we are not able to build the wall."

And our adversaries said, "They will neither know nor see anything, till we come into their midst and kill them and cause the work to cease."

So it was, when the Jews who dwelt near them came, that they told us ten times, "From whatever place you turn, *they will be* upon us."

Therefore I positioned *men* behind the lower parts of the wall, at the openings; and I set the people according to their families, with their swords, their spears, and their bows. And I looked, and arose and said to the nobles, to the leaders, and to the rest of the people, "Do not be afraid of them. Remember the Lord, great and awesome, and fight for your brethren, your sons, your daughters, your wives, and your houses."

And it happened, when our enemies heard that it was known to us, and *that* God had brought their plot to nothing, that all of us returned to the wall, everyone to his work. So it was, from that time on, *that* half of my servants worked at construction, while the other half held the spears, the shields, the bows, and *wore* armor; and the leaders *were* behind all the house of Judah. Those who built on the wall, and those who carried burdens, loaded themselves so that with one hand they worked at construction, and with the other held a weapon. Every one of the builders had his sword girded at his side as he built. And the one who sounded the trumpet *was* beside me.

Then I said to the nobles, the rulers, and the rest of the people, "The work *is* great and extensive, and we are separated far from one another on the wall. Wherever you hear the sound of the trumpet, rally to us there. Our God will fight for us."

Nehemiah 1–2; 4:7-20

WoRSHIP

You who love the LORD, hate evil!
He preserves the souls of His saints;
He delivers them out of the hand of the wicked.
Light is sown for the righteous,
And gladness for the upright in heart.
Rejoice in the LORD, you righteous,
And give thanks at the remembrance of His holy
name.

Psalm 97:10-12

WiSDoM

He who justifies the wicked, and he who
condemns the just,
Both of them alike *are* an abomination to the
LORD.

Proverbs 17:15

SW?! SO WHAT?
What does this tell me?

Nehemiah Completes The Wall

Now it happened when Sanballat, Tobiah, Geshem the Arab, and the rest of our enemies heard that I had rebuilt the wall, and *that* there were no breaks left in it (though at that time I had not hung the doors in the gates), that Sanballat and Geshem sent to me, saying, "Come, let us meet together among the villages in the plain of Ono." But they thought to do me harm.

So I sent messengers to them, saying, "I *am* doing a great work, so that I cannot come down. Why should the work cease while I leave it and go down to you?"

But they sent me this message four times, and I answered them in the same manner.

Then Sanballat sent his servant to me as before, the fifth time, with an open letter in his hand. In it *was* written:

It is reported among the nations, and Geshem says, *that* you and the Jews plan to rebel; therefore, according to these rumors, you are rebuilding the wall, that you may be their king. And you have also appointed prophets to proclaim concerning you at Jerusalem, saying, 'There is a king in Judah!' Now these matters will be reported to the king. So come, therefore, and let us consult together.

Then I sent to him, saying, "No such things as you say are being done, but you invent them in your own heart."

For they all *were trying to* make us afraid, saying, "Their hands will be weakened in the work, and it will not be done." Now therefore, *O God,* strengthen my hands.

Afterward I came to the house of Shemaiah the son of Delaiah, the son of Mehetabel, who *was* a secret informer; and he said, "Let us meet together in the house of God, within the temple, and let us close the doors of the temple, for they are coming to kill you; indeed, at night they will come to kill you."

And I said, "Should such a man as I flee? And who *is there* such as I who would go into the temple to save his life? I will not go in!" Then I perceived that God had not sent him at all, but that he pronounced *this* prophecy against me

because Tobiah and Sanballat had hired him. For this reason he *was* hired, that I should be afraid and act that way and sin, so *that* they might have *cause* for an evil report, that they might reproach me.

My God, remember Tobiah and Sanballat, according to these their works, and the prophetess Noadiah and the rest of the prophets who would have made me afraid.

So the wall was finished on the twenty-fifth *day* of Elul, in fifty-two days. And it happened, when all our enemies heard *of it,* and all the nations around us saw *these things,* that they were very disheartened in their own eyes; for they perceived that this work was done by our God.

Now all the people gathered together as one man in the open square that *was* in front of the Water Gate; and they told Ezra the scribe to bring the Book of the Law of Moses, which the LORD had commanded Israel. So Ezra the priest brought the Law before the assembly of men and women and all who *could* hear with understanding on the first day of the seventh month. Then he read from it in the open square that *was* in front of the Water Gate from morning until midday, before the men and women and those who could understand; and the ears of all the people *were attentive* to the Book of the Law.

Also Jeshua, Bani, Sherebiah, Jamin, Akkub, Shabbethai, Hodijah, Maaseiah, Kelita, Azariah, Jozabad, Hanan, Pelaiah, and the Levites, helped the people to understand the Law; and the people *stood* in their place. So they read distinctly from the book, in the Law of God; and they gave the sense, and helped *them* to understand the reading.

And Nehemiah, who *was* the governor, Ezra the priest *and* scribe, and the Levites who taught the people said to all the people, "This day *is* holy to the LORD your God; do not mourn nor weep." For all the people wept, when they heard the words of the Law.

Then he said to them, "Go your way, eat the fat, drink the sweet, and send portions to those for whom nothing is prepared; for *this* day *is* holy to our LORD. Do not sorrow, for the joy of the LORD is your strength."

So the Levites quieted all the people, saying, "Be still, for the day *is* holy; do not be grieved." And all the people went their way to eat and drink, to send portions and rejoice greatly, because they understood the words that were declared to them.

Now on the second day the heads of the fathers' *houses* of all the people, with the priests and Levites, were gathered to Ezra the scribe, in order to understand the words of the Law. And they found written in the Law, which the LORD had commanded by Moses, that the children of Israel should dwell in booths during the feast of the seventh month, and that they should announce and proclaim in all their cities and in Jerusalem, saying, "Go out to the mountain, and bring olive branches, branches of oil trees, myrtle branches, palm branches, and branches of leafy trees, to make booths, as *it is* written."

Then the people went out and brought *them* and made themselves booths, each one on the roof of his house, or in their courtyards or the courts of the house of God, and in the open square of the Water Gate and in the open square of the Gate of Ephraim. So the whole assembly of those who had returned from the captivity made booths and sat under the booths; for since the days of Joshua the son of Nun until that day the children of Israel had not done so. And there was very great gladness. Also day by day, from the first day until the last day, he read from the Book of the Law of God. And they kept the feast seven days; and on the eighth day *there was* a sacred assembly, according to the *prescribed* manner.

Now on the twenty-fourth day of this month the children of Israel were assembled with fasting, in sackcloth, and with dust on their heads. Then those of Israelite lineage separated themselves from all foreigners; and they stood and confessed their sins and the iniquities of their fathers. And they stood up in their place and read from the Book of the Law of the LORD their God *for one*-fourth of the day; and *for another* fourth they confessed and worshiped the LORD their God.

Then Jeshua, Bani, Kadmiel, Shebaniah, Bunni, Sherebiah, Bani, *and* Chenani stood on the stairs of the Levites and cried out with a loud voice to the LORD their God. And the Levites, Jeshua, Kadmiel, Bani, Hashabniah, Sherebiah, Hodijah, Shebaniah, *and* Pethahiah, said:

"Stand up *and* bless the LORD your God
Forever and ever!

"Blessed be Your glorious name,
Which is exalted above all blessing and praise!
You alone *are* the LORD;
You have made heaven,
The heaven of heavens, with all their host,

The earth and everything on it,
The seas and all that is in them,
And You preserve them all.
The host of heaven worships You.

"You *are* the LORD God,
Who chose Abram,
And brought him out of Ur of the Chaldeans,
And gave him the name Abraham;
You found his heart faithful before You,
And made a covenant with him
To give the land of the Canaanites,
The Hittites, the Amorites,
The Perizzites, the Jebusites,
And the Girgashites—
To give *it* to his descendants.
You have performed Your words,
For You *are* righteous."

Nehemiah 6:1-16; 8:1–3, 7–18; 9:1–8

WORSHIP

Oh, sing to the LORD a new song!
For He has done marvelous things;
His right hand and His holy arm have gained
   Him the victory.
The LORD has made known His salvation;
His righteousness He has revealed in the sight
   of the nations.
He has remembered His mercy and His
   faithfulness to the house of Israel;
All the ends of the earth have seen the salvation
   of our God.

Psalm 98:1-3

WISDOM

Why *is there* in the hand of a fool the purchase
   price of wisdom,
Since *he has* no heart *for it?*

Proverbs 17:16

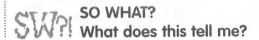

SO WHAT?
What does this tell me?

RENEWAL OF THE COVENANT AND DEDICATION OF THE WALL

Nehemiah 10:28-39; 12:27–13:3; Psalm 99:1-3; Proverbs 17:17

Now the rest of the people—the priests, the Levites, the gatekeepers, the singers, the Nethinim, and all those who had separated themselves from the peoples of the lands to the Law of God, their wives, their sons, and their daughters, everyone who had knowledge and understanding—these joined with their brethren, their nobles, and entered into a curse and an oath to walk in God's Law, which was given by Moses the servant of God, and to observe and do all the commandments of the LORD our Lord, and His ordinances and His statutes: We would not give our daughters as wives to the peoples of the land, nor take their daughters for our sons; *if* the peoples of the land brought wares or any grain to sell on the Sabbath day, we would not buy it from them on the Sabbath, or on a holy day; and we would forego the seventh year's *produce* and the exacting of every debt.

Also we made ordinances for ourselves, to exact from ourselves yearly one-third of a shekel for the service of the house of our God: for the showbread, for the regular grain offering, for the regular burnt offering of the Sabbaths, the New Moons, and the set feasts; for the holy things, for the sin offerings to make atonement for Israel, and all the work of the house of our God. We cast lots among the priests, the Levites, and the people, for *bringing* the wood offering into the house of our God, according to our fathers' houses, at the appointed times year by year, to burn on the altar of the LORD our God as *it is* written in the Law.

And *we made ordinances* to bring the firstfruits of our ground and the firstfruits of all fruit of all trees, year by year, to the house of the LORD; to bring the firstborn of our sons and our cattle, as *it is* written in the Law, and the firstborn of our herds and our flocks, to the house of our God, to the priests who minister in the house of our God; to bring the firstfruits of our dough, our offerings, the fruit from all kinds of trees, *the* new wine and oil, to the priests, to the storerooms of the house of our God; and to bring the tithes of our land to the Levites, for the Levites should receive the tithes in all our farming communities. And the priest, the descendant of Aaron, shall be with the Levites when the Levites receive tithes; and the Levites shall bring up a tenth of the tithes to the house of our God, to the rooms of the storehouse.

For the children of Israel and the children of Levi shall bring the offering of the grain, of the new wine and the oil, to the storerooms where the articles of the sanctuary *are, where* the priests who minister and the gatekeepers and the singers *are;* and we will not neglect the house of our God.

Now at the dedication of the wall of Jerusalem they sought out the Levites in all their places, to bring them to Jerusalem to celebrate the dedication with gladness, both with thanksgivings and singing, *with* cymbals and stringed instruments and harps. And the sons of the singers gathered together from the countryside around Jerusalem, from the villages of the Netophathites, from the house of Gilgal, and from the fields of Geba and Azmaveth; for the singers had built themselves villages all around Jerusalem. Then the priests and Levites purified themselves, and purified the people, the gates, and the wall.

So I brought the leaders of Judah up on the wall, and appointed two large thanksgiving choirs. *One* went to the right hand on the wall toward the Refuse Gate. After them went Hoshaiah and half of the leaders of Judah, and Azariah, Ezra, Meshullam, Judah, Benjamin, Shemaiah, Jeremiah, and some of the priests' sons with trumpets—Zechariah the son of Jonathan, the son of Shemaiah, the son of Mattaniah, the son of Michaiah, the son of Zaccur, the son of Asaph, and his brethren, Shemaiah, Azarel, Milalai, Gilalai, Maai, Nethanel, Judah, *and* Hanani, with the musical instruments of David the man of God. Ezra the scribe *went* before them. By the Fountain Gate, in front of them, they went up the stairs of the City of David, on the stairway of the wall, beyond the house of David, as far as the Water Gate eastward.

The other thanksgiving choir went the opposite *way*, and I *was* behind them with half of the people on the wall, going past the Tower of the Ovens as far as the Broad Wall, and above the Gate of Ephraim, above the Old Gate, above the Fish Gate, the Tower of Hananel, the Tower of the Hundred, as far as the Sheep Gate; and they stopped by the Gate of the Prison.

So the two thanksgiving choirs stood in the house of God, likewise I and the half of the rulers with me; and the priests, Eliakim, Maaseiah, Minjamin, Michaiah, Elioenai, Zechariah, *and* Hananiah, with trumpets; also Maaseiah, Shemaiah, Eleazar, Uzzi, Jehohanan, Malchijah, Elam, and Ezer. The singers sang loudly with Jezrahiah the director.

Also that day they offered great sacrifices, and rejoiced, for God had made them rejoice with great joy; the women and the children also rejoiced, so that the joy of Jerusalem was heard afar off.

And at the same time some were appointed over the rooms of the storehouse for the offerings, the firstfruits, and the tithes, to gather into them from the fields of the cities the portions specified by the Law for the priests and Levites; for Judah rejoiced over the priests and Levites who ministered. Both the singers and the gatekeepers kept the charge of their God and the charge of the purification, according to the command of David *and* Solomon his son. For in the days of David and Asaph of old *there were* chiefs of the singers, and songs of praise and thanksgiving to God. In the days of Zerubbabel and in the days of Nehemiah all Israel gave the portions for the singers and the gatekeepers, a portion for each day. They also consecrated *holy things* for the Levites, and the Levites consecrated *them* for the children of Aaron.

On that day they read from the Book of Moses in the hearing of the people, and in it was found written that no Ammonite or Moabite should ever come into the assembly of God, because they had not met the children of Israel with bread and water, but hired Balaam against them to curse them. However, our God turned the curse into a blessing. So it was, when they had heard the Law, that they separated all the mixed multitude from Israel.

Nehemiah 10:28-39; 12:27–13:3

WORSHIP

The LORD reigns;
Let the peoples tremble!
He dwells *between* the cherubim;
Let the earth be moved!
The LORD *is* great in Zion,
And He *is* high above all the peoples.
Let them praise Your great and awesome name—
He *is* holy.

Psalm 99:1-3

WISDOM

A friend loves at all times,
And a brother is born for adversity.

Proverbs 17:17

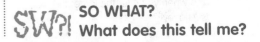

SO WHAT?
What does this tell me?

MALACHI'S MINISTRY IN NEHEMIAH'S ABSENCE

Malachi 1:1-11; 2:10–16; 3:1, 6; 4:4-6; Nehemiah 13:4-9, 30-31; Psalm 100:4-5; Proverbs 17:20

The burden of the word of the LORD to Israel by Malachi.

"I have loved you," says the LORD.
"Yet you say, 'In what way have You loved us?'
Was not Esau Jacob's brother?"
Says the LORD.
"Yet Jacob I have loved;
But Esau I have hated,
And laid waste his mountains and his
heritage
For the jackals of the wilderness."

Even though Edom has said,
"We have been impoverished,
But we will return and build the desolate
places,"

Thus says the LORD of hosts:

"They may build, but I will throw down;
They shall be called the Territory of
Wickedness,
And the people against whom the LORD
will have indignation forever.
Your eyes shall see,
And you shall say,
'The LORD is magnified beyond the border
of Israel.'

"A son honors *his* father,
And a servant *his* master.
If then I am the Father,
Where *is* My honor?
And if I *am* a Master,
Where *is* My reverence?
Says the LORD of hosts
To you priests who despise My name.
Yet you say, 'In what way have we
despised Your name?'

"You offer defiled food on My altar.
But say,
'In what way have we defiled You?'
By saying,
'The table of the LORD is contemptible.'
And when you offer the blind as a sacrifice,
Is it not evil?
And when you offer the lame and sick,
Is it not evil?

Offer it then to your governor!
Would he be pleased with you?
Would he accept you favorably?"
Says the LORD of hosts.

"But now entreat God's favor,
That He may be gracious to us.
While this is being *done* by your hands,
Will He accept you favorably?"
Says the LORD of hosts.
"Who *is there* even among you who would shut
the doors,
So that you would not kindle fire *on* My altar in
vain?
I have no pleasure in you,"
Says the LORD of hosts,
"Nor will I accept an offering from your hands.
For from the rising of the sun, even to its going
down,
My name *shall be* great among the Gentiles;
In every place incense *shall be* offered to My
name,
And a pure offering;
For My name shall be great among the
nations,"
Says the LORD of hosts.

Have we not all one Father?
Has not one God created us?
Why do we deal treacherously with one
another
By profaning the covenant of the fathers?
Judah has dealt treacherously,
And an abomination has been committed in
Israel and in Jerusalem,
For Judah has profaned
The LORD's holy *institution* which He loves:
He has married the daughter of a foreign god.
May the LORD cut off from the tents of Jacob
The man who does this, being awake and
aware,
Yet who brings an offering to the LORD of hosts!

And this is the second thing you do:
You cover the altar of the LORD with tears,
With weeping and crying;
So He does not regard the offering anymore,
Nor receive *it* with goodwill from your hands.

Yet you say, "For what reason?"
Because the LORD has been witness
Between you and the wife of your youth,
With whom you have dealt treacherously;
Yet she is your companion
And your wife by covenant.
But did He not make *them* one,
Having a remnant of the Spirit?
And why one?
He seeks godly offspring.
Therefore take heed to your spirit,
And let none deal treacherously with the wife
    of his youth.

"For the LORD God of Israel says
That He hates divorce,
For it covers one's garment with violence,"
Says the LORD of hosts.
"Therefore take heed to your spirit,
That you do not deal treacherously."

"Behold, I send My messenger,
And he will prepare the way before Me.
And the Lord, whom you seek,
Will suddenly come to His temple,
Even the Messenger of the covenant,
In whom you delight.
Behold, He is coming,"
Says the LORD of hosts.

"For I *am* the LORD, I do not change;
Therefore you are not consumed, O sons of
    Jacob.

"Remember the Law of Moses, My servant,
Which I commanded him in Horeb for all
    Israel,
With the statutes and judgments.
Behold, I will send you Elijah the prophet
Before the coming of the great and dreadful
    day of the LORD.
And he will turn
The hearts of the fathers to the children,
And the hearts of the children to their fathers,
Lest I come and strike the earth with a curse."

Now before this, Eliashib the priest, having authority over the storerooms of the house of our God, *was* allied with Tobiah. And he had prepared for him a large room, where previously they had stored the grain offerings, the frankincense, the articles, the tithes of grain, the new wine and oil, which were commanded *to be given* to the Levites and singers and gatekeepers, and the offerings for the priests. But during all this I [Nehemiah] was not in Jerusalem, for in the thirty-second year of Artaxerxes king of Babylon I had returned to the king. Then after certain days I obtained leave from the king, and I came to Jerusalem and discovered the evil that Eliashib had done for Tobiah, in preparing a room for him in the courts of the house of God. And it grieved me bitterly; therefore I threw all the household goods of Tobiah out of the room. Then I commanded them to cleanse the rooms; and I brought back into them the articles of the house of God, with the grain offering and the frankincense.

Thus I cleansed them of everything pagan. I also assigned duties to the priests and the Levites, each to his service, and *to bringing* the wood offering and the firstfruits at appointed times.
Remember me, O my God, for good!
Malachi 1:1-11; 2:10-16; 3:1, 6; 4:4-6;
Nehemiah 13:4-9, 30-31

WORSHIP

Enter into His gates with thanksgiving,
And into His courts with praise.
Be thankful to Him, *and* bless His name.
For the LORD *is* good;
His mercy *is* everlasting,
And His truth *endures* to all generations.
Psalm 100:4-5

WISDOM

He who has a deceitful heart finds no good,
And he who has a perverse tongue falls into
    evil.
Proverbs 17:20

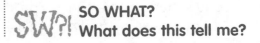
SO WHAT?
What does this tell me?

THE SOUNDS OF SILENCE

The four hundred years between the Old and New Testaments is often thought of as the silent age of Israel's history. This is especially true for most Protestant Christians, who do not regard as inspired the two books of Maccabees that record many of the historic events of this period. Protestant Bibles either don't contain these books at all, or they are found in a section of secondary writings called "the Apocrypha."

Although we might be tempted to skip over this mountain range and move directly into the New Testament, these 400 years of silence provide an important context for where the Old Testament ends and the New Testament begins. Although in terms of inspiration the 400 years of silence from heaven was remarkable, the earth below during this time was anything but quiet. This was an age of transition during which Greek culture, language, and philosophy gradually eclipsed predominantly Jewish customs.

The first major mountain peak in this period was the occupation of Phoenicia, Palestine, Egypt, and Persia by the Greek conqueror Alexander the Great. Having overrun the known world, Alexander died in Babylon in 323 B.C. at the young age of thirty-two.

After Alexander's death, some wanted to keep the empire intact and others wanted to divide it. After much infighting, it was decided to divide the empire among Alexander's four generals.

The Glory of God in His Patience

One of them, Ptolemy, was given the spoils of Palestine and Egypt and ruled until 198 B.C., when Palestine fell to the control of the Seleucids who ruled from Syria. The most famous of the Seleucid rulers was Antiochus IV Epiphanes, who sacrificed a pig on the holy altar in Jerusalem in 167 B.C. This slam in the face of Jewish religious sensibilities led to the Maccabean revolt. The Maccabeans fought Antiochus and the Seleucids for three years until they were able to liberate Jerusalem, cleanse the temple, and reestablish Jewish worship.

Another mountain peak in this period was the beginning of Roman rule in Palestine. This began in 63 B.C. when the Roman general Pompey arrived in Jerusalem and the Jewish people opened the gates of their city to him. The Roman Senate appointed Herod, an Idumean, as the "king of the Jews." Although it was an empty title at the time, Herod was determined to make the most of the opportunity. He raised an army and eventually brought all of Palestine under his authority. Herod had a long and successful political career and was a great builder who taxed the Jews heavily to support his many projects. His magnificent restoration of the temple was his crowning work. It was in the later days of Herod's rule that magi from the east arrived in Jerusalem saying, "Where is He who has been born king of the Jews?"

146,000 DAYS OF SILENCE

Think about your most intimate relationship. Sometimes your conversations are as trivial as "How's the weather?" Other times you share your deepest feelings. Your hopes. Your dreams. Your longings. Your pain. Your failures. Your joys. Your tears. Your laughter. Regardless of the topic, the time, or the season—you are "in touch." Hearing that person's voice, sensing their care, and feeling their touch in your life has become like oxygen to breathing lungs.

Now think about how you would feel if suddenly you didn't hear from this friend, this person in whose relationship you found intimacy, comfort, guidance, security, accountability, and direction. You call and there's no answer. You check your answering machine several times a day. Nothing. E-mails? Nothing. Mailbox? Nothing.

Days become weeks. Weeks become months. Months become years. No word, just the sounds of silence. How would you feel?

This hints at how the nation of Israel felt at the close of the Old Testament. For almost two thousand years they experienced the intimate presence of God—relating to them in a number of ways. You've spent the past two hundred and forty-four readings listening in on that relationship.

But here at the close of the Old Testament, the heavens are mute. For four hundred years the nation of Israel would not hear from God.

There is no Bible reading for today. No word. Imagine 146,000 days with no word. Imagine living the rest of your life crying out toward heaven but getting no answer. And as you do, consider this: How significant do you think the first word after such a lengthy period of silence would be?

You'll read about that "first word" tomorrow when God breaks the silence.

SW?! SO WHAT?
What does this tell me?

THE LIFE OF CHRIST

Eight summits rise from the range of Christ's life: His miraculous birth, His baptism and temptation, His offer of the Kingdom and rejection by the Jewish leaders, the Mount of Transfiguration, His entry into Jerusalem, His death, His resurrection and finally His ascension.

Jesus was conceived without a human father. This fulfilled the prophecy of Isaiah 7:14, "Behold, the virgin shall conceive and bear a Son." So significant was this event that history continues to be marked by time before Jesus' birth, "B.C." (for "before Christ"), and time after His birth, "A.D." (for "anno Domini," or "in the year of our Lord").

Jesus' baptism and temptation mark the beginning of His public ministry and empowerment by the Holy Spirit. Both events presented Jesus as the perfect Son of God and identified Him as the sinless Savior, the Messiah predicted by the Old Testament prophets.

The third peak in this range is Jesus' offer to establish the kingdom of heaven. His announcement that "the kingdom of God is at hand" (Mark 1:15) confirmed the angel Gabriel's words to Mary before Jesus was born that her Son would inherit the throne of David and rule God's kingdom forever (Luke 1:31-33). And though the evidence pointed to Jesus as Messiah, the Jewish religious leaders attributed His miracles to the power of Satan. After generations of studying and searching the writings of the Old Testament prophets to determine the identity of the promised Savior, Jesus was in their midst and they rejected

Him—a rejection that would ultimately lead to His crucifixion.

This was no surprise to Jesus, who began explaining the details of His impending death to His disciples. Their initial response was one of fear and concern that this also meant the death of His promises about the kingdom. The fourth peak occurred when Jesus appeared on the Mount of Transfiguration in the glorified presence of Moses and Elijah. Jesus calmed the disciples' fears and renewed their confidence that His death would not prevent His return in kingdom glory!

The royal entry of Jesus into Jerusalem was the official presentation of the Messiah to the nation of Israel. In spite of mounting opposition by the Jewish leaders, Jesus fulfilled prophecy by coming on the predicted day (Luke 19:42) and in the predicted way (Zechariah 9:9).

But the opposition to Jesus intensified, leading to the sixth peak in the life of Christ—His death on a cross for the sins of the world. The death of Jesus wasn't just any death. Jesus' death was the deliberate offering of the perfect Lamb of God to satisfy a holy and merciful God who had patiently endured His sinful creation since their rebellion against Him in the Garden of Eden.

Anyone could make the claims Jesus made. But Jesus went beyond words to action. Of all the miracles He performed, Jesus pointed to His resurrection as the ultimate proof that He was God in the flesh. After three days in the tomb, Jesus rose from the dead just like He said He would (Matthew 12:39).

The final peak in the earthly life of Christ was His ascension into heaven—evidence that His deity had not been diminished by His stay on earth, and confirmation that God the Father was pleased to accept His righteous sacrifice.

PROLOGUE: GOD TAKES ON HUMAN FLESH

John 1:1-18; Luke 1:5-38; Psalm 101:1-3; Proverbs 17:22

In the beginning was the Word, and the Word was with God, and the Word was God. He was in the beginning with God. All things were made through Him, and without Him nothing was made that was made. In Him was life, and the life was the light of men. And the light shines in the darkness, and the darkness did not comprehend it.

There was a man sent from God, whose name *was* John. This man came for a witness, to bear witness of the Light, that all through him might believe. He was not that Light, but *was sent* to bear witness of that Light. That was the true Light which gives light to every man coming into the world.

He was in the world, and the world was made through Him, and the world did not know Him. He came to His own, and His own did not receive Him. But as many as received Him, to them He gave the right to become children of God, to those who believe in His name: who were born, not of blood, nor of the will of the flesh, nor of the will of man, but of God.

And the Word became flesh and dwelt among us, and we beheld His glory, the glory as of the only begotten of the Father, full of grace and truth.

John bore witness of Him and cried out, saying, "This was He of whom I said, 'He who comes after me is preferred before me, for He was before me.' "

And of His fullness we have all received, and grace for grace. For the law was given through Moses, *but* grace and truth came through Jesus Christ. No one has seen God at any time. The only begotten Son, who is in the bosom of the Father, He has declared *Him.*

[*John's "first word" announces that Jesus, the Word, was with God before time and creation began. He was "in the beginning" with God, which takes us all the way back 245 readings to Genesis 1:1. This "first word" from John clearly proclaims that Jesus, before He took on human flesh, was God—and therefore, now in human flesh, is God.*]

There was in the days of Herod, the king of Judea, a certain priest named Zacharias, of the division of Abijah. His wife *was* of the daughters of Aaron, and her name *was* Elizabeth. And they were both righteous before God, walking in all the commandments and ordinances of the Lord blameless. But they had no child, because Elizabeth was barren, and they were both well advanced in years.

So it was, that while he was serving as priest before God in the order of his division, according to the custom of the priesthood, his lot fell to burn incense when he went into the temple of the Lord. And the whole multitude of the people was praying outside at the hour of incense. Then an angel of the Lord appeared to him, standing on the right side of the altar of incense. And when Zacharias saw *him,* he was troubled, and fear fell upon him.

But the angel said to him, "Do not be afraid, Zacharias, for your prayer is heard; and your wife Elizabeth will bear you a son, and you shall call his name John. And you will have joy and gladness, and many will rejoice at his birth. For he will be great in the sight of the Lord, and shall drink neither wine nor strong drink. He will also be filled with the Holy Spirit, even from his mother's womb. And he will turn many of the children of Israel to the Lord their God. He will also go before Him in the spirit and power of Elijah, 'to turn the hearts of the fathers to the children,' and the disobedient to the wisdom of the just, to make ready a people prepared for the Lord."

And Zacharias said to the angel, "How shall I know this? For I am an old man, and my wife is well advanced in years."

And the angel answered and said to him, "I am Gabriel, who stands in the presence of God, and was sent to speak to you and bring you these glad tidings. But behold, you will be mute and not able to speak until the day these things take place, because you did not believe my words which will be fulfilled in their own time."

And the people waited for Zacharias, and marveled that he lingered so long in the temple. But when he came out, he could not speak to them; and they perceived that he had seen a vision in the temple, for he beckoned to them and remained speechless.

So it was, as soon as the days of his service were completed, that he departed to his own house. Now after those days his wife Elizabeth conceived; and she hid herself five months, saying, "Thus the Lord has dealt with me, in the days when He looked on *me,* to take away my reproach among people."

Now in the sixth month the angel Gabriel was sent by God to a city of Galilee named Nazareth, to a virgin betrothed to a man whose name was Joseph, of the house of David. The virgin's name *was* Mary. And having come in, the angel said to her, "Rejoice, highly favored *one,* the Lord *is* with you; blessed *are* you among women!"

But when she saw *him,* she was troubled at his saying, and considered what manner of greeting this was. Then the angel said to her, "Do not be afraid, Mary, for you have found favor with God. And behold, you will conceive in your womb and bring forth a Son, and shall call His name Jesus. He will be great, and will be called the Son of the Highest; and the Lord God will give Him the throne of His father David. And He will reign over the house of Jacob forever, and of His kingdom there will be no end."

Then Mary said to the angel, "How can this be, since I do not know a man?"

And the angel answered and said to her, "*The* Holy Spirit will come upon you, and the power of the Highest will overshadow you; therefore, also, that Holy One who is to be born will be called the Son of God. Now indeed, Elizabeth your relative has also conceived a son in her old age; and this is now the sixth month for her who was called barren. For with God nothing will be impossible."

Then Mary said, "Behold the maidservant of the Lord! Let it be to me according to your word." And the angel departed from her.

John 1:1-18; Luke 1:5-38

WORSHIP

I will sing of mercy and justice;
To You, O LORD, I will sing praises.

I will behave wisely in a perfect way.
Oh, when will You come to me?
I will walk within my house with a perfect
    heart.

I will set nothing wicked before my eyes;
I hate the work of those who fall away;
It shall not cling to me.

Psalm 101:1-3

WISDOM

A merry heart does good, *like* medicine,
But a broken spirit dries the bones.

Proverbs 17:22

SW?! SO WHAT?
What does this tell me?

THE KING'S FORERUNNER IS BORN

Luke 1:39–80; Psalm 102:1-3;
Proverbs 17:24

Now Mary arose in those days and went into the hill country with haste, to a city of Judah, and entered the house of Zacharias and greeted Elizabeth. And it happened, when Elizabeth heard the greeting of Mary, that the babe leaped in her womb; and Elizabeth was filled with the Holy Spirit. Then she spoke out with a loud voice and said, "Blessed *are* you among women, and blessed *is* the fruit of your womb! But why *is* this *granted* to me, that the mother of my Lord should come to me? For indeed, as soon as the voice of your greeting sounded in my ears, the babe leaped in my womb for joy. Blessed *is* she who believed, for there will be a fulfillment of those things which were told her from the Lord."

And Mary said:

"My soul magnifies the Lord,
And my spirit has rejoiced in God my Savior.
For He has regarded the lowly state of His
    maidservant;
For behold, henceforth all generations will call
    me blessed.
For He who is mighty has done great things
    for me,
And holy *is* His name.
And His mercy *is* on those who fear Him
From generation to generation.
He has shown strength with His arm;
He has scattered *the* proud in the
    imagination of their hearts.
He has put down the mighty from *their*
    thrones,
And exalted *the* lowly.
He has filled *the* hungry with good things,
And *the* rich He has sent away empty.
He has helped His servant Israel,
In remembrance of *His* mercy,
As He spoke to our fathers,
To Abraham and to his seed forever."

And Mary remained with her about three months, and returned to her house.

Now Elizabeth's full time came for her to be delivered, and she brought forth a son. When her neighbors and relatives heard how the Lord had shown great mercy to her, they rejoiced with her.

So it was, on the eighth day, that they came to circumcise the child; and they would have called him by the name of his father, Zacharias. His mother answered and said, "No; he shall be called John."

But they said to her, "There is no one among your relatives who is called by this name." So they made signs to his father—what he would have him called.

And he asked for a writing tablet, and wrote, saying, "His name is John." So they all marveled. Immediately his mouth was opened and his tongue *loosed,* and he spoke, praising God. Then fear came on all who dwelt around them; and all these sayings were discussed throughout all the hill country of Judea. And all those who heard *them* kept *them* in their hearts, saying, "What kind of child will this be?" And the hand of the Lord was with him.

Now his father Zacharias was filled with the Holy Spirit, and prophesied, saying:

"Blessed *is* the Lord God of Israel,
For He has visited and redeemed His people,
And has raised up a horn of salvation for us
In the house of His servant David,
As He spoke by the mouth of His holy
    prophets,
Who *have been* since the world began,
That we should be saved from our enemies
And from the hand of all who hate us,
To perform the mercy *promised* to our fathers
And to remember His holy covenant,
The oath which He swore to our father
    Abraham:
To grant us that we,
Being delivered from the hand of our enemies,
Might serve Him without fear,
In holiness and righteousness before Him all
    the days of our life.

"And you, child, will be called the prophet of
    the Highest;
For you will go before the face of the Lord to
    prepare His ways,
To give knowledge of salvation to His people
By the remission of their sins,
Through the tender mercy of our God,
With which the Dayspring from on high has
    visited us;

To give light to those who sit in darkness and
the shadow of death,
To guide our feet into the way of peace."

So the child grew and became strong in spirit,
and was in the deserts till the day of his manifestation to Israel.

Luke 1:39-80

WORSHIP

Hear my prayer, O LORD,
And let my cry come to You.
Do not hide Your face from me in the day of
my trouble;
Incline Your ear to me;
In the day that I call, answer me speedily.

For my days are consumed like smoke,
And my bones are burned like a hearth.

Psalm 102:1-3

WISDOM

Wisdom *is* in the sight of him who has
understanding,
But the eyes of a fool *are* on the ends of the
earth.

Proverbs 17:24

SW?! **SO WHAT?**
What does this tell me?

JESUS THE KING IS BORN

Matthew 1:18-23; Luke 2:1-35; Psalm 102:12-15; Proverbs 17:25

Now the birth of Jesus Christ was as follows: After His mother Mary was betrothed to Joseph, before they came together, she was found with child of the Holy Spirit. Then Joseph her husband, being a just *man,* and not wanting to make her a public example, was minded to put her away secretly. But while he thought about these things, behold, an angel of the Lord appeared to him in a dream, saying, "Joseph, son of David, do not be afraid to take to you Mary your wife, for that which is conceived in her is of the Holy Spirit. And she will bring forth a Son, and you shall call His name JESUS, for He will save His people from their sins."

So all this was done that it might be fulfilled which was spoken by the Lord through the prophet, saying: "Behold, the virgin shall be with child, and bear a Son, and they shall call His name Immanuel," which is translated, "God with us."

And it came to pass in those days *that* a decree went out from Caesar Augustus that all the world should be registered. This census first took place while Quirinius was governing Syria. So all went to be registered, everyone to his own city.

Joseph also went up from Galilee, out of the city of Nazareth, into Judea, to the city of David, which is called Bethlehem, because he was of the house and lineage of David, to be registered with Mary, his betrothed wife, who was with child. So it was, that while they were there, the days were completed for her to be delivered. And she brought forth her firstborn Son, and wrapped Him in swaddling cloths, and laid Him in a manger, because there was no room for them in the inn.

Now there were in the same country shepherds living out in the fields, keeping watch over their flock by night. And behold, an angel of the Lord stood before them, and the glory of the Lord shone around them, and they were greatly afraid. Then the angel said to them, "Do not be afraid, for behold, I bring you good tidings of great joy which will be to all people. For there is born to you this day in the city of David a Savior, who is Christ the Lord. And this *will be* the sign to you: You will find a Babe wrapped in swaddling cloths, lying in a manger."

And suddenly there was with the angel a multitude of the heavenly host praising God and saying:

"Glory to God in the highest,
And on earth peace, goodwill toward men!"

So it was, when the angels had gone away from them into heaven, that the shepherds said to one another, "Let us now go to Bethlehem and see this thing that has come to pass, which the Lord has made known to us." And they came with haste and found Mary and Joseph, and the Babe lying in a manger. Now when they had seen *Him,* they made widely known the saying which was told them concerning this Child. And all those who heard *it* marveled at those things which were told them by the shepherds. But Mary kept all these things and pondered *them* in her heart. Then the shepherds returned, glorifying and praising God for all the things that they had heard and seen, as it was told them.

And when eight days were completed for the circumcision of the Child, His name was called JESUS, the name given by the angel before He was conceived in the womb.

Now when the days of her purification according to the law of Moses were completed, they brought Him to Jerusalem to present *Him* to the Lord (as it is written in the law of the Lord, "Every male who opens the womb shall be called holy to the LORD"), and to offer a sacrifice according to what is said in the law of the Lord, "A pair of turtledoves or two young pigeons."

And behold, there was a man in Jerusalem whose name was Simeon, and this man was just and devout, waiting for the Consolation of Israel, and the Holy Spirit was upon him. And it had been revealed to him by the Holy Spirit that he would not see death before he had seen the Lord's Christ. So he came by the Spirit into the temple. And when the parents brought in the Child Jesus, to do for Him according to the custom of the law, he took Him up in his arms and blessed God and said:

"Lord, now You are letting Your servant depart in peace,

According to Your word;
For my eyes have seen Your salvation
Which You have prepared before the face of
    all peoples,
A light to *bring* revelation to the Gentiles,
And the glory of Your people Israel."

And Joseph and His mother marveled at those things which were spoken of Him. Then Simeon blessed them, and said to Mary His mother, "Behold, this *Child* is destined for the fall and rising of many in Israel, and for a sign which will be spoken against (yes, a sword will pierce through your own soul also), that the thoughts of many hearts may be revealed."

Matthew 1:18-23; Luke 2:1-35

WORSHIP

But You, O Lord, shall endure forever,
And the remembrance of Your name to all
    generations.
You will arise *and* have mercy on Zion;
For the time to favor her,
Yes, the set time, has come.
For Your servants take pleasure in her stones,
And show favor to her dust.
So the nations shall fear the name of the Lord,
And all the kings of the earth Your glory.

Psalm 102:12-15

WISDOM

A foolish son *is* a grief to his father,
And bitterness to her who bore him.

Proverbs 17:25

SW?! **SO WHAT?**
What does this tell me?

Wise Men SEEK the Promised KING

Matthew 2:1-23; Luke 2:40-52; Psalm 102:25-27; Proverbs 17:27

Now after Jesus was born in Bethlehem of Judea in the days of Herod the king, behold, wise men from the East came to Jerusalem, saying, "Where is He who has been born King of the Jews? For we have seen His star in the East and have come to worship Him."

When Herod the king heard *this,* he was troubled, and all Jerusalem with him. And when he had gathered all the chief priests and scribes of the people together, he inquired of them where the Christ was to be born.

So they said to him, "In Bethlehem of Judea, for thus it is written by the prophet:

'But you, Bethlehem, *in* the land of Judah,
Are not the least among the rulers of Judah;
For out of you shall come a Ruler
Who will shepherd My people Israel.' "

Then Herod, when he had secretly called the wise men, determined from them what time the star appeared. And he sent them to Bethlehem and said, "Go and search carefully for the young Child, and when you have found *Him,* bring back word to me, that I may come and worship Him also."

When they heard the king, they departed; and behold, the star which they had seen in the East went before them, till it came and stood over where the young Child was. When they saw the star, they rejoiced with exceedingly great joy. And when they had come into the house, they saw the young Child with Mary His mother, and fell down and worshiped Him. And when they had opened their treasures, they presented gifts to Him: gold, frankincense, and myrrh.

Then, being divinely warned in a dream that they should not return to Herod, they departed for their own country another way.

Now when they had departed, behold, an angel of the Lord appeared to Joseph in a dream, saying, "Arise, take the young Child and His mother, flee to Egypt, and stay there until I bring you word; for Herod will seek the young Child to destroy Him."

When he arose, he took the young Child and His mother by night and departed for Egypt, and was there until the death of Herod, that it might be fulfilled which was spoken by the Lord through the prophet, saying, "Out of Egypt I called My Son."

Then Herod, when he saw that he was deceived by the wise men, was exceedingly angry; and he sent forth and put to death all the male children who were in Bethlehem and in all its districts, from two years old and under, according to the time which he had determined from the wise men. Then was fulfilled what was spoken by Jeremiah the prophet, saying:

"A voice was heard in Ramah,
Lamentation, weeping, and great mourning,
Rachel weeping *for* her children,
Refusing to be comforted,
Because they are no more."

Now when Herod was dead, behold, an angel of the Lord appeared in a dream to Joseph in Egypt, saying, "Arise, take the young Child and His mother, and go to the land of Israel, for those who sought the young Child's life are dead." Then he arose, took the young Child and His mother, and came into the land of Israel.

But when he heard that Archelaus was reigning over Judea instead of his father Herod, he was afraid to go there. And being warned by God in a dream, he turned aside into the region of Galilee. And he came and dwelt in a city called Nazareth, that it might be fulfilled which was spoken by the prophets, "He shall be called a Nazarene."

And the Child grew and became strong in spirit, filled with wisdom; and the grace of God was upon Him.

His parents went to Jerusalem every year at the Feast of the Passover. And when He was twelve years old, they went up to Jerusalem according to the custom of the feast. When they had finished the days, as they returned, the Boy Jesus lingered behind in Jerusalem. And Joseph and His mother did not know *it;* but supposing Him to have been in the company, they went a day's journey, and sought Him among *their* relatives and acquaintances. So when they did not find Him, they returned to

THE LIFE OF CHRIST

Jerusalem, seeking Him. Now so it was *that* after three days they found Him in the temple, sitting in the midst of the teachers, both listening to them and asking them questions. And all who heard Him were astonished at His understanding and answers. So when they saw Him, they were amazed; and His mother said to Him, "Son, why have You done this to us? Look, Your father and I have sought You anxiously."

And He said to them, "Why did you seek Me? Did you not know that I must be about My Father's business?" But they did not understand the statement which He spoke to them.

Then He went down with them and came to Nazareth, and was subject to them, but His mother kept all these things in her heart. And Jesus increased in wisdom and stature, and in favor with God and men.

Matthew 2:1-23; Luke 2:40-52

WORSHIP

Of old You laid the foundation of the earth,
And the heavens are the work of Your hands.
They will perish, but You will endure;
Yes, they will all grow old like a garment;
Like a cloak You will change them,
And they will be changed.
But You are the same,
And Your years will have no end.

Psalm 102:25-27

WISDOM

He who has knowledge spares his words,
And a man of understanding is of a calm
spirit.

Proverbs 17:27

SW?! **SO WHAT?**
What does this tell me?

JESUS IS BAPTIZED AND TEMPTED

Luke 3:1-22; 4:1-13; Psalm 103:1-4; Proverbs 17:28

Now in the fifteenth year of the reign of Tiberius Caesar, Pontius Pilate being governor of Judea, Herod being tetrarch of Galilee, his brother Philip tetrarch of Iturea and the region of Trachonitis, and Lysanias tetrarch of Abilene, while Annas and Caiaphas were high priests, the word of God came to John the son of Zacharias in the wilderness. And he went into all the region around the Jordan, preaching a baptism of repentance for the remission of sins, as it is written in the book of the words of Isaiah the prophet, saying:

"The voice of one crying in the wilderness:
'Prepare the way of the Lord;
Make His paths straight.
Every valley shall be filled
And every mountain and hill brought low;
The crooked places shall be made straight
And the rough ways smooth;
And all flesh shall see the salvation of God.' "

Then he said to the multitudes that came out to be baptized by him, "Brood of vipers! Who warned you to flee from the wrath to come? Therefore bear fruits worthy of repentance, and do not begin to say to yourselves, 'We have Abraham as *our* father.' For I say to you that God is able to raise up children to Abraham from these stones. And even now the ax is laid to the root of the trees. Therefore every tree which does not bear good fruit is cut down and thrown into the fire."

So the people asked him, saying, "What shall we do then?"

He answered and said to them, "He who has two tunics, let him give to him who has none; and he who has food, let him do likewise."

Then tax collectors also came to be baptized, and said to him, "Teacher, what shall we do?"

And he said to them, "Collect no more than what is appointed for you."

Likewise the soldiers asked him, saying, "And what shall we do?"

So he said to them, "Do not intimidate anyone or accuse falsely, and be content with your wages."

Now as the people were in expectation, and all reasoned in their hearts about John, whether he was the Christ *or* not, John answered, saying to all, "I indeed baptize you with water; but One mightier than I is coming, whose sandal strap I am not worthy to loose. He will baptize you with the Holy Spirit and fire. His winnowing fan *is* in His hand, and He will thoroughly clean out His threshing floor, and gather the wheat into His barn; but the chaff He will burn with unquenchable fire."

And with many other exhortations he preached to the people. But Herod the tetrarch, being rebuked by him concerning Herodias, his brother Philip's wife, and for all the evils which Herod had done, also added this, above all, that he shut John up in prison.

When all the people were baptized, it came to pass that Jesus also was baptized; and while He prayed, the heaven was opened. And the Holy Spirit descended in bodily form like a dove upon Him, and a voice came from heaven which said, "You are My beloved Son; in You I am well pleased."

Then Jesus, being filled with the Holy Spirit, returned from the Jordan and was led by the Spirit into the wilderness, being tempted for forty days by the devil. And in those days He ate nothing, and afterward, when they had ended, He was hungry.

And the devil said to Him, "If You are the Son of God, command this stone to become bread."

But Jesus answered him, saying, "It is written, 'Man shall not live by bread alone, but by every word of God.' "

Then the devil, taking Him up on a high mountain, showed Him all the kingdoms of the world in a moment of time. And the devil said to Him, "All this authority I will give You, and their glory; for *this* has been delivered to me, and I give it to whomever I wish. Therefore, if You will worship before me, all will be Yours."

And Jesus answered and said to him, "Get behind Me, Satan! For it is written, 'You shall worship the Lord your God, and Him only you shall serve.' "

Then he brought Him to Jerusalem, set Him on the pinnacle of the temple, and said to Him, "If You are the Son of God, throw Yourself down from here. For it is written:

'He shall give His angels charge over you,
To keep you,'
and,

'In their hands they shall bear you up,
Lest you dash your foot against a stone.' "

And Jesus answered and said to him, "It has been said, 'You shall not tempt the LORD your God.' "

Now when the devil had ended every temptation, he departed from Him until an opportune time.

Luke 3:1-22; 4:1-13

WORSHIP

Bless the LORD, O my soul;
And all that is within me, *bless* His holy name!
Bless the LORD, O my soul,
And forget not all His benefits:
Who forgives all your iniquities,
Who heals all your diseases,
Who redeems your life from destruction,
Who crowns you with lovingkindness and
tender mercies.

Psalm 103:1-4

WISDOM

Even a fool is counted wise when he holds his
peace;
When he shuts his lips, *he is considered*
perceptive.

Proverbs 17:28

SW?! **SO WHAT?**
What does this tell me?

JESUS BEGINS HIS MINISTRY
John 2:1-11; 3:1-30; Psalm 103:8-11; Proverbs 18:1

On the third day there was a wedding in Cana of Galilee, and the mother of Jesus was there. Now both Jesus and His disciples were invited to the wedding. And when they ran out of wine, the mother of Jesus said to Him, "They have no wine."

Jesus said to her, "Woman, what does your concern have to do with Me? My hour has not yet come."

His mother said to the servants, "Whatever He says to you, do *it.*"

Now there were set there six waterpots of stone, according to the manner of purification of the Jews, containing twenty or thirty gallons apiece. Jesus said to them, "Fill the waterpots with water." And they filled them up to the brim. And He said to them, "Draw *some* out now, and take *it* to the master of the feast." And they took *it.* When the master of the feast had tasted the water that was made wine, and did not know where it came from (but the servants who had drawn the water knew), the master of the feast called the bridegroom. And he said to him, "Every man at the beginning sets out the good wine, and when the *guests* have well drunk, then the inferior. You have kept the good wine until now!"

This beginning of signs Jesus did in Cana of Galilee, and manifested His glory; and His disciples believed in Him.

There was a man of the Pharisees named Nicodemus, a ruler of the Jews. This man came to Jesus by night and said to Him, "Rabbi, we know that You are a teacher come from God; for no one can do these signs that You do unless God is with him."

Jesus answered and said to him, "Most assuredly, I say to you, unless one is born again, he cannot see the kingdom of God."

Nicodemus said to Him, "How can a man be born when he is old? Can he enter a second time into his mother's womb and be born?"

Jesus answered, "Most assuredly, I say to you, unless one is born of water and the Spirit, he cannot enter the kingdom of God. That which is born of the flesh is flesh, and that which is born of the Spirit is spirit. Do not

marvel that I said to you, 'You must be born again.' The wind blows where it wishes, and you hear the sound of it, but cannot tell where it comes from and where it goes. So is everyone who is born of the Spirit."

Nicodemus answered and said to Him, "How can these things be?"

Jesus answered and said to him, "Are you the teacher of Israel, and do not know these things? Most assuredly, I say to you, We speak what We know and testify what We have seen, and you do not receive Our witness. If I have told you earthly things and you do not believe, how will you believe if I tell you heavenly things? No one has ascended to heaven but He who came down from heaven, *that is,* the Son of Man who is in heaven. And as Moses lifted up the serpent in the wilderness, even so must the Son of Man be lifted up, that whoever believes in Him should not perish but have eternal life. For God so loved the world that He gave His only begotten Son, that whoever believes in Him should not perish but have everlasting life. For God did not send His Son into the world to condemn the world, but that the world through Him might be saved.

"He who believes in Him is not condemned; but he who does not believe is condemned already, because he has not believed in the name of the only begotten Son of God. And this is the condemnation, that the light has come into the world, and men loved darkness rather than light, because their deeds were evil. For everyone practicing evil hates the light and does not come to the light, lest his deeds should be exposed. But he who does the truth comes to the light, that his deeds may be clearly seen, that they have been done in God."

After these things Jesus and His disciples came into the land of Judea, and there He remained with them and baptized. Now John also was baptizing in Aenon near Salim, because there was much water there. And they came and were baptized. For John had not yet been thrown into prison.

Then there arose a dispute between *some* of John's disciples and the Jews about purification. And they came to John and said to him, "Rabbi, He who was with you beyond the Jordan, to whom you have testified—behold, He is baptizing, and all are coming to Him!"

John answered and said, "A man can receive nothing unless it has been given to him from heaven. You yourselves bear me witness, that I said, 'I am not the Christ,' but, 'I have been sent before Him.' He who has the bride is the bridegroom; but the friend of the bridegroom, who stands and hears him, rejoices greatly because of the bridegroom's voice. Therefore this joy of mine is fulfilled. He must increase, but I *must* decrease."

John 2:1-11; 3:1-30

WORSHIP

The LORD *is* merciful and gracious,
Slow to anger, and abounding in mercy.
He will not always strive *with us,*
Nor will He keep *His anger* forever.
He has not dealt with us according to our sins,
Nor punished us according to our iniquities.

For as the heavens are high above the earth,
So great is His mercy toward those who fear
    Him.

Psalm 103:8-11

WISDOM

A man who isolates himself seeks his own
    desire;
He rages against all wise judgment.

Proverbs 18:1

SW?! SO WHAT?
What does this tell me?

JESUS PROVES HE IS FOR REAL

John 4:1-43; Psalm 103:19-22; Proverbs 18:2

Therefore, when the Lord knew that the Pharisees had heard that Jesus made and baptized more disciples than John (though Jesus Himself did not baptize, but His disciples), He left Judea and departed again to Galilee. But He needed to go through Samaria.

So He came to a city of Samaria which is called Sychar, near the plot of ground that Jacob gave to his son Joseph. Now Jacob's well was there. Jesus therefore, being wearied from *His* journey, sat thus by the well. It was about the sixth hour.

A woman of Samaria came to draw water. Jesus said to her, "Give Me a drink." For His disciples had gone away into the city to buy food.

Then the woman of Samaria said to Him, "How is it that You, being a Jew, ask a drink from me, a Samaritan woman?" For Jews have no dealings with Samaritans.

Jesus answered and said to her, "If you knew the gift of God, and who it is who says to you, 'Give Me a drink,' you would have asked Him, and He would have given you living water."

The woman said to Him, "Sir, You have nothing to draw with, and the well is deep. Where then do You get that living water? Are You greater than our father Jacob, who gave us the well, and drank from it himself, as well as his sons and his livestock?"

Jesus answered and said to her, "Whoever drinks of this water will thirst again, but whoever drinks of the water that I shall give him will never thirst. But the water that I shall give him will become in him a fountain of water springing up into everlasting life."

The woman said to Him, "Sir, give me this water, that I may not thirst, nor come here to draw."

Jesus said to her, "Go, call your husband, and come here."

The woman answered and said, "I have no husband."

Jesus said to her, "You have well said, 'I have no husband,' for you have had five husbands, and the one whom you now have is not your husband; in that you spoke truly."

The woman said to Him, "Sir, I perceive that You are a prophet. Our fathers worshiped on this mountain, and you *Jews* say that in Jerusalem is the place where one ought to worship."

Jesus said to her, "Woman, believe Me, the hour is coming when you will neither on this mountain, nor in Jerusalem, worship the Father. You worship what you do not know; we know what we worship, for salvation is of the Jews. But the hour is coming, and now is, when the true worshipers will worship the Father in spirit and truth; for the Father is seeking such to worship Him. God *is* Spirit, and those who worship Him must worship in spirit and truth."

The woman said to Him, "I know that Messiah is coming" (who is called Christ). "When He comes, He will tell us all things."

Jesus said to her, "I who speak to you am *He*."

And at this *point* His disciples came, and they marveled that He talked with a woman; yet no one said, "What do You seek?" or, "Why are You talking with her?"

The woman then left her waterpot, went her way into the city, and said to the men, "Come, see a Man who told me all things that I ever did. Could this be the Christ?" Then they went out of the city and came to Him.

In the meantime His disciples urged Him, saying, "Rabbi, eat."

But He said to them, "I have food to eat of which you do not know."

Therefore the disciples said to one another, "Has anyone brought Him *anything* to eat?"

Jesus said to them, "My food is to do the will of Him who sent Me, and to finish His work. Do you not say, 'There are still four months and *then* comes the harvest'? Behold, I say to you, lift up your eyes and look at the fields, for they are already white for harvest! And he who reaps receives wages, and gathers fruit for eternal life, that both he who sows and he who reaps may rejoice together. For in this the saying is true: 'One sows and another reaps.' I sent you to reap that for which you have not labored; others have labored, and you have entered into their labors."

And many of the Samaritans of that city believed in Him because of the word of the woman who testified, "He told me all that I *ever* did." So when the Samaritans had come to Him, they urged Him to stay with them; and He stayed there two days. And many more believed because of His own word.

Then they said to the woman, "Now we believe, not because of what you said, for we ourselves have heard *Him* and we know that this is indeed the Christ, the Savior of the world."

Now after the two days He departed from there and went to Galilee.

John 4:1-43

WORSHIP

The LORD has established His throne in heaven,
And His kingdom rules over all.

Bless the LORD, you His angels,
Who excel in strength, who do His word,
Heeding the voice of His word.
Bless the LORD, all *you* His hosts,
You ministers of His, who do His pleasure.
Bless the LORD, all His works,
In all places of His dominion.

Bless the LORD, O my soul!

Psalm 103:19-22

WISDOM

A fool has no delight in understanding,
But in expressing his own heart.

Proverbs 18:2

SW?! **SO WHAT?**
What does this tell me?

MOMENTUM BUILDS AND THE CROWDS ARE AMAZED
Mark 1:14-39; 2:1-12; Psalm 104:1-4; Proverbs 18:3

Now after John was put in prison, Jesus came to Galilee, preaching the gospel of the kingdom of God, and saying, "The time is fulfilled, and the kingdom of God is at hand. Repent, and believe in the gospel."

And as He walked by the Sea of Galilee, He saw Simon and Andrew his brother casting a net into the sea; for they were fishermen. Then Jesus said to them, "Follow Me, and I will make you become fishers of men." They immediately left their nets and followed Him.

When He had gone a little farther from there, He saw James the *son* of Zebedee, and John his brother, who also *were* in the boat mending their nets. And immediately He called them, and they left their father Zebedee in the boat with the hired servants, and went after Him.

Then they went into Capernaum, and immediately on the Sabbath He entered the synagogue and taught. And they were astonished at His teaching, for He taught them as one having authority, and not as the scribes.

Now there was a man in their synagogue with an unclean spirit. And he cried out, saying, "Let *us* alone! What have we to do with You, Jesus of Nazareth? Did You come to destroy us? I know who You are—the Holy One of God!"

But Jesus rebuked him, saying, "Be quiet, and come out of him!" And when the unclean spirit had convulsed him and cried out with a loud voice, he came out of him. Then they were all amazed, so that they questioned among themselves, saying, "What is this? What new doctrine *is* this? For with authority He commands even the unclean spirits, and they obey Him." And immediately His fame spread throughout all the region around Galilee.

Now as soon as they had come out of the synagogue, they entered the house of Simon and Andrew, with James and John. But Simon's wife's mother lay sick with a fever, and they told Him about her at once. So He came and took her by the hand and lifted her up, and immediately the fever left her. And she served them.

At evening, when the sun had set, they brought to Him all who were sick and those who were demon-possessed. And the whole city was gathered together at the door. Then He healed many who were sick with various diseases, and cast out many demons; and He did not allow the demons to speak, because they knew Him.

Now in the morning, having risen a long while before daylight, He went out and departed to a solitary place; and there He prayed. And Simon and those *who were* with Him searched for Him. When they found Him, they said to Him, "Everyone is looking for You."

But He said to them, "Let us go into the next towns, that I may preach there also, because for this purpose I have come forth."

And He was preaching in their synagogues throughout all Galilee, and casting out demons.

And again He entered Capernaum after *some* days, and it was heard that He was in the house. Immediately many gathered together, so that there was no longer room to receive *them,* not even near the door. And He preached the word to them. Then they came to Him, bringing a paralytic who was carried by four *men.* And when they could not come near Him because of the crowd, they uncovered the roof where He was. So when they had broken through, they let down the bed on which the paralytic was lying.

When Jesus saw their faith, He said to the paralytic, "Son, your sins are forgiven you."

And some of the scribes were sitting there and reasoning in their hearts, "Why does this *Man* speak blasphemies like this? Who can forgive sins but God alone?"

But immediately, when Jesus perceived in His spirit that they reasoned thus within themselves, He said to them, "Why do you reason about these things in your hearts? Which is easier, to say to the paralytic, '*Your* sins are forgiven you,' or to say, 'Arise, take up your bed and walk'? But that you may know that the Son of Man has power on earth to forgive sins"—He said to the paralytic, "I say to you, arise, take up your bed, and go to your house." Immediately he arose, took up the bed, and went out in the presence of them all, so that all were amazed and glorified God, saying, "We never saw *anything* like this!"

Mark 1:14-39; 2:1-12

WORSHIP

Bless the LORD, O my soul!

O LORD my God, You are very great:
You are clothed with honor and majesty,
Who cover *Yourself* with light as *with* a
    garment,
Who stretch out the heavens like a curtain.

He lays the beams of His upper chambers in
    the waters,
Who makes the clouds His chariot,
Who walks on the wings of the wind,
Who makes His angels spirits,
His ministers a flame of fire.

Psalm 104:1-4

WISDOM

When the wicked comes, contempt comes
    also;
And with dishonor *comes* reproach.

Proverbs 18:3

SW?! **SO WHAT?**
What does this tell me?

JESUS CLAIMS TO BE GOD

John 5:1-40; Psalm 104:14-17; Proverbs 18:4

After this there was a feast of the Jews, and Jesus went up to Jerusalem. Now there is in Jerusalem by the Sheep *Gate* a pool, which is called in Hebrew, Bethesda, having five porches. In these lay a great multitude of sick people, blind, lame, paralyzed, waiting for the moving of the water. For an angel went down at a certain time into the pool and stirred up the water; then whoever stepped in first, after the stirring of the water, was made well of whatever disease he had. Now a certain man was there who had an infirmity thirty-eight years. When Jesus saw him lying there, and knew that he already had been *in that condition* a long time, He said to him, "Do you want to be made well?"

The sick man answered Him, "Sir, I have no man to put me into the pool when the water is stirred up; but while I am coming, another steps down before me."

Jesus said to him, "Rise, take up your bed and walk." And immediately the man was made well, took up his bed, and walked.

And that day was the Sabbath. The Jews therefore said to him who was cured, "It is the Sabbath; it is not lawful for you to carry your bed."

He answered them, "He who made me well said to me, 'Take up your bed and walk.'"

Then they asked him, "Who is the Man who said to you, 'Take up your bed and walk'?" But the one who was healed did not know who it was, for Jesus had withdrawn, a multitude being in *that* place. Afterward Jesus found him in the temple, and said to him, "See, you have been made well. Sin no more, lest a worse thing come upon you."

The man departed and told the Jews that it was Jesus who had made him well.

For this reason the Jews persecuted Jesus, and sought to kill Him, because He had done these things on the Sabbath. But Jesus answered them, "My Father has been working until now, and I have been working."

Therefore the Jews sought all the more to kill Him, because He not only broke the Sabbath, but also said that God was His Fa-ther, making Himself equal with God. Then Jesus answered and said to them, "Most assuredly, I say to you, the Son can do nothing of Himself, but what He sees the Father do; for whatever He does, the Son also does in like manner. For the Father loves the Son, and shows Him all things that He Himself does; and He will show Him greater works than these, that you may marvel. For as the Father raises the dead and gives life to *them,* even so the Son gives life to whom He will. For the Father judges no one, but has committed all judgment to the Son, that all should honor the Son just as they honor the Father. He who does not honor the Son does not honor the Father who sent Him.

"Most assuredly, I say to you, he who hears My word and believes in Him who sent Me has everlasting life, and shall not come into judgment, but has passed from death into life. Most assuredly, I say to you, the hour is coming, and now is, when the dead will hear the voice of the Son of God; and those who hear will live. For as the Father has life in Himself, so He has granted the Son to have life in Himself, and has given Him authority to execute judgment also, because He is the Son of Man. Do not marvel at this; for the hour is coming in which all who are in the graves will hear His voice and come forth—those who have done good, to the resurrection of life, and those who have done evil, to the resurrection of condemnation. I can of Myself do nothing. As I hear, I judge; and My judgment is righteous, because I do not seek My own will but the will of the Father who sent Me.

"If I bear witness of Myself, My witness is not true. There is another who bears witness of Me, and I know that the witness which He witnesses of Me is true. You have sent to John, and he has borne witness to the truth. Yet I do not receive testimony from man, but I say these things that you may be saved. He was the burning and shining lamp, and you were willing for a time to rejoice in his light. But I have a greater witness than John's; for the works which the Father has given Me to finish—the very works that I do—bear witness of Me, that the Father has sent Me. And the Father Himself, who sent Me, has testified of Me. You have neither heard His voice at any time, nor seen His form. But you do not have His word abiding in you, because whom He sent, Him you do not believe. You search the Scriptures, for in them you think you have eternal life; and these are they which testify of Me. But you are not willing to come to Me that you may have life."

John 5:1-40

WORSHIP

He causes the grass to grow for the cattle,
And vegetation for the service of man,
That he may bring forth food from the earth,
And wine *that* makes glad the heart of man,
Oil to make *his* face shine,
And bread *which* strengthens man's heart.
The trees of the LORD are full *of sap,*
The cedars of Lebanon which He planted,
Where the birds make their nests;
The stork has her home in the fir trees.

Psalm 104:14-17

WISDOM

The words of a man's mouth *are* deep waters;
The wellspring of wisdom *is* a flowing brook.

Proverbs 18:4

SW?! **SO WHAT?**
What does this tell me?

JESUS DESCRIBES LIFE IN HIS KINGDOM

Luke 6:12–45; Matthew 7:24–29; Psalm 104:21–23; Proverbs 18:8

Now it came to pass in those days that He went out to the mountain to pray, and continued all night in prayer to God. And when it was day, He called His disciples to *Himself;* and from them He chose twelve whom He also named apostles: Simon, whom He also named Peter, and Andrew his brother; James and John; Philip and Bartholomew; Matthew and Thomas; James the *son* of Alphaeus, and Simon called the Zealot; Judas *the son* of James, and Judas Iscariot who also became a traitor.

And He came down with them and stood on a level place with a crowd of His disciples and a great multitude of people from all Judea and Jerusalem, and from the seacoast of Tyre and Sidon, who came to hear Him and be healed of their diseases, as well as those who were tormented with unclean spirits. And they were healed. And the whole multitude sought to touch Him, for power went out from Him and healed *them* all.

Then He lifted up His eyes toward His disciples, and said:

"Blessed *are you* poor,
    For yours is the kingdom of God.
Blessed *are you* who hunger now,
    For you shall be filled.
Blessed *are you* who weep now,
    For you shall laugh.
Blessed are you when men hate you,
    And when they exclude you,
    And revile *you,* and cast out your
        name as evil,
    For the Son of Man's sake.
Rejoice in that day and leap for joy!
    For indeed your reward *is* great in
        heaven,
    For in like manner their fathers did to
        the prophets.

"But woe to you who are rich,
    For you have received your
        consolation.
Woe to you who are full,
    For you shall hunger.
Woe to you who laugh now,
    For you shall mourn and weep.
Woe to you when all men speak well of you,

For so did their fathers to the false
    prophets.

"But I say to you who hear: Love your enemies, do good to those who hate you, bless those who curse you, and pray for those who spitefully use you. To him who strikes you on the *one* cheek, offer the other also. And from him who takes away your cloak, do not withhold *your* tunic either. Give to everyone who asks of you. And from him who takes away your goods do not ask *them* back. And just as you want men to do to you, you also do to them likewise.

"But if you love those who love you, what credit is that to you? For even sinners love those who love them. And if you do good to those who do good to you, what credit is that to you? For even sinners do the same. And if you lend *to those* from whom you hope to receive back, what credit is that to you? For even sinners lend to sinners to receive as much back. But love your enemies, do good, and lend, hoping for nothing in return; and your reward will be great, and you will be sons of the Most High. For He is kind to the unthankful and evil. Therefore be merciful, just as your Father also is merciful.

"Judge not, and you shall not be judged. Condemn not, and you shall not be condemned. Forgive, and you will be forgiven. Give, and it will be given to you: good measure, pressed down, shaken together, and running over will be put into your bosom. For with the same measure that you use, it will be measured back to you."

And He spoke a parable to them: "Can the blind lead the blind? Will they not both fall into the ditch? A disciple is not above his teacher, but everyone who is perfectly trained will be like his teacher. And why do you look at the speck in your brother's eye, but do not perceive the plank in your own eye? Or how can you say to your brother, 'Brother, let me remove the speck that *is* in your eye,' when you yourself do not see the plank that *is* in your own eye? Hypocrite! First remove the plank from your own eye, and then you will see clearly to remove the speck that is in your brother's eye.

"For a good tree does not bear bad fruit, nor does a bad tree bear good fruit. For every tree is known by its own fruit. For *men* do not gather figs from thorns, nor do they gather grapes from a bramble bush. A good man out of the good treasure of his heart brings forth good; and an evil man out of the evil treasure of his heart brings forth evil. For out of the abundance of the heart his mouth speaks."

"Therefore whoever hears these sayings of Mine, and does them, I will liken him to a wise man who built his house on the rock: and the rain descended, the floods came, and the winds blew and beat on that house; and it did not fall, for it was founded on the rock.

"But everyone who hears these sayings of Mine, and does not do them, will be like a foolish man who built his house on the sand: and the rain descended, the floods came, and the winds blew and beat on that house; and it fell. And great was its fall."

And so it was, when Jesus had ended these sayings, that the people were astonished at His teaching, for He taught them as one having authority, and not as the scribes.

Luke 6:12-45; Matthew 7:24-29

WORSHIP

The young lions roar after their prey,
And seek their food from God.
When the sun rises, they gather together
And lie down in their dens.
Man goes out to his work
And to his labor until the evening.

Psalm 104:21-23

WISDOM

The words of a talebearer *are* like tasty trifles,
And they go down into the inmost body.

Proverbs 18:8

SW?! SO WHAT?
What does this tell me?

THE BLIND SEE, THE LAME WALK, AND THE DEAD ARE RAISED

Luke 7:1-23, 36-50; Psalm 104:24-26; Proverbs 18:9

Now when He concluded all His sayings in the hearing of the people, He entered Capernaum. And a certain centurion's servant, who was dear to him, was sick and ready to die. So when he heard about Jesus, he sent elders of the Jews to Him, pleading with Him to come and heal his servant. And when they came to Jesus, they begged Him earnestly, saying that the one for whom He should do this was deserving, "for he loves our nation, and has built us a synagogue."

Then Jesus went with them. And when He was already not far from the house, the centurion sent friends to Him, saying to Him, "Lord, do not trouble Yourself, for I am not worthy that You should enter under my roof. Therefore I did not even think myself worthy to come to You. But say the word, and my servant will be healed. For I also am a man placed under authority, having soldiers under me. And I say to one, 'Go,' and he goes; and to another, 'Come,' and he comes; and to my servant, 'Do this,' and he does *it*."

When Jesus heard these things, He marveled at him, and turned around and said to the crowd that followed Him, "I say to you, I have not found such great faith, not even in Israel!" And those who were sent, returning to the house, found the servant well who had been sick.

Now it happened, the day after, *that* He went into a city called Nain; and many of His disciples went with Him, and a large crowd. And when He came near the gate of the city, behold, a dead man was being carried out, the only son of his mother; and she was a widow. And a large crowd from the city was with her. When the Lord saw her, He had compassion on her and said to her, "Do not weep." Then He came and touched the open coffin, and those who carried *him* stood still. And He said, "Young man, I say to you, arise." So he who was dead sat up and began to speak. And He presented him to his mother.

Then fear came upon all, and they glorified God, saying, "A great prophet has risen up among us"; and, "God has visited His people." And this report about Him went throughout all Judea and all the surrounding region.

Then the disciples of John reported to him concerning all these things. And John, calling two of his disciples to *him,* sent *them* to Jesus, saying, "Are You the Coming One, or do we look for another?"

When the men had come to Him, they said, "John the Baptist has sent us to You, saying, 'Are You the Coming One, or do we look for another?'" And that very hour He cured many of infirmities, afflictions, and evil spirits; and to many blind He gave sight.

Jesus answered and said to them, "Go and tell John the things you have seen and heard: that *the* blind see, *the* lame walk, *the* lepers are cleansed, *the* deaf hear, *the* dead are raised, *the* poor have the gospel preached to them. And blessed is *he* who is not offended because of Me."

Then one of the Pharisees asked Him to eat with him. And He went to the Pharisee's house, and sat down to eat. And behold, a woman in the city who was a sinner, when she knew that *Jesus* sat at the table in the Pharisee's house, brought an alabaster flask of fragrant oil, and stood at His feet behind *Him* weeping; and she began to wash His feet with her tears, and wiped *them* with the hair of her head; and she kissed His feet and anointed *them* with the fragrant oil. Now when the Pharisee who had invited Him saw *this,* he spoke to himself, saying, "This man, if He were a prophet, would know who and what manner of woman *this is* who is touching Him, for she is a sinner."

And Jesus answered and said to him, "Simon, I have something to say to you."

So he said, "Teacher, say it."

"There was a certain creditor who had two debtors. One owed five hundred denarii, and the other fifty. And when they had nothing with which to repay, he freely forgave them both. Tell Me, therefore, which of them will love him more?"

Simon answered and said, "I suppose the *one* whom he forgave more."

And He said to him, "You have rightly judged." Then He turned to the woman and said to Simon, "Do you see this woman? I entered your house; you gave Me no water for My feet, but she has washed My feet with her tears and wiped *them* with the hair of her head. You gave Me no kiss, but this woman has not ceased to kiss My feet since the time I came in. You did not anoint My head with oil, but this woman has anointed My feet with fragrant oil. Therefore I say to you, her sins, *which are* many, are forgiven, for she loved much. But to whom little is forgiven, *the same* loves little."

Then He said to her, "Your sins are forgiven."

And those who sat at the table with Him began to say to themselves, "Who is this who even forgives sins?"

Then He said to the woman, "Your faith has saved you. Go in peace."

Luke 7:1-23, 36-50

WORSHIP

O LORD, how manifold are Your works!
In wisdom You have made them all.
The earth is full of Your possessions—
This great and wide sea,
In which *are* innumerable teeming things,
Living things both small and great.
There the ships sail about;
There is that Leviathan
Which You have made to play there.

Psalm 104:24-26

WISDOM

He who is slothful in his work
Is a brother to him who is a great destroyer.

Proverbs 18:9

SW?! **SO WHAT?**
What does this tell me?

CONFLICT WITH THE RELIGIOUS LEADERS

Matthew 12:1-45; Psalm 104:31-34; Proverbs 18:10

At that time Jesus went through the grainfields on the Sabbath. And His disciples were hungry, and began to pluck heads of grain and to eat. And when the Pharisees saw *it,* they said to Him, "Look, Your disciples are doing what is not lawful to do on the Sabbath!"

But He said to them, "Have you not read what David did when he was hungry, he and those who were with him: how he entered the house of God and ate the showbread which was not lawful for him to eat, nor for those who were with him, but only for the priests? Or have you not read in the law that on the Sabbath the priests in the temple profane the Sabbath, and are blameless? Yet I say to you that in this place there is *One* greater than the temple. But if you had known what *this* means, 'I desire mercy and not sacrifice,' you would not have condemned the guiltless. For the Son of Man is Lord even of the Sabbath."

Now when He had departed from there, He went into their synagogue. And behold, there was a man who had a withered hand. And they asked Him, saying, "Is it lawful to heal on the Sabbath?"—that they might accuse Him.

Then He said to them, "What man is there among you who has one sheep, and if it falls into a pit on the Sabbath, will not lay hold of it and lift *it* out? Of how much more value then is a man than a sheep? Therefore it is lawful to do good on the Sabbath." Then He said to the man, "Stretch out your hand." And he stretched *it* out, and it was restored as whole as the other. Then the Pharisees went out and plotted against Him, how they might destroy Him.

But when Jesus knew *it,* He withdrew from there. And great multitudes followed Him, and He healed them all. Yet He warned them not to make Him known, that it might be fulfilled which was spoken by Isaiah the prophet, saying:

"Behold! My Servant whom I have chosen,
My Beloved in whom My soul is well
pleased!

I will put My Spirit upon Him,
And He will declare justice to the Gentiles.
He will not quarrel nor cry out,
Nor will anyone hear His voice in the streets.
A bruised reed He will not break,
And smoking flax He will not quench,
Till He sends forth justice to victory;
And in His name Gentiles will trust."

Then one was brought to Him who was demon-possessed, blind and mute; and He healed him, so that the blind and mute man both spoke and saw. And all the multitudes were amazed and said, "Could this be the Son of David?"

Now when the Pharisees heard *it* they said, "This *fellow* does not cast out demons except by Beelzebub, the ruler of the demons."

But Jesus knew their thoughts, and said to them: "Every kingdom divided against itself is brought to desolation, and every city or house divided against itself will not stand. If Satan casts out Satan, he is divided against himself. How then will his kingdom stand? And if I cast out demons by Beelzebub, by whom do your sons cast *them* out? Therefore they shall be your judges. But if I cast out demons by the Spirit of God, surely the kingdom of God has come upon you. Or how can one enter a strong man's house and plunder his goods, unless he first binds the strong man? And then he will plunder his house. He who is not with Me is against Me, and he who does not gather with Me scatters abroad.

"Therefore I say to you, every sin and blasphemy will be forgiven men, but the blasphemy *against* the Spirit will not be forgiven men. Anyone who speaks a word against the Son of Man, it will be forgiven him; but whoever speaks against the Holy Spirit, it will not be forgiven him, either in this age or in the *age* to come.

"Either make the tree good and its fruit good, or else make the tree bad and its fruit bad; for a tree is known by *its* fruit. Brood of vipers! How can you, being evil, speak good things? For out of the abundance of the heart the mouth speaks. A good man out of the good treasure of his heart brings forth good things, and an evil man out of the evil treasure brings forth evil things. But I say to you that

THE LIFE OF CHRIST

for every idle word men may speak, they will give account of it in the day of judgment. For by your words you will be justified, and by your words you will be condemned."

Then some of the scribes and Pharisees answered, saying, "Teacher, we want to see a sign from You."

But He answered and said to them, "An evil and adulterous generation seeks after a sign, and no sign will be given to it except the sign of the prophet Jonah. For as Jonah was three days and three nights in the belly of the great fish, so will the Son of Man be three days and three nights in the heart of the earth. The men of Nineveh will rise up in the judgment with this generation and condemn it, because they repented at the preaching of Jonah; and indeed a greater than Jonah *is* here. The queen of the South will rise up in the judgment with this generation and condemn it, for she came from the ends of the earth to hear the wisdom of Solomon; and indeed a greater than Solomon *is* here.

"When an unclean spirit goes out of a man, he goes through dry places, seeking rest, and finds none. Then he says, 'I will return to my house from which I came.' And when he comes, he finds *it* empty, swept, and put in order. Then he goes and takes with him seven other spirits more wicked than himself, and they enter and dwell there; and the last *state* of that man is worse than the first. So shall it also be with this wicked generation."

Matthew 12:1-45

WORSHIP

May the glory of the LORD endure forever;
May the LORD rejoice in His works.
He looks on the earth, and it trembles;
He touches the hills, and they smoke.

I will sing to the LORD as long as I live;
I will sing praise to my God while I have my
 being.
May my meditation be sweet to Him;
I will be glad in the LORD.

Psalm 104:31-34

WISDOM

The name of the LORD *is* a strong tower;
The righteous run to it and are safe.

Proverbs 18:10

SW?! **SO WHAT?**
What does this tell me?

STORIES ABOUT THE KINGDOM

Matthew 13:1-50; Psalm 105:1-4; Proverbs 18:11

On the same day Jesus went out of the house and sat by the sea. And great multitudes were gathered together to Him, so that He got into a boat and sat; and the whole multitude stood on the shore.

Then He spoke many things to them in parables, saying: "Behold, a sower went out to sow. And as he sowed, some *seed* fell by the wayside; and the birds came and devoured them. Some fell on stony places, where they did not have much earth; and they immediately sprang up because they had no depth of earth. But when the sun was up they were scorched, and because they had no root they withered away. And some fell among thorns, and the thorns sprang up and choked them. But others fell on good ground and yielded a crop: some a hundredfold, some sixty, some thirty. He who has ears to hear, let him hear!"

And the disciples came and said to Him, "Why do You speak to them in parables?"

He answered and said to them, "Because it has been given to you to know the mysteries of the kingdom of heaven, but to them it has not been given. For whoever has, to him more will be given, and he will have abundance; but whoever does not have, even what he has will be taken away from him. Therefore I speak to them in parables, because seeing they do not see, and hearing they do not hear, nor do they understand. And in them the prophecy of Isaiah is fulfilled, which says:

'Hearing you will hear and shall not
    understand,
And seeing you will see and not perceive;
For the hearts of this people have grown
    dull.
Their ears are hard of hearing,
And their eyes they have closed,
Lest they should see with *their* eyes and
    hear with *their* ears,
Lest they should understand with *their*
    hearts and turn,
So that I should heal them.'

But blessed *are* your eyes for they see, and your ears for they hear; for assuredly, I say to you that many prophets and righteous *men* desired to see what you see, and did not see *it,* and to hear what you hear, and did not hear *it.*

"Therefore hear the parable of the sower: When anyone hears the word of the kingdom, and does not understand *it,* then the wicked *one* comes and snatches away what was sown in his heart. This is he who received seed by the wayside. But he who received the seed on stony places, this is he who hears the word and immediately receives it with joy; yet he has no root in himself, but endures only for a while. For when tribulation or persecution arises because of the word, immediately he stumbles. Now he who received seed among the thorns is he who hears the word, and the cares of this world and the deceitfulness of riches choke the word, and he becomes unfruitful. But he who received seed on the good ground is he who hears the word and understands *it,* who indeed bears fruit and produces: some a hundredfold, some sixty, some thirty."

Another parable He put forth to them, saying: "The kingdom of heaven is like a man who sowed good seed in his field; but while men slept, his enemy came and sowed tares among the wheat and went his way. But when the grain had sprouted and produced a crop, then the tares also appeared. So the servants of the owner came and said to him, 'Sir, did you not sow good seed in your field? How then does it have tares?' He said to them, 'An enemy has done this.' The servants said to him, 'Do you want us then to go and gather them up?' But he said, 'No, lest while you gather up the tares you also uproot the wheat with them. Let both grow together until the harvest, and at the time of harvest I will say to the reapers, "First gather together the tares and bind them in bundles to burn them, but gather the wheat into my barn." ' "

Another parable He put forth to them, saying: "The kingdom of heaven is like a mustard seed, which a man took and sowed in his field, which indeed is the least of all the seeds; but when it is grown it is greater than the herbs and becomes a tree, so that the birds of the air come and nest in its branches."

Another parable He spoke to them: "The kingdom of heaven is like leaven, which a woman took and hid in three measures of meal till it was all leavened."

THE LIFE OF CHRIST

All these things Jesus spoke to the multitude in parables; and without a parable He did not speak to them, that it might be fulfilled which was spoken by the prophet, saying:

"I will open My mouth in parables;
I will utter things kept secret from the
foundation of the world."

Then Jesus sent the multitude away and went into the house. And His disciples came to Him, saying, "Explain to us the parable of the tares of the field."

He answered and said to them: "He who sows the good seed is the Son of Man. The field is the world, the good seeds are the sons of the kingdom, but the tares are the sons of the wicked *one*. The enemy who sowed them is the devil, the harvest is the end of the age, and the reapers are the angels. Therefore as the tares are gathered and burned in the fire, so it will be at the end of this age. The Son of Man will send out His angels, and they will gather out of His kingdom all things that offend, and those who practice lawlessness, and will cast them into the furnace of fire. There will be wailing and gnashing of teeth. Then the righteous will shine forth as the sun in the kingdom of their Father. He who has ears to hear, let him hear!

"Again, the kingdom of heaven is like treasure hidden in a field, which a man found and hid; and for joy over it he goes and sells all that he has and buys that field.

"Again, the kingdom of heaven is like a merchant seeking beautiful pearls, who, when he had found one pearl of great price, went and sold all that he had and bought it.

"Again, the kingdom of heaven is like a dragnet that was cast into the sea and gathered some of every kind, which, when it was full, they drew to shore; and they sat down and gathered the good into vessels, but threw the bad away. So it will be at the end of the age. The angels will come forth, separate the wicked from among the just, and cast them into the furnace of fire. There will be wailing and gnashing of teeth."

Matthew 13:1-50

WoRsHiP

Oh, give thanks to the LORD!
Call upon His name;
Make known His deeds among the peoples!
Sing to Him, sing psalms to Him;
Talk of all His wondrous works!
Glory in His holy name;
Let the hearts of those rejoice who seek the
    LORD!
Seek the LORD and His strength;
Seek His face evermore!

Psalm 105:1-4

WiSDoM

The rich man's wealth *is* his strong city,
And like a high wall in his own esteem.

Proverbs 18:11

SW?! **SO WHAT?**
What does this tell me?

JESUS CONTINUES TO BACK UP HIS CLAIMS
Mark 4:35–5:24, 37–43; Psalm 105:8-11; Proverbs 18:12

On the same day, when evening had come, He said to them, "Let us cross over to the other side." Now when they had left the multitude, they took Him along in the boat as He was. And other little boats were also with Him. And a great windstorm arose, and the waves beat into the boat, so that it was already filling. But He was in the stern, asleep on a pillow. And they awoke Him and said to Him, "Teacher, do You not care that we are perishing?"

Then He arose and rebuked the wind, and said to the sea, "Peace, be still!" And the wind ceased and there was a great calm. But He said to them, "Why are you so fearful? How *is it* that you have no faith?" And they feared exceedingly, and said to one another, "Who can this be, that even the wind and the sea obey Him!"

Then they came to the other side of the sea, to the country of the Gadarenes. And when He had come out of the boat, immediately there met Him out of the tombs a man with an unclean spirit, who had *his* dwelling among the tombs; and no one could bind him, not even with chains, because he had often been bound with shackles and chains. And the chains had been pulled apart by him, and the shackles broken in pieces; neither could anyone tame him. And always, night and day, he was in the mountains and in the tombs, crying out and cutting himself with stones.

When he saw Jesus from afar, he ran and worshiped Him. And he cried out with a loud voice and said, "What have I to do with You, Jesus, Son of the Most High God? I implore You by God that You do not torment me."

For He said to him, "Come out of the man, unclean spirit!" Then He asked him, "What *is* your name?"

And he answered, saying, "My name *is* Legion; for we are many." Also he begged Him earnestly that He would not send them out of the country.

Now a large herd of swine was feeding there near the mountains. So all the demons begged Him, saying, "Send us to the swine, that we may enter them." And at once Jesus gave them permission. Then the unclean spirits went out and entered the swine (there were about two thousand); and the herd ran violently down the steep place into the sea, and drowned in the sea.

So those who fed the swine fled, and they told *it* in the city and in the country. And they went out to see what it was that had happened. Then they came to Jesus, and saw the one *who had been* demon-possessed and had the legion, sitting and clothed and in his right mind. And they were afraid. And those who saw it told them how it happened to him *who had been* demon-possessed, and about the swine. Then they began to plead with Him to depart from their region.

And when He got into the boat, he who had been demon-possessed begged Him that he might be with Him. However, Jesus did not permit him, but said to him, "Go home to your friends, and tell them what great things the Lord has done for you, and how He has had compassion on you." And he departed and began to proclaim in Decapolis all that Jesus had done for him; and all marveled.

Now when Jesus had crossed over again by boat to the other side, a great multitude gathered to Him; and He was by the sea. And behold, one of the rulers of the synagogue came, Jairus by name. And when he saw Him, he fell at His feet and begged Him earnestly, saying, "My little daughter lies at the point of death. Come and lay Your hands on her, that she may be healed, and she will live." So *Jesus* went with him, and a great multitude followed Him and thronged Him.

And He permitted no one to follow Him except Peter, James, and John the brother of James. Then He came to the house of the ruler of the synagogue, and saw a tumult and those who wept and wailed loudly. When He came in, He said to them, "Why make this commotion and weep? The child is not dead, but sleeping."

And they ridiculed Him. But when He had put them all outside, He took the father and the mother of the child, and those *who were* with Him, and entered where the child was lying. Then He took the child by the hand, and said to her, "Talitha, cumi," which is translated, "Little girl, I say to you, arise." Immediately the girl arose and walked, for she was twelve years *of age*. And they were overcome with great amazement. But He commanded them strictly that no one should know it, and said that *something* should be given her to eat.

Mark 4:35–5:24, 37-43

WoRSHiP

He remembers His covenant forever,
The word *which* He commanded, for a
    thousand generations,
The covenant which He made with Abraham,
And His oath to Isaac,
And confirmed it to Jacob for a statute,
To Israel *as* an everlasting covenant,
Saying, "To you I will give the land of Canaan
As the allotment of your inheritance."

Psalm 105:8-11

WiSDoM

Before destruction the heart of a man is
    haughty,
And before honor *is* humility.

Proverbs 18:12

SW?! SO WHAT?
What does this tell me?

JESUS SENDS HIS DISCIPLES ON A MISSION

Matthew 9:35–10:42; Psalm 105:16-19; Proverbs 18:13

Then Jesus went about all the cities and villages, teaching in their synagogues, preaching the gospel of the kingdom, and healing every sickness and every disease among the people. But when He saw the multitudes, He was moved with compassion for them, because they were weary and scattered, like sheep having no shepherd. Then He said to His disciples, "The harvest truly *is* plentiful, but the laborers *are* few. Therefore pray the Lord of the harvest to send out laborers into His harvest."

And when He had called His twelve disciples to *Him,* He gave them power *over* unclean spirits, to cast them out, and to heal all kinds of sickness and all kinds of disease. Now the names of the twelve apostles are these: first, Simon, who is called Peter, and Andrew his brother; James the *son* of Zebedee, and John his brother; Philip and Bartholomew; Thomas and Matthew the tax collector; James the *son* of Alphaeus, and Lebbaeus, whose surname was Thaddaeus; Simon the Cananite, and Judas Iscariot, who also betrayed Him.

These twelve Jesus sent out and commanded them, saying: "Do not go into the way of the Gentiles, and do not enter a city of the Samaritans. But go rather to the lost sheep of the house of Israel. And as you go, preach, saying, 'The kingdom of heaven is at hand.' Heal the sick, cleanse the lepers, raise the dead, cast out demons. Freely you have received, freely give. Provide neither gold nor silver nor copper in your money belts, nor bag for *your* journey, nor two tunics, nor sandals, nor staffs; for a worker is worthy of his food.

"Now whatever city or town you enter, inquire who in it is worthy, and stay there till you go out. And when you go into a household, greet it. If the household is worthy, let your peace come upon it. But if it is not worthy, let your peace return to you. And whoever will not receive you nor hear your words, when you depart from that house or city, shake off the dust from your feet. Assuredly, I say to you, it will be more tolerable for the land of Sodom and Gomorrah in the day of judgment than for that city!

"Behold, I send you out as sheep in the midst of wolves. Therefore be wise as serpents and harmless as doves. But beware of men, for they will deliver you up to councils and scourge you in their synagogues. You will be brought before governors and kings for My sake, as a testimony to them and to the Gentiles. But when they deliver you up, do not worry about how or what you should speak. For it will be given to you in that hour what you should speak; for it is not you who speak, but the Spirit of your Father who speaks in you.

"Now brother will deliver up brother to death, and a father *his* child; and children will rise up against parents and cause them to be put to death. And you will be hated by all for My name's sake. But he who endures to the end will be saved. When they persecute you in this city, flee to another. For assuredly, I say to you, you will not have gone through the cities of Israel before the Son of Man comes.

"A disciple is not above *his* teacher, nor a servant above his master. It is enough for a disciple that he be like his teacher, and a servant like his master. If they have called the master of the house Beelzebub, how much more *will they call* those of his household! Therefore do not fear them. For there is nothing covered that will not be revealed, and hidden that will not be known.

"Whatever I tell you in the dark, speak in the light; and what you hear in the ear, preach on the housetops. And do not fear those who kill the body but cannot kill the soul. But rather fear Him who is able to destroy both soul and body in hell. Are not two sparrows sold for a copper coin? And not one of them falls to the ground apart from your Father's will. But the very hairs of your head are all numbered. Do not fear therefore; you are of more value than many sparrows.

"Therefore whoever confesses Me before men, him I will also confess before My Father who is in heaven. But whoever denies Me before men, him I will also deny before My Father who is in heaven.

"Do not think that I came to bring peace on

earth. I did not come to bring peace but a sword. For I have come to 'set a man against his father, a daughter against her mother, and a daughter-in-law against her mother-in-law'; and 'a man's enemies will be those of his *own* household.' He who loves father or mother more than Me is not worthy of Me. And he who loves son or daughter more than Me is not worthy of Me. And he who does not take his cross and follow after Me is not worthy of Me. He who finds his life will lose it, and he who loses his life for My sake will find it.

"He who receives you receives Me, and he who receives Me receives Him who sent Me. He who receives a prophet in the name of a prophet shall receive a prophet's reward. And he who receives a righteous man in the name of a righteous man shall receive a righteous man's reward. And whoever gives one of these little ones only a cup of cold *water* in the name of a disciple, assuredly, I say to you, he shall by no means lose his reward."

Matthew 9:35–10:42

WORSHIP

Moreover He called for a famine in the land;
He destroyed all the provision of bread.
He sent a man before them—
Joseph—*who* was sold as a slave.
They hurt his feet with fetters,
He was laid in irons.
Until the time that his word came to pass,
The word of the LORD tested him.

Psalm 105:16-19

WISDOM

He who answers a matter before he hears *it*,
It *is* folly and shame to him.

Proverbs 18:13

SO WHAT?
What does this tell me?

A CALL TO RADICAL FAITH

Matthew 14:1-33; John 6:22-40; Psalm 105:25-27; Proverbs 18:14

At that time Herod the tetrarch heard the report about Jesus and said to his servants, "This is John the Baptist; he is risen from the dead, and therefore these powers are at work in him." For Herod had laid hold of John and bound him, and put *him* in prison for the sake of Herodias, his brother Philip's wife. Because John had said to him, "It is not lawful for you to have her." And although he wanted to put him to death, he feared the multitude, because they counted him as a prophet.

But when Herod's birthday was celebrated, the daughter of Herodias danced before them and pleased Herod. Therefore he promised with an oath to give her whatever she might ask.

So she, having been prompted by her mother, said, "Give me John the Baptist's head here on a platter."

And the king was sorry; nevertheless, because of the oaths and because of those who sat with him, he commanded *it* to be given to *her*. So he sent and had John beheaded in prison. And his head was brought on a platter and given to the girl, and she brought *it* to her mother. Then his disciples came and took away the body and buried it, and went and told Jesus.

When Jesus heard *it,* He departed from there by boat to a deserted place by Himself. But when the multitudes heard it, they followed Him on foot from the cities. And when Jesus went out He saw a great multitude; and He was moved with compassion for them, and healed their sick. When it was evening, His disciples came to Him, saying, "This is a deserted place, and the hour is already late. Send the multitudes away, that they may go into the villages and buy themselves food."

But Jesus said to them, "They do not need to go away. You give them something to eat."

And they said to Him, "We have here only five loaves and two fish."

He said, "Bring them here to Me." Then He commanded the multitudes to sit down on the grass. And He took the five loaves and the two fish, and looking up to heaven, He blessed and broke and gave the loaves to the disciples; and the disciples gave to the multitudes. So they all ate and were filled, and they took up twelve baskets full of the fragments that remained. Now those who had eaten were about five thousand men, besides women and children.

Immediately Jesus made His disciples get into the boat and go before Him to the other side, while He sent the multitudes away. And when He had sent the multitudes away, He went up on the mountain by Himself to pray. Now when evening came, He was alone there. But the boat was now in the middle of the sea, tossed by the waves, for the wind was contrary.

Now in the fourth watch of the night Jesus went to them, walking on the sea. And when the disciples saw Him walking on the sea, they were troubled, saying, "It is a ghost!" And they cried out for fear.

But immediately Jesus spoke to them, saying, "Be of good cheer! It is I; do not be afraid."

And Peter answered Him and said, "Lord, if it is You, command me to come to You on the water."

So He said, "Come." And when Peter had come down out of the boat, he walked on the water to go to Jesus. But when he saw that the wind *was* boisterous, he was afraid; and beginning to sink he cried out, saying, "Lord, save me!"

And immediately Jesus stretched out *His* hand and caught him, and said to him, "O you of little faith, why did you doubt?" And when they got into the boat, the wind ceased.

Then those who were in the boat came and worshiped Him, saying, "Truly You are the Son of God."

On the following day, when the people who were standing on the other side of the sea saw that there was no other boat there, except that one which His disciples had entered, and that Jesus had not entered the boat with His disciples, but His disciples had gone away alone—however, other boats came from Tiberias, near the place where they ate bread after the Lord had given thanks—when the people therefore saw that Jesus was not there, nor His disciples, they also got into boats and came to Capernaum, seeking Jesus. And when they found Him on the other side of the sea, they said to Him, "Rabbi, when did You come here?"

Jesus answered them and said, "Most assuredly, I say to you, you seek Me, not because you saw the signs, but because you ate of the loaves and were filled. Do not labor for the food which perishes, but for the food which endures to everlasting life, which the Son of Man will give you, because God the Father has set His seal on Him."

Then they said to Him, "What shall we do, that we may work the works of God?"

Jesus answered and said to them, "This is the work of God, that you believe in Him whom He sent."

Therefore they said to Him, "What sign will You perform then, that we may see it and believe You? What work will You do? Our fathers ate the manna in the desert; as it is written, 'He gave them bread from heaven to eat.' "

Then Jesus said to them, "Most assuredly, I say to you, Moses did not give you the bread from heaven, but My Father gives you the true bread from heaven. For the bread of God is He who comes down from heaven and gives life to the world."

Then they said to Him, "Lord, give us this bread always."

And Jesus said to them, "I am the bread of life. He who comes to Me shall never hunger, and he who believes in Me shall never thirst. But I said to you that you have seen Me and yet do not believe. All that the Father gives Me will come to Me, and the one who comes to Me I will by no means cast out. For I have come down from heaven, not to do My own will, but the will of Him who sent Me. This is the will of the Father who sent Me, that of all He has given Me I should lose nothing, but should raise it up at the last day. And this is the will of Him who sent Me, that everyone who sees the Son and believes in Him may have everlasting life; and I will raise him up at the last day."

Matthew 14:1-33; John 6:22-40

WORSHIP

He turned their heart to hate His people,
To deal craftily with His servants.

He sent Moses His servant,
And Aaron whom He had chosen.
They performed His signs among them,
And wonders in the land of Ham.

Psalm 105:25-27

WISDOM

The spirit of a man will sustain him in sickness,
But who can bear a broken spirit?

Proverbs 18:14

SW?! SO WHAT?
What does this tell me?

IT'S THE HEART THAT MATTERS

Mark 7:1-23, 31-37; 8:1-21; Psalm 105:44-45; Proverbs 18:15

Then the Pharisees and some of the scribes came together to Him, having come from Jerusalem. Now when they saw some of His disciples eat bread with defiled, that is, with unwashed hands, they found fault. For the Pharisees and all the Jews do not eat unless they wash *their* hands in a special way, holding the tradition of the elders. *When they come* from the marketplace, they do not eat unless they wash. And there are many other things which they have received and hold, *like* the washing of cups, pitchers, copper vessels, and couches.

Then the Pharisees and scribes asked Him, "Why do Your disciples not walk according to the tradition of the elders, but eat bread with unwashed hands?"

He answered and said to them, "Well did Isaiah prophesy of you hypocrites, as it is written:

'This people honors Me with *their* lips,
But their heart is far from Me.
And in vain they worship Me,
Teaching *as* doctrines the commandments of men.'

For laying aside the commandment of God, you hold the tradition of men—the washing of pitchers and cups, and many other such things you do."

He said to them, "*All too* well you reject the commandment of God, that you may keep your tradition. For Moses said, 'Honor your father and your mother'; and, 'He who curses father or mother, let him be put to death.' But you say, 'If a man says to his father or mother, "Whatever profit you might have received from me *is* Corban"—' (that is, a gift *to God*), then you no longer let him do anything for his father or his mother, making the word of God of no effect through your tradition which you have handed down. And many such things you do."

When He had called all the multitude to *Himself,* He said to them, "Hear Me, everyone, and understand: There is nothing that enters a man from outside which can defile him; but the things which come out of him, those are the things that defile a man. If anyone has ears to hear, let him hear!"

When He had entered a house away from the crowd, His disciples asked Him concerning the parable. So He said to them, "Are you thus without understanding also? Do you not perceive that whatever enters a man from outside cannot defile him, because it does not enter his heart but his stomach, and is eliminated, *thus* purifying all foods?" And He said, "What comes out of a man, that defiles a man. For from within, out of the heart of men, proceed evil thoughts, adulteries, fornications, murders, thefts, covetousness, wickedness, deceit, lewdness, an evil eye, blasphemy, pride, foolishness. All these evil things come from within and defile a man."

Again, departing from the region of Tyre and Sidon, He came through the midst of the region of Decapolis to the Sea of Galilee. Then they brought to Him one who was deaf and had an impediment in his speech, and they begged Him to put His hand on him. And He took him aside from the multitude, and put His fingers in his ears, and He spat and touched his tongue. Then, looking up to heaven, He sighed, and said to him, "Ephphatha," that is, "Be opened."

Immediately his ears were opened, and the impediment of his tongue was loosed, and he spoke plainly. Then He commanded them that they should tell no one; but the more He commanded them, the more widely they proclaimed *it*. And they were astonished beyond measure, saying, "He has done all things well. He makes both the deaf to hear and the mute to speak."

In those days, the multitude being very great and having nothing to eat, Jesus called His disciples *to Him* and said to them, "I have compassion on the multitude, because they have now continued with Me three days and have nothing to eat. And if I send them away hungry to their own houses, they will faint on the way; for some of them have come from afar."

Then His disciples answered Him, "How can one satisfy these people with bread here in the wilderness?"

He asked them, "How many loaves do you have?"

And they said, "Seven."

So He commanded the multitude to sit down

on the ground. And He took the seven loaves and gave thanks, broke *them* and gave *them* to His disciples to set before *them;* and they set *them* before the multitude. They also had a few small fish; and having blessed them, He said to set them also before *them*. So they ate and were filled, and they took up seven large baskets of leftover fragments. Now those who had eaten were about four thousand. And He sent them away, immediately got into the boat with His disciples, and came to the region of Dalmanutha.

Then the Pharisees came out and began to dispute with Him, seeking from Him a sign from heaven, testing Him. But He sighed deeply in His spirit, and said, "Why does this generation seek a sign? Assuredly, I say to you, no sign shall be given to this generation."

And He left them, and getting into the boat again, departed to the other side. Now the disciples had forgotten to take bread, and they did not have more than one loaf with them in the boat. Then He charged them, saying, "Take heed, beware of the leaven of the Pharisees and the leaven of Herod."

And they reasoned among themselves, saying, "*It is* because we have no bread."

But Jesus, being aware of *it,* said to them, "Why do you reason because you have no bread? Do you not yet perceive nor understand? Is your heart still hardened? Having eyes, do you not see? And having ears, do you not hear? And do you not remember? When I broke the five loaves for the five thousand, how many baskets full of fragments did you take up?"

They said to Him, "Twelve."

"Also, when I broke the seven for the four thousand, how many large baskets full of fragments did you take up?"

And they said, "Seven."

So He said to them, "How *is it* you do not understand?"

Mark 7:1-23, 31-37; 8:1-21

WORSHIP

He gave them the lands of the Gentiles,
And they inherited the labor of the nations,
That they might observe His statutes
And keep His laws.

Praise the LORD!

Psalm 105:44-45

WISDOM

The heart of the prudent acquires knowledge,
And the ear of the wise seeks knowledge.

Proverbs 18:15

SO WHAT?
What does this tell me?

PETER STARTS TO GET THE PICTURE

Matthew 16:13–17:27; Psalm 106:1-3; Proverbs 18:16

When Jesus came into the region of Caesarea Philippi, He asked His disciples, saying, "Who do men say that I, the Son of Man, am?"

So they said, "Some *say* John the Baptist, some Elijah, and others Jeremiah or one of the prophets."

He said to them, "But who do you say that I am?"

Simon Peter answered and said, "You are the Christ, the Son of the living God."

Jesus answered and said to him, "Blessed are you, Simon Bar-Jonah, for flesh and blood has not revealed *this* to you, but My Father who is in heaven. And I also say to you that you are Peter, and on this rock I will build My church, and the gates of Hades shall not prevail against it. And I will give you the keys of the kingdom of heaven, and whatever you bind on earth will be bound in heaven, and whatever you loose on earth will be loosed in heaven."

Then He commanded His disciples that they should tell no one that He was Jesus the Christ.

From that time Jesus began to show to His disciples that He must go to Jerusalem, and suffer many things from the elders and chief priests and scribes, and be killed, and be raised the third day.

Then Peter took Him aside and began to rebuke Him, saying, "Far be it from You, Lord; this shall not happen to You!"

But He turned and said to Peter, "Get behind Me, Satan! You are an offense to Me, for you are not mindful of the things of God, but the things of men."

Then Jesus said to His disciples, "If anyone desires to come after Me, let him deny himself, and take up his cross, and follow Me. For whoever desires to save his life will lose it, but whoever loses his life for My sake will find it. For what profit is it to a man if he gains the whole world, and loses his own soul? Or what will a man give in exchange for his soul? For the Son of Man will come in the glory of His Father with His angels, and then He will reward each according to his works. Assuredly, I say to you, there are some standing here who shall not taste death till they see the Son of Man coming in His kingdom."

Now after six days Jesus took Peter, James, and John his brother, led them up on a high mountain by themselves; and He was transfigured before them. His face shone like the sun, and His clothes became as white as the light. And behold, Moses and Elijah appeared to them, talking with Him. Then Peter answered and said to Jesus, "Lord, it is good for us to be here; if You wish, let us make here three tabernacles: one for You, one for Moses, and one for Elijah."

While he was still speaking, behold, a bright cloud overshadowed them; and suddenly a voice came out of the cloud, saying, "This is My beloved Son, in whom I am well pleased. Hear Him!" And when the disciples heard *it,* they fell on their faces and were greatly afraid. But Jesus came and touched them and said, "Arise, and do not be afraid." When they had lifted up their eyes, they saw no one but Jesus only.

Now as they came down from the mountain, Jesus commanded them, saying, "Tell the vision to no one until the Son of Man is risen from the dead."

And His disciples asked Him, saying, "Why then do the scribes say that Elijah must come first?"

Jesus answered and said to them, "Indeed, Elijah is coming first and will restore all things. But I say to you that Elijah has come already, and they did not know him but did to him whatever they wished. Likewise the Son of Man is also about to suffer at their hands." Then the disciples understood that He spoke to them of John the Baptist.

And when they had come to the multitude, a man came to Him, kneeling down to Him and saying, "Lord, have mercy on my son, for he is an epileptic and suffers severely; for he often falls into the fire and often into the water. So I brought him to Your disciples, but they could not cure him."

Then Jesus answered and said, "O faithless and perverse generation, how long shall I be with you? How long shall I bear with you? Bring him here to Me." And Jesus rebuked the demon, and it came out of him; and the child was cured from that very hour.

Then the disciples came to Jesus privately and said, "Why could we not cast it out?"

So Jesus said to them, "Because of your unbe-

THE LIFE OF CHRIST

lief; for assuredly, I say to you, if you have faith as a mustard seed, you will say to this mountain, 'Move from here to there,' and it will move; and nothing will be impossible for you. However, this kind does not go out except by prayer and fasting."

Now while they were staying in Galilee, Jesus said to them, "The Son of Man is about to be betrayed into the hands of men, and they will kill Him, and the third day He will be raised up." And they were exceedingly sorrowful.

When they had come to Capernaum, those who received the *temple* tax came to Peter and said, "Does your Teacher not pay the *temple* tax?"

He said, "Yes."

And when he had come into the house, Jesus anticipated him, saying, "What do you think, Simon? From whom do the kings of the earth take customs or taxes, from their sons or from strangers?"

Peter said to Him, "From strangers."

Jesus said to him, "Then the sons are free. Nevertheless, lest we offend them, go to the sea, cast in a hook, and take the fish that comes up first. And when you have opened its mouth, you will find a piece of money; take that and give it to them for Me and you."

Matthew 16:13–17:27

WORSHIP

Praise the LORD!

Oh, give thanks to the LORD, for *He is* good!
For His mercy *endures* forever.

Who can utter the mighty acts of the LORD?
Who can declare all His praise?
Blessed *are* those who keep justice,
And he who does righteousness at all times!

Psalm 106:1-3

WISDOM

A man's gift makes room for him,
And brings him before great men.

Proverbs 18:16

SW?! **SO WHAT?**
What does this tell me?

LESSONS IN KINGDOM LIVING

Matthew 18; Psalm 106:9-12; Proverbs 18:19

A t that time the disciples came to Jesus, saying, "Who then is greatest in the kingdom of heaven?"

Then Jesus called a little child to Him, set him in the midst of them, and said, "Assuredly, I say to you, unless you are converted and become as little children, you will by no means enter the kingdom of heaven. Therefore whoever humbles himself as this little child is the greatest in the kingdom of heaven. Whoever receives one little child like this in My name receives Me.

Whoever causes one of these little ones who believe in Me to sin, it would be better for him if a millstone were hung around his neck, and he were drowned in the depth of the sea. Woe to the world because of offenses! For offenses must come, but woe to that man by whom the offense comes!

"If your hand or foot causes you to sin, cut it off and cast *it* from you. It is better for you to enter into life lame or maimed, rather than having two hands or two feet, to be cast into the everlasting fire. And if your eye causes you to sin, pluck it out and cast *it* from you. It is better for you to enter into life with one eye, rather than having two eyes, to be cast into hell fire.

"Take heed that you do not despise one of these little ones, for I say to you that in heaven their angels always see the face of My Father who is in heaven. For the Son of Man has come to save that which was lost.

"What do you think? If a man has a hundred sheep, and one of them goes astray, does he not leave the ninety-nine and go to the mountains to seek the one that is straying? And if he should find it, assuredly, I say to you, he rejoices more over that *sheep* than over the ninety-nine that did not go astray. Even so it is not the will of your Father who is in heaven that one of these little ones should perish.

"Moreover if your brother sins against you, go and tell him his fault between you and him alone. If he hears you, you have gained your brother. But if he will not hear, take with you one or two more, that 'by the mouth of two or three witnesses every word may be established.' And if he refuses to hear them, tell *it* to the church. But if he refuses even to hear the church, let him be to you like a heathen and a tax collector.

"Assuredly, I say to you, whatever you bind on earth will be bound in heaven, and whatever you loose on earth will be loosed in heaven.

"Again I say to you that if two of you agree on earth concerning anything that they ask, it will be done for them by My Father in heaven. For where two or three are gathered together in My name, I am there in the midst of them."

Then Peter came to Him and said, "Lord, how often shall my brother sin against me, and I forgive him? Up to seven times?"

Jesus said to him, "I do not say to you, up to seven times, but up to seventy times seven. Therefore the kingdom of heaven is like a certain king who wanted to settle accounts with his servants. And when he had begun to settle accounts, one was brought to him who owed him ten thousand talents. But as he was not able to pay, his master commanded that he be sold, with his wife and children and all that he had, and that payment be made. The servant therefore fell down before him, saying, 'Master, have patience with me, and I will pay you all.' Then the master of that servant was moved with compassion, released him, and forgave him the debt.

"But that servant went out and found one of his fellow servants who owed him a hundred denarii; and he laid hands on him and took *him* by the throat, saying, 'Pay me what you owe!' So his fellow servant fell down at his feet and begged him, saying, 'Have patience with me, and I will pay you all.' And he would not, but went and threw him into prison till he should pay the debt. So when his fellow servants saw what had been done, they were very grieved, and came and told their master all that had been done. Then his master, after he had called him, said to him, 'You wicked servant! I forgave you all that debt because you begged me. Should you not also have had compassion on your fellow servant, just as I had pity on you?' And his master was angry, and delivered him to the torturers until he should pay all that was due to him.

"So My heavenly Father also will do to you if

each of you, from his heart, does not forgive his brother his trespasses."

Matthew 18

WORSHIP

He rebuked the Red Sea also, and it dried up;
So He led them through the depths,
As through the wilderness.
He saved them from the hand of him who
     hated *them,*
And redeemed them from the hand of the
     enemy.
The waters covered their enemies;
There was not one of them left.
Then they believed His words;
They sang His praise.

Psalm 106:9-12

WISDOM

A brother offended *is harder to win* than a
     strong city,
And contentions *are* like the bars of a castle.

Proverbs 18:19

SW?! SO WHAT?
What does this tell me?

JESUS: A LIGHT IN DARKNESS, THE TRUTH THAT FREES

John 8:2-36; Psalm 106:13-15; Proverbs 18:21

Now early in the morning He came again into the temple, and all the people came to Him; and He sat down and taught them. Then the scribes and Pharisees brought to Him a woman caught in adultery. And when they had set her in the midst, they said to Him, "Teacher, this woman was caught in adultery, in the very act. Now Moses, in the law, commanded us that such should be stoned. But what do You say?" This they said, testing Him, that they might have *something* of which to accuse Him. But Jesus stooped down and wrote on the ground with *His* finger, as though He did not hear.

So when they continued asking Him, He raised Himself up and said to them, "He who is without sin among you, let him throw a stone at her first." And again He stooped down and wrote on the ground.

Then those who heard *it,* being convicted by *their* conscience, went out one by one, beginning with the oldest *even* to the last. And Jesus was left alone, and the woman standing in the midst. When Jesus had raised Himself up and saw no one but the woman, He said to her, "Woman, where are those accusers of yours? Has no one condemned you?"

She said, "No one, Lord."

And Jesus said to her, "Neither do I condemn you; go and sin no more."

Then Jesus spoke to them again, saying, "I am the light of the world. He who follows Me shall not walk in darkness, but have the light of life."

The Pharisees therefore said to Him, "You bear witness of Yourself; Your witness is not true."

Jesus answered and said to them, "Even if I bear witness of Myself, My witness is true, for I know where I came from and where I am going; but you do not know where I come from and where I am going. You judge according to the flesh; I judge no one. And yet if I do judge, My judgment is true; for I am not alone, but I *am* with the Father who sent Me. It is also written in your law that the testimony of two men is true. I am One who bears witness of Myself, and the Father who sent Me bears witness of Me."

Then they said to Him, "Where is Your Father?"

Jesus answered, "You know neither Me nor My Father. If you had known Me, you would have known My Father also."

These words Jesus spoke in the treasury, as He taught in the temple; and no one laid hands on Him, for His hour had not yet come.

Then Jesus said to them again, "I am going away, and you will seek Me, and will die in your sin. Where I go you cannot come."

So the Jews said, "Will He kill Himself, because He says, 'Where I go you cannot come'?"

And He said to them, "You are from beneath; I am from above. You are of this world; I am not of this world. Therefore I said to you that you will die in your sins; for if you do not believe that I am *He,* you will die in your sins."

Then they said to Him, "Who are You?"

And Jesus said to them, "Just what I have been saying to you from the beginning. I have many things to say and to judge concerning you, but He who sent Me is true; and I speak to the world those things which I heard from Him."

They did not understand that He spoke to them of the Father.

Then Jesus said to them, "When you lift up the Son of Man, then you will know that I am *He,* and *that* I do nothing of Myself; but as My Father taught Me, I speak these things. And He who sent Me is with Me. The Father has not left Me alone, for I always do those things that please Him." As He spoke these words, many believed in Him.

Then Jesus said to those Jews who believed Him, "If you abide in My word, you are My disciples indeed. And you shall know the truth, and the truth shall make you free."

THE LIFE OF CHRIST

They answered Him, "We are Abraham's descendants, and have never been in bondage to anyone. How *can* you say, 'You will be made free'?"

Jesus answered them, "Most assuredly, I say to you, whoever commits sin is a slave of sin. And a slave does not abide in the house forever, *but* a son abides forever. Therefore if the Son makes you free, you shall be free indeed."

John 8:2-36

WORSHIP

They soon forgot His works;
They did not wait for His counsel,
But lusted exceedingly in the wilderness,
And tested God in the desert.
And He gave them their request,
But sent leanness into their soul.

Psalm 106:13-15

WISDOM

Death and life *are* in the power of the tongue,
And those who love it will eat its fruit.

Proverbs 18:21

SW?! SO WHAT?
What does this tell me?

Lessons in KINGDOM Priorities

After these things the Lord appointed seventy others also, and sent them two by two before His face into every city and place where He Himself was about to go. Then He said to them, "The harvest truly *is* great, but the laborers *are* few; therefore pray the Lord of the harvest to send out laborers into His harvest. Go your way; behold, I send you out as lambs among wolves. Carry neither money bag, knapsack, nor sandals; and greet no one along the road. But whatever house you enter, first say, 'Peace to this house.' And if a son of peace is there, your peace will rest on it; if not, it will return to you. And remain in the same house, eating and drinking such things as they give, for the laborer is worthy of his wages. Do not go from house to house. Whatever city you enter, and they receive you, eat such things as are set before you. And heal the sick there, and say to them, 'The kingdom of God has come near to you.' But whatever city you enter, and they do not receive you, go out into its streets and say, 'The very dust of your city which clings to us we wipe off against you. Nevertheless know this, that the kingdom of God has come near you.' But I say to you that it will be more tolerable in that Day for Sodom than for that city."

"Woe to you, Chorazin! Woe to you, Bethsaida! For if the mighty works which were done in you had been done in Tyre and Sidon, they would have repented long ago, sitting in sackcloth and ashes. But it will be more tolerable for Tyre and Sidon at the judgment than for you. And you, Capernaum, who are exalted to heaven, will be brought down to Hades. He who hears you hears Me, he who rejects you rejects Me, and he who rejects Me rejects Him who sent Me."

Then the seventy returned with joy, saying, "Lord, even the demons are subject to us in Your name."

And He said to them, "I saw Satan fall like lightning from heaven. Behold, I give you the authority to trample on serpents and scorpions, and over all the power of the enemy, and nothing shall by any means hurt you. Nevertheless do not rejoice in this, that the spirits are subject to you, but rather rejoice because your names are written in heaven."

In that hour Jesus rejoiced in the Spirit and said, "I thank You, Father, Lord of heaven and earth, that You have hidden these things from *the* wise and prudent and revealed them to babes. Even so, Father, for so it seemed good in Your sight. All things have been delivered to Me by My Father, and no one knows who the Son is except the Father, and who the Father is except the Son, and *the one* to whom the Son wills to reveal *Him*."

Then He turned to *His* disciples and said privately, "Blessed *are* the eyes which see the things you see; for I tell you that many prophets and kings have desired to see what you see, and have not seen *it*, and to hear what you hear, and have not heard *it*."

And behold, a certain lawyer stood up and tested Him, saying, "Teacher, what shall I do to inherit eternal life?"

He said to him, "What is written in the law? What is your reading *of it*?"

So he answered and said, " 'You shall love the LORD your God with all your heart, with all your soul, with all your strength, and with all your mind,' and 'your neighbor as yourself.' "

And He said to him, "You have answered rightly; do this and you will live."

But he, wanting to justify himself, said to Jesus, "And who is my neighbor?"

Then Jesus answered and said: "A certain *man* went down from Jerusalem to Jericho, and fell among thieves, who stripped him of his clothing, wounded *him*, and departed, leaving *him* half dead. Now by chance a certain priest came down that road. And when he saw him, he passed by on the other side. Likewise a Levite, when he arrived at the place, came and looked, and passed by on the other side. But a certain Samaritan, as he journeyed, came where he was. And when he saw him, he had compassion. So he went to *him* and bandaged his wounds, pouring on oil and wine; and he set him on his own animal, brought him to an inn, and took care of him. On the next day, when he departed, he took out two denarii, gave *them* to the innkeeper, and said to him, 'Take care of him; and whatever more you spend, when I come again, I will repay you.' So which of these three do you think was neighbor to him who fell among the thieves?"

And he said, "He who showed mercy on him."

Then Jesus said to him, "Go and do likewise."

Now it happened as they went that He entered a certain village; and a certain woman named Martha welcomed Him into her house. And she had a sister called Mary, who also sat at Jesus' feet and heard His word. But Martha was distracted with much serving, and she approached Him and said, "Lord, do You not care that my sister has left me to serve alone? Therefore tell her to help me."

And Jesus answered and said to her, "Martha, Martha, you are worried and troubled about many things. But one thing is needed, and Mary has chosen that good part, which will not be taken away from her."

Luke 10

WORSHIP

They made a calf in Horeb,
And worshiped the molded image.
Thus they changed their glory
Into the image of an ox that eats grass.
They forgot God their Savior,
Who had done great things in Egypt.

Psalm 106:19-21

WISDOM

He who finds a wife finds a good *thing,*
And obtains favor from the LORD.

Proverbs 18:22

SW?! SO WHAT?
What does this tell me?

LESSONS IN KINGDOM PERSPECTIVES

Luke 11:1-13; 12:1-34; Psalm 106:28-31; Proverbs 18:24

ow it came to pass, as He was praying in a certain place, when He ceased, *that* one of His disciples said to Him, "Lord, teach us to pray, as John also taught his disciples."

So He said to them, "When you pray, say:

Our Father in heaven,
Hallowed be Your name.
Your kingdom come.
Your will be done
On earth as *it is* in heaven.
Give us day by day our daily bread.
And forgive us our sins,
For we also forgive everyone who is indebted
    to us.
And do not lead us into temptation,
But deliver us from the evil one."

And He said to them, "Which of you shall have a friend, and go to him at midnight and say to him, 'Friend, lend me three loaves; for a friend of mine has come to me on his journey, and I have nothing to set before him'; and he will answer from within and say, 'Do not trouble me; the door is now shut, and my children are with me in bed; I cannot rise and give to you'? I say to you, though he will not rise and give to him because he is his friend, yet because of his persistence he will rise and give him as many as he needs.

"So I say to you, ask, and it will be given to you; seek, and you will find; knock, and it will be opened to you. For everyone who asks receives, and he who seeks finds, and to him who knocks it will be opened. If a son asks for bread from any father among you, will he give him a stone? Or if *he asks* for a fish, will he give him a serpent instead of a fish? Or if he asks for an egg, will he offer him a scorpion? If you then, being evil, know how to give good gifts to your children, how much more will *your* heavenly Father give the Holy Spirit to those who ask Him!"

In the meantime, when an innumerable multitude of people had gathered together, so that they trampled one another, He began to say to His disciples first *of all*, "Beware of the leaven of the Pharisees, which is hypocrisy. For there is nothing covered that will not be revealed, nor hidden that will not be known. Therefore whatever you have spoken in the dark will be heard in the light, and what you have spoken in the ear in inner rooms will be proclaimed on the housetops.

"And I say to you, My friends, do not be afraid of those who kill the body, and after that have no more that they can do. But I will show you whom you should fear: Fear Him who, after He has killed, has power to cast into hell; yes, I say to you, fear Him!

"Are not five sparrows sold for two copper coins? And not one of them is forgotten before God. But the very hairs of your head are all numbered. Do not fear therefore; you are of more value than many sparrows.

"Also I say to you, whoever confesses Me before men, him the Son of Man also will confess before the angels of God. But he who denies Me before men will be denied before the angels of God.

"And anyone who speaks a word against the Son of Man, it will be forgiven him; but to him who blasphemes against the Holy Spirit, it will not be forgiven.

"Now when they bring you to the synagogues and magistrates and authorities, do not worry about how or what you should answer, or what you should say. For the Holy Spirit will teach you in that very hour what you ought to say."

Then one from the crowd said to Him, "Teacher, tell my brother to divide the inheritance with me."

But He said to him, "Man, who made Me a judge or an arbitrator over you?" And He said to them, "Take heed and beware of covetousness, for one's life does not consist in the abundance of the things he possesses."

Then He spoke a parable to them, saying: "The ground of a certain rich man yielded plentifully. And he thought within himself, saying, 'What shall I do, since I have no room to store my crops?' So he said, 'I will do this: I will pull down my barns and build greater, and there I will store all my crops and my goods. And I will say to my soul, "Soul, you have many goods laid up for many years; take your ease; eat, drink, *and* be merry." ' But God said to

THE LIFE OF CHRIST

him, 'Fool! This night your soul will be required of you; then whose will those things be which you have provided?'

"So *is* he who lays up treasure for himself, and is not rich toward God."

Then He said to His disciples, "Therefore I say to you, do not worry about your life, what you will eat; nor about the body, what you will put on. Life is more than food, and the body *is more* than clothing. Consider the ravens, for they neither sow nor reap, which have neither storehouse nor barn; and God feeds them. Of how much more value are you than the birds? And which of you by worrying can add one cubit to his stature? If you then are not able to do *the* least, why are you anxious for the rest? Consider the lilies, how they grow: they neither toil nor spin; and yet I say to you, even Solomon in all his glory was not arrayed like one of these. If then God so clothes the grass, which today is in the field and tomorrow is thrown into the oven, how much more *will He clothe* you, O *you* of little faith?

"And do not seek what you should eat or what you should drink, nor have an anxious mind. For all these things the nations of the world seek after, and your Father knows that you need these things. But seek the kingdom of God, and all these things shall be added to you.

"Do not fear, little flock, for it is your Father's good pleasure to give you the kingdom. Sell what you have and give alms; provide yourselves money bags which do not grow old, a treasure in the heavens that does not fail, where no thief approaches nor moth destroys. For where your treasure is, there your heart will be also."

Luke 11:1-13; 12:1-34

WORSHIP

They joined themselves also to Baal of Peor,
And ate sacrifices made to the dead.
Thus they provoked *Him* to anger with their
    deeds,
And the plague broke out among them.
Then Phinehas stood up and intervened,
And the plague was stopped.
And that was accounted to him for
    righteousness
To all generations forevermore.

Psalm 106:28-31

WISDOM

A man *who has* friends must himself be
    friendly,
But there is a friend *who* sticks closer than a
    brother.

Proverbs 18:24

SW?! **SO WHAT?**
What does this tell me?

HEALING SPIRITUAL BLINDNESS   John 9; Psalm 106:35-38; Proverbs 19:1

N ow as *Jesus* passed by, He saw a man who was blind from birth. And His disciples asked Him, saying, "Rabbi, who sinned, this man or his parents, that he was born blind?"

Jesus answered, "Neither this man nor his parents sinned, but that the works of God should be revealed in him. I must work the works of Him who sent Me while it is day; *the* night is coming when no one can work. As long as I am in the world, I am the light of the world."

When He had said these things, He spat on the ground and made clay with the saliva; and He anointed the eyes of the blind man with the clay. And He said to him, "Go, wash in the pool of Siloam" (which is translated, Sent). So he went and washed, and came back seeing.

Therefore the neighbors and those who previously had seen that he was blind said, "Is not this he who sat and begged?"

Some said, "This is he." Others *said,* "He is like him."

He said, "I am *he.*"

Therefore they said to him, "How were your eyes opened?"

He answered and said, "A Man called Jesus made clay and anointed my eyes and said to me, 'Go to the pool of Siloam and wash.' So I went and washed, and I received sight."

Then they said to him, "Where is He?" He said, "I do not know."

They brought him who formerly was blind to the Pharisees. Now it was a Sabbath when Jesus made the clay and opened his eyes. Then the Pharisees also asked him again how he had received his sight. He said to them, "He put clay on my eyes, and I washed, and I see."

Therefore some of the Pharisees said, "This Man is not from God, because He does not keep the Sabbath."

Others said, "How can a man who is a sinner do such signs?" And there was a division among them.

They said to the blind man again, "What do you say about Him because He opened your eyes?"

He said, "He is a prophet."

But the Jews did not believe concerning him, that he had been blind and received his sight, until they called the parents of him who had received his sight. And they asked them, saying, "Is this your son, who you say was born blind? How then does he now see?"

His parents answered them and said, "We know that this is our son, and that he was born blind; but by what means he now sees we do not know, or who opened his eyes we do not know. He is of age; ask him. He will speak for himself." His parents said these *things* because they feared the Jews, for the Jews had agreed already that if anyone confessed *that* He *was* Christ, he would be put out of the synagogue. Therefore his parents said, "He is of age; ask him."

So they again called the man who was blind, and said to him, "Give God the glory! We know that this Man is a sinner."

He answered and said, "Whether He is a sinner *or not* I do not know. One thing I know: that though I was blind, now I see."

Then they said to him again, "What did He do to you? How did He open your eyes?"

He answered them, "I told you already, and you did not listen. Why do you want to hear *it* again? Do you also want to become His disciples?"

Then they reviled him and said, "You are His disciple, but we are Moses' disciples. We know that God spoke to Moses; *as for* this *fellow,* we do not know where He is from."

The man answered and said to them, "Why, this is a marvelous thing, that you do not know where He is from; yet He has opened my eyes! Now we know that God does not hear sinners; but if anyone is a worshiper of God and does His will, He hears him. Since the world began it has been unheard of that anyone opened the eyes of one who was born blind. If this Man were not from God, He could do nothing."

They answered and said to him, "You were completely born in sins, and are you teaching us?" And they cast him out.

Jesus heard that they had cast him out; and when He had found him, He said to him, "Do you believe in the Son of God?"

He answered and said, "Who is He, Lord, that I may believe in Him?"

And Jesus said to him, "You have both seen Him and it is He who is talking with you."

Then he said, "Lord, I believe!" And he worshiped Him.

And Jesus said, "For judgment I have come into this world, that those who do not see may see, and that those who see may be made blind."

Then *some* of the Pharisees who were with Him heard these words, and said to Him, "Are we blind also?"

Jesus said to them, "If you were blind, you would have no sin; but now you say, 'We see.' Therefore your sin remains."

John 9

WORSHIP

But they mingled with the Gentiles
And learned their works;
They served their idols,
Which became a snare to them.
They even sacrificed their sons
And their daughters to demons,
And shed innocent blood,
The blood of their sons and daughters,
Whom they sacrificed to the idols of Canaan;
And the land was polluted with blood.

Psalm 106:35-38

WISDOM

Better *is* the poor who walks in his integrity
Than *one who is* perverse in his lips, and is a fool.

Proverbs 19:1

SW?! **SO WHAT?**
What does this tell me?

THE SHEPHERD OF LOST SHEEP

John 10; Psalm 106:47-48; Proverbs 19:8

"Most assuredly, I say to you, he who does not enter the sheepfold by the door, but climbs up some other way, the same is a thief and a robber. But he who enters by the door is the shepherd of the sheep. To him the door-keeper opens, and the sheep hear his voice; and he calls his own sheep by name and leads them out. And when he brings out his own sheep, he goes before them; and the sheep follow him, for they know his voice. Yet they will by no means follow a stranger, but will flee from him, for they do not know the voice of strangers." Jesus used this illustration, but they did not understand the things which He spoke to them.

Then Jesus said to them again, "Most assuredly, I say to you, I am the door of the sheep. All who *ever* came before Me are thieves and robbers, but the sheep did not hear them. I am the door. If anyone enters by Me, he will be saved, and will go in and out and find pasture. The thief does not come except to steal, and to kill, and to destroy. I have come that they may have life, and that they may have *it* more abundantly.

"I am the good shepherd. The good shepherd gives His life for the sheep. But a hireling, *he who is* not the shepherd, one who does not own the sheep, sees the wolf coming and leaves the sheep and flees; and the wolf catches the sheep and scatters them. The hireling flees because he is a hireling and does not care about the sheep. I am the good shepherd; and I know My *sheep*, and am known by My own. As the Father knows Me, even so I know the Father; and I lay down My life for the sheep. And other sheep I have which are not of this fold; them also I must bring, and they will hear My voice; and there will be one flock *and* one shepherd.

"Therefore My Father loves Me, because I lay down My life that I may take it again. No one takes it from Me, but I lay it down of Myself. I have power to lay it down, and I have power to take it again. This command I have received from My Father."

Therefore there was a division again among the Jews because of these sayings. And many of them said, "He has a demon and is mad. Why do you listen to Him?"

Others said, "These are not the words of one who has a demon. Can a demon open the eyes of the blind?"

Now it was the Feast of Dedication in Jerusalem, and it was winter. And Jesus walked in the temple, in Solomon's porch. Then the Jews surrounded Him and said to Him, "How long do You keep us in doubt? If You are the Christ, tell us plainly."

Jesus answered them, "I told you, and you do not believe. The works that I do in My Father's name, they bear witness of Me. But you do not believe, because you are not of My sheep, as I said to you. My sheep hear My voice, and I know them, and they follow Me. And I give them eternal life, and they shall never perish; neither shall anyone snatch them out of My hand. My Father, who has given *them* to Me, is greater than all; and no one is able to snatch *them* out of My Father's hand. I and *My* Father are one."

Then the Jews took up stones again to stone Him. Jesus answered them, "Many good works I have shown you from My Father. For which of those works do you stone Me?"

The Jews answered Him, saying, "For a good work we do not stone You, but for blasphemy, and because You, being a Man, make Yourself God."

Jesus answered them, "Is it not written in your law, 'I said, "You are gods" '? If He called them gods, to whom the word of God came (and the Scripture cannot be broken), do you say of Him whom the Father sanctified and sent into the world, 'You are blaspheming,' because I said, 'I am the Son of God'? If I do not do the works of My Father, do not believe Me; but if I do, though you do not believe Me, believe the works, that you may know and believe that the Father *is* in Me, and I in Him." Therefore they sought again to seize Him, but He escaped out of their hand.

And He went away again beyond the Jordan to the place where John was baptizing at first, and there He stayed. Then many came to Him and said, "John performed no sign, but all the things that

John spoke about this Man were true." And many believed in Him there.

John 10

WORSHIP

Save us, O LORD our God,
And gather us from among the Gentiles,
To give thanks to Your holy name,
To triumph in Your praise.

Blessed *be* the LORD God of Israel
From everlasting to everlasting!
And let all the people say, "Amen!"

Praise the LORD!

Psalm 106:47-48

WISDOM

He who gets wisdom loves his own soul;
He who keeps understanding will find good.

Proverbs 19:8

SW?! SO WHAT?
What does this tell me?

THE LOST ARE FOUND

Luke 14:25–15:32; Psalm 107:1-3; Proverbs 19:11

Now great multitudes went with Him. And He turned and said to them, "If anyone comes to Me and does not hate his father and mother, wife and children, brothers and sisters, yes, and his own life also, he cannot be My disciple. And whoever does not bear his cross and come after Me cannot be My disciple. For which of you, intending to build a tower, does not sit down first and count the cost, whether he has *enough* to finish *it*—lest, after he has laid the foundation, and is not able to finish, all who see *it* begin to mock him, saying, 'This man began to build and was not able to finish.' Or what king, going to make war against another king, does not sit down first and consider whether he is able with ten thousand to meet him who comes against him with twenty thousand? Or else, while the other is still a great way off, he sends a delegation and asks conditions of peace. So likewise, whoever of you does not forsake all that he has cannot be My disciple.

"Salt *is* good; but if the salt has lost its flavor, how shall it be seasoned? It is neither fit for the land nor for the dunghill, *but* men throw it out. He who has ears to hear, let him hear!"

Then all the tax collectors and the sinners drew near to Him to hear Him. And the Pharisees and scribes complained, saying, "This Man receives sinners and eats with them." So He spoke this parable to them, saying:

"What man of you, having a hundred sheep, if he loses one of them, does not leave the ninety-nine in the wilderness, and go after the one which is lost until he finds it? And when he has found *it,* he lays *it* on his shoulders, rejoicing. And when he comes home, he calls together *his* friends and neighbors, saying to them, 'Rejoice with me, for I have found my sheep which was lost!' I say to you that likewise there will be more joy in heaven over one sinner who repents than over ninety-nine just persons who need no repentance.

"Or what woman, having ten silver coins, if she loses one coin, does not light a lamp, sweep the house, and search carefully until she finds *it*? And when she has found *it,* she calls *her* friends and neighbors together, saying, 'Rejoice with me, for I have found the piece which I lost!' Likewise, I say to you, there is joy in the presence of the angels of God over one sinner who repents."

Then He said: "A certain man had two sons. And the younger of them said to *his* father, 'Father, give me the portion of goods that falls *to me.*' So he divided to them *his* livelihood. And not many days after, the younger son gathered all together, journeyed to a far country, and there wasted his possessions with prodigal living. But when he had spent all, there arose a severe famine in that land, and he began to be in want. Then he went and joined himself to a citizen of that country, and he sent him into his fields to feed swine. And he would gladly have filled his stomach with the pods that the swine ate, and no one gave him *anything*.

"But when he came to himself, he said, 'How many of my father's hired servants have bread enough and to spare, and I perish with hunger! I will arise and go to my father, and will say to him, "Father, I have sinned against heaven and before you, and I am no longer worthy to be called your son. Make me like one of your hired servants." '

"And he arose and came to his father. But when he was still a great way off, his father saw him and had compassion, and ran and fell on his neck and kissed him. And the son said to him, 'Father, I have sinned against heaven and in your sight, and am no longer worthy to be called your son.'

"But the father said to his servants, 'Bring out the best robe and put *it* on him, and put a ring on his hand and sandals on *his* feet. And bring the fatted calf here and kill *it,* and let us eat and be merry; for this my son was dead and is alive again; he was lost and is found.' And they began to be merry.

"Now his older son was in the field. And as he came and drew near to the house, he heard music and dancing. So he called one of the servants and asked what these things meant. And he said to him, 'Your brother has come, and because he has received him safe and sound, your father has killed the fatted calf.'

"But he was angry and would not go in. Therefore his father came out and pleaded with him. So he answered and said to *his* father, 'Lo, these many years I have been serving you; I never transgressed your commandment at any time; and yet you never gave me a young goat, that I might make merry with my friends. But as soon as this son of yours came, who has devoured your livelihood with harlots, you killed the fatted calf for him.'

"And he said to him, 'Son, you are always with me, and all that I have is yours. It was right that we should make merry and be glad, for your brother was dead and is alive again, and was lost and is found.'"

Luke 14:25–15:32

WORSHIP

Oh, give thanks to the LORD, for *He is* good!
For His mercy *endures* forever.
Let the redeemed of the LORD say *so,*
Whom He has redeemed from the hand of the
    enemy,
And gathered out of the lands,
From the east and from the west,
From the north and from the south.

Psalm 107:1-3

WISDOM

The discretion of a man makes him slow to
    anger,
And his glory *is* to overlook a transgression.

Proverbs 19:11

SW?! **SO WHAT?**
What does this tell me?

LIVING IN LIGHT OF ETERNITY

Luke 16:1–17:10; Psalm
107:6-9; Proverbs 19:14

e also said to His disciples: "There was a certain rich man who had a steward, and an accusation was brought to him that this man was wasting his goods. So he called him and said to him, 'What is this I hear about you? Give an account of your stewardship, for you can no longer be steward.'

"Then the steward said within himself, 'What shall I do? For my master is taking the stewardship away from me. I cannot dig; I am ashamed to beg. I have resolved what to do, that when I am put out of the stewardship, they may receive me into their houses.'

"So he called every one of his master's debtors to *him,* and said to the first, 'How much do you owe my master?' And he said, 'A hundred measures of oil.' So he said to him, 'Take your bill, and sit down quickly and write fifty.' Then he said to another, 'And how much do you owe?' So he said, 'A hundred measures of wheat.' And he said to him, 'Take your bill, and write eighty.' So the master commended the unjust steward because he had dealt shrewdly. For the sons of this world are more shrewd in their generation than the sons of light.

"And I say to you, make friends for yourselves by unrighteous mammon, that when you fail, they may receive you into an everlasting home. He who *is* faithful in *what is* least is faithful also in much; and he who is unjust in *what is* least is unjust also in much. Therefore if you have not been faithful in the unrighteous mammon, who will commit to your trust the true *riches*? And if you have not been faithful in what is another man's, who will give you what is your own?

"No servant can serve two masters; for either he will hate the one and love the other, or else he will be loyal to the one and despise the other. You cannot serve God and mammon."

Now the Pharisees, who were lovers of money, also heard all these things, and they derided Him. And He said to them, "You are those who justify yourselves before men, but God knows your hearts. For what is highly esteemed among men is an abomination in the sight of God.

"The law and the prophets *were* until John. Since that time the kingdom of God has been preached, and everyone is pressing into it. And it is easier for heaven and earth to pass away than for one tittle of the law to fail.

"Whoever divorces his wife and marries another commits adultery; and whoever marries her who is divorced from *her* husband commits adultery.

"There was a certain rich man who was clothed in purple and fine linen and fared sumptuously every day. But there was a certain beggar named Lazarus, full of sores, who was laid at his gate, desiring to be fed with the crumbs which fell from the rich man's table. Moreover the dogs came and licked his sores. So it was that the beggar died, and was carried by the angels to Abraham's bosom. The rich man also died and was buried. And being in torments in Hades, he lifted up his eyes and saw Abraham afar off, and Lazarus in his bosom.

"Then he cried and said, 'Father Abraham, have mercy on me, and send Lazarus that he may dip the tip of his finger in water and cool my tongue; for I am tormented in this flame.' But Abraham said, 'Son, remember that in your lifetime you received your good things, and likewise Lazarus evil things; but now he is comforted and you are tormented. And besides all this, between us and you there is a great gulf fixed, so that those who want to pass from here to you cannot, nor can those from there pass to us.'

"Then he said, 'I beg you therefore, father, that you would send him to my father's house, for I have five brothers, that he may testify to them, lest they also come to this place of torment.' Abraham said to him, 'They have Moses and the prophets; let them hear them.' And he said, 'No, father Abraham; but if one goes to them from the dead, they will repent.' But he said to him, 'If they do not hear Moses and the prophets, neither will they be persuaded though one rise from the dead.' "

Then He said to the disciples, "It is impossible that no offenses should come, but woe *to him* through whom they do come! It would be better for him if a millstone were hung around his neck, and he were thrown into the sea, than that he should of-

THE LIFE OF CHRIST

fend one of these little ones. Take heed to yourselves. If your brother sins against you, rebuke him; and if he repents, forgive him. And if he sins against you seven times in a day, and seven times in a day returns to you, saying, 'I repent,' you shall forgive him."

And the apostles said to the Lord, "Increase our faith."

So the Lord said, "If you have faith as a mustard seed, you can say to this mulberry tree, 'Be pulled up by the roots and be planted in the sea,' and it would obey you. And which of you, having a servant plowing or tending sheep, will say to him when he has come in from the field, 'Come at once and sit down to eat'? But will he not rather say to him, 'Prepare something for my supper, and gird yourself and serve me till I have eaten and drunk, and afterward you will eat and drink'? Does he thank that servant because he did the things that were commanded him? I think not. So likewise you, when you have done all those things which you are commanded, say, 'We are unprofitable servants. We have done what was our duty to do.' "

Luke 16:1–17:10

WORSHIP

Then they cried out to the LORD in their trouble,
And He delivered them out of their distresses.
And He led them forth by the right way,
That they might go to a city for a dwelling
    place.
Oh, that *men* would give thanks to the LORD *for*
    His goodness,
And *for* His wonderful works to the children of
    men!
For He satisfies the longing soul,
And fills the hungry soul with goodness.

Psalm 107:6-9

WISDOM

Houses and riches *are* an inheritance from
    fathers,
But a prudent wife *is* from the LORD.

Proverbs 19:14

SW?! SO WHAT?
What does this tell me?

JESUS DEMONSTRATES HIS POWER OVER DEATH
John 11:1-48, 53; Psalm 107:19-22; Proverbs 19:15

Now a certain *man* was sick, Lazarus of Bethany, the town of Mary and her sister Martha. It was *that* Mary who anointed the Lord with fragrant oil and wiped His feet with her hair, whose brother Lazarus was sick. Therefore the sisters sent to Him, saying, "Lord, behold, he whom You love is sick."

When Jesus heard *that,* He said, "This sickness is not unto death, but for the glory of God, that the Son of God may be glorified through it."

Now Jesus loved Martha and her sister and Lazarus. So, when He heard that he was sick, He stayed two more days in the place where He was. Then after this He said to *the* disciples, "Let us go to Judea again."

The disciples said to Him, "Rabbi, lately the Jews sought to stone You, and are You going there again?"

Jesus answered, "Are there not twelve hours in the day? If anyone walks in the day, he does not stumble, because he sees the light of this world. But if one walks in the night, he stumbles, because the light is not in him." These things He said, and after that He said to them, "Our friend Lazarus sleeps, but I go that I may wake him up."

Then His disciples said, "Lord, if he sleeps he will get well." However, Jesus spoke of his death, but they thought that He was speaking about taking rest in sleep.

Then Jesus said to them plainly, "Lazarus is dead. And I am glad for your sakes that I was not there, that you may believe. Nevertheless let us go to him."

Then Thomas, who is called the Twin, said to his fellow disciples, "Let us also go, that we may die with Him."

So when Jesus came, He found that he had already been in the tomb four days. Now Bethany was near Jerusalem, about two miles away. And many of the Jews had joined the women around Martha and Mary, to comfort them concerning their brother.

Now Martha, as soon as she heard that Jesus was coming, went and met Him, but Mary was sitting in the house. Then Martha said to Jesus, "Lord, if You had been here, my brother would not have died. But even now I know that whatever You ask of God, God will give You."

Jesus said to her, "Your brother will rise again."

Martha said to Him, "I know that he will rise again in the resurrection at the last day."

Jesus said to her, "I am the resurrection and the life. He who believes in Me, though he may die, he shall live. And whoever lives and believes in Me shall never die. Do you believe this?"

She said to Him, "Yes, Lord, I believe that You are the Christ, the Son of God, who is to come into the world."

And when she had said these things, she went her way and secretly called Mary her sister, saying, "The Teacher has come and is calling for you." As soon as she heard *that,* she arose quickly and came to Him. Now Jesus had not yet come into the town, but was in the place where Martha met Him. Then the Jews who were with her in the house, and comforting her, when they saw that Mary rose up quickly and went out, followed her, saying, "She is going to the tomb to weep there."

Then, when Mary came where Jesus was, and saw Him, she fell down at His feet, saying to Him, "Lord, if You had been here, my brother would not have died."

Therefore, when Jesus saw her weeping, and the Jews who came with her weeping, He groaned in the spirit and was troubled. And He said, "Where have you laid him?"

They said to Him, "Lord, come and see."

Jesus wept. Then the Jews said, "See how He loved him!"

And some of them said, "Could not this Man, who opened the eyes of the blind, also have kept this man from dying?"

Then Jesus, again groaning in Himself, came to the tomb. It was a cave, and a stone lay against it. Jesus said, "Take away the stone."

Martha, the sister of him who was dead, said to Him, "Lord, by this time there is a stench, for he has been *dead* four days."

Jesus said to her, "Did I not say to you that if

you would believe you would see the glory of God?" Then they took away the stone *from the place* where the dead man was lying. And Jesus lifted up *His* eyes and said, "Father, I thank You that You have heard Me. And I know that You always hear Me, but because of the people who are standing by I said *this*, that they may believe that You sent Me." Now when He had said these things, He cried with a loud voice, "Lazarus, come forth!" And he who had died came out bound hand and foot with graveclothes, and his face was wrapped with a cloth. Jesus said to them, "Loose him, and let him go."

Then many of the Jews who had come to Mary, and had seen the things Jesus did, believed in Him. But some of them went away to the Pharisees and told them the things Jesus did. Then the chief priests and the Pharisees gathered a council and said, "What shall we do? For this Man works many signs. If we let Him alone like this, everyone will believe in Him, and the Romans will come and take away both our place and nation."

Then, from that day on, they plotted to put Him to death.

John 11:1-48, 53

WORSHIP

Then they cried out to the LORD in their trouble,
And He saved them out of their distresses.
He sent His word and healed them,
And delivered *them* from their destructions.
Oh, that *men* would give thanks to the LORD *for*
His goodness,
And *for* His wonderful works to the children of
men!
Let them sacrifice the sacrifices of
thanksgiving,
And declare His works with rejoicing.

Psalm 107:19-22

WISDOM

Laziness casts *one* into a deep sleep,
And an idle person will suffer hunger.

Proverbs 19:15

SW?! SO WHAT?
What does this tell me?

ENTRANCE INTO THE KINGDOM
Luke 18:1-14; Mark 10:1-31; Psalm 107:23-25; Proverbs 19:18

Then He spoke a parable to them, that men always ought to pray and not lose heart, saying: "There was in a certain city a judge who did not fear God nor regard man. Now there was a widow in that city; and she came to him, saying, 'Get justice for me from my adversary.' And he would not for a while; but afterward he said within himself, 'Though I do not fear God nor regard man, yet because this widow troubles me I will avenge her, lest by her continual coming she weary me.' "

Then the Lord said, "Hear what the unjust judge said. And shall God not avenge His own elect who cry out day and night to Him, though He bears long with them? I tell you that He will avenge them speedily. Nevertheless, when the Son of Man comes, will He really find faith on the earth?"

Also He spoke this parable to some who trusted in themselves that they were righteous, and despised others: "Two men went up to the temple to pray, one a Pharisee and the other a tax collector. The Pharisee stood and prayed thus with himself, 'God, I thank You that I am not like other men—extortioners, unjust, adulterers, or even as this tax collector. I fast twice a week; I give tithes of all that I possess.' And the tax collector, standing afar off, would not so much as raise *his* eyes to heaven, but beat his breast, saying, 'God, be merciful to me a sinner!' I tell you, this man went down to his house justified *rather* than the other; for everyone who exalts himself will be humbled, and he who humbles himself will be exalted."

Then He arose from there and came to the region of Judea by the other side of the Jordan. And multitudes gathered to Him again, and as He was accustomed, He taught them again.

The Pharisees came and asked Him, "Is it lawful for a man to divorce *his* wife?" testing Him.

And He answered and said to them, "What did Moses command you?"

They said, "Moses permitted *a man* to write a certificate of divorce, and to dismiss *her.*"

And Jesus answered and said to them, "Because of the hardness of your heart he wrote you this precept. But from the beginning of the creation, God 'made them male and female.' 'For this reason a man shall leave his father and mother and be joined to his wife, and the two shall become one flesh'; so then they are no longer two, but one flesh. Therefore what God has joined together, let not man separate."

In the house His disciples also asked Him again about the same *matter.* So He said to them, "Whoever divorces his wife and marries another commits adultery against her. And if a woman divorces her husband and marries another, she commits adultery."

Then they brought little children to Him, that He might touch them; but the disciples rebuked those who brought *them.* But when Jesus saw *it,* He was greatly displeased and said to them, "Let the little children come to Me, and do not forbid them; for of such is the kingdom of God. Assuredly, I say to you, whoever does not receive the kingdom of God as a little child will by no means enter it." And He took them up in His arms, put *His* hands on them, and blessed them.

Now as He was going out on the road, one came running, knelt before Him, and asked Him, "Good Teacher, what shall I do that I may inherit eternal life?"

So Jesus said to him, "Why do you call Me good? No one *is* good but One, *that is,* God. You know the commandments: 'Do not commit adultery,' 'Do not murder,' 'Do not steal,' 'Do not bear false witness,' 'Do not defraud,' 'Honor your father and your mother.' "

And he answered and said to Him, "Teacher, all these things I have kept from my youth."

Then Jesus, looking at him, loved him, and said to him, "One thing you lack: Go your way, sell whatever you have and give to the poor, and you will have treasure in heaven; and come, take up the cross, and follow Me."

But he was sad at this word, and went away sorrowful, for he had great possessions.

Then Jesus looked around and said to His disciples, "How hard it is for those who have riches to enter the kingdom of God!" And the disciples were astonished at His words. But Jesus answered again and said to them, "Children, how hard it is for those who trust in riches to enter the kingdom of God! It is easier for a camel to go through the eye of a needle than for a rich man to enter the kingdom of God."

And they were greatly astonished, saying among themselves, "Who then can be saved?"

But Jesus looked at them and said, "With men *it is* impossible, but not with God; for with God all things are possible."

Then Peter began to say to Him, "See, we have left all and followed You."

So Jesus answered and said, "Assuredly, I say to you, there is no one who has left house or brothers or sisters or father or mother or wife or children or lands, for My sake and the gospel's, who shall not receive a hundredfold now in this time—houses and brothers and sisters and mothers and children and lands, with persecutions—and in the age to come, eternal life. But many *who are* first will be last, and the last first."

Luke 18:1-14; Mark 10:1-31

WORSHIP

Those who go down to the sea in ships,
Who do business on great waters,
They see the works of the LORD,
And His wonders in the deep.
For He commands and raises the stormy wind,
Which lifts up the waves of the sea.

Psalm 107:23-25

WISDOM

Chasten your son while there is hope,
And do not set your heart on his destruction.

Proverbs 19:18

SW?! SO WHAT?
What does this tell me?

THE FINAL JOURNEY TO JERUSALEM

Matthew 20:17-28; Luke 18:35–19:27; Psalm 107:31-32; Proverbs 19:20

Now Jesus, going up to Jerusalem, took the twelve disciples aside on the road and said to them, "Behold, we are going up to Jerusalem, and the Son of Man will be betrayed to the chief priests and to the scribes; and they will condemn Him to death, and deliver Him to the Gentiles to mock and to scourge and to crucify. And the third day He will rise again."

Then the mother of Zebedee's sons came to Him with her sons, kneeling down and asking something from Him.

And He said to her, "What do you wish?"

She said to Him, "Grant that these two sons of mine may sit, one on Your right hand and the other on the left, in Your kingdom."

But Jesus answered and said, "You do not know what you ask. Are you able to drink the cup that I am about to drink, and be baptized with the baptism that I am baptized with?"

They said to Him, "We are able."

So He said to them, "You will indeed drink My cup, and be baptized with the baptism that I am baptized with; but to sit on My right hand and on My left is not Mine to give, but *it is for those* for whom it is prepared by My Father."

And when the ten heard *it,* they were greatly displeased with the two brothers. But Jesus called them to *Himself* and said, "You know that the rulers of the Gentiles lord it over them, and those who are great exercise authority over them. Yet it shall not be so among you; but whoever desires to become great among you, let him be your servant. And whoever desires to be first among you, let him be your slave— just as the Son of Man did not come to be served, but to serve, and to give His life a ransom for many."

Then it happened, as He was coming near Jericho, that a certain blind man sat by the road begging. And hearing a multitude passing by, he asked what it meant. So they told him that Jesus of Nazareth was passing by. And he cried out, saying, "Jesus, Son of David, have mercy on me!"

Then those who went before warned him that he should be quiet; but he cried out all the more, "Son of David, have mercy on me!"

So Jesus stood still and commanded him to be brought to Him. And when he had come near, He asked him, saying, "What do you want Me to do for you?"

He said, "Lord, that I may receive my sight."

Then Jesus said to him, "Receive your sight; your faith has made you well." And immediately he received his sight, and followed Him, glorifying God. And all the people, when they saw *it,* gave praise to God.

Then *Jesus* entered and passed through Jericho. Now behold, *there was* a man named Zacchaeus who was a chief tax collector, and he was rich. And he sought to see who Jesus was, but could not because of the crowd, for he was of short stature. So he ran ahead and climbed up into a sycamore tree to see Him, for He was going to pass that *way.* And when Jesus came to the place, He looked up and saw him, and said to him, "Zacchaeus, make haste and come down, for today I must stay at your house." So he made haste and came down, and received Him joyfully. But when they saw *it,* they all complained, saying, "He has gone to be a guest with a man who is a sinner."

Then Zacchaeus stood and said to the Lord, "Look, Lord, I give half of my goods to the poor; and if I have taken anything from anyone by false accusation, I restore fourfold."

And Jesus said to him, "Today salvation has come to this house, because he also is a son of Abraham; for the Son of Man has come to seek and to save that which was lost."

Now as they heard these things, He spoke another parable, because He was near Jerusalem and because they thought the kingdom of God would appear immediately. Therefore He said: "A certain nobleman went into a far country to receive for himself a kingdom and to return. So he called ten of his servants, delivered to them ten minas, and said to them, 'Do business till I come.' But his citizens hated him, and sent a delegation after him, saying, 'We will not have this *man* to reign over us.'

"And so it was that when he returned, having

received the kingdom, he then commanded these servants, to whom he had given the money, to be called to him, that he might know how much every man had gained by trading. Then came the first, saying, 'Master, your mina has earned ten minas.' And he said to him, 'Well *done,* good servant; because you were faithful in a very little, have authority over ten cities.' And the second came, saying, 'Master, your mina has earned five minas.' Likewise he said to him, 'You also be over five cities.'

"Then another came, saying, 'Master, here is your mina, which I have kept put away in a handkerchief. For I feared you, because you are an austere man. You collect what you did not deposit, and reap what you did not sow.' And he said to him, 'Out of your own mouth I will judge you, *you* wicked servant. You knew that I was an austere man, collecting what I did not deposit and reaping what I did not sow. Why then did you not put my money in the bank, that at my coming I might have collected it with interest?'

"And he said to those who stood by, 'Take the mina from him, and give *it* to him who has ten minas.' (But they said to him, 'Master, he has ten minas.') 'For I say to you, that to everyone who has will be given; and from him who does not have, even what he has will be taken away from him. But bring here those enemies of mine, who did not want me to reign over them, and slay *them* before me.' "

Matthew 20:17-28; Luke 18:35–19:27

WoRSHiP

Oh, that *men* would give thanks to the LORD *for* His goodness,
And *for* His wonderful works to the children of men!
Let them exalt Him also in the assembly of the people,
And praise Him in the company of the elders.

Psalm 107:31-32

WiSDoM

Listen to counsel and receive instruction,
That you may be wise in your latter days.

Proverbs 19:20

SW?! SO WHAT?
What does this tell me?

JESUS BEGINS HIS FINAL DAYS

Luke 19:28-44; Matthew 21:12-17; John 12:20-46; Psalm 107:41-43; Proverbs 19:21

When He had said this, He went on ahead, going up to Jerusalem. And it came to pass, when He came near to Bethphage and Bethany, at the mountain called Olivet, *that* He sent two of His disciples, saying, "Go into the village opposite *you,* where as you enter you will find a colt tied, on which no one has ever sat. Loose it and bring *it* here. And if anyone asks you, 'Why are you loosing *it?*' thus you shall say to him, 'Because the Lord has need of it.' "

So those who were sent went their way and found *it* just as He had said to them. But as they were loosing the colt, the owners of it said to them, "Why are you loosing the colt?"

And they said, "The Lord has need of him." Then they brought him to Jesus. And they threw their own clothes on the colt, and they set Jesus on him. And as He went, *many* spread their clothes on the road.

Then, as He was now drawing near the descent of the Mount of Olives, the whole multitude of the disciples began to rejoice and praise God with a loud voice for all the mighty works they had seen, saying:

" 'Blessed *is* the King who comes in the
name of the Lord!'
Peace in heaven and glory in the
highest!"

And some of the Pharisees called to Him from the crowd, "Teacher, rebuke Your disciples."

But He answered and said to them, "I tell you that if these should keep silent, the stones would immediately cry out."

Now as He drew near, He saw the city and wept over it, saying, "If you had known, even you, especially in this your day, the things *that make* for your peace! But now they are hidden from your eyes. For days will come upon you when your enemies will build an embankment around you, surround you and close you in on every side, and level you, and your children within you, to the ground; and they will not leave in you one stone upon another, because you did not know the time of your visitation."

Then Jesus went into the temple of God and drove out all those who bought and sold in the temple, and overturned the tables of the money changers and the seats of those who sold doves. And He said to them, "It is written, 'My house shall be called a house of prayer,' but you have made it a 'den of thieves.' "

Then *the* blind and *the* lame came to Him in the temple, and He healed them. But when the chief priests and scribes saw the wonderful things that He did, and the children crying out in the temple and saying, "Hosanna to the Son of David!" they were indignant and said to Him, "Do You hear what these are saying?"

And Jesus said to them, "Yes. Have you never read,

'Out of the mouth of babes and nursing infants
You have perfected praise'?"

Then He left them and went out of the city to Bethany, and He lodged there.

Now there were certain Greeks among those who came up to worship at the feast. Then they came to Philip, who was from Bethsaida of Galilee, and asked him, saying, "Sir, we wish to see Jesus."

Philip came and told Andrew, and in turn Andrew and Philip told Jesus.

But Jesus answered them, saying, "The hour has come that the Son of Man should be glorified. Most assuredly, I say to you, unless a grain of wheat falls into the ground and dies, it remains alone; but if it dies, it produces much grain. He who loves his life will lose it, and he who hates his life in this world will keep it for eternal life. If anyone serves Me, let him follow Me; and where I am, there My servant will be also. If anyone serves Me, him *My* Father will honor.

"Now My soul is troubled, and what shall I say? 'Father, save Me from this hour'? But for this purpose I came to this hour. Father, glorify Your name."

Then a voice came from heaven, *saying,* "I have both glorified *it* and will glorify *it* again."

Therefore the people who stood by and heard *it* said that it had thundered. Others said, "An angel has spoken to Him."

Jesus answered and said, "This voice did not

come because of Me, but for your sake. Now is the judgment of this world; now the ruler of this world will be cast out. And I, if I am lifted up from the earth, will draw all *peoples* to Myself." This He said, signifying by what death He would die.

The people answered Him, "We have heard from the law that the Christ remains forever; and how *can* You say, 'The Son of Man must be lifted up'? Who is this Son of Man?"

Then Jesus said to them, "A little while longer the light is with you. Walk while you have the light, lest darkness overtake you; he who walks in darkness does not know where he is going. While you have the light, believe in the light, that you may become sons of light." These things Jesus spoke, and departed, and was hidden from them.

But although He had done so many signs before them, they did not believe in Him, that the word of Isaiah the prophet might be fulfilled, which he spoke:

"Lord, who has believed our report?
And to whom has the arm of the LORD been
	revealed?"

Therefore they could not believe, because Isaiah said again:

"He has blinded their eyes and hardened their
	hearts,
Lest they should see with *their* eyes,
Lest they should understand with *their* hearts
	and turn,
So that I should heal them."

These things Isaiah said when he saw His glory and spoke of Him.

Nevertheless even among the rulers many believed in Him, but because of the Pharisees they did not confess *Him,* lest they should be put out of the synagogue; for they loved the praise of men more than the praise of God.

Then Jesus cried out and said, "He who believes in Me, believes not in Me but in Him who sent Me. And he who sees Me sees Him who sent Me. I have come *as* a light into the world, that whoever believes in Me should not abide in darkness."

Luke 19:28-44; Matthew 21:12-17; John 12:20-46

WORSHIP

Yet He sets the poor on high, far from
	affliction,
And makes *their* families like a flock.
The righteous see *it* and rejoice,
And all iniquity stops its mouth.

Whoever *is* wise will observe these *things,*
And they will understand the lovingkindness of
	the LORD.

Psalm 107:41-43

WISDOM

There are many plans in a man's heart,
Nevertheless the LORD's counsel—that will
	stand.

Proverbs 19:21

SW?! SO WHAT?
What does this tell me?

THE RELIGIOUS ESTABLISHMENT CHALLENGES JESUS

Luke 20:1-26; Matthew 22:23-46; Psalm 108:3-5; Proverbs 19:22

Now it happened on one of those days, as He taught the people in the temple and preached the gospel, *that* the chief priests and the scribes, together with the elders, confronted *Him* and spoke to Him, saying, "Tell us, by what authority are You doing these things? Or who is he who gave You this authority?"

But He answered and said to them, "I also will ask you one thing, and answer Me: The baptism of John—was it from heaven or from men?"

And they reasoned among themselves, saying, "If we say, 'From heaven,' He will say, 'Why then did you not believe him?' But if we say, 'From men,' all the people will stone us, for they are persuaded that John was a prophet." So they answered that they did not know where *it was* from.

And Jesus said to them, "Neither will I tell you by what authority I do these things."

Then He began to tell the people this parable: "A certain man planted a vineyard, leased it to vinedressers, and went into a far country for a long time. Now at vintage-time he sent a servant to the vinedressers, that they might give him some of the fruit of the vineyard. But the vinedressers beat him and sent *him* away empty-handed. Again he sent another servant; and they beat him also, treated *him* shamefully, and sent *him* away empty-handed. And again he sent a third; and they wounded him also and cast *him* out.

"Then the owner of the vineyard said, 'What shall I do? I will send my beloved son. Probably they will respect *him* when they see him.' But when the vinedressers saw him, they reasoned among themselves, saying, 'This is the heir. Come, let us kill him, that the inheritance may be ours.' So they cast him out of the vineyard and killed *him*. Therefore what will the owner of the vineyard do to them? He will come and destroy those vinedressers and give the vineyard to others."

And when they heard *it* they said, "Certainly not!"

Then He looked at them and said, "What then is this that is written:

'The stone which the builders rejected
Has become the chief cornerstone'?

Whoever falls on that stone will be broken; but on whomever it falls, it will grind him to powder."

And the chief priests and the scribes that very hour sought to lay hands on Him, but they feared the people—for they knew He had spoken this parable against them.

So they watched *Him,* and sent spies who pretended to be righteous, that they might seize on His words, in order to deliver Him to the power and the authority of the governor.

Then they asked Him, saying, "Teacher, we know that You say and teach rightly, and You do not show personal favoritism, but teach the way of God in truth: Is it lawful for us to pay taxes to Caesar or not?"

But He perceived their craftiness, and said to them, "Why do you test Me? Show Me a denarius. Whose image and inscription does it have?"

They answered and said, "Caesar's."

And He said to them, "Render therefore to Caesar the things that are Caesar's, and to God the things that are God's."

But they could not catch Him in His words in the presence of the people. And they marveled at His answer and kept silent.

The same day the Sadducees, who say there is no resurrection, came to Him and asked Him, saying: "Teacher, Moses said that if a man dies, having no children, his brother shall marry his wife and raise up offspring for his brother. Now there were with us seven brothers. The first died after he had married, and having no offspring, left his wife to his brother. Likewise the second also, and the third, even to the seventh. Last of all the woman died also. Therefore, in the resurrection, whose wife of the seven will she be? For they all had her."

Jesus answered and said to them, "You are mistaken, not knowing the Scriptures nor the power of God. For in the resurrection they neither marry nor are given in marriage, but are like angels of God in heaven. But concerning the resurrection of the dead, have you not read what was spoken to you by God, saying, 'I am the God of Abraham, the God of Isaac, and the God of Jacob'? God is not the God of the dead, but of the living." And when the multitudes heard *this,* they were astonished at His teaching.

But when the Pharisees heard that He had silenced the Sadducees, they gathered together. Then one of them, a lawyer, asked *Him a question,* testing Him, and saying, "Teacher, which *is* the great commandment in the law?"

Jesus said to him, " 'You shall love the LORD your God with all your heart, with all your soul, and with all your mind.' This is *the* first and great commandment. And *the* second *is* like it: 'You shall love your neighbor as yourself.' On these two commandments hang all the Law and the Prophets."

While the Pharisees were gathered together, Jesus asked them, saying, "What do you think about the Christ? Whose Son is He?"

They said to Him, "*The Son* of David."

He said to them, "How then does David in the Spirit call Him 'Lord,' saying:

'The LORD said to my Lord,
"Sit at My right hand,
Till I make Your enemies Your footstool" '?

If David then calls Him 'Lord,' how is He his Son?" And no one was able to answer Him a word, nor from that day on did anyone dare question Him anymore.

Luke 20:1-26; Matthew 22:23-46

WORSHIP

I will praise You, O LORD, among the peoples,
And I will sing praises to You among the
    nations.
For Your mercy *is* great above the heavens,
And Your truth *reaches* to the clouds.

Be exalted, O God, above the heavens,
And Your glory above all the earth.

Psalm 108:3-5

WISDOM

What is desired in a man is kindness,
And a poor man is better than a liar.

Proverbs 19:22

SW?! SO WHAT?
What does this tell me?

JESUS CONDEMNS THE RELIGIOUS ESTABLISHMENT
Matthew 23:1-39; Mark 12:41-44; Psalm 108:10-13; Proverbs 19:23

Then Jesus spoke to the multitudes and to His disciples, saying: "The scribes and the Pharisees sit in Moses' seat. Therefore whatever they tell you to observe, *that* observe and do, but do not do according to their works; for they say, and do not do. For they bind heavy burdens, hard to bear, and lay *them* on men's shoulders; but they *themselves* will not move them with one of their fingers. But all their works they do to be seen by men. They make their phylacteries broad and enlarge the borders of their garments. They love the best places at feasts, the best seats in the synagogues, greetings in the marketplaces, and to be called by men, 'Rabbi, Rabbi.' But you, do not be called 'Rabbi'; for One is your Teacher, the Christ, and you are all brethren. Do not call anyone on earth your father; for One is your Father, He who is in heaven. And do not be called teachers; for One is your Teacher, the Christ. But he who is greatest among you shall be your servant. And whoever exalts himself will be humbled, and he who humbles himself will be exalted.

"But woe to you, scribes and Pharisees, hypocrites! For you shut up the kingdom of heaven against men; for you neither go in *yourselves,* nor do you allow those who are entering to go in. Woe to you, scribes and Pharisees, hypocrites! For you devour widows' houses, and for a pretense make long prayers. Therefore you will receive greater condemnation.

"Woe to you, scribes and Pharisees, hypocrites! For you travel land and sea to win one proselyte, and when he is won, you make him twice as much a son of hell as yourselves.

"Woe to you, blind guides, who say, 'Whoever swears by the temple, it is nothing; but whoever swears by the gold of the temple, he is obliged *to perform it.*' Fools and blind! For which is greater, the gold or the temple that sanctifies the gold? And, 'Whoever swears by the altar, it is nothing; but whoever swears by the gift that is on it, he is obliged *to perform it.*' Fools and blind! For which is greater, the gift or the altar that sanctifies the gift? Therefore he who swears by the altar, swears by it and by all things on it. He who swears by the temple, swears by it and by Him who dwells in it. And he who swears by heaven, swears by the throne of God and by Him who sits on it.

"Woe to you, scribes and Pharisees, hypocrites! For you pay tithe of mint and anise and cummin, and have neglected the weightier *matters* of the law: justice and mercy and faith. These you ought to have done, without leaving the others undone. Blind guides, who strain out a gnat and swallow a camel!

"Woe to you, scribes and Pharisees, hypocrites! For you cleanse the outside of the cup and dish, but inside they are full of extortion and self-indulgence. Blind Pharisee, first cleanse the inside of the cup and dish, that the outside of them may be clean also.

"Woe to you, scribes and Pharisees, hypocrites! For you are like whitewashed tombs which indeed appear beautiful outwardly, but inside are full of dead *men*'s bones and all uncleanness. Even so you also outwardly appear righteous to men, but inside you are full of hypocrisy and lawlessness.

"Woe to you, scribes and Pharisees, hypocrites! Because you build the tombs of the prophets and adorn the monuments of the righteous, and say, 'If we had lived in the days of our fathers, we would not have been partakers with them in the blood of the prophets.'

"Therefore you are witnesses against yourselves that you are sons of those who murdered the prophets. Fill up, then, the measure of your fathers' *guilt.* Serpents, brood of vipers! How can you escape the condemnation of hell? Therefore, indeed, I send you prophets, wise men, and scribes: *some* of them you will kill and crucify, and *some* of them you will scourge in your synagogues and persecute from city to city, that on you may come all the righteous blood shed on the earth, from the blood of righteous Abel to the blood of Zechariah, son of Berechiah, whom you murdered between the temple and the altar. Assuredly, I say to you, all these things will come upon this generation.

"O Jerusalem, Jerusalem, the one who kills the prophets and stones those who are sent to her!

How often I wanted to gather your children together, as a hen gathers her chicks under *her* wings, but you were not willing! See! Your house is left to you desolate; for I say to you, you shall see Me no more till you say, 'Blessed *is* He who comes in the name of the Lord!' "

Now Jesus sat opposite the treasury and saw how the people put money into the treasury. And many *who were* rich put in much. Then one poor widow came and threw in two mites, which make a quadrans. So He called His disciples to *Himself* and said to them, "Assuredly, I say to you that this poor widow has put in more than all those who have given to the treasury; for they all put in out of their abundance, but she out of her poverty put in all that she had, her whole livelihood."

Matthew 23:1-39; Mark 12:41-44

WORSHIP

Who will bring me *into* the strong city?
Who will lead me to Edom?
Is it not *You*, O God, *who* cast us off?
And *You*, O God, *who* did not go out with our
  armies?
Give us help from trouble,
For the help of man is useless.
Through God we will do valiantly,
For *it is* He *who* shall tread down our enemies.

Psalm 108:10-13

WISDOM

The fear of the Lord *leads* to life,
And *he who has it* will abide in satisfaction;
He will not be visited with evil.

Proverbs 19:23

**SW?! SO WHAT?
What does this tell me?**

JESUS PREDICTS HIS SECOND COMING

Mark 13:1-33; Matthew 25:31-46; Psalm 109:1-5; Proverbs 19:27

Then as He went out of the temple, one of His disciples said to Him, "Teacher, see what manner of stones and what buildings *are* here!"

And Jesus answered and said to him, "Do you see these great buildings? Not *one* stone shall be left upon another, that shall not be thrown down."

Now as He sat on the Mount of Olives opposite the temple, Peter, James, John, and Andrew asked Him privately, "Tell us, when will these things be? And what *will be* the sign when all these things will be fulfilled?"

And Jesus, answering them, began to say: "Take heed that no one deceives you. For many will come in My name, saying, 'I am *He*,' and will deceive many. But when you hear of wars and rumors of wars, do not be troubled; for *such things* must happen, but the end *is* not yet. For nation will rise against nation, and kingdom against kingdom. And there will be earthquakes in various places, and there will be famines and troubles. These *are* the beginnings of sorrows.

"But watch out for yourselves, for they will deliver you up to councils, and you will be beaten in the synagogues. You will be brought before rulers and kings for My sake, for a testimony to them. And the gospel must first be preached to all the nations. But when they arrest *you* and deliver you up, do not worry beforehand, or premeditate what you will speak. But whatever is given you in that hour, speak that; for it is not you who speak, but the Holy Spirit. Now brother will betray brother to death, and a father *his* child; and children will rise up against parents and cause them to be put to death. And you will be hated by all for My name's sake. But he who endures to the end shall be saved.

"So when you see the 'abomination of desolation,' spoken of by Daniel the prophet, standing where it ought not" (let the reader understand), "then let those who are in Judea flee to the mountains. Let him who is on the housetop not go down into the house, nor enter to take anything out of his house. And let him who is in the field not go back to get his clothes. But woe to those who are pregnant and to those who are nursing babies in those days! And pray that your flight may not be in winter. For *in* those days there will be tribulation, such as has not been since the beginning of the creation which God created until this time, nor ever shall be. And unless the Lord had shortened those days, no flesh would be saved; but for the elect's sake, whom He chose, He shortened the days.

"Then if anyone says to you, 'Look, here *is* the Christ!' or, 'Look, *He is* there!' do not believe it. For false christs and false prophets will rise and show signs and wonders to deceive, if possible, even the elect. But take heed; see, I have told you all things beforehand.

"But in those days, after that tribulation, the sun will be darkened, and the moon will not give its light; the stars of heaven will fall, and the powers in the heavens will be shaken. Then they will see the Son of Man coming in the clouds with great power and glory. And then He will send His angels, and gather together His elect from the four winds, from the farthest part of earth to the farthest part of heaven.

"Now learn this parable from the fig tree: When its branch has already become tender, and puts forth leaves, you know that summer is near. So you also, when you see these things happening, know that it is near—at the doors! Assuredly, I say to you, this generation will by no means pass away till all these things take place. Heaven and earth will pass away, but My words will by no means pass away.

"But of that day and hour no one knows, not even the angels in heaven, nor the Son, but only the Father. Take heed, watch and pray; for you do not know when the time is.

"When the Son of Man comes in His glory, and all the holy angels with Him, then He will sit on the throne of His glory. All the nations will be gathered before Him, and He will separate them one from another, as a shepherd divides *his* sheep from the goats. And He will set the sheep on His right hand, but the goats on the left. Then the King will say to those on His right hand, 'Come, you blessed of My Father, inherit the kingdom prepared for you from the foundation of the world: for I was hungry and you gave Me food; I was thirsty and you gave Me drink; I was a stranger and you took Me in; I *was* naked and you clothed Me; I was sick and you visited Me; I was in prison and you came to Me.'

"Then the righteous will answer Him, saying, 'Lord, when did we see You hungry and feed *You,* or thirsty and give *You* drink? When did we see You a stranger and take *You* in, or naked and clothe *You*? Or when did we see You sick, or in prison, and come to You?' And the King will answer and say to them, 'Assuredly, I say to you, inasmuch as you did *it* to one of the least of these My brethren, you did *it* to Me.'

"Then He will also say to those on the left hand, 'Depart from Me, you cursed, into the everlasting fire prepared for the devil and his angels: for I was hungry and you gave Me no food; I was thirsty and you gave Me no drink; I was a stranger and you did not take Me in, naked and you did not clothe Me, sick and in prison and you did not visit Me.'

"Then they also will answer Him, saying, 'Lord, when did we see You hungry or thirsty or a stranger or naked or sick or in prison, and did not minister to You?' Then He will answer them, saying, 'Assuredly, I say to you, inasmuch as you did not do *it* to one of the least of these, you did not do *it* to Me.' And these will go away into everlasting punishment, but the righteous into eternal life."

Mark 13:1-33; Matthew 25:31-46

WORSHIP

Do not keep silent,
O God of my praise!
For the mouth of the wicked and the mouth of
    the deceitful
Have opened against me;
They have spoken against me with a lying
    tongue.
They have also surrounded me with words of
    hatred,
And fought against me without a cause.
In return for my love they are my accusers,
But I *give myself to* prayer.
Thus they have rewarded me evil for good,
And hatred for my love.

Psalm 109:1-5

WISDOM

Cease listening to instruction, my son,
And you will stray from the words of
    knowledge.

Proverbs 19:27

SW?! **SO WHAT?**
What does this tell me?

THE PLOT TO KILL JESUS AND THE LAST SUPPER

Matthew 26:1-20; John 13:3-5, 12-19, 21; Matthew 26:22-30; Psalm 109:21-23; Proverbs 20:1

Now it came to pass, when Jesus had finished all these sayings, *that* He said to His disciples, "You know that after two days is the Passover, and the Son of Man will be delivered up to be crucified."

Then the chief priests, the scribes, and the elders of the people assembled at the palace of the high priest, who was called Caiaphas, and plotted to take Jesus by trickery and kill *Him*. But they said, "Not during the feast, lest there be an uproar among the people."

And when Jesus was in Bethany at the house of Simon the leper, a woman came to Him having an alabaster flask of very costly fragrant oil, and she poured *it* on His head as He sat *at the table*. But when His disciples saw *it,* they were indignant, saying, "Why this waste? For this fragrant oil might have been sold for much and given to *the* poor."

But when Jesus was aware of *it,* He said to them, "Why do you trouble the woman? For she has done a good work for Me. For you have the poor with you always, but Me you do not have always. For in pouring this fragrant oil on My body, she did *it* for My burial. Assuredly, I say to you, wherever this gospel is preached in the whole world, what this woman has done will also be told as a memorial to her."

Then one of the twelve, called Judas Iscariot, went to the chief priests and said, "What are you willing to give me if I deliver Him to you?" And they counted out to him thirty pieces of silver. So from that time he sought opportunity to betray Him.

Now on the first *day* of the *Feast of* the Unleavened Bread the disciples came to Jesus, saying to Him, "Where do You want us to prepare for You to eat the Passover?"

And He said, "Go into the city to a certain man, and say to him, 'The Teacher says, "My time is at hand; I will keep the Passover at your house with My disciples." ' "

So the disciples did as Jesus had directed them; and they prepared the Passover.

When evening had come, He sat down with the twelve.

Jesus, knowing that the Father had given all things into His hands, and that He had come from God and was going to God, rose from supper and laid aside His garments, took a towel and girded Himself. After that, He poured water into a basin and began to wash the disciples' feet, and to wipe *them* with the towel with which He was girded.

So when He had washed their feet, taken His garments, and sat down again, He said to them, "Do you know what I have done to you? You call me Teacher and Lord, and you say well, for *so* I am. If I then, *your* Lord and Teacher, have washed your feet, you also ought to wash one another's feet. For I have given you an example, that you should do as I have done to you. Most assuredly, I say to you, a servant is not greater than his master; nor is he who is sent greater than he who sent him. If you know these things, blessed are you if you do them.

"I do not speak concerning all of you. I know whom I have chosen; but that the Scripture may be fulfilled, 'He who eats bread with Me has lifted up his heel against Me.' Now I tell you before it comes, that when it does come to pass, you may believe that I am *He*."

When Jesus had said these things, He was troubled in spirit, and testified and said, "Most assuredly, I say to you, one of you will betray Me."

And they were exceedingly sorrowful, and each of them began to say to Him, "Lord, is it I?"

He answered and said, "He who dipped *his* hand with Me in the dish will betray Me. The Son of Man indeed goes just as it is written of Him, but woe to that man by whom the Son of Man is betrayed! It would have been good for that man if he had not been born."

Then Judas, who was betraying Him, answered and said, "Rabbi, is it I?"

He said to him, "You have said it."

And as they were eating, Jesus took bread, blessed and broke *it,* and gave *it* to the disciples and said, "Take, eat; this is My body."

Then He took the cup, and gave thanks, and

gave *it* to them, saying, "Drink from it, all of you. For this is My blood of the new covenant, which is shed for many for the remission of sins. But I say to you, I will not drink of this fruit of the vine from now on until that day when I drink it new with you in My Father's kingdom."

And when they had sung a hymn, they went out to the Mount of Olives.

Matthew 26:1-20; John 13:3-5, 12-19, 21;
Matthew 26:22-30

WORSHIP

But You, O GOD the Lord,
Deal with me for Your name's sake;
Because Your mercy *is* good, deliver me.
For I *am* poor and needy,
And my heart is wounded within me.
I am gone like a shadow when it lengthens;
I am shaken off like a locust.

Psalm 109:21-23

WISDOM

Wine *is* a mocker,
Strong drink *is* a brawler,
And whoever is led astray by it is not wise.

Proverbs 20:1

SW?! SO WHAT?
What does this tell me?

LAST WORDS AT THE LAST SUPPER: PART ONE

John 14:1–15:11; Psalm 109:26–28; Proverbs 20:4

"Let not your heart be troubled; you believe in God, believe also in Me. In My Father's house are many mansions; if *it were* not *so,* I would have told you. I go to prepare a place for you. And if I go and prepare a place for you, I will come again and receive you to Myself; that where I am, *there* you may be also. And where I go you know, and the way you know."

Thomas said to Him, "Lord, we do not know where You are going, and how can we know the way?"

Jesus said to him, "I am the way, the truth, and the life. No one comes to the Father except through Me.

"If you had known Me, you would have known My Father also; and from now on you know Him and have seen Him."

Philip said to Him, "Lord, show us the Father, and it is sufficient for us."

Jesus said to him, "Have I been with you so long, and yet you have not known Me, Philip? He who has seen Me has seen the Father; so how can you say, 'Show us the Father'? Do you not believe that I am in the Father, and the Father in Me? The words that I speak to you I do not speak on My own *authority;* but the Father who dwells in Me does the works. Believe Me that I *am* in the Father and the Father in Me, or else believe Me for the sake of the works themselves.

"Most assuredly, I say to you, he who believes in Me, the works that I do he will do also; and greater *works* than these he will do, because I go to My Father. And whatever you ask in My name, that I will do, that the Father may be glorified in the Son. If you ask anything in My name, I will do *it.*

"If you love Me, keep My commandments. And I will pray the Father, and He will give you another Helper, that He may abide with you forever—the Spirit of truth, whom the world cannot receive, because it neither sees Him nor knows Him; but you know Him, for He dwells with you and will be in you. I will not leave you orphans; I will come to you.

"A little while longer and the world will see Me no more, but you will see Me. Because I live, you will live also. At that day you will know that I *am* in My Father, and you in Me, and I in you. He who has My commandments and keeps them, it is he who loves Me. And he who loves Me will be loved by My Father, and I will love him and manifest Myself to him."

Judas (not Iscariot) said to Him, "Lord, how is it that You will manifest Yourself to us, and not to the world?"

Jesus answered and said to him, "If anyone loves Me, he will keep My word; and My Father will love him, and We will come to him and make Our home with him. He who does not love Me does not keep My words; and the word which you hear is not Mine but the Father's who sent Me.

"These things I have spoken to you while being present with you. But the Helper, the Holy Spirit, whom the Father will send in My name, He will teach you all things, and bring to your remembrance all things that I said to you. Peace I leave with you, My peace I give to you; not as the world gives do I give to you. Let not your heart be troubled, neither let it be afraid. You have heard Me say to you, 'I am going away and coming *back* to you.' If you loved Me, you would rejoice because I said, 'I am going to the Father,' for My Father is greater than I.

"And now I have told you before it comes, that when it does come to pass, you may believe. I will no longer talk much with you, for the ruler of this world is coming, and he has nothing in Me. But that the world may know that I love the Father, and as the Father gave Me commandment, so I do. Arise, let us go from here.

"I am the true vine, and My Father is the vinedresser. Every branch in Me that does not bear fruit He takes away; and every *branch* that bears fruit He prunes, that it may bear more fruit. You are already clean because of the word which I have spoken to you. Abide in Me, and I in you. As the branch cannot bear fruit of itself, unless it abides in the vine, neither can you, unless you abide in Me.

"I am the vine, you *are* the branches. He who abides in Me, and I in him, bears much fruit; for without Me you can do nothing. If anyone does not abide in Me, he is cast out as a branch and is withered; and they gather them and throw *them* into the fire, and they are burned. If you abide in Me, and My words abide in you, you will ask what you desire, and it shall be done for you. By this My Father is glorified, that you bear much fruit; so you will be My disciples.

"As the Father loved Me, I also have loved you; abide in My love. If you keep My commandments, you will abide in My love, just as I have kept My Father's commandments and abide in His love.

"These things I have spoken to you, that My joy may remain in you, and *that* your joy may be full."

John 14:1–15:11

WORSHIP

Help me, O LORD my God!
Oh, save me according to Your mercy,
That they may know that this *is* Your hand—
That You, LORD, have done it!
Let them curse, but You bless;
When they arise, let them be ashamed,
But let Your servant rejoice.

Psalm 109:26-28

WISDOM

The lazy *man* will not plow because of winter;
He will beg during harvest and *have* nothing.

Proverbs 20:4

SW?! SO WHAT?
What does this tell me?

LAST WORDS AT THE LAST SUPPER: PART TWO

John 15:12–16:33; Psalm 109:30–31; Proverbs 20:5

"This is My commandment, that you love one another as I have loved you. Greater love has no one than this, than to lay down one's life for his friends. You are My friends if you do whatever I command you. No longer do I call you servants, for a servant does not know what his master is doing; but I have called you friends, for all things that I heard from My Father I have made known to you. You did not choose Me, but I chose you and appointed you that you should go and bear fruit, and *that* your fruit should remain, that whatever you ask the Father in My name He may give you. These things I command you, that you love one another.

"If the world hates you, you know that it hated Me before *it hated* you. If you were of the world, the world would love its own. Yet because you are not of the world, but I chose you out of the world, therefore the world hates you. Remember the word that I said to you, 'A servant is not greater than his master.' If they persecuted Me, they will also persecute you. If they kept My word, they will keep yours also. But all these things they will do to you for My name's sake, because they do not know Him who sent Me. If I had not come and spoken to them, they would have no sin, but now they have no excuse for their sin. He who hates Me hates My Father also. If I had not done among them the works which no one else did, they would have no sin; but now they have seen and also hated both Me and My Father. But *this happened* that the word might be fulfilled which is written in their law, 'They hated Me without a cause.'

"But when the Helper comes, whom I shall send to you from the Father, the Spirit of truth who proceeds from the Father, He will testify of Me. And you also will bear witness, because you have been with Me from the beginning.

"These things I have spoken to you, that you should not be made to stumble. They will put you out of the synagogues; yes, the time is coming that whoever kills you will think that he offers God service. And these things they will do to you because they have not known the Father nor Me. But these things I have told you, that when the time comes, you may remember that I told you of them.

"And these things I did not say to you at the beginning, because I was with you.

"But now I go away to Him who sent Me, and none of you asks Me, 'Where are You going?' But because I have said these things to you, sorrow has filled your heart. Nevertheless I tell you the truth. It is to your advantage that I go away; for if I do not go away, the Helper will not come to you; but if I depart, I will send Him to you. And when He has come, He will convict the world of sin, and of righteousness, and of judgment: of sin, because they do not believe in Me; of righteousness, because I go to My Father and you see Me no more; of judgment, because the ruler of this world is judged.

"I still have many things to say to you, but you cannot bear *them* now. However, when He, the Spirit of truth, has come, He will guide you into all truth; for He will not speak on His own *authority*, but whatever He hears He will speak; and He will tell you things to come. He will glorify Me, for He will take of what is Mine and declare *it* to you. All things that the Father has are Mine. Therefore I said that He will take of Mine and declare *it* to you.

"A little while, and you will not see Me; and again a little while, and you will see Me, because I go to the Father."

Then *some* of His disciples said among themselves, "What is this that He says to us, 'A little while, and you will not see Me; and again a little while, and you will see Me'; and, 'because I go to the Father'?" They said therefore, "What is this that He says, 'A little while'? We do not know what He is saying."

Now Jesus knew that they desired to ask Him, and He said to them, "Are you inquiring among yourselves about what I said, 'A little while, and you will not see Me; and again a little while, and you will see Me'? Most assuredly, I say to you that you will weep and lament, but the world will rejoice; and you will be sorrowful, but your sorrow will be turned into joy. A woman, when she is in labor, has sorrow because her hour has come; but as soon as she has given birth to the child, she no longer remembers the anguish, for joy that a human being has been born into the world. Therefore you now have sorrow; but I will see you again and your heart will rejoice, and your joy no one will take from you.

"And in that day you will ask Me nothing. Most assuredly, I say to you, whatever you ask the Father in My name He will give you. Until now you have asked nothing in My name. Ask, and you will receive, that your joy may be full.

"These things I have spoken to you in figurative language; but the time is coming when I will no longer speak to you in figurative language, but I will tell you plainly about the Father. In that day you will ask in My name, and I do not say to you that I shall pray the Father for you; for the Father Himself loves you, because you have loved Me, and have believed that I came forth from God. I came forth from the Father and have come into the world. Again, I leave the world and go to the Father."

His disciples said to Him, "See, now You are speaking plainly, and using no figure of speech! Now we are sure that You know all things, and have no need that anyone should question You. By this we believe that You came forth from God."

Jesus answered them, "Do you now believe? Indeed the hour is coming, yes, has now come, that you will be scattered, each to his own, and will leave Me alone. And yet I am not alone, because the Father is with Me. These things I have spoken to you, that in Me you may have peace. In the world you will have tribulation; but be of good cheer, I have overcome the world."

John 15:12–16:33

WoRSHiP

I will greatly praise the LORD with my mouth;
Yes, I will praise Him among the multitude.
For He shall stand at the right hand of the poor,
To save *him* from those who condemn him.

Psalm 109:30-31

WiSDoM

Counsel in the heart of man *is like* deep water,
But a man of understanding will draw it out.

Proverbs 20:5

SW?! SO WHAT? What does this tell me?

JESUS PREPARES HIMSELF FOR THE CROSS IN PRAYER

John 17; Mark 14:26-42; Psalm 110:1-3; Proverbs 20:6

Jesus spoke these words, lifted up His eyes to heaven, and said: "Father, the hour has come. Glorify Your Son, that Your Son also may glorify You, as You have given Him authority over all flesh, that He should give eternal life to as many as You have given Him. And this is eternal life, that they may know You, the only true God, and Jesus Christ whom You have sent. I have glorified You on the earth. I have finished the work which You have given Me to do. And now, O Father, glorify Me together with Yourself, with the glory which I had with You before the world was.

"I have manifested Your name to the men whom You have given Me out of the world. They were Yours, You gave them to Me, and they have kept Your word. Now they have known that all things which You have given Me are from You. For I have given to them the words which You have given Me; and they have received *them,* and have known surely that I came forth from You; and they have believed that You sent Me.

"I pray for them. I do not pray for the world but for those whom You have given Me, for they are Yours. And all Mine are Yours, and Yours are Mine, and I am glorified in them. Now I am no longer in the world, but these are in the world, and I come to You. Holy Father, keep through Your name those whom You have given Me, that they may be one as We *are.* While I was with them in the world, I kept them in Your name. Those whom You gave Me I have kept; and none of them is lost except the son of perdition, that the Scripture might be fulfilled. But now I come to You, and these things I speak in the world, that they may have My joy fulfilled in themselves. I have given them Your word; and the world has hated them because they are not of the world, just as I am not of the world. I do not pray that You should take them out of the world, but that You should keep them from the evil one.

They are not of the world, just as I am not of the world. Sanctify them by Your truth. Your word is truth. As You sent Me into the world, I also have sent them into the world. And for their sakes I sanctify Myself, that they also may be sanctified by the truth.

"I do not pray for these alone, but also for those who will believe in Me through their word; that they all may be one, as You, Father, *are* in Me, and I in You; that they also may be one in Us, that the world may believe that You sent Me. And the glory which You gave Me I have given them, that they may be one just as We are one: I in them, and You in Me; that they may be made perfect in one, and that the world may know that You have sent Me, and have loved them as You have loved Me.

"Father, I desire that they also whom You gave Me may be with Me where I am, that they may behold My glory which You have given Me; for You loved Me before the foundation of the world. O righteous Father! The world has not known You, but I have known You; and these have known that You sent Me. And I have declared to them Your name, and will declare *it,* that the love with which You loved Me may be in them, and I in them."

And when they had sung a hymn, they went out to the Mount of Olives.

Then Jesus said to them, "All of you will be made to stumble because of Me this night, for it is written:

'I will strike the Shepherd,
And the sheep will be scattered.'

"But after I have been raised, I will go before you to Galilee."

Peter said to Him, "Even if all are made to stumble, yet I *will* not *be.*"

Jesus said to him, "Assuredly, I say to you that today, *even* this night, before the rooster crows twice, you will deny Me three times."

But he spoke more vehemently, "If I have to die with You, I will not deny You!"

And they all said likewise.

Then they came to a place which was named Gethsemane; and He said to His disciples, "Sit here while I pray." And He took Peter, James, and John with Him, and He began to be troubled and deeply distressed. Then He said to them, "My soul is exceedingly sorrowful, *even* to death. Stay here and watch."

He went a little farther, and fell on the ground, and prayed that if it were possible, the hour might pass from Him. And He said, "Abba, Father, all things *are* possible for You. Take this cup away from Me; nevertheless, not what I will, but what You *will*."

Then He came and found them sleeping, and said to Peter, "Simon, are you sleeping? Could you not watch one hour? Watch and pray, lest you enter into temptation. The spirit indeed *is* willing, but the flesh *is* weak."

Again He went away and prayed, and spoke the same words. And when He returned, He found them asleep again, for their eyes were heavy; and they did not know what to answer Him.

Then He came the third time and said to them, "Are you still sleeping and resting? It is enough! The hour has come; behold, the Son of Man is being betrayed into the hands of sinners. Rise, let us be going. See, My betrayer is at hand."

John 17; Mark 14:26-42

WORSHIP

The LORD said to my Lord,
"Sit at My right hand,
Till I make Your enemies Your footstool."
The LORD shall send the rod of Your strength
    out of Zion.
Rule in the midst of Your enemies!

Your people *shall be* volunteers
In the day of Your power;
In the beauties of holiness, from the womb of
    the morning,
You have the dew of Your youth.

Psalm 110:1-3

WISDOM

Most men will proclaim each his own
    goodness,
But who can find a faithful man?

Proverbs 20:6

SW?! SO WHAT?
What does this tell me?

JESUS IS BETRAYED, ARRESTED AND TRIED

Luke 22:47–23:11, 13-25; Psalm 110:4-7; Proverbs 20:7

And while He was still speaking, behold, a multitude; and he who was called Judas, one of the twelve, went before them and drew near to Jesus to kiss Him. But Jesus said to him, "Judas, are you betraying the Son of Man with a kiss?"

When those around Him saw what was going to happen, they said to Him, "Lord, shall we strike with the sword?" And one of them struck the servant of the high priest and cut off his right ear.

But Jesus answered and said, "Permit even this." And He touched his ear and healed him.

Then Jesus said to the chief priests, captains of the temple, and the elders who had come to Him, "Have you come out, as against a robber, with swords and clubs? When I was with you daily in the temple, you did not try to seize Me. But this is your hour, and the power of darkness."

Having arrested Him, they led *Him* and brought Him into the high priest's house. But Peter followed at a distance. Now when they had kindled a fire in the midst of the courtyard and sat down together, Peter sat among them. And a certain servant girl, seeing him as he sat by the fire, looked intently at him and said, "This man was also with Him."

But he denied Him, saying, "Woman, I do not know Him."

And after a little while another saw him and said, "You also are of them."

But Peter said, "Man, I am not!"

Then after about an hour had passed, another confidently affirmed, saying, "Surely this *fellow* also was with Him, for he is a Galilean."

But Peter said, "Man, I do not know what you are saying!"

Immediately, while he was still speaking, the rooster crowed. And the Lord turned and looked at Peter. And Peter remembered the word of the Lord, how He had said to him, "Before the rooster crows, you will deny Me three times." So Peter went out and wept bitterly.

Now the men who held Jesus mocked Him and beat Him. And having blindfolded Him, they struck Him on the face and asked Him, saying, "Prophesy! Who is the one who struck You?" And many other things they blasphemously spoke against Him.

As soon as it was day, the elders of the people, both chief priests and scribes, came together and led Him into their council, saying, "If You are the Christ, tell us."

But He said to them, "If I tell you, you will by no means believe. And if I also ask *you,* you will by no means answer Me or let *Me* go. Hereafter the Son of Man will sit on the right hand of the power of God."

Then they all said, "Are You then the Son of God?"

So He said to them, "You *rightly* say that I am."

And they said, "What further testimony do we need? For we have heard it ourselves from His own mouth."

Then the whole multitude of them arose and led Him to Pilate. And they began to accuse Him, saying, "We found this *fellow* perverting the nation, and forbidding to pay taxes to Caesar, saying that He Himself is Christ, a King."

Then Pilate asked Him, saying, "Are You the King of the Jews?"

He answered him and said, "*It is as* you say."

So Pilate said to the chief priests and the crowd, "I find no fault in this Man."

But they were the more fierce, saying, "He stirs up the people, teaching throughout all Judea, beginning from Galilee to this place."

When Pilate heard of Galilee, he asked if the Man were a Galilean. And as soon as he knew that He belonged to Herod's jurisdiction, he sent Him to Herod, who was also in Jerusalem at that time. Now when Herod saw Jesus, he was exceedingly glad; for he had desired for a long *time* to see Him, because he had heard many things about Him, and he hoped to see some miracle done by Him. Then he questioned Him with many words, but He answered him nothing. And the chief priests and scribes stood and vehemently accused Him. Then Herod, with his men of war, treated Him with contempt and mocked *Him,* arrayed Him in a gorgeous robe, and sent Him back to Pilate.

Then Pilate, when he had called together the chief priests, the rulers, and the people, said to them, "You have brought this Man to me, as one who misleads the people. And indeed, having examined *Him* in your presence, I have found no fault in this Man concerning those things of which you accuse Him; no, neither did Herod, for I sent you back to him; and indeed nothing deserving of death has been done by Him. I will therefore chastise Him and release *Him*" (for it was necessary for him to release one to them at the feast).

And they all cried out at once, saying, "Away with this *Man,* and release to us Barabbas"—who had been thrown into prison for a certain rebellion made in the city, and for murder.

Pilate, therefore, wishing to release Jesus, again called out to them. But they shouted, saying, "Crucify *Him,* crucify Him!"

Then he said to them the third time, "Why, what evil has He done? I have found no reason for death in Him. I will therefore chastise Him and let *Him* go."

But they were insistent, demanding with loud voices that He be crucified. And the voices of these men and of the chief priests prevailed. So Pilate gave sentence that it should be as they requested. And he released to them the one they requested, who for rebellion and murder had been thrown into prison; but he delivered Jesus to their will.

Luke 22:47–23:11, 13-25

WORSHIP

The LORD has sworn
And will not relent,
"You *are* a priest forever
According to the order of Melchizedek."

The Lord *is* at Your right hand;
He shall execute kings in the day of His
    wrath.
He shall judge among the nations,
He shall fill *the places* with dead bodies,
He shall execute the heads of many
    countries.
He shall drink of the brook by the wayside;
Therefore He shall lift up the head.

Psalm 110:4-7

WISDOM

The righteous *man* walks in his integrity;
His children *are* blessed after him.

Proverbs 20:7

SW?! **SO WHAT?**
What does this tell me?

JESUS IS BEATEN, CRUCIFIED AND BURIED
Matthew 27:27-66; Psalm 111:7-10; Proverbs 20:11

Then the soldiers of the governor took Jesus into the Praetorium and gathered the whole garrison around Him. And they stripped Him and put a scarlet robe on Him. When they had twisted a crown of thorns, they put *it* on His head, and a reed in His right hand. And they bowed the knee before Him and mocked Him, saying, "Hail, King of the Jews!" Then they spat on Him, and took the reed and struck Him on the head. And when they had mocked Him, they took the robe off Him, put His *own* clothes on Him, and led Him away to be crucified.

Now as they came out, they found a man of Cyrene, Simon by name. Him they compelled to bear His cross. And when they had come to a place called Golgotha, that is to say, Place of a Skull, they gave Him sour wine mingled with gall to drink. But when He had tasted *it,* He would not drink.

Then they crucified Him, and divided His garments, casting lots, that it might be fulfilled which was spoken by the prophet:

"They divided My garments among them,
And for My clothing they cast lots."

Sitting down, they kept watch over Him there. And they put up over His head the accusation written against Him:

THIS IS JESUS THE KING OF THE JEWS.

Then two robbers were crucified with Him, one on the right and another on the left.

And those who passed by blasphemed Him, wagging their heads and saying, "You who destroy the temple and build *it* in three days, save Yourself! If You are the Son of God, come down from the cross."

Likewise the chief priests also, mocking with the scribes and elders, said, "He saved others; Himself He cannot save. If He is the King of Israel, let Him now come down from the cross, and we will believe Him. He trusted in God; let Him deliver Him now if He will have Him; for He said, 'I am the Son of God.'"

Even the robbers who were crucified with Him reviled Him with the same thing.

Now from the sixth hour until the ninth hour there was darkness over all the land. And about the ninth hour Jesus cried out with a loud voice, saying, "Eli, Eli, lama sabachthani?" that is, "My God, My God, why have You forsaken Me?"

Some of those who stood there, when they heard *that,* said, "This Man is calling for Elijah!" Immediately one of them ran and took a sponge, filled *it* with sour wine and put *it* on a reed, and offered it to Him to drink.

The rest said, "Let Him alone; let us see if Elijah will come to save Him."

And Jesus cried out again with a loud voice, and yielded up His spirit.

Then, behold, the veil of the temple was torn in two from top to bottom; and the earth quaked, and the rocks were split, and the graves were opened; and many bodies of the saints who had fallen asleep were raised; and coming out of the graves after His resurrection, they went into the holy city and appeared to many.

So when the centurion and those with him, who were guarding Jesus, saw the earthquake and the things that had happened, they feared greatly, saying, "Truly this was the Son of God!"

And many women who followed Jesus from Galilee, ministering to Him, were there looking on from afar, among whom were Mary Magdalene, Mary the mother of James and Joses, and the mother of Zebedee's sons.

Now when evening had come, there came a rich man from Arimathea, named Joseph, who himself had also become a disciple of Jesus. This man went to Pilate and asked for the body of Jesus. Then Pilate commanded the body to be given to him. When Joseph had taken the body, he wrapped it in a clean linen cloth, and laid it in his new tomb which he had hewn out of the rock; and he rolled a large stone against the door of the tomb, and departed. And Mary Magdalene was there, and the other Mary, sitting opposite the tomb.

On the next day, which followed the Day of Preparation, the chief priests and Pharisees gathered together to Pilate, saying, "Sir, we remember, while He was still alive, how that deceiver said, 'After three days I will rise.' Therefore command that the tomb be made secure until the third day, lest His disciples come by night and steal Him *away,* and say to the people, 'He has risen from the dead.' So the last deception will be worse than the first."

Pilate said to them, "You have a guard; go your way, make *it* as secure as you know how." So they went and made the tomb secure, sealing the stone and setting the guard.

Matthew 27:27-66

WORSHIP

The works of His hands *are* verity and justice;
All His precepts *are* sure.
They stand fast forever and ever,
And are done in truth and uprightness.
He has sent redemption to His people;
He has commanded His covenant forever:
Holy and awesome *is* His name.

The fear of the LORD *is* the beginning of
wisdom;
A good understanding have all those who do
His commandments.
His praise endures forever.

Psalm 111:7-10

WISDOM

Even a child is known by his deeds,
Whether what he does *is* pure and right.

Proverbs 20:11

SW?! SO WHAT?
What does this tell me?

JESUS IS RAISED AND THE DISCIPLES ARE AMAZED
Matthew 28:1-15; Luke 24:13-35; John 20:19-29; Psalm 112:1-4; Proverbs 20:12

Now after the Sabbath, as the first *day* of the week began to dawn, Mary Magdalene and the other Mary came to see the tomb. And behold, there was a great earthquake; for an angel of the Lord descended from heaven, and came and rolled back the stone from the door, and sat on it. His countenance was like lightning, and his clothing as white as snow. And the guards shook for fear of him, and became like dead *men.*

But the angel answered and said to the women, "Do not be afraid, for I know that you seek Jesus who was crucified. He is not here; for He is risen, as He said. Come, see the place where the Lord lay. And go quickly and tell His disciples that He is risen from the dead, and indeed He is going before you into Galilee; there you will see Him. Behold, I have told you."

So they went out quickly from the tomb with fear and great joy, and ran to bring His disciples word.

And as they went to tell His disciples, behold, Jesus met them, saying, "Rejoice!" So they came and held Him by the feet and worshiped Him. Then Jesus said to them, "Do not be afraid. Go *and* tell My brethren to go to Galilee, and there they will see Me."

Now while they were going, behold, some of the guard came into the city and reported to the chief priests all the things that had happened. When they had assembled with the elders and consulted together, they gave a large sum of money to the soldiers, saying, "Tell them, 'His disciples came at night and stole Him *away* while we slept.' And if this comes to the governor's ears, we will appease him and make you secure." So they took the money and did as they were instructed; and this saying is commonly reported among the Jews until this day.

Now behold, two of them were traveling that same day to a village called Emmaus, which was seven miles from Jerusalem. And they talked together of all these things which had happened. So it was, while they conversed and reasoned, that Jesus Himself drew near and went with them. But their eyes were restrained, so that they did not know Him.

And He said to them, "What kind of conversation *is* this that you have with one another as you walk and are sad?"

Then the one whose name was Cleopas answered and said to Him, "Are You the only stranger in Jerusalem, and have You not known the things which happened there in these days?"

And He said to them, "What things?"

So they said to Him, "The things concerning Jesus of Nazareth, who was a Prophet mighty in deed and word before God and all the people, and how the chief priests and our rulers delivered Him to be condemned to death, and crucified Him. But we were hoping that it was He who was going to redeem Israel. Indeed, besides all this, today is the third day since these things happened. Yes, and certain women of our company, who arrived at the tomb early, astonished us. When they did not find His body, they came saying that they had also seen a vision of angels who said He was alive. And certain of those *who were* with us went to the tomb and found *it* just as the women had said; but Him they did not see."

Then He said to them, "O foolish ones, and slow of heart to believe in all that the prophets have spoken! Ought not the Christ to have suffered these things and to enter into His glory?" And beginning at Moses and all the Prophets, He expounded to them in all the Scriptures the things concerning Himself.

Then they drew near to the village where they were going, and He indicated that He would have gone farther. But they constrained Him, saying, "Abide with us, for it is toward evening, and the day is far spent." And He went in to stay with them.

Now it came to pass, as He sat at the table with them, that He took bread, blessed and broke *it,* and gave it to them. Then their eyes were opened and they knew Him; and He vanished from their sight.

And they said to one another, "Did not our heart burn within us while He talked with us on the road, and while He opened the Scriptures to us?"

So they rose up that very hour and returned to Jerusalem, and found the eleven and those *who were* with them gathered together, saying, "The Lord is risen indeed, and has appeared to Simon!" And they told about the things *that had happened* on the road, and how He was known to them in the breaking of bread.

Then, the same day at evening, being the first *day* of the week, when the doors were shut where the disciples were assembled, for fear of the Jews, Jesus came and stood in the midst, and said to them, "Peace *be* with you." When He had said this, He showed them *His* hands and His side. Then the disciples were glad when they saw the Lord.

So Jesus said to them again, "Peace to you! As the Father has sent Me, I also send you." And when He had said this, He breathed on *them,* and said to them, "Receive the Holy Spirit. If you forgive the sins of any, they are forgiven them; if you retain the *sins* of any, they are retained."

Now Thomas, called the Twin, one of the twelve, was not with them when Jesus came. The other disciples therefore said to him, "We have seen the Lord."

So he said to them, "Unless I see in His hands the print of the nails, and put my finger into the print of the nails, and put my hand into His side, I will not believe."

And after eight days His disciples were again inside, and Thomas with them. Jesus came, the doors being shut, and stood in the midst, and said, "Peace to you!" Then He said to Thomas, "Reach your finger here, and look at My hands; and reach your hand *here,* and put *it* into My side. Do not be unbelieving, but believing."

And Thomas answered and said to Him, "My Lord and my God!"

Jesus said to him, "Thomas, because you have seen Me, you have believed. Blessed *are* those who have not seen and *yet* have believed."

Matthew 28:1-15; Luke 24:13-35; John 20:19-29

WORSHIP

Praise the LORD!

Blessed *is* the man *who* fears the LORD,
Who delights greatly in His commandments.

His descendants will be mighty on earth;
The generation of the upright will be blessed.
Wealth and riches *will be* in his house,
And his righteousness endures forever.
Unto the upright there arises light in the
    darkness;
He is gracious, and full of compassion, and
    righteous.

Psalm 112:1-4

WISDOM

The hearing ear and the seeing eye,
The LORD has made them both.

Proverbs 20:12

SW?! SO WHAT?
What does this tell me?

JESUS APPEARS, COMMISSIONS AND ASCENDS

John 21:1-17; Matthew 28:16-20; Luke 24:44-53; John 20:30-31; Psalm 113:1-2; Proverbs 20:13

After these things Jesus showed Himself again to the disciples at the Sea of Tiberias, and in this way He showed *Himself:* Simon Peter, Thomas called the Twin, Nathanael of Cana in Galilee, the *sons* of Zebedee, and two others of His disciples were together. Simon Peter said to them, "I am going fishing."

They said to him, "We are going with you also." They went out and immediately got into the boat, and that night they caught nothing. But when the morning had now come, Jesus stood on the shore; yet the disciples did not know that it was Jesus. Then Jesus said to them, "Children, have you any food?"

They answered Him, "No."

And He said to them, "Cast the net on the right side of the boat, and you will find *some.*" So they cast, and now they were not able to draw it in because of the multitude of fish.

Therefore that disciple whom Jesus loved said to Peter, "It is the Lord!" Now when Simon Peter heard that it was the Lord, he put on *his* outer garment (for he had removed it), and plunged into the sea. But the other disciples came in the little boat (for they were not far from land, but about two hundred cubits), dragging the net with fish. Then, as soon as they had come to land, they saw a fire of coals there, and fish laid on it, and bread. Jesus said to them, "Bring some of the fish which you have just caught."

Simon Peter went up and dragged the net to land, full of large fish, one hundred and fifty-three; and although there were so many, the net was not broken. Jesus said to them, "Come *and* eat breakfast." Yet none of the disciples dared ask Him, "Who are You?"—knowing that it was the Lord. Jesus then came and took the bread and gave it to them, and likewise the fish.

This *is* now the third time Jesus showed Himself to His disciples after He was raised from the dead.

So when they had eaten breakfast, Jesus said to Simon Peter, "Simon, *son* of Jonah, do you love Me more than these?"

He said to Him, "Yes, Lord; You know that I love You."

He said to him, "Feed My lambs."

He said to him again a second time, "Simon, *son* of Jonah, do you love Me?"

He said to Him, "Yes, Lord; You know that I love You."

He said to him, "Tend My sheep."

He said to him the third time, "Simon, *son* of Jonah, do you love Me?" Peter was grieved because He said to him the third time, "Do you love Me?"

And he said to Him, "Lord, You know all things; You know that I love You."

Jesus said to him, "Feed My sheep."

Then the eleven disciples went away into Galilee, to the mountain which Jesus had appointed for them. When they saw Him, they worshiped Him; but some doubted.

And Jesus came and spoke to them, saying, "All authority has been given to Me in heaven and on earth. Go therefore and make disciples of all the nations, baptizing them in the name of the Father and of the Son and of the Holy Spirit, teaching them to observe all things that I have commanded you; and lo, I am with you always, *even* to the end of the age." Amen.

Then He said to them, "These *are* the words which I spoke to you while I was still with you, that all things must be fulfilled which were written in the Law of Moses and *the* Prophets and *the* Psalms concerning Me." And He opened their understanding, that they might comprehend the Scriptures.

Then He said to them, "Thus it is written, and thus it was necessary for the Christ to suffer and to rise from the dead the third day, and that repentance and remission of sins should be preached in His name to all nations, beginning at Jerusalem. And you are witnesses of these things. Behold, I send the Promise of My Father upon you; but tarry in the city of Jerusalem until you are endued with power from on high."

And He led them out as far as Bethany, and He lifted up His hands and blessed them. Now it came to pass, while He blessed them, that He was parted from them and carried up into heaven. And they worshiped Him, and returned to Jerusalem with great joy, and were continually in the temple praising and blessing God. Amen.

And truly Jesus did many other signs in the presence of His disciples, which are not written in this book; but these are written that you may believe that Jesus is the Christ, the Son of God, and that believing you may have life in His name.

John 21:1-17; Matthew 28:16-20; Luke 24:44-53; John 20:30-31

WORSHIP

Praise the LORD!

Praise, O servants of the LORD,
Praise the name of the LORD!
Blessed be the name of the LORD
From this time forth and forevermore!

Psalm 113:1-2

WISDOM

Do not love sleep, lest you come to poverty;
Open your eyes, *and* you will be satisfied with
bread.

Proverbs 20:13

SW?! SO WHAT?
What does this tell me?

APOSTLES AND THE CHURCH

The mountain range of the apostles and the development of the early church extends from the ascension of Christ to the destruction of Jerusalem a generation later in A.D. 70.

The most important peak in this range occurred just ten days after Jesus' ascension. It was on this day, the day of Pentecost, that the church received the indwelling ministry of the Holy Spirit which Jesus had promised His disciples (John 14:17).

The conversion of the apostle Paul marks a second peak in this range. Paul was a persecutor of Christians whose conversion on the road to Damascus turned him into a champion for Christ and prepared the way for the gospel to be preached to the Gentiles throughout the Roman world. Paul's travels and writings were foundational for the development of the early church and the theological formulations of biblical Christianity.

The martyrdom of James, the brother of John, is the third peak, for this event marked the beginning of the end for the apostles. Jesus warned them that they would be persecuted and martyred for their faith, and now those warnings were becoming reality. During the apostolic period, most of the apostles suffered and died advancing the kingdom of Christ.

Put two or more imperfect people in a room together and you don't get perfection, you get friction. As the early church grew, sparks began to fly. But the Jerusalem Council helped keep those sparks from becoming a firestorm. It was here on this fourth peak that Jewish believers were instructed to accept believing Gentiles into the church without demanding that they first be circumcised and observe the Jewish religion.

Other than the Book of Acts, which constitutes a narrative of the development of the early church, the rest of the story must be pieced together by reading someone else's mail. A large part of the readings in this range are letters called Epistles, the majority of which were written by Paul.

The apostles wrote these letters for the same reasons you often write a letter or an e-mail. They wrote to catch up with someone, update important information, rejoice over good news, grieve at bad news, encourage believers to hang tough through difficult trials, or to correct those who were living unwisely.

Paul's letter to the church in Rome is a mountain peak in this range that towers above the rest and casts a long shadow. On this peak, Paul systematically, thoroughly, and passionately explains that one is made right with God by grace through faith in Jesus, not by good works.

The sixth peak is the apostle John's description of the events before and after the future return of Jesus Christ to establish His kingdom reign on the earth. It's upon this peak that John describes a new heaven and a new earth where Jesus will dwell with His people forever—a place where there is no death, no tears, no mourning, and no pain.

The last great mountain peak for the apostolic period is the destruction of Jerusalem by the Romans in A.D. 70. While the death of Christ inaugurated the New Covenant, the destruction of Jerusalem and its temple effectively put an end to the Old Covenant pattern of sacrifice. No longer would the blood of Passover lambs be offered on the temple altar. As Paul wrote, "For indeed Christ, our Passover, was sacrificed for us" (1 Corinthians 5:7).

APOSTLES ARE EMPOWERED
Acts 1:1–2:13; Psalm 113:3–4;
Proverbs 20:14

The former account I made, O Theophilus, of all that Jesus began both to do and teach, until the day in which He was taken up, after He through the Holy Spirit had given commandments to the apostles whom He had chosen, to whom He also presented Himself alive after His suffering by many infallible proofs, being seen by them during forty days and speaking of the things pertaining to the kingdom of God.

And being assembled together with *them,* He commanded them not to depart from Jerusalem, but to wait for the Promise of the Father, "which," He said, "you have heard from Me; for John truly baptized with water, but you shall be baptized with the Holy Spirit not many days from now." Therefore, when they had come together, they asked Him, saying, "Lord, will You at this time restore the kingdom to Israel?" And He said to them, "It is not for you to know times or seasons which the Father has put in His own authority. But you shall receive power when the Holy Spirit has come upon you; and you shall be witnesses to Me in Jerusalem, and in all Judea and Samaria, and to the end of the earth."

Now when He had spoken these things, while they watched, He was taken up, and a cloud received Him out of their sight. And while they looked steadfastly toward heaven as He went up, behold, two men stood by them in white apparel, who also said, "Men of Galilee, why do you stand gazing up into heaven? This *same* Jesus, who was taken up from you into heaven, will so come in like manner as you saw Him go into heaven."

Then they returned to Jerusalem from the mount called Olivet, which is near Jerusalem, a Sabbath day's journey. And when they had entered, they went up into the upper room where they were staying: Peter, James, John, and Andrew; Philip and Thomas; Bartholomew and Matthew; James *the son* of Alphaeus and Simon the Zealot; and Judas *the son* of James. These all continued with one accord in prayer and supplication, with the women and Mary the mother of Jesus, and with His brothers.

And in those days Peter stood up in the midst of the disciples (altogether the number of names was about a hundred and twenty), and said, "Men *and* brethren, this Scripture had to be fulfilled, which the Holy Spirit spoke before by the mouth of David concerning Judas, who became a guide to those who arrested Jesus; for he was numbered with us and obtained a part in this ministry."

(Now this man purchased a field with the wages of iniquity; and falling headlong, he burst open in the middle and all his entrails gushed out. And it became known to all those dwelling in Jerusalem; so that field is called in their own language, Akel Dama, that is, Field of Blood.)

"For it is written in the book of Psalms:

'Let his dwelling place be desolate,
And let no one live in it';

and,

'Let another take his office.'

"Therefore, of these men who have accompanied us all the time that the Lord Jesus went in and out among us, beginning from the baptism of John to that day when He was taken up from us, one of these must become a witness with us of His resurrection."

And they proposed two: Joseph called Barsabas, who was surnamed Justus, and Matthias. And they prayed and said, "You, O Lord, who know the hearts of all, show which of these two You have chosen to take part in this ministry and apostleship from which Judas by transgression fell, that he might go to his own place." And they cast their lots, and the lot fell on Matthias. And he was numbered with the eleven apostles.

When the Day of Pentecost had fully come, they were all with one accord in one place. And suddenly there came a sound from heaven, as of a rushing mighty wind, and it filled the whole house where they were sitting. Then there appeared to them divided tongues, as of fire, and *one* sat upon each of them. And they were all filled with the Holy Spirit and began to speak with other tongues, as the Spirit gave them utterance.

And there were dwelling in Jerusalem Jews, devout men, from every nation under heaven. And when this sound occurred, the multitude came together, and were confused, because everyone heard them speak in his own language. Then they were all amazed and marveled, saying to one another, "Look, are not all these who speak Galileans? And how *is it that* we hear, each in our own language in which we were born? Parthians and Medes and Elamites, those dwelling in Mesopotamia, Judea and Cappadocia, Pontus and Asia, Phrygia and Pamphylia, Egypt and the parts of Libya adjoining Cyrene, visitors from Rome, both Jews and proselytes, Cretans and Arabs—we hear them speaking in our own tongues the wonderful works of God." So they were all amazed and perplexed, saying to one another, "Whatever could this mean?"

Others mocking said, "They are full of new wine."

Acts 1:1–2:13

WORSHIP

From the rising of the sun to its going down
The LORD's name *is* to be praised.

The LORD *is* high above all nations,
His glory above the heavens.

Psalm 113:3-4

WISDOM

"*It is* good for nothing," cries the buyer;
But when he has gone his way, then he boasts.

Proverbs 20:14

SW?! **SO WHAT?**
What does this tell me?

PETER DEMONSTRATES THE SPIRIT'S POWER

Acts 2:14–3:10; Psalm 114:1-3, 7-8; Proverbs 20:17

ut Peter, standing up with the eleven, raised his voice and said to them, "Men of Judea and all who dwell in Jerusalem, let this be known to you, and heed my words. For these are not drunk, as you suppose, since it is *only* the third hour of the day. But this is what was spoken by the prophet Joel:

'And it shall come to pass in the last days, says God,
That I will pour out of My Spirit on all flesh;
Your sons and your daughters shall prophesy,
Your young men shall see visions,
Your old men shall dream dreams.
And on My menservants and on My maidservants
I will pour out My Spirit in those days;
And they shall prophesy.
I will show wonders in heaven above
And signs in the earth beneath:
Blood and fire and vapor of smoke.
The sun shall be turned into darkness,
And the moon into blood,
Before the coming of the great and awesome day of the LORD.
And it shall come to pass
That whoever calls on the name of the LORD
Shall be saved.'

"Men of Israel, hear these words: Jesus of Nazareth, a Man attested by God to you by miracles, wonders, and signs which God did through Him in your midst, as you yourselves also know—Him, being delivered by the determined purpose and foreknowledge of God, you have taken by lawless hands, have crucified, and put to death; whom God raised up, having loosed the pains of death, because it was not possible that He should be held by it. For David says concerning Him:

'I foresaw the LORD always before my face,
For He is at my right hand, that I may not be shaken.
Therefore my heart rejoiced, and my tongue was glad;

Moreover my flesh also will rest in hope.
For You will not leave my soul in Hades,
Nor will You allow Your Holy One to see corruption.
You have made known to me the ways of life;
You will make me full of joy in Your presence.'

"Men *and* brethren, let *me* speak freely to you of the patriarch David, that he is both dead and buried, and his tomb is with us to this day. Therefore, being a prophet, and knowing that God had sworn with an oath to him that of the fruit of his body, according to the flesh, He would raise up the Christ to sit on his throne, he, foreseeing this, spoke concerning the resurrection of the Christ, that His soul was not left in Hades, nor did His flesh see corruption. This Jesus God has raised up, of which we are all witnesses. Therefore being exalted to the right hand of God, and having received from the Father the promise of the Holy Spirit, He poured out this which you now see and hear.

"For David did not ascend into the heavens, but he says himself:

'The LORD said to my Lord,
"Sit at My right hand,
Till I make Your enemies Your footstool." '

"Therefore let all the house of Israel know assuredly that God has made this Jesus, whom you crucified, both Lord and Christ."

Now when they heard *this,* they were cut to the heart, and said to Peter and the rest of the apostles, "Men *and* brethren, what shall we do?"

Then Peter said to them, "Repent, and let every one of you be baptized in the name of Jesus Christ for the remission of sins; and you shall receive the gift of the Holy Spirit. For the promise is to you and to your children, and to all who are afar off, as many as the Lord our God will call."

And with many other words he testified and exhorted them, saying, "Be saved from this perverse generation." Then those who gladly received his word were baptized; and that day about three thousand souls were added *to them.* And they continued steadfastly in the apostles' doctrine and fellowship, in the breaking of bread, and in prayers. Then fear came upon every soul, and many wonders and signs were done through the apostles. Now all who believed were together, and had all things in common, and sold their possessions and goods, and divided them among all, as anyone had need.

So continuing daily with one accord in the temple, and breaking bread from house to house, they ate their food with gladness and simplicity of heart, praising God and having favor with all the people. And the Lord added to the church daily those who were being saved.

Now Peter and John went up together to the temple at the hour of prayer, the ninth *hour*. And a certain man lame from his mother's womb was carried, whom they laid daily at the gate of the temple which is called Beautiful, to ask alms from those who entered the temple; who, seeing Peter and John about to go into the temple, asked for alms. And fixing his eyes on him, with John, Peter said, "Look at us." So he gave them his attention, expecting to receive something from them. Then Peter said, "Silver and gold I do not have, but what I do have I give you: In the name of Jesus Christ of Nazareth, rise up and walk." And he took him by the right hand and lifted *him* up, and immediately his feet and ankle bones received strength. So he, leaping up, stood and walked and entered the temple with them—walking, leaping, and praising God. And all the people saw him walking and praising God. Then they knew that it was he who sat begging alms at the Beautiful Gate of the temple; and they were filled with wonder and amazement at what had happened to him.

Acts 2:14–3:10

WORSHIP

When Israel went out of Egypt,
The house of Jacob from a people of strange language,
Judah became His sanctuary,
And Israel His dominion.

The sea saw *it* and fled;
Jordan turned back.

Tremble, O earth, at the presence of the Lord,
At the presence of the God of Jacob,
Who turned the rock *into* a pool of water,
The flint into a fountain of waters.

Psalm 114:1-3, 7-8

WISDOM

Bread gained by deceit *is* sweet to a man,
But afterward his mouth will be filled with gravel.

Proverbs 20:17

SW?! **SO WHAT?**
What does this tell me?

JAIL TIME FOR PETER AND JOHN

Acts 3:11–4:31; Psalm 115:1–3; Proverbs 20:18

Now as the lame man who was healed held on to Peter and John, all the people ran together to them in the porch which is called Solomon's, greatly amazed. So when Peter saw *it*, he responded to the people: "Men of Israel, why do you marvel at this? Or why look so intently at us, as though by our own power or godliness we had made this man walk? The God of Abraham, Isaac, and Jacob, the God of our fathers, glorified His Servant Jesus, whom you delivered up and denied in the presence of Pilate, when he was determined to let *Him* go. But you denied the Holy One and the Just, and asked for a murderer to be granted to you, and killed the Prince of life, whom God raised from the dead, of which we are witnesses. And His name, through faith in His name, has made this man strong, whom you see and know. Yes, the faith which *comes* through Him has given him this perfect soundness in the presence of you all.

"Yet now, brethren, I know that you did *it* in ignorance, as *did* also your rulers. But those things which God foretold by the mouth of all His prophets, that the Christ would suffer, He has thus fulfilled. Repent therefore and be converted, that your sins may be blotted out, so that times of refreshing may come from the presence of the Lord, and that He may send Jesus Christ, who was preached to you before, whom heaven must receive until the times of restoration of all things, which God has spoken by the mouth of all His holy prophets since the world began. For Moses truly said to the fathers, 'The LORD your God will raise up for you a Prophet like me from your brethren. Him you shall hear in all things, whatever He says to you. And it shall be *that* every soul who will not hear that Prophet shall be utterly destroyed from among the people.' Yes, and all the prophets, from Samuel and those who follow, as many as have spoken, have also foretold these days. You are sons of the prophets, and of the covenant which God made with our fathers, saying to Abraham, 'And in your seed all the families of the earth shall be blessed.' To you first, God, having raised up His Servant Jesus, sent Him to bless you, in turning away every one *of you* from your iniquities."

Now as they spoke to the people, the priests, the captain of the temple, and the Sadducees came upon them, being greatly disturbed that they taught the people and preached in Jesus the resurrection from the dead. And they laid hands on them, and put *them* in custody until the next day, for it was already evening. However, many of those who heard the word believed; and the number of the men came to be about five thousand.

And it came to pass, on the next day, that their rulers, elders, and scribes, as well as Annas the high priest, Caiaphas, John, and Alexander, and as many as were of the family of the high priest, were gathered together at Jerusalem. And when they had set them in the midst, they asked, "By what power or by what name have you done this?"

Then Peter, filled with the Holy Spirit, said to them, "Rulers of the people and elders of Israel: If we this day are judged for a good deed *done* to a helpless man, by what means he has been made well, let it be known to you all, and to all the people of Israel, that by the name of Jesus Christ of Nazareth, whom you crucified, whom God raised from the dead, by Him this man stands here before you whole. This is the 'stone which was rejected by you builders, which has become the chief cornerstone.' Nor is there salvation in any other, for there is no other name under heaven given among men by which we must be saved."

Now when they saw the boldness of Peter and John, and perceived that they were uneducated and untrained men, they marveled. And they realized that they had been with Jesus. And seeing the man who had been healed standing with them, they could say nothing against it. But when they had commanded them to go aside out of the council, they conferred among themselves, saying, "What shall we do to these men? For, indeed, that a notable miracle has been done through them *is* evident to all who dwell in Jerusalem, and we cannot deny *it*. But so that it spreads no further among the people, let us severely threaten them, that from now on they speak to no man in this name."

So they called them and commanded them not to speak at all nor teach in the name of Jesus. But Peter and John answered and said to them, "Whether it is right in the sight of God to listen to you more than to God, you judge. For we cannot but speak the things which we have seen and heard." So when they had further threatened them, they let them go, finding no way of punishing them, because of the people, since they all glorified God for what had been done. For the man was over forty years old on whom this miracle of healing had been performed.

And being let go, they went to their own *companions* and reported all that the chief priests and elders had said to them. So when they heard that, they raised their voice to God with one accord and said: "Lord, You *are* God, who made heaven and earth and the sea, and all that is in them, who by the mouth of Your servant David have said:

'Why did the nations rage,
And the people plot vain things?
The kings of the earth took their stand,
And the rulers were gathered together
Against the LORD and against His Christ.'

"For truly against Your holy Servant Jesus, whom You anointed, both Herod and Pontius Pilate, with the Gentiles and the people of Israel, were gathered together to do whatever Your hand and Your purpose determined before to be done. Now, Lord, look on their threats, and grant to Your servants that with all boldness they may speak Your word, by stretching out Your hand to heal, and that signs and wonders may be done through the name of Your holy Servant Jesus."

And when they had prayed, the place where they were assembled together was shaken; and they were all filled with the Holy Spirit, and they spoke the word of God with boldness.

Acts 3:11–4:31

WORSHIP

Not unto us, O LORD, not unto us,
But to Your name give glory,
Because of Your mercy,
Because of Your truth.
Why should the Gentiles say,
"So where *is* their God?"

But our God *is* in heaven;
He does whatever He pleases.

Psalm 115:1-3

WISDOM

Plans are established by counsel;
By wise counsel wage war.

Proverbs 20:18

SO WHAT?
What does this tell me?

A FATAL CONSEQUENCE BRINGS GREAT FEAR

Acts 4:32–5:32; Psalm 115:16-18; Proverbs 20:19

Now the multitude of those who believed were of one heart and one soul; neither did anyone say that any of the things he possessed was his own, but they had all things in common. And with great power the apostles gave witness to the resurrection of the Lord Jesus. And great grace was upon them all. Nor was there anyone among them who lacked; for all who were possessors of lands or houses sold them, and brought the proceeds of the things that were sold, and laid *them* at the apostles' feet; and they distributed to each as anyone had need.

And Joses, who was also named Barnabas by the apostles (which is translated Son of Encouragement), a Levite of the country of Cyprus, having land, sold *it,* and brought the money and laid *it* at the apostles' feet.

But a certain man named Ananias, with Sapphira his wife, sold a possession. And he kept back *part* of the proceeds, his wife also being aware *of it,* and brought a certain part and laid *it* at the apostles' feet. But Peter said, "Ananias, why has Satan filled your heart to lie to the Holy Spirit and keep back *part* of the price of the land for yourself? While it remained, was it not your own? And after it was sold, was it not in your own control? Why have you conceived this thing in your heart? You have not lied to men but to God."

Then Ananias, hearing these words, fell down and breathed his last. So great fear came upon all those who heard these things. And the young men arose and wrapped him up, carried *him* out, and buried *him.*

Now it was about three hours later when his wife came in, not knowing what had happened. And Peter answered her, "Tell me whether you sold the land for so much?"

She said, "Yes, for so much."

Then Peter said to her, "How is it that you have agreed together to test the Spirit of the Lord? Look, the feet of those who have buried your husband *are* at the door, and they will carry you out." Then immediately she fell down at his feet and breathed her last. And the young men came in and found her dead, and carrying *her* out, buried *her* by her husband. So great fear came upon all the church and upon all who heard these things.

And through the hands of the apostles many signs and wonders were done among the people. And they were all with one accord in Solomon's Porch. Yet none of the rest dared join them, but the people esteemed them highly. And believers were increasingly added to the Lord, multitudes of both men and women, so that they brought the sick out into the streets and laid *them* on beds and couches, that at least the shadow of Peter passing by might fall on some of them. Also a multitude gathered from the surrounding cities to Jerusalem, bringing sick people and those who were tormented by unclean spirits, and they were all healed.

Then the high priest rose up, and all those who *were* with him (which is the sect of the Sadducees), and they were filled with indignation, and laid their hands on the apostles and put them in the common prison. But at night an angel of the Lord opened the prison doors and brought them out, and said, "Go, stand in the temple and speak to the people all the words of this life."

And when they heard *that,* they entered the temple early in the morning and taught. But the high priest and those with him came and called the council together, with all the elders of the children of Israel, and sent to the prison to have them brought.

But when the officers came and did not find them in the prison, they returned and reported, saying, "Indeed we found the prison shut securely, and the guards standing outside before the doors; but when we opened them, we found no one inside!" Now when the high priest, the captain of the temple, and the chief priests heard these things, they wondered what the outcome would be. So one came and told them, saying, "Look, the men whom you put in prison are standing in the temple and teaching the people!"

APOSTLES AND THE CHURCH

Then the captain went with the officers and brought them without violence, for they feared the people, lest they should be stoned. And when they had brought them, they set *them* before the council. And the high priest asked them, saying, "Did we not strictly command you not to teach in this name? And look, you have filled Jerusalem with your doctrine, and intend to bring this Man's blood on us!"

But Peter and the *other* apostles answered and said: "We ought to obey God rather than men. The God of our fathers raised up Jesus whom you murdered by hanging on a tree. Him God has exalted to His right hand *to be* Prince and Savior, to give repentance to Israel and forgiveness of sins. And we are His witnesses to these things, and *so* also *is* the Holy Spirit whom God has given to those who obey Him."

Acts 4:32–5:32

WORSHIP

The heaven, *even* the heavens, *are* the LORD's;
But the earth He has given to the children of men.
The dead do not praise the LORD,
Nor any who go down into silence.
But we will bless the LORD
From this time forth and forevermore.

Praise the LORD!

Psalm 115:16-18

WISDOM

He who goes about *as* a talebearer reveals secrets;
Therefore do not associate with one who flatters with his lips.

Proverbs 20:19

SO WHAT?
What does this tell me?

STEPHEN PRESENTS HIS DEFENSE: PART ONE

Acts 5:33–7:19; Psalm 116:1-4; Proverbs 20:20

When they heard *this,* they were furious and plotted to kill them. Then one in the council stood up, a Pharisee named Gamaliel, a teacher of the law held in respect by all the people, and commanded them to put the apostles outside for a little while. And he said to them: "Men of Israel, take heed to yourselves what you intend to do regarding these men. For some time ago Theudas rose up, claiming to be somebody. A number of men, about four hundred, joined him. He was slain, and all who obeyed him were scattered and came to nothing. After this man, Judas of Galilee rose up in the days of the census, and drew away many people after him. He also perished, and all who obeyed him were dispersed. And now I say to you, keep away from these men and let them alone; for if this plan or this work is of men, it will come to nothing; but if it is of God, you cannot overthrow it—lest you even be found to fight against God."

And they agreed with him, and when they had called for the apostles and beaten *them,* they commanded that they should not speak in the name of Jesus, and let them go. So they departed from the presence of the council, rejoicing that they were counted worthy to suffer shame for His name. And daily in the temple, and in every house, they did not cease teaching and preaching Jesus *as* the Christ.

Now in those days, when *the number of* the disciples was multiplying, there arose a complaint against the Hebrews by the Hellenists, because their widows were neglected in the daily distribution. Then the twelve summoned the multitude of the disciples and said, "It is not desirable that we should leave the word of God and serve tables. Therefore, brethren, seek out from among you seven men of *good* reputation, full of the Holy Spirit and wisdom, whom we may appoint over this business; but we will give ourselves continually to prayer and to the ministry of the word."

And the saying pleased the whole multitude. And they chose Stephen, a man full of faith and the Holy Spirit, and Philip, Prochorus, Nicanor, Timon, Parmenas, and Nicolas, a proselyte from Antioch, whom they set before the apostles; and when they had prayed, they laid hands on them.

Then the word of God spread, and the number of the disciples multiplied greatly in Jerusalem, and a great many of the priests were obedient to the faith.

And Stephen, full of faith and power, did great wonders and signs among the people. Then there arose some from what is called the Synagogue of the Freedmen (Cyrenians, Alexandrians, and those from Cilicia and Asia), disputing with Stephen. And they were not able to resist the wisdom and the Spirit by which he spoke. Then they secretly induced men to say, "We have heard him speak blasphemous words against Moses and God." And they stirred up the people, the elders, and the scribes; and they came upon *him,* seized him, and brought *him* to the council. They also set up false witnesses who said, "This man does not cease to speak blasphemous words against this holy place and the law; for we have heard him say that this Jesus of Nazareth will destroy this place and change the customs which Moses delivered to us." And all who sat in the council, looking steadfastly at him, saw his face as the face of an angel.

Then the high priest said, "Are these things so?"

And he said, "Brethren and fathers, listen: The God of glory appeared to our father Abraham when he was in Mesopotamia, before he dwelt in Haran, and said to him, 'Get out of your country and from your relatives, and come to a land that I will show you.' Then he came out of the land of the Chaldeans and dwelt in Haran. And from there, when his father was dead, He moved him to this land in which you now dwell. And *God* gave him no inheritance in it, not even *enough* to set his foot on. But even when *Abraham* had no child, He promised to give it to him for a possession, and to his descendants after him. But God spoke in this way: that his descendants would dwell in a foreign land, and that they would bring them into bondage and oppress *them* four hundred years. 'And the nation to whom they will be in bondage I will judge,' said God, 'and after that they shall come out and serve Me in this place.' Then He gave him the covenant of circumcision; and so *Abraham* begot Isaac and circumcised him on the eighth day; and Isaac *begot* Jacob, and Jacob *begot* the twelve patriarchs.

"And the patriarchs, becoming envious, sold Joseph into Egypt. But God was with him and delivered him out of all his troubles, and gave him favor and wisdom in the presence of Pharaoh, king of Egypt; and he made him governor over Egypt and all his house. Now a famine and great trouble came over all the land of Egypt and Canaan, and our fathers found no sustenance. But when Jacob heard that there was grain in Egypt, he sent out our fathers first. And the second *time* Joseph was made known to his brothers, and Joseph's family became known to the Pharaoh. Then Joseph sent and called his father Jacob and all his relatives to *him,* seventy-five people. So Jacob went down to Egypt; and he died, he and our fathers. And they were carried back to Shechem and laid in the tomb that Abraham bought for a sum of money from the sons of Hamor, *the father* of Shechem.

"But when the time of the promise drew near which God had sworn to Abraham, the people grew and multiplied in Egypt till another king arose who did not know Joseph. This man dealt treacherously with our people, and oppressed our forefathers, making them expose their babies, so that they might not live."

Acts 5:33–7:19

WORSHIP

I love the LORD, because He has heard
My voice *and* my supplications.
Because He has inclined His ear to me,
Therefore I will call *upon Him* as long as I live.

The pains of death surrounded me,
And the pangs of Sheol laid hold of me;
I found trouble and sorrow.
Then I called upon the name of the LORD:
"O LORD, I implore You, deliver my soul!"

Psalm 116:1-4

WISDOM

Whoever curses his father or his mother,
His lamp will be put out in deep darkness.

Proverbs 20:20

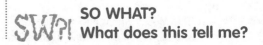

**SO WHAT?
What does this tell me?**

STEPHEN PRESENTS HIS DEFENSE: PART TWO

Acts 7:20–8:3; Psalm 116:5-7; Proverbs 20:21

APOSTLES AND THE CHURCH

"At this time Moses was born, and was well pleasing to God; and he was brought up in his father's house for three months. But when he was set out, Pharaoh's daughter took him away and brought him up as her own son. And Moses was learned in all the wisdom of the Egyptians, and was mighty in words and deeds.

"Now when he was forty years old, it came into his heart to visit his brethren, the children of Israel. And seeing one of *them* suffer wrong, he defended and avenged him who was oppressed, and struck down the Egyptian. For he supposed that his brethren would have understood that God would deliver them by his hand, but they did not understand. And the next day he appeared to two of them as they were fighting, and *tried to* reconcile them, saying, 'Men, you are brethren; why do you wrong one another?' But he who did his neighbor wrong pushed him away, saying, 'Who made you a ruler and a judge over us? Do you want to kill me as you did the Egyptian yesterday?' Then, at this saying, Moses fled and became a dweller in the land of Midian, where he had two sons.

"And when forty years had passed, an Angel of the Lord appeared to him in a flame of fire in a bush, in the wilderness of Mount Sinai. When Moses saw *it*, he marveled at the sight; and as he drew near to observe, the voice of the Lord came to him, *saying*, 'I *am* the God of your fathers—the God of Abraham, the God of Isaac, and the God of Jacob.' And Moses trembled and dared not look. 'Then the LORD said to him, "Take your sandals off your feet, for the place where you stand is holy ground. I have surely seen the oppression of my people who are in Egypt; I have heard their groaning and have come down to deliver them. And now come, I will send you to Egypt." '

"This Moses whom they rejected, saying, 'Who made you a ruler and a judge?' is the one God sent *to be* a ruler and a deliverer by the hand of the Angel who appeared to him in the bush. He brought them out, after he had shown wonders and signs in the land of Egypt, and in the Red Sea, and in the wilderness forty years.

"This is that Moses who said to the children of Israel, 'The LORD your God will raise up for you a Prophet like me from your brethren. Him you shall hear.'

"This is he who was in the congregation in the wilderness with the Angel who spoke to him on Mount Sinai, and *with* our fathers, the one who received the living oracles to give to us, whom our fathers would not obey, but rejected. And in their hearts they turned back to Egypt, saying to Aaron, 'Make us gods to go before us; *as for* this Moses who brought us out of the land of Egypt, we do not know what has become of him.' And they made a calf in those days, offered sacrifices to the idol, and rejoiced in the works of their own hands. Then God turned and gave them up to worship the host of heaven, as it is written in the book of the Prophets:

> 'Did you offer Me slaughtered animals and
>   sacrifices *during* forty years in the
>   wilderness,
> O house of Israel?
> You also took up the tabernacle of Moloch,
> And the star of your god Remphan,
> Images which you made to worship;
> And I will carry you away beyond Babylon.'

"Our fathers had the tabernacle of witness in the wilderness, as He appointed, instructing Moses to make it according to the pattern that he had seen, which our fathers, having received it in turn, also brought with Joshua into the land possessed by the Gentiles, whom God drove out before the face of our fathers until the days of David, who found favor before God and asked to find a dwelling for the God of Jacob. But Solomon built Him a house.

"However, the Most High does not dwell in temples made with hands, as the prophet says:

> 'Heaven *is* My throne,
> And earth *is* My footstool.

What house will you build for Me? says the
LORD,
Or what *is* the place of My rest?
Has My hand not made all these things?'

"*You* stiff-necked and uncircumcised in heart and ears! You always resist the Holy Spirit; as your fathers *did,* so *do* you. Which of the prophets did your fathers not persecute? And they killed those who foretold the coming of the Just One, of whom you now have become the betrayers and murderers, who have received the law by the direction of angels and have not kept *it.*"

When they heard these things they were cut to the heart, and they gnashed at him with *their* teeth. But he, being full of the Holy Spirit, gazed into heaven and saw the glory of God, and Jesus standing at the right hand of God, and said, "Look! I see the heavens opened and the Son of Man standing at the right hand of God!"

Then they cried out with a loud voice, stopped their ears, and ran at him with one accord; and they cast *him* out of the city and stoned *him.* And the witnesses laid down their clothes at the feet of a young man named Saul. And they stoned Stephen as he was calling on *God* and saying, "Lord Jesus, receive my spirit." Then he knelt down and cried out with a loud voice, "Lord, do not charge them with this sin." And when he had said this, he fell asleep.

Now Saul was consenting to his death.

At that time a great persecution arose against the church which was at Jerusalem; and they were all scattered throughout the regions of Judea and Samaria, except the apostles. And devout men carried Stephen *to his burial,* and made great lamentation over him.

As for Saul, he made havoc of the church, entering every house, and dragging off men and women, committing *them* to prison.

Acts 7:20–8:3

WORSHIP

Gracious *is* the LORD, and righteous;
Yes, our God *is* merciful.
The LORD preserves the simple;
I was brought low, and He saved me.
Return to your rest, O my soul,
For the LORD has dealt bountifully with you.

Psalm 116:5-7

WISDOM

An inheritance gained hastily at the beginning
Will not be blessed at the end.

Proverbs 20:21

SW?! SO WHAT?
What does this tell me?

SAUL SEES THE LIGHT

Acts 8:4-8, 14-17, 25-40; 9:1-19; Psalm 116:17-19; Proverbs 20:23

Therefore those who were scattered went everywhere preaching the word. Then Philip went down to the city of Samaria and preached Christ to them. And the multitudes with one accord heeded the things spoken by Philip, hearing and seeing the miracles which he did. For unclean spirits, crying with a loud voice, came out of many who were possessed; and many who were paralyzed and lame were healed. And there was great joy in that city.

Now when the apostles who were at Jerusalem heard that Samaria had received the word of God, they sent Peter and John to them, who, when they had come down, prayed for them that they might receive the Holy Spirit. For as yet He had fallen upon none of them. They had only been baptized in the name of the Lord Jesus. Then they laid hands on them, and they received the Holy Spirit.

So when they had testified and preached the word of the Lord, they returned to Jerusalem, preaching the gospel in many villages of the Samaritans.

Now an angel of the Lord spoke to Philip, saying, "Arise and go toward the south along the road which goes down from Jerusalem to Gaza." This is desert. So he arose and went. And behold, a man of Ethiopia, a eunuch of great authority under Candace the queen of the Ethiopians, who had charge of all her treasury, and had come to Jerusalem to worship, was returning. And sitting in his chariot, he was reading Isaiah the prophet. Then the Spirit said to Philip, "Go near and overtake this chariot."

So Philip ran to him, and heard him reading the prophet Isaiah, and said, "Do you understand what you are reading?"

And he said, "How can I, unless someone guides me?" And he asked Philip to come up and sit with him. The place in the Scripture which he read was this:

"He was led as a sheep to the
　　slaughter;

And as a lamb before its shearer *is* silent,
So He opened not His mouth.
In His humiliation His justice was taken away,
And who will declare His generation?
For His life is taken from the earth."

So the eunuch answered Philip and said, "I ask you, of whom does the prophet say this, of himself or of some other man?" Then Philip opened his mouth, and beginning at this Scripture, preached Jesus to him. Now as they went down the road, they came to some water. And the eunuch said, "See, *here is* water. What hinders me from being baptized?"

Then Philip said, "If you believe with all your heart, you may."

And he answered and said, "I believe that Jesus Christ is the Son of God."

So he commanded the chariot to stand still. And both Philip and the eunuch went down into the water, and he baptized him. Now when they came up out of the water, the Spirit of the Lord caught Philip away, so that the eunuch saw him no more; and he went on his way rejoicing. But Philip was found at Azotus. And passing through, he preached in all the cities till he came to Caesarea.

Then Saul, still breathing threats and murder against the disciples of the Lord, went to the high priest and asked letters from him to the synagogues of Damascus, so that if he found any who were of the Way, whether men or women, he might bring them bound to Jerusalem.

As he journeyed he came near Damascus, and suddenly a light shone around him from heaven. Then he fell to the ground, and heard a voice saying to him, "Saul, Saul, why are you persecuting Me?"

And he said, "Who are You, Lord?"

Then the Lord said, "I am Jesus, whom you are persecuting. It *is* hard for you to kick against the goads."

So he, trembling and astonished, said, "Lord, what do You want me to do?"

Then the Lord *said* to him, "Arise and go into the city, and you will be told what you must do."

And the men who journeyed with him stood speechless, hearing a voice but seeing no one. Then Saul arose from the ground, and when his eyes were opened he saw no one. But they led him by the hand and brought *him* into Damascus. And he was three days without sight, and neither ate nor drank.

Now there was a certain disciple at Damascus named Ananias; and to him the Lord said in a vision, "Ananias."

And he said, "Here I am, Lord."

So the Lord *said* to him, "Arise and go to the street called Straight, and inquire at the house of Judas for *one* called Saul of Tarsus, for behold, he is praying. And in a vision he has seen a man named Ananias coming in and putting *his* hand on him, so that he might receive his sight."

Then Ananias answered, "Lord, I have heard from many about this man, how much harm he has done to Your saints in Jerusalem. And here he has authority from the chief priests to bind all who call on Your name."

But the Lord said to him, "Go, for he is a chosen vessel of Mine to bear My name before Gentiles, kings, and the children of Israel. For I will show him how many things he must suffer for My name's sake."

And Ananias went his way and entered the house; and laying his hands on him he said, "Brother Saul, the Lord Jesus, who appeared to you on the road as you came, has sent me that you may receive your sight and be filled with the Holy Spirit." Immediately there fell from his eyes *something* like scales, and he received his sight at once; and he arose and was baptized.

So when he had received food, he was strengthened. Then Saul spent some days with the disciples at Damascus.

Acts 8:4-8, 14-17, 25-40; 9:1-19

WORSHIP

I will offer to You the sacrifice of thanksgiving, And will call upon the name of the Lord.

I will pay my vows to the Lord Now in the presence of all His people, In the courts of the Lord's house, In the midst of you, O Jerusalem.

Praise the Lord!

Psalm 116:17-19

WISDOM

Diverse weights *are* an abomination to the Lord, And dishonest scales *are* not good.

Proverbs 20:23

SW?! **SO WHAT?**
What does this tell me?

PETER'S UNUSUAL VISION

Immediately he preached the Christ in the synagogues, that He is the Son of God.

Then all who heard were amazed, and said, "Is this not he who destroyed those who called on this name in Jerusalem, and has come here for that purpose, so that he might bring them bound to the chief priests?"

But Saul increased all the more in strength, and confounded the Jews who dwelt in Damascus, proving that this *Jesus* is the Christ.

Now after many days were past, the Jews plotted to kill him. But their plot became known to Saul. And they watched the gates day and night, to kill him. Then the disciples took him by night and let *him* down through the wall in a large basket.

And when Saul had come to Jerusalem, he tried to join the disciples; but they were all afraid of him, and did not believe that he was a disciple. But Barnabas took him and brought *him* to the apostles. And he declared to them how he had seen the Lord on the road, and that He had spoken to him, and how he had preached boldly at Damascus in the name of Jesus. So he was with them at Jerusalem, coming in and going out. And he spoke boldly in the name of the Lord Jesus and disputed against the Hellenists, but they attempted to kill him. When the brethren found out, they brought him down to Caesarea and sent him out to Tarsus.

Then the churches throughout all Judea, Galilee, and Samaria had peace and were edified. And walking in the fear of the Lord and in the comfort of the Holy Spirit, they were multiplied.

There was a certain man in Caesarea called Cornelius, a centurion of what was called the Italian Regiment, a devout *man* and one who feared God with all his household, who gave alms generously to the people, and prayed to God always. About the ninth hour of the day he saw clearly in a vision an angel of God coming in and saying to him, "Cornelius!"

And when he observed him, he was afraid, and said, "What is it, lord?"

So he said to him, "Your prayers and your alms have come up for a memorial before God. Now send men to Joppa, and send for Simon whose surname is Peter. He is lodging with Simon, a tanner, whose house is by the sea. He will tell you what you must do." And when the angel who spoke to him had departed, Cornelius called two of his household servants and a devout soldier from among those who waited on him continually. So when he had explained all *these* things to them, he sent them to Joppa.

The next day, as they went on their journey and drew near the city, Peter went up on the housetop to pray, about the sixth hour. Then he became very hungry and wanted to eat; but while they made ready, he fell into a trance and saw heaven opened and an object like a great sheet bound at the four corners, descending to him and let down to the earth. In it were all kinds of four-footed animals of the earth, wild beasts, creeping things, and birds of the air. And a voice came to him, "Rise, Peter; kill and eat."

But Peter said, "Not so, Lord! For I have never eaten anything common or unclean."

And a voice *spoke* to him again the second time, "What God has cleansed you must not call common." This was done three times. And the object was taken up into heaven again.

Now while Peter wondered within himself what this vision which he had seen meant, behold, the men who had been sent from Cornelius had made inquiry for Simon's house, and stood before the gate. And they called and asked whether Simon, whose surname was Peter, was lodging there.

While Peter thought about the vision, the Spirit said to him, "Behold, three men are seeking you. Arise therefore, go down and go with them, doubting nothing; for I have sent them."

Then Peter went down to the men who had been sent to him from Cornelius, and said, "Yes, I am he whom you seek. For what reason have you come?"

And they said, "Cornelius *the* centurion, a just man, one who fears God and has a good reputation among all the nation of the Jews, was divinely instructed by a holy angel to summon you to his house, and to hear words from you." Then he invited them in and lodged *them*.

On the next day Peter went away with them, and some brethren from Joppa accompanied him.

And the following day they entered Caesarea. Now Cornelius was waiting for them, and had called together his relatives and close friends. As Peter was coming in, Cornelius met him and fell down at his feet and worshiped *him*. But Peter lifted him up, saying, "Stand up; I myself am also a man." And as he talked with him, he went in and found many who had come together. Then he said to them, "You know how unlawful it is for a Jewish man to keep company with or go to one of another nation. But God has shown me that I should not call any man common or unclean. Therefore I came without objection as soon as I was sent for. I ask, then, for what reason have you sent for me?"

So Cornelius said, "Four days ago I was fasting until this hour; and at the ninth hour I prayed in my house, and behold, a man stood before me in bright clothing, and said, 'Cornelius, your prayer has been heard, and your alms are remembered in the sight of God. Send therefore to Joppa and call Simon here, whose surname is Peter. He is lodging in the house of Simon, a tanner, by the sea. When he comes, he will speak to you.' So I sent to you immediately, and you have done well to come. Now therefore, we are all present before God, to hear all the things commanded you by God."

Acts 9:20-31; 10:1-33

WORSHIP

Praise the LORD, all you Gentiles!
Laud Him, all you peoples!
For His merciful kindness is great toward us,
And the truth of the LORD *endures* forever.

Praise the LORD!

Psalm 117

WISDOM

A man's steps *are* of the LORD;
How then can a man understand his own
   way?

Proverbs 20:24

SO WHAT?
What does this tell me?

PETER GRASPS THE WIDENESS OF GOD'S MERCY

Acts 10:34-43; 11:19-26; 12:1-25; Psalm 118:1-4; Proverbs 20:25

Then Peter opened *his* mouth and said: "In truth I perceive that God shows no partiality. But in every nation whoever fears Him and works righteousness is accepted by Him. The word which *God* sent to the children of Israel, preaching peace through Jesus Christ—He is Lord of all—that word you know, which was proclaimed throughout all Judea, and began from Galilee after the baptism which John preached: how God anointed Jesus of Nazareth with the Holy Spirit and with power, who went about doing good and healing all who were oppressed by the devil, for God was with Him. And we are witnesses of all things which He did both in the land of the Jews and in Jerusalem, whom they killed by hanging on a tree. Him God raised up on the third day, and showed Him openly, not to all the people, but to witnesses chosen before by God, *even* to us who ate and drank with Him after He arose from the dead. And He commanded us to preach to the people, and to testify that it is He who was ordained by God *to be* Judge of the living and the dead. To Him all the prophets witness that, through His name, whoever believes in Him will receive remission of sins."

Now those who were scattered after the persecution that arose over Stephen traveled as far as Phoenicia, Cyprus, and Antioch, preaching the word to no one but the Jews only. But some of them were men from Cyprus and Cyrene, who, when they had come to Antioch, spoke to the Hellenists, preaching the Lord Jesus. And the hand of the Lord was with them, and a great number believed and turned to the Lord.

Then news of these things came to the ears of the church in Jerusalem, and they sent out Barnabas to go as far as Antioch. When he came and had seen the grace of God, he was glad, and encouraged them all that with purpose of heart they should continue with the Lord. For he was a good man, full of the Holy Spirit and of faith. And a great many people were added to the Lord.

Then Barnabas departed for Tarsus to seek Saul. And when he had found him, he brought him to Antioch. So it was that for a whole year they assembled with the church and taught a great many people. And the disciples were first called Christians in Antioch.

Now about that time Herod the king stretched out *his* hand to harass some from the church. Then he killed James the brother of John with the sword. And because he saw that it pleased the Jews, he proceeded further to seize Peter also. Now it was *during* the Days of Unleavened Bread. So when he had arrested him, he put *him* in prison, and delivered *him* to four squads of soldiers to keep him, intending to bring him before the people after Passover.

Peter was therefore kept in prison, but constant prayer was offered to God for him by the church. And when Herod was about to bring him out, that night Peter was sleeping, bound with two chains between two soldiers; and the guards before the door were keeping the prison. Now behold, an angel of the Lord stood by *him,* and a light shone in the prison; and he struck Peter on the side and raised him up, saying, "Arise quickly!" And his chains fell off *his* hands. Then the angel said to him, "Gird yourself and tie on your sandals"; and so he did. And he said to him, "Put on your garment and follow me." So he went out and followed him, and did not know that what was done by the angel was real, but thought he was seeing a vision. When they were past the first and the second guard posts, they came to the iron gate that leads to the city, which opened to them of its own accord; and they went out and went down one street, and immediately the angel departed from him.

And when Peter had come to himself, he said, "Now I know for certain that the Lord has sent His angel, and has delivered me from the hand of Herod and *from* all the expectation of the Jewish people."

So, when he had considered *this,* he came to the house of Mary, the mother of John whose surname was Mark, where many were gathered together praying. And as Peter knocked at the door of the gate, a girl named Rhoda came to answer. When she recognized Peter's voice, because of *her* gladness she did not open the gate, but ran in and announced that Peter stood before the gate. But they said to her, "You are beside yourself!" Yet she kept insisting that it was so. So they said, "It is his angel."

Now Peter continued knocking; and when they opened *the door* and saw him, they were astonished. But motioning to them with his hand to keep silent, he declared to them how the Lord had brought him out of the prison. And he said, "Go, tell these things to James and to the brethren." And he departed and went to another place.

Then, as soon as it was day, there was no small stir among the soldiers about what had become of Peter. But when Herod had searched for him and not found him, he examined the guards and commanded that *they* should be put to death.

And he went down from Judea to Caesarea, and stayed *there*.

Now Herod had been very angry with the people of Tyre and Sidon; but they came to him with one accord, and having made Blastus the king's personal aide their friend, they asked for peace, because their country was supplied with food by the king's *country*.

So on a set day Herod, arrayed in royal apparel, sat on his throne and gave an oration to them. And the people kept shouting, "The voice of a god and not of a man!" Then immediately an angel of the Lord struck him, because he did not give glory to God. And he was eaten by worms and died.

But the word of God grew and multiplied.

And Barnabas and Saul returned from Jerusalem when they had fulfilled *their* ministry, and they also took with them John whose surname was Mark.

Acts 10:34-43; 11:19-26; 12:1-25

WORSHIP

Oh, give thanks to the LORD, for *He is* good! For His mercy *endures* forever.

Let Israel now say,
"His mercy *endures* forever."
Let the house of Aaron now say,
"His mercy *endures* forever."
Let those who fear the LORD now say,
"His mercy *endures* forever."

Psalm 118:1-4

WISDOM

It is a snare for a man to devote rashly
   something as holy,
And afterward to reconsider *his* vows.

Proverbs 20:25

SW?! **SO WHAT?**
What does this tell me?

REAL FAITH PRODUCES ACTION

James 1:1-27; 2:14-26; Psalm 118:6-9; Proverbs 20:27

James, a bondservant of God and of the Lord Jesus Christ,

To the twelve tribes which are scattered abroad:

Greetings.

My brethren, count it all joy when you fall into various trials, knowing that the testing of your faith produces patience. But let patience have *its* perfect work, that you may be perfect and complete, lacking nothing. If any of you lacks wisdom, let him ask of God, who gives to all liberally and without reproach, and it will be given to him. But let him ask in faith, with no doubting, for he who doubts is like a wave of the sea driven and tossed by the wind. For let not that man suppose that he will receive anything from the Lord; *he is* a double-minded man, unstable in all his ways.

Let the lowly brother glory in his exaltation, but the rich in his humiliation, because as a flower of the field he will pass away. For no sooner has the sun risen with a burning heat than it withers the grass; its flower falls, and its beautiful appearance perishes. So the rich man also will fade away in his pursuits.

Blessed *is* the man who endures temptation; for when he has been approved, he will receive the crown of life which the Lord has promised to those who love Him. Let no one say when he is tempted, "I am tempted by God"; for God cannot be tempted by evil, nor does He Himself tempt anyone. But each one is tempted when he is drawn away by his own desires and enticed. Then, when desire has conceived, it gives birth to sin; and sin, when it is full-grown, brings forth death.

Do not be deceived, my beloved brethren. Every good gift and every perfect gift is from above, and comes down from the Father of lights, with whom there is no variation or shadow of turning. Of His own will He brought us forth by the word of truth, that we might be a kind of firstfruits of His creatures.

So then, my beloved brethren, let every man be swift to hear, slow to speak, slow to wrath; for the wrath of man does not produce the righteousness of God.

Therefore lay aside all filthiness and overflow of wickedness, and receive with meekness the implanted word, which is able to save your souls.

But be doers of the word, and not hearers only, deceiving yourselves. For if anyone is a hearer of the word and not a doer, he is like a man observing his natural face in a mirror; for he observes himself, goes away, and immediately forgets what kind of man he was. But he who looks into the perfect law of liberty and continues *in it,* and is not a forgetful hearer but a doer of the work, this one will be blessed in what he does.

If anyone among you thinks he is religious, and does not bridle his tongue but deceives his own heart, this one's religion *is* useless. Pure and undefiled religion before God and the Father is this: to visit orphans and widows in their trouble, *and* to keep oneself unspotted from the world.

What *does it* profit, my brethren, if someone says he has faith but does not have works? Can faith save him? If a brother or sister is naked and destitute of daily food, and one of you says to them, "Depart in peace, be warmed and filled," but you do not give them the things which are needed for the body, what *does it* profit? Thus also faith by itself, if it does not have works, is dead.

But someone will say, "You have faith, and I have works." Show me your faith without your works, and I will show you my faith by my works. You believe that there is one God. You do well. Even the demons believe—and tremble! But do you want to know, O foolish man, that faith without works is dead? Was not Abraham our father justified by works when he offered Isaac his son on the altar? Do you see that faith was working together with his works, and by works faith was made perfect? And the Scripture was fulfilled which says, "Abraham believed God, and it was accounted to him for righteousness." And he was called the friend of God. You see then that a man is justified by works, and not by faith only.

Likewise, was not Rahab the harlot also justified by works when she received the messengers and sent *them* out another way?

For as the body without the spirit is dead, so faith without works is dead also.

James 1:1-27; 2:14-26

WORSHIP

The LORD *is* on my side;
I will not fear.
What can man do to me?
The LORD is for me among those who help me;
Therefore I shall see *my desire* on those who
    hate me.
It is better to trust in the LORD
Than to put confidence in man.
It is better to trust in the LORD
Than to put confidence in princes.

Psalm 118:6-9

WISDOM

The spirit of a man *is* the lamp of the LORD,
Searching all the inner depths of his heart.

Proverbs 20:27

SW?! SO WHAT?
What does this tell me?

THE INCREDIBLE POWER OF THE TONGUE

James 3:1–4:3, 13-17; 5:7-20; Psalm 118:15-17; Proverbs 20:29

My brethren, let not many of you become teachers, knowing that we shall receive a stricter judgment. For we all stumble in many things. If anyone does not stumble in word, he *is* a perfect man, able also to bridle the whole body. Indeed, we put bits in horses' mouths that they may obey us, and we turn their whole body. Look also at ships: although they are so large and are driven by fierce winds, they are turned by a very small rudder wherever the pilot desires. Even so the tongue is a little member and boasts great things.

See how great a forest a little fire kindles! And the tongue *is* a fire, a world of iniquity. The tongue is so set among our members that it defiles the whole body, and sets on fire the course of nature; and it is set on fire by hell. For every kind of beast and bird, of reptile and creature of the sea, is tamed and has been tamed by mankind. But no man can tame the tongue. *It is* an unruly evil, full of deadly poison. With it we bless our God and Father, and with it we curse men, who have been made in the similitude of God. Out of the same mouth proceed blessing and cursing. My brethren, these things ought not to be so. Does a spring send forth fresh *water* and bitter from the same opening? Can a fig tree, my brethren, bear olives, or a grapevine bear figs? Thus no spring yields both salt water and fresh.

Who *is* wise and understanding among you? Let him show by good conduct *that* his works *are done* in the meekness of wisdom. But if you have bitter envy and self-seeking in your hearts, do not boast and lie against the truth. This wisdom does not descend from above, but *is* earthly, sensual, demonic. For where envy and self-seeking *exist,* confusion and every evil thing *are* there. But the wisdom that is from above is first pure, then peaceable, gentle, willing to yield, full of mercy and good fruits, without partiality and without hypocrisy. Now the fruit of righteousness is sown in peace by those who make peace.

Where do wars and fights *come* from among you? Do *they* not *come* from your *desires for* pleasure that war in your members? You lust and do not have. You murder and covet and cannot obtain. You fight and war. Yet you do not have because you do not ask. You ask and do not receive, because you ask amiss, that you may spend *it* on your pleasures.

Come now, you who say, "Today or tomorrow we will go to such and such a city, spend a year there, buy and sell, and make a profit"; whereas you do not know what *will happen* tomorrow. For what *is* your life? It is even a vapor that appears for a little time and then vanishes away. Instead you *ought* to say, "If the Lord wills, we shall live and do this or that." But now you boast in your arrogance. All such boasting is evil.

Therefore, to him who knows to do good and does not do *it,* to him it is sin.

Therefore be patient, brethren, until the coming of the Lord. See *how* the farmer waits for the precious fruit of the earth, waiting patiently for it until it receives the early and latter rain. You also *be* patient. Establish your hearts, for the coming of the Lord is at hand.

Do not grumble against one another, brethren, lest you be condemned. Behold, the Judge is standing at the door! My brethren, take the prophets, who spoke in the name of the Lord, as an example of suffering and patience. Indeed we count them blessed who endure. You have heard of the perseverance of Job and seen the end *intended by* the Lord—that the Lord is very compassionate and merciful.

But above all, my brethren, do not swear, either by heaven or by earth or with any other oath. But let your "Yes," be "Yes," and *your* "No," "No," lest you fall into judgment.

Is anyone among you suffering? Let him pray. Is anyone cheerful? Let him sing psalms. Is anyone among you sick? Let him call for the elders of the church, and let them pray over him, anointing him with oil in the name of the Lord. And the prayer of faith will save the sick, and the Lord will raise him up. And if he has committed sins, he will be forgiven. Confess *your* trespasses to one another, and pray for one another, that you may be healed. The effective, fervent prayer of a righteous man avails much. Elijah was a man with a nature like ours, and he prayed earnestly that it would not rain; and it did not rain on the land for three years and six months. And he prayed again, and the heaven gave rain, and the earth produced its fruit.

Brethren, if anyone among you wanders from the truth, and someone turns him back, let him know that he who turns a sinner from the error of his way will save a soul from death and cover a multitude of sins.

James 3:1–4:3, 13-17; 5:7-20

WORSHIP

The voice of rejoicing and salvation
Is in the tents of the righteous;
The right hand of the LORD does valiantly.
The right hand of the LORD is exalted;
The right hand of the LORD does valiantly.
I shall not die, but live,
And declare the works of the LORD.

Psalm 118:15-17

WISDOM

The glory of young men *is* their strength,
And the splendor of old men *is* their gray
    head.

Proverbs 20:29

SO WHAT?
What does this tell me?

PAUL AND COMPANIONS HEAD FOR GALATIA

Acts 13:1-43; Psalm 118:22-26; Proverbs 21:1

Now in the church that was at Antioch there were certain prophets and teachers: Barnabas, Simeon who was called Niger, Lucius of Cyrene, Manaen who had been brought up with Herod the tetrarch, and Saul. As they ministered to the Lord and fasted, the Holy Spirit said, "Now separate to Me Barnabas and Saul for the work to which I have called them." Then, having fasted and prayed, and laid hands on them, they sent *them* away.

So, being sent out by the Holy Spirit, they went down to Seleucia, and from there they sailed to Cyprus. And when they arrived in Salamis, they preached the word of God in the synagogues of the Jews. They also had John as *their* assistant.

Now when they had gone through the island to Paphos, they found a certain sorcerer, a false prophet, a Jew whose name *was* Bar-Jesus, who was with the proconsul, Sergius Paulus, an intelligent man. This man called for Barnabas and Saul and sought to hear the word of God. But Elymas the sorcerer (for so his name is translated) withstood them, seeking to turn the proconsul away from the faith. Then Saul, who also *is called* Paul, filled with the Holy Spirit, looked intently at him and said, "O full of all deceit and all fraud, *you* son of the devil, *you* enemy of all righteousness, will you not cease perverting the straight ways of the Lord? And now, indeed, the hand of the Lord *is* upon you, and you shall be blind, not seeing the sun for a time."

And immediately a dark mist fell on him, and he went around seeking someone to lead him by the hand. Then the proconsul believed, when he saw what had been done, being astonished at the teaching of the Lord.

Now when Paul and his party set sail from Paphos, they came to Perga in Pamphylia; and John, departing from them, returned to Jerusalem. But when they departed from Perga, they came to Antioch in Pisidia, and went into the synagogue on the Sabbath day and sat down. And after the reading of the Law and the Prophets, the rulers of the synagogue sent to them, saying, "Men *and* brethren, if you have any word of exhortation for the people, say on."

Then Paul stood up, and motioning with *his* hand said, "Men of Israel, and you who fear God, listen: The God of this people Israel chose our fathers, and exalted the people when they dwelt as strangers in the land of Egypt, and with an uplifted arm He brought them out of it. Now for a time of about forty years He put up with their ways in the wilderness. And when He had destroyed seven nations in the land of Canaan, He distributed their land to them by allotment.

"After that He gave *them* judges for about four hundred and fifty years, until Samuel the prophet. And afterward they asked for a king; so God gave them Saul the son of Kish, a man of the tribe of Benjamin, for forty years. And when He had removed him, He raised up for them David as king, to whom also He gave testimony and said, 'I have found David the *son* of Jesse, a man after My *own* heart, who will do all My will.' From this man's seed, according to *the* promise, God raised up for Israel a Savior—Jesus—after John had first preached, before His coming, the baptism of repentance to all the people of Israel. And as John was finishing his course, he said, 'Who do you think I am? I am not *He*. But behold, there comes One after me, the sandals of whose feet I am not worthy to loose.'

"Men *and* brethren, sons of the family of Abraham, and those among you who fear God, to you the word of this salvation has been sent. For those who dwell in Jerusalem, and their rulers, because they did not know Him, nor even the voices of the Prophets which are read every Sabbath, have fulfilled *them* in condemning *Him*. And though they found no cause for death *in Him,* they asked Pilate that He should be put to death. Now when they had fulfilled all that was written concerning Him, they took *Him* down from the tree and laid *Him* in a tomb. But God raised Him from the dead. He was seen for many days by those who came up with Him from Galilee to Jerusalem, who are His witnesses to the people. And we declare to you glad

APOSTLES AND THE CHURCH

tidings—that promise which was made to the fathers. God has fulfilled this for us their children, in that He has raised up Jesus. As it is also written in the second Psalm:

'You are My Son,
Today I have begotten You.'

And that He raised Him from the dead, no more to return to corruption, He has spoken thus:

I will give you the sure mercies of David.'

Therefore He also says in another *Psalm:*

'You will not allow Your Holy One to see corruption.'

"For David, after he had served his own generation by the will of God, fell asleep, was buried with his fathers, and saw corruption; but He whom God raised up saw no corruption. Therefore let it be known to you, brethren, that through this Man is preached to you the forgiveness of sins; and by Him everyone who believes is justified from all things from which you could not be justified by the law of Moses. Beware therefore, lest what has been spoken in the prophets come upon you:

'Behold, you despisers,
Marvel and perish!
For I work a work in your days,
A work which you will by no means believe,
Though one were to declare it to you.' "

So when the Jews went out of the synagogue, the Gentiles begged that these words might be preached to them the next Sabbath. Now when the congregation had broken up, many of the Jews and devout proselytes followed Paul and Barnabas, who, speaking to them, persuaded them to continue in the grace of God.

Acts 13:1-43

WoRSHiP

The stone *which* the builders rejected
Has become the chief cornerstone.
This was the LORD's doing;
It *is* marvelous in our eyes.
This *is* the day the LORD has made;
We will rejoice and be glad in it.

Save now, I pray, O LORD;
O LORD, I pray, send now prosperity.
Blessed *is* he who comes in the name of the LORD!
We have blessed you from the house of the LORD.

Psalm 118:22-26

WiSDoM

The king's heart *is* in the hand of the LORD,
Like the rivers of water;
He turns it wherever He wishes.

Proverbs 21:1

SW?! **SO WHAT?**
What does this tell me?

A DOOR IS OPENED TO THE GENTILES
Acts 13:44–14:28; Psalm 119:1-3; Proverbs 21:2

On the next Sabbath almost the whole city came together to hear the word of God. But when the Jews saw the multitudes, they were filled with envy; and contradicting and blaspheming, they opposed the things spoken by Paul. Then Paul and Barnabas grew bold and said, "It was necessary that the word of God should be spoken to you first; but since you reject it, and judge yourselves unworthy of everlasting life, behold, we turn to the Gentiles. For so the Lord has commanded us:

'I have set you as a light to the Gentiles,
That you should be for salvation to the ends
of the earth.' "

Now when the Gentiles heard this, they were glad and glorified the word of the Lord. And as many as had been appointed to eternal life believed.

And the word of the Lord was being spread throughout all the region. But the Jews stirred up the devout and prominent women and the chief men of the city, raised up persecution against Paul and Barnabas, and expelled them from their region. But they shook off the dust from their feet against them, and came to Iconium. And the disciples were filled with joy and with the Holy Spirit.

Now it happened in Iconium that they went together to the synagogue of the Jews, and so spoke that a great multitude both of the Jews and of the Greeks believed. But the unbelieving Jews stirred up the Gentiles and poisoned their minds against the brethren. Therefore they stayed there a long time, speaking boldly in the Lord, who was bearing witness to the word of His grace, granting signs and wonders to be done by their hands.

But the multitude of the city was divided: part sided with the Jews, and part with the apostles. And when a violent attempt was made by both the Gentiles and Jews, with their rulers, to abuse and stone them, they became aware of it and fled to Lystra and Derbe, cities of Lycaonia, and to the surrounding region. And they were preaching the gospel there.

And in Lystra a certain man without strength in his feet was sitting, a cripple from his mother's womb, who had never walked. *This* man heard Paul speaking. Paul, observing him intently and seeing that he had faith to be healed, said with a loud voice, "Stand up straight on your feet!" And he leaped and walked. Now when the people saw what Paul had done, they raised their voices, saying in the Lycaonian *language*, "The gods have come down to us in the likeness of men!" And Barnabas they called Zeus, and Paul, Hermes, because he was the chief speaker. Then the priest of Zeus, whose temple was in front of their city, brought oxen and garlands to the gates, intending to sacrifice with the multitudes.

But when the apostles Barnabas and Paul heard this, they tore their clothes and ran in among the multitude, crying out and saying, "Men, why are you doing these things? We also are men with the same nature as you, and preach to you that you should turn from these useless things to the living God, who made the heaven, the earth, the sea, and all things that are in them, who in bygone generations allowed all nations to walk in their own ways. Nevertheless He did not leave Himself without witness, in that He did good, gave us rain from heaven and fruitful seasons, filling our hearts with food and gladness." And with these sayings they could scarcely restrain the multitudes from sacrificing to them.

Then Jews from Antioch and Iconium came there; and having persuaded the multitudes, they stoned Paul *and* dragged *him* out of the city, supposing him to be dead. However, when the disciples gathered around him, he rose up and went into the city. And the next day he departed with Barnabas to Derbe.

And when they had preached the gospel to that city and made many disciples, they returned to Lystra, Iconium, and Antioch, strengthening the souls of the disciples, exhorting *them* to continue in the faith, and *saying,* "We must through many tribulations enter the kingdom of God." So when they had appointed elders in every church, and prayed with fasting, they commended them to the Lord in whom they had believed. And after they had passed through Pisidia, they came to Pamphylia.

APOSTLES AND THE CHURCH

Now when they had preached the word in Perga, they went down to Attalia. From there they sailed to Antioch, where they had been commended to the grace of God for the work which they had completed.

Now when they had come and gathered the church together, they reported all that God had done with them, and that He had opened the door of faith to the Gentiles. So they stayed there a long time with the disciples.

Acts 13:44–14:28

WORSHIP

Blessed *are* the undefiled in the way,
Who walk in the law of the LORD!
Blessed *are* those who keep His testimonies,
Who seek Him with the whole heart!
They also do no iniquity;
They walk in His ways.

Psalm 119:1-3

WISDOM

Every way of a man *is* right in his own eyes,
But the LORD weighs the hearts.

Proverbs 21:2

SW?! SO WHAT?
What does this tell me?

THE COUNCIL AT JERUSALEM MAKES A DECREE

Acts 15; Psalm 119:9-11; Proverbs 21:3

And certain *men* came down from Judea and taught the brethren, "Unless you are circumcised according to the custom of Moses, you cannot be saved." Therefore, when Paul and Barnabas had no small dissension and dispute with them, they determined that Paul and Barnabas and certain others of them should go up to Jerusalem, to the apostles and elders, about this question.

So, being sent on their way by the church, they passed through Phoenicia and Samaria, describing the conversion of the Gentiles; and they caused great joy to all the brethren. And when they had come to Jerusalem, they were received by the church and the apostles and the elders; and they reported all things that God had done with them. But some of the sect of the Pharisees who believed rose up, saying, "It is necessary to circumcise them, and to command *them* to keep the law of Moses."

Now the apostles and elders came together to consider this matter. And when there had been much dispute, Peter rose up and said to them: "Men and brethren, you know that a good while ago God chose among us, that by my mouth the Gentiles should hear the word of the gospel and believe. So God, who knows the heart, acknowledged them by giving them the Holy Spirit, just as *He did* to us, and made no distinction between us and them, purifying their hearts by faith. Now therefore, why do you test God by putting a yoke on the neck of the disciples which neither our fathers nor we were able to bear? But we believe that through the grace of the Lord Jesus Christ we shall be saved in the same manner as they."

Then all the multitude kept silent and listened to Barnabas and Paul declaring how many miracles and wonders God had worked through them among the Gentiles. And after they had become silent, James answered, saying, "Men *and* brethren, listen to me: Simon has declared how God at the first visited the Gentiles to take out of them a people for His name. And with this the words of the prophets agree, just as it is written:

'After this I will return
And will rebuild the tabernacle of David, which
        has fallen down;
I will rebuild its ruins,
And I will set it up;
So that the rest of mankind may seek the LORD,
Even all the Gentiles who are called by My
        name,
Says the LORD who does all these things.'

"Known to God from eternity are all His works. Therefore I judge that we should not trouble those from among the Gentiles who are turning to God, but that we write to them to abstain from things polluted by idols, *from* sexual immorality, *from* things strangled, and *from* blood. For Moses has had throughout many generations those who preach him in every city, being read in the synagogues every Sabbath."

Then it pleased the apostles and elders, with the whole church, to send chosen men of their own company to Antioch with Paul and Barnabas, *namely,* Judas who was also named Barsabas, and Silas, leading men among the brethren.

They wrote this *letter* by them:

The apostles, the elders, and the brethren,

To the brethren who are of the Gentiles in Antioch, Syria, and Cilicia:

Greetings.

Since we have heard that some who went out from us have troubled you with words, unsettling your souls, saying, "*You must* be circumcised and keep the law"—to whom we gave no *such* commandment— it seemed good to us, being assembled with one accord, to send chosen men to you with our beloved Barnabas and Paul, men who have risked their lives for the name of our Lord Jesus Christ. We have therefore sent Judas and Silas, who will also report the same things by word of mouth. For it seemed good to the Holy Spirit, and to us, to lay upon you no greater burden than these necessary things: that you abstain from things

APOSTLES AND THE CHURCH

offered to idols, from blood, from things strangled, and from sexual immorality. If you keep yourselves from these, you will do well.

Farewell.

So when they were sent off, they came to Antioch; and when they had gathered the multitude together, they delivered the letter. When they had read it, they rejoiced over its encouragement. Now Judas and Silas, themselves being prophets also, exhorted and strengthened the brethren with many words. And after they had stayed *there* for a time, they were sent back with greetings from the brethren to the apostles.

However, it seemed good to Silas to remain there. Paul and Barnabas also remained in Antioch, teaching and preaching the word of the Lord, with many others also.

Then after some days Paul said to Barnabas, "Let us now go back and visit our brethren in every city where we have preached the word of the Lord, *and see* how they are doing." Now Barnabas was determined to take with them John called Mark. But Paul insisted that they should not take with them the one who had departed from them in Pamphylia, and had not gone with them to the work. Then the contention became so sharp that they parted from one another. And so Barnabas took Mark and sailed to Cyprus; but Paul chose Silas and departed, being commended by the brethren to the grace of God. And he went through Syria and Cilicia, strengthening the churches.

Acts 15

WORSHIP

How can a young man cleanse his way?
By taking heed according to Your word.
With my whole heart I have sought You;
Oh, let me not wander from Your
    commandments!
Your word I have hidden in my heart,
That I might not sin against You.

Psalm 119:9-11

WISDOM

To do righteousness and justice
Is more acceptable to the LORD than sacrifice.

Proverbs 21:3

SW?! SO WHAT?
What does this tell me?

Beware a DIFFERENT Gospel!   Galatians 1–2; Psalm 119:17-18, 24; Proverbs 21:5

Paul, an apostle (not from men nor through man, but through Jesus Christ and God the Father who raised Him from the dead), and all the brethren who are with me,

To the churches of Galatia:

Grace to you and peace from God the Father and our Lord Jesus Christ, who gave Himself for our sins, that He might deliver us from this present evil age, according to the will of our God and Father, to whom *be* glory forever and ever. Amen.

I marvel that you are turning away so soon from Him who called you in the grace of Christ, to a different gospel, which is not another; but there are some who trouble you and want to pervert the gospel of Christ. But even if we, or an angel from heaven, preach any other gospel to you than what we have preached to you, let him be accursed. As we have said before, so now I say again, if anyone preaches any other gospel to you than what you have received, let him be accursed.

For do I now persuade men, or God? Or do I seek to please men? For if I still pleased men, I would not be a bondservant of Christ.

But I make known to you, brethren, that the gospel which was preached by me is not according to man. For I neither received it from man, nor was I taught *it,* but *it came* through the revelation of Jesus Christ.

For you have heard of my former conduct in Judaism, how I persecuted the church of God beyond measure and *tried to* destroy it. And I advanced in Judaism beyond many of my contemporaries in my own nation, being more exceedingly zealous for the traditions of my fathers.

But when it pleased God, who separated me from my mother's womb and called *me* through His grace, to reveal His Son in me, that I might preach Him among the Gentiles, I did not immediately confer with flesh and blood, nor did I go up to Jerusalem to those *who were* apostles before me; but I went to Arabia, and returned again to Damascus.

Then after three years I went up to Jerusalem to see Peter, and remained with him fifteen days. But I saw none of the other apostles except James, the Lord's brother. (Now *concerning* the things which I write to you, indeed, before God, I do not lie.)

Afterward I went into the regions of Syria and Cilicia. And I was unknown by face to the churches of Judea which *were* in Christ. But they were hearing only, "He who formerly persecuted us now preaches the faith which he once *tried to* destroy." And they glorified God in me.

Then after fourteen years I went up again to Jerusalem with Barnabas, and also took Titus with *me.* And I went up by revelation, and communicated to them that gospel which I preach among the Gentiles, but privately to those who were of reputation, lest by any means I might run, or had run, in vain. Yet not even Titus who *was* with me, being a Greek, was compelled to be circumcised. And *this occurred* because of false brethren secretly brought in (who came in by stealth to spy out our liberty which we have in Christ Jesus, that they might bring us into bondage), to whom we did not yield submission even for an hour, that the truth of the gospel might continue with you.

But from those who seemed to be something—whatever they were, it makes no difference to me; God shows personal favoritism to no man—for those who seemed *to be something* added nothing to me. But on the contrary, when they saw that the gospel for the uncircumcised had been committed to me, as *the gospel* for the circumcised *was* to Peter (for He who worked effectively in Peter for the apostleship to the circumcised also worked effectively in me toward the Gentiles), and when James, Cephas, and John, who seemed to be pillars, perceived the grace that had been given to me, they gave me and Barnabas the right hand of fellowship, that we *should go* to the Gentiles and they to the circumcised. *They desired* only that we should remember the poor, the very thing which I also was eager to do.

Now when Peter had come to Antioch, I withstood him to his face, because he was to be blamed; for before certain men came from James, he would eat with the Gentiles; but when they came, he withdrew and separated himself, fearing those who were of the circumcision. And the rest of the Jews also played the hypocrite with him, so that even Barnabas was carried away with their hypocrisy.

But when I saw that they were not straightforward about the truth of the gospel, I said to Peter before *them* all, "If you, being a Jew, live in the manner of Gentiles and not as the Jews, why do you compel Gentiles to live as Jews? We *who are* Jews by nature, and not sinners of the Gentiles, knowing that a man is not justified by the works of the law but by faith in Jesus Christ, even we have believed in Christ Jesus, that we might be justified by faith in Christ and not by the works of the law; for by the works of the law no flesh shall be justified.

"But if, while we seek to be justified by Christ, we ourselves also are found sinners, *is* Christ therefore a minister of sin? Certainly not! For if I build again those things which I destroyed, I make myself a transgressor. For I through the law died to the law that I might live to God. I have been crucified with Christ; it is no longer I who live, but Christ lives in me; and the *life* which I now live in the flesh I live by faith in the Son of God, who loved me and gave Himself for me. I do not set aside the grace of God; for if righteousness *comes* through the law, then Christ died in vain."

Galatians 1–2

WORSHIP

Deal bountifully with Your servant,
That I may live and keep Your word.
Open my eyes, that I may see
Wondrous things from Your law.

Your testimonies also *are* my delight
And my counselors.

Psalm 119:17-18, 24

WISDOM

The plans of the diligent *lead* surely to plenty,
But *those of* everyone *who is* hasty, surely to poverty.

Proverbs 21:5

SW?! **SO WHAT?**
What does this tell me?

JUSTIFICATION COMES BY FAITH

Galatians 3:1-14, 21-29; 4:1-20;
Psalm 119:25-27; Proverbs 21:6

O foolish Galatians! Who has bewitched you that you should not obey the truth, before whose eyes Jesus Christ was clearly portrayed among you as crucified? This only I want to learn from you: Did you receive the Spirit by the works of the law, or by the hearing of faith? Are you so foolish? Having begun in the Spirit, are you now being made perfect by the flesh? Have you suffered so many things in vain—if indeed *it was* in vain?

Therefore He who supplies the Spirit to you and works miracles among you, *does He do it* by the works of the law, or by the hearing of faith?— just as Abraham "believed God, and it was accounted to him for righteousness." Therefore know that *only* those who are of faith are sons of Abraham. And the Scripture, foreseeing that God would justify the Gentiles by faith, preached the gospel to Abraham beforehand, *saying,* "In you all the nations shall be blessed." So then those who *are* of faith are blessed with believing Abraham.

For as many as are of the works of the law are under the curse; for it is written, "Cursed *is* everyone who does not continue in all things which are written in the book of the law, to do them." But that no one is justified by the law in the sight of God *is* evident, for "the just shall live by faith." Yet the law is not of faith, but "the man who does them shall live by them."

Christ has redeemed us from the curse of the law, having become a curse for us (for it is written, "Cursed *is* everyone who hangs on a tree"), that the blessing of Abraham might come upon the Gentiles in Christ Jesus, that we might receive the promise of the Spirit through faith.

Is the law then against the promises of God? Certainly not! For if there had been a law given which could have given life, truly righteousness would have been by the law. But the Scripture has confined all under sin, that the promise by faith in Jesus Christ might be given to those who believe. But before faith came, we were kept under guard by the law, kept for the faith which would afterward be revealed. Therefore the law was our tutor *to bring us* to Christ, that we might be justified by faith. But after faith has come, we are no longer under a tutor.

For you are all sons of God through faith in Christ Jesus. For as many of you as were baptized into Christ have put on Christ. There is neither Jew nor Greek, there is neither slave nor free, there is neither male nor female; for you are all one in Christ Jesus. And if you *are* Christ's, then you are Abraham's seed, and heirs according to the promise.

Now I say *that* the heir, as long as he is a child, does not differ at all from a slave, though he is master of all, but is under guardians and stewards until the time appointed by the father. Even so we, when we were children, were in bondage under the elements of the world. But when the fullness of the time had come, God sent forth His Son, born of a woman, born under the law, to redeem those who were under the law, that we might receive the adoption as sons.

And because you are sons, God has sent forth the Spirit of His Son into your hearts, crying out, "Abba, Father!" Therefore you are no longer a slave but a son, and if a son, then an heir of God through Christ.

But then, indeed, when you did not know God, you served those which by nature are not gods. But now after you have known God, or rather are known by God, how *is it that* you turn again to the weak and beggarly elements, to which you desire again to be in bondage? You observe days and months and seasons and years. I am afraid for you, lest I have labored for you in vain.

Brethren, I urge you to become like me, for I *became* like you. You have not injured me at all. You know that because of physical infirmity I preached the gospel to you at the first. And my trial which was in my flesh you did not despise or reject, but you received me as an angel of God, *even* as Christ Jesus. What then was the blessing you *enjoyed?* For I bear you witness that, if possible, you would have plucked out your own eyes and given them to me. Have I therefore become your enemy because I tell you the truth?

They zealously court you, *but* for no good; yes, they want to exclude you, that you may be zealous for them. But it is good to be zealous in a good thing always, and not only when I am present with you. My little children, for whom I labor in birth again until Christ is formed in you, I would like to be present with you now and to change my tone; for I have doubts about you.

Galatians 3:1-14, 21-29; 4:1-20

WORSHIP

My soul clings to the dust;
Revive me according to Your word.
I have declared my ways, and You answered me;
Teach me Your statutes.
Make me understand the way of Your precepts;
So shall I meditate on Your wondrous works.

Psalm 119:25-27

WISDOM

Getting treasures by a lying tongue
Is the fleeting fantasy of those who seek death.

Proverbs 21:6

SW?! SO WHAT?
What does this tell me?

FOLLOW THE SPIRIT TO FREEDOM

Galatians 5–6; Psalm 119:33–35, 37; Proverbs 21:13

Stand fast therefore in the liberty by which Christ has made us free, and do not be entangled again with a yoke of bondage. Indeed I, Paul, say to you that if you become circumcised, Christ will profit you nothing. And I testify again to every man who becomes circumcised that he is a debtor to keep the whole law. You have become estranged from Christ, you who *attempt to* be justified by law; you have fallen from grace. For we through the Spirit eagerly wait for the hope of righteousness by faith. For in Christ Jesus neither circumcision nor uncircumcision avails anything, but faith working through love.

You ran well. Who hindered you from obeying the truth? This persuasion does not *come* from Him who calls you. A little leaven leavens the whole lump. I have confidence in you, in the Lord, that you will have no other mind; but he who troubles you shall bear his judgment, whoever he is.

And I, brethren, if I still preach circumcision, why do I still suffer persecution? Then the offense of the cross has ceased. I could wish that those who trouble you would even cut themselves off!

For you, brethren, have been called to liberty; only do not *use* liberty as an opportunity for the flesh, but through love serve one another. For all the law is fulfilled in one word, *even* in this: "You shall love your neighbor as yourself." But if you bite and devour one another, beware lest you be consumed by one another!

I say then: Walk in the Spirit, and you shall not fulfill the lust of the flesh. For the flesh lusts against the Spirit, and the Spirit against the flesh; and these are contrary to one another, so that you do not do the things that you wish. But if you are led by the Spirit, you are not under the law.

Now the works of the flesh are evident, which are: adultery, fornication, uncleanness, lewdness, idolatry, sorcery, hatred, contentions, jealousies, outbursts of wrath, selfish ambitions, dissensions, heresies, envy, murders, drunkenness, revelries, and the like; of which I tell you beforehand, just as I also told *you* in time past, that those who practice such things will not inherit the kingdom of God.

But the fruit of the Spirit is love, joy, peace, longsuffering, kindness, goodness, faithfulness, gentleness, self-control. Against such there is no law. And those *who are* Christ's have crucified the flesh with its passions and desires. If we live in the Spirit, let us also walk in the Spirit. Let us not become conceited, provoking one another, envying one another.

Brethren, if a man is overtaken in any trespass, you who *are* spiritual restore such a one in a spirit of gentleness, considering yourself lest you also be tempted. Bear one another's burdens, and so fulfill the law of Christ. For if anyone thinks himself to be something, when he is nothing, he deceives himself. But let each one examine his own work, and then he will have rejoicing in himself alone, and not in another. For each one shall bear his own load.

Let him who is taught the word share in all good things with him who teaches.

Do not be deceived, God is not mocked; for whatever a man sows, that he will also reap. For he who sows to his flesh will of the flesh reap corruption, but he who sows to the Spirit will of the Spirit reap everlasting life. And let us not grow weary while doing good, for in due season we shall reap if we do not lose heart. Therefore, as we have opportunity, let us do good to all, especially to those who are of the household of faith.

See with what large letters I have written to you with my own hand! As many as desire to make a good showing in the flesh, these *would* compel you to be circumcised, only that they may not suffer persecution for the cross of Christ. For not even those who are circumcised keep the law, but they desire to have you circumcised that they may boast in your flesh. But God forbid that I should boast except in the cross of our Lord Jesus Christ, by whom the world has been crucified to me, and I to the world. For in Christ Jesus neither circumcision nor uncircumcision avails anything, but a new creation.

And as many as walk according to this rule, peace and mercy *be* upon them, and upon the Israel of God.

APOSTLES AND THE CHURCH

From now on let no one trouble me, for I bear in my body the marks of the Lord Jesus.

Brethren, the grace of our Lord Jesus Christ *be* with your spirit. Amen.

Galatians 5–6

WORSHIP

Teach me, O LORD, the way of Your statutes,
And I shall keep it *to* the end.
Give me understanding, and I shall keep Your
    law;
Indeed, I shall observe it with *my* whole heart.
Make me walk in the path of Your
        commandments,
For I delight in it.

Turn away my eyes from looking at worthless
    things,
And revive me in Your way.

Psalm 119:33-35, 37

WISDOM

Whoever shuts his ears to the cry of the poor
Will also cry himself and not be heard.

Proverbs 21:13

SW?! **SO WHAT?**
What does this tell me?

PAUL AND COMPANIONS HEAD FOR GREECE

Acts 16; Psalm 119:44–47; Proverbs 21:16

Then he came to Derbe and Lystra. And behold, a certain disciple was there, named Timothy, *the* son of a certain Jewish woman who believed, but his father *was* Greek. He was well spoken of by the brethren who were at Lystra and Iconium. Paul wanted to have him go on with him. And he took *him* and circumcised him because of the Jews who were in that region, for they all knew that his father was Greek. And as they went through the cities, they delivered to them the decrees to keep, which were determined by the apostles and elders at Jerusalem. So the churches were strengthened in the faith, and increased in number daily.

Now when they had gone through Phrygia and the region of Galatia, they were forbidden by the Holy Spirit to preach the word in Asia. After they had come to Mysia, they tried to go into Bithynia, but the Spirit did not permit them. So passing by Mysia, they came down to Troas. And a vision appeared to Paul in the night. A man of Macedonia stood and pleaded with him, saying, "Come over to Macedonia and help us." Now after he had seen the vision, immediately we sought to go to Macedonia, concluding that the Lord had called us to preach the gospel to them.

Therefore, sailing from Troas, we ran a straight course to Samothrace, and the next *day* came to Neapolis, and from there to Philippi, which is the foremost city of that part of Macedonia, a colony. And we were staying in that city for some days. And on the Sabbath day we went out of the city to the riverside, where prayer was customarily made; and we sat down and spoke to the women who met *there*. Now a certain woman named Lydia heard *us*. She was a seller of purple from the city of Thyatira, who worshiped God. The Lord opened her heart to heed the things spoken by Paul. And when she and her household were baptized, she begged *us,* saying, "If you have judged me to be faithful to the Lord, come to my house and stay." So she persuaded us.

Now it happened, as we went to prayer, that a certain slave girl possessed with a spirit of divination met us, who brought her masters much profit by fortune-telling. This girl followed Paul and us, and cried out, saying, "These men are the servants of the Most High God, who proclaim to us the way of salvation." And this she did for many days.

But Paul, greatly annoyed, turned and said to the spirit, "I command you in the name of Jesus Christ to come out of her." And he came out that very hour. But when her masters saw that their hope of profit was gone, they seized Paul and Silas and dragged *them* into the marketplace to the authorities.

And they brought them to the magistrates, and said, "These men, being Jews, exceedingly trouble our city; and they teach customs which are not lawful for us, being Romans, to receive or observe." Then the multitude rose up together against them; and the magistrates tore off their clothes and commanded *them* to be beaten with rods. And when they had laid many stripes on them, they threw *them* into prison, commanding the jailer to keep them securely. Having received such a charge, he put them into the inner prison and fastened their feet in the stocks.

But at midnight Paul and Silas were praying and singing hymns to God, and the prisoners were listening to them. Suddenly there was a great earthquake, so that the foundations of the prison were shaken; and immediately all the doors were opened and everyone's chains were loosed. And the keeper of the prison, awaking from sleep and seeing the prison doors open, supposing the prisoners had fled, drew his sword and was about to kill himself. But Paul called with a loud voice, saying, "Do yourself no harm, for we are all here."

Then he called for a light, ran in, and fell down trembling before Paul and Silas. And he brought them out and said, "Sirs, what must I do to be saved?"

So they said, "Believe on the Lord Jesus Christ, and you will be saved, you and your household." Then they spoke the word of the Lord to him and to all who were in his house. And he took them the same hour of the night and washed *their* stripes.

APOSTLES AND THE CHURCH

And immediately he and all his family were baptized. Now when he had brought them into his house, he set food before them; and he rejoiced, having believed in God with all his household.

And when it was day, the magistrates sent the officers, saying, "Let those men go."

So the keeper of the prison reported these words to Paul, saying, "The magistrates have sent to let you go. Now therefore depart, and go in peace."

But Paul said to them, "They have beaten us openly, uncondemned Romans, *and* have thrown *us* into prison. And now do they put us out secretly? No indeed! Let them come themselves and get us out."

And the officers told these words to the magistrates, and they were afraid when they heard that they were Romans. Then they came and pleaded with them and brought *them* out, and asked *them* to depart from the city. So they went out of the prison and entered *the house of* Lydia; and when they had seen the brethren, they encouraged them and departed.

Acts 16

WORSHIP

So shall I keep Your law continually,
Forever and ever.
And I will walk at liberty,
For I seek Your precepts.
I will speak of Your testimonies also before
      kings,
And will not be ashamed.
And I will delight myself in Your
      commandments,
Which I love.

Psalm 119:44-47

WISDOM

A man who wanders from the way of
      understanding
Will rest in the assembly of the dead.

Proverbs 21:16

SW?! **SO WHAT?**
What does this tell me?

TURNING THE WORLD UPSIDE DOWN

Acts 17:1–18:11; Psalm 119:53-55; Proverbs 21:17

Now when they had passed through Amphipolis and Apollonia, they came to Thessalonica, where there was a synagogue of the Jews. Then Paul, as his custom was, went in to them, and for three Sabbaths reasoned with them from the Scriptures, explaining and demonstrating that the Christ had to suffer and rise again from the dead, and *saying,* "This Jesus whom I preach to you is the Christ." And some of them were persuaded; and a great multitude of the devout Greeks, and not a few of the leading women, joined Paul and Silas.

But the Jews who were not persuaded, becoming envious, took some of the evil men from the marketplace, and gathering a mob, set all the city in an uproar and attacked the house of Jason, and sought to bring them out to the people. But when they did not find them, they dragged Jason and some brethren to the rulers of the city, crying out, "These who have turned the world upside down have come here too. Jason has harbored them, and these are all acting contrary to the decrees of Caesar, saying there is another king—Jesus." And they troubled the crowd and the rulers of the city when they heard these things. So when they had taken security from Jason and the rest, they let them go.

Then the brethren immediately sent Paul and Silas away by night to Berea. When they arrived, they went into the synagogue of the Jews. These were more fair-minded than those in Thessalonica, in that they received the word with all readiness, and searched the Scriptures daily *to find out* whether these things were so. Therefore many of them believed, and also not a few of the Greeks, prominent women as well as men. But when the Jews from Thessalonica learned that the word of God was preached by Paul at Berea, they came there also and stirred up the crowds. Then immediately the brethren sent Paul away, to go to the sea; but both Silas and Timothy remained there. So those who conducted Paul brought him to Athens; and receiving a command for Silas and Timothy to come to him with all speed, they departed.

Now while Paul waited for them at Athens, his spirit was provoked within him when he saw that the city was given over to idols. Therefore he reasoned in the synagogue with the Jews and with the *Gentile* worshipers, and in the marketplace daily with those who happened to be there. Then certain Epicurean and Stoic philosophers encountered him. And some said, "What does this babbler want to say?"

Others said, "He seems to be a proclaimer of foreign gods," because he preached to them Jesus and the resurrection.

And they took him and brought him to the Areopagus, saying, "May we know what this new doctrine *is* of which you speak? For you are bringing some strange things to our ears. Therefore we want to know what these things mean." For all the Athenians and the foreigners who were there spent their time in nothing else but either to tell or to hear some new thing.

Then Paul stood in the midst of the Areopagus and said, "Men of Athens, I perceive that in all things you are very religious; for as I was passing through and considering the objects of your worship, I even found an altar with this inscription:

TO THE UNKNOWN GOD.

Therefore, the One whom you worship without knowing, Him I proclaim to you: God, who made the world and everything in it, since He is Lord of heaven and earth, does not dwell in temples made with hands. Nor is He worshiped with men's hands, as though He needed anything, since He gives to all life, breath, and all things. And He has made from one blood every nation of men to dwell on all the face of the earth, and has determined their preappointed times and the boundaries of their dwellings, so that they should seek the Lord, in the hope that they might grope for Him and find Him, though He is not far from each one of us; for in Him we live and move and have our being, as also some of your own poets have said, 'For we are also His offspring.' Therefore, since we are the offspring of God, we ought not to think that the Divine Nature is like gold or silver or stone, something shaped by

art and man's devising. Truly, these times of ignorance God overlooked, but now commands all men
everywhere to repent, because He has appointed a
day on which He will judge the world in righteousness by the Man whom He has ordained. He has
given assurance of this to all by raising Him from
the dead."

And when they heard of the resurrection of the
dead, some mocked, while others said, "We will
hear you again on this *matter*." So Paul departed
from among them. However, some men joined him
and believed, among them Dionysius the Are-
opagite, a woman named Damaris, and others
with them.

After these things Paul departed from Athens
and went to Corinth. And he found a certain Jew
named Aquila, born in Pontus, who had recently
come from Italy with his wife Priscilla (because
Claudius had commanded all the Jews to depart
from Rome); and he came to them. So, because he
was of the same trade, he stayed with them and
worked; for by occupation they were tentmakers.
And he reasoned in the synagogue every Sabbath,
and persuaded both Jews and Greeks.

When Silas and Timothy had come from
Macedonia, Paul was compelled by the Spirit, and
testified to the Jews *that* Jesus *is* the Christ. But
when they opposed him and blasphemed, he
shook *his* garments and said to them, "Your blood
be upon your *own* heads; I *am* clean. From now on
I will go to the Gentiles." And he departed from
there and entered the house of a certain *man*
named Justus, *one* who worshiped God, whose
house was next door to the synagogue. Then Crispus, the ruler of the synagogue, believed on the
Lord with all his household. And many of the
Corinthians, hearing, believed and were baptized.

Now the Lord spoke to Paul in the night by a vision, "Do not be afraid, but speak, and do not keep
silent; for I am with you, and no one will attack you
to hurt you; for I have many people in this city." And
he continued *there* a year and six months, teaching
the word of God among them.

Acts 17:1–18:11

WoRSHiP

Indignation has taken hold of me
Because of the wicked, who forsake Your law.
Your statutes have been my songs
In the house of my pilgrimage.
I remember Your name in the night, O LORD,
And I keep Your law.

Psalm 119:53-55

WiSDoM

He who loves pleasure *will be* a poor man;
He who loves wine and oil will not be rich.

Proverbs 21:17

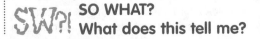

SO WHAT?
What does this tell me?

WALK WORTHY OF GOD'S CALLING

1 Thessalonians 1–3; Psalm 119:57-60; Proverbs 21:19

Paul, Silvanus, and Timothy,

To the church of the Thessalonians in God the Father and the Lord Jesus Christ:

Grace to you and peace from God our Father and the Lord Jesus Christ.

We give thanks to God always for you all, making mention of you in our prayers, remembering without ceasing your work of faith, labor of love, and patience of hope in our Lord Jesus Christ in the sight of our God and Father, knowing, beloved brethren, your election by God. For our gospel did not come to you in word only, but also in power, and in the Holy Spirit and in much assurance, as you know what kind of men we were among you for your sake.

And you became followers of us and of the Lord, having received the word in much affliction, with joy of the Holy Spirit, so that you became examples to all in Macedonia and Achaia who believe. For from you the word of the Lord has sounded forth, not only in Macedonia and Achaia, but also in every place. Your faith toward God has gone out, so that we do not need to say anything. For they themselves declare concerning us what manner of entry we had to you, and how you turned to God from idols to serve the living and true God, and to wait for His Son from heaven, whom He raised from the dead, *even* Jesus who delivers us from the wrath to come.

For you yourselves know, brethren, that our coming to you was not in vain. But even after we had suffered before and were spitefully treated at Philippi, as you know, we were bold in our God to speak to you the gospel of God in much conflict. For our exhortation *did* not *come* from error or uncleanness, nor *was it* in deceit.

But as we have been approved by God to be entrusted with the gospel, even so we speak, not as pleasing men, but God who tests our hearts. For neither at any time did we use flattering words, as you know, nor a cloak for covetousness—God *is* witness. Nor did we seek glory from men, either from you or from others, when we might have made demands as apostles of Christ. But we were gentle among you, just as a nursing *mother* cherishes her own children. So, affectionately longing for you, we were well pleased to impart to you not only the gospel of God, but also our own lives, because you had become dear to us. For you remember, brethren, our labor and toil; for laboring night and day, that we might not be a burden to any of you, we preached to you the gospel of God.

You *are* witnesses, and God *also,* how devoutly and justly and blamelessly we behaved ourselves among you who believe; as you know how we exhorted, and comforted, and charged every one of you, as a father *does* his own children, that you would walk worthy of God who calls you into His own kingdom and glory.

For this reason we also thank God without ceasing, because when you received the word of God which you heard from us, you welcomed *it* not *as* the word of men, but as it is in truth, the word of God, which also effectively works in you who believe. For you, brethren, became imitators of the churches of God which are in Judea in Christ Jesus. For you also suffered the same things from your own countrymen, just as they *did* from the Judeans, who killed both the Lord Jesus and their own prophets, and have persecuted us; and they do not please God and are contrary to all men, forbidding us to speak to the Gentiles that they may be saved, so as always to fill up *the measure of* their sins; but wrath has come upon them to the uttermost.

But we, brethren, having been taken away from you for a short time in presence, not in heart, endeavored more eagerly to see your face with great desire. Therefore we wanted to come to you—even I, Paul, time and again—but Satan hindered us. For what *is* our hope, or joy, or crown of rejoicing? *Is it* not even you in the presence of our Lord Jesus Christ at His coming? For you are our glory and joy.

Therefore, when we could no longer endure it, we thought it good to be left in Athens alone, and sent Timothy, our brother and minister of God, and our fellow laborer in the gospel of Christ, to establish you and encourage you concerning your faith, that no one should be shaken by these afflictions; for you yourselves know that we are appointed to this. For, in fact, we told you before when we were with you that we would suffer tribulation, just as it happened, and you know. For this reason, when I could no longer endure it, I sent to know your faith, lest by some means the tempter had tempted you, and our labor might be in vain.

But now that Timothy has come to us from you, and brought us good news of your faith and love, and that you always have good remembrance of us, greatly desiring to see us, as we also *to see* you—therefore, brethren, in all our affliction and distress we were comforted concerning you by your faith. For now we live, if you stand fast in the Lord.

For what thanks can we render to God for you, for all the joy with which we rejoice for your sake before our God, night and day praying exceedingly that we may see your face and perfect what is lacking in your faith?

Now may our God and Father Himself, and our Lord Jesus Christ, direct our way to you. And may the Lord make you increase and abound in love to one another and to all, just as we *do* to you, so that He may establish your hearts blameless in holiness before our God and Father at the coming of our Lord Jesus Christ with all His saints.

1 Thessalonians 1–3

WORSHIP

You are my portion, O LORD;
I have said that I would keep Your words.
I entreated Your favor with *my* whole heart;
Be merciful to me according to Your word.
I thought about my ways,
And turned my feet to Your testimonies.
I made haste, and did not delay
To keep Your commandments.

Psalm 119:57-60

WISDOM

Better to dwell in the wilderness,
Than with a contentious and angry woman.

Proverbs 21:19

SW?! **SO WHAT?**
What does this tell me?

EXCEL STILL MORE IN OBEDIENCE AND LOVE

1 Thessalonians 4–5; Psalm 119:69–72; Proverbs 21:21

Finally then, brethren, we urge and exhort in the Lord Jesus that you should abound more and more, just as you received from us how you ought to walk and to please God; for you know what commandments we gave you through the Lord Jesus.

For this is the will of God, your sanctification: that you should abstain from sexual immorality; that each of you should know how to possess his own vessel in sanctification and honor, not in passion of lust, like the Gentiles who do not know God; that no one should take advantage of and defraud his brother in this matter, because the Lord *is* the avenger of all such, as we also forewarned you and testified. For God did not call us to uncleanness, but in holiness. Therefore he who rejects *this* does not reject man, but God, who has also given us His Holy Spirit.

But concerning brotherly love you have no need that I should write to you, for you yourselves are taught by God to love one another; and indeed you do so toward all the brethren who are in all Macedonia. But we urge you, brethren, that you increase more and more; that you also aspire to lead a quiet life, to mind your own business, and to work with your own hands, as we commanded you, that you may walk properly toward those who are outside, and *that* you may lack nothing.

But I do not want you to be ignorant, brethren, concerning those who have fallen asleep, lest you sorrow as others who have no hope. For if we believe that Jesus died and rose again, even so God will bring with Him those who sleep in Jesus.

For this we say to you by the word of the Lord, that we who are alive *and* remain until the coming of the Lord will by no means precede those who are asleep. For the Lord Himself will descend from heaven with a shout, with the voice of an archangel, and with the trumpet of God. And the dead in Christ will rise first. Then we who are alive *and* remain shall be caught up together with them in the clouds to meet the Lord in the air. And thus we shall always be with the Lord. Therefore comfort one another with these words.

But concerning the times and the seasons, brethren, you have no need that I should write to you. For you yourselves know perfectly that the day of the Lord so comes as a thief in the night. For when they say, "Peace and safety!" then sudden destruction comes upon them, as labor pains upon a pregnant woman. And they shall not escape. But you, brethren, are not in darkness, so that this Day should overtake you as a thief. You are all sons of light and sons of the day. We are not of the night nor of darkness. Therefore let us not sleep, as others *do,* but let us watch and be sober. For those who sleep, sleep at night, and those who get drunk are drunk at night. But let us who are of the day be sober, putting on the breastplate of faith and love, and *as* a helmet the hope of salvation. For God did not appoint us to wrath, but to obtain salvation through our Lord Jesus Christ, who died for us, that whether we wake or sleep, we should live together with Him.

Therefore comfort each other and edify one another, just as you also are doing.

And we urge you, brethren, to recognize those who labor among you, and are over you in the Lord and admonish you, and to esteem them very highly in love for their work's sake. Be at peace among yourselves.

Now we exhort you, brethren, warn those who are unruly, comfort the fainthearted, uphold the weak, be patient with all. See that no one renders evil for evil to anyone, but always pursue what is good both for yourselves and for all.

Rejoice always, pray without ceasing, in everything give thanks; for this is the will of God in Christ Jesus for you.

Do not quench the Spirit. Do not despise prophecies. Test all things; hold fast what is good. Abstain from every form of evil.

Now may the God of peace Himself sanctify you completely; and may your whole spirit, soul, and body be preserved blameless at the coming of our Lord Jesus Christ. He who calls you *is* faithful, who also will do *it.*

Brethren, pray for us.

Greet all the brethren with a holy kiss.

I charge you by the Lord that this epistle be read to all the holy brethren.

The grace of our Lord Jesus Christ *be* with you. Amen.

1 Thessalonians 4–5

WORSHIP

The proud have forged a lie against me,
But I will keep Your precepts with *my* whole
    heart.
Their heart is as fat as grease,
But I delight in Your law.
It is good for me that I have been afflicted,
That I may learn Your statutes.
The law of Your mouth *is* better to me
Than thousands of *coins of* gold and silver.

Psalm 119:69-72

WISDOM

He who follows righteousness and mercy
Finds life, righteousness and honor.

Proverbs 21:21

SW?! SO WHAT?
What does this tell me?

STAND FIRM IN OUR TEACHING AND EXAMPLE

2 Thessalonians 1:1–3:16; Psalm 119:73-75; Proverbs 21:22

Paul, Silvanus, and Timothy,

To the church of the Thessalonians in God our Father and the Lord Jesus Christ:

Grace to you and peace from God our Father and the Lord Jesus Christ.

We are bound to thank God always for you, brethren, as it is fitting, because your faith grows exceedingly, and the love of every one of you all abounds toward each other, so that we ourselves boast of you among the churches of God for your patience and faith in all your persecutions and tribulations that you endure, *which is* manifest evidence of the righteous judgment of God, that you may be counted worthy of the kingdom of God, for which you also suffer; since *it is* a righteous thing with God to repay with tribulation those who trouble you, and to *give* you who are troubled rest with us when the Lord Jesus is revealed from heaven with His mighty angels, in flaming fire taking vengeance on those who do not know God, and on those who do not obey the gospel of our Lord Jesus Christ. These shall be punished with everlasting destruction from the presence of the Lord and from the glory of His power, when He comes, in that Day, to be glorified in His saints and to be admired among all those who believe, because our testimony among you was believed.

Therefore we also pray always for you that our God would count you worthy of *this* calling, and fulfill all the good pleasure of *His* goodness and the work of faith with power, that the name of our Lord Jesus Christ may be glorified in you, and you in Him, according to the grace of our God and the Lord Jesus Christ.

Now, brethren, concerning the coming of our Lord Jesus Christ and our gathering together to Him, we ask you, not to be soon shaken in mind or troubled, either by spirit or by word or by letter, as if from us, as though the day of Christ had come. Let no one deceive you by any means; for *that Day will not come* unless the falling away comes first, and the man of sin is revealed, the son of perdition, who opposes and exalts himself above all that is called God or that is worshiped, so that he sits as God in the temple of God, showing himself that he is God.

Do you not remember that when I was still with you I told you these things? And now you know what is restraining, that he may be revealed in his own time. For the mystery of lawlessness is already at work; only He who now restrains *will do so* until He is taken out of the way. And then the lawless one will be revealed, whom the Lord will consume with the breath of His mouth and destroy with the brightness of His coming. The coming of the *lawless one* is according to the working of Satan, with all power, signs, and lying wonders, and with all unrighteous deception among those who perish, because they did not receive the love of the truth, that they might be saved. And for this reason God will send them strong delusion, that they should believe the lie, that they all may be condemned who did not believe the truth but had pleasure in unrighteousness.

But we are bound to give thanks to God always for you, brethren beloved by the Lord, because God from the beginning chose you for salvation through sanctification by the Spirit and belief in the truth, to which He called you by our gospel, for the obtaining of the glory of our Lord Jesus Christ. Therefore, brethren, stand fast and hold the traditions which you were taught, whether by word or our epistle.

Now may our Lord Jesus Christ Himself, and our God and Father, who has loved us and given *us* everlasting consolation and good hope by grace, comfort your hearts and establish you in every good word and work.

Finally, brethren, pray for us, that the word of the Lord may run *swiftly* and be glorified, just as *it is* with you, and that we may be delivered from unreasonable and wicked men; for not all have faith.

But the Lord is faithful, who will establish you and guard *you* from the evil one. And we have confidence in the Lord concerning you, both that you do and will do the things we command you.

Now may the Lord direct your hearts into the love of God and into the patience of Christ.

But we command you, brethren, in the name of our Lord Jesus Christ, that you withdraw from every brother who walks disorderly and not according to the tradition which he received from us. For you yourselves know how you ought to follow us, for we were not disorderly among you; nor did we eat anyone's bread free of charge, but worked with labor and toil night and day, that we might not be a burden to any of you, not because we do not have authority, but to make ourselves an example of how you should follow us.

For even when we were with you, we commanded you this: If anyone will not work, neither shall he eat. For we hear that there are some who walk among you in a disorderly manner, not working at all, but are busybodies. Now those who are such we command and exhort through our Lord Jesus Christ that they work in quietness and eat their own bread.

But *as for* you, brethren, do not grow weary *in* doing good. And if anyone does not obey our word in this epistle, note that person and do not keep company with him, that he may be ashamed. Yet do not count *him* as an enemy, but admonish *him* as a brother.

Now may the Lord of peace Himself give you peace always in every way. The Lord *be* with you all.

2 Thessalonians 1:1–3:16

WORSHIP

Your hands have made me and fashioned me;
Give me understanding, that I may learn Your
    commandments.
Those who fear You will be glad when they
    see me,
Because I have hoped in Your word.
I know, O LORD, that Your judgments *are* right,
And *that* in faithfulness You have afflicted me.

Psalm 119:73-75

WISDOM

A wise *man* scales the city of the mighty,
And brings down the trusted stronghold.

Proverbs 21:22

SW?! **SO WHAT?**
What does this tell me?

THE GOOD NEWS IS BAD NEWS FOR THE EPHESIAN ECONOMY

Acts 18:18-23; 19:11-20:3; Psalm 119:81-83; Proverbs 21:25-26

So Paul still remained a good while. Then he took leave of the brethren and sailed for Syria, and Priscilla and Aquila *were* with him. He had *his* hair cut off at Cenchrea, for he had taken a vow. And he came to Ephesus, and left them there; but he himself entered the synagogue and reasoned with the Jews. When they asked *him* to stay a longer time with them, he did not consent, but took leave of them, saying, "I must by all means keep this coming feast in Jerusalem; but I will return again to you, God willing." And he sailed from Ephesus.

And when he had landed at Caesarea, and gone up and greeted the church, he went down to Antioch. After he had spent some time *there,* he departed and went over the region of Galatia and Phrygia in order, strengthening all the disciples.

Now God worked unusual miracles by the hands of Paul, so that even handkerchiefs or aprons were brought from his body to the sick, and the diseases left them and the evil spirits went out of them. Then some of the itinerant Jewish exorcists took it upon themselves to call the name of the Lord Jesus over those who had evil spirits, saying, "We exorcise you by the Jesus whom Paul preaches." Also there were seven sons of Sceva, a Jewish chief priest, who did so.

And the evil spirit answered and said, "Jesus I know, and Paul I know; but who are you?"

Then the man in whom the evil spirit was leaped on them, overpowered them, and prevailed against them, so that they fled out of that house naked and wounded. This became known both to all Jews and Greeks dwelling in Ephesus; and fear fell on them all, and the name of the Lord Jesus was magnified. And many who had believed came confessing and telling their deeds. Also, many of those who had practiced

magic brought their books together and burned *them* in the sight of all. And they counted up the value of them, and *it* totaled fifty thousand *pieces* of silver. So the word of the Lord grew mightily and prevailed.

When these things were accomplished, Paul purposed in the Spirit, when he had passed through Macedonia and Achaia, to go to Jerusalem, saying, "After I have been there, I must also see Rome." So he sent into Macedonia two of those who ministered to him, Timothy and Erastus, but he himself stayed in Asia for a time.

And about that time there arose a great commotion about the Way. For a certain man named Demetrius, a silversmith, who made silver shrines of Diana, brought no small profit to the craftsmen. He called them together with the workers of similar occupation, and said: "Men, you know that we have our prosperity by this trade. Moreover you see and hear that not only at Ephesus, but throughout almost all Asia, this Paul has persuaded and turned away many people, saying that they are not gods which are made with hands. So not only is this trade of ours in danger of falling into disrepute, but also the temple of the great goddess Diana may be despised and her magnificence destroyed, whom all Asia and the world worship."

Now when they heard *this,* they were full of wrath and cried out, saying, "Great *is* Diana of the Ephesians!" So the whole city was filled with confusion, and rushed into the theater with one accord, having seized Gaius and Aristarchus, Macedonians, Paul's travel companions. And when Paul wanted to go in to the people, the disciples would not allow him. Then some of the officials of Asia, who were his friends, sent to him pleading that he would not venture into the theater. Some therefore cried one thing and some another, for the assembly was confused, and most of them did not know why they had come together. And they drew Alexander out of the multitude, the Jews putting him forward. And Alexander motioned with his hand, and wanted to make his defense to the people. But when they found out that he was a Jew, all with one voice cried out for about two hours, "Great *is* Diana of the Ephesians!"

And when the city clerk had quieted the crowd, he said: "Men of Ephesus, what man is there who does not know that the city of the Ephesians is temple guardian of the great goddess Diana, and of the *image* which fell down from Zeus? Therefore, since these things cannot be denied, you ought to be quiet and do nothing rashly. For you have brought these men here who are neither robbers of temples nor blasphemers of your goddess. Therefore, if Demetrius and his fellow craftsmen have a case against anyone, the courts are open and there are proconsuls. Let them bring charges against one another. But if you have any other inquiry to make, it shall be determined in the lawful assembly. For we are in danger of being called in question for today's uproar, there being no reason which we may give to account for this disorderly gathering." And when he had said these things, he dismissed the assembly.

After the uproar had ceased, Paul called the disciples to *himself,* embraced *them,* and departed to go to Macedonia. Now when he had gone over that region and encouraged them with many words, he came to Greece and stayed three months. And when the Jews plotted against him as he was about to sail to Syria, he decided to return through Macedonia.

Acts 18:18-23; 19:11–20:3

WORSHIP

My soul faints for Your salvation,
But I hope in Your word.
My eyes fail *from searching* Your word,
Saying, "When will You comfort me?"
For I have become like a wineskin in smoke,
Yet I do not forget Your statutes.

Psalm 119:81-83

WISDOM

The desire of the lazy *man* kills him,
For his hands refuse to labor.
He covets greedily all day long,
But the righteous gives and does not spare.

Proverbs 21:25-26

SW?! SO WHAT?
What does this tell me?

PAUL SETS HIS SIGHTS ON JERUSALEM

From Miletus he sent to Ephesus and called for the elders of the church. And when they had come to him, he said to them: "You know, from the first day that I came to Asia, in what manner I always lived among you, serving the Lord with all humility, with many tears and trials which happened to me by the plotting of the Jews; how I kept back nothing that was helpful, but proclaimed it to you, and taught you publicly and from house to house, testifying to Jews, and also to Greeks, repentance toward God and faith toward our Lord Jesus Christ. And see, now I go bound in the spirit to Jerusalem, not knowing the things that will happen to me there, except that the Holy Spirit testifies in every city, saying that chains and tribulations await me. But none of these things move me; nor do I count my life dear to myself, so that I may finish my race with joy, and the ministry which I received from the Lord Jesus, to testify to the gospel of the grace of God.

"And indeed, now I know that you all, among whom I have gone preaching the kingdom of God, will see my face no more. Therefore I testify to you this day that I *am* innocent of the blood of all *men*. For I have not shunned to declare to you the whole counsel of God. Therefore take heed to yourselves and to all the flock, among which the Holy Spirit has made you overseers, to shepherd the church of God which He purchased with His own blood. For I know this, that after my departure savage wolves will come in among you, not sparing the flock. Also from among yourselves men will rise up, speaking perverse things, to draw away the disciples after themselves. Therefore watch, and remember that for three years I did not cease to warn everyone night and day with tears.

"So now, brethren, I commend you to God and to the word of His grace, which is able to build you up and give you an inheritance among all those who are sanctified. I have coveted no one's silver or gold or apparel. Yes, you yourselves know that these hands have provided for my necessities, and for those who were with me. I have shown you in every way, by laboring like this, that you must support the weak. And remember the words of the Lord Jesus, that He said, 'It is more blessed to give than to receive.' "

And when he had said these things, he knelt down and prayed with them all. Then they all wept freely, and fell on Paul's neck and kissed him, sorrowing most of all for the words which he spoke, that they would see his face no more. And they accompanied him to the ship.

Now it came to pass, that when we had departed from them and set sail, running a straight course we came to Cos, the following *day* to Rhodes, and from there to Patara. And finding a ship sailing over to Phoenicia, we went aboard and set sail. When we had sighted Cyprus, we passed it on the left, sailed to Syria, and landed at Tyre; for there the ship was to unload her cargo. And finding disciples, we stayed there seven days. They told Paul through the Spirit not to go up to Jerusalem. When we had come to the end of those days, we departed and went on our way; and they all accompanied us, with wives and children, till *we were* out of the city. And we knelt down on the shore and prayed. When we had taken our leave of one another, we boarded the ship, and they returned home.

And when we had finished *our* voyage from Tyre, we came to Ptolemais, greeted the brethren, and stayed with them one day. On the next *day* we who were Paul's companions departed and came to Caesarea, and entered the house of Philip the evangelist, who was *one* of the seven, and stayed with him. Now this man had four virgin daughters who prophesied. And as we stayed many days, a certain prophet named Agabus came down from Judea. When he had come to us, he took Paul's belt, bound his *own* hands and feet, and said, "Thus says the Holy Spirit, 'So shall the Jews at Jerusalem bind the man who owns this belt, and deliver *him* into the hands of the Gentiles.' "

Now when we heard these things, both we and those from that place pleaded with him not to go up to Jerusalem. Then Paul answered, "What do you mean by weeping and breaking my heart? For I am ready not only to be bound, but also to die at Jerusalem for the name of the Lord Jesus."

So when he would not be persuaded, we ceased, saying, "The will of the Lord be done."

And after those days we packed and went up to Jerusalem. Also some of the disciples from Caesarea went with us and brought with them a certain Mnason of Cyprus, an early disciple, with whom we were to lodge.

Acts 20:17–21:16

WORSHIP

Unless Your law *had been* my delight,
I would then have perished in my affliction.
I will never forget Your precepts,
For by them You have given me life.
I *am* Yours, save me;
For I have sought Your precepts.

Psalm 119:92-94

WISDOM

There is no wisdom or understanding
Or counsel against the LORD.

Proverbs 21:30

SW?! SO WHAT?
What does this tell me?

GOD MAKES FOOLISH THE WISDOM OF THE WORLD

1 Corinthians 1:1–2:5, 12-16; Psalm 119:97-100; Proverbs 21:31

Paul, called *to be* an apostle of Jesus Christ through the will of God, and Sosthenes *our* brother,

To the church of God which is at Corinth, to those who are sanctified in Christ Jesus, called *to be* saints, with all who in every place call on the name of Jesus Christ our Lord, both theirs and ours:

Grace to you and peace from God our Father and the Lord Jesus Christ.

I thank my God always concerning you for the grace of God which was given to you by Christ Jesus, that you were enriched in everything by Him in all utterance and all knowledge, even as the testimony of Christ was confirmed in you, so that you come short in no gift, eagerly waiting for the revelation of our Lord Jesus Christ, who will also confirm you to the end, *that you may be* blameless in the day of our Lord Jesus Christ. God *is* faithful, by whom you were called into the fellowship of His Son, Jesus Christ our Lord.

Now I plead with you, brethren, by the name of our Lord Jesus Christ, that you all speak the same thing, and *that* there be no divisions among you, but *that* you be perfectly joined together in the same mind and in the same judgment. For it has been declared to me concerning you, my brethren, by those of Chloe's *household,* that there are contentions among you. Now I say this, that each of you says, "I am of Paul," or "I am of Apollos," or "I am of Cephas," or "I am of Christ." Is Christ divided? Was Paul crucified for you? Or were you baptized in the name of Paul?

I thank God that I baptized none of you except Crispus and Gaius, lest anyone should say that I had baptized in my own name. Yes, I also baptized the household of Stephanas. Besides, I do not know whether I baptized any other. For Christ did not send me to baptize, but to preach the gospel, not with wisdom of words, lest the cross of Christ should be made of no effect.

For the message of the cross is foolishness to those who are perishing, but to us who are being saved it is the power of God. For it is written:

"I will destroy the wisdom of the wise,
And bring to nothing the understanding of the prudent."

Where *is* the wise? Where *is* the scribe? Where *is* the disputer of this age? Has not God made foolish the wisdom of this world? For since, in the wisdom of God, the world through wisdom did not know God, it pleased God through the foolishness of the message preached to save those who believe. For Jews request a sign, and Greeks seek after wisdom; but we preach Christ crucified, to the Jews a stumbling block and to the Greeks foolishness, but to those who are called, both Jews and Greeks, Christ the power of God and the wisdom of God. Because the foolishness of God is wiser than men, and the weakness of God is stronger than men.

For you see your calling, brethren, that not many wise according to the flesh, not many mighty, not many noble, *are called.* But God has chosen the foolish things of the world to put to shame the wise, and God has chosen the weak things of the world to put to shame the things which are mighty; and the base things of the world and the things which are despised God has chosen, and the things which are not, to bring to nothing the things that are, that no flesh should glory in His presence. But of Him you are in Christ Jesus, who became for us wisdom from God—and righteousness and sanctification and redemption—that, as it is written, "He who glories, let him glory in the LORD."

And I, brethren, when I came to you, did not come with excellence of speech or of wisdom declaring to you the testimony of God. For I determined not to know anything among you except Jesus Christ and Him crucified. I was with you in weakness, in fear, and in much trembling. And my speech and my preaching *were* not with persuasive words of human wisdom, but in demonstration of the Spirit and of power, that your faith should not be in the wisdom of men but in the power of God.

Now we have received, not the spirit of the world, but the Spirit who is from God, that we might know the things that have been freely given to us by God.

These things we also speak, not in words which man's wisdom teaches but which the Holy Spirit teaches, comparing spiritual things with spiritual. But the natural man does not receive the things of the Spirit of God, for they are foolishness to him; nor can he know *them,* because they are spiritually discerned. But he who is spiritual judges all things, yet he himself is *rightly* judged by no one. For "who has known the mind of the LORD that he may instruct Him?" But we have the mind of Christ.

1 Corinthians 1:1–2:5, 12-16

WORSHIP

Oh, how I love Your law!
It *is* my meditation all the day.
You, through Your commandments, make me
 wiser than my enemies;
For they *are* ever with me.
I have more understanding than all my
 teachers,
For Your testimonies *are* my meditation.
I understand more than the ancients,
Because I keep Your precepts.

Psalm 119:97-100

WISDOM

The horse *is* prepared for the day of battle,
But deliverance *is* of the LORD.

Proverbs 21:31

SW?! **SO WHAT?**
What does this tell me?

STEWARDS OF GOD'S MYSTERIES

1 Corinthians 3:1-17; 4:1-21; 5:9-13;
Psalm 119:105-107; Proverbs 22:1

And I, brethren, could not speak to you as to spiritual *people* but as to carnal, as to babes in Christ. I fed you with milk and not with solid food; for until now you were not able *to receive it,* and even now you are still not able; for you are still carnal. For where *there are* envy, strife, and divisions among you, are you not carnal and behaving like *mere* men? For when one says, "I am of Paul," and another, "I *am* of Apollos," are you not carnal?

Who then is Paul, and who *is* Apollos, but ministers through whom you believed, as the Lord gave to each one? I planted, Apollos watered, but God gave the increase. So then neither he who plants is anything, nor he who waters, but God who gives the increase. Now he who plants and he who waters are one, and each one will receive his own reward according to his own labor.

For we are God's fellow workers; you are God's field, *you are* God's building. According to the grace of God which was given to me, as a wise master builder I have laid the foundation, and another builds on it. But let each one take heed how he builds on it. For no other foundation can anyone lay than that which is laid, which is Jesus Christ. Now if anyone builds on this foundation *with* gold, silver, precious stones, wood, hay, straw, each one's work will become clear; for the Day will declare it, because it will be revealed by fire; and the fire will test each one's work, of what sort it is. If anyone's work which he has built on *it* endures, he will receive a reward. If anyone's work is burned, he will suffer loss; but he himself will be saved, yet so as through fire.

Do you not know that you are the temple of God and *that* the Spirit of God dwells in you? If anyone defiles the temple of God, God will destroy him. For the temple of God is holy, which *temple* you are.

Let a man so consider us, as servants of Christ and stewards of the mysteries of God. Moreover it is required in stewards that one be found faithful. But with me it is a very small thing that I should be judged by you or by a human court. In fact, I do not even judge myself. For I know of nothing against myself, yet I am not justified by this; but He who judges me is the Lord. Therefore judge nothing before the time, until the Lord comes, who will both bring to light the hidden things of darkness and reveal the counsels of the hearts. Then each one's praise will come from God.

Now these things, brethren, I have figuratively transferred to myself and Apollos for your sakes, that you may learn in us not to think beyond what is written, that none of you may be puffed up on behalf of one against the other. For who makes you differ *from another?* And what do you have that you did not receive? Now if you did indeed receive *it,* why do you boast as if you had not received *it?*

You are already full! You are already rich! You have reigned as kings without us—and indeed I could wish you did reign, that we also might reign with you! For I think that God has displayed us, the apostles, last, as men condemned to death; for we have been made a spectacle to the world, both to angels and to men. We *are* fools for Christ's sake, but you *are* wise in Christ! We *are* weak, but you *are* strong! You *are* distinguished, but we *are* dishonored! To the present hour we both hunger and thirst, and we are poorly clothed, and beaten, and homeless. And we labor, working with our own hands. Being reviled, we bless; being persecuted, we endure; being defamed, we entreat. We have been made as the filth of the world, the offscouring of all things until now.

I do not write these things to shame you, but as my beloved children I warn *you.* For though you might have ten thousand instructors in Christ, yet *you do* not *have* many fathers; for in Christ Jesus I have begotten you through the gospel. Therefore I urge you, imitate me. For this reason I have sent Timothy to you, who is my beloved and faithful son in the Lord, who will remind you of my ways in Christ, as I teach everywhere in every church.

Now some are puffed up, as though I were not coming to you. But I will come to you shortly, if the Lord wills, and I will know, not the word of those who are puffed up, but the power. For the kingdom of God *is* not in word but in power. What do you want? Shall I come to you with a rod, or in love and a spirit of gentleness?

I wrote to you in my epistle not to keep company with sexually immoral people. Yet *I* certainly *did* not *mean* with the sexually immoral people of this world, or with the covetous, or extortioners, or idolaters, since then you would need to go out of the world. But now I have written to you not to keep company with anyone named a brother, who is sexually immoral, or covetous, or an idolater, or a reviler, or a drunkard, or an extortioner—not even to eat with such a person.

For what *have* I *to do* with judging those also who are outside? Do you not judge those who are inside? But those who are outside God judges. Therefore "put away from yourselves the evil person."

1 Corinthians 3:1-17; 4:1-21; 5:9-13

WORSHIP

Your word *is* a lamp to my feet
And a light to my path.
I have sworn and confirmed
That I will keep Your righteous judgments.
I am afflicted very much;
Revive me, O LORD, according to Your word.
Psalm 119:105-107

WISDOM

A *good* name is to be chosen rather than
great riches,
Loving favor rather than silver and gold.
Proverbs 22:1

SW?! **SO WHAT?**
What does this tell me?

PRINCIPLES OF MORALITY AND MARRIAGE

1 Corinthians 6:12–7:16, 25-35, 39-40; Psalm 119:114-116; Proverbs 22:2

All things are lawful for me, but all things are not helpful. All things are lawful for me, but I will not be brought under the power of any. Foods for the stomach and the stomach for foods, but God will destroy both it and them. Now the body *is* not for sexual immorality but for the Lord, and the Lord for the body. And God both raised up the Lord and will also raise us up by His power.

Do you not know that your bodies are members of Christ? Shall I then take the members of Christ and make *them* members of a harlot? Certainly not! Or do you not know that he who is joined to a harlot is one body *with her*? For "the two," He says, "shall become one flesh." But he who is joined to the Lord is one spirit *with Him*.

Flee sexual immorality. Every sin that a man does is outside the body, but he who commits sexual immorality sins against his own body. Or do you not know that your body is the temple of the Holy Spirit *who is* in you, whom you have from God, and you are not your own? For you were bought at a price; therefore glorify God in your body and in your spirit, which are God's.

Now concerning the things of which you wrote to me:

It is good for a man not to touch a woman. Nevertheless, because of sexual immorality, let each man have his own wife, and let each woman have her own husband. Let the husband render to his wife the affection due her, and likewise also the wife to her husband. The wife does not have authority over her own body, but the husband *does*. And likewise the husband does not have authority over his own body, but the wife *does*. Do not deprive one another except with consent for a time, that you may give yourselves to fasting and prayer; and come together again so that Satan does not tempt you because of your lack of self-control. But I say this as a concession, not as a commandment. For I wish that all men were even as I myself. But each one has his own

gift from God, one in this manner and another in that.

But I say to the unmarried and to the widows: It is good for them if they remain even as I am; but if they cannot exercise self-control, let them marry. For it is better to marry than to burn *with passion*.

Now to the married I command, *yet* not I but the Lord: A wife is not to depart from *her* husband. But even if she does depart, let her remain unmarried or be reconciled to *her* husband. And a husband is not to divorce *his* wife.

But to the rest I, not the Lord, say: If any brother has a wife who does not believe, and she is willing to live with him, let him not divorce her. And a woman who has a husband who does not believe, if he is willing to live with her, let her not divorce him. For the unbelieving husband is sanctified by the wife, and the unbelieving wife is sanctified by the husband; otherwise your children would be unclean, but now they are holy. But if the unbeliever departs, let him depart; a brother or a sister is not under bondage in such *cases*. But God has called us to peace. For how do you know, O wife, whether you will save *your* husband? Or how do you know, O husband, whether you will save *your* wife?

Now concerning virgins: I have no commandment from the Lord; yet I give judgment as one whom the Lord in His merczy *has made* trustworthy. I suppose therefore that this is good because of the present distress—that *it is* good for a man to remain as he is: Are you bound to a wife? Do not seek to be loosed. Are you loosed from a wife? Do not seek a wife. But even if you do marry, you have not sinned; and if a virgin marries, she has not sinned. Nevertheless such will have trouble in the flesh, but I would spare you.

But this I say, brethren, the time *is* short, so that from now on even those who have wives should be as though they had none, those who weep as though they did not weep, those who rejoice as though they did not rejoice, those who buy as though they did not possess, and those who use this world as not misusing *it*. For the form of this world is passing away.

But I want you to be without care. He who is

unmarried cares for the things of the Lord—how he may please the Lord. But he who is married cares about the things of the world—how he may please *his* wife. There is a difference between a wife and a virgin. The unmarried woman cares about the things of the Lord, that she may be holy both in body and in spirit. But she who is married cares about the things of the world—how she may please *her* husband. And this I say for your own profit, not that I may put a leash on you, but for what is proper, and that you may serve the Lord without distraction.

A wife is bound by law as long as her husband lives; but if her husband dies, she is at liberty to be married to whom she wishes, only in the Lord. But she is happier if she remains as she is, according to my judgment—and I think I also have the Spirit of God.

1 Corinthians 6:12–7:16, 25-35, 39-40

WoRsHiP

You *are* my hiding place and my shield;
I hope in Your word.
Depart from me, you evildoers,
For I will keep the commandments of my God!
Uphold me according to Your word, that I may live;
And do not let me be ashamed of my hope.

Psalm 119:114-116

WiSDoM

The rich and the poor have this in common,
The Lord *is* the maker of them all.

Proverbs 22:2

SW?! **SO WHAT?**
What does this tell me?

HOW LOVE LIMITS LIBERTY

1 Corinthians 8–9; Psalm 119:123-125; Proverbs 22:3

Now concerning things offered to idols: We know that we all have knowledge. Knowledge puffs up, but love edifies. And if anyone thinks that he knows anything, he knows nothing yet as he ought to know. But if anyone loves God, this one is known by Him.

Therefore concerning the eating of things offered to idols, we know that an idol *is* nothing in the world, and that *there is* no other God but one. For even if there are so-called gods, whether in heaven or on earth (as there are many gods and many lords), yet for us *there is* one God, the Father, of whom *are* all things, and we for Him; and one Lord Jesus Christ, through whom *are* all things, and through whom we *live*.

However, *there is* not in everyone that knowledge; for some, with consciousness of the idol, until now eat *it* as a thing offered to an idol; and their conscience, being weak, is defiled. But food does not commend us to God; for neither if we eat are we the better, nor if we do not eat are we the worse.

But beware lest somehow this liberty of yours become a stumbling block to those who are weak. For if anyone sees you who have knowledge eating in an idol's temple, will not the conscience of him who is weak be emboldened to eat those things offered to idols? And because of your knowledge shall the weak brother perish, for whom Christ died? But when you thus sin against the brethren, and wound their weak conscience, you sin against Christ. Therefore, if food makes my brother stumble, I will never again eat meat, lest I make my brother stumble.

Am I not an apostle? Am I not free? Have I not seen Jesus Christ our Lord? Are you not my work in the Lord? If I am not an apostle to others, yet doubtless I am to you. For you are the seal of my apostleship in the Lord.

My defense to those who examine me is this: Do we have no right to eat and drink? Do we have no right to take along a believing wife, as *do* also the other apostles, the brothers of the Lord, and Cephas? Or *is it* only Barnabas and I *who* have no right to refrain from working? Who ever goes to war at his own expense? Who plants a vineyard and does not eat of its fruit? Or who tends a flock and does not drink of the milk of the flock?

Do I say these things as a *mere* man? Or does not the law say the same also? For it is written in the law of Moses, "You shall not muzzle an ox while it treads out the grain." Is it oxen God is concerned about? Or does He say *it* altogether for our sakes? For our sakes, no doubt, *this* is written, that he who plows should plow in hope, and he who threshes in hope should be partaker of his hope. If we have sown spiritual things for you, *is it* a great thing if we reap your material things? If others are partakers of *this* right over you, *are* we not even more?

Nevertheless we have not used this right, but endure all things lest we hinder the gospel of Christ. Do you not know that those who minister the holy things eat *of the things* of the temple, and those who serve at the altar partake of *the offerings of* the altar? Even so the Lord has commanded that those who preach the gospel should live from the gospel.

But I have used none of these things, nor have I written these things that it should be done so to me; for it *would be* better for me to die than that anyone should make my boasting void. For if I preach the gospel, I have nothing to boast of, for necessity is laid upon me; yes, woe is me if I do not preach the gospel! For if I do this willingly, I have a reward; but if against my will, I have been entrusted with a stewardship. What is my reward then? That when I preach the gospel, I may present the gospel of Christ without charge, that I may not abuse my authority in the gospel.

For though I am free from all *men,* I have made myself a servant to all, that I might win the more; and to the Jews I became as a Jew, that I might win Jews; to those *who are* under the law, as under the law, that I might win those *who are* under the law; to those *who are* without law, as without law (not being without law toward God, but under law toward Christ), that I might win those *who are* without law; to the weak I became as weak, that I might win the weak. I have become all things to all *men,* that I might by all means save some.

Now this I do for the gospel's sake, that I may be partaker of it with *you*.

Do you not know that those who run in a race all run, but one receives the prize? Run in such a way that you may obtain *it*. And everyone who competes *for the prize* is temperate in all things. Now they *do it* to obtain a perishable crown, but we *for* an imperishable *crown*. Therefore I run thus: not with uncertainty. Thus I fight: not as *one who* beats the air. But I discipline my body and bring *it* into subjection, lest, when I have preached to others, I myself should become disqualified.

1 Corinthians 8–9

WORSHIP

My eyes fail *from seeking* Your salvation
And Your righteous word.
Deal with Your servant according to Your
    mercy,
And teach me Your statutes.
I *am* Your servant;
Give me understanding,
That I may know Your testimonies.

Psalm 119:123-125

WISDOM

A prudent *man* foresees evil and hides
    himself,
But the simple pass on and are punished.

Proverbs 22:3

SW?! **SO WHAT?**
What does this tell me?

Do all THINGS to the glory of GOD

1 Corinthians 10:1-13, 23-33; 11:1-2, 23-34; Psalm 119:129-131; Proverbs 22:4

Moreover, brethren, I do not want you to be unaware that all our fathers were under the cloud, all passed through the sea, all were baptized into Moses in the cloud and in the sea, all ate the same spiritual food, and all drank the same spiritual drink. For they drank of that spiritual Rock that followed them, and that Rock was Christ. But with most of them God was not well pleased, for *their bodies* were scattered in the wilderness.

Now these things became our examples, to the intent that we should not lust after evil things as they also lusted. And do not become idolaters as *were* some of them. As it is written, "The people sat down to eat and drink, and rose up to play." Nor let us commit sexual immorality, as some of them did, and in one day twenty-three thousand fell; nor let us tempt Christ, as some of them also tempted, and were destroyed by serpents; nor complain, as some of them also complained, and were destroyed by the destroyer. Now all these things happened to them as examples, and they were written for our admonition, upon whom the ends of the ages have come.

Therefore let him who thinks he stands take heed lest he fall. No temptation has overtaken you except such as is common to man; but God *is* faithful, who will not allow you to be tempted beyond what you are able, but with the temptation will also make the way of escape, that you may be able to bear *it.*

All things are lawful for me, but not all things are helpful; all things are lawful for me, but not all things edify. Let no one seek his own, but each one the other's *well-being.*

Eat whatever is sold in the meat market, asking no questions for conscience' sake; for "the earth *is* the Lord's, and all its fullness."

If any of those who do not believe invites you *to dinner,* and you desire to go, eat whatever is set before you, asking no ques-

tion for conscience' sake. But if anyone says to you, "This was offered to idols," do not eat it for the sake of the one who told you, and for conscience' sake; for "the earth *is* the Lord's, and all its fullness." "Conscience," I say, not your own, but that of the other. For why is my liberty judged by another *man's* conscience? But if I partake with thanks, why am I evil spoken of for *the food* over which I give thanks?

Therefore, whether you eat or drink, or whatever you do, do all to the glory of God. Give no offense, either to the Jews or to the Greeks or to the church of God, just as I also please all *men* in all *things,* not seeking my own profit, but the *profit* of many, that they may be saved. Imitate me, just as I also *imitate* Christ.

Now I praise you, brethren, that you remember me in all things and keep the traditions just as I delivered *them* to you.

For I received from the Lord that which I also delivered to you: that the Lord Jesus on the *same* night in which He was betrayed took bread; and when He had given thanks, He broke *it* and said, "Take, eat; this is My body which is broken for you; do this in remembrance of Me." In the same manner *He* also *took* the cup after supper, saying, "This cup is the new covenant in My blood. This do, as often as you drink *it,* in remembrance of Me."

For as often as you eat this bread and drink this cup, you proclaim the Lord's death till He comes.

Therefore whoever eats this bread or drinks *this* cup of the Lord in an unworthy manner will be guilty of the body and blood of the Lord. But let a man examine himself, and so let him eat of the bread and drink of the cup. For he who eats and drinks in an unworthy manner eats and drinks judgment to himself, not discerning the Lord's body. For this reason many *are* weak and sick among you, and many sleep. For if we would judge ourselves, we would not be judged. But when we are judged, we are chastened by the Lord, that we may not be condemned with the world.

Therefore, my brethren, when you come together to eat, wait for one another. But if anyone is hungry, let him eat at home, lest you come together for judgment. And the rest I will set in order when I come.

1 Corinthians 10:1-13, 23-33; 11:1-2, 23-34

WORSHIP

Your testimonies are wonderful;
Therefore my soul keeps them.
The entrance of Your words gives light;
It gives understanding to the simple.
I opened my mouth and panted,
For I longed for Your commandments.

Psalm 119:129-131

WISDOM

By humility *and* the fear of the LORD
Are riches and honor and life.

Proverbs 22:4

SW?! SO WHAT?
What does this tell me?

THE MORE EXCELLENT WAY OF LOVE

1 Corinthians 12–13; Psalm 119:137-138, 144; Proverbs 22:6

Now concerning spiritual *gifts,* brethren, I do not want you to be ignorant: You know that you were Gentiles, carried away to these dumb idols, however you were led. Therefore I make known to you that no one speaking by the Spirit of God calls Jesus accursed, and no one can say that Jesus is Lord except by the Holy Spirit.

There are diversities of gifts, but the same Spirit. There are differences of ministries, but the same Lord. And there are diversities of activities, but it is the same God who works all in all. But the manifestation of the Spirit is given to each one for the profit *of all:* for to one is given the word of wisdom through the Spirit, to another the word of knowledge through the same Spirit, to another faith by the same Spirit, to another gifts of healings by the same Spirit, to another the working of miracles, to another prophecy, to another discerning of spirits, to another *different* kinds of tongues, to another the interpretation of tongues. But one and the same Spirit works all these things, distributing to each one individually as He wills.

For as the body is one and has many members, but all the members of that one body, being many, are one body, so also *is* Christ. For by one Spirit we were all baptized into one body—whether Jews or Greeks, whether slaves or free—and have all been made to drink into one Spirit. For in fact the body is not one member but many.

If the foot should say, "Because I am not a hand, I am not of the body," is it therefore not of the body? And if the ear should say, "Because I am not an eye, I am not of the body," is it therefore not of the body? If the whole body *were* an eye, where *would be* the hearing? If the whole *were* hearing, where *would be* the smelling? But now God has set the members, each one of them, in the body just as He pleased. And if they *were* all one member, where *would* the body *be?*

But now indeed *there are* many members, yet one body. And the eye cannot say to the hand, "I have no need of you"; nor

again the head to the feet, "I have no need of you." No, much rather, those members of the body which seem to be weaker are necessary. And those *members* of the body which we think to be less honorable, on these we bestow greater honor; and our unpresentable *parts* have greater modesty, but our presentable *parts* have no need. But God composed the body, having given greater honor to that *part* which lacks it, that there should be no schism in the body, but *that* the members should have the same care for one another. And if one member suffers, all the members suffer with *it;* or if one member is honored, all the members rejoice with *it.*

Now you are the body of Christ, and members individually. And God has appointed these in the church: first apostles, second prophets, third teachers, after that miracles, then gifts of healings, helps, administrations, varieties of tongues. *Are* all apostles? *Are* all prophets? *Are* all teachers? *Are* all workers of miracles? Do all have gifts of healings? Do all speak with tongues? Do all interpret? But earnestly desire the best gifts. And yet I show you a more excellent way.

Though I speak with the tongues of men and of angels, but have not love, I have become sounding brass or a clanging cymbal. And though I have *the gift of* prophecy, and understand all mysteries and all knowledge, and though I have all faith, so that I could remove mountains, but have not love, I am nothing. And though I bestow all my goods to feed *the poor,* and though I give my body to be burned, but have not love, it profits me nothing.

Love suffers long *and* is kind; love does not envy; love does not parade itself, is not puffed up; does not behave rudely, does not seek its own, is not provoked, thinks no evil; does not rejoice in iniquity, but rejoices in the truth; bears all things, believes all things, hopes all things, endures all things.

Love never fails. But whether *there are* prophecies, they will fail; whether *there are* tongues, they will cease; whether *there is* knowledge, it will vanish away. For we know in part and we prophesy in part. But when that which is perfect has come, then that which is in part will be done away.

When I was a child, I spoke as a child, I understood as a child, I thought as a child; but when I became a man, I put away childish things. For now we see in a mirror, dimly, but then face to face. Now I know in part, but then I shall know just as I also am known.

And now abide faith, hope, love, these three; but the greatest of these *is* love.

1 Corinthians 12–13

WORSHIP

Righteous *are* You, O LORD,
And upright *are* Your judgments.
Your testimonies, *which* You have
    commanded,
Are righteous and very faithful.

The righteousness of Your testimonies *is*
    everlasting;
Give me understanding, and I shall live.

Psalm 119:137-138, 144

WISDOM

Train up a child in the way he should go,
And when he is old he will not depart from it.

Proverbs 22:6

SW?! SO WHAT?
What does this tell me?

THE CERTAINTY OF THE RESURRECTION

1 Corinthians 14:1-33, 39-40; 15:1-11; Psalm 119:145-148; Proverbs 22:11

Pursue love, and desire spiritual *gifts,* but especially that you may prophesy. For he who speaks in a tongue does not speak to men but to God, for no one understands *him;* however, in the spirit he speaks mysteries. But he who prophesies speaks edification and exhortation and comfort to men. He who speaks in a tongue edifies himself, but he who prophesies edifies the church. I wish you all spoke with tongues, but even more that you prophesied; for he who prophesies *is* greater than he who speaks with tongues, unless indeed he interprets, that the church may receive edification.

But now, brethren, if I come to you speaking with tongues, what shall I profit you unless I speak to you either by revelation, by knowledge, by prophesying, or by teaching? Even things without life, whether flute or harp, when they make a sound, unless they make a distinction in the sounds, how will it be known what is piped or played? For if the trumpet makes an uncertain sound, who will prepare for battle? So likewise you, unless you utter by the tongue words easy to understand, how will it be known what is spoken? For you will be speaking into the air. There are, it may be, so many kinds of languages in the world, and none of them *is* without significance. Therefore, if I do not know the meaning of the language, I shall be a foreigner to him who speaks, and he who speaks *will be* a foreigner to me. Even so you, since you are zealous for spiritual *gifts, let it be* for the edification of the church *that* you seek to excel.

Therefore let him who speaks in a tongue pray that he may interpret. For if I pray in a tongue, my spirit prays, but my understanding is unfruitful. What is *the conclusion* then? I will pray with the spirit, and I will also pray with the understanding. I will sing with the spirit, and I will also sing with the understanding. Otherwise, if you bless with the spirit, how will he who occupies the place of the uninformed say "Amen" at your giving of thanks, since he does not understand what you say? For you indeed give thanks well, but the other is not edified.

I thank my God I speak with tongues more than you all; yet in the church I would rather speak five words with my understanding, that I may teach others also, than ten thousand words in a tongue.

Brethren, do not be children in understanding; however, in malice be babes, but in understanding be mature.

In the law it is written:

"With *men of* other tongues and other lips
I will speak to this people;
And yet, for all that, they will not hear Me,"

says the Lord.

Therefore tongues are for a sign, not to those who believe but to unbelievers; but prophesying is not for unbelievers but for those who believe. Therefore if the whole church comes together in one place, and all speak with tongues, and there come in *those who are* uninformed or unbelievers, will they not say that you are out of your mind? But if all prophesy, and an unbeliever or an uninformed person comes in, he is convinced by all, he is convicted by all. And thus the secrets of his heart are revealed; and so, falling down on *his* face, he will worship God and report that God is truly among you.

How is it then, brethren? Whenever you come together, each of you has a psalm, has a teaching, has a tongue, has a revelation, has an interpretation. Let all things be done for edification. If anyone speaks in a tongue, *let there be* two or at the most three, *each* in turn, and let one interpret. But if there is no interpreter, let him keep silent in church, and let him speak to himself and to God. Let two or three prophets speak, and let the others judge. But if *anything* is revealed to another who sits by, let the first keep silent. For you can all prophesy one by one, that all may learn and all may be encouraged. And the spirits of the prophets are subject to the prophets. For God is not *the author* of confusion but of peace, as in all the churches of the saints.

Therefore, brethren, desire earnestly to prophesy, and do not forbid to speak with tongues. Let all things be done decently and in order.

Moreover, brethren, I declare to you the gospel which I preached to you, which also you received and in which you stand, by which also you are saved, if you hold fast that word which I preached to you—unless you believed in vain.

For I delivered to you first of all that which I also received: that Christ died for our sins according to the Scriptures, and that He was buried, and that He rose again the third day according to the Scriptures, and that He was seen by Cephas, then by the twelve. After that He was seen by over five hundred brethren at once, of whom the greater part remain to the present, but some have fallen asleep. After that He was seen by James, then by all the apostles. Then last of all He was seen by me also, as by one born out of due time.

For I am the least of the apostles, who am not worthy to be called an apostle, because I persecuted the church of God. But by the grace of God I am what I am, and His grace toward me was not in vain; but I labored more abundantly than they all, yet not I, but the grace of God *which was* with me. Therefore, whether *it was* I or they, so we preach and so you believed.

1 Corinthians 14:1-33, 39-40; 15:1-11

WORSHIP

I cry out with *my* whole heart;
Hear me, O LORD!
I will keep Your statutes.
I cry out to You;
Save me, and I will keep Your testimonies.
I rise before the dawning of the morning,
And cry for help;
I hope in Your word.
My eyes are awake through the *night* watches,
That I may meditate on Your word.

Psalm 119:145-148

WISDOM

He who loves purity of heart
And has grace on his lips,
The king *will be* his friend.

Proverbs 22:11

SW?! **SO WHAT?**
What does this tell me?

THE CENTRALITY OF THE RESURRECTION

1 Corinthians 15:12-28, 35-58; 16:1-4, 13-14; Psalm 119:156, 159-160; Proverbs 22:14

Now if Christ is preached that He has been raised from the dead, how do some among you say that there is no resurrection of the dead? But if there is no resurrection of the dead, then Christ is not risen. And if Christ is not risen, then our preaching *is* empty and your faith *is* also empty. Yes, and we are found false witnesses of God, because we have testified of God that He raised up Christ, whom He did not raise up—if in fact the dead do not rise. For if *the* dead do not rise, then Christ is not risen. And if Christ is not risen, your faith *is* futile; you are still in your sins! Then also those who have fallen asleep in Christ have perished. If in this life only we have hope in Christ, we are of all men the most pitiable.

But now Christ is risen from the dead, *and* has become the firstfruits of those who have fallen asleep. For since by man *came* death, by Man also *came* the resurrection of the dead. For as in Adam all die, even so in Christ all shall be made alive. But each one in his own order: Christ the firstfruits, afterward those *who are* Christ's at His coming. Then *comes* the end, when He delivers the kingdom to God the Father, when He puts an end to all rule and all authority and power. For He must reign till He has put all enemies under His feet. The last enemy *that* will be destroyed *is* death. For "He has put all things under His feet." But when He says "all things are put under *Him*," *it is* evident that He who put all things under Him is excepted. Now when all things are made subject to Him, then the Son Himself will also be subject to Him who put all things under Him, that God may be all in all.

But someone will say, "How are the dead raised up? And with what body do they come?" Foolish one, what you sow is not made alive unless it dies. And what you sow, you do not sow that body that shall be, but mere grain—perhaps wheat or some other *grain*. But God gives it a body as He pleases, and to each seed its own body.

All flesh *is* not the same flesh, but *there is* one *kind of* flesh of men, another flesh of animals, another of fish, *and* another of birds.

There are also celestial bodies and terrestrial bodies; but the glory of the celestial *is* one, and the *glory* of the terrestrial *is* another. *There is* one glory of the sun, another glory of the moon, and another glory of the stars; for *one* star differs from *another* star in glory.

So also *is* the resurrection of the dead. *The body* is sown in corruption, it is raised in incorruption. It is sown in dishonor, it is raised in glory. It is sown in weakness, it is raised in power. It is sown a natural body, it is raised a spiritual body. There is a natural body, and there is a spiritual body. And so it is written, "The first man Adam became a living being." The last Adam *became* a life-giving spirit.

However, the spiritual is not first, but the natural, and afterward the spiritual. The first man *was* of the earth, *made* of dust; the second Man *is* the Lord from heaven. As *was* the *man* of dust, so also *are* those *who are made* of dust; and as *is* the heavenly *Man,* so also *are* those *who are* heavenly. And as we have borne the image of the *man* of dust, we shall also bear the image of the heavenly *Man.*

Now this I say, brethren, that flesh and blood cannot inherit the kingdom of God; nor does corruption inherit incorruption. Behold, I tell you a mystery: We shall not all sleep, but we shall all be changed—in a moment, in the twinkling of an eye, at the last trumpet. For the trumpet will sound, and the dead will be raised incorruptible, and we shall be changed. For this corruptible must put on incorruption, and this mortal *must* put on immortality. So when this corruptible has put on incorruption, and this mortal has put on immortality, then shall be brought to pass the saying that is written: "Death is swallowed up in victory."

"O Death, where *is* your sting?
O Hades, where *is* your victory?"

The sting of death *is* sin, and the strength of sin *is* the law. But thanks *be* to God, who gives us the victory through our Lord Jesus Christ.

Therefore, my beloved brethren, be steadfast, immovable, always abounding in the work of the Lord, knowing that your labor is not in vain in the Lord.

Now concerning the collection for the saints, as I have given orders to the churches of Galatia, so you must do also: On the first *day* of the week let each one of you lay something aside, storing up as he may prosper, that there be no collections when I come. And when I come, whomever you approve by *your* letters I will send to bear your gift to Jerusalem. But if it is fitting that I go also, they will go with me.

Watch, stand fast in the faith, be brave, be strong. Let all *that* you *do* be done with love.

1 Corinthians 15:12-28, 35-58; 16:1-4, 13-14

WORSHIP

Great *are* Your tender mercies, O LORD;
Revive me according to Your judgments.

Consider how I love Your precepts;
Revive me, O LORD, according to Your
    lovingkindness.
The entirety of Your word *is* truth,
And every one of Your righteous judgments
    endures forever.

Psalm 119:156, 159-160

WISDOM

The mouth of an immoral woman *is* a deep
    pit;
He who is abhorred by the LORD will fall there.

Proverbs 22:14

SW?! SO WHAT?
What does this tell me?

A LETTER WRITTEN ON TABLETS OF HUMAN HEARTS

2 Corinthians 1:1-14, 23-24; 2:1-4, 12-17; 3:1-18; Psalm 119:165-168; Proverbs 22:15

Paul, an apostle of Jesus Christ by the will of God, and Timothy our brother,

To the church of God which is at Corinth, with all the saints who are in all Achaia:

Grace to you and peace from God our Father and the Lord Jesus Christ.

Blessed be the God and Father of our Lord Jesus Christ, the Father of mercies and God of all comfort, who comforts us in all our tribulation, that we may be able to comfort those who are in any trouble, with the comfort with which we ourselves are comforted by God. For as the sufferings of Christ abound in us, so our consolation also abounds through Christ. Now if we are afflicted, it is for your consolation and salvation, which is effective for enduring the same sufferings which we also suffer. Or if we are comforted, it is for your consolation and salvation. And our hope for you is steadfast, because we know that as you are partakers of the sufferings, so also you will partake of the consolation.

For we do not want you to be ignorant, brethren, of our trouble which came to us in Asia: that we were burdened beyond measure, above strength, so that we despaired even of life. Yes, we had the sentence of death in ourselves, that we should not trust in ourselves but in God who raises the dead, who delivered us from so great a death, and does deliver us; in whom we trust that He will still deliver us, you also helping together in prayer for us, that thanks may be given by many persons on our behalf for the gift granted to us through many.

For our boasting is this: the testimony of our conscience that we conducted ourselves in the world in simplicity and godly sincerity, not with fleshly wisdom but by the grace of God, and more abundantly toward you. For we are not writing any other things to you than what you read or understand. Now I trust you will understand, even to the end (as also you have understood us in part), that we are your boast as you also are ours, in the day of the Lord Jesus.

Moreover I call God as witness against my soul, that to spare you I came no more to Corinth. Not that we have dominion over your faith, but are fellow workers for your joy; for by faith you stand.

But I determined this within myself, that I would not come again to you in sorrow. For if I make you sorrowful, then who is he who makes me glad but the one who is made sorrowful by me? And I wrote this very thing to you, lest, when I came, I should have sorrow over those from whom I ought to have joy, having confidence in you all that my joy is the joy of you all. For out of much affliction and anguish of heart I wrote to you, with many tears, not that you should be grieved, but that you might know the love which I have so abundantly for you.

Furthermore, when I came to Troas to preach Christ's gospel, and a door was opened to me by the Lord, I had no rest in my spirit, because I did not find Titus my brother; but taking my leave of them, I departed for Macedonia.

Now thanks be to God who always leads us in triumph in Christ, and through us diffuses the fragrance of His knowledge in every place. For we are to God the fragrance of Christ among those who are being saved and among those who are perishing. To the one we are the aroma of death leading to death, and to the other the aroma of life leading to life. And who is sufficient for these things? For we are not, as so many, peddling the word of God; but as of sincerity, but as from God, we speak in the sight of God in Christ.

Do we begin again to commend ourselves? Or do we need, as some others, epistles of commendation to you or letters of commendation from you? You are our epistle written in our hearts, known and read by all men; clearly you are an epistle of Christ, ministered by us, written not with ink but by the Spirit of the living God, not on tablets of stone but on tablets of flesh, that is, of the heart.

And we have such trust through Christ toward God. Not that we are sufficient of ourselves to think of anything as *being* from ourselves, but our sufficiency *is* from God, who also made us sufficient as ministers of the new covenant, not of the letter but of the Spirit; for the letter kills, but the Spirit gives life.

But if the ministry of death, written *and* engraved on stones, was glorious, so that the children of Israel could not look steadily at the face of Moses because of the glory of his countenance, which *glory* was passing away, how will the ministry of the Spirit not be more glorious? For if the ministry of condemnation *had* glory, the ministry of righteousness exceeds much more in glory. For even what was made glorious had no glory in this respect, because of the glory that excels. For if what is passing away *was* glorious, what remains *is* much more glorious.

Therefore, since we have such hope, we use great boldness of speech—unlike Moses, *who* put a veil over his face so that the children of Israel could not look steadily at the end of what was passing away. But their minds were blinded. For until this day the same veil remains unlifted in the reading of the Old Testament, because the *veil* is taken away in Christ. But even to this day, when Moses is read, a veil lies on their heart. Nevertheless when one turns to the Lord, the veil is taken away. Now the Lord is the Spirit; and where the Spirit of the Lord *is,* there *is* liberty. But we all, with unveiled face, beholding as in a mirror the glory of the Lord, are being transformed into the same image from glory to glory, just as by the Spirit of the Lord.

2 Corinthians 1:1-14, 23-24; 2:1-4, 12-17; 3:1-18

WORSHIP

Great peace have those who love Your law,
And nothing causes them to stumble.
LORD, I hope for Your salvation,
And I do Your commandments.
My soul keeps Your testimonies,
And I love them exceedingly.
I keep Your precepts and Your testimonies,
For all my ways *are* before You.

Psalm 119:165-168

WISDOM

Foolishness *is* bound up in the heart of a child;
The rod of correction will drive it far from him.

Proverbs 22:15

SW?! SO WHAT?
What does this tell me?

DISTINGUISH THE TEMPORARY FROM THE TIMELESS

2 Corinthians 4–5; Psalm 119:174-176; Proverbs 22:24-25

Therefore, since we have this ministry, as we have received mercy, we do not lose heart. But we have renounced the hidden things of shame, not walking in craftiness nor handling the word of God deceitfully, but by manifestation of the truth commending ourselves to every man's conscience in the sight of God. But even if our gospel is veiled, it is veiled to those who are perishing, whose minds the god of this age has blinded, who do not believe, lest the light of the gospel of the glory of Christ, who is the image of God, should shine on them. For we do not preach ourselves, but Christ Jesus the Lord, and ourselves your bondservants for Jesus' sake. For it is the God who commanded light to shine out of darkness, who has shone in our hearts to *give* the light of the knowledge of the glory of God in the face of Jesus Christ.

But we have this treasure in earthen vessels, that the excellence of the power may be of God and not of us. *We are* hard-pressed on every side, yet not crushed; *we are* perplexed, but not in despair; persecuted, but not forsaken; struck down, but not destroyed—always carrying about in the body the dying of the Lord Jesus, that the life of Jesus also may be manifested in our body. For we who live are always delivered to death for Jesus' sake, that the life of Jesus also may be manifested in our mortal flesh. So then death is working in us, but life in you.

And since we have the same spirit of faith, according to what is written, "I believed and therefore I spoke," we also believe and therefore speak, knowing that He who raised up the Lord Jesus will also raise us up with Jesus, and will present *us* with you. For all things *are* for your sakes, that grace, having spread through the many, may cause thanksgiving to abound to the glory of God.

Therefore we do not lose heart. Even though our outward man is perishing, yet the inward *man* is being renewed day by day. For our light affliction, which is but for a moment, is working for us a far more ex-

ceeding *and* eternal weight of glory, while we do not look at the things which are seen, but at the things which are not seen. For the things which are seen *are* temporary, but the things which are not seen *are* eternal.

For we know that if our earthly house, *this* tent, is destroyed, we have a building from God, a house not made with hands, eternal in the heavens. For in this we groan, earnestly desiring to be clothed with our habitation which is from heaven, if indeed, having been clothed, we shall not be found naked. For we who are in *this* tent groan, being burdened, not because we want to be unclothed, but further clothed, that mortality may be swallowed up by life. Now He who has prepared us for this very thing *is* God, who also has given us the Spirit as a guarantee.

So *we are* always confident, knowing that while we are at home in the body we are absent from the Lord. For we walk by faith, not by sight. We are confident, yes, well pleased rather to be absent from the body and to be present with the Lord.

Therefore we make it our aim, whether present or absent, to be well pleasing to Him. For we must all appear before the judgment seat of Christ, that each one may receive the things *done* in the body, according to what he has done, whether good or bad. Knowing, therefore, the terror of the Lord, we persuade men; but we are well known to God, and I also trust are well known in your consciences.

For we do not commend ourselves again to you, but give you opportunity to boast on our behalf, that you may have *an answer* for those who boast in appearance and not in heart. For if we are beside ourselves, *it is* for God; or if we are of sound mind, *it is* for you. For the love of Christ compels us, because we judge thus: that if One died for all, then all died; and He died for all, that those who live should live no longer for themselves, but for Him who died for them and rose again.

Therefore, from now on, we regard no one according to the flesh. Even though we have known Christ according to the flesh, yet now we know *Him* thus no longer. Therefore, if anyone *is* in Christ, *he is* a new creation; old things have passed away;

behold, all things have become new. Now all things *are* of God, who has reconciled us to Himself through Jesus Christ, and has given us the ministry of reconciliation, that is, that God was in Christ reconciling the world to Himself, not imputing their trespasses to them, and has committed to us the word of reconciliation.

Now then, we are ambassadors for Christ, as though God were pleading through us: we implore *you* on Christ's behalf, be reconciled to God. For He made Him who knew no sin *to be* sin for us, that we might become the righteousness of God in Him.

2 Corinthians 4–5

WORSHIP

I long for Your salvation, O LORD,
And Your law *is* my delight.
Let my soul live, and it shall praise You;
And let Your judgments help me.
I have gone astray like a lost sheep;
Seek Your servant,
For I do not forget Your commandments.

Psalm 119:174-176

WISDOM

Make no friendship with an angry man,
And with a furious man do not go,
Lest you learn his ways
And set a snare for your soul.

Proverbs 22:24-25

SW?! **SO WHAT?**
What does this tell me?

THE FRUIT AND BENEFIT OF GODLY SORROW

2 Corinthians 6:1–8:9; Psalm 120:1–2; Proverbs 22:26–27

We then, *as* workers together *with Him* also plead with *you* not to receive the grace of God in vain. For He says:

"In an acceptable time I have heard you,
And in the day of salvation I have helped you."

Behold, now *is* the accepted time; behold, now *is* the day of salvation.

We give no offense in anything, that our ministry may not be blamed. But in all *things* we commend ourselves as ministers of God: in much patience, in tribulations, in needs, in distresses, in stripes, in imprisonments, in tumults, in labors, in sleeplessness, in fastings; by purity, by knowledge, by longsuffering, by kindness, by the Holy Spirit, by sincere love, by the word of truth, by the power of God, by the armor of righteousness on the right hand and on the left, by honor and dishonor, by evil report and good report; as deceivers, and *yet* true; as unknown, and *yet* well known; as dying, and behold we live; as chastened, and *yet* not killed; as sorrowful, yet always rejoicing; as poor, yet making many rich; as having nothing, and *yet* possessing all things.

O Corinthians! We have spoken openly to you, our heart is wide open. You are not restricted by us, but you are restricted by your *own* affections. Now in return for the same (I speak as to children), you also be open.

Do not be unequally yoked together with unbelievers. For what fellowship has righteousness with lawlessness? And what communion has light with darkness? And what accord has Christ with Belial? Or what part has a believer with an unbeliever? And what agreement has the temple of God with idols? For you are the temple of the living God. As God has said:

"I will dwell in them
And walk among *them*.
I will be their God,
And they shall be My people."

Therefore

"Come out from among them
And be separate, says the Lord.
Do not touch what is unclean,
And I will receive you."
"I will be a Father to you,
And you shall be My sons and daughters,
Says the LORD Almighty."

Therefore, having these promises, beloved, let us cleanse ourselves from all filthiness of the flesh and spirit, perfecting holiness in the fear of God.

Open *your hearts* to us. We have wronged no one, we have corrupted no one, we have cheated no one. I do not say *this* to condemn; for I have said before that you are in our hearts, to die together and to live together. Great *is* my boldness of speech toward you, great *is* my boasting on your behalf. I am filled with comfort. I am exceedingly joyful in all our tribulation.

For indeed, when we came to Macedonia, our bodies had no rest, but we were troubled on every side. Outside *were* conflicts, inside *were* fears. Nevertheless God, who comforts the downcast, comforted us by the coming of Titus, and not only by his coming, but also by the consolation with which he was comforted in you, when he told us of your earnest desire, your mourning, your zeal for me, so that I rejoiced even more.

For even if I made you sorry with my letter, I do not regret it; though I did regret it. For I perceive that the same epistle made you sorry, though only for a while. Now I rejoice, not that you were made sorry, but that your sorrow led to repentance. For you were made sorry in a godly manner, that you might suffer loss from us in nothing. For godly sorrow produces repentance *leading* to salvation, not to be regretted; but the sorrow of the world produces death. For observe this very thing, that you sorrowed in a godly manner: What diligence it produced in you, *what* clearing *of yourselves, what* indignation, *what* fear, *what* vehement desire, *what* zeal, *what* vindication! In all *things* you proved yourselves to be clear in this matter. Therefore, although I wrote to you, *I did* not *do it* for the sake of him who had done the wrong, nor for the sake of him who suffered wrong, but that our care for you in the sight of God might appear to you.

Therefore we have been comforted in your comfort. And we rejoiced exceedingly more for the joy of Titus, because his spirit has been refreshed by you all. For if in anything I have boasted to him about you, I am not ashamed. But as we spoke all things to you in truth, even so our boasting to Titus was found true. And his affections are greater for you as he remembers the obedience of you all, how with fear and trembling you received him. Therefore I rejoice that I have confidence in you in everything.

Moreover, brethren, we make known to you the grace of God bestowed on the churches of Macedonia: that in a great trial of affliction the abundance of their joy and their deep poverty abounded in the riches of their liberality. For I bear witness that according to *their* ability, yes, and beyond *their* ability, *they were* freely willing, imploring us with much urgency that we would receive the gift and the fellowship of the ministering to the saints. And not *only* as we had hoped, but they first gave themselves to the Lord, and *then* to us by the will of God. So we urged Titus, that as he had begun, so he would also complete this grace in you as well. But as you abound in everything—in faith, in speech, in knowledge, in all diligence, and in your love for us—*see* that you abound in this grace also.

I speak not by commandment, but I am testing the sincerity of your love by the diligence of others. For you know the grace of our Lord Jesus Christ, that though He was rich, yet for your sakes He became poor, that you through His poverty might become rich.

2 Corinthians 6:1–8:9

WORSHIP

In my distress I cried to the LORD,
And He heard me.
Deliver my soul, O LORD, from lying lips
And from a deceitful tongue.

Psalm 120:1-2

WISDOM

Do not be one of those who shakes hands in a
   pledge,
One of those who is surety for debts;
If you have nothing *with which* to pay,
Why should he take away your bed from
   under you?

Proverbs 22:26-27

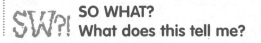

SO WHAT?
What does this tell me?

PRINCIPLES OF GIVING AND WARNINGS
OF FALSE PROPHETS

2 Corinthians 8:10-15; 9:6–11:4, 12-15; Psalm 120:5-7; Proverbs 22:29

And in this I give advice: It is to your advantage not only to be doing what you began and were desiring to do a year ago; but now you also must complete the doing *of it;* that as *there was* a readiness to desire *it,* so *there* also *may be* a completion out of what *you* have. For if there is first a willing mind, *it is* accepted according to what one has, *and* not according to what he does not have.

For I *do* not *mean* that others should be eased and you burdened; but by an equality, *that* now at this time your abundance *may supply* their lack, that their abundance also may supply your lack—that there may be equality. As it is written, "He who *gathered* much had nothing left over, and he who *gathered* little had no lack."

But this I *say:* He who sows sparingly will also reap sparingly, and he who sows bountifully will also reap bountifully. *So let* each one *give* as he purposes in his heart, not grudgingly or of necessity; for God loves a cheerful giver. And God *is* able to make all grace abound toward you, that you, always having all sufficiency in all *things,* may have an abundance for every good work. As it is written:

"He has dispersed abroad,
He has given to the poor;
His righteousness endures forever."

Now may He who supplies seed to the sower, and bread for food, supply and multiply the seed you have *sown* and increase the fruits of your righteousness, while *you are* enriched in everything for all liberality, which causes thanksgiving through us to God. For the administration of this service not only supplies the needs of the saints, but also is abounding through many thanksgivings to God, while, through the proof of this ministry, they glorify God for the obedience of your confession to the gospel of Christ, and for *your* liberal sharing with them and all *men,* and by their prayer for you, who long for you because of the exceeding grace of God in you. Thanks *be* to God for His indescribable gift!

Now I, Paul, myself am pleading with you by the meekness and gentleness of Christ—who in presence *am* lowly among you, but being absent am bold toward you. But I beg *you* that when I am present I may not be bold with that confidence by which I intend to be bold against some, who think of us as if we walked according to the flesh. For though we walk in the flesh, we do not war according to the flesh. For the weapons of our warfare *are* not carnal but mighty in God for pulling down strongholds, casting down arguments and every high thing that exalts itself against the knowledge of God, bringing every thought into captivity to the obedience of Christ, and being ready to punish all disobedience when your obedience is fulfilled.

Do you look at things according to the outward appearance? If anyone is convinced in himself that he is Christ's, let him again consider this in himself, that just as he *is* Christ's, even so we *are* Christ's. For even if I should boast somewhat more about our authority, which the Lord gave us for edification and not for your destruction, I shall not be ashamed—lest I seem to terrify you by letters. "For *his* letters," they say, "*are* weighty and powerful, but *his* bodily presence *is* weak, and *his* speech contemptible." Let such a person consider this, that what we are in word by letters when we are absent, such *we will* also *be* in deed when we are present.

For we dare not class ourselves or compare ourselves with those who commend themselves. But they, measuring themselves by themselves, and comparing themselves among themselves, are not wise. We, however, will not boast beyond measure, but within the limits of the sphere which God appointed us—a sphere which especially includes you. For we are not overextending ourselves (as though *our authority* did not extend to you), for it was to you that we came with the gospel of Christ; not boasting of things beyond measure, *that is,* in other men's labors, but having hope, *that* as your faith is increased, we shall be greatly enlarged by you in our sphere, to preach the gospel in the *regions* beyond you, *and* not to boast in another man's sphere of accomplishment.

But "he who glories, let him glory in the LORD." For not he who commends himself is approved, but whom the Lord commends.

Oh, that you would bear with me in a little folly—and indeed you do bear with me. For I am jealous for you with godly jealousy. For I have betrothed you to one husband, that I may present *you as* a chaste virgin to Christ. But I fear, lest somehow, as the serpent deceived Eve by his craftiness, so your minds may be corrupted from the simplicity that is in Christ. For if he who comes preaches another Jesus whom we have not preached, or *if* you receive a different spirit which you have not received, or a different gospel which you have not accepted—you may well put up with it!

But what I do, I will also continue to do, that I may cut off the opportunity from those who desire an opportunity to be regarded just as we are in the things of which they boast. For such *are* false apostles, deceitful workers, transforming themselves into apostles of Christ. And no wonder! For Satan himself transforms himself into an angel of light. Therefore *it is* no great thing if his ministers also transform themselves into ministers of righteousness, whose end will be according to their works.

2 Corinthians 8:10-15; 9:6–11:4, 12-15

WORSHIP

Woe is me, that I dwell in Meshech,
That I dwell among the tents of Kedar!
My soul has dwelt too long
With one who hates peace.
I *am for* peace;
But when I speak, they *are* for war.

Psalm 120:5-7

WISDOM

Do you see a man *who* excels in his work?
He will stand before kings;
He will not stand before unknown *men.*

Proverbs 22:29

SO WHAT?
What does this tell me?

PAUL'S APOSTOLIC CREDENTIALS AND FINAL COMMAND

2 Corinthians 11:16–12:10, 19-21; 13:1-11; Psalm 122:1-4; Proverbs 23:4-5

I say again, let no one think me a fool. If otherwise, at least receive me as a fool, that I also may boast a little. What I speak, I speak not according to the Lord, but as it were, foolishly, in this confidence of boasting. Seeing that many boast according to the flesh, I also will boast. For you put up with fools gladly, since you *yourselves* are wise! For you put up with it if one brings you into bondage, if one devours *you,* if one takes *from you,* if one exalts himself, if one strikes you on the face. To *our* shame I say that we were too weak for that! But in whatever anyone is bold—I speak foolishly—I am bold also.

Are they Hebrews? So *am* I. Are they Israelites? So *am* I. Are they the seed of Abraham? So *am* I. Are they ministers of Christ?—I speak as a fool—I *am* more: in labors more abundant, in stripes above measure, in prisons more frequently, in deaths often. From the Jews five times I received forty *stripes* minus one. Three times I was beaten with rods; once I was stoned; three times I was shipwrecked; a night and a day I have been in the deep; *in* journeys often, *in* perils of waters, *in* perils of robbers, *in* perils of *my own* countrymen, *in* perils of the Gentiles, *in* perils in the city, *in* perils in the wilderness, *in* perils in the sea, *in* perils among false brethren; in weariness and toil, in sleeplessness often, in hunger and thirst, in fastings often, in cold and nakedness—besides the other things, what comes upon me daily: my deep concern for all the churches. Who is weak, and I am not weak? Who is made to stumble, and I do not burn *with indignation?*

If I must boast, I will boast in the things which concern my infirmity. The God and Father of our Lord Jesus Christ, who is blessed forever, knows that I am not lying. In Damascus the governor, under Aretas the king, was guarding the city of the Damascenes with a garrison, desiring to arrest me; but I was let down in a basket through a window in the wall, and escaped from his hands.

It is doubtless not profitable for me to boast. I will come to visions and revelations of the Lord: I know a man in Christ who fourteen years ago—whether in the body I do not know, or whether out of the body I do not know, God knows—such a one was caught up to the third heaven. And I know such a man—whether in the body or out of the body I do not know, God knows—how he was caught up into Paradise and heard inexpressible words, which it is not lawful for a man to utter. Of such a one I will boast; yet of myself I will not boast, except in my infirmities. For though I might desire to boast, I will not be a fool; for I will speak the truth. But I refrain, lest anyone should think of me above what he sees me *to be* or hears from me.

And lest I should be exalted above measure by the abundance of the revelations, a thorn in the flesh was given to me, a messenger of Satan to buffet me, lest I be exalted above measure. Concerning this thing I pleaded with the Lord three times that it might depart from me. And He said to me, "My grace is sufficient for you, for My strength is made perfect in weakness." Therefore most gladly I will rather boast in my infirmities, that the power of Christ may rest upon me. Therefore I take pleasure in infirmities, in reproaches, in needs, in persecutions, in distresses, for Christ's sake. For when I am weak, then I am strong.

Again, do you think that we excuse ourselves to you? We speak before God in Christ. But *we do* all things, beloved, for your edification. For I fear lest, when I come, I shall not find you such as I wish, and *that* I shall be found by you such as you do not wish; lest *there be* contentions, jealousies, outbursts of wrath, selfish ambitions, backbitings, whisperings, conceits, tumults; lest, when I come again, my God will humble me among you, and I shall mourn for many who have sinned before and have not repented of the uncleanness, fornication, and lewdness which they have practiced.

APOSTLES AND THE CHURCH

This *will be* the third *time* I am coming to you. "By the mouth of two or three witnesses every word shall be established." I have told you before, and foretell as if I were present the second time, and now being absent I write to those who have sinned before, and to all the rest, that if I come again I will not spare—since you seek a proof of Christ speaking in me, who is not weak toward you, but mighty in you. For though He was crucified in weakness, yet He lives by the power of God. For we also are weak in Him, but we shall live with Him by the power of God toward you.

Examine yourselves *as to* whether you are in the faith. Test yourselves. Do you not know yourselves, that Jesus Christ is in you?—unless indeed you are disqualified. But I trust that you will know that we are not disqualified.

Now I pray to God that you do no evil, not that we should appear approved, but that you should do what is honorable, though we may seem disqualified. For we can do nothing against the truth, but for the truth. For we are glad when we are weak and you are strong. And this also we pray, that you may be made complete. Therefore I write these things being absent, lest being present I should use sharpness, according to the authority which the Lord has given me for edification and not for destruction.

Finally, brethren, farewell. Become complete. Be of good comfort, be of one mind, live in peace; and the God of love and peace will be with you.

2 Corinthians 11:16–12:10, 19-21; 13:1-11

WoRSHiP

I was glad when they said to me,
"Let us go into the house of the LORD."
Our feet have been standing
Within your gates, O Jerusalem!

Jerusalem is built
As a city that is compact together,
Where the tribes go up,
The tribes of the LORD,
To the Testimony of Israel,
To give thanks to the name of the LORD.

Psalm 122:1-4

WiSDoM

Do not overwork to be rich;
Because of your own understanding, cease!
Will you set your eyes on that which is not?
For *riches* certainly make themselves wings;
They fly away like an eagle *toward* heaven.

Proverbs 23:4-5

SW?! SO WHAT?
What does this tell me?

THE POWER OF THE GOSPEL AND THE PREDICAMENT OF THE UNRIGHTEOUS

Romans 1:1–2:11; Psalm 123:1, 3–4; Proverbs 23:13–14

Paul, a bondservant of Jesus Christ, called *to be* an apostle, separated to the gospel of God which He promised before through His prophets in the Holy Scriptures, concerning His Son Jesus Christ our Lord, who was born of the seed of David according to the flesh, *and* declared *to be* the Son of God with power according to the Spirit of holiness, by the resurrection from the dead. Through Him we have received grace and apostleship for obedience to the faith among all nations for His name, among whom you also are the called of Jesus Christ;

To all who are in Rome, beloved of God, called *to be* saints:

Grace to you and peace from God our Father and the Lord Jesus Christ.

First, I thank my God through Jesus Christ for you all, that your faith is spoken of throughout the whole world. For God is my witness, whom I serve with my spirit in the gospel of His Son, that without ceasing I make mention of you always in my prayers, making request if, by some means, now at last I may find a way in the will of God to come to you. For I long to see you, that I may impart to you some spiritual gift, so that you may be established—that is, that I may be encouraged together with you by the mutual faith both of you and me.

Now I do not want you to be unaware, brethren, that I often planned to come to you (but was hindered until now), that I might have some fruit among you also, just as among the other Gentiles. I am a debtor both to Greeks and to barbarians, both to wise and to unwise. So, as much as is in me, *I am* ready to preach the gospel to you who are in Rome also.

For I am not ashamed of the gospel of Christ, for it is the power of God to salvation for everyone who believes, for the Jew first and also for the Greek. For in it the righ-teousness of God is revealed from faith to faith; as it is written, "The just shall live by faith."

For the wrath of God is revealed from heaven against all ungodliness and unrighteousness of men, who suppress the truth in unrighteousness, because what may be known of God is manifest in them, for God has shown *it* to them. For since the creation of the world His invisible *attributes* are clearly seen, being understood by the things that are made, *even* His eternal power and Godhead, so that they are without excuse, because, although they knew God, they did not glorify *Him* as God, nor were thankful, but became futile in their thoughts, and their foolish hearts were darkened. Professing to be wise, they became fools, and changed the glory of the incorruptible God into an image made like corruptible man—and birds and four-footed animals and creeping things.

Therefore God also gave them up to uncleanness, in the lusts of their hearts, to dishonor their bodies among themselves, who exchanged the truth of God for the lie, and worshiped and served the creature rather than the Creator, who is blessed forever. Amen.

For this reason God gave them up to vile passions. For even their women exchanged the natural use for what is against nature. Likewise also the men, leaving the natural use of the woman, burned in their lust for one another, men with men committing what is shameful, and receiving in themselves the penalty of their error which was due.

And even as they did not like to retain God in *their* knowledge, God gave them over to a debased mind, to do those things which are not fitting; being filled with all unrighteousness, sexual immorality, wickedness, covetousness, maliciousness; full of envy, murder, strife, deceit, evil-mindedness; *they are* whisperers, backbiters, haters of God, violent, proud, boasters, inventors of evil things, disobedient to parents, undiscerning, untrustworthy, unloving, unforgiving, unmerciful; who, knowing the righteous judgment of God, that those who practice such things are deserving of death, not only do the same but also approve of those who practice them.

Therefore you are inexcusable, O man, whoever you are who judge, for in whatever you judge another you condemn yourself; for you who judge practice the same things. But we know that the judgment of God is according to truth against those who practice such things. And do you think this, O man, you who judge those practicing such things, and doing the same, that you will escape the judgment of God? Or do you despise the riches of His goodness, forbearance, and longsuffering, not knowing that the goodness of God leads you to repentance? But in accordance with your hardness and your impenitent heart you are treasuring up for yourself wrath in the day of wrath and revelation of the righteous judgment of God, who "will render to each one according to his deeds": eternal life to those who by patient continuance in doing good seek for glory, honor, and immortality; but to those who are self-seeking and do not obey the truth, but obey unrighteousness—indignation and wrath, tribulation and anguish, on every soul of man who does evil, of the Jew first and also of the Greek; but glory, honor, and peace to everyone who works what is good, to the Jew first and also to the Greek. For there is no partiality with God.

Romans 1:1–2:11

WORSHIP

Unto You I lift up my eyes,
O You who dwell in the heavens.

Have mercy on us, O LORD, have mercy on us!
For we are exceedingly filled with contempt.
Our soul is exceedingly filled
With the scorn of those who are at ease,
With the contempt of the proud.

Psalm 123:1, 3-4

WISDOM

Do not withhold correction from a child,
For *if* you beat him with a rod, he will not die.
You shall beat him with a rod,
And deliver his soul from hell.

Proverbs 23:13-14

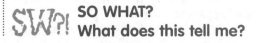

SO WHAT?
What does this tell me?

EVERYONE EVERYWHERE HAS A PROBLEM WITH SIN

Romans 2:12–3:20; Psalm 124:6-8; Proverbs 23:15-16

For as many as have sinned without law will also perish without law, and as many as have sinned in the law will be judged by the law (for not the hearers of the law *are* just in the sight of God, but the doers of the law will be justified; for when Gentiles, who do not have the law, by nature do the things in the law, these, although not having the law, are a law to themselves, who show the work of the law written in their hearts, their conscience also bearing witness, and between themselves *their* thoughts accusing or else excusing *them*) in the day when God will judge the secrets of men by Jesus Christ, according to my gospel.

Indeed you are called a Jew, and rest on the law, and make your boast in God, and know *His* will, and approve the things that are excellent, being instructed out of the law, and are confident that you yourself are a guide to the blind, a light to those who are in darkness, an instructor of the foolish, a teacher of babes, having the form of knowledge and truth in the law. You, therefore, who teach another, do you not teach yourself? You who preach that a man should not steal, do you steal? You who say, "Do not commit adultery," do you commit adultery? You who abhor idols, do you rob temples? You who make your boast in the law, do you dishonor God through breaking the law? For "the name of God is blasphemed among the Gentiles because of you," as it is written.

For circumcision is indeed profitable if you keep the law; but if you are a breaker of the law, your circumcision has become uncircumcision. Therefore, if an uncircumcised man keeps the righteous requirements of the law, will not his uncircumcision be counted as circumcision? And will not the physically uncircumcised, if he fulfills the law, judge you who, *even* with *your* written *code* and circumcision, *are* a transgressor of the law? For he is not a Jew who *is one* outwardly, nor *is* circumcision that which *is* outward in the flesh; but *he is* a Jew who *is one* inwardly; and circumcision *is that* of the heart, in the Spirit, not in the letter; whose praise *is* not from men but from God.

What advantage then has the Jew, or what *is* the profit of circumcision? Much in every way! Chiefly because to them were committed the oracles of God. For what if some did not believe? Will their unbelief make the faithfulness of God without effect? Certainly not! Indeed, let God be true but every man a liar. As it is written:

"That You may be justified in Your words,
And may overcome when You are judged."

But if our unrighteousness demonstrates the righteousness of God, what shall we say? *Is* God unjust who inflicts wrath? (I speak as a man.) Certainly not! For then how will God judge the world?

For if the truth of God has increased through my lie to His glory, why am I also still judged as a sinner? And *why* not *say*, "Let us do evil that good may come"?—as we are slanderously reported and as some affirm that we say. Their condemnation is just.

What then? Are we better *than they?* Not at all. For we have previously charged both Jews and Greeks that they are all under sin.

As it is written:

"There is none righteous, no, not one;
There is none who understands;
There is none who seeks after God.
They have all turned aside;
They have together become unprofitable;
There is none who does good, no, not one."
"Their throat *is* an open tomb;
With their tongues they have practiced deceit";
"The poison of asps *is* under their lips";
"Whose mouth *is* full of cursing and bitterness."
"Their feet *are* swift to shed blood;
Destruction and misery *are* in their ways;
And the way of peace they have not known."
"There is no fear of God before their eyes."

APOSTLES AND THE CHURCH

Now we know that whatever the law says, it says to those who are under the law, that every mouth may be stopped, and all the world may become guilty before God. Therefore by the deeds of the law no flesh will be justified in His sight, for by the law *is* the knowledge of sin.

Romans 2:12–3:20

WORSHIP

Blessed *be* the LORD,
Who has not given us *as* prey to their teeth.
Our soul has escaped as a bird from the snare
    of the fowlers;
The snare is broken, and we have escaped.
Our help *is* in the name of the LORD,
Who made heaven and earth.

Psalm 124:6-8

WISDOM

My son, if your heart is wise,
My heart will rejoice—indeed, I myself;
Yes, my inmost being will rejoice
When your lips speak right things.

Proverbs 23:15-16

SW?! SO WHAT?
What does this tell me?

JUSTIFICATION BY FAITH EXPLAINED AND ILLUSTRATED

Romans 3:21–4:25; Psalm 125:1-3; Proverbs 23:17-18

ut now the righteousness of God apart from the law is revealed, being witnessed by the Law and the Prophets, even the righteousness of God, through faith in Jesus Christ, to all and on all who believe. For there is no difference; for all have sinned and fall short of the glory of God, being justified freely by His grace through the redemption that is in Christ Jesus, whom God set forth *as* a propitiation by His blood, through faith, to demonstrate His righteousness, because in His forbearance God had passed over the sins that were previously committed, to demonstrate at the present time His righteousness, that He might be just and the justifier of the one who has faith in Jesus.

Where *is* boasting then? It is excluded. By what law? Of works? No, but by the law of faith. Therefore we conclude that a man is justified by faith apart from the deeds of the law. Or *is He* the God of the Jews only? *Is He* not also the God of the Gentiles? Yes, of the Gentiles also, since *there is* one God who will justify the circumcised by faith and the uncircumcised through faith. Do we then make void the law through faith? Certainly not! On the contrary, we establish the law.

What then shall we say that Abraham our father has found according to the flesh? For if Abraham was justified by works, he has *something* to boast about, but not before God. For what does the Scripture say? "Abraham believed God, and it was accounted to him for righteousness." Now to him who works, the wages are not counted as grace but as debt.

But to him who does not work but believes on Him who justifies the ungodly, his faith is accounted for righteousness, just as David also describes the blessedness of the man to whom God imputes righteousness apart from works:

"Blessed *are those* whose lawless deeds are forgiven,

And whose sins are covered;

Blessed *is the* man to whom the LORD shall not impute sin."

Does this blessedness then *come* upon the circumcised *only*, or upon the uncircumcised also? For we say that faith was accounted to Abraham for righteousness. How then was it accounted? While he was circumcised, or uncircumcised? Not while circumcised, but while uncircumcised. And he received the sign of circumcision, a seal of the righteousness of the faith which *he had while still* uncircumcised, that he might be the father of all those who believe, though they are uncircumcised, that righteousness might be imputed to them also, and the father of circumcision to those who not only *are* of the circumcision, but who also walk in the steps of the faith which our father Abraham *had while still* uncircumcised.

For the promise that he would be the heir of the world *was* not to Abraham or to his seed through the law, but through the righteousness of faith. For if those who are of the law *are* heirs, faith is made void and the promise made of no effect, because the law brings about wrath; for where there is no law *there is* no transgression.

Therefore *it is* of faith that *it might be* according to grace, so that the promise might be sure to all the seed, not only to those who are of the law, but also to those who are of the faith of Abraham, who is the father of us all (as it is written, "I have made you a father of many nations") in the presence of Him whom he believed—God, who gives life to the dead and calls those things which do not exist as though they did; who, contrary to hope, in hope believed, so that he became the father of many nations, according to what was spoken, "So shall your descendants be." And not being weak in faith, he did not consider his own body, already dead (since he was about a hundred years old), and the deadness of Sarah's womb. He did not waver at the promise of God through unbelief, but was strengthened in faith, giving glory to God, and being fully convinced that what He had promised He was also able to perform. And therefore "it was accounted to him for righteousness."

Now it was not written for his sake alone that it was imputed to him, but also for us. It shall be imputed to us who believe in Him who raised up Jesus our Lord from the dead, who was delivered up because of our offenses, and was raised because of our justification.

Romans 3:21–4:25

WORSHIP

Those who trust in the LORD
Are like Mount Zion,
Which cannot be moved, but abides forever.
As the mountains surround Jerusalem,
So the LORD surrounds His people
From this time forth and forever.

For the scepter of wickedness shall not rest
On the land allotted to the righteous,
Lest the righteous reach out their hands to
    iniquity.

Psalm 125:1-3

WISDOM

Do not let your heart envy sinners,
But be zealous for the fear of the LORD all the
    day;
For surely there is a hereafter,
And your hope will not be cut off.

Proverbs 23:17-18

SW?! **SO WHAT?**
What does this tell me?

JUSTIFICATION BY FAITH DEALS A BLOW TO THE SIN PROBLEM

Romans 5:1–6:14; Psalm 126:1-3; Proverbs 23:23

Therefore, having been justified by faith, we have peace with God through our Lord Jesus Christ, through whom also we have access by faith into this grace in which we stand, and rejoice in hope of the glory of God. And not only *that,* but we also glory in tribulations, knowing that tribulation produces perseverance; and perseverance, character; and character, hope. Now hope does not disappoint, because the love of God has been poured out in our hearts by the Holy Spirit who was given to us.

For when we were still without strength, in due time Christ died for the ungodly. For scarcely for a righteous man will one die; yet perhaps for a good man someone would even dare to die. But God demonstrates His own love toward us, in that while we were still sinners, Christ died for us. Much more then, having now been justified by His blood, we shall be saved from wrath through Him. For if when we were enemies we were reconciled to God through the death of His Son, much more, having been reconciled, we shall be saved by His life. And not only *that,* but we also rejoice in God through our Lord Jesus Christ, through whom we have now received the reconciliation.

Therefore, just as through one man sin entered the world, and death through sin, and thus death spread to all men, because all sinned—(For until the law sin was in the world, but sin is not imputed when there is no law. Nevertheless death reigned from Adam to Moses, even over those who had not sinned according to the likeness of the transgression of Adam, who is a type of Him who was to come. But the free gift *is* not like the offense. For if by the one man's offense many died, much more the grace of God and the gift by the grace of the one Man, Jesus Christ, abounded to many. And the gift *is* not like *that which came* through the one who sinned. For the judgment *which came*

from one *offense resulted* in condemnation, but the free gift *which came* from many offenses *resulted* in justification. For if by the one man's offense death reigned through the one, much more those who receive abundance of grace and of the gift of righteousness will reign in life through the One, Jesus Christ.)

Therefore, as through one man's offense *judgment* came to all men, resulting in condemnation, even so through one Man's righteous act *the free gift came* to all men, resulting in justification of life. For as by one man's disobedience many were made sinners, so also by one Man's obedience many will be made righteous.

Moreover the law entered that the offense might abound. But where sin abounded, grace abounded much more, so that as sin reigned in death, even so grace might reign through righteousness to eternal life through Jesus Christ our Lord.

What shall we say then? Shall we continue in sin that grace may abound? Certainly not! How shall we who died to sin live any longer in it? Or do you not know that as many of us as were baptized into Christ Jesus were baptized into His death? Therefore we were buried with Him through baptism into death, that just as Christ was raised from the dead by the glory of the Father, even so we also should walk in newness of life.

For if we have been united together in the likeness of His death, certainly we also shall be *in the likeness* of *His* resurrection, knowing this, that our old man was crucified with *Him,* that the body of sin might be done away with, that we should no longer be slaves of sin. For he who has died has been freed from sin. Now if we died with Christ, we believe that we shall also live with Him, knowing that Christ, having been raised from the dead, dies no more. Death no longer has dominion over Him. For *the death* that He died, He died to sin once for all; but *the life* that He lives, He lives to God. Likewise you also, reckon yourselves to be dead indeed to sin, but alive to God in Christ Jesus our Lord.

Therefore do not let sin reign in your mortal body, that you should obey it in its lusts. And do not present your members *as* instruments of unrighteousness to sin, but present yourselves to God as being alive from the dead, and your members *as* instruments of righteousness to God. For sin shall not have dominion over you, for you are not under law but under grace.

Romans 5:1–6:14

WORSHIP

When the LORD brought back the captivity of Zion,
We were like those who dream.
Then our mouth was filled with laughter,
And our tongue with singing.
Then they said among the nations,
"The LORD has done great things for them."
The LORD has done great things for us,
And we are glad.

Psalm 126:1-3

WISDOM

Buy the truth, and do not sell *it,*
Also wisdom and instruction and
understanding.

Proverbs 23:23

SW?! SO WHAT?
What does this tell me?

Jesus Sets us FREE
Romans 6:15–7:25; Psalm 127:3-5; Proverbs 23:24-25

What then? Shall we sin because we are not under law but under grace? Certainly not! Do you not know that to whom you present yourselves slaves to obey, you are that one's slaves whom you obey, whether of sin *leading* to death, or of obedience *leading* to righteousness? But God be thanked that *though* you were slaves of sin, yet you obeyed from the heart that form of doctrine to which you were delivered. And having been set free from sin, you became slaves of righteousness. I speak in human *terms* because of the weakness of your flesh. For just as you presented your members *as* slaves of uncleanness, and of lawlessness *leading* to *more* lawlessness, so now present your members *as* slaves *of* righteousness for holiness.

For when you were slaves of sin, you were free in regard to righteousness. What fruit did you have then in the things of which you are now ashamed? For the end of those things *is* death. But now having been set free from sin, and having become slaves of God, you have your fruit to holiness, and the end, everlasting life. For the wages of sin *is* death, but the gift of God *is* eternal life in Christ Jesus our Lord.

Or do you not know, brethren (for I speak to those who know the law), that the law has dominion over a man as long as he lives? For the woman who has a husband is bound by the law to *her* husband as long as he lives. But if the husband dies, she is released from the law of *her* husband. So then if, while *her* husband lives, she marries another man, she will be called an adulteress; but if her husband dies, she is free from that law, so that she is no adulteress, though she has married another man. Therefore, my brethren, you also have become dead to the law through the body of Christ, that you may be married to another—to Him who was raised from the dead, that we should bear fruit to God. For when we were in the flesh, the sinful passions which were aroused by the law were at work in our members to bear fruit to death. But now we have been delivered from the law, having died to what

we were held by, so that we should serve in the newness of the Spirit and not *in* the oldness of the letter.

What shall we say then? *Is* the law sin? Certainly not! On the contrary, I would not have known sin except through the law. For I would not have known covetousness unless the law had said, "You shall not covet." But sin, taking opportunity by the commandment, produced in me all *manner of* evil desire. For apart from the law sin *was* dead. I was alive once without the law, but when the commandment came, sin revived and I died. And the commandment, which *was* to *bring* life, I found to *bring* death. For sin, taking occasion by the commandment, deceived me, and by it killed *me*. Therefore the law *is* holy, and the commandment holy and just and good.

Has then what is good become death to me? Certainly not! But sin, that it might appear sin, was producing death in me through what is good, so that sin through the commandment might become exceedingly sinful. For we know that the law is spiritual, but I am carnal, sold under sin. For what I am doing, I do not understand. For what I will to do, that I do not practice; but what I hate, that I do. If, then, I do what I will not to do, I agree with the law that *it is* good. But now, *it is* no longer I who do it, but sin that dwells in me. For I know that in me (that is, in my flesh) nothing good dwells; for to will is present with me, but *how* to perform what is good I do not find. For the good that I will *to do,* I do not do; but the evil I will not *to do,* that I practice. Now if I do what I will not *to do,* it is no longer I who do it, but sin that dwells in me.

I find then a law, that evil is present with me, the one who wills to do good. For I delight in the law of God according to the inward man. But I see another law in my members, warring against the law of my mind, and bringing me into captivity to the law of sin which is in my members. O wretched man that I am! Who will deliver me from this body of death? I thank God—through Jesus Christ our Lord!

So then, with the mind I myself serve the law of God, but with the flesh the law of sin.

Romans 6:15–7:25

WORSHIP

Behold, children *are* a heritage from the LORD,
The fruit of the womb *is* a reward.
Like arrows in the hand of a warrior,
So *are* the children of one's youth.
Happy *is* the man who has his quiver full of
    them;
They shall not be ashamed,
But shall speak with their enemies in the gate.
Psalm 127:3-5

WISDOM

The father of the righteous will greatly rejoice,
And he who begets a wise *child* will delight in
    him.
Let your father and your mother be glad,
And let her who bore you rejoice.
Proverbs 23:24-25

SW?! **SO WHAT?**
What does this tell me?

ENJOYING THE INDESTRUCTIBLE LOVE OF CHRIST

Romans 8; Psalm 128:1-4; Proverbs 24:3-4

There is therefore now no condemnation to those who are in Christ Jesus, who do not walk according to the flesh, but according to the Spirit. For the law of the Spirit of life in Christ Jesus has made me free from the law of sin and death. For what the law could not do in that it was weak through the flesh, God *did* by sending His own Son in the likeness of sinful flesh, on account of sin: He condemned sin in the flesh, that the righteous requirement of the law might be fulfilled in us who do not walk according to the flesh but according to the Spirit. For those who live according to the flesh set their minds on the things of the flesh, but those *who live* according to the Spirit, the things of the Spirit. For to be carnally minded *is* death, but to be spiritually minded *is* life and peace. Because the carnal mind *is* enmity against God; for it is not subject to the law of God, nor indeed can be. So then, those who are in the flesh cannot please God.

But you are not in the flesh but in the Spirit, if indeed the Spirit of God dwells in you. Now if anyone does not have the Spirit of Christ, he is not His. And if Christ *is* in you, the body *is* dead because of sin, but the Spirit *is* life because of righteousness. But if the Spirit of Him who raised Jesus from the dead dwells in you, He who raised Christ from the dead will also give life to your mortal bodies through His Spirit who dwells in you.

Therefore, brethren, we are debtors—not to the flesh, to live according to the flesh. For if you live according to the flesh you will die; but if by the Spirit you put to death the deeds of the body, you will live. For as many as are led by the Spirit of God, these are sons of God. For you did not receive the spirit of bondage again to fear, but you received the Spirit of adoption by whom we cry out, "Abba, Father." The Spirit Himself bears witness with our spirit that we are children of God, and if children, then heirs—heirs of God and joint heirs with Christ, if indeed we suffer with *Him,* that we may also be glorified together.

For I consider that the sufferings of this present time are not worthy *to be compared* with the glory which shall be revealed in us. For the earnest expectation of the creation eagerly waits for the revealing of the sons of God. For the creation was subjected to futility, not willingly, but because of Him who subjected *it* in hope; because the creation itself also will be delivered from the bondage of corruption into the glorious liberty of the children of God. For we know that the whole creation groans and labors with birth pangs together until now. Not only *that,* but we also who have the firstfruits of the Spirit, even we ourselves groan within ourselves, eagerly waiting for the adoption, the redemption of our body. For we were saved in this hope, but hope that is seen is not hope; for why does one still hope for what he sees? But if we hope for what we do not see, we eagerly wait for *it* with perseverance.

Likewise the Spirit also helps in our weaknesses. For we do not know what we should pray for as we ought, but the Spirit Himself makes intercession for us with groanings which cannot be uttered. Now He who searches the hearts knows what the mind of the Spirit *is,* because He makes intercession for the saints according to *the will of* God.

And we know that all things work together for good to those who love God, to those who are the called according to *His* purpose. For whom He foreknew, He also predestined *to be* conformed to the image of His Son, that He might be the firstborn among many brethren. Moreover whom He predestined, these He also called; whom He called, these He also justified; and whom He justified, these He also glorified.

What then shall we say to these things? If God *is* for us, who *can be* against us? He who did not spare His own Son, but delivered Him up for us all, how shall He not with Him also freely give us all things? Who shall bring a charge against God's elect? *It is* God who justifies. Who *is* he who condemns? *It is* Christ who died, and furthermore is also risen, who is even at the right hand of God, who also makes intercession for us. Who shall separate us from the love of Christ? *Shall* tribulation, or distress, or persecution, or famine, or nakedness, or peril, or sword? As it is written:

"For Your sake we are killed all day long;
    We are accounted as sheep for the slaughter."

Yet in all these things we are more than conquerors through Him who loved us. For I am persuaded that neither death nor life, nor angels nor principalities nor powers, nor things present nor things to come, nor height nor depth, nor any other created thing, shall be able to separate us from the love of God which is in Christ Jesus our Lord.

Romans 8

WORSHIP

Blessed *is* every one who fears the LORD,
Who walks in His ways.

When you eat the labor of your hands,
You *shall be* happy, and *it shall be* well with
    you.
Your wife *shall be* like a fruitful vine
In the very heart of your house,
Your children like olive plants
All around your table.
Behold, thus shall the man be blessed
Who fears the LORD.

Psalm 128:1-4

WISDOM

Through wisdom a house is built,
And by understanding it is established;
By knowledge the rooms are filled
With all precious and pleasant riches.

Proverbs 24:3-4

SW?! **SO WHAT?**
What does this tell me?

PAUL'S HEART AND GOD'S PLAN FOR ISRAEL: PART ONE

Romans 9:1–10:11; Psalm 129:1–4; Proverbs 24:5–6

I tell the truth in Christ, I am not lying, my conscience also bearing me witness in the Holy Spirit, that I have great sorrow and continual grief in my heart. For I could wish that I myself were accursed from Christ for my brethren, my countrymen according to the flesh, who are Israelites, to whom *pertain* the adoption, the glory, the covenants, the giving of the law, the service *of God,* and the promises; of whom *are* the fathers and from whom, according to the flesh, Christ *came,* who is over all, *the* eternally blessed God. Amen.

But it is not that the word of God has taken no effect. For they *are* not all Israel who *are* of Israel, nor *are they* all children because they are the seed of Abraham; but, "In Isaac your seed shall be called." That is, those who *are* the children of the flesh, these *are* not the children of God; but the children of the promise are counted as the seed. For this *is* the word of promise: "At this time I will come and Sarah shall have a son."

And not only *this,* but when Rebecca also had conceived by one man, *even* by our father Isaac (for *the children* not yet being born, nor having done any good or evil, that the purpose of God according to election might stand, not of works but of Him who calls), it was said to her, "The older shall serve the younger." As it is written, "Jacob I have loved, but Esau I have hated."

What shall we say then? *Is there* unrighteousness with God? Certainly not! For He says to Moses, "I will have mercy on whomever I will have mercy, and I will have compassion on whomever I will have compassion." So then *it is* not of him who wills, nor of him who runs, but of God who shows mercy. For the Scripture says to the Pharaoh, "For this very purpose I have raised you up, that I may show My power in you, and that My name may be declared in all the earth."

Therefore He has mercy on whom He wills, and whom He wills He hardens.

You will say to me then, "Why does He still find fault? For who has resisted His will?" But indeed, O man, who are you to reply against God? Will the thing formed say to him who formed *it,* "Why have you made me like this?" Does not the potter have power over the clay, from the same lump to make one vessel for honor and another for dishonor?

What if God, wanting to show *His* wrath and to make His power known, endured with much long-suffering the vessels of wrath prepared for destruction, and that He might make known the riches of His glory on the vessels of mercy, which He had prepared beforehand for glory, *even* us whom He called, not of the Jews only, but also of the Gentiles?

As He says also in Hosea:

"I will call them My people, who were not My
    people,
And her beloved, who was not beloved."
"And it shall come to pass in the place where it
    was said to them,
'You *are* not My people,'
There they shall be called sons of the living
    God."

Isaiah also cries out concerning Israel:

"Though the number of the children of Israel be
    as the sand of the sea,
The remnant will be saved.
For He will finish the work and cut *it* short in
    righteousness,
Because the LORD will make a short work upon
    the earth."

And as Isaiah said before:

"Unless the LORD of Sabaoth had left us a seed,
We would have become like Sodom,
And we would have been made like
    Gomorrah."

What shall we say then? That Gentiles, who did not pursue righteousness, have attained to righteousness, even the righteousness of faith; but Israel, pursuing the law of righteousness, has not attained to the law of righteousness. Why? Because *they did* not *seek it* by faith, but as it were, by the works of the law. For they stumbled at that stumbling stone. As it is written:

"Behold, I lay in Zion a stumbling stone and rock of offense,
And whoever believes on Him will not be put to shame."

Brethren, my heart's desire and prayer to God for Israel is that they may be saved. For I bear them witness that they have a zeal for God, but not according to knowledge. For they being ignorant of God's righteousness, and seeking to establish their own righteousness, have not submitted to the righteousness of God. For Christ *is* the end of the law for righteousness to everyone who believes.

For Moses writes about the righteousness which is of the law, "The man who does those things shall live by them." But the righteousness of faith speaks in this way, "Do not say in your heart, 'Who will ascend into heaven?' " (that is, to bring Christ down *from above*) or, " 'Who will descend into the abyss?' " (that is, to bring Christ up from the dead). But what does it say? "The word is near you, in your mouth and in your heart" (that is, the word of faith which we preach): that if you confess with your mouth the Lord Jesus and believe in your heart that God has raised Him from the dead, you will be saved. For with the heart one believes unto righteousness, and with the mouth confession is made unto salvation. For the Scripture says, "Whoever believes on Him will not be put to shame."

Romans 9:1–10:11

WORSHIP

"Many a time they have afflicted me from my youth,"
Let Israel now say—
"Many a time they have afflicted me from my youth;
Yet they have not prevailed against me.
The plowers plowed on my back;
They made their furrows long."
The LORD *is* righteous;
He has cut in pieces the cords of the wicked.

Psalm 129:1-4

WISDOM

A wise man *is* strong,
Yes, a man of knowledge increases strength;
For by wise counsel you will wage your own war,
And in a multitude of counselors *there is* safety.

Proverbs 24:5-6

SW?! SO WHAT?
What does this tell me?

PAUL'S HEART AND GOD'S PLAN FOR ISRAEL: PART TWO

Romans 10:12–11:36; Psalm 130:1-4; Proverbs 24:19-20

For there is no distinction between Jew and Greek, for the same Lord over all is rich to all who call upon Him. For "whoever calls on the name of the LORD shall be saved."

How then shall they call on Him in whom they have not believed? And how shall they believe in Him of whom they have not heard? And how shall they hear without a preacher? And how shall they preach unless they are sent? As it is written:

> "How beautiful are the feet of those who
> preach the gospel of peace,
> Who bring glad tidings of good things!"

But they have not all obeyed the gospel. For Isaiah says, "LORD, who has believed our report?" So then faith *comes* by hearing, and hearing by the word of God.

But I say, have they not heard? Yes indeed:

> "Their sound has gone out to all the
> earth,
> And their words to the ends of the
> world."

But I say, did Israel not know? First Moses says:

> "I will provoke you to jealousy by *those
> who are* not a nation,
> I will move you to anger by a foolish
> nation."

But Isaiah is very bold and says:

> "I was found by those who did not seek
> Me;
> I was made manifest to those who did
> not ask for Me."

But to Israel he says:

> "All day long I have stretched out My
> hands
> To a disobedient and contrary people."

I say then, has God cast away His people? Certainly not! For I also am an Israelite, of the seed of Abraham, *of* the tribe of Benjamin. God has not cast away His people whom He foreknew. Or do you not know what the Scripture says of Elijah, how he pleads with God against Israel, saying, "LORD, they have killed Your prophets and torn down Your altars, and I alone am left, and they seek my life"? But what does the divine response say to him? "I have reserved for Myself seven thousand men who have not bowed the knee to Baal." Even so then, at this present time there is a remnant according to the election of grace. And if by grace, then *it is* no longer of works; otherwise grace is no longer grace. But if *it is* of works, it is no longer grace; otherwise work is no longer work.

What then? Israel has not obtained what it seeks; but the elect have obtained it, and the rest were blinded. Just as it is written:

> "God has given them a spirit of stupor,
> Eyes that they should not see
> And ears that they should not hear,
> To this very day."

And David says:

> "Let their table become a snare and a trap,
> A stumbling block and a recompense to them.
> Let their eyes be darkened, so that they do not
> see,
> And bow down their back always."

I say then, have they stumbled that they should fall? Certainly not! But through their fall, to provoke them to jealousy, salvation *has come* to the Gentiles. Now if their fall *is* riches for the world, and their failure riches for the Gentiles, how much more their fullness!

For I speak to you Gentiles; inasmuch as I am an apostle to the Gentiles, I magnify my ministry, if by any means I may provoke to jealousy *those who are* my flesh and save some of them. For if their being cast away *is* the reconciling of the world, what *will* their acceptance *be* but life from the dead?

For if the firstfruit *is* holy, the lump *is* also *holy*; and if the root *is* holy, so *are* the branches. And if some of the branches were broken off, and you, being a wild olive tree, were grafted in among them, and with them became a partaker of the root and fatness of the olive tree, do not boast against the branches. But if you do boast, *remember that* you do not support the root, but the root supports you.

You will say then, "Branches were broken off that I might be grafted in." Well *said.* Because of unbelief they were broken off, and you stand by faith. Do not be haughty, but fear. For if God did not spare the natural branches, He may not spare you either. Therefore consider the goodness and severity of God: on those who fell, severity; but toward you, goodness, if you continue in *His* goodness. Otherwise you also will be cut off. And they also, if they do not continue in unbelief, will be grafted in, for God is able to graft them in again. For if you were cut out of the olive tree which is wild by nature, and were grafted contrary to nature into a cultivated olive tree, how much more will these, who *are* natural *branches,* be grafted into their own olive tree?

For I do not desire, brethren, that you should be ignorant of this mystery, lest you should be wise in your own opinion, that blindness in part has happened to Israel until the fullness of the Gentiles has come in. And so all Israel will be saved, as it is written:

"The Deliverer will come out of Zion,
And He will turn away ungodliness from
    Jacob;
For this *is* My covenant with them,
When I take away their sins."

Concerning the gospel *they are* enemies for your sake, but concerning the election *they are* beloved for the sake of the fathers. For the gifts and the calling of God *are* irrevocable. For as you were once disobedient to God, yet have now obtained mercy through their disobedience, even so these also have now been disobedient, that through the mercy shown you they also may obtain mercy. For God has committed them all to disobedience, that He might have mercy on all.

Oh, the depth of the riches both of the wisdom and knowledge of God! How unsearchable *are* His judgments and His ways past finding out!

"For who has known the mind of the LORD?
Or who has become His counselor?"
"Or who has first given to Him
And it shall be repaid to him?"

For of Him and through Him and to Him *are* all things, to whom *be* glory forever. Amen.
Romans 10:12–11:36

WORSHIP

Out of the depths I have cried to You, O LORD;
Lord, hear my voice!
Let Your ears be attentive
To the voice of my supplications.
If You, LORD, should mark iniquities,
O Lord, who could stand?
But *there is* forgiveness with You,
That You may be feared.
Psalm 130:1-4

WISDOM

Do not fret because of evildoers,
Nor be envious of the wicked;
For there will be no prospect for the evil *man;*
The lamp of the wicked will be put out.
Proverbs 24:19-20

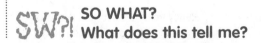

**SO WHAT?
What does this tell me?**

PROVING THE WILL OF GOD BY YOUR SERVICE AND LOVE

Romans 12:1–14:12; Psalm 131:1-3; Proverbs 24:21-22

I beseech you therefore, brethren, by the mercies of God, that you present your bodies a living sacrifice, holy, acceptable to God, *which is* your reasonable service. And do not be conformed to this world, but be transformed by the renewing of your mind, that you may prove what *is* that good and acceptable and perfect will of God.

For I say, through the grace given to me, to everyone who is among you, not to think *of himself* more highly than he ought to think, but to think soberly, as God has dealt to each one a measure of faith. For as we have many members in one body, but all the members do not have the same function, so we, *being* many, are one body in Christ, and individually members of one another. Having then gifts differing according to the grace that is given to us, *let us use them:* if prophecy, *let us prophesy* in proportion to our faith; or ministry, *let us use it in our* ministering; he who teaches, in teaching; he who exhorts, in exhortation; he who gives, with liberality; he who leads, with diligence; he who shows mercy, with cheerfulness.

Let love *be* without hypocrisy. Abhor what is evil. Cling to what is good. *Be* kindly affectionate to one another with brotherly love, in honor giving preference to one another; not lagging in diligence, fervent in spirit, serving the Lord; rejoicing in hope, patient in tribulation, continuing steadfastly in prayer; distributing to the needs of the saints, given to hospitality.

Bless those who persecute you; bless and do not curse. Rejoice with those who rejoice, and weep with those who weep. Be of the same mind toward one another. Do not set your mind on high things, but associate with the humble. Do not be wise in your own opinion.

Repay no one evil for evil. Have regard for good things in the sight of all men. If it is possible, as much as depends on you, live peaceably with all men. Beloved, do not avenge yourselves, but *rather* give place to wrath; for it is written, "Vengeance *is* Mine, I will repay," says the Lord. Therefore

"If your enemy is hungry, feed him;
If he is thirsty, give him a drink;
For in so doing you will heap coals of fire on his head."

Do not be overcome by evil, but overcome evil with good.

Let every soul be subject to the governing authorities. For there is no authority except from God, and the authorities that exist are appointed by God. Therefore whoever resists the authority resists the ordinance of God, and those who resist will bring judgment on themselves. For rulers are not a terror to good works, but to evil. Do you want to be unafraid of the authority? Do what is good, and you will have praise from the same. For he is God's minister to you for good. But if you do evil, be afraid; for he does not bear the sword in vain; for he is God's minister, an avenger to *execute* wrath on him who practices evil. Therefore *you* must be subject, not only because of wrath but also for conscience' sake. For because of this you also pay taxes, for they are God's ministers attending continually to this very thing. Render therefore to all their due: taxes to whom taxes *are due,* customs to whom customs, fear to whom fear, honor to whom honor.

Owe no one anything except to love one another, for he who loves another has fulfilled the law. For the commandments, "You shall not commit adultery," "You shall not murder," "You shall not steal," "You shall not bear false witness," "You shall not covet," and if *there is* any other commandment, are *all* summed up in this saying, namely, "You shall love your neighbor as yourself." Love does no harm to a neighbor; therefore love *is* the fulfillment of the law.

And *do* this, knowing the time, that now *it is* high time to awake out of sleep; for now our salva-

APOSTLES AND THE CHURCH

tion *is* nearer than when we *first* believed. The night is far spent, the day is at hand. Therefore let us cast off the works of darkness, and let us put on the armor of light. Let us walk properly, as in the day, not in revelry and drunkenness, not in lewdness and lust, not in strife and envy. But put on the Lord Jesus Christ, and make no provision for the flesh, to *fulfill its* lusts.

Receive one who is weak in the faith, *but* not to disputes over doubtful things. For one believes he may eat all things, but he who is weak eats *only* vegetables. Let not him who eats despise him who does not eat, and let not him who does not eat judge him who eats; for God has received him. Who are you to judge another's servant? To his own master he stands or falls. Indeed, he will be made to stand, for God is able to make him stand.

One person esteems *one* day above another; another esteems every day *alike*. Let each be fully convinced in his own mind. He who observes the day, observes *it* to the Lord; and he who does not observe the day, to the Lord he does not observe *it*. He who eats, eats to the Lord, for he gives God thanks; and he who does not eat, to the Lord he does not eat, and gives God thanks. For none of us lives to himself, and no one dies to himself. For if we live, we live to the Lord; and if we die, we die to the Lord. Therefore, whether we live or die, we are the Lord's. For to this end Christ died and rose and lived again, that He might be Lord of both the dead and the living. But why do you judge your brother? Or why do you show contempt for your brother? For we shall all stand before the judgment seat of Christ. For it is written:

"As I live, says the LORD,
Every knee shall bow to Me,
And every tongue shall confess to God."

So then each of us shall give account of himself to God.

Romans 12:1–14:12

WoRSHiP

LORD, my heart is not haughty,
Nor my eyes lofty.
Neither do I concern myself with great matters,
Nor with things too profound for me.

Surely I have calmed and quieted my soul,
Like a weaned child with his mother;
Like a weaned child *is* my soul within me.
O Israel, hope in the LORD
From this time forth and forever.

Psalm 131:1-3

WiSDoM

My son, fear the LORD and the king;
Do not associate with those given to change;
For their calamity will rise suddenly,
And who knows the ruin those two can bring?

Proverbs 24:21-22

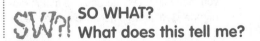

SO WHAT?
What does this tell me?

PAUL'S PASSION TO PREACH THE GOSPEL

Romans 14:13–15:21; 16:17-20, 25-27; Psalm 132:1-5; Proverbs 24:24-25

Therefore let us not judge one another anymore, but rather resolve this, not to put a stumbling block or a cause to fall in *our* brother's way.

I know and am convinced by the Lord Jesus that *there is* nothing unclean of itself; but to him who considers anything to be unclean, to him *it is* unclean. Yet if your brother is grieved because of *your* food, you are no longer walking in love. Do not destroy with your food the one for whom Christ died. Therefore do not let your good be spoken of as evil; for the kingdom of God is not eating and drinking, but righteousness and peace and joy in the Holy Spirit. For he who serves Christ in these things *is* acceptable to God and approved by men.

Therefore let us pursue the things *which make* for peace and the things by which one may edify another. Do not destroy the work of God for the sake of food. All things indeed *are* pure, but *it is* evil for the man who eats with offense. *It is* good neither to eat meat nor drink wine nor *do anything* by which your brother stumbles or is offended or is made weak. Do you have faith? Have *it* to yourself before God. Happy *is* he who does not condemn himself in what he approves. But he who doubts is condemned if he eats, because *he does* not *eat* from faith; for whatever *is* not from faith is sin.

We then who are strong ought to bear with the scruples of the weak, and not to please ourselves. Let each of us please *his* neighbor for *his* good, leading to edification. For even Christ did not please Himself; but as it is written, "The reproaches of those who reproached You fell on Me." For whatever things were written before were written for our learning, that we through the patience and comfort of the Scriptures might have hope. Now may the God of patience and comfort grant you to be like-minded toward one another, according to Christ Jesus, that you may with one mind *and* one mouth glorify the God and Father of our Lord Jesus Christ.

Therefore receive one another, just as Christ also received us, to the glory of God. Now I say that Jesus Christ has become a servant to the circumcision for the truth of God, to confirm the promises *made* to the fathers, and that the Gentiles might glorify God for *His* mercy, as it is written:

> "For this reason I will confess to You among the Gentiles,
> And sing to Your name."

And again he says:

> "Rejoice, O Gentiles, with His people!"

And again:

> "Praise the LORD, all you Gentiles!
> Laud Him, all you peoples!"

And again, Isaiah says:

> "There shall be a root of Jesse;
> And He who shall rise to reign over the Gentiles,
> In Him the Gentiles shall hope."

Now may the God of hope fill you with all joy and peace in believing, that you may abound in hope by the power of the Holy Spirit.

Now I myself am confident concerning you, my brethren, that you also are full of goodness, filled with all knowledge, able also to admonish one another. Nevertheless, brethren, I have written more boldly to you on *some* points, as reminding you, because of the grace given to me by God, that I might be a minister of Jesus Christ to the Gentiles, ministering the gospel of God, that the offering of the Gentiles might be acceptable, sanctified by the Holy Spirit. Therefore I have reason to glory in Christ Jesus in the things *which pertain* to God. For I will not dare to speak of any of those things which Christ has not accomplished through me, in word and deed, to make the Gentiles obedient—in mighty signs and wonders, by the power of the Spirit of God, so that from Jerusalem and round about to Illyricum I have fully preached the gospel of Christ. And so I have made it my aim to preach the gospel, not where Christ was named, lest I should build on another man's foundation, but as it is written:

APOSTLES AND THE CHURCH

"To whom He was not announced, they shall
see;
And those who have not heard shall
understand."

Now I urge you, brethren, note those who cause divisions and offenses, contrary to the doctrine which you learned, and avoid them. For those who are such do not serve our Lord Jesus Christ, but their own belly, and by smooth words and flattering speech deceive the hearts of the simple. For your obedience has become known to all. Therefore I am glad on your behalf; but I want you to be wise in what is good, and simple concerning evil. And the God of peace will crush Satan under your feet shortly.

The grace of our Lord Jesus Christ *be* with you. Amen.

Now to Him who is able to establish you according to my gospel and the preaching of Jesus Christ, according to the revelation of the mystery kept secret since the world began but now made manifest, and by the prophetic Scriptures made known to all nations, according to the commandment of the everlasting God, for obedience to the faith—to God, alone wise, *be* glory through Jesus Christ forever. Amen.

Romans 14:13–15:21; 16:17-20, 25-27

WORSHIP

LORD, remember David
And all his afflictions;
How he swore to the LORD,
And vowed to the Mighty One of Jacob:
"Surely I will not go into the chamber of my
house,
Or go up to the comfort of my bed;
I will not give sleep to my eyes
Or slumber to my eyelids,
Until I find a place for the LORD,
A dwelling place for the Mighty One of Jacob."
Psalm 132:1-5

WISDOM

He who says to the wicked, "You *are*
righteous,"
Him the people will curse;
Nations will abhor him.
But those who rebuke *the wicked* will have
delight,
And a good blessing will come upon them.
Proverbs 24:24-25

SW?! **SO WHAT?**
What does this tell me?

PAUL CREATES CONFUSION IN JERUSALEM

Acts 21:17–22:22; Psalm 132:10-12; Proverbs 25:3

And when we had come to Jerusalem, the brethren received us gladly. On the following day Paul went in with us to James, and all the elders were present. When he had greeted them, he told in detail those things which God had done among the Gentiles through his ministry. And when they heard *it,* they glorified the Lord. And they said to him, "You see, brother, how many myriads of Jews there are who have believed, and they are all zealous for the law; but they have been informed about you that you teach all the Jews who are among the Gentiles to forsake Moses, saying that they ought not to circumcise *their* children nor to walk according to the customs. What then? The assembly must certainly meet, for they will hear that you have come. Therefore do what we tell you: We have four men who have taken a vow. Take them and be purified with them, and pay their expenses so that they may shave *their* heads, and that all may know that those things of which they were informed concerning you are nothing, but *that* you yourself also walk orderly and keep the law. But concerning the Gentiles who believe, we have written *and* decided that they should observe no such thing, except that they should keep themselves from *things* offered to idols, from blood, from things strangled, and from sexual immorality."

Then Paul took the men, and the next day, having been purified with them, entered the temple to announce the expiration of the days of purification, at which time an offering should be made for each one of them.

Now when the seven days were almost ended, the Jews from Asia, seeing him in the temple, stirred up the whole crowd and laid hands on him, crying out, "Men of Israel, help! This is the man who teaches all *men* everywhere against the people, the law, and this place; and furthermore he also brought Greeks into the temple and has defiled this holy place." (For they had previously seen Trophimus the Ephesian with him in the city, whom they supposed that Paul had brought into the temple.)

And all the city was disturbed; and the people ran together, seized Paul, and dragged him out of the temple; and immediately the doors were shut. Now as they were seeking to kill him, news came to the commander of the garrison that all Jerusalem was in an uproar. He immediately took soldiers and centurions, and ran down to them. And when they saw the commander and the soldiers, they stopped beating Paul. Then the commander came near and took him, and commanded *him* to be bound with two chains; and he asked who he was and what he had done. And some among the multitude cried one thing and some another.

So when he could not ascertain the truth because of the tumult, he commanded him to be taken into the barracks. When he reached the stairs, he had to be carried by the soldiers because of the violence of the mob. For the multitude of the people followed after, crying out, "Away with him!"

Then as Paul was about to be led into the barracks, he said to the commander, "May I speak to you?"

He replied, "Can you speak Greek? Are you not the Egyptian who some time ago stirred up a rebellion and led the four thousand assassins out into the wilderness?"

But Paul said, "I am a Jew from Tarsus, in Cilicia, a citizen of no mean city; and I implore you, permit me to speak to the people."

So when he had given him permission, Paul stood on the stairs and motioned with his hand to the people. And when there was a great silence, he spoke to *them* in the Hebrew language, saying,

"Brethren and fathers, hear my defense before you now." And when they heard that he spoke to them in the Hebrew language, they kept all the more silent.

Then he said: "I am indeed a Jew, born in Tarsus of Cilicia, but brought up in this city at the feet of Gamaliel, taught according to the strictness of our fathers' law, and was zealous toward God as you all are today. I persecuted this Way to the death, binding and delivering into prisons both men and women, as also the high priest bears me witness, and all the council of the elders, from whom I also received letters to the brethren, and went to Damascus to bring in chains even those who were there to Jerusalem to be punished.

"Now it happened, as I journeyed and came near Damascus at about noon, suddenly a great light from heaven shone around me. And I fell to the ground and heard a voice saying to me, 'Saul, Saul, why are you persecuting Me?' So I answered, 'Who are You, Lord?' And He said to me, 'I am Jesus of Nazareth, whom you are persecuting.'

"And those who were with me indeed saw the light and were afraid, but they did not hear the voice of Him who spoke to me. So I said, 'What shall I do, Lord?' And the Lord said to me, 'Arise and go into Damascus, and there you will be told all things which are appointed for you to do.' And since I could not see for the glory of that light, being led by the hand of those who were with me, I came into Damascus.

"Then a certain Ananias, a devout man according to the law, having a good testimony with all the Jews who dwelt *there*, came to me; and he stood and said to me, 'Brother Saul, receive your sight.' And at that same hour I looked up at him. Then he said, 'The God of our fathers has chosen you that you should know His will, and see the Just One, and hear the voice of His mouth. For you will be His witness to all men of what you have seen and heard. And now why are you waiting? Arise and be baptized, and wash away your sins, calling on the name of the Lord.'

"Now it happened, when I returned to Jerusalem and was praying in the temple, that I was in a trance and saw Him saying to me, 'Make haste and get out of Jerusalem quickly, for they will not receive your testimony concerning Me.' So I said, 'Lord, they know that in every synagogue I imprisoned and beat those who believe on You. And when the blood of Your martyr Stephen was shed, I also was standing by consenting to his death, and guarding the clothes of those who were killing him.' Then He said to me, 'Depart, for I will send you far from here to the Gentiles.' "

And they listened to him until this word, and *then* they raised their voices and said, "Away with such a *fellow* from the earth, for he is not fit to live!"
Acts 21:17–22:22

WORSHIP

For Your servant David's sake,
Do not turn away the face of Your Anointed.

The LORD has sworn *in* truth to David;
He will not turn from it:
"I will set upon your throne the fruit of your
    body.
If your sons will keep My covenant
And My testimony which I shall teach them,
Their sons also shall sit upon your throne
    forevermore."
Psalm 132:10-12

WISDOM

As the heavens for height and the earth for
    depth,
So the heart of kings *is* unsearchable.
Proverbs 25:3

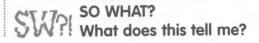

SO WHAT?
What does this tell me?

JEWISH LEADERS CONSPIRE TO KILL PAUL

Acts 22:23–23:35; Psalm 133:1-3; Proverbs 25:11-12

Then, as they cried out and tore off *their* clothes and threw dust into the air, the commander ordered him to be brought into the barracks, and said that he should be examined under scourging, so that he might know why they shouted so against him. And as they bound him with thongs, Paul said to the centurion who stood by, "Is it lawful for you to scourge a man who is a Roman, and uncondemned?"

When the centurion heard *that,* he went and told the commander, saying, "Take care what you do, for this man is a Roman."

Then the commander came and said to him, "Tell me, are you a Roman?"

He said, "Yes."

The commander answered, "With a large sum I obtained this citizenship."

And Paul said, "But I was born *a citizen.*"

Then immediately those who were about to examine him withdrew from him; and the commander was also afraid after he found out that he was a Roman, and because he had bound him.

The next day, because he wanted to know for certain why he was accused by the Jews, he released him from *his* bonds, and commanded the chief priests and all their council to appear, and brought Paul down and set him before them.

Then Paul, looking earnestly at the council, said, "Men *and* brethren, I have lived in all good conscience before God until this day." And the high priest Ananias commanded those who stood by him to strike him on the mouth. Then Paul said to him, "God will strike you, *you* whitewashed wall! For you sit to judge me according to the law, and do you command me to be struck contrary to the law?"

And those who stood by said, "Do you revile God's high priest?"

Then Paul said, "I did not know, brethren, that he was the high priest; for it is written, 'You shall not speak evil of a ruler of your people.'"

But when Paul perceived that one part were Sadducees and the other Pharisees, he cried out in the council, "Men *and* brethren, I am a Pharisee, the son of a Pharisee; concerning the hope and resurrection of the dead I am being judged!"

And when he had said this, a dissension arose between the Pharisees and the Sadducees; and the assembly was divided. For Sadducees say that there is no resurrection—and no angel or spirit; but the Pharisees confess both. Then there arose a loud outcry. And the scribes of the Pharisees' party arose and protested, saying, "We find no evil in this man; but if a spirit or an angel has spoken to him, let us not fight against God."

Now when there arose a great dissension, the commander, fearing lest Paul might be pulled to pieces by them, commanded the soldiers to go down and take him by force from among them, and bring *him* into the barracks.

But the following night the Lord stood by him and said, "Be of good cheer, Paul; for as you have testified for Me in Jerusalem, so you must also bear witness at Rome."

And when it was day, some of the Jews banded together and bound themselves under an oath, saying that they would neither eat nor drink till they had killed Paul. Now there were more than forty who had formed this conspiracy. They came to the chief priests and elders, and said, "We have bound ourselves under a great oath that we will eat nothing until we have killed Paul. Now you, therefore, together with the council, suggest to the commander that he be brought down to you tomorrow, as though you were going to make further inquiries concerning him; but we are ready to kill him before he comes near."

So when Paul's sister's son heard of their ambush, he went and entered the barracks and told Paul. Then Paul called one of the centurions to *him* and said, "Take this young man to the commander, for he has something to tell him." So he took him and brought *him* to the commander and said, "Paul the prisoner called me to *him* and asked *me* to bring this young man to you. He has something to say to you."

Then the commander took him by the hand,

went aside and asked privately, "What is it that you have to tell me?"

And he said, "The Jews have agreed to ask that you bring Paul down to the council tomorrow, as though they were going to inquire more fully about him. But do not yield to them, for more than forty of them lie in wait for him, men who have bound themselves by an oath that they will neither eat nor drink till they have killed him; and now they are ready, waiting for the promise from you."

So the commander let the young man depart, and commanded *him*, "Tell no one that you have revealed these things to me."

And he called for two centurions, saying, "Prepare two hundred soldiers, seventy horsemen, and two hundred spearmen to go to Caesarea at the third hour of the night; and provide mounts to set Paul on, and bring *him* safely to Felix the governor." He wrote a letter in the following manner:

Claudius Lysias,

To the most excellent governor Felix:

Greetings.

This man was seized by the Jews and was about to be killed by them. Coming with the troops I rescued him, having learned that he was a Roman. And when I wanted to know the reason they accused him, I brought him before their council. I found out that he was accused concerning questions of their law, but had nothing charged against him deserving of death or chains. And when it was told me that the Jews lay in wait for the man, I sent him immediately to you, and also commanded his accusers to state before you the charges against him.

Farewell.

Then the soldiers, as they were commanded, took Paul and brought *him* by night to Antipatris. The next day they left the horsemen to go on with him, and returned to the barracks. When they came to Caesarea and had delivered the letter to the governor, they also presented Paul to him. And when the governor had read *it,* he asked what province he was from. And when he understood that *he was* from Cilicia, he said, "I will hear you when your accusers also have come." And he commanded him to be kept in Herod's Praetorium.

Acts 22:23–23:35

WORSHIP

Behold, how good and how pleasant *it is*
For brethren to dwell together in unity!

It is like the precious oil upon the head,
Running down on the beard,
The beard of Aaron,
Running down on the edge of his garments.
It is like the dew of Hermon,
Descending upon the mountains of Zion;
For there the LORD commanded the blessing—
Life forevermore.

Psalm 133:1-3

WISDOM

A word fitly spoken *is like* apples of gold
In settings of silver.
Like an earring of gold and an ornament of
fine gold
Is a wise rebuker to an obedient ear.

Proverbs 25:11-12

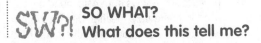

SO WHAT?
What does this tell me?

PAUL'S DEFENSE BEFORE FELIX AND FESTUS

Acts 24:1-5, 9-27; 25:1-22; Psalm 134:1-3; Proverbs 25:13

ow after five days Ananias the high priest came down with the elders and a certain orator *named* Tertullus. These gave evidence to the governor against Paul.

And when he was called upon, Tertullus began his accusation, saying: "Seeing that through you we enjoy great peace, and prosperity is being brought to this nation by your foresight, we accept *it* always and in all places, most noble Felix, with all thankfulness. Nevertheless, not to be tedious to you any further, I beg you to hear, by your courtesy, a few words from us. For we have found this man a plague, a creator of dissension among all the Jews throughout the world, and a ringleader of the sect of the Nazarenes."

And the Jews also assented, maintaining that these things were so.

Then Paul, after the governor had nodded to him to speak, answered: "Inasmuch as I know that you have been for many years a judge of this nation, I do the more cheerfully answer for myself, because you may ascertain that it is no more than twelve days since I went up to Jerusalem to worship. And they neither found me in the temple disputing with anyone nor inciting the crowd, either in the synagogues or in the city. Nor can they prove the things of which they now accuse me. But this I confess to you, that according to the Way which they call a sect, so I worship the God of my fathers, believing all things which are written in the Law and in the Prophets. I have hope in God, which they themselves also accept, that there will be a resurrection of *the* dead, both of *the* just and *the* unjust. This *being* so, I myself always strive to have a conscience without offense toward God and men.

"Now after many years I came to bring alms and offerings to my nation, in the midst of which some Jews from Asia found me purified in the temple, neither with a mob nor with tumult. They ought to have been here

before you to object if they had anything against me. Or else let those who are *here* themselves say if they found any wrongdoing in me while I stood before the council, unless *it is* for this one statement which I cried out, standing among them, 'Concerning the resurrection of the dead I am being judged by you this day.' "

But when Felix heard these things, having more accurate knowledge of *the* Way, he adjourned the proceedings and said, "When Lysias the commander comes down, I will make a decision on your case." So he commanded the centurion to keep Paul and to let *him* have liberty, and told him not to forbid any of his friends to provide for or visit him.

And after some days, when Felix came with his wife Drusilla, who was Jewish, he sent for Paul and heard him concerning the faith in Christ. Now as he reasoned about righteousness, self-control, and the judgment to come, Felix was afraid and answered, "Go away for now; when I have a convenient time I will call for you." Meanwhile he also hoped that money would be given him by Paul, that he might release him. Therefore he sent for him more often and conversed with him.

But after two years Porcius Festus succeeded Felix; and Felix, wanting to do the Jews a favor, left Paul bound.

Now when Festus had come to the province, after three days he went up from Caesarea to Jerusalem. Then the high priest and the chief men of the Jews informed him against Paul; and they petitioned him, asking a favor against him, that he would summon him to Jerusalem—while *they* lay in ambush along the road to kill him. But Festus answered that Paul should be kept at Caesarea, and that he himself was going *there* shortly. "Therefore," he said, "let those who have authority among you go down with *me* and accuse this man, to see if there is any fault in him."

And when he had remained among them more than ten days, he went down to Caesarea. And the next day, sitting on the judgment seat, he commanded Paul to be brought. When he had come, the Jews who had come down from Jerusalem stood about and laid many serious complaints against Paul, which they could not prove, while he answered for himself, "Neither against the law of the Jews, nor against the temple, nor against Caesar have I offended in anything at all."

But Festus, wanting to do the Jews a favor, answered Paul and said, "Are you willing to go up to Jerusalem and there be judged before me concerning these things?"

So Paul said, "I stand at Caesar's judgment seat, where I ought to be judged. To the Jews I have done no wrong, as you very well know. For if I am an offender, or have committed anything deserving of death, I do not object to dying; but if there is nothing in these things of which these men accuse me, no one can deliver me to them. I appeal to Caesar."

Then Festus, when he had conferred with the council, answered, "You have appealed to Caesar? To Caesar you shall go!"

And after some days King Agrippa and Bernice came to Caesarea to greet Festus. When they had been there many days, Festus laid Paul's case before the king, saying: "There is a certain man left a prisoner by Felix, about whom the chief priests and the elders of the Jews informed *me,* when I was in Jerusalem, asking for a judgment against him. To them I answered, 'It is not the custom of the Romans to deliver any man to destruction before the accused meets the accusers face to face, and has opportunity to answer for himself concerning the charge against him.' Therefore when they had come together, without any delay, the next day I sat on the judgment seat and commanded the man to be brought in. When the accusers stood up, they brought no accusation against him of such things as I supposed, but had some questions against him about their own religion and about a certain Jesus, who had died, whom Paul affirmed to be alive. And because I was uncertain of such questions, I asked whether he was willing to go to Jerusalem and there be judged concerning these matters. But when Paul appealed to be reserved for the decision of Augustus, I commanded him to be kept till I could send him to Caesar."

Then Agrippa said to Festus, "I also would like to hear the man myself."

"Tomorrow," he said, "you shall hear him."

Acts 24:1-5, 9-27; 25:1-22

WORSHIP

Behold, bless the LORD,
All *you* servants of the LORD,
Who by night stand in the house of the LORD!
Lift up your hands *in* the sanctuary,
And bless the LORD.

The LORD who made heaven and earth
Bless you from Zion!

Psalm 134:1-3

WISDOM

Like the cold of snow in time of harvest
Is a faithful messenger to those who send him,
For he refreshes the soul of his masters.

Proverbs 25:13

SW?! **SO WHAT?**
What does this tell me?

PAUL TAKES AGRIPPA TO THE EDGE OF FAITH

Acts 25:23–26:32; Psalm 135:5-7; Proverbs 25:14

So the next day, when Agrippa and Bernice had come with great pomp, and had entered the auditorium with the commanders and the prominent men of the city, at Festus' command Paul was brought in. And Festus said: "King Agrippa and all the men who are here present with us, you see this man about whom the whole assembly of the Jews petitioned me, both at Jerusalem and here, crying out that he was not fit to live any longer. But when I found that he had committed nothing deserving of death, and that he himself had appealed to Augustus, I decided to send him. I have nothing certain to write to my lord concerning him. Therefore I have brought him out before you, and especially before you, King Agrippa, so that after the examination has taken place I may have something to write. For it seems to me unreasonable to send a prisoner and not to specify the charges against him."

Then Agrippa said to Paul, "You are permitted to speak for yourself."

So Paul stretched out his hand and answered for himself: "I think myself happy, King Agrippa, because today I shall answer for myself before you concerning all the things of which I am accused by the Jews, especially because you are expert in all customs and questions which have to do with the Jews. Therefore I beg you to hear me patiently.

"My manner of life from my youth, which was spent from the beginning among my own nation at Jerusalem, all the Jews know. They knew me from the first, if they were willing to testify, that according to the strictest sect of our religion I lived a Pharisee. And now I stand and am judged for the hope of the promise made by God to our fathers. To this *promise* our twelve tribes, earnestly serving *God* night and day, hope to attain. For this hope's sake, King Agrippa, I am accused by the Jews. Why should it be thought incredible by you that God raises the dead?

"Indeed, I myself thought I must do many things contrary to the name of Jesus of Nazareth. This I also did in Jerusalem, and many of the saints I shut up in prison, having received authority from the chief priests; and when they were put to death, I cast my vote against *them.* And I punished them often in every synagogue and compelled *them* to blaspheme; and being exceedingly enraged against them, I persecuted *them* even to foreign cities.

"While thus occupied, as I journeyed to Damascus with authority and commission from the chief priests, at midday, O king, along the road I saw a light from heaven, brighter than the sun, shining around me and those who journeyed with me. And when we all had fallen to the ground, I heard a voice speaking to me and saying in the Hebrew language, 'Saul, Saul, why are you persecuting Me? *It is* hard for you to kick against the goads.' So I said, 'Who are You, Lord?' And He said, 'I am Jesus, whom you are persecuting. But rise and stand on your feet; for I have appeared to you for this purpose, to make you a minister and a witness both of the things which you have seen and of the things which I will yet reveal to you. I will deliver you from the *Jewish* people, as well as *from* the Gentiles, to whom I now send you, to open their eyes, *in order* to turn *them* from darkness to light, and *from* the power of Satan to God, that they may receive forgiveness of sins and an inheritance among those who are sanctified by faith in Me.'

"Therefore, King Agrippa, I was not disobedient to the heavenly vision, but declared first to those in Damascus and in Jerusalem, and throughout all the region of Judea, and *then* to the Gentiles, that they should repent, turn to God, and do works befitting repentance. For these reasons the Jews seized me in the temple and tried to kill *me.* Therefore, having obtained help from God, to this day I stand, witnessing both to small and great, saying no other things than those which the prophets and Moses said would come—that the Christ would suffer, that He would be the first to rise from the dead, and would proclaim light to the *Jewish* people and to the Gentiles."

Now as he thus made his defense, Festus said

with a loud voice, "Paul, you are beside yourself! Much learning is driving you mad!"

But he said, "I am not mad, most noble Festus, but speak the words of truth and reason. For the king, before whom I also speak freely, knows these things; for I am convinced that none of these things escapes his attention, since this thing was not done in a corner. King Agrippa, do you believe the prophets? I know that you do believe."

Then Agrippa said to Paul, "You almost persuade me to become a Christian."

And Paul said, "I would to God that not only you, but also all who hear me today, might become both almost and altogether such as I am, except for these chains."

When he had said these things, the king stood up, as well as the governor and Bernice and those who sat with them; and when they had gone aside, they talked among themselves, saying, "This man is doing nothing deserving of death or chains."

Then Agrippa said to Festus, "This man might have been set free if he had not appealed to Caesar."

Acts 25:23–26:32

WORSHIP

For I know that the LORD *is* great,
And our Lord *is* above all gods.
Whatever the LORD pleases He does,
In heaven and in earth,
In the seas and in all deep places.
He causes the vapors to ascend from the ends
 of the earth;
He makes lightning for the rain;
He brings the wind out of His treasuries.

Psalm 135:5-7

WISDOM

Whoever falsely boasts of giving
Is like clouds and wind without rain.

Proverbs 25:14

SW?! SO WHAT?
What does this tell me?

A PERILOUS VOYAGE ENDS IN SHIPWRECK

Acts 27; Psalm 135:13-14; Proverbs 25:19

A nd when it was decided that we should sail to Italy, they delivered Paul and some other prisoners to *one* named Julius, a centurion of the Augustan Regiment. So, entering a ship of Adramyttium, we put to sea, meaning to sail along the coasts of Asia. Aristarchus, a Macedonian of Thessalonica, was with us. And the next *day* we landed at Sidon. And Julius treated Paul kindly and gave *him* liberty to go to his friends and receive care. When we had put to sea from there, we sailed under *the shelter of* Cyprus, because the winds were contrary. And when we had sailed over the sea which is off Cilicia and Pamphylia, we came to Myra, *a city* of Lycia. There the centurion found an Alexandrian ship sailing to Italy, and he put us on board.

When we had sailed slowly many days, and arrived with difficulty off Cnidus, the wind not permitting us to proceed, we sailed under *the shelter of* Crete off Salmone. Passing it with difficulty, we came to a place called Fair Havens, near the city *of* Lasea.

Now when much time had been spent, and sailing was now dangerous because the Fast was already over, Paul advised them, saying, "Men, I perceive that this voyage will end with disaster and much loss, not only of the cargo and ship, but also our lives." Nevertheless the centurion was more persuaded by the helmsman and the owner of the ship than by the things spoken by Paul. And because the harbor was not suitable to winter in, the majority advised to set sail from there also, if by any means they could reach Phoenix, a harbor of Crete opening toward the southwest and northwest, *and* winter *there.*

When the south wind blew softly, supposing that they had obtained *their* desire, putting out to sea, they sailed close by Crete. But not long after, a tempestuous head wind arose, called Euroclydon. So when the ship was caught, and could not head into the wind, we let *her* drive. And running under *the shelter of* an island called Clauda, we secured the skiff with difficulty. When they

had taken it on board, they used cables to undergird the ship; and fearing lest they should run aground on the Syrtis *Sands,* they struck sail and so were driven. And because we were exceedingly tempest-tossed, the next *day* they lightened the ship. On the third *day* we threw the ship's tackle overboard with our own hands. Now when neither sun nor stars appeared for many days, and no small tempest beat on *us,* all hope that we would be saved was finally given up.

But after long abstinence from food, then Paul stood in the midst of them and said, "Men, you should have listened to me, and not have sailed from Crete and incurred this disaster and loss. And now I urge you to take heart, for there will be no loss of life among you, but only of the ship. For there stood by me this night an angel of the God to whom I belong and whom I serve, saying, 'Do not be afraid, Paul; you must be brought before Caesar; and indeed God has granted you all those who sail with you.' Therefore take heart, men, for I believe God that it will be just as it was told me. However, we must run aground on a certain island."

Now when the fourteenth night had come, as we were driven up and down in the Adriatic *Sea,* about midnight the sailors sensed that they were drawing near some land. And they took soundings and found *it* to be twenty fathoms; and when they had gone a little farther, they took soundings again and found *it* to be fifteen fathoms. Then, fearing lest we should run aground on the rocks, they dropped four anchors from the stern, and prayed for day to come. And as the sailors were seeking to escape from the ship, when they had let down the skiff into the sea, under pretense of putting out anchors from the prow, Paul said to the centurion and the soldiers, "Unless these men stay in the ship, you cannot be saved." Then the soldiers cut away the ropes of the skiff and let it fall off.

And as day was about to dawn, Paul implored *them* all to take food, saying, "Today is the fourteenth day you have waited and continued without food, and eaten nothing. Therefore I urge you to take nourishment, for this is for your survival, since not a hair will fall from the head of any of you." And when he had said these things, he took bread and gave thanks to God in the presence of them all; and when he had broken *it* he began to eat. Then they were all encouraged, and also took food themselves. And in all we were two hundred and seventy-six persons on the ship. So when they had eaten enough, they lightened the ship and threw out the wheat into the sea.

When it was day, they did not recognize the land; but they observed a bay with a beach, onto which they planned to run the ship if possible. And they let go the anchors and left *them* in the sea, meanwhile loosing the rudder ropes; and they hoisted the mainsail to the wind and made for shore. But striking a place where two seas met, they ran the ship aground; and the prow stuck fast and remained immovable, but the stern was being broken up by the violence of the waves.

And the soldiers' plan was to kill the prisoners, lest any of them should swim away and escape. But the centurion, wanting to save Paul, kept them from *their* purpose, and commanded that those who could swim should jump *overboard* first and get to land, and the rest, some on boards and some on *parts* of the ship. And so it was that they all escaped safely to land.

Acts 27

WORSHIP

Your name, O LORD, *endures* forever,
Your fame, O LORD, throughout all generations.
For the LORD will judge His people,
And He will have compassion on His servants.

Psalm 135:13-14

WISDOM

Confidence in an unfaithful *man* in time of trouble
Is like a bad tooth and a foot out of joint.

Proverbs 25:19

SW?! **SO WHAT?**
What does this tell me?

PAUL PREACHES AND TEACHES IN ROME
Acts 28; Psalm 135:19-21; Proverbs 25:25

Now when they had escaped, they then found out that the island was called Malta. And the natives showed us unusual kindness; for they kindled a fire and made us all welcome, because of the rain that was falling and because of the cold. But when Paul had gathered a bundle of sticks and laid *them* on the fire, a viper came out because of the heat, and fastened on his hand. So when the natives saw the creature hanging from his hand, they said to one another, "No doubt this man is a murderer, whom, though he has escaped the sea, yet justice does not allow to live." But he shook off the creature into the fire and suffered no harm. However, they were expecting that he would swell up or suddenly fall down dead. But after they had looked for a long time and saw no harm come to him, they changed their minds and said that he was a god.

In that region there was an estate of the leading citizen of the island, whose name was Publius, who received us and entertained us courteously for three days. And it happened that the father of Publius lay sick of a fever and dysentery. Paul went in to him and prayed, and he laid his hands on him and healed him. So when this was done, the rest of those on the island who had diseases also came and were healed. They also honored us in many ways; and when we departed, they provided such things as were necessary.

After three months we sailed in an Alexandrian ship whose figurehead was the Twin Brothers, which had wintered at the island. And landing at Syracuse, we stayed three days. From there we circled round and reached Rhegium. And after one day the south wind blew; and the next day we came to Puteoli, where we found brethren, and were invited to stay with them seven days. And so we went toward Rome. And from there, when the brethren heard about us, they came to meet us as far as Appii Forum and Three Inns. When Paul saw them, he thanked God and took courage.

Now when we came to Rome, the centurion delivered the prisoners to the captain of the guard; but Paul was permitted to dwell by himself with the soldier who guarded him.

And it came to pass after three days that Paul called the leaders of the Jews together. So when they had come together, he said to them: "Men *and* brethren, though I have done nothing against our people or the customs of our fathers, yet I was delivered as a prisoner from Jerusalem into the hands of the Romans, who, when they had examined me, wanted to let *me* go, because there was no cause for putting me to death. But when the Jews spoke against *it,* I was compelled to appeal to Caesar, not that I had anything of which to accuse my nation. For this reason therefore I have called for you, to see *you* and speak with *you,* because for the hope of Israel I am bound with this chain."

Then they said to him, "We neither received letters from Judea concerning you, nor have any of the brethren who came reported or spoken any evil of you. But we desire to hear from you what you think; for concerning this sect, we know that it is spoken against everywhere."

So when they had appointed him a day, many came to him at *his* lodging, to whom he explained and solemnly testified of the kingdom of God, persuading them concerning Jesus from both the Law of Moses and the Prophets, from morning till evening. And some were persuaded by the things which were spoken, and some disbelieved. So when they did not agree among themselves, they departed after Paul had said one word: "The Holy Spirit spoke rightly through Isaiah the prophet to our fathers, saying,

'Go to this people and say:
"Hearing you will hear, and shall not
    understand;
And seeing you will see, and not perceive;
For the hearts of this people have grown dull.
Their ears are hard of hearing,
And their eyes they have closed,
Lest they should see with *their* eyes and hear
    with *their* ears,
Lest they should understand with *their* hearts
    and turn,
So that I should heal them." '

"Therefore let it be known to you that the salvation of God has been sent to the Gentiles, and they will hear it!" And when he had said these words, the Jews departed and had a great dispute among themselves.

Then Paul dwelt two whole years in his own rented house, and received all who came to him, preaching the kingdom of God and teaching the things which concern the Lord Jesus Christ with all confidence, no one forbidding him.

Acts 28

WoRSHiP

Bless the LORD, O house of Israel!
Bless the LORD, O house of Aaron!
Bless the LORD, O house of Levi!
You who fear the LORD, bless the LORD!
Blessed be the LORD out of Zion,
Who dwells in Jerusalem!

Praise the LORD!

Psalm 135:19-21

WiSDoM

As cold water to a weary soul,
So *is* good news from a far country.

Proverbs 25:25

SW?! **SO WHAT?**
What does this tell me?

SPIRITUAL FOUNDATIONS OF A WALK WITH CHRIST

Ephesians 1–2; Psalm 136:1-4; Proverbs 25:28

Paul, an apostle of Jesus Christ by the will of God,

To the saints who are in Ephesus, and faithful in Christ Jesus:

Grace to you and peace from God our Father and the Lord Jesus Christ.

Blessed *be* the God and Father of our Lord Jesus Christ, who has blessed us with every spiritual blessing in the heavenly *places* in Christ, just as He chose us in Him before the foundation of the world, that we should be holy and without blame before Him in love, having predestined us to adoption as sons by Jesus Christ to Himself, according to the good pleasure of His will, to the praise of the glory of His grace, by which He made us accepted in the Beloved.

In Him we have redemption through His blood, the forgiveness of sins, according to the riches of His grace which He made to abound toward us in all wisdom and prudence, having made known to us the mystery of His will, according to His good pleasure which He purposed in Himself, that in the dispensation of the fullness of the times He might gather together in one all things in Christ, both which are in heaven and which are on earth—in Him. In Him also we have obtained an inheritance, being predestined according to the purpose of Him who works all things according to the counsel of His will, that we who first trusted in Christ should be to the praise of His glory.

In Him you also *trusted,* after you heard the word of truth, the gospel of your salvation; in whom also, having believed, you were sealed with the Holy Spirit of promise, who is the guarantee of our inheritance until the redemption of the purchased possession, to the praise of His glory.

Therefore I also, after I heard of your faith in the Lord Jesus and your love for all the saints, do not cease to give thanks for you, making mention of you in my prayers: that the God of our Lord Jesus Christ, the Fa-

ther of glory, may give to you the spirit of wisdom and revelation in the knowledge of Him, the eyes of your understanding being enlightened; that you may know what is the hope of His calling, what are the riches of the glory of His inheritance in the saints, and what *is* the exceeding greatness of His power toward us who believe, according to the working of His mighty power which He worked in Christ when He raised Him from the dead and seated *Him* at His right hand in the heavenly *places,* far above all principality and power and might and dominion, and every name that is named, not only in this age but also in that which is to come.

And He put all *things* under His feet, and gave Him *to be* head over all *things* to the church, which is His body, the fullness of Him who fills all in all.

And you *He made alive,* who were dead in trespasses and sins, in which you once walked according to the course of this world, according to the prince of the power of the air, the spirit who now works in the sons of disobedience, among whom also we all once conducted ourselves in the lusts of our flesh, fulfilling the desires of the flesh and of the mind, and were by nature children of wrath, just as the others.

But God, who is rich in mercy, because of His great love with which He loved us, even when we were dead in trespasses, made us alive together with Christ (by grace you have been saved), and raised *us* up together, and made *us* sit together in the heavenly *places* in Christ Jesus, that in the ages to come He might show the exceeding riches of His grace in *His* kindness toward us in Christ Jesus. For by grace you have been saved through faith, and that not of yourselves; *it is* the gift of God, not of works, lest anyone should boast. For we are His workmanship, created in Christ Jesus for good works, which God prepared beforehand that we should walk in them.

Therefore remember that you, once Gentiles in the flesh—who are called Uncircumcision by what is called the Circumcision made in the flesh by hands—that at that time you were without Christ, being aliens from the commonwealth of Israel and strangers from the covenants of promise, having no hope and without God in the world. But now in Christ Jesus you who once were far off have been brought near by the blood of Christ.

For He Himself is our peace, who has made both one, and has broken down the middle wall of separation, having abolished in His flesh the enmity, *that is,* the law of commandments *contained* in ordinances, so as to create in Himself one new man *from* the two, *thus* making peace, and that He might reconcile them both to God in one body through the cross, thereby putting to death the enmity. And He came and preached peace to you who were afar off and to those who were near. For through Him we both have access by one Spirit to the Father.

Now, therefore, you are no longer strangers and foreigners, but fellow citizens with the saints and members of the household of God, having been built on the foundation of the apostles and prophets, Jesus Christ Himself being the chief corner*stone,* in whom the whole building, being fitted together, grows into a holy temple in the Lord, in whom you also are being built together for a dwelling place of God in the Spirit.

Ephesians 1–2

WoRSHIP

Oh, give thanks to the LORD, for *He is* good!
For His mercy *endures* forever.
Oh, give thanks to the God of gods!
For His mercy *endures* forever.
Oh, give thanks to the Lord of lords!
For His mercy *endures* forever:

To Him who alone does great wonders,
For His mercy *endures* forever.

Psalm 136:1-4

WiSDoM

Whoever *has* no rule over his own spirit
Is like a city broken down, without walls.

Proverbs 25:28

SW?! **SO WHAT?**
What does this tell me?

WALKING THE WALK IN THE CHURCH

For this reason I, Paul, the prisoner of Christ Jesus for you Gentiles—if indeed you have heard of the dispensation of the grace of God which was given to me for you, how that by revelation He made known to me the mystery (as I have briefly written already, by which, when you read, you may understand my knowledge in the mystery of Christ), which in other ages was not made known to the sons of men, as it has now been revealed by the Spirit to His holy apostles and prophets: that the Gentiles should be fellow heirs, of the same body, and partakers of His promise in Christ through the gospel, of which I became a minister according to the gift of the grace of God given to me by the effective working of His power.

To me, who am less than the least of all the saints, this grace was given, that I should preach among the Gentiles the unsearchable riches of Christ, and to make all see what *is* the fellowship of the mystery, which from the beginning of the ages has been hidden in God who created all things through Jesus Christ; to the intent that now the manifold wisdom of God might be made known by the church to the principalities and powers in the heavenly *places,* according to the eternal purpose which He accomplished in Christ Jesus our Lord, in whom we have boldness and access with confidence through faith in Him. Therefore I ask that you do not lose heart at my tribulations for you, which is your glory.

For this reason I bow my knees to the Father of our Lord Jesus Christ, from whom the whole family in heaven and earth is named, that He would grant you, according to the riches of His glory, to be strengthened with might through His Spirit in the inner man, that Christ may dwell in your hearts through faith; that you, being rooted and grounded in love, may be able to comprehend with all the saints what *is* the width and length and depth and height— to know the love of Christ which passes knowledge; that you may be filled with all the fullness of God.

Now to Him who is able to do exceed-ingly abundantly above all that we ask or think, according to the power that works in us, to Him *be* glory in the church by Christ Jesus to all generations, forever and ever. Amen.

I, therefore, the prisoner of the Lord, beseech you to walk worthy of the calling with which you were called, with all lowliness and gentleness, with longsuffering, bearing with one another in love, endeavoring to keep the unity of the Spirit in the bond of peace.

And He Himself gave some *to be* apostles, some prophets, some evangelists, and some pastors and teachers, for the equipping of the saints for the work of ministry, for the edifying of the body of Christ, till we all come to the unity of the faith and of the knowledge of the Son of God, to a perfect man, to the measure of the stature of the fullness of Christ; that we should no longer be children, tossed to and fro and carried about with every wind of doctrine, by the trickery of men, in the cunning craftiness of deceitful plotting, but, speaking the truth in love, may grow up in all things into Him who is the head—Christ—from whom the whole body, joined and knit together by what every joint supplies, according to the effective working by which every part does its share, causes growth of the body for the edifying of itself in love.

This I say, therefore, and testify in the Lord, that you should no longer walk as the rest of the Gentiles walk, in the futility of their mind, having their understanding darkened, being alienated from the life of God, because of the ignorance that is in them, because of the blindness of their heart; who, being past feeling, have given themselves over to lewdness, to work all uncleanness with greediness.

But you have not so learned Christ, if indeed you have heard Him and have been taught by Him, as the truth is in Jesus: that you put off, concerning your former conduct, the old man which grows corrupt according to the deceitful lusts, and be renewed in the spirit of your mind, and that you put on the new man which was created according to God, in true righteousness and holiness.

Therefore, putting away lying, "Let each one *of you* speak truth with his neighbor," for we are members of one another. "Be angry, and do not sin": do not let the sun go down on your wrath, nor give place to the devil. Let him who stole steal no longer, but rather let him labor, working with *his* hands what is good, that he may have something to give him who has need. Let no corrupt word proceed out of your mouth, but what is good for necessary edification, that it may impart grace to the hearers. And do not grieve the Holy Spirit of God, by whom you were sealed for the day of redemption. Let all bitterness, wrath, anger, clamor, and evil speaking be put away from you, with all malice. And be kind to one another, tenderhearted, forgiving one another, even as God in Christ forgave you.

Ephesians 3:1–4:3, 11-32

WORSHIP

Oh, give thanks to the LORD, for *He is* good!
    For His mercy *endures* forever.

To Him who struck Egypt in their firstborn,
    For His mercy *endures* forever;
And brought out Israel from among them,
    For His mercy *endures* forever;
With a strong hand, and with an outstretched
        arm,
    For His mercy *endures* forever.

Psalm 136:1, 10-12

WISDOM

As snow in summer and rain in harvest,
So honor is not fitting for a fool.

Proverbs 26:1

SO WHAT?
What does this tell me?

WALKING THE WALK AT HOME
Ephesians 5:1–6:4, 10-20; Psalm 136:1, 23-25; Proverbs 26:11

Therefore be imitators of God as dear children. And walk in love, as Christ also has loved us and given Himself for us, an offering and a sacrifice to God for a sweet-smelling aroma.

But fornication and all uncleanness or covetousness, let it not even be named among you, as is fitting for saints; neither filthiness, nor foolish talking, nor coarse jesting, which are not fitting, but rather giving of thanks. For this you know, that no fornicator, unclean person, nor covetous man, who is an idolater, has any inheritance in the kingdom of Christ and God. Let no one deceive you with empty words, for because of these things the wrath of God comes upon the sons of disobedience. Therefore do not be partakers with them.

For you were once darkness, but now *you are* light in the Lord. Walk as children of light (for the fruit of the Spirit *is* in all goodness, righteousness, and truth), finding out what is acceptable to the Lord. And have no fellowship with the unfruitful works of darkness, but rather expose *them*. For it is shameful even to speak of those things which are done by them in secret. But all things that are exposed are made manifest by the light, for whatever makes manifest is light. Therefore He says:

"Awake, you who sleep,
Arise from the dead,
And Christ will give you light."

See then that you walk circumspectly, not as fools but as wise, redeeming the time, because the days are evil.

Therefore do not be unwise, but understand what the will of the Lord *is*. And do not be drunk with wine, in which is dissipation; but be filled with the Spirit, speaking to one another in psalms and hymns and spiritual songs, singing and making melody in your heart to the Lord, giving thanks always for all things to God the Father in the name of our Lord Jesus Christ, submitting to one another in the fear of God.

Wives, submit to your own husbands, as to the Lord. For the husband is head of the wife, as also Christ is head of the church; and He is the Savior of the body. Therefore, just as the church is subject to Christ, so *let* the wives *be* to their own husbands in everything.

Husbands, love your wives, just as Christ also loved the church and gave Himself for her, that He might sanctify and cleanse her with the washing of water by the word, that He might present her to Himself a glorious church, not having spot or wrinkle or any such thing, but that she should be holy and without blemish. So husbands ought to love their own wives as their own bodies; he who loves his wife loves himself. For no one ever hated his own flesh, but nourishes and cherishes it, just as the Lord *does* the church. For we are members of His body, of His flesh and of His bones. "For this reason a man shall leave his father and mother and be joined to his wife, and the two shall become one flesh." This is a great mystery, but I speak concerning Christ and the church. Nevertheless let each one of you in particular so love his own wife as himself, and let the wife *see* that she respects *her* husband.

Children, obey your parents in the Lord, for this is right. "Honor your father and mother," which is the first commandment with promise: "that it may be well with you and you may live long on the earth."

And you, fathers, do not provoke your children to wrath, but bring them up in the training and admonition of the Lord.

Finally, my brethren, be strong in the Lord and in the power of His might. Put on the whole armor of God, that you may be able to stand against the wiles of the devil. For we do not wrestle against flesh and blood, but against principalities, against powers, against the rulers of the darkness of this age, against spiritual *hosts* of wickedness in the heavenly *places*. Therefore take up the whole armor of God, that you may be able to withstand in the evil day, and having done all, to stand.

Stand therefore, having girded your waist with truth, having put on the breastplate of righteousness, and having shod your feet with the preparation of the gospel of peace; above all, taking the shield of faith with which you will be able to quench

APOSTLES AND THE CHURCH

all the fiery darts of the wicked one. And take the helmet of salvation, and the sword of the Spirit, which is the word of God; praying always with all prayer and supplication in the Spirit, being watchful to this end with all perseverance and supplication for all the saints—and for me, that utterance may be given to me, that I may open my mouth boldly to make known the mystery of the gospel, for which I am an ambassador in chains; that in it I may speak boldly, as I ought to speak.

Ephesians 5:1–6:4, 10-20

WORSHIP

Oh, give thanks to the LORD, for *He is* good!
    For His mercy *endures* forever.

Who remembered us in our lowly state,
    For His mercy *endures* forever;
And rescued us from our enemies,
    For His mercy *endures* forever;
Who gives food to all flesh,
    For His mercy *endures* forever.

Psalm 136:1, 23-25

WISDOM

As a dog returns to his own vomit,
So a fool repeats his folly.

Proverbs 26:11

SW?! **SO WHAT?**
What does this tell me?

THE GREATNESS OF JESUS CHRIST

Colossians 1:1-23, 28-29; 2:6-23; Psalm 137:4-6; Proverbs 26:16

Paul, an apostle of Jesus Christ by the will of God, and Timothy our brother,

To the saints and faithful brethren in Christ *who are* in Colosse:

Grace to you and peace from God our Father and the Lord Jesus Christ.

We give thanks to the God and Father of our Lord Jesus Christ, praying always for you, since we heard of your faith in Christ Jesus and of your love for all the saints; because of the hope which is laid up for you in heaven, of which you heard before in the word of the truth of the gospel, which has come to you, as *it has* also in all the world, and is bringing forth fruit, as *it is* also among you since the day you heard and knew the grace of God in truth; as you also learned from Epaphras, our dear fellow servant, who is a faithful minister of Christ on your behalf, who also declared to us your love in the Spirit.

For this reason we also, since the day we heard it, do not cease to pray for you, and to ask that you may be filled with the knowledge of His will in all wisdom and spiritual understanding; that you may walk worthy of the Lord, fully pleasing *Him,* being fruitful in every good work and increasing in the knowledge of God; strengthened with all might, according to His glorious power, for all patience and longsuffering with joy; giving thanks to the Father who has qualified us to be partakers of the inheritance of the saints in the light. He has delivered us from the power of darkness and conveyed *us* into the kingdom of the Son of His love, in whom we have redemption through His blood, the forgiveness of sins.

He is the image of the invisible God, the firstborn over all creation. For by Him all things were created that are in heaven and that are on earth, visible and invisible, whether thrones or dominions or principalities or powers. All things were created through Him and for Him. And He is before all things, and in Him all things consist. And He is the head of the body, the church, who is the beginning, the firstborn from the dead, that in all things He may have the preeminence.

For it pleased *the Father that* in Him all the fullness should dwell, and by Him to reconcile all things to Himself, by Him, whether things on earth or things in heaven, having made peace through the blood of His cross.

And you, who once were alienated and enemies in your mind by wicked works, yet now He has reconciled in the body of His flesh through death, to present you holy, and blameless, and above reproach in His sight—if indeed you continue in the faith, grounded and steadfast, and are not moved away from the hope of the gospel which you heard, which was preached to every creature under heaven, of which I, Paul, became a minister.

Him we preach, warning every man and teaching every man in all wisdom, that we may present every man perfect in Christ Jesus. To this *end* I also labor, striving according to His working which works in me mightily.

As you therefore have received Christ Jesus the Lord, so walk in Him, rooted and built up in Him and established in the faith, as you have been taught, abounding in it with thanksgiving.

Beware lest anyone cheat you through philosophy and empty deceit, according to the tradition of men, according to the basic principles of the world, and not according to Christ. For in Him dwells all the fullness of the Godhead bodily; and you are complete in Him, who is the head of all principality and power.

In Him you were also circumcised with the circumcision made without hands, by putting off the body of the sins of the flesh, by the circumcision of Christ, buried with Him in baptism, in which you also were raised with *Him* through faith in the working of God, who raised Him from the dead. And you, being dead in your trespasses and the uncircumcision of your flesh, He has made alive together with Him, having forgiven you all trespasses, having wiped out the handwriting of requirements that was against us, which was contrary to us. And He has taken it out of the way, having nailed it to the cross. Having disarmed principalities and powers, He made a public spectacle of them, triumphing over them in it.

So let no one judge you in food or in drink, or regarding a festival or a new moon or sabbaths, which are a shadow of things to come, but the substance is of Christ. Let no one cheat you of your reward, taking delight in *false* humility and worship of angels, intruding into those things which he has not seen, vainly puffed up by his fleshly mind, and not holding fast to the Head, from whom all the body, nourished and knit together by joints and ligaments, grows with the increase *that is* from God.

Therefore, if you died with Christ from the basic principles of the world, why, as *though* living in the world, do you subject yourselves to regulations— "Do not touch, do not taste, do not handle," which all concern things which perish with the using—according to the commandments and doctrines of men? These things indeed have an appearance of wisdom in self-imposed religion, *false* humility, and neglect of the body, *but are* of no value against the indulgence of the flesh.

Colossians 1:1-23, 28-29; 2:6-23

WORSHIP

How shall we sing the LORD's song
In a foreign land?
If I forget you, O Jerusalem,
Let my right hand forget *its skill!*
If I do not remember you,
Let my tongue cling to the roof of my mouth—
If I do not exalt Jerusalem
Above my chief joy.

Psalm 137:4-6

WISDOM

The lazy *man is* wiser in his own eyes
Than seven men who can answer sensibly.

Proverbs 26:16

**SW?! SO WHAT?
What does this tell me?**

DEAD TO SELF AND ALIVE TO CHRIST

Colossians 3–4; Psalm 138:1-3; Proverbs 26:17

If then you were raised with Christ, seek those things which are above, where Christ is, sitting at the right hand of God. Set your mind on things above, not on things on the earth. For you died, and your life is hidden with Christ in God. When Christ *who is* our life appears, then you also will appear with Him in glory.

Therefore put to death your members which are on the earth: fornication, uncleanness, passion, evil desire, and covetousness, which is idolatry. Because of these things the wrath of God is coming upon the sons of disobedience, in which you yourselves once walked when you lived in them.

But now you yourselves are to put off all these: anger, wrath, malice, blasphemy, filthy language out of your mouth. Do not lie to one another, since you have put off the old man with his deeds, and have put on the new *man* who is renewed in knowledge according to the image of Him who created him, where there is neither Greek nor Jew, circumcised nor uncircumcised, barbarian, Scythian, slave *nor* free, but Christ *is* all and in all.

Therefore, as *the* elect of God, holy and beloved, put on tender mercies, kindness, humility, meekness, longsuffering; bearing with one another, and forgiving one another, if anyone has a complaint against another; even as Christ forgave you, so you also *must do.* But above all these things put on love, which is the bond of perfection. And let the peace of God rule in your hearts, to which also you were called in one body; and be thankful. Let the word of Christ dwell in you richly in all wisdom, teaching and admonishing one another in psalms and hymns and spiritual songs, singing with grace in your hearts to the Lord. And *whatever* you do in word or deed, *do* all in the name of the Lord Jesus, giving thanks to God the Father through Him.

Wives, submit to your own husbands, as is fitting in the Lord.

Husbands, love your wives and do not be bitter toward them.

Children, obey your parents in all things, for this is well pleasing to the Lord.

Fathers, do not provoke your children, lest they become discouraged.

Bondservants, obey in all things your masters according to the flesh, not with eyeservice, as menpleasers, but in sincerity of heart, fearing God. And whatever you do, do it heartily, as to the Lord and not to men, knowing that from the Lord you will receive the reward of the inheritance; for you serve the Lord Christ. But he who does wrong will be repaid for what he has done, and there is no partiality.

Masters, give your bondservants what is just and fair, knowing that you also have a Master in heaven.

Continue earnestly in prayer, being vigilant in it with thanksgiving; meanwhile praying also for us, that God would open to us a door for the word, to speak the mystery of Christ, for which I am also in chains, that I may make it manifest, as I ought to speak.

Walk in wisdom toward those *who are* outside, redeeming the time. *Let* your speech always *be* with grace, seasoned with salt, that you may know how you ought to answer each one.

Tychicus, a beloved brother, faithful minister, and fellow servant in the Lord, will tell you all the news about me. I am sending him to you for this very purpose, that he may know your circumstances and comfort your hearts, with Onesimus, a faithful and beloved brother, who is *one* of you. They will make known to you all things which *are happening* here.

Aristarchus my fellow prisoner greets you, with Mark the cousin of Barnabas (about whom you received instructions: if he comes to you, welcome him), and Jesus who is called Justus. These *are my* only fellow workers for the kingdom of God who are of the circumcision; they have proved to be a comfort to me.

Epaphras, who is *one* of you, a bondservant of Christ, greets you, always laboring fervently for you in prayers, that you may stand perfect and complete in all the will of God. For I bear him witness that he has a great zeal for you, and those who are in Laodicea, and those in Hierapolis. Luke the beloved physician and Demas greet you. Greet the brethren who are in Laodicea, and Nymphas and the church that *is* in his house.

APOSTLES AND THE CHURCH

Now when this epistle is read among you, see that it is read also in the church of the Laodiceans, and that you likewise read the epistle from Laodicea. And say to Archippus, "Take heed to the ministry which you have received in the Lord, that you may fulfill it."

This salutation by my own hand—Paul. Remember my chains. Grace *be* with you. Amen.

Colossians 3–4

WoRSHiP

I will praise You with my whole heart;
Before the gods I will sing praises to You.
I will worship toward Your holy temple,
And praise Your name
For Your lovingkindness and Your truth;
For You have magnified Your word above all
    Your name.
In the day when I cried out, You answered me,
And made me bold *with* strength in my soul.

Psalm 138:1-3

WiSDoM

He who passes by *and* meddles in a quarrel
    not his own
Is like one who takes a dog by the ears.

Proverbs 26:17

SW?! **SO WHAT?**
What does this tell me?

THE HUMBLE EXAMPLE OF JESUS

Philippians 1:1–2:11; Psalm 139:7-10; Proverbs 26:22

Paul and Timothy, bondservants of Jesus Christ,

To all the saints in Christ Jesus who are in Philippi, with the bishops and deacons:

Grace to you and peace from God our Father and the Lord Jesus Christ.

I thank my God upon every remembrance of you, always in every prayer of mine making request for you all with joy, for your fellowship in the gospel from the first day until now, being confident of this very thing, that He who has begun a good work in you will complete *it* until the day of Jesus Christ; just as it is right for me to think this of you all, because I have you in my heart, inasmuch as both in my chains and in the defense and confirmation of the gospel, you all are partakers with me of grace. For God is my witness, how greatly I long for you all with the affection of Jesus Christ.

And this I pray, that your love may abound still more and more in knowledge and all discernment, that you may approve the things that are excellent, that you may be sincere and without offense till the day of Christ, being filled with the fruits of righteousness which *are* by Jesus Christ, to the glory and praise of God.

But I want you to know, brethren, that the things *which happened* to me have actually turned out for the furtherance of the gospel, so that it has become evident to the whole palace guard, and to all the rest, that my chains are in Christ; and most of the brethren in the Lord, having become confident by my chains, are much more bold to speak the word without fear.

Some indeed preach Christ even from envy and strife, and some also from goodwill: The former preach Christ from selfish ambition, not sincerely, supposing to add affliction to my chains; but the latter out of love, knowing that I am appointed for the defense of the gospel. What then? Only *that* in every way, whether in pretense or in truth, Christ is preached; and in this I rejoice, yes, and will rejoice.

For I know that this will turn out for my deliverance through your prayer and the supply of the Spirit of Jesus Christ, according to my earnest expectation and hope that in nothing I shall be ashamed, but with all boldness, as always, so now also Christ will be magnified in my body, whether by life or by death. For to me, to live *is* Christ, and to die *is* gain. But if *I* live on in the flesh, this *will mean* fruit from *my* labor; yet what I shall choose I cannot tell. For I am hard-pressed between the two, having a desire to depart and be with Christ, *which is* far better. Nevertheless to remain in the flesh *is* more needful for you. And being confident of this, I know that I shall remain and continue with you all for your progress and joy of faith, that your rejoicing for me may be more abundant in Jesus Christ by my coming to you again.

Only let your conduct be worthy of the gospel of Christ, so that whether I come and see you or am absent, I may hear of your affairs, that you stand fast in one spirit, with one mind striving together for the faith of the gospel, and not in any way terrified by your adversaries, which is to them a proof of perdition, but to you of salvation, and that from God. For to you it has been granted on behalf of Christ, not only to believe in Him, but also to suffer for His sake, having the same conflict which you saw in me and now hear *is* in me.

Therefore if *there is* any consolation in Christ, if any comfort of love, if any fellowship of the Spirit, if any affection and mercy, fulfill my joy by being likeminded, having the same love, *being* of one accord, of one mind. *Let* nothing *be done* through selfish ambition or conceit, but in lowliness of mind let each esteem others better than himself. Let each of you look out not only for his own interests, but also for the interests of others.

Let this mind be in you which was also in Christ Jesus, who, being in the form of God, did not consider it robbery to be equal with God, but made Himself of no reputation, taking the form of a bondservant, *and* coming in the likeness of men. And being found in appearance as a man, He humbled Himself and became obedient to *the point of* death, even the death of the cross. Therefore God also has highly exalted Him and given Him the name which is above every name, that at the name of Jesus every knee should bow, of those in heaven, and of those on earth, and of those under the earth, and *that* every tongue should confess that Jesus Christ *is* Lord, to the glory of God the Father.

Philippians 1:1–2:11

WoRShiP

Where can I go from Your Spirit?
Or where can I flee from Your presence?
If I ascend into heaven, You *are* there;
If I make my bed in hell, behold, You *are there.*
If I take the wings of the morning,
And dwell in the uttermost parts of the sea,
Even there Your hand shall lead me,
And Your right hand shall hold me.

Psalm 139:7-10

WiSDoM

The words of a talebearer *are* like tasty trifles,
And they go down into the inmost body.

Proverbs 26:22

SW?! SO WHAT?
What does this tell me?

HOW KNOWING CHRIST WILL CHANGE YOUR LIFE
Philippians 2:12–16; 3:1–4:1, 4–20; Psalm 139:13–16; Proverbs 27:1

Therefore, my beloved, as you have always obeyed, not as in my presence only, but now much more in my absence, work out your own salvation with fear and trembling; for it is God who works in you both to will and to do for *His* good pleasure.

Do all things without complaining and disputing, that you may become blameless and harmless, children of God without fault in the midst of a crooked and perverse generation, among whom you shine as lights in the world, holding fast the word of life, so that I may rejoice in the day of Christ that I have not run in vain or labored in vain.

Finally, my brethren, rejoice in the Lord. For me to write the same things to you *is* not tedious, but for you *it is* safe.

Beware of dogs, beware of evil workers, beware of the mutilation! For we are the circumcision, who worship God in the Spirit, rejoice in Christ Jesus, and have no confidence in the flesh, though I also might have confidence in the flesh. If anyone else thinks he may have confidence in the flesh, I more so: circumcised the eighth day, of the stock of Israel, *of* the tribe of Benjamin, a Hebrew of the Hebrews; concerning the law, a Pharisee; concerning zeal, persecuting the church; concerning the righteousness which is in the law, blameless.

But what things were gain to me, these I have counted loss for Christ. Yet indeed I also count all things loss for the excellence of the knowledge of Christ Jesus my Lord, for whom I have suffered the loss of all things, and count them as rubbish, that I may gain Christ and be found in Him, not having my own righteousness, which *is* from the law, but that which *is* through faith in Christ, the righteousness which is from God by faith; that I may know Him and the power of His resurrection, and the fellowship of His sufferings, being conformed to His death, if, by any means, I may attain to the resurrection from the dead.

Not that I have already attained, or am already perfected; but I press on, that I may lay hold of that for which Christ Jesus has also laid hold of me. Brethren, I do not count myself to have apprehended; but one thing *I do,* forgetting those things which are behind and reaching forward to those things which are ahead, I press toward the goal for the prize of the upward call of God in Christ Jesus.

Therefore let us, as many as are mature, have this mind; and if in anything you think otherwise, God will reveal even this to you. Nevertheless, to *the degree* that we have already attained, let us walk by the same rule, let us be of the same mind.

Brethren, join in following my example, and note those who so walk, as you have us for a pattern. For many walk, of whom I have told you often, and now tell you even weeping, *that they are* the enemies of the cross of Christ: whose end *is* destruction, whose god *is their* belly, and *whose* glory *is* in their shame—who set their mind on earthly things. For our citizenship is in heaven, from which we also eagerly wait for the Savior, the Lord Jesus Christ, who will transform our lowly body that it may be conformed to His glorious body, according to the working by which He is able even to subdue all things to Himself.

Therefore, my beloved and longed-for brethren, my joy and crown, so stand fast in the Lord, beloved.

Rejoice in the Lord always. Again I will say, rejoice!

Let your gentleness be known to all men. The Lord *is* at hand.

Be anxious for nothing, but in everything by prayer and supplication, with thanksgiving, let your requests be made known to God; and the peace of God, which surpasses all understanding, will guard your hearts and minds through Christ Jesus.

Finally, brethren, whatever things are true, whatever things *are* noble, whatever things *are* just, whatever things *are* pure, whatever things *are* lovely, whatever things *are* of good report, if *there is* any virtue and if *there is* anything praiseworthy—meditate on these things. The things which you

APOSTLES AND THE CHURCH

learned and received and heard and saw in me, these do, and the God of peace will be with you.

But I rejoiced in the Lord greatly that now at last your care for me has flourished again; though you surely did care, but you lacked opportunity. Not that I speak in regard to need, for I have learned in whatever state I am, to be content: I know how to be abased, and I know how to abound. Everywhere and in all things I have learned both to be full and to be hungry, both to abound and to suffer need. I can do all things through Christ who strengthens me.

Nevertheless you have done well that you shared in my distress. Now you Philippians know also that in the beginning of the gospel, when I departed from Macedonia, no church shared with me concerning giving and receiving but you only. For even in Thessalonica you sent *aid* once and again for my necessities. Not that I seek the gift, but I seek the fruit that abounds to your account. Indeed I have all and abound. I am full, having received from Epaphroditus the things *sent* from you, a sweet-smelling aroma, an acceptable sacrifice, well pleasing to God. And my God shall supply all your need according to His riches in glory by Christ Jesus. Now to our God and Father *be* glory forever and ever. Amen.

Philippians 2:12-16; 3:1–4:1, 4-20

WORSHIP

For You formed my inward parts;
You covered me in my mother's womb.
I will praise You, for I am fearfully *and*
    wonderfully made;
Marvelous are Your works,
And *that* my soul knows very well.
My frame was not hidden from You,
When I was made in secret,
And skillfully wrought in the lowest parts of the
    earth.
Your eyes saw my substance, being yet
    unformed.
And in Your book they all were written,
The days fashioned for me,
When *as yet there were* none of them.

Psalm 139:13-16

WISDOM

Do not boast about tomorrow,
For you do not know what a day may bring
    forth.

Proverbs 27:1

SW?! SO WHAT?
What does this tell me?

How to Conduct Yourself IN THE Church

1 Timothy 1:1-17; 2:1-4, 8-15, 3:1-15; Psalm 139:17-18, 23-24; Proverbs 27:2

Paul, an apostle of Jesus Christ, by the commandment of God our Savior and the Lord Jesus Christ, our hope,

To Timothy, a true son in the faith:

Grace, mercy, *and* peace from God our Father and Jesus Christ our Lord.

As I urged you when I went into Macedonia—remain in Ephesus that you may charge some that they teach no other doctrine, nor give heed to fables and endless genealogies, which cause disputes rather than godly edification which is in faith. Now the purpose of the commandment is love from a pure heart, *from* a good conscience, and *from* sincere faith, from which some, having strayed, have turned aside to idle talk, desiring to be teachers of the law, understanding neither what they say nor the things which they affirm.

But we know that the law *is* good if one uses it lawfully, knowing this: that the law is not made for a righteous person, but for *the* lawless and insubordinate, for *the* ungodly and for sinners, for *the* unholy and profane, for murderers of fathers and murderers of mothers, for manslayers, for fornicators, for sodomites, for kidnappers, for liars, for perjurers, and if there is any other thing that is contrary to sound doctrine, according to the glorious gospel of the blessed God which was committed to my trust.

And I thank Christ Jesus our Lord who has enabled me, because He counted me faithful, putting *me* into the ministry, although I was formerly a blasphemer, a persecutor, and an insolent man; but I obtained mercy because I did *it* ignorantly in unbelief. And the grace of our Lord was exceedingly abundant, with faith and love which are in Christ Jesus. This *is* a faithful saying and worthy of all acceptance, that Christ Jesus came into the world to save sinners, of whom I am chief. However, for this reason I obtained mercy, that in me first Jesus Christ might show all longsuffering, as a pattern to those who are going to believe on Him for everlasting life. Now to the King eternal, immortal, invisible, to God who alone is wise, *be* honor and glory forever and ever. Amen.

Therefore I exhort first of all that supplications, prayers, intercessions, *and* giving of thanks be made for all men, for kings and all who are in authority, that we may lead a quiet and peaceable life in all godliness and reverence. For this *is* good and acceptable in the sight of God our Savior, who desires all men to be saved and to come to the knowledge of the truth.

I desire therefore that the men pray everywhere, lifting up holy hands, without wrath and doubting; in like manner also, that the women adorn themselves in modest apparel, with propriety and moderation, not with braided hair or gold or pearls or costly clothing, but, which is proper for women professing godliness, with good works. Let a woman learn in silence with all submission. And I do not permit a woman to teach or to have authority over a man, but to be in silence. For Adam was formed first, then Eve. And Adam was not deceived, but the woman being deceived, fell into transgression. Nevertheless she will be saved in childbearing if they continue in faith, love, and holiness, with self-control.

This *is* a faithful saying: If a man desires the position of a bishop, he desires a good work. A bishop then must be blameless, the husband of one wife, temperate, sober-minded, of good behavior, hospitable, able to teach; not given to wine, not violent, not greedy for money, but gentle, not quarrelsome, not covetous; one who rules his own house well, having *his* children in submission with all reverence (for if a man does not know how to rule his own house, how will he take care of the church of God?); not a novice, lest being puffed up with pride he fall into the *same* condemnation as the devil. Moreover he must have a good testimony among those who are outside, lest he fall into reproach and the snare of the devil.

Likewise deacons *must be* reverent, not double-tongued, not given to much wine, not greedy for money, holding the mystery of the faith with a pure conscience. But let these also first be tested; then let them serve as deacons, being *found* blameless. Likewise *their* wives *must be* reverent, not slanderers, temperate, faithful in all things. Let deacons be the husbands of one wife, ruling *their* children and their own houses well. For those who have served well as deacons obtain for themselves a good standing and great boldness in the faith which is in Christ Jesus.

These things I write to you, though I hope to come to you shortly; but if I am delayed, *I write* so that you may know how you ought to conduct yourself in the house of God, which is the church of the living God, the pillar and ground of the truth.

1 Timothy 1:1-17; 2:1-4, 8-15, 3:1-15

WORSHIP

How precious also are Your thoughts to me,
  O God!
How great is the sum of them!
If I should count them, they would be more in
  number than the sand;
When I awake, I am still with You.

Search me, O God, and know my heart;
Try me, and know my anxieties;
And see if *there is any* wicked way in me,
And lead me in the way everlasting.

Psalm 139:17-18, 23-24

WISDOM

Let another man praise you, and not your own
  mouth;
A stranger, and not your own lips.

Proverbs 27:2

SW?! SO WHAT?
What does this tell me?

How TO fight THE good fight OF faith

1 Timothy 4:1–5:4, 17-22; 6:3-21; Psalm 140:6-8; Proverbs 27:6

Now the Spirit expressly says that in latter times some will depart from the faith, giving heed to deceiving spirits and doctrines of demons, speaking lies in hypocrisy, having their own conscience seared with a hot iron, forbidding to marry, *and commanding* to abstain from foods which God created to be received with thanksgiving by those who believe and know the truth. For every creature of God *is* good, and nothing is to be refused if it is received with thanksgiving; for it is sanctified by the word of God and prayer.

If you instruct the brethren in these things, you will be a good minister of Jesus Christ, nourished in the words of faith and of the good doctrine which you have carefully followed. But reject profane and old wives' fables, and exercise yourself toward godliness. For bodily exercise profits a little, but godliness is profitable for all things, having promise of the life that now is and of that which is to come. This *is* a faithful saying and worthy of all acceptance. For to this *end* we both labor and suffer reproach, because we trust in the living God, who is *the* Savior of all men, especially of those who believe. These things command and teach.

Let no one despise your youth, but be an example to the believers in word, in conduct, in love, in spirit, in faith, in purity. Till I come, give attention to reading, to exhortation, to doctrine. Do not neglect the gift that is in you, which was given to you by prophecy with the laying on of the hands of the eldership. Meditate on these things; give yourself entirely to them, that your progress may be evident to all. Take heed to yourself and to the doctrine. Continue in them, for in doing this you will save both yourself and those who hear you.

Do not rebuke an older man, but exhort *him* as a father, younger men as brothers, older women as mothers, younger women as sisters, with all purity.

Honor widows who are really widows. But if any widow has children or grandchildren, let them first learn to show piety at home and to repay their parents; for this is good and acceptable before God.

Let the elders who rule well be counted worthy of double honor, especially those who labor in the word and doctrine. For the Scripture says, "You shall not muzzle an ox while it treads out the grain," and, "The laborer *is* worthy of his wages." Do not receive an accusation against an elder except from two or three witnesses. Those who are sinning rebuke in the presence of all, that the rest also may fear.

I charge *you* before God and the Lord Jesus Christ and the elect angels that you observe these things without prejudice, doing nothing with partiality. Do not lay hands on anyone hastily, nor share in other people's sins; keep yourself pure.

If anyone teaches otherwise and does not consent to wholesome words, *even* the words of our Lord Jesus Christ, and to the doctrine which accords with godliness, he is proud, knowing nothing, but is obsessed with disputes and arguments over words, from which come envy, strife, reviling, evil suspicions, useless wranglings of men of corrupt minds and destitute of the truth, who suppose that godliness is a *means of* gain. From such withdraw yourself.

Now godliness with contentment is great gain. For we brought nothing into *this* world, *and it is* certain we can carry nothing out. And having food and clothing, with these we shall be content. But those who desire to be rich fall into temptation and a snare, and *into* many foolish and harmful lusts which drown men in destruction and perdition. For the love of money is a root of all *kinds of* evil, for which some have strayed from the faith in their greediness, and pierced themselves through with many sorrows.

But you, O man of God, flee these things and pursue righteousness, godliness, faith, love, patience, gentleness. Fight the good fight of faith, lay hold on eternal life, to which you were also called and have confessed the good confession in the presence of many witnesses. I urge you in the sight of God who gives life to all things, and *before* Christ Jesus who witnessed the good confession before Pontius Pilate, that you keep *this* commandment without spot, blameless until our Lord Jesus Christ's appearing, which He will manifest in His own time, *He who is* the blessed and only Potentate, the King of kings and Lord of lords, who alone has immortality, dwelling in unapproachable light, whom no man has seen or can see, to whom *be* honor and everlasting power. Amen.

Command those who are rich in this present age not to be haughty, nor to trust in uncertain riches but in the living God, who gives us richly all things to enjoy. *Let them* do good, that they be rich in good works, ready to give, willing to share, storing up for themselves a good foundation for the time to come, that they may lay hold on eternal life.

O Timothy! Guard what was committed to your trust, avoiding the profane *and* idle babblings and contradictions of what is falsely called knowledge—by professing it some have strayed concerning the faith.

Grace *be* with you. Amen.

1 Timothy 4:1–5:4, 17-22; 6:3-21

WORSHIP

I said to the LORD: "You *are* my God;
Hear the voice of my supplications, O LORD.
O GOD the Lord, the strength of my salvation,
You have covered my head in the day of
   battle.
Do not grant, O LORD, the desires of the wicked;
Do not further his *wicked* scheme,
Lest they be exalted."   Selah

Psalm 140:6-8

WISDOM

Faithful *are* the wounds of a friend,
But the kisses of an enemy *are* deceitful.

Proverbs 27:6

SW?! **SO WHAT?**
What does this tell me?

LIVING SENSIBLY IN THIS PRESENT AGE
Titus 1:1–3:11, 13-14; Psalm 140:9-10, 12-13; Proverbs 27:15-16

Paul, a bondservant of God and an apostle of Jesus Christ, according to the faith of God's elect and the acknowledgment of the truth which accords with godliness, in hope of eternal life which God, who cannot lie, promised before time began, but has in due time manifested His word through preaching, which was committed to me according to the commandment of God our Savior;

To Titus, a true son in *our* common faith:

Grace, mercy, *and* peace from God the Father and the Lord Jesus Christ our Savior.

For this reason I left you in Crete, that you should set in order the things that are lacking, and appoint elders in every city as I commanded you—if a man is blameless, the husband of one wife, having faithful children not accused of dissipation or insubordination. For a bishop must be blameless, as a steward of God, not self-willed, not quick-tempered, not given to wine, not violent, not greedy for money, but hospitable, a lover of what is good, sober-minded, just, holy, self-controlled, holding fast the faithful word as he has been taught, that he may be able, by sound doctrine, both to exhort and convict those who contradict.

For there are many insubordinate, both idle talkers and deceivers, especially those of the circumcision, whose mouths must be stopped, who subvert whole households, teaching things which they ought not, for the sake of dishonest gain. One of them, a prophet of their own, said, "Cretans *are* always liars, evil beasts, lazy gluttons." This testimony is true. Therefore rebuke them sharply, that they may be sound in the faith, not giving heed to Jewish fables and commandments of men who turn from the truth. To the pure all things are pure, but to those who are defiled and unbelieving nothing is pure; but even their mind and conscience are defiled. They profess to know God, but in works they deny Him, being abominable, disobedient, and disqualified for every good work.

But as for you, speak the things which are proper for sound doctrine: that the older men be sober, reverent, temperate, sound in faith, in love, in patience; the older women likewise, that they be reverent in behavior, not slanderers, not given to much wine, teachers of good things—that they admonish the young women to love their husbands, to love their children, to be discreet, chaste, homemakers, good, obedient to their own husbands, that the word of God may not be blasphemed.

Likewise, exhort the young men to be sober-minded, in all things showing yourself *to be* a pattern of good works; in doctrine *showing* integrity, reverence, incorruptibility, sound speech that cannot be condemned, that one who is an opponent may be ashamed, having nothing evil to say of you.

Exhort bondservants to be obedient to their own masters, to be well pleasing in all *things,* not answering back, not pilfering, but showing all good fidelity, that they may adorn the doctrine of God our Savior in all things.

For the grace of God that brings salvation has appeared to all men, teaching us that, denying ungodliness and worldly lusts, we should live soberly, righteously, and godly in the present age, looking for the blessed hope and glorious appearing of our great God and Savior Jesus Christ, who gave Himself for us, that He might redeem us from every lawless deed and purify for Himself *His* own special people, zealous for good works.

Speak these things, exhort, and rebuke with all authority. Let no one despise you.

Remind them to be subject to rulers and authorities, to obey, to be ready for every good work, to speak evil of no one, to be peaceable, gentle, showing all humility to all men. For we ourselves were also once foolish, disobedient, deceived, serving various lusts and pleasures, living in malice and envy, hateful and hating one another. But when the kindness and the love of God our Savior toward man appeared, not by works of righteousness which we have done, but according to His mercy He saved us, through the washing of regeneration and renewing of the Holy Spirit, whom He poured out on us abundantly through Jesus Christ our Savior, that having been justified by His grace we should become heirs according to the hope of eternal life.

This is a faithful saying, and these things I want you to affirm constantly, that those who have believed in God should be careful to maintain good works. These things are good and profitable to men.

But avoid foolish disputes, genealogies, contentions, and strivings about the law; for they are unprofitable and useless. Reject a divisive man after the first and second admonition, knowing that such a person is warped and sinning, being self-condemned.

Send Zenas the lawyer and Apollos on their journey with haste, that they may lack nothing. And let our *people* also learn to maintain good works, to *meet* urgent needs, that they may not be unfruitful.

Titus 1:1–3:11, 13-14

WORSHIP

"*As for* the head of those who surround me,
Let the evil of their lips cover them;
Let burning coals fall upon them;
Let them be cast into the fire,
Into deep pits, that they rise not up again."

I know that the Lord will maintain
The cause of the afflicted,
And justice for the poor.
Surely the righteous shall give thanks to Your
 name;
The upright shall dwell in Your presence.

Psalm 140:9-10, 12-13

WISDOM

A continual dripping on a very rainy day
And a contentious woman are alike;
Whoever restrains her restrains the wind,
And grasps oil with his right hand.

Proverbs 27:15-16

SW?! **SO WHAT?**
What does this tell me?

A CALL TO HOLINESS 1 Peter 1:1–2:20; Psalm 141:1-4; Proverbs 27:17

eter, an apostle of Jesus Christ,

To the pilgrims of the Dispersion in Pontus, Galatia, Cappadocia, Asia, and Bithynia, elect according to the foreknowledge of God the Father, in sanctification of the Spirit, for obedience and sprinkling of the blood of Jesus Christ:

Grace to you and peace be multiplied.

Blessed *be* the God and Father of our Lord Jesus Christ, who according to His abundant mercy has begotten us again to a living hope through the resurrection of Jesus Christ from the dead, to an inheritance incorruptible and undefiled and that does not fade away, reserved in heaven for you, who are kept by the power of God through faith for salvation ready to be revealed in the last time.

In this you greatly rejoice, though now for a little while, if need be, you have been grieved by various trials, that the genuineness of your faith, *being* much more precious than gold that perishes, though it is tested by fire, may be found to praise, honor, and glory at the revelation of Jesus Christ, whom having not seen you love. Though now you do not see *Him,* yet believing, you rejoice with joy inexpressible and full of glory, receiving the end of your faith— the salvation of *your* souls.

Of this salvation the prophets have inquired and searched carefully, who prophesied of the grace *that would come* to you, searching what, or what manner of time, the Spirit of Christ who was in them was indicating when He testified beforehand the sufferings of Christ and the glories that would follow. To them it was revealed that, not to themselves, but to us they were ministering the things which now have been reported to you through those who have preached the gospel to you by the Holy Spirit sent from heaven—things which angels desire to look into.

Therefore gird up the loins of your mind, be sober, and rest *your* hope fully upon the grace that is to be brought to you at the revelation of Jesus Christ; as obedient

children, not conforming yourselves to the former lusts, *as* in your ignorance; but as He who called you *is* holy, you also be holy in all *your* conduct, because it is written, "Be holy, for I am holy."

And if you call on the Father, who without partiality judges according to each one's work, conduct yourselves throughout the time of your stay *here* in fear; knowing that you were not redeemed with corruptible things, *like* silver or gold, from your aimless conduct *received* by tradition from your fathers, but with the precious blood of Christ, as of a lamb without blemish and without spot. He indeed was foreordained before the foundation of the world, but was manifest in these last times for you who through Him believe in God, who raised Him from the dead and gave Him glory, so that your faith and hope are in God.

Since you have purified your souls in obeying the truth through the Spirit in sincere love of the brethren, love one another fervently with a pure heart, having been born again, not of corruptible seed but incorruptible, through the word of God which lives and abides forever, because

"All flesh *is* as grass,
And all the glory of man as the flower of the
      grass.
The grass withers,
And its flower falls away,
But the word of the LORD endures forever."

Now this is the word which by the gospel was preached to you.

Therefore, laying aside all malice, all deceit, hypocrisy, envy, and all evil speaking, as newborn babes, desire the pure milk of the word, that you may grow thereby, if indeed you have tasted that the Lord *is* gracious.

Coming to Him *as to* a living stone, rejected indeed by men, but chosen by God *and* precious, you also, as living stones, are being built up a spiritual house, a holy priesthood, to offer up spiritual sacrifices acceptable to God through Jesus Christ. Therefore it is also contained in the Scripture,

"Behold, I lay in Zion
A chief cornerstone, elect, precious,
And he who believes on Him will by no means
      be put to shame."

APOSTLES AND THE CHURCH

Therefore, to you who believe, *He is* precious; but to those who are disobedient,

"The stone which the builders rejected
Has become the chief cornerstone,"

and

"A stone of stumbling
And a rock of offense."

They stumble, being disobedient to the word, to which they also were appointed.

But you *are* a chosen generation, a royal priesthood, a holy nation, His own special people, that you may proclaim the praises of Him who called you out of darkness into His marvelous light; who once *were* not a people but *are* now the people of God, who had not obtained mercy but now have obtained mercy.

Beloved, I beg *you* as sojourners and pilgrims, abstain from fleshly lusts which war against the soul, having your conduct honorable among the Gentiles, that when they speak against you as evildoers, they may, by *your* good works which they observe, glorify God in the day of visitation.

Therefore submit yourselves to every ordinance of man for the Lord's sake, whether to the king as supreme, or to governors, as to those who are sent by him for the punishment of evildoers and *for the* praise of those who do good. For this is the will of God, that by doing good you may put to silence the ignorance of foolish men—as free, yet not using liberty as a cloak for vice, but as bondservants of God. Honor all *people.* Love the brotherhood. Fear God. Honor the king.

Servants, *be* submissive to *your* masters with all fear, not only to the good and gentle, but also to the harsh. For this *is* commendable, if because of conscience toward God one endures grief, suffering wrongfully. For what credit *is it* if, when you are beaten for your faults, you take it patiently? But when you do good and suffer, if you take it patiently, this *is* commendable before God.

1 Peter 1:1–2:20

WORSHIP

LORD, I cry out to You;
Make haste to me!
Give ear to my voice when I cry out to You.
Let my prayer be set before You *as* incense,
The lifting up of my hands *as* the evening
sacrifice.

Set a guard, O LORD, over my mouth;
Keep watch over the door of my lips.
Do not incline my heart to any evil thing,
To practice wicked works
With men who work iniquity;
And do not let me eat of their delicacies.

Psalm 141:1-4

WISDOM

As iron sharpens iron,
So a man sharpens the countenance of his
friend.

Proverbs 27:17

SW?! **SO WHAT?**
What does this tell me?

SUFFERING: THE PATH TO HOLINESS

1 Peter 2:21–3:12; 4:1–5:11;
Psalm 142:5–7; Proverbs 27:19

For to this you were called, because Christ also suffered for us, leaving us an example, that you should follow His steps:

"Who committed no sin,
Nor was deceit found in His mouth";

who, when He was reviled, did not revile in return; when He suffered, He did not threaten, but committed *Himself* to Him who judges righteously; who Himself bore our sins in His own body on the tree, that we, having died to sins, might live for righteousness—by whose stripes you were healed. For you were like sheep going astray, but have now returned to the Shepherd and Overseer of your souls.

Wives, likewise, *be* submissive to your own husbands, that even if some do not obey the word, they, without a word, may be won by the conduct of their wives, when they observe your chaste conduct *accompanied* by fear. Do not let your adornment be *merely* outward—arranging the hair, wearing gold, or putting on *fine* apparel—rather *let it be* the hidden person of the heart, with the incorruptible *beauty* of a gentle and quiet spirit, which is very precious in the sight of God. For in this manner, in former times, the holy women who trusted in God also adorned themselves, being submissive to their own husbands, as Sarah obeyed Abraham, calling him lord, whose daughters you are if you do good and are not afraid with any terror.

Husbands, likewise, dwell with *them* with understanding, giving honor to the wife, as to the weaker vessel, and as *being* heirs together of the grace of life, that your prayers may not be hindered.

Finally, all *of you be* of one mind, having compassion for one another; love as brothers, *be* tenderhearted, *be* courteous; not returning evil for evil or reviling for reviling, but on the contrary blessing, knowing that you were called to this, that you may inherit a blessing. For

"He who would love life
And see good days,

Let him refrain his tongue from evil,
And his lips from speaking deceit.
Let him turn away from evil and do good;
Let him seek peace and pursue it.
For the eyes of the LORD *are* on the righteous,
And His ears *are* open to their prayers;
But the face of the LORD *is* against those who do evil."

Therefore, since Christ suffered for us in the flesh, arm yourselves also with the same mind, for he who has suffered in the flesh has ceased from sin, that he no longer should live the rest of *his* time in the flesh for the lusts of men, but for the will of God. For we *have spent* enough of our past lifetime in doing the will of the Gentiles—when we walked in lewdness, lusts, drunkenness, revelries, drinking parties, and abominable idolatries. In regard to these, they think it strange that you do not run with *them* in the same flood of dissipation, speaking evil of *you.* They will give an account to Him who is ready to judge the living and the dead. For this reason the gospel was preached also to those who are dead, that they might be judged according to men in the flesh, but live according to God in the spirit.

But the end of all things is at hand; therefore be serious and watchful in your prayers. And above all things have fervent love for one another, for "love will cover a multitude of sins." *Be* hospitable to one another without grumbling. As each one has received a gift, minister it to one another, as good stewards of the manifold grace of God. If anyone speaks, *let him speak* as the oracles of God. If anyone ministers, *let him do it* as with the ability which God supplies, that in all things God may be glorified through Jesus Christ, to whom belong the glory and the dominion forever and ever. Amen.

Beloved, do not think it strange concerning the fiery trial which is to try you, as though some strange thing happened to you; but rejoice to the extent that you partake of Christ's sufferings, that when His glory is revealed, you may also be glad with exceeding joy. If you are reproached for the name of Christ, blessed *are you,* for the Spirit of glory and of God rests upon you. On their part He is blasphemed, but on your part He is glorified. But let none of you suffer as a murderer, a thief, an evildoer, or as a busybody in other people's matters. Yet if *anyone suffers* as a Christian, let him not be ashamed, but let him glorify God in this matter.

For the time *has come* for judgment to begin at the house of God; and if *it begins* with us first, what will *be* the end of those who do not obey the gospel of God? Now

"If the righteous one is scarcely saved,
Where will the ungodly and the sinner
appear?"

Therefore let those who suffer according to the will of God commit their souls *to Him* in doing good, as to a faithful Creator.

The elders who are among you I exhort, I who am a fellow elder and a witness of the sufferings of Christ, and also a partaker of the glory that will be revealed: Shepherd the flock of God which is among you, serving as overseers, not by compulsion but willingly, not for dishonest gain but eagerly; nor as being lords over those entrusted to you, but being examples to the flock; and when the Chief Shepherd appears, you will receive the crown of glory that does not fade away.

Likewise you younger people, submit yourselves to *your* elders. Yes, all of *you* be submissive to one another, and be clothed with humility, for

"God resists the proud,
But gives grace to the humble."

Therefore humble yourselves under the mighty hand of God, that He may exalt you in due time, casting all your care upon Him, for He cares for you.

Be sober, be vigilant; because your adversary the devil walks about like a roaring lion, seeking whom he may devour. Resist him, steadfast in the faith, knowing that the same sufferings are experienced by your brotherhood in the world. But may the God of all grace, who called us to His eternal glory by Christ Jesus, after you have suffered a while, perfect, establish, strengthen, and settle *you*. To Him *be* the glory and the dominion forever and ever. Amen.

1 Peter 2:21–3:12; 4:1–5:11

WORSHIP

I cried out to You, O LORD:
I said, "You *are* my refuge,
My portion in the land of the living.
Attend to my cry,
For I am brought very low;
Deliver me from my persecutors,
For they are stronger than I.
Bring my soul out of prison,
That I may praise Your name;
The righteous shall surround me,
For You shall deal bountifully with me."

Psalm 142:5-7

WISDOM

As in water face *reflects* face,
So a man's heart *reveals* the man.

Proverbs 27:19

SW?! SO WHAT?
What does this tell me?

STIRRING YOUR MIND TO BE ON GUARD FOR ERROR

2 Peter 1:1–2:3; 3:1-18; Psalm 143:7-9; Proverbs 27:20

Simon Peter, a bondservant and apostle of Jesus Christ,

To those who have obtained like precious faith with us by the righteousness of our God and Savior Jesus Christ:

Grace and peace be multiplied to you in the knowledge of God and of Jesus our Lord, as His divine power has given to us all things that *pertain* to life and godliness, through the knowledge of Him who called us by glory and virtue, by which have been given to us exceedingly great and precious promises, that through these you may be partakers of the divine nature, having escaped the corruption *that is* in the world through lust.

But also for this very reason, giving all diligence, add to your faith virtue, to virtue knowledge, to knowledge self-control, to self-control perseverance, to perseverance godliness, to godliness brotherly kindness, and to brotherly kindness love. For if these things are yours and abound, *you will be* neither barren nor unfruitful in the knowledge of our Lord Jesus Christ. For he who lacks these things is shortsighted, even to blindness, and has forgotten that he was cleansed from his old sins.

Therefore, brethren, be even more diligent to make your call and election sure, for if you do these things you will never stumble; for so an entrance will be supplied to you abundantly into the everlasting kingdom of our Lord and Savior Jesus Christ.

For this reason I will not be negligent to remind you always of these things, though you know and are established in the present truth. Yes, I think it is right, as long as I am in this tent, to stir you up by reminding *you,* knowing that shortly I *must* put off my tent, just as our Lord Jesus Christ showed me. Moreover I will be careful to ensure that you always have a reminder of these things after my decease.

For we did not follow cunningly devised fables when we made known to you the power and coming of our Lord Jesus Christ, but were eyewitnesses of His majesty. For He received from God the Father honor and glory when such a voice came to Him from the Excellent Glory: "This is My beloved Son, in whom I am well pleased." And we heard this voice which came from heaven when we were with Him on the holy mountain.

And so we have the prophetic word confirmed, which you do well to heed as a light that shines in a dark place, until the day dawns and the morning star rises in your hearts; knowing this first, that no prophecy of Scripture is of any private interpretation, for prophecy never came by the will of man, but holy men of God spoke *as they were* moved by the Holy Spirit.

But there were also false prophets among the people, even as there will be false teachers among you, who will secretly bring in destructive heresies, even denying the Lord who bought them, *and* bring on themselves swift destruction. And many will follow their destructive ways, because of whom the way of truth will be blasphemed. By covetousness they will exploit you with deceptive words; for a long time their judgment has not been idle, and their destruction does not slumber.

Beloved, I now write to you this second epistle (in *both of* which I stir up your pure minds by way of reminder), that you may be mindful of the words which were spoken before by the holy prophets, and of the commandment of us, the apostles of the Lord and Savior, knowing this first: that scoffers will come in the last days, walking according to their own lusts, and saying, "Where is the promise of His coming? For since the fathers fell asleep, all things continue as *they were* from the beginning of creation." For this they willfully forget: that by the word of God the heavens were of old, and the earth standing out of water and in the water, by which the world *that* then existed perished, being flooded with water. But the heavens and the earth *which* are now preserved by the same word, are reserved for fire until the day of judgment and perdition of ungodly men.

But, beloved, do not forget this one thing, that with the Lord one day *is* as a thousand years, and a thousand years as one day. The Lord is not slack concerning *His* promise, as some count slackness, but is longsuffering toward us, not willing that any should perish but that all should come to repentance.

But the day of the Lord will come as a thief in the night, in which the heavens will pass away with a great noise, and the elements will melt with fervent heat; both the earth and the works that are in it will be burned up. Therefore, since all these things will be dissolved, what manner *of persons* ought you to be in holy conduct and godliness, looking for and hastening the coming of the day of God, because of which the heavens will be dissolved, being on fire, and the elements will melt with fervent heat? Nevertheless we, according to His promise, look for new heavens and a new earth in which righteousness dwells.

Therefore, beloved, looking forward to these things, be diligent to be found by Him in peace, without spot and blameless; and consider *that* the longsuffering of our Lord *is* salvation—as also our beloved brother Paul, according to the wisdom given to him, has written to you, as also in all his epistles, speaking in them of these things, in which are some things hard to understand, which untaught and unstable *people* twist to their own destruction, as *they do* also the rest of the Scriptures.

You therefore, beloved, since you know *this* beforehand, beware lest you also fall from your own steadfastness, being led away with the error of the wicked; but grow in the grace and knowledge of our Lord and Savior Jesus Christ.

To Him *be* the glory both now and forever. Amen.

2 Peter 1:1–2:3; 3:1-18

WORSHIP

Answer me speedily, O LORD;
My spirit fails!
Do not hide Your face from me,
Lest I be like those who go down into the pit.
Cause me to hear Your lovingkindness in the
    morning,
For in You do I trust;
Cause me to know the way in which I should
    walk,
For I lift up my soul to You.

Deliver me, O LORD, from my enemies;
In You I take shelter.

Psalm 143:7-9

WISDOM

Hell and Destruction are never full;
So the eyes of man are never satisfied.

Proverbs 27:20

SW?! SO WHAT?
What does this tell me?

GUARD THE TREASURE THAT HAS BEEN ENTRUSTED TO YOU

2 Timothy 1–2; Psalm 143:10-11; Proverbs 28:5

Paul, an apostle of Jesus Christ by the will of God, according to the promise of life which is in Christ Jesus,

To Timothy, a beloved son:

Grace, mercy, *and* peace from God the Father and Christ Jesus our Lord.

I thank God, whom I serve with a pure conscience, as *my* forefathers *did,* as without ceasing I remember you in my prayers night and day, greatly desiring to see you, being mindful of your tears, that I may be filled with joy, when I call to remembrance the genuine faith that is in you, which dwelt first in your grandmother Lois and your mother Eunice, and I am persuaded is in you also. Therefore I remind you to stir up the gift of God which is in you through the laying on of my hands. For God has not given us a spirit of fear, but of power and of love and of a sound mind.

Therefore do not be ashamed of the testimony of our Lord, nor of me His prisoner, but share with me in the sufferings for the gospel according to the power of God, who has saved us and called *us* with a holy calling, not according to our works, but according to His own purpose and grace which was given to us in Christ Jesus before time began, but has now been revealed by the appearing of our Savior Jesus Christ, *who* has abolished death and brought life and immortality to light through the gospel, to which I was appointed a preacher, an apostle, and a teacher of the Gentiles. For this reason I also suffer these things; nevertheless I am not ashamed, for I know whom I have believed and am persuaded that He is able to keep what I have committed to Him until that Day.

Hold fast the pattern of sound words which you have heard from me, in faith and love which are in Christ Jesus. That good thing which was committed to you, keep by the Holy Spirit who dwells in us.

This you know, that all those in Asia have turned away from me, among whom are Phygellus and Hermogenes. The Lord grant mercy to the household of Onesiphorus, for he often refreshed me, and was not ashamed of my chain; but when he arrived in Rome, he sought me out very zealously and found *me.* The Lord grant to him that he may find mercy from the Lord in that Day—and you know very well how many ways he ministered *to me* at Ephesus.

You therefore, my son, be strong in the grace that is in Christ Jesus. And the things that you have heard from me among many witnesses, commit these to faithful men who will be able to teach others also. You therefore must endure hardship as a good soldier of Jesus Christ. No one engaged in warfare entangles himself with the affairs of *this* life, that he may please him who enlisted him as a soldier. And also if anyone competes in athletics, he is not crowned unless he competes according to the rules. The hardworking farmer must be first to partake of the crops. Consider what I say, and may the Lord give you understanding in all things.

Remember that Jesus Christ, of the seed of David, was raised from the dead according to my gospel, for which I suffer trouble as an evildoer, *even* to the point of chains; but the word of God is not chained. Therefore I endure all things for the sake of the elect, that they also may obtain the salvation which is in Christ Jesus with eternal glory. *This is* a faithful saying:

For if we died with *Him,*
    We shall also live with *Him.*
If we endure,
    We shall also reign with *Him.*
If we deny *Him,*
    He also will deny us.
If we are faithless,
    He remains faithful;
He cannot deny Himself.

Remind *them* of these things, charging *them* before the Lord not to strive about words to no profit, to the ruin of the hearers. Be diligent to present yourself approved to God, a worker who does not need to be ashamed, rightly dividing the word of truth. But shun profane *and* idle babblings, for they will increase to more ungodliness. And their message will spread like cancer. Hymenaeus and Philetus are of this sort, who have strayed concerning the truth, saying that the resurrection is already past; and they overthrow the faith of some. Nevertheless the solid foundation of God stands, having this seal: "The Lord knows those who are His," and, "Let everyone who names the name of Christ depart from iniquity."

But in a great house there are not only vessels of gold and silver, but also of wood and clay, some for honor and some for dishonor. Therefore if anyone cleanses himself from the latter, he will be a vessel for honor, sanctified and useful for the Master, prepared for every good work. Flee also youthful lusts; but pursue righteousness, faith, love, peace with those who call on the Lord out of a pure heart. But avoid foolish and ignorant disputes, knowing that they generate strife. And a servant of the Lord must not quarrel but be gentle to all, able to teach, patient, in humility correcting those who are in opposition, if God perhaps will grant them repentance, so that they may know the truth, and *that* they may come to their senses *and escape* the snare of the devil, having been taken captive by him to *do* his will.

2 Timothy 1–2

WORSHIP

Teach me to do Your will,
For You *are* my God;
Your Spirit *is* good.
Lead me in the land of uprightness.

Revive me, O LORD, for Your name's sake!
For Your righteousness' sake bring my soul out
    of trouble.

Psalm 143:10-11

WISDOM

Evil men do not understand justice,
But those who seek the LORD understand all.

Proverbs 28:5

SW?! **SO WHAT?**
What does this tell me?

LAST WORDS FROM A MENTOR TO HIS PROTÉGÉ

2 Timothy 3:1–4:18; Psalm 144:1–4; Proverbs 28:13

But know this, that in the last days perilous times will come: For men will be lovers of themselves, lovers of money, boasters, proud, blasphemers, disobedient to parents, unthankful, unholy, unloving, unforgiving, slanderers, without self-control, brutal, despisers of good, traitors, headstrong, haughty, lovers of pleasure rather than lovers of God, having a form of godliness but denying its power. And from such people turn away! For of this sort are those who creep into households and make captives of gullible women loaded down with sins, led away by various lusts, always learning and never able to come to the knowledge of the truth. Now as Jannes and Jambres resisted Moses, so do these also resist the truth: men of corrupt minds, disapproved concerning the faith; but they will progress no further, for their folly will be manifest to all, as theirs also was.

But you have carefully followed my doctrine, manner of life, purpose, faith, longsuffering, love, perseverance, persecutions, afflictions, which happened to me at Antioch, at Iconium, at Lystra—what persecutions I endured. And out of *them* all the Lord delivered me. Yes, and all who desire to live godly in Christ Jesus will suffer persecution. But evil men and impostors will grow worse and worse, deceiving and being deceived. But you must continue in the things which you have learned and been assured of, knowing from whom you have learned *them,* and that from childhood you have known the Holy Scriptures, which are able to make you wise for salvation through faith which is in Christ Jesus.

All Scripture *is* given by inspiration of God, and *is* profitable for doctrine, for reproof, for correction, for instruction in righteousness, that the man of God may be complete, thoroughly equipped for every good work.

I charge *you* therefore before God and the Lord Jesus Christ, who will judge the living and the dead at His appearing and His kingdom: Preach the word! Be ready in season *and* out of season. Convince, rebuke, exhort, with all longsuffering and teaching. For the time will come when they will not endure sound doctrine, but according to their own desires, *because* they have itching ears, they will heap up for themselves teachers; and they will turn *their* ears away from the truth, and be turned aside to fables. But you be watchful in all things, endure afflictions, do the work of an evangelist, fulfill your ministry.

For I am already being poured out as a drink offering, and the time of my departure is at hand. I have fought the good fight, I have finished the race, I have kept the faith. Finally, there is laid up for me the crown of righteousness, which the Lord, the righteous Judge, will give to me on that Day, and not to me only but also to all who have loved His appearing.

Be diligent to come to me quickly; for Demas has forsaken me, having loved this present world, and has departed for Thessalonica—Crescens for Galatia, Titus for Dalmatia. Only Luke is with me. Get Mark and bring him with you, for he is useful to me for ministry. And Tychicus I have sent to Ephesus. Bring the cloak that I left with Carpus at Troas when you come—and the books, especially the parchments.

Alexander the coppersmith did me much harm. May the Lord repay him according to his works. You also must beware of him, for he has greatly resisted our words.

At my first defense no one stood with me, but all forsook me. May it not be charged against them.

But the Lord stood with me and strengthened me, so that the message might be preached fully through me, and *that* all the Gentiles might hear. Also I was delivered out of the mouth of the lion. And the Lord will deliver me from every evil work and preserve *me* for His heavenly kingdom. To Him *be* glory forever and ever. Amen!

2 Timothy 3:1–4:18

APOSTLES AND THE CHURCH

WORSHIP

Blessed *be* the LORD my Rock,
Who trains my hands for war,
And my fingers for battle—
My lovingkindness and my fortress,
My high tower and my deliverer,
My shield and *the One* in whom I take refuge,
Who subdues my people under me.

LORD, what *is* man, that You take knowledge of
    him?
Or the son of man, that You are mindful of
    him?
Man is like a breath;
His days *are* like a passing shadow.

Psalm 144:1-4

WISDOM

He who covers his sins will not prosper,
But whoever confesses and forsakes *them* will
    have mercy.

Proverbs 28:13

SW?! **SO WHAT?**
What does this tell me?

CHRIST: SUPERIOR TO THE ANGELS

Hebrews 1:1–2:18; 3:12-19; Psalm 144:9-11; Proverbs 28:23

God, who at various times and in various ways spoke in time past to the fathers by the prophets, has in these last days spoken to us by *His* Son, whom He has appointed heir of all things, through whom also He made the worlds; who being the brightness of *His* glory and the express image of His person, and upholding all things by the word of His power, when He had by Himself purged our sins, sat down at the right hand of the Majesty on high, having become so much better than the angels, as He has by inheritance obtained a more excellent name than they.

For to which of the angels did He ever say:

"You are My Son,
Today I have begotten You"?

And again:

"I will be to Him a Father,
And He shall be to Me a Son"?

But when He again brings the firstborn into the world, He says:

"Let all the angels of God worship Him."

And of the angels He says:

"Who makes His angels spirits
And His ministers a flame of fire."

But to the Son *He says:*

"Your throne, O God, *is* forever and ever;
A scepter of righteousness *is* the scepter of Your Kingdom.
You have loved righteousness and hated lawlessness;
Therefore God, Your God, has anointed You
With the oil of gladness more than Your companions."

And:

"You, LORD, in the beginning laid the foundation of the earth,

And the heavens are the work of Your hands.
They will perish, but You remain;
And they will all grow old like a garment;
Like a cloak You will fold them up,
And they will be changed.
But You are the same,
And Your years will not fail."

But to which of the angels has He ever said:

"Sit at My right hand,
Till I make Your enemies Your footstool"?

Are they not all ministering spirits sent forth to minister for those who will inherit salvation?

Therefore we must give the more earnest heed to the things we have heard, lest we drift away. For if the word spoken through angels proved steadfast, and every transgression and disobedience received a just reward, how shall we escape if we neglect so great a salvation, which at the first began to be spoken by the Lord, and was confirmed to us by those who heard *Him,* God also bearing witness both with signs and wonders, with various miracles, and gifts of the Holy Spirit, according to His own will?

For He has not put the world to come, of which we speak, in subjection to angels. But one testified in a certain place, saying:

"What is man that You are mindful of him,
Or the son of man that You take care of him?
You have made him a little lower than the angels;
You have crowned him with glory and honor,
And set him over the works of Your hands.
You have put all things in subjection under his feet."

For in that He put all in subjection under him, He left nothing *that is* not put under him. But now we do not yet see all things put under him. But we see Jesus, who was made a little lower than the angels, for the suffering of death crowned with glory and honor, that He, by the grace of God, might taste death for everyone.

For it was fitting for Him, for whom *are* all things and by whom *are* all things, in bringing many sons to glory, to make the captain of their salvation perfect through sufferings. For both He who sanctifies and those who are being sanctified *are* all of one, for which reason He is not ashamed to call them brethren, saying:

> "I will declare Your name to My brethren;
> In the midst of the assembly I will sing praise to You."

And again:

> "I will put My trust in Him."

And again:

> "Here am I and the children whom God has given Me."

Inasmuch then as the children have partaken of flesh and blood, He Himself likewise shared in the same, that through death He might destroy him who had the power of death, that is, the devil, and release those who through fear of death were all their lifetime subject to bondage. For indeed He does not give aid to angels, but He does give aid to the seed of Abraham. Therefore, in all things He had to be made like *His* brethren, that He might be a merciful and faithful High Priest in things *pertaining* to God, to make propitiation for the sins of the people. For in that He Himself has suffered, being tempted, He is able to aid those who are tempted.

Beware, brethren, lest there be in any of you an evil heart of unbelief in departing from the living God; but exhort one another daily, while it is called "Today," lest any of you be hardened through the deceitfulness of sin. For we have become partakers of Christ if we hold the beginning of our confidence steadfast to the end, while it is said:

> "Today, if you will hear His voice,
> Do not harden your hearts as in the rebellion."

For who, having heard, rebelled? Indeed, *was it* not all who came out of Egypt, *led* by Moses? Now with whom was He angry forty years? *Was it* not with those who sinned, whose corpses fell in the wilderness? And to whom did He swear that they would not enter His rest, but to those who did not obey? So we see that they could not enter in because of unbelief.

Hebrews 1:1–2:18; 3:12-19

WORSHIP

I will sing a new song to You, O God;
On a harp of ten strings I will sing praises to
   You,
The One who gives salvation to kings,
Who delivers David His servant
From the deadly sword.

Rescue me and deliver me from the hand of
   foreigners,
Whose mouth speaks lying words,
And whose right hand *is* a right hand of
   falsehood.

Psalm 144:9-11

WISDOM

He who rebukes a man will find more favor
   afterward
Than he who flatters with the tongue.

Proverbs 28:23

SW?! **SO WHAT?**
What does this tell me?

CHRIST: THE PERFECT HIGH PRIEST

Hebrews 4:1–5:10; 7:26-28; 10:19-25, 32-39; Psalm 145:1-5; Proverbs 28:25

APOSTLES AND THE CHURCH

Therefore, since a promise remains of entering His rest, let us fear lest any of you seem to have come short of it. For indeed the gospel was preached to us as well as to them; but the word which they heard did not profit them, not being mixed with faith in those who heard *it*. For we who have believed do enter that rest, as He has said:

"So I swore in My wrath,
'They shall not enter My rest,' "

although the works were finished from the foundation of the world. For He has spoken in a certain place of the seventh *day* in this way: "And God rested on the seventh day from all His works"; and again in this *place:* "They shall not enter My rest."

Since therefore it remains that some *must* enter it, and those to whom it was first preached did not enter because of disobedience, again He designates a certain day, saying in David, "Today," after such a long time, as it has been said:

"Today, if you will hear His voice,
Do not harden your hearts."

For if Joshua had given them rest, then He would not afterward have spoken of another day. There remains therefore a rest for the people of God. For he who has entered His rest has himself also ceased from his works as God *did* from His.

Let us therefore be diligent to enter that rest, lest anyone fall according to the same example of disobedience. For the word of God *is* living and powerful, and sharper than any two-edged sword, piercing even to the division of soul and spirit, and of joints and marrow, and is a discerner of the thoughts and intents of the heart. And there is no creature hidden from His sight, but all things *are* naked and open to the eyes of Him to whom we *must give* account.

Seeing then that we have a great High Priest who has passed through the heavens, Jesus the Son of God, let us hold fast *our* confession. For we do not have a High Priest who cannot sympathize with our weaknesses, but was in all *points* tempted as *we are, yet* without sin. Let us therefore come boldly to the throne of grace, that we may obtain mercy and find grace to help in time of need.

For every high priest taken from among men is appointed for men in things *pertaining* to God, that he may offer both gifts and sacrifices for sins. He can have compassion on those who are ignorant and going astray, since he himself is also subject to weakness. Because of this he is required as for the people, so also for himself, to offer *sacrifices* for sins. And no man takes this honor to himself, but he who is called by God, just as Aaron *was*.

So also Christ did not glorify Himself to become High Priest, *but it* was He who said to Him:

"You are My Son,
Today I have begotten You."

As *He* also *says* in another *place:*

"You *are* a priest forever
According to the order of Melchizedek";

who, in the days of His flesh, when He had offered up prayers and supplications, with vehement cries and tears to Him who was able to save Him from death, and was heard because of His godly fear, though He was a Son, *yet* He learned obedience by the things which He suffered. And having been perfected, He became the author of eternal salvation to all who obey Him, called by God as High Priest "according to the order of Melchizedek."

For such a High Priest was fitting for us, *who is* holy, harmless, undefiled, separate from sinners, and has become higher than the heavens; who does not need daily, as those high priests, to offer up sacrifices, first for His own sins and then for the people's, for this He did once for all when He offered up Himself. For the law appoints as high priests men who have weakness, but the word of the oath, which came after the law, *appoints* the Son who has been perfected forever.

Therefore, brethren, having boldness to enter the Holiest by the blood of Jesus, by a new and living way which He consecrated for us, through the veil, that is, His flesh, and *having* a High Priest over the house of God, let us draw near with a true heart in full assurance of faith, having our hearts sprinkled from an evil conscience and our bodies washed with pure water. Let us hold fast the confession of *our* hope without wavering, for He who promised *is* faithful. And let us consider one another in order to stir up love and good works, not forsaking the assembling of ourselves together, as *is* the manner of some, but exhorting *one another*, and so much the more as you see the Day approaching.

But recall the former days in which, after you were illuminated, you endured a great struggle with sufferings: partly while you were made a spectacle both by reproaches and tribulations, and partly while you became companions of those who were so treated; for you had compassion on me in my chains, and joyfully accepted the plundering of your goods, knowing that you have a better and an enduring possession for yourselves in heaven. Therefore do not cast away your confidence, which has great reward. For you have need of endurance, so that after you have done the will of God, you may receive the promise:

> "For yet a little while,
>   *And* He who is coming will come and will not
>   tarry.
> Now the just shall live by faith;
> But if *anyone* draws back,
> My soul has no pleasure in him."

But we are not of those who draw back to perdition, but of those who believe to the saving of the soul.
Hebrews 4:1–5:10; 7:26-28; 10:19-25, 32-39

WoRSHiP

I will extol You, my God, O King;
And I will bless Your name forever and ever.
Every day I will bless You,
And I will praise Your name forever and ever.
Great *is* the LORD, and greatly to be praised;
And His greatness *is* unsearchable.

One generation shall praise Your works to
    another,
And shall declare Your mighty acts.
I will meditate on the glorious splendor of Your
    majesty,
And on Your wondrous works.

Psalm 145:1-5

WiSDoM

He who is of a proud heart stirs up strife,
But he who trusts in the LORD will be
    prospered.

Proverbs 28:25

SW?! **SO WHAT?**
What does this tell me?

FAITH'S HALL OF FAME: PORTRAITS OF GOD PLEASERS

Hebrews 11:1–12:3; Psalm 145:8-10; Proverbs 29:1

ow faith is the substance of things hoped for, the evidence of things not seen. For by it the elders obtained a *good* testimony.

By faith we understand that the worlds were framed by the word of God, so that the things which are seen were not made of things which are visible.

By faith Abel offered to God a more excellent sacrifice than Cain, through which he obtained witness that he was righteous, God testifying of his gifts; and through it he being dead still speaks.

By faith Enoch was taken away so that he did not see death, "and was not found, because God had taken him"; for before he was taken he had this testimony, that he pleased God. But without faith *it is* impossible to please *Him,* for he who comes to God must believe that He is, and *that* He is a rewarder of those who diligently seek Him.

By faith Noah, being divinely warned of things not yet seen, moved with godly fear, prepared an ark for the saving of his household, by which he condemned the world and became heir of the righteousness which is according to faith.

By faith Abraham obeyed when he was called to go out to the place which he would receive as an inheritance. And he went out, not knowing where he was going. By faith he dwelt in the land of promise as *in* a foreign country, dwelling in tents with Isaac and Jacob, the heirs with him of the same promise; for he waited for the city which has foundations, whose builder and maker *is* God.

By faith Sarah herself also received strength to conceive seed, and she bore a child when she was past the age, because she judged Him faithful who had promised. Therefore from one man, and him as good as dead, were born *as many* as the stars of the sky in multitude—innumerable as the sand which is by the seashore.

These all died in faith, not having received the promises, but having seen them afar off were assured of them, embraced *them* and confessed that they were strangers and pilgrims on the earth. For those who say such things declare plainly that they seek a homeland. And truly if they had called to mind that *country* from which they had come out, they would have had opportunity to return. But now they desire a better, that is, a heavenly *country.* Therefore God is not ashamed to be called their God, for He has prepared a city for them.

By faith Abraham, when he was tested, offered up Isaac, and he who had received the promises offered up his only begotten *son,* of whom it was said, "In Isaac your seed shall be called," concluding that God *was* able to raise *him* up, even from the dead, from which he also received him in a figurative sense.

By faith Isaac blessed Jacob and Esau concerning things to come.

By faith Jacob, when he was dying, blessed each of the sons of Joseph, and worshiped, *leaning* on the top of his staff.

By faith Joseph, when he was dying, made mention of the departure of the children of Israel, and gave instructions concerning his bones.

By faith Moses, when he was born, was hidden three months by his parents, because they saw *he was* a beautiful child; and they were not afraid of the king's command.

By faith Moses, when he became of age, refused to be called the son of Pharaoh's daughter, choosing rather to suffer affliction with the people of God than to enjoy the passing pleasures of sin, esteeming the reproach of Christ greater riches than the treasures in Egypt; for he looked to the reward.

By faith he forsook Egypt, not fearing the wrath of the king; for he endured as seeing Him who is invisible. By faith he kept the Passover and the sprinkling of blood, lest he who destroyed the firstborn should touch them.

By faith they passed through the Red Sea as by

APOSTLES AND THE CHURCH

dry *land, whereas* the Egyptians, attempting *to do* so, were drowned.

By faith the walls of Jericho fell down after they were encircled for seven days. By faith the harlot Rahab did not perish with those who did not believe, when she had received the spies with peace.

And what more shall I say? For the time would fail me to tell of Gideon and Barak and Samson and Jephthah, also *of* David and Samuel and the prophets: who through faith subdued kingdoms, worked righteousness, obtained promises, stopped the mouths of lions, quenched the violence of fire, escaped the edge of the sword, out of weakness were made strong, became valiant in battle, turned to flight the armies of the aliens. Women received their dead raised to life again.

Others were tortured, not accepting deliverance, that they might obtain a better resurrection. Still others had trial of mockings and scourgings, yes, and of chains and imprisonment. They were stoned, they were sawn in two, were tempted, were slain with the sword. They wandered about in sheepskins and goatskins, being destitute, afflicted, tormented—of whom the world was not worthy. They wandered in deserts and mountains, *in* dens and caves of the earth.

And all these, having obtained a good testimony through faith, did not receive the promise, God having provided something better for us, that they should not be made perfect apart from us.

Therefore we also, since we are surrounded by so great a cloud of witnesses, let us lay aside every weight, and the sin which so easily ensnares *us*, and let us run with endurance the race that is set before us, looking unto Jesus, the author and finisher of *our* faith, who for the joy that was set before Him endured the cross, despising the shame, and has sat down at the right hand of the throne of God.

For consider Him who endured such hostility from sinners against Himself, lest you become weary and discouraged in your souls.

Hebrews 11:1–12:3

WoRSHIP

The LORD *is* gracious and full of compassion,
Slow to anger and great in mercy.
The LORD *is* good to all,
And His tender mercies *are* over all His works.
All Your works shall praise You, O LORD,
And Your saints shall bless You.

Psalm 145:8-10

WiSDoM

He who is often rebuked, *and* hardens *his* neck,
Will suddenly be destroyed, and that without remedy.

Proverbs 29:1

SW?! SO WHAT?
What does this tell me?

CHRIST'S UNSHAKABLE KINGDOM AND CHANGELESS CHARACTER

Hebrews 12:4-17, 25-29; 13:1-22; Psalm 145:17-19, 21; Proverbs 29:9

You have not yet resisted to bloodshed, striving against sin. And you have forgotten the exhortation which speaks to you as to sons:

"My son, do not despise the chastening of the LORD,
Nor be discouraged when you are rebuked by Him;
For whom the LORD loves He chastens,
And scourges every son whom He receives."

If you endure chastening, God deals with you as with sons; for what son is there whom a father does not chasten? But if you are without chastening, of which all have become partakers, then you are illegitimate and not sons. Furthermore, we have had human fathers who corrected *us,* and we paid *them* respect. Shall we not much more readily be in subjection to the Father of spirits and live? For they indeed for a few days chastened *us* as seemed *best* to them, but He for *our* profit, that *we* may be partakers of His holiness. Now no chastening seems to be joyful for the present, but painful; nevertheless, afterward it yields the peaceable fruit of righteousness to those who have been trained by it.

Therefore strengthen the hands which hang down, and the feeble knees, and make straight paths for your feet, so that what is lame may not be dislocated, but rather be healed.

Pursue peace with all *people,* and holiness, without which no one will see the Lord: looking carefully lest anyone fall short of the grace of God; lest any root of bitterness springing up cause trouble, and by this many become defiled; lest there *be* any fornicator or profane person like Esau, who for one morsel of food sold his birthright. For you know that afterward, when he wanted to inherit the blessing, he was rejected, for he found no place for repentance, though he sought it diligently with tears.

See that you do not refuse Him who speaks. For if they did not escape who refused Him who spoke on earth, much more *shall we not escape* if we turn away from Him who *speaks* from heaven, whose voice then shook the earth; but now He has promised, saying, "Yet once more I shake not only the earth, but also heaven." Now this, "Yet once more," indicates the removal of those things that are being shaken, as of things that are made, that the things which cannot be shaken may remain.

Therefore, since we are receiving a kingdom which cannot be shaken, let us have grace, by which we may serve God acceptably with reverence and godly fear. For our God *is* a consuming fire.

Let brotherly love continue. Do not forget to entertain strangers, for by so *doing* some have unwittingly entertained angels. Remember the prisoners as if chained with them—those who are mistreated—since you yourselves are in the body also.

Marriage *is* honorable among all, and the bed undefiled; but fornicators and adulterers God will judge.

Let your conduct *be* without covetousness; *be* content with such things as you have. For He Himself has said, "I will never leave you nor forsake you." So we may boldly say:

"The LORD *is* my helper;
I will not fear.
What can man do to me?"

Remember those who rule over you, who have spoken the word of God to you, whose faith follow, considering the outcome of *their* conduct. Jesus Christ *is* the same yesterday, today, and forever. Do not be carried about with various and strange doctrines. For *it is* good that the heart be established by grace, not with foods which have not profited those who have been occupied with them.

We have an altar from which those who serve the tabernacle have no right to eat. For the bodies of those animals, whose blood is brought into the sanctuary by the high priest for sin, are burned outside the camp. Therefore Jesus also, that He might sanctify the people with His own blood, suffered outside the gate. Therefore let us go forth to Him, outside the camp, bearing His reproach. For here we have no continuing city, but we seek the one to come. Therefore by Him let us continually offer the sacrifice of praise to God, that is, the fruit of *our* lips, giving thanks to His name. But do not forget to do good and to share, for with such sacrifices God is well pleased.

Obey those who rule over you, and be submissive, for they watch out for your souls, as those who must give account. Let them do so with joy and not with grief, for that would be unprofitable for you.

Pray for us; for we are confident that we have a good conscience, in all things desiring to live honorably. But I especially urge *you* to do this, that I may be restored to you the sooner.

Now may the God of peace who brought up our Lord Jesus from the dead, that great Shepherd of the sheep, through the blood of the everlasting covenant, make you complete in every good work to do His will, working in you what is well pleasing in His sight, through Jesus Christ, to whom *be* glory forever and ever. Amen.

And I appeal to you, brethren, bear with the word of exhortation, for I have written to you in few words.

Hebrews 12:4-17, 25-29; 13:1-22

WORSHIP

The LORD *is* righteous in all His ways,
Gracious in all His works.
The LORD *is* near to all who call upon Him,
To all who call upon Him in truth.
He will fulfill the desire of those who fear Him;
He also will hear their cry and save them.

My mouth shall speak the praise of the LORD,
And all flesh shall bless His holy name
Forever and ever.

Psalm 145:17-19, 21

WISDOM

If a wise man contends with a foolish man,
Whether *the fool* rages or laughs, *there is* no
    peace.

Proverbs 29:9

SW?! SO WHAT?
What does this tell me?

CONTENDING FOR THE FAITH AND CONFESSING OUR SIN

Jude; 1 John 1:1–2:11; Psalm 146:1-5; Proverbs 29:11

Jude, a bondservant of Jesus Christ, and brother of James,

To those who are called, sanctified by God the Father, and preserved in Jesus Christ:

Mercy, peace, and love be multiplied to you.

Beloved, while I was very diligent to write to you concerning our common salvation, I found it necessary to write to you exhorting you to contend earnestly for the faith which was once for all delivered to the saints. For certain men have crept in unnoticed, who long ago were marked out for this condemnation, ungodly men, who turn the grace of our God into lewdness and deny the only Lord God and our Lord Jesus Christ.

But I want to remind you, though you once knew this, that the Lord, having saved the people out of the land of Egypt, afterward destroyed those who did not believe. And the angels who did not keep their proper domain, but left their own abode, He has reserved in everlasting chains under darkness for the judgment of the great day; as Sodom and Gomorrah, and the cities around them in a similar manner to these, having given themselves over to sexual immorality and gone after strange flesh, are set forth as an example, suffering the vengeance of eternal fire.

Likewise also these dreamers defile the flesh, reject authority, and speak evil of dignitaries. Yet Michael the archangel, in contending with the devil, when he disputed about the body of Moses, dared not bring against him a reviling accusation, but said, "The Lord rebuke you!" But these speak evil of whatever they do not know; and whatever they know naturally, like brute beasts, in these things they corrupt themselves. Woe to them! For they have gone in the way of Cain, have run greedily in the error of Balaam for profit, and perished in the rebellion of Korah.

These are spots in your love feasts, while they feast with you without fear, serving *only* themselves. *They are* clouds without water, carried about by the winds; late autumn trees without fruit, twice dead, pulled up by the roots; raging waves of the sea, foaming up their own shame; wandering stars for whom is reserved the blackness of darkness forever.

Now Enoch, the seventh from Adam, prophesied about these men also, saying, "Behold, the Lord comes with ten thousands of His saints, to execute judgment on all, to convict all who are ungodly among them of all their ungodly deeds which they have committed in an ungodly way, and of all the harsh things which ungodly sinners have spoken against Him."

These are grumblers, complainers, walking according to their own lusts; and they mouth great swelling *words*, flattering people to gain advantage. But you, beloved, remember the words which were spoken before by the apostles of our Lord Jesus Christ: how they told you that there would be mockers in the last time who would walk according to their own ungodly lusts. These are sensual persons, who cause divisions, not having the Spirit.

But you, beloved, building yourselves up on your most holy faith, praying in the Holy Spirit, keep yourselves in the love of God, looking for the mercy of our Lord Jesus Christ unto eternal life.

And on some have compassion, making a distinction; but others save with fear, pulling *them* out of the fire, hating even the garment defiled by the flesh.

Now to Him who is able to keep you from
    stumbling,
And to present *you* faultless
Before the presence of His glory with
    exceeding joy,
To God our Savior,
Who alone is wise,
Be glory and majesty,
Dominion and power,

Both now and forever.
Amen.

That which was from the beginning, which we have heard, which we have seen with our eyes, which we have looked upon, and our hands have handled, concerning the Word of life—the life was manifested, and we have seen, and bear witness, and declare to you that eternal life which was with the Father and was manifested to us—that which we have seen and heard we declare to you, that you also may have fellowship with us; and truly our fellowship *is* with the Father and with His Son Jesus Christ. And these things we write to you that your joy may be full.

This is the message which we have heard from Him and declare to you, that God is light and in Him is no darkness at all. If we say that we have fellowship with Him, and walk in darkness, we lie and do not practice the truth. But if we walk in the light as He is in the light, we have fellowship with one another, and the blood of Jesus Christ His Son cleanses us from all sin.

If we say that we have no sin, we deceive ourselves, and the truth is not in us. If we confess our sins, He is faithful and just to forgive us *our* sins and to cleanse us from all unrighteousness. If we say that we have not sinned, we make Him a liar, and His word is not in us.

My little children, these things I write to you, so that you may not sin. And if anyone sins, we have an Advocate with the Father, Jesus Christ the righteous. And He Himself is the propitiation for our sins, and not for ours only but also for the whole world.

Now by this we know that we know Him, if we keep His commandments. He who says, "I know Him," and does not keep His commandments, is a liar, and the truth is not in him. But whoever keeps His word, truly the love of God is perfected in him. By this we know that we are in Him. He who says he abides in Him ought himself also to walk just as He walked.

Brethren, I write no new commandment to you, but an old commandment which you have had from the beginning. The old commandment is the word which you heard from the beginning. Again, a new commandment I write to you, which thing is true in Him and in you, because the darkness is passing away, and the true light is already shining.

He who says he is in the light, and hates his brother, is in darkness until now. He who loves his brother abides in the light, and there is no cause for stumbling in him. But he who hates his brother is in darkness and walks in darkness, and does not know where he is going, because the darkness has blinded his eyes.

Jude; 1 John 1:1–2:11

WORSHIP

Praise the LORD!

Praise the LORD, O my soul!
While I live I will praise the LORD;
I will sing praises to my God while I have my
    being.

Do not put your trust in princes,
Nor in a son of man, in whom *there is* no help.
His spirit departs, he returns to his earth;
In that very day his plans perish.

Happy *is* he who *has* the God of Jacob for his
    help,
Whose hope *is* in the LORD his God.

Psalm 146:1-5

WISDOM

A fool vents all his feelings,
But a wise *man* holds them back.

Proverbs 29:11

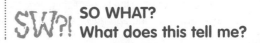

SO WHAT?
What does this tell me?

LEARNING TO LOVE IN DEED AND TRUTH

1 John 2:12–3:24; Psalm 147:1-3; Proverbs 29:15

I write to you, little children,

Because your sins are forgiven you for His
name's sake.
I write to you, fathers,
Because you have known Him *who is* from the
beginning.
I write to you, young men,
Because you have overcome the wicked one.
I write to you, little children,
Because you have known the Father.
I have written to you, fathers,

    Because you have known Him *who is*
      from the beginning.
I have written to you, young men,

    Because you are strong, and the word
      of God abides in you,
    And you have overcome the wicked
      one.

Do not love the world or the things in the world. If anyone loves the world, the love of the Father is not in him. For all that *is* in the world—the lust of the flesh, the lust of the eyes, and the pride of life—is not of the Father but is of the world. And the world is passing away, and the lust of it; but he who does the will of God abides forever.

Little children, it is the last hour; and as you have heard that the Antichrist is coming, even now many antichrists have come, by which we know that it is the last hour. They went out from us, but they were not of us; for if they had been of us, they would have continued with us; but *they went out* that they might be made manifest, that none of them were of us.

But you have an anointing from the Holy One, and you know all things. I have not written to you because you do not know the truth, but because you know it, and that no lie is of the truth.

Who is a liar but he who denies that Jesus is the Christ? He is antichrist who denies the Father and the Son. Whoever denies the Son does not have the Father either; he who acknowledges the Son has the Father also. Therefore let that abide in you which

you heard from the beginning. If what you heard from the beginning abides in you, you also will abide in the Son and in the Father. And this is the promise that He has promised us—eternal life.

These things I have written to you concerning those who *try to* deceive you. But the anointing which you have received from Him abides in you, and you do not need that anyone teach you; but as the same anointing teaches you concerning all things, and is true, and is not a lie, and just as it has taught you, you will abide in Him.

And now, little children, abide in Him, that when He appears, we may have confidence and not be ashamed before Him at His coming. If you know that He is righteous, you know that everyone who practices righteousness is born of Him.

Behold what manner of love the Father has bestowed on us, that we should be called children of God! Therefore the world does not know us, because it did not know Him. Beloved, now we are children of God; and it has not yet been revealed what we shall be, but we know that when He is revealed, we shall be like Him, for we shall see Him as He is. And everyone who has this hope in Him purifies himself, just as He is pure.

Whoever commits sin also commits lawlessness, and sin is lawlessness. And you know that He was manifested to take away our sins, and in Him there is no sin. Whoever abides in Him does not sin. Whoever sins has neither seen Him nor known Him.

Little children, let no one deceive you. He who practices righteousness is righteous, just as He is righteous. He who sins is of the devil, for the devil has sinned from the beginning. For this purpose the Son of God was manifested, that He might destroy the works of the devil. Whoever has been born of God does not sin, for His seed remains in him; and he cannot sin, because he has been born of God.

In this the children of God and the children of the devil are manifest: Whoever does not practice righteousness is not of God, nor *is* he who does not love his brother. For this is the message that you heard from the beginning, that we should love one another, not as Cain *who* was of the wicked one and murdered his brother. And why did he murder him? Because his works were evil and his brother's righteous.

Do not marvel, my brethren, if the world hates you. We know that we have passed from death to life, because we love the brethren. He who does not love *his* brother abides in death. Whoever hates his brother is a murderer, and you know that no murderer has eternal life abiding in him.

By this we know love, because He laid down His life for us. And we also ought to lay down *our* lives for the brethren. But whoever has this world's goods, and sees his brother in need, and shuts up his heart from him, how does the love of God abide in him?

My little children, let us not love in word or in tongue, but in deed and in truth. And by this we know that we are of the truth, and shall assure our hearts before Him. For if our heart condemns us, God is greater than our heart, and knows all things. Beloved, if our heart does not condemn us, we have confidence toward God. And whatever we ask we receive from Him, because we keep His commandments and do those things that are pleasing in His sight. And this is His commandment: that we should believe on the name of His Son Jesus Christ and love one another, as He gave us commandment.

Now he who keeps His commandments abides in Him, and He in him. And by this we know that He abides in us, by the Spirit whom He has given us.

1 John 2:12–3:24

WORSHIP

Praise the LORD!
For *it is* good to sing praises to our God;
For *it is* pleasant, *and* praise is beautiful.

The LORD builds up Jerusalem;
He gathers together the outcasts of Israel.
He heals the brokenhearted
And binds up their wounds.

Psalm 147:1-3

WISDOM

The rod and rebuke give wisdom,
But a child left *to himself* brings shame to his
   mother.

Proverbs 29:15

SW?! SO WHAT?
What does this tell me?

THE CERTAIN ASSURANCE OF ETERNAL LIFE

1 John 4–5; Psalm 147:7-11; Proverbs 29:18

Beloved, do not believe every spirit, but test the spirits, whether they are of God; because many false prophets have gone out into the world. By this you know the Spirit of God: Every spirit that confesses that Jesus Christ has come in the flesh is of God, and every spirit that does not confess that Jesus Christ has come in the flesh is not of God. And this is the *spirit* of the Antichrist, which you have heard was coming, and is now already in the world.

You are of God, little children, and have overcome them, because He who is in you is greater than he who is in the world. They are of the world. Therefore they speak *as* of the world, and the world hears them. We are of God. He who knows God hears us; he who is not of God does not hear us. By this we know the spirit of truth and the spirit of error.

Beloved, let us love one another, for love is of God; and everyone who loves is born of God and knows God. He who does not love does not know God, for God is love. In this the love of God was manifested toward us, that God has sent His only begotten Son into the world, that we might live through Him. In this is love, not that we loved God, but that He loved us and sent His Son *to be* the propitiation for our sins. Beloved, if God so loved us, we also ought to love one another.

No one has seen God at any time. If we love one another, God abides in us, and His love has been perfected in us. By this we know that we abide in Him, and He in us, because He has given us of His Spirit. And we have seen and testify that the Father has sent the Son *as* Savior of the world. Whoever confesses that Jesus is the Son of God, God abides in him, and he in God. And we have known and believed the love that God has for us. God is love, and he who abides in love abides in God, and God in him.

Love has been perfected among us in this: that we may have boldness in the day of judgment; because as He is, so are we in this world. There is no fear in love; but perfect love casts out fear, because fear involves torment. But he who fears has not been made perfect in love. We love Him because He first loved us.

If someone says, "I love God," and hates his brother, he is a liar; for he who does not love his brother whom he has seen, how can he love God whom he has not seen? And this commandment we have from Him: that he who loves God *must* love his brother also.

Whoever believes that Jesus is the Christ is born of God, and everyone who loves Him who begot also loves him who is begotten of Him. By this we know that we love the children of God, when we love God and keep His commandments. For this is the love of God, that we keep His commandments. And His commandments are not burdensome. For whatever is born of God overcomes the world. And this is the victory that has overcome the world—our faith. Who is he who overcomes the world, but he who believes that Jesus is the Son of God?

This is He who came by water and blood—Jesus Christ; not only by water, but by water and blood. And it is the Spirit who bears witness, because the Spirit is truth. For there are three that bear witness in heaven: the Father, the Word, and the Holy Spirit; and these three are one. And there are three that bear witness on earth: the Spirit, the water, and the blood; and these three agree as one.

If we receive the witness of men, the witness of God is greater; for this is the witness of God which He has testified of His Son. He who believes in the Son of God has the witness in himself; he who does not believe God has made Him a liar, because he has not believed the testimony that God has given of His Son. And this is the testimony: that God has given us eternal life, and this life is in His Son. He who has the Son has life; he who does not have the Son of God does not have life. These things I have written to you who believe in the name of the Son of God, that you may know that you have eternal life, and that you may *continue to* believe in the name of the Son of God.

Now this is the confidence that we have in Him, that if we ask anything according to His will, He hears us. And if we know that He hears us,

APOSTLES AND THE CHURCH

whatever we ask, we know that we have the petitions that we have asked of Him.

If anyone sees his brother sinning a sin *which does* not *lead* to death, he will ask, and He will give him life for those who commit sin not *leading* to death. There is sin *leading* to death. I do not say that he should pray about that. All unrighteousness is sin, and there is sin not *leading* to death.

We know that whoever is born of God does not sin; but he who has been born of God keeps himself, and the wicked one does not touch him.

We know that we are of God, and the whole world lies *under the sway of* the wicked one.

And we know that the Son of God has come and has given us an understanding, that we may know Him who is true; and we are in Him who is true, in His Son Jesus Christ. This is the true God and eternal life.

Little children, keep yourselves from idols. Amen.

1 John 4–5

WORSHIP

Sing to the LORD with thanksgiving;
Sing praises on the harp to our God,
Who covers the heavens with clouds,
Who prepares rain for the earth,
Who makes grass to grow on the mountains.
He gives to the beast its food,
And to the young ravens that cry.

He does not delight in the strength of the
    horse;
He takes no pleasure in the legs of a man.
The LORD takes pleasure in those who fear
    Him,
In those who hope in His mercy.

Psalm 147:7-11

WISDOM

Where *there is* no revelation, the people cast
    off restraint;
But happy *is* he who keeps the law.

Proverbs 29:18

SO WHAT?
What does this tell me?

MESSAGES TO SEVEN CHURCHES: PART ONE

Revelation 1:1–2:17; Psalm 147:12-15; Proverbs 29:25

The Revelation of Jesus Christ, which God gave Him to show His servants—things which must shortly take place. And He sent and signified *it* by His angel to His servant John, who bore witness to the word of God, and to the testimony of Jesus Christ, to all things that he saw. Blessed *is* he who reads and those who hear the words of this prophecy, and keep those things which are written in it; for the time *is* near.

John, to the seven churches which are in Asia:

Grace to you and peace from Him who is and who was and who is to come, and from the seven Spirits who are before His throne, and from Jesus Christ, the faithful witness, the firstborn from the dead, and the ruler over the kings of the earth.

To Him who loved us and washed us from our sins in His own blood, and has made us kings and priests to His God and Father, to Him *be* glory and dominion forever and ever. Amen.

Behold, He is coming with clouds, and every eye will see Him, even they who pierced Him. And all the tribes of the earth will mourn because of Him. Even so, Amen.

"I am the Alpha and the Omega, *the* Beginning and *the* End," says the Lord, "who is and who was and who is to come, the Almighty."

I, John, both your brother and companion in the tribulation and kingdom and patience of Jesus Christ, was on the island that is called Patmos for the word of God and for the testimony of Jesus Christ. I was in the Spirit on the Lord's Day, and I heard behind me a loud voice, as of a trumpet, saying, "I am the Alpha and the Omega, the First and the Last," and, "What you see, write in a book and send *it* to the seven churches which are in Asia: to Ephesus, to Smyrna, to Pergamos, to Thyatira, to Sardis, to Philadelphia, and to Laodicea."

Then I turned to see the voice that spoke with me. And having turned I saw seven golden lampstands, and in the midst of the seven lampstands *One* like the Son of Man, clothed with a garment down to the feet and girded about the chest with a golden band. His head and hair *were* white like wool, as white as snow, and His eyes like a flame of fire; His feet *were* like fine brass, as if refined in a furnace, and His voice as the sound of many waters; He had in His right hand seven stars, out of His mouth went a sharp two-edged sword, and His countenance *was* like the sun shining in its strength. And when I saw Him, I fell at His feet as dead. But He laid His right hand on me, saying to me, "Do not be afraid; I am the First and the Last. I *am* He who lives, and was dead, and behold, I am alive forevermore. Amen. And I have the keys of Hades and of Death. Write the things which you have seen, and the things which are, and the things which will take place after this. The mystery of the seven stars which you saw in My right hand, and the seven golden lampstands: The seven stars are the angels of the seven churches, and the seven lampstands which you saw are the seven churches.

"To the angel of the church of Ephesus write,

'These things says He who holds the seven stars in His right hand, who walks in the midst of the seven golden lampstands: "I know your works, your labor, your patience, and that you cannot bear those who are evil. And you have tested those who say they are apostles and are not, and have found them liars; and you have persevered and have patience, and have labored for My name's sake and have not become weary. Nevertheless I have *this* against you, that you have left your first love. Remember therefore from where you have fallen; repent and do the first works, or else I will come to you quickly and remove your lampstand from its place—unless you repent. But this you have, that you hate the deeds of the Nicolaitans, which I also hate.

"He who has an ear, let him hear what the Spirit says to the churches. To him who overcomes I will give to eat from the tree of life, which is in the midst of the Paradise of God." '

"And to the angel of the church in Smyrna write,

'These things says the First and the Last, who was dead, and came to life: "I know your works, tribulation, and poverty (but you are rich); and *I know* the blasphemy of those who say they are Jews and are not, but *are* a synagogue of Satan. Do not fear any of those things which you are about to suffer. Indeed, the devil is about to throw *some* of you into prison, that you may be tested, and you will have tribulation ten days. Be faithful until death, and I will give you the crown of life.

"He who has an ear, let him hear what the Spirit says to the churches. He who overcomes shall not be hurt by the second death." '

"And to the angel of the church in Pergamos write,

'These things says He who has the sharp two-edged sword: "I know your works, and where you dwell, where Satan's throne *is*. And you hold fast to My name, and did not deny My faith even in the days in which Antipas *was* My faithful martyr, who was killed among you, where Satan dwells. But I have a few things against you, because you have there those who hold the doctrine of Balaam, who taught Balak to put a stumbling block before the children of Israel, to eat things sacrificed to idols, and to commit sexual immorality. Thus you also have those who hold the doctrine of the Nicolaitans, which thing I hate. Repent, or else I will come to you quickly and will fight against them with the sword of My mouth.

"He who has an ear, let him hear what the Spirit says to the churches. To him who overcomes I will give some of the hidden manna to eat. And I will give him a white stone, and on the stone a new name written which no one knows except him who receives *it*." ' "

Revelation 1:1–2:17

WORSHIP

Praise the LORD, O Jerusalem!
Praise your God, O Zion!
For He has strengthened the bars of your
    gates;
He has blessed your children within you.
He makes peace *in* your borders,
And fills you with the finest wheat.

He sends out His command *to the* earth;
His word runs very swiftly.

Psalm 147:12-15

WISDOM

The fear of man brings a snare,
But whoever trusts in the LORD shall be safe.

Proverbs 29:25

SW?! SO WHAT?
What does this tell me?

Messages to Seven Churches: PART Two

Revelation 2:18–3:22; Psalm 148:1-3; Proverbs 30:7-9

"And to the angel of the church in Thyatira write,

'These things says the Son of God, who has eyes like a flame of fire, and His feet like fine brass: "I know your works, love, service, faith, and your patience; and *as* for your works, the last *are* more than the first. Nevertheless I have a few things against you, because you allow that woman Jezebel, who calls herself a prophetess, to teach and seduce My servants to commit sexual immorality and eat things sacrificed to idols. And I gave her time to repent of her sexual immorality, and she did not repent. Indeed I will cast her into a sickbed, and those who commit adultery with her into great tribulation, unless they repent of their deeds. I will kill her children with death, and all the churches shall know that I am He who searches the minds and hearts. And I will give to each one of you according to your works.

"Now to you I say, and to the rest in Thyatira, as many as do not have this doctrine, who have not known the depths of Satan, as they say, I will put on you no other burden. But hold fast what you have till I come. And he who overcomes, and keeps My works until the end, to him I will give power over the nations—

'He shall rule them with a rod of iron;
They shall be dashed to pieces like the potter's vessels'—

as I also have received from My Father; and I will give him the morning star.

"He who has an ear, let him hear what the Spirit says to the churches." '

"And to the angel of the church in Sardis write,

'These things says He who has the seven Spirits of God and the seven stars: "I know your works, that you have a name that you are alive, but you are dead. Be watchful, and strengthen the things which remain, that are ready to die, for I have not found your works perfect before God. Remember therefore how you have received and heard;

hold fast and repent. Therefore if you will not watch, I will come upon you as a thief, and you will not know what hour I will come upon you. You have a few names even in Sardis who have not defiled their garments; and they shall walk with Me in white, for they are worthy. He who overcomes shall be clothed in white garments, and I will not blot out his name from the Book of Life; but I will confess his name before My Father and before His angels.

"He who has an ear, let him hear what the Spirit says to the churches." '

"And to the angel of the church in Philadelphia write,

'These things says He who is holy, He who is true, "He who has the key of David, He who opens and no one shuts, and shuts and no one opens": "I know your works. See, I have set before you an open door, and no one can shut it; for you have a little strength, have kept My word, and have not denied My name. Indeed I will make *those* of the synagogue of Satan, who say they are Jews and are not, but lie—indeed I will make them come and worship before your feet, and to know that I have loved you. Because you have kept My command to persevere, I also will keep you from the hour of trial which shall come upon the whole world, to test those who dwell on the earth. Behold, I am coming quickly! Hold fast what you have, that no one may take your crown. He who overcomes, I will make him a pillar in the temple of My God, and he shall go out no more. I will write on him the name of My God and the name of the city of My God, the New Jerusalem, which comes down out of heaven from My God. And *I will write on him* My new name.

"He who has an ear, let him hear what the Spirit says to the churches." '

"And to the angel of the church of the Laodiceans write,

'These things says the Amen, the Faithful and True Witness, the Beginning of the creation of God: "I know your works, that you are neither cold nor hot. I could wish you were cold or hot. So then, because you are lukewarm, and neither cold nor hot, I will vomit you out of My mouth. Because you say, 'I am rich, have become wealthy, and have need of nothing'—and do not know that you are wretched, miserable, poor, blind, and naked—I counsel you to buy from Me gold refined in the fire, that you may be rich; and white garments, that you may be clothed, *that* the shame of your nakedness may not be revealed; and anoint your eyes with eye salve, that you may see. As many as I love, I rebuke and chasten. Therefore be zealous and repent. Behold, I stand at the door and knock. If anyone hears My voice and opens the door, I will come in to him and dine with him, and he with Me. To him who overcomes I will grant to sit with Me on My throne, as I also overcame and sat down with My Father on His throne.

"He who has an ear, let him hear what the Spirit says to the churches." ' "

Revelation 2:18–3:22

WORSHIP

Praise the LORD!

Praise the LORD from the heavens;
Praise Him in the heights!
Praise Him, all His angels;
Praise Him, all His hosts!
Praise Him, sun and moon;
Praise Him, all you stars of light!

Psalm 148:1-3

WISDOM

Two *things* I request of You
(Deprive me not before I die):
Remove falsehood and lies far from me;
Give me neither poverty nor riches—
Feed me with the food allotted to me;
Lest I be full and deny *You,*
And say, "Who *is* the LORD?"
Or lest I be poor and steal,
And profane the name of my God.

Proverbs 30:7-9

SW?! **SO WHAT?**
What does this tell me?

THE CURTAINS OF HEAVEN ARE PEELED BACK

Revelation 4–6; Psalm 148:13-14; Proverbs 30:18-19

After these things I looked, and behold, a door *standing* open in heaven. And the first voice which I heard *was* like a trumpet speaking with me, saying, "Come up here, and I will show you things which must take place after this."

Immediately I was in the Spirit; and behold, a throne set in heaven, and *One* sat on the throne. And He who sat there was like a jasper and a sardius stone in appearance; and *there was* a rainbow around the throne, in appearance like an emerald.

Around the throne *were* twenty-four thrones, and on the thrones I saw twenty-four elders sitting, clothed in white robes; and they had crowns of gold on their heads. And from the throne proceeded lightnings, thunderings, and voices. Seven lamps of fire *were* burning before the throne, which are the seven Spirits of God.

Before the throne *there was* a sea of glass, like crystal. And in the midst of the throne, and around the throne, *were* four living creatures full of eyes in front and in back. The first living creature *was* like a lion, the second living creature like a calf, the third living creature had a face like a man, and the fourth living creature *was* like a flying eagle. *The* four living creatures, each having six wings, were full of eyes around and within. And they do not rest day or night, saying:

"Holy, holy, holy,
Lord God Almighty,
Who was and is and is to come!"

Whenever the living creatures give glory and honor and thanks to Him who sits on the throne, who lives forever and ever, the twenty-four elders fall down before Him who sits on the throne and worship Him who lives forever and ever, and cast their crowns before the throne, saying:

"You are worthy, O Lord,
To receive glory and honor and power;
For You created all things,
And by Your will they exist and were created."

And I saw in the right *hand* of Him who sat on the throne a scroll written inside and on the back, sealed with seven seals. Then I saw a strong angel proclaiming with a loud voice, "Who is worthy to open the scroll and to loose its seals?" And no one in heaven or on the earth or under the earth was able to open the scroll, or to look at it.

So I wept much, because no one was found worthy to open and read the scroll, or to look at it. But one of the elders said to me, "Do not weep. Behold, the Lion of the tribe of Judah, the Root of David, has prevailed to open the scroll and to loose its seven seals."

And I looked, and behold, in the midst of the throne and of the four living creatures, and in the midst of the elders, stood a Lamb as though it had been slain, having seven horns and seven eyes, which are the seven Spirits of God sent out into all the earth. Then He came and took the scroll out of the right hand of Him who sat on the throne.

Now when He had taken the scroll, the four living creatures and the twenty-four elders fell down before the Lamb, each having a harp, and golden bowls full of incense, which are the prayers of the saints. And they sang a new song, saying:

"You are worthy to take the scroll,
And to open its seals;
For You were slain,
And have redeemed us to God by Your blood
Out of every tribe and tongue and people and nation,
And have made us kings and priests to our God;
And we shall reign on the earth."

Then I looked, and I heard the voice of many angels around the throne, the living creatures, and the elders; and the number of them was ten thousand times ten thousand, and thousands of thousands, saying with a loud voice:

"Worthy is the Lamb who was slain
To receive power and riches and wisdom,
And strength and honor and glory and blessing!"

And every creature which is in heaven and on the earth and under the earth and such as are in the sea, and all that are in them, I heard saying:

"Blessing and honor and glory and power

Be to Him who sits on the throne,
And to the Lamb, forever and ever!"

Then the four living creatures said, "Amen!" And the twenty-four elders fell down and worshiped Him who lives forever and ever.

Now I saw when the Lamb opened one of the seals; and I heard one of the four living creatures saying with a voice like thunder, "Come and see." And I looked, and behold, a white horse. He who sat on it had a bow; and a crown was given to him, and he went out conquering and to conquer.

When He opened the second seal, I heard the second living creature saying, "Come and see." Another horse, fiery red, went out. And it was granted to the one who sat on it to take peace from the earth, and that *people* should kill one another; and there was given to him a great sword.

When He opened the third seal, I heard the third living creature say, "Come and see." So I looked, and behold, a black horse, and he who sat on it had a pair of scales in his hand. And I heard a voice in the midst of the four living creatures saying, "A quart of wheat for a denarius, and three quarts of barley for a denarius; and do not harm the oil and the wine."

When He opened the fourth seal, I heard the voice of the fourth living creature saying, "Come and see." So I looked, and behold, a pale horse. And the name of him who sat on it was Death, and Hades followed with him. And power was given to them over a fourth of the earth, to kill with sword, with hunger, with death, and by the beasts of the earth.

When He opened the fifth seal, I saw under the altar the souls of those who had been slain for the word of God and for the testimony which they held. And they cried with a loud voice, saying, "How long, O Lord, holy and true, until You judge and avenge our blood on those who dwell on the earth?" Then a white robe was given to each of them; and it was said to them that they should rest a little while longer, until both *the number of* their fellow servants and their brethren, who would be killed as they *were*, was completed.

I looked when He opened the sixth seal, and behold, there was a great earthquake; and the sun became black as sackcloth of hair, and the moon became like blood. And the stars of heaven fell to the earth, as a fig tree drops its late figs when it is shaken by a mighty wind. Then the sky receded as a scroll when it is rolled up, and every mountain and island was moved out of its place. And the kings of the earth, the great men, the rich men, the commanders,

the mighty men, every slave and every free man, hid themselves in the caves and in the rocks of the mountains, and said to the mountains and rocks, "Fall on us and hide us from the face of Him who sits on the throne and from the wrath of the Lamb! For the great day of His wrath has come, and who is able to stand?"

Revelation 4–6

WORSHIP

Let them praise the name of the LORD,
For His name alone is exalted;
His glory *is* above the earth and heaven.
And He has exalted the horn of His people,
The praise of all His saints—
Of the children of Israel,
A people near to Him.

Praise the LORD!

Psalm 148:13-14

WISDOM

There are three *things which* are too wonderful
    for me,
Yes, four *which* I do not understand:
The way of an eagle in the air,
The way of a serpent on a rock,
The way of a ship in the midst of the sea,
And the way of a man with a virgin.

Proverbs 30:18-19

SW?! SO WHAT?
What does this tell me?

SUMMARY: REVELATION 7–18

The catastrophic events in Revelation chapters 7–18 are of such a magnitude and severity that John's vocabulary and descriptive ability are stretched to the limit. In fact, when you read of a third of the earth burning, man-killing locusts, a star falling from heaven, a great red dragon with seven heads and ten horns, or one hundred pound hailstones falling from heaven, you may be tempted to think John has not just been stretched, but that he is hallucinating.

He isn't. He is describing in terms and images familiar to him things no man has ever witnessed. Think of it this way.

continued on page 760

How difficult might it have been for someone in Jesus' day to describe putting a man on the moon, or the flight of the space shuttle? Or how about that same person explaining how a surgeon uses a laser in eye surgery, or how he replaces a valve on the human heart? Or even how music is placed on a small silver disc and then comes out very loud from black boxes with tiny holes?

You see, Revelation is "apocalyptic" literature and as such is characterized by symbolic language, terrifying visions, dreadful judgments. Everything is of titanic proportions.

John's dictionary may be limited as he describes the consummation of history, but all of time and creation will end just as he describes . . . he has gotten every detail down pat.

THE KING OF KINGS COMES TO CONSUMMATE HISTORY

Revelation 19:1–21:8; Psalm 149:1-4; Proverbs 31:10-12

After these things I heard a loud voice of a great multitude in heaven, saying, "Alleluia! Salvation and glory and honor and power *belong* to the Lord our God! For true and righteous *are* His judgments, because He has judged the great harlot who corrupted the earth with her fornication; and He has avenged on her the blood of His servants *shed* by her." Again they said, "Alleluia! Her smoke rises up forever and ever!" And the twenty-four elders and the four living creatures fell down and worshiped God who sat on the throne, saying, "Amen! Alleluia!" Then a voice came from the throne, saying, "Praise our God, all you His servants and those who fear Him, both small and great!"

And I heard, as it were, the voice of a great multitude, as the sound of many waters and as the sound of mighty thunderings, saying, "Alleluia! For the Lord God Omnipotent reigns! Let us be glad and rejoice and give Him glory, for the marriage of the Lamb has come, and His wife has made herself ready." And to her it was granted to be arrayed in fine linen, clean and bright, for the fine linen is the righteous acts of the saints.

Then he said to me, "Write: 'Blessed *are* those who are called to the marriage supper of the Lamb!'" And he said to me, "These are the true sayings of God." And I fell at his feet to worship him. But he said to me, "See *that you do* not *do that!* I am your fellow servant, and of your brethren who have the testimony of Jesus. Worship God! For the testimony of Jesus is the spirit of prophecy."

Now I saw heaven opened, and behold, a white horse. And He who sat on him *was* called Faithful and True, and in righteousness He judges and makes war. His eyes *were* like a flame of fire, and on His head *were* many crowns. He had a name written that no one knew except Himself. He *was* clothed with a robe dipped in blood, and His name is called The Word of God. And the armies in heaven, clothed in fine linen, white and clean, followed Him on white horses. Now out of His mouth goes a sharp sword, that with it He should strike the nations. And He Himself will rule them with a rod of iron. He Himself treads the winepress of the fierceness and wrath of Almighty God. And He has on *His* robe and on His thigh a name written:

KING OF KINGS AND LORD OF LORDS.

Then I saw an angel standing in the sun; and he cried with a loud voice, saying to all the birds that fly in the midst of heaven, "Come and gather together for the supper of the great God, that you may eat the flesh of kings, the flesh of captains, the flesh of mighty men, the flesh of horses and of those who sit on them, and the flesh of all *people,* free and slave, both small and great."

And I saw the beast, the kings of the earth, and their armies, gathered together to make war against Him who sat on the horse and against His army. Then the beast was captured, and with him the false prophet who worked signs in his presence, by which he deceived those who received the mark of the beast and those who worshiped his image. These two were cast alive into the lake of fire burning with brimstone. And the rest were killed with the sword which proceeded from the mouth of Him who sat on the horse. And all the birds were filled with their flesh.

Then I saw an angel coming down from heaven, having the key to the bottomless pit and a great chain in his hand. He laid hold of the dragon, that serpent of old, who is *the* Devil and Satan, and bound him for a thousand years; and he cast him into the bottomless pit, and shut him up, and set a seal on him, so that he should deceive the nations no more till the thousand years were finished. But after these things he must be released for a little while.

And I saw thrones, and they sat on them, and judgment was committed to them. Then *I saw* the souls of those who had been beheaded for their witness to Jesus and for the word of God, who had not worshiped the beast or his image, and had not received *his* mark on their foreheads or on their hands. And they lived and reigned with Christ for a thousand years. But the rest of the dead did not live again until the thousand years were finished. This *is* the first resurrection. Blessed and holy *is* he who has part in the first resurrection. Over such the second death has no power, but they shall be priests of God and of Christ, and shall reign with Him a thousand years.

Now when the thousand years have expired, Satan will be released from his prison and will go out to deceive the nations which are in the four corners of the earth, Gog and Magog, to gather them together to battle, whose number *is* as the sand of the sea. They went up on the breadth of the earth and surrounded the camp of the saints and the beloved city. And fire came down from God out of heaven and devoured them. The devil, who deceived them, was cast into the lake of fire and brimstone where the beast and the false prophet *are*. And they will be tormented day and night forever and ever.

Then I saw a great white throne and Him who sat on it, from whose face the earth and the heaven fled away. And there was found no place for them. And I saw the dead, small and great, standing before God, and books were opened. And another book was opened, which is *the Book* of Life. And the dead were judged according to their works, by the things which were written in the books. The sea gave up the dead who were in it, and Death and Hades delivered up the dead who were in them. And they were judged, each one according to his works. Then Death and Hades were cast into the lake of fire. This is the second death. And anyone not found written in the Book of Life was cast into the lake of fire.

Now I saw a new heaven and a new earth, for the first heaven and the first earth had passed away. Also there was no more sea. Then I, John, saw the holy city, New Jerusalem, coming down out of heaven from God, prepared as a bride adorned for her husband. And I heard a loud voice from heaven saying, "Behold, the tabernacle of God *is* with men, and He will dwell with them, and they shall be His people. God Himself will be with them *and be* their God. And God will wipe away every tear from their eyes; there shall be no more death, nor sorrow, nor crying. There shall be no more pain, for the former things have passed away."

Then He who sat on the throne said, "Behold, I make all things new." And He said to me, "Write, for these words are true and faithful."

And He said to me, "It is done! I am the Alpha and the Omega, the Beginning and the End. I will give of the fountain of the water of life freely to him who thirsts. He who overcomes shall inherit all things, and I will be his God and he shall be My son. But the cowardly, unbelieving, abominable, murderers, sexually immoral, sorcerers, idolaters, and all liars shall have their part in the lake which burns with fire and brimstone, which is the second death."

Revelation 19:1–21:8

WORSHIP

Praise the LORD!

Sing to the LORD a new song,
And His praise in the assembly of saints.

Let Israel rejoice in their Maker;
Let the children of Zion be joyful in their King.
Let them praise His name with the dance;
Let them sing praises to Him with the timbrel
    and harp.
For the LORD takes pleasure in His people;
He will beautify the humble with salvation.

Psalm 149:1-4

WISDOM

Who can find a virtuous wife?
For her worth *is* far above rubies.
The heart of her husband safely trusts her;
So he will have no lack of gain.
She does him good and not evil
All the days of her life.

Proverbs 31:10-12

SO WHAT?
What does this tell me?

HOW IT ALL BEGINS AGAIN, FOREVER!

Revelation 21:9–22:21; Psalm 150:1-2, 6; Proverbs 31:30-31

Then one of the seven angels who had the seven bowls filled with the seven last plagues came to me and talked with me, saying, "Come, I will show you the bride, the Lamb's wife." And he carried me away in the Spirit to a great and high mountain, and showed me the great city, the holy Jerusalem, descending out of heaven from God, having the glory of God. Her light *was* like a most precious stone, like a jasper stone, clear as crystal. Also she had a great and high wall with twelve gates, and twelve angels at the gates, and names written on them, which are *the names* of the twelve tribes of the children of Israel: three gates on the east, three gates on the north, three gates on the south, and three gates on the west.

Now the wall of the city had twelve foundations, and on them were the names of the twelve apostles of the Lamb. And he who talked with me had a gold reed to measure the city, its gates, and its wall. The city is laid out as a square; its length is as great as its breadth. And he measured the city with the reed: twelve thousand furlongs. Its length, breadth, and height are equal. Then he measured its wall: one hundred *and* forty-four cubits, *according* to the measure of a man, that is, of an angel. The construction of its wall was *of* jasper; and the city *was* pure gold, like clear glass. The foundations of the wall of the city *were* adorned with all kinds of precious stones: the first foundation *was* jasper, the second sapphire, the third chalcedony, the fourth emerald, the fifth sardonyx, the sixth sardius, the seventh chrysolite, the eighth beryl, the ninth topaz, the tenth chrysoprase, the eleventh jacinth, and the twelfth amethyst. The twelve gates *were* twelve pearls: each individual gate was of one pearl. And the street of the city *was* pure gold, like transparent glass.

But I saw no temple in it, for the Lord God Almighty and the Lamb are its temple. The city had no need of the sun or of the moon to shine in it, for the glory of God illuminated it. The Lamb *is* its light. And the nations of those who are saved shall walk in its light, and the kings of the earth bring their glory and honor into it. Its gates shall not be shut at all by day (there shall be no night there). And they shall bring the glory and the honor of the nations into it. But there shall by no means enter it anything that defiles, or causes an abomination or a lie, but only those who are written in the Lamb's Book of Life.

And he showed me a pure river of water of life, clear as crystal, proceeding from the throne of God and of the Lamb. In the middle of its street, and on either side of the river, *was* the tree of life, which bore twelve fruits, each *tree* yielding its fruit every month. The leaves of the tree *were* for the healing of the nations. And there shall be no more curse, but the throne of God and of the Lamb shall be in it, and His servants shall serve Him. They shall see His face, and His name *shall be* on their foreheads. There shall be no night there: They need no lamp nor light of the sun, for the Lord God gives them light. And they shall reign forever and ever.

Then he said to me, "These words *are* faithful and true." And the Lord God of the holy prophets sent His angel to show His servants the things which must shortly take place.

"Behold, I am coming quickly! Blessed *is* he who keeps the words of the prophecy of this book."

Now I, John, saw and heard these things. And when I heard and saw, I fell down to worship before the feet of the angel who showed me these things.

Then he said to me, "See *that you do* not *do that.* For I am your fellow servant, and of your brethren the prophets, and of those who keep the words of this book. Worship God." And he said to me, "Do not seal the words of the prophecy of this book, for the time is at hand. He who is unjust, let him be unjust still; he who is filthy, let him be filthy still; he who is righteous, let him be righteous still; he who is holy, let him be holy still."

"And behold, I am coming quickly, and My reward *is* with Me, to give to every one according to his work. I am the Alpha and the Omega, *the* Beginning and *the* End, the First and the Last."

Blessed *are* those who do His commandments, that they may have the right to the tree of

APOSTLES AND THE CHURCH

life, and may enter through the gates into the city. But outside *are* dogs and sorcerers and sexually immoral and murderers and idolaters, and whoever loves and practices a lie.

"I, Jesus, have sent My angel to testify to you these things in the churches. I am the Root and the Offspring of David, the Bright and Morning Star."

And the Spirit and the bride say, "Come!" And let him who hears say, "Come!" And let him who thirsts come. Whoever desires, let him take the water of life freely.

For I testify to everyone who hears the words of the prophecy of this book: If anyone adds to these things, God will add to him the plagues that are written in this book; and if anyone takes away from the words of the book of this prophecy, God shall take away his part from the Book of Life, from the holy city, and *from* the things which are written in this book.

He who testifies to these things says, "Surely I am coming quickly."

Amen. Even so, come, Lord Jesus!

The grace of our Lord Jesus Christ *be* with you all. Amen.

Revelation 21:9–22:21

WORSHIP

Praise the LORD!

Praise God in His sanctuary;
Praise Him in His mighty firmament!

Praise Him for His mighty acts;
Praise Him according to His excellent
   greatness!

Let everything that has breath praise the LORD.

Praise the LORD!

Psalm 150:1-2, 6

WISDOM

Charm *is* deceitful and beauty *is* passing,
But a woman *who* fears the LORD, she shall be
   praised.
Give her of the fruit of her hands,
And let her own works praise her in the gates.

Proverbs 31:30-31

SW?! SO WHAT?
What does this tell me?

PEAKS AND
SCRIPTURE INDEX

PEAKS

The Bible contains not only major divisions or Ranges, but also Peaks, which are the high points of the Bible story. Below are listed the Peaks and the days on which they can be seen.

SCRIPTURE INDEX

Chapters of the Bible from which selections have been taken are shown with the days on which the selections can be found.